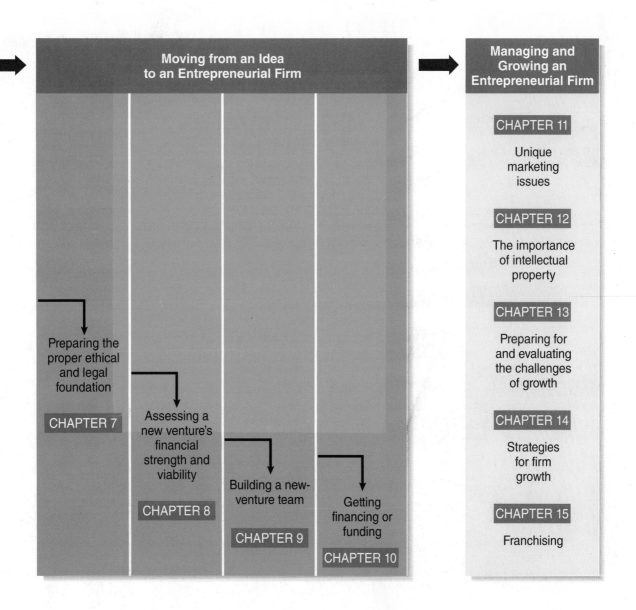

Moving from an Idea to an Entrepreneurial Firm

Preparing the proper ethical and legal foundation

CHAPTER 7

Assessing a new venture's financial strength and viability

CHAPTER 8

Building a new-venture team

CHAPTER 9

Getting financing or funding

CHAPTER 10

Managing and Growing an Entrepreneurial Firm

CHAPTER 11

Unique marketing issues

CHAPTER 12

The importance of intellectual property

CHAPTER 13

Preparing for and evaluating the challenges of growth

CHAPTER 14

Strategies for firm growth

CHAPTER 15

Franchising

Where a great idea meets a great process

University
Library

Entrepreneurship

SUCCESSFULLY LAUNCHING NEW VENTURES

FIFTH EDITION

GLOBAL EDITION

Bruce R. Barringer
Oklahoma State University

R. Duane Ireland
Texas A & M University

PEARSON

Boston Columbus Indianapolis New York San Francisco Amsterdam Cape Town
Dubai London Madrid Milan Munich Paris Montréal Toronto
Delhi Mexico City São Paulo Sydney Hong Kong Seoul Singapore Taipei Tokyo

Vice President, Business Publishing: Donna Battista
Editor in Chief: Stephanie Wall
Acquisitions Editor: Daniel Tylman
Program Management Lead: Ashley Santora
Program Manager: Claudia Fernandes
Editorial Assistant: Linda Albelli
Senior Acquisitions Editor, Global Editions: Steven Jackson
Project Editor, Global Editions: Suchismita Ukil
Editorial Assistant, Global Editions: Alice Dazeley
Vice President, Product Marketing: Maggie Moylan
Director of Marketing, Digital Services and Products: Jeanette Koskinas
Executive Product Marketing Manager: Anne Fahlgren
Field Marketing Manager: Lenny Ann Raper
Senior Strategic Marketing Manager: Erin Gardner

Project Management Lead: Judy Leale
Project Manager: Ann Pulido
Media Production Manager, Global Editions: M. Vikram Kumar
Senior Production Controller, Global Editions: Trudy Kimber
Procurement Specialist: Diane Peirano
VP, Director of Digital Strategy & Assessment: Paul Gentile
Manager of Learning Applications: Paul Deluca
Digital Editor: Brian Surette
Digital Studio Manager: Diane Lombardo
Digital Studio Project Manager: Robin Lazrus
Digital Studio Project Manager: Alana Coles
Digital Studio Project Manager: Monique Lawrence
Digital Studio Project Manager: Regina DaSilva
Text Designer: Integra-Chicago
Cover Image: © Anna-Mari West/Shutterstock
Full-Service Project Management: Alverne Ball/Integra-Chicago

Pearson Education Limited
Edinburgh Gate
Harlow
Essex CM20 2JE
England

and Associated Companies throughout the world

Visit us on the World Wide Web at:
www.pearsonglobaleditions.com

© Pearson Education Limited 2016

ISBN 10: 1-292-09537-7
ISBN 13: 978-1-292-09537-0

British Library Cataloguing-in-Publication Data
A catalogue record for this book is available from the British Library

10 9 8 7 6 5 4
19 18 17

Typeset in 10/12 ITC Bookman Std by Integra Software Services

Printed in Malaysia (CTP-VVP)

Dedication

To my wife, Jan. Thanks for your never-ending encouragement and support. Without you, this book would have never been possible. Also, thanks to all the student entrepreneurs who contributed to the chapter opening features in the book. Your stories are both insightful and inspiring.

—*Bruce R. Barringer*

To my family: I am so proud of each of you and so blessed by your perseverance and never-ending love and support. I know that sometimes it seems as though "we lose ourselves in work to do and bills to pay and that it's a ride, ride, ride without much cover." But you are always in my heart, a gift for which I remain deeply grateful.

—*R. Duane Ireland*

Brief Contents

Preface   13

PART 1   **Decision to Become an Entrepreneur   23**

CHAPTER 1   **Introduction to** *Entrepreneurship*   **25**

PART 2   **Developing Successful Business Ideas   61**

CHAPTER 2   **Recognizing** *Opportunities* **and Generating Ideas   63**
CHAPTER 3   **Feasibility** *Analysis*   **97**
CHAPTER 4   **Developing an** *Effective* **Business Model   133**
CHAPTER 5   **Industry and Competitor** *Analysis*   **171**
CHAPTER 6   **Writing a** *Business* **Plan   203**

PART 3   **Moving from an Idea to an Entrepreneurial Firm   239**

CHAPTER 7   **Preparing the Proper** *Ethical and Legal* **Foundation   241**
CHAPTER 8   **Assessing a New Venture's** *Financial Strength* **and Viability   281**
CHAPTER 9   **Building a** *New-Venture* **Team   317**
CHAPTER 10   **Getting** *Financing* **or Funding   349**

PART 4   **Managing and Growing an Entrepreneurial Firm   385**

CHAPTER 11   **Unique** *Marketing* **Issues   387**
CHAPTER 12   **The Importance of** *Intellectual* **Property   425**
CHAPTER 13   **Preparing for and** *Evaluating* **the Challenges of Growth   463**
CHAPTER 14   **Strategies for** *Firm Growth*   **495**
CHAPTER 15   **Franchising   529**

Glossary   570
Name Index   580
Company Index   582
Subject Index   586

Contents

Preface   13

PART 1   **Decision to Become an Entrepreneur   23**

CHAPTER 1   **Introduction to Entrepreneurship   25**

Opening Profile—SUPERJAM: The Classic Entrepreneurial Story   25

Introduction to Entrepreneurship   27

What Is Entrepreneurship and Why Is It Important?   28

Why Do People Become Entrepreneurs?   29

Be Their Own Boss   29

Pursue Their Own Ideas   30

Pursue Financial Rewards   30

Characteristics of Successful Entrepreneurs   31

Passion for the Business   31

WHAT WENT WRONG? Prim: How a Lack of Passion and Resolve Can Kill a Business   33

Product/Customer Focus   34

Tenacity Despite Failure   34

Execution Intelligence   35

SAVVY ENTREPRENEURIAL FIRM: Pandora: What's Possible When an Entire Company Has "Tenacity"   36

Common Myths About Entrepreneurs   36

Myth 1: Entrepreneurs Are Born, Not Made   37

Myth 2: Entrepreneurs Are Gamblers   37

Myth 3: Entrepreneurs Are Motivated Primarily by Money   38

Myth 4: Entrepreneurs Should Be Young and Energetic   39

Myth 5: Entrepreneurs Love the Spotlight   39

Types of Start-Up Firms   40

PARTNERING FOR SUCCESS: Start-up Incubators and Accelerators: A New Way of Gaining Access to Mentors, Partners, Investors, and Other Critical Start-up Resources   41

Changing Demographics of Entrepreneurs   42

Women Entrepreneurs   42

Minority Entrepreneurs   43

Senior Entrepreneurs   43

Young Entrepreneurs   43

The Positive Effects of Entrepreneurship and Entrepreneurial Firms   44

Economic Impact of Entrepreneurial Firms   44

Entrepreneurial Firms' Impact on Society   46

Entrepreneurial Firms' Impact on Larger Firms   46

The Entrepreneurial Process   47

Decision to Become an Entrepreneur (Chapter 1)   47

Developing Successful Business Ideas (Chapters 2–6)   47

Moving from an Idea to an Entrepreneurial Firm (Chapters 7–10)   48

Managing and Growing an Entrepreneurial Firm (Chapters 11–15)   48

Chapter Summary   50 | Key Terms   51
Review Questions   51 | Application Questions   52
You Be the VC 1.1   53 | You Be the VC 1.2   53
CASE 1.1   54 | CASE 1.2   57
Endnotes   59

PART 2   **Developing Successful Business Ideas   61**

CHAPTER 2   **Recognizing Opportunities and Generating Ideas   63**

Opening Profile—ICRACKED: Solving a Problem and Building a Business in an Exploding Industry   63

The Differences Between Opportunities and Ideas   65

Three Ways to Identify Opportunities   66

Observing Trends   66

SAVVY ENTREPRENEURIAL FIRM: How to Learn About Emerging Trends Through the Effective Use of Social Media   72

Solving a Problem   72

Finding Gaps in the Marketplace   75

Personal Characteristics of the Entrepreneur   76

WHAT WENT WRONG? Why a Company that Solved a Problem With a Great Product Went Out of Business   77

Prior Experience   78

Cognitive Factors   78

Social Networks   79

Creativity   79

Techniques for Generating Ideas   81

Brainstorming   81

Focus Groups   82

Library and Internet Research   83

Other Techniques   84

Encouraging the Development of New Ideas   84

   Establishing a Focal Point for Ideas   84

   Encouraging Creativity at the Firm Level   84

   PARTNERING FOR SUCCESS: Want Help Fine-Tuning a Business Idea? Find a Mentor   85

Chapter Summary   86 | Key Terms   87
Review Questions   87 | Application Questions   88
You Be the VC 2.1   89 | You Be the VC 2.2   89
CASE 2.1   90 | CASE 2.2   92

Endnotes   94

CHAPTER 3   **Feasibility *Analysis*   97**

Opening Profile—LUMINAID: The Value of Validating a Business Idea   97

Feasibility Analysis   99

Product/Service Feasibility Analysis   100

   Product/Service Desirability   100

   Product/Service Demand   105

Industry/Target Market Feasibility Analysis   107

   SAVVY ENTREPRENEURIAL FIRM: How Learning from Customers Caused a Successful Firm to Make a 180-Degree Turn on the Positioning of a Product   108

   Industry Attractiveness   109

   Target Market Attractiveness   110

Organizational Feasibility Analysis   111

   Management Prowess   111

   Resource Sufficiency   111

   WHAT WENT WRONG? How Feasible Was Standout Jobs from the Beginning?   112

   PARTNERING FOR SUCCESS: Finding the Right Business Partner   113

Financial Feasibility Analysis   114

   Total Start-Up Cash Needed   114

   Financial Performance of Similar Businesses   115

   Overall Financial Attractiveness of the Proposed Venture   116

A Feasibility Analysis Template   116

Chapter Summary   117 | Key Terms   118
Review Questions   119 | Application Questions   119
You Be the VC 3.1   121 | You Be the VC 3.2   121
CASE 3.1   122 | CASE 3.2   124

Appendix 3.1   127

Appendix 3.2   129

Endnotes   131

CHAPTER 4   **Developing an *Effective* Business Model   133**

Opening Profile—HER CAMPUS MEDIA: Executing on an Established Business Model and Preparing for the Future   133

Business Models and Their Importance   135

SAVVY ENTREPRENEURIAL FIRM: Quirky: How One Company Creates, Delivers, and Captures Value for Its Stakeholders   136

General Categories of Business Models   137

   Standard Business Models   137

   WHAT WENT WRONG? Peer-to-Peer Business Models: Good for Some, Not So Good for Others   139

   Disruptive Business Models   140

The Barringer/Ireland Business Model Template   141

   Core Strategy   142

   Resources   146

   Financials   148

   Operations   151

   PARTNERING FOR SUCCESS: Odesk, Elance, and Guru: Platforms That Facilitate the Forming of Partnerships with Freelancers   154

Chapter Summary   155 | Key Terms   156
Review Questions   156 | Application Questions   157
You Be the VC 4.1   158 | You Be the VC 4.2   158
CASE 4.1   159 | CASE 4.2   163

Appendix 1   167

Endnotes   168

CHAPTER 5   **Industry and Competitor *Analysis*   171**

Opening Profile—GREENVELOPE: Occupying a Unique Position in an Evolving Industry—and Thriving   171

Industry Analysis   173

   Studying Industry Trends   174

   PARTNERING FOR SUCCESS: Three Ts That Are Important for Becoming Active in an Industry: Trade Associations, Trade Shows, and Trade Journals   175

The Five Forces Model   176

   Threat of Substitutes   177

   Threat of New Entrants   178

   Rivalry Among Existing Firms   179

   Bargaining Power of Suppliers   180

   Bargaining Power of Buyers   181

The Value of the Five Forces Model   182

Industry Types and the Opportunities They Offer   184

   Emerging Industries   185

   Fragmented Industries   185

   Mature Industries   185

   Declining Industries   186

   Global Industries   187

Competitor Analysis   187

   Identifying Competitors   187

   Sources of Competitive Intelligence   188

SAVVY ENTREPRENEURIAL FIRM: Thriving in a Crowded Industry by Creating Meaningful Value and Differentiation from Competitors 189

Completing a Competitive Analysis Grid 190

WHAT WENT WRONG? Digg: A Start-up That Lost Its Way and Its Place in Its Industry 192

Chapter Summary 193 | Key Terms 194
Review Questions 194 | Application Questions 195
You Be the VC 5.1 196 | You Be the VC 5.2 196
CASE 5.1 197 | CASE 5.2 199

Endnotes 201

CHAPTER 6 **Writing a *Business* Plan 203**

Opening Profile—TEMPORUN: Proceeding on the Strength of a Winning Business Plan 203

The Business Plan 205

Reasons for Writing a Business Plan 205

Who Reads the Business Plan—and What Are They Looking for? 207

A Firm's Employees 207

Investors and Other External Stakeholders 207

Guidelines for Writing a Business Plan 208

Structure of the Business Plan 208

Content of the Business Plan 209

Outline of the Business Plan 211

Exploring Each Section of the Plan 212

SAVVY ENTREPRENEURIAL FIRM: Know When to Hold Them, Know When to Fold Them 213

PARTNERING FOR SUCCESS: Types of Partnerships That Are Common in Business Plans 217

WHAT WENT WRONG? What EventVue Learned the Hard Way About Making Assumptions 224

Presenting the Business Plan to Investors 225

The Oral Presentation of a Business Plan 225

Questions and Feedback to Expect from Investors 227

Chapter Summary 227 | Key Terms 228
Review Questions 228 | Application Questions 229
You Be the VC 6.1 231 | You Be the VC 6.2 231
CASE 6.1 232 | CASE 6.2 234

Endnotes 238

PART 3 Moving from an Idea to an Entrepreneurial Firm 239

CHAPTER 7 **Preparing the Proper *Ethical and Legal* Foundation 241**

Opening Profile—TEMPERED MIND: Proceeding on a Firm Legal Foundation 241

Establishing a Strong Ethical Culture for a Firm 243

Lead by Example 244

Establish a Code of Conduct 245

Implement an Ethics Training Program 246

Dealing Effectively with Legal Issues 247

Choosing an Attorney for a Firm 247

WHAT WENT WRONG? Fitbit Force Recall: Did Fitbit React Quickly Enough? 248

Drafting a Founders' Agreement 250

Avoiding Legal Disputes 250

SAVVY ENTREPRENEURIAL FIRM: Vesting Ownership in Company Stock: A Sound Strategy for Start-Ups 251

PARTNERING FOR SUCCESS: Patagonia and Build-A-Bear Workshop: Picking Trustworthy Partners 254

Obtaining Business Licenses and Permits 255

Federal Licenses and Permits 255

State Licenses and Permits 255

Local Licenses and Permits 256

Choosing a Form of Business Organization 257

Sole Proprietorship 258

Partnerships 260

Corporations 261

Limited Liability Company 264

Chapter Summary 265 | Key Terms 266
Review Questions 266 | Application Questions 267
You Be the VC 7.1 269 | You Be the VC 7.2 269
CASE 7.1 270 | CASE 7.2 273

Appendix 7.1 276

Endnotes 278

CHAPTER 8 **Assessing a New Venture's *Financial Strength* and Viability 281**

Opening Profile—GYMFLOW: Managing Finances Prudently 281

Introduction to Financial Management 283

Financial Objectives of a Firm 284

The Process of Financial Management 284

PARTNERING FOR SUCCESS: Organizing Buying Groups to Cuts Costs and Maintain Competitiveness 285

Financial Statements 287

Historical Financial Statements 287

SAVVY ENTREPRENEURIAL FIRM: Know the Facts Behind the Numbers 290

Forecasts 295

Sales Forecast 295

Forecast of Costs of Sales and Other Items 297

Pro Forma Financial Statements 299

Pro Forma Income Statement 300

WHAT WENT WRONG? Be Careful What You Wish For: How Growing Too Quickly Overwhelmed One Company's Cash Flow 301

Pro Forma Balance Sheet 301

Pro Forma Statement of Cash Flows 302

Ratio Analysis 305

Chapter Summary 306 | Key Terms 307
Review Questions 307 | Application Questions 308
You Be the VC 8.1 309 | You Be the VC 8.2 309
CASE 8.1 310 | CASE 8.2 312

Endnotes 314

CHAPTER 9 **Building a *New-Venture* Team 317**

Opening Profile—NEXT BIG SOUND: Hitting the Ground Running 317

Liability of Newness as a Challenge 319

Creating a New-Venture Team 319

PARTNERING FOR SUCCESS: **To Overcome the Liabilities of Newness, Consider Joining a Start-up Accelerator 320**

The Founder or Founders 321

WHAT WENT WRONG? **Devver: How Miscues in Regard to the Composition and Management of a New-Venture Team Can Kill a Start-up 324**

The Management Team and Key Employees 325

SAVVY ENTREPRENEURIAL FIRM: **Overcoming a Lack of Business Experience 326**

The Roles of the Board of Directors 329

Rounding Out the Team: The Role of Professional Advisers 332

Board of Advisors 332

Lenders and Investors 333

Other Professionals 335

Consultants 335

Chapter Summary 336 | Key Terms 337
Review Questions 337 | Application Questions 337
You Be the VC 9.1 339 | You Be the VC 9.2 339
CASE 9.1 340 | CASE 9.2 343

Endnotes 346

CHAPTER 10 **Getting *Financing* or Funding 349**

Opening Profile—ROOMINATE: Raising Money Carefully and Deliberately 349

The Importance of Getting Financing or Funding 351

Why Most New Ventures Need Funding 351

Cash Flow Challenges 351

Capital Investments 352

Lengthy Product Development Cycles 352

PARTNERING FOR SUCCESS: **Startup Weekend: A Fertile Place to Meet Business Cofounders 353**

Sources of Personal Financing 354

Personal Funds 354

Friends and Family 354

Bootstrapping 355

Preparing to Raise Debt or Equity Financing 356

Sources of Equity Funding 359

Business Angels 359

Venture Capital 360

Initial Public Offering 362

WHAT WENT WRONG? **How One Start-up Caught the Attention of VCs, Gained 25,000 Daily Users, and Still Failed 363**

Sources of Debt Financing 365

Commercial Banks 365

SBA Guaranteed Loans 366

Other Sources of Debt Financing 367

Creative Sources of Financing and Funding 367

Crowdfunding 367

Leasing 368

SBIR and STTR Grant Programs 369

Other Grant Programs 370

SAVVY ENTREPRENEURIAL FIRM: **Working Together: How Biotech Firms and Large Drug Companies Bring Pharmaceutical Products to Market 371**

Strategic Partners 371

Chapter Summary 372 | Key Terms 373
Review Questions 373 | Application Questions 374
You Be the VC 10.1 376 | You Be the VC 10.2 376
CASE 10.1 377 | CASE 10.2 380

Endnotes 383

PART 4 Managing and Growing an Entrepreneurial Firm 385

CHAPTER 11 **Unique *Marketing* Issues 387**

Opening Profile—WINK NATURAL COSMETICS: Creating a New Brand in the Cosmetics Industry 387

Selecting a Market and Establishing a Position 389

Segmenting the Market 389

Selecting a Target Market 390

Crafting a Unique Market Position 391

Branding 392

The 4Ps of Marketing for New Ventures 395

Product 395

PARTNERING FOR SUCCESS: **How Co-Branding Is Combining the Strengths of Two Already Successful Brands 396**

Price 398

Promotion 399

WHAT WENT WRONG? **What Start-ups Can Learn About Marketing from Missteps at JCPenney 400**

SAVVY ENTREPRENEURIAL FIRM: How Airbnb Used Blogs as a Stepping-Stone to Generate Substantial Buzz About Its Service 405

Place (or Distribution) 408

Sales Process and Related Issues 409

Chapter Summary 412 | Key Terms 413
Review Questions 413 | Application Questions 414
You Be the VC 11.1 415 | You Be the VC 11.2 415
CASE 11.1 416 | CASE 11.2 419

Endnotes 422

CHAPTER 12 **The Importance of Intellectual Property 425**

Opening Profile—DRIPCATCH: The Key Role of Intellectual Property Early In a Firm's Life and Its Ongoing Success 425

The Importance of Intellectual Property 427

Determining What Intellectual Property to Legally Protect 429

The Four Key Forms of Intellectual Property 429

Patents 430

Types of Patents 432

Who Can Apply for a Patent? 433

The Process of Obtaining a Patent 434

Patent Infringement 436

Trademarks 436

SAVVY ENTREPRENEURIAL FIRM: Knowing the Ins and Outs of Filing a Provisional Patent Application 437

The Four Types of Trademarks 438

PARTNERING FOR SUCCESS: Individual Inventors and Large Firms: Partnering to Bring New Products to Market 439

What Is Protected Under Trademark Law? 440

Exclusions from Trademark Protection 441

The Process of Obtaining a Trademark 441

Copyrights 443

What Is Protected by a Copyright? 443

Exclusions from Copyright Protection 444

How to Obtain a Copyright 444

Copyright Infringement 445

Copyright and the Internet 446

WHAT WENT WRONG? GoldieBlox vs. Beastie Boys: The Type of Fight That No Start-up Wants to Be a Part Of 447

Trade Secrets 448

What Qualifies for Trade Secret Protection? 449

Trade Secret Disputes 449

Trade Secret Protection Methods 450

Conducting an Intellectual Property Audit 451

Why Conduct an Intellectual Property Audit? 451

The Process of Conducting an Intellectual Property Audit 451

Chapter Summary 452 | Key Terms 454
Review Questions 454 | Application Questions 455
You Be the VC 12.1 456 | You Be the VC 12.2 456
CASE 12.1 457 | CASE 12.2 459

Endnotes 460

CHAPTER 13 **Preparing for and Evaluating the Challenges of Growth 463**

Opening Profile—BIG FISH PRESENTATIONS: Growing in a Cautious, Yet Deliberate Manner 463

Preparing for Growth 465

Appreciating the Nature of Business Growth 465

Staying Committed to a Core Strategy 467

PARTNERING FOR SUCCESS: How Threadless Averted Collapse by Bringing on a Partner with Back-End Operational Expertise 468

Planning for Growth 469

Reasons for Growth 470

Capturing Economies of Scale 471

Capturing Economies of Scope 471

Market Leadership 471

Influence, Power, and Survivability 471

Need to Accommodate the Growth of Key Customers 472

Ability to Attract and Retain Talented Employees 472

Managing Growth 472

Knowing and Managing the Stages of Growth 473

SAVVY ENTREPRENEURIAL FIRM: Safesforce.com Crosses the Chasm 476

Challenges of Growth 477

Managerial Capacity 477

Day-to-Day Challenges of Growing a Firm 478

WHAT WENT WRONG? How Trying to Build Out Its Own Capabilities in a Key Area Contributed to the Failure of a Promising Firm 480

Chapter Summary 481 | Key Terms 482
Review Questions 483 | Application Questions 483
You Be the VC 13.1 485 | You Be the VC 13.2 485
CASE 13.1 486 | CASE 13.2 489

Endnotes 492

CHAPTER 14 **Strategies for Firm Growth 495**

Opening Profile—SHAKE SMART: Maintaining Consistent Strategies for Growth 495

Internal Growth Strategies 497

New Product Development 497

SAVVY ENTREPRENEURIAL FIRM: SwitchFlops: How to Create Built-in Avenues for Future Growth 499

Additional Internal Product-Growth
Strategies   501

Improving an Existing Product or Service   501

Increasing the Market Penetration of an Existing Product
or Service   501

Extending Product Lines   502

Geographic Expansion   502

International Expansion   503

WHAT WENT WRONG? Lessons for Growth-Minded
Start-ups from Crumbs Bake Shop's Failure   504

Assessing a Firm's Suitability for Growth Through
International Markets   505

Foreign Market Entry Strategies   506

Selling Overseas   506

External Growth Strategies   507

Mergers and Acquisitions   507

Licensing   511

Strategic Alliances and Joint Ventures   512

PARTNERING FOR SUCCESS: Three Steps to Alliance
Success   514

Chapter Summary   516 | Key Terms   517
Review Questions   517 | Application Questions   518
You Be the VC 14.1   520 | You Be the VC 14.2   520
CASE 14.1   521 | CASE 14.2   524

Endnotes   526

CHAPTER 15   **Franchising   529**

Opening Profile—UPTOWN CHEAPSKATE: Franchising
as a Form of Business Ownership and Growth   529

What Is Franchising and How Does
It Work?   532

What Is Franchising?   532

How Does Franchising Work?   532

Establishing a Franchise System   535

When to Franchise   536

Steps to Franchising a Business   536

SAVVY ENTREPRENEURIAL FIRM: Wahoo's Fish
Taco: A Moderate-Growth Yet Highly Successful
Franchise Organization   537

Selecting and Developing Effective Franchisees   539

Advantages and Disadvantages of Establishing a
Franchise System   540

Buying a Franchise   542

Is Franchising Right for You?   542

WHAT WENT WRONG? Trouble at Curves
International   543

The Cost of a Franchise   545

Finding a Franchise   546

PARTNERING FOR SUCCESS: Using Co-Branding to
Reduce Costs and Boost Sales   547

Advantages and Disadvantages of Buying a
Franchise   548

Steps in Purchasing a Franchise   550

Watch Out! Common Misconceptions About
Franchising   551

Legal Aspects of the Franchise Relationship   552

Federal Rules and Regulations   552

State Rules and Regulations   553

More About Franchising   555

Franchise Ethics   555

International Franchising   556

The Future of Franchising   557

Chapter Summary   558 | Key Terms   559
Review Questions   559 | Application Questions   560
You Be the VC 15.1   562 | You Be the VC 15.2   562
CASE 15.1   563 | CASE 15.2   565

Endnotes   568

Glossary   570

Name Index   580

Company Index   582

Subject Index   586

Preface

What Is New to This Edition?

This fifth edition is a thorough revision of our book. Each chapter was revised to reflect examples of current entrepreneurial firms and the latest thinking about entrepreneurship from academic journals and practitioner publications. Specifically, the following is new to the fifth edition.

Opening Profile   Each chapter begins with a profile of an entrepreneurial firm that was started while the founders were in college. A total of 14 of the 15 Opening Profiles (one for each chapter) are new to this edition. Each profile is specific to the chapter's topic. The profiles are based on personal interviews with the student entrepreneurs involved.

Updated Boxed Features   The majority of the "What Went Wrong?" "Savvy Entrepreneurial Firm," and "Partnering for Success" features are new to this edition. These features not only alert students and readers to contemporary issues facing entrepreneurial firms, but are meant to be helpful to them in a practical sense as well. Select features focus on topics such as how to find a mentor, how to select a business co-founder, and how to avoid the types of mistakes that typify unsuccessful entrepreneurial ventures. The two "You Be the VC" features at the end of each chapter have been a staple of the book since its inception. A total of 25 of the 30 "You be the VC" features in the fifth edition are new.

Barringer/Ireland Business Model Template   One of the strongest additions to the fifth edition is the inclusion and thorough explanation of the Barringer/Ireland Business Model Template. We introduce this template to you in Chapter 4. It provides a nicely designed way for students to think through and articulate the business model for a proposed or existing firm. The template, which is similar in its intent and usefulness to the popular Business Model Canvas created by Alexander Osterwalder and Yves Pigneur, contains four sections and 11 parts. Chapter 4 fully explains each section and part. An enlarged version of the template is included in the Appendix to Chapter 4. It can be photocopied and used to assist students in completing business models for proposed or existing firms.

New and Updated Cases   The majority of end-of-chapter cases are new to this edition. Those that were retained have been completely updated. The cases were carefully selected to illustrate the principles introduced in their respective chapters. The questions included at the end of each case can be used to stimulate classroom discussion or for quizzes or tests.

Updated References   The amount of academic research examining entrepreneurship-related topics continues to grow. To provide the most recent insights from academic journals, we draw upon recent research from journals such as *Strategic Entrepreneurship Journal*, *Entrepreneurship Theory and Practice*, *Journal of Business Venturing*, and *Academy of Management Journal*. Similarly, we relied on the most current articles appearing in business publications such as *The Wall Street Journal* and *Entrepreneur* among others, to present you with examples of the actions being taken by today's entrepreneurs as they lead their ventures.

Introduction to Entrepreneurship

There is tremendous interest in entrepreneurship on college campuses and around the world. One indicator of this interest is the fact that of the approximately 2,000 colleges and universities in the United States, about two-thirds of the total now offer a course in entrepreneurship. As a result, a growing number of students are forgoing traditional careers and starting their own businesses. Ordinary people across the world are equally interested in launching entrepreneurial careers. According to the 2013 Global Entrepreneurship Monitor, in the United States a total of 12.7 percent of the adult population is starting a business or has started a business in the past three-and-a-half years. There are regions of the world where the percentage is even higher. In Brazil, for example, 17.3 percent of the adult population is starting or has started a business in the past three-and-a-half years. The percentage is 24.3 percent in Chile.

The lure of entrepreneurship is the ability to create products and services that enhance people's lives. You'll see this through the many examples of entrepreneurial firms provided in the book. Particularly inspiring are the examples of businesses started while the founders were still in college. We begin each chapter of this book with a profile of a business that was founded while the founders were still in college. Several of the end-of-chapter cases are focused on student-founded businesses as well. The opening profile for Chapter 3, for example, focuses on LuminAid, a business started by Andrea Sreshta and Anna Stork, two students at Columbia University. The three children pictured on the front page of Part I are looking at what Sreshta and Stork created—solar powered pillows that provide light for people in disaster relief situations. What we hope to accomplish via the profiles and cases about businesses that were started while their founders were still in college is to inspire the students who are using the book. Hopefully they'll look at students like Sreshta and Stork and realize that they aren't too different from them, and that they have the capacity to conceive a business idea and launch a successful company too.

Many of the examples of student-inspired businesses provided in the book are both instructive and heartwarming. For example, Case 3.2 focuses on a company named Embrace, which was started by four Stanford University students. Embrace makes a product, called the Embrace Baby Warmer, which literally saves the lives of premature babies born in remote villages in developing countries. It looks like a small sleeping bag and contains a warming element that when turned on emulates the heat provided by a more sophisticated incubator in a hospital. No one can read the case without being inspired and somewhat awed by what a motivated group of college students, surrounded by a supportive university and dedicated faculty and mentors, were able to accomplish when they set their sights on becoming entrepreneurs. A photo of the Embrace Baby Warmer is provided in the case. We invite you to go to Case 3.2 now to glance at the Embrace Baby Warmer.

There is one caveat to successful entrepreneurship, and it's a big one. People, regardless of age, need a process to follow to successfully navigate the entrepreneurial journey. This is where our book offers unique value. The book describes entrepreneurship as a four step process, beginning with the decision to become an entrepreneur and culminating with managing and growing a successful firm. There is a lot in between, as you'll see. Entrepreneurship is not easy, which is a sentiment that we express throughout the book. But it is doable, as evidenced by the many success stories provided. The process, pictured nearby, provides a framework or roadmap of the entrepreneurial process that many professors, students, and others that have used the book have told us has been particularly helpful to them. In the book, we're also careful to talk about failures as well as successes. Each chapter includes a boxed feature titled "What Went Wrong?" The feature contains a real-life example of something that went wrong with an entrepreneurial firm. Professors have commented to us that they appreciate having failure stories as well as success stories as teaching tools in their classrooms. At the other extreme, each chapter also includes a boxed feature called "Savvy Entrepreneurial Firm." In these features, we describe actions entrepreneurial firms have taken that contributed to their success. Complementing these features is a third one that is presented in each chapter. Called "Partnering for Success," these features discuss relationships entrepreneurial firms form with various parties (such as suppliers and distributors) in order to increase the likelihood of being successful.

We sincerely hope that college and university students and their professors as well as others who choose to read this book will find it thoughtful, instructive, helpful, and inspiring. Our goal is to place into your hands—our readers— a book with the ability to both inspire and lead you through the steps in the entrepreneurial process.

How Is This Book Organized?

As mentioned above, the book is organized around the entrepreneurial process. The four parts of the entrepreneurial process are as follows:

Part 1: Decision to Become an Entrepreneur

Part 2: Developing Successful Business Ideas

Part 3: Moving from an Idea to an Entrepreneurial Firm

Part 4: Managing and Growing an Entrepreneurial Firm

The book mirrors this process. It is laid out in four parts and 15 chapters. The nearby figure depicts the parts of the process and the chapters that are included in each part.

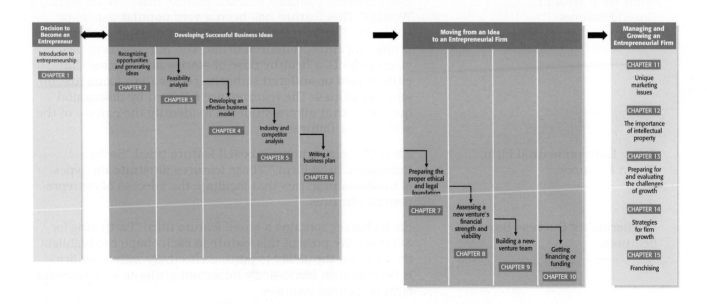

What Are the Unique Aspects of the Book?

While using the book, we think you'll find several unique features to be particularly helpful. The following table lays out the most unique features of the book followed by an explanation.

Unique Feature of the Book	Explanation
Focus on opportunity recognition, feasibility analysis, and the developing of an effective business model.	The book opens with strong chapters on the front end of the entrepreneurial process, including opportunity recognition, feasibility analysis, and the development of an effective business model. These are activities that must be completed early when investigating the merits of a business idea.
First Screen (template for completing feasibility analysis).	Chapter 3 (Appendix 3.1) provides a template for completing a feasibility analysis. The template can be copied and used to complete a feasibility analysis for a business idea.
Internet Resource Table.	Chapter 3 (Appendix 3.2) contains a table of Internet resources that can be used in completing a feasibility analysis and in other aspects of investigating the merits of a business idea.
Barringer/Ireland Business Model Template.	The Barringer/Ireland Business Model Template is a nicely designed template for helping students think through and articulate the business model for a proposed or existing firm. Each section of the template is fully explained in Chapter 4. The template can be easily copied and used by those wishing to develop a business model for an entrepreneurial venture.
Opening Profiles.	Each chapter starts with a profile of an entrepreneurial firm started while the founder of founders were still in college. Photos of the entrepreneurs and a Q&A format that allows readers to get to know a little about each of the student entrepreneurs personally are included. All 15 opening profiles are unique to the fifth edition.
What Went Wrong? Boxed Features.	Each chapter contains a boxed feature titled "What Went Wrong?" This feature has been a very popular aspect of the book. The features explain the missteps of seemingly promising entrepreneurial firms. The purpose is to provide students a healthy dose of stories about firms that either failed or suffered setbacks rather than focus just on success stories. The features are followed by discussion questions that allows students to identify the causes of the setbacks or failures.
Savvy Entrepreneurial Firm Boxed Features.	Each chapter contains a boxed feature titled "Savvy Entrepreneurial Firm." These features illustrate the types of business practices that facilitate the success of entrepreneurial ventures.
Partnering for Success Boxed Features.	Each chapter contains a boxed feature titled "Partnering for Success." We present this feature in each chapter to highlight the fact that the ability to partner effectively with other firms is becoming an increasingly important attribute for successful entrepreneurial ventures.

You Be the VC end of chapter features	Two features, titled "You be the VC," are provided at the end of each chapter. These features present a "pitch" for funding for an emerging entrepreneurial venture. The features are designed to stimulate classroom discussion by sparking debate on whether a particular venture should or shouldn't receive funding. All of the firms featured are real-life entrepreneurial ventures.
End of chapter cases	Two medium-length cases, written by the authors of the book, are featured at the end of each chapter. The cases are designed to stimulate classroom discussion and illustrate the issued discussed in the chapter.

Instructor Resources

At the Instructor Resource Center, www.pearsonglobaleditions.com/barringer, instructors can easily register to gain access to a variety of instructor resources available with this text in downloadable format. If assistance is needed, our dedicated technical support team is ready to help with the media supplements that accompany this text. Visit http://247.pearsoned.com for answers to frequently asked questions and toll-free user support phone numbers.

The following supplements are available with this text:

- **Instructor's Resource Manual**
- **Test Bank**
- **TestGen® Computerized Test Bank**
- **PowerPoint Presentation**
- **Image Library**

Feedback

If you have questions related to this book about entrepreneurship, please contact our customer service department online at http://247.pearsoned.com.

Acknowledgments

We are pleased to express our sincere appreciation to four groups of people for helping bring both editions of our book to life.

Pearson Education Professionals   A number of individuals at Pearson Education have worked with us conscientiously and have fully supported our efforts to create a book that will work for those both studying and teaching the entrepreneurial process. From Pearson Education, we want to extend our sincere appreciation to our Acquisitions Editor, Dan Tylman; our Senior Strategic Marketing Manager, Erin Gardner; and our Editorial Program Manager, Claudia Fernandes. Each individual provided us invaluable guidance and support, and we are grateful for their contribution.

Student Entrepreneurs   We want to extend a heartfelt "thank you" to the student entrepreneurs who contributed to the opening features in our book. Our conversations with these individuals were both informative and inspiring. We enjoyed getting to know these bright young entrepreneurs, and wish them nothing but total success as they continue to build their ventures.

Academic Reviewers   We want to thank our colleagues who participated in reviewing individual chapters of the book while they were being written. We gained keen insight from these individuals (each of whom teaches courses in entrepreneurship) and incorporated many of the suggestions of our reviewers into the final version of the book.

Thank you to these professors who participated in reviews:

Dr. Richard Bartlett, *Columbus State Community College*

Greg Berezewski, *Robert Morris College*

Jeff Brice, Jr., *Texas Southern University*

Ralph Jagodka, *Mt. San Antonio College*

Christina Roeder, *James Madison University*

Aron S. Spencer, *New Jersey Institute of Technology*

Vincent Weaver, *Greenville Technical College*

Lisa Zidek, *Florida Gulf Coast University*

Academic Colleagues   We thank this large group of professors whose thoughts about entrepreneurial education have helped shape our book's contents and presentation structure:

David C. Adams, *Manhattanville College*

Sol Ahiarah, *SUNY—Buffalo State College*

Frederic Aiello, *University of Southern Maine*

James J. Alling Sr., *Augusta Technical College*

Jeffrey Alstete, *Iona College*

Jeffrey Alves, *Wilkes University*

Joe Aniello, *Francis Marion University*

Mary Avery, *Ripon College*

Jay Azriel, *Illinois State University*

Richard Barker, *Upper Iowa University*

Jim Bell, *Texas State University*

Robert J. Berger, *SUNY Potsdam*

James Bloodgood, *Kansas State University*

Jenell Bramlage, *University of Northwestern Ohio*

Michael Brizek, *South Carolina State University*

Barb Brown, *Southwestern Community College*

James Burke, *Loyola University—Chicago*

Lowell Busenitz, *University of Oklahoma*

John Butler, *University of Texas—Austin*

Jane Byrd, *University of Mobile*

Art Camburn, *Buena Vista University*

Carol Carter, *Louisiana State University*

Gaylen Chandler, *Wichita State University*

James Chrisman, *Mississippi State University*

Delena Clark, *Plattsburgh State University*

Dee Cole, *Middle Tennessee State University*

Roy Cook, *Fort Lewis College*

Andrew Corbett, *Babson College*

Simone Cummings, *Washington University School of Medicine*

Suzanne D'Agnes, *Queensborough Community College*

Douglas Dayhoff, *Indiana University*

Frank Demmler, *Carnegie Mellon University*

David Desplaces, *University of Hartford/Barney*

Vern Disney, *University of South Carolina—Sumter*

Dale Eesley, *University of Toledo*

Alan Eisner, *Pace University*

Susan Everett, *Clark State Community College*

Henry Fernandez, *North Carolina Central University*

Charles Fishel, *San Jose State University*

Dana Fladhammer, *Phoenix College*

Brenda Flannery, *Minnesota State University*

John Friar, *Northeastern University*

Barbara Fuller, *Winthrop University*

Barry Gilmore, *University of Memphis*

Caroline Glackin, *Delaware State University*

Cheryl Gracie, *Washtenaw Community College*

Frederick Greene, *Manhattan College*

Lee Grubb, *East Carolina University*

Brad Handy, *Springfield Technical Community College*

Carnella Hardin, *Glendale College*

Ashley Harmon, *Southeastern Technical College*

Steve Harper, *University of North Carolina at Wilmington*

Alan Hauff, *University of Missouri—St. Louis*

Gordon Haym, *Lyndon State College*

Andrea Hershatter, *Emory University*

Richard Hilliard, *Nichols College*

Jo Hinton, *Copiah Lincoln Community College*

Dennis Hoagland, *LDS Business College*

Kathie Holland, *University of Central Florida*

Frank Hoy, *Worcester Polytechnic Institute*

Jeffrey Jackson, *Manhattanville College*

Grant Jacobsen, *Northern Virginia Community College–Woodbridge*

Susan Jensen, *University of Nebraska—Kearney*

Alec Johnson, *University of St. Thomas*

James M. Jones, *University of the Incarnate Word, ERAU, Del Mar College*

Jane Jones, *Mountain Empire Community College*

Joy Jones, *Ohio Valley College*

Tom Kaplan, *Fairleigh Dickinson University—Madison*

Elizabeth Kisenwether, *Penn State University*

James Klingler, *Villanova University*

Edward Kuljian, *Saint Joseph's University*

James Lang, *Virginia Tech University*

Allon Lefever, *Eastern Mennonite University*

Anita Leffel, *University of Texas—San Antonio*

Gary Levanti, *Polytechnic University—LI Campus*

Benjamin Lichtenstein, *University of Massachusetts, Boston*

Bruce Lynskey, *Vanderbilt University*

Janice Mabry, *Mississippi Gulf Coast Community College*

Jeffrey Martin, *University of Alabama*

Greg McCann, *Stetson University*

Elizabeth McCrea, *Pennsylvania State—Great Valley*

Brian McKenzie, *California State University—Hayward*

Chris McKinney, *Vanderbilt University*

Dale Meyer, *University of Colorado*

Steven C. Michael, *University of Illinois Urbana—Champaign*

Angela Mitchell, *Wilmington College*

Bryant Mitchell, *University of Maryland—Eastern Shore*

Rob Mitchell, *Western University—Canada*

Patrick Murphy, *DePaul University*

Charlie Nagelschmidt, *Champlain College*

William Naumes, *University of New Hampshire*

Connie Nichols, *Odessa College*

Gary Nothnagle, *Nazareth College*

Edward O'Brien, *Scottsdale Community College*

David Orozco, *Florida State University*

Haesun Park, *Louisiana State University*

John Pfaff, *University of the Pacific*

Joseph Picken, *University of Texas at Dallas*

Emmeline de Pillis, *University of Hawaii—Hilo*

Carol Reeves, *University of Arkansas*

John Richards, *Brigham Young University*

Christo Roberts, *University of Minnesota—Twin Cities*

George Roorbach, *Lyndon State College*

Michael Rubach, *University of Central Arkansas*

Janice Rustia, *University of Nebraska Medical Center*

James Saya, *The College of Santa Fe*

William Scheela, *Bemidji State University*

Gerry Scheffelmaier, *Middle Tennessee State University*

Gerald Segal, *Florida Gulf Coast University*

Cynthia Sheridan, *St. Edward's University*

Donald Shifter, *Fontbonne University*

C. L. J. Spencer, *Kapi'olani Community College*

Joseph Stasio, *Merrimack College*

Deborah Streeter, *Cornell University*

Dara Szyliowicz, *University of Denver*

Clint B. Tankersley, *Syracuse University*

Craig Tunwall, *Empire State College*

Barry Van Hook, *Arizona State University*

George Vozikis, *California State University—Fresno*

David Wilemon, *Syracuse University*

Charlene Williams, *Brewton Parker College*

Doug Wilson, *University of Oregon*

Diana Wong, *Eastern Michigan University*

Finally, we want to express our appreciation to our home institutions (Oklahoma State University and Texas A&M University) for creating environments in which ideas are encouraged and supported.

We wish each of you—our readers—all the best in your study of the entrepreneurial process. And, of course, we hope that each of you will be highly successful entrepreneurs as you pursue the ideas you'll develop at different points in your careers.

Pearson would like to thank and acknowledge the following people for their work on the Global Edition:

Contributor

Anushia Chelvarayan, *Multimedia University, Malaysia*

Reviewers

Evelyn Toh Bee Hwa, *Sunway University, Malaysia*

Hussin Jose Hejase, *American University of Science and Technology, Lebanon*

Man Tsun Jimmy Chang, *The Hong Kong Polytechnic University, Hong Kong*

Hamed Shamma, *The American University in Cairo, Egypt*

Robin Cheng, *Taylor's University, Malaysia*

About the Authors

Bruce R. Barringer Bruce R. Barringer is the Head of the School of Entrepreneurship at Oklahoma State University, and holds the N. Malone Mitchell Jr. Chair and the Student Ventures Chair. He earned his PhD from the University of Missouri and his MBA from Iowa State University. His research interests include feasibility analysis, firm growth, corporate entrepreneurship, and the impact of interorganizational relationships on business organizations. Over the years, he has worked with a number of technology-based incubators and student-led entrepreneurship activities and clubs.

Bruce's research has been published in *Strategic Management Journal, Journal of Management, Journal of Business Venturing, Journal of Small Business Management* and other academic outlets. He is the author or coauthor of five books, including Entrepreneurship Successfully Launching New Ventures, Preparing Effective Business Plans, Launching a Business: The First 100 Days, The Truth About Starting a Business, and What's Stopping You? Shatter the 9 Most Common Myths Keeping You From Starting a Business.

Bruce's outside interests include running, trail biking, and swimming.

R. Duane Ireland R. Duane Ireland is a University Distinguished Professor and holds the Conn Chair in New Ventures Leadership in the Mays Business School, Texas A&M University. Previously, he served on the faculties at University of Richmond, Baylor University, and Oklahoma State University. His research interests include strategic entrepreneurship, corporate entrepreneurship, strategic alliances, and effectively managing organizational resources.

Duane's research has been published in journals such as *Academy of Management Journal, Academy of Management Review, Academy of Management Executive, Strategic Management Journal, Administrative Science Quarterly, Journal of Management, Journal of Business Venturing, Entrepreneurship Theory and Practice*, and *Strategic Entrepreneurship Journal* among others. He is a coauthor of both scholarly books and textbooks, including best-selling strategic management texts. Along with Dr. Mike Morris (University of Florida), Duane serves as a co-editor for the Prentice Hall Entrepreneurship Series. These books offer in-depth treatments of specific entrepreneurship topics, such as *Business Plans for Entrepreneurs* (authored by Bruce Barringer).

Duane has served or is serving on the editorial review boards for a number of journals, including *AMJ, AMR, AME, JOM, JBV*, and *ETP*. He just completed a term as Editor for *AMJ*. He has completed terms as an associate editor for *AME* and as a consulting editor for *ETP* and has served as a guest co-editor for special issues of a number of journals including *AMR, AME*, and *SMJ*. He is a Fellow of the Academy of Management and a Fellow of the Strategic Management Society. He recently completed a term as the President of the Academy of Management.

Duane's outside interests include running, reading, listening to a variety of music, and playing with his grandson.

About the Authors

PART 1 Decision to Become an Entrepreneur

LuminAID Lab, LLC

CHAPTER 1 **Introduction to *Entrepreneurship* 25**

Getting Personal with SUPERJAM

Founder

FRASER DOHERTY

BS in Economics,
University of Wisconsin, 2009

AUSTIN STOFFERS

BS in Real Estate,
University of Wisconsin, 2011

JORDAN SCHAU

BS in Computer Science,
Columbia University, 2011

MICHAEL FISHMAN

BS in Real Estate,
University of Wisconsin, 2011

Dialogue with Fraser Doherty

BEST ADVICE I'VE RECEIVED
Go with your passion. Makes it so much easier! I love bikes, and it makes my job infinitely easier.

MY BIGGEST WORRY AS AN ENTREPRENEUR
That we're not innovating fast enough to keep ahead of the competition

WHAT I DO WHEN I'M NOT WORKING
Drive my 40-year-old VW camper van round the countryside!

MY FAVORITE SMARTPHONE APP
SuperJam's Recipe App

MY FIRST ENTREPRENEURIAL EXPERIENCE
Hatching chickens on top of the TV, age 10, and selling their eggs

FAVORITE PERSON I FOLLOW ON TWITTER
Has to be Stephen Fry.

Introduction to *Entrepreneurship*

OPENING PROFILE

SUPERJAM
The Classic Entrepreneurial Story

• Web: http://www.superjam.co.uk • Facebook: SuperJam 100% Fruit Spread • SuperJam's Recipe App

Growing up in Scotland, Fraser Doherty spent his childhood coming up with ideas for new products. Not all his money-making ideas were a success—indeed his fledgling egg-selling enterprise ended abruptly when a fox ate all his chickens—but he had a hunger to set up a business.

At the age of 14, Doherty gave jam-making a try. He had always enjoyed the jam his grandmother made and thought there might be an opportunity here. After making a batch and selling it door-to-door, he discovered people really liked it, and Doherty's jam enterprise gradually spread into local shops and farmers' markets. A feature in the *Edinburgh Evening News* brought in even more orders from further afield.

After resolving to expand the business, Doherty did some research and found that sales of jam had been in decline for the past few decades. Jam had acquired an old-fashioned image and people preferred healthier alternatives on their toast.

The solution the young Scottish entrepreneur came up with was a jam for the modern world. Doherty's SuperJam would be made using traditional recipes, completely from fruit juice. The jars would contain no sugar and no artificial flavorings. He also boldly resolved to target supermarkets to sell his products.

Fraser faced a number of challenges. At this point, he was making hundreds of jars of jam every week in his parents' kitchen. Apart from the fact his parents were struggling to get in there to cook their dinner, the business clearly couldn't grow any further.

At the age of 17, he was in no position to start a factory and he did not have any money to pay a design agency to create a brand either. He also did not have a clue how to approach supermarkets. In fact, all he had was a passion about his product and a great recipe.

The first supermarket Fraser approached was Waitrose on a "meet the buyer" day. Fraser pitched his idea to the senior jam buyer who liked it, but said it had a long way to go. He advised Fraser that he had to set up a production facility and create a brand before coming back with a well-priced product.

Fraser set off around the United Kingdom trying to convince food manufacturers to believe in his 100 percent fruit jam. He told them that he didn't have any money to

LEARNING OBJECTIVES

After studying this chapter you should be ready to:

1. Describe entrepreneurship, corporate entrepreneurship, and the characteristics of entrepreneurial firms.

2. Discuss three main reasons people decide to become entrepreneurs.

3. Identify four main characteristics of successful entrepreneurs.

4. Explain five common myths regarding entrepreneurship.

5. Describe the three types of start-up firms.

6. Discuss the changing demographics of entrepreneurs in the United States.

7. Discuss the positive effects of entrepreneurship and entrepreneurial firms on economies and societies.

8. Explain the entrepreneurial process.

invest, but if they took the long-term view, then they too would reap the benefit. He did the same with a string of advertising agencies to persuade them to help him create a brand. Eventually, after two years of persistence, Doherty finally convinced a factory and an advertising agency to work with him.

SuperJam is exhibited in the National Museum of Scotland as an "Iconic Scottish Brand" alongside Irn-Bru and Tunnock's and Baxters, two other brands synonymous with Scotland. In 2010, Fraser shared his jam making secrets with the world in the SuperJam Cook, following this in 2011 with his autobiography and jam story, SuperBusiness. Since 2010, Fraser has been the entrepreneur-in-residence at the London Metropolitan University where he delivers presentations and lecturers on aspects of entrepreneurship.

Doherty has kept close to his customers throughout SuperJam's meteoric rise and is conscious of the part technology and, in particular, social networks play in his business and in retaining a meaningful conversation with his customers.

Against a backdrop of digital social networking, SuperJam Tea Parties are about as far removed from the virtual world as you could imagine. The company runs these events for elderly people who live alone, primarily in care homes or sheltered accommodation. To date, they have run over 125 events across the UK. The mix of live music, dancing, a heavy dose of scones, and SuperJam attract up to 600 people to each event.

From humble beginnings working at his kitchen table to grow his entrepreneurial venture, Fraser now supplies over 2,000 supermarkets around the world with SuperJam and has won a variety of awards for the range. Fraser has now scooped over 20 prestigious awards, including Bighearted Scotland Business Person of The Year (2009), Smarta 100 Award (2010), and Inc Magazine 30 under 30 Award (2010). He made the finals for "Times Young Power List" (2011), NatWest Enterprise Awards Finalist (2012) and Ben & Jerry's "Join our Core" Finalist (2012).[1]

I n this first chapter of your book about the successful launching of an entrepreneurial venture or firm, we define entrepreneurship and discuss why some people decide to become entrepreneurs. We then look at successful entrepreneurs' characteristics, the common myths surrounding entrepreneurship, the different types of start-up firms, and the changing demographics of entrepreneurs in the United States and in nations throughout the world. We then examine entrepreneurship's importance, including the economic and social impact of new firms as well as the importance of entrepreneurial firms to larger businesses. To close this chapter, we introduce you to the entrepreneurial process. This process, which we believe is the foundation for successfully launching a start-up firm, is the framework we use to present the book's materials to you.

Introduction to Entrepreneurship

There is tremendous interest in entrepreneurship around the world. Although this statement may seem bold, there is evidence supporting it, some of which is provided by the Global Entrepreneurship Monitor (GEM). GEM, which is a joint research effort by Babson College, London Business School, Universidad del Desarrollo (Santiago, Chile), and Universiti Tun Abdul Razak (Malaysia), tracks entrepreneurship in 70 countries, including the United States. Of particular interest to GEM is early stage entrepreneurial activity, which consists of businesses that are just being started and businesses that have been in existence for less than three and a half years. A sample of the rate of early-stage entrepreneurial activity in countries included in the GEM study is shown in Table 1.1. While the highest rates of entrepreneurial start-up activities occur in low-income countries, where good jobs are not plentiful, the rates are also impressive in high-income countries such as Germany (5.0 percent), United Kingdom (7.1 percent), and the United States (12.7 percent). What the 12.7 percent means for the United States is that almost 1 out of every 8 American adults is actively engaged in starting a business or is the owner/manager of a business that is less than three-and-a-half-years old.[2]

The GEM study also identifies whether its respondents are starting a new business to take advantage of an attractive opportunity or because of necessity to earn an income. The majority of people in high-income countries are drawn to entrepreneurship to take advantage of attractive opportunities. The reverse is true of people in low-income countries, who tend to be drawn to entrepreneurship primarily because of necessity (resulting from a lack of career prospects).[3]

One criticism of entrepreneurship, which is often repeated in the press, is that the majority of new businesses fail. It simply isn't true. The often used statistic that 9 out of 10 businesses fail in their first few years is an exaggeration. For example, evidence indicates that the three-year survival rates for entrepreneurial ventures established in Denmark is 53.5 percent, while it is up to 66.9 percent in other parts of Europe.[4] Historically, survival rates of entrepreneurial firms

TABLE 1.1   Rates of Early-Stage Entrepreneurial Activity (Ages 18 to 64)

Country	Percent of Population Starting a New Business
Argentina	15.9%
Brazil	17.3%
Chile	24.3%
China	14.0%
France	4.6%
Germany	5.0%
Nigeria	39.9%
Russia	5.8%
United Kingdom	7.1%
United States	12.7%

Source: Based on J. E. Amoros and N. Bosma, *Global Entrepreneurship Monitor 2013 Global Report* (Babson College, Universidad del Desarrollo, Universiti Tun Abdul Razak, and London Business School, 2013).

launched in the United States have been as high as 50 percent after four years. While overall these figures are heartening, the percentage of firms that do fail in Europe, the United States, and throughout the world shows that a motivation to start and run a business isn't enough; it must be coupled with a solid business idea, good financial management, and effective execution to maximize chances for success. In this book, we'll discuss many examples of entrepreneurial firms and the factors separating successful new ventures from unsuccessful ones.

Many people see entrepreneurship as an attractive career path. Think about your friends and others you know. In all probability, you are acquainted with at least one or two people who want to become an entrepreneur—either now or at some point in the future. The number of books dealing with starting one's own business is another indication entrepreneurship is growing in popularity. Amazon.com, for example, currently lists over 36,900 books and other items dealing with entrepreneurship and over 89,900 books concerned with small businesses. The number of books on small business is up from 62,700 just three years ago.

What Is Entrepreneurship and Why Is It Important?

LEARNING OBJECTIVE

1. Describe entrepreneurship, corporate entrepreneurship, and the characteristics of entrepreneurial firms.

The word *entrepreneur* derives from the French words *entre*, meaning "between," and *prendre*, meaning "to take." The word was originally used to describe people who "take on the risk" between buyers and sellers or who "undertake" a task such as starting a new venture.[5] Inventors and entrepreneurs differ from each other. An inventor creates something new. An entrepreneur assembles and then integrates all the resources needed—the money, the people, the business model, the strategy, and the risk-bearing ability—to transform the invention into a viable business.[6]

Entrepreneurship is defined as the process by which individuals pursue opportunities without regard to resources they currently control for the purpose of exploiting future goods and services.[7] Others, such as venture capitalist Fred Wilson, define it more simply, seeing entrepreneurship as the art of turning an idea into a business. In essence, an entrepreneur's behavior finds him or her trying to identify opportunities and putting useful ideas into practice.[8] The tasks called for by this behavior can be accomplished by either an individual or a group and typically require creativity, drive, and a willingness to take risks. Zach Schau, the cofounder of Pure Fix Cycles, exemplifies all these qualities. Zach saw an *opportunity* to create a new type of bicycle and a new type of bicycling experience for riders, he *risked* his career by passing up alternatives to work on Pure Fix Cycles full time, and he's now *working hard* to put Pure Fix Cycles in a position to deliver a *creative* and *useful* product to its customers.

In this book, we focus on entrepreneurship in the context of an entrepreneur or team of entrepreneurs launching a new business. However, ongoing firms can also behave entrepreneurially. Typically, established firms with an entrepreneurial emphasis are proactive, innovative, and risk-taking. For example, Google is widely recognized as a firm in which entrepreneurial behaviors are clearly evident. Larry Page, one of Google's cofounders, is at the heart of Google's entrepreneurial culture. With his ability to persuade and motivate others' imaginations, Page continues to inspire Google's employees as they develop innovative product after innovative product. To consider the penetration Google has with some of its innovations, think of how often you and people you know use the Google search engine, Gmail, Google Maps, or Google Earth. Google is currently working on a bevy of far-reaching innovations, such as Google Glasses and self-driving cars. Similarly, studying Facebook or Dropbox's ability to grow and succeed reveals a history of entrepreneurial behavior at multiple levels within the firms.[9] In addition, many of the firms traded on the NASDAQ, such as Amgen, Intuit, Apple, and Green Mountain Coffee Roasters, are commonly thought of as entrepreneurial firms. The NASDAQ is the largest U.S. electronic stock market, with nearly 5,000 companies listed on the exchange.

We want to note here that established firms with an orientation toward acting entrepreneurially practice **corporate entrepreneurship**.[10] All firms fall along a conceptual continuum that ranges from highly conservative to highly entrepreneurial. The position of a firm on this continuum is referred to as its **entrepreneurial intensity**.[11] As we mentioned previously, entrepreneurial firms are typically proactive innovators and are not averse to taking calculated risks. In contrast, conservative firms take more of a "wait and see" posture, are less innovative, and are risk averse.

One of the most persuasive indications of entrepreneurship's importance to an individual or to a firm is the degree of effort undertaken to behave in an entrepreneurial manner. Firms with higher entrepreneurial intensity regularly look for ways to cut bureaucracy. For example, Virgin Group, the large British conglomerate, works hard to keep its units small and instill in them an entrepreneurial spirit. Virgin is one of the most recognized brands in Britain and is involved in businesses as diverse as airlines and music. In the following quote, Sir Richard Branson, the founder and CEO of Virgin, describes how his company operates in an entrepreneurial manner:

> Convention ... dictates that "big is beautiful," but every time one of our ventures gets too big we divide it up into smaller units. I go to the deputy managing director, the deputy sales director, and the deputy marketing director and say, "Congratulations. You're now MD [managing director], sales director and marketing director—of a new company." Each time we've done this, the people involved haven't had much more work to do, but necessarily they have a greater incentive to perform and a greater zeal for their work. The results for us have been terrific. By the time we sold Virgin Music, we had as many as 50 subsidiary record companies, and not one of them had more than 60 employees.[12]

Why Do People Become Entrepreneurs?

The three primary reasons that people become entrepreneurs and start their own firms are to be their own boss, pursue their own ideas, and realize financial rewards.

Be Their Own Boss

The first of these reasons—being one's own boss—is given most commonly. This doesn't mean, however, that entrepreneurs are difficult to work with or that they have trouble accepting authority. Instead, many entrepreneurs want to be their own boss because either they have had a long-time ambition to own their own firm or because they have become frustrated working in traditional jobs. The type of frustration that some entrepreneurs feel working in conventional jobs is exemplified by Wendy DeFeudis, the founder of VeryWendy, a company that makes customized social invitations. Commenting on how her experiences working for herself have been more satisfying than working for a large firm, DeFeudis remarked:

> I always wanted to be my own boss. I felt confined by the corporate structure. I found it frustrating and a complete waste of time—a waste to have to sell my ideas to multiple people and attend all kinds of internal meetings before moving forward with a concept.[13]

Some entrepreneurs transition from a traditional job to owning their own business more gradually, by starting their business part time to begin with. While this approach isn't possible in all situations, by starting a business part

LEARNING OBJECTIVE

2. Discuss three main reasons people decide to become entrepreneurs.

time individuals can gain valuable experience, tuck away the money they earn, and find out if they really like the business before deciding to leave their job. In some businesses, such as catering or financial planning, it takes time to build a client list. Some entrepreneurs will time their departure from their job with the point in time where their client list is large enough and profitable enough to support a full-time business.[14]

Pursue Their Own Ideas

The second reason people start their own firms is to pursue their own ideas.[15] Some people are naturally alert, and when they recognize ideas for new products or services, they have a desire to see those ideas realized. Corporate entrepreneurs who innovate within the context of an existing firm typically have a mechanism for their ideas to become known. Established firms, however, often resist innovation. When this happens, employees are left with good ideas that go unfulfilled.[16] Because of their passion and commitment, some employees choose to leave the firm employing them in order to start their own business as the means to develop their own ideas.

This chain of events can take place in non-corporate settings, too. For example, some people, through a hobby, leisure activity, or just everyday life, recognize the need for a product or service that is not available in the marketplace. If the idea is viable enough to support a business, they commit tremendous time and energy to convert the idea into a part-time or full-time firm. In Chapters 2 and 3, we focus on how entrepreneurs spot ideas and determine if their ideas represent viable business opportunities.

An example of a person who left a job to pursue an idea is Melissa Pickering, the founder of iCreate to Educate, a company that is developing software apps that allows students to build, express, and share their creativity through animated videos. Pickering started her career as a mechanical engineer at Walt Disney Corp., a role that she said is more commnonly referred to as an imagineer or a roller coaster engineer. She was struck by the fact that even at Dinsey, a place that some may refer to as the ultimate creative group, there weren't many people who were female or close to her own age, and young engineers didn't seem to be seeking out a Disney career. Her attention shifted to creativity and kids. Commenting on what happened next, she said:

> My hunch was kids are not getting enough hands-on opportunities in the classroom to express and engage their creativity and problem solving skills. At that point I sought to launch an education technology business that would provide kids with the tools to create and explore, fostering the natural innovator within.[17]

iCreate to Eductate is currently building a portfolio of products, which includes both an iPhone and an iPad app. All of the firm's products are centered on helping kids better develop and express their creativity.[18]

Pursue Financial Rewards

Finally, people start their own firms to pursue financial rewards. This motivation, however, is typically secondary to the first two and often fails to live up to its hype. The average entrepreneur does not make more money than someone with a similar amount of responsibility in a traditional job. The financial lure of entrepreneurship is its upside potential. People such as Jeff Bezos of Amazon.com, Mark Zuckerberg of Facebook, and Larry Page and Sergey Brin of Google made hundreds of millions of dollars building their firms. Money is also a unifier. Making a profit and increasing the value of a company is a solidifying goal that people can rally around. But money is rarely the primary motivation behind the launch of an entrepreneurial firm. Some entrepreneurs even report that the financial rewards associated with entrepreneurship can be bittersweet if they are accompanied by losing control of their firm. For example, Sir Richard Branson, after selling Virgin Records, wrote, "I remember walking down the street [after the sale was completed]. I was crying. Tears ... [were] streaming down my face. And there I was holding a check for a billion dollars.... If you'd have seen me, you would have thought I was loony. A billion dollars."[19] For Branson, it wasn't just the money—it was the thrill of building the business and of seeing the success of his initial idea.

Characteristics of Successful Entrepreneurs

Although many behaviors have been ascribed to entrepreneurs, several are common to those who are successful. Those in new ventures and those who are already part of an entrepreneurial firm share these qualities, which are shown in Figure 1.1 and described in the following section.

LEARNING OBJECTIVE

3. Identify four main characteristics of successful entrepreneurs.

Passion for the Business

The number-one characteristic shared by successful entrepreneurs is a **passion for their business**, whether it is in the context of a new firm or an existing business. This passion typically stems from the entrepreneur's belief that the business will positively influence people's lives. Making a difference in people's lives is also the primary motivator behind many social enterprises, which are often started by people who set aside promising careers to pursue a social goal. This was the case with John Wood, who founded Room to Read and is the author of the book *Leaving Microsoft to Change the World*. Wood's deep passion to help children in the developing world caused him to start cashing in small amounts of Microsoft stock to buy books and build schools, even before he left the company. In excerpts from an interview published by *Forbes* magazine, Wood said:

> During my travels, I met so many children in the poorest parts of the world, lacking access to school, books, and libraries, that I began cashing in small amounts of stocks to help them. Two hundred shares of Microsoft stock was enough to build an entire school in rural Nepal.[20]

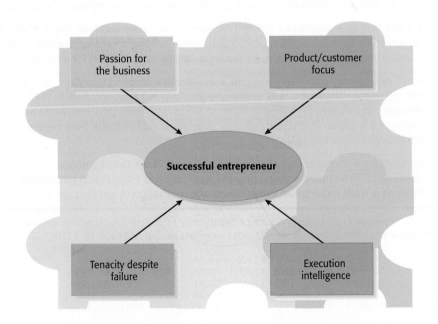

FIGURE 1.1
Four Primary Characteristics of Successful Entrepreneurs

Wood eventually left Microsoft to work on Room to Read full time. Since its inception in 2000, Room to Read has built 1,450 schools, established 12,522 libraries, distributed over 10 million children's books, and funded 13,662 long-term girls' schlorships in developing parts of the world.[21]

Passion is particularly important for both for-profit and not-for-profit entrepreneurial organizations because although rewarding, the process of starting a firm or building a social enterprise is demanding. There are five primary reasons passion is important, as reflected in Table 1.2. Each of these reasons reflects a personal attribute that passion engenders. Removing just one of these qualities would make it much more difficult to launch and sustain a successful entrepreneurial organization.

A note of caution is in order here: While entrepreneurs should have passion, they should not wear rose-colored glasses. It would be a mistake to believe that all one needs is passion and anything is possible. It is important to be enthusiastic about a business idea, but it is also important to understand its potential flaws and risks. In addition, entrepreneurs should understand that the most effective business ideas take hold when their passion is consistent with their skills and is in an area that represents a legitimate business opportunity.

To illustrate the importance of passion, as well as other factors that are critical in determining a firm's success or failure, we include a boxed feature titled "What Went Wrong?" in each chapter. The feature for this chapter shows how Prim, a laundry and pick-up and delivery service, ultimately failed in part because its founders were not able to remain passionate about their business idea.

TABLE 1.2 Five Primary Reasons Passion Is Important for the Launch of a Successful Entrepreneurial Organization

Reason Passion Is Important	Explanation
1. The ability to learn and iterate	Founders don't have all the answers. It takes passion and drive to solicit feedback, make necessary changes, and move forward. The changes won't always be obvious. Passion makes the search for the right answers invigorating and fun.
2. A willingness to work hard for an extended period of time	Commonly, entrepreneurs work longer hours than people with traditional jobs. You can only do that, on a sustained basis, if you're passionate about what you're doing.
3. Ability to overcome setbacks and "no's"	It's rare that an entrepreneur doesn't experience setbacks and hear many "no's" from potential customers, investors, and others while building an entrepreneurial business or social enterprise. The energy to continue comes from passion for an idea.
4. The ability to listen to feedback on the limitations of your organization and yourself	You'll meet plenty of people along the way—some with good intentions and some without—who will tell you how to improve your organization and how to improve yourself. You have to be willing to listen to the people with good intentions and make changes if it helps. You have to be able to brush aside feedback from people with bad intentions without letting them get you down.
5. Perseverance and persistence when the going gets tough	Perseverance and persistence come from passion. As an entrepreneur, you'll have down days. Building an entrepreneurial organization is fraught with challenges. Passion is what provides an entrepreneur the motivation to get through tough times.

Source: Based on A. Sack, "Why Is Passion So Important to a Startup?" A Sack of Seattle blog, http://asack.typepad.com/a_sack_of_seattle/2010/03/why-is-passion-so-important-to-a-startup.html (accessed May 22, 2011, originally posted on March 16, 2010).

WHAT WENT WRONG?

Prim: How a Lack of Passion and Resolve Can Kill a Business

Prim's idea was to disrupt the laundry industry. A growing number of people in the United States are using laundry services to wash and fold their clothes. The problems with these services is that they are a hassle. In most instances customers have to bag their laundry, drop them off at the laundry service, and then pick them up later. Many services have lines at the busiest times of the day, which result in drivers having to wait to drop off or pick up their laundry.

Prim's launched in mid-2013, after passing through the prestigueous Y-Combiator business accelerator program earlier that year. Here's how Prim's laundry service worked. A customer bagged her/his laundry, and then went online to choose a pickup and delivery time. The price was $25 for the first bag and $15 for each additional bag. The bags would be picked up by a driver recruited by a third-party delivery service. (Rickshaw was the name of the delivery service in the city where Prim started). Everything would be back, washed and folded, later that day or early the next day. No cash changed hands between the customer and the pickup or delivery drivers. Everything was paid for through Prim's website. Prim gained favorable press and early momentum. When it closed, it was handling 1,000 pounds of laundry a day from 40 clients and was growing. What went wrong?

Two things went wrong with Prim. First, once Prim got your clothes, it went from a innovative disruptor to an old-school company. It would take your clothes to a laundry service and utilize its wash and fold services. Prim negotiated volume discounts with several laundry services, but the discounts were verbal and were not in writing. What Prim didn't count on was the partnerships going sour. While the laundry services were initially receptive to working with Prim, they had their own delivery services and eventually saw Prim as siphoning off their customers and revenue. During its short history, Prim churned through three different laundry services.

The second thing that went wrong with Prim was a lack of passion and resolve on the part of its founders. Faced with the reality that working with local laundry services was a fragile business model, Prim's founders, Yin Yin Wu and Xuwen Cao, had a decision to make. Should they build or lease their own laundry service? This was a daunting prospect, given the hundreds of thousands of dollars necessary to build and staff a high-volume laundry wash and fold facility. Even more daunting was the prospect that this step would need to be repeated in each new market Prim entered. After two months of deliberation, Wu and Cao pulled the plug. While they estimated that by constructing their own laundry service they could build a profitable business in 5 to 10 years, with revenues of $10 million to $15 million, it was a direction they simply did not want to pursue. Both were computer science students in college and had no direct experience in the laundry business. In an article published by CNNMoney, Garry Tan, a partner with Y-Combinator, reflecting on why Wu and Cao closed Prim, said, "They didn't want to actually have to wash the laundry—they wanted to be the connector."

Questions for Critical Thinking

1. Why is passion such a critical part of entrepreneurial success? Prim's founders were apparently passionate about building a company but not passionate about the laundry business specifically. In what ways is this combination problematic?

2. How could Prim's co-founders have better anticipated that laundry services would eventually see Prim as siphoning off their own business and be reluctant to work with them?

3. Rather than employ its own drivers to pick up and deliver laundry for its customers, Prim relied on the use of third-party delivery services. In what ways do you think this approach could have limited Prim's growth in other markets?

4. San Francisco, the city in which Prim launched, has several innovative laundry services. These services include LaundryLocker, where you drop your clothes in a public locker, Sfwash, a delivery service where you pay by the pound, and Sudzee, which requires special lockable bags. Spend some time studying LaundryLocker (https://laundrylocker.com), Sfwash (https://sfwash.com), and Sudzee (https://sudzee.com). Select the service that you think has the most potential and explain the rationale for your selection. Compare the service to Prim's approach.

Sources: J. P. Mangalindan, "Prim: Anatomy of a Folded Startup," CNNMoney, available at http://tech.fortune.com/2014/01/22-prim-anatomy-of-a-folded-startup, posted January 22, 2014, accessed March 14, 2014; J. Constine, "Prim Laundry Startup Throws in the Towel," Techcrunch, available at http://techcrunch.com/2014/01/06/prim-laundry-shuts-down, posted Jan 6, 2014, accessed March 14, 2014.

Product/Customer Focus

A second defining characteristic of successful entrepreneurs is a **product/customer focus**. This quality is exemplified by Steven Jobs, the late co-founder of Apple Inc., who wrote, "The computer is the most remarkable tool we've ever built ... but the most important thing is to get them in the hands of as many people as possible."[22] This sentiment underscores an understanding of the two most important elements in any business—products and customers. While it's important to think about management, marketing, finance, and the like, none of those functions makes any difference if a firm does not have good products with the capability to satisfy customers.

This philosophy is affirmed by Alex Algard, the founder of WhitePages.com. WhitePages.com started in 1997 to provide consumers a free, accurate, and fast online alternative to telephone directory assistance. It is one of the most trusted and comprehensive sources for consumers to quickly find relevant, accurate contact information in North America. When asked how he was able to grow WhitePages.com from a one person operation in 1997 to the multimillion-dollar company it is today, Algard's reply reflected not only his feelings about the importance of providing value to both users and customers but also how a company measures if the value is being successfully delivered:

> The philosopny that we as a company have always stuck to is that everything we build has to provide real value to both our users and customers. The best measurement of whether or not we are successful at delivering something valuable is if our customers, advertisers in our case, are willing to pay.[23]

A product/customer focus also involves the diligence to spot product opportunities and to see them through to completion. The idea for the Apple Macintosh, for example, originated in the early 1980s when Steven Jobs and several other Apple employees took a tour of a Xerox research facility. They were astounded to see computers that displayed graphical icons and pull-down menus. The computers also allowed users to navigate desktops using a small, wheeled device called a mouse. Jobs decided to use these innovations to create the Macintosh, the first user-friendly computer. Throughout the two and a half years the Macintosh team developed this new product, it maintained an intense product/customer focus, creating a high-quality computer that is easy to learn, fun to use, and meets the needs of a wide audience of potential users.[24]

Tenacity Despite Failure

Because entrepreneurs are typically trying something new, the possibility of failure exists. In addition, the process of developing a new business is somewhat similar to what a scientist experiences in the laboratory. A chemist, for example, typically has to try multiple combinations of chemicals before finding an optimal combination that can accomplish a certain objective. In a similar fashion, developing a new business idea may require a certain degree of experimentation before a success is attained. Setbacks and failures inevitably occur during this process. The litmus test for entrepreneurs is their ability to persevere through setbacks and failures.

An example of the degree of tenacity it sometimes takes to launch a successful firm is provided by Jerry Stoppelman and Russel Simmons, the founders of Yelp, the popular online review site. The original idea for Yelp, which was founded in 2004, is that when people are looking for a new restaurant, dentist, or plumber they normally ask their friends for recommendations. Yelp was launched to give people the ability to e-mail a list of their friends and ask for a recommendation. The message included a link that allowed the friend to easily respond. The business plan didn't work. People started complaining that they were getting too many e-mail messages from friends who often didn't have a recommendation to provide. Yelp could have died at this point. Instead, Stoppelman and Simmons demonstrated the tenacity it often takes to keep a business alive. Curiously, the one aspect of Yelp's business plan that did work was the ability to write your own review—a feature that had been included by Stoppelman and Simmons almost as an afterthought. Rather than responding to a friend's request for a recommendation, people seemed to enjoy sharing information about their favorite restaurant or hair salon without being asked. In 2005, Yelp pivoted and revised its business plan. The new plan dropped the "e-mail your friend idea" and focused on providing a platform for people to proactively write reviews of local businesses. Today, Yelp is one of the most popular review sites on the Internet.

An additional example of tenacity, which involved all the employees of Pandora,[25] is provided in the boxed feature titled "Savvy Entrepreneurial Firm." In each chapter, this feature will provide an illustration of the exemplary behavior of one or more entrepreneurial firms or will provide an example of a tool or technique that well-managed entrepreneurial firms use to improve their performance.

Execution Intelligence

The ability to fashion a solid idea into a viable business is a key characteristic of successful entrepreneurs. Commonly, this ability is thought of as **execution intelligence**.[26] In many cases, execution intelligence is the factor that determines whether a start-up is successful or fails. An ancient Chinese saying warns, "To open a business is very easy; to keep it open is very difficult."

The ability to effectively execute a business idea means developing a business model, putting together a new venture team, raising money, establishing partnerships, managing finances, leading and motivating employees, and so on. It also demands the ability to translate thought, creativity, and imagination into action and measurable results. As Jeff Bezos, the founder of Amazon.com, once said, "Ideas are easy. It's execution that's hard."[27] For many entrepreneurs, the hardest time is shortly after they launch their firm. This reality was expressed by Jodi Gallaer, the founder of a lingerie company, who said, "The most challenging part of my job is doing everything for the first time."[28]

To illustrate solid execution, let's look at Starbucks. The business idea of Howard Schultz, the entrepreneur behind the success of Starbucks, was his recognition of the fact that most Americans didn't have a place to enjoy coffee in a comfortable, quiet setting. Seeing a great opportunity to satisfy customers' needs, Schultz attacked the marketplace aggressively to make Starbucks the industry leader and to establish a national brand. First, he hired a seasoned management team, constructed a world-class roasting facility to supply his outlets with premium coffee beans, and focused on building an effective organizational infrastructure. Then Schultz recruited a management information systems expert from McDonald's to design a point-of-sale system capable of tracking consumer purchases across 300 outlets. This decision was crucial to the firm's ability to sustain rapid growth over the next several years. Starbucks succeeded because Howard Schultz knew how to execute a business idea.[29] He built a seasoned management team, implemented an effective strategy, and used information technology wisely to make his business thrive.[30] These fundamental aspects of execution excellence should serve Schultz and Starbucks when it comes to dealing with the competitive challenges facing the firm in 2014 and beyond. In mid-2014, over 21,000 Starbucks' locations had been established in 65 countries.

SAVVY ENTREPRENEURIAL FIRM

Pandora: What's Possible When an Entire Company Has "Tenacity"

Web: www.pandora.com; Facebook: Pandora, Twitter: @pandora_radio

Most everyone is familiar with Pandora, the Internet radio station. The service plays music of a certain genre based on the artist or type of music the user selects. The user then provides positive or negative feedback for songs chosen by Pandora, which are taken into account when the service selects future songs. While listening, users are offered the opportunity to buy the songs or albums at online retailers. Over 400 different musical attributes are considered when selecting the next song for a user. The goal is to provide the user the precise type of music that s/he wants to hear. Pandora has two subscription plans: a free service supported by ads and a fee-based service without ads. Pandora went public on June 15, 2011, and is now traded on the New York Stock Exchange. As of that date, Pandora had 800,000 songs from over 80,000 artists in its music library and 80 million users. A year later it reported it had 150 million users.

Impressive, isn't it? But, as the old saying goes, wait until you hear the rest of the story. Pandora was founded in 1999 by Tim Westergren, a musician and film composer. The company raised $1 million just before the Internet bubble burst. At that time, Pandora's business model was to license its technology to other companies. The initial investment lasted about a year, which gave Westergren and his team enough time to build a prototype and have a product to show to potential customers. Then the money ran out. Pandora spent the next two and a half years essentially broke, earning only enough to keep the lights on. What was needed was an additional investment. Westergren pitched over 300 venture capitalists before one finally said yes. Pandora eventually shifted its business model to offer the Internet radio streaming service that it features today. Fast forward to the present: Today Pandora has over 250 million registered users.

So how did Pandora do it? How did it survive two and a half years with essentially no money? The answer: Its employees agreed to work for no pay. They agreed to a deferred compensation plan, meaning they would get paid if and when the company raised money. Some used credit cards to survive, some had working spouses or significant others, and others worked two jobs. Reflecting on this period in Pandora's history, Westergren, who was the first person to go without pay, said the employees agreed to the plan for two reasons. First, they believed in Pandora and its idea. They also believed that Pandora would ultimately raise money and become a successful business. Second, the employees felt a sense of responsibility for one another. If one left, the burden would be greater on the others. As time went on, Westergren believes, those relationships deepened and the employees ultimately stuck it out for one another.

When the funding did come through each employee was given his/her entire back pay. This is a very unusual outcome in the funding world. Usually, new money isn't used to solve old problems, it's used to build for the future. Westergren credits his investors for the outcome. He's said that what the investors were investing in was the *tenacity* of the Pandora team.

Lesson Learned: This is what can be accomplished when an entire company demonstrates the tenacity necessary to build a successful entrepreneurial firm.

Questions for Critical Thinking

1. How do you think Westergren was able to persevere through 300 rejections before an investor finally said yes to Pandora's attempts to raise additional money?
2. If you had been a Pandora employee during the time the firm was essentially broke, would you have agreed to work for no money? Westergren provided two reasons that the employees present at the time were willing to work without pay. Would these reasons have been good enough for you? Explain your answer.
3. Think of a time in your life where you showed tenacity and the tenacity produced positive outcomes. Briefly relate the story and what you learned from the experience to your classmates.
4. What lesson or lessons can other entrepreneurial start-ups learn from Pandora's story?

Sources: W. Wei, "How Pandora Survived More Than 300 VC Rejections," *Business Insider*, July 14, 2010, available at www.businessinsider.com/pandora-vc-2010-7

Common Myths About Entrepreneurs

LEARNING OBJECTIVE

4. Explain the five common myths regarding entrepreneurship.

There are many misconceptions about who entrepreneurs are and what motivates them to launch firms to develop their ideas. Some misconceptions are because of the media covering atypical entrepreneurs, such as a couple of college students who obtain venture capital to fund a small business that they grow into a multimillion-dollar company. Such articles rarely state that these

You might describe an entrepreneur as an independent thinker, an innovator, or perhaps a risk taker. These young entrepreneurs are passionate enough to work at a hectic pace if that's what it takes to get their company up and running.

Laura Doss/Fancy/Corbis

entrepreneurs are the exception rather than the norm and that their success is a result of carefully executing an appropriate plan to commercialize what inherently is a solid business idea. Indeed, the success of many of the entrepreneurs we study in each chapter's Opening Profile is a result of carefully executing the different aspects of the entrepreneurial process. Let's look at the most common myths and the realities about entrepreneurs.

Myth 1: Entrepreneurs Are Born, Not Made

This myth is based on the mistaken belief that some people are genetically predisposed to be entrepreneurs. The consensus of many hundreds of studies on the psychological and sociological makeup of entrepreneurs is that entrepreneurs are not genetically different from other people. This evidence can be interpreted as meaning that no one is "born" to be an entrepreneur and that everyone has the potential to become one. Whether someone does or doesn't is a function of environment, life experiences, and personal choices.[31] However, there are personality traits and characteristics commonly associated with entrepreneurs; these are listed in Table 1.3. These traits are developed over time and evolve from an individual's social context. For example, studies show that people with parents who were self-employed are more likely to become entrepreneurs.[32] After witnessing a father's or mother's independence in the workplace, an individual is more likely to find independence appealing.[33] Similarly, people who personally know an entrepreneur are more than twice as likely to be involved in starting a new firm as those with no entrepreneur acquaintances or role models.[34] The positive impact of knowing an entrepreneur is explained by the fact that direct observation of other entrepreneurs reduces the ambiguity and uncertainty associated with the entrepreneurial process.

Myth 2: Entrepreneurs Are Gamblers

A second myth about entrepreneurs is that they are gamblers and take big risks. The truth is, entrepreneurs are usually **moderate risk takers**, as are

TABLE 1.3   **Common Traits and Characteristics of Entrepreneurs**

A moderate risk taker	Optimistic disposition
Persuasive	A networker
Promoter	Achievement motivated
Resource assembler/leverager	Alert to opportunities
Creative	Self-confident
Self-starter	Decisive
Tenacious	Energetic
Tolerant of ambiguity	A strong work ethic
Visionary	Lengthy attention span

most people.[35] This finding is affirmed by The Hartford's 2013 Small Business Success Study. The study conducted a survey of 2,600 business owners. A total of 79 percent of the participants rated themselves as conservative rather than risky.[36] The idea that entrepreneurs are gamblers originates from two sources. First, entrepreneurs typically have jobs that are less structured, and so they face a more uncertain set of possibilities than managers or rank-and-file employees.[37] For example, an entrepreneur who starts a social network consulting service has a less stable job than one working for a state governmental agency. Second, many entrepreneurs have a strong need to achieve and often set challenging goals, a behavior that is sometimes equated with risk taking.

Myth 3: Entrepreneurs Are Motivated Primarily by Money

It is naïve to think that entrepreneurs don't seek financial rewards. As discussed previously, however, money is rarely the primary reason entrepreneurs start new firms and persevere. The importance and role of money in a start-up is put in perspective by Colin Angle, the founder and CEO of iRobot, the maker of the popular Roomba robotic vacuum cleaner. Commenting on his company's mission statement, Angle said:

> Our, "Build Cool Stuff, Deliver Great Products, Have Fun, Make Money, Change the World" (mission statement) kept us (in the early days of the Company) unified with a common purpose while gut-wrenching change surrounded us. It reminded us that our goal was to have fun and make money. Most importantly, it reminded us that our mission was not only to make money, but to change the world in the process.[38]

Some entrepreneurs warn that the pursuit of money can be distracting. Media mogul Ted Turner said, "If you think money is a real big deal … you'll be too scared of losing it to get it."[39] Similarly, Sam Walton, commenting on all the media attention that surrounded him after he was named the richest man in America by *Forbes* magazine in 1985, said:

> Here's the thing: money never has meant that much to me, not even in the sense of keeping score…. We're not ashamed of having money, but I just don't believe a big showy lifestyle is appropriate for anywhere, least of all here in Bentonville

where folks work hard for their money. We all know that everyone puts on their trousers one leg at a time.... I still can't believe it was news that I get my hair cut at the barbershop. Where else would I get it cut? Why do I drive a pickup truck? What am I supposed to haul my dogs around in, a Rolls-Royce?[40]

Myth 4: Entrepreneurs Should Be Young and Energetic

Entrepreneurial activity is fairly evenly spread out over age ranges. The age distribution of business owners, determined by the Kauffman Foundation and LegalZoom 2012 Startup Environment Index, is shown in Table 1.4. As shown, the majority of individuals who start companies are in their thirties and forties. Not suprisingly, given this age distribution, the majoity of business owners have work experience prior to launching a new venture.[41] Although it is important to be energetic, investors often cite the strength of the entrepreneur (or team of entrepreneurs) as their most important criterion in the decision to fund new ventures.[42] In fact, a sentiment that venture capitalists often express is that they would rather fund a strong entrepreneur with a mediocre business idea than fund a strong business idea and a mediocre entrepreneur. What makes an entrepreneur "strong" in the eyes of an investor is experience in the area of the proposed business, skills and abilities that will help the business, a solid reputation, a track record of success, and passion about the business idea. The first four of these five qualities favor older rather than younger entrepreneurs.

Myth 5: Entrepreneurs Love the Spotlight

Indeed, some entrepreneurs are flamboyant; however, the vast majority of them do not attract public attention. In fact, many entrepreneurs, because they are working on proprietary products or services, avoid public notice. Consider that entrepreneurs are the source of the launch of many of the 5,000 companies listed on the NASDAQ, and many of these entrepreneurs are still actively involved with their firms. But how many of these entrepreneurs can you name? Perhaps three or four? Most of us could come up with Jeff Bezos of Amazon.com, Mark Zuckerberg of Facebook, and maybe Larry Page and Sergey Brin of Google or Larry Ellison of Oracle. Whether or not they sought attention, these are the entrepreneurs who are often in the news. But few of us could name the founders of Netflix, Twitter, or DIRECTV, even though we

TABLE 1.4 Age Distribution of Business Owners

Age	Percentage of Business Owners
18-29	17.5
30-39	25
40-49	24
50-59	21
60+	12.5

Source: The Kauffman Foundation and LegalZoom 2102 Startup Environment Index, The Ewing Marion Kauffman Foundation, February 2013. The numbers are based on a survey of 1,431 individuals who formed a business through LegalZoom in 2012.

frequently use these firms' services. These entrepreneurs, like most, have either avoided attention or been passed over by the popular press. They defy the myth that entrepreneurs, more so than other groups in our society, love the spotlight.

Types of Start-Up Firms

LEARNING OBJECTIVE

5. Describe the three types of start-up firms.

As shown in Figure 1.2, there are three types of start-up firms: salary-substitute firms, lifestyle firms, and entrepreneurial firms.

Salary-substitute firms are small firms that yield a level of income for their owner or owners that is similar to what they would earn when working for an employer. Dry cleaners, convenience stores, restaurants, accounting firms, retail stores, and hairstyling salons are examples of salary-substitute firms. The vast majority of small businesses fit into this category. Salary-substitute firms offer common, easily available and not particularly innovative products or services to customers.

Lifestyle firms provide their owner or owners the opportunity to pursue a particular lifestyle and earn a living while doing so. Lifestyle firms include personal trainers, golf and tennis pros, the owners of bed & breakfasts, and tour guides. These firms are not innovative, nor do they grow quickly. Commonly, lifestyle companies promote a particular sport, hobby, or pastime and may employ only the owner or just a handful of people.

Entrepreneurial firms bring new products and services to market. As we noted earlier in this chapter, the essence of entrepreneurship is creating value and then disseminating that value to customers. In this context, **value** refers to worth, importance, or utility. Entrepreneurial firms bring new products and services to market by creating and then seizing opportunities. Dropbox, Facebook, and LinkedIn are well-known, highly successful examples of entrepreneurial firms. Having recognized an opportunity, the entrepreneurs leading companies of this type create products and services that have worth, are important to their customers, and provide a measure of usefulness to their customers that they wouldn't have otherwise.

One characteristic of entrepreneurial firms, which will be explored throughout this book, is that they partner with other firms and organizations, often to obtain the boost they need to realize their full potential. In each chapter, look for the boxed feature titled "Partnering for Success," which illustrates how entepreneurial firms used partnerships to increase their chances for success. This feature in this chapter discusses how entreprenurs and their firms are engaging business incubators and accelerators to gain access to mentors, partners, investors, and other critical start-up resources.

Next, we describe the newly emerging characteristics of today's entrepreneurs. You may be surprised to learn about the types of individuals who are choosing to become entrepreneurs! While reading these characteristics, think about people you know who are accurately described by these characteristics. Do you think any of these people will choose to become entrepreneurs?

FIGURE 1.2
Types of Start-Up Firms

Salary-Substitute Firms	Lifestyle Firms	Entrepreneurial Firms
Firms that basically provide their owner or owners a similar level of income to what they would be able to earn in a conventional job	Firms that provide their owner or owners the opportunity to pursue a particular lifestyle, and make a living at it	Firms that bring new products and services to the market by creating and seizing opportunities regardless of the resources they currently control

PARTNERING FOR SUCCESS

Start-up Incubators and Accelerators: A New Way of Gaining Access to Mentors, Partners, Investors, and Other Critical Start-up Resources

The number of start-up incubator and accelerator programs in the United States continues to grow. These are programs for which entrepreneurs must apply. In some cases, the programs require that the entrepreneur or team of entrepreneurs surrender a small amount of equity for a similarly small amount of seed funding. In other cases, the start-ups pay a modest amount for participation or rent but do not surrender equity in their firms. The greatest advantage of getting into one of these programs is the mentorship opportunities they provide. Start-up incubators and accelerators are also fertile places for entrepreneurs to meet potential co-founders, business partners, and/or equity investors.

The two most well-known accelerator programs are Y-Combinator and Tech Stars. Y-Combinator is located in the Silicon Valley. It provides seed stage funding, mentorship, and networking opportunities to its participants in two, three-month sessions per year. Started in Boulder, Colorado, TechStars is similar to Y-Combinator in that it provides seed stage funding in three-month membership programs. TechStars has now expanded to Austin, Boston, Chicago, London, New York City, and Seattle.

While admission to Y-Combinator and TechStars is very competitive and requires a start-up to be physically present where Y-Combinator and TechStars is locted, there are a growing number of start-up incubators and accelerators in most American cities. To illustrate this point, the following is a list of the incubator and accelerator programs available in Austin, Texas. While Austin may offer an above-average number of programs, a little digging turns up a surprising number of similar programs in medium-sized and large American cities and on college campuses.

DreamIt Austin: A three-month program that provides the entrepreneurs it selects with pre-seed funding (up to $25,000), mentoring from seasoned entrepreneurs, access to follow-on capital, and work space in a creative, rigorous start-up environment.

Capital Factory: Offers an accelerator program and co-working space and hosts meetups and other events for aspiring entrepreneurs. The accelerator program matches $50,000 angel investments and then targets select portfolio companies for $250,000 follow-on investments.

Tech Ranch: A for-profit incubator that offers co-working space along with consulting services and specialized programs to help entrepreneurs launch their ventures. Its flagship programs include Venture Start, which is a one-day program, Venture Forth, an 8-week bootcamp, and Venture Builder, a 26-week partnership between Tech Ranch and business founders to launch promising entrepreneurial firms.

TechStars Austin: A three-month accelerator program that puts seed money into start-ups in exchange for a small amount of equity. TechStars provides participating start-ups workspace in a stimulating environment, along with access to top-quality mentors.

Incubation Station: An accelerator program focused on consumer goods companies. Selected start-ups participate in intensive 12- to 14-week mentoring programs designed to maximize the potential for success. Provides participants access to high-quality mentors and other forms of industry-relevant support.

Austin Technology Incubator: The start-up incubator at the University of Texas at Austin. It is affiliated with the university's IC2 Institute.

Texas Venture Labs: Supports business start-ups on the University of Texas at Austin campus via mentoring, team building, market and business plan validation, technology commercialization, and domain knowledge needed to start and grow entrepreneurial ventures.

Longhorn Startup: A semester-long program for undergraduate students on the University of Texas at Austin campus. It places students in interdisciplinary teams to start real companies. Each semester ends with participating students pitching to investors at a Demo Day.

SXSW Accelerator: Competition takes place during South by Southwest, which is an annual film, music, and interactive (technology) conference held in March of each year. The judges choose 18 finalists, who give a final pitch, and then the winners are chosen.

Questions for Critical Thinking

1. If you were starting a new venture, do you think you would benefit from participating in a business incubator or accelerator program? If so, what do you think the primary benefits would be?
2. Find an example of a start-up incubator or accelerator at the college or university you are attending or in the town you live in or a nearby city. Describe the program. Which one of the Austin, Texas, programs does it most resemble?
3. If a student has a promising business idea, what can s/he do while in college to improve his or her chances of being accepted into a well-regarded incubator or accelerator program?
4. Make a list of the types of business partnerships that participants in a business incubator or accelerator program are likely to fashion.

Changing Demographics of Entrepreneurs

LEARNING OBJECTIVE

6. Discuss the changing demographics of entrepreneurs in the United States.

Over the past 10 years, the demographic makeup of entrepreneurial firms has changed in the United States and around the world. Of the 23 million businesses in the United States,[43] women, minorities, seniors, and young people own an increasingly larger number of them. This is an exciting development for the entrepreneurial sector of the U.S. economy.

Women Entrepreneurs

While men are still more likely to start businesses than women, the number of women-owned businesses is increasing. According to a study commissioned by American Express OPEN, there were 8.6 million women-owned businesses in the United States in 2013, generating over $1.3 trillion in revenues and employing nearly 7.8 million people. In addition, between 1997 and 2013, the number of women who owned businesses increased at a rate of one-and-a-half times the national average. Particularly impressive is the growth in the number of firms owned by women who are minorities. A total of 33 percent of women-owned firms are now owned by minorities, up from 17 percent 16 years ago.[44]

Additional data is available from the 2007 U.S. Census Beureau's report on Women Owned Business (the most recent year the data was collected). According to the report, in some industries, women control a significant share of the business. For example, women-owned businesses accounted for 52 percent of all businesses in the health care and social assistance sector. The three states with the highest number of women-owned businesses in 2007 were California, Texas, and New York. There were 141,893 women-owned businesses earning more than $1 million in 2007.[45]

The number of groups that support and advocate for women-owned businesses continues to increase. An example of these groups is Count Me In (www.countmein.org), which is the leading national not-for-profit provider of resources, business education, and community support for women entrepreneurs.[46]

These are the faces of the entrepreneurs of the future. Collectively they will be older, more ethnically diverse, and will include more women than any time in the past.

Andriy Popov/123RF

Minority Entrepreneurs

There has been a substantial increase in minority entrepreneurs in the United States. The most comprehensive statistics are reported by the Minority Business Development Agency (www.mbda.gov). According to the MBDA, between 2002 and 2007 (the most recent years the data was collected), minority-owned firms outpaced the growth of non-minority firms in gross receipts, employment, and number of firms. In 2007, there were 5.8 million minority-owned firms. Minorities represented 36 percent of the U.S. population in 2010, and will become the majority of the population by 2042.[47]

In 2007, there were about 1.9 million African American–owned firms in the United States. The African American firms with employees had average receipts of over $911,000 and average employment of 9 workers. Similarly, in 2007 there were 1.5 million Asian American–owned firms. The Asian American firms with employees had average receipts of more than $1.1 million and 7 employees. Finally, in 2007, there were about 2.3 million Hispanic-owned firms in the United States. The Hispanic firms with employees had average receipts of $1.1 million and 8 workers.[48]

Similar to women entrepreneurs, an important factor facilitating the growth of minority entrepreneurs is the number of organizations that promote and provide assistance. Examples include the Latin Business Association, Black Business Association, National Indian Business Association, The National Council of Asian American Business Associations, and the Minority Business Development Agency, which is part of the United States Department of Commerce.

Senior Entrepreneurs

The number of seniors (those 50 years of age and older) starting businesses is substantial and growing. According to the Kauffman Foundation and LegalZoom study cited earlier in the chapter, in 2012, 20 percent of new businesses were started by people between 50 and 59 years old while another 12.5 percent were founded by individuals 60 years old and older.[49] This increase is attributed to a number of factors, including corporate downsizing, an increasing desire among older workers for more personal fulfillment in their lives, and growing worries among seniors that they need to earn additional income to pay for future health care services and other expenses. Many people in the 50 and older age range have substantial business experience, financial resources that they can draw upon, and excellent vigor and health, which make them ideal candidates to start businesses in many industries. In addition, the steady increase in life expectancy means that Americans are not only living longer, but are living healthier longer, and are likely to remain engaged in either a job or an entrepreneurial venture longer in their lives than earlier generations.

Young Entrepreneurs

A desire to pursue an entrepreneurial career is high among young people. According to a recent Gallop survey, about 4 in 10 kids in grades 5–12 say they plan to start their own business. Interestingly, the percentage is higher among girls (46 percent) than boys (40 percent). About 59 percent of students in grades 5–12 say their school offers classes in how to start a business. This percentage represents a 9 percent jump from 2011 to 2012. About one-third (32 percent) of young people say their parents or guardians have started a business, which provides them a firsthand look at the entrepreneurial lifestyle.[50]

A number of organizations are involved in spurring interest in entrepreneurship among young people. The Network for Teaching Entrepreneurship (NFTE), for example, provides entrepreneurship education programs to young people from low-income communities. A nonprofit organization called Lemonade Day, sponsored in part by Google, is a 14-step process that walks young people from a business concept to a business plan and beyond. The idea is to expose young people to entrepreneurial concepts by helping them start and operate their own business—a lemonade stand. Launched in 2007, Lemonade Day has grown from 2,700 kids in Houston, Texas, to more than 200,000 kids in cities across the United States. The organization's goal is to eventually provide this experience to 1 million kids in 100 cities each year.[51]

In addition to organizations targeting elementary and middle-aged school kids, a growing number of colleges and universities are offering entrepreneurship-focused programs for high school students. Babson College, for example, offers a five-week summer program for high school juniors and seniors. The program, called the Babson Entrepreneurial Development Experience, allows students to work together on new business ideas. The students can earn college credit and learn from top-ranked faculty in a challenging college atmosphere.[52]

On university and college campuses, interest in entrepreneurship education is at an all-time high. More than 2,300 colleges and universities in the United States offer at least one course in entrepreneurship at the undergraduate or graduate level.[53] Although the bulk of entrepreneurship education takes place within business schools, many other colleges and departments are offering entrepreneurship courses as well—including engineering, agriculture, law, hospitality management, and nursing.

A growing number of organizations are popping up that focus on helping college student entrepreneurs. These organizations range from the Dorm Room Fund, which is a student-run venture fund that invests in student-initiatied start-ups, to Startup Weekend, which helps students organize teams and launch start-ups in 54 hours. A sample of these organizations is shown in Table 1.5.

The Positive Effects of Entrepreneurship and Entrepreneurial Firms

Entrepreneurship's importance to an economy and the society in which it resides was expertly articulated in 1934 by Joseph Schumpeter, an Austrian economist who did the majority of his work at Harvard University. In his book *The Theory of Economic Development*, Schumpeter argued that entrepreneurs develop new products and technologies that over time make current products and technologies obsolete. Schumpeter called this process **creative destruction**. Because new products and technologies are typically better than those they replace and the availability of improved products and technologies increases consumer demand, creative destruction stimulates economic activity. The new products and technologies may also increase the productivity of all elements of a society.[54]

The creative destruction process is initiated most effectively by start-up ventures that improve on what is currently available. Small firms that practice this art are often called "innovators" or "agents of change." The process of creative destruction is not limited to new products and technologies; it can include new pricing strategies (e.g., Netflix in DVDs), new distribution channels (such as e-books for books), or new retail formats (such as IKEA in furniture and Whole Foods Market in groceries).

Now let's look more closely at entrepreneurship's importance.

Economic Impact of Entrepreneurial Firms

For two reasons, entrepreneurial behavior has a strong impact on an economy's strength and stability.

TABLE 1.5 Organizations that Help College Students Learn More About Entrepreneurship and/or Advance Their Business Ideas

Organization	Description	Website Address
3-Day Startup	Offers a 3-day program that helps students kick-start companies and build entrepreneurial capabilities.	http://3daystartup.org
CEO (Collegiate Entrepreneurs' Organization)	Premier entrepreneurship network with chapters on more than 240 college campuses.	www.c-e-o.org
CollabFinder	A Web platform that students across the country are using to team up on start-ups and other projects. A business student, for example, can use the platform to find an engineering student to collaborate on a business idea.	www.collabFinder.com
College Startup	An independent start-up news site dedicated to covering entrepreneurial people, companies, and events emerging from college campuses.	www.collegestartup.org
Dorm Room Fund	Student-run venture fund that invests in student-initiated start-ups. Backed by First Round Capital.	http://dormroomfund.com
Entrepreneurs' Organization	Global business network of 9,500+ business owners. Runs the annual Global Student Entrepreneur Award program.	www.gsea.org
Startup Weekend	Start-up weekends are 54-hour events where developers, marketers, product managers, and start-up enthusiasts come together to share ideas, form teams, build products, and launch start-ups.	http://startupweekend.org
UFunded	A crowdfunding site for college-student start-ups.	www.unfunded.com
VentureWell	A nonprofit organization that funds and trains faculty and student innovators to create new businesses.	www:venturewell.org
YoungEntreprenuer.com	Website and blog devoted to sharing business tools and other resources for young entrepreneurs.	www.youngentreprenur.com

One of the most satisfying things about an entrepreneurial career is bringing products to life that enhance people's lives. This young woman is enjoying music provided by an online streaming music service started by two entrepreneurs.

Dean Drobot/Shutterstock

Innovation   **Innovation** is the process of creating something new, which is central to the entrepreneurial process.[55] According to the Small Business Administration (SBA) Office of Advocacy, small innovative firms are 16 times more productive than large innovative firms in terms of patents per employee. Small firms tend to be particularly innovative in certain industries, as measured by patent activity. For example, small firms account for more than 32 percent of patents in both smart grids and solar energy and 15 percent of patents in batteries and fuel cells.[56]

Job Creation   According to the SBA, small businesses create a substantial number of net new jobs in the United States. Firms with 500 or fewer employees create 65 percent of new jobs on an annual basis, while firms with 50 or fewer employees create 32 percent of new jobs. The only downside of small business jobs is that employee pay tends to be less than is the case in larger companies. According to the SBA, weekly wages averaged $679 at businesses with 5 to 9 employees, $815 at businesses with 50 to 99 employees, and $1,000 for firms with over 250 employees.[57] Still, small businesses are held in high regard in terms of job creation.

Entrepreneurial Firms' Impact on Society

Entrepreneurial firms' innovations have a dramatic impact on a society. Think of all the new products and services that make our lives easier, enhance our productivity at work, improve our health, and entertain us. For example, Amgen, an entrepreneurial firm that helped pioneer the biotechnology industry, has produced a number of drugs that have dramatically improved people's lives. An example is NEUPOGEN, a drug that decreases the incidence of infection in cancer patients who are undergoing chemotherapy treatment. In addition to improved health care, consider smartphones, social networks, Internet shopping, overnight package delivery, and digital photography. All these products are new to this generation, yet it's hard to imagine our world without them.

However, innovations do create moral and ethical issues with which societies are forced to grapple. For example, bar-code scanner technology and the Internet have made it easier for companies to track the purchasing behavior of their customers, a fact that raises privacy concerns. Similarly, bioengineering has made it easier to extend the shelf life of many food products, but some researchers and consumers question the long-term health implications of bioengineered foods.

Entrepreneurial Firms' Impact on Larger Firms

In addition to the impact that entrepreneurial firms have on economies and societies, they also positively impact the effectiveness of larger firms. For example, some entrepreneurial firms are original equipment manufacturers, producing parts that go into products that larger firms manufacture and sell. Thus, many exciting new products, such as smartphones, digital cameras, and improved prescription drugs, are not solely the result of the efforts of larger companies with strong brand names, such as Samsung, Apple, and Johnson & Johnson. They were produced with the cutting-edge component parts or research-and-development efforts provided by entrepreneurial firms.

The evidence shows that many entrepreneurial firms have built their entire business models around producing products and services that increase the efficiency or effectiveness of larger firms. For example, an increasing number of U.S. firms are competing in foreign markets. These initiatives often require firms to employ translators to help them communicate with their foreign counterparts. SpeakLike, a 2008 start-up, has created an online service that provides real-time translation services for two or more people who speak different languages. This cost of this service is considerably below what it costs to employ human translators. A large percentage of SpeakLike's customers are large firms. Similarly, Box is an entreprenurial start-up that allows clients to store data files in the cloud. The majority of *Fortune* 500 companies are now Box subscribers.

The Entrepreneurial Process

The entrepreneurial process we discuss in this book consists of four steps:

LEARNING OBJECTIVE
8. Explain the entrepreneurial process.

Step1 Deciding to become an entrepreneur

Step2 Developing successful business ideas

Step3 Moving from an idea to an entrepreneurial firm

Step4 Managing and growing the entrepreneurial firm

Figure 1.3 models the entrepreneurial process you'll study while reading this text. This process is the guide or framework around which we develop this book's contents. The double-headed arrow between the decision to become an entrepreneur and the development of successful business ideas indicates that sometimes the opportunity to develop an idea prompts a person to become an entrepreneur. Each section of Figure 1.3 is explained in the following sections.

Decision to Become an Entrepreneur (Chapter 1)

As discussed earlier, people become entrepreneurs to be their own bosses, to pursue their own ideas, and to realize financial rewards. Usually, a **triggering event** prompts an individual to become an entrepreneur.[58] For example, an individual may lose her job and decide that the time is right to start her own business. Or a person might receive an inheritance and for the first time in his life have the money to start his own company. Lifestyle issues may also trigger entrepreneurial careers. For example, a woman may wait until her youngest child is in school before she decides to launch her own entrepreneurial venture.

Developing Successful Business Ideas (Chapters 2–6)

Many new businesses fail not because the entrepreneur didn't work hard but because there was no real opportunity to begin with. Developing a successful business idea includes opportunity recognition, feasibility analysis, the development of an effective business model, industry analysis, and writing a business plan. Chapter 2 takes a scientific look at how entrepreneurs recognize opportunities and describes how the opportunity recognition process typically unfolds. Chapter 3 focuses on feasibility analysis: the way to determine whether an idea represents a viable business opportunity. Chapter 4 focuses on the important topic of developing an effective business model. A firm's **business model** is its plan or receipe for how it creates, delivers, and captures value for its stakeholders. Entrepreneurial firms need to have a crystal clear understanding of the issues concerned with creating, delivering, and capturing value if they are to be successful. Industry and competitor analysis is our concern in Chapter 5. Knowing the industry in which a firm will choose to compete is crucial to an entrepreneur's success. In Chapter 6, we describe how to write a business plan. A **business plan** is a written document that describes all the aspects of a business venture in a concise manner. It is usually necessary to have a written business plan to raise money and attract high-quality business partners. Some entrepreneurs

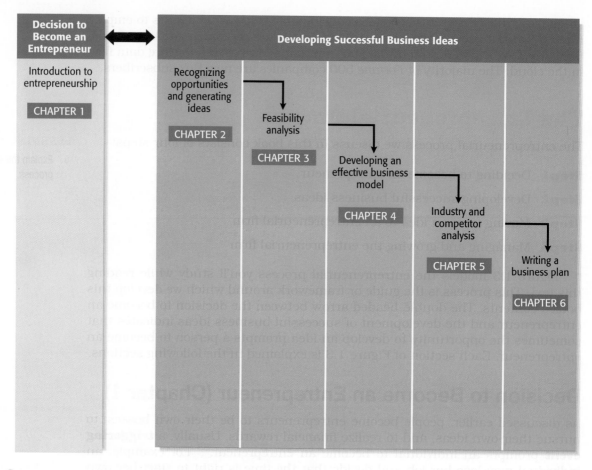

FIGURE 1.3
Basic Model of the
Entrepreneurial Process

are impatient and don't want to spend the time it takes to write a business plan.[59] This approach is usually a mistake. Writing a business plan forces an entrepreneur to think carefully through all the aspects of a business venture. It also helps a new venture establish a set of milestones that can be used to guide the early phases of the business rollout.

Moving from an Idea to an Entrepreneurial Firm (Chapters 7–10)

The first step in turning an idea into reality is to prepare a proper ethical and legal foundation for a firm, including selecting an appropriate form of business ownership. These issues are discussed in Chapter 7. Chapter 8 deals with the important topic of assessing a new venture's financial strength and viability-. Important information is contained in this chapter about completing and analyzing both historical and pro forma financial statements. Chapter 9 focuses on building a new-venture team. Chapter 10 highlights the important task of getting financing or funding and identifies the options a firm has for raising money.

Managing and Growing an Entrepreneurial Firm (Chapters 11–15)

Given today's competitive environment, all firms must be managed and grown properly to ensure their ongoing success. This is the final stage of the entrepreneurial process.

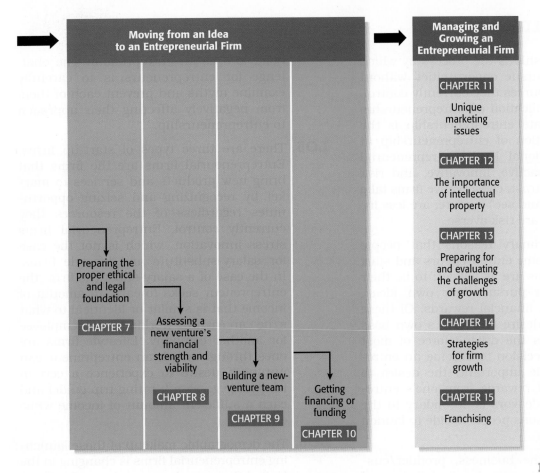

FIGURE 1.3
Continued

Chapter 11 focuses on the unique marketing issues facing entrepreneurial firms, including selecting an appropriate target market, building a brand, and the four Ps—product, price, promotion, and place (or distribution). Chapter 12 examines the important role of intellectual property in the growth of entrepreneurial firms. More and more, the value of "know-how" exceeds the value of a company's physical assets. In addition, we will talk about protecting business ideas through intellectual property statutes, such as patents, trademarks, copyrights, and trade secrets.

Preparing for and evaluting the challenges of growth is the topic of Chapter 13. We'll look at the characteristics and behaviors of successful growth firms. In Chapter 14, we'll study strategies for growth, ranging from new product development to mergers and acquisitions. We conclude with Chapter 15, which focuses on franchising. Not all franchise organizations are entrepreneurial firms, but franchising is a growing component of the entrepreneurial landscape. When you finish studying these 15 chapters, you will have been exposed to all components of the entrepreneurial process—a process that is vital to entrepreneurial success.

Chapter Summary

LO1. Entrepreneurship is the process by which individuals pursue opportunities without regard to resources they currently control. A specific application of entrepreneurship called corporate entrepreneurship is the conceptualization of entrepreneurship at the organizational level. Entrepreneurial firms are proactive, innovative, and risk taking. In contrast, conservative firms take a more "wait and see" posture, are less innovative, and are risk averse.

LO2. The three primary reasons that people decide to become entrepreneurs and start their own firms are as follows: to be their own boss, to pursue their own ideas, and to realize financial rewards. Of these reasons, the desire to be one's own boss or manager is the driving force of most individuals' decision to become an entrepreneur. While important, the desire to reap financial rewards from one's entrepreneurial endeavors is secondary to the other two reasons people decide to launch their own firm.

LO3. Passion for the business, product/customer focus, tenacity despite failure, and execution intelligence are the four primary characteristics of successful entrepreneurs. Of these four, being passionate about the firm the entrepreneur intends to launch is the most common characteristic shared among successful entrepreneurs. Commonly, the entrepreneur's passion is demonstrated by a belief that her/his firm will make a difference in people's lives. Always concentrating on the product or service as a means of satisfying a customer need, being tenancious in pursuing an entrepreneurial opportunity, and the ability to craft a business idea into a viable business operation are the other key characteristics associated with successful entrepreneurs.

LO4. The five most common myths regarding entrepreneurship are that entrepreneurs are born, not made; that entrepreneurs are gamblers; that entrepreneurs are motivated primarily by money; that entrepreneurs should be young and energetic; and that entrepreneurs love the spotlight. The issue with myths is that, if unchecked, they can affect an individual's orientation toward and subsequent behaviors as an entrepreneur. The challenge for entrepreneurs is to carefully examine myths and prevent each of them from negatively affecting their approach to entrepreneurship.

LO5. There are three types of start-up firms. Entrepreneurial firms are the firms that bring new products and services to market by recognizing and seizing opportunities regardless of the resources they currently control. Entrepreneurial firms stress innovation, which is not the case for salary-substitute and lifestyle firms. In the case of a salary-substitue firm, the entrepreneur seeks to earn an amount of income that is similar or identical to what s/he can earn by working as an employee for another company. Lifestyle firms are ones through which an entrepreneur can pursue a desire to experience a certain lifestyle (e.g., as a hunting trip guide) and earn a sufficient amount of income while doing so.

LO6. The demographic makeup of those launching entrepreneurial firms is changing in the United States and around the world. There is growing evidence that an increasing number of women, minorities, seniors, and young people are becoming actively involved in the entrepreneurial process. Evidence suggests that each of these groups of entrepreneurs are capable of appropriately using the entrepreneurial process as a foundation for developing a successful entrepreneurial venture.

LO7. There is strong evidence that entrepreneurship and the entrepreneurial behavior associated with it have significantly positive impacts on the stability and strength of economies throughout the world. The areas in which entrepreneurial firms contribute the most are innovation and job creation. Entrepreneurial behavior also has a dramatic impact on society. It's easy to think of new products and services that have helped make our lives easier, that have made us more productive at work, that have improved our health, and that have entertained us in new ways. In addition, entrepreneurial firms have a positive impact on the effectiveness of larger firms. There are many entrepreneurial firms that have built their entire business models around producing products and services that help larger firms increase their efficiency and effectiveness.

LO8. The four distinct elements of the entrepreneurial process, pictured in Figure 1.3, are deciding to become an entrepreneur, developing successful business ideas,

moving from an idea to establishing an entrepreneurial firm, and managing and growing an entrepreneurial firm. Each of these elements plays a critical role in entrepreneurial success. As a result, we carefully examine these elements in the book's remaining chapters.

Key Terms

business model, **47**
business plan, **47**
corporate entrepreneurship, **29**
creative destruction, **44**
entrepreneurial firms, **40**
entrepreneurial intensity, **29**

entrepreneurship, **28**
execution intelligence, **35**
innovation, **46**
lifestyle firms, **40**
moderate risk takers, **37**
passion for their business, **31**

product/customer focus, **34**
salary-substitute firms, **40**
triggering event, **47**
value, **40**

Review Questions

1-1. What are the characteristics of firms with higher entrepreneurial intensity and how would you manage this?

1-2. What key insights does the GEMS study provide us about entrepreneurship?

1-3. What does evidence show us about the rate of failure associated with entrepreneurial ventures?

1-4. What is entrepreneurship?

1-5. In what ways is an entrepreneur who just launched a restaurant different from someone who just took a job as the general manager of a restaurant owned by a major restaurant chain?

1-6. What are the three main attributes of firms that pursue high levels of corporate entrepreneurship?

1-7. What are the three primary reasons people become entrepreneurs?

1-8. Of the three primary reasons people become entrepreneurs, which one is given most commonly and why?

1-9. What are the four primary traits and characteristics of successful entrepreneurs?

1-10. Why is passion such an important characteristic of successful entrepreneurs?

1-11. What is it about passion that makes it particularly compatible with the entrepreneurial process?

1-12. What are the skills and abilities required to effectively execute a business idea?

1-13. What are the startup types available to someone looking to start their own business?

1-14. What are the five common myths of entrepreneurship?

1-15. How would you debunk the myth that entrepreneurs are motivated primarily by money?

1-16. What are the four distinctive parts of the entrepreneurial process and what is the relationship among the parts?

1-17. How would you characterize the risk-taking propensity of most entrepreneurs?

1-18. How do entrepreneurial firms have a positive impact on larger firms?

1-19. What did Joseph Schumpeter mean by the term *creative destruction*?

1-20. In general, what effects does entrepreneurship have on economies and societies throughout the world?

1-21. What are the changes to the demographic makeup of entrepreneurs in the United States that are described in this chapter?

Application Questions

1-22. After rereading the opening case, identify all of the effective or smart moves Zac Schau and his co-founders made in the early days of building Pure Fix Cycles.

1-23. You have been invited by a local community college to talk to the students on how to develop entrepreneurial skills. However, some of your colleagues are against the idea as they believe that entrepreneurial skills can only be acquired through life experiences and firsthand knowledge. Prepare a speech on the key elements of being a successful entrepreneur to convince both the students and your colleagues.

1-24. As a business lecturer, Peter has asked students in his class to present in groups a few business ideas that they are planning to pursue after their graduation. One particular group has caught his attention. Their business idea on developing an ecotourism center in their neighborhood seems possible and realistic. It might be a good opportunity for them to take this to the next level. However, when Peter spoke to them it became clear that they had many misconceptions about being entrepreneurs and were afraid to pursue this as a career. How can Peter ease their fears and convince them to follow their dreams?

1-25. One question that is often asked by people thinking about launching an entrepreneurial venture is "what should first-time entrepreneurs know before they launch?" Based on information featured in Chapter 1, what should entrepreneurs know before they commit to launching their firm?

1-26. A friend came up to you for advice. She has been contemplating for some time now to start a new venture. She has been employed in the corporate sector for the past 15 years, and has finally decided to pursue her dream of being self-employed and start a wellness center with a focus on healthy living. However, she is still a little confused. She is looking to learn the positive effects of entrepreneurship. Help her decide why she should undertake this process?

1-27. A group of new students in your entrepreneurship class was heard arguing that being an entrepreneur positively affects the entrepreneur in question only. They do not believe that an entrepreneur benefits the society and the nation as well. They do not understand that creative destruction stimulates economic activity and increases the productivity of all elements of a society. Explain to them the positive effects of entrepreneurship and entrepreneurial firms on economies and societies.

YOU BE THE VC 1.1 COMPANY: Wello

• Web: www.wello.com • Facebook: Wello • Twitter: @WeAreWello

Business Idea: Create an online platform that allows people to connect with personal trainers via live, interactive video, and participate in one-on-one or group training sessions.

Pitch: Many people are interested in engaging a personal trainer, to not only plan and lead their workouts but to provide motivation, feedback, and accountability. The problem is that people are busy and often don't have the time to meet a personal trainer at a gym when the trainer is available. Meeting with a personal trainer is even more difficult for people who travel frequently, particularly if their travel schedule varies from week to week.

Wello was designed to solve this problem. It is an online platform that allows anyone with a Web camera and Internet access to meet with a personal trainer online to conduct a workout. Workouts are available on a one-to-one basis or in a group setting. You have the same interactive, personalized experience but from the comfort of your home, office, hotel room, or wherever you work out. Wello has personal trainers available that offer sessions in yoga, Pilates, aerobics, general training, sports/performance, martial arts, and therapy/rehab.

Here's how Wello works. You go to the firm's website and select the type of training you desire. You then indicate the day you'd like the workout, and Wello will provide you a list of the trainers that are available that day and when they are available. Each trainer has a profile page that includes a bio, a list of health and wellness certifications, a video introduction, and customer reviews. All trainers are vetted to check out their certifications and references and are also run through trial sessions to

see how they do in a streaming-video context. A typical customer review consists of something like "Donny was punctual, very professional, and prepared. During the session he challenged me but kept a close eye to make sure I wasn't overdoing it or messing up my form. He was motivational without being cheesy. I plan to book another session with him soon." You can also send direct messages to trainers, to ask questions or to see if they can schedule a workout at a time other than what they have listed as available. Once you enroll you have your own profile page that keeps track of your workouts and your progress over time. One-on-one classes cost between $14 and $25 per workout, depending on how many workouts you buy at a time. Group classes, which can include up to five people, cost between $7 and $12 per class. Classes last between 30 and 60 minutes. You can select the people you include in your group workout (five maximum). As a result, you can participate in the same workout as friends or family members regardless of where they live.

Wello makes money by taking a percentage of every transaction that takes place on its site. The company is currently focused on fitness but has plans to extend its platform and business model to other areas.

1-28. Based on the material covered in this chapter, what questions would you ask the firm's founders before making your funding decision? What answers would satisfy you?

1-29. If you had to make your decision on just the information provided in the pitch and on the company's website, would you fund this company? Why or why not?

YOU BE THE VC 1.2 COMPANY: Brain Sentry

• Web: www.brainsentry.com • Facebook: Brain Sentry - Impact Sensors • Twitter: @BrainSentry

Business Idea: Create a device that helps coaches, athletic trainers, officials, and parents recognize when an athlete has received a blow to the head strong enough that it may have caused a concussion.

Pitch: Approximately 135 million Americans play organized team sports each year. One of the biggest fears of sports participants is receiving a blow to the head that results in a concussion. A problem with concussions is that unlike a ligament tear or a shoulder sprain, a concussion is not always apparent or detectable. As a result, athletes often receive a blow to the head and continue playing without knowing that they are at risk for further injury. When a blow to the head is observed

by a coach or parent, it is also hard to know if it was severe enough to cause concern. Sometimes athletes will actually downplay the severity of a blow to the head because they don't want to be removed from a game.

The potential impact of sport-related concussions is heart-wrenching. The big fear in an athlete continuing to play after suffering a concussion is the possibility of experiencing second impact syndrome (SIS), which can occur if the athlete sustains a second blow. The second blow may be relatively minor and can cause rapid brain swelling, respiratory failure, permanent brain damage, and possible death. Tragically, athletes less than 18 years old are the most susceptible to SIS.

Brain Sentry was founded to make it easier to detect sports-related concussions. The company makes an unobtrusive helmet-mounted device that signals an alert when an athlete suffers a rapid and potentially dangerous acceleration to the head. The sensor is placed at the base of the rear of the helmet. In the event of a big acceleration to the head, a bright red LED light illuminates and blinks every three seconds. Once the sensor flashes a red light, the player should be taken off the field and examined for the possibility of a head injury prior to returning to play. If the player is cleared to play, the coach or other designated adult simply resets the sensor to turn off the blinking light. The sensor keeps track of how many times it has been activated. If, within 30 days of the first alert, a second big impact is detected, the red light will flash quickly twice every three seconds. The sensor detects approximately 2 percent of the hardest hits, so it does not significantly affect the flow of the game. The sensor is light (one ounce), fully sealed, and is waterproof. It runs on a battery that doesn't need to be recharged during the course of a regular sports season. The Brain Sentry

monitor costs approximately $50 per helmet. It has to be replaced each season.

Brain Sentry is initially targeting football, hockey, and lacrosse, the three most popular helmeted sports. It is also developing sensors for biking, alpine, and other helmeted activities. The company has gained some early traction. In 2013, the Louisiana State University football team used Brain Sentry–equipped helmets during practices and scrimmages, and the Arena Football League is reportedly adopting Brain Sentry for all its teams. The Brain Sentry device was used by the Newcastle, Oklahoma, high school football team during the 2013 season.

1-30. Based on the material covered in this chapter, what questions would you ask the firm's founders before making your funding decision? What answers would satisfy you?

1-31. If you had to make your decision on just the information provided in the pitch and on the company's website, would you fund this company? Why or why not?

CASE 1.1

GoPro: A Classic Entrepreneurial Tale

• *Web: www.gopro.com* • *Facebook: GoPro* • *Twitter: @GoPro*

Bruce R. Barringer, *Oklahoma State University*

R. Duane Ireland, *Texas A&M University*

Introduction

GoPro sells a line of wearable, mountable, and reasonably affordable HD video cameras. Although they're now used for a variety of purposes, they were orginally designed for extreme sports enthusiasts, such as surfers and snow skiers, who wanted to shoot videos of their activities. About two inches wide, the cameras look like tiny gray boxes. Despite their size, they're packed with amazing capabilities. They can be mounted almost anywhere and shoot video that was previously impossible to get. If you've never seen what a GoPro camera can do, set this case aside for a few minutes and go to YouTube on your computer or smartphone. Type in the search box "Flying eagle point of view #1." The video was shot by a GoPro camera mounted on the back of an eagle. You get to see what the eagle sees flying through a beautiful mountain canyon. The video has been viewed almost 8 million times.

GoPro (technically Woodman Labs) is an enormously successful company. Currently, the firm is generating over $500 million in annual sales, and its cameras have become the gold standard for self-documenting extreme sports experiences. But it wasn't always this way. GoPro started with a single entrepreneur, working out of his parent's house, who was passionate about a specific idea. It's a good story—one from which any

student of entrepreneurship can learn and find takeaways that they can apply to their own start-up idea.

Nick Woodman

GoPro was started by Nick Woodman, who gew up in northern California. In high school, he played football and baseball before becoming infatuated with surfing. For college, he picked the University of California, San Diego, because of its proximity to the beach. Woodman knew early on that he wanted to be an entrepreneur. Before starting GoPro, he had two start-ups, both of which failed. The first, a website called EmpowerAll.com, tried to sell electronic products for no more than a $2 markup. It barely got off the ground. The second start-up, Funbug, was a game and marketing platform that gave users the chance to win cash prizes. It was launched in 1999, the height of the dot-com bubble, and raised $3.9 million in funding. The company failed a year later, never having gained traction.

Woodman was shaken by the failure of Funbug, and he decided to take some time off. He traveled to Australia and Indonesia to surf, thinking that when he returned he would find a normal job. It was in Australia that the idea for GoPro first emerged. Woodman had brought a makeshift strap that he used to tether a Kodak disposable camera to his wrist so he could photograph himself and others surfing. It didn't work well. What he needed was a strap that was durable enough to take the wear and tear of ocean waves, and still be comfortable enough to wear. Woodman experimented with different strap designs during the trip. When he returned to California, he decided to pursue the idea of designing a wrist strap for cameras full time. Years later, reflecting on the trip, Woodman told *Forbes* magazine, "I remember my parents not being very supportive of it (the trip). But if I (hadn't) followed my passion for surfing … I would have never come up with the concept to make a wrist camera."

Protoyping and First Sale

Woodman moved into his parents' house and started building prototypes. He was determined to bootstrap his start-up this time, still smarting from losing $3.9 million of his investors' money on Funbug. To support himself, he made money traveling up and down the California coast selling bead-and-shell belts he bought in Indonesia for $2.50 and was able to sell in California for as much as $60. Using an improvised set of tools and his mom's sewing machine, he gained confidence that he could make a strap that was better than anything currently available for tethering a camera to a surfer's wrist. His thinking evolved to selling not only the strap, but a combination of the strap, a camera, and casings (to protect the camera from water and other debris). After borrowing money from his parents, he moved to a cottage in the redwood forest near Pesadero, California, where he worked nonstop testing fabrics, designing marketing materials, and writing patent applications. Getting the strap right wasn't an easy task. He needed to find the perfect tightness and perfect fabric, so it didn't make you sweat, didn't make you sore, and wouldn't break down in water. He had no expertise in camera design, so knew he'd

have to license a camera from an existing manufacturer. He settled on an inexpensive 35-millimeter model made in China. He finally had what he wanted—a camera, casings, and a durable and comfortable strap. He decided to call the combination GoPro.

To test the market for his product, Woodman and his roommate and first hire, Neil Dana, hit the trade show circuit. The moment start-up founders dream about happened at the first show, which turned out to be the 2004 Action Sports Retailer show in San Diego. GoPro got its first order for 100 units from a Japanese distributor.

Growth Years

GoPro grossed $350,000 its first year. Woodman and Dana visited surf shops across the country trying to convince them to carry the product. In 2005, Woodman appeared on QVC three times. GoPro slowly built momentum. Woodman also didn't stop innovating. Along with surfing, Woodman had an interest in race car driving. He treated himself to driving lessons at Infineon Raceway in Sonoma, California. On a hunch, he strapped a GoPro wrist cam to the car's roll bar, which is in front of the driver. That led to an inspirational moment. GoPro would make mounts for its cameras so people could point them back at themselves.

Woodman also broadened his vision and started attending trade shows in all the action sports and consumer electronics markets. By this time, GoPro was manufacturing its own cameras. Although GoPro was getting into surf shops and sportings goods stores, it hadn't yet penetrated a major retailer. Woodman started engaging executives at REI, an outdoors and sporting goods chain. At one point, he was sending them an e-mail once a month updating them on GoPro's activities. Eventually, GoPro broke into REI and Dick's Sportings Goods. In 2010, GoPro's big break happened. After

This young man is a mountain hiker. He is using a GoPro camera, mounted on his forehead, to record himself ascending and descending challenging mountain trails.

Gerhard Zwerger Schoner/Glow Images

(continued)

reaching out to Best Buy repeatedly with no luck, Best Buy approached GoPro. After beating sales targets in several test stores, GoPro's cameras were placed in all Best Buy locations. GoPro also got a little lucky. The Flip camera was a big seller for Best Buy, but its appeal evaporated when smartphones obtained video capability. In 2011, the Flip camera was pulled from Best Buy's shelves. That left a void in Best Buy's camera line that GoPro was able to fill.

As is the case for most start-up ventures, GoPro has had some scary moments. In 2007, revenue was in the low seven figures and Woodman was concerned. He wondered if GoPro would grow beyond its extreme sports niche, and considered turning the company over to a group of outside investors. The financial crisis of 2008 prevented that from happening, and GoPro moved on.

The Influence of Social Media

A fascinating part of the GoPro story is the influence of social media on the firm's success. From the beginning, extreme sports enthusiasts who bought GoPro cameras posted their videos. Many went viral and posted millions of views. This situation created the best possible scenario for GoPro. Its brand was being promoted not by the firm itself, but by its users. Piggybacking on its users' appetite for stunning videos, GoPro sponsored several well-known extreme sports athletes, including American skateboarder and snowboarder Shaun White. For a fun experience, go to YouTube and type in "Shaun White GoPro." There will be several videos. You can see exactly what Shaun White sees when he tackles an X Games halfpipe or a particularly difficult run, all captured by helmet-mounted GoPro cameras. GoPro is also a little edgy in its sponsorships. When Felix Baumgartner set a sky-diving record by jumping from the edge of space, he wore five GoPro cameras on the way down.

To GoPro's credit, in part it has made its own luck when it comes to social media. Its $300 cameras produce video that rivals that of professionally created content, so it's fun to shoot and post. For instance, Woodman and his team knew that to produce truly satisfying video the sound quality would have to be good. Viewers would want to hear, for example, a snowboard crunching through snow to get the full impact of a thrilling descent. Wind noise rushing into a camera's microphone is a problem in this type of setting and can easily drown out everything else. By riding bikes that are nearly silent, Woodman and his engineers were able to record almost pure wind noise in a natural environment.

They then developed firmware that isolates the sound of wind and eliminates distracting sound from GoPro recordings.

As a result of all of this, GoPro says it has over 222 million views on its YouTube channel and 4.7 million likes on Facebook.

The Road Ahead

Not everyone is widely optimistic about GoPro's future. Maintaining its momentum may be tough. Major brands such as Sony, Coleman, and Swann have started selling sports cameras that are similar to GoPro's. Other tech heavyweights, such as Apple and Google, are working on wearable devices with video and photo capabilities. The wildcard is smartphones, and how good their video capabilities will eventually become. If a smartphone will eventually be able to do everything that a GoPro camera is able to do, that doesn't project a bright future for GoPro, at least in its current form.

GoPro, of course, is aware of these challenges. In May 2011, Woodman broke his vow to never take outside funding and raised $88 million in a series A round. The round involved several venture capital firms, some with deep ties in the entertainment and technology industries. Woodman says that the momey was raised in part to build an experienced board of directors to help GoPro navigate the future. As for the money itself, Woodman has remained mum about how it will be used. That causes one to speculate that GoPro may have future generations of products in its pipeline.

Discussion Questions

1-32. Which of the characteristics of a successful entrepreneur, discussed in the chapter, do you see in Nick Woodman? To what degree do you think these characteristics have contributed to GoPro's success?

1-33. How does GoPro's basic business idea "add value" in the lives of its customers?

1-34. How do Nick Woodman's entrepreneurial actions debunk the myth that most entrepreneurs are motivated by money?

1-35. What are the most significant challenges GoPro faces in the future? Do you think GoPro will able to meet the challenges or do you think the company's future is in doubt? Explain your answer.

Sources: L. Chapman, "Extreme Sports Gets a Camera," *The Wall Street Journal*, B7, June 20, 2013; R. Mac, "The Mad Billionaire Behind GoPro: The World's Hottest Camera Company," *Forbes*, March 25, 2013; T. Foster, "The GoPro Army," *Inc.*, January 26, 2012.

CASE 1.2

PatientsLikeMe: Allowing People with Serious Diseases to Connect with One Another and Exchange Support and Advice

• *Web: www.patientslikeme.com* • *Facebook: PatientsLikeMe* • *Twitter: @patientslikeme*

Bruce R. Barringer, *Oklahoma State University*

R. Duane Ireland, *Texas A&M University*

Introduction

It's a sad yet heartwarming story. In 1998, Stephen Heywood, a strong 28-year-old carpenter who was building his dream house in California, got the worst possible news. He was diagnosed with amyotrophic lateral sclerosis (ALS), or Lou Gehrig's disease. His brothers, Jamie and Ben, stood by his side as he doggedly fought his disease and pursued a cure. Stephen eventually succumbed to ALS, but his courageous journey will always be remembered through an autobiographical movie, *So Much So Fast*, and a book, *His Brother's Keeper,* by Pulitzer Prize–winning author Jonathan Weiner.

Helping Stephen deal with the day-to-day challenges of his disease and experiencing firsthand the decisions that have to be made and the lack of information that's often available profoundly changed the direction of Jamie and Ben Heywood's lives. In 1999, Jamie Haywood launched an organization called the ALS Therapy Development Foundation, to help Stephen and others fight ALS. Today, it remains well funded and staffed and supports a number of research efforts. In 2005, Jamie and his brother Ben took an additional step and launched PatientsLikeMe, a Web-based company that allows people with life-changing diseases to converse with one another, share their experiences, and learn techniques from each other that help them better cope with their diseases.

Since its launch, PatientsLikeMe has achieved remarkable success. Any patient with any medical condition can join the site. As a result, the company now has hundreds of thousands of patients sharing their experiences with respect to over 500 conditions. At the heart of PatientsLikeMe's success is a truly unique value proposition—a platform that encourages patients to interact in ways that are very meaningful for them. PatientsLikeMe is also a bold company, in that one of its goals is to change the way that the medical industry thinks about patients and patient care. To facilitate that goal, PatientsLikeMe is working with, rather than against, the medical industry. In fact, its primary revenue driver is to sell aggregated data that it collects from its online patient communities to medical companies to enable them to factor the "voice of the patient" into all aspects of their product decisions.

Value Proposition

PatientsLikeMe's value proposition is the opposite of what you might expect, in that conventional thinking is that a person's medical information is private and should be kept confined to a tight circle of family and health care providers. PatientsLikeMe advocates that people openly share their experiences to help others. It's inspirational in that most of its members have illnesses that consume a great deal of their own time and energy, yet are willing to expend time and effort to share information to improve the lives of others.

Here's how it works. Say someone you care about has been diagnosed with Parkinson's disease, a neurological disorder. On PatientsLikeMe, that person will be able to interact with people who have been living with Parkinson's disease for 3 years, 5 years, 10 years, or more. Your friend or loved one will be able to ask, "What's it like after 3 years? What will I be able to do and not do? What's the scariest part of the disease?" Your friend or loved one will also be able to ask the number-one question that people with diseases have, which is: "Given my status, what's the best outcome I can hope for and how can I get there?" This question will be answered by someone who has the disease and who truly understands all the emotions and fears rather than being answered by a medical professional.

PatientsLikeMe's service is unique in that it not only facilitates these types of interactions but also collects detailed information from its members about the symptoms they're experiencing, medications they're on, and how their diseases are affecting their lives. It then displays this data in aggregate form for its members and others to see. It also drills deeper. It allows patients to share the experiences they're having with a particular drug, for example, including how long they've been on the drug, what the side effects have been, whether they feel the drug has been effective, and so forth. This is information that people who have just been prescribed a drug are anxious to see. Members can also interact directly with each other regarding their experiences. For example, Carbidopa-Levodopa is a drug commonly prescribed to Parkinson's disease patients. Someone named "Mary O." may have reported on her profile that "When I first started taking Carbidopa-Levodopa it made me

(continued)

sleepy, but over time my body adjusted and I no longer have that side effect." If you've just been prescribed Carbidopa-Levodopa, you can send a message to Mary O. and ask her, "How sleepy did you get? Was it so bad you couldn't go to work? How long did it take before your body adjusted? Did you try caffeine? Did it help?" Mary O. would then respond and answer the questions. In addition, as a result of this exchange, you and Mary O. may start to regularly correspond, and Mary O. may become for you an important source of information and support.

What's remarkable about PatientsLikeMe's value proposition is that the information its members exchange and the manner in which it aggregates and displays data aren't available anywhere else. The degree to which its members are willing to be transparent about very personal health-related issues is also compelling. Along with maintaining its website and member communities, PatientsLikeMe has also become an authoritative voice in the medical community. It has published over 30 peer-reviewed research studies. In 2013, PatientsLikeMe's vice president for advocacy, Sally Okun, made a highly visible presentation at TEDMED about the idea of building a "patient lexicon" to make it as easy for patients to talk about their conditions and compare notes as it is for doctors. The eight-minute talk titled "Does Anyone in Healthcare Want to Be Understood?" is available at www.tedmed.com. Simply type "Sally Okun" into the search bar.

Revenue Driver

Although its services are free to users, PatientsLikeMe is a for-profit entrepreneurial venture. The company makes money by aggregating the information its members share and selling it to its partners. Its partners include members of the medical community such as drug companies, medical-device companies, insurance companies, and health care providers. For example, the aggregate data of how patients with Parkinson's disease are reacting to a particular medication would be of interest to the company that makes that medication. The sharing of this information then circles back and helps patients. For example, if the maker of the Parkinson's drug finds that a large percentage of people who take the drug experience fatigue, the drug can potentially be tweaked to remedy that issue. For patients, not experiencing fatigue as a side effect of the drug may not only translate into feeling better, but may mean fewer days missed from work or even the ability to maintain a job rather than having to quit. Because of these types of outcomes, most patients are eager to have their personal data included in larger databases and passed along to companies in the medical industry. Finally, their experiences and their voices become part of the data that medical companies study when making decisions about patients and their care. PatientsLikeMe is very transparent about the fact that it sells its patients' data, and it sees the sharing of data as integral to its mission. It does not share or sell

personally identifiable information without the explicit consent of the member.

There are no ads or sponsorships on PatientsLikeMe's website. The company's sole intention is to align the interests of its members with the medical community.

Challenges Ahead

PatientsLikeMe is expanding its reach. While its site originally focused exclusively on life-threatening diseases, it now supports communities that focus on issues such as infertility (for both men and women), mood conditions (including depression), and hearing loss. Rapid growth is a challenge for all firms, and PatientsLikeMe is in a rapid-growth phase. In fact, at the time this case was written, PatientsLikeMe was supporting communities for more than 500 conditions.

There are also several worries that surround a service such as PatientsLikeMe. The company openly acknowledges these worries but believes the benefits outweigh the risks. One worry is that some employers may not want to employ people with a high-cost or high-risk disease. Again, it's possible that some people may reveal the existence of a disease on their PatientsLikeMe profiles that may jeopardize current or future employment opportunities. Another worry is the unknowns about changes to health care policies and the overall health care system in the United States as a result of the passage of the Affordable Care Act. How changes brought about by that act will affect how information about patients is distributed and to whom is still not entirely clear.

For now, PatientsLikeMe is aggressively moving forward. The company's overarching goal, along with providing the value it currently provides, is to shift the thinking of companies in the medical industry by providing them access to data they never had before. By better knowing the journey that patients are on, the hope is that the medical community will increasingly go beyond treating their patients' core diseases and create products that will impact all aspects—physical, social, and mental—of their lives.

Discussion Questions

1-36. Of the three reasons articulated in Chapter 1 that movitate people to start businesses, which of the three reasons was the primary motivation behind Jamie and Ben Heywood's decision to launch PatientsLikeMe?

1-37. How do those who are leading PatientsLikeMe practice "execution intelligence?"

1-38. What type of start-up firm is PatientsLikeMe?

Sources: PatientsLikeMe website, www.patientslikeme.com (accessed March 14, 2014); J. Comstock, "PatientsLikeMe Has 200K Users, Calls for New Lexicon," mobihealthnews, April 17, 2013, available at http://mobihealthnews.com/21671/patients-likeme-has-200k-users-calls-for-new-lexicon/ (accessed March 15, 2014); R. Bradley, "Rethinking Health Care with PatientsLikeMe," *Fortune*, April 15, 2013.

Endnotes

1. SuperJam homepage, www.superjam.co.uk; "Fraser Doherty: 'How I Set Up SuperJam,'" Newbusiness. co.uk, www.newbusiness.co.uk/articles/entrepreneurs/fraser-doherty-how-i-set-superjam (accessed September 5, 2011, originally posted December 21, 2009); "Q&A: Fraser Doherty—SuperJam," Inspiresme.co.uk, www.inspiresme.co.uk/interviews/q-a—fraser-doherty—superjam (accessed September 5, 2011, originally posted May 31, 2011).

2. J. E. Amoros and N. Bosma, *Global Entrepreneurship Monitor 2013 Global Report* (Babson College and Universidad del Desarrollo, 2013). London, England.

3. S. F. Gohmann and J. M. Fernandez, "Proprietorship and Unemployment in the United States," *Journal of Business Venturing* 29, no. 2 (2014): 289–309.

4. T. Astebro and J. Chen, "The Entrepreneurial Earnings Puzzle: Mismeasurement or Real?" *Journal of Business Venturing* 29, no. 1 (2014): 88–105.

5. T. Tyszka, J. Cieslie, A. Domurat, and A. Macko, "Motivation, Self-Efficacy, and Risk Attitudes Among Entrepreneurs During Transition to a Market Economy," *Journal of Socio-Economics* 40, no. 2 (2011): 124–31.

6. D. Grichnik, J. Brinckmann, L. Singh, and S. Manigart, "Beyond Environmental Scarcity: Human and Social Capital as Driving Forces of Bootstrapping Activities," *Journal of Business Venturing* 29, no. 2 (2014): 310–326.

7. C. S. Hayter, "Conceptualizing Knowledge-Based Entrepreneurship Networks: Perspectives from the Literature," *Small Business Economics* 41, no. 4 (2013): 899–911.

8. S. A. Alvarez and J. B. Barney, "Entrepreneurial Opportunities and Poverty Alleviation," *Entrepreneurship Theory and Practice* 38, no. 1 (2014): 159–184.

9. M. Frese, D. M. Rousseau, and J. Wiklund, "The Emergence of Evidence-Based Entrepreneurship," *Entrepreneurship Theory and Practice* 38, no. 2 (2014): 209–216.

10. G. D. Bruton, I. Filatotchev, S. Si, and M. Wright, "Entrepreneurship and Strategy in Emerging Economies," *Strategic Entrepreneurship Journal* 7, no. 3 (2013): 169–180.

11. M. A. Uy, M.-D. Foo, and R. Ilies, "Perceived Progress Variability and Entrepreneurila Effort Intensity: The Moderating Role of Venture Goal Commitment," *Journal of Business Venturing* 2014, in press.

12. R. Branson, *Losing My Virginity* (New York: Time Warner, 1999).

13. Ladies Who Launch home page, www.ladieswho-launch.com (accessed March 5, 2014).

14. B. Barringer, *The Truth About Starting a Business* (Upper Saddle River, NJ: Financial Times, 2009).

15. T. J. Bae, S. Qian, C. Miao, and J. O. Fiet, "The Relationship Between Entrepreneurship Education and Entrepreneurial Intentions: A Meta-Analytic Review," *Entrepreneurship Theory and Practice* 38, no. 2 (2014): 217–254.

16. D. Courpasson, F. Dany, and I. Marti, "Organizational Entrepreneurship as Active Resistance: A Struggle Against Outsourcing," *Entrepreneurship Theory and Practice* 2014, in press.

17. M. Sullivan, "Interview with Melissa Pickering," Business Inerviews.com, accessed March 5, 2014.

18. iCreate to Educate home page, www.icreatetoeducate.com, accessed March 1, 2014.

19. D. Carnoy, "Richard Branson," *Success*, April 1998, 62–63.

20. J. Wood, "John Wood, 43, Founder of Room to Read and Author of Leaving Microsoft to Change the World," in K. Finneran, "In Pictures: The Greatest Risk They Ever Took," *Forbes*, January 20, 2010.

21. Wikipedia, "Room to Read," www.Wikipedia.org, accessed March 1, 2014.

22. K. Farrell and L. C. Farrell, *Entrepreneurial Age* (New York: Allworth Press, 2001).

23. M. Sullivan, "Interview with Alex Algar, Founder, WhitePages.com," BusinessInverviews.com, accessed March 5, 2014.

24. R. D. Jager and R. Ortiz, *In the Company of Giants* (New York: McGraw-Hill, 2007).

25. W. Wei, "How Pandora Survived More Than 300 VC Rejections," *Business Insider*, July 14, 2010.

26. P. H. Kim, K. C. Longest, and S. Lippmann, "The Tortoise Versus the Hare; Progress and Business Viability Differences Between Conventional and Leisure-Based Founders," *Journal of Business Venturing* 2014, in press.

27. L. Hazleton, "Profile: Jeff Bezos," *Success*, July 1998: 60.

28. Ladies Who Launch home page, www.ladieswholaunch.com, accessed April 16, 2006.

29. N. Koehn, *Brand New: How Entrepreneurs Earned Consumers' Trust from Wedgwood to Dell* (Boston: Harvard Business School Press, 2001).

30. Koehn, *Brand New*.

31. M. Lofstrom, T. Bates, and S. C. Parker, "Why Are Some People More Likely to Become Small-Business Owners Than Others: Entrepreneurship Entry and Industry-Specific Barriers," *Journal of Business Venturing* 29, no. 2 (2014): 232–251.

32. G. N. Powell and K. A. Eddleston, "Linking Family-to-Business Enrichment and Support to Entrepreneurial Success: Do Female and Male Entrepreneurs Experience Different Outcomes?" *Journal of Business Venturing* 28, no. 2 (2013): 261–280.

33. H. A. Ndofor and R. L. Priem, "Immigrant Entrepreneurs, the Ethnic Enclave Strategy, and Venture Performance," *Journal of Management* 37, no. 3 (2011): 790–818.

34. M. R. Marvel, "Human Capital and Search-Based Discovery: A Study of High-Tech Entrepreneurship," *Entrepreneurship Theory and Practice* 37, no. 2 (2013): 403–419.

35. J. P. J. de Jong, S. K. Parter, S. Wennekers, and C.-H. Wu, "Entrepreneurial Behavior

in Organizations: Does Job Design Matter?" *Entrepreneurship Theory and Practice* 2014, in press; R. A. Baron and J. Tang, "The Role of Entrepreneurs in Firm-Level Innovation: Joint Effects of Positive Affect, Creativity, and Environmental Dynamism," *Journal of Business Venturing* 26, no. 1 (2011): 49–60.

36. The Hartford 2013 Small Business Success Study, October 13, 2013. Available at http://www.thehartford.com/our-company/success-study-2013. Accessed March 13, 2014.

37. D. Miller and C. Sardais, "Bifurcating Time: How Entrepreneurs Reconcile the Paradoxical Demands of the Job," *Entrepreneurship Theory and Practice* 2014, in press.

38. C. Angle, "Iterate Again," in D. Cohen and B. Feld (eds.), *Do More Faster* (Hoboken, NJ: John Wiley & Sons, Inc., 2011), 50.

39. C. Williams, *Lead, Follow, or Get Out of the Way* (New York: Times Books, 1981), 111.

40. S. Walton, *Made in America: My Story* (New York: Doubleday, 1992).

41. The Kauffman Foundation and LegalZoom Startup Environment Index 2012, Ewing Marion Kauffman Foundation, February 2013.

42. D. H. Hsu and R. H. Ziedonis, "Resources as Dual Sources of Advantage: Implications for Valuing Entrepreneurial-Firm Patents," *Strategic Management Journal* 34, no. 7 (2013): 761–781; J. Zhang, "The Advantage of Experienced Start-Up Founders in Venture Capital Acquisition: Evidence from Serial Entrepreneurs," *Small Business Economics* 36, no. 2 (2010): 187–208.

43. SBA, Small Business Trends, available at www.sba.gov/content/small-business-trends, accessed March 13, 2014.

44. American Express OPEN, "The 2013 State of Women-Owned Business Report, American Express Corp.

45. U.S. Census Bureau, www.census.gov, accessed March 13, 2014.

46. Count Me In home page, www.countmein.org, accessed March 13, 2014.

47. MBDA, "Minority-Owned Business Growth & Global Reach," MBDA, available at www.mbda.gove, accessed March 13, 2014.

48. MBDA, "Minority-Owned Business Growth & Global Reach," MBDA, available at www.mbda.gove, accessed March 13, 2014.

49. The Kauffman Foundation and LegalZoom Startup Environment Index 2012, Ewing Marion Kauffman Foundation, February 2013.

50. Gallup, "U.S. Students' Entrepreneurial Aspirations Still Undeveloped," available at http://www.gallup.com/poll/160040/students-entrepreneurial-aspirations-undeveloped.aspx, accessed March 14, 2014.

51. Lemonade Day home page, http://lemonadeday.org, accessed March 14, 2014.

52. Babson College home page, www.babson.edu, accessed March 14, 2014.

53. Entrepreneur, "With Entrepreneurship in Vogue, Colleges Beef up Offerings (Infographic)," available at www.entrepreneur.com/article/printthis/230274.html, accessed March 14, 2014.

54. J. A. Schumpeter, *The Theory of Economic Development* (Cambridge, MA: Harvard University Press, 1994).

55. R. Klingebiel and C. Rammer, "Resource Allocation Strategy for Innovation Portfolio Management," *Strategic Management Journal* 35, no. 2 (2014): 246–268; W. J. Baumol, "Formal Microeconomic Structure for Innovative Entrepreneurship Theory," *Entrepreneurship Research Journal* 1, no. 1 (2011): 1–3.

56. SBA, "Small Businesses Lead the Way in Green Technology Innovation," available at www.sba.gov/advocacy/809/29201, accessed March 14, 2014.

57. C. Bialik, "Sizing up the Small-Business Jobs Machine," *Wall Street Journal*, October 15, 2011, A2.

58. A. D. Cruz, C. Howorth, and E. Hamilton, "Intrafamily Entrepreneurship: The Formation and Membership of Family Entrepreneurial Teams," *Entrepreneurship Theory and Practice* 37, no. 1 (2013): 17–46.

59. B. Barringer, *Preparing Effective Business Plans* (Upper Saddle River, NJ: Prentice Hall, 2009).

PART 2 Developing Successful Business Ideas

LuminAID Lab, LLC

CHAPTER 2 **Recognizing *Opportunities* and Generating Ideas 63**

CHAPTER 3 **Feasibility *Analysis* 97**

CHAPTER 4 **Developing an *Effective* Business Model 133**

CHAPTER 5 **Industry and Competitor *Analysis* 171**

CHAPTER 6 **Writing a Business Plan 203**

Getting Personal

with **ICRACKED**

Co-Founders

AJ FORSYTHE

BS, Business Economics, UC Santa Barbara, 2010

ANTHONY MARTIN

BS, Psychology, Cal Poly-San Luis Obispo, 2011

Dialogue with
Anthony Martin

▼

MY BIGGEST WORRY AS AN ENTREPRENEUR
Not moving fast enough/Hiring awesome people.

MY ADVICE FOR NEW ENTREPRENEURS
If you wait for your product to be perfect before you launch, you've waited too long.

FIRST ENTREPRENEURIAL EXPERIENCE
Selling Mistletoe outside my house during the holidays at 10 years old. (Gold Mine)

MY FAVORITE SMARTPHONE APP
Uber—I click a button and a driver is there to pick me up. How cool is that?

MY BIGGEST SURPRISE AS AN ENTREPRENEUR
You don't to have to have all the answers figured out to start a company. You need to have intellectual curiosity and a passion for what you're doing.

BEST PART OF BEING A STUDENT
It's really not real life—Enjoy the parties and take the time to find your passion.

CHAPTER 2

Recognizing *Opportunities* and Generating Ideas

OPENING PROFILE

ICRACKED

Solving a Problem and Building a Business in an Exploding Industry

• *WEB: www.icracked.com* • *Facebook: iCracked* • *Twitter: @icracked*

n mid-2009, AJ Forsythe had a problem. While a student at California-Poly San Luis Obispo, he broke his iPhone twice within two days. The first time occurred when he was exiting his car. He dropped his iPhone and cracked the screen. That accident cost him $200 and an hour's trip to the Apple store. A few days later the same phone broke again, when his roommate casually tossed it to him and it hit a ceiling fan. Determined to fix the phone himself this time, Forsythe got help from some engineering students and used a small screwdriver and dental pick to replace the phone's shattered screen. Incredibly, shortly after these two incidents, Forsythe's roommate broke his iPhone. At that point, Forsythe realized that repairing iPhones was a promising idea for pursuing a business opportunity.

To start, Forsythe gave a friend $20 to design a flyer, and began putting the flyers up around campus. Within two weeks, he had his first customer. Forsythe set up a Facebook page and a Twitter account to generate additional awareness and sales, and the business—which he named iCracked—started to take shape. Profit margins were good. At $75 a phone, Forsythe was making about $40 for less than an hour's work.

From the outset, Forsythe saw iCracked as a business that could be replicated on other college campuses. He spent the summer of 2010 in Dallas, his hometown, pitching the idea to local campuses. Forsythe brought on a partner in the fall of 2010, Anthony Martin. The two met through a mutual friend. Martin's best friend in high school was Forsythe's best friend in college. At the time, Martin was running a textbook exchange platform at UC Santa Barbara. Martin and Forsythe were both college entrepreneurs and enjoyed talking to each other about business. Martin liked the opportunity Forsythe was pursuing, particularly given Apple's growing market share in the smartphone industry. Martin put the first investment into iCracked to buy inventory and set up a website. The two began putting job listings on college campuses across the United States. Within 30 days, they had their first website up and 23 repair technicians on college campuses across the country. They called their repair technicians "iTechs." In the nearby photo, Anthony Martin appears on the left while AJ Forsythe is on the right.

LEARNING OBJECTIVES

After studying this chapter you should be ready to:

1. Explain the difference between opportunities and ideas.

2. Describe the three general approaches entrepreneurs use to identify opportunities.

3. Discuss the personal characteristics of entrepreneurs that contribute to their ability to recognize business opportunities.

4. Identify and describe techniques entrepreneurs use to generate ideas.

5. Discuss actions to take to encourage continuous development of new ideas in entrepreneurial firms.

Since that time, iCracked has continued to expand, and the company now has over 500 iTechs spread over most of the United States and eight foreign countries. Initially, a customer would be put in touch with an iTech technician, and they agree on a place to meet. Starting in late 2013, the service improved, and the iTechs now travel directly to the customer. They repair broken screens, LCDs, bad batteries and all other small parts problems, as well as water damage for Apple iPhone, iPad, and iPod models. As long as the logic board is intact, which it usually is, the repair can be made. The repairs typically take between 10 and 30 minutes and cost between $70 and $170. They also purchase used iPhone, iPad, and iPod devices. The iTechs aren't full-time employees of iCracked. The firm makes money by selling parts to the iTechs and connecting them to customers. iCracked is extremely diligent about who becomes an iTech. Every applicant is subject to a five-step interview process and a background check. Thousands apply, but only 2 percent of applicants are accepted. The firm adds 50-70 new iTechs each month. Over time, iCracked technicians have seen all manner of iPhone catastrophes, from pet pigs stomping on them, to iPhones being run over by trucks, to phones falling out of the hands of skydivers. Often badly damaged, the phones can usually be repaired and restored. Offering insurance on iPhones is a new product line iCracked is considering. The insurance is expected to cost around $6 a month, with a $20 deductible. For people in areas where iTech technicians aren't yet available, iCracked offers the option of sending the broken phone to the company's headquarters, where it will be fixed and sent back the same day. iCracked also continues to sell its do-it-yourself iPhone Screen Repair Kit.

iCracked believes it is just getting started. The company had sales of around $2 million in 2012 and $10 million in 2013. It sees additional opportunities in its core business and in other areas. In regard to its core business, it's estimated that within the next five years, there will be five billion smartphones in the world. About 30 percent of smartphones are damaged and at some point need repairs. iCracked has already positioned itself as the world's largest and most efficient iPhone repair and buyback service. It plans to soon extend its service to Android-equipped phones. As a result, iCracked is positioned to dramatically increase its revenue in smartphone repairs, buy-backs, and additional services. Its smartphone insurance service is also expected to significantly add to the firm's sales revenue.

In regard to other areas, in early 2012, Forsythe and Martin were admitted to Y Combinator, based on the strength of their company's early traction. Y Combinator is a business accelerator that provides seed money, mentoring and connections to promising technology startups. The three-month Y Combinator experience challenged Forsythe and Martin to see iCracked in a new light and as a much bigger potential opportunity. Forsythe and Martin believe their network of iTech technicians is the company's most valuable asset. They foresee the technicians eventually providing repairs, installations, and additional service across a variety of industries for a wide range of clientele.

In this chapter, we discuss the importance of understanding the difference between ideas and opportunities. While ideas are interesting and can intrigue us as possibilities, not every idea is in fact the source of an opportunity for an entrepreneur to pursue. In addition to describing the differences between ideas and opportunities, this chapter also discusses approaches entrepreneurs use to spot opportunities, as well as factors or conditions in the external environment that may result in opportunities. As you will see, too, certain characteristics seem to be associated with individuals who are adept at spotting viable business opportunities.

The Differences Between Opportunities and Ideas

Essentially, entrepreneurs recognize an opportunity and turn it into a successful business.[1] An **opportunity** is a favorable set of circumstances that creates a need for a new product, service, or business. Most entrepreneurial ventures are started in one of two ways. Some ventures are externally stimulated. In this instance, an entrepreneur decides to launch a firm, searches for and recognizes an opportunity, and then starts a business, as Jeff Bezos did when he created Amazon.com. In 1994, Bezos quit his lucrative job at a New York City investment firm and headed for Seattle with a plan to find an attractive opportunity and launch an e-commerce company. Other firms are internally stimulated, like iCracked. An entrepreneur recognizes a problem or an **opportunity gap** and creates a business to address the problem or fill the identified gap.

Regardless of which of these two ways an entrepreneur starts a new business, opportunities are tough to spot. Identifying a product, service, or business opportunity that isn't merely a different version of something already available is difficult. A common mistake entrepreneurs make in the opportunity recognition process is picking a currently available product or service that they like or are passionate about and then trying to build a business around a slightly better version of it. Although this approach seems sensible, such is usually not the case. The key to opportunity recognition is to identify a product or service that people need and are willing to buy, not one that an entrepreneur wants to make and sell.

As shown in Figure 2.1, an opportunity has four essential qualities: It is (1) attractive, (2) timely, (3) durable, and (4) anchored in a product, service, or business that creates or adds value for its buyer or end-user. For an entrepreneur to capitalize on an opportunity, its **window of opportunity** must be open. The term *window of opportunity* is a metaphor describing the time period in which a firm can realistically enter a new market. Once the market for a new product is established, its window of opportunity opens. As the market grows, firms enter and try to establish a profitable position. At some point, the market matures, and the window of opportunity closes. This is the case with Internet search engines. Yahoo, the first search engine, appeared in 1995, and the market grew quickly, with the addition of Lycos, Excite, and several others. Google entered the market in 1998, sporting advanced search technology. Since then, the search engine market has matured, and the window of opportunity is less prominent. Today, it would be very difficult for a new start-up search engine firm to be successful unless it offered compelling

LEARNING OBJECTIVE

1. Explain the difference between opportunities and ideas.

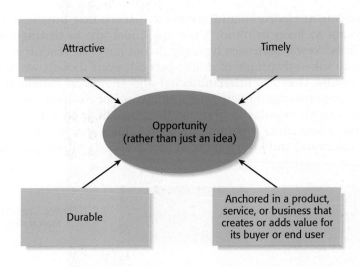

FIGURE 2.1
Four Essential Qualities of an Opportunity

advantages over already established competitors or targeted a niche market in an exemplary manner. Bing, Microsoft's search engine, is gaining ground with approximately 18 percent market share (compared to 67 percent for Google), but only after Microsoft has exerted an enormous amount of effort in head-to-head competition with Google.[2]

It is important to understand that there is a difference between an opportunity and an idea. An **idea** is a thought, an impression, or a notion. An idea may or may not meet the criteria of an opportunity. This is a critical point because many entrepreneurial ventures fail not because the entrepreneurs that launched them didn't work hard, but rather because there was no real opportunity to begin with. Before getting excited about a business idea, it is crucial to understand whether the idea fills a need and meets the criteria for an opportunity.

Three Ways to Identify Opportunities

LEARNING OBJECTIVE

2. Describe the three general approaches entrepreneurs use to identify opportunities.

There are three approaches entrepreneurs use to identify an opportunity their new venture can choose to pursue (see Figure 2.2). Once an entrepreneur understands the importance of each approach, s/he will be much more likely to look for opportunities and ideas that fit each profile. We discuss the three approaches in the next three sections.

Observing Trends

The first approach to identifying opportunities is to observe trends and study how they create opportunities for entrepreneurs to pursue. The most important trends to follow are economic trends, social trends, technological advances, and political action and regulatory changes. As an entrepreneur or potential entrepreneur, it's important to remain aware of changes in these areas. This sentiment is affirmed by Michael Yang, the founder of Become.com, a comparison shopping site, who believes that keen observation skills and a willingness to stay on top of changing environmental trends are key attributes of successful entrepreneurs:

> One of the most important attributes of a good entrepreneur is having a keen observation ability. Basically seeing what's needed in people's everyday lives and coming up with innovative new ideas and services that meet those needs ... I always believe the entrepreneurs that anticipate trends and maintain observations of what's needed ... to solve those needs will have a higher chance of succeeding in the marketplace.[3]

When looking at environmental trends to discern new business ideas, there are two caveats to keep in mind. First, it's important to distinguish between trends and fads. New businesses typically do not have the resources to ramp up fast enough to take advantage of a fad. Second, even though we discuss each trend individually, they are interconnected and should be considered simultaneously when brainstorming new business ideas. For example, one reason that smartphones are so popular is because they benefit from several trends converging at the same time, including an increasingly mobile population (social trend), the continual miniaturization of electronics (technological trend), and

FIGURE 2.2
Three Ways to Identify
an Opportunity

| Observing Trends | Solving a Problem | Finding Gaps in the Marketplace |

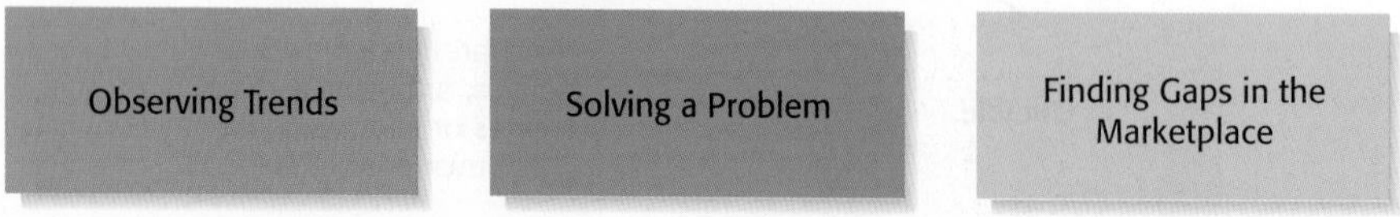

As baby boomers age, opportunities will grow for firms that provide unique services to the age group. Look for the resulting expansion in organic foods, specialty wines, insurance, and travel.

Rick Gomez/Comet/Corbis

their ability to help users better manage their money via online banking and comparison shopping (economic trend). If any of these trends weren't present, smartphones wouldn't be as successful as they are and wouldn't hold as much continuing promise to be even more successful in the future.

Figure 2.3 provides a summary of the relationship between the environmental factors just mentioned and identifying opportunity gaps. Next, let's look at how entrepreneurs can study each of these factors to help them spot business, product, and service opportunity gaps.

Economic Forces   Understanding economic trends is helpful in determining areas that are ripe for new business ideas, as well as areas to avoid.[4] When

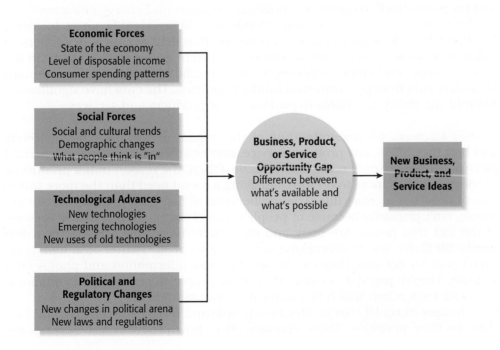

FIGURE 2.3
Environmental Trends Suggesting Business or Product Opportunity Gaps

the economy is strong, people have more money to spend and are willing to buy discretionary products and services that enhance their lives. In contrast, when the economy is weak, not only do people have less money to spend, they are typically more reluctant to spend the money they have, fearing the economy may become even worse, and that in turn, they might lose their jobs because of a weakening economy. Paradoxically, a weak economy provides business opportunities for start-ups that help consumers and businesses save money. Examples include GasBuddy and GasPriceWatch.com, two companies started to help consumers save money on gasoline. A similar example is WaterSmart Software, a 2009 start-up. WaterSmart Software sells software to water utilities that makes it easier for their customers to save water and money.

When studying how economic forces affect business opportunities, it is important to evaluate who has money to spend and what they spend it on. For example, an increase in the number of women in the workforce and their related increase in disposable income is largely responsible for the number of online retailers and boutique clothing stores targeting professional women that have opened the past several years. Similarly, the increased buying power of minority populations has resulted in an upswing of ethnic restaurants and ethnic supermarkets in the United States. Baby boomers are another potential group to examine. These individuals, who were born between 1946 and 1964, are retiring in large numbers and will be retiring in even larger numbers over the next five years or so. The expectation is that these people will redirect a sizeable portion of their assets to products and services that facilitate their retirement. This trend will invariably spawn new businesses in many areas, largely because baby boomers have greater disposable income relative to previous generations. For example, baby boomers tend to take pride in their homes and lawns. Recent data indicates that baby boomers who own homes are 21 percent more likely than all American adults to have spent $10,000 or more on home improvements.[5] Other areas that baby boomers spend heavily on include health care, travel, and consumer packaged goods. The high cost of energy, coupled with a desire to be socially responsible, has also spawned a growing number of startups that are developing products and services that help business and consumers become more energy efficient. An example is Nest Labs (www.nest.com), a 2010 startup. Nest Labs—which was acquired by Google in 2014—makes the world's first learning thermostat. The thermostat, which can be used in homes or businesses, learns from your temperature adjustments and programs itself to optimize a building's comfort and energy efficiency.[6]

An understanding of economic trends also helps identify areas to avoid. For example, a decision to launch a company that sells products or services to public schools was not a wise one during the recent economic downturn. In the United States—and other countries, as well—public schools have been hit hard by budget cuts from governmental funding agencies. The cuts have significantly reduced the ability of schools to purchase new products and services.

Social Forces An understanding of the impact of social forces on trends and how they affect new product, service, and business ideas is a fundamental piece of the opportunity recognition puzzle. Often, the reason that a product or service exists has more to do with satisfying a social need than the more transparent need the product fills. The proliferation of fast-food restaurants, for example, isn't primarily because of people's love of fast food, but rather because of the fact that people are busy and often don't have time to cook their own meals. Similarly, social networking sites like Facebook, Twitter, and Instagram aren't popular because they can be used to post information and photos on a website. They're popular because they allow people to connect and communicate with each other, which is a natural human tendency.

Changes in social trends alter how people and businesses behave and how they set their priorities. These changes affect how products and services are built and sold. Here is a sample of the social trends that are currently affecting how individuals behave and set their priorities:

- Aging of the population
- The increasing diversity of the workforce
- Increased participation in social networks
- Growth in the use of mobile devices
- An increasing focus on health and wellness
- Emphasis on clean forms of energy, including wind, solar, biofuels, and others
- Continual migration of people from small towns and rural areas to cities
- Desire for personalization (which creates a need for products and services that people can tailor to their own tastes and needs)

Each of these trends is providing the impetus for new business ideas. The continual migration of people from small towns and rural areas to cities, for example, is creating more congestion in cities. Businesses like Zipcar, a car-sharing service, and Alta Bicycle Share, a bicycle-sharing service, were started in part to address this problem. Similarly, the aging of the population is creating business opportunities from vision care to home health care to senior dating sites. An example is Glaukos, a company that's developing a new approach for treating glaucoma, which is an age-related eye disorder.

The proliferation of smartphones is a social trend that's opening business opportunities for entrepreneurs across the globe. More than 1.75 billion people worldwide owned mobile phones in 2014, and that number is expected grow to 2.5 billion by 2017. By 2017, nearly 50 percent of mobile phones will be smartphones, like the Apple iPhone and Android-equipped devices. The proliferation of smartphones will spawn new businesses both in the United States and throughout the world. Sometimes social trends converge to create a particuarly compelling business idea. For example, CareZone, a 2012 startup, was launched by Johathan Schwartz, who was looking for ways to better manage the care of five aging parents and in-laws. CareZone is an app for smartphones, tablets, or computers that allows those involved in a person's care to share and save information in a secure, online setting. CareZone's potential is bolstered by two societal trends: the aging of the population and the growth in the use of smartphone apps and other connected devices.

The increasing interest in social networking sites such as Facebook, Twitter, and LinkedIn is a highly visible social trend. A total of 69 percent of men and 78 percent of women use one or more social networking sites.[7] In addition to providing people new ways to communicate and interact with each other, social networks also act as platforms for other businesses to build on. Zynga, for example, the maker of popular online games like FarmVille and Scramble, became popular by making browser-based games that worked as application widgets on Facebook. Similarly, entrepreneurs have launched businesses for the purpose of starting social networks that cater to specific niches. An example is PatientsLikeMe, the subject of Case 1.2, which is a social networking site for people with serious diseases.

Technological Advances Advances in technology frequently dovetail with economic and social changes to create opportunities. For example, there are many overlaps between an increased focus on health and wellness and technology. Wearable devices, like the Fitbit Flex and the Jawbone Up, help people maintain a healthy lifestyle by monitoring their movements and sleep. In fact, ABI Research projects that 90 million wearable computing devices will be shipped in 2014.[8] There are a growing number of mobile apps and activity trackers that beam the data they collect to their health care providers so they can keep tabs on their activities and inform treatments. Insurance companies and corporations are increasingly partnering with technology companies like RedBrick Health and Audax Health, which establish programs to help encourage healthy lifestyles.

Technological advances also provide opportunities to help people perform everyday tasks in better or more convenient ways. For example, OpenTable.com is a website that allows users to make restaurant reservations online and now covers most of the United States. If you're planning a trip to Boston, for example, you can access OpenTable.com, select the area of the city you'll be visiting, and view descriptions, reviews, customer ratings, and in most cases the menus of the restaurants in the area. You can then make a reservation at the restaurant and print a map and the directions to it. The basic tasks that OpenTable.com helps people perform have always been done: looking for a restaurant, comparing prices and menus, soliciting advice from people who are familiar with competing restaurants, and getting directions. What OpenTable.com does is help people perform these tasks in a more convenient and expedient manner.

Another aspect of technological advances is that once a technology is created, products often emerge to advance it. For example, the creation of the Apple iPod, iPhone, iPad, and similar devices has in turned spawned entire industries that produce compatible devices. For example, Rokit is a high-end mobile accessories company that makes smartphone cases, headphones, portable USB device chargers and Bluetooth speakers. Rokit wouldn't exist if it weren't for the advent of the smartphone industry. Similarly, there are a growing number of start-ups working on smartphone apps. An example is Ubersense, the subject of the You Be the VC 5.2 feature. Ubersense has made a smartphone and tablet app that allows athletes, coaches, and parents to shoot video of an athlete's move or competition, and then analyze the video in a variety of ways.

Political Action and Regulatory Changes Political and regulatory changes also provide the basis for business ideas. For example, new laws often spur start-ups that are launched to take advantage of their specifications. This is currently happening as a result of the passage of the Affordable Care Act (Obamacare). The combination of new regulations, incentives for doctors and hospitals to shift to electronic records, and the release of mountains of data held by the Department of Health and Human Services (on topics such as hospital quality and nursing home patient satisfaction), is motivating entrepreneurs to launch electronic medical records start-ups, apps to help patients monitor their medications, and similar companies.[9]

On some occassions, entire industries hinge on whether certain government regulations evolve in a manner that is favorable to the industry. For example, there are several start-ups poised to commercialize the use of drones, or Aerial UAV's. Drones can be used for a number of domestic purposes, such as helping farmers determine the optimal level of fertilizer to place on crops or helping filmmakers shoot overhead scenes. Amazon.com created quite a bit of buzz in late 2013 when it suggested it would like to use drones for package delivery. As of spring 2014, the FAA permitted drones to be used for personal use, and restricted their use to below 400 feet, within eyesight of the controller and away from airports and populated areas. Drone start-ups, like 3D Robotics, are waiting for the FAA to develop more liberal rules and standards that will allow drones to be used for expanded purposes.[10]

Political change also engenders new business and product opportunities. For example, global political instability and the threat of terrorism have resulted in many firms becoming more security-conscious. These companies need new products and services to protect their physical assets and intellectual property, as well as to protect their customers and employees. The backup data storage industry, for example, is expanding because of this new trend in the tendency to feel the need for data to be more protected than in the past. An example of a start-up in this area is Box.net, which was funded by Mark Cuban, the owner of the Dallas Mavericks. Box.net allows its customers to store data "offsite" on Box.net servers, and access it via any Internet connection.

Table 2.1 offers additional examples of changes in environmental trends that provided fertile soil for opportunities and subsequent concepts to take advantage of them.

One thing entrepreneurs invarably do when a changing environmental trend prompts them to think about a business opportunity is to learn more about the trend in an effort to shape and mold their idea. The "Savvy Entrepreneurial Firm" feature in this chapter focuses on how to learn more about specific environmental trends through the effective use of social media.

TABLE 2.1 Examples of How Changes in Environmental Trends Provide Openings for New Business and Product Opportunities

Changing Environmental Trend	Resulting New Business, Product, and Service Opportunities	Companies That Resulted
Economic Trends		
Search for alternatives to traditional fossil fuels like gasoline	Ethanol, biodiesel, solar power, wind-generated power	Noesis Energy, Effortless Energy, eMeter, Nest Labs
Aging of the population	In-home care, health and wellness apps, financial services for older people, travel-related services for older people	CareLinx, Mango Health, Elder Life Financial Services, Senior Travel Services, Inc.
Social Trends		
Increased interest in different, tastier, and healthier food	Healthy-fare restaurants, ethnic packaged foods, craft beer, functional beverages	Naked Pizza, Brooklyn Brewery, Hint (bottled water), Popchips
Increased interest in fitness as the result of new medical information warning of the hazards of being overweight	Fitness centers, pilates and yogo studios, exercise apps, weight-loss programs and apps	Snap Fitness, Wello, Yogaview (Chicago), Fitbit, Noom Weight Loss Coach
Technological Advances		
Smartphones	Smartphone operating systems, smartphone apps, smartphone accessories	Android, Instagram, Mango Health, iSkin, OnTrion
Wearable technology	Wearable fitness devices, wearable life-sytle devices (like Google Glasses), and wearable tech gadgets.	Fitbit, Pebble Technologies, Oculus Rift, Recon Jet, Sensoria
Political and Regulatory Changes		
Increased EPA and OSHA standards	Consulting companies, software to monitor compliance	PrimeTech, Compliance Consulting Services, SafeSoft
Affordable Care Act (Obamacare)	Electronic medical records, doctor-patient matching services, physician social networks	CareCloud, One Touch EMR, ZocDoc, PracticeFusion, Sermo

SAVVY ENTREPRENEURIAL FIRM

How to Learn About Emerging Trends Through the Effective Use of Social Media

Often, as a result of a changing environmental trend, individuals have the seeds of a business idea, but need to know more about the trend before their idea can fully take shape. For example, one environmental trend, the continual migration of people from small towns and rural areas to cities, has resulted in cities becoming more congested. To help relieve congestion, many large cities are implementing bike-sharing programs. The programs typically allow a person to pick up a bike at Point A and then drop it off at Point B. The idea is that if someone has a short commute to work, or plans to make a short trip, s/he might opt to ride a bike rather than drive their car. The fewer cars there are on the street, the less congestion there will be.

Say you had the idea to start a for-profit company to manage bike-sharing programs for mid-sized cities. This potentially could be a viable idea, given that to date, most of the programs are in large cities. A mid-sized city would be a city like Tulsa, OK, or Little Rock, AR. You have the idea, but you now need to learn as much as you can about the migration of people from small towns and rural areas to cities, as well as how bike-sharing programs work. You're just in the idea stage here, collecting information and looking for insights. Many people try to use social media to learn about emerging trends, but go about it in a haphazard manner. Here are some suggestions for effectively using social media to study environmental trends and business ideas associated with those trends.

■ Facebook Groups. Look for Facebook Groups that pertain to the topics in which you have an interest. You can find Facebook groups by simply accessing Facebook's main page and typing the appropriate keywords in the search bar. Once you start typing for a term like "bike sharing," you'll see a list of suggestions pop up beneath the search bar. You can then look at the groups in which you have an interest. Simply "like" the groups that you want to follow, and you'll start getting notifications of new posts. Most groups will ask you to join (by clicking the join button) if you want to post information or make comments on others' posts.

■ LinkedIn Groups. LinkedIn also has groups. To find a group, simply go to LinkedIn's homepage,

and to the left of the search bar, access the dropdown menu and select Groups. You can then search to see if groups exist that match your topic. When writing this feature, there were several LinkedIn groups on bike-sharing. There were also groups that dealt with urban congestion. By typing "urban congestion" into the search bar, LinkedIn suggested the group "Creating Healthy, Liveable Cities," among others. Similar to Facebook, most LinkedIn groups will want you to join to participate in the discussions.

■ Twitter. You can search for topics on Twitter, along with people, businesses, and organizations. You simply place the hashtag (#) in front of the topic. For example, for the business idea proposed above, you might want to search for the following topics: #bikesharing, #urbancongestion, #urbanqualityoflife, #healthycities, etc. Your searches will result in the most current tweets of people talking about those topics. This is a good way to both consume content on a topic in which you are interested and to identify people or organizations that you might want to follow on a consistent basis. Twitter does not support groups. Some third-party Twitter tools, like Tweetdeck, do allow you to form or join groups of Twitter followers that are interested in a specific topic.

■ Blogs. To check to see if there is a blog on a topic of interest, seach Google Blogs at www.google.com/blogsearch. A quick search identified a blog named The Bike-Sharing Blog at www.bike-sharing.blogspot.com. It also identified a website on Healthy Cities at www.healthycities.org.

■ Tumblr. Tumblr is a popular microblogging platform and social networking website owned by Yahoo. Simply go to Tumblr (www.tumblr.com) and type your query into the search bar. You'll see what Tumblr has to offer. You can try many different combinations of terms, such as "bike sharing," "healthy cities," "migrations to cities," etc. You can then periodically view or follow the Tumblr microblogs that interest you the most.

Solving a Problem

The second approach to identifying opportunities is to recognize problems and find ways to solve them. Problems can be recognized by observing the challenges that people encounter in their daily lives and through more simple means, such as intuition, serendipity, or chance. There are many problems

One of the most pressing problems facing the United States and other countries is finding alternatives to fossil fuels. A large number of entrepreneurial firms are being launched to take on this challenge. Among potential solutions is wind-generated energy.

Winslow Productions/Tetra Images/Corbis

that have yet to be solved. Commenting on this issue and how noticing problems can lead to recognizing business ideas, Philip Kotler, a marketing expert, said:

> Look for problems. People complain about it being hard to sleep through the night, get rid of clutter in their homes, find an affordable vacation, trace their family origins, get rid of garden weeds, and so on. As the late John Gardner, founder of Common Cause, observed: "Every problem is a brilliantly disguised opportunity."[11]

Consistent with this observation, many companies have been started by people who have experienced a problem in their own lives, and then realized that the solution to the problem represented a business opportunity. For example, in 1991, Jay Sorensen dropped a cup of coffee in his lap because the paper cup was too hot. This experience led Sorensen to invent an insulating cup sleeve and to start a company to sell it. Since launching his venture, the company, Java Jacket, has sold over four billion cup sleeves. Similarly, after watching countless women walk home barefoot after a long night in heels, New York University finance students Katie Shea and Susie Levitt started a company named CitySlips to make easily portable, comfortable shoes. They created a pair of flats that fold up to fit into a pocket-size zip pouch, which easily fits into most women's purses. When a woman pops on the shoes, the pouch unfurles into a tote bag to carry the high heels. The two began selling CitySlips in 2009; today, their product is carried in over 500 stores.[12]

Advances in technology often result in problems for people who can't use the technology in the way it is sold to the masses. For example, some older people find traditional cell phones hard to use: the buttons are small, the text is hard to read, and it's often difficult to hear someone on a cell phone in a noisy room. To solve these problems, GreatCall, Inc. is producing a cell phone called the Jitterbug, which is designed specifically for older users. The Jitterbug features a large keypad that makes dialing easy, powerful speakers that deliver clear sound, easy-to-read text, and simple text-messaging capability. Another company, Firefly Mobile, has created a cell phone designed specifically for kids and tweens. The phone weighs only 2 ounces, and is designed to fit in a kid's hand. The phone includes a full-color screen, built-in games, built-in parental controls that allow parents to restrict incoming and outgoing calls as well as limit or restrict texting, and special speed dials for mom and dad.

If you're having difficulty solving a particular problem, one technique that is useful is to find an instance where a similar problem was solved and then apply that solution to your problem. For example, Yogitoes, a company that makes nonslip rugs for yoga enthusiasts, was started in this manner. Several yoga positions require participants to strike poses where they balance their weight on their feet at an angle. In this position, it is easy to slip when using a regular yoga mat. The company's founder, Susan Nicols, looked for a yoga mat that would prevent her from slipping, but found that no one knew how to make one. So she started looking for an example of a product that was designed specifically to prevent it from slipping on a hard floor, to study how it functioned. Eventually, she came across a dog bowl with rubber nubs on the bottom to prevent it from sliding when a large dog ate or drank from it. Using the dog bowl as a model, Nichols found a manufacturer who helped her develop a rug with small PVC nubs that prevents yoga participants from slipping when they perform yoga moves. Nichols started Yogitoes to sell the rugs, patented her solution, and has now been in business for more than 10 years.[13]

Some business ideas are gleaned by recognizing problems that are associated with emerging trends. For example, SafetyWeb has created a Web-based service that helps parents protect their children's online reputation, privacy, and safety. The social trend toward more online activity by children resulted in the need for this service. Similarly, the proliferation of smartphones enables people to stay better connected, but results in problems when people aren't able to access electricity to recharge their phones for a period of time. A number of companies have solved this problem in innovative ways. Examples include BioLite, which is a stove for campers that uses wood to create energy to recharge smartphones, and BikeCharge, which is a set of devices that are placed near the rear wheels of your bike and on your handlebars that charges your smartphone while you ride.

Additional examples of people who launched businesses to solve problems are included in Table 2.2.

TABLE 2.2 Businesses Created to Solve a Problem

Entrepreneur(s)	Year	Problem	Solution	Name of Business That Resulted
Alison Johnson Rue and Dan Johnson	2012	There is no easy way for a student to connect with an online tutor.	Create an online platform that makes it possible for any student to connect with a tutor at any time.	InstaEdu (www.instaedu.com)
Greg Goff and Hesky Kutscher	2010	People traveling do not have ready access to their children's medical records, which may be needed if the child gets injured or sick.	Create an online platform that can be pulled up from any Web browser or on a smartphone that provides access to a child's full medical history.	MotherKnows (www.motherknows.com)
Jason Kiesel	2009	There is no easy way for residents of a city to report quality-of-life issues, such as graffiti or an abandoned car.	Create a mobile app that allows a resident to take a photo of the problem, send it to a central clearinghouse in city government, who will alert the appropriate city agency to fix the problem.	CitySourced (www.citysourced.com)

(Continued)

TABLE 2.2 Continued

Entrepreneur(s)	Year	Problem	Solution	Name of Business That Resulted
Roger Marsh	2009	Concrete block construction takes time and requires water; a building built with concrete blocks cannot be occupied immediately because the building's mortar needs time to cure.	Alter traditional methods of concrete block construction to enable the assembly of the block to be completed in a manner that requires no water, has immediate occupancy, and is faster than current procedures.	Bolt-A-Blok Systems
Perry Chen, Yancey Strickler, and Charles Adler	2009	No easy-to-access platform for funding creative projects, like indie films, record albums, or food-related projects.	Create a Web-based "crowdfunding" platform that helps artists, musicians, and people involved in other creative projects raise money from the public.	Kickstarter

Finding Gaps in the Marketplace

Gaps in the marketplace are the third source of business opportunities. There are many examples of products that consumers need or want that aren't available in a particular location or aren't available at all. Part of the problem is created by large retailers, like Wal-Mart and Costco, that compete primarily on price and offer the most popular items targeted toward mainstream consumers. While this approach allows the large retailers to achieve economies of scale, it leaves gaps in the marketplace. This is the reason that clothing boutiques, specialty shops, and e-commerce websites exist. These businesses are willing to carry merchandise that doesn't sell in large enough quantities for Wal-Mart and Costco to carry.

Product gaps in the marketplace represent potentially viable business opportunities. For example, Tish Cirovolo realized that there were no guitars on the market made specifically for women. To fill this gap, she started Daisy Rock guitars, a company that makes guitars just for women. Daisy Rock guitars are stylish, come in feminine colors, and incorporate design features that accommodate a woman's smaller hand and build. In a related manner, Southpaw Guitars located in Houston, Texas, carries only guitars that are designed and produced for left-handed players. Another company that is filling a gap in the marketplace is ModCloth, a firm selling vintage and vintage-inspired clothing for 18- to 32-year-old women, which is a surprisingly large market. A start-up in a completely different industry is GreenJob Spider. GreenJob Spider fills a gap in the online recruiting industry by supporting a job site for employers and prospective employees in "green" industries such as solar, wind, recycling, green buildings, and LED lighting.

Additional examples of companies started to fill gaps in the marketplace are provided in Table 2.3.

A common way that gaps in the marketplace are recognized is when people become frustrated because they can't find a product or service that they need and recognize that other people feel the same way. This scenario played out for Lorna Ketler and Barb Wilkins, who became frustrated when they couldn't find stylish "plus-sized" clothing that fit. In response to their frustration, they started Bodacious, a store that sells fun and stylish "plus-size" clothing that fits. Ketler and Wilkins's experience illustrates how compelling a business idea can be when it strikes just the right chord by filling a gap that deeply resonates with a specific clientele. Reflecting on the success of Bodacious, Wilkins said:

> It's so rewarding when you take a risk and it pays off for you and people are telling you every single day, "I am so glad you are here." We've had people cry in our store. It happens a lot. They're crying because they're so happy (that they're

TABLE 2.3   Businesses Created to Fill a Gap in the Marketplace

Gap in the Marketplace	Resulting New Business Opportunity	Name of Businesses That Resulted
No fitness centers that are open 24 hours a day	24-hour fitness centers to accommodate people who work odd hours	Anytime Fitness, 24 Hour Fitness
Lack of toys and toy stores that focus on a child's intellectual development	Toy stores, toy manufacturers, websites that sell educational toys, and toy and smartphone app combinations	Launchpad Toys, Little Bits, Modular Robotics, Ubolly
Too few women pursuing careers in engineering	For-profit and non-profit organizations that teach older girls to code, after-school programs that engage school-age girls in engineering-related projects, interactive books and games that interest young girls in engineering	Girls Who Code, Engineering for Kids, GoldieBlox, Roominate
Shortage of clothing stores that sell fashionable clothing for hard-to-fit people	Boutiques and retail stores that sell fashionable clothing for hard-to-fit people, including plus-sized clothing, maternity clothes, or clothing for tall or short people	Casual Male, Fashions to Figure, Motherhood Maternity

finding clothes that fit). One woman put on a pair of jeans that fit her, and she called me an hour later and said, "They still look good, even at home!" Sometimes people have a body change that happens, whether they have been ill or had a baby, and there's lots of emotion involved in it. If you can go and buy clothes that fit, that helps people feel good about themselves.[14]

A related technique for generating new business opportunities is to take an existing product or service and create a new category by targeting a completely different target market. This approach essentially involves creating a gap and filling it. An example is PopCap Games, a company that was started to create a new category in the electronic games industry called "casual games." The games are casual and relaxing rather than flashy and action-packed, and are made for people who want to wind down after a busy day.

One thing that entrepreneurs must remain mindful of in pursuing business opportunities, regardless of whether the opportunity results from changing environmental trends, solving a problem, or finding gaps in the marketplace, is that the opportunity must ultimately be fashioned into a successful business. The nearby "What Went Wrong?" feature focuses on Everpix, a company that resulted from its founders' frustration regarding the lack of a good service to store and organize photos. Regrettably, the founder spent too much time focused on the opportunity at the expenses of the business, as you'll see in the feature.

Personal Characteristics of the Entrepreneur

LEARNING OBJECTIVE
3. Discuss the personal characteristics of entrepreneurs that contribute to their ability to recognize business opportunities.

How did Michael Dell come up with the idea of a "build it yourself" computer company? How did Dave Roberts, the founder of PopCap Games, figure out that there is a large and growing market for "casual" electronic games?

Researchers have identified several characteristics that tend to make some people better at recognizing opportunities than others. We've already defined an opportunity as a favorable set of circumstances that create the need for a new product, service, or business, but the term **opportunity recognition**

WHAT WENT WRONG?

Why a Company that Solved a Problem With a Great Product Went Out of Business

In 2009, Pierre-Olivier Latour spent some time traveling through Asia with a friend. He became frustrated with how difficult it was to store and organize all the photos he was taking. When he returned to the United States, he discussed his frustration with Kevin Quennesson, a fellow French engineer. Quennesson had a different frustration with photos, noting that the more photos he took, the less likely he was to go back and look at them. Quennesson saw this likelihood as a paradox. The more he documented his life, the less likely he was to enjoy what he had created.

Latour and Quennesson saw the combination of their frustrations as a problem. There wasn't a good solution on the market to store and organize photos in a manner that would encourage people to go back and look at them. The two decided to start a business and build a prototype of a photo storing and organizing service that potentially solved the problem. In June 2011 they met Wayne Fan, who was working at a San Francisco firm doing interaction and visual design, and brought him in as a co-founder. The three spent the next several months building a prototype of their service, which they named Everpix. The service seamlessly found and uploaded photos from your desktop and from online services, then organized them to highlight the best ones. The service was fast, the design was clean, and it was simple to use.

Everpix raised a total of $1.8 million from angel investors and continued to work on the product. The first version of Everpix 1.0 rolled out in March 2013. A free option let you see all your photos from the past year or longer if you connected to Everpix's app. For $4.99 a month or $49 a year, the service would let you store an unlimited amount of photos. One cool feature, called Flashbacks, sent users daily email messages of their photos from the same day in prior years. The overall service got rave reviews, and its users seemed to love it. The Everpix app had a 4.5-star average rating (on a scale of 1-5) out of more than 1,000 reviews. It seemed as though the founders were solving the problem they had set out to solve, with an attractive and solid product. Then, in the summer of 2013, Everpix closed. What went wrong?

In a nutshell, Everpix's founders spent too much time and energy perfecting their service at the expense of building a business. The service wasn't viral, meaning it wasn't easy for Everpix subscribers to share photos with friends and encourage them to become Everpix members. The Everpix team realized this was a problem and kicked around ways to make the service more viral. One idea was to require a subscriber's friends to create an account to download any photos that the subscriber shared with them, but the idea was killed as just the type of self-serving design choice that the team prided itself in avoiding. It also spent almost nothing on advertising or promotions. It had spent the $1.8 million it raised building the service. So at the time when other photo apps were attracting millions of users, Everpix had fewer than 19,000 sign-ups.

In the weeks prior to closing, Everpix's founders scrambled to raise additional funding. Because they were well-connected in the angel investing and venture capital world, they got a number of meetings. They were consistently praised on the quality of their product and the quality of the team they had assembled, but the business was the problem. Investors were getting spooked, in part, by the sheer number of apps that were being created and the ease with which consumers could switch between them. In addition, a number of Everpix's competitors were giving their services away for free, while Everpix's business model relied on paid subscriptions. One by one, the investors turned them down. Several overtures were made to potential acquirers, but none panned out. Eventually, Everpix ran out of money and didn't have the capacity to continue.

Questions for Critical Thinking

1. In the context of this chapter, make a list of three "takeaways" from this feature that you can learn from and try to avoid if you set out to solve a problem by launching a business.
2. To what degree is there a difference between pursuing an opportunity to solve a problem and building a business? In what ways did Everpix fail to do both?
3. According to the feature, Everpix spent almost nothing on advertising and promotions. How large of a role do you think that decision played in Everpix's failure?
4. Venture capitalists are often accused of swinging for the fences—in other words, they don't invest in firms that are hitting signals, doubles, or triples. They want home runs. In hindsight, do you think Everpix was building a business that had the potential to hit singles, doubles, or triples, or a business that had the potential to be a home run? Explain your answer.

Sources: C. Newton, "Out of the Picture: Why the World's Best Photo Startup is Going Out of Business." The Verge, orginally posted on November 5, 2013, Available at http://www.theverge.com/2013/11/5/5039216/everpix-life-and-death-inside-the-worlds-best-photo-startup, accessed March 19, 2014; The Sublog, "Everpix, Snapchat, and The Startup Life," November 7, 2013, Available at http://subimage.com/blog/2013/11/07/everpix-snapchat-and-the-startup-lie/#.Uym15qMo670, accessed March 19, 2014.

refers to the process of *perceiving* the possibility of a profitable new business or a new product or service. That is, an opportunity cannot be pursued until it's *recognized*. Now let's look at some specific characteristics shared by those who excel at recognizing an opportunity.

Prior Experience

Several studies show that prior experience in an industry helps entrepreneurs recognize business opportunities. For example, evidence over time about the founders of firms appearing on the *Inc.* 500 list shows that well over 40 percent of those studied got the idea for their new businesses while working as employees for companies in the same industries.[15] This finding is consistent with those reported by scholars studying the relationship between industry experience and being able to recognize opportunities.[16] There are several explanations for these findings. By working in an industry, an individual may spot a market niche that is underserved. It is also possible that while working in a particular area, an individual builds a network of social contacts in that industry that may provide insights that lead to opportunities.[17]

Although prior experience is important in an industry in most instances, there is anecdotal evidence suggesting that people outside an industry can sometimes enter it with a new set of eyes, and as a result innovate in ways that people with prior experience might find difficult. An example is provided by Sam Calagione, the founder of Dogfish Head Craft Brewery, a very successful brewery based in Milton, Delaware. As indicated in the following quote, Milton set aside current industry best practices to craft some of his most popular products:

> In the mid-'90s, some beer enthusiasts and experts called us heretics for brewing beers with ingredients outside of the "traditional" water, yeast, hops, and barley. So, I started researching ancient brewing cultures and learned that long ago, brewers in every corner of the world made beer with whatever was beautiful and natural and grew beneath the ground they lived on. We (Dogfish Brewery) now make a whole series of Ancient Ales inspired by historic and molecular evidence found in tombs and dig sites.[18]

Cognitive Factors

Opportunity recognition may be an innate skill or a cognitive process.[19] There are some who think that entrepreneurs have a "sixth sense" that allows them to see opportunities that others miss. This sixth sense is called **entrepreneurial alertness**, which is formally defined as the ability to notice things without engaging in deliberate search.[20] Most entrepreneurs see themselves in this light, believing they are more "alert" than others. Alertness is largely a learned skill, and people who have more knowledge of an area tend to be more alert to opportunities in that area than others. A computer engineer, for example, would be more alert to needs and opportunities within the computer industry than a lawyer would be.

The research findings on entrepreneurial alertness are mixed. Some researchers conclude that alertness goes beyond noticing things and involves a more purposeful effort. For example, one scholar believes that the crucial difference between opportunity finders (i.e., entrepreneurs) and nonfinders is their relative assessments of the marketplace.[21] In other words, entrepreneurs may be better than others at sizing up the marketplace and inferring the likely implications.

Social Networks

The extent and depth of an individual's social network affects opportunity recognition.[22] People who build a substantial network of social and professional contacts will be exposed to more opportunities and ideas than people with sparse networks. This exposure can lead to new business starts. Research results over time consistently suggest that somewhere between 40 percent and 50 percent of those who start businesses got their ideas through social contacts.[23] In a related study, the differences between **solo entrepreneurs** (those who identified their business ideas on their own) and **network entrepreneurs** (those who identified their ideas through social contacts) were examined. The researchers found that network entrepreneurs identified significantly more opportunities than solo entrepreneurs, but were less likely to describe themselves as being particularly alert or creative.[24]

An important concept that sheds light on the importance of social networks to opportunity recognition is the differential impact of strong-tie versus weak-tie relationships. Relationships with other people are called "ties." We all have ties. **Strong-tie relationships** are characterized by frequent interaction, such as ties between coworkers, friends, and spouses. **Weak-tie relationships** are characterized by infrequent interaction, like ties between casual acquaintances. According to research in this area, it is more likely that an entrepreneur will get a new business idea through a weak-tie than a strong-tie relationship, because strong-tie relationships —which typically form between like-minded individuals —tend to reinforce insights and ideas the individuals already have.[25] Weak-tie relationships, on the other hand, which form between casual acquaintances, are not as apt to be between like-minded individuals, so one person may say something to another that sparks a completely new idea. An example might be an electrician explaining to a restaurant owner how he solved a business problem. After hearing the solution, the restaurant owner might say, "I would never have heard that solution from someone in my company or industry. That insight is completely new to me and just might help me solve my problem."

Creativity

Creativity is the process of generating a novel or useful idea. Opportunity recognition may be, at least in part, a creative process. On an anecdotal basis, it is easy to see the creativity involved in forming many products, services, and businesses. Increasingly, teams of entrepreneurs working within a company are sources of creativity for their firm.[26]

For an individual, the creative process can be broken into five stages, as shown in Figure 2.4.[27] Let's examine how these stages relate to the opportunity recognition process. In the figure, the horizontal arrows that point from box to box suggest that the creative process progresses through five stages. The vertical arrows suggest that if at any stage an individual (such as an entrepreneur) gets "stuck" or doesn't have enough information or insight to continue, the

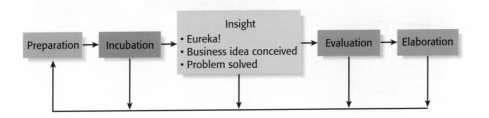

FIGURE 2.4
Five Steps to Generating Creative Ideas

best choice is to return to the preparation stage—to obtain more knowledge or experience before continuing to move forward.

Preparation. Preparation is the background, experience, and knowledge that an entrepreneur brings to the opportunity recognition process. Just as an athlete must practice to excel, an entrepreneur needs experience to spot opportunities. Over time, the results of research suggest that as much as 50 to 90 percent of start-up ideas emerge from a person's prior work experience.

Incubation. Incubation is the stage during which a person considers an idea or thinks about a problem; it is the "mulling things over" phase. Sometimes incubation is a conscious activity, and sometimes it is unconscious and occurs while a person is engaged in another activity. One writer characterized this phenomenon by saying that "ideas churn around below the threshold of consciousness."

Insight. Insight is the flash of recognition when the solution to a problem is seen or an idea is born. It is sometimes called the "eureka" experience. In a business context, this is the moment an entrepreneur recognizes an opportunity. Sometimes this experience pushes the process forward, and sometimes it prompts an individual to return to the preparation stage. For example, an entrepreneur may recognize the potential for an opportunity, but may feel that more knowledge and thought is required before pursuing it.

Evaluation. Evaluation is the stage of the creative process during which an idea is subjected to scrutiny and analyzed for its viability. Many entrepreneurs mistakenly skip this step and try to implement an idea before they've made sure it is viable. Evaluation is a particularly challenging stage of the creative process because it requires an entrepreneur to take a candid look at the viability of an idea. We discuss how to evaluate the feasibility of new business ideas in Chapter 3.

Elaboration. Elaboration is the stage during which the creative idea is put into a final form: The details are worked out and the idea is transformed into something of value, such as a new product, service, or business concept. In the case of a new business, this is the point at which a business plan is written.

Figure 2.5 illustrates the opportunity recognition process. As shown in the figure, there is a connection between an awareness of emerging trends and

FIGURE 2.5
The Opportunity
Recognition Process

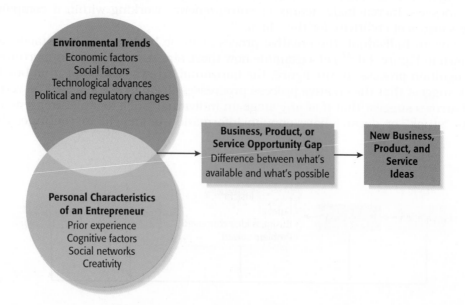

the personal characteristics of the entrepreneur because the two facets of opportunity recognition are interdependent. For example, an entrepreneur with a well-established social network may be in a better position to recognize emerging technological trends than an entrepreneur with a poorly established social network. Or the awareness of an emerging technology trend, such as digitization, may prompt an entrepreneur to attend conferences or workshops to learn more about the topic, expanding the social network.

Techniques for Generating Ideas

In general, entrepreneurs identify more ideas than opportunities because many ideas are typically generated to find the best way to capitalize on an opportunity.[28] Several techniques can be used to stimulate and facilitate the generation of new ideas for products, services, and businesses. Let's take a look at some of them.

LEARNING OBJECTIVE

4. Identify and describe techiques entrepreneurs use to generate ideas.

Brainstorming

A common way to generate new business ideas is through **brainstorming**. In general, brainstorming is simply the process of generating several ideas about a specific topic. The approaches range from a person sitting down with a yellow legal pad and jotting down interesting business ideas to formal "brainstorming sessions" led by moderators that involve a group of people.

In a formal brainstorming session, the leader of the group asks the participants to share their ideas. One person shares an idea, another person reacts to it, another person reacts to the reaction, and so on. A flip chart or an electronic whiteboard is typically used to record all the ideas. A productive session is freewheeling and lively. The session is not used for analysis or decision making—the ideas generated during a brainstorming session need to be filtered and analyzed, but this is done later. We show the four strict rules for conducting a formal brainstorming session in Table 2.4. As you'll see, the number one rule for a brainstorming session is that no criticism is allowed, including chuckles, raised eyebrows, or facial expressions that express skepticism or doubt. Criticism stymies creativity and inhibits the free flow of ideas.

Some organizations use "brainstorming walls" for people to jot down ideas. By putting ideas on walls, people can stand back and view multiple ideas simultaneously, and make connections that they otherwise would not have made.

Hiya Images/Fancy/Corbis

TABLE 2.4 Rules for a Formal Brainstorming Session

Rule	Explanation
1	No criticism is allowed, including chuckles, raised eyebrows, or facial expressions that express skepticism or doubt. Criticism stymies creativity and inhibits the free flow of ideas.
2	Freewheeling, which is the carefree expression of ideas free from rules or restraints, is encouraged; the more ideas, the better. Even crazy or outlandish ideas may lead to a good idea or a solution to a problem.
3	The session moves quickly, and nothing is permitted to slow down its pace. For example, it is more important to capture the essence of an idea than to take the time to write it down neatly.
4	Leapfrogging is encouraged. This means using one idea as a means of jumping forward quickly to other ideas.

Brainstorming sessions dedicated to generating new business ideas are often less formal. For example, while creating Proactiv, a popular acne treatment product, Dr. Katie Rodan, one of the company's founders, hosted dinner parties at her house and conducted brainstorming sessions with guests. The guests included business executives, market researchers, marketing consultants, an FDA regulatory attorney, and others. Rodan credits this group with helping her and her co-founder brainstorm a number of ideas that helped shape Proactiv and move the process of starting the company forward.[29] Similarly, Sharelle Klaus—the founder of Dry Soda, a company that makes an all-natural soda that's paired with food the way wine is in upscale restaurants—tested her idea by first talking to her husband's colleagues, who were in the food industry, and then tapped into the professional network of a friend who owned a bottled water company. Through the process, she met a chemist, who was instrumental in helping her develop the initial recipes for her beverage. Klaus also went directly to restaurant owners and chefs to ask them to sample early versions of her product.[30] While this approach only loosely fits the definition of brainstorming, the spirit is the same. Klaus was bouncing ideas and early prototypes of her product off others to get their reactions and generate additional ideas.

An individual's imagination is the only limiting factor to brainstorming. Asking students to complete a **bug report** is a popular technique that is used in classrooms to teach brainstorming. To compile a bug report, students are instructed to list 50 to 75 conditions or "things" that "bug" them in their everyday lives. Asking students to identify a number of conditions or things that bug them reduces the likelihood that they will specify only obvious things that bug them (e.g., campus parking, dorm food, and untidy roommates). Students can also be encouraged to hold focus groups with friends to brainstorm conditions that can be included on their "bug" list.

Focus Groups

A **focus group** is a gathering of 5 to 10 people who are selected because of their relationship to the issue being discussed. Focus groups are used for a variety of purposes, including the generation of new business ideas.

Focus groups typically involve a group of people who are familiar with a topic, are brought together to respond to questions, and shed light on an issue through the give-and-take nature of a group discussion. Focus groups usually work best as a follow-up to brainstorming, when the general idea for a business has been formulated—such as casual electronic games for adults—but further refinement of the idea is needed. Usually, focus groups are conducted by trained moderators. The moderator's primary goals are to keep the group "focused" and to generate lively discussion. Much of the effectiveness of a focus group session depends on the moderator's ability to ask questions and keep the discussion on track. For example, a retail establishment in which coffee is sold, such as Starbucks, might conduct a focus group consisting of 7 to 10 frequent customers and ask the group, "What is it that you *don't* like about our coffee shop?" A customer may say, "You sell 1-pound bags of your specialty ground coffees for people to brew at home. That's okay, but I often run out of the coffee in just a few days. Sometimes it's a week before I get back to the shop to buy another bag. If you sold 3-pound or 5-pound bags, I'd actually use more coffee because I wouldn't run out so often. I guess I could buy two or three 1-pound bags at the same time, but that gets a little pricey. I'd buy a 3- or 5-pound bag, however, if you'd discount your price a little for larger quantities." The moderator may then ask the group, "How many people here would buy 3-pound or 5-pound bags of our coffee if they were available?" If five hands shoot up, the coffee shop may have just uncovered an idea for a new product line.

A relatively new service called Napkin Labs helps companies funnel followers from Facebook and other sites into more intimate, more structured online communities intended to serve as focus groups. For example, Modify, the subject of Case 3.1, is a company that creates custom watches. The watches have interchangable faces, straps, and sliders and come in two sizes. Modify uses Napkin Labs to get people to chime in on what new colors and designs they'd like to see, and where they'd like to see the watches sold. Each lab poses a challenge, such as "where should our watches be sold?" A dialogue is created among the participants. Each participant knows what the other ones are saying and can react to their comments. According to Aaron Schwartz, Modify's founder, one lab showed a surprisingly big interest in seeing his company's watches sold in surf shops. Other online companies, such as UserVoice and Get Satisfaction, help firms connect with their users in a similar manner.[31]

Library and Internet Research

A third approach to generating new business ideas is to conduct library and Internet research. A natural tendency is to think that an idea should be chosen, and the process of researching the idea should then begin. This approach is too linear. Often, the best ideas emerge when the general notion of an idea—like creating casual electronic games for adults—is merged with extensive library and Internet research, which might provide insights into the best type of casual games to create.

Libraries are often an underutilized source of information for generating business ideas. The best approach to utilizing a library is to discuss your general area of interest with a reference librarian, who can point out useful resources, such as industry-specific magazines, trade journals, and industry reports. Simply browsing through several issues of a trade journal on a topic can spark new ideas. Very powerful search engines and databases are also available through university and large public libraries, which would cost hundreds or thousands of dollars to access on your own. An example is IBISWorld (www.ibisworld.com), a company that publishes market research on all major industries and subcategories within industries.

Internet research is also important. If you are starting from scratch, simply typing "new business ideas" into Google or Bing will produce links to newspaper and magazine articles about the "hottest" and "latest" new business ideas. Although these types of articles are general in nature, they represent a starting point if you're trying to generate new business ideas from scratch. If you have a specific idea in mind, a useful technique is to set up a Google "email alert" using keywords that pertain to your topic of interest. Google email alerts are email updates of the latest Google results including press releases, news articles, and blog posts based on your topic. This technique, which is available for free, will feed you a daily stream of news articles and blog postings about specific topics. Another approach is to follow business leaders and experts in the industries you're interested in on Twitter. The best way to locate people on Twitter you might be interested in following is by typing into the search bar relevant keywords preceded by the "#" sign. For example, if you're interested in solar power, type "#solarpower" into the search bar. All the results will be people or companies who tweet about solar power topics.

Once an entrepreneur has an idea, it often needs to be shaped and fine-tuned. One way to do this—in conjunction with the suggestions made previously—is to enlist a mentor to help. An explanation of how to use a mentor in this regard, and where mentors can be found, is described in the "Partnering for Success" feature.

Other Techniques

Firms use a variety of other techniques to generate ideas. Some companies set up **customer advisory boards** that meet regularly to discuss needs, wants, and problems that may lead to new ideas. Other companies conduct varying forms of anthropological research, such as **day-in-the-life research**. Intuit, the maker of Quicken, Quickbooks, and TurboTax, practices day-in-the life research. The company routinely sends teams of testers to the homes and businesses of its users to see how its products are working and to seek insights for new product ideas.

Encouraging the Development of New Ideas

LEARNING OBJECTIVE

5. Discuss actions to take to encourage continuous development of new ideas in entrepreneurial firms.

In many firms, idea generation is a haphazard process. However, entrepreneurial ventures can take certain concrete steps to build an organization that encourages and protects new ideas. Let's see what these steps are.

Establishing a Focal Point for Ideas

Some firms meet the challenge of encouraging, collecting, and evaluating ideas by designating a specific person to screen and track them—for if it's everybody's job, it may be no one's responsibility.[32] Another approach is to establish an **idea bank** (or vault), which is a physical or digital repository for storing ideas. An example of an idea bank would be a password-protected location on a firm's **intranet** that is available only to qualified employees. It may have a file for ideas that are being actively contemplated and a file for inactive ideas. Other firms do not have idea banks, but instead encourage employees to keep journals of their ideas.

Encouraging Creativity at the Firm Level

There is an important distinction between creativity and innovation. As indicated in Chapter 1, innovation refers to the successful introduction of new outcomes by a firm. In contrast, creativity is the process of generating a novel or useful idea; however, creativity does not require implementation of an idea. In other words, creativity is the raw material that goes into innovation. A team of employees may come up with a hundred legitimate creative ideas for a new product or service, but only one may eventually be implemented. Of course, it may take a hundred creative ideas to discover the one that ideally satisfies an opportunity.

PARTNERING FOR SUCCESS

Want Help Fine-Tuning a Business Idea? Find a Mentor

Fine-tuning a business idea isn't easy. While fairly course-grained ideas are rather easy to develop, like creating a smartphone that's designed specifically for elderly people, fleshing out the details is where experience helps. This reality puts first-time entrepreneurs at a disadvantage. While there are many books and websites about new business ideas, what many first-time entrepreneurs find most helpful in the idea generation and perfecting stage is to find a mentor to guide them through the process.

A **mentor** is someone who is more experienced than you and is willing to be your counselor, confidant, and go-to person for advice. There are two ways to find a mentor. First, you can work with your network of acquaintances—professors, business owners, coaches—to determine if there is someone available that you trust, has experience helping first-time entrepreneurs, and is willing to become your mentor. Many first-time entrepreneurs are surprised by the number of talented and experienced people who are eager to share their expertise and enter into a mentoring relationship. The second way is to utilize one of the growing numbers of websites and organizations that help match business founders with people who are willing to become mentors. One website is MicroMentor.org, which is a nonprofit that matches business founders with mentors. You can go to the site and fill out a profile about yourself and your goals, and then search profiles of potential mentors who match your needs. Once a match is made, the mentoring can take place through email, via Web conferencing, over the phone, or in person. There is a tab on MicroMentor's website that provides access to "success stories" of business founders who have had excellent results using its service. A number of organizations provide a similar service. For example, the National Association for Women Business Owners (NAWBO) has over 5,000 members in 60 chapters across the United States. Some chapters sponsor mentorship programs.

Another useful suggestion is to reach out to somone in your college or university's alumni network. Alumni are often looking for a way to "give back" to the instIution from which they graduated and are frequently willing to connect with others as a way of doing so. Alumni often serve as judges for college-sponsored pitch or business plan competitions, so that's one way to connect. A particularly useful resource is to do an Advanced People Search on LinkedIn. You can do this by accessing the Advanced People Search function in LinkedIn (www.linkedin.com/search?trk=advsrch). You type in a title and your university. For example, if what you're looking for is a mentor that can help navigate you through the process of raising money for your start-up and you're a student at Oklahoma State University, you might type into the search bar "CFO Oklahoma State University." The results will list everyone with a LinkedIn profile who identifies themself as the CFO (Chief Financial Officer) of an organization and is a graduate of Oklahoma State University. You can then connect with the person through the private email service within LinkedIn. Most people have fond memories of their college days. As a result, even experienced entrepreneurs and executives are often delighted to connect with a student at their alma mater.

The ideal situation is to find a mentor in your own community so you can meet face-to-face, whether it's an alumni of your university of someone else. Still, the online options provide a wide range of mentors to choose from, which may result in a better match. Online mentoring and counseling relationships are becoming increasingly common. For example, a sizeable percent of all the counseling and mentoring done by SCORE counselors is now done online.

Similar to any relationship, a business founder should be careful and only share private information with a mentor once a trusting relationship has been established.

Questions for Critical Thinking

1. If you were working on fine-tuning a business idea, would you check out one of these online options or an association in your area that provides mentoring and advice for business founders? Why or why not?
2. To what degree do you believe that having a mentor can make the difference between an entrepreneur succeeding or failing? In what areas of the entrepreneurial process do you believe that mentors are called on the most?
3. Make a list of the organizations in your area that provide mentorship and advice for business founders. Which organizations make the most sense to reach out to for someone who is still in the opportunity recognition stage of the start-up process?
4. How do you know what to do with a mentor's advice? If you get advice from several mentors or counselors at organizations like SCORE and local Small Business Development Centers, how can you best sort through the advice and know which advice to take and which advice to set aside?

Source: P. Ryckman, "How to Choose and Work with a Mentor," *New York Times*, www.nytimes.com/2010/09/02/business/smallbusiness/02sbiz.html?_r=2&emc=eta1 (accessed April 2, 2011, originally posted on September 1, 2010).

An employee may exhibit creativity in a number of ways, including solving a problem or taking an opportunity and using it to develop a new product or service idea. Although creativity is typically thought of as an individual attribute, it can be encouraged or discouraged at the firm level. The extent to which an organization encourages and rewards creativity affects the creative output of its employees.[33] Table 2.5 provides a list of actions and behaviors that encourage and discourage creativity at both the organizational level and the individual supervisor level.

TABLE 2.5 Actions and Behaviors That Encourage and Discourage Creativity

Organizational Level	*Inhibitors of Creativity*	▪ Failing to hire creative people ▪ Maintaining an organizational culture that stifles people ▪ Retaining people in the same job for years, preventing them from broad and deep experiences ▪ Promoting a mentality suggesting that the best solutions to all problems are known
	Facilitators of Creativity	▪ Supporting and highlighting creativity's importance in all parts of the firm ▪ Overtly rewarding those demonstrating creativity in their work ▪ Investing in resources for the purpose of helping employees become more creative ▪ Hiring people with different skills and viewpoints compared to current employees
Individual Supervisory Level	*Inhibitors of Creativity*	▪ Being pessimistic, judgmental, and critical ▪ Punishing people for failed ideas ▪ Insisting on precision and certainty early in the creative process ▪ Being inattentive, acting distant, and remaining silent when employees want to discuss new ideas
	Facilitators of Creativity	▪ Listening attentively for the purpose of openly acknowledging and supporting ideas early in their development ▪ Treating employees as equals for the purpose of demonstrating that status isn't important ▪ Speculating, being open, and building on others' ideas ▪ Protecting people who make honest mistakes and commit to learning from them

Chapter Summary

LO1. An idea is a thought, an impression, or a notion. An opportunity is an idea that has the qualities of being attractive, durable, and timely and is anchored in a product or service that creates value for its buyers or end-users. Not all ideas are opportunities. Once an opportunity is recognized, a window opens, and the market to fill the opportunity grows. At some point, the market matures and becomes saturated with competitors, and the window of opportunity closes.

LO2. Observing trends, solving a problem, and finding gaps in the marketplace are the three general approaches entrepreneurs use to identify a business opportunity. Economic forces, social forces, technological advances, and political action and regulatory changes are the four environmental trends that are most instrumental in creating opportunities. Through the second approach, entrepreneurs identify problems that they and others encounter in various parts of the lives and then go about developing a good or service that is intended to solve the identified problem. Carefully observing people and the actions they take is an excellent way to find problems that, when solved, would create value for a customer. Finding gaps in the marketplace is the third way to spot a business opportunity. Typically, the way this works is that an entrepreneur recognizes that some people are interested in buying more specialized products, such as guitars that are made for left-handed players or scissors for people who are dominant left-handers.

LO3. Over time, research results and observations of entrepreneurs in action indicate that some people are better at recognizing opportunities than others. Prior experience, cognitive factors, social networks, and creativity are the main personal characteristics researchers have identified and that observation indicates tend to make some people better at recognizing business opportunities than others.

LO4. Entrepreneurs use several techniques for the purpose of identifying ideas for new products and services. Brainstorming is one of these. More specifically, brainstorming is a technique used to quickly generate a large number of ideas and solutions to problems. One reason to conduct a brainstorming session is to generate ideas that might represent product, service, or business opportunities. A focus group, a second technique entrepreneurs use, is a gathering of 5 to 10 people who have been selected on the basis of their common characteristics relative to the issue being discussed. One reason to conduct a focus group is to generate ideas that might represent product or business opportunities. Careful and extensive searches of a physical library's holdings and of Internet sites are a third technique. Here, the entrepreneur uses an open mind to sort through large amounts of information and data to see if s/he can identify a problem that could be solved by creating an innovative product or service.

LO5. Entrepreneurs and their firms engage in several actions to encourage the development and retention of business ideas. Creativity is central to a firm's efforts to innovate; as such, firms take actions to nurture creativity. More specifically, entrepreneurs and their firms encourage creativity at the firm level through both organizational and individual supervisory level facilitators of creativity. Examples of organizational level facilitators of creativity include supporting creativity's importance and hiring people with different skills and viewpoints than those of current employees. Examples of individual supervisory level facilitators of creativity include listening attentively for the purpose of acknowledging and supporting ideas early in their development and protecting people who make honest mistakes and commit to learning from them. Ideas flowing from the exercise of creativity are stored in an idea bank, which is a physical or digital repository for storing ideas generated throughout an entrepreneurial venture.

Key Terms

brainstorming, **81**
bug report, **82**
creativity, **79**
customer advisory boards, **84**
day-in-the-life research, **84**
entrepreneurial alertness, **78**
focus group, **82**

idea, **66**
idea bank, **84**
intranet, **84**
mentor, **85**
network entrepreneurs, **79**
opportunity, **65**
opportunity gap, **65**

opportunity recognition, **76**
solo entrepreneurs, **79**
strong-tie relationships, **79**
weak-tie relationships, **79**
window of opportunity, **65**

Review Questions

2-1. What is a product opportunity gap?

2-2. How can an entrepreneur tell if a product opportunity gap exists?

2-3. What are the four essential qualities of an opportunity?

2-4. What are the qualities of an opportunity, and why is each quality important?

2-5. What four environmental trends are most instrumental in creating business opportunities? Provide an example of each environmental trend and the type of business opportunity it might help create.

2-6. How can "solving a problem" create a business opportunity for an entrepreneur to pursue?

2-7. How can finding a gap in the marketplace create a business opportunity?

2-8. What is the meaning of the term opportunity recognition?

2-9. What are the two caveats that an entrepreneur should keep in mind when observing environmental trends to create new business opportunities?

2-10. What is entrepreneurial alertness and why is it important to entrepreneurs?

2-11. How does an extensive social network provide an entrepreneur an advantage in recognizing business opportunities?

2-12. What is the difference between a weak-tie and a strong-tie relationship? Which type of tie is most likely to help an entrepreneur find an idea and why?

2-13. What is brainstorming?

2-14. How does creativity contribute to the opportunity recognition process?

2-15. What are the five stages of the creative process for an individual?

2-16. What are the differences between an opportunity and an idea and why are those differences important for entrepreneurs?

2-17. What are some of the innovative methods of teaching brainstorming?

2-18. How is a focus group used to generate new business ideas?

2-19. How does a firm encourage and protect new ideas?

2-20. What is the purpose of an idea bank?

2-21. How do businesses encourage creativity at the firm level?

Application Questions

2-22. Sean Parker has decided to start his own business. He plans to find an attractive opportunity and start an e-commerce company, just as Jeff Bezos did when he created Amazon.com. As a new entrepreneur fresh out of college, he needs to recognize a problem or an opportunity gap and create a business to address the problem or fill the identified gap. However, he still does not understand the difference between an idea and an opportunity. How can he ensure that his new idea is an opportunity for him instead of just an idea?

2-23. Identify three start-ups, other than those discussed in this chapter or listed in Table 2.2, that were started to solve a problem. Briefly describe the problems the three start-ups are solving and how they are going about doing so.

2-24. Marshall Hanson, the founder of Santa Fe Hitching Rail, a chain of nine steak restaurants in New Mexico, is considering expanding his menu, which is currently restricted to steak, hamburger, potatoes, and fries. He has just read a book about entrepreneurship and learned that entrepreneurs should study social trends to help identify new product opportunities. What are some current social trends that might help Marshall choose items to add to his menu? Given the trends you list, what items do you suggest Marshall add to expand his restaurant's menu?

2-25. As the founder of Masie's Ice-Cream Parlor, James North has newly appointed a creative manager for his outlet. He needs to advise his new manager to keep a look-out for new ideas and opportunities that can be introduced to his business. What are the key-points he needs to mention to his manager?

2-26. As mentioned in this chapter, "prior experience" in an industry helps entrepreneurs recognize business opportunities. This concept of "help" extends to prior experience in any aspect of life—whether it is in sports, music, or a volunteer activity. In what areas to you have a good amount of prior experience? How could this prior experience position you to start a business?

2-27. Make a list of your strong-tie and weak-tie realtionships. Include at least five names on each list. Select two names from your list of weak-tie relationships and speculate on the types of new business ideas you think these individuals would be uniquely qualified to help you contemplate.

2-28. Haley Branson, an enthusiastic young entrepreneur, has tried to establish a business based on ideas in her area of interest a couple of times. However, all her previous ventures have failed. She is quite upset as a result, especially since she believed her ideas were good. You need to advise her that ideas alone do not work, and that she needs to acquire certain characteristics that make some people better at recognizing opportunities than others.

2-29. Jonathan Reed has been asked to prepare a bug report for his Creative Class based on the problems faced by him in his daily campus life. What are the techniques that can be used by Jonathan to prepare this report?

YOU BE THE VC 2.1 COMPANY: NatureBox

• Web: www.naturebox.com • Facebook: NatureBox • Twitter: @naturebox

Business Idea: Launch a monthly subscription service that delivers healthy snacks to subscribers at their doorsteps for a low monthly fee.

Pitch: Snacking is a part of everyday life. As Americans become more health conscious, they are continually looking for healthier snacks. NatureBox provides a subscription service where it delivers a box of healthy snacks to its subscribers on a monthly basis. The boxes come in three sizes: individual, family, and office. The individual box contains five snacks, the family box 10 snacks, and the office box 15 snacks. The boxes contain packages of snack items such as dried fruit strips, harvest nut mix, cranberry almond bits, and roasted kettle kernels. Each package is a NatureBox-branded product that is formulated in-house by NatureBox's nutritional specialists.

With a mission of "Discover a Healthier You," NatureBox's selling proposition is that it provides consumers with a variety of healthy snacks without having to go to the store, walk the aisles, and read the labels on snack selections to make sure they are nutritious. Since snacks are consumed, they need to be regularly replenished, which is facilitated by NatureBox's monthly deliveries. The company also sells full-sized versions of the snacks that it includes in its monthly subscription boxes on its website. A customer can customize his or her monthly subscription box or let NatureBox surprise them. For those that allow NatureBox to surprise them, the service contains an element of anticipation and fun as customers await their monthly box and then discovers what's inside. All of NatureBox's snacks are sourced from local growers and independent food suppliers across the United States. Every NatureBox snack is guaranteed nutritious and is free from high-fructose corn syrup, hydrogenated oils, trans fats, and artificial sweeteners, flavors, and colors.

While NatureBox views the subscription model as a powerful form of distribution, it realizes that not all consumers want to subscribe to a product or service. As a result, the company's goal is to build a brand of nutritious snack foods that can be sold both within and outside the subscription framework. The company's intentions are to continue to sell online. Only 2 percent of all food products are currently sold online. NatureBox believes that as people become increasingly comfortable conducting the majority of their purchases online, that 2 percent number will increase and consumers will be drawn to brands that sell predominately online and are distinctive and unique, such as NatureBox's tasty, nutritious snacks.

NatureBox is spreading the word about its subscription service and products primarily via social media. It currently has more than 786,000 Facebook likes and says that many of its sales come from pass-alongs and word-of-mouth referrals.

2-30. Based on the material covered in this chapter, what questions would you ask the firm's founders before making your funding decision? What answers would satisfy you?

2-31. If you had to make your decision on just the information provided in the pitch and on the company's website, would you fund this company? Why or why not?

YOU BE THE VC 2.2 COMPANY: Parking Panda

• Web: www.parkingpanda.com • Facebook: Parking Panda • Twitter: @ParkingPanda

Business Idea: Create a service that allows motorists to find parking spots on a regular basis or for special events, and allow parking space owners (both individuals and commercial lots) a way of connecting with drivers to rent underutilized parking spaces.

Pitch: Finding convenient parking in a city or for a major sporting event or concert is a frustration that almost every motorist has experienced. Trouble finding parking is also a major cause of congestion. Experts estimate that 30 percent of urban traffic is caused by motorists trying to find parking. At the same time, commercial lots and garages often have underutilized parking spaces because people can't find them or mistakenly assume they are full. In most cases, there are also homes and businesses within a short walking distance from where people are looking for parking with spaces that are vacant during large portions of the day.

Parking Panda has created a solution for this problem. It is a website and app that connects drivers looking for parking with commercial lots and individuals who have spaces to rent. Here's how it works. In areas where Parking Panda is available (70 cities and counting), drivers that are already on the road can enter their location, and Parking Panda will show them the nearest available spaces. If you're planning ahead, you can browse a collection of parking spots based on price and location, and reserve one. You can search by neighborhood, restaurant, hotel, nightclub, music venue, or stadium. When you arrive at your destination, your spot will be available, even if the ramp or lot is sold out. You gain admittance by showing the reservation on your smartphone to the attendant. If the lot is gated and does not have an attendant, you gain admittance by using the Parking Panda app to scan a code at the entrance, which opens the gate. You exit the lot in the same manner. Parking spots can be reserved on a one-time basis or can be reserved for regular use. Parking Panda collects the fee at the time the reservation is made and then reimburses the owner of the spot.

Parking Panda makes money by taking a commission on each spot that is rented. It negotiates directly with commercial lots and garages. Individuals and businesses that have parking spaces available simply upload a picture of

their spot and set a price. Parking Panda lets the owner know when a spot has been rented and handles the payment. Parking Panda also has arrangements with sports leagues such as the National Basketball Association (NBA) and the National Hockey Association (NHL) to facilitate parking for their events.

2-32. Based on the material covered in this chapter, what questions would you ask the firm's founders before making your funding decision? What answers would satisfy you?

2-33. If you had to make your decision on just the information provided in the pitch and on the company's website, would you fund this company? Why or why not?

CASE 2.1

Dropbox: Solving a Compelling Problem in a Smooth Manner

• *Web: www.dropbox.com* • *Facebook: Dropbox* • *Twitter: @Dropbox*

Bruce R. Barringer, *Oklahoma State University*

R. Duane Ireland, *Texas A&M University*

Introduction

In early 2007, Drew Houston was on a bus from Boston to New York City. He was excited because he had four hours to work on his laptop. All of a sudden, he had a feeling in the pit of his stomach that something was wrong. He searched through his pockets and discovered that he had forgotten his USB memory stick. He was now stuck on the bus with nothing to work on. Frustrated, he immediately starting building technology to synch files over the Web. Fast forward to the present. Houston's eventual solution, Dropbox, has over 200 million users. Dropbox allows users to create a special folder on each of their devices. Once a piece of digital content is placed in a folder (Word file, Excel file, photo, video, etc.), Dropbox automatically syncs it across all the users' devices, permitting the content to be retrieved and updated from any device. The content also appears in a file on Dropbox's website. And if you make a change to a file in one location, that file is updated across all devices. Dropbox completely solves the problem of working on a file on one device, such as an office computer, and then not having it available on another device, like a laptop at home. You can even invite others to view these files, making the sharing of files easy. It's like having a magic pocket that contains all your digital content and is always with you, with the ability to share the digital content with whomever you want.

Although Dropbox's service is easy to use, it wasn't easy to build or even easy to explain at the outset. It's a story of two determined entrepreneurs who set out to solve a problem, build an elegant solution, and then did a lot of things right in executing on their business idea.

Drew Houston

The Dropbox story starts when Houston was young. He started writing code in his early teens. At 14, he signed up to beta test an online game, and began identifying security flaws. The company soon hired him as their networking programmer, in exchange for equity. Houston worked at start-ups through high school and college. By the time he got to MIT, most of his time was spent coding. He knew that to start businesses, he'd need to know more than just coding, so he starting reading business books. He read books on finance, management, negotiations, etc.

After graduating from college, Houston took a job with a tech firm. The day on the bus from Boston to New York City took place about a year into the new job. Four months later, he flew to San Francisco to pitch the idea for Dropbox to Paul Graham of business accelerator Y Combinator. Graham insisted that Houston have a co-founder, even to pitch. Houston was soon introduced to Arash Ferdowsi, who was a junior engineering student at MIT, and the two hit it off. They decided to work on Dropbox together. They were soon admitted and went through Y Combinator in 2007.

Minimal Viable Product and Solving a Problem People Didn't Know They Had

After their Y Combinator experience finished, Houston and Ferdowsi raised $1.2 million in funding. A challenge they faced from the beginning is that they were solving a problem that most people didn't know they had. There were ways for people to transfer files from one device to another, such as USB memory sticks, e-mailing files to yourself, and so forth. The idea of a service that would sync your files across all your devices didn't exist, so no one knew to ask for it. This reality posed a problem. To gain traction, it wouldn't do any good to buy Google AdWords, for example, because no one was searching for a file syncing service.

To test demand and get feedback on early versions of Dropbox, Houston and Ferdowsi opted for a novel solution. They made two short product videos. The first video, which was made just before Y Combinator, appeared on Dropbox's Homepage. It was a simple, 2-minute-and-17-second stick figure video showing what the service did—nothing complicated, just a guy who loses stuff and goes on a trip to Africa. The second video was a year later. It was a bland, simple three-minute demonstration of Dropbox as it was meant to work, targeted at a community of technology early adopters. Houston narrated the video. It was both informative and playful. If you look closly, you'll notice that the files that Houston is moving around (on the video) are full of humorous references that were appreciated by the audience to whom he was talking.

At the time of the videos, Dropbox was available only to a small group of beta-users. Houston and Ferdowsi were reluctant to release the product to a wider audience because it wasn't completely ready. As noted by Eric Riese in a TechCrunch article titled "How DropBox Started As a Minimal Viable Product," the videos were essentially the minimal viable product—they provided sufficient detail to test whether there was a market for the service. The videos did the trick, with the second one driving hundreds of thousands of people to Dropbox's website. Its waiting list for beta users went from 5,000 people to 75,000 people overnight. Dropbox was off and running.

If you'd like to watch the videos, they are available on YouTube. For the first video, go to YouTube and type in the search box "Original Dropbox Video." For the second video, type in the search box "Dropbox Digg Video." (It was originally posted on the website Digg.)

Building a Company

In Dropbox's early days, Houston and Ferdowsi were the only employees. They didn't hire anyone until they got their first round of funding. Two years later, long after the second video was released, Dropbox had 200,000 customers, but only nine employees. In 2011, Dropbox grossed more than three times per employee than Google. All of the early hires were engineers. Despite Dropbox's seeming simplicity, it required significant technical expertise to build.

Houston and Ferdowsi have always believed in keeping Dropbox lean, which remains a central element in the firm's culture today. The company has raised substantial venture capital funding. Dropbox utilizes a freemium business model, where users are offered a free account with a set storage size and paid subscriptions for accounts with more capaticy. Along the way, Houston and Ferdowsi have done several clever things to spur Dropbox's growth. The freemium model itself drives user adoption. The company also has a referal system to get new user

sign-ups. A current user could get additional memory for free by making a referral. Interestingly, almost 96 percent of Dropbox's users pay nothing. They utilize the free service. The 4 percent that do pay represent a large enough critial mass of subscribers to fund Dropbox's operations and its growth. Dropbox is a private company, so it doesn't reveal its financial results.

Compelling Nature of Service

More than anything else, Dropbox's success can be attributed to the compelling nature of its service. Early in the company's history, there was a sign in its corporate office that said "It simply works!" Here are some specific facts and figures about Dropbox's service that illustrate the compelling nature of what it has to offer.

- Install the Dropbox application, and a Dropbox folder appears on your desktop. Anything you drag into the folder is uploaded automatically to the Dropbox service and is then instantly replicated across all your computers, smartphones, and other devices. How cool is that?
- Dropbox folders are extremely convenient for group projects.
- The service is easy and simple to learn. Most people upload and start using the service without ever referring to the instructions. The Dropbox team knew that with millions of people using its service, it had to be simple.
- It is supported on all platforms. Apple iCloud, for example, is a comparable service, but it only works for Apple devices. Dropbox has vowed to remain neutral and support all platforms.
- In April 2012, Dropbox announced a new feature allowing users to automatically upload (to their Dropbox account) photos and videos from cameras, tablets, SD cards, and smartphones.
- In September 2012, Facebook and Dropbox integrated to allow group users to share files to Facebook Groups using Dropbox's cloud-based storage system.

The Advent of the Smartphone

The advent of the smartphone, including the Apple iPhone and Android-equipped devices, has created an interesting point of differentiation for Dropbox. Prior to the smartphone, Dropbox was a nice to have, but not necessarily a have-to-have product. People could still transfer information using USB memory sticks. Memory sticks can't be attached to smartphones. Apple allows users to upload the data on their smartphones to iCloud, but iCloud is limited to Apple devices, as mentioned above. If people want to have all the digital content they own, including what's on their smartphone in one place, the clear choice is Dropbox.

Challenges Ahead

Despite its impressive success, Dropbox has vexing challenges ahead. Some observers feel the long-term

(continued)

potential of Dropbox will be determined by how they meet these challenges.

There are two primary challenges that Dropbox is facing. First, it deals with enormous complexity. Its 200 million users save one billion files every 24 hours. In addition, anytime a device manufacturer tweaks the software or hardware associated with their device, the Dropbox team must remain on top of the change to make sure that its service will still work for that device. Second, Dropbox is facing an increasing number of competitors. Apple iCloud is an example. Dropbox has an edge over iCloud because it's available across platforms, but more challenging competition may be coming. If Google, Apple, or Samsung, for example, decided to go head-to-head with Dropbox, those companies would have the technological chops to give Dropbox a go. Many believe Dropbox is up to the challenge. In January 2014, *Fast Compay* magazine listed Dropbox as the most innovative company in America in the category of Productivity.

Discussion Questions

2-34. What environmental trends are working in Dropbox's favor as the firm seeks to operate profitably? What environmental trends may work against Dropbox and why?

2-35. What personal characteristics does Drew Houston possess that suggest he may have what it takes to be a successful entrepreneur?

2-36. What *problem* did Dropbox's founders solve with the service they developed?

Sources: Dropbox Homepage, www.dropbox.com, accessed March 24, 2014; *Forbes*, "Dropbox: The Inside Story of Tech's Hottest Startup," November 7, 2011; E. Ries, "How Dropbox Started As a Minimal Viable Product," available at http://techcrunch.com/2011/10/19/dropbox-minimal-viable-product; A. Walsh, "Dropbox: A Social Web Business Case Study,"Social Web Q&A Homepage, available at http:socialwebquanda.com, posted August 26, 2012, accessed March 21, 2014.

CASE 2.2

Rover.com: Don't Chuckle: This Is One Impressive Business Idea

* *Web: www.rover.com* * *Facebook: Rover.com* * *Twitter: @RoverDotCom*

Bruce R. Barringer, *Oklahoma State University*

R. Duane Ireland, *Texas A&M University*

Introduction

Jill is a 26-year-old sales rep for a technology company. She lives in a two-bedroom townhouse with her Golden Retriever Rex. Jill travels about twice a month, and when she's gone, she has three options regarding care for Rex. Option #1—She can ask a neighbor to watch him, but that's hit-and-miss, and she hasn't found anyone she can depend on; Option # 2—She can take him to her parents' house, but they live about an hour away; and Option #3—She can take Rex to one of the two kennels that are close to where Jill lives. There is nothing wrong with them, but they are typical kennels. The dogs are cooped up most of the day, and a month ago, Rex came home from the kennel with a cough he picked up from another dog.

Jill loves Rex and has no plans to give him up, but every time she travels, it's a problem to decide what to do with Rex.

A Bad Experience at a Kennel Leads to a Business Idea

Many people are just like Jill. They either have trouble finding suitable arrangements for their dog when they travel, or they feel bad when they're packing for an exciting trip with their dog's big, sad eyes staring at them. The idea for Rover.com—a service that connects

dog owners with dog sitters—occurred to Greg Gottesman after his yellow Labrador Ruby Tuesday had a bad experience at a traditional kennel. To see if the idea had legs, Gottesman pitched it at a Startup Weekend event in Seattle in 2011. Startup Weekends are events that are held across the country. Anyone can pitch a business idea and get feedback from peers. Gottesman's idea received top prize, and six months later, he launched Rover.com.

While Gottesman may have had a good pitch, a little research helps validate the business idea. The dog boarding/sitting market is about $6 billion a year. More encouraging is that the market could be much larger. Many people don't travel because there is no one they can trust to watch their dog(s). In addition, a survey of 1,000 dog owners by PetCare.com indicated that 80 percent worry about the care their dogs are getting while they're away, and 66 percent are unhappy with their current boarding situation. A total of 70 percent said they would travel more if they had a trusted dog sitter. To get a sense of just how deeply some people care about their pets, a survey of dog owners (commissioned by Rover.com) found that 76 percent of dog owners self-identify themselves as "pet parents," as opposed to "dog owners." A growing number of people see their dogs as "family members" rather than pets. The American Veterinary Medical Association found that people who consider their dogs to be family members spend twice as much money on them annually ($438 vs. $190) as those who view pets as property.

How Rover.com Works

Rover.com's service is run through its website. If you're a dog owner, you simply follow the prompts on the website, which asks you to identify your location and select the dates you need your dog to be watched. You can indicate whether you'd like your dog to be watched at your home or the sitter's household. You're then provided profiles of Rover.com-approved dog sitters in the area. The profile includes prices (per night), photos, reviews, certifications, and a full description of the sitter. The reviews are particularly helpful. For example, a Rover.com customer wrote the following about Jennifer, a Rover.com sitter in Central Florida: "I boarded my 1-year old Beagle with Jennifer for eight nights while on a cruise. She took great care of him and e-mailed us every night with an update. I highly recommend her and will definitely be using her in the future." Some sitters send text and photo updates along with e-mails. Rover sitters charge between $25 and $75 per night. In San Francisco, Rover.com's biggest market, there are over 500 sitters registered on the site.

The profiles also reveal the nature of the sitter. Some are professionals who watch dogs on a full-time basis. Others are large families with their own dogs. Some have rural property with park-like settings. Still, others are elderly people who enjoy watching dogs in their homes.

If you'd like to become a Rover.com sitter, the website walks you through the application process. You must create a profile and must be approved by Rover.com. The company says that it approves only 10 percent of the sitters who apply. Rover also encourages a "meet-and-greet" session before a dog owner tries a sitter. This suggestion recommends that the dog owners (with their dog in tow) meet the dog sitter at a mutually agreeable time and place to talk before they try each other out. The meet-and-greet can be arranged through Rover.com's website. Rover helps sitters get started by providing them access to $20 coupons to provide to new clients. A sitter can get up to 250 of the coupons, and Rover pays the bill.

Rover handles client billing. It takes a 15 percent commission for its part. Many Rover.com sitters leave successful careers to dog-sit full time. While critics chuckle when they hear statements like this, Rover.com can be a serious business. There are now over 25,000 dog sitters with profiles on Rover.com's website. Top Rover.com sitters earn several thousand dollars a month. A Rover sitter can also work as much or as little as they want. A sitter's profile includes a calendar indicating when the sitter is available. The average stay for a dog at a sitter's home is just over four days.

Rover tries to take care of both the dog owner and dog sitter by offering additional layers of protection. For example, every stay booked through Rover includes premium insurance for emergency vet bills, property damage, liability, and more. Rover offers additional services for dog owners, an area of its business that is destined to grow. Rover subscribers can currently purchase an annual $49.99 protection package that includes a 24/7 vet consultation and special Rover tags for extra safety and security.

Making Things Fun

Rover.com also makes things fun for both its dog owners and dog sitters. Its website features RoverCam, which is a camera inside Rover.com's Seattle

To reassure dog owners and make things fun, Rover.com has an app that allows sitters to send photos of the dogs they are watching during their stay.

Martin Novak/Shutterstock

(continued)

headquarters aimed at the part of the building where Rover.com's employees let their dogs hang out. The day this case was written, there were six dogs in-house, including Carmel, Georgie Girl, Gus, Charlie, Oscar, and another Gus. Oscar, for example, is a three-year, one-month-old Miniature Schnauzer. He was lounging on a comfy chair the day the case was written. Rover's sitters are also equipped with some cool technology. The company's app allows sitters to send photos of the dogs they are watching to their owners while they're away.

In late 2013, Rover.com introduced Rover Reel, which offers Rover customers free videos of their dog's experience during their stay with a Rover.com sitter. Sitters simply submit sufficient photos of a dog they're watching, and they will receive a personalized video (Rover Reel) of the dog's stay to share with the owner.

Growth Plans & Venture Capital

Rover.com's potential has garnered plenty of attention. In 2013, the company increased its revenue by 800 percent and currently has about 200,000 dog owners listed on its site. Incredibly, as of January 2014, the 43-person company had raised $25 million in funding from top-shelf venture capital firms and pet retailer PetCo. The numbers in the pet industry are staggering. Americans spent $53 billion on their pets in 2012. Currently, there are roughly 78 million dogs in the United States (this number is an all-time high).

In light of these statistics and what it has learned in its three years of existence, Rover.com has a three-prong growth strategy, as follows:

1. Spread geographically, including in international markets.
2. Provide new services, including dog grooming and dog walking.
3. Add other animals, such as cats, horses, and reptiles.

Rover.com's CEO Aaron Easterly, a passionate dog lover, believes the company is only a fraction of the size it can become.

Discussion Questions

2-37. In the United States, what environmental trends are supporting the development of Rover.com's business?
2-38. How might Rover.com use focus groups to gain a better understanding of its current and potential customers and their needs?
2-39. In this chapter, we noted that a true business opportunity is attractive, durable, timely, and anchored in a product or service that creates value for a buyer. To what extent does Rover.com's service satisfy each of these criteria?

Sources: Rover.com Homepage, www.rover.com, accessed March 21, 2014; C. Garnick, "Rover.com Lands $12 Million More in Financing," The Seattle Times," March 12, 2014; "Rover: A Dog's Tale," Strictly VC, available at http://www.strictlyvc.com/2013/10/03/rover-dogs-tale, posted October 3, 2013, accessed March 22, 2014; Sources: Startupbeat.com, "Dog 2.0: This Time is Different (Really), available at http://startupbeat.com/2013/09/10/dog-2-0-this-time-is-different-really-id3433/. posted September 10, 2013, accessed March 21, 2013.

Endnotes

1. H. Yang, Y. Zheng, and X. Zhao, "Exploration or exploitation? Small firms' alliance strategies with large firms," *Strategic Management Journal* 35, no. 1 (2014): 146-157.
2. comScore, "comScore Releases 2013 U.S. Search Engine Results," November 13, 2013, available at http://www.comscore.com/Insights/Press_Releases/2013/11/comScore_Releases_October_2013_US_Search_Engine_Rankings, (accessed March 18, 2014).
3. M. Yang, "Interview with Michael Yang, CEO of Become.com," npost, originally posted on April 24, 2006, available at http://www.npost.com/?s=become.com, (accessed on March 18, 2014).
4. P.A. Coomes, J. Fernandez, and S. F. Gohmann, "The Rate of Proprietorship among Metropolitan Areas: The Impact of the Local Economic Environment and Capital Resources," *Entrepreneurship Theory, and Practice*, 37, no. 4 (2013): 745-770.
5. Immersion Active, "Resources 50+ Fact and Fiction," available at http://www.immersionactive.com/resources/50-plus-facts-and-fiction/, (accessed March 18, 2014).
6. Nest Labs Homepage, www.nest.com, accessed on March 18, 2014.
7. Pew Research Internet Project, "Social Networking Fact Sheet," available at http://www.pewinternet.org/fact-sheets/social-networking-fact-sheet/, posted December 27, 2013, (accessed March 18, 2014).
8. ABIresearch, "Ninety Million Wearable Computing Devices Will be Shipped in 2014 Driven by Sports, Health and Fitness," ABIresearch Homepage, www.aibresearch.com, Accessed March 18, 2014.
9. T. Freeman, "Obamacare's Other Surprise," *The New York Times*, May 25, 2013.
10. J. Nicas, "Drones Find Fans among Farmers, Filmmakers," *The Wall Street Journal*, March 10, 2014.
11. P. Kotler, *Marketing Insights from A to Z* (New York: John Wiley & Sons, 2003), 128.
12. CitySlips Homepage, www.cityslips.com, (accessed March 18, 2014).
13. Yogitoes Homepage, http://yogitoes.com/, (accessed March 18, 2014).
14. Ladies Who Launch homepage, www.ladieswholaunch.com, (accessed March 18, 2014).

15. A. G. Lafley and R. Charan, "Innovation: Making Inspiration Routine," *Inc.*, www.inc.com, June 1, 2008; J. Case, "The Origins of Entrepreneurship," *Inc.*, June, 1989.

16. M. V. Jones and L. Casulli, "International Entrepreneurship: Exploring the Logic and Utility of Individual Experience through Comparative Reasoning Approaches," *Entrepreneurship Theory and Practice* 38, no. 1 (2014): 45-69; M. R. Marvel, "Human Capital and Search-Based Discovery: A Study of High-Tech Entrepreneurship," *Entrepreneurship Theory and Practice* 37, no. 2 (2013): 403-419.

17. E. Mollick, "The Dynamics of Crowdfunding: An Exploratory Study," *Journal of Business Venturing* 29, no. 1 (2014): 1-16; S. L. Newbert, E. T. Tornikoski, & N. R. Quigley, "Exploring the Evolution of Supporter Networks in the Creation of New Organizations," *Journal of Business Venturing* 28, no. 2 (2014): 281-298.

18. "How to Come Up With a Great Idea," *The Wall Street Journal*, April 29, 2013, R1.

19. J. Y.-K. Lim, L. W. Busenitz, and L. Chidambaram, "New Venture Teams and the Quality of Business Opportunities Identified: Faultlines between Subgroups of Founders and Inventors," *Entrepreneurship Theory and Practice* 37, no. 1 (2013): 47-467; I. P. Vaghely and P.-A. Julien, "Are Opportunities Recognized or Constructed? An Information Perspective on Entrepreneurial Opportunity Identification," *Journal of Business Venturing* 25, no. 1 (2010): 73–86.

20. M. McCaffrey, "On the Theory of Entrepreneurial Incentives and Alertness," *Entrepreneurship Theory and Practice* 2014: in press, D. Valliere, "Towards a Schematic Theory of Entrepreneurial Alertness," *Journal of Business Venturing* 28, no. 3 (2013): 430-442. I. M. Kirzner, *Perception, Opportunity, and Profit: Studies in the Theory of Entrepreneurship* (Chicago: University of Chicago Press, 1979).

21. I. M. Kirzner, "The Primacy of Entrepreneurial Discovery," in *The Prime Mover of Progress*, ed. A. Seldon (London: Institute of Economic Affairs, 1980), 5–30.

22. A. J. Kacperczyk, "Social Influence and Entrepreneurship: The Effect of University Peers on Entrepreneurial Entry," *Organization Science* 24, no. 3 (2013): 664-683; J. M. Haynie, D. Shepherd, E. Mosakowski, and P. C. Earley, "A Situated Metacognitive Model of the Entrepreneurial Mindset," *Journal of Business Venturing* 25, no. 2 (2010): 217–29; S. C. Parker, "The Economics of Formal Business Networks," *Journal of Business Venturing* 23, no. 6 (2008): 627–40.

23. L. Harris and A. Rae, "The Online Connection: Transforming Marketing Strategy for Small Businesses," *Journal of Business Strategy* 31, no. 2 (2010): 4–12.

24. G. E. Hills, C. M. Hultman, S. Kraus, and R. Schulte, "History, Theory and Evidence of Entrepreneurial Marketing—An Overview," *International Journal of Entrepreneurship and Innovation Management* 11, no. 1 (2010): 3–18.

25. J.-L. Arregle, B. Batjargal, M. A. Hitt, J. W. Webb, T. Miller, and A. S. Tsui, "Family Ties in Entrepreneurs' Social Networks and New Venture Growth," *Entrepreneurship Theory and Practice*, 2014: in press; Y. Zhang, "The Contingent Value of Social Resources: Entrepreneurs' Use of Debt-Financing Sources in Western China," *Journal of Business Venturing*, 2014: in press.

26. A. C. Klotz, K. M. Hmieleski, B. H. Bradley, and L. W. Busenitz, "New Venture Teams: A Review of the Literature and Roadmap for Future Research," *Journal of Management* 40, no. 1 (2014): 226-255;D. De Clercq, D. Dimov, and N. Thongpapanl, "Organizational Social Capital, Formalization, and Internal Knowledge Sharing in Entrepreneurial Orientation Formation," *Entrepreneurship Theory and Practice* 37, no. 3 (2013): 505-537.

27. N. Anderson, K. Potocnik, and J. Zhou, "Innovation and Creativity in Organizations: A State-of-the-Art Review, Prospective Commentary, and Guiding Framework," *Journal of Management* (2014): in press; P. Criscuolo, A. Salter, and An L. J. Ter Wal, "Going Underground: Bootlegging and Individual Innovation Performance," *Organization Science* (2014): in press; J. J. Kao, *Entrepreneurship, Creativity, and Organization* (Upper Saddle River, NJ: Prentice Hall, 1989).

28. S. A. Alvarez, J. B. Barney, and P. Anderson, "Forming and Exploiting Opportunities: The Implications of Discovery and Creation Processes for Entrepreneurial and Organizational Research," *Organization Science* 24, no. 1 (2013): 301-317.

29. K. Rodan, Entrepreneurial Thought Leaders Podcast, Stanford Technology Ventures Program, http://stvp.stanford.edu, (accessed March 18, 2014).

30. G. Galant and S. Klaus, "VV Show #35," *Venture Voice Podcast*, www.venturevoice.com, originally posted on June 14, 2006, (accessed March 18, 2014).

31. D. Freeman, "Turning Facebook Followers into Online Focus Groups," *The New York Times*, January 5, 2012.

32. J. P. J. de Jong, "The Decision to Exploit Opportunities for Innovation: A Study of High-Tech Small-Business Owners," *Entrepreneurship Theory and Practice* 37, no. 2 (2013): 281-301.

33. Y. Gong, T.-Y. Kim, D.-R. Lee, and J. Zhu, "A Multilevel Model of Team Goal Orientation, Information Exchange, and Creativity," *Academy of Management Journal* 56, no. 3 (2013): 827-851.

Getting
Personal with LUMINAID

Co-Founders

ANDREA SRESHTA

Master's in Architecture, Columbia University, 2011

ANNA STORK

Master's in Architecture, Columbia University, 2011

Dialogue with
Andrea Sreshta

▼

FIRST ENTREPRENEURIAL EXPERIENCE
Selling homemade jewelry in the driveway when I was 12

MY BIGGEST WORRY AS AN ENTREPRENEUR
Making sure we have enough cash in the bank to finance the next round of growth

MY FAVORITE SMARTPHONE APP
Quickbooks for Android

FAVORITE BAND ON MY SMARTPHONE MUSIC LIST
Coldplay

MY ADVICE FOR NEW ENTREPRENEURS
Fail smart. Which, to me, means that each time you try something that does not work out, learn from actual data about what not to do the next time around

BEST PART OF BEING A STUDENT
You have an entire class and faculty at a school ready to give you honest feedback about your business idea

CHAPTER 3

Feasibility *Analysis*

OPENING PROFILE

LUMINAID
The Value of Validating a Business Idea

• Web: www.luminaid.com • Facebook: LuminAid • Twitter: @LuminAid

At 4:53 P.M. on January 12, 2010, Haiti experienced a devastating earthquake. The epicenter of the 7.0 magnitude quake was near Leogane, approximately 16 miles west of Port-au-Prince, Haiti's capital and largest city. The Haitian government later reported that 316,000 people were killed, 300,000 were injured, and approximately 1 million were left homeless.

Two weeks later in New York City, Anna Stork and Andrea Sreshta, master's in architecture students at Columbia University, were tasked with a project to design solutions for disaster relief aid as part of their design studio course. In the nearby photo, Andrea Sreshta is on the left and Anna Stork is on the right. Design studio courses within Columbia's architecture school are open ended and without prescriptive assignments, and students are given the freedom to define and execute their projects to a large degree. Both Stork and Sreshta were deeply affected by the Haiti earthquake, and decided to focus their project on redesigning disaster relief aid to better serve people in emergency situations. They had read and heard about the dangerous conditions in the tent cities erected in Haiti to provide shelter for homeless people. It occurred to them that light—something we take for granted—is often unavailable in emergency situations. They also learned that more broadly, 1.6 billion people across the globe lack access to reliable electricity. Many of these people use kerosene lanterns to light their homes. This is dangerous, in that kerosene lamps are a fire hazard and produce toxic fumes.

The convergence of these two factors led Stork and Sreshta to the idea for their project—something they nicknamed the "solar pillow." The idea was to create a simple, affordable source of light that could be easily and affordably shipped to disaster locations. As part of their research, Stork and Sreshta looked at the small-scale solar products currently on the market. There were many, which prompted them to ask the question "Is there a need for another product in the mix?" The answer ultimately was yes, largely because many of the existing products, while useful, could not be easily and affordably shipped to disaster locations. Stork and Sreshta's solution was an inflatable plastic bag, about the size of a small pillow, that had a rectangular pouch in the middle. The pouch contained a solar panel, three LEDs, and a rechargeable battery. When inflated, the bag became a diffuser for the LED light. Because the solar pillow was inflatable, it packs and ships flat. That provides it an advantage, particularly in a disaster situation. For

LEARNING OBJECTIVES

After studying this chapter you should be ready to:

1. Explain what a feasibility analysis is and why it's important.

2. Describe a product/service feasibility analysis, explain its purpose, and discuss the two primary issues that a proposed business should consider in this area.

3. Describe an industry/market feasibility analysis, explain its purpose, and discuss the two primary issues to consider when completing this analysis.

4. Explain what an organizational feasibility analysis is and its purpose and discuss the two primary issues to consider when completing this analysis.

5. Describe what a financial feasibility analysis is, explain its importance, and discuss the most critical issues to consider when completing this analysis.

6. Describe a feasibility analysis template and explain why it is important for entrepreneurs to use this template.

every eight flashlights packed in a box, a total of 50 solar pillows could be placed into the same container. Once set in the sun for a few hours, the solar pillow could produce a substantial amount of reliable light.

A second factor that was part of Stork and Sreshta's thinking is a principle they called "here and there." The same product—the solar pillow—could be used by someone who is camping or pursuing any form of outdoor recreation as easily as someone in a disaster situation or a developing country using the solar pillow as an alternative to a kerosene lantern. That facet of the device provided the solar pillow a more robust market than a product designed exclusively for a disaster situation or to be used in developing countries.

The design studio class eventually ended, but Stork and Sreshta couldn't let go of the solar pillow idea. Through the summer and fall of 2010, they entered their idea, now called LuminAID, into several business plan competitions. They also shipped 50 early prototypes of the device to places like Haiti, Ghana, and Nicaragua for feedback and advice. They continued to work on the device while finishing school. During that time, the initial prototype evolved to reduce the cost, make it more durable, and brighten the light. In November 2011, Stork and Sreshta launched an Indiegogo crowdfunding campaign titled "LuminAID: An Inflatable Solar Light." The campaign included a short 2-minute, 51-second video that explained the device and the entrepreneurs' passion to bring it to market. If you'd like to see the video and hear directly from Stork and Sreshta, simply go to Indiegogo.com and type in the search bar "LuminAID." The goal of the Indiegogo campaign was threefold: test interest and demand for the device, raise money for the initial product run (assuming sufficient interest existed), and get feedback and advice. One thing that is helpful about running an Indiegogo campaign (the same is true for Kickstarter) is that anyone can write a comment about the campaign, during and after the campaign is concluded. Stork and Sreshta's campaign generated over 500 comments, some of which were helpful to them in tweaking the LuminAid device. The campaign was a hit, raising $51,829, more than five times the original goal. Stork and Sreshta were not only heartened by the overall response, but were pleased to see pledges come in from several developing countries. The pledges from the developing countries, in particular, affirmed in their minds the potential for their device.

Stork and Sreshta managed a successful production run of the LuminAid device and fulfilled their Indiegogo commitments. They used the shipping of the devices as another opportunity to obtain feedback. The e-mail they posted on Indiegogo when the devices were shipped was addressed to "Dear Friends." In part, the e-mail said "When you receive the light, we would greatly value your feedback. This is our first manufacturing run and your comments will help us to improve the product and develop additional products. Please e-mail us at info@luminAIDlab.com with questions or suggestions." After providing instructions on how to use the LuminAID device, the e-mail ended with: "We included instructions with each LuminAID. Feel free to email us if you have any questions and don't forget to send us pictures and stories of the LuminAID in use."

The Indiegogo campaign concluded in late 2012, and the devices were shipped in early 2013 to over 25 countries! LuminAID is now moving forward, but at a measured pace. Stork is working on LuminAID full time, and at the time this feature was written, March 2014, Sreshta was an MBA student at the University of Chicago Booth School of Business. Upon graduation, she plans to work on LuminAID full time. The LuminAID device is now available via the company's website, Amazon.com, LLBean, and several similar outlets. Stork and Sreshta have and are continuing to establish partnerships with relief agencies to utilize the LuminAID solution in disaster situations and in developing countries.

n this chapter, we'll discuss the importance of feasibility analysis. Conducting a well-crafted feasibility analysis, prior to developing a business model, is a critical step in discerning the merits of a business idea. The front cover of this book, along with the pages that introduce each of the four parts of the book, include a depiction of three children in a developing country utilizing a LuminAID device. Note the sense of wonder on their faces. The devices provide a surprising amount of light given their relatively simple design and attractive price-point.

Feasibility Analysis

Feasibility analysis is the process of determining if a business idea is viable (see Figure 3.1). If a business idea falls short on one or more of the four components of feasibility analysis, it should be dropped or rethought, as shown in the figure. Many entrepreneurs make the mistake of identifying a business idea and then jumping directly to developing a business model (see Chapter 4) to describe and gain support for the idea. This sequence often omits or provides little time for the important step of testing the feasibility of a business idea.

A mental transition must be made when completing a feasibility analysis from thinking of a business idea as just an idea to thinking of it as a business. A feasibility analysis is an assessment of a potential business rather than strictly a product or service idea. The sequential nature of the steps shown in Figure 3.1 cleanly separates the investigative portion of thinking through the merits of a business idea from the planning and selling portion of the process. Feasibility analysis is investigative in nature and is designed to critique the merits of a proposed business. A business plan (see Chapter 6) is more focused on planning and selling. The reason it's important to complete the entire process, according to John W. Mullins, the author of the highly regarded book *The New Business Road Test*, is to avoid falling into the "everything about my opportunity is wonderful" mode. In Mullins's view, failure to properly investigate the merits of a business idea before developing a business model and a business plan is written runs the risk of blinding an entrepreneur to inherent risks associated with the potential business and results in too positive of a plan.[1]

This chapter provides a methodology for conducting a feasibility analysis by describing its four key areas: product/service feasibility, industry/target market feasibility, organizational feasibility, and financial feasibility. We introduce supplemental material in two appendixes to the chapter. Appendix 3.1 contains a tool called First Screen, which is a template for completing a feasibility analysis. Appendix 3.2 contains an Internet Resource Table that provides information on Internet resources that are helpful in completing First Screen.

An outline for the approach to feasibility analysis we describe in this chapter is provided in Table 3.1. Completing a feasibility analysis requires both primary

LEARNING OBJECTIVE

1. Explain what a feasibility analysis is and why it's important.

FIGURE 3.1
Role of Feasibility Analysis in Developing Successful Business Ideas

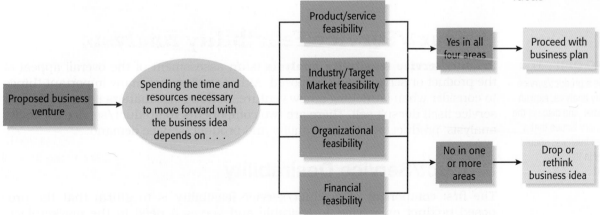

TABLE 3.1   Feasibility Analysis

Part 1: Product/Service Feasibility

  A. Product/service desirability

  B. Product/service demand

Part 2: Industry/Target Market Feasibility

  A. Industry attractiveness

  B. Target market attractiveness

Part 3: Organizational Feasibility

  A. Management prowess

  B. Resource sufficiency

Part 4: Financial Feasibility

  A. Total start-up cash needed

  B. Financial performance of similar businesses

  C. Overall financial attractiveness of the proposed venture

Overall Assessment

and secondary research. **Primary research** is research that is collected by the person or persons completing the analysis. It normally includes talking to prospective customers, getting feedback from industry experts, conducting focus groups, and administering surveys. **Secondary research** probes data that is already collected. The data generally includes industry studies, Census Bureau data, analyst forecasts, and other pertinent information gleaned through library and Internet research. The Internet Resource Table in Appendix 3.2 is useful for conducting secondary research.

It should be emphasized that while a feasibility analysis tests the merits of a specific idea, it allows ample opportunity for the idea to be revised, altered, and changed as a result of the feedback that is obtained and the analysis that is conducted. The key objective behind feasibility analysis is to put an idea to the test—by eliciting feedback from potential customers, talking to industry experts, studying industry trends, thinking through the financials, and scrutinizing it in other ways. These types of activities not only help determine whether an idea is feasible but also help shape and mold the idea.

Now let's turn our attention to the four areas of feasibility analysis. The first area we'll discuss is product/service feasibility.

Product/Service Feasibility Analysis

LEARNING OBJECTIVE

2. Describe a product/service feasibility analysis, explain its purpose, and discuss the two primary issues that a proposed business should consider in this area.

Product/service feasibility analysis is an assessment of the overall appeal of the product or service being proposed. Although there are many important things to consider when launching a new venture, nothing else matters if the product or service itself doesn't sell. There are two components to product/service feasibility analysis: product/service desirability and product/service demand.

Product/Service Desirability

The first component of product/service feasibility is to affirm that the proposed product or service is desirable and serves a need in the marketplace.

Bill Varie/Corbis/Glow Images

One of the most effective techniques for discerning the feasibility of a product or service idea is to get out and talk to prospective users. Here, a young entrepreneur is explaining a product idea to a potential customer.

You should ask yourself, and others, the following questions to determine the basic appeal of the product or service:

- ◼ Does it make sense? Is it reasonable? Is it something real customers will buy?
- ◼ Does it take advantage of an environmental trend, solve a problem, or fill a gap in the marketplace?
- ◼ Is this a good time to introduce the product or service to the market?
- ◼ Are there any fatal flaws in the product or service's basic design or concept?

The proper mind-set at the feasibility analysis stage is to get a general sense of the answers to these and similar questions, rather than to try to reach final conclusions. The best way to achieve this is to "get out of the building" and talk to potential customers. This sentiment is the primary mantra of the lean startup movement, referred to in more detail in Chapter 6. A tool that is particularly useful in soliciting feedback and advice from prospective customers is to administer a concept test.

Concept Test A **concept test** involves showing a preliminary description of a product or service idea, called a **concept statement**, to industry experts and prospective customers to solicit their feedback. It is a one-page document that normally includes the following:

- ◼ A description of the product or service. This section details the features of the product or service; many include a sketch of it as well.
- ◼ The intended target market. This section lists the consumers or businesses who are expected to buy the product or service.
- ◼ The benefits of the product or service. This section describes the benefits of the product or service and includes an account of how the product or service adds value and/or solves a problem.

■ A description of how the product or service will be positioned relative to competitors. A company's position describes how its product or service is situated relative to its rivals.

■ A brief description of the company's management team.

After the concept statement is developed, it should be shown to at least 20 people who are familiar with the industry that the firm plans to enter and who can provide informed feedback. The temptation to show it to family members and friends should be avoided because these people are predisposed to give positive feedback. Instead, it should be distributed to people who will provide candid and informed feedback and advice.

The concept statement for a fictitious company named New Venture Fitness Drinks is provided in Figure 3.2. New Venture Fitness Drinks sells a line of nutritious fitness drinks and targets sports enthusiasts. Its strategy is to place small restaurants, similar to smoothie restaurants, near large sports complexes. It is important to keep a concept statement relatively short (no more than one page) to increase the likelihood that it will be read. The concept statement is followed by a short buying intentions survey. The information gleaned from the survey should be tabulated and carefully read. If time permits, the statement can be used in an iterative manner to strengthen the product or service idea. For example, you might show the statement to a group of prospective customers, receive their feedback, tweak the idea, show it to a second group of customers, tweak the idea some more, and so on.

FIGURE 3.2
New Venture Fitness Drinks' Concept Statement

New Business Concept
New Venture Fitness Drinks Inc.

Product

New Venture Fitness Drinks will sell delicious, nutrition-filled, all-natural fitness drinks to thirsty sports enthusiasts. The drinks will be sold through small storefronts (600 sq. ft.) that will be the same size as popular smoothie restaurants. The drinks were formulated by Dr. William Peters, a world-renowned nutritionist, and Dr. Michelle Smith, a sports medicine specialist, on behalf of New Venture Fitness Drinks and its customers.

Target Market

In the first three years of operation, New Venture Fitness Drinks plans to open three or four restaurants. They will all be located near large sports complexes that contain soccer fields and softball diamonds. The target market is sports enthusiasts.

Why New Venture Fitness Drinks?

The industry for sports drinks continues to grow. New Venture Fitness Drinks will introduce exciting new sports drinks that will be priced between $1.50 and $2.50 per 16-ounce serving. Energy bars and other over-the-counter sports snacks will also be sold. Each restaurant will contain comfortable tables and chairs (both inside and outside) where sports enthusiasts can congregate after a game. The atmosphere will be fun, cheerful, and uplifting.

Special Feature—No Other Restaurant Does This

As a special feature, New Venture Fitness Drinks will videotape select sporting events that take place in the sports complexes nearest its restaurants and will replay highlights of the games on video monitors in their restaurants. The "highlight" film will be a 30-minute film that will play continuously from the previous day's sporting events. This special feature will allow sports enthusiasts, from kids playing soccer to adults in softball leagues, to drop in and see themselves and their teammates on television.

Management Team

New Venture Fitness Drink is led by its cofounders, Jack Petty and Peggy Wills. Jack has 16 years of experience with a national restaurant chain, and Peggy is a certified public accountant with seven years of experience at a Big 4 accounting firm.

The problem with not talking to potential customers prior to starting a business is that it's hard to know if a product is sufficiently desirable based simply on gut instinct or secondary research. A common reason new businesses fail is that there isn't a large enough market for the venture's product. This scenario played out for Matt Cooper, who was a partner in a business called Soggy Bottom Canoe and Kayak Rental. It was his first start-up and turned out to be, as Cooper put it, an "unmitigated disaster." Cooper and his partner owned 10 acres near a national forest in Mississippi, where they decided to launch a canoe rental business. They invested heavily in finishing out the facilities on the property and bought 32 canoes, 16 kayaks, 4 trailers, and 2 vans. They opened on a July 4th weekend and everything was immaculate. The following is what happened, in Cooper's words:

> "In our quest to have the best facilities and equipment, we neglected to speak to a single prospective customer. No Boy Scout troops, no church youth groups, no fraternities from Southern Mississippi University. As a result, I can count on only one hand the number of times, in the seven years that we owned the business, that we reached even half of our booking capacity.[2]

Cooper goes on to admit that he's learned his lesson. Reflecting on his Soggy Bottom Canoe and Kayak Rental experience he said:

> "Today, I still fight against the urge to make big investments before we've "beta tested." Every time that urge pops up, I picture gleaming new canoes hitched up to sad empty passenger vans."[3]

Rather than developing a formal concept statement, some entrepreneurs conduct their initial product/service feasibility analysis by simply talking through their ideas with prospective customers or conducting focus groups to solicit feedback. The ideal combination is to do both—distribute a concept statement to 20 or more people who can provide informed feedback and engage in verbal give-and-take with as many industry experts and prospective customers as possible. There are also a growing number of online tools that help entrepreneurs quickly and inexpensively make contact with prospective customers and complete other steps in the feasibility analysis process. These tools range from services like Quirky, which provides direct feedback on product ideas, to 3D printing services like Shapeways, which converts CAD drawings of product ideas into physical prototypes that you can show to potential customers. We provide a sample of the online tools that are available in Table 3.2.

TABLE 3.2   Online Tools Available for Completing Feasibility Analysis

Tool	Brief Description	URL
3D Printing Services		
i.materialise	Allows you to convert your ideas into physical objects via a 3D printing service. Also provides a platform for sharing and selling your designs.	http://i.materalise.com
Shapeways	Provides a platform for converting ideas into physical objects to use as product prototypes or to sell through the Shapeways community.	www.shapeways.com
A/B Split Testing		
PickFu	Provides instant market feedback, A/B testing, and polls directed toward early users of your product.	www.pickfu.com
Ubounce	Allows you to create simple landing pages and conduct A/B split testing.	www.ubounce.com

(Continued)

TABLE 3.2 **Continued**

Tool	Brief Description	URL
Feedback on Business Ideas		
Foundersuite	Allows you to submit an executive summary of a business idea and get feedback from potential customers, advisers, and others.	http://foundersuite.com
Quirky	Allows you to submit product ideas to a community that vets and provides feedback on the ideas.	www.quirky.com
Unassumer	Allows you to test your ideas and assumptions about what people want.	www.unassumer.com
Landing Pages		
LaunchRock	Allows you to create a "coming soon" landing page in seconds and collect e-mail addresses of potential early users of your product.	www.launchrock.com
Market Research		
AskYourTargetMarket	Allows you to setup surveys that reach a specific target market.	www.aytm.com
CrowdPicker	Allows you to ask a "crowd" of potential customers which logo, tagline, company name, packaging design, etc. is the best choice for your start-up.	www.crowdpicker.com
Google Trends	Allows you to enter a search term (such as running or swimming) and see if it's trending upwards or downwards in Google search queries.	www.google.com/trends
Facebook Ads	Allows you to put together a Facebook ad campaign to assess how a specific target market responds to a new product idea. Can be something as simple as "fill out this form to be one of our first beta testers."	www.facebook.com/ads
Google AdWords	Allows you to put together an AdWords campaign, which usually directs prospective customers to landing pages that assess the demand for a new product or service idea.	www.google.com/adwords
Online Whiteboard		
RealTimeBoard	Allows you to create a whiteboard on your computer (with the capability to draw and erase) and collaborate with team members in real time.	http://realtimeboard.com
Prototyping Service		
Proto Labs	Get prototypes built from CAD drawings.	www.protolabs.com
Stratasys	Offers design validation and rapid prototyping from CAD drawings.	www.stratasys.com
Q&A Sites		
Quora	Platform allows you to ask any business-related question and get answers from the Quora community.	www.quora.com
Stack Overflow	Q&A site for programmers.	www.stackoverflow.com
Surveys		
Google Consumer Surveys	An easy, quick, and inexpensive way to create online surveys.	www.google.com/consumersurveys
Survey.io	A customer development platform that helps start-ups quickly learn what customers like and don't like about their product offerings.	www.survey.io
Survey Monkey	A popular and inexpensive way to create and distribute online surveys.	www.surveymonkey.com
Website Usability Testing		
Usertesting	The company's network of testers will review your website and provide audio commentary while they are using it.	www.usertesting.com
Verify	The company's testers provide feedback on the design and functionality on early to completed versions of your website.	www.verifyapp.com

Product/Service Demand

The second component of product/service feasibility analysis is to determine if there is demand for the product or service. Three commonly utilized methods for doing this include (1) talking face-to-face with potential customers, (2) utilizing online tools, such as Google Adwords and landing pages, to assess demand, and (3) library, Internet, and gumshoe research.

Talking Face-to-Face with Potential Customers The only way to know if your product or service is what people want is by talking to them. Curiously, this often doesn't happen. One study of 120 business founders revealed that more than half fully developed their products without getting feedback from potential buyers.[4] In hindsight, most viewed it as a mistake. The authors of the study quoted one of the participants as saying "You'll learn more from talking to five customers than you will from hours of market research (at a computer)." The idea is to gauge customer reaction to the general concept of what you want to sell. Entrepreneurs are often surprised to find out that a product idea that they think solves a compelling problem gets a lukewarm reception when they talk to actual customers.

In some instances, you have to pause and think carefully about who the potential customer is. For example, in health care the "customer" is typically not the patient who will use the drugs or benefit from a medical procedure. Instead the actual customer, or the entity that will be paying the bill, is often an insurance company, hospital, or Medicare or Medicaid. You should also talk to as many of the relevant players in an industry as possible. Sometimes this involves a complex list of people, but it is necessary to fully vet the initial feasibility of an idea. For example, say you were thinking about launching an innovative new type of home health care service. The service would allow elderly people to stay in their homes longer before going into assisted living or a nursing home, and it would help people remember to take their medicine on time and provide other health care monitoring services. Table 3.3 contains a list of the categories of people that you might want to talk to as part of your product/service feasibility analysis. While the list is long, imagine the rich insight that you could get on your business idea from people in these categories.

TABLE 3.3   **Categories of People to Talk to as Part of Product/Service Feasibility Analysis for a New Type of Home Health Care Service**

Category of people to talk to

1. Potential users of the service

2. Family members of potential users of the service

3. Physicians

4. Nurses

5. Health insurance companies

6. Medicare and Medicaid personnel

7. Pharmaceutical companies

8. Owners/managers of assisted living facilities and nursing homes

9. Hospital and physician office administrators

10. Founders of other companies in the home health care industry

One approach to finding qualified people to talk to about a product or service idea or to react to a concept statement is to contact trade associations and/or attend industry trade shows. If your product idea is in the digital media space, for example, you may be able to call the Digital Media Association (which is a national trade association devoted primarily to the online audio and video industries) and get a list of members who live in your area. Attending trade shows in the industry you're interested in will place you in direct contact with numerous people who might be of assistance. A website that provides a directory of trade associations is included in the Internet Resource Table in Appendix 3.2. Online surveys are also useful to reach a large number of people quickly. Services such as SurveyMonkey and AYTM are making it increasingly easy to survey specific target markets and receive detailed analytics for a very affordable price.

Utilizing Online Tools, Such as Google AdWords and Landing Pages, to Assess Demand   Another common approach to assessing product demand is to use online tools, such as Google AdWords and landing pages. The way this works is as follows. Suppose you've developed a new type of sunglasses for snowboarders and want to assess likely demand. One way of doing this is to buy keywords on the Google search page like "snowboarding" and "sunglasses." You can purchase the keywords through Google's AdWords program. Once you buy the keywords, when someone searches for the term "snowboarding" or "sunglasses" a link to an ad you've prepared will show up either at the top or to the right of the organic search results. The text below the link will say something such as "Innovative new sunglasses for snowboarders." If someone clicks on the link, they'll be taken to what online marketers call a **landing page**. A **landing page** is a single Web page that typically provides direct sales copy, like "click here to buy a Hawaiian vacation." Your landing page, which can be inexpensively produced through a company like LaunchRock (see Table 3.2), will show an artist's depiction of your innovative new sunglasses, provide a brief explanation, and will then say something like "Coming Soon—Please Enter Your E-mail Address for Updates." How often your ad appears will depend on what you purchase through Google's automated AdWord's keyword auction. Google will provide you analytics regarding how many people click on the ad and how many follow through and provide their e-mail address. You can also capture the e-mail addresses that are provided.

The beauty of using Google AdWords is that the people who click on the ad were either searching for the term "snowboarding" or "sunglasses" or they wouldn't have seen the ad. So you're eliciting responses from a self-selected group of potential buyers. The overarching purpose is to get a sense of interest in your product. If, over a three-day period, 10,000 people click on the ad and 4,000 provide their e-mail address to you, that might signal a fairly strong interest in the product. On the other hand, if only 500 people click on the ad and 50 give you their e-mail address, that's a much less affirming response. It's strictly a judgment call regarding how many clicks represent an encouraging response to your product idea. Normally, utilizing an AdWords and landing page campaign wouldn't be the only thing you'd do to assess demand. You'd still want to talk to prospective customers face-to-face, as discussed earlier. Running an AdWords and landing page campaign is, however, a practical and often surprisingly affordable way to get another data point in regard to assessing demand for a new product or service idea.

Library, Internet, and Gumshoe Research   The third way to assess demand for a product or service idea is by conducting library, Internet, and gumshoe research. While talking to prospective customers is critical, collecting secondary data on an industry is also helpful. For example, Spring Toys makes super-safe, environmentally friendly, educational toys for children.

Sounds like a good idea. But "sounds like a good idea," as mentioned in previous sections, isn't enough. We need feedback from prospective customers and industry-related data to make sure. Industry-related data can help us answer the following types of questions: What's the trajectory of the toy industry? What do industry experts say are the most important factors that parents consider when they buy their children toys? Is there an "educational toy" segment within the larger toy industry? If so, is this segment growing or shrinking? Is there a trade association for the makers of educational toys that already has statistics about the market demand for educational toys?

The overarching point is that for your particular product or service you need archival as well as primary forms of research to assess likely demand. Your university or college library is a good place to start, and the Internet is a marvelous resource. The Internet Resource Table in Appendix 3.2 provides specific recommendations of online resources to utilize. For example, IBISWorld, which is available for free through most university libraries, provides current industry reports on hundreds of industries. Its report on the toy industry, which is frequently updated, is titled "Toy, Doll and Game Manufacturing in the US (NAICS 33993)." This report would be a good place to start in terms of understanding relevant industry trends. More general Internet research is also often helpful. Simply typing a query into the Google or Bing search bar such as "market demand for educational toys" will often produce helpful articles and industry reports.

Simple gumshoe research is also important for gaining a sense of the likely demand for a product or service idea. A gumshoe is a detective or an investigator that scrounges around for information or clues wherever they can be found. Don't be bashful. Ask people what they think about your product or service idea. If your idea is to sell educational toys, spend a week volunteering at a day care center and watch how children interact with toys. Take the owner of a toy store to lunch and discuss your ideas. Spend some time browsing through toy stores and observe the types of toys that get the most attention. If you actually launch a business, there is simply too much at stake to rely on gut instincts and cursory information to assure you that your product or service will sell. Collect as much information as you can within reasonable time constraints.

The importance of library, Internet, and gumshoe research doesn't wane once a firm is launched. It's important to continually assess the strength of product or service ideas and learn from users. A colorful example of the value of ongoing gumshoe research is provided in the "Savvy Entrepreneurial Firm" feature. In this feature, a successful company made a 180-degree turn regarding how to position a particular product simply by watching how customers interacted with the product in retail stores.

Industry/Target Market Feasibility Analysis

Industry/target market feasibility is an assessment of the overall appeal of the industry and the target market for the product or service being proposed. There is a distinct difference between a firm's industry and its target market; having a clear understanding of this difference is important. An **industry** is a group of firms producing a similar product or service, such as computers, children's toys, airplanes, or social networks. A firm's **target market** is the limited portion of the industry that it goes after or to which it wants to appeal. Most firms, and certainly entrepreneurial start-ups, typically do not try to service an entire industry. Instead, they select or carve out a specific target market and try to service that group of customers particularly well. Sprig Toys, for example, is not trying to target the entire children's toy industry. Its target market

SAVVY ENTREPRENEURIAL FIRM

How Learning from Customers Caused a Successful Firm to Make a 180-Degree Turn on the Positioning of a Product

Bill Gross is both a serial entrepreneur and the founder of Idealab, an incubator-type organization that has launched over 75 companies. He's also an Internet pioneer and the creator of the pay-per-click model of Internet advertising. In speaking to groups about entrepreneurship and in working with start-ups at Idealab, there is a story that Gross likes to tell about the importance of feasibility analysis and getting close to customers. It's an experience that has shaped his views about how important it is to learn from the potential users of your product.

In the early 1990s Gross started a software company named Knowledge Adventure. It started by making educational CD-ROM products for children, such as Space Adventure and Dinosaur Adventure. The firm also launched a line of products under the JumpStart brand. These products help kids with topics they encounter in school, such as math and science.

One Christmas, in the early 1990s, Gross really wanted his company to excel, so he decided to have employees spend weekends in places where Knowledge Adventure products were sold, to demo the products to parents and hopefully boost sales. So the company's 65 employees took turns traveling to electronics stores, where they would set up booths at the end of aisles to demo their firm's products. Each Monday, following a weekend when employees were in stores, the employees met to talk about their experiences. One interesting theme emerged from these meetings. When looking at educational software products, parents were often confused about whether a particular product was age-appropriate for their child. They would often look at the back of the box (software was sold on CDs in boxes in those days), look at their child, look back at the box, and appear puzzled about whether the software was a good match for their child. Many companies, Knowledge Adventure included, would put wide age ranges on their products to broaden their appeal. Apparently, this practice inadvertently caused parents to wonder whether a product with a wide age range was really a good match for their particular child.

Thinking through what the employees had observed, Gross and his team came up with a novel idea. What if they produced educational software products that were targeted for a specific grade—like one for preschoolers, one for kindergarteners, one for first grade students, and so forth, to try to avoid confusion for parents trying to determine if a product was age-appropriate for their child. Gross remembers that there was a big fight in his company over this idea. The sales force said, "We can't convince stores to sell software for one age group. They'll never sell enough product." After listening to all the arguments, Gross concluded it was worth a try. So Knowledge Adventure created JumpStart Pre-School and JumpStart Kindergarten to test the concept. The result: The products sold 20 to 50 times the company's other products. Parents loved it—now they knew exactly what product was right for their child. There was even an aspirational quality to the products. Parents would see a product like JumpStart Kindergarten and buy it for their preschool child hoping to give them a head start in kindergarten. Knowledge Adventure has sold over 20 million copies of its grade-specific JumpStart products, and they are still for sale today.

What Gross likes to emphasize when telling this story is that he and his team would have never discovered the confusion that parents had in trying to determine if particular software products were age-appropriate for their children without directly observing them in stores. As a result of this experience, Gross is now a passionate advocate of start-ups directly interacting with potential users of their products.

Questions for Critical Thinking

1. In putting wide age ranges on their products (e.g., suitable for ages 4 through 7), do you think that software companies prior to the advent of JumpStart's grade-specific products ever thought that the wide age range caused parents angst in trying to determine if a particular product was suitable for their child? If your answer is "no," how could companies have missed such a fundamental factor? What is the broader implication of this lesson?

2. Could Gross and his team have gleaned the same type of insights they gained via directly observing parents shopping for educational software for their kids through surveys and focus groups? Explain your answer.

3. Design a program for August Smart Lock, the subject of the "You Be the VC 3.1" feature, to directly observe its customers use its service. How should August Smart Lock go about it? What type of insights might emerge from this initiative?

4. How can a start-up that hasn't already launched apply the lessons learned from Gross's experience with JumpStart and grade-specific software products?

Source: B. Gross, "A Devotion to New Ideas," Stanford Technology Ventures Entrepreneurial Thought Leaders Podcast (accessed April 4, 2014, originally posted on February 23, 2011).

Information pertaining to industry growth rates, trends, and future prospects is available via online databases like the one accessed here. IBISWorld and BizMiner are additional databases that provide particularly helpful information.

Andrey Popov/Shutterstock

is parents who are willing to pay a premium for super-safe, environmentally friendly, educational toys.

There are two components to industry/target market feasibility analysis: industry attractiveness and target market attractiveness.

Industry Attractiveness

Industries vary in terms of their overall attractiveness.[5] In general, the most attractive industries have the characteristics depicted in Table 3.4. The top three factors are particularly important. Industries that are young rather than old, are early rather than late in their life cycle, and are fragmented rather than concentrated are more receptive to new entrants than industries with the opposite characteristics. You also want to pick an industry that is structurally attractive—meaning start-ups can enter the industry (in various target markets) and compete effectively. Some industries are characterized by such high barriers to entry or the presence of one or two dominant players that potential new entrants are essentially shut out.

TABLE 3.4 Characteristics of Attractive Industries

■ Are young rather than old

■ Are early rather than late in their life cycle

■ Are fragmented rather than concentrated

■ Are growing rather than shrinking

■ Are selling products or services that customers "must have" rather than "want to have"

■ Are not crowded

■ Have high rather than low operating margins

■ Are not highly dependent on the historically low price of a key raw material, like gasoline or flour, to remain profitable

Other factors are also important. For example, the degree to which environmental and business trends are moving in favor rather than against the industry are important for the industry's long-term health and its capacity to spawn new target or niche markets. Are changing economic and societal trends helping or hurting industry incumbents? Are profit margins increasing or falling? Is innovation accelerating or waning? Are input costs going up or down? Are new markets for the industry's staple products opening up or are current markets being shut down by competing industries? You can't cover every facet of an industry, but you should gain a sense of whether the industry you're entering is a good one or a poor one for start-ups.

Information that addresses each of these issues is available via industry reports published by IBISWorld, Mintel, Bizminer, and similar fee-based databases that are typically free if accessed through a university or large public library's website. These resources are listed in the Internet Resource Table in Appendix 3.2. The First Screen, which is the feasibility analysis template included in Appendix 3.1, includes a section that draws attention to the most important issues to focus on regarding industry attractiveness during the feasibility analysis stage of investigating a business idea.

Target Market Attractiveness

We noted previously that a target market is a place within a larger market segment that represents a narrower group of customers with similar needs. Most start-ups simply don't have the resources needed to participate in a broad market, at least initially. Instead, by focusing on a smaller target market, a firm can usually avoid head-to-head competition with industry leaders and can focus on serving a specialized market very well. It's also not realistic, in most cases, for a start-up to introduce a completely original product idea into a completely new market. In most instances, it's just too expensive to be a pioneer in each area. Most successful start-ups either introduce a new product into an existing market (like Sprig Toys introducing new toys into the existing toy market) or introduce a new market to an existing product (like Wello is introducing Web-based, real-time fitness instruction, which is a new market for an existing product offered by personal trainers, yoga instructors, etc.).

The challenge in identifying an attractive target market is to find a market that's large enough for the proposed business but yet is small enough to avoid attracting larger competitors at least until the entrepreneurial venture can get off to a successful start. Tommy John, a maker of men's undershirts, is an example of a company that has targeted a market that meets these criteria. Tommy John began in 2008 by making custom-fitted men's undershirts, and has now expanded to men's briefs and men's socks. The undershirts are sold under the brand name Second Skin, based on the idea that they fit so well they feel like a "second skin" when worn. Tommy John started by selling through a single retailer and eventually persuaded Neiman Marcus to give its undershirts a try. Today, Tommy John undershirts are sold in Neiman Marcus stores nationwide and are making their way into other retailers as well. Although Tommy John operates in the worldwide market for men's undershirts, it has carved out a specialized target or niche market for itself and is gaining momentum. One key to its success is that it has remained laser-focused on a clearly defined target market. The number one question the company gets is "when will it start producing women's undergarments?" So far it's resisted, preferring to remain focused on its Second Skin line of men's undershirts.[6]

While it's generally easy to find good information to assess the attractiveness of an entire industry, discerning the attractiveness of a small target market within an industry is tougher, particularly if the start-up is pioneering the target market. Often, under these circumstances, information from more than one industry and/or market must be collected and synthesized to make an informed judgment. For example, say you were developing new, innovative sunglasses for snowboarders, consistent with the illustration provided earlier. The question for a product like this is what market to assess? Obviously, a combination of markets must be studied, including the market for sunglasses and the market for snowboarding. It would be important to not only know how well sunglasses are selling but whether the market for snowboarding accessories (and the number of people who participate in snowboarding) is on the rise or decline. If the market for sunglasses is on an upward trajectory but the market for snowboarding accessories is on a sharp decline, the target market you would be pursuing would be much less attractive than if both markets were on the rise.

A failure to fully understand both the broad HR/recruitment industry and the specific markets it was targeting contributed to the problems encountered by Standout Jobs, a company that developed an innovative recruitment portal in 2008. The Standout Jobs story, which is rich in lessons about the importance of feasibility analysis, is included in the nearby "What Went Wrong" feature.

Organizational Feasibility Analysis

Organizational feasibility analysis is conducted to determine whether a proposed business has sufficient management expertise, organizational competence, and resources to successfully launch.[7] There are two primary issues to consider in this area: management prowess and resource sufficiency.

Management Prowess

A proposed business should evaluate the prowess, or ability, of its initial management team, whether it is a sole entrepreneur or a larger group.[8] This task requires the individuals starting the firm to be honest and candid in their self-assessments. Two of the most important factors in this area are the passion that the solo entrepreneur or the management team has for the business idea and the extent to which the management team or solo entrepreneur understands the markets in which the firm will participate.[9] There are no practical substitutes for strengths in these areas.[10]

A collection of additional factors help define management prowess. Managers with extensive professional and social networks have an advantage in that they are able to reach out to colleagues and friends to help them plug experience or knowledge gaps. In addition, a potential new venture should have an idea of the type of new-venture team that it can assemble. A **new-venture team** is the group of founders, key employees, and advisers that either manage or help manage a new business in its start-up years. If the founder or founders of a new venture have identified several individuals they believe will join the firm after it is launched and these individuals are highly capable, that knowledge lends credibility to the organizational feasibility of the potential venture. The same rationale applies for highly capable people a new venture believes would be willing to join its board of directors or board of advisers.

One thing that many potential business founders find while assessing management prowess is that they may benefit from finding one or more partners to help them launch their business. Tips for finding an appropriate business partner are provided in the "Partnering for Success" feature.

Resource Sufficiency

The second area of organizational feasibility analysis is to determine whether the proposed venture has or is capable of obtaining sufficient resources to move forward. The focus in organizational feasibility analysis is on nonfinancial

LEARNING OBJECTIVE

4. Explain what an organizational feasibility analysis is and its purpose and discuss the two primary issues to consider when completing this analysis.

WHAT WENT WRONG?

How Feasible Was Standout Jobs from the Beginning?

The idea for Standout Jobs emerged in 2007, when its founders, Ben Yoskovitz, Fred Ngo, and Austin Hill, saw an opportunity to revitalize the job recruitment process. At the time, most companies recruited by placing static position descriptions on job boards and hoping for the best. The idea behind Standout Jobs was to create more energy in the recruitment process. To do that, Standout Jobs built a customizable recruitment platform, named RECEPTION, that enabled companies to showcase their culture and team to job candidates. The platform was built on social media tools, such as video, blogs, and a variety of widgets, to make the recruting process dynamic and engaging, and help the company's clients "stand out" from the competition.

Standout Jobs launched at the DEMO conference in early 2008. It raised $1.58 million in venture funding and picked up some early traction. It also seemed to have substantial upside potential. In early 2008, one of its initial investors, John Elton, partner with iNovia Capital, made the following remarks about Standout Jobs: "We believe in the team and Standout Jobs' market potential because they are changing the way companies recruit great employees." Elton went on to observe that at the time, the recruitment sector represented about one-fourth of all online advertising, and that many companies were dissatisfied with the results they were getting. Standout Jobs, in Elton's opinion, helped companies approach online recruiting in a fresh and promising manner.

In 2010, Standout Jobs was sold to Talent Technology, another recruitment company. It wasn't a financial success. After the sale, one of Standout Jobs' founders, Ben Yoskovitz, wrote a thoughtful blog post on why Standout Jobs essentially failed, and the lessons he took away from his Standout Jobs experience. Yoskovitz highlighted five reasons, several of which are directly related to the need to complete a thorough feasibility analysis before a company launches.

First, the company's timing was bad. The company launched in 2008, just before the U.S. economy went sour. Most companies weren't hiring. In fact, Yoskovitz said that he got feedback on sales calls like this: "That's a great product, really love it, but we won't be hiring for another 18 months or so. You have anything to help us fire people?" Obviously, Standout Jobs couldn't help that the economy turned sour, but in retrospect, Yoskovitz feels that the company didn't react fast enough. When things weren't working, he didn't sound alarm bells, and the company continued doing what it was doing.

Second, Yoskovitz believes that prior to launch, he didn't have a strong enough understanding of the HR/recruitment market. He indicated that he looked at the market and thought he could fix it, only to find out that when he was in neck-deep there were a lot of issues that he didn't understand. He did do a lot of networking in the industry and brand building among industry evangelists. But that can create a false sense of success, Yoskovitz now believes. Indusry evangelists

aren't necessarily buyers. It's important to do as much homework as possible, he now urges, about an industry upfront, before you launch a company.

Third, Yoskovitz feels that his team didn't get its product in the hands of customers fast enough and iterate based on their feedback. It's easier, Yoskovitz learned, to build a product to specifications rather than deal with the constant tweaking that occurs when soliciting customer feedback. In the future, Yoskovitz is committed to building a minimum viable product (MVP) and getting it into the hands of customers as early as possible. He's also committed to soliciting real, hard feedback from them.

Fourth, Yoskovitz learned that you can't shove a solution down your customers' throats. In the blog post, Yoskovitz said then when Standout Jobs did get its product into the hands of customers, the customers weren't using it as actively as the Standout Jobs team had expected. It boils down to changing behavior. The Standout Jobs team underestimated just how hard it is to change people's behavior, even if you think you're providing them a much better solution to problems they face.

Finally, Yoskovitz feels that Standout Jobs raised too much money, too early. Looking back, he feels the company didn't have the validation needed to justify raising the money they did. Raising money also comes with strings attached. Because Standout Jobs raised money, it quickly built a big product, based on assumptions that weren't tested in the marketplace. Raising money also takes time—time that could be spent building and validating a product. Yoskovitz found that raising money isn't a validation that something works and has a market. It's a validation that someone will write a check.

Questions for Critical Thinking

1. Of the five reasons that Standout Jobs didn't reach its full potential, which reason do you think damaged the company's chances of success the most? Explain your answer.
2. Describe the difference between Standout Jobs as an idea and an actual business. Is it possible for something to be an exciting idea but a poor business?
3. Make a list of the categories of people that the founders of Standout Jobs should have talked to prior to launching the firm. Based on the experience that the company had, what do you think some of the feedback would have been? Do you think the founders would have received any feedback that might have caused them to dramatically change their business idea or consider shelving the idea all together?
4. What can a start-up learn from Standout Jobs' experience about the importance of feasibility analysis?

Sources: B. Yoskovitz, "A Postmortem Analysis of Standout Jobs," available at http://www.instigatorblog.com/postmortem-analysis-of-standout-jobs/2010/10/05/, posted on October 5, 2010, accessed on April 4, 2014; Standout Jobs, "Standout Jobs Raises $2 Million Financing from iNovia Capital," www.prnewswire.com, accessed April 4, 2014.

PARTNERING FOR SUCCESS

Finding the Right Business Partner

One thing that becomes clear to many potential business founders while conducting organizational feasibility analysis is that they need one or more partners to help launch their business. You might be a computer programmer who has a great idea for a cooking website, for example, but have no experience in marketing or sales. In this instance, you may need to find a partner with marketing and sales experience to successfully launch and run the firm. There are five key criteria to look for in a business partner. You want to get this right because picking the wrong partner or partners can lead to a lot of heartaches and business challenges.

1. **Know the skills and experiences you need.** Make an honest assessment of the skills and experience you bring to the business and the gaps that remain. Pick someone who fills the gaps. For example, if you're an experienced computer programmer you probably don't want to partner with another experienced computer programmer. Pick someone who brings other competencies that you need to the venture, such as marketing or finance.
2. **Make sure your personalities and work habits are compatible.** While you don't need someone who is just like yourself, you do need to be comfortable with the person you'll be in business with. For example, if you'd rather work 16 hours a day if that is what it takes to finish a project on time, and your partner would rather quit after 8 hours a day and try to renegotiate the due date for the project, that difference in work styles will invariably cause conflict. Similarly, if you like to wear a coat and tie when meeting with clients and your partner thinks wearing blue jeans is fine, obvious disagreements could arise.
3. **Make sure you and your partner have common goals and aspirations.** Be sure that you and your partner are shooting for the same target. For example, if your goal is to build a billion-dollar company but your partner would be perfectly satisfied growing the company to $10 million in sales and then selling out, obvious problems could ensue.
4. **Look in the right places.** If you don't have someone already in mind, it's important to know where to look

for a potential partner. Generic networking events, like Chamber of Commerce mixers, are usually ineffective for finding a business partner. Instead, if you're looking for an engineer, contact engineering trade associations for leads or attend engineering trade fairs. Social networking sites for professionals, such as LinkedIn, can be an effective way to make contacts. Most cities have startup networking events. There are also websites and events specifically designed to help bring people together to start companies. Examples include Startup Weekend (http://startupweekend.org), Founder2Be (www.founder2be.com), and CofoundersLab (www.cofounderslab.com).

5. **Hire a lawyer.** When you have identified a potential partner and you're confident that the first four criteria we've discussed have been satisfied, you should hire a lawyer to sit down with the two (or more) of you to help hammer out the details. You should decide what each partner will contribute to the business, how the equity in the business will be split, what form of business ownership to select, what each partner's role in the company will be, and so forth. It's important to hire someone who's not loyal to any specific partner (even if it's you). Hire someone who is impartial and everyone feels good about.

Questions for Critical Thinking

1. Think about your personality and work habits. What type of person (in terms of personality and work habits) do you think you'd work well with and what type of person do you think you'd be in constant conflict with?
2. Do you think it's a good idea or a bad idea to form a business partnership with a close friend? How could you go about discerning if a good friend would make a good business partner?
3. Provide some suggestions, other than those mentioned in the feature, for places (online or offline) for finding a business partner.
4. Spend some time looking at LinkedIn. How could you use LinkedIn to help find a business partner?

resources. The objective is to identify the most important nonfinancial resources and assess their availability. An example is a start-up that will require employees with specialized skills. If a firm launches in a community that does not have a labor pool that includes people with the skill sets the firm needs, a serious resources sufficiency problem exists.

Another key resource sufficiency issue is the ability to obtain intellectual property protection on key aspects of the business. This issue doesn't apply to all start-ups; but, it is critical for companies that have invented a new product or are introducing a new business process that adds value to the way a product is manufactured or a service is delivered. One quick test a start-up can administer is to see if a patent has already been filed for its product or business process idea. Google Patents (www.google.com/patents) is a user-friendly way to search for patents. Although it isn't a substitute for utilizing a patent attorney, this approach can give a start-up a quick assessment of whether someone has beaten them to the punch regarding a particular product or business process idea.

To test resource sufficiency, a firm should list the 6 to 12 most critical nonfinancial resources that it will need to move its business idea forward and determine if those resources are available. Table 3.5 provides a list of the types of nonfinancial resources that are critical to many start-ups' success.

Financial Feasibility Analysis

LEARNING OBJECTVE

5. Describe what a financial feasibility analysis is, explain its importance, and discuss the most critical issues to consider in this area when completing this analysis.

Financial feasibility analysis is the final component of a comprehensive feasibility analysis. For feasibility analysis, a preliminary financial assessment is usually sufficient; indeed, additional rigor at this point is typically not required because the specifics of the business will inevitably evolve, making it impractical to spend a lot of time early on preparing detailed financial forecasts.

The most important issues to consider at this stage are total start-up cash needed, financial performance of similar businesses, and the overall financial attractiveness of the proposed venture.

If a proposed new venture moves beyond the feasibility analysis stage, it will need to complete pro forma (or projected) financial statements that demonstrate the firm's financial viability for the first one to three years of its existence. In Chapter 8, we'll provide you with specific instructions for preparing these statements.

Total Start-Up Cash Needed

This first issue refers to the total cash needed to prepare the business to make its first sale. An actual budget should be prepared that lists all the anticipated capital purchases and operating expenses needed to get the business up and running. After determining a total figure, an explanation of where the money will come from should be provided. Avoid cursory explanations such as "I plan to bring investors on board" or "I'll borrow the money." Although you may ultimately involve investors or lenders in your business, a more thoughtful account is required of how you'll provide for your initial cash needs. We'll cover funding and financing in Chapter 10.

If the money will come from friends and family or is raised through other means, such as credit cards or a home equity line of credit, a reasonable plan should be stipulated to repay the money. Showing how a new venture's

TABLE 3.5 **Types of Nonfinancial Resources That Are Critical to Many Start-Ups' Success**

- Affordable office space
- Lab space, manufacturing space, or space to launch a service business
- Contract manufacturers or service providers
- Key management employees (now and in the future)
- Key support personnel (now and in the future)
- Key equipment needed to operate the business (computers, machinery, delivery vehicles)
- Ability to obtain intellectual property protection on key aspects of the business
- Support of local governments and state government if applicable for business launch
- Ability to form favorable business partnerships

start-up costs will be covered and repaid is an important issue. Many new ventures look promising as ongoing concerns but have no way of raising the money to get started or are never able to recover from the initial costs involved. When projecting start-up expenses, it is better to overestimate rather than underestimate the costs involved. Murphy's Law is prevalent in the start-up world—things will go wrong. It is a rare start-up that doesn't experience some unexpected expenses during the start-up phase.

There are worksheets posted online that help entrepreneurs determine the start-up costs to launch their respective businesses. Start-up cost worksheets are available via SCORE (www.score.org) and the Small Business Administration (www.sba.gov).

Financial Performance of Similar Businesses

The second component of financial feasibility analysis is estimating a proposed start-up's potential financial performance by comparing it to similar, already established businesses. Obviously, this effort will result in approximate rather than exact numbers. There are several ways of doing this, all of which involve a little gumshoe labor.

First, substantial archival data, which offers detailed financial reports on thousands of individual firms, is available online. The easiest data to obtain is on publicly traded firms through Hoovers or a similar source. These firms are typically too large, however, for meaningful comparisons to proposed new ventures. The challenge is to find the financial performance of small, more comparable firms. Samples of websites that are helpful in this regard are provided in the Internet Resource table in Appendix 3.2. IBISWorld, BizMiner, and Mintel provide data on the average sales and profitability for the firms in the industries they track. Reference USA provides revenue estimates for many private firms, but fewer libraries subscribe to its service. (This resource is more commonly available at large city libraries.) On the expense side, a very useful website is BizStats.com, where an entrepreneur can type in the projected revenue of his or her firm, by industry classification (not all industries are covered), and receive a mock income statement in return that shows the average profitability and expense percentages of U.S. businesses in the same category. IBISWorld also normally provides a chart of the average expenses (as a percentage of sales) for major items such as wages, rent, office and administrative expenses, and utilities for firms in the industries they follow. Another source to help estimate a firm's sales and net profit is BizMiner (www.bizminer.com). BizMiner provides a printout of the average sales and profitability for firms in the industries it follows and provides more detail than similar reports. It is a fee-based site but is free if accessed through a university library that subscribes to the service.[11]

There are additional ways to obtain financial data on smaller firms. If a start-up entrepreneur identifies a business that is similar to the one he or she wants to start, and the business isn't likely to be a direct competitor, it's perfectly acceptable to ask the owner or manager of the business to share sales and income data. Even if the owner or manager is only willing to talk in general terms (e.g., our annual sales are in the $3 million range, and we're netting around 9 percent of sales), that information is certainly better than nothing. Simple Internet, ProQuest, and LexisNexis Academic searches are also helpful. If you're interested in the sports apparel industry, simply typing "sports apparel industry sales" and "sports apparel industry profitability" will invariably result in links to stories about sports apparel companies that will mention their sales and profitability.

Simple observation and legwork is a final way to obtain sales data for similar businesses. This approach is suitable in some cases and in others it isn't. For example, if you were proposing to open a new smoothie shop, you could gauge the type of sales to expect by estimating the number of people who patronize similar smoothie shops in your area, along with the average purchase per visit. A very basic way to do this is to frequent these stores and count the number of customers who come in and out of the stores during various times of the day.

Overall Financial Attractiveness of the Proposed Venture

A number of other factors are associated with evaluating the financial attractiveness of a proposed venture. These evaluations are based primarily on a new venture's projected sales and rate of return (or profitability), as just discussed. At the feasibility analysis stage, the projected return is a judgment call. A more precise estimation can be computed by preparing pro forma (or projected) financial statements, including one- to three-year pro forma statements of cash flow, income statements, and balance sheets (along with accompanying financial ratios). This work can be done if time and circumstances allow, but is typically done at the business plan stage rather than the feasibility analysis stage of a new venture's development.

To gain perspective, a start-up's projected rate of return should be weighed against the following factors to assess whether the venture is financially feasible:

■ The amount of capital invested

■ The risks assumed in launching the business

■ The existing alternatives for the money being invested

■ The existing alternatives for the entrepreneur's time and efforts

As promising as they seem on the surface, some opportunities simply may not be worth it financially. For example, it makes no economic sense for a group of entrepreneurs to invest $10 million in a capital-intense, risky start-up that offers a relatively low return (say around 3 percent) on the capital the entrepreneurs are investing. The adequacy of returns also depends on the alternatives the individuals involved have. For example, an individual who is thinking about leaving a $150,000-per-year job to start a new firm requires a higher rate of return than the person thinking about leaving a $50,000-per-year job.[12]

Other factors used to weigh the overall financial attractiveness of a new business are listed in Table 3.6.

LEARNING OBJECTIVE

6. Describe a feasibility analysis template and explain why it is important for entrepreneurs to use this template.

A Feasibility Analysis Template

First Screen, shown in Appendix 3.1, is a template entrepreneurial firms use to complete a feasibility analysis. It is called First Screen because a feasibility analysis is an entrepreneur's (or a group of entrepreneurs') initial pass at

TABLE 3.6 Financial Feasibility

■ Steady and rapid growth in sales during the first five to seven years in a clearly defined market niche

■ High percentage of recurring revenue—meaning that once a firm wins a client, the client will provide recurring sources of revenue

■ Ability to forecast income and expenses with a reasonable degree of certainty

■ Internally generated funds to finance and sustain growth

■ Availability of an exit opportunity (such as an acquisition or an initial public offering) for investors to convert equity into cash determining the feasibility of a business idea. If a business idea cuts muster at this stage, the next step is to complete a business plan.

The mechanics for filling out the First Screen worksheet are straightforward. It maps the four areas of feasibility analysis described in the chapter, accentuating the most important points in each area. The final section of the worksheet, "Overall Potential," includes a section that allows for suggested revisions to a business idea to improve its potential or feasibility. For example, a business might start out planning to manufacture its own product, but through the process of completing First Screen, learn that the capital needed to set up a manufacturing facility is prohibitive in terms of both the money that would need to be raised and the extended time to break even for the business. As a result, two of five items in Part 5, "Initial Capital Investment" and "Time to Break Even," might be rated "low potential." This doesn't need to be the end of the story, however. In the column labeled "Suggestions for Improving the Potential," the founders of the business might write, "Consider contract manufacturing or outsourcing as an alternative to manufacturing the product ourselves." The value of the First Screen worksheet is that it draws attention to issues such as this one and forces the founders to think about alternatives. If this particular suggestion is realistic and is determined to be a better way to proceed, a revised version of First Screen might rate the two factors referred to previously, "Initial Capital Requirements" and "Time to Break Even," as "high potential" rather than "low potential" because of the change in the business concept that was made. Business ideas at the feasibility analysis stage should always be seen as fluid and subject to change. Little is lost if several versions of First Screen are completed for the same business idea; however, there is much more to be lost if a start-up gets halfway through writing a business plan and concludes that the business isn't feasible, or actually launches a business without having at least most of the kinks worked out.

Although completing First Screen does take some research and analysis, it is not meant to be a lengthy process. It is also not meant to be a shot in the dark. The best ideas are ones that emerge from analysis that is based on facts and good information, rather than speculation and guesses, as emphasized throughout the chapter. Appendix 3.2 contains the Internet Resource Table that may be particularly helpful in completing a First Screen analysis. It is well worth your time to learn how to use these resources—they are rich in terms of their content and analysis.

It's important to be completely candid when completing First Screen for your business idea. No business scores "high potential" on every item. There is also no definitive way of discerning, after the worksheet is completed, if an idea is feasible. First Screen, like the feasibility analysis itself, is meant to convey an overall impression or sense of the feasibility of a business idea.

Chapter Summary

LO1. Feasibility analysis is the process of determining whether a business idea is viable. It is a preliminary evaluation of a business idea, conducted for the purpose of determining whether the idea is worth pursuing. The proper time to conduct a feasibility analysis is early in thinking through the prospects for a new business idea. It follows opportunity recognition but comes before the development of a business model and a business plan.

LO2. A product/service feasibility analysis is an assessment of the overall appeal of the product or service being proposed. The two components of product/service feasibility analysis are product desirability and product demand. A concept statement, which is a preliminary description of a product idea, is developed during this particular aspect of the feasibility analysis process to see if the proposed product or service makes sense to potential customers and if it has any fatal flaws that require immediate attention. Using online tools such as Google AdWords and Landing Pages and conducing library, Internet, and gumshoe research are techniques entrepreneurs use to assess the likely demand for a product or service.

LO3. An industry/market feasibility analysis is an assessment of the overall appeal of the market for the product or service being proposed. For feasibility analysis, there are two primary issues that a business should consider in this area: industry attractiveness and target market attractiveness. A target market is a place within a larger market segment that represents a narrower group of customers with similar needs. Most start-ups simply don't have the resources needed to participate in a broad market, at least initially. Instead, by focusing on a smaller target market, a firm can usually avoid head-to-head competition with industry leaders and can focus on serving a specialized market very well. An attractive industry has several desirable characteristics for a new venture, including those of being (a) "young" rather than old or very well established, (b) in the early rather than the late stage of the product life cycle, and (c) fragmented (where a large number of firms are competing but no single firm has a dominate market position) rather than highly concentrated (where a few large firms dominate competition).

LO4. An organizational feasibility analysis is conducted to determine whether a proposed business has sufficient management expertise, organizational competence, and resources to successfully launch its business. There are two primary issues to consider in this area: management prowess and resource sufficiency. With respect to management prowess, the intention is to determine the ability of the proposed venture's initial management team. In terms of analysis, resource sufficiency is concerned with determining if the proposed venture would have the resources required to compete successfully.

LO5. A financial feasibility analysis is a preliminary financial analysis of whether a business idea is worth pursuing. The most important areas to consider are the total start-up cash needed, financial performance of similar businesses, and the overall financial attractiveness of the proposed business.

LO6. First Screen is a template for completing a feasibility analysis. It is called First Screen because a feasibility analysis is an entrepreneur's (or group of entrepreneurs') initial pass at determining the feasibility of a business idea.

Key Terms

concept statement, **101**
concept test, **101**
feasibility analysis, **99**
financial feasibility
    analysis, **114**
industry, **107**

industry/target market
    feasibility, **107**
landing page, **106**
new-venture team, **111**
organizational feasibility
    analysis, **111**

primary research, **100**
product/service feasibility
    analysis, **100**
secondary research, **100**
target market, **107**

Review Questions

3-1. How would you describe the four areas that a properly executed feasibility analysis explores?

3-2. What is a product/service feasibility analysis?

3-3. What is the difference between primary research and secondary research?

3-4. What is a concept test?

3-5. What are the two ways that entrepreneurs assess the likely product demand for the proposed product or service they are analyzing?

3-6. What is gumshoe research in the context of product/service feasibility analysis?

3-7. What is an industry/target market feasibility analysis?

3-8. Why do we need to have face-to-face conversations with potential customers?

3-9. What is the purpose of an industry feasibility analysis and what must be considered?

3-10. Why do most start-ups focus on relatively small target markets to begin with rather than larger markets with more substantial demand?

3-11. What are some of the ways to determine the attractiveness of a small target market within a larger industry?

3-12. What is an organizational feasibility analysis?

3-13. What are the two primary issues to consider when conducting an organizational feasibility analysis?

3-14. What is a new venture team?

3-15. What is a financial feasibility analysis?

3-16. What are the three separate components of financial feasibility analysis?

3-17. What are some of the techniques a start-up can use to estimate its potential financial performance by comparing it to similar, already established businesses?

3-18. What are the essential non-financial resources needed for a business to start up?

3-19. Why is the feasibility analysis template called "First Screen," and what is included in the final part of the first screen analysis?

Application Questions

3-20. Jackson Reed, a friend of yours, just told you an interesting story. He was at his parents' house over the weekend. While there, his father saw your entrepreneurship book laying to the side of your backpack. He looked through the book and spent a bit of time studying Chapter 3. After doing so, he said to Jackson, "When you were growing up, I launched and sold three successful businesses and never once completed a feasibility analysis. What do you think the authors of your text would say about that?" What would you suggest that Jackson say in response to his father's question?

3-21. In a recent entrepreneurship class, Steven Milton has been assigned by his professor to conduct a product/service feasibility analysis. He is to propose a product or service that might be useful to students on campus. The analysis should include an assessment of the overall appeal of the product or service being proposed. Steven should include the following questions in his analysis to determine the appeal of his product or service. Does the product/service make sense? Does it solve a problem or fill a gap in the market? Is it suitable to introduce the product/service right now? Are there any flaws? As a friend to Steven, help him to propose a suitable product/service to the intended target market and conduct a product/service feasibility analysis based on his proposal.

3-22. If you were one of the recipients of New Venture Fitness Drink's concept statement, as presented earlier in the chapter, what type of feedback would you have given the company about the viability of its product idea?

3-23. Linda Toombs, who has considerable experience in the home security industry, is planning to launch a new line of home security alarms that she believes would be superior to other products in the market. Linda knows how to develop a concept statement and administer a buying intentions survey but is less clear about the type of library and Internet research that might help her assess the demand for her product. If Linda asked you about this, what advice would you give to her about how to conduct successful library and Internet searches?

3-24. Marie Finn is planning to start up a business in home cleaning services. List out the potential methods of marketing analysis that Marie should conduct for her new venture.

3-25. If you were interested in opening a musical instruments store near the college or university you are attending in order to sell guitars, drums, and other types of musical instruments, what online resources would you draw on to conduct secondary research regarding the industry/target market feasibility of your business idea?

3-26. You bumped into your ex-colleague Allen Smith at a nearby supermarket. He was so glad to meet you and the conversation was all about his upcoming business. He is in the middle of planning to start up a fitness center in your neighborhood. Throughout your conversation with him, you noticed that he did not have a proper financial feasibility analysis. He was blindly pursuing his dreams with no proper planning, especially none on financial matters. As a friend, advise him on the most critical issues to consider in the financial area when completing this analysis.

3-27. In a group of three, prepare a First Screen analysis on a proposed business idea. You may refer to appendix 3.1 and 3.2 for assistance. Once completed, please share with your class if the proposed idea can proceed to the next stage, i.e., preparing the business plan.

3-28. What are some of the red flags that would suggest that the overall financial attractiveness of a proposed new venture is poor? Which of the red flags you identified would suggest that realistically, a proposed venture isn't feasible?

3-29. A friend of yours just completed a First Screen analysis for an e-commerce site that she hopes to launch to sell horse riding supplies such as saddles, tacks, lead ropes, and feed buckets. She's disappointed because she rated 10 of the 25 items included in First Screen as having either low or moderate potential. After thinking about this, your friend says to you, "Well that's that. Good thing I completed a feasibility analysis. I definitely do not want to start the business I was thinking about." Is your friend correct in reaching this conclusion? How would you advise her to interpret the results of her First Screen analysis?

YOU BE THE VC 3.1 COMPANY: August Smart Lock

• Web: www.august.com • Facebook: August Smart Lock • Twitter: @AugustSmartLock

Business Idea: Develop a safer, simpler, and more social way to lock and unlock the front door of a home or an apartment.

Pitch: Conventional door locks have several downsides. First, they require a key that can be lost or misplaced. Second, if the owner of a house wants to provide access during the middle of the day to someone such as a dog walker or housekeeper, it creates a problem. The person accessing the house has to be given a key or a key has to be hidden somewhere, like under the flower pot near the door (which is the first place a burglar would look). Finally, if a friend stops by to drop something off and the house is locked, s/he may have made a wasted trip.

The August Smart Lock solves all these problems. It is an attractive hardware device that retrofits over an existing single-cylinder deadbolt lock, which is the type of lock found on the majority of front doors for homes and apartments. The August Smart Lock fits on the interior portion of the door. It does not affect the ability to use the same key that has always been used to lock and unlock the door.

Once the August Smart Lock is installed, it allows the door to be locked and unlocked via a smartphone app. The app allows you to send a virtual key to anyone you choose to have access to your home or apartment. Your guest then uses their smartphone to gain access to the residence without the need to exchange physical keys. You can specify the duration that the August virtual key

is active, and the key can be disabled at any time. For example, if someone walks your dog from 1:00 P.M. to 1:30 P.M. every day, access to the home can be granted to that specific person for that time each day.

The August Smart Lock is easy to install. It is completely self-sufficient, meaning that it does not need access to electricity or Wi-Fi, like more complicated keyless door lock systems. It literally takes 10 minutes to install. The August Smart Lock app is compatible with the iPhone and Android-based products, and will soon be adding BlackBerry and Windows Phone 8. If you lose your phone you can log onto august.com and remove access authorization for that device. The system is completely safe and will not allow entry for people who do not have a virtual or physical key. The virtual key function uses the same secure communications technology used by financial institutions. August has additional safety features. For example, for guests who are provided a virtual key, August keeps track of how many times they enter your home and keeps track of the duration of each visit.

3-30. Based on the material covered in this chapter, what questions would you ask the firm's founders before making your funding decision? What answers would satisfy you?

3-31. If you had to make your decision on just the information provided in the pitch and on the company's website, would you fund this company? Why or why not?

YOU BE THE VC 3.2 COMPANY: CADI Scientific—SmartSense

• Web: www.cadi.com.sg • Facebook: CADI Scientific • Twitter: @cadismartsense

Business Idea: Produce and sell the first wireless patient monitoring system, enhancing patient care by continuously measuring vital medical data, and transmitting the information to health practitioners.

Pitch: Monitoring a sick patient can be a delicate balancing act. Although they need uninterrupted sleep to aid their recovery, medical staff must also regularly check vital signs such as temperature and blood pressure. The two needs are not always fine bedfellows.

Four entrepreneurial scientists have come up with a solution: a wireless gadget called SmartSense, which is now being used in hospitals in Singapore, Bangkok, Taipei, and the Middle East. The 1.2-inch wide SmartSense is taped to a patient's body to continuously measure vital signs. Radio frequency technology then transfers the

data wirelessly via ceiling-mounted transmitters to computers in the nurses' station.

The inspiration for the idea came out of a coffee break conversation between CADI Scientific founder Zenton Goh and a colleague. The colleague had a sick child and said he and his wife were waking the infant every two hours through the night to take her temperature. Goh thought of the idea of an automated wireless sensing system to monitor a baby's body temperature, so that both parents and children could enjoy uninterrupted sleep. The idea evolved into SmartSense.

Nurses can now dispense with the task of manually checking temperatures and blood pressure every few hours, and patients get uninterrupted rest. SmartSense also cuts down on any possibility of human error in the checks and reduces nurses' workload. Doctors can check on the data on-the-go too via WiFi-enabled digital assistants, or on PCs anywhere in the hospital.

Another bonus to introducing this system into crowded wards is it is now very easy to quickly spot clusters of patients developing a fever at the same time. At a time of growing incidences of hospital-acquired infections, this is an important early warning signal. Since then, consumer versions of SmartSense have

been produced, such as an Infrared Ear and Forehead Thermometer, to allow people to monitor temperature and blood pressure at home.

3-32. Based on the material covered in this chapter, what questions would you ask the firm's founders before making your funding decision? What answers would satisfy you?

3-33. If you had to make your decision on just the information provided in the pitch and on the company's website, would you fund this firm? Why or why not?

CASE 3.1

How "Listening to Customers" Has Shaped Modify Watches

• *Web: www.modifywatches.com* • *Facebook: Modify Watches* • *Twitter: @ModifyWatches*

Bruce R. Barringer, *Oklahoma State University*

R. Duane Ireland, *Texas A&M University*

Introduction

Modify Watches was started by Aaron Schwartz and Gary Coover, shortly after the two received their MBAs from UC-Berkeley's Hass School of Business in 2010. While in college, Schwartz started a sustainability business called Refill Revolution. He also took a class from Steve Blank and Eric Ries—champions of the lean start-up movement. The class was called "Customer Development in High-Tech Enterprises." The staple concepts underlying the class were "building a minimal viable product" and "get out of the building." Building a minimal viable product means that a start-up's initial product should include just enough core features to allow early adopters to provide feedback. The start-up can then iterate based on the feedback. "Get out of the building" refers to the notion that it's impossible to know what customers really want without talking to them.

Blank and Ries's class impacted Schwartz. He realized that Refill Revolution, which he eventually sold, wasn't built utilizing Blank and Ries's principles. Instead, he and his co-founders built a service based on what they thought was right, rather than on what customers

told them they wanted. Luckily, they found a buyer that was able to take advantage of the Refill Revolution platform. The company itself wouldn't have been successful as a stand-alone business.

Giving Steve Blank and Eric Ries's Philosophy a Try

Modify Watches started from a different premise. The general idea was to sell affordable watches that have interchangeable faces and bands. That approach would give customers the ability to switch their watch face and band to match their clothing or mood. Rather than pushing forward, the firm chose to give Blank and Ries's philosophy a try. They knew the idea rested on a core hypothesis: people would buy interchangeable watch parts. To test the hypothesis, they went to eBay and bought cheap interchangeable watches. They then built an inexpensive website, using Weebly.com, that featured jokes, images of the watch parts, nicknames for every single watch-color combination, and "Buy Now" buttons. The inexpensive watches were their minimal viable product. They just wanted to see how people

A sample of Modify Watches

Modify Industries, Inc.

would buy. The test validated the idea that they could sell interchangeable watch faces and brands.

Company Launch

Modify Watches launched soon afterwards. It didn't take the company long to develop a certain character, which was customer focused. They called their customers "The ModiFamily." When people complimented them on their products, they referred to their motto, which is "We're not craftsmen, we're just good listeners." Not everything went swimmingly, though. Coover left Modify in August 2010 to join a strategy team with Samsung in South Korea. Schwartz, like Coover, had planned to resume a full time job but decided to commit to Modify full-time. Schwartz, like Coover, planned to resume a full-time job but decided to commit to Modify on a full-time basis instead. He did not take a salary the first year to help the company get up and running, and the company was initially run out of his apartment. A big break occurred shortly after launch when Schwartz was on a cross-country flight. He met a business executive on the plane and ended up selling him 2,500 watches. That sale earned Schwartz the blessing of his family and advisers to stick with the business. Schwartz also started surrounding himself with a talented team. He hired Ashil Parag, who he describes as an A+ designer. As his tech director he hired a UC-Berkeley student named Sean Linehan, whom Schwartz described as "as talented as anyone I have ever met."

The company's focus on customers wasn't forced. In fact, in an article Schwartz wrote for *Startup America* he said that "interacting with customers gives us (the Modify Watch team) happiness on a daily basis." Similarly, in an article Schwartz wrote for *Forbes*, he provided the following advice for business founders: "Think of your customers as family and friends. It sounds silly, but when you believe that folks you care about rely on your product or service, you will work harder to make sure they are treated well." Schwartz's actions indicated that his sentiments are real. From the beginning, for example, whoever does the packing for a Modify Watches order includes their business card. The card includes the team member's e-mail address and their cell phone number, just in case a customer wants to give them a shout. The more Modify's team members interact with customers, Schwartz figures, the better the company will be able to design watches that their customers want.

Modify Watches

From the get-go, Modify Watches tapped into the customization movement. Its line of watches includes multiple faces and straps, all of which are interchangeable, so you can design any style you'd like. To fully appreciate the number of watch faces and bands the company offers, pause for a moment and visit its website. The watches come in two sizes, big and bigger. They're water resistant and made of stainless steel and plastic. Changing straps is very simple. If you have a large enough collection of straps and faces, you can have a different daily look on your wrist for some time. The least

expensive combination of face and strap costs $40 plus shipping. The company also has a license with the Major League Baseball Player's Association, so you can get a watch face with your favorite baseball team's logo on it.

Modify has continued to involve customers every step of the way, often in very substantive manners. An illustrative example is an initiative launched in November 2011. Modify rolled out crowd-sourcing platform Napkin Labs' (www.napkinlabs.com) brainstorming app to its Facebook page. The app allows companies to create virtual, interactive focus groups with its customers. Modify ran a competition that asked customers to submit suggestions for co-branding products. An idea to co-brand a watch with the Wounded Warrior Project won. Modify had to push back the deadline for the competition because of the large number of submissions it received.

Kickstarter

Modify Watches' current initiative is its Mod-to-Order campaign. It is an initiative that will allow the company to produce individual customized watches for people. So if you'd like a watch with your best friend's image on it, Modify Watch will be able to do that for you. To raise money for the machinery and staff needed to make individually customized watches, Modify ran a Kickstarter campaign in early 2014. If you'd really like to get a sense of what Modify Watches is all about, go to www.kickstarter.com, type Modify in the search bar, and watch the videos that the company made to promote the campaign. They are expertly done and fully convey Modify Watches' culture and values. Modify reached its goal and received contributions from 790 backers. Of course, while the outward purpose of the campaign was to raise $50,000 to buy equipment and hire people, the campaign had another purpose. Harkening back to Blank and Ries's philosophy of launching a minimal viable product, the Kickstarter campaign and its accompanying videos were the minimal viable product for Mod-to-Order. The $54,873 in pledges from 790 backers was the validation needed to move the idea forward.

The Difference Listening to Customers Makes

One thing Schwartz likes to emphasize is that listening to customers makes a difference. Along with the practices mentioned above, Modify surveys its fans at least quarterly, and its entire team has calls with customers every week. In a guest post written on the Tech Cocktail blog, Schwartz noted the following substantive changes the company has made strictly as a result of listening to customers.

- Business model change. A good share of Modify's business comes from customizing watches for brands. The idea to do this came from a Google employee who contacted Modify and asked if they could make a Goole Chrome watch. Modify said yes, and a new product line was born. It now designs branded watches for Google, Facebook, the Pac 12 conference, and a number of other businesses and organizations.

(continued)

- The right product improvements. Modify reaches out to customers in a variety of ways to ask what they want (and don't want) in their watches. At one point, Modify assumed that people would want the watches to be water resistant, have a stopwatch, and have a backlight. A total of 95 percent wanted the watches to be water resistant while less than 10 percent wanted a stopwatch and even fewer wanted a backlight.
- Adding brand-name licensing. Modify's fans asked early and often for licensed properties like Major League Baseball. The company took the feedback, and it has been rewarded with significant product sales.
- Design decisions. Before Modify launches a new limited-edition watch, it always asks its fans to vote on what should be made.

Discussion Questions

3-34. What type of research did those leading Modify Watches conduct when completing a product/service feasibility analysis and what additional research might the founders have pursued when assessing the feasibility of their firm's product?

3-35. What target market is Modify Watches seeking to serve and how attractive is that market?

3-36. What evidence can you provide from the case to support the view that Schwartz is very interested in understanding customers' reactions to Modify's products?

3-37. If you were asked to complete an organizational analysis of Modify, what conclusions would you reach regarding the firm's management prowess and resource sufficiency at the time the firm launched and immediately thereafter?

Sources: Modify Watch home page, www.modifywatches.com, accessed April 5, 2014; A. Schwartz, "Lean Methodology: Building a Product Company with the Lessons of Steve Blank and Eric Ries," http:tech.co, available at http://tech.co/lean-methodology-steve-blank-eric-ries-2013-06, posted June 13, 2013, accessed April 4, 2014; A. Schwartz, "3 Keys to Startup Success: Hustle, Follow-Through and Curiosity," *Forbes*, January 26, 2012; A. Schwartz, "Six Startup Lessons Learned by Modify Watches Co-Founder, Aaron Schwarts," available at http://www.s.co/content/todays-featured-startup-modify-watches, accessed April 4, 2014.

CASE 3.2

Embrace Infant Warmer: Sometimes a Business Start Is a Matter of Life and Death

• *Web: http://embraceglobal.org* • *Facebook: Embrace* • *Twitter: @embracewarmer*

Introduction

When Rahul Panicker, Jane Chen, and Linus Liang enrolled in Design for Extreme Affordability, a course taught in the Design School at Stanford University, little did they know that the class would change their lives. And little did they know that a short three years later, premature babies born in rural India, who often don't survive because of hypothermia, would have a new chance at life because of a product they designed.

The Design for Extreme Affordability class draws students from across the Stanford campus. The goal of the class is to develop solutions for formidable, real-world problems. The project Panicker, Chen, and Liang were assigned was to develop a low-cost infant incubator for use in developing countries. This was a topic that the three knew nothing about. They were electrical engineering, MBA, and computer science students, respectively. To get started, they did some simple Google searches. They learned that millions of permature babies are born annually in developing countries. About a million of them die, often within 24 hours. The biggest cause of death is hypothermia. Premature babies don't have enough fat to regulate their body temperature. As a result, they can literally freeze to death in a room that is at room temperature. Nearly half of the world's low-birth-weight babies are born in India. Hospitals have incubators that provide consistent, life-saving heat to premature babies. But incubators cost up to $20,000 a piece.

The obvious solution was to drive down the cost of incubators. The team could systematically reduce the cost of traditional incubators by eliminating nonessential parts and using cheaper materials. Rather than moving forward, Liang got funding for a trip to Nepal to study incubators in developing countries. While visiting a hospital he noticed something that was odd. Many of the incubators were empty. He then learned the sad truth. About 80 percent of the premature babies born in the developing world are born in rural villages. They never are brought to a hospital and placed in an incubator. Even when they are, they're often taken home before the baby is ready to leave due to family needs back at the village.

Back at Stanford, the team grappled with what to do with the insight. The easier road ahead would be to redesign the traditional incubator, to make them more affordable. But that wasn't the answer. The harder challenge was to find a solution for saving premature babies where they were born—in rural villages.

Early Prototypes

The team tackled the harder challenge: How to create a baby-warming device that doctors and parents in rural villages could use to save premature babies? The team set to work and started creating rough prototypes of an original design. The earliest prototypes were made using old sleeping bags, baby dolls, and blankets. The design was a portable infant warmer that looks like a tiny sleeping bag. The warmer opens in the front, allowing mothers to nurse their babies and maintain intimate contact. The bag contained a pouch of wax-like phase-change material that keeps the baby warm for up to six hours at regular body temperatures. It required just 30 minutes of electricity to heat the pouch, an ideal situation for areas where the availability of electricity is spotty. To provide additional warmth, mothers would be instructed to hold their babies as much as possible against their skin. This activity prompted the team to call the product "Embrace."

The class ended and the team had a decision to make. All had promising prospects. In the end, the team members couldn't walk away. The lives of premature babies were at stake. They would move forward and continue to work on what was now known as the Embrace Infant Warmer.

Embrace Infant Warmer

The team, now joined by a fourth Stanford student, Naganand Murty, took the prototye to India to solicit customer feedback. They used rapid prototyping techniques to iterate on feedback and zero in on the attributes that are of highest relevance and value in a rural setting. Some of what they found out was suprising, and would have never been learned had they remained in California. For example, they found that women in India believe that Western medicine is very powerful, so they routinely cut back on the recommended dosages of Western medicines, just to be safe. That knowledge impacted early prototypes of the Embrace Infant Warmer. The early prototypes instructed mothers to set the temperature at 37 degrees Celsius. What they found was that the devices were being set at about 30 degrees. To solve the problem, they preprogrammed the ideal temperature into the device and just put an OK and Not OK switch on it. Commenting on the decision to go to India rather than remain at Stanford to build out the Embrace Infant Warmer, Chen told Helen Walters, who wrote an article on Embrace, "There are so many nuances that are critical to design and effective implementation, so many nuances that you don't understand unless you're there and living and breathing the culture every day."

Talking to potential customers raised other issues. For example, they learned that villagers wanted different pricing options—like an option to rent the device. Commenting on changes that were made as a result of feedback from rural villagers, Chen said in an *HBR* blog post, "Entrepreneurs often fall in love with their original product idea or business model and fail to listen

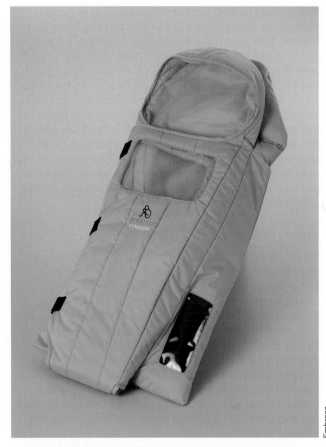

Embrace Infant Warmer

to customers. We (meaning the Embrace team), on the other hand, have no qualms about modifying our product features and pricing again and again until we find a solution that delivers the highest value to our customers at the lowest cost for them."

Gaining Momentum

The initial prototypes of the Embrace Infant Warmer were a success, which emboldened the team to keep working. Additional field resarch took place, involving village mothers in every aspect of design, from the straps on the warmer to the instructions printed on its front. Spending time in homes in rural India produced additional insights. "Oftentimes the mother-in-law is the decision maker," Chen said in the same interview as the one cited above. As a result, they determined a way to involve mother-in-laws in the process of using the Embrace Infant Warmer. In December of 2010, Embrace was featured in a segment of the ABC News show *20/20*. The show contained images of a five-pound baby girl in India named Nisha, the first child to use the Embrce Infant Warmer in a clinical trial—and maybe the first life saved by the device.

The Embrace Infant Warmer was formally launched in April 2011, after completing clinical trials. It went through more than 60 iterations before a final

(continued)

design was settled on. All manufacturing is done in Bangalore, India. Some of the parts are outsourced, but the final assembly and quality testing is done by the company. To ensure distribution, Embrace is partnering with multinational medical devices companies like GE Healthcare and with local NGOs. An organizational structure has also emerged. Embrace has both a nonprofit arm, which donates its baby warmer to those in need and runs educational programs, and a for-profit side, which sells the baby warmers to government entities and private clinics. It's a two-pronged approach that the founders hope will allow the company to prosper, grow, and save an increasing number of premature babies.

Embrace Today

As of the end of 2013, roughly two and a half years after launch, the Embrace Infant Warmer had been used on about 10,000 babies. Panicker and Chen lead Embrace, while their Stanford classmates and co-founders have moved on. The company is private and doesn't disclose financial information, other than to say that its margins are sufficient to keep growing and try additional products. The Embrace Infant Warmer is not only used in rural villages. Its also used in hospitals and clinics, to move premature babies from location to location and to use when a premature baby is born and all of the traditional incubators are already in use.

In addition to continuing to improve the Embrace Infant Warmer, the company has aspirations to tackle some of the other factors that cause infant mortality. Other potentially fatal conditions include meningitis, pneumonia, infections such as sepsis, and diarrhea.

To fully appreciate the heart of Embrace and the company's goals, visit its website at http://embraceglobal.org or Facebook page at Embrace. A particualy heart-warming portion of its website is titled "Spread the Warmth with Embrace." A $25 donation provides the life-saving warmth of an Embrace warmer to one low-birth-weight or premature baby.

Discussion Questions

3-38. What target market does Embrace seek to serve and how attractive is that market?

3-39. What examples of primary research that Embrace's founders completed appear in the case?

3-40. What actions did Embrace's founders take to solicit feedback from prospective customers and what did they learn from these efforts?

3-41. If you were asked to conduct a financial feasibility analysis for Embrace, what issues would you consider to complete this analysis and why are those important?

Sources: T. Kelley and D. Kelley, *Creative Confidence,* New York: Random House Publishing, 2013; S. K. Narang and K. R. Balasubramanyam, "Saving Preemie Lives, Business Today," available at http://businesstoday.intoday.in/story/portable-warmer-by-students-helping-premature-babies-survive/1/201084.html, posted on December 22, 2013, accessed April 5, 2014; H. Walters, "Mother Knows Best: Re-Making the Embrace Baby Warmer for Moms," TED Blog, available at http://blog.ted.com/2013/12/18/mother-knows-best-re-making-the-embrace-baby-warmer-for-moms/, posted December 18, 2013, acessed April 4, 2014; N. Radjou, J. Prabhu, and S. Ahuja, "When Ingenuity Saves Lives," HBR Blog Network, posted May 17, 2012, accessed April 4, 2014.

APPENDIX 3.1 **First Screen**

Part 1: Strength of Business Idea

For each item, circle the most appropriate answer and make note of the (–1), (0), or (+1) score.

	Low Potential (–1)	Moderate Potential (0)	High Potential (+1)
1. Extent to which the idea: • Takes advantage of an environmental trend • Solves a problem • Addresses an unfilled gap in the marketplace	Weak	Moderate	Strong
2. Timeliness of entry to market	Not timely	Moderately timely	Very timely
3. Extent to which the idea "adds value" for its buyer or end user	Low	Medium	High
4. Extent to which the customer is satisfied by competing products that are already available	Very satisfied	Moderately satisfied	Not very satisfied or ambivalent
5. Degree to which the idea requires customers to change their basic practices or behaviors	Substantial changes required	Moderate changes required	Small to no changes required

Part 2: Industry-Related Issues

	Low Potential (–1)	Moderate Potential (0)	High Potential (+1)
1. Number of competitors	Many	Few	None
2. Stage of industry life cycle	Maturity phase or decline phase	Growth phase	Emergence phase
3. Growth rate of industry	Little or no growth	Moderate growth	Strong growth
4. Importance of industry's products and/or services to customers	"Ambivalent"	"Would like to have"	"Must have"
5. Industry operating margins	Low	Moderate	High

Part 3: Target Market and Customer-Related Issues

	Low Potential (–1)	Moderate Potential (0)	High Potential (+1)
1. Identification of target market for the proposed new venture	Difficult to identify	May be able to identify	Identified
2. Ability to create "barriers to entry" for potential competitors	Unable to create	May or may not be able to create	Can create
3. Purchasing power of customers	Low	Moderate	High
4. Ease of making customers aware of the new product or service	Low	Moderate	High
5. Growth potential of target market	Low	Moderate	High

Part 4: Founder- (or Founders-) Related Issues

	Low Potential (–1)	Moderate Potential (0)	High Potential (+1)
1. Founder's or founders' experience in the industry	No experience	Moderate experience	Experienced
2. Founder's or founders' skills as they relate to the proposed new venture's product or service	No skills	Moderate skills	Skilled

(continued)

	Low Potential (–1)	Moderate Potential (0)	High Potential (+1)
3. Extent of the founder's or founders' professional and social networks in the relevant industry	None	Moderate	Extensive
4. Extent to which the proposed new venture meets the founder's or founders' personal goals and aspirations	Weak	Moderate	Strong
5. Likelihood that a team can be put together to launch and grow the new venture	Unlikely	Moderately likely	Very likely

Part 5: Financial Issues

	Low Potential (–1)	Moderate Potential (0)	High Potential (+1)
1. Initial capital investment	High	Moderate	Low
2. Number of revenue drivers (ways in which the company makes money)	One	Two to three	More than three
3. Time to break even	More than two years	One to two years	Less than one year
4. Financial performance of similar businesses	Weak	Modest	Strong
5. Ability to fund initial product (or service) development and/or initial start-up expenses from personal funds or via bootstrapping	Low	Moderate	High

Overall Potential

Each part has five items. Scores will range from –5 to +5 for each part. The score is a guide—there is no established rule of thumb for the numerical score that equates to high potential, moderate potential, or low potential for each part. The ranking is a judgment call.

Score (–5 to +5)	Overall Potential of the Business Idea Based on Each Part	Suggestions for Improving the Potential
Part 1: Strength of Business Idea	High potential Moderate potential Low potential	
Part 2: Industry-Related Issues	High potential Moderate potential Low potential	
Part 3: Target Market and Customer Related Issues	High potential Moderate potential Low potential	
Part 4: Founder- (or Founders-) Related Issues	High potential Moderate potential Low potential	
Part 5: Financial Issues	High potential Moderate potential Low potential	
Overall Assessment	High potential Moderate potential Low potential	

Summary

Briefly summarize your justification for your overall assessment:

APPENDIX 3.2   Internet Resource Table

Resources to Help Complete the First Screen Worksheet in Appendix 3.1

Source	Description	Applicable Parts of First Screen	Cost/Availability
American Factfinder (www.factfinder2.census.gov)	An easy-to-use portal for obtaining census data. One quick way to retrieve data is to get a "Fact Sheet" on a geographic area (by city, county, or zip code), which provides population, median household income, demographic breakdown (age, gender, race), and other information.	Part 3	Free
A-Z Index of Trade Associations (www.usa.gov/directory/tradeassc/index.shtml)	Directory provides access to the phone numbers and website addresses of trade associations in all industries. Trade associations can be contacted to obtain information on all areas of feasibility analysis.	Parts 1, 2, 3, 4, and 5.	Free
BizMiner (www.bizminer.com)	Industry statistics, sample pro forma financial statements by industry (and size of business), business start activity and failure rates by industry, and similar information. Provides data on small private firms.	Parts 2, 3, and 5	Fee based (more affordable than most); typically free if accessed through a university library
BizStats (www.bizstats.com)	Has a variety of detailed financial data on various retail categories. On the site, a user can type in the projected income of a firm, by industry, and receive a mock income statement in return.	Parts 2 and 5	Free
City-Data.com (www.city-data.com)	Contains detailed information on cities, including median resident age, median household income, ethnic mix of residents, and aerial photos.	Part 3	Free
County Business Patterns (www.census.gov/econ/cbp)	Good resources for looking at business activity, including the number of competitors, at a city, county, or state level. For example, you can find the number of dry cleaners (or any other business) in a specific zip code or city.	Parts 2 and 3	Free
Factiva (www.factiva.com)	Robust search engine that aggregates content from more than 36,000 sources such as newspapers, magazines, journals, photos, and radio and television transcripts.	Parts 1, 2, 3, 4, and 5	Fee based; typically free if accessed through a university library website
FedStats (www.fedstats.gov)	Provides easy access to information generated by over 100 federal agencies.	Parts 1, 2, 3, 4, and 5.	Free
Hoovers Online (www.hoovers.com)	Brief histories and financial information on companies, industries, people, and products. Premium service provides access to detailed financial information and 10-K reports for publicly traded firms.	Parts 2, 3, and 5	Free; premium version available on a fee basis or typically for free if accessed through a university library
IBISWorld (www.ibisworld.com)	Detailed reports available on hundreds of industries, including industry statistics, trends, buyer behavior, and expected returns.	Parts 1, 2, 3, and 5	Fee based; typically free if accessed through a university library

(continued)

Source	Description	Applicable Parts of First Screen	Cost/Availability
LexisNexis Academic (www.lexisnexis.com)	Provides access to sales data for public and private firms, which can be searched in a number of useful ways. Helps start-ups estimate the financial performance of similar businesses. Go to "Business" and then "Company Financial."	Part 5	Fee based; typically free if accessed through a university library
MagPortal.com (www.magportal.com)	Search engine and directory for finding online magazine articles. Helps start-ups by providing access to magazine articles about their product/service and industry of interest. This information may be helpful in all areas of feasibility analysis.	Parts 1, 2, 3, 4, and 5	Free
Mergent Online (www.mergentonline.com.)	Provides near instant access to financial data, including income statements, balance sheets, and cash flows, on more than 10,000 U.S. public corporations.	Parts 2 and 5	Fee based; typically free if accessed through a university library
Mintel (www.mintel.com)	Detailed reports available on hundreds of industries, including industry statistics, trends, buyer behavior, and expected returns.	Parts 1, 2, 3, and 5	Fee based; typically free if accessed through a university library
ProQuest (http://proquest.com)	Very robust search engine for searching publications such as the *Wall Street Journal* and the *New York Times*. Useful for all areas of feasibility analysis.	Parts 1, 2, 3, 4, and 5	Fee based; typically free if accessed through a university library
Quickfacts (http://quickfacts.census.gov)	A very quick way to access census bureau data, including population, median household income, census breakdowns by age and other demographic characteristics, and so on.	Parts 2 and 3	Free
ReferenceUSA (www.referenceusa.com)	Provides contact information, estimated annual sales, credit rating score, year established, news, and other information on both public and private companies. Contains more information on private firms than many similar sites. Helps start-ups estimate the financial performance of similar businesses.	Part 5	Fee based; typically free if accessed through a university library
Salary.com	Useful resources for determining salary ranges for positions (such as computer programming) in a specific city or zip code.	Part 5	Free
SimilarWeb (www.similarweb.com)	Allows users to assess the website traffic for any URL. Information can be helpful in assessing the attractiveness of a similar business idea.	Part 1	Free
Standard & Poor's NetAdvantage (www.netadvantage.standardpoor.com)	Detailed reports available on hundreds of industries, including industry statistics, trends, buyer behavior, and expected returns.	Parts 1, 2, 3, and 5	Free; premium version available on a fee basis or typically free if accessed through a university library
Thomas Register of American Manufacturers	Search engine for sourcing components, equipment, raw materials, and customer manufacturing services. Helpful in determining how much it will cost to manufacture a product.	Part 5	Free

Source	Description	Applicable Parts of First Screen	Cost/Availability
U.S. Small Business Administration (www.sba.com)	Describes loan availability, eligibility, sources of grants, etc. Helpful in determining the financial feasibility of a business idea.	Part 5	Free
Yahoo! Industry Center (http://biz.yahoo.com/ic)	Provides a directory of industries, along with a list of the companies in each industry, the latest industry-related news, and performance data on the top companies in an industry.	Parts 2, 3, and 5	Free

Endnotes

1. J. Mullins, *The New Business Road Test* (London: Prentice Hall, 2003).
2. M. Cooper, "Bootstrapping Lessons from a Startup Disaster," *Inc.*, November 6, 2013.
3. M. Cooper, "Bootstrapping Lessons from a Startup Disaster," *Inc.*, November 6, 2013.
4. V. Onyemah, M. R. Pesquera, and A. Ali, "What Entrepreneurs Get Wrong," *Harvard Business Review*, May 2013.
5. M. Lofstrom, T. Bates, and S. C. Parker, "Why Are Some People More Likely to Become Small-Business Owners Than Others: Entrepreneurship Entry and Industry-Specific Barriers," *Journal of Business Venturing* 29, no. 2 (2014): 232–251; D. A. Shepherd, H. Patzelt, and R. A. Baron, "I Care About Nature, But... .: Disengaging Values in Assessing Opportunities That Cause Harm," *Academy of Management Journal* 56, no. 5 (2013): 1251–1273.
6. B. Freed and T. Patterson, "Tom Patterson, Inventory & Founder of Tommy John Show," Got Invention Radio Podcast, http://gotinvention.com/pastshows.php?g=tom+patterson&d= (accessed March 20, 2014, originally posted on July 15, 2010).
7. W. Drover, M. S. Wood, and G. T. Payne, "The Effects of Perceived Control on Venture Capitalist Investment Decisions: A Configurational Perspective," *Entrepreneurship Theory and Practice*, in press; J. J. Ebbers, "Networking Behavior and Contracting Relationships Among Entrepreneurs in Business Incubators," *Entrepreneurship Theory and Practice*, in press.
8. E. Mollick, "The Dynamics of Crowdfunding: An Exploratory Study," *Journal of Business Venturing* 29, no. 1 (2014): 1–16; L. Schjoedt, E. Monsen, A. Pearson, T. Barnett, and J. J. Chrisman, "New Venture and Family Business Teams: Understanding Team Formation, Composition, Behaviors, and Performance," *Entrepreneurship Theory and Practice* 37, no. 1 (2013): 1–15.
9. M. A. Uy, M.-D. Foo, and R. Ilies, "Perceived Progress Variability and Entrepreneurial Effort Intensity: The Moderating Role of Venture Goal Commitment," *Journal of Business Venturing*, in press.
10. G. Casser, "Industry and Startup Experience on Entrepreneur Forecast Performance in New Firms," *Journal of Business Venturing* 29, no. 2 (2014): 137–151.
11. BizMiner home page, www.bizminer.com, (accessed April 3, 2014).
12. T. Astebro and J. Chen, "The Entrepreneurial Earnings Puzzle: Mismeasurement or Real? *Journal of Business Venturing* 29, no. 1 (2014): 88–105.

Getting Personal with HER CAMPUS MEDIA

Co-Founders

STEPHANIE KAPLAN
BA, Psychology, Harvard University, 2010

ANNIE WANG
Currently on leave from Harvard University

WINDSOR HANGER
BA, History and Science, Harvard University, 2010

Dialogue with
Stephanie Kaplan

FAVORITE BAND ON MY SMARTPHONE MUSIC LIST
Carrie Underwood

BEST ADVICE I'VE RECEIVED
Whether you think you can or you think you can't, you're right.

MY ADVICE FOR NEW ENTREPRENEURS
Don't delay—start NOW!

FIRST ENTREPRENEURIAL EXPERIENCE
In high school, my best friend and I baked goods and then sold them to local bakeries and businesses to resell.

MY FAVORITE SMARTPHONE APP
AnyList—I'm obsessed with to-do lists, and this houses all of mine for me!

MY BIGGEST WORRY AS AN ENTREPRENEUR
Letting down our employees if things don't go well.

CHAPTER 4

Developing an *Effective* Business Model

OPENING PROFILE

HER CAMPUS MEDIA
Executing on an Established Business Model and Preparing for the Future

• Web: www.hercampus.com • Facebook: HerCampus • Twitter: @HerCampus

f you're a female college student and are looking for an enriching experience, you might consider plugging into your college campus's Her Campus chapter. Her Campus is the number-one online community for college women. Written entirely by 4,000-plus college journalists and supported by a dedicated staff at its Boston headquarters, Her Campus features national content on style, beauty, health, love, life, and career, supplemented by local content from 250-plus campus chapters across the world. In addition, Her Campus offers slideshows, videos, memes, gifts, quizzes, giveaways, e-commerce, a daily e-mail newsletter, and social media communities. It's like nothing else available for college-aged women.

Her Campus was started in 2009 by three Harvard University undergraduates: Stephanie Kaplan, Annie Wang, and Windsor Hanger. The women met in 2007 while working on a separate Harvard publication. In the nearby photo, Stephanie Kaplan is on the left, Annie Wang is in the middle, and Windsor Hanger is on the right. In January 2009, Kaplan, Wang, and Hanger entered the i3 Innovation Challenge, a business plan competition held on the Harvard campus, proposing a national online magazine for college women, with student chapters at colleges and universities across the United States. After the business plan received the Harvard Student Agencies Investment Award, Her Campus was born. The award secured national attention, along with free office space for a period of time.

Her Campus, the flagship site of the company, which is formally named Her Campus Media, features a vibrant online magazine, with feature articles targeted toward all aspects of college life and survival. The website is divided into six categories: style, beauty, health, love, life, and career. The content is wholesome and upbeat, and speaks to the daily challenges, concerns, dilemmas, and triumphs that college-aged women experience. In addition to a staff of full-time editors, designers, and managers working at the company's Boston headquarters, Her Campus is represented by students at 250-plus college campuses. These campuses are known as My Campus chapters. Each chapter has a president/editor-in-chief, and a staff of volunteer correspondents who develop feature articles, photos, and other content specific to their particular university. Her Campus also has a team of national contributing writers who "pitch" articles to run on the Her Campus national website. The

LEARNING OBJECTIVES

After studying this chapter you should be ready to:

1. Describe business models and discuss their importance.

2. Identify and describe the two general types of business models—standard and disruptive business models.

3. Explain the components of the Barringer/Ireland Business Model Template that entrepreneurs can use to develop a business model for their firm.

133

local chapters compete to reach certain levels of distinction within the Her Campus community. The highest level is the Pink Level. To reach the Pink Level a local chapter has to demonstrate flawless writing and formatting, update their site every day, post several times a day on social media sites, host events, and reach 40 percent of the undergraduate female population on their campus. An example of a local chapter, the My Campus chapter at the University of Central Florida, is available at www. hercampus.com/ucf. Toward the end of 2014, Her Campus was receiving approximately 3.5 million monthly unique visitors, 15 million monthly page views, and was operating with 20 full-time employees.

Of paramount importance to Kaplan, Wang, and Hanger from the outset was developing an effective business model for their company. The company's core competency is developing compelling content at a low cost and displaying the content in an attractive and accessible manner. The 4,000-plus local chapter correspondents are all volunteers, who write for Her Campus to obtain experience and hone their journalistic skills rather than make money. The same applies to interns in the company's Boston headquarters. The company's mission is crystal clear: to produce, on a daily basis, the "Collegiette's Guide to Life." The word "collegiette" can't be found in the dictionary, at least not yet. It's a word made up by the founders of Her Campus to describe the women in their target audience. According to Stephanie Kaplan, a collegiette is "a college girl who is on top of her game—strategically career-minded, distinctly fashionable, socially connected, academically driven, and smartly health-conscious, who endeavors to get the most out of her college experience on every level." In early 2012, Her Campus received a trademark on the word "collegiette" from the U.S. Patent and Trademark office. Her Campus is now the only company that can use that word in a business context.

On the revenue side, Her Campus's business model focuses on connecting companies with college females. The key to making this work is Her Campus's unparalleled access to college-aged women. Part of their business model is native advertising, or sponsored content. The way sponsored content works is that Her Campus will run an article that is sponsored by a brand and that promotes that brand to its audience. This arrangement allows brands to connect with Her Campus's audience. Her Campus's client list includes Victoria's Secret PINK, New Balance, Pinkberry, and many other national brands. Her Campus also generates revenue from other types of advertising and sponsorships, which is often visible on its website and additional platforms. Other revenue generators include product sampling and on-campus and event-based marketing programs.

In regard to expansion, Her Campus is steadily increasing its number of My Campus local chapters. It is also interested in overseas markets. In late 2013, Her Campus acquired HerUni.com, a similar online magazine for college-aged women in England. The acquisition of HerUni.com will strengthen Her Campus's presence throughout the United Kingdom. The company is also thinking about broadening its audience to include men, including the possibility of a His Campus site. The founders would have to think carefully about how that possibility would affect their current business model and future prospects.

In this chapter, we introduce you to the concept of the business model. A **business model** is a firm's plan or recipe for how it creates, delivers, and captures value for its stakeholders.[1] Business models are foundational to a firm's ability to succeed both in the short and long term, especially when it is the first one to introduce a new product or service to customers.[2] Dropbox, for example, has what's referred to as a freemium business model. It offers its customers a free account with a set amount of storage space, and makes money by selling premium accounts with more capacity. Dropbox could charge all of its users a monthly fee based on the amount of storage that they use, but that's not its business model. Its business model is based on the belief that by introducing users to its service through a free account, it will ultimately sign up more paid users. To further illustrate what a business model is, the Savvy Entrepreneurial Firm feature focuses on Quirky, an interesting company that helps bring peoples' inventions to life. The feature illustrates how Quirky creates, delivers, and captures value for its stakeholder.

The proper time to determine a company's business model is following the initial validation of the business idea and prior to fleshing out the operational details of the firm.[3] This sequence, which is depicted in Figure 4.1, nicely parallels the chapters in the book. Chapter 1 dealt with the decision to become an entrepreneur. Chapters 2–3 considered the initial validation of the business idea. This chapter deals with determining a business model, while Chapters 5–15 deal with the topics needed to implement a firm's business model and grow the firm.

In this chapter we'll first discuss business models and their importance. We then introduce and discuss a template for developing a business model. The template, called the Barringer/Ireland Business Model Template, consists of 4 categories and 12 items that make up a firm's business model. The template, which can be completed on an 8 ½ by 11 sheet of paper or blown up and placed on the wall, provides a nice visual mechanism to think through and display the elements of a firm's business model.

A critical factor is that similar to feasibility analysis, a firm's business model should not be completed in isolation. The founders of a firm should "get out of the building" and talk to potential customers as a firm's business model takes shape.[4] This is a facet of developing an effective business model that we stress throughout the chapter.

Business Models and Their Importance

As stated above, a firm's business model is its plan or recipe for how it creates, delivers, and captures value for its stakeholders. Glance ahead to Figure 4.2, the Barringer/Ireland Business Model Template. As you can see by looking at the template, a firm's business model represents the core aspects of its business. It also describes how the core aspects fit together and support one another. For example, three important elements of a firm's business model are its target market, its basis for differentiation, and its key assets. In Her Campus's case, its target market is college-aged females, it differentiates itself by focusing on six topics that college-aged females care about (style, beauty, health, love, life, and career), and its key assets include 4,000-plus college females volunteering in Her Campus chapters across the country writing articles that they believe other college females will be interested in. This example illustrates a nicely designed business model, at least as it pertains to the three elements mentioned above. Each element supports the others. It's also a business model that would be difficult to copy. It would take a tremendous effort on the part of a competitor to match Her Campus's network of 4,000-plus volunteers on college campuses.

LEARNING OBJECTIVE

1. Describe business models and discuss their importance.

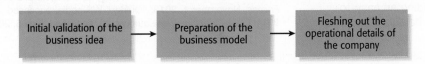

FIGURE 4.1

Proper Time to Determine a Company's Business Model

SAVVY ENTREPRENEURIAL FIRM

Quirky: How One Company Creates, Delivers, and Captures Value for Its Stakeholders

Web: www.quirky.com; Facebook: Quirky; Twitter: @Quirky

Quirky is an interesting company. It was conceived by Ben Kauffman, a young entrepreneur who launched his first company when he was 18. Kauffman's first company, Mophie, designed accessories for Apple products. In 2006, Mophie won Best in Show at Macworld for a modular case accessory system for the iPod Nano. The next year at the same conference, Kaufman and his company did an unusual thing. Instead of bringing their hottest new products to showcase, they brought next to nothing. Instead, they set up a booth made out of two-by-fours, and handed out scratch pads to 30,000 people, asking the Macworld community for new product suggestions. The sketch that got the most attention, and was repeatedly exposed to the community for improvements, was a case/bottle opener for the iPod Shuffle. The product was built, and with this amazing story behind it, became a hit, selling in 28 countries worldwide.

This and similar experiences became the inspiration for Quirky, which was launched in 2009. In a nutshell, Quirky is an invention company that allows people to submit product ideas (mostly household items and kitchen gadgets) that are then vetted by the Quirky community. The best ideas are selected for prototype development and possible sale. It's become quite a success. Over 550,000 people are now part of the Quirky "community," and participate in pitching, refining, or voting on product ideas. The process has created several hit products, including Pivot Power (a flexible power strip that bends to fit large three-prong plugs in each outlet) and Crates (modular plastic milk crates used as shelving). Quirky's products are sold via its website and in big-box stores such as Target and Home Depot. The system is a win-win for everyone involved. The inventors and community members who help with the product get a cut of the profit. In 2012, Quirky launched 121 new products—all invented by ordinary people.

Quirky accomplishes what it does via its business model. As we noted above, a business model is a firm's plan or recipe for how it creates, delivers, and captures value for its stakeholders. Here is how Quirky accomplishes each of these key elements:

- Quirky *creates* value by allowing ordinary people to submit product ideas. Ordinary people often have good product ideas, but don't have the wherewithal to start a company. As a result, the ideas generally never come to fruition. Now, because of Quirky, anyone with an idea for a household product or a kitchen gadget has a shot at seeing the idea become a reality.

- Quirky *delivers* value by providing an easy-to-navigate process for ideas to be submitted and vetted by the Quirky community. The most promising ideas are fashioned into products that are sold. By creating this process, Quirky has brought down the barriers that prevent most people from seeing their ideas realized. Quirky has just what a good idea needs—product designers, prototype specialists, manufacturing capabilities, and relationships with retailers to get products on store shelves.

- Quirky *captures* value for its stakeholders via the profits that it realizes on the products that are sold. For every product that is sold, Quirky takes 60 percent of the revenue and returns 40 percent to the original inventor and the community members (called Influencers) that help shape the idea. To minimize risk, Quirky only fully develops products that have a certain level of pre-sales. Quirky has relationships with a growing number of retailers to maximize revenue from the best-selling items.

The attractiveness of Quirky's business model is that as the company grows, it can expand into new product categories. Quirky is also a business that would be difficult to copy. It has raised over $91 million in venture capital and as noted above, has over 550,000 people in its network. It has also built relationships with organizations up and down the manufacturing and retail supply chains.

Questions for Critical Thinking

1. Do you think Quirky's basic business model is sound and fair? If you could suggest any changes, what would they be?
2. To what degree does Quirky's business reflect the attributes of a sound business idea as described in Chapter 2?
3. In what other product areas would Quirky's business model work the best?
4. Think of the challenges in your own life that might represent a product idea for Quirky. If you don't think of something right away, don't give up. All of us encounter problems and challenges in our everyday lives that might represent the basis of a promising idea. Be prepared to describe to others one of the challenges or problems you encounter and how a solution to the problem could be fashioned into a product idea to submit to Quirky.

Source: "How Quirky Uses Technology to Disrupt Manufacturing," *Forbes*, November 1, 2013; "Quirky," Wikipedia, accessed June 5, 2014; Quirky website, www.quirky.com, accessed June 5, 2014.

General Categories of Business Models

There are two general categories of business models: standard business models and disruptive business models.[5] Next, we provide details about each model.

Standard Business Models

The first category is standard business models. This type of model is used commonly by existing firms as well as by those launching an entrepreneurial venture. **Standard business models** depict existing plans or recipes firms can use to determine how they will create, deliver, and capture value for their stakeholders. There are a number of standard or common business models. An abbreviated list is shown in Table 4.1. Most of the standard business models, with the exception of the freemium model, have been in place for some time. In fact, many of the business models utilized by online firms were originally developed by offline firms, and simply transferred to the Internet. For example, Amazon did not invent a new business model. It took the mail order business model, pioneered years ago by Sears Roebuck and Company, and moved it online. Similarly, eBay did not invent the auction business model—that has been in existence for centuries. It moved the auction format online. What Amazon.com and eBay did do, however, which is common among successful start-ups, is adopt a standard business model and build upon it in one or more meaningful ways to produce a new way of creating value. Birchbox, for example, adopted the subscription business model and then built upon it in novel ways. This firm provides its subscribers a monthly assortment of cosmetic and skin care samples in hopes of enticing them to buy full-sized versions of the same products. Its cost structure is low because it operates via the Internet and many of the samples that it distributes are provided for free by companies that want to get their products in front of Birchbox's unique clientele. The other elements of Birchbox's business model are supportive of its basic premise. The multifaceted "value" that Birchbox's business model creates is that it presents products to women that they wouldn't have otherwise tried. Through this model, Birchbox creates two revenue streams for itself (i.e., the subscription service and online sales), and it creates additional sales for the companies that provide the samples that Birchbox disseminates to its subscribers. You can read more about Birchbox in Case 6.1.

It is important to understand that there is no perfect business model.[6] Each of the standard models has inherent strengths and weaknesses. For example, the strength of the subscription business model is recurring revenue. Birchbox has approximately 400,000 subscribers who pay $10 per month. As a result, if Birchbox maintains its subscriber base, it would know that it had a minimum of $4 million in revenue each month. The disadvantage of the subscription business model is "churn." **Churn** refers to the number of subscribers that a subscription-based business loses each month. If Birchbox loses 10 percent of its subscribers each month, it will need to recruit 40,000 new subscribers each month just to stay even. This is why companies that feature a subscription-based business model normally offer a high level of customer service. They want to retain as high a percentage of their subscribers as they can to lower churn and avoid the expenses involved with replacing existing customers.

It's important to note that a firm's business model takes it beyond its own boundaries. Her Campus's business model, for example, is based on the idea that female college students will form My Campus chapters and voluntarily contribute content to their chapter's website and the main Her Campus portal. The trick to getting something like this to work is to provide sufficient incentive for partners to participate. In Her Campus's case, the local My Campus members contribute because they want to obtain experience, hone their journalistic skills, and build their résumés. Apparently, Her Campus is providing these individuals a rich enough experience that it's worth their time to participate. Many

LEARNING OBJECTIVE

2. Identify and describe the two general types of business models—standard and disruptive business models

TABLE 4.1 Standard Business Models

Name	Description	Examples of Entrepreneurial Firms (or Types of Firm) Utilizing This Model
Advertising Business Model	Business model based on providing advertisers access to highly targeted customer niches.	Google, Facebook, YouTube
Auction Business Model	Currently synonymous with eBay, the auction business model has been around since 500 BC. The idea is to provide a platform for individuals and businesses to sell items in an auction format.	eBay, uBid.com
Bricks and Clicks Business Model	A business model by which a company integrates both offline (bricks) and online (clicks) presences.	Apple, Barnes & Noble, J. Crew
Franchise Business Model	A business model in which a firm that has a successful product or service (franchisor) licenses its trademark and method of doing business to other businesses (franchisees).	24 Hour Fitness, Panera Bread, School of Rock
Freemium Business Model	A business model in which a firm provides a basic version of its service for free, and makes money by selling a premium version of the service.	Dropbox, Evernote, Pandora
Low-Cost Business Model	A well-established business model that relies on driving down costs and making money by servicing a large number of customers.	Southwest Airlines, Warby Parker
Manufacturer/Retailer Business Model	A business model in which a manufacturer both produces and sells (online, offline, or both) a product.	Apple, Fitbit, Tesla Motors
Peer-to-Peer Business Model	A model in which a business acts as a matchmaker between individuals with a service to offer and others who want the service.	Airbnb, Getaround, Task Rabbit
Razor and Blades Business Model	This model involves the sales of dependent goods for different prices—one good (a razor) is sold at a discount, with the dependent good (blades) sold at a considerably higher margin.	Game Consoles and Games, Mobile Phones and Air Time, Printers and Ink Cartridges
Subscription Business Model	A business model where the customer pays a monthly, quarterly, or yearly subscription fee to have access to a product or service.	Birchbox, Blue Apron, Netflix
Traditional Retailer Business Model	A business model calling for a firm to sell its products or services, made by others, directly to consumers at a markup from the original price. Can be sold online or offline.	Amazon, Whole Foods Markets, Zappos

companies feature the participation of others as an integral part of their business models. An example is Apple, and in particular the Apple App Store. As of December 2013, more than 1 million apps were available through the Apple App Store, created by over 262,000 publishers. About 140 new apps are added each day. It's a win-win situation for both Apple and the developers. The developers get access to a platform to sell their apps, while Apple shares in the revenue that's generated. Positive scenarios like this often allow businesses to not only strengthen but to expand their business models. As a result of the success of its app store, Apple launched iAd, a platform that allows app developers to sell advertising on the apps they make available via the Apple App Store. Apple shares in the revenue generated by the advertising.

Regardless of the business model a start-up is rolling out, one thing that new companies should guard themselves against is thinking that one particular business model is a "homerun" regardless of circumstances.[7] In this sense, the issues discussed in Chapters 1–3 still apply, meaning, for example, that the strength of the opportunity must be assessed and the feasibility of the idea must be validated. The What Went Wrong feature nearby draws attention to

WHAT WENT WRONG?

Peer-to-Peer Business Models: Good for Some, Not So Good for Others

Peer-to-Peer business models are hot. Airbnb, Uber, and Lyft, three of the most successful firms in the peer-to-peer business model space, are growing and are worth hundreds of millions of dollars. Peer-to-peer businesses act as matchmaker between individuals with a service to offer and others who want the service. Airbnb, for example, matches people who are looking for a place to stay (for a day or two or longer) with people who have an extra room that they're willing to rent. Relying to some degree on smartphone technology's capabilities, Lyft and Uber match people who need a ride with people who are willing to provide rides. The success of Airbnb, Uber, Lyft, and others has captured the attention of investors, who are generally bullish on the peer-to-peer concept. Sam Altman, president of Y Combinator, a start-up accelerator, was quoted in a *Wall Street Journal* article saying "We're bullish on the sharing economy (a catchall term for peer-to-peer businesses), and we'll definitely make more investment in it."

Despite the promise of the peer-to-peer business model, several high-profile peer-to-peer business have failed. The failures include BlackJet, a service that matched the owners of private jets with people who wanted a seat on a private jet for a trip, Ridejoy, a carpooling service, and Neighborrow.com, a service that allowed people to list household items for rent, such as vacuum cleaners, tools, and food mixers. So, what went wrong? On the surface, BlackJet, Ridejoy, and Neighborrow.com seem very similar to Airbnb, Uber, and Lyft in that they matched people wanting a particular service with someone willing to offer it.

BlackJet's basic premise was that once a person joined the service, s/he could book a seat on a private jet within minutes for a ride to a desired location. The idea was that BlackJet would sign up a large number of owners of private jets, who would let BlackJet know when they were making a trip. If a seat was open on the jet, it would be made available to a BlackJet member who was looking for a ride to the same destination. For those seeking rides, BlackJet charged a $2,500 yearly membership fee and up to $4,000 per ride. As it turned out, there just weren't enough people willing to pay that stiff of a fee for the service. In addition, a private jet ride isn't something people need frequently, so BlackJet wasn't an option that was foremost on people's minds. "If you have to reacquire the customer every six months, they'll forget you," said Howard Morgan, co-founder of First Round Capital, in the same *Wall Street Journal* article mentioned above. Further compounding BlackJet's challenge, there are readily available substitutes for BlackJet's service. Anyone can book a first-class seat on an airline and ride in relative luxury, without having to pay a yearly membership fee. BlackJet closed in late 2013, after only about a year in service.

Ridejoy was a carpooling service that focused on connecting people that wanted to share rides for long distances, such as Los Angeles to San Francisco. Lyft and Uber, mentioned earlier, focus on short rides. Ridejoy experienced early success. During its first year, 2011, its user base grew about 30 percent a month, with more than 25,000 drivers signed up and an estimated 10,000 rides completed. But it didn't grow fast enough to satisfy its investors. In addition, it had competition from free alternatives, such as carpooling forums on college websites. Also, some riders started cutting Ridejoy out once they got to know one another. Instead of paying Ridejoy its 10 percent transaction fee for a trip from Portland to San Francisco, for example, the car owner and riders would just exchange cash among each other instead of paying by credit card on Ridejoy's website or mobile app. Ridejoy shut down in the summer of 2013, returning about half of its funding to its investors.

Neighborrow.com would let people list household items for rent, such as vacuum cleaners, cameras, tools, and electronics. The idea was that if you only use a power saw or a high-end camera once or twice a year, why buy one if your next-door neighbor has exactly what you need and would be willing to rent it to you for a modest fee. The site got plenty of publicity when it launched, including a story in *USA Today* and a spot on NBC's early morning program, the *Today Show*. It also had thousands of people sign up and list their items. The problem: very few people actually used the service. What the company eventually found is that people don't like borrowing things. In addition, borrowing an item such as a power drill isn't typically an urgent need, so people didn't tend to think "Oh, I could get that through Neighborrow.com." Although they may have read about the company in *USA Today* or seen it featured on television, they soon forgot about the service. Neighborrow.com folded in 2011, after a five-year run.

Questions for Critical Thinking

1. Prior to launching their firms, how could BlackJet, Ridejoy, and Neighborrow.com have better anticipated the issues that ultimately caused them to fail?

2. In regard to putting together an effective business model, what can other peer-to-peer business model start-ups learn from the failures of BlackJet, Ridejoy, and Neighborrow.com?

3. Spend some time looking at Lyft, one of the successful peer-to-peer business model companies mentioned in this feature. Why do you think Lyft has been successful while BlackJet, Ridejoy, and Neighborrow.com failed?

(continued)

4. What role do you think the industry that a start-up is in plays in its suceess or failure as a peer-to-peer business? Are some industries more receptive to peer-to-peer business model start-ups than others? Explain your answers.

Sources: S. Needleman and A. Loten, "Startups Want to Be the Next Airbnb, Uber," *Wall Street Journal,* May 8, 2014, B4; N. Tiku, "JayZ and Ashton Kutcher-Backed 'Uber for Planes' Grinds to a Halt," ValleyWag, posted on November 20, 2013, available at http://valleywag.gawker.com/jay-z-and-ashton-kutcher-backed-uber-for-planes-grind-1467083423, accessed on May 31, 2014; Ridejoy (the blog), posted on December 16, 2013, available at http://blog.ridejoy.com/from-carpool-to-deadpool-ridejoys-startup-journey/, accessed on May 31, 2014; D. Kander, "Lessons from Failure: Borrowing Tools from Your Neighbors," Entrepreneurship.org, available at http://www.entrepreneurship.org/resource-center/lessons-from-failure-borrowing-tools-from-your-neighbors.aspx, accessed on May 31, 2014.

this point. Even though the peer-to-peer business model is currently hot, with homeruns such as Airbnb and Uber, utilizing the peer-to-peer business model is not sufficient to guarantee firm success.

Disruptive Business Models

The second category is disruptive business models. **Disruptive business models**, which are rare, are ones that do not fit the profile of a standard business model, and are impactful enough that they disrupt or change the way business is conducted in an industry or an important niche within an industry.[8] In Table 4.2, we describe actual disruptive business models that were used by four different companies.

There are three types of disruptive business models. The first type is called new market disruption. A **new market disruption** addresses a market that previously wasn't served. An example is Google and its AdWords program. AdWords allows an advertiser to buy keywords on Google's home page, which triggers text-based ads to the side of (and sometimes above) the search results when the keyword is used. So, if you type the words "organic snacks" into the Google search bar, you will see ads paid for by companies that have organic snacks to sell. The ads are usually paid for on a pay-per-click basis. The cost of keywords varies depending on the popularity of the word. Prior to the advent of AdWords, online advertising was cost prohibitive for small businesses. At one time Yahoo, for example, required advertisers to spend at least $5,000 creating a compelling banner ad and $10,000 for a minimum ad buy. AdWords changed that. Its customers could set up a budget and spend as little as $1 per day (depending on the keywords that they purchased). Thus, AdWords was a new market-disruptive business model in that it provided a way for small businesses, in large numbers, to advertise online.

The second type of disruptive business model is referred to as a **low-end market disruption**. This is a type of disruption that was elegantly written about by Harvard professor Clayton Christensen in the book *The Innovator's Dilemma.*[9] Low-end disruption is possible when the firms in an industry continue to improve products or services to the point where they are actually better than a sizable portion of their clientele needs or desires. This "performance oversupply" creates a vacuum that provides an opportunity for simple, typically low-cost business models to exist. Examples here include Southwest Airlines in the United States and Ryanair in Europe. Southwest created its point-to-point, low-cost, no-frills business model as an alternative to higher-end service offerings provided by legacy carriers such as United and American. By actually offering what some would conclude is inferior service relative to its competitors, Southwest was able to attract a large clientele that still wanted a safe and comfortable ride, but were willing to trade off amenities for a lower fare. Low-end disruptive business models are also introduced to offer a simpler, cheaper, or more convenient way to perform an everyday task. If a start-up goes this route, the advantages must be compelling and the company must strike a nerve for disruption to take place. An example of

TABLE 4.2 Four Disruptive Business Models

Company	Disruptive Business Model and Description	Standard Business Model That Was Disrupted
Dell	Direct-to-consumer computer sales model, which allowed consumers to customize their computers Introduced the notion of buying a computer first over the phone and then via the Web. The customer would configure the computer and pay for it before the computer was assembled. Delivery via UPS or FedEx.	Computers that were assembled, shipped to a store, and then sat on shelves until someone bought them. No customization was possible because the computer was assembled before the customer bought it.
Google	AdWords (online advertising product) Introduced text advertising, which appears to the right or the top of organic search results, that when clicked takes the searcher to an advertiser's website or landing page. The text ads could be bought for as little at $1. Google's initial customers were small businesses who couldn't afford Yahoo's service.	Traditional banner advertising, provided by companies such as Yahoo. Some services required a minimum $10,000 ad buy for a company to advertise on the Internet.
Salesforce.com	SaaS (Software as a Service) provider of customer relationships management (CRM) software First company to offer CRM software as a SaaS product, making CRM affordable to small companies for the first time. By moving CRM to the cloud, it also enabled salespeople to access their CRM service anywhere they had an Internet connection.	Traditional installed CRM software, which required large licensing fees, provided by vendors such as Siebel Systems and PeopleSoft
Uber	Quickly connects riders with the owners of private cars who are willing to provide rides First company to provide riders with an app that connects them with the owners of private cars who are willing to provide rides. Advantages include: cleaner cars, avoiding the frustration of trying to hail a cab, direct billing via Uber so no money changes hands between the passenger and driver, and Uber knows the location of the nearest driver so pickup time is often reduced.	Local taxis and town-car services

a firm that's pulled this off is Uber, a 2009 start-up that connects people needing a ride with the owners of private cars willing to provide rides. Uber, which is the subject of Case 14.1, provides a compelling set of features—cars are ordered by sending a text message or via an app, customers can track their reserved car's location, payment is made through the app so no cash trades hands between the passenger and the driver, and Uber maintains strict quality standards for the cars and drivers that participate in its service. Uber not only offers a cheaper and more convenient way to perform an everyday task (i.e., getting a ride), but has also struck a nerve.[10] The taxi industry scores low on most measures of customer satisfaction, so consumers were eager to try something new. Uber also appeals to technologically savvy people, who see a big advantage in using an app to order a ride as opposed to the often frustrating process of hailing a cab.

The Barringer/Ireland Business Model Template

Although not everyone agrees precisely on the components of a business model, many agree that a successful business model has a common set of attributes. These attributes are often laid out in a visual framework or template

LEARNING OBJECTIVE

3. Explain the components of the Barringer/Ireland Business Model Template that entrepreneurs can use to develop a business model for their firm.

Many entrepreneurs enlarge their business model templates and place them on a whiteboard. This practice provides a means to step back and look at how all the parts of a prospective business model fit together.

Helen King/Bridge/Corbis

so it is easy to see the individual parts and their interrelationships. One widely-used framework is the Business Model Canvas, popularized by Alexander Osterwalder and Yves Pigneur in their book, *Business Model Generation*.[11] The Business Model Canvas consists of nine basic parts that show the logic of how a firm intends to create, deliver, and capture value for its stakeholders. You can view the Business Model Canvas via a simple Google search.

The business model framework used here, the Barringer/Ireland Business Model Template, is shown in Figure 4.2. It is slightly more comprehensive than the Business Model Canvas in that it consists of 4 major categories and 12 individual parts. The 12 parts make up a firm's business model. The job of the entrepreneur, or team of entrepreneurs, is to configure their firm's business model in a manner that produces a viable and exciting business. The Barringer/Ireland Business Model Template is a tool that allows an entrepreneur to describe, project, revise, and pivot a business model until all 12 parts are decided upon. Appendix 4.1 contains an expanded version of the Barringer/Ireland Template shown here. The 12 parts are spread out, which provides space for ideas to be recorded, scratched out, and recorded again as ideas morph and change. Feel free to copy and use the template to help formulate the business model for an individual firm.

Next, we discuss each of the 4 categories and the 12 individual elements of a firm's business model. We will refer frequently to Figure 4.2 throughout the discussion.

Core Strategy

The first component of a business model is core strategy. A **core strategy** describes how the firm plans to compete relative to its competitors.[12] The primary elements of core strategy are: business mission, basis of differentiation, target market, and product/market scope.

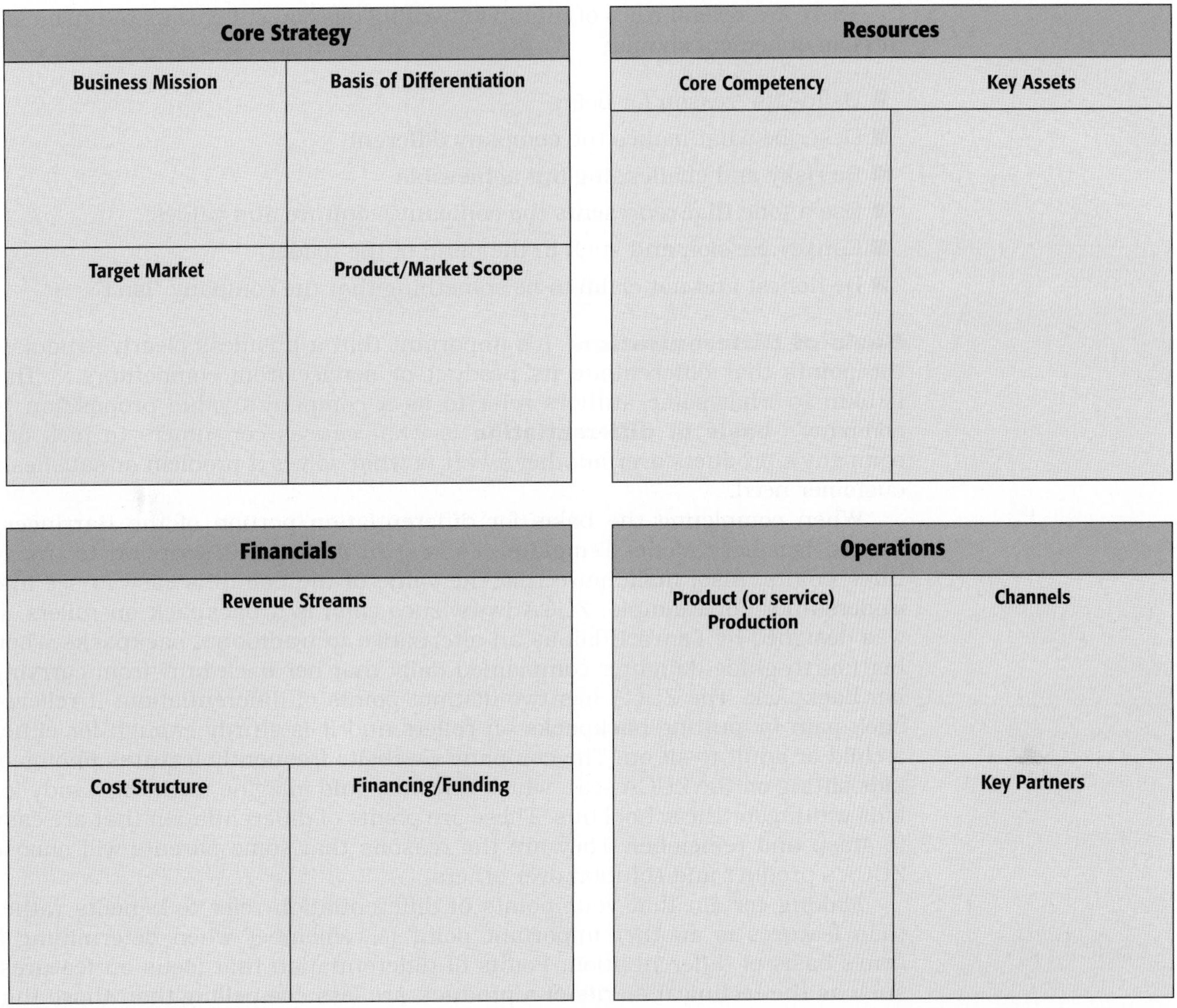

Core Strategy	
Business Mission	**Basis of Differentiation**
Target Market	**Product/Market Scope**

Resources	
Core Competency	**Key Assets**

Financials	
Revenue Streams	
Cost Structure	**Financing/Funding**

Operations	
Product (or service) Production	**Channels**
	Key Partners

FIGURE 4.2
Barringer/Ireland
Business Model
Template

© 2014 Bruce R. Barringer
and R. Duane Ireland

Business Mission   A business's **mission or mission statement** describes why it exists and what its business model is supposed to accomplish.[13] If carefully written and used properly, a mission statement can articulate a business's overarching priorities and act as its financial and moral compass. A firm's mission is the first box that should be completed in the business model template. A well-written mission statement is something that a business can continually refer back to as it makes important decisions in other elements of its business model.

At a 50,000-foot level, a mission statement indicates how a firm intends to create value for stakeholders. For example, Zynga's mission is "Connecting the world through games." Zynga is a producer of social games, such as FarmVille and Texas HoldEm Poker, which can be played through its website and social networking platforms such as Facebook and Google+. Although Zynga's mission statement is short and to the point, it provides direction for how the other elements of its business model should be configured. The company will focus on games, as opposed to other business pursuits, and its games will be social, meaning that they will be designed to be played with other people. The remaining 11 parts of Zynga's business model should support these basic premises.

There are several rules of thumb for writing mission statements. A business's mission statement should:

- Define its "reason for being"
- Describe what makes the company different
- Be risky and challenging but achievable
- Use a tone that represents the company's culture and values
- Convey passion and stick in the mind of the reader
- Be honest and not claim to be something that the company "isn't"

Basis of Differentiation It's important that a business clearly articulate the points that differentiate its product or service from competitors.[14] This is akin to what some authors refer to as a company's value proposition. A company's **basis of differentiation** is what causes consumers to pick one company's products over another's.[15] It is what solves a problem or satisfies a customer need.

When completing the basis for differentiation portion of the Barringer/Ireland Business Model Template, it's best to limit the description to two to three points. Also, make sure that the value of the points is easy to see and understand. For example, ZUCA (www.zuca.com) is a backpack on rollers. It was designed by Laura Udall as an alternative to traditional backpacks when her fourth-grade daughter complained daily that her back hurt from carrying her backpack. The ZUCA has two distinct points of differentiation: It relieves back pain by putting backpacks on rollers and it is sturdy enough for either a child or adult to sit on. The company's website frequently features photos of kids sitting on the ZUCA seat, which anyone could imagine might be handy for kids waiting for the school bus. These are points of differentiation that are easy to grasp and remember. They are the reasons that some parents will choose ZUCA's product and solution over others.

Making certain that your points of differentiation refer to benefits rather than features is another important point to remember when determining a firm's basis of differentiation. Points of differentiation that focus on features, such as the technical merits of a product, are less compelling than those that focus on benefits, which is what a product can do. For example, when Laura Udall introduced the ZUCA, she could have focused on the features of the product and listed its points of differentiation as follows: (1) is pulled like a suitcase rather than worn on the back, (2) includes a sturdy aluminum frame, and (3) is available in six colors. While features are nice, they typically don't entice someone to buy a product. A better approach for Udall would have been to focus on the benefits of the product: (1) relieves back pain by putting backpacks on rollers, (2) is sturdy enough for either an adult or child to sit on, and (3) strikes the ideal balance between functionality and "cool" for kids. This set of points focuses on benefits. It tells parents how buying the product will enhance their son or daughter's life.

Target Market The identification of the target market in which the firm will compete is extremely important.[16] As explained in Chapter 3, a **target market** is a place within a larger market segment that represents a narrower group of customers with similar interests.[17] Most new businesses do not start by selling to broad markets. Instead, most start by identifying an emerging or underserved niche within a larger market.[18]

A firm's target market should be made explicit on the business model template. Her Campus's target market is active college females. Zynga's target market is online game enthusiasts. A target market can be based on any relevant variable, as long as it identifies for a firm the group of like-minded customers that it will try to appeal to. For example, Hayley Barna and Katia

Beauchamp, the founders of Birchbox, wrote the following about their company's target market:

> From the start, we've always said that our target market isn't a specific demographic, but instead a psychographic—we believe that Birchbox appeals to women of all ages and backgrounds as long as they are excited to try new things and learn through discovery.[19]

This type of awareness of a firm's intended market, and the people who are the most likely to respond positively to a firm's product or service, is helpful in building out all the elements of a firm's business model. For example, targeting women of all ages and backgrounds who are excited to try new things and learn through discovery requires a certain set of core competencies (we define core competencies in the next section). It requires identifying and hiring people who have the ability to build anticipation and can locate partners and suppliers that have exciting new products that appeal to all age groups. If Barna and Beauchamp had instead identified Birchbox's target market as females ages 16–31, and left the "try new things and learn through discovery" part out, a different set of core competencies may have been needed for Birchbox's overall business model to work. The same philosophy applies across the business model template. The target market a firm selects affects everything it does, from the key assets it acquires to the financing or funding it will need to the partnerships it forms.

Product/Market Scope The fourth element of core strategy is product/market scope. A company's **product/market scope** defines the products and markets on which it will concentrate. Most firms start narrow and pursue adjacent product and market opportunities as the company grows and becomes financially secure. As explained earlier, new firms typically do not have the resources to produce multiple products and pursue multiple markets simultaneously.

An example is Dropbox, the online data storage company profiled in Case 2.1. When Dropbox was pitching its business idea, a challenge it had was that it was solving a problem that most people didn't know they had. There were ways for people to transfer files from one device to another, such as USB memory sticks, e-mailing files to yourself, and so forth. Dropbox's solution was much more elegant. Its service allows users to create a special folder on each of their devices, and sync and store data across devices. Dropbox completely solved the problem of working on a file on one device, such as an office computer, and then not having it available on another device, such as a laptop at home. When Dropbox launched in 2008, it had a single product—its online data storage service. The initial market it pursued was tech-savvy people in the Silicon Valley. Since then, Dropbox's market has expanded to all computer and Internet users; the firm now has 200 million customers. But for the first five years of its existence, it stuck to its initial product, preferring to continually improve the quality of its online data storage service rather than developing new services. It wasn't until 2013 that Dropbox added a second product through the acquisition of Mailbox, an e-mail processing service for mobile devices. Recently, the firm announced a third product, Carousel, which will be a digital gallery that will allow users to share their entire life's memories. So in terms of product/market scope, Dropbox has progressed as follows:

- Launch—Single product/Silicon Valley tech-savvy users
- 1-2 years into existence—Single product/Growing number of Silicon Valley tech-savvy users and people they told about the service
- 3-4 years into existence—Single product/All computer and Internet users
- 5 years into existence—Two products/All computer and Internet users
- 6 years into existence—Three products/All computer and Internet users

This example illustrates a well-thought-out and executed expansion of product/market scope.

In completing the Barringer/Ireland Business Model Template, a company should be very clear about its initial product/market scope and project 3-5 years in the future in terms of anticipated expansion. A bullet-point format, as shown for Dropbox above, is acceptable. Similar to all aspects of a company's business model, its product/market scope will affect other elements of the model.

Resources

The second component of a business model is resources. **Resources** are the inputs a firm uses to produce, sell, distribute, and service a product or service.[20] At a basic level, a firm must have a sufficient amount of resources to enable its business model to work.[21] For example, a firm may need a patent (i.e., a key asset) to protect its basis of differentiation. Similarly, a business may need expertise in certain areas (i.e., core competencies) to understand the needs of its target market. At a deeper level a firm's most important resources, both tangible and intangible, must be both difficult to imitate and hard to find a substitute for in order for the company's business model to be competitive over the long term. A tangible resource that fits this criterion is Her Campus's network of 4,000-plus volunteers. As mentioned earlier, it would take a tremendous effort for a competitor to amass a similar number of volunteers. In addition, there is no practical substitute for the work that 4,000-plus volunteers can do. An example of an intangible resource that fits the criterion is Zappos's reputation for customer service. Zappos is consistently viewed very favorably for its ability to deliver a high level of customer service that is both difficult to imitate and hard to find a substitute for.

Resources are developed and accumulated over a period of time.[22] As a result, when completing the Barringer/Ireland Business Plan Template, the current resources a company possesses should be the resources that are noted, but aspirational resources should be kept in mind. For example, it took time for Her Campus to recruit 4,000-plus volunteers. The company may have had 100 volunteers if and when it completed its first business model template. As a result, the proper notation under the Key Assets portion of the Barringer/Ireland Business Model Template would have been "100 volunteers" (with the goal of adding 100 volunteers a month) or whatever the exact number might have been.

Core Competencies A **core competency** is a specific factor or capability that supports a firm's business model and sets it apart from its rivals.[23] A core competency can take on various forms, such as technical know-how, an efficient process, a trusting relationship with customers, expertise in product design, and so forth. It may also include factors such as passion for a business idea and a high level of employee morale. A firm's core competencies largely determine what it can do. For example, many firms that sell physical products do not do their own manufacturing because manufacturing is not a core competency. Instead, their core competencies may be in areas such as product design and marketing. The key idea is that to be competitive a business must be particularly good at certain things, and those certain things must be supportive of all elements of its business model. For example, Netflix is particularly good at supply chain management, which was essential during the years that Netflix's business model was geared primarily towards delivering DVDs to customers via the mail. Without a core competency in supply chain management, Netflix's entire business model would not have worked.

Most start-ups will list two to three core competencies on the business model template. Consistent with the information provided above, a core competency is compelling if it not only supports a firm's initiatives, but is also difficult

Start-ups vary in terms of their core competencies. Here, two members of a start-up team are designing a new product. The startup's core competency is product design.

Monkey Business Images/Shutterstock

to imitate and substitute. Few start-ups have core competencies in more than two to three areas. For example, Her Campus has three core competencies:

■ Creating content of interest to active college-aged females
■ Recruiting and managing a volunteer network
■ Connecting active college-aged females with major brands

Similar to the Netflix and supply chain management example, Her Campus's entire business model would be untenable absent these three core competencies. In Her Campus's case, an added advantage is that its core competencies are, at varying levels, difficult to imitate and hard to find substitutes for.

Key Assets **Key assets** are the assets that a firm owns that enable its business model to work.[24] The assets can be physical, financial, intellectual, or human. Physical assets include physical space, equipment, vehicles, and distribution networks. Intellectual assets include resources such as patents, trademarks, copyrights, and trade secrets, along with a company's brand and its reputation. Financial assets include cash, lines of credit, and commitments from investors. Human assets include a company's founder or founders, its key employees, and its advisors.

Firms vary regarding the key assets they prioritize and accumulate. All companies require financial assets to varying degrees. Retailers such as Whole Foods Markets and Amazon rely heavily on physical assets—Whole Foods because of its stores and Amazon because of its warehouses and distribution network. Companies such as Uber rely almost exclusively on intellectual assets. Uber does not employ the drivers that provide its customers rides or own the cars they ride in. It simply provides a technology-based platform that connects people wanting rides with people willing to provide them. As a result, Uber's key assets are an app, its brand, and the relationships it has with its customers, drivers, and the communities in which it operates. Many companies rely heavily on human assets. The success of Zynga's business model, for example, relies heavily on its ability to attract and retain a group of game producers and programmers who are creative enough and proficient enough to continually come up with online games that are engaging and social.

Obviously, different key resources are needed depending on the business model that a firm conceives. In filling out the Barringer/Ireland Business Model Template, a firm should list the three to four key assets that it possesses that support its business model as a whole. In some cases, the ongoing success of a firm's business model hinges largely on a single key resource. For example, Zynga has historically maintained an agreement with Facebook that provided Zynga a privileged position on Facebook's platform. In 2013, that agreement came to end, which weakened Zynga's business model and dimmed its future prospects.

Financials

The third component of a business model focuses on its financials. This is the only section of a firm's business model that describes how it earns money—thus, it is extremely important. For most businesses, the manner in which it makes money is one of the most fundamental aspects around which its business model is built.[25] The primary aspects of financials are: revenue streams, cost structure, and financing/funding.

Revenue Streams A firm's **revenue streams** describe the ways in which it makes money.[26] Some businesses have a single revenue stream, while others have several. For example, most restaurants have a single revenue stream. Their customers order a meal and pay for it when they're finished eating. Other restaurants have several revenue streams. They may operate a restaurant, offer a catering service, and sell products at their counter, such as bottled barbeque sauce in the case of a barbeque restaurant. The nature of the way businesses make money also varies. Some businesses make money via one-time customer payments, while others receive recurring revenue by selling a subscription service. Some businesses are very creative in the ways in which they make money. For example, many providers of online games offer the basic game for free, and generate most of their revenue from a small number of users who purchase premium products such as time-saving shortcuts, special weapons, and other features to enhance play.

The most common revenue streams are shown in Table 4.3. As noted above, many businesses have more than one revenue stream, primarily to leverage the value they are creating for their customers. For example, Birchbox has two revenue streams—its subscription service and its online store. For $10 a month, its subscribers receive four to five product samples. If a customer wants to buy a full-sized version of one of the samples, it is available via Birchbox's online store. For Birchbox, having two revenue streams makes perfect sense. The product samples introduce subscribers to products that they might not have known about otherwise. If a subscriber likes a particular product and wants a full-sized version, it is available via Birchbox's website. The arrangement is good for the subscriber and is good for Birchbox. It provides the subscriber a convenient way to buy a product that he or she just sampled, and provides Birchbox dual revenue streams.

The number and nature of a business's revenue streams has a direct impact on the other elements of its business model. All for-profit businesses need at least one revenue stream to fund their operations. Whether additional revenue streams add or subtract value depends on the nature of the business and the other elements of its business model. It makes sense for Birchbox to have two revenue streams, as explained above. It also makes sense for a retail store, such as a bicycle shop, to not only sell bicycles (Revenue Stream #1), but to sell bicycle accessories (Revenue Stream #2), offer bicycle repair services (Revenue

TABLE 4.3 Most Common Revenue Streams

Revenue Stream	Description
Advertising	Revenue generated from advertising a particular product or service in a newspaper, magazine, website, or in some other manner.
Commissions	Revenue generated by bringing two parties together to complete a sale. Etsy and eBay generate revenue in this manner. The money usually comes from taking a small percentage of the sale price.
Download Fee	Revenue generated by allowing a user to download a digital product, such as a smartphone app, an e-book, or a software product.
Licensing	Revenue generated from charging for the use of a protected intellectual property, such as a software product.
Matchmaking	Revenue generated by matching someone who wants temporary access to an asset or competency with someone who owns an asset or has a competency and is willing to make it available. This is how peer-to-peer networks work. Examples include Airbnb, TaskRabbit, and Uber.
Product Sale	Selling a physical good—such as a product in a retail store or on a website.
Renting/Leasing	Revenue generated by renting or leasing an asset such as a rental car, a copy machine, or a piece of specialized machinery.
Service Sale	Selling a service—such as a meal in a restaurant or a car repair.
Subscription Service	Selling a subscription—such as Netflix for DVDs or streaming of content, or Birchbox for lifestyle samples.

Stream #3), and sponsor local bicycle races (Revenue Stream #4). In contrast, the seller of a smartphone app may charge a one-time download fee (Revenue Stream #1) and offer product upgrades (Revenue Stream #2). But the seller may stop short of selling online advertising (Potential Revenue Stream #3), fearing that online advertising would detract from the experience of playing the game and lead to poorer user reviews and ultimately fewer downloads.

In filling out the Barringer/Ireland Business Model Template, you should clearly identify your revenue streams. Placing them in bullet-point format is preferable.

Cost Structure A business's **cost structure** describes the most important costs incurred to support its business model.[27] It costs money to establish a basis of differentiation, develop core competencies, acquire or develop key assets, form partnerships, and so on. Generally, the goal for this box in a firm's business model template is threefold: identify whether the business is a cost-driven or value-driven business, identify the nature of the business's costs, and identify the business's major cost categories.

Initially, it is important to determine the role of costs in a business. Businesses can be categorized as cost-driven or value-driven. Cost-driven businesses focus on minimizing costs wherever possible. An example is Warby Parker, the subject of Case 5.2. Warby Parker sells prescription glasses for $95, which is well below the price charged by stores like Pearle Vision and LensCrafters. To do this, Warby Parker's entire business model is based on cost containment. Its glasses are designed in-house, manufactured overseas, and sold via the Web, eliminating many of the costs associated with traditional glasses manufacturing and retailing. Instead of concentrating on driving costs lower and lower relative to rivals' cost structures, value-driven business models focus on offering a high-quality product (or experience) and personalized service. Optometrists routinely sell prescription glasses in the $400 to $500 price range.

The additional value they provide is a wide selection, personalized service selecting and fitting the glasses, and free follow-on services if the glasses need to be adjusted or repaired.

Next, it's important to identify the nature of a business's costs. Most businesses have a mainly fixed-cost or variable-cost structure. **Fixed costs** are costs that remain the same despite the volume of goods or services provided. **Variable costs** vary proportionally with the volume of goods or services produced. The reason that it's important to know this is that it impacts the other elements of a firm's business model. Developing smartphone apps, for example, involves large fixed costs (i.e., the coding and development of the app) and small variable costs (i.e., the incremental costs associated with each additional app that is sold). As a result, a large amount of money will be needed up front, to fund the initial development, but not so much downstream, to fund the ongoing sales of the app. In contrast, a business such as a sub sandwich shop may have low fixed costs and high variable costs. The initial cost to set up the business may be modest, particularly if it is located in a leased facility, but the cost of labor and ingredients needed to prepare and serve the sandwiches may be high relative to the prices charged. This type of business may need a smaller up-front investment but may require a line of credit to fund its ongoing operations. Other elements of the business model may also be affected. For example, a business with substantial fixed costs, such as an airline, has typically made a major investment in key assets. A service-based company may have few key assets but may have core competencies and a partnership network that allows it to source raw materials, prepare products, and reliably deliver the finished products to its customers.

The third element of cost structure is to identify the business's major cost categories. At the business model stage, it is not necessary to establish a budget or prepare pro-forma financial projections. It is necessary, however, to have a sense of a firm's major categories of costs. For example, Facebook's major categories of costs are data center costs, marketing and sales, research and development, and general and administrative. This type of breakdown helps a business understand where its major costs will be incurred. It will also provide anyone looking at the business model template a sense of the major cost items that a company's business model relies on.

Financing/Funding   Finally, many business models rely on a certain amount of financing or funding to bring their business model to life. For example, Birchbox's business model may have looked elegant on paper, but the firm needed an infusion of investment dollars to get up and running. Most businesses incur costs prior to the time they generate revenue. Think of a business such as SuperJam, the subject of the opening feature in Chapter 1. Prior to earning revenue the company had to design its product, arrange for manufacturing, purchase inventory, acquire customers, and ship its product to its customers. This sequence, which is common, typically necessitates an infusion of up-front capital for the business to be feasible. Absent the capital, the entire business model is untenable.

Some entrepreneurs are able to draw from personal resources to fund their business. In other cases, the business may be simple enough that it is funded from its own profits from day one. In many cases, however, an initial infusion of funding or financing is required, as described above. In these cases, the business model template should indicate the approximate amount of funding that will be needed and where the money is most likely to come from.

Similar to cost structure, at the business model stage projections do not need to be completed to determine the exact amount of money that is needed. An approximation is sufficient. There are three categories of costs to consider: capital costs, one-time expenses, and provisions for ramp-up expenses. In regard to capital costs, this category includes real estate, buildings, equipment, vehicles, furniture, fixtures, and similar capital purchases. These costs vary considerably depending on the business. A restaurant or retail store may have substantial capital costs, while a service business may have little or no capital costs. The second category includes one-time expenses such as legal expenses to launch the business, website design, procurement of initial inventory, and similar one-time expenses and fees. All businesses incur at least some of these expenses. Finally, a business must allow for ramp-up expenses. Many businesses require a ramp-up period in which they lose money until they are fully up to speed and reach profitability. For example, it usually takes a new fitness center several months to reach its membership goals and achieve profitability. It's important to have cash set aside to make it through this period.

Operations

The final quadrant in a firm's business model focuses on operations. **Operations** are both integral to a firm's overall business model and represent the day-to-day heartbeat of a firm. The primary elements of operations are: product (or service) production, channels, and key partners.

Product (or Service) Production This section focuses on how a firm's products and/or service are produced. If a firm sells physical products, the products can be manufactured or produced in-house, by a contract manufacturer, or via an outsource provider. This decision has a major impact on all aspects of a firm's business model. If it opts to produce in-house, it will need to develop core competencies in manufacturing and procure key assets related to the production process. It will also require substantial up-front investment. If a firm that produces a physical product opts to use a contract manufacturer or an outsource provider, then a critical aspect of its business model is its ability to locate a suitable contract manufacturer or outsource provider. This is not a trivial activity. It's often difficult to find a contract manufacturer or outsource provider that will take a chance on a start-up. As a result, in the Barringer/Ireland Business Model Template, it is not sufficient to complete this box by simply saying "Manufacturing will be completed by a contract manufacturer." The exact name of the manufacturer is not necessary, but a general sense of what part of the world the manufacturer is located in and the type of arrangement that will be forged with the manufacturer is needed.

If a firm is providing a service rather than a physical product, a brief description of how the service will be produced should be provided. For example, Rover.com, the subject of Case 2.2, is a service that matches people who need their dogs watched while they are out of town with individuals who are willing to watch and care for dogs. The business model template needs to briefly report how this works. The explanation does not need to be lengthy, but it needs to be substantive. For example, an acceptable description for Rover.com is as follows:

> Rover.com will connect dog owners and dog sitters via a website. The dog sitters will be screened to ensure a quality experience. Customer support will be provided 24/7 to troubleshoot any problems that occur. Pet insurance is provided that covers any medical bills that a dog has while in the care of a Rover.com sitter.

This brief statement provides a great deal of information about how Rover.com works and how the elements of its business model need to be configured. This is information that isn't provided in another box in the business model template.

Channels A company's **channels** describe how it delivers its product or service to its customers.[28] Businesses sell direct, through intermediaries, or through a combination of both.

Many businesses sell direct, through a storefront and/or online. For example, Warby Parker sells its eyewear via its website and in a small number of company-owned stores. It does not sell via intermediaries, such as distributors and wholesalers. In contrast, SuperJam sells direct, via its website, and also through supermarkets throughout the country. It utilizes distributors and wholesalers to get its bikes into stores. Some companies sell strictly through intermediaries. For example, some of the manufacturers that sell via Zappos and Amazon do not maintain a storefront or sell via a website of their own. They strictly rely on broadly trafficked sites such as Zappos and Amazon to sell their products.

The same holds true for firms that sell services. Hotels, for example, sell their services (typically rooms) directly through their websites and telephone reservation services, and also through intermediaries such as travel agents, tour operators, airlines, and so forth. For example, if you were planning a trip to San Francisco, you could book your flight, rental car, and hotel through Travelocity, Expedia, or many other similar services. In this instance, Travelocity and the others act as intermediaries for the service providers.

A firm's selection of channels affects other aspects of its business model. Warby Parker maintains a simple channels strategy, selling strictly through its website and a small number of company-owned stores. Its price point is low enough that it must capture 100 percent of its margins for itself for its business model to work. In contrast, GoPro sells its cameras through its website, via online outlets such as Amazon and BestBuy.com, and through hundreds of retail stores in the United States and abroad. It utilizes intermediaries, such as wholesalers and distributors, to help it find new outlets. GoPro has a value-driven cost structure, so it can afford to share some of its margins with channel partners. The advantage of GoPro's approach is wide dissemination of its products both online and in retail outlets.

Some firms employ a sales force that calls on potential customers to try to close sales. This is an expensive strategy but necessary in some instances. For example, if a firm is selling a new piece of medical equipment that needs to be demonstrated to be sold, fielding a sales force may be the only realistic option.

Key Partners The final element of a firm's business model is key partners. Start-ups, in particular, typically do not have sufficient resources (or funding) to perform all the tasks needed to make their business models work, so they rely on partners to perform key roles. In most cases, a business does not want to do everything itself because the majority of tasks needed to build a product or deliver a service are outside a business's core competencies or areas of expertise.

The first partnerships that many businesses forge are with suppliers. A **supplier** (or vendor) is a company that provides parts or services to another company. Almost all firms have suppliers who play vital roles in the functioning of their business models. Traditionally, firms maintained an arm's-length relationship with their suppliers and viewed them almost as adversaries. Producers needing a component part would negotiate with several suppliers to find the best price. Today, firms are moving away from this approach and are developing more cooperative relationships with suppliers. More and more, managers are focusing on supply chain management, which is the coordination of the flow of all information, money, and material that moves through a product's supply chain. The more efficiently an organization can manage its supply chain, the more effectively its entire business model will work.

Along with suppliers, firms partner with other companies to make their business models work. The most common types of relationships, which include strategic alliances and joint ventures, are shown in Table 4.4. The advantages of participating in partnerships include: gaining access to a particular resource, risk and cost sharing, speed to market, and learning.[29] An example is a partnership between Zynga, the online games company, and Hasbro, a long-time maker of board games. In 2012, the two companies formed a partnership, which resulted in the production of Zynga-themed adaptations of classic Hasbro games. Hasbro now makes a board game called FarmVille Hungry Hungry Herd, which is an adaptation of Zynga's popular FarmVille online game. The partnership is good for both Zynga and Hasbro. It provides Zynga a new source of revenue and entry into a new industry, board games, and it provides Hasbro a fresh new game to sell to its customers.[30] Partnerships also have potential disadvantages.[31] The disadvantages include loss of proprietary information, management complexities, and partial loss of decision autonomy.[32]

When completing the Barringer/Ireland Business Model Template, you should identify your primary supplier partnerships and other partnerships. Normally, a start-up begins with a fairly small number of partnerships, which grows over time.

One trend in partnering, utilized by all types of businesses, is to use freelancers to do jobs that are outside their core competencies. A freelancer is an independent contractor that has skills in a certain area, such as software development or website design. There are several Web platforms that are making it increasingly easy to identify and find qualified freelancers. These platforms are highlighted in the Partnering for Success boxed feature.

TABLE 4.4 The Most Common Types of Business Partnerships

Partnership Form	Description
Joint venture	An entity created by two or more firms pooling a portion of their resources to create a separate, jointly-owned organization
Network	A hub-and-wheel configuration with a local firm at the hub organizing the interdependencies of a complex array of firms
Consortia	A group of organizations with similar needs that band together to create a new entity to address those needs
Strategic alliance	An arrangement between two or more firms that establishes an exchange relationship but has no joint ownership involved
Trade associations	Organizations (typically nonprofit) that are formed by firms in the same industry to collect and disseminate trade information, offer legal and technical advice, furnish industry-related training, and provide a platform for collective lobbying

Source: B. Barringer and J. S. Harrison, "Walking a Tightrope: Creating Value Through Interorganizational Relationships," *Journal of Management* 26, no. 3 (2000): 367–403.

PARTNERING FOR SUCCESS

Odesk, Elance, and Guru: Platforms That Facilitate the Forming of Partnerships with Freelancers

Odesk: Web: www.odesk.com; Facebook: oDesk; Twitter @oDesk
Elance: Web: www.elance.com; Facebook: Elance; Twitter: @Elance
Guru: Web: www.guru.com; Facebook: Guru.com; Twitter: @Guru_com

A freelancer is an independent contractor that has skills in a certain area, such as website design, search engine optimization (SEO), or marketing. Start-ups hire freelancers for two reasons. First, they fill gaps that companies have in their expertise. For example, a business may need to develop a social media strategy, but lack capabilities in that area. There are freelancers who are social media specialists, who can quickly and effectively help a business design a social media strategy. Second, freelancers can be hired on an "as needed" basis, so they are typically cheaper than hiring a part-time employee. In addition, if a business hires a freelancer for a project and it doesn't work out, a decision can be made to not hire the same person again. It is more difficult to separate from a part-time or full-time employee.

There are a growing number of Web-based platforms that make it easy to identify and hire experienced freelancers. Odesk (www.odesk.com), Elance (www.elance.com), and Guru (www.guru.com) are popular examples. The platforms are services that allow freelancers to identify themselves and allow anyone needing a freelancer to browse through the listings to find a good fit. For example, Guru lists freelancers by category, which includes IT & Programming, Design & Multimedia, Writing and Translation, Sales & Marketing, and several others. The freelancers post their photo, an explanation of their expertise, an overview of their experience and job history, their hourly rate, and a portfolio of their work. Elance posts statistics that reflect the freelancers' ratings from previous jobs, the number of jobs that have been obtained through Elance, and comments from previous clients. For example, at the time this feature was written a freelancer named Chris S. had completed five jobs through Elance with a perfect five-star rating from clients. One of his clients wrote, "Chris did again a great job on a PHP/WordPress type project. Great communication and turn around as usual." This type of feedback provides future clients assurance that Chris might be worth a try for a similar project. Chris charges $46 per hour. While that number may seem high, if Chris is a proficient programmer and designer, and turns around work on time, he may be well worth it. He'll also only charge for the number of hours it takes him to complete a job.

Over time, companies often become comfortable with individual freelancers, and the relationship becomes more of a partnership than an arms-length arrangement. The platforms make money by taking a percentage of the money that the freelancers are paid. The amounts vary—Odesk takes 10 percent, while Elance charges 8.75 percent. There are protections built into the services to prevent freelancers from taking money and not completing a job. Sites such as Elance and Guru, which initially focused on IT freelancers, have expanded their offerings. Companies can now find qualified freelancers to reliably plug almost any skill gap that they have.

Questions for Critical Thinking

1. Imagine that you are the founder of a company and need help setting up QuickBooks for your company. QuickBooks is an accounting and bookkeeping platform for small businesses. Search Guru, Elance, and Odesk for QuickBooks freelancers. Select the one that you think represents the best combination of expertise, experience, and cost. Summarize the key attributes of the person you selected.
2. To what degree is it appropriate or inappropriate to hire freelancers to fulfill some of the core competencies of a business?
3. Make a bullet-point list of the advantages of hiring freelancers to do short-term projects for a start-up.
4. In what ways do you believe that a freelancer could become a partner of a company rather than an arms-length independent contractor?

Chapter Summary

LO1. A business model is a firm's recipe for how it intends to create, deliver, and capture value for stakeholders. In essence, a business model deals with the core aspects of how a firm will conduct business and try to succeed in the marketplace. The quality of the business model a firm develops, as well as the quality of how that model is executed, affect the firm's performance in both the short and long term. How well the different parts or elements of a business model fit together and are mutually supportive affects its quality. The best business models are developed and executed in ways that are difficult for competitors to understand and imitate. Moreover, the greater the difference between a firm's business model and those of its competitors, and assuming that the model has been effectively developed, the stronger the likelihood a firm will be competitively successful. Thus, an entrepreneurial firm wants to develop a business model that clearly specifies how the firm intends to be uniquely different from its competitors and create value for stakeholders as a result.

LO2. There are several types of business models. However, it is important for an entrepreneur to understand that no particular type of business model is inherently superior to any other model. The "best" business model is the one that allows a firm to effectively describe the value it intends to create for stakeholders and appropriately details the actions it will take to create that value. Standard and disruptive business models are two well recognized categories of business models. We say "categories" because there are several types of standard models (see Table 4.1) and two types of disruptive models (discussed below). Standard business models depict or reveal plans or recipes firms can use to determine how they will create, deliver, and capture value for stakeholders. Many of the standard models have been in existence for many years. When selecting a standard business model, an entrepreneurial venture believes that it can integrate the elements of that model uniquely as a means of creating value while competing against rivals. Disruptive business models, which are rare, are ones that do not fit the profile of a standard business model and are impactful enough that they disrupt or change the way business is conducted in an industry or in an important segment or niche of an industry. A new market disruption and a low-end market disruption are the two types of disruptive models. A new market disruption finds a firm using a business model through which it is able to address a market that wasn't previously served (think of Google as an example). A low-end market disruption is possible when firms already competing in an industry are providing customers with products or services that exceed their expectations or desires. This "performance oversupply" creates an opportunity for an entrepreneurial venture to enter an industry for the purpose of providing customers with the product or service functionality that more closely approximates what they want. Low-cost business models are often used to create a low-end market disruption (think of Southwest Airlines in the United States and Ryanair in Europe as examples).

LO3. Comprehensive in scope, the Barringer/Ireland Business Model Template features 4 major categories and 12 individual parts (see Figure 4.2). As a tool, entrepreneurs can use this business model template to describe, project, revise, and pivot its intended actions until they are convinced that the model's elements are integrated in a way that will yield an exciting and viable business firm. Core strategy, which describes how the firm plans to compete relative to rivals, is the first of the four major categories. The firm's mission, basis of differentiation, target market, and product/market scope are the parts of the core strategy category. Resources, the second category, are the inputs a firm intends to use to sell, distribute, and service its product or service. Core competency, which is a specific factor or capability that supports a firm's business model and differentiates it from competitors and key assets, or the assets a firm owns that enable its business model to work, are the critical resources a firm needs to execute as called for by its chosen core strategy. The third category, financials, is concerned with how the firm intends to earn money. Revenue streams, which deal with the exact ways a firm earns revenue, cost structure, which includes the most important costs (both fixed and variable costs) the firm will incur to support the execution of its business model, and funding/financing (dealing with how the firm will support or cover its costs) are the parts of the financials category. Operations is the fourth and final category featured in the Barringer/Ireland Business Model Template. The product (or service) production part of this category details the firm's intended production methods. The channels part specifies how products or services will be delivered to customers, while the key partners part identifies others with whom the firm intends to collaborate as a means of supporting its operations.

Key Terms

basis of differentiation, **144**
business model, **134**
channels, **152**
churn, **137**
core competency, **146**
core strategy, **142**
cost structure, **149**

disruptive business models, **140**
fixed costs, **150**
key assets, **147**
low-end market disruption, **140**
mission or mission statement, **143**
new market disruption, **140**

operations, **151**
product/market scope, **145**
resources, **146**
revenue streams, **148**
standard business models, **137**
supplier, **152**
target market, **144**
variable costs, **150**

Review Questions

4-1. What is a business model?
4-2. How does a freemium business model work?
4-3. What is the best time for a firm to develop its business model?
4-4. What is a standard business model and what is a disruptive business model?
4-5. What are the four major categories that comprise the Barringer/Ireland Business Template?
4-6. How are a firm's core strategy and its mission related to each other as parts of a business template?
4-7. What is the difference between a new market disruption and a low-end market disruption?
4-8. Why do most entrepreneurial firms initially choose to compete within a narrow target market?
4-9. What is a "churn" and how does it affect a firm?
4-10. Why are the resources a firm possesses a critical part of its business model?

4-11. What is a core competency?
4-12. How many core competencies do most start-ups have?
4-13. What is a business's cost structure?
4-14. What are the differences between a firm's physical assets and its intellectual assets?
4-15. What is a revenue stream and why is it so important to a firm's short- and long-term success?
4-16. What are the most common revenue streams for certain business firms?
4-17. What are the primary elements of the Operations component of the Barringer/Ireland Business Model Template?
4-18. Who are "key partners" and why are they important to the success of an entrepreneurial venture?
4-19. What are the different ways a firm may choose to deliver its product or service to its customers?
4-20. Who are "freelancers" and why are these individuals potentially attractive as partners for an entrepreneurial venture?

Application Questions

4-21. Hans Bliss knows that he needs to establish partnerships with other companies to ensure that his business model works. Unfortunately, apart from his supplier, he is not sure of the types of alliances on which he may gain assistance in future. What are the types of partnerships that Hans can consider for future needs?

4-22. Sean Johansen is looking to establish a fast food outlet that serves healthy organic food. His outlet aims to be an ideal place for all weight-watchers and calorie-counters. Advise him on how to prepare a business model, and explain to him why a good business model would benefit his outlet.

4-23. Core competency is a specific factor or capability that supports a firm's business model and sets it apart from its rivals. Walk around your neighborhood. Choose three different restaurants located in your neighborhood and visit them. Prepare a list of core competencies that each of the restaurant may have that makes them different from their competitors.

4-24. Twitter (http://twitter.com) is a free networking and micro-blogging service that allows its users to send and read other users' updates, called "tweets." Although Twitter has millions of users and is growing rapidly, the firm has been criticized for not having a viable long-term business model. Spend some time studying how Twitter does business. How does the company earn money? Does it or does it not have a business model with long-term potential?

4-25. Debra McGahan, a close friend of yours, mentioned to you that to complete a project in one of the courses she is taking this semester, she needs to describe a firm that is using an effective business model. Your immediate response is to recall that you just read this chapter and learned about Quirky's successful business model while reading this chapter's Savvy Entrepreneurial firm feature. Describe Quirky's business model to Debra for the purpose of explaining to her how this particular model allows Quirky to create value for the firm's stakeholders.

4-26. Resources and core competencies are both important parts of the Barringer/Ireland Business Model Template. What are the differences between resources and core competencies and why must an entrepreneurial firm have both resources and core competencies in order to develop an effective business model?

4-27. What are some examples of instances in which location is an important part of a firm's business model?

4-28. What are the basic resources needed by Steven Gerald, who plans to start a 24-hour laundry mart? Create a list of the necessary resources to assist Steven.

4-29. Basis of differentiation is part of the Barringer/Ireland Business Model Template. This term was defined in the chapter as "what causes consumers to pick one company's products over another's." What is Apple's basis of differentiation?

YOU BE THE VC 4.1 COMPANY: Secret Recipe Cakes and Café

• Web: www.secretrecipe.com.my • Facebook: Secret Recipe Malaysia • Twitter: @SecretRecipe_My

Business Idea: A café chain that integrates both local and international flavors for food enthusiasts all over the world.

Pitch: Secret Recipe Cakes and Café is no stranger to food enthusiasts, particularly in Malaysia. It has become a household name since its first establishment in 1997. With quality cakes, fusion food, and distinctive service as its core strategy, Secret Recipe has already developed a winning recipe for success. It is one of the leading and largest café chains in the country with more than 150 outlets in Malaysia serving a variety of dishes and desserts that appeal to a wide range of customers. Serving more than 20 types of fusion food, 40 different types of cake creations, and an assortment of pastries, designer ice creams, and beverages, Secret Recipe has won the hearts of many Malaysians and has successfully established its brand name in the region.

The Secret Recipe business formula has also been successfully replicated internationally with more outlets located in Thailand, Singapore, Indonesia, the Philippines, China, Pakistan, and Brunei. In 14 years, Secret Recipe has expanded to a network of more than 250 cafés.

Building a sustainable business with a strong brand was not an easy task for Secret Recipe. To be different, it had to identify features of its brand that could extend beyond one store or one country. Differentiation, innovation, adaptability, research and development, consistency, identity, and brand promise were the key ingredients that have allowed Secret Recipe to enjoy worldwide success. Secret Recipe is one of the most successful home-grown café chains in the country, having won several awards, including the Homegrown Franchise of the Year, International Franchisor of the Year, Franchise of the Year Best Sales Growth Award, and Best Brand Food & Beverage Café Award. Moreover, Secret Recipe has also grabbed several international awards, such as the Best Casual Dining Restaurant of the Year 2007/2008 in the Philippines, and Philippine Tatler's Best Restaurant 2008. More recently Secret Recipe won the 2013 Putra Brand Award, which included the Most Enterprising Brand of the Year and the Silver Award in the category of retail food and beverage.

Secret Recipe is not only a café that offers a wide variety of cakes but it also offers a flexible menu with different items available in different countries. However, to identify itself as a truly Malaysian brand, a customer will be able to find Malaysian all-time favorites like *nasi lemak* (rice with spicy gravy) and *mee goreng* (fried noodles) in some of the overseas outlets as well. Secret Recipe will continue striving to surpass its own accomplishments and aims to be recognized as a leader in the industry both locally and globally.

4-30. Based on the material covered in this chapter, what questions would you ask the firm's founders before making your funding decision? What answers would satisfy you?

4-31. If you had to make your decision on just the information provided in the pitch and on the company's website, would you fund this company? Why or why not?

YOU BE THE VC 4.2 COMPANY: Mango Health

• Web: www.mangohealth.com • Facebook: Mango Health • Twitter: @MangoHealth

Business Idea: Create a smartphone app that reminds people to take medicine and nutritional supplements on time, warns users of potentially dangerous interactions, and uses gaming techniques to motivate people to remain engaged with the app and meet their personal health goals.

Pitch: One of the toughest issues facing American health care providers is motivating patients to take their medication on time. While 80 percent of adults in America take a combination of prescription drugs, over-the-counter medications, and nutritional supplements, 75 percent do not take their medications or supplements on time. Failure to take medication on time increases health care costs and exacts a significant human toll. It's associated with increased physician visits, increased hospitalizations, increased nursing home admissions, and increases in avoidable health care costs. Some experts have estimated that nationwide, not taking medicine on time costs the United States health care system $300 billion per year.

Mango Health is a smartphone app designed to tackle this problem. After downloading the app, a user simply enters the medications and supplements s/he is taking, pertinent information such as patient name, type of medication (tablets, syrup, etc.), how much is in the container, and how often the medicine and/or supplements are to be taken. There are several additional core features. The app will tell users if any potentially dangerous interactions exist among the drugs, supplements, and food and beverage products they are consuming. The app also allows users to maintain a health journal, where they can keep a log of their personal health activity and compare themselves to others taking the same medications or who have similar conditions. The app sends users a reminder when it's time to take a medication. When the reminder goes off, the user is not allowed to ignore it. The app most be opened and the user must verify that "I took it" or additional reminders will be sent.

An attribute that separates Mango Health from similar apps is its gamification aspects. Each time a user takes a medicine or supplement on time, he or she earns points. There are eight different levels that can be achieved, depending on the number of points a user accumulates. Each level is associated with a prize, such as a gift card to Whole Foods, Gap, or Target, or a donation to the user's favorite charity. The rewards are used to incentivize people to keep taking their medications and supplements on time. The brands that offer the rewards benefit by bringing people into their stores that care about health and wellness.

Mango Health plans to create a range of consumer health apps, all of which will include some form of gamification incentives.

4-32. Based on the material covered in this chapter, what questions would you ask the firm's founders before making your funding decision? What answers would satisfy you?

4-33. If you had to make your decision on just the information provided in the pitch and on the company's website, would you fund this company? Why or why not?

CASE 4.1

Etsy: Breaking Down a Business Model
• *Web: www.etsy.com* • *Facebook: Etsy* • *Twitter: @Etsy*

Introduction

Etsy is an e-commerce website that focuses on handmade or vintage items, as well as unique factory-manufactured products. These items cover a wide range of product types, including jewelry, furniture, housewares, kitchen gadgets, clothing, and art. The site resembles an open craft fair, where sellers (mostly small merchants and local artisans) set up Etsy stores and sell their products to buyers, who are people that want unique, mostly handmade products from small/local producers. Etsy launched in 2005. As of late 2013, 30 million buyers and nearly one million sellers were registered on the Etsy website.

History

The idea for Etsy originated in a woodworking shop. Rob Kalin, who earned a college degree in the classics, bypassed the traditional job market to focus on his woodworking talents. He created a unique product, a computer encased in wood, but couldn't find a marketplace to sell it. So he, along with Chris Maguire, Jared Tarbell, and Haim Schoppik, launched Etsy, an online marketplace for crafts where hobbyists and artisans could connect with people interested in buying handmade goods.

From the beginning, Etsy championed the idea of community. The company saw itself as an advocate of small merchants and artisans. It also took steps to engage its community and empower its sellers. Every Monday evening Etsy sponsored craft night, where 50 to 80 people came to its office in Brooklyn to make crafts. The company also sponsored employee craft nights where its employees would hone their craft-making talents. At the same time, Kalin started holding virtual town hall meetings with Etsy sellers to provide tips to them on how to increase their sales. All this was done in part to build community, but there was a broader purpose. Kalin and his team knew that Etsy's financial success hinged on how much commerce flowed through its site.

Since it launched in 2005, Etsy has grown steadily. It currently employs more than 400 people in the United States and abroad and facilitates transactions in nearly 200 countries. Etsy is still private, so it is not required to release financial data; but, the estimate is that approximately $1 billion worth of sales take place through Etsy's website each year.

How Etsy Works

To sell on Etsy, a seller registers and creates an online Etsy store. Creating a store is free. Each item in the store costs 20 cents to list. The prices in the store are determined by the seller. Etsy takes a 3.5 percent commission on each sale. An example of an Etsy store is AHeirloom, which can be seen at https://www.etsy.com/shop/AHeirloom. AHeirloom sells handmade wood items. One of its most popular items is kitchen cutting boards that come in the shape of states. At the time this case was written, AHeirloom had 209 items listed, ranging in price from $2 to $48. When a sale is made, AHeirloom collects the money and delivers the item to the buyer. Etsy bills AHeirloom and its others sellers once a month for its listing and commission fees.

To buy on Etsy, a customer can either use the search bar on Etsy's home page to search for an item or can browse through a list of categories that includes Art, Home & Living, Jewelry, Women, Men, Kids, Vintage, Weddings, and Craft Supplies. A select number of items

(continued)

Etsy's platform is designed to help people sell hand-made items. This photo contains a collection of headbands and other hair accessories made by an Etsy seller.

DreamBig/Shutterstock

are also featured each day on Etsy's home page. When a buyer enters an Etsy online store, he or she can read reviews from past buyers and see how the seller stacks up on a five-star scale. AHeirloom, for example, has over 3,600 reviews and nearly a perfect five-star rating.

Business Model Breakdown

At the heart of Etsy's success is its business model. A business model is a firm's plan or recipe for how it creates, delivers, and captures value for its stakeholders. The Barringer/Ireland Business Model Template, completed for what Etsy looks like today, is shown nearby. The following is a breakdown of each of the four major categories of Etsy's business model. What is particularly instructive is the way the model fits together. As you read through the description of each category, notice how it affects the other categories and Etsy's business model as a whole.

Core Strategy

Etsy's mission is ambitious. It wants to "re-imagine commerce in ways that build a more fulfilling and lasting world." To do this, Etsy has built its business around the neighborhood feel. Its focus is on constructing a way to shop that is meaningful to both sellers and buyers. To illustrate this point, Etsy CEO Chad Dickerson said, "Etsy, technologically and culturally, is a platform that provides meaning to people, and an opportunity to validate their art, their craft." To further articulate Etsy's core values Dickerson said, "At the end of each transaction you get something real from a real person. There is existential satisfaction to that." In addition to this set of values, Etsy is an advocate for small merchants and artisans. These are two categories of businesses that have been hurt by

mass production and the advent of the big-box store. Etsy is helping bring back these businesses by providing them a platform to sell their products to a sizeable audience of buyers.

Etsy's basis of differentiation flows from its mission to focus on handmade goods, the number of buyers and sellers on its site, and the sense of community that it has created. Although its website is easy to navigate, that's not what differentiates Etsy from its rivals. Many online businesses have websites that are easy to navigate. What differentiates Etsy are the factors mentioned above. It's instructive to note that Etsy's points of differentiation are made possible by its core competencies and key assets. From the beginning, Etsy has excelled at helping its sellers increase sales via Web-based tools, educational materials, and offline events. It also set its business up in a way that encourages its sellers to build awareness of Etsy in general. Each seller has its own Etsy store. As sellers promote their Etsy stores, they introduce people to Etsy more broadly, which is a key factor that has enabled Etsy to grow so quickly.

Etsy has two target markets—its sellers and its buyers. Its sellers are the producers of handmade goods. Its buyers are people drawn to the site because they want something unique, something that has a story. They want something that they enjoy telling other people about. It's a different motivation for buying than shopping at Walmart or on Amazon.com. This is what Etsy means by "re-imagining" commerce. Etsy's product/market scope has expanded since its inception. While the majority of items are still handmade, on October 1, 2013, Etsy announced that it would allow factory-made goods on its site. This move, according to the company, was necessary to allow its most successful sellers to expand their businesses and keep them from leaving

Core Strategy	
Business Mission	**Basis of Differentiation**
• Re-imagine commerce in ways that build a more fulfilling and lasting world	• Focus on handmade goods • Largest number of registered buyers and sellers of handmade goods in the world • Sense of community associated with its site
Target Customer(s)	**Product/Market scope**
• Buyers—A global clientele that wants unique, hand-made products from small/local producers • Sellers—Small merchants, home-based businesses and local artisans who want to sell their goods online	• Handmade goods • Manufactured goods that meet strict guidelines • Global audience of both buyers and sellers

Resources	
Core Competencies	**Key Assets**
• Developing and maintaining a vibrant community of buyers and sellers • Development of tools and educational materials to empower sellers • Generating word-of-mouth aware-ness of their business	• Intuitive and easy-to-navigate Web-based platform • Etsy's community of both buyers and sellers • Continual inflow of high-quality hand-made products • Is a Certified B Corporation

Financials	
Revenue Streams	
• Sales commissions—3.5% on each item sold via the Etsy website • 20 cent listing fee for each item listed • Showcase—Etsy's advertising program for its sellers	
Cost Structure	**Financing/Funding**
• Cost-driven business • High fixed/low variable costs • Major categories of costs: Web-based platform development; staff salaries and general administrative; seller education initiatives	• $97.3 million in angel and venture capital funding since the company founding in 2005 • Funding from operations

Operations	
Product (or service) Production	**Channels**
• Etsy's secure platform allows small merchants and artisans that have products to sell to connect with people interested in buying hand-made goods • Etsy's platform was built and is maintained by an in-house staff of IT professionals	• Esty website • Retail partners • Temporary holiday storefronts
	Key Partners
	• Third-party developers • Local organizations and businesses • Community and business alliances

Etsy: Barringer/Ireland Business Model Template

© 2014 Bruce R. Barringer and R. Duane Ireland

the site. There are restrictions. The seller must design the product, or hire someone to design it, and be open about where it is made. Some controversy was caused by this move, but Etsy's numbers continue to grow.

Resources

Etsy has three core competencies—the development of tools and educational materials to empower sellers, the growth of a vibrant community of buyers and sellers, and the ability to generate word-of-mouth awareness of its business. The first, which has been developed over time, includes tools and educational material to empower Etsy sellers. A key to Etsy's success has been a recognition that its sellers, which it affectionately calls Etsians, must be successful for the site to work. As a result, from the beginning Etsy has focused on developing tools, edu-cational materials, and offline events to assist its sellers. For example, each year Etsy sponsors an event called the Etsy Success Symposium, which is a physical and online gathering of Etsy sellers for the purpose of helping one another increase sales. Etsy produces a number of publications, including the Etsy Seller's Handbook and the Etsy Success Newsletter, both geared towards helping

Etsy newbies and veterans boost their clientele. Etsy Labs organizes community events for Etsy sellers, facilitates online workshops, and assembles Etsy teams, which are groups of sellers that organize around a particular loca-tion or craft. These efforts have enabled Etsy to build and maintain a vibrant community of buyers and sellers.

As mentioned earlier, Etsy's website is constructed in a way that has led to a core competency in generating word-of-mouth awareness of its business. As sellers promote their Etsy stores, they promote Etsy more broadly. Etsy has also been a leader in social media, including major pres-ences on both Facebook and Twitter. The combination of these factors has been instrumental in Etsy's growth.

In regard to key assets, Etsy's platform is intuitive and easy to navigate. Its community of buyers and sell-ers continues to grow. Its sellers populate its site with a continual influx of fresh new products, which keeps its buyers coming back. Etsy takes deliberate steps to add to its key assets in ways that support its mission and provide people another reason to engage in its site. For example, in early 2012 Etsy became a Certified B Corporation. B Corporations are a new type of company that uses the power of business to solve social and envi-ronmental problems.

(continued)

Financials

Etsy has three revenue streams, including a 20 cent listing fee for each item listed on its site, a 3.5 percent commission on each item sold, and Search Ads, an advertising program that allows Etsy sellers to promote items in their online stores. This mix of revenue streams makes sense given Etsy's core strategy and its resources. The larger and more engaged a community it builds, the more revenue it will earn from listing fees and commissions. Etsy's cost structure is based on cost containment and a high fixed/low variable cost model. Etsy has high infrastructure costs, driven by the network capacity and data storage necessary to service 30 million registered buyers and one million registered sellers, and the nearly one billion dollars of commerce that flows through its site each year. It also has a staff of 400 that manages the site and maintains the Etsy community. To support its core strategy, the firm has people with job titles that don't exist in most businesses, such as Head of Seller Education (currently Danielle Maveal). Etsy's variable costs are low. It costs Etsy very little to add another buyer or seller to its site.

Notable is the amount of funding that Etsy has raised—$97.3 million. The funding has been used to build out the company's infrastructure, add employees, invest in strategies for expansion, and fund seller education initiatives. Etsy is reported to be profitable. If this is the case, it is funding its operations in part through its own revenues.

Operations

Etsy's website was built and is maintained by an in-house staff of IT professionals. The site has a homespun rather than a highly polished look. This is intentional, although some critics have urged Etsy to up its game some in terms of site design and functionality. In terms of channels, Etsy's main channel is its website. As mentioned earlier, Etsy is strictly a platform that brings buyers and sellers together. While a seller's Etsy store resides on Etsy's website, all of the logistics involved with the sales process are handled by the seller. This includes stocking the store, processing orders, collecting payment, and shipping the merchandise. This arrangement relieves Etsy of the cost and responsibility of providing for those functions.

In terms of channels, the majority of sales flow through Etsy's website. Etsy is experimenting with some additional channels. It has partnered with select retail chains, such as West Elm and Nordstrom, to sell some Etsy products in its stores. It also has tried some special promotional events, such as setting up temporary physical storefronts in New York City during the Christmas season to feature products made by Etsy sellers.

Etsy has several key partners, or groups of partners, which improve its operations and help expand sales. In terms of operations, by publishing its API (Application Programming Interface), Etsy has enabled third-party developers to create tools that help Etsy sellers more efficiently manage their inventory and track their shipments. Etsy works with a number of organizations and businesses to support crafts and homemade products. An example is Etsy's involvement in New York's annual Renegade Craft Fair, which is an event that features and champions the work of artisans and small merchants. Etsy is also branching into areas that enable it to support small businesses and entrepreneurship in more general ways. For example, in 2013 Etsy announced plans to collaborate with local communities to teach entrepreneurship skills to residents. By doing this, Etsy is helping seed the next generation of Etsy sellers. All of these efforts are consistent with Etsy's mission of reimagining commerce and acquainting as many people as possible with Etsy and the marketplace it facilitates.

Challenges Ahead

Etsy's primary challenge will be to maintain the integrity of its business model while trying to grow. The complexity of this challenge is starting to show. Many Etsy sellers, for example, were not happy with the company's decision to allow the sale of manufactured goods. But providing this option has allowed some of Etsy's most successful sellers to effectively grow their businesses. A limitation of producing handmade goods is that it's labor intensive. When artisans make something that sells well (such as a piece of jewelry or furniture), if they can't offload some of the actual production of the good, their sales will be limited by the time they have to make it themselves. Sellers complain about rising fees, which may be an artifact of Etsy's need to produce sufficient profits to satisfy investors. Its initial listing fee was 10 cents per item, and it's now 20 cents. Some also complain about the lack of traditional marketing and would like to see Etsy take a more active role in driving traffic to its site. Recall that Etsy takes the opposite approach. It relies on its sellers to promote their Etsy stores, and benefits when the customers of individual sellers learn about Etsy more broadly.

Discussion Questions

4-34. What is Etsy's core strategy, or how the firm intends to compete in the marketplace?

4-35. What evidence can you provide to demonstrate that Etsy's founders, Rob Kalin, Chris Maguird, Jared Tarbell, and Haim Schoppik, developed a disruptive business model as the foundation for launching their firm?

4-36. In thinking about the firm's "basis of differentiation" as part of its business model, what does differentiate Etsy from its competitors?

4-37. What are Etsy's three core competencies and how do these help the firm in its efforts to be successful?

Sources: Etsy home page, available at www.etsy.com, accessed June 3, 2014; O. Malik, "Meet the Man Behind New York's Other Billion Dollar Internet Company. This One Makes Money," Gigaom, available at https://gigaom.com/2013/08/23/meet-the-man-behind-new-yorks-other-billion-dollar-internet-company-this-one-makes-money/, posted on August 23, 2013, accessed on June 3, 2014; "The 'Etsy Economy' and Changing the Way We Shop," *Entrepreneur,* March 22, 2013. "Etsy," Wikipedia, www.wikipedia.com, accessed June 4, 2014.

CASE 4.2

TOMS's One-for-One Business Model: Is it Sustainable for the Future?

• *Web: www.toms.com* • *Facebook: TOMS* • *Twitter: @TOMS*

Introduction

In 2005 Blake Mycoskie, a serial entrepreneur, needed a break. After starting 5 companies in 12 years, he traveled to Argentina looking for some time to relax. He met some expatriates who were doing social work in villages on the outskirts of Buenos Aires and asked if he could tag along. In one village in particular, he noticed that most of the children didn't have shoes. He stopped a few of the kids to look at their feet and saw cuts, abrasions, and infections. He knew the villagers were poor and couldn't afford to buy their children shoes and wondered what he could do to help. He also knew there was an inexpensive shoe in Argentina called the alpargata. What would be the best way to provide poor Argentinean children alpargata shoes?

Mycoskie thought about starting a charity but felt the charity model wouldn't work. He envisioned himself asking his family and friends for contributions, and knew they would contribute once, or twice, or maybe even several times. But it would be hard to continue to ask. What he needed was an approach that would sustain itself by selling a product that people needed to buy anyway. The approach Mycoskie came up with he later dubbed "one for one." He would create a for-profit business to sell alpargata shoes, and for every pair sold he'd donate a pair to a child in need.

Mycoskie returned to the United States and set up shop in Santa Monica, California. He started TOMS with no shoe industry experience. The company was originally called Shoes for Tomorrow but was quickly shortened to TOMS. To get started, Mycoskie went from one retail store to another with his unique business idea. A few Los Angeles boutiques agreed to sell the shoes. His first break came when the *Los Angeles Times* ran an article about his business. To Mycoskie's surprise, the article spurred $88,000 in orders in a single weekend.

Fast forward to today. TOMS is now an international brand. It's one for one model has been expanded to include shoes, eyewear, and coffee. As of mid-2014, TOMS had given away 10 million pairs of shoes in 60 countries, had helped restore sight for 200,000 people in 13 countries, and is providing clean water and sanitation to villagers in 5 countries. The one-to-one model has been tweaked some, but the intention is the same. TOMS still gives away a pair of shoes for ever pair it sells. Eyewear was added in 2011. Rather than donating a pair of glasses for every pair its sells, TOMS donates an equivalent amount of money that is used for sight-saving measures, such as eye surgery, medical treatment, or a new pair of prescription glasses. Coffee was added in 2014. For every bag of coffee that's sold, TOMS donates an equivalent amount of money to provide clean water and sanitation for people who need it the most.

TOMS's Business Model

TOMS is known for pioneering the one-to-one business model. A firm's business model is a plan or recipe for how it creates, captures, and delivers value to its stakeholders. TOMS's business model is unique in that it combines the goals of a for-profit company with the ambitions of a philanthropic organization. TOMS's business model template is shown nearby. The following is a brief overview of each of the major sections of the business model template.

Core Strategy

TOMS's mission is "One for One." The mission is made possible by the way TOMS is structured. TOMS has two parts. TOMS is a for-profit company that manages the overall operations and logistics. Friends of TOMS is a nonprofit organization that assembles volunteers, delivers the shoes, and coordinates the eyewear/site restoration and coffee/clean water initiatives.

An important decision Mycoskie and his team made early on, when TOMS was strictly a shoe company, was that the cost of providing shoes to children in need would be built into the shoes' selling price. The same approach now applies to eyewear and coffee. As a result, as long as TOMS sells its products, it can fulfill its philanthropic mission. It does not need to rely on donations, as most charities and nonprofits do, to sustain itself.

TOMS's strategy is built on selling practical products. Shoes, eyewear, and coffee are products that are sold widely. Its shoes are pricey ($54 to $80 for a pair of simple slip-ons), but people know that when they buy TOMS shoes they are paying for a pair that will be donated to a child in need. TOMS relies heavily on volunteers, interns, and partners to do much of its work. Many of the people who volunteer and work with TOMS are motivated by the company's mission, which changes lives. In some countries, shoes are required in order to attend school. Owning a pair of shoes provides a child a chance to be educated and to have a better life. TOMS is not reluctant to share these types of realities, which deeply resonate with volunteers and customers. TOMS has almost as many interns, for example, working in its facilities as employees. Friends of TOMS works with nonprofits and NGOs to distribute its products. It does this

(continued)

Core Strategy	
Business Mission	**Basis of Differentiation**
• "One for One"	• Strong brand • Business structure: TOMS (for profit) and its collaboration with Friends of TOMS (non profit subsidiary) • Products (shoes, eyewear, coffee) that resonate with consumers) • TOMS volunteers • Ability to change lives
Target Customer(s)	**Product/Market Scope**
• Consumers who resonate with TOMS one-for-one approach and the company's combined for-profit/philanthropic persona	• Shoes, eyewear, and coffee • Branded products (t-shirts, caps) • Misc items sold via the TOMS marketplace • TOMS products are sold worldwide. Shoes have been distributed to 60 countries, eyewear 13, and clean water provided in five

Resources	
Core Competencies	**Key Assets**
• Pioneered the one-for-one business model; diligence in execution has created a strong brand • Creation and management of for-profit/philanthropic business strategy that is sustainable • Ability to create passion and excitement about what TOMS is doing in others (nonprofit partners, TOMS volunteers, Interns, etc.) • Willingness to learn (i.e., responding to critics who point out how TOMS could be doing things better by adopting the best suggestions)	• Blake Mycoskie • Corporate culture • Relationships with nonprofits that help TOMS distribute products to children and people in need • TOMS volunteers • Interns (that work in TOMS facilities) • Campus clubs • Day Without Shoes campaign

Financials	
Revenue Streams	
• Product sales, which include shoes, eyewear, and coffee • TOMS branded products (t-shirts, sweatshirts, caps, and TOMS flags) • Misc items available via the TOMS Marketplace, including Accessories, Home & Bath Products, and a small number of Tech Products • All sales trigger a commensurate gift to people in need.	
Cost Structure	**Financing/Funding**
• Cost-driven business • Low fixed/high variable costs • Major categories of costs: Product manufacturer, distribution of products to people in need, salaries and general administrative	• Initial capital infusion of $500,000 from founder Blake Mycoskie • Profits from business operations • TOMS customers/supporters volunteer their time to get products to adults and children in need and to spread the word about TOMS.

Operations	
Product (or service) Production	**Channels**
• Products (shoes, eyewear, & coffee) are made by contract manufacturers which are carefully selected and monitored • Products are shipped directly to retailers or online outlets for sale to their customers (TOMS does not dropship) • TOMS collaborates with nonprofits to distribute the shoes and eyewear and to provide clean water for those in need	• Online (TOMS.com, Zappos.com, etc.) • Retailers (Nordstrom, Whole Foods, etc.) • Products distributed to children and adults in need via Friends of TOMS, nonprofit partners, and TOMS volunteers
	Key Partners
	• Friends of TOMS • Nonprofit partners • TOMS volunteers • Top brands, such as Ralph Lauren and Element Skateboard • Affiliates (via the TOMS affiliate program)

Toms: Barringer/Ireland Business Model Template

© 2014 Bruce R. Barringer and R. Duane Ireland

in part because local organizations, already embedded in a country, know the needs better than TOMS does and can direct the company. An example is TOMS's partnership with the Seva Foundation to implement its eyewear/restore sight program. The Seva Foundation runs sight programs in Nepal, Tibet, and Cambodia. It is uniquely equipped to help TOMS make the best use of its dollars.

TOMS's product/market scope now includes shoes, eyewear, and coffee. The company also has a "Marketplace" that sells a variety of items, including jewelry, household items, and tech products. The company's "one for one" mission still applies, just in a different form. If you buy a $140 Turquoise Alba Necklace, for example, your purchase will get you the necklace and provide 11 meals for a child in need.

Resources

TOMS has been diligent in the execution of its one-to-one model. Its products are appealing, its philanthropic efforts are making a difference, and it involves a lot of people in what it does. These factors have enabled TOMS to build a strong brand. Its core strategy is also working. It has remained sustainable without needing donations. TOMS has also excelled at creating excitement and passion in others for what it is doing. It does a lot to elicit this. For example, every two weeks a group of TOMS volunteers travels to Argentina or another part of the world to make a "shoe drop," which is the term that TOMS uses for distributing shoes. Anyone can apply for the trip, and for many it is a life-changing experience. Every shoe TOMS gives away is placed on a child's foot by a TOMS volunteer. Volunteers pay their own travel expenses, but the trips are organized by TOMS.

TOMS also listens. It has both proponents and critics that are vocal in their feedback. Rather than ignoring the feedback, TOMS reacts, which encourages additional feedback. For example, one source of criticism that TOMS has faced is that when it gives a child a pair of shoes, it is a one-time event. The child will eventually grow out of the shoes and be right back to where he or she started. TOMS acknowledged this criticism as a valid point, and has responded by putting a program in place that tracks the children to whom shoes have been provided. It makes sure the children receive additional shoes when needed.

TOMS has a number of key assets. It has a healthy corporate culture, which draws people in. It has an entire apparatus to get people involved in its initiatives, including community groups, students, educators, and others. You can see TOMS's work in this area by accessing the TOMS Community website (www.tom-community.com). TOMS also frequently touts the work of its volunteers on its Twitter account, which is available at @TOMS. TOMS also organizes events, which are heartfelt and draw attention to its products and causes. The most popular event is its One Day Without Shoes campaign. This campaign was started in 2008 to raise public awareness of the importance of shoes. It asks ordinary people to go one day without shoes, just to see how it feels. The point is to instill in people what a difference a simple pair of shoes can make, particularly for children. The campaign grows every year. You can see highlights of the most recent year's campaign at www.toms.com/daywithoutshoes. In past years, people from over 25 countries have participated. Participants have included Kris Ryan, Charlize Theron, the Dallas Cowboys Cheerleaders, and employees from Nordstrom, Microsoft, and AOL.

Financials

TOMS's revenue comes from product sales. TOMS is a cost-driven business. It contains costs via its partnerships, volunteer network, and by avoiding traditional marketing. TOMS does very little traditional marketing, such as print media, radio, and television. Instead, it relies on word-of-mouth, social media, and prominent placements in retail stores by its retail partners. TOMS does not manufacture its products. Instead, it relies on contract manufacturers and growers (for its coffee) spread throughout the world. TOMS's approach to manufacturing has raised eyebrows because it produces products in China, where labor practices are suspect. TOMS aggressively polices its manufacturers and other suppliers. It maintains strict standards that everyone in its supply chain is obligated to adhere to, particularly when it comes to fairness to workers. TOMS's employees regularly visit its manufacturers to monitor compliance.

TOMS funds it operations from profits. It also benefits from the work of its volunteers.

Operations

To produce its products, TOMS manages a global supply chain. Its shoes are made in low-wage countries such as China, Argentina, and Ethiopia. Its eyewear is made in Italy. Its coffee beans are sourced from growers across the world and are roasted in the United States. Some of its most popular selections come from growers in Rwanda, Malawi, and Guatemala. In regard to distribution, TOMS delivers its products to its retail and online partners, who in turn sell to their customers. TOMS does not drop ship or sell on a consignment basis.

Manufacturing and selling is only the first step in TOMS's overall process. Its philanthropic efforts come next. To distribute its shoes, TOMS partners with nonprofits and NGOs in the countries in which it distributes products. These organizations are called "Giving Partners." The Giving Partners identify the children in need. The process of actually distributing the shoes is referred to as Shoe Drops. Friends of TOMS helps coordinate the Shoe Drops. TOMS's eyewear/restore sight and its coffee/clean water initiatives are executed in a similar manner. TOMS works with Friends of TOMS and local organizations to make the distributions.

In regard to channels, TOMS sells its products through both retail and online outlets. Over 500 retailers around the world now carry TOMS shoes. Its distribution network for eyewear and coffee is growing. A string of TOMS café-stores is on the drawing boards. The café-stores will sell TOMS coffee in a coffee house setting and will sell TOMS shoes, eyewear, and other products in an adjacent retail setting. TOMS's business model would not be possible without key partners. Its most important partners are Friends of TOMS (its nonprofit subsidiary), the nonprofits and NGOs that distribute its products, and its volunteers. TOMS also has a robust affiliate program.

Criticisms of TOMS

For some, it may be hard to imagine that TOMS has critics, but it does. Its critics point out flaws in TOMS's approach, which some go as far as to say threaten the firm's future.

The criticism focuses on three main issues. First, critics argue that TOMS, along with similar organizations, makes people in poor countries dependent on the good will of others rather than creating opportunities for them to take care of themselves. Many social entrepreneurs believe that the best way to create sustainable change in an impoverished country is through education, job creation, and trade, rather than aid, which is what TOMS does. In fact, a mantra among some social entrepreneurs is "trade not aid." Microfinance, which provides loans to people in developing countries to start their own businesses, is based on these principles. The second criticism is that TOMS has manufacturing facilities in China and elsewhere where human rights violations have been documented. The third criticism is that by pouring a large number of free shoes into countries such as Argentina and Ethiopia, TOMS is inadvertently stymieing local entrepreneurship. The idea is that by providing shoes for free, TOMS takes potential business away from local companies, which provide not only shoes but jobs.

TOMS is aware of these criticisms, and in each case has responded in a proactive manner.

(continued)

Is TOMS's Business Model Sustainable?

The question is, "Is TOMS's business model sustainable for the future?" The primary threats to its business model stem from the criticisms it receives, its reliance on people continuing to pay a premium for its products, and whether the one-for-one movement will continue to resonate with volunteers and nonprofit partners. Another threat is the nature of the products that TOMS sells. On the one hand, selling a physical product mitigates TOMS's risk because it does not have to rely on donations to fulfill its mission. On the other hand, TOMS has the dual challenge of managing a global supply chain while at the same time leading a worldwide philanthropic effort. The complexity of this challenge will grow as TOMS continues to scale its business. No company has attempted to scale a one-to-one business model to the extent that TOMS is contemplating.

Discussion Questions

4-38. What is TOMS's target market? How might this market change in the future?

4-39. What revenue streams does TOMS have that support how the firm competes? How sustainable are these revenue streams?

4-40. What key assets does TOMS possess and how sustainable are those assets?

4-41. What are the major challenges TOMS faces as the firm continues implementing its business model as a means of reaching its mission? Which of these challenges is the most serious and why?

Sources: TOMS website, www.toms.com, accessed June 5, 2014; TOMS, Wikipedia, www.wikipedia.com, accessed June 5, 2014; A. Spaulding, S. Fernandez, and J. Sawayda, "TOMS: One for One Movement," Daniels Fund Ethics Initiative, University of New Mexico, http://danielsethics.mgt.umn.edu

Company Name _____

Core Strategy	
Business Mission	**Basis of Differentiation**
Target Customer	**Product/Market Scope**

Resources	
Core Competency	**Key Assets**

Financials	
Revenue Streams	
Cost Structure	**Financing/Funding**

Operations	
Product (or service) Production	**Channels**
	Key Partners

Barringer/Ireland Business Model Template

Key

Business Mission	A business's mission or mission statement describes why it exists and what its business model is supposed to accomplish.
Basis of Differentiation	A company's basis of differentiation is what separates it from its competitors. It is what causes consumers to pick one company's products or services over another's.
Target Market	A target market is a place within a larger market segment that represents a narrower group of customers with similar interests. This is the market in which the firm will compete.
Product/Market Scope	A company's product/market scope defines the products and markets on which it will concentrate.
Core Competencies	A core competency is a specific factor or capability that supports a firm's business model and sets it apart from its rivals.
Key Assets	Key assets are assets that a firm owns that enable its business model to work. The assets can be physical, financial, intellectual, or human.
Revenue Streams	A firm's revenue streams describe the ways in which it makes money. Some businesses have a single revenue stream, while others have several.
Cost Structure	A business's cost structure describes the most important costs incurred to support its business model.
Financing or Funding	This box describes how a business will finance its business model.
Product (or Service) Production	This section focuses on how a firm's product and/or service are produced.
Channels	A company's channels describe how it delivers its product or service to its customers.
Key Partners	This box describes the key partnerships that a firm's business model relies on.

Endnotes

1. M. Malmstrom, J. Johansoon, and J. Wincent, "Cognitive Constructions of Low-Profit and High-Profit Business Models: A Repertory Grid Study of Serial Entrepreneurs," *Entrepreneurship Theory and Practice*, 2014, in press; D.J. Teece, "Business Models, Business Strategy and Innovation," *Long Range Planning* 43, no. 2–3 (2010): 172–194.

2. C. Markides and L. Sosa, "Pioneering and First Mover Advantages: The Importance of Business Models," *Long Range Planning*, 46 no. 4–5 (2013): 325–334.

3. R. Garud, H. A. Schildt, and T. K. Lant, "Entrepreneurial Storytelling, Future Expectations, and the Paradox of Legitimacy," *Organization Science*, 2014, in press.

4. S. Blank and B. Dorf, *The Startup Owner's Manual* (Pescadero, CA: K&S Ranch Press, 2012).

5. P. Andries, K. Debackere, and B. van Looy, "Simultaneous Experimentation as a Learning Strategy: Business Model Development Under Uncertainty," *Strategic Entrepreneurship Journal* 7, no. 4 (2013): 288–310.

6. G. N. Chandler, J. C. Broberg, and T. H. Allison, "Customer Value Propositions in Declining Industries: Differences Between Industry Representative and High-Growth Firms," *Strategic Entrepreneurship Journal*, 2014, in press.

7. C. Baden-Fuller and S. Haefliger, "Business Models and Technological Innovation," *Long Range Planning* 46, no. 6 (2013): 419–426.

8. A. Konig, N. Kammerlander, and A. Enders, "The Family Innovator's Dilemma: How Family Influence Affects the Adoption of Discontinuous Technologies by Incumbent Firms," *Academy of Management Review* 38, no. 3 (2013): 418–441.

9. C. M. Christensen, *The Innovator's Dilemma: The Revolutionary Book That Will Change the Way You Do Business* (New York: Harper Business, 2011).

10. E. M. Rusli and D. Macmillan, "Uber Gets an Uber-Valuation," *Wall Street Journal Online*, www.wsj.com, June 6, 2014.

11. A. Osterwalder and Y. Pigneur, *Business Model Generation: A Handbook for Visionaries, Game Changers, and Challengers* (New York: John Wiley & Co., 2010).

12. N. J. Foss and S. Lindenberg, "Microfoundations for Strategy: A Goal-Framing Perspective on the Drivers of Value Creation," *Academy of Management Perspectives*, 27, no. 2 (2013): 85–102.

13. R. I. Williams Jr., D. L. Morrell, and J. V. Mullane, "Reinvigorating the Mission Statement Through Top Management Commitment," *Management Decision* 52, no. 3 (2014): 27–39.

14. M.-J. Chen and D. Miller, "Reconceptualizing Competitive Dynamics: A Multidimensional Framework," *Strategic Management Journal*, 2014, in press.

15. E. Fischer and A. R. Reuber, "Online Entrepreneurial Communication: Mitigating Uncertainty and Increasing Differentiation via Twitter," *Journal of Business Venturing* 29, no. 4 (2014): 565–583.

16. J. Y.-K. Lim, L. W. Busenitz, and L. Chidambaram, "New Venture Teams and the Quality of Business Opportunities Identified: Faultlines Between Subgroups of Founders and Investors," *Entrepreneurship Theory and Practice* 37, no. 1 (2013): 47–67.

17. G. N. Chandler, J. C. Broberg, and T. H. Allison, "Customer Value Propositions in Declining Industries: Differences Between Industry Representation and High-Growth Firms." *Strategic Entrepreneurship Journal*, 2014, in press.

18. K. M. Kuhn and T. L. Galloway, "With a Little Help from My Competitors: Peer Networking Among Artisan Entrepreneurs," *Entrepreneurship Theory and Practice*, 2014, in press.

19. Birchbox corporate blog, "Behind the Box: Birthday Thoughts," available at http://blog.birchbox.com/post/10202608110/behind-the-box-birthday-thoughts," posted on September 15, 2011, (accessed on May 20, 2014).

20. M. A. Hitt, R. D. Ireland, and R. E. Hoskisson, *Strategic Management: Competitiveness and Globalization*, 11th edition (Cincinnati, OH: Cengage Learning, 2015).

21. R. Garcia-Castron and R. V. Aguilera, "Incremental Value Creation and Appropriation in a World with Multiple Stakeholders," *Strategic Management Journal*, 2014, in press.

22. G. D. Bruton, I. Filatotchev, S. Si, and M. Wright, "Entrepreneurship and Strategy in Emerging Economies," *Strategic Entrepreneurship Journal* 7, no. 3 (2013): 169–180.

23. P. Dimitratos, I. Liouka, and S. Young, "A Missing Operationalization: Entrepreneurial Competencies in Multinational Enterprise Subsidiaries," *Long Range Planning* 47, no. 1–2 (2014): 64–75.

24. W. E. Gillis, J. G. Combs, and D. J. Ketchen Jr., "Using Resource-Based Theory to Help Explain Plural Form Franchising," *Entrepreneurship Theory and Practice* 38, no. 3 (2014): 449–472.

25. R. Casadesus-Masanell and F. Zhu, "Business Model Innovation and Competitive Imitation: The Case of Sponsor-Based Business Models," *Strategic Management Journal* 34, no. 4 (2013): 464–482.

26. M. H. Morris, G. Shirokova, and A. Shatalov, "The Business Model and Firm Performance: The Case of Russian Food Service Vendors," *Journal of Small Business Management* 51, no. 1 (2013): 46–65.

27. G. Cassar, "Industry and Startup Experience on Entrepreneur Forecast Performance in New Firms," *Journal of Business Venturing* 29, no. 1 (2014): 137–151.

28. R. Chandy and K. Ramdas, "The M in Future," *Business Strategy Review* 24, no. 1 (2013): 30–43.

29. D. Li, "Multilateral R&D Alliances by New Ventures," *Journal of Business Venturing* 28, no. 2 (2013): 241–260; B. Barringer and J. S. Harrison, "Walking a Tightrope: Creating Value Through Interorganizational Relationships," *Journal of Management* 26, no. 3 (2000): 367–403.

30. M. Thompson, "Hasbro's Zynga-Branded Merchandise Coming to Stores Next Week," InsideSocialGames, posted September 25, 2012, available at http://www.insidesocialgames.com/2012/09/25/hasbros-zynga-branded-mer-chandise-coming-to-stores-next-week/, (accessed May 22, 2014).

31. H. Yang, Y. Zheng, and X. Zhao, "Exploration or Exploitation: Small Firms' Alliance Strategies with Large Firms," *Strategic Management Journal* 35, no. 1 (2014): 146–157.

32. B. Barringer and J. S. Harrison, "Walking a Tightrope: Creating Value Through Interorganizational Relationships," *Journal of Management* 26, no. 3 (2000): 367–403.

Getting Personal with GREENVELOPE

Founder

SAM FRANKLIN

Business Degree, Washington University (St. Louis, Missouri), undecided

Dialogue with
Sam Franklin

WHAT I DO WHEN I'M NOT WORKING
Enjoy the outdoors to climb, fish, and ski!

FAVORITE BAND ON MY SMARTPHONE LIST
Beat Connection

MY ADVICE FOR NEW ENTREPRENEURS
Trust your data and make data-driven decisions.

FIRST ENTREPRENEURIAL EXPERIENCE
Knocking on neighborhood doors and pressure washing driveways—the initial Greenvelope funding!

BEST ADVICE I'VE RECEIVED
Quality over quantity

MY FAVORITE SMARTPHONE APP
Spotify

CHAPTER 5

Industry and Competitor *Analysis*

OPENING PROFILE

GREENVELOPE

Occupying a Unique Position in an Evolving Industry—and Thriving

• Web: www.greenvelope.com • Facebook: Greenvelope • Twitter: @Greenvelope

t was one of those moments in time when a business idea was born. Sam Franklin's family received a wedding invitation in the mail, which was printed on card stock. Card stock is a type of paper that is thicker and more durable than normal writing paper. Because most wedding invitations are ultimately thrown away, that got Franklin thinking there might be a better way. At roughly the same time, Franklin read an article in *USA Today* about wedding invitations. The article said that in the previous year, 1.2 million wedding invitations were sent out by the free online service Evite. While Evite is free, the invitations include ads, which to Franklin seemed a little unseemly. Franklin's idea was to create a paid solution for sending wedding invitations online that didn't include ads and would be a cleaner and a more elegant experience for everyone involved.

That was mid-2008. Franklin took a year off from school so he could build on his idea. He entered Washington University in St. Louis, Missouri, as a freshman in 2009. He followed through with the idea and launched Greenvelope, the name he chose for the company, literally from his dorm room. He invested $50,000 in start-up funds—half from a loan from a family member and half from savings he accumulated during high school—and created the back end of the company's website and 20 templates for wedding invitations. He also developed software that mimicked the experience of opening a traditional printed invitation. Greenvelope's first customers were secured by buying Google AdWords for people who were searching for terms like "e-mail wedding invitations" or "e-mail save the date." The company initially gave away e-mail "save the date" messages and made money by encouraging people to upgrade to paid invitations. An added benefit of Greenvelope's offering was cost savings. At the time, it cost couples about $650 (on average) to print and mail invitations for a 100-guest wedding. Greenvelope offered template packages starting at $100 for up to 300 guests.

When Franklin started analyzing his initial sales data, he realized that engaged couples were only part of his customer base. To his surprise, businesses and individuals were customizing the wedding templates to send invitations for a variety of purposes, including corporate events. That realization prompted Franklin to widen his vision for Greenvelope, adding business templates to the company's offerings as a result.

Midway through his degree program at Washington University, Franklin returned to Seattle, his hometown, to work on Greenvelope full time. The way the Greenvelope

LEARNING OBJECTIVES

After studying this chapter you should be ready to:

1. Explain the purpose of an industry analysis.

2. Identify and discuss the five competitive forces that determine industry profitability.

3. Explain the value that entrepreneurial firms create by successfully using the five forces model.

4. Identify the five primary industry types and the opportunities they offer.

5. Explain the purpose of a competitor analysis and a competitive analysis grid.

site works is that a customer creates an account, selects an invitation, and then loads the e-mail invitation list into a spreadsheet. The invitations are then delivered via e-mail in a personalized spinning envelope (with the guest's name on the front) that emulates the fun and excitement of opening a traditional paper invitation. The digital invitations look like real paper. An advanced RSVP tracking system allows customers to see which invites have been opened, which haven't been opened, and which were undeliverable for whatever reason. When guests RSVP, they can select meal options, make song requests, write a note to the bride or groom, or respond to any question that the customer sets up. If someone is on the invitation list that doesn't have an e-mail address or never opens the electronic invitation, a paper version of the invitation can be printed from the Greenvelope site. The invitation can then be sent by regular mail.

Greenvelope currently has five full-time employees with part-time employees used as needed. An in-house design staff works with freelance designers and artists who create the invitation and are paid a commission when their designs are picked. Many of the designs are stylish and inviting and objectively rival handmade invitations. Currently, roughly 60 percent of Greenvelope's sales are for wedding invitations, with the remaining 40 percent being for graduation announcements, baby showers, birthdays, corporate events, and a variety of other purposes.

An integral part of Greenvelope's offering is the opportunity to participate in environmental sustainability. Sam Franklin grew up in Seattle, and spent his childhood camping, fishing, and hiking. Through those experiences, he gained a deep appreciation for the outdoors. Greenvelope donates 1 percent of its revenue each quarter to Mountains to Sound, a nonprofit organization that supports the greenway along the I-90 corridor in northwest Washington State. These donations were made even before the firm was earning profits. The fact that the company's electronic invitations replace paper invitations, which is an environmental plus, is also a key facet of how it operates.

Greenvelope's main competitors include Paperless Post, a recently launched venture-capital-funded electronic invitation start-up, Evite, and old-fashioned snail mail. The company feels that it has sufficiently differentiated itself through its diverse collection of designs, its outstanding customer service, and its brand. An interesting facet of what Greenvelope does is the viral nature of its offering. Towards the bottom of each of its invitations is an unobtrusive statement that says "Powered by Greenvelope" with the Greenvelope logo. If recipients click on the logo, they are directed to the Greenvelope website. This is the manner in which Greenvelope obtains many of its new customers.

Greenvelope envisions a bright future. As time moves on, the company believes that people will become increasing comfortable performing the majority of their tasks online—which bodes well for its online electronic invitation service. Greenvelope also believes that sufficient barriers to entry have been put in place that will enable it to maintain a leadership position in the invitation industry. The strength of its brand, its network of freelance designers, its social mission, and the functionality of its website are all factors that place Greenvelope in an enviable position in the invitation industry.

Greenvelope is a success in part because of Sam Franklin's ability to analyze the invitation industry and precisely position Greenvelope within it. In this chapter, we'll look at industry analysis and competitor analysis. The first section of the chapter considers **industry analysis**, which is business research that focuses on the potential of an industry. An **industry** is a group of firms producing a similar product or service, such as music, pilates and yoga studios, and solar panel manufacturing. Once it is determined that a new venture is feasible in regard to the industry and the target market in which it intends to compete, a more in-depth analysis is needed to learn the "ins and outs" of the chosen industry. The in-depth analysis helps a firm determine if the niche or target markets it identified during its feasibility analysis are accessible and which ones represent the best point of entry for the new firm.

We focus on competitor analysis in the chapter's second section. A **competitor analysis** is a detailed evaluation of a firm's competitors. Once a firm decides to enter an industry and chooses a market in which to compete, it must gain an understanding of its competitive environment. We'll look at how a firm identifies its competition and the importance of completing a competitive analysis grid.

Industry Analysis

LEARNING OBJECTIVE

1. Explain the purpose of an industry analysis.

When studying an industry, an entrepreneur must answer three questions before pursuing the idea of starting a firm. First, is the industry accessible—in other words, is it a realistic place for a new venture to enter? Second, does the industry contain markets that are ripe for innovation or are underserved? Third, are there positions in the industry that will avoid some of the negative attributes of the industry as a whole? It is useful for a new venture to think about its **position** at both the company level and the product or service level. At the company level, a firm's position determines how the company is situated relative to its competitors, as discussed in Chapter 4. For example, Fresh Healthy Vending has positioned itself as a vending machine provider that specializes in healthy alternatives to traditional vending machine snack foods and beverages. The company's refrigerated machines offer carrots, yogurt, smoothies, granola bars, and beverages such as milk, juice, and teas. This is a much different position than the vending machine providers that offer the standard fare such as chips, pretzels, salted peanuts, candy bars, sports drinks, and sodas.

The importance of knowing the competitive landscape, which is what an industry is, may have been first recognized in the fourth century BC by Sun Tzu, a Chinese philosopher. Reputedly he wrote *The Art of War* to help generals prepare for battle. However, the ideas in the book are still used today to help managers prepare their firms for the competitive wars of the marketplace. The following quote from Sun Tzu's work points out the importance of industry analysis:

> We are not fit to lead an army on the march unless we are familiar with the face of the country—its pitfalls and precipices, its marshes and swamps.[1]

These words serve as a reminder to entrepreneurs that regardless of how eager they are to start a business, they are not adequately prepared until they are "familiar with the face of the country"—that is, until they understand the industry or industries they plan to enter and in which they intend to compete.

It's also important to know that some industries are simply more attractive than others in terms of their annual growth rate and other factors. For example, according to IBISWorld the industry for e-book publishing is expected to grow at an annual rate of 7.5 percent over the next five years. For the same period, the industry for traditional book publishing is expected to grow at an annual rate of 0.7 percent. What this means is that the conditions for growing a company are significantly more favorable in the e-book industry than in the traditional book publishing industry.[2] These types of differences exist for comparisons across other types of industries. The differences can be mitigated some by firm-level factors, including a company's products, culture, reputation, and other resources.[3] Still, in various studies researchers have found that from 8 to 30 percent of the variation in firm profitability is directly attributable to the industry in which a firm competes.[4] As a result, the overall attractiveness of an industry should be part of the equation when an entrepreneur decides whether to pursue a particular opportunity. Studying industry trends and using the five forces model are two techniques entrepreneurs have available for assessing industry attractiveness.

Studying Industry Trends

The first technique that an entrepreneur has available to discern the attractiveness of an industry is to study industry trends. Environmental and business trends are the two most important trends for entrepreneurs to evaluate.

Environmental Trends   As discussed in Chapter 2, environmental trends are very important. The strength of an industry often surges or wanes not so much because of the management skills of those leading firms in a particular industry, but because environmental trends shift in favor or against the products or services sold by firms in the industry.

Economic trends, social trends, technological advances, and political and regulatory changes are the most important environmental trends for entrepreneurs to study. For example, companies in industries selling products to seniors, such as the eyeglasses industry and the hearing aid industry, benefit from the social trend of the aging of the population. In contrast, industries selling food products that are high in sugar, such as the candy industry and the sugared soft-drink industry, suffer as the result of a renewed emphasis on health and fitness. Sometimes there are multiple environmental changes at work that set the stage for an industry's future. This point is illustrated in the following statement from IBISWorld's assessment of the future of the motorcycle dealership and repair industry. After first reporting that motorcycle sales are anticipated to increase at an annualized rate of 2.3 percent between 2014 and 2018 to reach a sales volume of $25.2 billion, the report goes on to say:

> With more money in their pockets, consumers will head to motorcycle lots again; with favorable consumer sentiment about the future of the economy, consumers will resume purchasing industry products. Furthermore, the tight lending standards of the past are projected to dissipate and more financing will be available for consumers to use when purchasing a motorcycle. High fuel prices will also feed into industry demand as some consumers switch from cars to motorcycles.[5]

This short assessment about sales in the motorcycle industry illustrates the degree to which environmental trends affect an industry's prospects. Note that nothing is said about improvements in the management of motorcycle dealerships or innovation in the motorcycle industry. The somewhat positive assessment of the motorcycle industry's future is tied to an improved U.S. economy, a loosening of tight credit standards, and high fuel prices. High fuel prices work to the advantage of the motorcycle industry because motorcycles use less fuel than cars. Similar forces are at work in all industries.

Business Trends   Other trends affect industries that aren't environmental trends per se but are important to mention. For example, the firms in some industries benefit from an increasing ability to outsource manufacturing or service functions to lower-cost foreign labor markets, while firms in other industries don't share this advantage. In a similar fashion, the firms in some industries are able to move customer procurement and service functions online, at considerable cost savings, while the firms in other industries aren't able to capture this advantage. Trends such as these favor some industries over others.

It's important that start-ups stay on top of both environmental and business trends in their industries. One way to do this is via participation in industry trade associations, trade shows, and trade journals, as illustrated in the "Partnering for Success" feature.

PARTNERING FOR SUCCESS

Three Ts That Are Important for Becoming Active in an Industry: Trade Associations, Trade Shows, and Trade Journals

One thing that's important for a start-up is to become active in the industry it's entering. Activity leads to learning about and understanding the industry, finding business partners, and becoming recognized as an industry leader. Three important Ts that lead to industry activity are trade associations, trade shows, and trade journals. Start-ups should consider utilizing these Ts as a part of their early and ongoing activities.

Trade Associations

A trade association (or trade group) is an organization that firms in the same industry form for the purpose of collecting and disseminating trade information, offering legal and technical advice, furnishing industry-related training, and providing a platform for collective lobbying. In addition to promoting industry-related issues, trade associations typically provide a variety of other services to their members. For example, the American Watchmakers-Clockmakers Institute, which is a trade association of watchmakers and clockmakers, provides its members with training, a database of hard-to-find parts, technical support for watch and clock repair, bulletins with up-to-date product information, and an extensive library of industry-specific educational material.[6]

Trade associations are typically governed by a paid staff and a volunteer board. Busy CEOs and entrepreneurs are motivated to serve on trade association boards, not only to influence the direction of the associations but because their service provides them visibility and a platform to network closely with other members of the association. These types of interactions can lead to businesses forming partnerships and working together in other ways.

There are 7,600 national trade associations in the United States. The vast majority have websites that list their activities and their members.

Trade Shows

A trade show (or a trade fair) is an exhibition organized to create opportunities for companies in an industry to showcase and demonstrate their products and services. Some trade shows are open to the public, while others can only be attended by company representatives and members of the press. Over 10,000 trade shows are held annually in the United States. There are several on-line directories, such as the Trade Show News Network (www.tsnn.com), that help organizers, attendees, and marketers identify the most appropriate trade shows to attend. The largest trade show in the United States is the International Consumer Electronics Trade Show, which is held every January in Las Vegas, and is not open to the public. In 2014, it included more than 2,700 exhibitors, 150,000 attendees, and 5,000 tech journalists.

Along with displaying their products and services, businesses attend trade shows to study their rivals, meet members of the press, and network with industry participants. Companies must rent exhibit space at trade shows. Some of the high-quality shows, which usually last just under a week, cost upward of $20,000 to attend. Small companies are often able to share exhibit space and split the cost. Trade shows offer prime opportunities for networking in order to generate business and to establish new relationships and nurture existing ones. In fact, there are many articles and "how-to" guides published in periodicals and posted on websites that teach businesses how to maximize their time at trade shows and establish business relationships.

Trade Journals

Trade journals or magazines are usually published by trade associations and contain articles and advertising focused on a specific industry. Very little general-audience advertising appears in trade journals. They may also include industry-specific job notices and classified advertising.

Some trade journals are available to the general public, while others are very specifically controlled—meaning that you must be an industry participant to receive the journal. This practice ensures advertisers that their ads will be viewed by people in their target audience. Many of the articles in trade journals are written about companies in the industry. It enhances the stature and visibility of a company to have a favorable article written about it in a premier industry trade journal.

Along with trade journals, some industries have peer-reviewed journals that contain both technical articles and heavy advertising content. The articles are often co-authored by people who work for vendors that advertise in the journal. *BioTechniques,* which is concerend with the life sciences area, is an example of an industry-specific peer-reviewed journal that follows this format. These journals blur the distinction somewhat between trade journals and peer-reviewed journals.

Although trade journals do not provide the direct networking opportunities that trade associations and trade shows do, the visibility a company can obtain by being featured in an article or by running ads can result in multiple positive outcomes.

Questions for Critical Thinking

1. Pick an industry in which you have an interest. Make a list of the premier trade associations, trade shows, and trade journals associated with that industry.
2. How can an entrepreneur assess whether offering to serve in a leadership capacity in a trade association,

(continued)

on a voluntary basis, will be worth the time and effort? Establish a set of criteria that you would follow if making this type of decision.

3. Spend some time looking at the Organic Trade Association. Make a list of networking opportunities available via membership in this organization.

4. What are the risks involved with networking? For example, are there risks involved with sharing information with industry participants about how your firm competes? How can a company strike the

right balance between giving out enough information about itself to attract the attention of potential partners without divulging too much proprietary information?

Sources: American Watchmakers-Clockmakers Institute home page, www.awci.com (accessed February 18, 2014); B. Barringer and J. Harrison, "Walking a Tightrope: Creating Value Through Interorganizational Relationships," *Journal of Management* 26, no. 3, 1999: 367–403; Organic Trade Association home page, www.craftandhobby.org (accessed February 18, 2014).

The Five Forces Model

LEARNING OBJECTIVE

2. Identify and discuss the five competitive forces that determine industry profitability.

The five forces model is a framework entrepreneurs use to understand an industry's structure. Professor Michael Porter developed this important tool. Shown in Figure 5.1, the framework is comprised of the forces that determine industry profitability.[7] These forces—the threat of substitutes, the threat of new entrants (that is, new competitors), rivalry among existing firms, the bargaining power of suppliers, and the bargaining power of buyers—determine the average rate of return for the firms competing in a particular industry (e.g., the restaurant industry) or a particular segment of an industry (e.g., the fast-casual segment of the restaurant industry).

Each of Porter's five forces affects the average rate of return for the firms in an industry by applying pressure on industry profitability. Well-managed companies try to position their firms in a way that avoids or diminishes these forces—in an attempt to beat the average rate of return for the industry. For example, the rivalry among existing firms in the wedding invitation industry is high. Greenvelope has diminished the impact of this threat to its profitability by selling customized wedding invitations online. Compared to traditional wedding invitation services, this approach lowers the cost to the consumer and provides a high profit margin per order for Greenvelope.

In his book *Competitive Advantage*, Porter points out that industry profitability is not a function of *only* a product's features. Although the book was published in 1980 and the dynamics of the industries mentioned have changed, Porter's essential points still offer important insights for entrepreneurs such as the insight suggested by the following quote:

> Industry profitability is not a function of what the product looks like or whether it embodies high or low technology but of industry structure. Some very mundane industries such as postage meters and grain trading are extremely profitable, while some more glamorous, high-technology industries such as personal computers and cable television are not profitable for many participants.[8]

The five competitive forces that determine industry profitability are described next. As mentioned in previous chapters, industry reports, produced by companies such as IBISWorld, Mintel, and Standard & Poor's NetAdvantage,

FIGURE 5.1
Forces That Determine Industry Profitability

provide substantive information for analyzing the impact of the five forces on specific industries. All three of these resources are available free through many university library websites and are highlighted in the Internet Resources Table in Appendix 3.2.

Threat of Substitutes

In general, industries are more attractive when the threat of substitutes is low. This means that products or services from other industries can't easily serve as substitutes for the products or services being made and sold in the focal firm's industry. For example, there are few if any substitutes for prescription medicines, which is one of the reasons the pharmaceutical industry has historically been so profitable. When people are sick, they typically don't quibble with the pharmacist about the price of a medicine. In contrast, when close substitutes for a product do exist, industry profitability is suppressed because consumers will opt not to buy when the price is too high. Consider the price of airplane tickets. If the price gets too high, businesspeople will increasingly switch to videoconferencing services such as Skype and GoToMeeting as a substitute for travel. This problem is particularly acute if the substitutes are free or nearly free. For example, if the price of express mail gets too high, people will increasingly attach documents to e-mail messages rather than sending them via UPS or FedEx.

The extent to which substitutes suppress the profitability of an industry depends on the propensity for buyers to substitute alternatives. This is why the firms in an industry often offer their customers amenities to reduce the likelihood they'll switch to a substitute product, even in light of a price increase. Let's look at the coffee restaurant industry as an example of this. The coffee sold at Starbucks is relatively expensive. A consumer could easily find a less expensive cup of coffee at a convenience store or brew coffee at home rather than pay more at Starbucks. To decrease the likelihood that customers will choose either of these alternatives, Starbucks offers high-quality fresh coffee, a pleasant atmosphere (often thought of as part of the "Starbucks experience"), and good service. Starbucks doesn't do this just so its customers don't go to a different

This independently owned coffee shop doesn't just sell coffee. It also offers its patrons a convenient and pleasant place to meet, socialize, and study. The shop offers these amenities in part to decrease the likelihood that its customers will "substitute" coffee at this shop for a less expensive alternative.

Lucky Business/Shutterstock

coffee restaurant. It offers the service so its customers won't switch to substitute products as well. Although this strategy is still working for Starbucks, there have been times (such as during the recent economic slowdown) when its effectiveness was reduced. Because of this, Starbucks is now experimenting with offering less expensive coffees while maintaining its commitment to quality and providing customers with what the firm believes is the unique Starbucks experience.

Threat of New Entrants

In general, industries are more attractive when the threat of entry is low. This means that competitors cannot easily enter the industry and successfully copy what the industry incumbents are doing to generate profits. There are a number of ways that firms in an industry can keep the number of new entrants low. These techniques are referred to as barriers to entry. A **barrier to entry** is a condition that creates a disincentive for a new firm to enter an industry.[9] Let's look at the six major sources of barriers to entry:

- **Economies of scale:** Industries that are characterized by large economies of scale are difficult for new firms to enter, unless they are willing to accept a cost disadvantage. **Economies of scale** occur when mass-producing a product results in lower average costs. For example, Intel has huge microprocessor factories that produce vast quantities of computer chips, thereby reducing the average cost of each chip produced. It would be difficult for a new entrant to match Intel's advantage in this area. There are instances in which the competitive advantage generated by economies of scale can be overcome. For example, many microbreweries have successfully entered the beer industry by brewing their beer locally and relying on a local niche market clientele. By offering locally brewed, high-quality products, successful microbreweries counter the enormous economies of scale (and the lower price to consumers they permit) of major and often global brewers, such as Anheuser-Busch InBev, which manages a portfolio of over 200 beer brands.[10]

- **Product differentiation:** Industries such as the soft-drink industry that are characterized by firms with strong brands are difficult to break into without spending heavily on advertising. For example, imagine how costly it would be to compete head-to-head against PepsiCo (owner of the Pepsi brands) or Coca-Cola Company. Product innovation is another way a firm can differentiate its good or service from competitors' offerings. Apple is an example of a company that has differentiated itself in laptop computers by regularly improving the features on its line of MacBooks, such as the MacBook Air, as well as the unqiuness of the accessories customers can buy to enhance their experience as users. It does this to not only keep existing customers and win new ones, but also to deter competitors from making a big push to try to win market share from Apple in the laptop computer industry.

- **Capital requirements:** The need to invest large amounts of money to gain entrance to an industry is another barrier to entry. The automobile industry is characterized by large capital requirements, although Tesla, which launched in 2003, was able to overcome this barrier and raise substantial funds by winning the confidence of investors through its expertise and innovations in electric car technology. Current evidence suggests that this firm may have potential to achieve long-term success. In early 2014 for example, Tesla reported results for the fourth quarter of 2013 that exceeded analysts' expectations and projected that sales of its Model S electric sedan would increase by 55 percent in 2014 compared to 2013.[11]

■ **Cost advantages independent of size:** Entrenched competitors may have cost advantages not related to size that are not available to new entrants. Commonly, these advantages are grounded in the firm's history. For example, the existing competitors in an industry may have purchased land and equipment in the past when the cost was far less than new entrants would have to pay for the same assets at the time of their entry.

■ **Access to distribution channels:** Distribution channels are often hard to crack. This is particularly true in crowded markets, such as the convenience store market. For a new sports drink to be placed on a convenience store shelf, it typically has to displace a product that is already there. If Greenvelope decided to start producing traditional wedding invitations and greeting cards, it would find it difficult to gain shelf space in stationery stores where a large number of offerings from major producers are already available to consumers.

■ **Government and legal barriers:** In knowledge-intensive industries, such as biotechnology and software, patents, trademarks, and copyrights form major barriers to entry. Other industries, such as banking and broadcasting, require the granting of a license by a public authority.

When start-ups create their own industries or create new niche markets within existing industries, they must create barriers to entry of their own to reduce the threat of new entrants. It is difficult for start-ups to create barriers to entry that are expensive, such as economies of scale, because money is usually tight. The biggest threat to a new firm's viability, particularly if it is creating a new market, is that larger, better-funded firms will step in and copy what it is doing. The ideal barrier to entry is a patent, trademark, or copyright, which prevents another firm from duplicating what the start-up is doing. Companies like Greenvelope typically have trade secrets associated with the functionality of their websites; in turn, trade secrets create a barrier to entry for a firm thinking about emulating the service provided by firms holding those secrets. The strength of Greenvelope's brand and the network of freelance designers and artists that it has assembled to create its invitations are also aspects of its business model that would be difficult to copy. Apart from these types of options, however, start-ups have to rely on nontraditional barriers to entry to discourage new entrants, such as assembling a world-class management team that would be difficult for another company to replicate. In Table 5.1, we provide a list of nontraditional barriers to entry that are particularly suited to start-up firms.

Rivalry Among Existing Firms

In most industries, the major determinant of industry profitability is the level of competition among the firms already competing in the industry. Some industries are fiercely competitive to the point where prices are pushed below the level of costs. When this happens, industry-wide losses occur. In other industries, competition is much less intense and price competition is subdued. For example, the airline industry is fiercely competitive and profit margins hinge largely on fuel prices and consumer demand. In contrast, the market for specialized medical equipment is less competitive, and profit margins are higher.

There are four primary factors that determine the nature and intensity of the rivalry among existing firms in an industry:

■ **Number and balance of competitors:** With a larger number of competitors, it is more likely that one or more will try to gain customers by cutting prices. Price-cutting causes problems throughout the industry and occurs more often when all the competitors in an industry are about the same size and when there is no clear market leader.

TABLE 5.1 Nontraditional Barriers to Entry

Barrier to Entry	Explanation	Example
Strength of management team	If a start-up puts together a world-class management team, it may give potential rivals pause in taking on the start-up in its chosen industry.	Square
First-mover advantage	If a start-up pioneers an industry or a new concept within an existing industry, the name recognition the start-up establishes may create a formidable barrier to entry.	Facebook
Passion of management team and employees	If the key employees of a start-up are highly motivated by its unique culture, are willing to work long hours because of their belief in what they are doing, and anticipate large financial gains through stock options, this is a combination that cannot be replicated by a larger firm. Think of the employees of a biotech firm trying to find a cure for a disease.	Amgen
Unique business model	If a start-up is able to construct a unique business model and establish a network of relationships that make the business model work, this set of advantages creates a barrier to entry.	Netflix
Internet domain name	Some Internet domain names are so "spot-on" in regard to a specific product or service that they give a start-up a meaningful leg up in terms of e-commerce opportunities. Think of www.1800flowers.com, www.1800gotjunk.com, and www.bodybuilding.com.	www.1800contacts.com
Inventing a new approach to an industry and executing the idea in an exemplary fashion	If a start-up invents a new approach to an industry and executes it in an exemplary fashion, these factors create a barrier to entry for potential imitators.	Cirque du Soleil

- **Degree of difference between products:** The degree to which products differ from one producer to another affects industry rivalry. For example, commodity industries such as paper products producers tend to compete on price because there is no meaningful difference between one manufacturer's products and another's.
- **Growth rate of an industry:** The competition among firms in a slow-growth industry is stronger than among those in fast-growth industries. Slow-growth industry firms, such as insurance, must fight for market share, which may tempt them to lower prices or increase quality to obtain customers. In fast-growth industries, such as e-book publishing, there are enough customers to satisfy most firms' production capacity, making price-cutting less likely.
- **Level of fixed costs:** Firms that have high fixed costs must sell a higher volume of their product to reach the break-even point than firms with low fixed costs. Once the break-even point is met, each additional unit sold contributes directly to a firm's bottom line. Firms with high fixed costs are anxious to fill their capacity, and this anxiety may lead to price-cutting.

Bargaining Power of Suppliers

In general, industries are more attractive when the bargaining power of suppliers is low. In some cases, suppliers can suppress the profitability of the industries to which they sell by raising prices or reducing the quality of the components they provide. If a supplier reduces the quality of the components it supplies, the quality of the finished product will suffer, and the manufacturer will eventually have to lower its price. If the suppliers are powerful relative to the firms in the industry to which they sell, industry profitability can suffer.[12] For example, Intel, with its Pentium chip, is a powerful supplier to the PC industry. Because most PCs feature Pentium chips, Intel can command a premium price from the PC manufacturers, thus directly affecting the overall profitability of the PC industry. Several factors have an impact on the ability of suppliers to exert pressure on buyers and suppress the profitability of the industries they serve. These include the following:

- **Supplier concentration:** When there are only a few suppliers to provide a critical product to a large number of buyers, the supplier has an advantage. This is the case in the pharmaceutical industry, where relatively few drug manufacturers are selling to thousands of doctors and their patients.

- **Switching costs:** Switching costs are the fixed costs that buyers encounter when switching or changing from one supplier to another. If switching costs are high, a buyer will be less likely to switch suppliers. For example, suppliers often provide their largest buyers with specialized software that makes it easy to buy their products. After the buyer spends time and effort learning the supplier's ordering and inventory management systems, it will be less likely to want to spend time and effort learning another supplier's system.

- **Attractiveness of substitutes:** Supplier power is enhanced if there are no attractive substitutes for the products or services the supplier offers. For example, there is little the computer industry can do when Microsoft and Intel raise their prices, as there are relatively few substitutes for these firms' products (although this is less true today than has been the case historically).

- **Threat of forward integration:** The power of a supplier is enhanced if there is a credible possibility that the supplier might enter the buyer's industry. For example, Microsoft's power as a supplier of computer operating systems is enhanced by the threat that it might enter the PC industry if PC makers balk too much at the cost of its software or threaten to use an operating system from a different software provider.

Bargaining Power of Buyers

In general, industries are more attractive when the bargaining power of buyers (a start-up's customers) is low. Buyers can suppress the profitability of the industries from which they purchase by demanding price concessions or increases in quality. For example, even in light of the problems it has encountered over the past several years, the automobile industry remains dominated by a handful of large automakers that buy products from thousands of suppliers in different industries. This enables the automakers to suppress the profitability of the industries from which they buy by demanding price reductions. Similarly, if the automakers insisted that their suppliers provide better-quality parts for the same price, the profitability of the suppliers would suffer. Several factors affect buyers' ability to exert pressure on suppliers and suppress the profitability of the industries from which they buy. These include the following:

- **Buyer group concentration:** If the buyers are concentrated, meaning that there are only a few large buyers, and they buy from a large number of suppliers, they can pressure the suppliers to lower costs and thus affect the profitability of the industries from which they buy.

- **Buyer's costs:** The greater the importance of an item is to a buyer, the more sensitive the buyer will be to the price it pays. For example, if the component sold by the supplier represents 50 percent of the cost of the buyer's product, the buyer will bargain hard to get the best price for that component.

- **Degree of standardization of supplier's products:** The degree to which a supplier's product differs from its competitors' offering affects the buyer's bargaining power. For example, a buyer who is purchasing a standard or undifferentiated product from a supplier, such as the corn syrup that goes into a soft drink, can play one supplier against another until it gets the best combination of features such as price and service.
- **Threat of backward integration:** The power of a buyer is enhanced if there is a credible threat that the buyer might enter the supplier's industry. For example, the PC industry can keep the price of computer monitors down by threatening to make its own monitors if the price gets too high.

The Value of the Five Forces Model

LEARNING OBJECTIVE

3. Explain the value that entrepreneurial firms create by successfully using the five forces model.

Along with helping a firm understand the dynamics of the industry it plans to enter, the five forces model can be used in two ways: (1) to help a firm determine whether it should enter a particular industry and (2) whether it can carve out an attractive position in that industry. Let's examine these two positive outcomes.

First, the five forces model can be used to assess the attractiveness of an industry or a specific position within an industry by determining the level of threat to industry profitability for each of the forces, as shown in Table 5.2. This analysis of industry attractiveness should be more in-depth than the less rigorous analysis conducted during feasibility analysis. For example, if a firm filled out the form shown in Table 5.2 and several of the threats to industry profitability were high, the firm may want to reconsider entering the industry or think carefully about the position it will occupy in the industry. In the restaurant industry, for example, the threat of substitute products, the threat of new entrants, and the rivalry among existing firms are high. For certain restaurants, such as fresh-seafood restaurants, the bargaining power of suppliers

TABLE 5.2 Determining the Attractiveness of an Industry Using the Five Forces Model

	Threat to Industry Profitability		
Competitive Force	**Low**	**Medium**	**High**
Threat of substitutes			
Threat of new entrants			
Rivalry among existing firms			
Bargaining power of suppliers			
Bargaining power of buyers			

Instructions:

Step 1 Select an industry.
Step 2 Determine the level of threat to industry profitability for each of the forces (low, medium, or high).
Step 3 Use the table to develop an overall feel for the attractiveness of the industry.
Step 4 Use the table to identify the threats that are most often relevant to industry profitability.

may also be high (the number of seafood suppliers is relatively small compared to the number of beef and chicken suppliers). Thus, a firm that enters the restaurant industry has several forces working against it simply because of the nature of the industry. To help sidestep or diminish these threats, it must establish a favorable position. One firm that has accomplished this is Panera Bread, as discussed in Case 5.1 at the end of this chapter. By studying the restaurant industry, Panera found that some consumers have tired of fast food but don't always have the time to eat at a sit-down restaurant. To fill the gap, Panera helped to pioneer a new category called "fast casual," which combines relatively fast service with high-quality food. Panera has been very successful in occupying this unique position in the restaurant industry. You'll learn more about Panera Bread's success while reading Case 5.1.

The second way a new firm can apply the five forces model to help determine whether it should enter an industry is by using the model pictured in Figure 5.2 to answer several key questions. By doing so, a new venture can assess the thresholds it may have to meet to be successful in a particular industry:

Question 1: Is the industry a realistic place for our new venture to enter? This question can be answered by looking at the overall attractiveness of an industry, as depicted in Table 5.2, and by assessing whether the window of opportunity is open. It's up to the entrepreneur to determine if the window of opportunity for the industry is open or closed.

Question 2: If we do enter the industry, can our firm do a better job than the industry as a whole in avoiding or diminishing the impact of the forces that suppress industry profitability? Entering an industry with a fresh brand, innovative ideas, and a world-class management team and performing better than the industry incumbents increases the likelihood a new venture will be successful. This was the case when Google entered the Internet search engine industry and displaced Yahoo as the market leader. Outperforming industry incumbents can also be achieved if a new venture brings an attractive new product to market that is patented, preventing others from duplicating it for a period of time.

Question 3: Is there a unique position in the industry that avoids or diminishes the forces that suppress industry profitability? As we've described, this is the advantage that both Greenvelope and Panera Bread have captured.

Question 4: Is there a superior business model that can be put in place that would be hard for industry incumbents to duplicate? Keep in mind that the five forces model provides a picture of an industry "as is," which isn't necessarily the way a new venture has to approach it. Sometimes the largest firms in an industry are trapped by their own strategies and contractual obligations, providing an opening for a start-up to try something new. For example, when Dell started selling computers directly to consumers, its largest rivals—Hewlett-Packard, Compaq, and IBM—were not able to respond quickly and effectively. They were locked into a strategy of selling through retailers. If they had tried to mimic Dell and sell directly to end users or customers, they would have alienated their most valuable partners—retailers such as Sears and Best Buy. However, with the passage of time, Dell's competitors have learned how to effectively and efficiently sell directly to consumers, largely erasing Dell's historic advantage in the process of doing so.

The steps involved in answering these questions are pictured in Figure 5.2. If the founders of a new firm believe that a particular industry is a realistic place for their new venture, a positive response to one or more of the questions posed in Figure 5.2 increases the likelihood that the new venture will be successful.

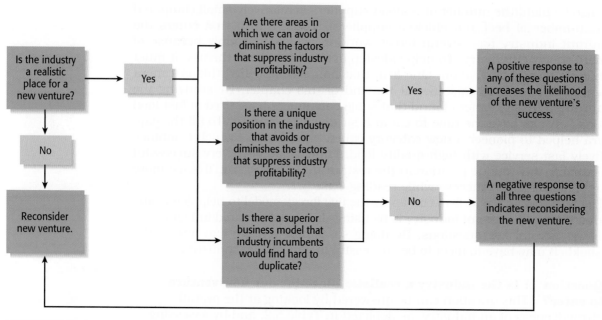

FIGURE 5.2
Using the Five Forces Model to Pose Questions to Determine the Potential Success of a New Venture

Industry Types and the Opportunities They Offer

LEARNING OBJECTIVE

4. Identify the five primary industry types and the opportunities they offer.

Along with studying the factors discussed previously, it is helpful for a new venture to study industry types to determine the opportunities they offer.[13] The five most prevalent industry types, depicted in Table 5.3, are emerging industries, fragmented industries, mature industries, declining industries, and global industries.[14] There are unique opportunities associated with each type of industry.

Home health care is an example of a fragmented industry. A fragmented industry is fertile ground for an entrepreneurial start-up.

TABLE 5.3 Industry Structure and Opportunities

Industry Type	Industry Characteristics	Opportunities	Examples of Entrepreneurial Firms Exploiting These Opportunities
Emerging industries	Recent changes in demand or technology; new industry standard operating procedures have yet to be developed	First-mover advantage	■ Brain Sentry's device to help detect sports-related concussions ■ Windspire in small-scale wind-generated power ■ Buzzy's procedure that helps relieve the pain and anxiety associated with getting a shot
Fragmented industries	Large number of firms of approximately equal size	Consolidation	■ Chipotle Mexican Grill in fast-casual restaurants ■ 1-800-GOT-JUNK? in junk removal ■ Modcloth in women's clothing
Mature industries	Slow increases in demand, numerous repeat customers, and limited product innovation	Process and after-sale service innovation	■ Justin's in peanut butter ■ SuperJam in fruit jams ■ Flings Bins in trash bags
Declining industries	Consistent reduction in industry demand	Leaders, niche, harvest, and divest	■ Nucor in steel ■ JetBlue in airlines ■ Cirque du Soleil in circuses
Global industries	Significant international sales	Multinational and global	■ PharmaJet in needleless injection systems ■ d.light in solar-powered lanterns

Emerging Industries

An **emerging industry** is a new industry in which standard operating procedures have yet to be developed. The firm that pioneers or takes the leadership of an emerging industry often captures a first-mover advantage. A **first-mover advantage** is a sometimes insurmountable advantage gained by the first company to establish a significant position in a new market.

Because a high level of uncertainty characterizes emerging industries, any opportunity that is captured may be short-lived. Still, many new ventures enter emerging industries because barriers to entry are usually low and there is no established pattern of rivalry.

Fragmented Industries

A **fragmented industry** is one that is characterized by a large number of firms of approximately equal size. The primary opportunity for start-ups in fragmented industries is to consolidate the industry and establish industry leadership as a result of doing so. The most common way to do this is through a **geographic roll-up strategy**, in which one firm starts acquiring similar firms that are located in different geographic areas.[15] This is an often observed path for growth for businesses such as auto repair shops and beauty salons. It is difficult for them to generate additional income in a single location, so they grow by expanding into new geographic areas via either organic growth or by acquiring similar firms.

Mature Industries

A **mature industry** is an industry that is experiencing slow or no increase in demand, has numerous repeat (rather than new) customers, and has limited product innovation. Occasionally, entrepreneurs introduce new product innovations to mature industries, surprising incumbents who thought nothing new was possible in their industries. An example is Steve Demos, the founder of White Wave, a company that makes vegetarian food products. White Wave introduced a new product—Silk Soymilk—into a mature industry—consumer milk. Silk Soymilk became the best-selling soymilk in the country. Soymilk isn't really milk at all—it's a soybean-based beverage that looks like milk and has a similar texture. Still, it has made its way into the dairy section of most supermarkets in the United States and has positioned itself as a healthy substitute for milk. Who would have thought that a major innovation was possible in the milk industry?

The lure of mature industries, for start-ups, is that they're often large industries with seemingly vast potential if product and/or process innovations can be effectively introduced and the industry can be revitalized. This is the hope for a company such as Beyond Meat, the subject of the You Be the VC 5.1 feature. Beyond Meat is producing a plant-based substitute for chicken strips, called Chichen-Free Strips, that replicate the look, taste, and sensory experience of eating meat. The company is not targeting people who are ultra careful about what they eat, but a more mainstream market of people who are trying to eat healthier. Beyond Meat is now working on a similarly healthy substitute for ground beef. Meat is a mature industry. If Beyond Meat's products can be effectively introduced into the marketplace and it is successful in revitilizing the meat industry, the firm's market potential is huge.

Declining Industries

A **declining industry** is an industry or a part of an industry that is experiencing a reduction in demand. The renting of DVDs and video games by mail and producing and distributing hard copy textbooks are examples of products associated with industries or segments of an industry that are in some state of decline. Typically, entrepreneurs shy away from declining industries because the firms in the industry do not meet the tests of an attractive opportunity as we described in Chapter 2. There are occasions, however, when a start-up will do just the opposite of what conventional wisdom would suggest and, by doing so, stakes out a position in a declining industry that isn't being hotly contested. That is what Cirque du Soleil did in the circus industry.

Entrepreneurial firms employ three different strategies in declining industries. The first is to adopt a **leadership strategy**, in which the firm tries to become the dominant player in the industry. This is a rare strategy for a start-up in a declining industry. The second is to pursue a **niche strategy**, which focuses on a narrow segment of the industry that might be encouraged to grow through product or process innovation. The third is a **cost reduction strategy**, which is accomplished through achieving lower costs than industry incumbents through process improvements. Achieving lower costs allows a firm to sell its product or service at a lower price, creating value for consumers in the process of doing so. Initially a small firm but now quite large as a result of its success, Nucor Steel revolutionized the steel industry through the introduction of the "minimill" concept, and is an example of an entrepreneurially minded firm that pursued this strategy. Historically, most steel mills in the United States used large blast furnaces to produce a wide line of products; however, the scale of these furnaces meant that firms had to produce and sell significant quantities of their products in order to be profitable. In contrast, Nucor's then-innovative minimills were smaller and were used to produce a narrower range of products. Of great importance too is the fact that minimills are energy efficient and make high-quality steel.[16] Nucor proved its concept and quickly found growth markets within the largely declining U.S. steel industry.

Global Industries

A **global industry** is an industry that is experiencing significant international sales. Many start-ups enter global industries and from day one try to appeal to international rather than just domestic markets. The two most common strategies pursued by firms in global industries are the multidomestic strategy and the global strategy. Firms that pursue a **multidomestic strategy** compete for market share on a country-by-country basis and vary their product or service offerings to meet the demands of the local market. In contrast, firms pursuing a **global strategy** use the same basic approach in all foreign markets. The choice between these two strategies depends on how similar consumers' tastes are from market to market. For example, food companies typically are limited to a multidomestic strategy because food preferences vary significantly from country to country. Firms that sell more universal products, such as athletic shoes, have been successful with global strategies. Entrepreneurial firms can use both strategies successfully. The key to achieving success is gaining a clear understanding of customers' needs and interests in each market in which the firm intends to compete.[17]

Competitor Analysis

After a firm has gained an understanding of the industry and the target market in which it plans to compete, the next step is to complete a competitor analysis. A competitor analysis is a detailed analysis of a firm's competition. It helps a firm understand the positions of its major competitors and the opportunities that are available to obtain a competitive advantage in one or more areas. These are important issues, particularly for new ventures.[18] In the words of Sun Tzu, quoted earlier in this chapter, "Time spent in reconnaissance is seldom wasted."

LEARNING OBJECTIVE

5. Explain the purpose of a competitor analysis and a competitive analysis grid.

First we'll discuss how a firm identifies its major competitors. We'll then look at the process of completing a competitive analysis grid, which is a tool for organizing the information a firm collects about its primary competitors.

Identifying Competitors

The first step in a competitive analysis is to determine who the competition is. This is more difficult than one might think. For example, take a company such as 1-800-FLOWERS. Primarily, the company sells flowers. But 1-800-FLOWERS is not only in the flower business; in fact, because flowers are often given for gifts, the company is also in the gift business. If the company sees itself in the gift business rather than just the flower business, it has a broader set of competitors and opportunities to consider. In addition, some firms sell products or services that straddle more than one industry. For example, a company that makes computer software for dentists' offices operates in both the computer software industry and the health care industry. Again, this type of company has more potential competitors but also more opportunities to consider.

The different types of competitors a business will face are shown in Figure 5.3. The challenges associated with each of these groups of competitors are described here:

- **Direct competitors:** These are businesses that offer products or services that are identical or highly similar to those of the firm completing the analysis. These competitors are the most important because they are going after the same customers as the new firm. A new firm faces winning over the loyal followers of its major competitors, which is difficult to do, even when the new firm has a better product.

FIGURE 5.3
Types of Competitors
New Ventures Face

Direct Competitors	Indirect Competitors	Future Competitors
Businesses offering identical or similar products	Businesses offering close substitute products	Businesses that are not yet direct or indirect competitors but could be at any time

- **Indirect competitors:** These competitors offer close substitutes to the product the firm completing the analysis sells. These firms' products are also important in that they target the same basic need that is being met by the new firm's product. For example, when people told Roberto Goizueta, the late CEO of Coca-Cola, that Coke's market share was at a maximum, he countered by saying that Coke accounted for less than 2 percent of the 64 ounces of fluid that the average person drinks each day. "The enemy is coffee, milk, tea [and] water," he once said.[19]

- **Future competitors:** These are companies that are not yet direct or indirect competitors but could move into one of these roles at any time. Firms are always concerned about strong competitors moving into their markets. For example, think of how the world has changed substantially for Barnes & Noble and other brick-and-mortar bookstores since Amazon.com was founded. These changes are perhaps especially dramatic for Borders, which filed for bankruptcy in 2011. Former competitor Barnes & Noble bought Borders's remaining assets (primarily its brand name) later in that year. But this story has yet to reach a conclusion, in that in February of 2014, investment firm G Asset Management offered "to acquire a majority interest in Barnes & Noble Inc." If this transaction takes place, G Asset intends to split Barnes & Noble's retail and e-reader businesses into separate operations.[20] And, think of how smartphone technology continues to change the nature of competition for a variety of firms, including those selling entertainment services, telephone services, and the like.

It is impossible for a firm to identify all its direct and indirect competitors, let alone its future competitors. However, identifying its top 5 to 10 direct competitors and its top 5 to 10 indirect and future competitors makes it easier for the firm to complete its competitive analysis grid.

If a firm does not have a direct competitor, it shouldn't forget that the status quo can be the toughest competitor of all. In general, people are resistant to change and can always keep their money rather than spend it.[21] A product or service's utility must rise above its cost, not only in monetary terms but also in terms of the hassles associated with switching or learning something new, to motivate someone to buy a new product or service.[22]

Creating meaningful value and sharp differentiation from competitors are actions small firms in crowded industries can take to remain competitive and gain market share. Three firms that have successfully accomplished this are profiled in the "Savvy Entrepreneurial Firm" feature.

Sources of Competitive Intelligence

To complete a meaningful competitive analysis grid, a firm must first understand the strategies and behaviors of its competitors. The information that is gathered by a firm to learn about its competitors is called **competitive intelligence**. Obtaining sound competitive intelligence is not always a simple task.

SAVVY ENTREPRENEURIAL FIRM

Thriving in a Crowded Industry by Creating Meaningful Value and Differentiation from Competitors

Hipmunk: Web: www.hipmunk.com; Facebook: Hipmunk; Twitter: @thehipmunk
Element Bars: Web: www.elementbars.com; Facebook: Element Bars; Twitter: @elementbars
BenchPrep: Web: www.benchprep.com; Facebook: BenchPrep; Twitter: @benchprep

Firms do well in a crowded industry when two conditions exist: (1) they create meaningful value for customers at a fair price and (2) they effectively differentiate themselves from competitors. In fact, diminishing the impact of three of Porter's five forces rests largely on these factors. A firm is able to withstand rivalry among existing firms and is able to deter substitutes and new entrants by creating value for its customers and offering something that people can't get anywhere else.

The following are examples of three businesses that are creating unique value in their industries and have differentiated themselves from their competitors. Each industry is very competitive, yet these companies are growing and thriving.

Hipmunk

Talk about a crowded industry, consider the options a consumer has for booking an airline flight. Choices include tavel agents, airline websites, and online travel sites like Travelocity or Orbitz. Never mind—Hipmunk, an online travel service, launched in 2010, offering travelers what they believe is an improved way to plan travel. Hipmunk's premise is that existing travel sites provide too much information in a less-than-optimal format. It differentiates itself by tackling that problem and displaying results in a more appealing manner.

Here's how it works. For airline travel you go to Hipmunk's site and enter your departure airport, arrival location, departure date, and return date just like any other travel site. Then things change. Instead of offering pages of results, Hipmunk displays its results on a single page. The flights are color coded—each color represents a different airline. The flights are displayed as bars, and the length of the flight corresponds to the width of the bar. Flights can be sorted by price, time of day, and "agony," which is a score based on the best combination of price, duration, and number of stops. The flights with the least amount of agony are shown first. Flights that are similar to the ones displayed, but are more expensive or have a higher agony score, are automatically removed from the results. Thus, the only results shown are the ones that make the most sense to purchase.

Hipmunk doesn't release booking numbers, but it is reportedly gaining momemtum in the travel industry. A similar easy-to-use interface is available for booking hotel rooms. Hipmunk is aggressively moving into the mobile market, and its app is highly ranked in the Apple App Store.

Element Bars

Another tough industry is protien bars. Seriously, how many choices does a consumer have for buying protein bars at a store? In 2007 Element Bars launched with a new twist in the energy bar market. The company would differentiate itself by offering fresh, nutritious bars that could be sold online and "customized" by its customers.

Here's how Element Bars was orginally set up, and how the company operates today. Customers log on to Element Bars's website, and in five steps they can "build" their own energy bar. They are first asked to pick a basic texture, with options such as Chewy, Crispy, and Datey. They then add their choice of fruits, nuts, sweets, and boosts (such as whey protein or fiber) to create their customized bar. A nutrition label on the right portion of the screen changes as ingredients are added, so the creator can see how different ingredients affect the calories or the grams of saturated fat in the bar. After the bar is built, the final step is for the consumer to name the bar whatever he or she wants. Once the order is placed, the bar is made and is shipped in just a few days.

Along with selling customizable energy bars via the Internet, Element Bars sells directly to speciality retailers who want to create their own branded energy bars. Its difficlut for fitness centers, for example, to sell well-known bars like Clif bars at a premium, when their members can buy the same bars at Walmart or a similar type of outlet. By branding their own bar via Element Bars, a fitness center can sell the bars for a premium and capture higher margins.

BenchPrep

BenchPrep is competing in the hyper-competitive test prep industry. For standardized tests such as the SAT, GRE, GMAT, LSAT, and MCAT, there are many print test preparation guides, online courses, smartphone apps, and face-to-face short courses taught on college and university campuses to help students prepare for the tests. BenchPrep differentiates itself by selling cross-platform test prep courses. What this means is that not only can students access their courses on their computers and mobile devices, they can also sync their progresss so they can pick up right where they left off regardless of what device they're using. As a result, a student could start a practice test on her/his laptop in the morning, answer a few questions during the day on an iPhone, and finish the test in the evening on a desktop computer.

(continued)

BenchPrep differentiates itself in additional ways. The company partners with the world's top publishers, authors, and subject matter experts in preparing its courses. BenchPrep's test preps give students progress reports to show where they are excelling and where performance needs to be improved. In addition, the test preps have social features, and allow students to study their progress and performance against other students preparing for the same test.

Questions for Critical Thinking

1. What are the common attributes across the three companies in this feature? How do these attributes help the companies thrive in otherwise competitive industries?

2. In what ways are each company's features redefining the customer experience in their industries?

3. Of the three companies featured, which one do you think has the most potential to remain competitive? Which company do you think is the most vulnerable to increased competition from competitors? Explain your answers.

4. Find an example of another company that is thriving in a highly competitive industry. Analyze the company and discern what sets it apart from its competitors.

Sources: Hipmunk, Hipmunk home page, www.hipmunk.com (accessed February 19, 2014); Element Bars home page, www.elementbars.com (accessed February 19, 2014); BenchPrep home page, www.benchprep.com (accessed February 19, 2014); B. Sherr, "App Watch: Making Test Preparation Mobile, Social," *Wall Street Journal*, November 1, 2010.

If a competitor is a publicly traded firm, a description of the firm's business and its financial information is available through annual reports filed with the Securities and Exchange Commission (SEC). These reports are public records and are available at the SEC's website (www.sec.gov). If one or more of the competitors is a private company, the task is more difficult, given that private companies are not required to divulge information to the public. There are a number of ways that a firm can ethically obtain information about its competitors. A sample of the most common techniques is shown in Table 5.4.

Completing a Competitive Analysis Grid

As we mentioned previously, a **competitive analysis grid** is a tool for organizing the information a firm collects about its competitors. It can help a firm see how it stacks up against its competitors, provide ideas for markets to

TABLE 5.4 Sources of Competitive Intelligence

Source	Description/Benefit
Attend conferences and trade shows	Participants talk about the latest trends in the industry and display their most current products.
Purchase competitors' products	Purchasing and using a competitor's products can provide insight into their benefits and shortcomings. The purchase process itself can provide data about how a competitor treats its customers.
Study competitors' websites and social media pages	Many companies put a lot of information on their websites, including product information and the latest news about the company. The same goes for a company's pages on social media outlets, such as Facebook and Twitter.
Set up Google e-mail alerts	Google e-mail alerts are updates of the latest Google results, including press releases, news articles, and blog posts, on any keywords of interest. You can set up e-mail alerts using your company's name or the name of a competitor.
Read industry-related books, magazines, websites, and blogs	Many of these sources contain articles or features that have information about competitors.
Talk to customers about what motivated them to buy your product as opposed to your competitor's product	Customers can provide a wealth of information about the advantages and disadvantages of competing products.

pursue, and, perhaps most importantly, identify its primary sources of competitive advantage. To be a viable company, a new venture must have at least one clear competitive advantage over its major competitors.

An example of a competitive analysis grid is provided in Table 5.5. This grid is for Greenvelope, the online wedding invitation start-up featured at the beginning of the chapter. The main competitive factors in the industry, which include online and traditional wedding invitation services, are cost, selection, customizable, presentation to invitee, turnaround time, no ads, green, and social consciousness/philanthropy. Some industry participants, such as Greenvelope, also engage in philanthropy. (As highlighted previously, Greenvelope gives 1 percent of its revene each quarter to Moutains to Sound, a nonprofit organization that supports the greenway along the I-90 corridor of Northwest Washington State.) These factors are placed on the vertical axis of Greenvelope's competitive analysis grid. The horizontal axis contains Greenvelope and its four main competitors. In each box, Greenvelope rates itself against its main competitors. The purpose of this exercise is for a company to see how it stacks up against its competitors and to illustrate the areas in which it has an advantage (and has a disadvantage). For example, Greenvelope rates itself as superior to its competitors in terms of presentation to invitee and social consciousness/philanthropy. It will likely use this information in its advertising and promotions. An additional benefit of completing a competitive analysis grid is that it helps a company fine-tune its offering. For example, Greenvelope rates itself as "even" with its competitors on several criteria. It might use that knowledge to look for ways to up its game on one or more of these criteria to increase its overall competitiveness in relation to its competitors.

As this discussion shows, analyzing competitors is a complex and challenging process. But, the link between understanding competitors and how an entrepreneurial venture stacks up against them and the new firm's success in both the short and long term is clear and strong. In the "What Went Wrong?" feature, we describe the experiences of Digg. Once one of the hottest Internet sites, this firm competed in a rapidly emerging industry. While reading about Digg, keep in mind the actions firms should take to understand their competitors and to form a competitive analysis grid. In an overall sense, might more effective work in terms of understanding its competitors and their actions increase the likelihood of Digg's competitive success?

TABLE 5.5 Competitive Analysis Grid for Greenvelope

Name	Greenvelope (electronic)	Evite (electronic)	Paperless Post (electronic)	Minted (traditional)	Local Stationery Store (traditional)
Cost	Even	Advantage	Even	Disadvantage	Disadvantage
Selection	Even	Even	Even	Even	Disadvantage
Customizable	Even	Even	Even	Even	Even
Presentation to Invitee	Advantage	Even	Even	Even	Even
Turnaround Time	Even	Even	Even	Disadvantage	Disadvantage
No Ads	Even	Disadvantage	Even	Even	Even
Green	Even	Even	Even	Disadvantage	Disadvantage
Social Consciousness/ Philanthropy	Advantage	Disadvantage	Disadvantage	Disadvantage	Disadvantage

WHAT WENT WRONG?

Digg: A Start-up That Lost Its Way and Its Place in Its Industry

At one time, Digg was one of the hottest sites on the Internet. The site's primary purpose was to allow users to discover, share, and recommend Web content. A user could submit an article or anything posted on the Internet for consideration. Other users either voted the article or page up ("dig") or down ("bury"). Although the voting took place on digg.com, many websites added "dig" buttons to their pages, allowing users to vote as they surfed the Web. The end product was a vibrant website with wide-ranging, constantly changing lists of popular and trending content from around the Internet.

Digg launched on December 4, 2004. At the height of its popularity, 2007-2008, it was attracting over 236 million visitors annually. It had grown large enough that it affected the traffic experienced by other websites. If an article was submitted to Digg, and it made it to the front page of digg.com (by enough users "digging" it), the site the article was posted on would see a spike in traffic. This phenomenon was referred to as the "Digg effect." In 2008, Digg was valued at more than $160 million. The sky seemed to be the limit for Digg, its users, and its investors. Incredibly, by July 2012, Digg was a shadow of its former self and was sold to Betaworks, a technology development company, for pennies on the dollar. What went wrong?

Several things went wrong with Digg, which caused the firm to lose its way and its place in the Internet social media industry. First, at the same time Digg was enjoying its height of popularity, Facebook and Twitter were gaining momentum. Eventually, Facebook and Twitter started eating away at Digg's traffic, as they morphed into places where people discovered the most up-to-date news and Internet gossip, the main reason for coming to Digg. Rather than remaining true to its identity, Digg started emulating the best features of Facebook, Twitter, and other social media websites. To make matters worse, Digg started falling behind Facebook and Twitter in terms of functionality. It took several steps to post a link on Digg, whereas Facebook and Twitter were simpler.

A second thing that hampered Digg was a poorly executed relaunch. In early 2010 Digg announced that its site would undergo an extensive overhaul, to freshen it up and make it more user-friendly. Digg was losing traffic and was desperate to win some back. The company was experiencing a technical problem concerning the difficulty in scaling its MySQL database software,

so it decided to switch over to another open-source system called Cassandra. Digg's relaunch on August 25, 2010, was tarnished by site-wide bugs and glitches. For weeks, the site frequently wasn't available or was unstable at best, and when users finally reached the site, they complained about the new design and the removal of many features that they liked. Reflecting on this period in a 2012 *Wall Street Journal* article, Kevin Rose, Digg's founder and CEO, characterized the 2010 relaunch as botched and said that the company was slow to respond to criticism.

A third problem Digg encountered was that while it was supposedly "democratizing the Web" by allowing users to vote on the articles that would appear on its front page rather than editors selecting them, people claimed that it was easy to game Digg's system. Anyone could submit an article, rally his friends, co-workers, and others to vote up the story, and see the story rise to the top of Digg's rankings. Once this practice became widely known, users originally attracted to Digg thinking they could submit an article and have it advance to Digg's front page strictly on its merits became disillusioned and less interested in the site.

Questions for Critical Thinking

1. What lessons does Digg's failure have for entrepreneurs who are studying entering the social media industry?
2. Would you characterize the "Rivalry Among Existing Firms" in the industry Digg competed in as high, moderate, or low? To what degree was Digg able to effectively diminish or suppress the negative effects of the rivalry it experienced? What, if anything, should Digg have done differently in this area?
3. If Digg had completed a competitive analysis grid shortly before it relaunched in 2010, what factors would you have placed on the vertical axis of the grid and what companies would you have compared Digg against? To what degree do you think Digg would have favorably compared to its competitors?
4. What steps could Digg have taken, throughout the life of its business, that may have enabled it to remain competitive and still be a successful firm today?

Sources: S. E. Ante and J. Walker, "Digg Admits Missteps," *Wall Street Journal*, July 16, 2010, B7; M. Elgin, "Elgan: Why Digg Failed." *Computerworld*, March 19, 2011.

Chapter Summary

LO1. To compete successfully, a firm needs to understand the industry in which it intends to compete. Industry analysis is a business research framework or tool that focuses on an industry's potential. The knowledge gleaned from this analysis helps a firm decide whether to enter an industry and if it can carve out a position in that industry that will provide it a competitive advantage. Environmental trends and business trends are the two main components of "industry trends" that firms should study. Environmental trends include economic trends, social trends, technological advances, and political and regulatory changes. Business trends include other business-related trends that aren't environmental trends but are important to recognize and understand.

LO2. Firms use the "five forces model" to understand an industry's structure. The parts of Porter's five forces model are threat of substitutes, threat of new entrants, rivalry among existing firms, bargaining power of suppliers, and bargaining power of buyers.

LO3. What entrepreneurs should understand is that each individual force has the potential to affect the ability of any firm to generate profits while competing in the industry or a segment of an industry. The challenge is to find a position within an industry or a segment of an industry in which the probability of the firm being negatively affected by the five forces is reduced. Additionally, successfully examining an industry yields valuable information to those starting a business. Armed with the information it has collected, firms are prepared to consider four industry-related questions that should be examined before deciding to enter an industry. These questions are: Is the industry a realistic place for a new venture? If we do enter the industry, can our firm do a better job than the industry as a whole in avoiding or diminishing the threats that suppress industry profitability? Is there a unique position in the industry that avoids or diminishes the forces that suppress industry profitability? Is there a superior business model that can be put in place that would be hard for industry incumbents to duplicate?

LO4. There are five primary industry types entrepreneurial firms consider when choosing the industry in which they will compete. These industry types and the opportunities they offer are as follows: emerging industry/first-mover advantage; fragmented industry/consolidation; mature industry/emphasis on service and process innovation; declining industry/leadership, niche, harvest, and divest; and global industry/multidomestic strategy or global strategy.

LO5. A competitor analysis is a detailed analysis of a firm's competition. It helps a firm understand the positions of its major competitors and the opportunities that are available to obtain a competitive advantage in one or more areas. Direct competitors, indirect competitors, and future competitors are the three groups of competitors a new firm faces.

Successful competition demands that a firm understand its competitors and the actions they may take in the future. There are a number of ways a firm can ethically obtain the information it seeks to have about its competitors, including attending conferences and trade shows; purchasing competitors' products; studying competitors' websites; setting up Google e-mail alerts; reading industry-related books, magazines, and websites; and talking to customers about what motivated them to buy your product as opposed to your competitor's product.

A competitive analysis grid is a tool for organizing the information a firm collects about its competitors. This grid can help a firm see how it stacks up against its competitors, provide ideas for markets to pursue, and, perhaps most importantly, identify its primary sources of competitive advantage.

Key Terms

barrier to entry, **178**
competitive analysis grid, **190**
competitive intelligence, **188**
competitor analysis, **173**
cost reduction strategy, **186**
declining industry, **186**
economies of scale, **178**

emerging industry, **185**
first-mover advantage, **185**
fragmented industry, **185**
geographic roll-up strategy, **185**
global industry, **187**
global strategy, **187**

industry, **172**
industry analysis, **172**
leadership strategy, **186**
mature industry, **185**
multidomestic strategy, **187**
niche strategy, **186**
position, **173**

Review Questions

5-1. What is an industry?

5-2. What is an industry analysis and why is it important for a new firm to analyze the industry in which it may choose to compete?

5-3. How can startups stay on top of environmental and business trends in their industries?

5-4. What are the five forces that determine an industry's profitability?

5-5. How can the threat of substitute products suppress an industry's profitability?

5-6. How can the threat of new entrants suppress an industry's profitability?

5-7. What are the major determinants of profitability in most industries?

5-8. How does rivalry among existing firms have the potential to suppress an industry's profitability?

5-9. What are the two values created by firms when they successfully use the five forces model?

5-10. How does the bargaining power of suppliers have the potential to suppress an industry's profitability?

5-11. What are the five primary industry types and what are the opportunities they offer?

5-12. How does the bargaining power of buyers have the potential to suppress an industry's profitability?

5-13. What are the nontraditional barriers to entry that are particularly suitable for entrepreneurial firms to study when selecting an industry in which to compete?

5-14. How can a start-up avoid or sidestep the pressure applied by one of the five forces on industry profitability by establishing a unique "position" in an industry?

5-15. What are the characteristics of a fragmented industry?

5-16. What is the primary opportunity for new firms in fragmented industries?

5-17. What are the characteristics of a mature industry?

5-18. What is the primary opportunity for new firms in a mature industry?

5-19. What is a global industry?

5-20. What are the two most common strategies pursued by firms in global industries?

5-21. What is the purpose of a competitor analysis?

5-22. What are the differences among direct competitors, indirect competitors, and future competitors?

5-23. What is the meaning of the term *competitive intelligence*?

5-24. Why is it important for firms to collect intelligence about their competitors?

5-25. What are the three different strategies that may be adopted by a firm in a declining industry?

5-26. What is the purpose of completing a competitive analysis grid?

Application Questions

5-27. Linda Henricks is thinking about starting a firm in the home health care provider industry. When asked by a potential investor if she had studied the industry, Linda replied, "With the aging of the population and the fact that people are living longer than ever, the home health care provider industry is so full of potential, it doesn't require formal analysis." In what ways will Linda limit her possibilities with the potential investor if her current attitude about the importance of industry analysis doesn't change?

5-28. The "You Be the VC 5.2" feature focuses on Ubersense, a company in the sports coaching industry. What environmental trends and business trends favor Ubersense's unique approach and service?

5-29. Eric Andrews has been investigating the possibility of starting a service that will partner with grocery stores to provide a delivery service for their customers. The idea is that after purchasing their groceries, customers could go to a kiosk in the store, pay a small fee, and have their groceries delivered to their homes within 60 minutes. Which of the five forces in Porter's five forces model do you anticipate will most strongly affect Eric's potential business and why?

5-30. Read Case 5.1, which focuses on Panera Bread. What are some of the barriers to entry a firm would have to deal with and try to overcome if it tried to compete against Panera Bread in the casual dining segment of the restaurant industry?

5-31. In groups of two, choose a new venture of your interest. It is helpful for a new business to study industry types and determine the opportunities that they offer. Identify your chosen industry type and the opportunities offered. You may use Table 5.3 in the chapter as a guide for your analysis.

5-32. A friend of yours came to you for advice. She was in the middle of preparing a competitive analysis grid for her online clothing business. She understands that in order for her to prepare the analysis grid, she needs to first understand the strategies and behaviors of her competitors, and this information is also known as competitive intelligence. However, she does not know how to ethically obtain sensitive information on her competitors. Advise her.

5-33. Trends in the motorcycle industry are presented early in this chapter. Revisit this issue by identifying the effects of economic, demographic, and regulatory changes that may affect the motorcycle industry at the time you are reading this book.

5-34. Ben Jose is an established entrepreneur in your neighborhood. He has been running an Italian restaurant for the last 10 years and has enjoyed great profits due to his good relationship with his suppliers. However, recently he noticed a drop in his profits that he couldn't explain initially. After thorough investigation, he noticed that the problem was caused by his suppliers. He was able to identify several factors that impacted the ability of his suppliers to exert pressure on him, and suppress the profitability of his business directly and the industry indirectly. As his business advisor, explain to him the effect suppliers can have on a business.

5-35. Stella Marie has just ventured into the flower business. Her core business is to sell flowers. However, she is aware that her competitors are not only those shops that sell flowers. She needs to do a competitive analysis to face the competition better. The first step in a competitive analysis is to determine who the competition is. What are the different types of competitors that Stella will face in the business of selling flowers?

YOU BE THE VC 5.1 COMPANY: Beyond Meat

• Web: www.beyondmeat.com • Facebook: Beyond Meat • Twitter: @BeyondMeat

Business Idea: Provide consumers with plant-based protein foods that take the animal out of meat—without sacrificing the taste, chew, or satisfaction.

Pitch: A number of factors motivate people to seek out meat substitutes. Health benefits, animal welfare, lowering greenhouse gas emissions, and bad press about the poor conductions under which some animals raised for slaughter are kept are some of these factors. Many of the most common meat substitutes—tofu, bean burgers, vegetable cutlets, and so on—lack bite, chew, juiciness, and flavor. As a result, people try them for a while and then return to traditional meat products. A parallel problem exists regarding the demand for meat. Global demand for meat has tripled in the last 40 years, driven by population growth and an upward trend in per-capita consumption of meat. Producing meat has significant environmental implications. Animal agriculture is said to be responsible for about 14.5 percent of human-induced greenhouse gas emissions, more than the transportation sector. All of these factors suggest that there is a big opportunity for a company that can produce a tasty and affordable plant-based substitute for meat, and can do it in a way that is friendlier to the environment than traditional meat production.

Beyond Meat is positioning itself to be that company. On the taste and healthfulness side, the company's first product line, Chicken-Free Strips, are made with plant-based proteins that legitimately replicate the sensory experience of eating meat. The product is also gluten-free and is free of trans and saturated fat, cholesterol, dairy, eggs, hormones, and antibiotics, so it's better for you than actual chicken. On the cost and environmental side, Beyond Meat's Chicken-Free Strips require less land and water to raise than real chickens and, when produced at a sufficient scale, cost less to make.

Beyond Meat's products are the result of more than 15 years of research conducted by two scientists at the University of Missouri-Columbia, Fu-Hung Hsieh and Harold Huff. The company's Chicken-Free Strips have been precisely engineered to look like chicken, taste like chicken, and especially to feel like chicken when you take a bite. The company is presently working on a Beyond Meat substitute for ground beef that can be worked into tacos, lasagna, or any other meal in which beef is included. Beyond Meat's Chicken-Free Strips are being introduced to the marketplace through Whole Foods Markets and similar health-conscious food stores.

5-36. Based on the material covered in this chapter, what questions would you ask the firm's founders before making your funding decision? What answers would satisfy you?

5-37. If you had to make your decision on just the information provided in the pitch and on the company's website, would you fund this company? Why or why not?

YOU BE THE VC 5.2 COMPANY: Ubersense

• Web: www.ubersense.com • Facebook: Ubersense Goal Coach • Twitter: @ubersense.com

Business Idea: Coaches have long used video to evaluate their athletes' performances to try to help make improvements. Video equipment, however, is cumbersome, and the equipment varies in regard to its ability to replay videos in slow motion, whether a video can be shown side by side against another athlete, or whether the video can be easily e-mailed to someone else to solicit feedback and advice.

Pitch: Ubersense has created a smartphone and tablet app that makes each of the tasks referred to above seamless and easy, and adds additional functionality. The app allows athletes, coaches, and parents to shoot video of an athlete's move or competition (e.g., golf swing, tennis stroke, 100 meter dash, basketball shot, high jump) and then analyze the video in a variety of ways. The video can be analyzed in slow motion or frame by frame. Drawing tools are included to allow coaches to analyze form and posture and share their analysis with their athletes. A timeline feature allows users to look through videos that have been shot over time to see where improvements have been made. A video can also be placed side by side against a professional athlete performing the same move or act, such as a golf swing or a gymnastics routine. Ubersesense's most powerful feature is its innovative video-based feedback tool called Uberview. An Uberview, which can easily be shared with others, can contain a coach's audio critique, instructive drawings, alterations to video playback, and even comparisons of the athlete that is the focus of the evaluation with other athletes. For example, a gymnastics coach could create an Uberview of a balance beam routine of an aspiring female gymnast and then compare the routine against a similar routine performed by an Olympic gymnast.

There are additional functionalities that make Uberview useful. There is a note function that allows anyone to comment on a video, so an athlete can distribute a video to solicit written feedback. A video can be connected to a big screen so a group of people can benefit from an evaluation or critique. Ubersense also includes a host of social features. Videos can easily be shared with others via e-mail and can be posted to Facebook, Twitter, YouTube, or Dropbox. An athlete can also create a profile, post videos of him or herself on the profile, and ask for feedback from the broader Ubersense community. In turn, an athlete can view videos posted by others and offer feedback, encouragement, and support.

The Ubersense app can be downloaded for free. The company has several ways of making money, including selling drill videos and connecting athletes with coaches to get advanced help.

5-38. Based on the material covered in this chapter, what questions would you ask the firm's founders before making your funding decision? What answers would satisfy you?

5-39. If you had to make your decision on just the information provided in the pitch and on the company's website, would you fund this company? Why or why not?

CASE 5.1

Panera Bread: Occupying a Favorable Position in a Highly Competitive Industry

• *Web: www.panerabread.com* • *Facebook: Panera Bread* • *Twitter: @panerabread*

Bruce R. Barringer, *Oklahoma State University*

R. Duane Ireland, *Texas A&M University*

Introduction

If you analyzed the restaurant industry using Porter's five forces model, you wouldn't be favorably impressed with the results. Three of the threats to profitability—the threat of substitutes, the threat of new entrants, and rivalry among existing firms—are high. Despite these threats to industry profitability, one restaurant chain is moving forward in a very positive direction. St. Louis–based Panera Bread, a chain of specialty bakery-cafés, has grown from 602 company-owned and franchised units in 2003 to 1,770 in early 2014. In 2013, system-wide sales reached $2.4 billion, up 12 percent from the previous year. These numbers reflect a strong performance for a restaurant chain, particularly during a difficult economic period. So what's Panera's secret? How is it that this company flourishes while its industry as a whole is experiencing difficulty? As we'll see, Panera Bread's success can be explained in two words: positioning and execution.

Changing Consumer Tastes

Panera's roots go back to 1981, when it was founded under the name of Au Bon Pain Co. and consisted of three Au Bon Pain bakery-cafés and one cookie store. The company grew slowly until the mid-1990s, when it acquired Saint Louis Bread Company, a chain of 20 bakery-cafés located in the St. Louis area. About that time, the owners of the newly combined companies observed that people were increasingly looking for products that were "special"—meaning that they differed from run-of-the-mill restaurant food. Second, they noted that although consumers were tiring of standard fast-food fare, they didn't want to give up the convenience of quick service. This trend led the company to conclude that consumers wanted the convenience of fast food combined with a higher-quality experience. In slightly different words, they wanted good food served quickly in an enjoyable environment.

The Emergence of Fast Casual

As a result of these changing consumer tastes, a new category in the restaurant industry, called "fast casual," emerged. This category provided consumers the alternative they wanted by capturing the advantage of both the fast-food category (speed) and the casual dining category (good food), with no significant disadvantages. The owners of Au Bon Pain and Saint Louis Bread Company felt that they could help pioneer this new category, so they repositioned their restaurants and named them Panera Bread. The position that Panera moved into is depicted in the graphic titled "Positioning Strategy of Various Restaurant Chains." A market positioning grid provides a visual representation of the positions of various companies in an industry. About Panera's category, industry expert T. J. Callahan said, "I don't think fast casual is a fad; I think it's a structural change starting to happen in the restaurant industry."

Panera's Version of Fast Casual

To establish itself as the leader in the fast-casual category and to distinguish itself from its rivals, Panera

(continued)

Positioning Strategy of
Various Restaurant Chains

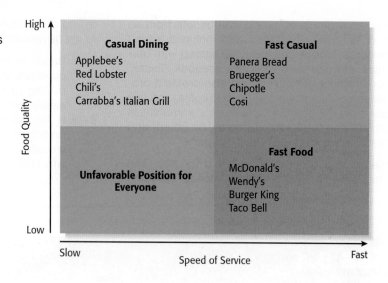

(which is Latin for "time for bread") added a bonus to the mix—specialty food. The company has become known as the nation's bread expert and offers a variety of artisan and other specialty breads, along with bagels, pastries, and baked goods. Panera Bread's restaurants are open for breakfast, lunch, and dinner, and also offer hand-tossed salads, signature sandwiches, and hearty soups served in edible sourdough bread bowls, along with hot and cold coffee drinks and other beverages. The company also provides catering services. Its restaurants present customers with an inviting neighborly atmosphere and relaxing decor, adding to their appeal. Panera even suggests a new time of day to eat specialty foods, calling the time between lunch and dinner "chill-out" time.

With high hopes for future expansion, Panera Bread is an acknowledged leader in the fast-casual category. Its unique blend of fast-casual service and specialty foods also continues to gain momentum. This sentiment is captured in the following quote from Mark von Waaden, an investor and restaurateur who signed an agreement to open 20 Panera Bread restaurants in the Houston, Texas, area early in the company's recent growth spurt. Commenting on why he was attracted to Panera Bread as opposed to other restaurant chains, von Waaden said, "My wife, Monica, and I fell in love with the fresh-baked breads and the beautiful bakery-cafés. We think the Panera Bread concept of outstanding bread coupled with a warm, inviting environment is a natural fit with the sophistication that the Houston market represents."

The spirit of von Waaden's statement captures the essence of Panera's advantage. It isn't just another restaurant. By observing trends and listening to customers, its leaders helped the firm carve out a unique and favorable position in a difficult industry.

Present Status and Goal for the Future

Panera's leadership in the fast-casual category and its financial performance have drawn considerable attention. The company employs more than 75,000 people, serves millions of customers a year, and is currently one of the largest restaurant chains in the United States. It also continues to innovate and evolve. In 2012, Panera Bread introduced antibiotic-free roasted turkey, which both tastes better and appeals to health-conscious consumers. Other recent introductions include it's new Roasted Turkey & Avocado BLT sandwich, Chopped Chicken Cobb Salad with Avocado, and Roasted Turkey Orchard Harvest Salad. Panera Bread is counting on its unique positioning strategy, its commitment to serving food that its customers feel good about eating and serving their families, and savvy execution to continue its positive momentum.

Discussion Questions

5-40. How has Panera Bread established a unique position in the restaurant industry?

5-41. How has Panera Bread's unique position in the restaurant industry contributed to the firm's success?

5-42. What barriers to entry has Panera Bread created for potential competitors?

5-43. What are Panera Bread's primary sources of competitive advantage?

5-44. What are the ways that Panera Bread can conduct ethical and proper forms of competitive analysis to learn about potential competitors entering the fast-casual category?

Sources: Panera Bread home page, www.panerabread.com, (accessed February 20, 2014); Panera Bread Annual Report 2012; "Industry by Industry: A Look at the Start, Their Stocks—and Their Latest Picks," *Wall Street Journal*, May 12, 2003, R8.

CASE 5.2

How Warby Parker Broke Through Formable Barriers to Entry and Disrupted the Eyeglasses Industry

• *Web: www.warbyparker.com* • *Facebook: Warby Parker* • *Twitter:@WarbyParker*

Bruce R. Barringer, *Oklahoma State University*
R. Duane Ireland, *Texas A&M University*

Introduction

It started in business school. In the fall of 2008, Neil Blumenthal and David Gilboa, both 28, were in the first year of their MBA program at the University of Pennsylvania's Wharton School. They were in a computer lab kicking around business ideas with classmates Andrew Hunt and Jeffrey Raider. The topic of eyeglasses came up. Gilboa had recently lost his glasses, and was shocked to learn that a replacement pair would cost $700. He recalled thinking that his iPhone cost $200. He thought how could an iPhone, that can do unimaginable things, cost $200 and a simple pair of glasses cost $700?

Blumenthal thought he had the answer. He had spent time working for VisionSpring, a nonprofit that distributes eyewear to low-income people in developing countries. While at VisionSpring, he learned that the global eyewear industry was dominated by a single company, Luxottica. Luxottica is the world's largest eyewear company, and controls over 80 percent of the world's major eyewear brands. It owns Oakley, Persol, Ray-Ban, Sunglass Hut, LensCrafters, and Pearle Vision. It also owns the eyewear stores located inside several major retail chains, including Sears Optical and Target Optical. Luxottica's near-monopoly status was the reason for the $700 glasses. That was the "aha" moment. The four thought that if VisionSpring could outfox Luxottica by manufacturing its own glasses for people in developing countries, why couldn't four business students do the same thing for people just like themselves?

Industry Analysis

Before jumping ahead, Blumenthal and his three friends spent some time studying the eyewear industry. The term "eyewear" includes glasses, contacts, and sunglasses. They discovered four interesting characteristics about the industry. First, the industry had experienced very little innovation. Buying eyewear today isn't much different than it was 20 years ago. Second, there were virtually no brands on the market that evoked passion or that people were excited to be associated with. Third, only 1 percent of eyeglasses were bought online. They figured this was because people like to try on glasses before they buy them. Finally, they learned that eyeglasses can do tremendous good. The University of Michigan conducted a study to evaluate the impact of VisionSpring's efforts to provide eyeglasses to people who couldn't afford them in "Base of the Pyramid" countries. The study found that a pair of VisionSpring eyelgasses increased the monthly income of the user by 20 percent and overall productivity by 35 percent on average. These are staggeringly positive numbers for a social initiative.

Blumenthal and his classmates concluded that the eyewear industry, which is projected to reach a total of $95.5 billion in revenue by 2015, was ripe for disruption. What was needed was a company that (1) had the courage to do an end-run around Luxottica by manufacturing its own glasses, (2) could lower the price by selling online, (3) knew how to create a brand that people could get passionate about, and (4) was willing to give away a pair of glasses to low-income people in the developing world for every pair the firm sold. As emerging entrepreneurs, they concluded that a company could earn money, inspire customers, and do good at the same time.

Warby Parker

Warby Parker launched in 2010 as an online eyewear company, based on the criteria shown above. All four founders were involved at lauch, but soon afterward Hunt and Raider moved on. Hunt joined a venture capital firm and Raider founded a company called Harry's, which is trying to disrupt the online razor business. The name Warby Parker comes from characters in Jack Kerouac books, Warby Pepper and Zagg Parker. Here's how the company was set up.

Blumenthal and Gilboa secured Chinese manufacturers to produce frames and an Italian company to make lenses, allowing them to make the glasses and frames themselves. At the start, the glasses were sold strictly online, for $95 a pair. The $95 price point was possible because the glasses were designed in-house, manufactured overseas, and sold via the Web, eliminating many of the costs associated with traditional glasses manufacturing and retailing. Also, when traditional glasses bear a brand name, such as Coach or Polo Ralph Lauren, they include a licensing fee that can run as high as 15 percent. Warby Parker's approach to selling glasses works like this. A customer submits his/her prescrption and begins browsing Warby Parker's site. To ensure a proper fit, the customer can upload a photo of him or herself and "try on" frames through a virtual system. The company's Home-Try-On program allows the customer to pick five frames, which s/he then receives to try on at home for five days, free of charge. The $95 includes the frame and the prescription lenses.

(continued)

From the beginning the company set out to create a hip urban brand, targeting 18 to 34 year olds. They wanted to pick a market and evoke excitement and passion. The website had (and still has) a distinct, funky tone, with women who looked like grad students or magazine editors and men who appeared to be architects, artists, or jazz musicians. The company didn't spend much on promotions, with one exception. Early on they hired a top fashion PR firm, Brandbury Lewis, to help them get press coverage. Soon they were featured in *Vogue* and *GQ*, which boosted Warby Parker's visibility among its hip target market. The glasses themselves were part of the branding strategy. They had simple frames with slightly chunky temples that feature subdued colors: gray, blue, and burgundy. The glasses have preppy, country names like Sibley, Winston, Ellsworth, and Ames. As shown in the table below, the descriptions of Warby Parker's glasses are purposefully playful.

Sample of Warby Parker Men's Glasses

Name of Frame	Description
Wilkie	There's no reason to mess with a good thing. Wilkie is our version of a never-fail frame, with a sloped rectangular eyeframe that flatters any face.
Ames	With a bold brow line and generous width, Ames transitions easily from mornings in the quad to nights on the town.
Greeley	A sleek architectural frame with contrast temple arms, Greeley is an everyday frame with dress-up potential.
Roosevelt	A modern classic, Roosevelt is a large, masculine frame with a keyhole bridge that immediately inspires confidence.
Ellsworth	With its slender temples and narrow silhouette, Ellsworth is a bright, to-anywhere frame that flatters all face shapes.

Warby Parker's tone, product, and price resonated with its target market, young urban hipsters, almost immediately and the company experienced success. Although the company doesn't release sales figures, it is estimated that it had sold more than 300,000 pairs of glasses by the end of 2012.

Social Mission

An important component of what Warby Parker stands for is encompassed by its social mission. It gives away a pair of glasses for each pair it sells. While the company's efforts appear to be heartfelt, it has also been good for business. According to a recent study, about 80 percent of Americans are likely to switch brands, if price and quality are the same, if a company supports a compelling social cause.

Companies that support social causes are also more naturally viral. People generally feel good about recommending a company that not only has an attractive product but also supports a meaningful social cause. A portion of Warby Parker's website is dedicated to a section labeled "Do Good." It has three parts labeled "Buy a Pair, Give a Pair," "Good Company," and "WP Stories." The "WP Stories" section provides hearthwearming stories of how Warby Parker and the organizations the company partners with have changed the lives of people in devleoping countries.

The Road Ahead

Warby Parker envisions an exciting future. At the time this feature was written, in February 2014, the company's website indicated that it had given away 500,000 pairs of glasses. Since the company gives away a pair of glasses for every one it sells, that means it has sold 500,000 pairs of glasses since 2010, which represents over $47.5 million in sales. The company has evolved since its 2010 beginnings. In the last two years, it has partnered with boutiques to open "stores within stores" in cities such as Los Angeles, Nashville, and San Francisco. In 2013, Warby Parker opened its first store in New York City. The company acknowledgs that some people are skittish about buying glasses online. The store is an experiment to see if a physical store will bring in new buyers. The store has the same quirky appeal as Warby Parker's website. It's 2,500-squre-foot space is lined with books and old-school rolling library ladders. An in-store optometrist is on hand to perform eye exams for $50. Shoppers can track their appointments on an appointment board. A second store is planned for Boston.

A question for Warby Parker is whether the company will expand to products beyond glasses, using its distinct approach to business to do so. The company is studying possibilities, but no decision has been made.

Discussion Questions

5-45. What environmental trends and business trends are working both for and against Warby Parker?

5-46. How has Warby Parker's social mission contributed to the firm's success?

5-47. What are some reasons that would support a decision by Warby Parker to expand into products beyond glasses?

5-48. What are some reasons that would support a decision by Warby Parker to *not* expand to products beyond glasses?

5-49. What actions has Warby Parker taken that have allowed the firm to at least in part successfully disrupt a large industry that had been dominated by a single company, Luxottica?

5-50. What can an entrepreneur learn, regardless of the industry he or she is entering, by how Warby Parker redefined the customer experience in its industry?

Sources: Warby Parker website, www.warbyparker.com (accessed February 20, 2014); VisionSpring website, www.visionspring.org (accessed February 20, 2014); J. Pressler, "20/30 Vision," *New York Magazine,* August 11, 2013; H. Bennett, "Social Commerce Cast Study: Warby Parker," available at http://insparq.com/social-commerce.case.study-warby-parker, posted November 28, 2012 (accessed February 20, 2014).

Endnotes

1. Sun Tzu, *The Art of War* (Mineola, NY: Dover Publications, 2002), ch. 7.
2. IBISWorld, 2014.
3. B. Batjargal, M. A. Hitt, A. S. Tsui, J.-L. Arregle, J. W. Webb, and T. L. Miller, "Institutional Polycentrism, Entrepreneurs' Social Networks, and New Venture Growth," *Academy of Management Journal* 56, no. 4 (2013): 1024–1049; C. Boone, F. C. Wezel, and A. van Witteloostuijn, "Joining the Pack or Going Solo? A Dynamic Theory of New Firm Positioning," *Journal of Business Venturing* 28, no. 4 (2013): 511–527; D. R. King and R. J. Slotegraaf, "Industry Implications of Value Creation and Appropriation Investment," *Decision Sciences* 42, no. 2 (2011): 511–529.
4. A. Pe'er and T. Keil, "Are All Startups Affected Similarly by Clusters? Agglomeration, Competition, Firm Heterogeneity, and Survival," *Journal of Business Venturing* 28, no. 3 (2013): 354–372; Y. E. Spanos, G. Zaralis, and S. Lioukas, "Strategy and Industry Effects on Profitability: Evidence from Greece," *Strategic Management Journal* 25 (2004): 139–165.
5. B. Ruiz, "Motorcycle Dealership and Repair in the U.S." IBISWorld Industry Report 44122a, October 2013.
6. About Us, American Watchmakers-Clockmakers Institute, February 2014, www.wci.com.
7. M. Porter, *Competitive Strategy: Techniques for Analyzing Industries and Competitors* (New York: Free Press, 1980).
8. Porter, *Competitive Strategy.*
9. S. A. Alvarez and J. B. Barney, "Entrepreneurial Opportunities and Poverty Alleviation," *Entrepreneurship Theory and Practice* 38, no. 1 (2014): 159–184; M. Lofstrom, T. Bates, and S. C. Parker, "Why Are Some People More Likely to Become Small-Businesses Owners Than Others: Entrepreneurship Entry and Industry-Specific Barriers," *Journal of Business Venturing* 29, no. 2 (2014): 232–251.
10. About Us, Anheuser-Busch InBev, February 2014, www.ab-inbev.com.
11. N. Groom, "Tesla Gives Strong 2014 Outlook, Shares Jump 12 Percent," *Reuters*, February 19, 2014, www.reuters.com.
12. C. Bellavitis, I. Filatotchev, and D. S. Kamuriwo, "The Effects of Intra-Industry and Extra-Industry Networks on Performance: A Case of Venture Capital Portfolio Firms," *Managerial and Decision Economics* 35, no. 2 (2014): 129–144; T. Jambulingam, R. Kathuria, and J. R. Nevin, "Fairness-Trust-Loyalty Relationship Under Varying Conditions of Supplier-Buyer Interdependence," *Journal of Marketing Theory and Practice* 19, no.1 (2011): 39–56.
13. W. Stam, S. Arzianian, and T. Elfring, "Social Capital of Entrepreneurs and Small Firm Performance: A Meta-Analysis of Contextual and Methodological Moderators," *Journal of Business Venturing* 29, no. 1 (2014): 152–173; Y. L. Zhao, M. Song, and G. L. Storm, "Founding Team Capabilities and New Venture Performance: The Mediating Role of Strategic Positional Advantages," *Entrepreneurship Theory and Practice* 37, no. 4 (2013): 789–814.
14. P. G. Klein, D. S. Siegel, N. Wilson, and M. Wright, "The Effects of Alternative Investments on Entrepreneurship, Innovation, and Growth," *Managerial and Decision Economics* 35, no. 2 (2014): 67–72; J. P. Murmann, "The Coevolution of Industries and Important Features of Their Environments," *Organization Science* 24, no. 1 (2013): 58–78.
15. D. A. Aaker, *Aaker on Branding: 20 Principles That Drive Success* (New York, NY: Morgan James Publishing, 2014); F. Salmon, "The Financial-Media Rollup Strategy," *Reuters*, November 15, 2013, www.blogs.reuters.com.
16. Our Story, Nucor Corporation, February 2014, www.nucor.com; J. Rodengen, *The Legend of Nucor Corporation* (Ft. Lauderdale, FL: Write Stuff Enterprises, 1997).
17. G. Abhishek, "Small Businesses as Multinational Companies: Overcoming Barriers and Finding Opportunities," *Asian Journal of Research in Banking and Finance* 3, no. 11 (2013): 33–42; S. A. Fernhaber and D. Li, "International Exposure Through Network Relationships: Implications for New Venture Internationalization," *Journal of Business Venturing* 28, no. 2 (2013): 316–334.
18. P. C. Patel and S. A. Fernhaber, "Beating Competitors to International Markets: The Value of Geographically Balanced Networks for Innovation," *Strategic Management Journal*, 2014, in press; K.-Y. Hsieh, W. Tsai, and M.-C. Chen, "If They Can Do It, Why Not Us? Competitors as Reference Points for Justifying Escalation of Commitment," *Academy of Management Journal*, 2014, in press ; M.-J. Chen, K.-H. Su, and W. Tsai, "Competitive Tension: The Awareness-Motivation-Capability Perspective," *Academy of Management Journal* 50, no. 1 (2007): 101–118; M.-J. Chen, "Competitor Analysis and Inter-Firm Rivalry: Toward a Theoretical Integration," *Academy of Management Review* 21, no. 1 (1996): 100–134.
19. P. Kotler, *Marketing Insights from A to Z* (Hoboken, NJ: Wiley, 2003), 23.
20. A. Prior, "G Asset Management Offers to Buy 51% of Barnes & Noble," *Wall Street Journal*, February 21, 2014, www.wsj.com.
21. D. Grichnik, J. Brinckmann, L. Singh, and S. Manigart, "Beyond Environmental Scarcity: Human and Social Capital as Driving Forces of Bootstrapping Activities," *Journal of Business Venturing* 29, no. 2 (2014): 310–326; C. Baumann, G. Elliott, and H. Hamin, "Modelling Customer Loyalty in Financial Services: A Hybrid of Formative and Reflective Constructs," *International Journal of Bank Marketing* 29, no. 3 (2011): 247–267.
22. K.-H. Huarng and D. E. Ribeiro-Soriano, "Developmental Management: Theories, Methods, and Applications in Entrepreneurship, Innovation, and Sensemaking," *Journal of Business Research* 67, no. 5 (2014): 657–662; C. Boone, F. C. Wezel, and A. van Witteloostuijn, "Joining the Pack or Going Solo? A Dynamic Theory of New Firm Positioning," *Journal of Business Venturing* 28, no. 4 (2013): 511–527; L. Grzybowski and P. Pereira, "Subscription Choices and Switching Costs in Mobile Telephony," *Review of Industrial Organization* 38, no. 1 (2011): 23–42.

Getting
Personal with TEMPORUN

Co-Founders

JOSH LEIDER
Eli Broad College of Business,
Michigan State University, 2013

BENNY EBERT-ZAVOS
Eli Broad College of Business,
Michigan State University, 2013

ADAM PROSCHK
College of Engineering,
Michigan State University, 2014

PHIL GATZEN
College of Engineering,
Michigan State University, 2014

Dialogue with
Josh Leider

MY FAVORITE SMARTPHONE APP
Snapchat

BEST ADVICE I'VE RECEIVED
Don't postpone joy.

MY ADVICE FOR NEW ENTREPRENEURS
Take your time. Many entrepreneurs just want to get their product out as soon as possible. But you need time to test, not only your idea, but your team.

MY BIGGEST SURPRISE AS AN ENTREPRENEUR
The love and support you get from other entrepreneurs.

BEST PART OF BEING A STUDENT
Resources, resources, resources.

WHAT I DO WHEN I'M NOT WORKING
I love to run, hike, and camp.

CHAPTER 6

Writing a *Business* Plan

OPENING PROFILE

TEMPORUN
Proceeding on the Strength of a Winning Business Plan

• *Web: www.temporun.com*

In August of 2012 Josh Leider was on a run. He was listening to "Lose Yourself" by Eminem on his iPhone. The tempo of the song matched his running pace perfectly. Then "Lose Yourself" ended and another song started. The tempo was entirely different, throwing off Leider's run as a result. He thought, "Why can't you always run to the tempo of your music?" Hence, the idea of TempoRun, a smartphone app, was born.

Leider shared the idea with Benny Ebert-Zavos, a friend of his and a serious runner. Ebert-Zavos loved the idea, and the two of them decided to pursue it further. The pair found that there were apps on the market that adjust song tempos as a runner's pace changes, but none that did exactly what Leider and Ebert-Zavos envisioned, which was an app that categorized music according to tempo. Leider had worked on several business ideas and had a sense of how to proceed. He and Ebert-Zavos contacted the Computer Science department at Michigan State, the university they were attending, and a professor in the department hooked them up with two students, Adam Proschek and Phil Gatzen, who were good at coding and development. The group of four decided to form a business and build the app, using the name TempoRun for both.

One thing the partners did from the outset is utilize the resources of Michigan State. Leider was a marketing and economics major in the Eli Broad College of Business, while Ebert-Zavos was a student in the School of Hospitality Business. Both Proschek and Gatzen were in Computer Science. They wrote a business plan for TempoRun and, in December of 2012, entered the first Broad Pitch Competition, which was held in the college of business. Instead of wearing business attire, they pitched in running clothes, in part to show their passion for their business idea. Incredibly, they won the competition. The win included a $5,000 first prize and access to The Hatch, a student business accelerator in partnership with MSU's Entrepreneurship Network. The partners used the $5,000 and a grant from a campus businesses association to buy computers, trademark their idea, and create a limited liability company (LLC). They also utilized pro bono resources available through MSU's Entrepreneurship Network, such as interns who designed a logo and worked on TempoRun's marketing and legal efforts.

At the suggestion of a professor, in early 2013 they entered TempoRun in Student Startup Madness, a pitch competition for college digital projects at the South by Southwest Music and Media Conference in Austin, Texas. Michigan State funded the trip. They were competing against tech start-ups from universities across the country, including Stanford and Harvard, and ended up winning. Leider characterized the competition,

LEARNING OBJECTIVES

After studying this chapter you should be ready to:

1. Explain the purpose of a business plan.

2. Describe who reads a business plan and what they're looking for.

3. Discuss the guidelines to follow to write an effective business plan.

4. Identify and describe a suggested outline of a business plan.

5. Explain how to effectively present a business plan to potential investors.

and in particular the judging, as *Shark Tank* times 10. The judges were executives and well-known entrepreneurs from companies like Google, Square, and TechStars. Leider summed up the experience by saying that "We went into the competition thinking we knew everything but found that we knew very little." This was actually a positive comment on Leider's part. He was referring to the learning that took place as a result of the rigor of the judges' questions and their feedback. The South by Southwest win also netted TempoRun $5,000 in Google Cloud Platform credit and acquainted the entrepreneurs with people they would have had no way of coming into contact with otherwise. The nearby photo was taken just after the win at the South by Southwest competition. The team, from left to right, included Phil Gatzen, Benny Ebert-Zavos, Adam Proschek, and Josh Leider.

To gain visibility and prepare for launch, the TempoRun team sponsored a charity 5K at Michigan State in April of 2013. The proceeds went to support breast cancer research. The company formally launched in the Apple App Store in May 2013. The way the app works is that it helps users run at their preferred pace by categorizing the music on their iPhone from Level 1 (walking) to Level 10 (sprinting). It also incorporates music from a streaming Internet music station. The user selects a level, which can be changed with arrows on a simple interface. The app also keeps track of basic running analytics, such as distance run, pace, and calories burned. TempoRun, which charged a one-time download fee of $2.99 when it first launched, had 2,000 downloads its first day of launch. The company has experienced a steady pace of downloads since.

Looking back, Leider credits the time his team spent in The Hatch, the Michigan State student accelerator, and the business plan and pitch competitions in which they participated as pivotal to their success. Leider says that the value of a business plan or pitch competition is that it "gets your ideas down on paper and causes you to ask questions of yourself that you would have never thought of before—questions about your business, your revenue streams, and more." Another ingredient to TempoRun's success is that Leider and Elbert-Zavos are very involved in the running community. Because they are consumers of their own product, they are able to make tweaks to the product based on their own observations and listen to suggestions from runners whom they know and who are also TempoRun users.

TempoRun is not yet a full-time job for the four founders, but they hope this will soon be the case. They envision extending TempoRun's basic approach to other sports, such as cycling and swimming.

This chapter discusses the importance of writing a business plan. Although some new ventures simply "wing it" and start doing business without the benefit of formal planning, it is hard to find an expert who doesn't recommend preparing a business plan. A **business plan** is a written narrative, typically 25 to 35 pages long, that describes what a new business intends to accomplish and how it intends to accomplish it. For most new ventures, the business plan is a dual-purpose document that is used both inside and outside the firm. Inside the firm, the plan helps the company develop a "road map" to follow to execute its strategies and plans. Outside the firm, it introduces potential investors and other stakeholders to the business opportunity the firm is pursuing and how it plans to pursue it.[1]

To begin this chapter, we discuss issues with which entrepreneurs often grapple when facing the challenge of writing a business plan. Topics included in the chapter's first section are reasons for writing a business plan, a description of who reads the business plan and what they're looking for, and guidelines to follow when preparing a written business plan. In the chapter's second section, we present an outline of a business plan with a description of the material in each section of the plan. The third section of the chapter deals with strategies for how to present the business plan to potential investors and others.

The Business Plan

As illustrated in the basic model of the entrepreneurial process shown in Chapter 1, writing a business plan is the last activity completed in the step of the entrepreneurial process titled "Developing Successful Business Ideas." It is a mistake to write a business plan too early. The business plan must be substantive enough and have sufficient details about the merits of the new venture in order to convince the reader that the new business is exciting and should receive support. Much of this detail is accumulated in the feasibility analysis stage of investigating the merits of a potential new venture.

In spite of conventional wisdom suggesting the need to do so, a relatively large percentage of entrepreneurs do not write business plans for their new ventures. In fact, a 2010–2012 study of 350 entrepreneurs found that of those that had successful exits (i.e., an IPO or sale to another firm), only about 30 percent started with a business plan.[2] That number is similar to the results of a 2011 survey by The Hartford. According to The Hartford's 2011 Small Business Success Study, which surveyed 2,000 business owners, only 35 percent of the owners said that they have a business plan.[3] Similarly, in a 2002 study, *Inc.* magazine asked the founders of the firms that make up the *Inc.* 500 that year whether they had written a formal business plan before they launched their companies. A total of 60 percent did not.[4] These statistics should not deter an entrepreneur from writing a business plan. Indeed, ample evidence supports the notion that writing a business plan is an extremely good investment of an entrepreneur's time and money.

Reasons for Writing a Business Plan

We show the two primary reasons to write a business plan in Figure 6.1. First, writing a business plan forces a firm's founders to systematically think through each aspect of their new venture.[5] This is not a trivial effort—it usually takes several days or weeks to complete a well-developed business plan—and the founders will usually meet regularly to work on the plan during this period. An example of how much work is sometimes involved, and how a well-planned new business unfolds, is provided by Gwen Whiting and Lindsey Wieber, the co-founders of The Laundress, a company that sells specially formulated laundry detergents and other fabric care products. Whiting and Wieber met at Cornell University while studying fabrics, and after graduating the pair decided to start a business together. The following vignette comes from an interview they gave to Ladies Who Launch, a website that highlights the accomplishments of female entrepreneurs:

> *Gwen*: Lindsey and I went to college and studied textiles at Cornell together and always wanted to be in business together. We knew it was going to happen. We always talked about ideas. We were talking about this concept, and it was the right time for us. The first thing we did was the business plan and then a cash flow analysis. We wanted to do as much research as possible before developing the products.

LEARNING OBJECTIVE

1. Explain the purpose of a business plan.

Internal Reason	External Reason
Forces the founding team to systematically think through every aspect of its new venture	Communicates the merits of a new venture to outsiders, such as investors and bankers

FIGURE 6.1
Two Primary Reasons for Writing a Business Plan

This group of young entrepreneurs plans to launch a website that features educational toys for children. Here, they are discussing how to integrate the results of their feasibility analysis into their business plan. A business plan is more compelling if it contains primary research conducted by the entrepreneurs launching the business.

Lindsey: We spent Memorial Day weekend (2003) doing our business plan. We spent the Fourth of July weekend doing our cash flow. After we had our ideas on paper, we went back to Cornell, met with a professor there, and had a crash course in chemistry. She worked with us on the formulation of the products.

Gwen: I found a manufacturer on Columbus Day. Every piece of free time we had, we dedicated to the business. We weren't at the beach with our friends anymore.[6]

The payoff for this level of dedication and hard work, which involved the preparation of a formal business plan, is that Whiting and Wieber have now had a successful business for 10-plus years. Their products are sold through their website and in many stores.

Consistent with Whiting and Wieber's experience, writing a business plan forces a firm's founders to intently study every aspect of their business, a process that's hard to replicate in any other way. Imagine the following. Two friends are thinking about opening a seafood restaurant. They spend the next two months meeting four nights a week to hash out every detail of the business. They study the restaurant industry, identify their target market, develop a marketing plan, settle on a hiring schedule, identify the type of people they want to employ, plan their facility, determine what their start-up expenses will be, and put together five years of pro forma (projected) financial statements. After 32 meetings and several drafts, they produce a 30-page business plan that explains every aspect of their business. Regardless of how conscientious the founders of a business are, it's difficult to discipline oneself to cover this level of detail absent writing a business plan. As stated earlier, writing a business plan forces a business's founders to systematically think through every aspect of their business and develop a concrete blueprint to follow.

The second reason to write a business plan is to create a selling document for a company. It provides a mechanism for a young company to present itself to potential investors, suppliers, business partners, key job candidates, and others. Imagine that you have enough money to invest in one new business.[7] You chat informally with several entrepreneurs at a conference for start-ups and decide that there are two new ventures that you would like to know more about.

You contact the first entrepreneur and ask for a copy of his business plan. The entrepreneur hesitates a bit and says that he hasn't prepared a formal business plan but would love to get together with you to discuss his ideas. You contact the second entrepreneur and make the same request. This time, the entrepreneur says that she would be glad to forward you a copy of a 30-page business plan, along with a 10-slide PowerPoint presentation that provides an overview of the plan. An hour or two later, the PowerPoint presentation is in your e-mail in-box with a note that the business plan will arrive the next morning. You look through the slides, which are crisp and to the point and do an excellent job of outlining the strengths of the business opportunity. The next day, the business plan arrives just as promised and is equally impressive.

Which entrepreneur has convinced you to invest in his or her business? All other things being equal, the answer is obvious—the second entrepreneur. The fact that the second entrepreneur has a business plan not only provides you with detailed information about the venture but also suggests that the entrepreneur has thought through each element of the business and is committed enough to the new venture to invest the time and energy necessary to prepare the plan. Having a business plan also gives an investor something to which s/he can react. Very few, if any, investors will free up time to "listen" to your idea for a new business, at least initially.

Who Reads the Business Plan— and What Are They Looking for?

There are two primary audiences for a firm's business plan. Let's look at each of them.

LEARNING OBJECTIVE

2. Describe who reads a business plan and what they're looking for.

A Firm's Employees

A clearly written business plan, one that articulates the vision and future plans of a firm, is important for both the management team and the rank-and-file employees. Some experts argue that it's a waste of time to write a business plan because the marketplace changes so rapidly that any plan will become quickly outdated. Although it's true that marketplaces can and often do change rapidly, the process of writing the plan may be as valuable as the plan itself.

A clearly written business plan also helps a firm's rank-and-file employees operate in sync and move forward in a consistent and purposeful manner. The existence of a business plan is particularly useful for the functional department heads of a young firm. For example, imagine that you are the newly hired vice president for management information systems for a rapidly growing start-up. The availability of a formal business plan that talks about all aspects of the business and the business's future strategies and goals can help you make sure that what you're doing is consistent with the overall plans and direction of the firm.

Investors and Other External Stakeholders

External stakeholders who are being recruited to join a firm, such as investors, potential business partners, and key employees, are the second audience for a business plan. To appeal to this group, the business plan must be realistic and not reflective of overconfidence on the firm's part. Overly optimistic statements or projections undermine a business plan's credibility, so it is foolish to include them. At the same time, the plan must clearly demonstrate that the business idea is viable and offers potential investors financial returns greater than lower-risk investment alternatives. The same is true for potential business partners, customers, and key recruits. Unless the new business can show that it has impressive potential, investors have little reason to become involved with it.

Investors vary in terms of the reliance they place on formal business plans.[8] Initially, many investors ask for a PowerPoint deck or the executive summary of a business plan. A PowerPoint deck is a short set of PowerPoint slides that describe a business idea, and an executive summary is a one- to two-page overview of the full plan. If their interest is sufficiently peaked, in some cases investors will ask for a full business plan, and in other cases they won't. It's still necessary to have a business plan, however. If an investor commits, in most cases a business plan will be required during the due diligence phase. Due diligence refers to the process investors go through after they tentatively commit to an investment.[9] The commitment is based on a thorough investigation of the merits of the venture, whether any legal complications exist, and whether the claims made in the business plan are accurate and realistic.

A firm must validate the feasibility of its business idea and have a good understanding of its competitive environment prior to presenting its business plan to others. Sophisticated investors, potential business partners, and key recruits will base their assessment of a proposed firm's future prospects on facts, not guesswork or platitudes, as emphasized in Chapter 3. The most compelling facts a company can provide in its business plan are the results of its own feasibility analysis and the articulation of a distinctive and competitive business model. A business plan rings hollow if it is based strictly on an entrepreneur's predictions of a business's future prospects. Modify Watches, a retailer of customizable watches, is an example of a business that laid a firm foundation for its business plan via the feasibility analysis that it conducted very early on. Modify Watches is the focus of Case 3.1.

In addition to the previously mentioned attributes, a business plan should disclose all resource limitations that the business must address before it is ready to start earning revenues. For example, a firm may need to hire service people before it can honor the warranties for the products it sells. It is foolhardy for a new venture to try to downplay or hide its resource needs. One of the main reasons new ventures seek out investors is to obtain the capital needed to hire key personnel, further develop their products or services, lease office space, or fill some other gap in their operations. Investors understand this, and experienced investors are typically willing to help the firms they fund plug resource or competency gaps.

Guidelines for Writing a Business Plan

LEARNING OBJECTIVE

3. Discuss the guidelines to follow to write an effective business plan.

There are several important guidelines that should influence the writing of a business plan. It is important to remember that a firm's business plan is typically the first aspect of a proposed venture that an investor will see. If the plan is incomplete or looks sloppy, it is easy for an investor to infer that the venture itself is incomplete and sloppy.[10] It is important to be sensitive to the structure, content, and style of a business plan before sending it to an investor or anyone else who may be involved with the new firm. Table 6.1 lists some of the "red flags" that are raised when certain aspects of a business plan are insufficient or miss the mark.

Structure of the Business Plan

To make the best impression, a business plan should follow a conventional structure, such as the outline shown in the next section. Although some entrepreneurs want to demonstrate creativity in everything they do, departing

TABLE 6.1   Red Flags in Business Plans

Red Flag	Explanation
Founders with none of their own money at risk	If the founders aren't willing to put their own money at risk, why should anyone else?
A poorly cited plan	A plan should be built on hard evidence and sound research, not guesswork or what an entrepreneur "thinks" will happen. The sources for all primary and secondary research should be cited.
Defining the market size too broadly	Defining the market for a new venture too broadly shows that the true target market has not been clearly identified. For example, saying that a new venture will target the global pharmaceutical industry isn't helpful. The market opportunity needs to be better defined. Obviously, the new venture will target a segment or a specific market within the industry.
Overly aggressive financials	Many investors skip directly to this portion of the plan. Projections that are poorly reasoned or unrealistically optimistic lose credibility. In contrast, sober, well-reasoned statements backed by sound research and judgment gain credibility quickly.
Sloppiness in any area	It is never a good idea to make a reader wade through typos, balance sheets that don't balance, or sloppiness in any area. These types of mistakes are seen as inattention to detail and hurt the entrepreneur's credibility.

from the basic structure of the conventional business plan format is usually a mistake. Typically, investors are very busy people and want a plan where they can easily find critical information. If an investor has to hunt for something because it is in an unusual place or just isn't there, he or she might simply give up and move on to the next plan.[11]

Many software packages are available that employ an interactive, menu-driven approach to assist in the writing of a business plan. Some of these programs are very helpful.[12] However, entrepreneurs should avoid a boilerplate plan that looks as though it came from a "canned" source. The software package may be helpful in providing structure and saving time, but the information in the plan should still be tailored to the individual business. Some businesses hire consultants or outside advisers to write their business plans. Although there is nothing wrong with getting advice or making sure that a plan looks as professional as possible, a consultant or outside adviser shouldn't be the primary author of the plan. Along with facts and figures, a business plan needs to project a sense of anticipation and excitement about the possibilities that surround a new venture—a task best accomplished by the creators of the business themselves.[13]

Content of the Business Plan

The business plan should give clear and concise information on all the important aspects of the proposed new venture. It must be long enough to provide sufficient information, yet short enough to maintain reader interest. For most plans, 25 to 35 pages (and typically closer to 25 than 35 pages) are sufficient. Supporting information, such as the résumés of the founding entrepreneurs, can appear in an appendix.

After a business plan is completed, it should be reviewed for spelling, grammar, and to make sure that no critical information has been omitted. There are numerous stories about business plans sent to investors that left out important information, such as significant industry trends, how much money the company needed, or how the money was going to be used. One investor even told the authors of this book that he once received a business plan that didn't include any contact information for the entrepreneur. Apparently, the entrepreneur was so focused on the content of the plan that he or she simply forgot to provide contact information on the business plan itself. This was a shame, because the investor was interested in learning more about the business idea.[14]

Style or Format of the Business Plan The plan's appearance must be carefully thought out. It should look sharp but not give the impression that a lot of money was spent to produce it. Those who read business plans know that entrepreneurs have limited resources and expect them to act accordingly. A plastic spiral binder including a transparent cover sheet and a back sheet to support the plan is a good choice. When writing the plan, avoid getting carried away with the design elements included in word-processing programs, such as boldfaced type, italics, different font sizes and colors, clip art, and so forth. Overuse of these tools makes a business plan look amateurish rather than professional.[15]

One of the most common questions that the writers of business plans ask is, "How long and detailed should it be?" The answer to this question depends on the type of business plan that is being written. There are three types of business plans, each of which has a different rule of thumb regarding length and level of detail. Presented in Figure 6.2, the three types of business plans are as follows:

- **Summary plan:** A **summary business plan** is 10 to 15 pages and works best for companies that are very early in their development and are not prepared to write a full plan. The authors may be asking for funding to conduct the analysis needed to write a full plan. Ironically, summary business plans are also used by very experienced entrepreneurs who may be thinking about a new venture but don't want to take the time to write a full business plan. For example, if someone such as Drew Houston, the co-founder of Dropbox, was thinking about starting a new business, he might write a summary business plan and send it out to selected investors to get feedback on his idea. Most investors know about Houston's success with Dropbox and don't need detailed information. Dropbox, the subject of Case 2.1, is a free file hosting service that was founded in 2007 and is now being used by more than 200 million people across the world.

- **Full business plan:** A **full business plan** is typically 25 to 35 pages long. This type of plan spells out a company's operations and plans in much more detail than a summary business plan, and it is the format that is usually used to prepare a business plan for an investor.

- **Operational business plan:** Some established businesses will write an **operational business plan**, which is intended primarily for an internal audience. An operational business plan is a blueprint for a company's operations. Commonly running between 40 and 100 pages in length, these plans can obviously feature a great amount of detail that provides guidance to operational managers.

FIGURE 6.2
Types of Business Plans

Summary Business Plan	Full Business Plan	Operational Business Plan
10–15 pages	25–35 pages	40–100 pages
Works best for new ventures in the early stages of development that want to "test the waters" to see if investors are interested in their idea	Works best for new ventures that are at the point where they need funding or financing; serves as a "blueprint" for the company's operations	Is meant primarily for an internal audience; works best as a tool for creating a blueprint for a new venture's operations and providing guidance to operational managers

If an investor asks you for a PowerPoint deck or the executive summary of your business plan rather than the complete plan, don't be alarmed. This is a common occurrence. If the investor's interest is piqued, he or she will ask for more information. Most investors believe the process of writing a full business plan is important, even if they don't ask for one initially. This sentiment is affirmed by Brad Feld, a venture capitalist based in Boulder, Colorado, who wrote:

> Writing a good business plan is hard. At one point it was an entry point for discussion with most funding sources (angels and VCs). Today, while a formal business plan is less critical to get in the door, the exercise of writing a business plan is incredibly useful. As an entrepreneur, I was involved in writing numerous business plans. It's almost always tedious, time consuming, and difficult but resulted in me having a much better understanding of the business I was trying to create.[16]

A cover letter should accompany a business plan sent to an investor or other stakeholders through the mail. The cover letter should briefly introduce the entrepreneur and clearly state why the business plan is being sent to the individual receiving it. As discussed in Chapter 10, if a new venture is looking for funding, a poor strategy is to obtain a list of investors and blindly send the plan to everyone on the list. Instead, each person who receives a copy of the plan should be carefully selected on the basis of being a viable investor candidate.

Recognizing the Elements of the Plan May Change A final guideline for writing a business plan is to recognize that the plan will usually change as it is being written and as the business evolves. New insights invariably emerge when entrepreneurs immerse themselves in writing the plan and start getting feedback from others. This process continues throughout the life of a company, and it behooves entrepreneurs to remain alert and open to new insights and ideas.

Because business plans usually change while being written, there is an emerging school of thought that opposes the idea of writing a business plan and advocates experimentation and trial-and-error learning gleaned through customer feedback over formal planning.[17] This approach, which is associated with the Lean Startup movement, espouses many excellent ideas, particularly in the area of soliciting feedback directly from prospective customers prior to settling on a business idea and business model to execute on the idea. In this book, we take the opposite position, arguing that a business plan, proceeded by a feasibility analysis, represents an important starting point for a new venture and serves many useful purposes. In this sense, those developing a business plan should understand that it is not intended to be a static document written in isolation at a desk. Instead, it is anticipated that the research conducted to complete the plan, and the preceding feasibility analysis, will place the founders in touch with potential customers, suppliers, business partners, and others, and that the feedback obtained from these key people will cause the plan to change as it's being written.[18] It's also anticipated that the business itself will iterate and change after it's launched, based on additional feedback. Some businesses will change more than others, based on the quality of their initial feasibility analysis and the newness and volatility of their industry. These issues and related ones are considered in the "Savvy Entrepreneurial Firm" feature.

Outline of the Business Plan

A suggested outline of the full business plan appears in Table 6.2. Specific plans may vary, depending on the nature of the business and the personalities of the founding entrepreneurs. Most business plans do not include all the elements introduced in Table 6.2; we include them here for the purpose of completeness.

LEARNING OBJECTIVE
4. Identify and describe a suggested outline of a business plan.

TABLE 6.2   **Business Plan Outline**

Cover Page
Table of Contents

I. Executive Summary
II. Industry Analysis
  Industry Size, Growth Rate,
  and Sales Projections
  Industry Structure
  Nature of Participants
  Key Success Factors
  Industry Trends
  Long-Term Prospects
III. Company Description
  Company History
  Mission Statement
  Products and Services
  Current Status
  Legal Status and Ownership
  Key Partnerships (if any)
IV. Market Analysis
  Market Segmentation and Target Market Selection
  Buyer Behavior
  Competitor Analysis
  Estimates of Annual Sales and Market Share
V. The Economics of the Business
  Revenue Drivers and Profit Margins
  Fixed and Variable Costs
  Operating Leverage and Its Implications
  Start-up Costs
  Break-Even Chart and Calculation
VI. Marketing Plan
  Overall Marketing Strategy

  Product, Price, Promotions, and Distribution
  Sales Process (or Cycle)
  Sales Tactics
VII. Design and Development Plan
  Development Status and Tasks
  Challenges and Risks
  Projected Development Costs
  Proprietary Issues (Patents, Trademarks,
    Copyrights, Licenses, Brand Names)
VIII. Operations Plan
  General Approach to Operations
  Business Location
  Facilities and Equipment
IX. Management Team and Company
    Structure
  Management Team (Including a Skills
    Profile)
  Board of Directors
  Board of Advisors
  Company Structure
X. Overall Schedule
XI. Financial Projections
  Sources and Uses of Funds Statement
  Assumptions Sheet
  Pro Forma Income Statements
  Pro Forma Balance Sheets
  Pro Forma Cash Flows
  Ratio Analysis
Appendices

Exploring Each Section of the Plan

Cover Page and Table of Contents   The cover page should include the company's name, address, and phone number; the date; the contact information for the lead entrepreneur; and the company's website address if it has one. The company's Facebook page and Twitter name can also be included. The contact information should include a land-based phone number, an e-mail address, and a smartphone number. This information should be centered at the top of the page. Because the cover letter and the business plan could get separated, it is wise to include contact information in both places. The bottom of the cover page should include information alerting the reader to the confidential nature of the plan. If the company already has a distinctive trademark, it should be placed somewhere near the center of the page. A table of contents should follow the cover letter. It should list the sections and page numbers of the business plan and the appendices.

Executive Summary   The **executive summary** is a short overview of the entire business plan; it provides a busy reader with everything she needs to know about the new venture's distinctive nature.[19] As mentioned earlier, in

SAVVY ENTREPRENEURIAL FIRM

Know When to Hold Them, Know When to Fold Them

Songkick: Web: www.songkick.com; Facebook: Songkick; Twttter: @songkick
GrubHub: Web: www.grubhub.com; Facebook: GrubHub; Twitter: @GrubHub
Instagram: Web: http://instagram.com; Facebook: Instagram; Twitter: @Instagram

One of the challenges business owners have is determining how closely to stick to their business plan once the business is launched and they start receiving customer feedback. In almost all cases, some changes will need to be made to the firm's plan. But the degree to which business plans pan out as their founders envisioned varies. In some cases, a business plan is spot-on and the worst thing a founder could do is vary from the plan. In other cases, a plan needs to be significantly tweaked, and in still other cases it needs to be thrown out the window and the business needs to start over. The following are brief descriptions of businesses that have experienced these various outcomes.

Songkick—No Changes Needed

Songkick was founded in 2007 by Pete Smith, Michelle You, and Ian Hogarth. The problem the company solves is music lovers missing out on seeing their favorite bands because they didn't know they were in their area. Concertgoers try to avoid this problem by subscribing to venue e-mail lists, checking band websites, and surfing through generic concert newsletters. This is a clumsy process and doesn't ensure that music fans won't miss a concert they'd like to see. To solve this problem, Songkick indexes a large number of ticket vendors, venue websites, and local newspapers to create the most comprehensive database of upcoming concerts available. Its mission is to know about every concert that's happening in every location—from an indie band playing at a local nightclub to Beyoncé playing at Madison Square Garden. Users can track the performers they like, and Songkick will send them a personalized concert alert when those performers announce a tour date in their area. Songkick makes money by selling concert tickets on its website. While Songkick has enhanced its service offerings over the years, its business plan has remained unchanged. The site now has over 8 million users per month.

GrubHub—Minor Change Needed

GrubHub began in 2004 as a simple resaurant listing website. The idea was to set up a website that listed all the restaurants that deliver to a particular user's home or office address. The initial business plan was based on a "freemium" pricing model. GrubHub would list restaurants for free and make money by charging a subscription fee for restaurants that wanted to be placed in a premium position on its website. The idea was that the restaurants placed in a premium position would get more orders from existing customers, and would have a better chance being "discovered" by new customers. As time went on, the founders of GrubHub realized that restaurants loved what they were doing, but weren't comfortable with paying up front for sales that might or might not happen. Its customers were clear that they only wanted to pay GrubHub when a GrubHub user placed an order. These insights prompted GrubHub to revise its business plan. The company switched from a subscription pricing model, where they charged restaurants for a premium place, to a transactional model where they collected a commission for each order placed. After the change was made, GrubHub saw a dramatic increase in restaurants asking to be placed on its website.

Instagram—Major Changes Needed

Instagram almost wasn't Instagram at all. Before Instagram became the photo-sharing hit that it is, co-founders Kevin Systrom and Mike Krieger were working on a check-in service called Burbn. Burbn was a location-based service similar to Foursquare. Users could check in to locations, earn points for hanging out with their friends, and share pictures inside the app. Systrom and Krieger worked on Burbn for over a year. It was completely done, had generated buzz, and had $500,000 in funding. The only problem—Systrom and Krieger didn't like it. To them it felt cluttered and overrun with features. They also worried about its competitiveness. Two similar services, Foursquare and Gowalla, already existed. They would have to fight it out with Foursquare and Gowalla for market share. So they stepped back and reconsidered. They concluded that the best approach was to pick a single feature and execute on it extremely well. So, they stripped Burbn down to the one group or feature they liked and felt they could contribute to the most. As it turned out, it was the photo-sharing, comment, and like capabilities. What was left was Instagram. Instagram is now a widely popular online photo-sharing, video-sharing, and social networking service that allows its users to take pictures and videos, and apply digital filters to them. Instagram was acquired by Facebook in 2012 for approximately $1 billion.

Questions for Critical Thinking

1. Despite all the changes that have happened with the Internet since 2007, when Songkick was founded, why do you think the company has been able to successfully stick with its original business plan?
2. What do you think would have happened to GrubHub if it hadn't changed its business plan?

(continued)

3. Why do you think some start-ups find it difficult to change their business plan, even when presented with evidence that their current business plan isn't working?
4. Look at the "You Be the VC" features at the end of Chapter 3, which focus on August Smart Locks and Blue Apron, and the "You Be the VC" features at the end of this chapter, which focus on Buzzy and Flings Bins. From the information in the features and on each company's website, which company do you think will have the easiest time sticking to its original business

plan? Which company do you think will have the hardest time? Explain your selections.

Sources: Songkick home page, www.songkick.com, accessed February 28, 2014; GrubHub home page, www.grubhub.com, accessed February 28, 2014; Instagram home page, http://instagram, accessed February 28, 2014; B. Barringer and R. D. Ireland, *Entrepreneurship: Successfully Launching New Ventures,* 3rd edition, 2010; M. G. Siegler, "A Pivotal Point," Techcrunch, available at http://techcrunch.com/2010/11/08/instagram-a-pivotal-point, accessed February 28, 2014.

many instances an investor will first ask for a copy of a firm's PowerPoint deck or executive summary and will request a copy of the full business plan only if the PowerPoint deck or executive summary is sufficiently convincing. Thus, certainly when requested, the executive summary arguably becomes the most important section of the business plan.[20] The most critical point to remember when writing an executive summary is that it is not an introduction or preface to the business plan; instead, it is meant to be a summary of the plan itself.

An executive summary shouldn't exceed two single-spaced pages. The cleanest format for an executive summary is to provide an overview of the business plan on a section-by-section basis. The topics should be presented in the same order as they are presented in the business plan. Two identical versions of the executive summary should be prepared—one that's part of the business plan and one that's a stand-alone document. The stand-alone document should be used to accommodate people who ask to see the executive summary before they decide whether they want to see the full plan.

Even though the executive summary appears at the beginning of the business plan, it should be written last. The plan itself will evolve as it's written, so not everything is known at the outset. In addition, if you write the executive summary first, you run the risk of trying to write a plan that fits the executive summary rather than thinking through each piece of the plan independently.[21]

Industry Analysis   The main body of the business plan begins by describing the industry in which the firm intends to compete. This description should include data and information about various characteristics of the industry, such as its size, growth rate, and sales projections. It is important to focus strictly on the business's industry and not its industry and target market simultaneously. Before a business selects a target market, it should have a good grasp of its industry—including where its industry's promising areas are and where its points of vulnerability are located.

Industry structure refers to how concentrated or fragmented an industry is.[22] Fragmented industries are more receptive to new entrants than industries that are dominated by a handful of large firms. You should also provide your reader a feel for the nature of the participants in your industry. Issues such as whether the major participants in the industry are innovative or conservative and are quick or slow to react to environmental changes are the types of characteristics to convey. You want your reader to visualize how your firm will fit in or see the gap that your firm will fill. The key success factors in an industry are also important to know and convey. Most industries have 6 to 10 key factors in which all participants must establish competence as a foundation for competing successfully against competitors. Most participants try to then differentiate themselves by excelling in two or three areas.

If you plan to start a company in the nursery and garden industry, it's important to document the health and future potential of the industry. A careful analysis of a firm's industry lays out what is realistically possible and what isn't realistically possible for a start-up to achieve.

Mike Kemp/Blend Images/Corbis

Industry trends should be discussed, which include both environmental and business trends. The most important environmental trends are economic trends, social trends, technological advances, and political and regulatory changes. Business trends include issues such as whether profit margins in the industry are increasing or declining and whether input costs are going up or down. The industry analysis should conclude with a brief statement of your beliefs regarding the long-term prospects for the industry.

Company Description   This section begins with a general description of the company. Although at first glance this section may seem less critical than others, it is extremely important in that it demonstrates to your reader that you know how to translate an idea into a business.

The company history section should be brief, but should explain where the idea for the company came from and the driving force behind its inception. If the story of where the idea for the company came from is heartfelt, tell it. For example, the opening feature for Chapter 3 focuses on LuminAid, a solar light company that was started by Andrea Sreshta and Anna Stork, two Columbia University students. Sreshta and Stork's motivation to design the light was spurred by their concern for people affected by a major earthquake that took place in Haiti in 2010. They experienced firsthand how a disaster can negatively impact the lives of millions. One thing most disaster victims suffer from is a lack of light. Sreshta and Stork started LuminAid to solve this problem. The LuminAid solar light is unique in that it can be shipped flat, and inflates when used to produce a portable, renewable source of light. The company's goal is to make the LuminAid light a part of the supplies commonly sent as part of disaster relief efforts.

Sreshta and Stork's story is heartfelt and is one with which anyone can relate. It might even cause one to pause and think, "That is a fantastic idea.

That's just the type of solution that people recovering from a natural disaster like an earthquake need."

A **mission statement** defines why a company exists and what it aspires to become.[23] If carefully written and used properly, a mission statement can define the path a company takes and act as its financial and moral compass. Some businesses also include a tagline in their business plan. A **tagline** is a phrase that a business plans to use to reinforce its position in the marketplace. For example, Wello's tagline is "Bye, Bye Gym Hello Convenience." Wello is an online platform that allows participants to arrange workouts with trainers via Skype or another online means, which avoids having to make a trip to a gym to receive the same service.

The products and services section should include an explanation of your product or service. Include a description of how your product or service is unique and how you plan to position it in the marketplace. A product or service's **position** is how it is situated relative to its rivals. If you plan to open a new type of smoothie shop, for example, you should explain how your smoothie shop differs from others and how it will be positioned in the market in terms of the products it offers and the clientele it attracts. This section is the ideal place for you to start reporting the results of your feasibility analysis. If the concept test, buying intentions survey, and library, Internet, and gumshoe research produced meaningful results, they should be reported here.

The current status section should reveal how far along your company is in its development. A good way to frame this discussion is to think in terms of milestones. A **milestone** is a noteworthy or significant event. If you have selected and registered your company's name, completed a feasibility analysis, developed a business model, and established a legal entity, you have already cleared several important milestones. The legal status and ownership section should indicate who owns the business and how the ownership is split up. You should also indicate what your current form of business ownership is (i.e., LLC, Subchapter S Corp., etc.) if that issue has been decided. We provide a full discussion of the different forms of business ownership in Chapter 7.

A final item a business should cover in this opening section is whether it has any key partnerships that are integral to the business. Many business plans rely on the establishment of partnerships to make them work. Examples of the types of partnerships that are common in business plans are shown in the "Partnering for Success" feature.

Market Analysis   The market analysis is distinctly different from the industry analysis. Whereas the industry analysis focuses on the industry in which a firm intends to compete (e.g., toy industry, fitness center industry, men's clothing industry), the **market analysis** breaks the industry into segments and zeroes in on the specific segment (or target market) to which the firm will try to appeal. As mentioned in Chapter 3, most start-ups focus on servicing a specific target market within an industry.

The first task that's generally tackled in a market analysis is to segment the industry the business will be entering and then identify the specific target market on which it will focus. This is done through **market segmentation**, which is the process of dividing the market into distinct segments. Markets can be segmented in many ways, such as by geography (city, state, country), demographic variables (age, gender, income), psychographic variables (personality, lifestyle, values), and so forth. Sometimes a firm segments its market based on more than one dimension in order to drill down to a specific segment that the firm thinks it is uniquely capable of serving. For example, in its market analysis, GreatCall, the cell phone service provided especially for older people, probably segmented the cell phone market by age and by benefits sought. Some start-ups create value by finding a new way to segment an industry.

PARTNERING FOR SUCCESS

Types of Partnerships That Are Common in Business Plans

Because new businesses are resource constrained, they often make partnering an essential part of their business plans. As illustrated throughout this book, effective partnering can help a start-up in many ways. The following are examples of the types of partnering scenarios that are common in business plans.

Smaller Companies Partnering with Larger Companies to Bring Their Products to Market

Because the cost of bringing a new drug to market is so high, biotech companies commonly partner with large pharmaceutical companies to bring their products to market. Biotech companies specialize in discovering and developing new drugs—it's what they're good at. In most cases, however, they have neither the money nor the experience to bring the products to market. In contrast, the large drug companies, like Merck and Pfizer, specialize in marketing and selling drugs and in providing information to doctors about them. It's what they're good at. As a result, most biotech firms' business plans plainly state that their mission is to discover, develop, and patent new drugs and that they'll partner with larger pharmaceutical companies to bring the products to market.

Smaller Companies Partnering with Larger Companies to Produce, Fulfill, and/or Ship Their Products

Many new firms, from the get-go, structure their business plans on the notion that partners will produce, fulfill, and ship their products. As a result, a start-up that develops a new type of board game may have the game made by a contract manufacturer in China, have it shipped from China to a warehouse and fulfillment company in the United States, and when an order is placed (by a retailer such as Barnes & Noble or Walmart) the warehouse and fulfillment company ships the product to the buyer. While there are costs involved at every step in the process, this arrangement frees the board game company to focus on designing and marketing products and reduces its initial capital requirements. A variation of this approach, for catalog and Web-based companies that sell other manufacturers' products, is a method called drop shipping. Drop shippers like eBags, which is an online retailer that sells luggage, backpacks, and similar items, do not warehouse anything they sell. Instead, when eBags receives an order it passes the order on to the original manufacturer (or distributor), which fulfills the order, often in an eBags box with an eBags packing list so it looks as though it came directly from eBags. This arrangement costs eBags money, but it is integral to eBags's business plan of offering a wide selection of products to customers at affordable prices and not getting caught with outdated merchandise.

Smaller Companies Outsourcing Human Resources Management Tasks

An increasingly common feature in business plans is to outsource human resource management tasks that are labor intensive and require specialized expertise. Some start-ups outsource only administrative tasks, such as payroll processing and benefits administration. These firms partner with payroll accounting firms such as Paychex or TriNet. Other start-ups outsource a broader range of their human resource management functions and partner with a company such as ADP or Administaff. These companies are called professional employer organizations (PEOs) and act as an off-site human resource department for a start-up or other firm. Along with doing everything that Paychex and TriNet does, PEOs can help a start-up with hiring, firing, training, regulatory compliance, and other more in-depth human resource–related issues. Outsourcing these tasks can minimize a firm's investment in human resources management personnel and support (such as software products) and frees a company to focus on other core activities.

Questions for Critical Thinking

1. What factors in the business environment encourage firms to partner to compete?
2. What risks do small firms face when partnering with large, successful companies? What risks do large companies take when they partner with small start-ups?
3. Describe two reasons (that aren't mentioned in this feature) why a small firm would partner with another firm. Provide an example of a partnership that fits one of the reasons.
4. The "You Be the VC 6.1" feature focuses on Buzzy, a company that has created a device that helps relieve the pain and axiety associated with getting a shot. What types of partnerships could Buzzy form to lower its capital requirements and allow its top management team to focus on its distinctive competencies?

For example, before Tish Ciravolo started Daisy Rock Guitar, a company that makes guitars just for women, the guitar industry had not been segmented by gender. Daisy Rock Guitar's competitive advantage is that it makes guitars that accommodate a woman's smaller hands and build.

It's important to include a section in the market analysis that deals directly with the behavior of the consumers in a firm's target market. The more a start-up knows about the consumers in its target market, the more it can gear products or services to accommodate their needs. Many start-ups find it hard to sell products to public schools, for example, because purchase decisions are often made by committees (which draws out the decision-making process), and the funding often has to go through several levels of administrators before it can be approved. A **competitor analysis**, which is a detailed analysis of a firm's competitors, should be included. We provided a thorough explanation of how to complete a competitor analysis in Chapter 5.

The final section of the market analysis estimates a firm's annual sales and market share. There are four basic ways for a new firm to estimate its initial sales. If possible, more than one method should be used to complete this task. The most important outcome is to develop an estimate that is based on sound assumptions and seems both realistic and attainable. We show the four methods entrepreneurs can use to estimate sales in Table 6.3.

The Economics of the Business   This section begins the financial analysis of a business, which is further fleshed out in the financial projections. It addresses the basic logic of how profits are earned in the business and how many units of a business's product or service must be sold for the business to "break even" and then start earning a profit.

The major revenue drivers, which are the ways a business earns money, should be identified. If a business sells a single product and nothing else, it has one revenue driver. If it sells a product plus a service guarantee, it has two revenue drivers, and so on. The size of the overall gross margin for each revenue driver should be determined. The gross margin for a revenue driver is the selling price minus the cost of goods sold or variable costs. The **costs of goods sold** are the materials and direct labor needed to produce the revenue driver.

TABLE 6.3   The Four Methods for Estimating a New Firm's Initial Sales

Method	Explanation
Utilize the Multiplication Method	There are two approaches that fit this category. Start-ups that plan to sell a product on a national basis normally use a top-down approach. This involves trying to estimate the total number of users of the product, estimate the average price customers pay, and estimate what percentage of the market your business will garner. Start-ups that plan to sell locally normally use more of a bottom-up approach. This approach involves trying to determine how many customers to expect and the average amount each customer will spend.
Find a Comparable Firm	Find a comparable firm and ask for an estimate of annual sales. For example, if you are planning to open a women's clothing boutique, try to find a boutique that is similar to yours (and is not in your trade area) and simply call the owner and ask for a chance to talk to him or her about the business. Once a relationship has been established, you can ask for an estimate of the business's annual sales.
Contact Industry Trade Associations	Contact the premier trade associations in your industry and ask if they track the sales numbers for businesses that are similar to your business. If the trade association doesn't track actual sales numbers for comparable businesses, ask if there are other rules of thumb or metrics that help new companies estimate sales. For example, many industries collect statistics such as "average sales per square foot" or "average sales per employee" for firms in their industry.
Conduct Internet Searches	Internet searches often reveal magazine and newspaper articles as well as blog entries that focus on firms in your industry. On occasion, these articles and blog entries will talk about the sales experiences of a similar early-stage firm. If you know of a firm that is comparable to your firm, target that firm first in your search. You may get lucky and find an article or entry that says, "XYZ firm earned gross revenues of $250,000 per year its first three years." If the source of this data is credible and XYZ firm is comparable to your firm, you've just found useful information.

So, if a product sells for $100 and the cost of goods sold is $40 (labor and materials), the gross margin is $60 or 60 percent. The $60 is also called the **contribution margin**. This is the amount per unit of sale that's left over and is available to "contribute" to covering the business's fixed costs and producing a profit. If your business has more than one revenue driver, you should figure the contribution margin for each. If you have multiple products in a given revenue driver category, you can calculate the contribution margin for each product and take an average. (For example, if you're opening an office supply store, you may have several different computer printers under the revenue driver "printers.") You can then calculate the weighted average contribution margin for each of the company's revenue drivers by weighing the individual contribution margin of each revenue driver based on the percentage of sales expected to come from that revenue driver.

The next section should provide an analysis of the business's fixed and variable costs. The variable costs (or costs of goods sold) for each revenue driver was figured previously. Add a projection of the business's fixed costs. A firm's **variable costs** vary by sales, while its **fixed costs** are costs a company incurs whether it sells something or not. The company's operating leverage should be discussed next. A firm's **operating leverage** is an analysis of its fixed versus variable costs. Operating leverage is highest in companies that have a high proportion of fixed costs relative to their variable costs. In contrast, operating leverage is lowest in companies that have a low proportion of fixed costs relative to variable costs. The implications of the firm's projected operating leverage should be discussed. For example, a firm with a high operating leverage takes longer to reach break-even; however, once break-even is reached, more of its revenues fall to the bottom line.

The business's one-time start-up costs should be estimated and put in a table. These costs include legal expenses, fees for business licenses and permits, website design, business logo design, and similar one-time expenses. Normal operating expenses should not be included.

This section should conclude with a break-even analysis, which is an analysis of how many units of its product a business must sell before it breaks even and starts earning a profit. In Chapter 8, we explain how to compute a break-even analysis.

Marketing Plan The marketing plan focuses on how the business will market and sell its product or service. It deals with the nuts and bolts of marketing in terms of price, promotion, distribution, and sales. For example, GreatCall, a firm producing cell phones for older users, may have a great product, a well-defined target market, and a good understanding of its customers and competitors, but it still has to find customers and persuade them to buy its product.

The best way to describe a company's marketing plan is to start by articulating its marketing strategy, positioning, and points of differentiation, and then talk about how these overall aspects of the plan will be supported by price, promotional mix and sales process, and distribution strategy. Obviously, it's not possible to include a full-blown marketing plan in the four to five pages permitted in a business plan for the marketing section, but you should hit the high points as best as possible.

A firm's **marketing strategy** refers to its overall approach for marketing its products and services. A firm's overall approach typically boils down to how it positions itself in its market and how it differentiates itself from competitors. GoldieBlox, the toy company introduced in Chapter 2, is positioning itself as a company that introduces girls to the field of engineering. Only about 10 percent of engineering jobs in the United States are held by women. Beginning with the assumption that storytelling will increase a young girl's connection with the act of building, the company has created a set of toys intended to be used to solve problems while reading about adventures. The ultimate goal is to connect girls with the art of building and encourage young women to pursue careers in engineering. As we see with the example of GoldieBlox, the marketing strategy sets the tone and provides guidance for how the company should reach its target market via its product, pricing, promotions, and distribution tactics. For example, it will invariably promote and advertise its products in places that young women and their parents are most likely to see. Similarly, it will most likely sell its products through specialty toy stores and its own website, along with mass merchandisers such as Toys"R"Us.

The next section should deal with your company's approach to product, price, promotion, and distribution. If your product has been adequately explained already, you can move directly to price. Price, promotion, and distribution should all be in sync with your positioning and points of differentiation, as described previously. Price is a particularly important issue because it determines how much money a company can make. It also sends an important message to a firm's target market. If GoldieBlox advertised its toys as high-quality toys that are both educationally sound and environmentally friendly but also charged a low price, people in its target market would be confused. They would think, "This doesn't make sense. Are GoldieBlox toys high quality or aren't they?" In addition, the lower price wouldn't generate the profits that GoldieBlox needs to further develop its toys. You should also briefly discuss your plans regarding promotions and distribution.

The final section should describe the company's sales process or cycle and specific sales tactics it will employ. It's surprising how many business plans describe a business's overall marketing strategies, but never comment on how a product or service will actually be sold.

Product (or Service) Design and Development Plan   If you're developing a completely new product or service, you need to include a section in your business plan that focuses on the status of your development efforts. Many seemingly promising start-ups never get off the ground because their product development efforts stall or the actual development of the product or service turns out to be more difficult than expected.

The first issue to address is to describe the present stage of the development of your product or service. Most products follow a logical path of development that includes product conception, prototyping, initial production, and full production. You should describe specifically the point that your product or service is at and provide a timeline that describes the remaining steps. If you are in the very early stages of your business and only have an idea, you should carefully explain how a prototype, which is the first physical depiction of a new product or service, will be produced. A **product prototype** is the first physical manifestation of a new product, often in a crude or preliminary form. The idea is to solicit feedback and then iterate. For example, a prototype of a product, like one of GoldieBlox's toys, might consist of a preliminary version of the product for users to test and then report their experiences. GoldieBlox would then modify or tweak the toy based on the users' experiences. Similarly, a prototype for a Web-based company might consist of a preliminary or beta version of the site, with sufficient functionality built into the site for users to test it and then provide feedback. In some instances a virtual prototype is sufficient. A **virtual prototype** is a computer-generated 3D image of a product or service idea. It displays the idea as a 3D model that can be viewed from all sides and rotated 360 degrees.

A section labeled "Challenges and Risks" should be included and disclose any major anticipated design and development challenges and risks that will be involved in bringing the product or service to market. While you want to remain upbeat, the last thing you want to do is paint an overly rosy picture of how quickly and effortlessly your design and development process will unfold.

Experienced readers know that product and service development is an inherently bumpy and challenging process, and they will want insights into the challenges and risks you anticipate with your particular offering.

A final section should describe any patents, trademarks, copyrights, or trade secrets that you have secured or plan to secure relative to the products or services you are developing. If your start-up is still in the early stages and you have not taken action regarding intellectual property issues yet, you should get legal advice so you can, at a minimum, discuss your plans in these areas. Intellectual property is discussed in Chapter 12.

Operations Plan The operations plan section of the business plan outlines how your business will be run and how your product or service will be produced. You have to strike a careful balance between adequately describing this topic and providing too much detail. Your readers will want an overall sense of how the business will be run, but they generally will not be looking for detailed explanations. As a result, it is best to keep this section short and crisp.

A useful way to illustrate how your business will be run is to first articulate your general approach to operations in terms of what's most important and what the make-or-break issues are. You can then frame the discussion in terms of "back stage," or behind-the-scenes activities, and "front stage," or what the customer sees and experiences. For example, if you're opening a new fitness center, the back-stage and the front-stage issues might be broken down as follows:

Back Stage (Behind-the-Scenes Activities)	Front Stage (What the Members See)
■ Staff selection	■ Member tours
■ Operations manual	■ Operating hours
■ Relationships with suppliers	■ Staff assistance
■ Relationships with city government	■ Fitness classes and programs
■ Development of marketing materials	■ Fitness machines
■ Employee orientation and training	■ Workshops
■ Emergency plans	■ Monthly newsletter

Obviously you can't comment on each issue in the three to four pages you have for your operations plan, but you can lay out the key back-stage and front-stage activities and address the most critical ones.

The next section of the operations plan should describe the geographic location of your business. In some instances location is an extremely important issue, and in other instances it isn't. For example, one of the reasons Jeff Bezos decided to locate Amazon.com in Seattle is that this city is a major distribution hub for several large book publishers. By locating near these distribution facilities, Amazon.com has enjoyed a cost advantage that it wouldn't have had otherwise. On a more fine-grained level, for restaurants and retail businesses, the specific location within a mall or shopping center, or a certain side of a busy street, may make a dramatic difference.

This section should also describe a firm's facilities and equipment. You should list your most important facilities and equipment and briefly describe how they will be (or have been) acquired, in terms of whether they will be purchased, leased, or acquired through some other means. If you will be producing a product and will contract or outsource your production, you should comment on how that will be accomplished. If your facilities are nondescript, such as a generic workspace for computer programmers, it isn't necessary to provide a detailed explanation.

Management Team and Company Structure   Many investors and others who read business plans look first at the executive summary and then go directly to the management team section to assess the strength of the people starting the firm. Investors read more business plans with interesting ideas and exciting markets than they are able to finance. As a result, it's often not the idea or market that wins funding among competing plans, but the perception that one management team is better prepared to execute its idea than the others.

The management team of a new firm typically consists of the founder or founders and a handful of key management personnel. A brief profile of each member of the management team should be provided, starting with the founder or founders of the firm. Each profile should include the following information:

- ■ Title of the position
- ■ Duties and responsibilities of the position
- ■ Previous industry and related experience
- ■ Previous successes
- ■ Educational background

Although they should be kept brief, the profiles should illustrate why each individual is qualified and will uniquely contribute to the firm's success. Certain attributes of a management team should be highlighted if they apply in your case. For example, investors and others tend to prefer team members who've worked together before. The thinking here is that if people have worked together before and have decided to partner to start a new firm, it usually means that they get along personally and trust one another.[24] You should also identify the gaps that exist in the management team and your plans and timetable for filling them. The complete résumés of key management team personnel can be placed in an appendix to the business plan.

If a start-up has a board of directors and/or a board of advisors, their qualifications and the roles they play should be explained and they should be included as part of your management team. A **board of directors** is a panel of individuals elected by a corporation's shareholders to oversee the management of the firm, as explained in more detail in Chapter 9. A **board of advisors** is a panel of experts asked by a firm's management to provide counsel and advice on an ongoing basis. Unlike a board of directors, a board of advisors possesses no legal responsibility for the firm and gives nonbinding advice.[25] Many start-ups ask people who have specific skills or expertise to serve on their board of advisors to help plug competency gaps until the firm can afford to hire additional personnel. For example, if a firm is started by two Web designers and doesn't have anyone on staff with marketing expertise, the firm might place one or two people on its board of advisors with marketing expertise to provide guidance and advice.

The final portion of this section of your business plan focuses on how your company will be structured. Even if you are a start-up, you should outline how the company is currently structured and how it will be structured as it grows. It's important that the internal structure of a company makes sense and that the lines of communication and accountability are clear. Including a description of your company's structure also reassures the people who read the plan that you know how to translate your business idea into a functioning firm.

The most effective way to illustrate how a company will be structured and the lines of authority and accountability that will be in place is to include an organizational chart in the plan. An **organizational chart** is a graphic representation of how authority and responsibility are distributed within the company. The organizational chart should be presented in graphical format if possible.

Overall Schedule A schedule should be prepared that shows the major events required to launch the business. The schedule should be in the format of milestones critical to the business's success, such as incorporating the venture, completion of prototypes, rental of facilities, obtaining critical financing, starting the production of operations, obtaining the first sale, and so forth. An effectively prepared and presented schedule can be extremely valuable in convincing potential investors that the management team is aware of what needs to take place to launch the venture and has a plan in place to get there.

Financial Projections The final section of a business plan presents a firm's pro forma (or projected) financial projections. Having completed the previous sections of the plan, it's easy to see why the financial projections come last. They take the plans you've developed and express them in financial terms.

The first thing to include is a **sources and uses of funds statement**, which is a document that lays out specifically how much money a firm needs (if the intention of the business plan is to raise money), where the money will come from, and how the money will be used. The next item to include is an **assumptions sheet**, which is an explanation of the most critical assumptions on which the financial statements are based. Some assumptions will be based on general information, and no specific sources will be cited to substantiate the assumption. For example, if you believe that the U.S. economy will gain strength over the next three to five years, and that's an underlying assumption driving your sales projections, then you should state that assumption. In this instance, you wouldn't cite a specific source—you're reflecting a consensus view. (It's then up to your reader to agree or disagree.) Other assumptions will be based on very specific information, and you should cite the source for your assumptions. For example, if GoldieBlox has credible data showing that the educational segment of the children's toy industry is expected to grow at a certain percentage each year for the foreseeable future, and this figure plays a large role in its belief that it can increase its sales every year, then it should cite the sources of its information.

The importance of identifying the most critical assumptions that a business is based on and thoroughly vetting the assumptions is illustrated in the "What Went Wrong" feature. EventVue, the company that is the focus of the feature, failed largely because several of the key assumptions that business was based on turned out to be incorrect.

The **pro forma (or projected) financial statements** are the heart of the financial section of a business plan. Although at first glance preparing financial statements appears to be a tedious exercise, it's a fairly straightforward process if the preceding sections of your plan are thorough. The financial statements also represent the finale of the entire plan. As a result, it's interesting to see how they turn out.

A firm's pro forma financial statements are similar to the historical statements an established firm prepares, except they look forward rather than track the past. Pro forma financial statements include the pro forma income statement, the pro forma balance sheet, and the pro forma cash flow statement. They are usually prepared in this order because information flows logically from one to the next. Most experts recommend three to five years of pro forma statements. If the company you're writing your plan for already exists, you should also include three years of historical financial statements. Most business plan writers interpret or make sense of a firm's historical or pro forma financial statements through **ratio analysis**. Ratios, such as return on assets and return on sales, are computed by taking numbers out of financial statements and forming ratios with them. Each ratio has a particular meaning in regard to the potential of the business.

We present a complete explanation of how to complete pro forma financial statements and ratio analysis in Chapter 8.

WHAT WENT WRONG?

What EventVue Learned the Hard Way About Making Assumptions

EventVue was a product that was intended to improve the experience of people who attend conferences. It started as a private social network that helped conference attendees network more effectively. It pivoted twice, once to rollout a widget that would bring more people to specific conferences, and then to an app that promised to be the best way for conference attendees to disscuss what was taking place in real time. EventVue launched with promise but failed in early 2010. What went wrong?

Several things, all of which have to do with incorrect assumptions. The first assumption was that conference organizers would see EventVue as an invaluable asset. They didn't. While EventVue saw itself as essential, conference organizers saw it more as "a vitamin rather than a pain pill." It was something that event organizers said they liked, but none of them saw it as essential. It didn't make their lives easier, make them more money, reduce their costs, or boost the profile of an event. It was simply nice to have. Although EventVue's platform made it easier for conference attendees to network with one another, it wasn't clear what was in it for the organizers, who were the ones being asked to pay for it. What the founders of EventVue found was that conference organizers care first and foremost about one thing—selling tickets. Anthing that doesn't sell tickets is a secondary consideration.

After disappointing initial results, EventVue pivoted to offer a widget that would help bring more people to conferences. This, the company founders assumed, would get the attention of conference organizers. The widget would let people know who was registered for an event. The idea was that if a prospective attendee saw that a friend or someone they admired was registered for a conference, they would be more likely to register for the event conference as well. Incredibly, the widget had the opposite effect. A rule of thumb for conferences is that the majority of sales come in the last two weeks before the conference is scheduled to take place. As a result, when people looked at the registration list—particularly if they looked at it more than two weeks out from the event—and saw that none of their friends or people that they admired were registered,

they were less likely to register themselves. Therefore, rather than making conference organizers money, the EventVue widget actually cost them money. EventVue tried out several other ideas, but eventually ran out of ideas, persistence, and money.

There are two key takeaways from the EventVue story for business plan writers. First, a business should test its assumptions prior to launching. This lesson illustrates the need to complete a comprehesive feasibility analysis prior to writing a business plan and moving forward with a business idea, as illustrated in Chapter 3. Second, it's essential that a business understand its customers' needs. EventVue never found a way to help conference organizers sell more tickets. It found a way to help conference attendees better network with others, but conference attendees were not EventVue's customers.

Questions for Critical Thinking

1. Briefly map out the feasibility analysis that EventVue's founders should have conducted prior to launching the company. Of the four forms of feasibility analysis described in Chapter 3, which of the forms should have been emphasized the most? Explain your answer.

2. If EventVue had conducted a comprehensive feasibility analysis prior to launch, what do you think the company would have looked like?

3. Do some Internet research to see if there are companies that are providing social networks for conference attendees. If so, what are they doing differently than what EventVue tried to do? Try to discern why they have been able to stay in business while EventVue failed.

4. The "You Be the VC 3.1" feature focuses on August Smart Locks, a company that will enable users to control the locks on their homes or apartments via a smartphone. What are some of the main assumptions that August's business plan is based on?

Source: J. Fraser, "A Few Words About EventVue," Online Aspect, available at www.onlineaspect.com/2010/10/26/a-few-words-about-eventvue, accessed February 28, 2014.

Appendix Any material that does not easily fit into the body of a business plan should appear in an appendix—résumés of the top management team, photos or diagrams of product or product prototypes, certain financial data, and market research projections. The appendix should not be bulky and add significant length to the business plan. It should include only the additional information vital to the plan but not appropriate for the body of the plan itself.

Putting It All Together In evaluating and reviewing the completed business plan, the writers should put themselves in the reader's shoes to determine if the most important questions about the viability of their business venture have been answered. Table 6.4 lists the 10 most important questions a business plan should answer. It's a good checklist for any business plan writer.

Presenting the Business Plan to Investors

If the business plan successfully elicits the interest of a potential investor, the next step is to meet with the investor and present the plan in person. The investor will typically want to meet with the firm's founders. Because investors ultimately fund only a few ventures, the founders of a new firm should make as positive an impression on the investor as possible.

The first meeting with an investor is generally very short, about one hour.[26] The investor will typically ask the firm to make a 15- to 20-minute presentation using PowerPoint slides and use the rest of the time to ask questions. If the investor is impressed and wants to learn more about the venture, the presenters will be asked back for a second meeting to meet with the investor and his or her partners. This meeting will typically last longer and will require a more thorough presentation.

LEARNING OBJECTIVE

5. Explain how to effectively present a business plan to potential investors.

The Oral Presentation of a Business Plan

When asked to meet with an investor, the founders of a new venture should prepare a set of PowerPoint slides that will fill the time slot allowed for the presentation portion of the meeting. The same format applies to most business plan competitions. The first rule in making an oral presentation is to follow instructions. If an investor tells an entrepreneur that he or she has one hour and that the hour will consist of a 20-minute presentation and a 40-minute question-and-answer period, the presentation shouldn't last more than 20 minutes. The presentation should be smooth and well-rehearsed. The slides should be sharp and not cluttered with material.

The entrepreneur should arrive at the appointment on time and be well prepared. If any audiovisual equipment is needed, the entrepreneur should be prepared to supply the equipment if the investor doesn't have it. These arrangements should be made prior to the meeting. The presentation should consist of plain talk and should avoid technical jargon. Start-up

---

TABLE 6.4 **The 10 Most Important Questions a Business Plan Should Answer**

1. Is the business just an idea, or is it an opportunity with real potential?

2. Is the product or service viable? Does it add significant value to the customer? Has a feasibility analysis been completed? If so, what are the results?

3. Is the business entering an exciting, growing industry, and has the firm identified an attractive position within the industry?

4. Does the business have a well-defined target market?

5. Does the business have points of differentiation that truly separate it from its competitors? Are these points of differentiation sustainable?

6. Does the business have a sound marketing plan?

7. Is the management team experienced, skilled, and up to the task of launching the new firm?

8. Is the business's operations plan appropriate and sound?

9. Are the assumptions that the firm is basing its financial projections on realistic?

10. Are the financial projections completed correctly, and do they project a bright future for the firm?

entrepreneurs may mistakenly spend too much time talking about the technology that will go into a new product or service and not enough time talking about the business itself. The most important issues to cover in the presentation and how to present them are shown in Table 6.5. This presentation format calls for the use of 12 slides. A common mistake entrepreneurs make is to prepare too many slides and then try to rush through them during a 20-minute presentation.

TABLE 6.5 Twelve PowerPoint Slides to Include in an Investor Presentation

Topic	Explanation
1. Title slide	Introduce the presentation with your company's name, the names of the founders, and the company logo if available.
2. Problem	Briefly state the problem to be solved or the need to be filled.
3. Solution	Explain how your firm will solve the problem or how it will satisfy the need to be filled.
4. Opportunity and target market	Articulate your specific target market. Talk about business and environmental trends that are providing your target market momentum.
5. Technology	This slide is optional but is normally included. Talk about your technology or any unusual aspects of your product or service. Don't talk in an overly technical manner. Make your descriptions easy to understand and interesting.
6. Competition	Explain specifically the firm's competitive advantage in the marketplace and how it will compete against more established competitors.
7. Marketing and sales	Describe your overall marketing strategy. Talk about your sales process. If you've conducted primary research regarding how people feel about your product, report the results here.
8. Management team	Describe your existing management team. Explain how the team came together and how their backgrounds and expertise are keys to the success of your firm. If you have a board of advisors or board of directors, briefly mention the key individuals involved. If you have gaps in your team, explain how and when they will be filled.
9. Financial projections	Briefly discuss the financials. Stress when the firm will achieve profitability, how much capital it will take to get there, and when its cash flow will break even. Use additional slides if needed to properly display your information, but don't go overboard.
10. Current status	Describe the current status of your firm in the context of the milestones you've achieved to date. Don't diminish the value of your accomplishments.
11. Financing sought	Lay out specifically how much financing you're seeking and how you'll use the money.
12. Summary	Bring the presentation to a close. Summarize the strongest points of your venture and your team. Solicit feedback from your audience.

Source: B. Barringer, *Preparing Effective Business Plans: An Entrepreneurial Approach,* 1st Edition, © 2009, pp. 242–253. Adapted by permission of Pearson Education, Inc., Upper Saddle River, NJ.

Questions and Feedback to Expect from Investors

Whether in the initial meeting or on subsequent occasions, an entrepreneur will be asked a host of questions by potential investors. The smart entrepreneur has a solid idea of what to expect and is prepared for these queries. Because investors often come across as being very critical,[27] it is easy for an entrepreneur to become discouraged, particularly if the investor seems to be poking holes in every aspect of the business plan. The same dynamic typifies the question-and-answer sessions that follow presentations in business plan competitions. In fact, an investor who is able to identify weaknesses in a business plan or presentation does a favor for the entrepreneur. This is because the entrepreneur can take the investor's feedback to heart and use it to improve the business plan and/or the presentation.

In the first meeting, investors typically focus on whether a real opportunity exists and whether the management team has the experience and skills to pull off the venture. The investor will also try to sense whether the managers are highly confident in their own venture. The question-and-answer period is extremely important. Here investors are typically looking for how well entrepreneurs think on their feet and how knowledgeable they are about the business venture. Michael Rovner, a partner of Rob Adam's at AV Labs, put it this way: "We ask a lot of peripheral questions. We might not want answers—we just want to evaluate the entrepreneur's thought process."[28]

Chapter Summary

LO1. A business plan is a written narrative that describes what a new business intends to accomplish and how it plans to achieve its goals. For most new businesses, the business plan is a dual-purpose document that is used both inside and outside the firm. Inside the firm, it helps the company develop a road map to follow in executing its strategies. Outside the firm, it acquaints potential investors and other stakeholders with the business opportunity the firm is pursuing and describes how the business will pursue that opportunity.

LO2. The two primary audiences for a firm's business plan are its employees and potential investors and other external stakeholders. There are different kinds of business plans. For example, a summary business plan is 10 to 15 pages and works best for companies in the early stages of development. These companies don't have the information needed for a full business plan but may put together a summary business plan to see if potential investors are interested in their idea. A full business plan, typically 25 to 35 pages, spells out a company's operations and plans in much more detail than a summary business plan and is the usual format for a business plan prepared for an investor. An operational business plan is usually prepared for an internal audience. It is 40 to 100 pages long and provides a blueprint for a company's operations.

LO3. Guidelines are available for those writing a business plan to follow. Adhering to these guidelines increases the probability that an entrepreneur will develop an effective business plan. The structure of the plan is the first guideline to consider. The advice here is that a conventional structure should be used to develop a business plan. Doing this allows business investors to focus on the parts of a plan that are critical to their decision-making process. Second, a business plan should be concise and clear in its development. All important aspects of the proposed venture should be included in the plan. Once written, the plan should be checked for grammar errors, spelling mistakes, and to verify that all vital information is in fact included. The plan's style and format are the issues around which the third guideline is framed. The plan's appearance should be carefully evaluated; however, it should be consistent with a conventional structure (as noted earlier) and should not suggest to the potential investor that a great deal of money was spent to prepare the plan itself.

LO4. A business plan has multiple parts, the first of which is the executive summary. The executive summary is a quick overview of the entire business plan and provides busy readers with everything they need to know about the distinctive nature of the new venture. In many instances, an investor will ask for a copy of a firm's executive summary and will request a copy of the full business plan only when the executive summary is sufficiently convincing. The industry analysis, which is another part of the business plan, describes the industry a business will enter. The market analysis part of the plan breaks the industry analysis into segments and zeros in on the specific segments (or target markets) to which the firm will seek to appeal. The management team and company structure section of a business plan is critical. Many investors and others who read business plans look first at the executive summary and then go directly to the management team section to assess the strength of the people starting the firm. The sources and uses of funds statement is a document that lays out specifically how much money a firm needs (if it is raising money), where the money will come from, and what it will be used for. An assumptions sheet is an explanation of the most critical assumptions that a business's financial analysis is based on.

LO5. After writing the business plan, the entrepreneur must prepare to present it effectively to potential investors and possibly others as well. The oral presentation of a business plan typically consists of 20 minutes of formal remarks, accompanied by approximately 12 PowerPoint slides, and 40 minutes of questions and answers. The presentation should be smooth and well-rehearsed. The slides should be sharp and not cluttered with material.

Key Terms

assumptions sheet, **223**
board of advisors, **222**
board of directors, **222**
business plan, **204**
competitor analysis, **218**
contribution margin, **219**
costs of goods sold, **218**
executive summary, **212**
fixed costs, **219**
full business plan, **210**
market analysis, **216**

market segmentation, **216**
marketing strategy, **219**
milestone, **216**
mission statement, **216**
operating leverage, **219**
operational business
   plan, **210**
organizational chart, **222**
position, **216**
pro forma (or projected)
   financial statements, **223**

product prototype, **220**
ratio analysis, **223**
sources and uses of funds
   statement, **223**
summary business
   plan, **210**
tagline, **216**
variable costs, **219**
virtual prototype, **220**

Review Questions

6-1. What is a business plan?
6-2. What are the advantages of preparing a business plan for a new venture?
6-3. When is the appropriate time to write a business plan?
6-4. What are the two primary reasons for those starting a new venture to write a business plan?

6-5. Why is writing a business plan the last activity to be completed in the entrepreneurial process?
6-6. Who reads the business plan and what are they looking for when doing so?
6-7. How will investors typically react if they think a business plan is based on

estimates and predictions rather than on careful analysis and facts?

6-8. Why is it important for a business plan to follow a conventional structure rather than be highly innovative and creative?

6-9. What are the differences among a summary business plan, a full business plan, and an operational business plan?

6-10. Why should the executive summary, which is one of the first things that appears in a business plan, be written last?

6-11. What is the difference between the industry analysis section and the market analysis section of a business plan?

6-12. Why should an entrepreneur keep an open mind about the elements of a business plan changing?

6-13. What is the purpose of "The Economics of the Business" section of a business plan?

6-14. If you're developing a completely new product or service, what type of information should you include in your business plan regarding the status of the development efforts?

6-15. What is the purpose of the "Operations Plan" section of a business plan?

6-16. Why is the "Management Team and Company Structure" section of a business plan often touted as one of the most important sections?

6-17. What is the purpose of an executive summary?

6-18. What is the purpose of a mission statement?

6-19. What is the difference between a product prototype and a virtual prototype?

6-20. What is the number-one rule in making an investor presentation?

Application Questions

6-21. Travis Ryan is one of four cofounders of a skateboard company. The cofounders have decided to write a business plan to obtain funding for their venture. During a recent meeting, Travis said, "I know that we're all really busy, so I'd like to volunteer to write our business plan. A friend of mine has a house on a lake near where we are going to school. If the three of you agree, I'll take my laptop to my friend's house for a couple of days and knock out our business plan. Any objections?" If you were one of Travis's co-founders, what would you say? What alternative approaches to writing a business plan would you propose and why?

6-22. A good friend of yours, Andrew Waters, has decided to leave his corporate job in order to launch a private SEO (search engine optimization) consulting firm. He is putting together a business plan for this venture and says the following to you: "I've read several books and articles about how to write a business plan, and there is a point about which I am still a bit confused. Is a business plan written more for learning and discovering or is it written more for pitching and selling?" What would you say to Andrew in response to his question?

6-23. Josh White has a brilliant idea of starting up an e-payment business using online payment kiosks. However, he is looking for investors to fund his business. As you are a good friend to Josh, he called you to seek advice on writing a good business plan to attract potential investors. He needs a structured plan detailing how to achieve the potential of his ideas so that his plan doesn't look hastily put together. Advise Josh on some of the "red flags" that he should avoid while preparing the plan.

6-24. Ginny Welch needs to prepare a market analysis for her business plan for a loan provider which is due in the next two weeks. However, she does not know what to write and who her target market is. All she knows is that her potential customers are those who are seeking a healthy lifestyle, as she is proposing to start a wellness center. She has completed her industry analysis but only recently learned the difference between market analysis and industry analysis. What is the next step she should take to complete the market analysis?

6-25. The entrepreneurship class you are taking meets for four hours once per week. A break of 10 minutes or so takes place after the first two hours of each class.

During a recent break, you overhead one of your classmates say to another person that in her opinion, the teacher is over-selling the importance to potential investors of a start-up's management team. "After all," the classmate says, "A good product outweighs any deficiency a firm may have in terms of managers and their abilities." Given what you have learned about business plans, what would you say to your classmate to convince her that she needs to rethink her view about potential investors' views about the quality of a proposed venture's management team?

6-26. Shane Hanks has prepared a business plan for his phone app Mobil Gym, and needs a few tips on how to effectively present the business plan to his potential investors. His business plan has a couple of investors interested and now he needs to meet them in person and present to his plan. Guide Shane.

6-27. Michael Graves and Jill Simpson just left their jobs with Microsoft to launch a business that will sell a new type of fax machine. They wrote a full business plan that they've asked you to review. When reading the plan, you noticed that several key sections begin with the phrase "We believe...." Is any knowledgable person who reads this business plan going to know what "We believe..." really means? What is the problem with including the phrase "We believe...." to introduce key sections of a business plan?

6-28. Recently, Megan, Jennifer, and Mark, the cofounders of a medical products company, presented their business plan to a group of investors in the hopes of receiving funding for their venture. One of the investors asked the three, "How much of your personal money do each of you have invested in this firm?" Is this a legitimate question for the potential investor to ask? Why would an investor want to know how much of their own money each cofounder has committed to the proposed new venture?

6-29. Janine Morris has prepared a business plan for her online shoe business. She has approached an angel investor to support her business financially. Being a close friend, she showed you her business plan and asked for your opinion. After reading through her plan, you noticed that her plan did not include the important elements that the investor would be looking for. Moreover, her business plan was very vague and did not clearly state the real intention of starting the business. Advise Janine.

YOU BE THE VC 6.1 COMPANY: Buzzy

• Web: www.buzzy.com • Facebook: Buzzy • Twitter: @Buzzy4shots

Business Idea: Create a device that helps relieve the pain and anxiety associated with getting a shot and other needle sticks like IV starts, blood draws, and finger pricks.

Pitch: While no one looks forward to getting a shot or finger prick, some people are so afraid of the experience that they are literally needle phobic. Needle phobic people are so fearful of getting a shot that it keeps them from donating blood, getting immunizations like flu shots, and receiving regular health care. Buzzy founder Amy Baxter, an emergency room physician and pain researcher, found herself dealing firsthand with this situation. Her son had a really bad shot experience and became needle phobic. She knew right away that she had to do something so her son would no longer be afraid to go to the doctor and receive appropriate treatments.

After some research and experimentation, and aided by a $1 million grant from the National Institutes of Health (NIH), Dr. Baxter invented Buzzy, a bee-shaped, palm-sized device. Buzzy operates on a pain management theory called gait control. Researchers have long suspected that various kinds of sensory simulation could actually interrupt pain signals traveling up the spinal cord, before they reach the brain. After experimenting with different kinds of stimulations, Dr. Baxter settled on a combination of cold temperature with high-speed vibration. The cold and the vibration crowds out the pain caused by a shot by literally sending stronger motion

and temperature sensations up the nerve pathways than are produced by the pain. It's kind of like rubbing a cut under cold water or the dentist jiggling your cheek before giving you a shot. The vibrating bee attaches to thin ice packs that look like wings. The device is then placed between the injection site and the brain to block the pain from the injection. It also blocks the burning sensation that some medications cause after a shot is administered.

Buzzy's efficacy has been verified by independent testing and research. Along with helping people who get an occasional shot, Buzzy is particularly beneficial for people who must receive regular shots as the result of a chronic condition. Buzzy is sold to doctors' offices, hospitals, and clinics. A fully FDA-compliant version is also available for home use and is priced at $39.95. The home version can be used by people who inject themselves as part of a physician-supervised home health care regime, or can be taken to the doctor's office when the need for a shot is anticipated. The Buzzy device is reusable.

6-30. Based on the material covered in this chapter, what questions would you ask the firm's founders before making your funding decision? What answers would satisfy you?

6-31. If you had to make your decision on just the information provided in the pitch and on the website, would you fund this company? Why or why not?

YOU BE THE VC 6.2 COMPANY: Flings Bins

• Web: www.flingsbins.com • Facebook: Flings Pop-Up Recycling and Trash Bins • Twitter: No Twitter account at the time this case was written

Business Idea: Create a pop-up, disposable trash bin that makes the process of recycling and collecting trash, particularly at parties and events that are held away from everyday garbage and recycling receptacles, simpler, cleaner, and more fun.

Pitch: Most people want to do what is "right" when it comes to handling trash and recycling, but obstacles get in their way. Trash bags are often flimsy and hard to deal with. Recycling containers can quickly get dirty and unsightly. And handling trash and recycling can be difficult at parties and events that are held away from a person's home or business. These types of complications cause many people angst. Imagine throwing a party at a park, a beach, or a facility that you're not familiar with. It's easy for soda cans and beer bottles to pile up and for garbage cans to overflow. Even if you're throwing a party in your own home, household

garbage cans and recycling containers are often too small to handle the job.

Flings Bins were created to address these problems. Flings is a freestanding pop-up container and trash bag in one. You can set up several Flings containers around the house and not have to worry about taking out trash in the middle of the party. They are portable and can be brought outdoors to picnics, campsites, and tailgating parties where there is no trash can nearby. They are disposable and 100 percent biodegradable, but are sturdy enough to be emptied and used again if the trash inside wasn't particularly messy. They also dress up a party or event rather than create an eyesore, as is the case with most trash containers. They are available in many different colors and patterns, such as patriotic colors for a Fourth of July party, red and white gingham for a barbeque, or confetti and balloons for a New Year's

Eve party. While people don't normally think of impressing their guests with their trash or garbage containers, Flings Bins are quite stylish. Flings Bins are also available that are completely covered in the recycle symbol and are labeled "Please Recycle Here." There are boxes that can be checked with a marker or sharpie that say "cans," "plastics," "glass," and so on, so a host can opt to set up recycling bins for different purposes.

Flings containers come flat and pop up for use. As a result, they are easy to transport and store. As the company says,

"Pop It! Fill It! Toss It! Or Recycle and Reuse!" Each bin has a 13-gallon capacity (which holds about 60 cans or bottles), and a drawstring that makes them easy to close and carry.

6-32. Based on the material covered in this chapter, what questions would you ask the firm's founders before making your funding decision? What answers would satisfy you?

6-33. If you had to make your decision on just the information provided in the pitch and on the company's website, would you fund this company? Why or why not?

CASE 6.1

Birchbox: Leveraging the College Experience to Write a Business Plan and Launch a Winning Start-up

• *Web: www.birchbox.com* • *Facebook: Birchbox* • *Twitter: @birchbox*

Bruce R. Barringer, *Oklahoma State University*

R. Duane Ireland, *Texas A&M University*

Introduction

Katie Beauchamp and Hayley Barna met on their first day at Harvard Business School. They volunteered to co-coordinate a spring holiday for themselves and 50 of their classmates. Through the experience they realized that they worked well together as a team, but at that time, they had no thought of co-founding a business. That all changed just over a year later, when Beauchamp and Barna launched Birchbox, a beauty samples subscription service that now has over 400,000 monthly subscribers.

The College Experience

Beauchamp and Barna quickly became friends. They were also in the same MBA cohort and took many of their classes together. The idea for Birchbox emerged gradually. One class was particularly instrumental. It was a class on disruptive innovation taught by Harvard professor Clayton Christensen. The class challenged the students to think of a big idea that's an industry game changer. Beauchamp and Barna's first idea concerned the beauty industry, which hadn't experienced significant innovation for many years. A personal dynamic also nudged them

Birchbox Co-founders
Hayley Barna and Katie
Beauchamp

towards a business idea in the beauty industry. Barna's best friend, Mollie Chen, was a beauty editor. Beauchamp would notice that Barna always had the best beauty products, and when asked where she got them, she would always say that Chen (the beauty editor) had recommended them. It got Beauchamp and Barna thinking "wouldn't every woman like to have a best friend that was a beauty editor and could recommend beauty products to them?"

Beauchamp and Barna's thoughts coalesced in the last semester of their two-year MBA program. For the first time, they were thinking about starting a business together. They saw a void in the marketplace ripe to be filled. Companies had come up with great ways to sell many products online, including fashion, but not beauty products. Beauty products are tough to sell online because they have a touch, try, and feel element to them. To capitalize on the opportunity of selling beauty products online, and get around the hesitation that people have for buying beauty products without touching and seeing them first, Beauchamp and Barna's idea was an online monthly subscription service that consisted of a small box of beauty product samples that qualified customers could try out. They would then offer full-sized versions of the samples on their website for sale. The major brands were already making samples that they handed out in stores. Beauchamp and Barna decided to call their business Birchbox.

Last Semester at Harvard—A Testing Ground for Birchbox

Rather than let the clock run out on their college experience and then try to launch Birchbox, Beauchamp and Barna did everything they could to leverage their college status. They negotiated with their professors so their final project in each class would be Birchbox. They also used their student status as a way of getting their foot in the door with suppliers and customers. For Birchbox to work, Beauchamp and Barna had to answer three fundamental questions. First, would beauty brands work with them, in regard to providing samples? Second, would women pay for curated boxes of samples? And third, would samples drive full-sized purchases? The only way, they figured, to answer these questions was to go

straight to the sources. First, they built a prototype of the box in which they would send the monthly samples and determined how the samples would be presented in the box. They then thought through the rest of the business. Each month, the box would contain five beauty product samples. Information would be put on their website and YouTube channel about each product, so the customer could learn more about them. They would then offer full-sized versions of the products for sale. To get buy-in, they "cold-called" beauty and cosmetics companies. They never hid the fact that they were still in college. Instead, they framed it as an advantage (they had a readymade audience of their target market right in their classes). Incredibly, several of the companies, including Benefits, Nars, and Keihl's signed on. Second, they created a beta version of their website and incented 200 subscribers to pay them $20 a month to test their concept. They used feedback from the users to improve the original Birchbox in several key areas. At this point, Beauchamp and Barna had more than an idea. They had suppliers, a preliminary list of potential customers, results, and data.

After completing these steps, Beauchamp and Barna entered Birchbox into the HBS business plan competition. They won second place, which further bolstered their confidence. The competition provided tremendous exposure for Birchbox and for Beauchamp and Barna as nascent entrepreneurs. They met people who became advisers and mentors. The competition was judged by venture capitalists, and several of them offered the pair money. They passed on the offers, thinking it would be best to keep Birchbox lean.

Birchbox officially launched in September 2010. At the outset, it remained lean and reflected a college student's lifestyle. After graduation, Beauchamp and Barna moved Birchbox to Brooklyn to be closer to their suppliers. Their first office was unpretentious and had IKEA furniture. Beauchamp and Barna learned many lessons the hard, and sometimes fun, way. For example, when they made their first product video they tried to recruit volunteers in Union Square (a popular area in Manhattan). They soon found that it's impossible to get busy New Yorkers to volunteer, so they, along with a couple of early employees, dressed up and starred in the video themselves. By the end of 2010, Birchbox had 10,000 subscribers.

Each monthly Birchbox for Women includes a small collection of high-quality beauty, grooming, and lifestyle product samples. The product samples are similar to the ones shown here.

Christopher Hall/Shutterstock

(continued)

Birchbox Today

Birchbox today is operating on all cylinders. The company has 400,000 monthly subscribers. Its monthly subscription service for women, which costs $10 per month, is much the same as it was when the company originally launched, except that subscribers now fill out a beauty profile and several versions of the monthly box are sent out. In 2012, the company launched Birchbox Man, a $20 box filled with men's grooming supplies and lifestyle products. It also started testing a limited edition "home box" for $58 a month that will include home décor products and items such as seasonal napkins and decorations. In September 2012, Birchbox acquired JolieBox, a Paris-based competitor. The acquisition will allow Birchbox to more effectively enter European markets. Along the way the company has grown to 140 employees and raised almost $12 million in funding.

The company's performance metrics are also strong. The number of monthly subscribers in all of its categories continues to grow. More than half of its monthly subscribers make purchases from the firm's e-commerce store, and the e-commerce store now represents a quarter of its revenue. Birchbox's online store even attracts business from nonsubscribers. About 15 percent of the company's orders come from customers who don't get the monthly box of sample products.

Birchbox's model is also working out for its suppliers. Traditionally, beauty suppliers have tried to acquire customers by handing out samples at their counters and in other parts of stores and malls. Birchbox's customers, in stark contrast, actually pay to be acquired through the monthly subscription service. They in effect opt-in and explicitly want to be sampled. When Birchbox sells a full-sized version of something that was sampled through its subscription service, it shares the revenue with the supplier.

Challenges Ahead

Despite its success, Birchbox has significant challenges. It may at some point plateau in terms of subscribers for its staple women's subscription service. New markets may be more difficult to grow. For example, the number of products and product samples made for men's grooming and lifestyle supplies is much lower than those made for women. It may also be difficult to find as large a following for products like home décor as for women's beauty suppliers.

Another challenge Birchbox faces is growing competition. A number of start-ups have replicated Birchbox's monthly subscription service for beauty product samples for women. While Birchbox remains the clear leader in this space, the number of competitors it is attracting is somewhat worrisome. Interestingly, while it doesn't directly impact Birchbox's business, the company has also inspired a wave of companies selling monthly boxed products in almost every conceivable area, including fishing, food, crafts, kids' toys, products for dogs, and wine.

Discussion Questions

6-34. How effectively do you think Katie Beauchamp and Hayley Barna used their time in college to advance their business idea?

6-35. In what ways is Birchbox's business approach a win-win for both its suppliers and its customers?

6-36. How was writing a business plan and preparing for a business plan competition helpful to Katie Beauchamp and Hayley Barna while Birchbox was still in the planning, testing, and prototyping stage?

6-37. Going forward, what are the most serious challenges facing Birchbox? Which of these challenges do you believe is the most threatening to the firm's success? Why?

Sources: Birchbox home page, www.birchbox.com, accessed March 1, 2014; A. Groth, "Exclusive Q&A: Birchbox Co-Founder on HSB and the Advice They Got from Investors," *Business Insider,* www.businessinsider.com, acessed March 1, 2014; A. Dizik, "MBA Enrepreneurs Think Outside the Box for Beauty Business," *Financial Times,* March 3, 2013; T. Baldwin, "Entrepreneur's Corner: Birchbox," *The Wharton Journal,* February 28, 2014.

CASE 6.2

d.light: How Bringing Its Business Plan to Life Helped a Social Enterprise Get Off to a Strong Start

• *Web: dlightdesign.com* • *Facebook: D.lightDesign* • *Twitter: @dlightdesign*

Bruce R. Barringer, *Oklahoma State University*

R. Duane Ireland, *Texas A&M University*

Introduction

Imagine the following. You're in the audience of a business plan competition. The next team up to present is d.light, a for-profit social enterprise that plans to bring light to people without access to reliable electricity. Two young men introduce themselves as the founders of d.light, and say they're going to start their presentation with a demonstration. The lights go out. In a few seconds, you see a dim light at the front of the room, and smell smoke and burning kerosene. After about 30 seconds, your eyes start to water and it becomes slightly uncomfortable to breathe. The lights switch back on and the smoke clears. The young men apologize for the lack of light and the smoke, but say the demonstration was staged to illustrate a point. Around 1.6 billion people, or more than one fifth of the world's population, have no access to electricity, and about a billion more have an unreliable or intermittent supply. A large share of these people use kerosene to light their homes at night. Kerosene fumes are extremely unhealthy, even fatal. In fact, the United Nations estimates that kerosene fumes kill 1.5 million people per year, and cause countless health complications for others.

Sam Goldman and the Origins of d.light

The scene described here actually took place—several times. It's the way Sam Goldman and Ned Tozun, the co-founders of d.light, introduced the company at business plan competitions and when they pitched investors. d.light is an international consumer products company serving "base of the pyramid" consumers who don't have access to reliable electricity. Although d.light technically started in a class at Stanford University, its beginning can be traced to Sam Goldman's youth and early adulthood. Growing up, Goldman's parents worked for the United States Agency for International Development (USAID), a government agency that provides economic and humanitarian assistance in countries across the globe. Goldman lived in Pakistan, Peru, India, Canada, and several other countries. As a young adult, while working for the Peace Corps, he lived for four years in a West African village that had no electricity. A neighbor boy was badly burned in a kerosene fire, an event that deeply impacted Goldman. At one point during his time in the village, Goldman was given a battery-powered LED headlamp, and was struck by the dramatic difference that simply having light at night can make in a person's life. He could now cook, read, and do things at night that were unimaginable without the benefits reliable lighting provides.

Impacted by this experience, Goldman sought out a graduate program that would provide him the opportunity to start thinking about creating a business to take light to people without access to reliable electricity. He landed at Stanford, which was starting a program in social enterprise. A pivotal class was Jim Patelli's 2006–2007 Entrepreneurial Design course. The class was divided into teams, and each team was challenged to address a significant issue in the developing world. Goldman was teamed up with Ned Tozun, a business classmate, and two engineering students, Erica Estrade and Xian Wu. The team tackled the problem of light for people without access to reliable electricity, and developed a rough prototype of a portable LED light that could be recharged via solar power. That spring, the team traveled to Burma for the purpose of going into villages that didn't have access to electricity to introduce their device. Villagers told them they spent up to 40

percent of their income on kerosene. When shown how their crude prototype could provide light at night and be recharged during the day simply by deploying small solar panels on their homes, the villagers were so taken that one woman actually wept. According to one account of the team's trip, in one village the local police confiscated the prototypes. They, too, needed light at night.

Design and Distribution

After completing the Entrepreneurial Design course, the teammates headed their separate directions for the summer. In the fall, they reunited, determined to continue to work on their business concept. The concept of using solar power to recharge portable lights in poor rural areas wasn't new. In fact, it had been tried many times. The problem, in Goldman and his team's estimation, was a combination of design and distribution. Previous models relied either on NGOs and governments "giving" fairly expensive lights to people without access to electricity, which they couldn't afford to replace when used up or if broken, or commercial enterprises buying extremely inexpensive lights in China and exporting them to Africa and elsewhere, where they performed poorly. It was clear to Goldman that neither of these models was sustainable.

So Goldman and his team, driven by the possibility of changing literally millions of people's lives throughout the world, recruited talented engineers and distribution experts, who worked on a near pro bono basis, to help with the project. The goal was to produce a solar-powered portable LED light that was exactly what rural villagers needed—nothing more and nothing less. It also had to be cheap enough that villagers could afford it yet capable of being produced in a way that yielded sufficient margins for d.light to be profitable. The decision was made early on that d.light would be a for-profit company. The company's goal was not to impact 100,000 people or a million people but to impact hundreds of millions of people. Goldman and his team knew that their lofty ambitions would take cash and additional R&D efforts, which would require private-sector investment capital.

During this period, which covered the summer of 2007 until early 2008, Goldman and his co-founders continued traveling to remote areas for the purpose of obtaining feedback about their prototype. During Christmas break, instead of traveling home to see his family, Goldman was in the middle of Myanmar doing research. The team thinned some in early 2008, with Goldman, Tozan, and Wu continuing. d.light was now up-and-running and opened its first international offices in India, China, and Tanzania.

Business Plan Competitions and Investor Presentations

One thing Goldman stresses during talks about d.light is the instrumental role that the company's business plan played in helping the company take shape and

(continued)

in raising investment capital. Early on, d.light entered several business plan competitions. It the spring of 2007, it took second place in the University of California, Berkley's Social Venture Competition and won first prize at Stanford's Social E-Challenge. A big breakthrough happened in May 2007, when the team claimed the $250,000 first prize in the prestigious Draper Fisher Jurvetson Venture Challenge competition. This money provided seed funding for much of the work that was completed during the summer and fall of 2007.

What's particularly interesting is Goldman's reflections about why d.light was so successful in business plan competitions and eventually with investor presentations. These reflections are instructive for entrepreneurs as they think about how to design and then successfully launch their ventures. As shown in the nearby table, there are six reasons that account for d.light's success, specifically with business plan competitions. Collectively, the attributes shown in the table present d.light as an organization with a compelling idea, a strong management team, large markets to serve, an intense product focus, and a coherent, resolute, and extremely admirable vision for the future.

d.light Today

Today, d.light is having the impact that its founders envisioned it could. The nearby chart shows the numbers on d.light's social impact dashboard, which is

updated frequently. These numbers reflect the impact of the availability of light, produced by d.light solar lanterns, for people who didn't previously have access to reliable electricity and light. The numbers are remarkable, particularly in terms of lives empowered, school-aged children reached with solar lighting, and savings in energy-related expenses. The numbers reflect the good that a well-managed social enterprise can create.

d.light's Social Impact Dashboard

Number	Category
28,785,844	Lives empowered
7,196,461	School-aged children reached with solar lighting
$905,549,027	Saved in energy-related expenses
9,276,143,334	Productive hours created for working and studying
2,125,754	Tons of CO2, offset
37,590,326	kWh generated from renewable energy source

d.light sells its product through a number of channels in more than 30 countries. One strategy that has worked well is to employ "rural entrepreneurs" to sell the product. d.light likes to employ indigenous personnel, who know the local customs, people, and language, to sell its product on a commission basis. It also has partnerships with NGOs, microfinance organizations, and social enterprise start-ups that are producing solar lanterns to achieve the same goals it is striving towards. In 2013, d.light entered into a major partnership with Total, a French oil and gas company that sells d.light's products as part of the "Access to Energy Program" throughout Africa. As a result of the Total partnership, and its initiatives across the world, d.light now makes more than 500,000 of its solar lanterns per month. The first few years of its existence, d.light's production was more in the neighborhood of 20,000 to 30,000 units per month. d.light has funded its operations and growth through both investment capital and earnings. d.light is also continually updating its products. For example, its newest design incorporates a smartphone charger, knowing smartphones are the lifeline of many small business owners and others in developing countries.

Challenges Ahead

As it continues to grow, d.light faces a host of challenges. The problem it is trying to solve, to provide a reliable source of light to people without access to electricity, is as large as ever. The United Nations now estimates that over 2 billion people in the world do not have access to reliable electricity. Incredibly, that number is higher than when d.light was founded in 2007. Its for-profit status is also periodically challenged. A

Archivo particular GDA Photo Service/Newscom

Indian mother of three with her d.light solar-powered lamp.

Six Key Reasons d.light Was Successful in Business Plan Competitions

Told Stories and Showed Pictures	While many teams enter business plan competitions with impressive PowerPoint slides and bullet points, d.light focused on telling stories and showing pictures. The company's founders showed photographs of rural villagers using their device, and shared their testimonials. In one interview, Goldman remarked that no matter how many plans or pitches a group of judges or investors heard during a day, he was confident they remembered d.light's presentation.
All In	The founders were fully committed to d.light. They passed on corporate jobs and focused on d.light full time. Along with "talking the talk," they also "walked the walk." Instead of saying that they planned to travel to remote villages to test their device, they just went out and did it. Some of the trips came before the business plan presentations.
Right Team	d.light put together a strong team, with a balance of business and engineering expertise. The team was well-suited for launching a global initiative. Goldman had lived overseas the majority of his life, in places like India and Pakistan. Other team members had demonstrated that they had no inhibitions about traveling to remote villages to talk about their device.
Big Market	d.light was tackling a large market, which investors like. To make their financials work, the team would have to scale the business and sell millions of units. While the challenge was great, so was the potential payoff.
Product Focus	The company iterated its device multiple times before settling on its first solar-powered portable LED light, called the Nova. The Nova sold for a U.S. equivalent of around $25. Early feedback indicated that the price was still too high, so more iterations took place.
Strong Vision	Although d.light was a social enterprise, it unashamedly presented itself as a for-profit venture. The team was resolute that getting to scale could only be accomplished via private-sector capital. d.light also measured its success by the number of families it positively impacted. This sense of purpose and vision permeated the organization.

d.light lantern costs the equivalent of 30 U.S. dollars, an amount that remains beyond the reach of many people in underdeveloped countries. Some observers believe that companies like d.light should be nonprofits and give their lanterns away. d.light's counter to this argument is that the only way to effectively tackle the worldwide shortage of reliable lighting is to stimulate business activity through the private sector. How can an entrepreneur in Kenya, the company argues, make a living selling solar lights if a nearby NGO is giving them away for free?

d.light also continues to face the challenge of convincing hesistant customers with a little extra income to invest in unfamiliar technology. Although kerosene has many harmful side effects, it is an integral part of many villagers' lives. It often takes an influential person in a village buying a d.light lantern for others to follow suit. d.light is also continually trying to lower the price point of its basic lanterns.

d.light's efforts have clearly made a difference in the lives of millions of people. The firm has received numerous awards to recognize what it has accomplished. One particularly nice distinction is its place in the British Museum's History of the World in 100 Objects. d.light's basic lantern, the S250, is object number 100 in the collection.

d.light's stated goal is to impact the lives of at least 100 million people by 2020. It appears to be well on its way to achieving the goal.

Discussion Questions

6-38. Why is the problem of bringing light to people who don't have access to reliable electricity not being tackled in a meaningful way by a large lighting company, such as GE (General Electric) or Philips?

6-39. What qualities do Sam Goldman and his team have that will help them solve the problem of providing light to the billions of people in the world who lack access to reliable electricity?

6-40. Why does Sam Goldman go out of his way to talk about the importance of d.light's business plan? In what ways do you think having a meticulously created business helped d.light in its launch efforts?

6-41. If you were one of d.light's founders, what would your marketing strategy be? How would you go about educating people in remote areas of the world about your product and the beneifts associated with purchasing it?

Sources: d.light home page, www.dlightdesign.com, accessed February 28, 2014; W. Eggers and P. M. Dowser, "Meet the Social Entrepreneurs Completely Disrupting the World of Philanthropy," *The Huffington Post*, www.huffingtonpost.com, accessed March 1, 2014; A. Zweynert, "What Happens When a Social Enterprise and an Oil Giant Join Forces?" *The Christian Science Monitor*, www.csmonitor.com, accessed March 1, 2014; J. Wiener, "d.light's Lofty Goals Meet Practical Challenges in India," *Stanford Business Magazine*, May 24, 2010; S. Sethuraman and S. Goldman, "Lighting the Way to Economic Development," *Social Innovation Conversations Podcast*, http://sic.conversationsnetwork.org/shows/detail4238.html, September 8, 2009.

Endnotes

1. S. A. Alvarez and J. B. Barney, "Entrepreneurial Opportunities and Poverty Alleviation," *Entrepreneurship Theory and Practice* 38, no. 1 (2014): 159–184.

2. A. Tjan, R. Harrington, and Tsun-Yan Hsieh, *Heart, Smarts, Guts and Luck* (Boston, MA: Harvard Business Review Press, 2012).

3. The Hartford *Small Business Success Study*, 2011. Available at http://newsroom.thehartford.com, (accessed March 1, 2014).

4. S. Barlett, "Seat of the Pants," *Inc.*, October 2002.

5. J. Brinckmann, D. Grichnik, and D. Kapsa, "Should Entrepreneurs Plan or Just Storm the Castle? A Meta-analysis on Contextual Factors Impacting the Business Planning-Performance Relationship in Small Firms," *Entrepreneurship Theory and Practice* 25, no. 1 (2010): 24–40.

6. "Meet Lindsey Wieber and Gwen Whiting," Ladies Who Launch, www.ladieswholaunch.com, (accessed July 20, 2007), originally posted January 16, 2007.

7. A. Parhankangas and M. Ehrlich, "How Entrepreneurs Seduce Business Angels: An Impression Management Approach," *Journal of Business Venturing*, 2014, in press.

8. R. Zachary and C. S. Mishra, "Research on Angel Investments: The Intersection of Equity Investments and Entrepreneurship," *Entrepreneurship Research Journal* 3, no. 2 (2013): 160–170.

9. H. Scarbrough, J. Swan, K. Amaeshi, and T. Briggs, "Exploring the Role of Trust in the Deal-Making Process for Early-Stage Technology Ventures," *Entrepreneurship Theory and Practice* 37, no. 5 (2013): 1203–1228.

10. G. Sutton, *Writing Winning Business Plans: How to Prepare a Business Plan That Investors Will Want to Read—and Invest In* (Scottsdale, AZ: BZK Press LLC, 2012).

11. W. Drover, M. S. Wood, and G. T. Payne, "The Effects of Perceived Control on Venture Capitalist Investment Decisions: A Configurational Perspective," *Entrepreneurship Theory and Practice*, 2014, in press.

12. M. W. Lawless, "Entrepreneurial Risk: Jordan Baltimore and Oyster Digital Media," *Entrepreneurship Theory and Practice* 37, no. 5 (2013): 1229–1245.

13. P. M. Getty, *The 12 Magic Slides* (New York, NY: APress, 2014).

14. Personal conversation with Michael Heller, January 20, 2002.

15. L. Essig, "Ownership, Failure, and Experience: Goals and Evaluation Metrics of University-Based Arts Venture Incubators," *Entrepreneurship Research Journal* 4, no. 1 (2014): 117–135.

16. B. Feld, "Should You Hire Someone to Write Your Business Plan?" Ask the VC, http://www.ask-thevc.com/wp/archives/2007/02/should-you-hire-someone-to-write-your-business-plan.html, accessed February 27, 2014.

17. S. Blank, "Why the Lean Start-up Changes Everything," *Harvard Business Review* 91, no. 5 (2013): 110–112.

18. G. Clydesdale, *Entrepreneurial Opportunity* (New York, NY: Routledge, 2010).

19. M. J. Bliemel, "Getting Entrepreneurship Education Out of the Classroom and Into Students' Heads," *Entrepreneurship Research Journal*, 2014, in press.

20. U.S. Small Business Administration, "Executive Summary," www.sba.gov, (accessed March 10, 2014).

21. M. Jenkin, "Small Business Tips: How to Write a Business Plan Executive Summary," *The Guardian*, www.theguardian.com, February 22, 2014.

22. C. A. Bartel and B. M. Wiesenfeld, "The Social Negotiation of Group Prototype Ambiguity in Dynamic Organizational Contexts," *Academy of Management Review* 38, no. 4 (2013): 503–524.

23. D. L. King, C. J. Case, and M. Kathleen, "2012 Mission Statements: A Ten Country Global Analysis," *Academy of Strategic Management Journal* 12, no. 1 (2013): 77–93.

24. E. R. Crawford and J. A. LePine, "A Configural Theory of Team Processes: Accounting for the Structure of Taskwork and Teamwork," *Academy of Management Review* 38, no. 1 (2013): 32–48.

25. J. J. Chrisman, P. Sharma, L. P. Steier, and J. H. Chua, "The Influence of Family Goals, Governance, and Resources on Firm Outcomes," *Entrepreneurship Theory and Practice* 37, no. 6 (2013): 1249–1261.

26. T. Vanacker, S. Maingart, and M. Meuleman, "Path-Dependent Evolution Versus Intentional Management of Investment Ties in Science-Based Entrepreneurial Firms," *Entrepreneurship Theory and Practice* 38, 2014, in press.

27. M. Renko, "Early Challenges of Nascent Social Entrepreneurs," *Entrepreneurship Theory and Practice* 37, no. 5 (2013): 1045–1069.

28. R. Adams, *A Good Hard Kick in the Ass* (New York, NY: Crown Books, 2002), 150.

PART 3 Moving from an Idea to an Entrepreneurial Firm

LuminAID Lab, LLC

CHAPTER 7 **Preparing the Proper *Ethical and Legal* Foundation 241**

CHAPTER 8 **Assessing a New Venture's *Financial Strength* and Viability 281**

CHAPTER 9 **Building a *New-Venture* Team 317**

CHAPTER 10 **Getting *Financing* or Funding 349**

Getting Personal with TEMPERED MIND

Founder
JOHN HARDEN

Master's in Entrepreneurship, Spears School of Business, Oklahoma State University, 2013

Dialogue with
John Harden

FAVORITE PERSON I FOLLOW ON TWITTER
Jane McGonigal

WHAT I DO WHEN I'M NOT WORKING
Spend time with my family

MY BIGGEST WORRY AS AN ENTREPRENEUR
That I didn't spend enough time validating my assumptions

MY FAVORITE SMARTPHONE APP
Call to Knowledge: FLV

MY ADVICE FOR NEW ENTREPRENEURS
Find qualified advisers early on

FAVORITE BAND ON MY SMARTPHONE LIST
A Perfect Circle

CHAPTER 7

Preparing the Proper *Ethical and Legal* Foundation

OPENING PROFILE

TEMPERED MIND
Proceeding on a Firm Legal Foundation

• Web: www.temperedmind.com • Facebook: Tempered Mind • Twitter: @temperedmind

John Harden enlisted in the United States Air Force on September 11, 2001. He entered the Air Force as an Airman, which is an enlisted rank, as a computer systems operator. While serving a deployment in Qatar, he developed an interest in studying Japanese. He was eventually assigned duty in Japan, where he was disappointed in his inability to converse more fluently with the local population. The disappointment led Harden to check out several foreign language instruction programs, none of which he found to be particularly impressive.

In August 2004 Harden took a leave from active duty to enter the Air Force ROTC program at Oklahoma State University. While at Oklahoma State, he studied Japanese for two years, earning an A in each of his classes. Harden graduated from Oklahoma State in December 2007, and reentered the Air Force as second lieutenant and became a public affairs officer shortly thereafter.

Harden's interest in foreign language grew. He tried a number of foreign language instruction apps, but none maintained his interest. In his free time, he enjoyed playing games on apps or the Internet— the types of games where you have to slay dragons or perform some other feat to advance to higher levels. In fact, when trying to use a foreign language instruction program, Harden often caught himself switching back and forth from the language program to games, as he found them more engaging.

This was the inspiration for Tempered Mind, the mobile app company Harden launched in early 2012. The idea was to create a foreign language instruction platform that would combine both of his interests—foreign language and gaming. Rather than "gamify" educational material—using game mechanics in non-game contexts to engage users in solving problems—Harden sought to make studying and learning a primary requirement to progress through a fully-developed game. His approach is intended to leverage people's natural desire for competition, achievement, status, and self-expression while simultaneously keeping them engaged in learning new material. Harden decided to start with a program that would teach French, German, and Spanish. Those languages represent 93 percent of the foreign language instruction that is provided by U.S. public schools.

LEARNING OBJECTIVES

After studying this chapter you should be ready to:

1. Discuss the actions founders can take to establish a strong ethical culture in their entrepreneurial ventures.

2. Describe actions taken in new firms to effectively deal with legal issues.

3. Provide an overview of the business licenses and permits that a start-up must obtain before it begins operating.

4. Identify and describe the different forms of organization available to new firms.

The way in which Tempered Mind's app was developed, and the company was built, is an interesting story. Also interesting is the work that was done to place Tempered Mind on a sound ethical and legal foundation from the beginning.

Tempered Mind was created primarily by Harden, with some assistance from his brother, Dan Harden, and a family friend. Dan Harden is a certified financial planner (CFP) and is Tempered Mind's chief financial officer (CFO). The work on Tempered Mind began in early 2012, when Harden obtained the Internet domain name, www.temperedmind.com, which was available. To build the back end of the app, Harden used contract labor, found primarily on Odesk.com. Harden provided the overall vision for the game and managed the development process. To learn more about entrepreneurship, and the new venture creation process, Harden separated from the Air Force in spring 2012 and entered the Master's in Entrepreneurship program at Oklahoma State. One course, in particular, titled "Launching a Business: The First 100 Days," was instrumental in helping Harden actually start the business. The course is a very nuts-and-bolts class that walks students through the steps necessary to launch a new firm. Partly because of this course, and also as a result of his own initiative, one thing Harden prioritized was making sure Tempered Mind started on a firm ethical and legal foundation. Here are the specific steps that Harden took, some before the class and some after, to make this priority a reality.

- Obtained the appropriate Internet domain name (mentioned above)
- Obtained a Federal Tax Identification Number
- Obtained a DUNS Number (which is a nine-digit identification number used by Dun & Bradstreet for credit reporting purposes)
- Registered Tempered Mind as a C-Corporation
- Engaged an intellectual property attorney to obtain the appropriate copyrights and trademarks
- Created nondisclosure agreements for contractors
- Opened a bank account

These items placed Tempered Mind on a solid legal foundation. Business ethics was also a concern. There are several temptations that mobile app developers have to be careful to avoid. One is to essentially pay people to write positive reviews. Another is to exaggerate the potential and efficacy of the game. Harden was mindful of these temptations and vowed from the outset to avoid them. His posture was to create and run Tempered Mind in as ethical a manner as possible.

Tempered Mind is now up and running, and the app is available via the Apple App Store. Any review posted is from a legitimate user. The app is targeted towards the 13–22 age range. The hope is that Tempered Mind will be adopted by both traditional and online schools. At the time this featured was written, the company was on target to pilot its app in one school district in fall 2014. Although he is pleased with how Tempered Mind has progressed, Harden does have some suggestions for other entrepreneurs, particular in the area of establishing a legal foundation. He believes that having a full-time co-founder would have made the process easier. Tempered Mind has not engaged an attorney, other than to do the legal work necessary to obtain copyrights and trademarks. In retrospect, Harden felt that utilizing an attorney would have been helpful.

W e begin this chapter with a discussion of the most important initial ethical and legal issues facing a new firm, including establishing a strong ethical organizational culture, choosing a lawyer, drafting a founders' agreement, and avoiding litigation. Next, we discuss the different forms of business organization, including sole proprietorships, partnerships, corporations, and limited liability companies.

In Chapter 12, we discuss the protection of intellectual property through patents, trademarks, copyrights, and trade secrets. This topic, which is also a legal issue, is becoming increasingly important as entrepreneurs rely more on intellectual property rather than physical property as a source of a competitive advantage. Chapter 15 discusses legal issues pertaining to franchising. The chapter next discusses the licenses and permits that may be needed to launch a business, along with the different forms of business organization, including sole proprietorships, partnerships, corporations, and limited liability companies.

As the opening feature about Tempered Mind suggests, new ventures must deal with important ethical and legal issues at the time of their launching. As a company grows, the legal environment becomes more complex. A reevaluation of a company's ownership structure usually takes place when investors become involved. In addition, companies that go public in the United States are required to comply with a host of Securities and Exchange Commission (SEC) regulations. Of course, firms established in nations throughout the world must comply with regulations that are specific to those countries.

Against this backdrop, the following sections discuss several of the most important ethical and legal issues facing the founders of new firms.

Establishing a Strong Ethical Culture for a Firm

One of the most important things the founders of an entrepreneurial venture can do is establish a strong ethical culture for their firms. The data regarding business ethics are both encouraging and discouraging. The most recent version of the National Business Ethics Survey was published in 2013. This survey is the only longitudinal study that tracks the experiences of employees within organizations regarding business ethics. According to the survey, 41 percent of the 6,420 employees surveyed reported that they had observed misconduct or unethical behavior in the past year. Of the employees who observed misconduct, 63 percent reported their observation to a supervisor or another authority in their firm.[1] The 10 most common types of misconduct or unethical behavior observed by the employees surveyed are shown in Table 7.1.

While the percentage of employees who have observed misconduct or unethical behavior (41 percent) is discouraging, it's encouraging that 63 percent of employees reported the behavior. Support, trust, and transparency also make a difference. Employees who reported that their supervisor conducts his or her personal life in an ethical manner reported ethical misconduct at a rate of 74 percent, compared to a 51 percent reporting rate for employees who are less confident about their direct supervisor's personal ethical conduct. Similarly, a total of 72 percent of employees who said they received positive feedback from their supervisor for their ethical conduct reported ethical misconduct when observed compared to only 51 percent that did not receive similar support.[2] Both of these comparisons indicate that an employee's supervisor makes a major difference in regard to whether an employee reports ethical misconduct or not.

In analyzing the results of its survey, the Ethics Resource Center concluded that the most important thing an organization can do to combat ethical misconduct is to establish a strong ethical culture.[3] But strong ethical cultures don't emerge by themselves. It takes entrepreneurs who make ethics a priority and

LEARNING OBJECTIVE

1. Discuss the actions founders can take to establish a strong ethical culture in their entrepreneurial ventures.

TABLE 7.1 **Percentage of U.S. Workforce Observing Specific Forms of Misconduct or Unethical Behavior (Based on 2013 National Business Ethics Survey)**

Form of Misconduct or Unethical Behavior	Percentage of U.S. Workforce Observing Behavior
Abusive behavior or behavior that creates a hostile work environment	18%
Lying to employees	17%
A conflict of interest—that is, behavior that places an employee's interests over the company's interests	12%
Violating company policies related to Internet use	12%
Discriminating against employees	12%
Violations of health or safety regulations	10%
Lying to customers, vendors, or the public	10%
Retaliation against someone who has reported misconduct	10%
Falsifying time reports or hours worked	10%
Stealing or theft	9%

Source: 2013 National Business Ethics Survey Ethics in the Recession (Washington, DC: Ethics Resource Center, 2013).

organizational policies and procedures that encourage ethical behavior (and punish unethical behavior) to make it happen. The following are specific steps that an entrepreneurial organization can take to build a strong ethical culture.

Lead by Example

Leading by example is the most important thing that any entrepreneur, manager, or supervisor can do to build a strong ethical culture in their organization. In strong ethical cultures, entrepreneurs, managers, and supervisors:

- Communicate ethics as a priority
- Set a good example of ethical conduct
- Keep commitments
- Provide information about what is going on
- Support following organizational standards[4]

Employees also have responsibilities. The most important things that employees can do to support a strong ethical culture in an organization are to:

- Consider ethics in making decisions
- Talk about ethics in the work (they) do
- Set a good example of ethical conduct
- Support following organizational standards[5]

In companies where these attributes are present, a stronger ethical culture exists. This reality demonstrates the important role that everyone involved with a start-up plays in developing a strong ethical culture for their firm.

Establish a Code of Conduct

A **code of conduct** (or code of ethics) is a formal statement of an organization's values on certain ethical and social issues.[6] The advantage of having a code of conduct is that it provides specific guidance to entrepreneurs, managers, and employees regarding expectations of them in terms of ethical behavior. Consider what Google has done in this area. The company's informal corporate motto is "Don't be evil," but it also has a formal code of conduct, which explicitly states what is and isn't permissible in the organization. The table of contents for Google's code of conduct is shown in Table 7.2. It illustrates the ethical issues that Google thinks can be bolstered and better explained to employees via a written document to which they are required to adhere. A copy of Google's full code of conduct is available at http://investor.google.com/conduct.html.

TABLE 7.2 Table of Contents of Google's Code of Conduct

1. **Serve Our Users**

   1. Integrity

   2. Usefulness

   3. Privacy, Security and Freedom of Expression

   4. Responsiveness

   5. Take Action

2. **Respect Each Other**

   1. Equal Opportunity Employment

   2. Positive Environment

   3. Drugs and Alcohol

   4. Safe Workplace

   5. Dog Policy

3. **Avoid Conflicts of Interest**

   1. Personal Investments

   2. Outside Employment, Advisory Roles, Board Seats and Starting Your Own Business

   3. Business Opportunities Found Through Work

   4. Inventions

   5. Friends and Relatives; Co-Worker Relationships

   6. Accepting Gifts, Entertainment and Other Business Courtesies

   7. Use of Google Products and Services

4. **Preserve Confidentiality**

   1. Confidential Information

   2. Google Partners

   3. Competitors/Former Employees

   4. Outside Communications and Research

(continued)

TABLE 7.2 Continued

5. Protect Google's Assets

    1. Intellectual Property

    2. Company Equipment

    3. The Network

    4. Physical Security

    5. Use of Google's Equipment and Facilities

    6. Employee Data

6. Ensure Financial Integrity and Responsibility

    1. Spending Google's Money

    2. Signing a Contract

    3. Recording Transactions

    4. Reporting Financial or Accounting Irregularities

    5. Hiring Suppliers

    6. Retaining Records

7. Obey the Law

    1. Trade Controls

    2. Competition Laws

    3. Insider Trading Laws

    4. Anti-Bribery Laws

8. Conclusion

Source: Google website, http://investor.google.com/corporate/code-of-conduct.html (accessed June 20, 2014). Google Code of Conduct © Google Inc.; used with permission.

In practice, some codes of conduct are very specific, like Google's. Other codes of conduct set out more general principles about an organization's beliefs on issues such as product quality, respect for customers and employees, and social responsibility. In all cases though, codes of conduct are intended to influence people to behave in ways that are consistent with a firm's ethical orientation.

Implement an Ethics Training Program

Firms also use ethics training programs to promote ethical behavior. **Ethics training programs** teach business ethics to help employees deal with ethical dilemmas and improve their overall ethical conduct. An **ethical dilemma** is a situation that involves doing something that is beneficial to oneself or the organization, but may be unethical. Most employees confront ethical dilemmas at some point during their careers.

Ethics training programs can be provided by outside vendors or can be developed in-house. For example, one organization, Character Training International (CTI), provides ethics training programs for both large organizations and smaller entrepreneurial firms. The company offers a variety of ethics-related training services, including ethics training videos/DVD programs, ethics online courses, train-the-trainer curriculum, and consulting services. A distinctive attribute of

CTI is its focus on the moral and ethical roots of workplace behavior. In workshops, participants talk about the reasons behind ethical dilemmas and are provided practical, helpful information about how to prevent problems and how to deal appropriately with the ethical problems and temptations that do arise. The hope is that this training will significantly cut down on employee misconduct and fraud and will increase morale.[7]

In summary, ethical cultures are built through both strong ethical leadership and administrative tools that reinforce and govern ethical behavior in organizations. Building an ethical culture motivates employees to behave ethically and responsibly from the inside out, rather than relying strictly on laws that motivate behavior from the outside in.[8] There are many potential payoffs to organizations that act and behave in an ethical manner. A sample of the potential payoffs appears in Figure 7.1.

The strength of a firm's ethical culture and fortitude is put to the test when it faces a crisis or makes a mistake and has to determine how to respond. Fitbit provides an example of this, as described in the nearby "What Went Wrong?" feature. In early 2014 Fitbit, the maker of wearable devices that measure data such as number of steps walked, quality of sleep, and other personal metrics, was forced to recall its newest product, the Fitbit Force. A number of users reported skin irritations from wearing the device (the Fitbit Force is worn on a user's wrist). Observers vary regarding whether Fitbit reacted quickly enough, and whether the episode tells us that Fitbit has a strong or weak ethical culture. After reading the case, you will be ready to decide for yourself.

Dealing Effectively with Legal Issues

LEARNING OBJECTIVE

2. Describe actions taken in new firms to effectively deal with legal issues.

Those leading entrepreneurial ventures can also expect to encounter a number of important legal issues when launching and then, at least initially, operating their firm. We discuss a number of these issues next.

Choosing an Attorney for a Firm

It is important for an entrepreneur to select an attorney as early as possible when developing a business venture. Selecting an attorney was instrumental in helping Tempered Mind, the company profiled in the opening feature, establish a firm legal foundation. Table 7.3 provides guidelines to consider when selecting an attorney. It is critically important that the attorney be familiar with start-up issues and that he or she has successfully shepherded entrepreneurs through the start-up process before. It is not wise to select an attorney just

FIGURE 7.1
Potential Payoffs for Establishing a Strong Ethical Culture

WHAT WENT WRONG?

Fitbit Force Recall: Did Fitbit React Quickly Enough?

Web: www.fitbit.com; Facebook: Fitbit; Twitter: @Fitbit

It's every business owner's nightmare. Your company launches a new product, the reviews are good, sales take off, and then, out of nowhere, people using your product start getting sick. The question quickly becomes: what to do? It's the type of question that tests a company's ethical culture and its moral fiber. In Fitbit's case, some observers feel the company met the challenge by putting its customer's health concerns first. Others feel Fitbit could have reacted more swiftly and decisively. Here's what happened.

Fitbit was launched in 2007. The company makes wearable activity trackers that measure data such as number of steps walked, quality of sleep, and other personal metrics. Fitbit has grown quickly and is the clear leader in the wearable activity tracker industry. Its market share is around 50 percent, well ahead of Jawbone and Nike, its main competitors in the industry.

Since its launch in 2007, Fitbit has produced a string of progressively better products, including the Fitbit Ultra, the Fitbit One, the Fitbit Zip, and the Fitbit Flex. On October 10, 2013, the company introduced the Fitbit Force, its newest product. The Fitbit Force tracks a number of statistics in real time, including steps taken, distance traveled, calories burned, stairs climbed, and active minutes throughout the day. It also tracks sleep quality at night. Initial reviews were both positive and enthusiastic.

Shortly after the Force went on sale, Fitbit started getting reports that a small fraction of users were experiencing skin irritations while wearing the device (the Force is worn around the user's wrist). Symptoms ranged from red, itchy skin to painful blisters that would ooze or bleed. Some users sought medical attention, and were typically prescribed prednisone (used to treat allergic reactions) and antibiotics. On January 14, 2014, Fitbit issued a statement indicating that it was looking into reports of users experiencing skin irritations as a result of wearing the Force. It suggested that the irritations were possibly a result of an allergic reaction to nickel, an element of the stainless steel used in the device. Fitbit offered an immediate refund or replacement with a different Fitbit device to anyone affected. It concluded the statement by saying:

"We are sorry that even a few customers have experienced these problems and assure you that we are looking at ways to modify the product so that anyone can wear the Fitbit Force comfortably."

Reports of problems continued, with no definitive resolution of why the Force was causing skin irritations. On February 20, 2014, Fitbit issued a statement saying that it was halting sales of the Fitbit Force, and issued a voluntary recall of the device. The same day, Fitbit co-founder and CEO James Pak issued another statement. The statement said, in part:

"Recently, some Force users have reported skin irritation. While only 1.7% of Force users have reported any type of skin irritation, we care about every one of our customers. On behalf of the entire Fitbit team, I want to apologize to anyone affected."

The statement went on to provide a bullet-point list of what the company knew about the causes of the irritations. The most likely cause, according to an independent lab, was allergic contact dermatitis. Allergic contact dermatitis is a catch-all term for red or inflamed skin brought on by allergies or irritants.

On March 12, 2014, the Consumer Products Safety Commission (CPSC) took action. It announced a recall of the one million Fitbit Force units sold in the United States and the 28,000 sold in Canada. It also made it illegal to sell the Fitbit Force. As a result, anyone who had the Force for sale on Craigslist, eBay, or a similar site had to take it down. The CPSC reported that it had received about 9,000 complaints of the wristband causing skin irritations and about 250 reports of blistering.

The reaction to how Fitbit handled the Fitbit Force situation has been mixed. Some have praised Fitbit for showing concern for its customers and for relatively quickly issuing a voluntary recall. For example, a March 2, 2014, editorial in *Entrepreneur* magazine was titled "How Fitbit, Like Tylenol Before It, Handled a Recall the Right Way." Others have been critical, feeling that Fitbit should have reacted more swiftly. Some Force users also feel that Fitbit hasn't come completely clean on the exact causes of the skin irritations. They'd like to know whether there will be any long-term adverse health consequences caused by the irritations. An example is a man who lives in Bozeman, Montana, and bought a Fitbit Force for his girlfriend. His reaction, as reported on ABC News's health blog, was as follows:

"The bigger issue is dealing with the unknown. Is this a carcinogen reaction? Will it affect her immune system? I'm sick over this," he wrote in an e-mail. "A gift that was meant to promote health has turned into a nightmare."

Questions for Critical Thinking

1. What does the Fitbit Force incident tell you about Fitbit's ethical culture?
2. On a scale of 1-10 (10 is high), how well do you think Fitbit handled the Fitbit Force situation? After reading this feature, if you were shopping for a wearable fitness tracker, would you be more inclined or less inclined to buy a Fitbit product and why?

3. To what degree, if any, do you think the Fitbit Force incident will negatively affect consumer confidence in wearable technologies in general?
4. What lessons can start-up firms learn, both positive and negative, from the Fitbit Force story?

Sources: Fitbit website (www.fitbit.com, accessed June 22, 2014); K. Roseman, "Fitbit to Stop Selling and Recall Its Force Wristband,"

Wall Street Journal, Feb. 21, 2014; T. Stenovec, "Fitbit Apologizes to Customers Who've Experienced Skin Reactions," *The Huffington Post*, available at http://www.huffingtonpost.com/2014/01/14/fitbit-apologies-_n_4599193.html, posted on Jan. 14, 2014, accessed on June 22, 2014; "Reports of Rashes Spur Fitbit Recall," ABC News Health Blog, available at http://abcnews.go.com/blogs/health/2014/03/13/reports-of-fierce-rashes-spur-fitbit-recall/, posted on May 13, 2014, accessed on June 23, 2014.

because she is a friend or because you were pleased with the way she prepared your will. For issues dealing with intellectual property protection, it is essential to use an attorney who specializes in this field; such as a patent attorney when filing a patent application.[9]

While hiring an attorney is advisable, it is not the only option available for researching, preparing, and filing the necessary forms to get a business up and running legally. Most business owners can do much of the preliminary work on their own, and they rely on an attorney for guidance and advice. If you're particularly tight on money and feel as though you can handle portions of the legal process on your own (which is not generally recommended but may apply in some cases), there are online companies that can help you with the necessary forms and filings. Examples include LegalZoom (www.legalzoom.com), Rocket Lawyer (www.rocketlawyer.com), and Nolo (www.nolo.com). All three companies provide a comprehensive menu of legal services for business owners, including the ability to ask a lawyer questions either for free or for a modest fee. It's a judgment call as to whether to hire a lawyer to do your legal work, utilize a service such as LegalZoom, RocketLawyer, or Nolo, or pursue a blended approach. A blended approach might involve hiring an attorney to obtain legal advice (such as determining your form of business ownership) and then utilizing one of the online services to prepare the documents and file them with the appropriate governmental agencies on your behalf.

TABLE 7.3 How to Select an Attorney

1. Contact the local bar association and ask for a list of attorneys who specialize in business start-ups in your area.
2. Interview several attorneys. Check references. Ask your prospective attorney whom he or she has guided through the start-up process before and talk to the attorney's clients. If an attorney is reluctant to give you the names of past or present clients, select another attorney.
3. Select an attorney who is familiar with the start-up process. Make sure that the attorney is more than just a legal technician. Most entrepreneurs need an attorney who is patient and is willing to guide them through the start-up process.
4. Select an attorney who can assist you in raising money for your venture. This is a challenging issue for most entrepreneurs, and help in this area can be invaluable.
5. Make sure your attorney has a track record of completing his or her work on time. It can be very frustrating to be prepared to move forward with a business venture, only to be stymied by delays on the part of an attorney.
6. Talk about fees. If your attorney won't give you a good idea of what the start-up process will cost, keep looking.
7. Trust your intuition. Select an attorney who you think understands your business and with whom you will be comfortable spending time and having open discussions about the dreams you have for your entrepreneurial venture.
8. Learn as much about the process of starting a business yourself as possible. It will help you identify any problems that may exist or any aspect that may have been overlooked. Remember, it's your business start-up, not your attorney's. Stay in control.

Drafting a Founders' Agreement

If two or more people start a business, it is important that they have a founders' (or shareholders') agreement. A **founders' agreement** is a written document that deals with issues such as the relative split of the equity among the founders of the firm, how individual founders will be compensated for the cash or the "sweat equity" they put into the firm, and how long the founders will have to remain with the firm for their shares to fully vest.[10]

The items typically included in a founders' agreement are shown in Table 7.4.

An important issue addressed by most founders' agreements is what happens to the equity of a founder if the founder dies or decides to leave the firm. Most founders' agreements include a **buyback clause**, which legally obligates departing founders to sell to the remaining founders their interest in the firm if the remaining founders are interested.[11] In most cases, the agreement also specifies the formula for computing the dollar value to be paid. The presence of a buyback clause is important for at least two reasons. First, if a founder leaves the firm, the remaining founders may need the shares to offer to a replacement person. Second, if founders leave because they are disgruntled, the buyback clause provides the remaining founders a mechanism to keep the shares of the firm in the hands of people who are fully committed to a positive future for the venture.

Vesting ownership in company stock is another topic most founders' agreements address. The idea behind vesting is that when a firm is launched, instead of issuing stock outright to the founder or founders, it is distributed over a period of time, typically three to four years, as the founder or founders "earn" the stock. Not only does vesting keep employees motivated and engaged, but it also solves a host of potential problems that can result if employees are given their stock all at once. More on the concept of vesting ownership in company stock is provided in the "Savvy Entrepreneurial Firm" feature.

Avoiding Legal Disputes

Most legal disputes are the result of misunderstandings, sloppiness, or a simple lack of knowledge of the law. Getting bogged down in legal disputes is something that an entrepreneur should work hard to avoid. It is important

TABLE 7.4   Items Included in a Founders' (or Shareholders') Agreement

- Nature of the prospective business
- Identity and proposed titles of the founders
- Legal form of business ownership
- Apportionment of stock (or division of ownership)
- Consideration paid for stock or ownership share of each of the founders (may be cash or "sweat equity")
- Identification of any intellectual property signed over to the business by any of the founders
- Description of how the founders will be compensated and how the profits of the business will be divided
- Basic description of how the business will be operated and who will be responsible for what
- Description of the outside business activities that the founders will not be allowed to engage in (e.g., you wouldn't want a founder to engage in an outside business that directly competed with your business)
- Provisions for resolving disputes (many founders' agreements include a stipulation that disputes will be resolved via mediation or arbitration rather than through the courts)
- Buyback clause, which explains how a founder's shares will be disposed of if she or he dies, wants to sell, or is forced to sell by court order

SAVVY ENTREPRENEURIAL FIRM

Vesting Ownership in Company Stock: A Sound Strategy for Start-Ups

If you're not familiar with vesting, the idea is that when a firm is launched, instead of issuing stock outright to the founders, the stock is distributed over a period of time, typically three to four years, as the founder or founders "earn" the stock. The same goes for employees who join the firm later and receive company stock. Instead of giving someone stock all at once, the stock is distributed over a period of time.

The reason vesting is a smart move is that although everyone is normally healthy and on the same page when launching an entrepreneurial venture, you never know what might happen. You want everyone involved with the firm to stay engaged. You also want a way of determining the price of a departing employee's stock, if the firm has a "buyback" clause in its corporate bylaws and wants to repurchase a departing employee's shares. Vesting provides a mechanism for accomplishing both of these objectives. A typical start-up's vesting schedule lasts 36 to 48 months and includes a 12-month cliff. The cliff represents the period of time that the person must work for the company in order to leave with any ownership interest. Thus, if a company has a 48-month vesting schedule and offers 1,000 shares of stock to an employee, if the employee leaves after 10 months, the employee keeps no equity. If the employee leaves after 28 months, the employee gets to keep 28/48 of the equity promised, or 583 of the 1,000 shares. The shares will be issued at a specific price. If an employee leaves and the company is entitled to buy back the employee's shares, normally the buyback clause will stipulate that the shares can be repurchased at the price at which they were issued.

Vesting avoids three problems. First, it helps keep employees motivated and engaged. If the employee in the example mentioned in the previous paragraph received his or her entire allotment of 1,000 shares on day one, the employee could walk away from the firm at any point and keep all the shares. Second, if an employee's departure is acrimonious, there isn't any squabbling about how many shares the employee will leave with—the answer to this question is spelled out in the vesting schedule. In addition, if a buyback clause is in place and it stipulates the formula for determining the value of the departing employee's stock, the company can repurchase the shares without an argument. It's never a good thing to have a former employee, particularly one that left under less than ideal conditions, remain a partial owner of the firm. Finally, investors are generally reluctant to invest in a firm if a block of stock is owned by a former employee. It just spells trouble, which investors are eager to avoid.

Questions for Critical Thinking

1. Investors are often criticized for insisting that a vesting schedule be put in place for stock that's issued to employees. After reading this feature, do you think this criticism is justified? If a company anticipated that it will never take money from an investor, is it still a good idea to establish a vesting schedule? Explain your answer.

2. Why do you think start-ups launch and distribute stock to founders and others members of their new-venture team without vesting schedules?

3. Is it typically necessary to hire an attorney to set up a vesting schedule for a firm, or can the firm do it on its own?

4. If a company started with a single founder and no employees, is it necessary to set up a vesting schedule for the founder?

early in the life of a new business to establish practices and procedures to help avoid legal disputes. Legal snafus, particularly if they are coupled with management mistakes, can be extremely damaging to a new firm.

There are several steps entrepreneurs can take to avoid legal disputes and complications, as discussed next.

Meet All Contractual Obligations It is important to meet all contractual obligations on time. This includes paying vendors, contractors, and employees as agreed and delivering goods or services as promised. If an obligation cannot be met on time, the problem should be communicated to the affected parties as soon as possible. It is irritating for vendors, for example, when they are not paid on time; largely because of the other problems the lack of prompt payments creates. The following comments dealing with construction companies demonstrate this situation: "Not getting paid on time can be devastating to construction companies that have costs to (their) vendors and employees that sometimes require payment weekly. Cash flow problems can send a company into a hole from which they will often not recover."[12] Being forthright with vendors or creditors

One of the simplest ways to avoid misunderstandings and ultimately legal disputes is to get everything in writing.

if an obligation cannot be met and providing the affected party or parties a realistic plan for repaying the money is an appropriate path to take and tends to maintain productive relationships between suppliers and vendors.

Avoid Undercapitalization If a new business is starved for money, it is much more likely to experience financial problems that will lead to litigation.[13] A new business should raise the money it needs to effectively conduct business or should stem its growth to conserve cash. Many entrepreneurs face a dilemma regarding this issue. Most entrepreneurs have a goal of retaining as much of the equity in their firms as possible, but equity must often be shared with investors to obtain sufficient investment capital to support the firm's growth. This issue is discussed in more detail in Chapter 10.

Get Everything in Writing Many business disputes arise because of the lack of a written agreement or because poorly prepared written agreements do not anticipate potential areas of dispute.[14] Although it is tempting to try to show business partners or employees that they are "trusted" by downplaying the need for a written agreement, this approach is usually a mistake. Disputes are much easier to resolve if the rights and obligations of the parties involved are in writing. For example, what if a new business agreed to pay a Web design firm $5,000 to design its website? The new business should know what it's getting for its money, and the Web design firm should know when the project is due and when it will receive payment for its services. In this case, a dispute could easily arise if the parties simply shook hands on the deal and the Web design firm promised to have a "good-looking website" done "as soon as possible." The two parties could easily later disagree over the quality and functionality of the finished website and the project's completion date.

The experiences and perspectives of Maxine Clark, the founder of Build-A-Bear Workshop, provide a solid illustration of the practical benefits of putting things in writing, even when dealing with a trusted partner:

While I prefer only the necessary contracts (and certainly as few pages as possible), once you find a good partner you can trust, written up-front agreements are often a clean way to be sure all discussed terms are acceptable to all parties. It's also a good idea after a meeting to be sure someone records the facts and agree-to points, and distributes them to all participants in writing. E-mail is a good method for doing this. Steps like this will make your life easier. After all, the bigger a business gets, the harder it is to remember all details about every vendor, contract, and meeting. Written records give you good notes for doing follow-up, too.[15]

There are also two important written agreements that the majority of firms ask their employees to sign. A **nondisclosure agreement** binds an employee or another party (such as a supplier) to not disclose a company's trade secrets. A **noncompete agreement** prevents an individual from competing against a former employer for a specific period of time. A sample nondisclosure and noncompete agreement is shown in Figure 7.2.

Set Standards   Organizations should also set standards that govern employees' behavior beyond what can be expressed via a code of conduct. For example, four of the most common ethical problem areas that occur in an organization are human resource ethical problems, conflicts of interest, customer confidence, and inappropriate use of corporate resources. Policies and procedures should be established to deal with these issues. In addition, as reflected in the "Partnering for Success" boxed features throughout this book, firms are increasingly partnering with others to achieve their objectives. Because of this, entrepreneurial ventures should be vigilant when selecting their alliance partners. A firm falls short in terms of establishing high ethical standards if it is willing to partner with firms that behave in a contrary manner. This chapter's "Partnering for Success" feature illustrates how two firms, Patagonia and Build-A-Bear Workshop, deal with this issue.

When legal disputes do occur, they can often be settled through negotiation or mediation, rather than more expensive and potentially damaging litigation. **Mediation** is a process in which an impartial third party (usually a professional mediator) helps those involved in a dispute reach an agreement.

FIGURE 7.2
Sample Nondisclosure and Noncompete Agreement

Nondisclosure and Noncompetition. (a) At all times while this agreement is in force and after its expiration or termination, [employee name] agrees to refrain from disclosing [company name]'s customer lists, trade secrets, or other confidential material. [Employee name] agrees to take reasonable security measures to prevent accidental disclosure and industrial espionage.

(b) While this agreement is in force, the employee agrees to use [his/her] best efforts to [describe job] and to abide by the nondisclosure and noncompetition terms of this agreement; the employer agrees to compensate the employee as follows: [describe compensation]. After expiration or termination of this agreement, [employee name] agrees not to compete with [company name] for a period of [number] years within a [number] mile radius of [company name and location]. This prohibition will not apply if this agreement is terminated because [company] violated the terms of this agreement.

Competition means owning or working for a business of the following type: [specify type of business employee may not engage in].

(c) [Employee name] agrees to pay liquidated damages in the amount of $[dollar amount] for any violation of the covenant not to compete contained in subparagraph (b) of this paragraph.

IN WITNESS WHEREOF, [company name] and [employee name] have signed this agreement.

_____

[company name]

_____

[employee's name]

Date: _____

PARTNERING FOR SUCCESS

Patagonia and Build-A-Bear Workshop: Picking Trustworthy Partners

Patagonia: Web: www.patagonia.com; Twitter: @Patagonia; Facebook: Patagonia
Build-A-Bear Workshop: Web: www.buildabear.com; Twitter: @buildabear; Facebook: Build a Bear

Patagonia

Patagonia sells rugged clothing and gear to mountain climbers, skiers, and other extreme-sport enthusiasts. The company is also well known for its environmental stands and its commitment to product quality. Patagonia has never owned a fabric mill or a sewing shop. Instead, to make a ski jacket, for example, it buys fabric from a mill, and zippers and facings from other manufacturers, and then hires a sewing shop to complete the garment. To meet its own environmental standards and ensure product quality, it works closely with each partner to make sure the jacket meets its rigid standards.

As a result of these standards, Patagonia does as much business as it can with as few partners as possible and chooses its relationships carefully. The first thing the company looks for in a partner is the quality of its work. It doesn't look for the lowest-cost provider, who might sew one day for a warehouse store such as Costco and try to sew the next day for Patagonia. Contractors that sew on the lowest-cost basis, the company reasons, wouldn't hire sewing operators of the skill required or welcome Patagonia's oversight of its working conditions and environmental standards. What Patagonia looks for, more than anything, is a good fit between itself and the companies it partners with. It sees its partners as an extension of its own business, and wants partners that convey Patagonia's own sense of product quality, business ethics, and environmental and social concern.

Once a relationship is established, Patagonia doesn't leave adherence to its principles to chance. Its production department monitors its partners on a consistent basis. The objective is for both sides to prosper and win. In fact, in describing the company's relationship with its partners, Patagonia founder Yvon Chouinard says, "We become like friends, family—mutually selfish business partners; what's good for them is good for us."

Build-A-Bear Workshop

A similar set of beliefs and actions describe Build-A-Bear Workshop. Build-A-Bear lets its customers, who are usually children, design and build their own stuffed animals, in a sort of Santa's workshop setting. Like Patagonia, Build-A-Bear is a very socially conscious organization, and looks for partners that reflect its values. Affirming

this point, Maxine Clark, the company's founder, said, "The most successful corporate partnerships are forged between like-minded companies with similar cultures that have come together for a common goal, where both sides benefit from the relationship."

Also similar to Patagonia, Build-A-Bear thinks of its partners as good friends. Reflecting on her experiences in this area, Clark said, "I tend to think of partners as good business friends—companies and people who would do everything they could to help us succeed and for whom I would do the same." In a book she wrote about founding and building Build-A-Bear into a successful company, Clark attributes having good partners to careful selection. She also likens business partnership to a marriage, which has many benefits but also takes hard work: "Good business partnerships are like successful marriages. To work, they require compatibility, trust and cooperation. Both parties need to be invested in one another's well-being and strive for a common goal."

Both Patagonia and Build-A-Bear make extensive use of partnerships and are leaders in their respective industries.

Questions for Critical Thinking

1. To what extent do you believe that Patagonia and Build-A-Bear Workshop's ethical cultures drive their views on partnering?
2. Assume you were assigned the task of writing a code of conduct for Patagonia. Write the portion of the code of conduct that deals with business partnership relationships.
3. What similarities do you see between the partnership philosophies of Patagonia and Build-A-Bear Workshop?
4. Spend some time studying Patagonia by looking at the company's website and its Facebook page, and via other Internet searches. Describe Patagonia's general approach to business ethics, social responsibility, and environmental concerns. What, if anything, can start-ups learn from Patagonia's philosophies and its experiences?

Sources: M. Clark, *The Bear Necessities of Business* (New York: Wiley, 2006); Y. Chouinard, *Let My People Go Surfing* (New York: The Penguin Press, 2005).

At times, legal disputes can also be avoided by a simple apology and a sincere pledge on the part of the offending party to make amends. Yale professor Constance E. Bagley illustrates this point.[16] Specifically, in regard to the role a simple apology plays in resolving legal disputes, Professor Bagley refers to a *Wall Street Journal* article in which the writer commented about a jury awarding $2.7 million to a woman who spilled scalding hot McDonald's coffee on her lap. The *Wall Street Journal* writer noted that "A jury awarded $2.7 million to a woman who spilled scalding hot McDonald's coffee on her lap. Although this case is often cited as an example of a tort (legal) system run amok, the *Wall Street Journal* faulted McDonald's for not only failing to respond to prior scalding incidents but also for mishandling the injured woman's complaints by not apologizing."[17]

A final issue important in promoting business ethics involves the manner in which entrepreneurs and managers demonstrate accountability to their investors and shareholders. This issue, which we discuss in greater detail in Chapter 10, is particularly important in light of the corporate scandals observed during the early 2000s, as well as scandals that may surface in future years.

Obtaining Business Licenses and Permits

Many businesses require licenses and permits to operate. Depending on the nature of the business, licenses and permits may be required at the federal, state, and/or local levels. There are three ways for those leading a business to determine the licenses and permits that are necessary. The first is to ask someone who is running a similar business, and they will usually be able to point you in the right direction. The second is to contact the secretary of state's office in the state where the business will be launched. In most cases, they'll be able to help you identify the federal, state, and local licenses that you'll need. The third is to use one of the search tools available online. An example is the SBA's *Permit Me* search tool, available at www.sba.gov/licenses-and-permits. This very useful search tool allows you to search by zip code and type of business for the licenses and permits that are needed to open a particular business.

The number-one rule is that if you're uncertain, ask. Severe penalties can be levied if you start running a business without the proper licenses in place. The following is an overview of the licenses and permits that are required in the United States at the federal, state, and local levels for business organizations.

LEARNING OBJECTIVE

3. Provide an overview of the business licenses and permits that a start-up must obtain before it begins operating.

Federal Licenses and Permits

Most businesses do not require a federal license to operate, although some do. Table 7.5 contains a partial list of the business activities that require a federal license or permit, along with the federal agency to contact and its website address. Seemingly simple businesses sometimes require more licenses and permits than one might think. For example, if you prepare tax returns for others you are required by the IRS to register and obtain a tax preparer tax identification number (PTIN). Similarly, if you make beer that is sold, you'll need a federal permit and a state liquor license. You do not need a federal permit or a state liquor license if you make beer strictly for personal consumption.

State Licenses and Permits

In most states, there are three different categories of licenses and permits that you may need to operate a business. Most states have start-up guides that walk you through the steps of setting up a business in the state. For example, the guide for starting a business in Oregon, called the Startup Toolkit, is available at www.oregon.gov/business/Pages/toolkit.aspx. It provides step-by-step instructions for starting a business in Oregon.

Business Registration Requirements   Some states require all new businesses to register with the state. For example, the State of Oklahoma requires new businesses to complete a document titled "Oklahoma Business Registration

TABLE 7.5   Partial List of Businesses That Require a Federal License or Permit to Operate

Business Activity	Federal Agency
Animals—Import or transfer of animals, animal products, or plants across state lines	U.S. Department of Agriculture (www.usda.gov)
Alcohol, Tobacco, Firearms, and Explosives—Including microbreweries and small wineries	U.S. Treasury Alcohol and Tobacco Tax and Trade Bureau (www.ttb.gov)
Aviation—Including businesses that operate aircraft, transport goods or people by air, or provide aircraft maintenance	FAA (www.faa.gov)
Commercial Fisheries	NOAA Fisheries Service (http://www.fisheries.noaa.gov/)
Firearms, Ammunition, and Explosives	Bureau of Alcohol, Tobacco, Firearms and Explosives (www.atf.gov)
Fish and Wildlife—Businesses involved in any wildlife activity	U.S. Fish and Wildlife Service (www.fws.gov)
Income Tax Preparation	IRS (www.irs.gov)
Maritime Transportation	Federal Maritime Commission (www.fmc.gov)
Radio and Television Broadcasting	The Federal Communication Commission (www.fcc.gov)

Application" prior to commencing business. The purpose of the document is to (1) register the business, (2) place the business on the radar screen of the tax authorities, and (3) make sure the business is aware of and complies with certain regulations, such as the need to withhold state and federal taxes from the paychecks of employees. The best way to determine if your state has a similar document is to ask a business owner or contact your secretary of state's office.

Sales Tax Permits   Most states and communities require businesses that sell goods, and in some cases services, to collect sales tax and submit the tax to the proper state authorities. If you're obligated to collect sales tax, you must get a permit from your state. Most states have online portals that make it easy to obtain a sales tax permit. For example, if you are opening a business in Texas, you can obtain your Texas Sales Tax Permit at www.window.state.tx.us/taxpermit/.

Professional and Occupational Licenses and Permits   In all states, there are laws that require people in certain professions to pass a state examination and maintain a professional license to conduct business. Examples include barbers, chiropractors, nurses, tattoo artists, land surveyors, and real estate agents. There are also certain businesses that require a state occupational license or permit to operate. Examples include plumbers, daycare centers, trucking companies, and insurance agencies.

Local Licenses and Permits

On the local level, there are two categories of licenses and permits that may be needed.

The first is a permit to operate a certain type of business. Examples include child care, barber shops and salons, automotive repair, and hotels and motels. Many cities have quirky requirements, so it's important to check, prior to launching a business, if a specific permit is required. For example, in Atlanta you need a permit to operate a business that involves billiard or pool rooms. In Baltimore, you need a permit to operate a dance academy.

The second category is permits for engaging in certain types of activities. Examples include the following:

- Building permit: Typically required if you are constructing or modifying your place of business
- Health permit: Normally required if you are involved in preparing or selling food
- Signage permit: May be required to erect a sign
- Street vendor permit: May be required for anyone wanting to sell food products or merchandise on a city street
- Sidewalk café permit: May be required if tables and chairs are placed in a city right-of-way
- Alarm permit: Sometimes required if you have installed a burglar or fire alarm
- Fire permit: May be required if a business sells or stores highly flammable material or handles hazardous substances

In addition to obtaining the proper licenses and permits, if you plan to use a fictitious name for your business, you'll need to obtain a fictitious business name permit (also called dba or doing business as). A **fictitious business name permit** allows a business to legally operate under a fictitious name, like Gold Coast Sea Food or Red Rock Bakery. Selecting a name for a business and obtaining a fictitious business name permit if needed is an important task, not only to comply with the law but because a business's name is a critical part of its identity and its branding strategy. It's also one of the first things that people associate with a business. Appendix 7.1 contains a set of guidelines and suggestions for picking a business's name. As illustrated in the appendix, it is important that a business choose a name that facilitates rather than hinders how it wants to differentiate itself in the marketplace.

Finally, all businesses, other than sole proprietorships that do not have employees, are required to obtain a **Federal Employee Identification Number** (normally called the Employer Identification Number or EIN). The easiest and quickest way to obtain an EIN is to go to www.irs.com and click on Apply for an EIN Online. A business's EIN is similar to an individual's social security number. It is used by the IRS to track the business for tax compliance purposes.

Choosing a Form of Business Organization

When a business is launched, a form of legal entity must be chosen. Sole proprietorships, partnerships, corporations, and limited liability companies are the most common legal entities from which entrepreneurs make a choice. Choosing a legal entity is not a one-time event. As a business grows and matures, it is necessary to periodically review whether the current form of business organization remains appropriate.

LEARNING OBJECTIVE

4. Identify and describe the different forms of organization available to new firms.

There is no single form of business organization that works best in all situations. It's up to the owners of a firm and their attorney to select the legal entity that best meets their needs. The decision typically hinges on several factors, which are shown in Figure 7.3. It is important to be careful in selecting a legal entity for a new firm because each form of business organization involves trade-offs among these factors and because an entrepreneur wants to be sure to achieve the founders' specific objectives.

This section describes the four forms of business organization and discusses the advantages and disadvantages of each. A comparison of the four legal entities, based on the factors that are typically the most important in making a selection, is provided in Table 7.6.

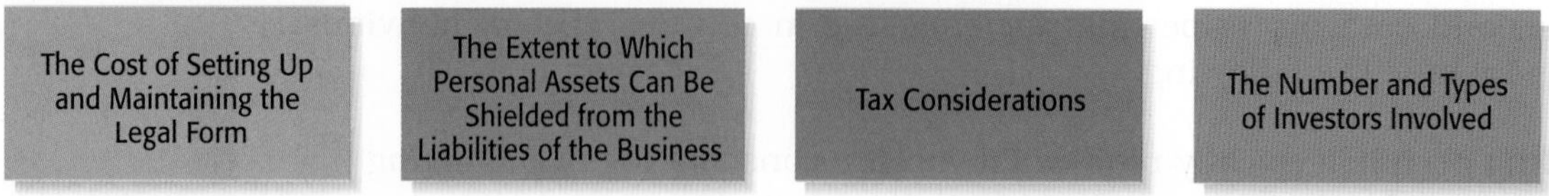

The Cost of Setting Up and Maintaining the Legal Form	The Extent to Which Personal Assets Can Be Shielded from the Liabilities of the Business	Tax Considerations	The Number and Types of Investors Involved

FIGURE 7.3
Factors Critical in Selecting a Form of Business Organization

Sole Proprietorship

The simplest form of business entity is the sole proprietorship. A **sole proprietorship** is a form of business organization involving one person, and the person and the business are essentially the same. Sole proprietorships are the most prevalent form of business organization. The two most important advantages of a sole proprietorship are that the owner maintains complete control over the business and that business losses can be deducted against the owner's personal tax return.[18]

Setting up a sole proprietorship is cheap and relatively easy compared to the other forms of business ownership. The only legal requirement, in most states, is to obtain the appropriate license and permits to do business, as described in the previous section of the chapter.

If the business will be operated under a trade name (e.g., West Coast Graphic Design) instead of the name of the owner (e.g., Sam Ryan), the owner will have to file an assumed or fictitious name certificate with the appropriate local government agency, as mentioned earlier. This step is required to ensure that there is only one business in an area using the same name and provides a public record of the owner's name and contact information.

A sole proprietorship is not a separate legal entity. For tax purposes, the profit or loss of the business flows through to the owner's personal tax return document and the business ends at the owner's death or loss of interest in the business. The sole proprietor is responsible for all the liabilities of the business, and this is a significant drawback. If a sole proprietor's business is sued, the owner could theoretically lose all the business's assets along with personal assets. The liquidity of an owner's investment in a sole proprietorship is typically low. **Liquidity** is the ability to sell a business or other asset quickly at a price that is close to its market value.[19] It is usually difficult for a sole proprietorship to raise investment capital because the ownership of the business cannot be shared. Unlimited liability and difficulty raising investment capital are the primary reasons entrepreneurs typically form corporations or limited liability companies as opposed to sole proprietorships. Most sole proprietorships are salary-substitute or lifestyle firms (as described in Chapter 1) and are typically a poor choice for an aggressive entrepreneurial firm.

To summarize, the primary advantages and disadvantages of a sole proprietorship are as follows:

Advantages of a Sole Proprietorship

- Creating one is easy and inexpensive.
- The owner maintains complete control of the business and retains all the profits.
- Business losses can be deducted against the sole proprietor's other sources of income.
- It is not subject to double taxation (explained later).
- The business is easy to dissolve.

TABLE 7.6 **Comparison of Forms of Business Ownership**

Factor	Sole Proprietorship	Partnership		Corporation		Limited Liability Company
		General	Limited	C Corporation	S Corporation	
Number of owners allowed	1	Unlimited number of general partners allowed	Unlimited number of general and limited partners allowed	Unlimited	Up to 100	Unlimited number of "members" allowed
Cost of setting up and maintaining	Low	Moderate	Moderate	High	High	High
Personal liability of owners	Unlimited	Unlimited for all partners	Unlimited for general partners; limited partners only to extent of investment	Limited to amount of investment	Limited to amount of investment	Limited to amount of investment
Continuity of business	Ends at death of owner	Death or withdrawal of one partner unless otherwise specified	Death or withdrawal of general partner	Perpetual	Perpetual	Typically limited to a fixed amount of time
Taxation	Not a taxable entity; sole proprietor pays all taxes	Not a taxable entity; each partner pays taxes on his or her share of income and can deduct losses against other sources of income	Not a taxable entity; each partner pays taxes on his or her share of income and can deduct losses against other sources of income	Separate taxable entity	No tax at entity level; income/loss is passed through to the shareholders	No tax at entity level if properly structured; income/loss is passed through to the members
Management control	Sole proprietor is in full control	All partners share control equally, unless otherwise specified	Only general partners have control	Board of directors elected by the shareholders	Board of directors elected by the shareholders	Members share control or appoint manager
Method of raising capital	Must be raised by sole proprietor	Must be raised by general partners	Sale of limited partnerships, depending on terms of operating agreement	Sell shares of stock to the public	Sell shares of stock to the public	It's possible to sell interests, depending on the terms of the operating agreement
Liquidity of investment	Low	Low	Low	High, if publicly traded	Low	Low
Subject to double taxation	No	No	No	Yes	No	No

Disadvantages of a Sole Proprietorship

- Liability on the owner's part is unlimited.
- The business relies on the skills and abilities of a single owner to be successful. Of course, the owner can hire employees who have additional skills and abilities.
- Raising capital can be difficult.
- The business ends at the owner's death or loss of interest in the business.
- The liquidity of the owner's investment is low.

Partnerships

If two or more people start a business, they must organize as a partnership, corporation, or limited liability company. Partnerships are organized as either general or limited partnerships.

General Partnerships   A **general partnership** is a form of business organization where two or more people pool their skills, abilities, and resources to run a business. The primary advantage of a general partnership over a sole proprietorship is that the business isn't dependent on a single person for its survival and success. In fact, in most cases, the partners have equal say in how the business is run. Most partnerships have a partnership agreement, which is a legal document that is similar to a founders' agreement. A **partnership agreement** details the responsibilities and the ownership shares of the partners involved with an organization. The business created by a partnership ends at the death or withdrawal of a partner, unless otherwise stated in the partnership agreement. General partnerships are typically found in service industries. In many states, a general partnership must file a certificate of partnership or similar document as evidence of its existence. Similar to a sole proprietorship, the profit or loss of a general partnership flows through to the partner's personal tax returns. If a business has four general partners and they all have equal ownership in the business, then one-fourth of the profits or losses would flow through to each partner's individual tax return.[20] The partnership files an informational tax return only.

The primary disadvantage of a general partnership is that the individual partners are liable for all the partnership's debts and obligations. If one partner is negligent while conducting business on behalf of the partnership, all the partners may be liable for damages. Although the non-negligent partners may later try to recover their losses from the negligent one, the joint liability of all partners to the injured party remains. It is typically easier for a general partnership to raise money than a sole proprietorship simply because more than one person is willing to assume liability for a loan. One way a general partnership can raise investment capital is by adding more partners. Investors are typically reluctant to sign on as general partners, however, because of the unlimited liability that follows each one.

In summary, the primary advantages and disadvantages of a general partnership are as follows:

Advantages of a General Partnership

- Creating one is relatively easy and inexpensive compared to a corporation or limited liability company.
- The skills and abilities of more than one individual are available to the firm.
- Having more than one owner may make it easier to raise funds.
- Business losses can be deducted against the partners' other sources of income.
- It is not subject to double taxation (explained later).

Disadvantages of a General Partnership

■ Liability on the part of each general partner is unlimited.

■ The business relies on the skills and abilities of a fixed number of partners. Of course, similar to a sole proprietorship, the partners can hire employees who have additional skills and abilities.

■ Raising capital can be difficult.

■ Because decision making among the partners is shared, disagreements can occur.

■ The business ends at the death or withdrawal of one partner unless otherwise stated in the partnership agreement.

■ The liquidity of each partner's investment is low.

Limited Partnerships A **limited partnership** is a modified form of a general partnership. The major difference between the two is that a limited partnership includes two classes of owners: general partners and limited partners. There are no limits on the number of general or limited partners permitted in a limited partnership. Similar to a general partnership, the general partners are liable for the debts and obligations of the partnership, but the limited partners are liable only up to the amount of their investment. The limited partners may not exercise any significant control over the organization without jeopardizing their limited liability status.[21] Similar to general partnerships, most limited partnerships have partnership agreements. A **limited partnership agreement** sets forth the rights and duties of the general and limited partners, along with the details of how the partnership will be managed and eventually dissolved.

A limited partnership is usually formed to raise money or to spread out the risk of a venture without forming a corporation. Limited partnerships are common in real estate development, oil and gas exploration, and motion picture ventures.[22]

Corporations

A **corporation** is a separate legal entity organized under the authority of a state. Corporations are organized as either C corporations or subchapter S corporations. The following description pertains to C corporations, which are what most people think of when they hear the word *corporation*. Subchapter S corporations are explained later.

C Corporations A **C corporation** is a separate legal entity that, in the eyes of the law, is separate from its owners. In most cases, the corporation shields its owners, who are called **shareholders**, from personal liability for the debts and obligations of the corporation. A corporation is governed by a board of directors, which is elected by the shareholders (more about this in Chapter 9). In most instances, the board hires officers to oversee the day-to-day management of the organization. It is usually easier for a corporation to raise investment capital than a sole proprietorship or a partnership because the shareholders are not liable beyond their investment in the firm. It is also easier to allocate partial ownership interests in a corporation through the distribution of stock. Most C corporations have two classes of stock: common and preferred. **Preferred stock** is typically issued to conservative investors who have preferential rights over common stockholders in regard to dividends and to the assets of the corporation in the event of liquidation. **Common stock** is issued more broadly than preferred stock. The common stockholders have voting rights and elect the board of directors of the firm. The common stockholders are typically the last to get paid in the event of the liquidation of the corporation; that is, after the creditors and the preferred stockholders.[23]

Establishing a corporation is more complicated than a sole proprietorship or a partnership. A corporation is formed by filing **articles of incorporation** with the secretary of state's office in the state of incorporation. The articles of incorporation typically include the corporation's name, purpose, authorized number of stock shares, classes of stock, and other conditions of operation.[24] In most states, corporations must file papers annually, and state agencies impose annual fees. It is important that a corporation's owners fully comply with these regulations. If the owners of a corporation don't file their annual paperwork, neglect to pay their annual fees, or commit fraud, a court could ignore the fact that a corporation has been established and the owners could be held personally liable for actions of the corporation. This chain of effects is referred to as "**piercing the corporate veil**."[25]

A corporation is taxed as a separate legal entity. In fact, the "C" in the title "C corporation" comes from the fact that regular corporations are taxed under subchapter C of the Internal Revenue Code. A disadvantage of corporations is that they are subject to **double taxation**, which means that a corporation is taxed on its net income and, when the same income is distributed to shareholders in the form of dividends, is taxed again on shareholders' personal income tax returns. This complication is one of the reasons that entrepreneurial firms often retain their earnings rather than paying dividends to their shareholders. The firm can use the earnings to fuel future growth and at the same time avoid double taxation. The hope is that the shareholders will ultimately be rewarded by an appreciation in the value of the company's stock.

The ease of transferring stock is another advantage of corporations. It is often difficult for a sole proprietor to sell a business and even more awkward for a partner to sell a partial interest in a general partnership. If a corporation is listed on a major stock exchange, such as the New York Stock Exchange or the NASDAQ, an owner can sell shares at almost a moment's notice. This advantage of incorporating, however, does not extend to corporations that are not listed on a major stock exchange. There are approximately 2,800 companies listed on the New York Stock Exchange (with a market capitalization of approximately $18 trillion dollars) and 3,100 on the NASDAQ. These firms are **public corporations**. The stockholders of these 5,900 companies enjoy a **liquid market** for their stock, meaning that the stock can be bought and sold fairly easily through an organized marketplace. It is much more difficult to sell stock in closely held or private corporations. In a **closely held corporation**, the voting stock is held by a small number of individuals and is very thinly or infrequently traded.[26] A **private corporation** is one in which all the shares are held by a few shareholders, such as management or family members, and are not publicly traded.[27] The vast majority of the corporations in the United States are private corporations. The stock in both closely held and private corporations is fairly **illiquid**, meaning that it typically isn't easy to find a buyer for the stock.

A final advantage of organizing as a C corporation is the ability to share stock with employees as part of an employee incentive plan. Because it's easy to distribute stock in small amounts, many corporations, both public and private, distribute stock as part of their employee bonus or profit-sharing plans. Such incentive plans are intended to help firms attract, motivate, and retain high-quality employees.[28] **Stock options** are a special form of incentive compensation. These plans provide employees the option or right to buy a certain number of shares of their company's stock at a stated price over a certain period of time. The most compelling advantage of stock options is the potential rewards to participants when (and if) the stock price increases.[29] Many employees receive stock options at the time they are hired and then periodically receive additional options. As employees accumulate stock options, the link between their potential reward and their company's stock price becomes increasingly clear. This link provides a powerful inducement for employees to exert extra effort on behalf of their firm in hopes of positively affecting the stock price.[30]

To summarize, the advantages and disadvantages of a C corporation are as follows:

Advantages of a C Corporation

- Owners are liable only for the debts and obligations of the corporation up to the amount of their investment.
- The mechanics of raising capital is easier.
- No restrictions exist on the number of shareholders, which differs from subchapter S corporations.
- Stock is liquid if traded on a major stock exchange.
- The ability to share stock with employees through stock option or other incentive plans can be a powerful form of employee motivation.

Disadvantages of a C Corporation

- Setting up and maintaining one is more difficult than for a sole proprietorship or a partnership.
- Business losses cannot be deducted against the shareholders' other sources of income.
- Income is subject to double taxation, meaning that it is taxed at the corporate and the shareholder levels.
- Small shareholders typically have little voice in the management of the firm.

Subchapter S Corporation A **subchapter S corporation** combines the advantages of a partnership and a C corporation. It is similar to a partnership in that the profits and losses of the business are not subject to double taxation. The subchapter S corporation does not pay taxes; instead, the profits or losses of the business are passed through to the individual tax returns of the owners. The S corporation must file an information tax return. An S corporation is similar to a C corporation in that the owners are not subject to personal liability for the behavior of the business. An additional advantage of the subchapter S corporation pertains to self-employment tax. By electing the subchapter S corporate status, only the earnings actually paid out as salary are subject to payroll taxes. The ordinary income that is disbursed by the business to the shareholders is not subject to payroll taxes or self-employment tax.

Because of these advantages, many entrepreneurial firms start as subchapter S corporations. There are strict standards that a business must meet to qualify for status as a subchapter S corporation:

- The business cannot be a subsidiary of another corporation.
- The shareholders must be U.S. citizens. Partnerships and C corporations may not own shares in a subchapter S corporation. Certain types of trusts and estates are eligible to own shares in a subchapter S corporation.
- It can have only one class of stock issued and outstanding (either preferred stock or common stock).
- It can have no more than 100 members. Husbands and wives count as one member, even if they own separate shares of stock. In some instances, family members count as one member.
- All shareholders must agree to have the corporation formed as a subchapter S corporation.

The primary disadvantages of a subchapter S corporation are restrictions in qualifying, expenses involved with setting up and maintaining the subchapter S status, and the fact that a subchapter S corporation is limited to 100 shareholders.[31] If a subchapter S corporation wants to include more than 100 shareholders, it must convert to a C corporation or a limited liability company.

Limited Liability Company

The **limited liability company (LLC)** is a form of business organization that is rapidly gaining popularity in the United States. The concept originated in Germany and was first introduced in the United States in the state of Wyoming in 1978. Along with the subchapter S corporation, it is a popular choice for start-up firms. As with partnerships and corporations, the profits of an LLC flow through to the tax returns of the owners and are not subject to double taxation. The main advantage of the LLC is that all partners enjoy limited liability. This differs from regular and limited partnerships, where at least one partner is liable for the debts of the partnership. The LLC combines the limited liability advantage of the corporation with the tax advantages of the partnership.[32]

Some of the terminology used for an LLC differs from the other forms of business ownership. For example, the shareholders of an LLC are called "members," and instead of owning stock, the members have "interests." The LLC is more flexible than a subchapter S corporation in terms of number of owners and tax-related issues. An LLC must be a private business—it cannot be publicly traded. If at some point the members want to take the business public and be listed on one of the major stock exchanges, it must be converted to a C corporation.

The LLC is rather complex to set up and maintain, and in some states the rules governing the LLC vary. Members may elect to manage the LLC themselves or may designate one or more managers (who may or may not be members)

These two entrepreneurs just opened a baby store. Before they opened, they obtained the necessary licenses and permits and organized as a limited liability company.

Dann Tardif/LWA/Corbis

to run the business on a day-to-day basis. The profits and losses of the business may be allocated to the members anyway they choose. For example, if two people owned an LLC, they could split the yearly profits 50–50, 75–25, 90–10, or any other way they choose.[33]

In summary, the advantages and disadvantages of an LLC are as follows:

Advantages of a Limited Liability Company

- Members are liable for the debts and obligations of the business only up to the amount of their investment.
- The number of shareholders is unlimited.
- An LLC can elect to be taxed as a sole proprietor, partnership, S corporation, or corporation, providing much flexibility.
- Because profits are taxed only at the shareholder level, there is no double taxation.

Disadvantages of a Limited Liability Company

- Setting up and maintaining one is more difficult and expensive.
- Tax accounting can be complicated.
- Some of the regulations governing LLCs vary by state.
- Because LLCs are a relatively new type of business entity, there is not as much legal precedent available for owners to anticipate how legal disputes might affect their businesses.
- Some states levy a franchise tax on LLCs—which is essentially a fee the LLC pays the state for the benefit of limited liability.

Chapter Summary

LO1. Establishing a strong ethical culture in their firms is the single most important thing the founders of an entrepreneurial venture can do. Three important ways to do this are (1) lead by example, (2) establish a code of conduct (also known as a code of ethics), and (3) implement an ethics training program. In the context of "leading by example," three keys to building a strong ethical culture in a firm are (1) having leaders who intentionally make ethics a part of their daily conversations and decision making, (2) supervisors who emphasize integrity when working with their direct reports, and (3) peers who encourage each other to act ethically. A code of conduct and an ethics training program are two techniques entrepreneurs use to promote high standards of business ethics in their firms. A code of conduct describes the general value system, moral principles, and specific ethical rules that govern a firm. An ethics training program provides employees with instructions for how to deal with ethical dilemmas when they occur.

LO2. We show the criteria that are important for selecting an attorney for a new firm in Table 7.3. Critical issues include selecting an attorney familiar with the start-up process, selecting an attorney who can assist you in raising money, and making certain that the attorney has a track record of completing work on time. It is important to ensure that a venture's founders agree on their relative interests in the venture and their commitment to its future. A founders' (or shareholders') agreement is a written document dealing with issues such as the split of equity between or among the founders of the firm, how individual founders will be compensated for the cash or the "sweat equity" they put into the firm, and how long the founders will have to stay with the firm for their shares to fully vest. Suggestions for how new firms can avoid litigation include meeting all contractual obligations, avoiding undercapitalization, getting everything in writing, and promoting business ethics in the firm. A nondisclosure agreement is a promise made by an employee or another party (such as a supplier) not to disclose a company's trade secrets. A noncompete agreement prevents an individual from competing against a former employer for a specific period of time.

LO3. Before a business is launched, a number of licenses and permits are typically needed. The required licenses and permits vary by city, county, and state, as well as by type of business, so it's important to study local regulations carefully. In most communities, a business needs a license to operate. Along with obtaining the appropriate licenses, some businesses may need to obtain one or more permits.

LO4. The major differences among sole proprietorships, partnerships, corporations, and limited liability companies are shown in Table 7.6. These forms of business organization differ in terms of the number of owners allowed, cost of setting up and maintaining, personal liability of owners, continuity of the business, methods of taxation, degree of management control, ease of raising capital, and ease of liquidating investments. Fast-growth firms tend to organize as corporations or limited liability companies for two main reasons: to shield the owners from personal liability for the behavior of the firm and to make it easier to raise capital.

Key Terms

articles of incorporation, **262**
buyback clause, **250**
C corporation, **261**
closely held corporation, **262**
code of conduct, **245**
common stock, **261**
corporation, **261**
double taxation, **262**
ethical dilemma, **246**
ethics training programs, **246**
federal employee identification number (EIN), **257**

fictitious business name permit, **257**
founders' agreement, **250**
general partnership, **260**
illiquid, **262**
limited liability company (LLC), **264**
limited partnership, **261**
limited partnership agreement, **261**
liquid market, **262**
liquidity, **258**
mediation, **253**

noncompete agreement, **253**
nondisclosure agreement, **253**
partnership agreement, **260**
piercing the corporate veil, **262**
preferred stock, **261**
private corporation, **262**
public corporation, **262**
shareholders, **261**
sole proprietorship, **258**
stock options, **262**
subchapter S corporation, **263**

Review Questions

7-1. When should your friend, who is considering launching a consulting firm to provide financial services to small businesses, think about the ethical climate she wants to establish in her venture?

7-2. Based on the information included in this chapter, in general, do entrepreneurs tend to overestimate or underestimate their knowledge of the laws that pertain to starting a new firm, and why?

7-3. What are the prerequisites for building a strong ethical culture in a firm?

7-4. What are some of the specific steps that can be taken in an entrepreneurial venture for the purpose of building a strong ethical culture?

7-5. What is the purpose of a *code of conduct*?

7-6. What is the purpose of establishing and using an *ethics training* program in an entrepreneurial firm?

7-7. What are some of the more important criteria to consider when selecting an attorney for a new firm?

7-8. What is a founders' agreement and why is it important for a team of entrepreneurs to have one in place when launching a venture?

7-9. What is the purpose of a nondisclosure agreement and the purpose of a noncompete agreement?

7-10. How can entrepreneurial ventures avoid legal disputes?

7-11. What is mediation and how do entrepreneurs use it to resolve disputes?

7-12. At what point, during the process of starting a firm, does a business need to focus on the business licenses and permits that it needs, and why at that point?

7-13. Why is it important for a firm's founders to think carefully about the name they pick for their company?

7-14. Why isn't choosing a legal entity a one-time event?

7-15. What might trigger a firm's decision to change how it is legally organized?

7-16. What are the advantages and disadvantages of organizing a new firm as a sole proprietorship?

7-17. Is a sole proprietorship a separate legal entity? Why or why not?

7-18. What are the differences between a general partnership and a limited partnership?

7-19. What are the major advantages and disadvantages of a C corporation?

7-20. Why is a C corporation a separate entity?

7-21. How is a subchapter S corporation similar to a partnership arrangement?

7-22. What is meant by the term *piercing the corporate veil* and what are the implications for the owners of a corporation if the corporate veil is pierced?

7-23. What are the differences between a public corporation, a closely held corporation, and a private corporation?

7-24. How can a limited liability company be made public and listed on a major stock exchange?

7-25. What are the advantages and disadvantages of a limited liability company?

7-26. Is a limited liability company an appropriate form of ownership for an aggressive entrepreneurial firm, and why might this be so?

Application Questions

7-27. Under what conditions should ethical considerations be part of a company's business plan? Should a company periodically measure its ethical performance? If so, what are the best ways for a firm to do this?.

7-28. Tom Andersen owns an electronics firm in Wichita, Kansas. He has told you that he has been suffering some cash flow problems recently, but has avoided having to borrow money by letting some of his firm's bills run late. When you raised your eyebrows in response to hearing these comments from Tom, he said, "Don't worry. I'm really not nervous about this situation in that I have some large orders coming in soon. I'll use the cash from these orders to catch up on my bills." Does what Tom has told you seem to be a sound strategy for him to follow? What are the downsides associated with how Tom is approaching his cash flow issues?

7-29. Martha Young has recently developed a business in laundry services. She has done her groundwork and is very confident of her business plan. Recently you met her over lunch; she was happily discussing her business and the steps she has taken to ensure the success of her new venture. When asked about her attorney, she mentioned to you that she is considering her sister Stella, a fresh graduate from law school, to be her legal advisor. Do you think that Martha has made the right choice by appointing her sister, especially since she is new to this industry?

7-30. Friends of your parents are having dinner in your home. The friends are interested in launching an entrepreneurial venture and are expressing some of their views about doing so to your parents. You've been asked to join the conversation given that you are pursuing a major in entrepreneurship at your local university. As it turns out, your parents' friends are involved with two other couples who will join them as founders of the proposed venture. They indicate to you that the other couples have expressed a desire to establish a founders' agreement as part of the launch effort. They also say though that they see no reason to establish such an agreement given that the three couples are close friends and have been for years. How would you respond to the position about a founders' agreement that your parents' friends are taking? What would you say to them to encourage the establishment of a founders' agreement?

7-31. The "You Be the VC 7.1" feature focuses on Velib, a company that is encouraging people to give up their cars in favour of pedal power with an easy-to-use, selfservice, bike-for-hire system. Spend some time studying Velib. Other than the ethical and legal issues that confront all firms, what special issues do you think Velib should be particularly attentive to?

7-32. PillPack is the focus of the "You Be the VC" 7.2 feature. Assume that this firm's founders have asked you to help them write a code of conduct for their firm. Given your understanding of PillPack's business model and its priorities, put together a table of contents for the firm's code of conduct.

7-33. Sam Anderson is deciding to start a Mexican food restaurant in your neighborhood. However, he is unaware of the types of permits and licenses that are necessary for his business. His restaurant is scheduled to start operating within the next three months. Since you are associated with the local municipal council, he came to seek your advice on the two categories of licenses and permits that may be needed for his business. Help Sam.

7-34. Stephen Martin and James Canton came up with an idea of starting a business called "Bicycle for Hire." They found a good location in the town center and decided to open a shop where people can park their car and rent a bicycle to travel around town. This idea came about because they themselves found it difficult to travel in the town as the roads were always congested with traffic. Since Stephen and James have been the best of friends for over two decades, they have decided not to sully their bond by having a Founders' Agreement. Do you think it's a good idea to not sign the Founders' Agreement? Why?

7-35. Laura Simpson just took a job with Cisco Systems in San Jose, California. One of the attractions of this job is the stock option plan Cisco offers to its employees. What is meant by the term "stock option?" Why would Cisco as well as other companies choose to offer stock options to its employees?

7-36. Your good friend, Celia Walsh needs your advice on the type of business organization she should form for her fast food outlet. Advise her.

YOU BE THE VC 7.1 COMPANY: Velib

• Web: www.velib.paris.fr • Facebook: Vélib' • Twitter: @Velib

Business Idea: Reduce traffic congestion, air pollution, and wear and tear on the nation's highways by introducing an easy-to-use, self-service, bike-for-hire system.

Pitch: Traffic congestion is stressful; it causes air pollution and costs millions in tax revenue to keep roads in good repair. Now one company is encouraging people to give up their cars in favor of pedal power. Velib, located in Paris, France, is pioneering the concept of a public bicycle rental program. On July 15, 2007, 10,000 bicycles were introduced to the city, along with 750 automated rental stations, which hold 15 bicycles each. Customers pay a deposit of $200 for an unlimited number of rentals and are then given a charge card, which also detaches the bikes from the cycle racks. The rental is $1.80, for unlimited access for 24 hours a day, or $8.50 for a seven-day pass. The bike does not need to be returned to the same pick-up point. Customers can pick up one of the distinctive gray bicycles from a rack near the Eiffel Tower, cycle to the Pantheon, and leave it at the nearest Velib stand there. Twenty trucks are used each night to redistribute the machines to high-demand stations.

Theft is kept to a minimum by the heavy design of the bikes. The parking facilities are also secure, and the credit card deposit system deters users from "forgetting" to return the bikes, because fines can be collected directly from the card. The service is primarily aimed at people who are making short journeys. Each bicycle is used on average 30 times a day, and the average trip time is just 18 minutes. To date, nearly 200 million journeys have been made with an average of 90,000 per day. Visitors to the city can take out short-term subscriptions by simply using their credit cards directly at the cycle rack terminals.

The service is financed by family-controlled advertising company JCDecaux that provides the bikes in return for an exclusive contract to sell outdoor advertising in prime locations around Paris. JCDecaux paid start-up costs of around $115 million. The Paris City Council pays the $500 replacement cycle costs estimated at around $2 million per year.

Since the launch, the number of bicycles available for hire has doubled to 20,000, and the number of rental stations has increased to 1,800. City officials say traffic has been reduced by 5 percent in the French capital.

7-37. Based on the material covered in this chapter, what questions would you ask the firm's founders before making your funding decision? What answers would satisfy you?

7-38. If you had to make your decision on just the information provided in the pitch and on the company's website, would you fund this firm? Why, or why not?

YOU BE THE VC 7.2 COMPANY: PillPack

• Web: www.pillpack.com • Facebook: PillPack • Twitter: @PillPack

Business Idea: Create an online pharmacy that is easier to navigate than traditional pharmacies by (1) syncing all prescriptions so they can be refilled at the same time, (2) delivering exactly what each customer is required to take for the next two weeks by mail, and (3) sorting each customer's medications into a chain of small plastic envelopes that contain the exact medications that a customer needs to take labeled by day and time of day.

Pitch: Approximately 10.6 percent of the American population, or 30 million people, take five or more prescription drugs per day. Many people in this category visit their pharmacy multiple times per month because their prescriptions aren't synced. Once they get home, they have to sort their medications into daily doses. This task can be difficult for elderly patients, who may be taking different meds at different times of the day. It's also hard for people who have hands that shake or poor eyesight, and find it difficult to sort medications into pill boxes.

PillPack, which is an online pharmacy, has developed a system that provides a solution to these problems. First, the company syncs all of its customers' prescriptions so they can be refilled at the same time. Second, the prescriptions are delivered by mail every two weeks in a small, discreet, tamper-evident box. Third, inside the box is a recyclable plastic dispenser—a PillPack—with a large decal on the side displaying images and descriptions of each of the medications inside. Rolled inside each PillPack is chain of small plastic envelopes, each of which holds the specific prescriptions, over-the-counter medications, and vitamins that a customer is supposed to take, labeled by day and time of day. Each envelope can easily be torn from the chain. No more sorting. No more pill boxes. No more waiting in line at the pharmacy. PillPack applied design thinking principles to make the ordering and taking of medications as simple and error-free as possible.

PillPack's target market is individuals who take five or more prescription drugs a day. It was conceived by J. Parker, who grew up working in his father's family-owned pharmacy. He often delivered medications to his father's customers, and the sight of customers with piles of pill bottles and computer spreadsheets taped to refrigerator doors (to help them sort and remember to take their medications on time) convinced him there had to be a better way. After graduating from the Massachusetts College of Pharmacy and Health Sciences in 2012, Parker started the process of creating PillPack.

PillPack, which launched in early 2014, is a full-service pharmacy available in 34 states. It charges $20 per month for its service, and its prices for prescription medications are on-par with traditional pharmacies. Once enrolled, PillPack handles all the logistics for its customers, including transferring their medications, confirming the medications and start date, shipping the medications right to their door, and contacting their doctor for refills.

7-39. Based on the material covered in this chapter, what questions would you ask the firm's founders before making your funding decision? What answers would satisfy you?

7-40. If you had to make your decision on just the information provided in the pitch and on the company's website, would you fund this company? Why or why not?

CASE 7.1

Preparing a Proper Legal Foundation: A Start-up Fable

Bruce R. Barringer, *Oklahoma State University*

R. Duane Ireland, *Texas A&M University*

Introduction

Jack Peterson and Sarah Jones are planning to start a business. Their plan is to locate and operate 10 kiosks in malls and other high-traffic areas to sell accessories for Apple iPhones, iPads, and iPods. To complement their accessory sales, the two have created a series of short videos that help users learn how to make better use of their iPhones, iPads, and iPods. The videos will be available on Jack and Sarah's website for a one-time fee of $5.99 or on an app they are developing for a $5.99 one-time download fee. Both the website and the mobile app will include promotions to buy additional iPhone, iPad, and iPod accessories via Jack and Sarah's kiosks or through their online store.

iUser Accessories is the tentative name for the business. Jack and Sarah like to use the word *tentative* because they aren't completely sold on the name. The Internet domain name, www.iuseraccessories.com, was available, so they registered it on GoDaddy.com. Part of their start-up funding will be used to hire a trademark attorney to do a formal trademark search before they use the name or do any advertising.

Jack and Sarah met in an introduction to entrepreneurship course at their local university. They hit it off while working on the initial business plan for iUser Accessories, which they completed as an assignment for the class. Their senior year, they refined the plan by working on it during a business planning class. They took first place in a university-wide business plan competition just before graduation. The win netted them $10,000 in cash and $10,000 in "in-kind" services for the business. Their plan was to use the money to establish a relationship with an accountant affiliated with the university.

Feasibility Analysis and Business Plan

As part of their business plan, Jack and Sarah completed a product feasibility analysis for iUser Accessories. They first developed a concept statement and distributed it to a total of 20 people, including professors; electronic store owners; iPhone, iPad, and iPod users; and the parents of young iPhone, iPad, and iPod users. The responses were both positive and instructive. The idea to distribute videos dealing with how to better use your iPhone, iPad, and iPod via streaming video over the Internet or via the mobile app came directly from one of the concept-statement participants. Jack and Sarah's original idea was to distribute this material in a more conventional manner. The person who came up with the idea wrote on the bottom of the concept statement, "Not only will this approach save you money (by not having to distribute actual DVDs) but it will drive traffic to your website and your app and provide you with additional e-commerce opportunities."

Following the concept statement, Jack and Sarah surveyed 410 people in their target market, which is 15- to 35-year-olds. They did this by approaching people wherever they could and politely asking them to complete the survey. They persuaded one of their marketing professors to help them with the survey's design, to make sure it generalized to a larger population. They learned that 58 percent of the people in their target market own an iPod or iPhone or plan to buy one soon. The survey also listed a total of 36 iPhone, iPad, and iPod accessories, which are available through vendors to which Jack and Sarah have access. The results affirmed Jack and Sarah's notion that the vast majority of people in their target market don't realize the number of iPhone, iPad, and iPod accessories that exist, let alone know where to get them. They also were pleased with the high degree of interest expressed by the survey participants in learning more about many of the accessories.

Start-up Capital

As part of their business plan, Jack and Sarah completed one- and three-year pro forma financial statements, which demonstrate the potential viability of their business. They have commitments for $66,000 of funding from friends and family. According to their projections, they should be cash-flow positive within four months and will not need any additional infusions of cash, unless they expand the business beyond the scope of their original business plan. The projections include salaries of $35,000 per year for both Jack and Sarah, who will both work more than 40 hours a week manning the kiosks and running the business.

Jack and Sarah are fortunate in that they are able to each contribute $3,000 to the business personally and were able to gain commitments of $30,000 each from their respective groups of friends and family. A year or so ago they participated in a class offered by their local Small Business Development Center (SBDC) about how to start a business and remembered an attorney saying that it's all right to talk to people about funding prior to talking to an attorney, but don't actually accept any money until you have your legal ducks in order. As a result, other than their own money, Jack and Sarah don't actually have the $66,000 yet. They can accumulate it within 30 days once they are confident that the business is a go.

Preparing for the Meeting with the Attorney

Jack and Sarah plan to launch their business on September 15, just a couple of months prior to the start of the busy Christmas season. They spent some time asking around the business school and the technology incubator attached to their university to identify the name of a good small-business attorney. They identified an attorney and made the appointment. The appointment was scheduled for 2:15 P.M. on July 16 at the attorney's office.

Another takeaway that Jack and Sarah gleaned from the SBDC class was to plan carefully the time you spend with an attorney, in order to make best use of your time and minimize expenses. As a result, prior to the meeting, Jack and Sarah planned to spend several evenings at a local Barnes & Nobel bookstore, looking at books that deal with forms of business ownership and other legal issues and making a concise list of issues to discuss with the attorney. They had also gone over this material in preparing their business plan. In the meeting

Jack and Sarah preparing for the meeting with the attorney.

Wavebreakmedia/Shutterstock

(continued)

with the attorney, they want to be as well informed as possible and actually lead the discussion and make recommendations. Sarah's dad is a real estate agent and had dealt with many attorneys during his career. One thing he told her, in helping her prepare for this meeting, is that attorneys are helpful and necessary but shouldn't make your decisions for you. Sarah shared this insight with Jack, and they were both determined to follow that advice in their upcoming meeting.

Jack and Sarah's Recommendations

To put their list on paper and get started, Jack created a document (shown nearby) for the purposing of listing issues they wanted to discuss with the attorney.

Jack and Sarah spent the next several evenings completing this list and talking about their business. When they made the call to set up the meeting with the attorney, the attorney told them that she wasn't an intellectual property lawyer, and if it looked like the business was a go after their meeting, she could arrange for them to talk to one of her partners who specialized in patent and trademark law. As a result, Jack and Sarah knew that this meeting would focus more on forms of business ownership and general legal issues, and they would address their intellectual property questions at another meeting.

Jack Peterson and Sarah Jones

Founders, iUser Accessories
List of Legal Issues to Discuss with Attorney

Issue	Jack and Sarah's Recommendation

The Day Arrives

The day for the meeting arrived, and Jack and Sarah met at the attorney's office at 2:15 P.M. They had e-mailed the attorney their list of issues along with their recommendations a week prior to the meeting. The attorney greeted them with a firm handshake and opened a file labeled "iUser Accessories, Jack Peterson and Sarah Jones." Seeing their names like that, on an attorney's file, made it seem like their company was already real. The attorney looked at both of them and placed a copy of the list they had e-mailed in front of her. The list already had a number of handwritten notes on it. The attorney smiled and said to Jack and Sarah, "Let's get started."

Discussion Questions

7-41. Complete Jack and Sarah's list for them, including the issues you think they will place on the list along with their recommendations. Which of the issues do you think will stimulate the most discussion with the attorney, and which issues do you think will stimulate the least?

7-42. What are some of the actions Jack and Sarah took prior to meeting with the attorney that are appropriate for them to have taken?

7-43. Is it too early for Jack and Sarah to begin laying an ethical foundation for their proposed venture? If not, what steps could they take now as a foundation for an ethical culture within their firm?

7-44. What advantages do Jack and Sarah have starting iUser Accessories together, rather than one of them starting it as a sole entrepreneur?

7-45. Based on information featured in the case, what challenges do you think Jack and Sarah will have keeping their partnership together?

CASE 7.2

CoachUp and Charity: Water: How For-Profit and Nonprofit Start-ups Build Credibility and Trust

- *CoachUp: www.coachup.com* • *Facebook: CoachUp* • *Twitter: @CoachUp*
- *charity: water: Web: www.charitywater.org* • *Facebook: charity: water* • *Twitter: @charitywater*

Bruce R. Barringer, *Oklahoma State University*

R. Duane Ireland, *Texas A&M University*

Introduction

Credibility is a vital part of any start-up's persona. Whether a prospective customer in a for-profit context or a prospective donor in a nonprofit context, it's important that the company or organization presents itself in a manner that builds credibility and trust during first encounters. Both consumers and donors have multiple options for allocating their money. As a result, it's essential that a start-up make a favorable first impression and give its patrons reasons to trust it.

How Companies and Organizations Build Credibility and Trust

There are several ways companies and organizations can build credibility and trust. We present eight techniques that are essential in nearly all cases in the following list.

The following are examples of how two organizations—one for-profit and one nonprofit—are building credibility and trust via these techniques.

Techniques for Engendering Credibility, Legitimacy, and Trust

Technique	Explanation
1. Have an attractive logo, corporate e-mail address, and professional looking website.	Prospective customers and donors have a mental image of what *real* companies and organizations looks like. If your logo, website, or e-mail address look amateurish or suspect, the game is up. Always have a corporate.com or .org e-mail address. A Gmail or Yahoo! e-mail address makes a company or organization look amateurish.
2. Receive media coverage.	Display prominently on your website the media coverage you've received. If you're new, start by asking bloggers in your industry to cover you. Media coverage is a tacit sign of legitimacy and support.
3. Obtain expert testimonials.	Get expert testimonials and feature them on your website and in your literature. An expert doesn't have to be someone who is famous. If you're selling surgery-related software, ask a surgeon to test it and comment. If you're starting a nonprofit to provide a place for at-risk kids to hang out after school, ask the local police chief or a school principal to comment on your service.
4. Obtain customer testimonials.	Ask customers, donors, or recipients of the good or service you provide to test that good or service and then to comment about their experiences. Include their pictures if possible. Positive quotes from real people are often the most persuasive.
5. Give people a reason to care.	Make sure to convey your start-up's relevance, but don't use buzz words like you're "revolutionary," or "are the industry's best." These terms are too slick. Instead, be genuine. Explain in everyday language why your customers or donors should care.
6. Tell your story.	Why do you care? There is nothing that builds credibility and trust faster than a founder telling the sincere story of why he or she is launching a company or starting a nonprofit. Include your picture and put a real e-mail address next to it.
7. Have a presence on Twitter, Facebook, or both.	Like it or not, people will look for you on Twitter and Facebook. If you're not there, it's a red flag. Establish a presence on one or both sites and provide frequent updates.
8. Tell people how you'll use and/or protect their money.	If you're a for-profit business, offer a money-back guarantee. If you're a nonprofit, explain in specific terms how your donor's money will be spent.

(continued)

CoachUp

Launched in 2012, CoachUp is a service that connects athletes with private coaches. The company believes strongly that private coaching is the secret to reaching the next level in sports and life. CoachUp was founded by Jordan Fliegel. Fliegel was an average high school basketball player until has father hired a private coach for him, Greg Kristof, who had been the captain of the Brandeis University team. The sessions with Kristof helped Fliegel make his own high school basketball team, and he went on to play in college and in a professional league overseas. CoachUp's website matches athletes, in all major sports, with coaches that are willing to work with them. Over 60,000 athletes have connected with more than 12,000 coaches since the site was launched. CoachUp vets all coaches for necessary coaching experience. The average cost of a coaching session is $40-$60 per hour. CoachUp makes money by taking a small percentage of the coaching fees charged through its site.

That's the service that CoachUp offers. Here's how CoachUp is building credibility and trust via the eight techniques described previously.

1. It has a professional logo design, beautiful website, and a corporate e-mail address.
2. It has attracted considerable press and has been featured on ABC, CNN, and CBS SportsRadio. Articles about CoachUp have appeared in *The Huffington Post, Forbes, The Wall Street Journal*, and *USA Today*.
3. CoachUp has established partnerships with the National High School Basketball Association, the Positive Coaching Alliance, and the Sports Legacy Institute. Its advisory board includes Philadelphia 76ers center Nerleans Noel and Boston Bruins president Cam Neely. The company has raised money from private investors Paul English (co-founder of Kayak.com) and Albert Dobron (managing director of Providence Equity Partners) and venture capital firms Point Judith Capital and General Catalyst Partners.
4. CoachUp maintains an archive of customer testimonials on its website. The testimonials are provided by coaches, athletes, and the parents of athletes.
5. The company routinely posts videos on the front page of its website that depict the benefits of private coaching. The videos connect potential clients with CoachUp's core belief—that coaching is the secret to reaching the next level in both sports and life.
6. CoachUp founder Jordan Fliegel is very transparent about his story—of being a mediocre high school basketball player who, through the efforts of a private coach, made his high school team, played in college, and played professional basketball overseas. The company's core values are also very visible and transparent. CoachUp believes that private coaching helps boost the performance and life skills of athletes and provides extraordinarily rewarding experiences for coaches.
7. The company is active on both Twitter and Facebook. As of June 2014, it had 4,780 Twitter followers and a very active Facebook page.
8. CoachUp offers a 100 percent money back guarantee on all sessions. CoachUp also provides a phone number on its website (1-888-680-4750) and encourages its clients or prospective clients to call at any time with questions or concerns.

CoachUp prominently features this information on its website. It's tastefully done, provides useful information, conveys the company's values, and provides multiple opportunities (i.e., FAQ, blog, Twitter, Facebook) for prospective customers to get to know the company before trying it out. While these techniques serve multiple purposes, they're essential in helping CoachUp build credibility and trust with its target market.

Charity: Water

Charity: Water is a nonprofit organization bringing safe and clean drinking water to people in developing countries. Founded in 2006, it has helped fund over 11,700 water projects in 22 countries.

Charity: Water was started by Scott Harrison. Harrison developed a passion for helping alleviate the plight of the 1-plus billion people in the world who do not have access to clean water. The company started when Harrison asked a large group of family, friends, and acquaintances to attend his 31st birthday party. Instead of giving him a gift, he asked each invitee to pledge $31 to help him start a nonprofit to focus on clean water. A total of 700 people attended, and the money was used to fund the drilling of six wells in a refugee camp in Uganda. Charity: Water has grown and is now active across the world. It has done many things to bring the urgency of its cause to the attention of the public, including setting up an outdoor exhibition in New York City in which it displayed tanks of water that were similar in appearance and quality to the poor-quality water consumed daily in many parts of the world. In 2012 alone, Charity: Water raised $33 million and funded more than 2,000 water projects. Its projects vary from country to country depending on water sources, the nature of the terrain, and the local population. Its solutions range from drilled wells to rainwater catchments (gutters on rooftops that catch rain water and place it in sanitary holding tanks) to spring protections (a system captures and safely stores pure water from a natural spring).

That's what Charity: Water is about. Like any charity, it relies on the trust and support of its donors. Here's how Charity: Water covers the eight techniques shown previously for building credibility and support.

1. It has a professional logo design, beautiful website, and a .org e-mail address.
2. It's attracted considerable press and has been featured on MSNBC, ABC, CNN, and Fox News. Articles have been written about it in *The New York Times, USA Today, The New Yorker*, and other outlets.
3. A number of high-profile people have raised money for Charity: Water, including Tony Hawk, Justin Bieber, and Dr. Oz. In each area of the world it enters, Charity: Water collaborates with local partners to complete its work.

4. In 2012, 90,057 people donated money to Charity: Water for an average donation of $187.90. A section of Charity: Water's website is titled "Stories from the Field." The stories provide contributors a personal view of what it's like for someone to get clean water for the first time, and the difference their donations are making to real people across the world.

5. The statistics that Charity: Water disseminates about the hazards of unsafe drinking water are both compelling and heart-wrenching. Unsafe drinking water represents a health crisis in many parts of the world. A total of 90 percent of the 30,000 deaths that occur each week from unsafe water and unhygienic living conditions are children under five years old.

6. Charity: Water's website provides extensive information about why the organization was started and who's behind it.

7. Charity: Water is active on both Twitter and Facebook. As of June 2014, it had 1.43 million Twitter followers and a very active Facebook page.

8. Since day one, Charity: Water has believed in proving its work to its supporters. Much of the money raised by Charity: Water is raised via campaigners, which are schools, churches, and others who are interested in helping provide clean water for people in need. Once a campaigner's project is funded and finished, they are sent a completion report with photos and GPS coordinates of their project.

Discussion Questions

7-46. What actions have CoachUp and Charity: Water taken to establish trust and credibility with various groups?

7-47. How can building trust and credibility help start-up firms avoid legal disputes and problems?

7-48. As related to ethics and ethical behavior, what are the characteristics you anticipate are associated with the cultures at CoachUp and Charity: Water?

7-49. Describe actions the founders of CoachUp (Jordan Fliegel) and Charity: Water (Scott Harrison) took to lead by example with respect to establishing an ethical culture.

Sources: CoachUp website, www.coachup.com (accessed June 19, 2014); Charity: Water website, www.charitywater.org (accessed June 19, 2014).

APPENDIX 7.1 What's in a Business Name?: A Lot of Trouble If You Aren't Careful

Introduction

While at first glance naming a business may seem like a minor issue, it is an extremely important one. A company's name is one of the first things people associate with a business, and it is a word or phrase that will be said thousands or hundreds of thousands of times during the life of a firm. A company's name is also the most critical aspect of its branding strategy. A company brand is the unique set of attributes that allows consumers to separate it from its competitors. As a result, it is important that a business choose its name carefully so that it will facilitate rather than hinder how the business wants to differentiate itself in the marketplace.

If an entrepreneur isn't careful, the process of naming a business can also result in a peck of trouble. There are a number of legal issues involved in naming a business, which should be taken seriously. If a business selects a name and later finds out that it has already been legally taken, the business may have to (1) amend its articles of incorporation, (2) change its Internet domain name, (3) obtain new listings in telephone and other directories, (4) purchase new stationery and business cards, (5) redo signage and advertising, and (6) incur the expense and potential embarrassment of introducing a new name to its customers. These are complications that no entrepreneur wants to endure. The following case describes the strategies for naming a business, along with the legal issues involved.

Strategies for Naming a Business

The primary consideration in naming a company is that the name should complement the type of business the company plans to be. It is helpful to divide companies into four categories to discuss this issue.

Consumer-Driven Companies

If a company plans to focus on a particular type of customer, its name should reflect the attributes of its clientele. For example, a high-end clothing store that specializes in small sizes for women is called La Petite Femme. Similarly, a company named Local Dirt helps food retailers connect with local producers of produce, meats, and other food products. These companies have names that were chosen to appeal specifically to their target market or clientele.

Product- or Service-Driven Companies

If a company plans to focus on a particular product or service, its name should reflect the advantages that its product or service brings to the marketplace. Examples include Jiffy Print, Anytime Fitness, and 1-800-FLOWERS. These names were chosen to reflect the distinctive attributes of the product or service the company offers, regardless of the clientele.

Industry-Driven Companies

If a company plans to focus on a broad range of products or services in a particular industry, its name should reflect the category in which it participates. Examples include General Motors, Bed Bath & Beyond, and Home Depot. These companies have names that are intentionally broad and are not limiting in regard to target market or product selection.

Personality- or Image-Driven Companies

Some companies are founded by individuals who put such an indelible stamp on the company that it may be smart to name the company after the founder. Examples include Liz Claiborne, Walt Disney, Charles Schwab, and Magic Johnson Enterprises. These companies have names that benefit from a positive association with a popular or distinctive founder. Of course, this strategy can backfire if the founder falls out of favor in the public's eye.

While names come to some business owners easily, for others it's a painstaking process. It was a painstaking process for JetBlue, as described in the book *Blue Streak*, which is a chronology of the early years of JetBlue. According to Barbara Peterson, the book's author, David Neeleman, the founder of JetBlue, and his initial management team agonized over what to name the company and considered literally hundreds of names before settling on JetBlue. JetBlue was launched in 1999. Neeleman felt that a strong brand would surmount the handicap of being a new airline and believed that the company's name was the key to building its brand. A list of some of the alternative names that Neeleman and his management team seriously considered for JetBlue is shown in a nearby feature. Today, it's hard to think of JetBlue as anything other than JetBlue, which illustrates the power of branding.

Names That Were Seriously Considered for JetBlue

Air Hop	Egg
Scout Air	It
Competition	Blue
Home	Fair Air
Air Taxi	Scout
Avenues	Hi! Way
Civilization Airways	True Blue

Legal Issues Involved in Naming a Business

The general rule for business names is that they must be unique. In other words, in most instances, there may not be more than one business per name per state. In addition, a business may not have a name that is confusingly similar to another business. This regulation prevents a software company from naming itself Macrosoft, for example, which Microsoft would undoubtedly claim is confusingly similar to its name.

To determine if a name is available in a particular state, the entrepreneur must usually contact the secretary of state's office to see if a particular name is available. The inquiry can typically be accomplished online or over the phone. If the name is available, the next step is to reserve it in the manner recommended by the secretary of state's office. Many attorneys and incorporation services include this step in the fee-based services they offer to entrepreneurs and their ventures.

Once a name that is available has been chosen, it should be trademarked. The process for obtaining a trademark is straightforward and relatively inexpensive, given the protection it provides. A full explanation of how to obtain a trademark is provided in Chapter 12 of this book.

The entire process of naming a business is often very frustrating for entrepreneurs, because it is becoming increasingly difficult to find a name that isn't already taken. For example, if an entrepreneur was planning to open a new quick-printing service, almost every possible permutation of the word *printing* with words like *quick, swift, fast, rapid, speedy, jiffy, express, instant*, and so forth are taken. In addition, sometimes names that work in one culture don't work in another, which is something that should be taken into consideration. The classic example of this is the Chevy Nova. After much advertising and fanfare, the car received a very cool reception in Mexico. It turned out that the phrase *No va* in Spanish means "Doesn't Go." Not surprisingly, the Nova didn't sell well in Mexico.

As a result of these complications, and for other reasons, entrepreneurs use a variety of other strategies when naming their business. Some names are simply made up, because the firm wants a name that is catchy or distinctive, or because it needs to make up a name to get an Internet domain name that isn't already taken (more about this later). Examples of names that were made up include Wello, Verizon, eBay, Google, and Fitbit. Some of these names are made up with the help of marketing research firms that use sophisticated methodologies such as an evaluation of the "linguistic properties" (will a consumer read the name properly?), the "phonetic transparency" (is it spelled as it sounds?), and the "multilingual functionality" (is it as intelligible in Japanese as in English?) of a particular name. All of these issues are potentially important. Several years ago Anderson Consulting changed its name to Accenture. The pronunciation of "Accenture" isn't obvious, which has been a problem for the firm ever since.

Internet Domain Names

A final complicating factor in selecting a name for a company is registering an Internet domain name. A domain name is a company's Internet address (e.g., www.facebook.com). Most companies want their domain name to be the same as their company's name. It is easy to register a domain name through an online registration service such as GoDaddy.com (www.godaddy.com). The standard fee for registering and maintaining a domain name is about $13 per year.

Because no two domain names can be exactly the same, frustrations often arise when a company tries to register its domain name and the name is already taken. There are two reasons that a name may already be taken. First, a company may find that another company with the same name has already registered it. For example, if an entrepreneur started a company called Delta Semiconductor, it would find that the domain name www.delta.com is already taken by Delta Airlines. This scenario plays itself out every day and represents a challenge for new firms that have chosen fairly ordinary names. The firm can either select another domain name (such as www.deltasemiconductor.com) or try to acquire the name from its present owner. However, it is unlikely that Delta Airlines would give up www.delta.com for any price. The second reason that a domain name may already be taken is that it might be in the hands of someone who has registered the name with the intention of using it at a later date or of someone who simply collects domain names in hopes that someone will want to buy the name at a higher price.

Still, a little imagination goes a long way in selecting a company name and an Internet domain name. For example, we (your book's authors) made up the name iUser Accessories for the business described in Case 7.1. The Internet domain name www.iuseraccessories.com was available, which we registered on GoDaddy.com for $13 per year. What might we do with this Internet domain name? We aren't certain. But, another party deciding to launch an entrepreneurial venture with this name will discover that the hoped-for name is already registered.

Endnotes

1. *2013 National Business Ethics Survey, Ethics in the Recession* (Washington, DC: Ethics Resource Center, 2013).

2. *2013 National Business Ethics Survey, Ethics in the Recession* (Washington, DC: Ethics Resource Center, 2013).

3. *2013 National Business Ethics Survey, Ethics in the Recession* (Washington, DC: Ethics Resource Center, 2013).

4. *2013 National Business Ethics Survey, Ethics in the Recession* (Washington, DC: Ethics Resource Center, 2013).

5. *2013 National Business Ethics Survey, Ethics in the Recession* (Washington, DC: Ethics Resource Center, 2013).

6. M. Frese, D. M. Rousseau, and J. Wiklund, "The Emergence of Evidence-Based Entrepreneurship," *Entrepreneurship Theory and Practice* 38, no. 2 (2014): 209–216; T. W. Moss, D. O. Neubaum, and M. Meyskens, "The Effect of Virtuous and Entrepreneurial Orientations on Microfinance Lending and Repayment: A Signaling Theory Perspective," *Entrepreneurship Theory and Practice*, 2014, in press.

7. Character Training International home page, www.character-ethics.org (accessed June 20, 2014).

8. G. Stahl and M. Sully de Luque, "Antecedents of Responsible Leader Behavior: A Research Synthesis, Conceptual Framework, and Agenda for Future Research," *Academy of Management Perspectives*, 2014, in press.

9. T. Fischer and P. Ringler, "What Patents Are Used as Collateral? An Empirical Analysis of Patent Reassignment Data," *Journal of Business Venturing*, 2014, in press; D. H. Hsu and R. H. Ziedonis, "Resources as Dual Sources of Advantage: Implications for Valuing Entrepreneurial-Firm Patents," *Strategic Management Journal* 34, no. 7 (2013): 761–781.

10. A. Rauch and S. A. Rijsdijk, "The Effects of General and Specific Human Capital on Long-Term Growth and Failure of Newly Founded Businesses," *Entrepreneurship Theory and Practice* 37, no. 4 (2013): 923–941; E. Gimmon and J. Levie, "Founder's Human Capital, External Investment and the Survival of New High Technology Ventures," *Research Policy* 39, no. 9 (2010): 1214–1226.

11. S. Arcot, "Participating Convertible Preferred Stock in Venture Capital Exits," *Journal of Business Venturing* 29, no. 1 (2014): 72–87; T. M. Marcum and E. S. Blair, "Entrepreneurial Decisions and Legal Issues in Early Venture Stages: Advice That Shouldn't Be Ignored," *Business Horizons* 54, no. 2 (2011): 143–152.

12. J. Poole, "What to Do If You're Not Getting Paid," *Constructonomics*, www.constructonomics.com, July 5, 2010.

13. D. Cumming and N. Dai, "Why Do Entrepreneurs Switch Lead Venture Capitalists?" *Entrepreneurship Theory and Practice* 37, no. 5 (2013): 999–1017; N. Rosenbusch, J. Broinckmann, and V. Muller, "Does Acquiring Venture Capital Pay Off for the Funded Firms? A Meta-Analysis on the Relationship Between Venture Capital Investment and Funded Firm Financial Performance," *Journal of Business Venturing* 28, no. 3 (2013): 335–353.

14. W. O. Peake and W. Watson, "Ties That Bind? A Mediation Analysis Exploring Contract Use in Family Versus Nonfamily Firms," *Journal of Small Business Management*, 2014, in press.

15. M. Clark, *The Bear Necessities of Business* (New York: Wiley, 2006), 112.

16. C. E. Bagley, *Legal Aspects of Entrepreneurship: A Conceptual Framework* (Cambridge, MA: Harvard Business School Publishing, 2002), 17.

17. A. Gerlin, "A Matter of Degree: How a Jury Decided That a Coffee Spill Is Worth $2.7 Million," *Wall Street Journal*, September 1, 1994.

18. P. A. Coomes, J. Fernandez, and S. F. Gohmann, "The Rate of Proprietorship Among Metropolitan Areas: The Impact of the Local Economic Environment and Capital Resources," *Entrepreneurship Theory and Practice* 37, no. 4 (2013): 745–770; H. R. Cheeseman, *The Legal Environment of Business and Online Commerce*, 6th ed. (Upper Saddle River, NJ: Pearson Education, 2009).

19. J. C. Leach and R. W. Mellcher, *Entrepreneurial Finance*, 4th ed. (Cincinnati: Cengage Learning, 2012).

20. V. Gerasymenko and J. D. Arthurs, "New Insights into Venture Capitalists' Activity: IPO and Time-To-Exit Forecast as Antecedents of Their Post-Investment Involvement," *Journal of Business Venturing* 29, no. 3 (2014): 405–420; R. L. Miller and G. A. Jentz, *Business Law Today*, 9th ed. (Cincinnati: Cengage Learning, 2012).

21. J. E. Adamson and A. Morrison, *Law for Business and Personal Use*, 19th ed. (Cincinnati: Cengage Learning, 2012).

22. B. A. Sensoy, Y. Wang, and M. S. Weisbach, "Limited Partner Performance and the Maturing of the Private Equity Industry," *Journal of Financial Economics* 112, no. 3 (2014): 320–324; D. J. McKenzie, R. M. Betts, and C. A. Jensen, *Essentials of Real Estate Economics* (Cincinnati: Cengage Learning, 2011).

23. W. Lazonick, "Innovative Enterprise and Shareholder Value," *Law and Financial Markets Review* 8, no. 1 (2014): 52–64.

24. J. Dammann and M. Schundein, "The Incorporation Choices of Privately Held Corporations," *Journal of Law, Economics and Organization* 27, no. 1 (2011): 79–112.

25. A. Mandaraka-Sheppard, "New Trends in Piercing the Corporate Veil: The Conservative Versus the Liberal Approaches," *Business Law Review* 35, no. 1 (2014): 2–14; F. B. Cross and R. L. Miller, *The Legal Environment of Business*, 8th ed. (Cincinnati: Cengage Learning, 2012).

26. Investorwords.com home page, www.investorwords.com (accessed June 27, 2014).

27. Investorwords.com home page, www.investorwords.com (accessed June 27, 2014).

28. R. El Houcine and A. Boubaker, "Share Repurchasing and the Policies of Stock-Options," *International Journal of Academic Research in Accounting, Finance and Management Sciences* 4, no. 1 (2014): 175–187.

29. R. Krause, K. A. Whitler, and M. Semadeni, "Power to the Principals! An Experimental Look at Shareholder Say-On-Pay Voting," *Academy of Management Journal* 57, no. 1 (2014): 94–115; M. Abudy and S. Benniga, "Taxation and the Value of Employee Stock Options," *International Journal of Managerial Finance* 7, no. 1 (2011): 9–37; E. J. McElvaney, "The Benefits of Promoting Employee Ownership Incentives to Improve Employee Satisfaction, Company Productivity and Profitability," *International Review of Business Research Papers* 7, no. 1 (2011): 201–210.

30. J. Harris, D. Souder, and S. Johnson, "Model Theoretic Knowledge Accumulation: The Case of Agency Theory and Incentive Alignment," *Academy of Management Review*, 2014, in press; A. Pendleton and A. Robinson, "Employee Share Ownership, Involvement, and Productivity: An Interaction-Based Approach," *Industrial & Labor Relations Review* 46, no. 1 (2010): 3–29.

31. C. H. Green, *The SBA Loan Book*, 3rd ed. (Avon, MA: Adams Business, 2011).

32. A. Mancuso, *Your Limited Liability Company: An Operating Manual*, 7th ed. (Brainerd, MN: Bang Printing, 2013); J. M. Malcomson, "Do Managers with Limited Liability Take More Risky Decisions? An Information Acquisition Model," *Journal of Economics & Management Strategy* 20, no. 1 (2011): 83–120.

33. B. Frfeudenberg, "Advisors' Understanding of Tax Compliance for Choice of Business Form," *Global Review of Accounting and Finance* 4, no. 1 (2013): 1–12; L. Gray, "The Three Forms of Governance: A New Approach to Family Wealth Transfer and Asset Protection, Part III," *Journal of Wealth Management* 14, no. 1 (2011): 41–54.

Getting
Personal with GYMFLOW

Co-Founders

JIMMY LIU

BS in Entrepreneurship and Finance, University of Southern California, Summer 2013

JIANGYANG ZHANG

PhD in Engineering, University of Southern California, Spring 2014

Dialogue with
Jimmy Liu

BEST ADVICE I'VE RECEIVED
Fail hard, fail fast

MY BIGGEST WORRY AS AN ENTREPRENEUR
Making it to the next month

MY BIGGEST SURPRISE AS AN ENTREPRENEUR
How little "guarding the company's secrets" matters

FIRST ENTREPRENEURIAL EXPERIENCE
Selling paper airplanes for $0.10 apiece in 1st grade

BEST PART OF BEING A STUDENT
Playing the student card with potential customers

CHAPTER 8

Assessing a New Venture's *Financial Strength* and Viability

OPENING PROFILE

GYMFLOW
Managing Finances Prudently

• *Web: www.mygymflow.com* • *Facebook: Gymflow* • *Twitter: @mygymflow*

Have you ever gone to a gym only to have your heart sink because the machines you planned to work out on were already in use? If so, you would be interested in joining a gym that features GymFlow. GymFlow is a mobile app that helps people determine before they show up just how crowded a gym is. It works by tapping into a gym's IT center to provide real-time traffic data.

GymFlow is the creation of Jimmy Liu and Jiangyang Zhang, two USC students. In the nearby photo, Jiangyang Zhang is on the left and Jimmy Liu is on the right. Liu was a double major in entrepreneurship and finance, while Zhang was a PhD student in engineering. The two met in fall 2012, in USC's Viterbi School of Engineering's "Building the High Tech Startup" course. The course combines business and engineering students to conceive and develop new product ideas. Liu and Zhang identified a two-sided problem that gyms face. Gym members are often frustrated when they show up at the gym and it's more crowded than they anticipated. At the same time, gym owners are frustrated by low retention rates. About 40 percent of the people who belong to gyms turn over every year. This is a huge problem for gyms. If a gym has 1,000 members, it must gain 400 new members a year just to stay even.

To solve the two-sided problem that gyms and its members face, Liu and Zhang developed a mobile app called GymFlow. Although there are now over one million apps in the Apple App Store alone, Liu and Zhang found a gap. There was no app that accurately showed how busy a gym was at any given point in time. GymFlow was set up to do two things. First, show the user in real time how crowded a particular gym is. And second, forecast future traffic flows to help the user plan workouts and avoid waiting time for equipment at the gym. The benefit to the gym would be more satisfied users, a smoothing out of when people come to the gym, and higher member retention. The app would be free to the member. Gyms would be charged for the back-end technology needed to make the system work. The app would have no ads. Liu and Zhang wanted the user experience to be as high quality as possible.

LEARNING OBJECTIVES

After studying this chapter you should be ready to:

1. Learn about the importance of understanding the financial management of an entrepreneurial firm.

2. Identify the four main financial objectives of entrepreneurial ventures.

3. Describe the process of financial management as used in entrepreneurial firms.

4. Explain the difference between historical and pro forma financial statements.

5. Describe the different historical financial statements and their purposes.

6. Discuss the role of forecasts in projecting a firm's future income and expenses.

7. Explain the purpose of pro forma financial statements.

After the class concluded, Liu and Zhang decided to pursue GymFlow further. From the beginning, they were mindful of the costs and financials involved. To make sure they were on the right track, the two talked to both gyms and gym members prior to spending any money. They found that gym members saw the value of the app instantly. Gym owners were a tougher sell. Still, the feedback was sufficiently positive to move forward. Early 2013 was spent building the app. Zhang, a former Google employee, had programming skills that he used to write the code for the app himself. The pair's first funding was $20,000 in cash from the Virerbi Startup Garage, a start-up accelerator affiliated with USC. GymFlow was one of 10 USC start-ups, out of 100 applicants, accepted into the accelerator. Beyond the money, the accelerator program provided Liu and Zhang access to mentors and an entrepreneurial network to plug into. An additional $5,000 came from an innovation grant and another $5,000 came from winning a pitch competition.

To avoid loan payments or pressure to grow quickly from investors, Liu and Zhang decided to rely on the money mentioned above and bootstrap the remaining costs needed to get GymFlow up and running. While their initial plan was to work on GymFlow full time, they decided to pursue the venture part time and maintain jobs on the side. Prior to marketing GymFlow beyond USC, Liu and Zhang conducted a pilot study at USC's Lyon Recreational Center. The first month that GymFlow was available it was downloaded by 2,000 USC students and was used over 20,000 times. The pilot test was successful and provided Liu and Zhang the confidence to press forward and market GymFlow to a wider audience.

As of August 2014, GymFlow was in seven gyms on three college campuses, all in Southern California. The company has encouraging prospects for expansion, not only in the United States but abroad. Liu and Zhang remain focused on GymFlow's finances. One thing that's helped them, particularly from a cash flow standpoint, is that the app required very little capital to build and the company started earning revenue as soon as the first GymFlow system was deployed. As a result, GymFlow has not experienced the type of cash-flow gaps that B2B (business-to-business) companies often experience when they incur substantial up-front expenses for a product run or job, and then have to wait 30 to 60 days to get paid. While Liu and Zhang did not write a formal business plan, they did complete financial projections, which they felt were useful. They have found that projecting future income is one of their most difficult challenges. They've also found that this is one of the most important things an entrepreneur can do. Other things have worked to Liu and Zhang's advantage when it comes to managing finances. For example, selling via the Apple App Store and Google Play (primary source for Android Apps) is an advantage for an app-based company. Apple and Google Play essentially act as GymFlow's distributor for the app. This relieves a company like GymFlow of the financial burden of building its own distribution platform.

In terms of overall financial management, Liu and Zhang are comfortable with where GymFlow is today. Many lessons have been learned, however, about the importance of cash flow and the need for sharp financial management for a growing company.

In this chapter, we'll look at how new ventures manage their finances and assess their financial strength and viability. For the purposes of completeness, we'll look at how both existing firms and entrepreneurial ventures accomplish these tasks. First, we'll consider general financial management and discuss the financial objectives of a firm and the steps involved in the financial management process. **Financial management** deals with two activities: raising money and managing a company's finances in a way that achieves the highest rate of return.[1] We cover the process of raising money in Chapter 10. This chapter focuses on how a company manages its finances in an effort to increase its financial strength and earn the highest rate of return. Next, we'll examine how existing firms track their financial progress through preparing, analyzing, and maintaining past financial statements. Finally, we'll discuss how both existing firms and start-up ventures forecast future income and expenses and how the forecasts are used to prepare pro forma (i.e., projected) financial statements. Pro forma financial statements, which include the pro forma income statement, the pro forma balance sheet, and the pro forma statement of cash flows, are extremely helpful to firms in financial planning.

Introduction to Financial Management

An entrepreneur's ability to pursue an opportunity and turn the opportunity into a viable entrepreneurial firm hinges largely on the availability of money. Regardless of the quality of a product or service, a company can't be viable in the long run unless it is successful financially. Money either comes from external sources (such as investors or lenders) or is internally generated through earnings. It is important for a firm to have a solid grasp of how it is doing financially. One of the most common mistakes young entrepreneurial firms make is not emphasizing financial management and putting in place appropriate forms of financial controls.[2]

LEARNING OBJECTIVE

1. Learn about the importance of understanding the financial management of an entrepreneurial firm.

Entrepreneurs and those managing established companies must be aware of how much money they have in the bank and if that amount is sufficient to satisfy their firm's financial obligations. Just because a firm is successful doesn't mean that it doesn't face financial challenges.[3] For example, many of the small firms that sell their products to larger companies such as Apple, General Electric (GE), and The Home Depot aren't paid for 30 to 60 days from the time they make a sale. Think about the difficulty this scenario creates. The small firm must buy parts, pay its employees, pay its routine bills, build and ship its products, and then wait for one to two months for payment. Unless a firm manages its money carefully, it is easy to run out of cash, even if its products or services are selling like hotcakes.[4] Similarly, as a company grows, its cash demands often increase to service a growing clientele. It is important for a firm to accurately anticipate whether it will be able to fund its growth through earnings or if it will need to look for investment capital or borrowing to raise needed cash.

The financial management of a firm deals with questions such as the following on an ongoing basis:

■ How are we doing? Are we making or losing money?

■ How much cash do we have on hand?

■ Do we have enough cash to meet our short-term obligations?

■ How efficiently are we utilizing our assets?

■ How do our growth and net profits compare to those of our industry peers?

■ Where will the funds we need for capital improvements come from?

■ Are there ways we can partner with other firms to share risk and reduce the amount of cash we need?

■ Overall, are we in good shape financially?

A properly managed firm stays on top of the issues suggested by these questions through the tools and techniques that we'll discuss in this chapter.

Financial Objectives of a Firm

Most entrepreneurial firms—whether they have been in business for several years or they are start-ups—have four main financial objectives: profitability, liquidity, efficiency, and stability. Understanding these objectives sets a firm on the right financial course and helps it track the answers to the previously posed questions. Figure 8.1 describes each of these objectives.

Profitability is the ability to earn a profit. Many start-ups are not profitable during their first one to three years, while they are training employees and building their brands, but a firm must become profitable to remain viable and provide a return to its owners.

Liquidity is a company's ability to meet its short-term financial obligations. Even if a firm is profitable, it is often a challenge to keep enough money in the bank to meet its routine obligations in a timely manner. To do so, a firm must keep a close watch on accounts receivable and inventories. A company's **accounts receivable** is money owed to it by its customers. Its **inventory** is its merchandise, raw materials, and products waiting to be sold. If a firm allows the levels of either of these assets to get too high, it may not be able to keep sufficient cash on hand to meet its short-term obligations.[5]

Efficiency is how productively a firm utilizes its assets relative to its revenue and its profits. Southwest Airlines, for example, uses its assets very productively. Its turnaround time, or the time that its airplanes sit on the ground while they are being unloaded and reloaded, is the lowest in the airline industry. As Southwest officials are quick to point out, "Our planes don't make any money sitting on the ground—we have to get them back into the air."[6]

Stability is the strength and vigor of the firm's overall financial posture. For a firm to be stable, it must not only earn a profit and remain liquid but also keep its debt in check. If a firm continues to borrow from its lenders and its **debt-to-equity ratio**, which is calculated by dividing its long-term debt by its shareholders' equity, gets too high, it may have trouble meeting its obligations and securing the level of financing needed to fuel its growth.

An increasingly common way that small companies improve their prospects across several of these areas is to join buying groups or co-ops, where businesses band together to attain volume discounts on products and services. Gaining access to products and services this way facilitates smaller firms' efforts to compete on more of a "level playing field" with larger, more established companies. The way buying groups work, and how they're able to help businesses cut costs without adversely affecting their competitiveness, is described in this chapter's "Partnering for Success" feature.

The Process of Financial Management

To assess whether its financial objectives are being met, firms rely heavily on analyses of financial statements, forecasts, and budgets. A **financial statement** is a written report that quantitatively describes a firm's financial health.

FIGURE 8.1
Primary Financial Objectives of Entrepreneurial Firms

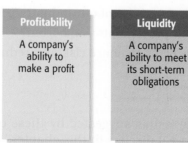
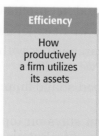

Profitability	Liquidity	Efficiency	Stability
A company's ability to make a profit	A company's ability to meet its short-term obligations	How productively a firm utilizes its assets	The overall health of the financial structure of the firm, particularly as it relates to its debt-to-equity ratio

PARTNERING FOR SUCCESS

Organizing Buying Groups to Cuts Costs and Maintain Competitiveness

One challenge that businesses confront is cutting costs in ways that don't erode their ability to remain competitive. Many cost-cutting techniques, such as scaling back on hiring, lowering marketing expenses, or reducing inventory, may save money but may also decrease a business's chances to remain competitive. One technique that can help to conserve a product-based business's financial assets without adverse side effects is to join or organize a buying group.

A buying group, or buying co-op, is a partnership that bands small businesses and start-up firms together to attain volume discounts on products and services. In the UK and the Republic of Ireland, the Toymaster Group has been in operation since 1977 and now has around 250 members. They are all small, independent toys and games stores that operate under the name Toymaster and benefit from the combined buying power of all of the members. Some 55 percent of an average toy shop's revenue comes in during the pre-Christmas period and just 15 percent for each of the other three quarters of the year. This means accounting and money management is tightly controlled and this is what a buying group offers.

Suma is the UK's largest independent co-operative wholefood wholesaler/distributor. They specialize in vegetarian, fairly traded, organic, ethical and natural products. They provide a unique, niche service as they are 100 percent vegetarian and stock no animal products or products derived from animals. They have close relationships with the growers and suppliers and cite that they have real commitment to fair trade rather than simply using it as a marketing device.

The beauty of buying groups is that they generally allow businesses to obtain the exact same product for a lower price, with no undesirable impact (other than the membership fee) on the other parts of their operations. The money that's freed up can go directly to a business's bottom line or be used to invest in customer service or other methods to increase competitiveness. There is no national directory of industry buying groups. The best way to find out whether there are buying groups servicing an industry is to conduct an Internet research and ask among industry participants.

Questions for Critical Thinking

1. Which of the four financial objectives of a firm—profitability, liquidity, efficiency, or stability—does participating in a buying cooperative contribute to the most?

2. Do some Internet and/or library research to discern whether there is a small business buying group or groups that New Venture Fitness Drinks, the fictitious company introduced in Chapter 3 and used as an example throughout this chapter, could benefit from. New Venture Fitness Drinks' products contain all the ingredients used to make smoothies and similar fitness drinks and shakes.

3. Identify three ways, other than buying cooperatives, that small businesses partner with other small businesses to cut costs without sacrificing their competitiveness?

4. In an effort to improve the financial position of their firms, do you think the majority of entrepreneurs spend an equal amount of time focusing on (1) cost cutting and (2) increasing revenues? If not, which of the two do you think they spend more time on and why?

The income statement, the balance sheet, and the statement of cash flows are the financial statements entrepreneurs use most commonly. **Forecasts** are an estimate of a firm's future income and expenses, based on its past performance, its current circumstances, and its future plans.[7] New ventures typically base their forecasts on an estimate of sales and then on industry averages or the experiences of similar start-ups regarding the cost of goods sold (based on a percentage of sales) and on other expenses. **Budgets** are itemized forecasts of a company's income, expenses, and capital needs and are also an important tool for financial planning and control.[8]

The process of a firm's financial management is shown in Figure 8.2. It begins by tracking the company's past financial performance through the preparation and analysis of financial statements. These statements organize and report the firm's financial transactions. They tell a firm how much money it is making or losing (income statement), the structure of its assets and liabilities (balance sheet), and where its cash is coming from and going (statement of cash flows). The statements also help a firm discern how it stacks up against its competitors and industry norms. Most firms look at two to three years of past financial statements when preparing forecasts.

FIGURE 8.2

The Process of
Financial Management

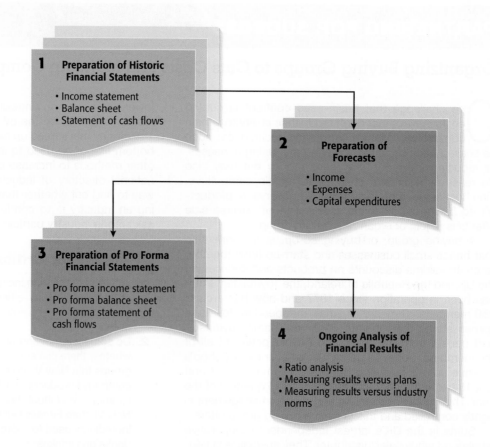

The next step is to prepare forecasts for two to three years in the future. In turn, forecasts are used to prepare a firm's pro forma financial statements, which, along with its more fine-tuned budgets, constitute its financial plan.

The final step in the process is the ongoing analysis of a firm's financial results. **Financial ratios**, which depict relationships between items on a firm's financial statements, are used to discern whether a firm is meeting its financial objectives and how it stacks up against its industry peers. These ratios are also used to assess trends. Obviously, a completely new venture would start at step 2 in Figure 8.2. It is important that a new venture be familiar with the entire process, however. Typically, new ventures prepare financial statements quarterly so that as soon as the first quarter is completed, the new venture will have historic financial statements to help prepare forecasts and pro forma statements for future periods.

It is important for a firm to evaluate how it is faring relative to its industry. Sometimes raw financial ratios that are not viewed in context are deceiving. For example, a firm's past three years' income statements may show that it is increasing its sales at a rate of 15 percent per year. This number may seem impressive—until one learns that the industry in which the firm competes is growing at a rate of 30 percent per year, showing that the firm is steadily losing market share.

Many experienced entrepreneurs stress the importance of keeping on top of the financial management of a firm. In the competitive environments in which most firms exist, it's simply not good enough to shoot from the hip when making financial decisions. Reinforcing this point, Bill Gates, the founder of Microsoft, said,

The business side of any company starts and ends with hard-core analysis of its numbers. Whatever else you do, if you don't understand what's happening in your business factually and you're making business decisions based on anecdotal data or gut instinct, you'll eventually pay a big price.[9]

Financial Statements

Historical financial statements reflect past performance and are usually prepared on a quarterly and annual basis. Publicly traded firms are required by the Securities and Exchange Commission (SEC) to prepare financial statements and make them available to the public. The statements are submitted to the SEC through a number of required filings. The most comprehensive filing is the **10-K**, which is a report similar to the annual report except that it contains more detailed information about the company's business.[10] The 10-K for any publicly traded firm is available at www.freeedgar.com.

Pro forma financial statements are projections for future periods based on forecasts and are typically completed for two to three years in the future. Pro forma financial statements are strictly planning tools and are not required by the SEC. In fact, most companies consider their pro forma statements to be confidential and reveal them to outsiders, such as lenders and investors, only on a "need-to-know" basis.

To illustrate how these financial instruments are prepared, let's look at New Venture Fitness Drinks, the fictitious sports drink company to which you were introduced in Chapter 3. New Venture Fitness Drinks has been in business for five years. Targeting sports enthusiasts, the company sells a line of nutritional fitness drinks. It opened a single location in 2012, added a second location in 2014, and plans to add a third in 2015. The company's strategy is to place small restaurants, similar to smoothie restaurants, near large outdoor sports complexes. The company is profitable and is growing at a rate of 25 percent per year.

LEARNING OBJECTIVE

4. Explain the difference between historical and pro forma financial statements.

Historical Financial Statements

Historical financial statements include the income statement, the balance sheet, and the statement of cash flows. The statements are usually prepared in this order because information flows logically from one to the next. In start-ups, financial statements are typically scrutinized closely to monitor the financial progress of the firm. On the rare occasion when a company has not used financial

LEARNING OBJECTIVE

5. Describe the different historical financial statements and their purposes.

Keeping good records is the first step toward prudent financial management. This entrepreneur, who is the owner of a barbeque restaurant, takes a minute at the end of a busy day to add several receipts to his records.

DreamPictures/Blend Images/Corbis

statements in planning, it should prepare and maintain them anyway. If a firm goes to a banker or investor to raise funds, the banker or investor will invariably ask for copies of past financial statements to analyze the firm's financial history. If a firm does not have these statements, it may be precluded from serious consideration for an investment or a loan. Let's look at each of these statements.

Income Statement   The **income statement** reflects the results of the operations of a firm over a specified period of time.[11] It records all the revenues and expenses for the given period and shows whether the firm is making a profit or is experiencing a loss (which is why the income statement if often referred to as the "profit-and-loss statement"). Income statements are typically prepared on a monthly, quarterly, and annual basis. Most income statements are prepared in a multiyear format, making it easy to spot trends.

The consolidated income statement for the past three years for New Venture Fitness Drinks is shown in Table 8.1. The value of the multi period format is clear. It's easy to see that the company's sales are increasing at the rate of about 25 percent per year, it is profitable, and its net income is increasing. The numbers are used to evaluate the effect of past strategies and to help project future sales and earnings.

The three numbers that receive the most attention when evaluating an income statement are the following:

- **Net sales: Net sales** consist of total sales minus allowances for returned goods and discounts.
- **Cost of sales (or cost of goods sold): Cost of sales** includes all the direct costs associated with producing or delivering a product or service, including the material costs and direct labor. In the case of New Venture

TABLE 8.1   **Consolidated Income Statements for New Venture Fitness Drinks, Inc.**

	December 31, 2014	December 31, 2013	December 31, 2012
Net sales	$586,600	$463,100	$368,900
Cost of sales	268,900	225,500	201,500
Gross profit	317,700	237,600	167,400
Operating expenses			
Selling, general, and administrative expenses	117,800	104,700	90,200
Depreciation	13,500	5,900	5,100
Operating income	186,400	127,000	72,100
Other income			
Interest income	1,900	800	1,100
Interest expense	(15,000)	(6,900)	(6,400)
Other income (expense), net	10,900	(1,300)	1,200
Income before income taxes	184,200	119,600	68,000
Income tax expense	53,200	36,600	18,000
Net income	131,000	83,000	50,000
Earnings per share	1.31	0.83	0.50

Fitness Drinks, this would include the ingredients that go into the fitness drinks and the labor needed to produce them.

■ **Operating expenses: Operating expenses** include marketing, administrative costs, and other expenses not directly related to producing a product or service.

One of the most valuable things that entrepreneurs and managers do with income statements is to compare the ratios of cost of sales and operating expenses to net sales for different periods. For example, the cost of sales for New Venture Fitness Drinks, which includes the ingredients for its fitness drinks and the labor needed to make them, has been 55, 49, and 46 percent of sales for 2012, 2013, and 2014, respectively. This is a healthy trend. It shows that the company is steadily decreasing its material and labor costs per dollar of sales. This is the type of trend that can be noticed fairly easily by looking at a firm's multiyear income statements.

Profit margin is a ratio that is of particular importance when evaluating a firm's income statements. A firm's **profit margin**, or return on sales, is computed by dividing net income by net sales. For the years 2012, 2013, and 2014, the profit margin for New Venture Fitness Drinks has been 13.6, 17.9, and 22.3 percent, respectively. This is also a healthy trend. A firm's profit margin tells it what percentage of every dollar in sales contributes to the bottom line. An increasing profit margin means that a firm is either boosting its sales without increasing its expenses or that it is doing a better job of controlling its costs. In contrast, a declining profit margin means that a firm is losing control of its costs or that it is slashing prices to maintain or increase sales.

One ratio that will not be computed for New Venture Fitness Drinks is **price-to-earnings ratio, or P/E ratio**. New Venture Fitness Drinks is incorporated, so it has stock, but its stock is not traded on a public exchange such as the NASDAQ or the New York Stock Exchange. P/E is a simple ratio that measures the price of a company's stock against its earnings.[12] Generally, the higher a company's price-to-earnings ratio goes, the greater the market thinks it will grow. In 2014, New Venture Fitness Drinks earned $1.31 per share. If it was listed on the NASDAQ and its stock was trading at $20 per share, its P/E would be 15.3. This is what is meant when you hear that a company is selling for "15 times earnings."

The importance of looking at several years of income statements rather than just one is illustrated in this chapter's "Savvy Entrepreneurial Firm" feature.

Balance Sheet Unlike the income statement, which covers a specified *period* of time, a **balance sheet** is a snapshot of a company's assets, liabilities, and owners' equity at a specific *point* in time.[13] The left-hand side of a balance sheet (or the top, depending on how it is displayed) shows a firm's assets, while the right-hand side (or bottom) shows its liabilities and owners' equity. The assets are listed in order of their "liquidity," or the length of time it takes to convert them to cash. The liabilities are listed in the order in which they must be paid. A balance sheet must always "balance," meaning that a firm's assets must always equal its liabilities plus owners' equity.[14]

The major categories of assets listed on a balance sheet are the following:

■ **Current assets: Current assets** include cash plus items that are readily convertible to cash, such as accounts receivable, marketable securities, and inventories.

■ **Fixed assets: Fixed assets** are assets used over a longer time frame, such as real estate, buildings, equipment, and furniture.

■ **Other assets: Other assets** are miscellaneous assets, including accumulated goodwill.

SAVVY ENTREPRENEURIAL FIRM

Know the Facts Behind the Numbers

Let's say that New Venture Fitness Drinks was interested in hiring a new chief executive officer (CEO) and was interviewing the CEOs of three small restaurant chains. To get a sense of how savvy each candidate was at managing a firm's finances, the board of directors of New Venture Fitness Drinks asked each person to submit the 2014 income statement for his or her current firm. An analysis of an abbreviated version of each firm's income statement is shown here.

	Candidate 1: CEO of New Venture Soup and Salad	Candidate 2: CEO of New Venture Beef	Candidate 3: CEO of New Venture Sea Food
Net sales	$326,400	$281,200	$486,700
Cost of sales	150,500	143,900	174,700
Gross profit	175,900	137,300	312,000
All expenses, including taxes and depreciation	114,200	112,400	150,000
Net income	61,700	24,900	162,000

By glancing at these statements, it would appear that the shrewdest financial manager of the three is the CEO of New Venture Sea Food. The company's net income is more than double that of the other two firms. In addition, New Venture Sea Food's cost of sales was 35.9 percent of net sales in 2014, compared to 46.1 percent for New Venture Soup and Salad and 51 percent for New Venture Beef. Similarly, New Venture Sea Food's expenses were 30.9 percent of sales, compared to 35.0 percent for New Venture Soup and Salad and 40 percent for New Venture Beef.

Fortunately, one of the board members of New Venture Fitness Drinks asked a series of questions during the personal interviews of the candidates and uncovered some revealing information. As it turns out, New Venture Sea Food was in the hottest segment of the restaurant industry in 2014. Seafood restaurants of comparable size produced about 1.5 times as much net income as New Venture Sea Food did. So if candidate 3 had done his job properly, his company's net income should have been in the neighborhood of $240,000 instead of $162,000. New Venture Soup and Salad was in a slow-growth area and at midyear feared that it might not meet its financial targets. So the CEO pulled several of his best people off projects and reassigned them to marketing to develop new menu items. In other words, the company borrowed from its future to make its numbers work today.

As for New Venture Beef, the CEO found herself in a market that was losing appeal. Several reports that gained national publicity were published early in the year warning consumers of the risks of eating red meat. To compensate, the CEO quickly implemented a productivity improvement program and partnered with a local beef promotion board to counter the bad press with more objective research results about beef's nutritional value. The company also participated in several volunteer efforts in its local community to raise the visibility of its restaurants in a positive manner. If the CEO of New Venture Beef hadn't moved quickly to take these actions, its 2014 performance would have been much worse.

Ultimately, New Venture Fitness Drinks decided that candidate 2, the CEO of New Venture Beef, was the best candidate for its job. This example illustrates the need to look at multiple years of an income statement rather than a single year to fairly assess how well a firm is performing financially. It also illustrates the need to look beyond the numbers and understand the circumstances that surround a firm's financial results.

Questions for Critical Thinking

1. Show the income statements for the three candidates to two or three friends who are majoring in business. Ask them to select the best CEO from among these three people on the basis of these income statements. In addition, ask your friends to explain their choices to you. Did your friends choose the same candidate? If not, what do you think caused the differences in their choices?
2. Based on material presented in this chapter, earlier chapters in this book, and your general business knowledge, where would you go to find information about the growth of the different segments of the restaurant industry? Where would you go to find information about the profitability of the restaurant industry in general?
3. What would have been the appropriate financial information to request from the three candidates for the job?
4. What are the three most important insights you gained from studying this feature? Which of these insights surprised you, and why?

The major categories of liabilities listed on a balance sheet are the following:

- **Current liabilities: Current liabilities** include obligations that are payable within a year, including accounts payable, accrued expenses, and the current portion of long-term debt.
- **Long-term liabilities: Long-term liabilities** include notes or loans that are repayable beyond one year, including liabilities associated with purchasing real estate, buildings, and equipment.
- **Owners' equity: Owners' equity** is the equity invested in the business by its owners plus the accumulated earnings retained by the business after paying dividends.

Balance sheets are somewhat deceiving. First, a company's assets are recorded at cost rather than fair market value. A firm may have invested $500,000 in real estate several years ago that is worth $1 million today, but the value that is reflected on the firm's current balance sheet is the $500,000 purchase price rather than the $1 million fair market value. Second, intellectual property, such as patents, trademarks, and copyrights, receive value on the balance sheet in some cases and in some cases they don't, depending on the circumstances involved. In many cases, a firm's intellectual property will receive no value on its balance sheet even though it may be very valuable from a practical standpoint.[15] Third, intangible assets, such as the amount of training a firm has provided to its employees and the value of its brand, are not recognized on its balance sheet. Finally, the goodwill that a firm has accumulated is not reported on its balance sheet, although this may be the firm's single most valuable asset.

The consolidated balance sheet for New Venture Fitness Drinks is shown in Table 8.2. Again, multiple years are shown so that trends can be easily spotted. When evaluating a balance sheet, the two primary questions are whether a firm has sufficient short-term assets to cover its short-term debts and whether it is financially sound overall. There are two calculations that provide the answer to the first question. In 2014, the **working capital** of New Venture Fitness Drinks, defined as its current assets minus its current liabilities, was $82,500. This number represents the amount of liquid assets the firm has available. Its **current ratio**, which equals the firm's current assets divided by its current liabilities, provides another picture of the relationship between its current assets and current liabilities and can tell us more about the firm's ability to pay its short-term debts.

New Venture Fitness Drinks's current ratio is 3.06, meaning that it has $3.06 in current assets for every $1.00 in current liabilities. This is a healthy number and provides confidence that the company will be able to meet its current liabilities. The company's trend in this area is also positive. For the years 2012, 2013, and 2014, its current ratio has been 2.35, 2.26, and 3.06, respectively.

Computing a company's overall debt ratio will give us the answer to the second question, as it is a means of assessing a firm's overall financial soundness. A company's debt ratio is computed by dividing its total debt by its total assets. The present debt ratio for New Venture Fitness Drinks is 39.7 percent, meaning that 39.7 percent of its total assets are financed by debt and the remaining 60.3 percent by owners' equity. This is a healthy number for a young firm. The trend for New Venture Fitness Drinks in this area is also encouraging. For the years 2012, 2013, and 2014, its debt ratio has been 42.3, 37.4, and 39.7 percent, respectively. These figures indicate that over time, the company is relying less on debt to finance its operations. In general, less debt creates more freedom for the entrepreneurial firm in terms of taking different actions.

TABLE 8.2   Consolidated Balance Sheets for New Venture Fitness Drinks, Inc.

Assets	December 31, 2014	December 31, 2013	December 31, 2012
Current assets			
Cash and cash equivalents	$63,800	$54,600	$56,500
Accounts receivable, less allowance for doubtful accounts	39,600	48,900	50,200
Inventories	19,200	20,400	21,400
Total current assets	122,600	123,900	128,100
Property, plant, and equipment			
Land	260,000	160,000	160,000
Buildings and equipment	412,000	261,500	149,000
Total property, plant, and equipment	672,000	421,500	309,000
Less: accumulated depreciation	65,000	51,500	45,600
Net property, plant, and equipment	607,000	370,000	263,400
Total assets	729,600	493,900	391,500
Liabilities and shareholders' equity			
Current liabilities			
Accounts payable	30,200	46,900	50,400
Accrued expenses	9,900	8,000	4,100
Total current liabilities	40,100	54,900	54,500
Long-term liabilities			
Long-term debt	249,500	130,000	111,000
Long-term liabilities	249,500	130,000	111,000
Total liabilities	289,600	184,900	165,500
Shareholders' equity			
Common stock (100,000 shares)	10,000	10,000	10,000
Retained earnings	430,000	299,000	216,000
Total shareholders' equity	440,000	309,000	226,000
Total liabilities and shareholders' equity	729,600	493,900	391,500

The numbers across all the firm's financial statements are consistent with one another. Note that the $131,000 net income reported by New Venture Fitness Drinks on its 2014 income statement shows up as the difference between its 2014 and 2013 retained earnings on its 2014 balance sheet. This number would have been different if New Venture Fitness Drinks had paid dividends to its stockholders, but it paid no dividends in 2014. The company retained all of its $131,000 in earnings.

Statement of Cash Flows   The **statement of cash flows** summarizes the changes in a firm's cash position for a specified period of time and details why the change occurred. The statement of cash flows is similar to a month-end bank statement. It reveals how much cash is on hand at the end of the month as well as how the cash was acquired and spent during the month.

The statement of cash flows is divided into three separate activities: operating activities, investing activities, and financing activities. These activities, which are explained in the following list, are the activities from which a firm obtains and uses cash:

- **Operating activities: Operating activities** include net income (or loss), depreciation, and changes in current assets and current liabilities other than cash and short-term debt. A firm's net income, taken from its income statement, is the first line on the corresponding period's cash flow statement.
- **Investing activities: Investing activities** include the purchase, sale, or investment in fixed assets, such as real estate, equipment, and buildings.
- **Financing activities: Financing activities** include cash raised during the period by borrowing money or selling stock and/or cash used during the period by paying dividends, buying back outstanding stock, or buying back outstanding bonds.

Interpreting and analyzing cash flow statements takes practice. On the statement, the *uses* of cash are recorded as negative figures (which are shown by placing them in parentheses) and the *sources* of cash are recorded as positive figures. An item such as depreciation is shown as a positive figure on the statement of cash flows because it was deducted from net income on the income statement but was not a cash expenditure. Similarly, a decrease in accounts payable shows up as a negative figure on the cash flow statement because the firm used part of its cash to reduce its accounts payable balance from one period to the next.

The statement of cash flows for New Venture Fitness Drinks is shown in Table 8.3. As a management tool, it is intended to provide perspective on the following questions: Is the firm generating excess cash that could be used to pay down debt or returned to stockholders in the form of dividends? Is the firm generating enough cash to fund its investment activities from earnings, or is it relying on lenders or investors? Is the firm generating sufficient cash to pay down its short-term liabilities, or are its short-term liabilities increasing as the result of an insufficient amount of cash?

Again, a multi period statement is created so that trends can easily be spotted. A large increase in a firm's cash balance is not necessarily a good sign. It could mean that the firm is borrowing heavily, is not paying down its short-term liabilities, or is accumulating cash that could be put to work for a more productive purpose. On the other hand, it is almost always prudent for a young firm to have a healthy cash balance.

Table 8.3 shows the consolidated statement of cash flows for New Venture Fitness Drinks for two years instead of three because it takes three years of balance sheets to produce two years of cash flow statements. The statements show that New Venture Fitness Drinks is funding its investment activities from a combination of debt and earnings while at the same time it is slowly decreasing its accounts receivable and inventory levels (which is good—these items are major drains on a company's cash flow). It is also steadily increasing its cash on hand. These are encouraging signs for a new venture.

Ratio Analysis The most practical way to interpret or make sense of a firm's historical financial statements is through ratio analysis. Table 8.4 is a summary of the ratios used to evaluate New Venture Fitness Drinks during the time period covered by the previously provided financial statements.

TABLE 8.3   Consolidated Statement of Cash Flows for New Venture Fitness Drinks, Inc.

	December 31, 2014	December 31, 2013
Cash flows from operating activities		
Net income	$131,000	$83,000
Additions (sources of cash)		
Depreciation	13,500	5,900
Decreases in accounts receivable	9,300	1,300
Increase in accrued expenses	1,900	3,900
Decrease in inventory	1,200	1,000
Subtractions (uses of cash)		
Decrease in accounts payable	(16,700)	(3,500)
Total adjustments	9,200	8,600
Net cash provided by operating activities	140,200	91,600
Cash flows from investing activities		
Purchase of building and equipment	(250,500)	(112,500)
Net cash flows provided by investing activities	(250,500)	(112,500)
Cash flows from financing activities		
Proceeds from increase in long-term debt	119,500	19,000
Net cash flows provided by financing activities		19,000
Increase in cash	9,200	(1,900)
Cash and cash equivalents at the beginning of each year	54,600	56,500
Cash and cash equivalents at the end of each year	63,800	54,600

The ratios are divided into profitability ratios, liquidity ratios, and overall financial stability ratios. These ratios provide a means of interpreting the historical financial statements for New Venture Fitness Drinks and provide a starting point for forecasting the firm's financial performance and capabilities for the future.

Comparing a Firm's Financial Results to Industry Norms
Comparing its financial results to industry norms helps a firm determine how it stacks up against its competitors and if there are any financial "red flags" requiring attention. This type of comparison works best for firms that are of similar size, so the results should be interpreted with caution by new firms. Many sources provide industry-related information. For example, both Hoover's premium service and BizMiner provide industry norms to which a new firm can compare itself and are typically free of charge if accessed via a university library. BizMiner (www.bizminer.com) is particularly good for providing comparison data for private firms. Several suggestions for obtaining comparison data for private firms are provided in Chapter 3.

TABLE 8.4   Ratio Analysis for New Venture Fitness Drinks, Inc.

Ratio	Formula	2014	2013	2012
Profitability ratios: associate the amount of income earned with the resources used to generate it				
Return on assets	ROA = net income/average total assets[a]	21.4%	18.7%	14.7%
Return on equity	ROE = net income/average shareholders' equity[b]	35.0%	31.0%	24.9%
Profit margin	Profit margin = net income/net sales	22.3%	17.9%	13.6%
Liquidity ratios: measure the extent to which a company can quickly liquidate assets to cover short-term liabilities				
Current	Current assets/current liabilities	3.06	2.26	2.35
Quick	Quick assets/current liabilities	2.58	1.89	1.96
Overall financial stability ratio: measures the overall financial stability of a firm				
Debt	Total debt/total assets	39.7%	37.4%	42.3%
Debt to equity	Total liabilities/owners' equity	65.8%	59.8%	73.2%

[a] Average total assets = beginning total assets + ending total assets ÷ 2.
[b] Average shareholders' equity = beginning shareholders' equity + ending shareholders' equity ÷ 2.

Forecasts

As depicted in Figure 8.2, the analysis of a firm's historical financial statement is followed by the preparation of forecasts. **Forecasts** are predictions of a firm's future sales, expenses, income, and capital expenditures. A firm's forecasts provide the basis for its pro forma financial statements. A well-developed set of pro forma financial statements helps a firm create accurate budgets, build financial plans, and manage its finances in a proactive rather than a reactive manner.

As mentioned earlier, completely new firms typically base their forecasts on a good-faith estimate of sales and on industry averages (based on a percentage of sales) or the experiences of similar start-ups for cost of goods sold and other expenses. As a result, a completely new firm's forecast should be preceded in its business plan by an explanation of the sources of the numbers for the forecast and the assumptions used to generate them. This explanation is called an **assumptions sheet**, as mentioned in Chapter 6. Investors typically study assumptions sheets like hawks to make sure the numbers contained in the forecasts and the resulting financial projections are realistic. For example, the assumptions sheet for a new venture may say that its forecasts are based on selling 500 units of its new product the first year, 1,000 units the second year, and 1,500 units the third year, and that its cost of goods sold will remain stable (meaning that it will stay fixed at a certain percentage of net sales) over the three-year period. It's up to the reader of the plan to determine if these numbers are realistic.[16] If the reader feels they are not, then the credibility of the entire plan is called into question.

Sales Forecast

A **sales forecast** is a projection of a firm's sales for a specified period (such as a year), though most firms forecast their sales for two to five years into the future.[17] It is the first forecast developed and is the basis for most of the other

LEARNING OBJECTIVE

6. Discuss the role of forecasts in projecting a firm's future income and expenses.

forecasts.[18] A sales forecast for an existing firm is based on (1) its record of past sales, (2) its current production capacity and product demand, and (3) any factor or factors that will affect its future production capacity and product demand. To demonstrate how a sales forecast works, Figure 8.3 is a graph of the past sales and the forecasted future sales for New Venture Fitness Drinks. The company's sales increased at a rate of about 26 percent per year from 2012 to 2014 as the company became established and more people became aware of its brand. In forecasting its sales for 2015 and 2016, the company took into consideration the following factors:

- The fitness craze in America continues to gain momentum and should continue to attract new people to try its fitness drinks.

- The interest in intramural sports, especially soccer, baseball, and softball, should continue to provide a high level of traffic for its restaurants, which are located near large intramural sports complexes.

- The company expanded from a single location in 2011 to two locations in 2014 (the second restaurant was added in November 2014), and this should increase its capacity to serve fitness drinks by approximately 50 percent. The second restaurant is smaller than the first and is located in an area where the company is not as well known. The company will be actively promoting the new restaurant but knows it will take time to win market share.

- The general economy in the city where the company is located is flat—it is neither growing nor shrinking. However, layoffs are rumored for a larger employer near the location of the new restaurant.

The combination of these factors results in a forecast of a 40 percent increase in sales from 2014 to 2015 and a 25 percent increase in sales from 2015 to 2016. It is extremely important for a company such as New Venture Drinks to forecast future sales as accurately as possible. If it overestimates the demand for its products, it might get stuck with excess inventory and spend too much on overhead. If it underestimates the demand for its product, it might have to turn away business, and some of its potential customers might get into the habit of buying other firms' fitness drinks.

Note that sophisticated tools are available to help firms project their future sales. One approach is to use **regression analysis**, which is a statistical technique used to find relationships between variables for the purpose of predicting future values.[19] For example, if New Venture Fitness Drinks felt that its future sales were a function of its advertising expenditures, the number of

FIGURE 8.3
Historical and
Forecasted Annual
Sales for New Venture
Fitness Drinks

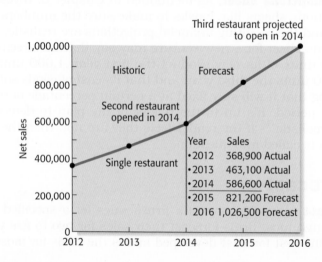

people who participate in intramural sports at the sports complexes near its restaurants, and the price of its drinks, it could predict future sales using regression analysis as long as it had historical data for each of these variables. If the company used simpler logic and felt that its future sales would increase a certain percentage over its current sales, regression analysis could be used to generate a more precise estimate of future sales than was predicted from the information contained in Figure 8.3. For a new firm that has limited years of "annual data," monthly data could be used to project sales.

Forecast of Costs of Sales and Other Items

After completing its sales forecast, a firm must forecast its cost of sales (or cost of goods sold) and the other items on its income statement. The most common way to do this is to use the **percent-of-sales method**, which is a method for expressing each expense item as a percentage of sales.[20] For example, in the case of New Venture Fitness Drinks, its cost of sales has averaged 47.5 percent over the past two years. In 2014, its sales were $586,600 and its cost of sales was $268,900. The company's sales are forecast to be $821,200 in 2015. Therefore, based on the percent-of-sales method, its cost of sales in 2015 will be $390,000, or 47.5 percent of projected sales. The same procedure could be used to forecast the cost of each expense item on the company's income statement.

Once a firm completes its forecast using the percent-of-sales method, it usually goes through its income statement on an item-by-item basis to see if there are opportunities to make more precise forecasts. For example, a firm can closely estimate its depreciation expenses, so it wouldn't be appropriate to use the percent-of-sales method to make a forecast for this item. In addition, some expense items are not tied to sales. For those items, the firm makes reasonable estimates.

Obviously, a firm must apply common sense in using the percent-of-sales method. If a company is implementing cost-cutting measures, for example, it might be able to justify projecting a smaller percentage increase in expenses as opposed to sales. Similarly, if a firm hires an upper-level manager, such as a chief financial officer, toward the end of the year and plans to pay the person $100,000 the next year, that $100,000 may not have an immediate impact on sales. In this case, the firm's forecast for administrative expenses may have to be adjusted upward beyond what the percent-of-sales method would suggest.

If a firm determines that it can use the percent-of-sales method and it follows the procedure described previously, then the net result is that each expense item on its income statement (with the exception of those items that may be individually forecast, such as depreciation) will grow at the same rate as sales. This approach is called the **constant ratio method of forecasting**. This approach will be used in preparing the pro forma financial statements for New Venture Fitness Drinks in the next section.

A summary of the forecasts used to prepare the pro forma financial statements for New Venture Fitness Drinks is provided in Table 8.5.

In addition to computing sales forecasts, when a company like New Venture Fitness Drinks considers opening a new restaurant or producing a new product, it often calculates a break-even analysis to determine if the proposed initiative is feasible. The **break-even point** for a new restaurant or product is the point where total revenue received equals total costs associated with the output of the restaurant or the sale of the product.[21] In the case of opening a new restaurant, New Venture Fitness Drinks could use break-even analysis as one way of determining whether the proposed initiative is feasible. The formula for break-even analysis is as follows: Total fixed costs/(price – average variable costs). In most instances, average variable cost is the same number as average cost of goods sold. As a result, if the total fixed cost associated with opening

TABLE 8.5   **Forecasts Used to Prepare Pro Forma Financial Statements for New Venture Fitness Drinks, Inc.**

Pro Forma Income Statements

Net sales

Historic	Average sales increase of 25% per year
2015	Increase to 40% as the result of increased brand awareness and the opening of a second service location
2016	Increase to 25% as the result of increased brand awareness (a third service location will be opened late in the year)

Cost of goods sold (COGS)

Historic	Average of 47.5% of sales the past two years
2015	47.5% of sales
2016	47.5% of sales

Selling, general, and administrative expenses

Historic	Average 22% of sales the past two years
2015	Increase to 25% of sales as the result of the opening of a second service location (the increase will not be any larger as the result of increased operating efficiencies)
2016	25% of sales

Interest expense

Historic	6% to 7% of long-term debt
2015	7% of long-term debt
2016	7% of long-term debt

Other income

Historic	Licensing income of $10,900 per year
2015	Licensing income will increase to $20,000 as the result of the renegotiation of the licensing contract
2016	Licensing income will be $20,000

Pro Forma Balance Sheets

Accounts receivable

Historic	Accounts receivable have trended down to 6.8% of sales in 2014 from 13.6% of sales in 2013
2015	7% of sales
2016	7% of sales

Inventories

Historic	Inventories have trended down to 3.3% of sales in 2014 from 4.4% of sales in 2013
2015	4% of sales (reflecting slight increase over 2014 as the result of the opening of a second service location)
2016	4% of sales

(continued)

TABLE 8.5 **Continued**

Land, buildings, and equipment

2015	$100,000 in equipment purchases and capital improvements made to existing buildings
2016	$275,000 in capital improvements, including a $100,000 real estate purchase and $175,000 in buildings and equipment

Accounts payable

Historic	Accounts payable have trended down to 5.1% of sales in 2014 from 13.6% of sales in 2013 because of the implementation of more effective collection methods (a slightly higher level of accounts payable will be projected for the future)
2015	7% of sales
2016	7% of sales

Long-term debt

2015	$75,000 reduction in long-term debt from earnings
2016	$150,000 will be borrowed to finance $275,000 to acquire land, equipment, and buildings (the balance of the acquisition costs will be funded from earnings)

a new restaurant is $101,000 per year, the average price for a fitness drink is $2.75, and the variable cost (or cost of goods sold) for each drink is $1.10, then the break-even point for the new restaurant is as follows:

$101,000 (total fixed costs)/($2.75 − $1.10) or $1.65 = 61,212 units

This number means that the new restaurant will have to sell 61,212 "units," or fitness drinks, per year to "break even" at the current price of the drinks. That number breaks down to the sale of 170 fitness drinks per day, on average, based on a 360-day year. To determine whether opening the new restaurant is feasible, the managers of New Venture Fitness Drinks would compare this number against the historic sales figures for their other restaurants, making adjustments as appropriate (e.g., the new restaurant may have a better or worse location than the existing restaurants). If selling 170 fitness drinks per day seems unrealistic, then the managers of New Fitness Drinks might opt to not open the new restaurant, or find ways to lower fixed or variable costs or increase revenues. An obvious way to increase revenues is to raise the price of the fitness drinks, if that option is realistic given the competitive nature of the marketplace.

Pro Forma Financial Statements

A firm's pro forma financial statements are similar to its historical financial statements except that they look forward rather than track the past. New ventures typically offer pro forma statements, but well-managed established firms also maintain these statements as part of their routine financial planning process and to help prepare budgets. The preparation of pro forma statements also helps firms rethink their strategies and make adjustments if necessary. For example, if the pro forma statements predict a downturn in profitability, a firm can make operational changes, such as increasing prices or decreasing expenses, to help prevent the decrease in profitability from actually happening.[22]

LEARNING OBJECTIVE

7. Explain the purpose of pro forma financial statements.

Pro forma financial statements look forward rather than backwards. They help entrepreneurs establish budgets and plan for the future.

2/John Lamb/Ocean/Corbis

A firm's pro forma financial statements should not be prepared in isolation. Instead, they should be created in conjunction with the firm's overall planning activities. For example, it's often critical to have a good sense of how quickly a firm can raise money. Sometimes a firm has a good product or service, good demand, and knows how much capital it needs to maintain a sufficient cash flow, but it can't raise the money in time. This is what happened to Wise Acre Frozen Treats, as illustrated in this chapter's "What Went Wrong?" feature. The Wide Acre Frozen Treats case is a good example of how one aspect of financial management (i.e., raising money) can have a dramatic impact on another aspect of financial management (i.e., maintaining a sufficient cash flow).

The following sections explain the development of pro forma financial statements for New Venture Fitness Drinks.

Pro Forma Income Statement

Once a firm forecasts its future income and expenses, the creation of the **pro forma income statement** is merely a matter of plugging in the numbers. Table 8.6 shows the pro forma income statement for New Venture Fitness Drinks. Recall that net sales for New Venture Fitness Drinks are forecast to increase by 40 percent from 2014 to 2015 and by 25 percent from 2015 to 2016, and that its cost of sales has averaged 47.5 percent of net sales. In the pro forma income statement, the constant ratio method of forecasting is used to forecast the cost of sales and general and administrative expenses, meaning that these items are projected to remain at the same percentage of sales in the future as they were in the past (which is the mathematical equivalent of saying that they will increase at the same rate of sales). Depreciation, other income, and several other items that are not directly tied to sales are figured separately—using reasonable estimates. The most dramatic change is "other income," which jumps significantly from 2014 to 2015. New Venture Fitness Drinks anticipates a significant increase in this category as the result of the renegotiation of a licensing agreement for one of its fitness drinks that is sold by another company.

WHAT WENT WRONG?

Be Careful What You Wish For: How Growing Too Quickly Overwhelmed One Company's Cash Flow

When Jim Picariello started Wise Acre Frozen Treats, no other company was making organic popsicles from unrefined sweeteners. Working out of a makeshift kitchen in 2006, Picariello developed his recipes using maple syrup and honey. He worked alone for a year and a half before hiring his first employee. About that time, his frozen popsicles really took off; by 2008, Wise Acre Frozen Treats had 15 employees, a 3,000-square-foot manufacturing facility, and was distributing its product to natural food stores and supermarkets across the East Coast. The company was awarded a contract to distribute to the West Coast. Then, abruptly, Wise Acre Frozen Treats failed. What went wrong?

Here's what happened. In its first year, Wise Acre Frozen Treats grew at a measured pace. It was filling orders for eight stores for a few hundred dollars each, nothing Picariello couldn't handle. Early in its second year, it won the "Most Innovative Product" award out of more than 2,000 products at a large food show called Expo East. That award increased Wise Acre Frozen Treats's profile, and it landed a contract with United National Foods, a huge national distributor, for freezer space in premier stores like Whole Foods and Wegmans. At that time, it seemed that things couldn't have worked out better.

Picariello knew he'd need to raise capital to cover the increased pace of activity. Operating expenses including labor, equipment, ingredients, packaging material, insurance, and design and marketing would all increase. Picariello obtained $300,000 from a local bank and $200,000 from an investment firm. But because Wise Acre Frozen Treats had so many orders to fill, it needed about $1 million to make things work. Picariello approached a local high-net-worth individual who agreed to invest $1 million, and who assured Picariello that he could put together the money quickly. Based on that promise, Picariello placed orders for the additional material and equipment Wise Acre Frozen Treats needed.

The timing of the investor's promise couldn't have been worse. In short order, the economy tanked and the investor reneged on his promise. At that point, Picariello characterized his life as a mad dash between running the company and meeting with potential investors. In regard to potential investors, Wise Acre Frozen Treats found itself in somewhat of a no-man's-land. Although its future was bright, the entrepreneurial venture wasn't big enough yet for investors to take notice. As time went on, serious cash flow difficulties kicked in. According to a blog post that Picariello wrote about Wise Acre Frozen Treats's failure, the company was burning through about $30,000 a month at its peak but didn't have the capital to back it up.

In retrospect, many things lined up well for Wise Acre Frozen Treats. It had a product that sold well, it had national distribution, and it had a business plan that indicated that it would take about two years for the company to break even. Its fatal flaw was that it didn't raise the money it needed before it hit major milestones, like getting the big orders. It literally went from eight stores to dozens to hundreds in a matter of months. From a cash standpoint, the firm lacked what it needed to keep up with its growth.

Questions for Critical Thinking

1. What lessons can be learned from Jim Picariello's agreement with the high-net-worth individual, who agreed to invest $1 million in Wise Acre Frozen Treats and then reneged on the agreement when the economy turned sour?
2. Why is it that a company can grow too fast? If Wise Acre Frozen Treats significantly increased its sales, why wouldn't its increased income provide more than enough cash to even out its cash flow?
3. Besides cash flow difficulties, what other problems can a firm experience by growing too quickly?
4. If Jim Picariello starts another company, make a list of the things you think he'll do differently as a result of his Wise Acre Frozen Treats experience.

Sources: J. Picariello, "My Company Grew Too Fast—and Went Out of Business," CBS Moneywatch, available at http://www.cbsnews.com/news/my-company-grew-too-fast-and-went-out-of-business/, posted on August 12, 2010, accessed on August 28, 2014; L. Petrecca, "Fast Growth Isn't Always Good: A Big Influx of Orders Can Be Overwhelming," *USA Today*, September 13, 2010, 1B.

Pro Forma Balance Sheet

The **pro forma balance sheet** provides a firm a sense of how its activities will affect its ability to meet its short-term liabilities and how its finances will evolve over time. It can also quickly show how much of a firm's money will be tied up in accounts receivable, inventory, and equipment. The pro forma balance sheet is also used to project the overall financial soundness of a company. For example, a firm may have a very aggressive set of pro forma income

TABLE 8.6   **Pro Forma Income Statement for New Venture Fitness Drinks, Inc.**

	2014 Actual	2015 Projected	2016 Projected
Net sales	$586,600	$821,200	$1,026,500
Cost of sales	268,900	390,000	487,600
Gross profit	317,700	431,200	538,900
Operating expenses			
Selling, general, and administrative expenses	117,800	205,300	256,600
Depreciation	13,500	18,500	22,500
Operating income	186,400	207,400	259,800
Other income			
Interest income	1,900	2,000	2,000
Interest expense	(15,000)	(17,500)	(17,000)
Other income (expense), net	10,900	20,000	20,000
Income before income taxes	184,200	211,900	264,800
Income tax expense	53,200	63,600	79,400
Net income	131,000	148,300	185,400
Earnings per share	1.31	1.48	1.85

statements that project rapidly increasing growth and profitability. However, if this rapid growth and profitability push the firm's debt ratio to 75 percent (which is extremely high), investors may conclude that there is too much risk involved for the firm to be an attractive investment.

The pro forma balance sheet for New Venture Fitness Drinks is shown in Table 8.7. Note that the company's projected change in retained earnings each year is consistent with its projected net income for the same period on its pro forma income statements. The same approach was used to construct the pro forma balance sheets as the pro forma income statements. For each item listed under current assets and current liabilities, the item's historical percentage of sales was used to project its future percentage of sales. Several of the numbers were adjusted slightly upward, such as inventory levels and accounts payable, to reflect the potential impact of the opening of the second restaurant.

In regard to property, plant, and equipment, New Venture Fitness Drinks plans to invest $100,000 in 2015 and $275,000 in 2016. The pro forma balance sheet shows a corresponding increase in valuation in this category for 2015 and 2016, respectively. The company's projected long-term debt for 2015 and 2016 reflects changes resulting from principal reductions from cash flow and increased borrowing to fund the property, plant, and equipment purchases just mentioned. These transactions are reflected in the pro forma statement of cash flows for New Venture Fitness Drinks.

Pro Forma Statement of Cash Flows

The **pro forma statement of cash flows** shows the projected flow of cash into and out of the company during a specified period. The most important function of the pro forma statement of cash flows is to project whether the firm will

TABLE 8.7 **Pro Forma Balance Sheets for New Venture Fitness Drinks, Inc.**

Assets	December 31, 2014	Projected 2015	Projected 2016
Current assets			
Cash and cash equivalents	$63,800	$53,400	$80,200
Accounts receivable, less allowance for doubtful accounts	39,600	57,500	71,900
Inventories	19,200	32,900	41,000
Total current assets	122,600	143,800	193,100
Property, plant, and equipment			
Land	260,000	260,000	360,000
Buildings and equipment	412,000	512,000	687,000
Total property, plant, and equipment	672,000	772,000	1,047,000
Less: accumulated depreciation	65,000	83,500	106,000
Net property, plant, and equipment	607,000	688,500	941,000
Total assets	729,600	832,300	1,134,100
Liabilities and shareholders' equity			
Current liabilities			
Accounts payable	30,200	57,500	71,900
Accrued expenses	9,900	12,000	14,000
Total current liabilities	40,100	69,500	85,900
Long-term liabilities			
Long-term debt	249,500	174,500	274,500
Total long-term liabilities	249,500	174,500	274,500
Total liabilities	289,600	244,000	360,400
Shareholders' equity			
Common stock (100,000 shares)	10,000	10,000	10,000
Retained earnings	430,000	578,300	763,700
Total shareholders' equity	440,000	588,300	773,700
Total liabilities and shareholders' equity	729,600	832,300	1,134,100

have sufficient cash to meet its needs. As with the historical statement of cash flows, the pro forma statement of cash flows is broken into three activities: operating activities, investing activities, and financing activities. Close attention is typically paid to the section on operating activities because it shows how changes in the company's accounts receivable, accounts payable, and inventory levels affect the cash that it has available for investing and finance activities. If any of these items increases at a rate that is faster than the company's annual increase in sales, it typically raises a red flag. For example, an increase in accounts receivable, which is money that is owed to a company by its customers, decreases the amount of cash that it has available for investment or finance activities. If accounts receivable gets out of hand, it may jeopardize a company's ability to fund its growth or service its debt.

The pro forma consolidated statement of cash flows for New Venture Fitness Drinks is shown in Table 8.8. The figures appearing on the statement come directly, or are calculated directly, from the pro forma income statement and the pro forma balance sheet. The one exception is that the last line of each statement of cash flows, which reflects the company's cash balance at the end of the period, becomes the first line of the company's balance sheet for the next period. The pro forma statement of cash flows for New Venture Fitness Drinks shows healthy cash balances at the end of each projected period and shows that investment activities are being funded more by earnings than by debt. This scenario reflects a company that is generating sufficient cash flow to fund the majority of its growth without overly relying on debt or investment capital.

In regard to dividends, the pro forma statement of cash flows shows that New Venture Fitness Drinks is not planning to pay a dividend to its stockholders in 2015 and 2016. Recall that New Venture Fitness Drinks is incorporated and has stockholders even though it is not traded on an organized exchange. If New Venture Fitness Drinks were planning to pay a dividend, the projected dividend payments would show up under financing activities and would

TABLE 8.8   Pro Forma Statement of Cash Flows for New Venture Fitness Drinks, Inc.

	December 31, 2014	Projected 2015	Projected 2016
Cash flows from operating activities			
Net income	$131,000	$148,300	$185,400
Changes in working capital			
Depreciation	13,500	18,500	22,500
Increase (decrease) in accounts receivable	9,300	(17,900)	(14,400)
Increase (decrease) in accrued expenses	1,900	2,100	2,000
Increase (decrease) in inventory	1,200	(13,700)	(8,100)
Increase (decrease) in accounts payable	(16,700)	27,300	14,400
Total adjustments	9,200	16,300	16,400
Net cash provided by operating activities	140,200	164,600	201,800
Cash flows from investing activities			
Purchase of building and equipment	(250,500)	(100,000)	(275,000)
Net cash flows provided by investing activities	(250,500)	(100,000)	(275,000)
Cash flows from financing activities			
Proceeds from increase in long-term debt	119,500	—	100,000
Principle reduction in long-term debt		(75,000)	
Net cash flows provided by financing activities			
Increase in cash	9,200	(10,400)	26,800
Cash and cash equivalents at the beginning of the year	54,600	63,800	53,400
Cash and cash equivalents at the end of the year	63,800	53,400	80,200

reduce the amount of cash available for investing and financing activities. It is common for a new firm to invest the majority of its cash in activities that fund its growth, such as property, plant, and equipment purchases, rather than pay dividends.

Ratio Analysis

The same financial ratios used to evaluate a firm's historical financial statements should be used to evaluate the pro forma financial statements. This work is completed so the firm can get a sense of how its projected financial performance compares to its past performance and how its projected activities will affect its cash position and its overall financial soundness.

The historical financial ratios and projected ratios for New Venture Fitness Drinks are shown in Table 8.9. The profitability ratios show a slight decline from the historical period to the projected. This indicates that the projected increase in assets and corresponding sales will not produce income quite as efficiently as has been the case historically. Still, the numbers are strong, and no dramatic changes are projected.

The liquidity ratios show a consistently healthy ratio of current assets to current liabilities, suggesting that the firm should be able to cover its short-term liabilities without difficulty. The overall financial stability ratios indicate promising trends. The debt ratio drops from an actual of 39.7 percent in 2014 to a projected 31.8 percent in 2016. The debt-to-equity ratio shows an even more dramatic drop, indicating that an increasing portion of the firm's assets is being funded by equity rather than debt.

In summary, it is extremely important for a firm to understand its financial position at all times and for new ventures to base their financial projections on solid numbers. As mentioned earlier, regardless of how successful a firm is in other areas, it must succeed financially to remain strong and viable.

TABLE 8.9 **Ratio Analysis of Historical and Pro Forma Financial Statements for New Venture Fitness Drinks, Inc.**

	Historical			Projected	
Ratio	2012	2013	2014	2015	2016
Profitability ratios					
Return on assets	14.7%	18.7%	21.4%	19.0%	18.9%
Return on equity	24.9%	31.0%	35.0%	28.9%	27.2%
Profit margin	13.6%	17.9%	22.3%	18.1%	18.1%
Liquidity ratios					
Current	2.35	2.26	3.05	2.07	2.24
Quick	1.96	1.89	2.58	1.60	1.78
Overall financial stability ratios					
Debt	42.3%	37.4%	39.7%	29.3%	31.8%
Debt to equity	73.2%	59.8%	65.8%	41.5%	46.6%

Chapter Summary

LO1. To pursue an opportunity and to turn that pursuit into a viable venture, entrepreneurs require financial capital. Financial management deals with this reality. More specifically, financial management is concerned with two activities: raising money and managing a company's finances in a way that achieves the highest rate of return.

LO2. Profitability, liquidity, efficiency, and stability are the four main financial objectives of entrepreneurial firms. Profitability is the ability of a firm to earn a profit, liquidity is the ability of a company to meet or satisfy its short-term obligations, efficiency deals with how productively a firm uses its assets relative to its revenue and profits, and stability is the strength and vigor of the firm's overall financial standing.

LO3. The process of financial management includes the activities a firm takes to determine if its financial objectives are being met. Several documents are foundational to an entrepreneur's efforts to assess the degree to which a firm's financial objectives are being satisfied. These documents, as follows, are prepared regularly: (1) financial statements (a written report that describes a firm's health from a quantitative perspective), (2) forecasts (which are estimates of a firm's future income and expenses, based on its past performance, current situation, and its future plans), and (3) budgets (which are itemized forecasts of a firm's income, expenses, and capital requirements).

LO4. Historical financial statements reflect past performance. Typically, these documents are prepared on a quarterly and annual basis. The Securities and Exchange Commission (SEC) requires that publicly traded firms prepare and submit these documents. Pro forma financial statements are projections for expected performance in future periods. These projections are based on forecasts and are usually completed for two or three years into the future. Unlike historical financial statements, firms are not required to make their pro forma statements publicly available.

LO5. Historical financial statements include an income statement, a balance sheet, and a statement of cash flow. An income statement reflects the results of a firm's operations over a specified period of time. It records all the revenues and expenses for the given period and shows whether the firm is making a profit or is experiencing a loss. A balance sheet is a snapshot of a company's assets, its liabilities, and owners' equity. While income statements cover a specified period of time, a balance sheet is a snapshot of the firm at a specific point in time. A statement of cash flows summarizes the changes in a firm's cash position for a specified period of time and details why the changes occurred. This statement allows a firm to understand how much cash it has on hand and how its cash was used over a period of time.

LO6. Forecasts are predictions of a firm's future sales, expenses, income, and capital expenditures. A firm's forecasts provide the basis for its pro forma financial statements. When developed effectively, forecasts provide the foundation for a firm to prepare its future-oriented pro forma financial statements. Completely new firms typically base their forecasts on a good-faith estimate of sales and on industry averages (based on a percentage of sales) or the experiences of similar start-ups for cost of goods sold and other expenses. Once a firm has completed its sales forecast, it must forecast its costs of sales as well as the other items on its income statement. The most common way to do this is to use the percent-of-sales method, which is a method for expressing each expense item as a percentage of sales.

LO7. Pro forma financial statements are similar to historical financial statements except that they look forward rather than backward. Preparing pro forma statements helps entrepreneurs think about the quality of the strategies being implemented by their firm and to make adjustments to those strategies if necessary. Considered to be part of a firm's planning efforts, firms prepare a pro forma income statement, a pro forma balance sheet, and a pro forma statement of cash flows to help them anticipate and prepare for future activities and their anticipated outcomes.

Key Terms

10-K, **287**
accounts receivable, **284**
assumptions sheet, **295**
balance sheet, **289**
break-even point, **297**
budgets, **285**
constant ratio method of forecasting, **297**
cost of sales, **288**
current assets, **289**
current liabilities, **291**
current ratio, **291**
debt-to-equity ratio, **284**
efficiency, **284**
financial management, **283**
financial ratios, **286**
financial statement, **284**

financing activities, **293**
fixed assets, **289**
forecasts, **295**
historical financial statements, **287**
income statement, **288**
inventory, **284**
investing activities, **293**
liquidity, **284**
long-term liabilities, **291**
net sales, **288**
operating activities, **293**
operating expenses, **289**
other assets, **289**
owners' equity, **291**
percent-of-sales method, **297**

price-to-earnings (P/E) ratio, **289**
pro forma balance sheet, **301**
pro forma financial statements, **287**
pro forma income statement, **300**
pro forma statement of cash flows, **302**
profit margin, **289**
profitability, **284**
regression analysis, **296**
sales forecast, **295**
stability, **284**
statement of cash flows, **292**
working capital, **291**

Review Questions

8-1. What are the two primary functions of the financial management of a firm?

8-2. What are the four main financial objectives of a firm?

8-3. What is the difference between historical and pro forma financial statements?

8-4. What is meant by the term *efficiency* as it relates to the financial management of a firm?

8-5. What is meant by the term *stability* as it relates to the financial management of a firm?

8-6. What is the purpose of a forecast? What factors does a firm use to create its forecasts of future income and expenses?

8-7. On what factors or conditions do completely new firms base their forecasts?

8-8. What is the purpose of an income statement? What are the three numbers that receive the most attention when evaluating an income statement? Why are these numbers important?

8-9. Why do we need to compare a firm's financial ratio to industry norms?

8-10. How does a firm compute its price-to-earnings ratio? Why does a high price-to-earnings ratio indicate that the stock market thinks the firm will grow?

8-11. What is the purpose of a balance sheet?

8-12. What are the major categories of assets and liabilities on a balance sheet? Briefly explain each category.

8-13. How do you compute a firm's debt ratio? What is the significance of this ratio?

8-14. How does a firm compute its current ratio? Is this a relatively important or unimportant financial ratio? Explain your answer.

8-15. What is the purpose of a statement of cash flows?

8-16. What are the three separate categories of activities that are reflected on a firm's statement of cash flows? Briefly explain the importance of each activity.

8-17. What is the purpose of financial ratios? Why are financial ratios particularly useful in helping a firm interpret its financial statements?

8-18. What is a "break-even point"?

8-19. Why is a firm's sales forecast the basis for most of its other forecasts?

8-20. Why do firms prepare pro forma balance sheets?

Application Questions

8-21. Kirsten, a friend of yours, plans to open a fashion boutique that will sell women's clothing and accessories. She told you that she leafed through several books on how to prepare forecasts and pro forma financial statements but that the books were geared toward existing firms that have several years of historical financial statements on which to base their projections. If Kirsten asked for your advice about how to prepare forecasts for a completely new women's fashion boutique, what would you tell her?

8-22. Suppose a friend of yours showed you the pro forma income statements for his start-up and exclaimed excitedly that during the first three years of operations his firm will make a net income of $150,000 per year, which is just the amount of money ($450,000) the firm will need to pay off a three-year loan. Given your study of this chapter, why is it that your friend may not actually have $450,000 in cash, even though his pro forma income statements say that he will earn that amount of money?

8-23. Sammy Hench has savings of $50,000 and is planning to invest in a business that will give him good returns. For the last six months, he has been investigating all types of business ventures and has finally decided to buy over an existing company. However, Sammy does not have any entrepreneurial or financial background that can assist him in making the right decision. His friends have advised him to look at a potential business's historical financial statements. Is this advice helpful? How can you assist Sammy and explain to him why should he do so?

8-24. In groups of three, visit a business outlet in your vicinity. With the owner or the manager's consent, prepare a sales forecast for the years 2015 and 2016 based on the outlet's sales from 2012 to 2014. You may present the answer in class.

8-25. As a lecturer for the class on Entrepreneurship Studies, you have been invited by the Business Society to share your subject knowledge with the club members. They have requested you to present on the importance of understanding financial management of an entrepreneurial firm. Share some of the key points to be highlighted during your presentation.

8-26. Jorge Martinez is thinking about buying an existing printing business and has been carefully studying the records of the business to get a good handle on its historical financial performance. Jorge heard that you are taking a class in entrepreneurship and asks you, "What suggestions do you have for me to make the best use of this financial information (i.e., three years of audited income statements, balance sheets, and statements of cash flow)?" What suggestions would you give Jorge for making the maximum use of the financial statements?

8-27. A friend came to you for advice. She needs to prepare a business plan for her potential investor. She has prepared a very detailed financial plan and is quite confident of it. However, she is not sure of what is to be included in the section on financial objectives of her firm. Advise her.

8-28. What items on the left side (or top) and what items on the right side (or bottom) of a firm's balance sheet should receive the greatest scrutiny? In regard to each of these items, what are the most important factors that a new venture should focus on to maintain its overall financial health?

8-29. Suppose a colleague of yours is gearing up to write a business plan for a business she intends to start. She told you she plans to prepare the financial statements first to get that job out of the way before she tackles the rest of the plan. What is the flaw in your colleague's logic as described to you?

YOU BE THE VC 8.1 COMPANY: Spindrift Soda

• Web: www.spindriftfresh.com • Facebook: Spindriftfresh • Twitter: @Spindriftfresh

Business Idea: Make a specialty soda that is made entirely from just fresh-squeezed fruit juice, cane sugar, and carbonated water rather than sweetened syrup, juice concentrates, and preservatives.

Pitch: The knocks leveled against traditional sodas, like Coke and Pepsi, have created a market for small, specialty sodas such as Jones's and Boylan's. Still, most specialty sodas are made from sweetened syrups, and in many ways they are not that dissimilar from the major brands. Spindrift Soda provides a healthy and refreshing alternative. It is a carbonated beverage that is made from triple-purified sparkling water, fresh-squeezed fruit or berry puree (pulp and all), and cane sugar. Unlike almost every other soda on the market, it contains no syrups, no juice concentrates, no additives, and no preservatives. It's also light, bright, and tastes great.

Spindrift Soda is made every four to six weeks in small batches, and is shipped cold. It took nearly a year for Spindrift's founder, Bill Creelman, to figure out how to make it. Lots of people make fresh-squeezed juices on a small scale, and serve them to their families or sell them at a farmer's market. The challenge was to incorporate fresh-squeezed juices into a carbonated beverage at scale. Temperature-sensitive juices can't sit in vats the way syrups can. They have to be delivered in small jugs, stored properly, and then opened at the last minute and mixed in by hand. They're also hard to distribute to stores. Most sodas ship warm, like in the Coke or Pepsi trucks you see on the road. Spindrift Soda ships cold, which preserves its freshness. Creelman found distributors of fish, produce, and cheese willing to carry his product on their trucks. An added benefit of using fresh distributors is that they deliver daily, which allows them to quickly replenish Spindrift Soda inventories in stores when the stores are running low.

Spindrift's mission is to change how America experiences soda. Spindrift sodas come in six flavors including Blackberry, Sparking Orange Mango, Sparkling Lemonade, Sparkling Grapefruit, Cranberry Raspberry, and Half and Half. Spindrift also makes three flavors of bottled water including Tangerine, Lemon, and Raspberry Lime. Its beverages are truly fresh. For example, Spindrift Sparkling Grapefruit contains the following ingredients: triple-filtered sparkling water, fresh-squeezed juices (fresh pink grapefruit juice, fresh lemon juice), cane sugar, natural flavor, fruit, and vegetable juice for color. Now that's a list of ingredients that anyone can feel good about serving their family.

8-30. Based on the material covered in this chapter, what questions would you ask the firm's founders before making your funding decision? What answers would satisfy you?

8-31. If you had to make your decision on just the information provided in the pitch and on the company's website, would you fund this company? Why or why not?

YOU BE THE VC 8.2 COMPANY: How Do You Roll?

• Web: www.howdoyouroll.com • Facebook: HDYRsushi • Twitter: @How_Do_You_Roll

Business Idea: Create a sushi restaurant that allows customers to "build their own sushi" by allowing them to select their own kind of wrap, rice, veggies, proteins, and toppings.

Pitch: People who like sushi have two choices. They can go to a fancy sushi restaurant and pay a fancy bill. Or they can go to a grocery store and buy sushi that is supposedly made daily. Now there is a third option. How Do You Roll? is a fast-casual sushi restaurant that combines the quality of a high-end restaurant with the convenience of a grocery store.

How Do You Roll? is the brainchild of two brothers, Yuen Yung and Peter Yung. Both grew up in the restaurant industry. Their parents had several Chinese restaurants, and at the tender age of eight or nine they both started working in their parents' restaurants. How Do You Roll? launched with a single store in Austin, Texas. It lets the customer be the chef by allowing customers to pick their own ingredients. The customer approaches a counter and is led through four steps:

Step 1 Choose Your Wrap: Traditional (seaweed) or modern (soy)

Step 2 Eat Your Veggies: Choose up to three healthy vegetables

Step 3 Stuff Your Roll: Choose one or more of our fresh meats

Step 4 Top It Off: Indulge in one or more of our specialty toppings or sides

Through this process customers personalize their sushi rolls. The meal, which consists of a six-piece sushi roll and a fountain drink, costs an average of $8 to $11. How Do You Roll's business model is also designed to make sushi accessible to people who won't touch raw ingredients or even fish. There is cooked chicken and beef available as substitutes. Along with sushi, each restaurant also sells miso soup, seaweed salad, and green tea ice cream. It is an experience that is totally unique in the sushi industry. It also provides fast-casual food patrons an alternative to the standard fare of burgers and chicken sandwiches.

How Do You Roll? is growing via franchising. It currently has eight franchise units and two company-owned stores. It has penned several development agreements, which may add up to 70 additional franchise units over the next 10 years. According to the company, it costs between $304,295 and $508,780 to open a How Do You Roll? restaurant. The initial franchise fee is $30,000, and the ongoing royalty is 7 percent of gross sales.

In spring 2013, Yuen Yung and Peter Yung pitched the business on the popular ABC show *Shark Tank.* Along with a $1 million investment from shark Kevin O'Leary, Yung said restaurant sales jumped 30 percent. In addition, he and his brother received more than 600 inquiries from potential franchisees interested in opening How Do You Roll? restaurants.

8-32. Based on the material covered in this chapter, what questions would you ask the firm's founders before making your funding decision? What answers would satisfy you?

8-33. If you had to make your decision on just the information provided in the pitch and on the company's website, would you fund this firm? Why or why not?

CASE 8.1

Fundbox: Designed to Help Small Businesses Minimize Cash Flow Shortfalls

• *Web: www.fundbox.com* • *Facebook: Fundbox* • *Twitter: @fundbox*

Introduction

Fundbox is an entrepreneurial start-up that offers 12-week loans to small businesses. The loans are tied to specific invoices that the businesses have outstanding. Payment for the loans (including principle, interest, and fees) is deducted from a company's bank account in 12 equal amounts on a weekly basis. Once the money for the invoice comes in, the loan can be paid in full. There is no penalty for early payment.

Fundbox was launched in 2012 by Yuval Ariav, Eyal Shinar, and Tomer Michael, who are technological innovators and financial professionals. The firm's mission is to offer small businesses a common-sense approach to cash-flow management.

The Problem

Almost all small businesses experience cash flow shortfalls. Think of how business works. Businesses often win a contract, purchase the materials and supplies that are needed to produce the firm's product or service, pay employees, and then have to wait 30 to 60 days to receive payment from the customer. This scenario causes even healthy businesses to be short on cash at times. There are two traditional solutions to the problem. The first is to maintain a line of credit at a bank. A line of credit allows a business to borrow up to a certain amount of money and pay it down when money comes in. The problem with this solution is that banks are increasingly reluctant to establish lines of credit for small businesses. Banks also don't like to make short-term loans for specific amounts. The second solution is invoice factoring. With invoice factoring, a company sells its invoices to a factoring company in

exchange for a lump sum of money (say $4,500 for a $5,000 invoice). The factoring company then proceeds to collect the money from the company's customer. Many businesses don't like this alternative because it involves a third party having a direct relationship with their customer. If the factoring company becomes aggressive in trying to collect the invoice, it could affect the business's relationship with its customer.

To further complicate things, Days Sales Outstanding (DSO), or the time between when a business issues an invoice and the payment is received, has been increasing across the board in recent years.

Fundbox

Fundbox offers a novel solution to the problem. When an invoice comes in, it will issue a 12-week loan for the amount of the invoice. Because the loan is matched with a specific receivable, it prevents the repayment of the loan from creating a new cash flow problem for the business. The interest rate on the loan is tied to both the creditworthiness of the borrower and the company that owes the amount on the invoice. This practice encourages borrowers to borrow money on invoices that they are confident will be paid. For example, say a business does $10,000 of work for Home Depot. It knows Home Depot will pay the invoice, but Home Depot may operate on a net 30 or net 60 day payment schedule (meaning that it has 30 days or 60 days to make the payment). If the business has an account with Fundbox, it could get the $10,000 right away, minus Fundbox's fee. Weekly payments would start immediately. When Home Depot paid the invoice, the loan to Fundbox would be paid in full. This scenario allows a business to get its money sooner rather than later and avoid short-term gaps in its cash flow. The interest rate for Fundbox's service varies. According to a review published by the FitSmall Business blog, rates range from 0.7 percent to 3 percent per month, with the typical borrower at about 2 percent per month. About 40 percent of businesses that apply are accepted by Fundbox.

Fundbox uses sophisticated data analytics to build a picture of a potential borrower's overall financial health and likelihood of repayment. Fundbox doesn't talk much about how this actually works. It is a core feature of their business and considered to be a trade secret.

Partnerships with Bookkeeping Companies

To make it easy for clients, Fundbox has established partnerships with many of the top online bookkeeping programs, including Quickbooks, Freshbooks, Xero, and Harvest. For Freshbooks, for example, once a business-person creates a Fundbox account (sign-up is free), it can easily be tied to the business's Freshbooks account. When an invoice is entered into Freshbooks, Fundbox will analyze all pertinent data to see if a 12-week loan to cover the amount of the invoice can be made. The business will receive an e-mail message indicating whether a loan can be made. The business can then evaluate the terms of the loan and either accept or pass on the offer. If the offer is accepted, the funds will be deposited in the business's bank account, usually within a day. Fundbox only works with the borrower. In the Home Depot example provided above, if the borrower defaulted on Fundbox's loan, Fundbox would not try to collect the loan amount from Home Depot. Each borrower is given a maximum line of credit from Fundbox, so offers will not be made on all invoices.

B2B Players

Fundbox's loans are most suitable for business to business (B2B) companies. These are businesses that do work for other businesses and issue invoices for the work they do. Most business to consumer companies (B2C) are paid at the point of sale. For example, when you eat at a restaurant or buy a book from Amazon.com, you pay for it right away. The B2B category includes freelancers who do work for businesses. These are individuals who may benefit especially from Fundbox's service. For example, an independent software developer may spend 100 hours developing a mobile app for a small business and invoice the business $15,000. If the payment terms are net 60, the business will have 60 days to pay the bill. Via Fundbox, the independent software developer could get his money right away. For a freelancer, getting money sooner rather than later may make the difference in making rent or paying a mortgage on time.

Fundbox's Future

According to TechCrunch, Fundbox launched in stealth mode, presumably to test its service and work the bugs out. Since it has gone live, it has signed up thousands of active users (mostly small businesses) and clears tens of thousands of invoices daily in 42 states.

Fundbox is among a growing number of "alternative lenders" that small businesses are relying on, largely because banks have pulled back from small business lending. Firms offering services that are similar to those provided by Fundbox include Kabbage, OnDeck, and Lending Club. What is unique about Fundbox is that it connects loans to specific invoices, which helps small businesses minimize cash flow challenges.

Fundbox has partnerships with many of the top online bookkeeping programs. If a business has a Freshbooks account, for example, it can easily be tied to the business's Fundbox's account.

Creativa Images/Shutterstock

(continued)

The downside to using Fundbox as a fix for cash flow gaps is the costs involved. While the loans are short-term, an interest rate of between 0.7 percent and 3 percent per month, as reported above, results in a high annual APR. The best thing for any small business to do is to check with an accountant regarding the wisdom of using Fundbox or a similar product to minimize cash flow shortfalls.

Fundbox has raised $17.5 million from a collection of venture capitalists to fund and grow its operations.

Discussion Questions

8-34. Toward the beginning of this case, the following statement appears: "Almost all small businesses experience cash flow shortfalls." What is cash flow? Why is cash flow so critical to an entrepreneurial firm's success? Why do almost all small businesses experience cash flow shortfalls?

8-35. As explained in this chapter, a firm's statement of cash flows is divided into three separate activities. Which of the activities from the statement of cash flows would be affected by a firm's decision to use Fundbox's service? What are some of the potential effects of a small entrepreneurial firm's decision to use Fundbox on the components of that firm's statement of cash flows?

8-36. If Fundbox's co-founders (Yuval Ariav, Eyal Shinar, and Tomer Michael) were to ask your advice about the importance of pro forma statements to their firm's continuing success, what would you say to them? What pro forma statements would you recommend the co-founders develop and why?

8-37. As a young entrepreneur, what lessons about the financial management of a firm can you learn from the actions taken by the three cofounders of Fundbox?

Sources: L. Rao, "Lending Startup Fundbox Raises $17.5 from Khosla to Help SMBs Improve Cash Flow," TechCrunch, available at http://techcrunch.com/2014/04/10/lending-startup-fundbox-raises-17-5m-from-khosla-to-help-smbs-improve-cash-flow/, posted on April 10, 2014, accessed on August 29, 2014; M. Prosser, "Fundbox: An Alternative to Invoice Factoring or Discounting," FitSmallBusiness, available at http://fitsmallbusiness.com/fundbox/, posted on August 6, 2014, accessed on August 29, 2014; R. Shafaghi, "Meet: Fundbox—Turn Unpaid Invoices into Cash," available at http://www.freshbooks.com/blog/2014/05/28/meet-fundbox-turn-unpaid-invoices-into-cash/, posted on May 28, 2014, accessed on August 29, 2014.

CASE 8.2

Dell Inc.: How Its Business Model Sweetens Its Financial Statements

• *Web: www.dell.com* • *Facebook: Dell* • *Twitter: @Dell*

Bruce R. Barringer, *Oklahoma State University*

R. Duane Ireland, *Texas A&M University*

Introduction

There are many reasons that Dell Inc. has, for the most part, been successful over the years. Two of the most compelling reasons are its direct sales model and its ultra-efficient global supply chain. While a start-up can't quickly emulate what Dell has done, there are lessons to be learned from Dell's experiences that any start-up can benefit from. Historically at least, Dell's approach to business made it the preferred computer brand for many businesses and consumers. Additionally, the business approach has sweetened Dell's financial statements and its ability to make money.

Dell's Hybrid Sales Approach (Combining Direct Sales and Retail Sales)

Dell was founded in 1988 touting a direct sales model. Rather than selling through stores like Sears and Best Buy, Dell sold direct, first over the phone and then via the Internet. Its business model not only allowed businesses and consumers to "customize" their computers, but also had profound positive effects on Dell's supply chain and financial activities. For a period of time after Dell launched its business model, other PC manufacturers, like Hewlett-Packard, had to forecast demand, build computers, ship them to retailers, hope they'd sell, and then wait 30 days or more for payment. Dell sidestepped all of this via its direct sales model. It received orders, built computers, and then shipped them to the buyers via UPS or FedEx. There was no "forecasting" of demand because demand was determined in real time, and Dell never got stuck with outdated computers because it maintained no inventory. Its customers also essentially financed its operations by paying in advance.

Dell maintained this business model from 1988 until 2007, when it shifted its sales strategy. Rather than selling exclusively directly, it decided to transition to a hybrid model, where it would continue to emphasize direct sales, but also sell a portion of its product line through retailers such as Best Buy, Staples, and Walmart. The main reason for the change was that Dell was shifting its emphasis from targeting businesses to targeting businesses, consumers, and international markets. The thinking was that it needed to have its computers side-by-side with its competitors in consumer channels if it hoped to become the preferred computer vendor for consumers along with businesses. It was also problematic to sell exclusively directly in some international markets.

Dell doesn't disclose the percentage of its sales that originate through its website or over the phone (its original direct-sales model) versus the percentage of its sales that come through retail outlets. It's clear, though, that a significant portion of its sales now occur online and over the phone and an increasing percentage of its sales are generated through retail outlets.

Dell's Supply Chain and Manufacturing Strategy

Dell's hybrid sales model has a significant impact on its supply chain and manufacturing strategy. It can produce computers in a highly efficient manner, because it does not have to forecast demand and keep excess inventory on hand for a large percentage of its sales. In fact, when Dell receives an order, via the Internet or on the phone, its suppliers are alerted in real time and, periodically throughout the day, deliver parts to Dell's assembly facilities where the computers are assembled, configured, and shipped. It also searches on a worldwide basis to find the best combinations of quality and cost for parts, which results in a complex yet highly efficient supply chain. In fact, in his 2005 book *The World Is Flat,* Thomas Friedman asked Dell to retrace the supply chain for his laptop computer, to determine where it was made, how many suppliers were involved, and how it reached his front door. The total supply chain for Friedman's Dell Inspiron 600m notebook computer, including suppliers of suppliers, involved about 400 companies in North America, Europe, and primarily Asia. The computer was codesigned in Austin, Texas, in Taiwan by a team of Dell engineers, and by a team of Taiwanese notebook designers (a globally distributed team can work 24 hours a day). Its final assembly was in a Dell factory in Penang, Malaysia. It was flown from Penang, Malaysia, to Nashville, Tennessee, on a China Airlines 747, the only 747 that lands in Nashville, other than when Air Force One is in town. It was delivered to Friedman's home via UPS.

To further increase efficiencies and reduce the amount of capital it must maintain, Dell is currently transitioning from this model and is relying increasingly on contract manufacturers.

Financial Advantages of Dell's Hybrid Sales Approach and Its Supply Chain and Manufacturing Strategy

There are direct financial benefits to Dell's hybrid sales approach and its approach to supply chain management and manufacturing. One of the biggest advantages is its inventory turnover. Dell turns its inventory over 31.4 times a year, compared to 13.9 times a year for Hewlett-Packard and 14.6 times a year for the S&P 500 average. Inventory turnover is determined by the following formula (the higher the number the better):

$$\text{Inventory Turnover} = \frac{\text{Cost of Goods Sold}}{\text{Average Inventories}}$$

A high inventory turnover means that a company is converting its inventory into cash quickly. Turning its inventory over quickly allows Dell to generate cash that's used to fund its growth, and to not get caught with out-of-date inventory. An often-told joke in the PC industry is that unsold inventory is like unsold vegetables—it spoils quickly. So maintaining a favorable inventory turnover ratio is critical.

Another ratio that's important is the asset turnover ratio. Asset turnover reflects the amount of sales generated for every dollar's worth of assets. It's calculated using the following formula (the higher the number the better):

$$\text{Asset Turnover} = \frac{\text{Sales}}{\text{Assets}}$$

Dell's asset turnover ratio is 1.26, compared to 1.06 for Hewlett-Packard and 0.34 for the S&P 500 average. Asset turnover denotes the amount of sales generated for every dollar's worth of assets. It's a measure of efficiency in regard to a firm's ability to use its assets to generate sales.

Along with crunching numbers, savvy managers assess the impact of their financial strategies on their overall goals and levels of customer satisfaction. Ultimately, it doesn't matter that a company has attractive-looking financial statements if its customers are starting to go elsewhere. Dell's hybrid sales approach and its supply chain and manufacturing strategy shine in this area too. Because it turns its inventory over quickly, it offers its customers the latest technologies rather than saddling them with products that likely will soon be outdated. It can also pass along the advantages of falling component costs quicker than its competitors can.

The Downside of Pushing Cost Savings Too Far

Although the majority of the decisions that Dell has made have both sweetened its financial statements and pleased its customers, Dell is learning the hard way that cost savings can be pushed too far. In the early 1990s, partly in response to the challenges imposed by its rapid growth, Dell started outsourcing the majority of its call center activities to low-wage countries in Asia and Central America. This strategy led to a chorus of growing complaints about long wait times for customer service calls and poor post-sales support. In response, Dell has spent over $100 million to revive its customer service, including an effort to increase the percentage of full-time Dell employees who staff customer service support lines and reduce its use of part-time and

(continued)

contract workers. The jury is still out on whether Dell has done enough to stem the tide of customer dissatisfaction. Another downside is that Dell pushes its suppliers hard. While most suppliers respond positively, it's hard to gauge the long-term impact in supplier relations by Dell's appearing to assume the role of "taskmaster" in its relationships with its suppliers.

It's also unclear how long Dell's hybrid sales approach will maintain an advantage. Although its inventory turnover number is still strong, it's not as outstanding as it was when Dell sold primarily online and over the phone. In 2004, Dell's inventory turnover was 107.1, but it is 31.4 today. Dell also has a formable competitor in Apple. Apple's inventory turnover is 63.0. It may be unfair to compare Dell directly to Apple, given that Apple is a more diversified company, but the comparison highlights the fact that Dell is no longer a trendsetter in inventory management efficiency. Another challenge that all computer manufacturers face is a global decline in personal computer sales. In slightly different words, global declines in computer sales is the reality of the day, even for premier firms like Dell, Hewlett-Packard, and Apple.

Discussion Questions

8-38. Investigate the financial ratio of inventory turnover. Find current information about Dell (www.hoovers.com is a good starting place) and report whether its inventory turnover is still as impressive as the number mentioned in the case. How does Dell's current inventory turnover ratio compare to that of some of its competitors such as Apple and Hewlett-Packard? Do the same for Dell's asset turnover ratio.

8-39. Locate Dell's most recent 10-K report and either locate or compute what you believe are the three most important financial ratios for Dell. Are the ratios impressive or do they provide you reason for concern?

8-40. If you were the CEO of Dell Inc., what expectations would you reflect when preparing a pro forma income statement for your company?

8-41. What lessons can a young entrepreneurial firm learn from Dell's experiences?

Sources: Dell 10-K report, available at www.sec.gov, for the fiscal year ending February 1, 2013; Financial data, including Inventory Turnover and Asset Turnover ratios, available at www.csimarket.com B. Breen, "Living in Dell Time," *Fast Company*, December 19, 2007.

Endnotes

1. R. C. Moyer, J. R. McGuigan, and R. P. Rao, *Contemporary Financial Management*, 13th ed. (Cincinnati, OH: SouthWestern Cengage Learning, 2015).

2. W. Drover, M. S. Wood, and G. T. Payne, "The Effects of Perceived Control on Venture Capitalist Investment Decisions: A Configurational Perspective," *Entrepreneurship Theory and Practice* 38, no. 4 (2014): 833–861; J. Brinckmann, S. Salomo, and H. G. Gemuenden, "Financial Management Competence of Founding Teams and Growth of New Technology-Based Firms," *Entrepreneurship Theory and Practice* 35, no. 2 (2011): 217–243.

3. W. R. Kerr, J. Lerner, and A. Schoar, "The Consequences of Entrepreneurial Finance: Evidence from Angel Financings," *Review of Financial Studies* 27, no. 1 (2014): 20–55; C. Koropp, D. Grichnik, and F. Kellermanns, "Financial Attitudes in Family Firms: The Moderating Role of Family Commitment," *Journal of Small Business Management* 51, no. 1 (2013): 114–137.

4. G. Michalski, *Value-Based Working Capital Management: Determining Liquid Asset Levels in Entrepreneurial Environments* (New York, NY: Palgrave Macmillan, 2014).

5. J. C. Leach and R. W. Melicher, *Entrepreneurial Finance*, 5th ed. (Cincinnati, OH: SouthWestern Cengage Learning, 2015).

6. J. H. Gittell, *The Southwest Airlines Way* (New York, NY: McGraw-Hill, 2003), 7.

7. G. Cassar, "Industry and Startup Experience on Entrepreneur Forecast Performance in New Firms," *Journal of Business Venturing* 29, no. 1 (2014): 137–151.

8. E. F. Brigham and J. F. Houston, *Fundamentals of Financial Management*, 14th ed. (Cincinnati, OH: SouthWestern Cengage Learning, 2016).

9. B. Gates, *Business @ the Speed of Thought* (New York, NY: Time Warner, 1999), 214.

10. SEC home page, www.sec.gov (accessed August 23, 2014).

11. P. J. Adelman and A. M. Marks, *Entrepreneurial Finance*, 6th ed. (Upper Saddle River, NJ: Prentice Hall, 2014).

12. A. M. Ormiston and L. M. Fraser, *Understanding Financial Statements*, 10th ed. (Upper Saddle River, NJ: Prentice Hall, 2013).

13. L. J. Gitman and C. J. Zutter, *Principles of Managerial Finance*, 7th ed. (Upper Saddle River, NJ: Prentice Hall, 2014); H. Van Auken and S. M. Carraher, "How Do Small Firms Use Financial Statements?" *Academy of Accounting and Financial Studies Proceedings* 16, no. 1 (2011): 35–42.

14. K. P. Schoenebeck and M. P. Holtzman, *Interpreting and Analyzing Financial Statements*, 6th ed. (Upper Saddle River, NJ: Prentice Hall, 2013).

15. S. Anokhin and J. Wincent, "Technological Arbitrage Opportunities and Interindustry Differences in Entry Rates," *Journal of Business Venturing* 29, no. 3 (2014): 437–452; J. H. Block, G. De Vries, J. H. Schumann, and P. Sander, "Trademarks and Venture Capital Evaluation,"

Journal of Business Venturing 29, no. 4 (2014): 525–542.

16. D. M. Cain, D. A. Moore, and U. Haran, "Making Sense of Overconfidence in Market Entry," *Strategic Management Journal*, 2014, in press; T. C. Flatten, A. Engelen, T. Moller, and M. Brettel, "How Entrepreneurial Firms Profit from Pricing Capabilities: An Examination of Technology-Based Ventures," *Entrepreneurship Theory and Practice*, 2014, in press.

17. S. Carraher and H. Van Auken, "The Use of Financial Statements for Decision Making by Small Firms," *Journal of Small Business & Entrepreneurship* 26, no. 3 (2013): 323–336.

18. J. C. Dencker and M. Gruber, "The Effects of Opportunities and Founder Experience on New Firm Performance," *Strategic Management Journal*, 2014, in press.

19. N. D. Sharpe, R. D. De Veaux, and P. Velleman, *Business Statistics*, 3rd ed. (Upper Saddle River, NJ: Prentice Hall, 2014).

20. J. Berk, P. DeMarzo, and J. Harford, *Fundamentals of Corporate Finance*, 3rd ed. (Upper Saddle River, NJ: Prentice Hall, 2014).

21. C. M. Rambo, "Time Required to Break-Even for Small and Medium Enterprises: Evidence from Kenya," *International Journal of Management and Marketing Research* 6, no. 1 (2013): 81–94.

22. R. N. Lussier, J. Corman, and D. C. Kimball, *Entrepreneurial New Venture Skills*, 3rd ed. (New York, NY: Routledge, 2015).

Getting Personal

with **NEXT BIG SOUND**

Co-Founders

DAVID HOFFMAN
BA, School of Education and Social Policy, Northwestern University, 2009

ALEX WHITE
BA, School of Education and Social Policy, Northwestern University, 2010

SAMIR RAYANI
BS, McCormick School of Engineering, Northwestern University, 2009

Dialogue with
David Hoffman

MY BIGGEST SURPRISE AS AN ENTREPRENEUR
Most overnight (success) stories were actually five-plus years

BEST ADVICE I'VE RECEIVED
Trust but verify

MY FAVORITE SMARTPHONE APP
Moves is pretty great

MY BIGGEST WORRY AS AN ENTREPRENEUR
Not building things people love

FAVORITE PERSON I FOLLOW ON TWITTER
@EdwardTufte

WHAT I DO WHEN I'M NOT WORKING
Get curious about the rest of the world

CHAPTER 9

Building a *New-Venture* Team

NEXT BIG SOUND
Hitting the Ground Running

• Web: www.nextbigsound • Facebook: Next Big Sound • Twitter: @nextbigsound

The idea for Next Big Sound started in Troy Henikoff's entrepreneurship class at Northwestern University. It was 2008, and three of the students in the class, Alex White, David Hoffman, and Samir Rayani, hatched an idea for a business in the music industry. Rayani and White had met earlier when White was running the concert booking group on campus. Rayani's job was to sign off on White's spending to bring in acts like Flight of the Conchords and Kanye West. White and Hoffman's paths had crossed earlier, too, in that they both were organizational change majors at Northwestern. In the nearby photo, Alex White is on the left, David Hoffman is in the middle, and Samir Rayani is on the right.

The idea was for a fantasy network for music. Users would create their own fantasy record label, sign artists they believed would become popular, and compete against each other. As part of the class, students presented their ideas to venture capitalists. White, Hoffman, and Rayani pitched the idea for their fantasy music network, which they called Next Big Sound, and landed $25,000 in seed money. The three continued to work on the idea following graduation. Next Big Sound gained traction and applied for TechStars. TechStars is a mentorship-driven business accelerator in Boulder, Colorado, that holds 13-week programs. They were turned down. Rather than becoming discouraged, the three stuck with the idea, and in the summer of 2008 participated in an accelerator program in Illinois. When the application date for TechStars in 2009 rolled around, they decided to give it a second try. This time they were accepted. They were the same team with the same idea, but this time their product had been built and launched, they had thousands of users, they had press (including a feature in *The New York Times*), and the three had proven that they could work together as a team.

In early 2009, White, Hoffman, and Rayani left Chicago for Boulder, reportedly making the 1,000-mile trip in Hoffman's Volkswagen Rabbit. TechStars is a heavily mentorship-driven program, so the three had access to high-quality mentors from the beginning. They quickly realized that their idea, the fantasy network for music, wasn't sustainable. It just didn't have a revenue model. That caused the three to pivot. They spent a lot of time talking to mentor Jason Mendelson, who is a partner in Foundry Group, a Boulder-based venture capital firm. Next Big Sound's team characterizes their TechStars experience as worth its weight in gold. They emerged

LEARNING OBJECTIVES

After studying this chapter you should be ready to:

1. Explain the concept called *liability of newness*.

2. Describe a new-venture team and discuss the primary elements that form such a team.

3. Identify professional advisers and explain their role with a new-venture team.

4. Explain why a new-venture team might use consultants to obtain advice.

from the program with a much sounder business concept and direction for how to move forward.

Next Big Sound is now a music analytics company. The premise of the company is to mine data to help the music industry make decisions, like whom to bet on in regard to the next big act. For years record sales information and radio play data were the only factors available to help music executives discern who the up-and-coming bands were. But now there are many sources of data, such as music sites like Spotify and Pandora, social networks like Facebook and Twitter, and video-sharing sites like YouTube, that help identify which songs and musicians are trending. Next Big Sound takes all the data and packages it into one central dashboard per artist or band. They sell access to the dashboard for a monthly subscription fee. With the data it collects, Next Big Sound says it can forecast record sales for 85 percent of artists, within a 20 percent accuracy range. The company's data is useful for additional purposes. For example, it can tell the areas of the country in which an artist is the most popular. That helps the artist plan tours and special promotions. Similarly, it can tell which activities an artist or band engages in provide the biggest bang for the buck. Appearing on some late-night talk shows, for instance, translates into more record sales than others. Having access to this type of information helps an artist or band make informed judgments when requests for appearances come in.

In regard to building a new venture team, the Next Big Sound team is unique in that it has three co-founders, which is above average in the start-up world. When asked how they get along with one another, David Hoffman indicated that they have healthy debates, but are able to come to consensus and get along well and trust one another. They also have complementary rather than redundant skills. When it came time to designate one of the three co-founders as the company's CEO, Hoffman indicated that it seemed only natural that Alex White would assume the role, which he did when Next Big Sound launched in 2009, and he remains in that role today. Next Big Sound's founders have had multiple mentors along the way, which they credit for much of their success. Hoffman recommends that the best way to get a mentor is not to ask for one. Instead, he suggests establishing a mutually beneficial relationship with someone, where each party has something to offer to the other. The mentorship will then come more naturally.

In the summer of 2012, Next Big Sound moved from Boulder, Colorado, to New York City, where the firm now has offices in Chelsea, an area on the west side of midtown Manhattan. The move brought Next Big Sound closer to its major customers and the music industry in general. The company continues to gain momentum and stature in the music industry.

In this chapter, we focus on how the founders of an entrepreneurial venture build a new-venture team as well as the importance of the team to the firm's overall success. A **new-venture team** is the group of founders, key employees, and advisers that move a new venture from an idea to a fully functioning firm.[1] Usually, the team doesn't come together all at once. Instead, it is built as the new firm can afford to hire additional personnel. The team also involves more than paid employees. Many firms have a board of directors, a board of advisors, investors, and other professionals on whom they rely for direction and advice.

In this chapter's first section, we discuss the role of an entrepreneurial venture's founder or founders and emphasize the substantial effect that founders have on their firm's future. We then turn our attention to a discussion about how the founders build a new-venture team, including the recruitment and selection of key employees and the forming of a board of directors. The chapter's second section examines the important role of advisors, lenders and investors, and other professionals in shaping and rounding out a new-venture team.

Liability of Newness as a Challenge

As we note throughout this textbook, new ventures have a high propensity to fail. The high failure rate is due in part to what is known as the **liability of newness**, which refers to the fact that companies often falter because the people who start them aren't able to adjust quickly enough to their new roles and because the firm lacks a "track record" with outside buyers and suppliers.[2] Assembling a talented and experienced new-venture team is one path firms can take to overcome these limitations. Indeed, experienced management teams that get up to speed quickly are much less likely to make a novice's mistakes. In addition, firms able to persuade high-quality individuals to join them as directors or advisers quickly gain legitimacy with a variety of people, such as some of those working inside the venture as well as some outside the venture (e.g., suppliers, customers, and investors). In turn, legitimacy opens doors that otherwise would be closed.

Another way entrepreneurs overcome the liability of newness is by attending entrepreneurship-focused workshops and events, such as Startup Weekend, hackathons, boot camps, and so on. These types of activities are sponsored by local universities, small business development centers, and economic development commissions. Another route to overcoming the liabilities of newness is joining one of the growing number of start-up accelerators that are popping up across the country. Start-up accelerators provide entrepreneurs access to mentors, investors, subject matter experts (such as attorneys and accountants), and other entrepreneurs. More information about start-up accelerators and the benefits they provide new businesses is explored in the "Partnering for Success" boxed feature. Entrepreneurs should remember that, at the end of the day, the faster they can overcome the liabilities associated with launching a new venture, the greater the likelihood they will achieve success with their firm.

Creating a New-Venture Team

Those who launch or found an entrepreneurial venture have an important role to play in shaping the firm's business model. Stated even more directly, it is widely known that a well-conceived business plan, one that flows from the firm's previously established business model, cannot get off the ground unless a firm has the leaders and personnel to carry it out. As some experts put it, "People are the one factor in production ... that animates all the others."[3] Often, several start-ups develop what is essentially the same idea at the same time. When this happens, the key to success is not the idea but rather the ability of the initial founder or founders to assemble a team that can execute the idea better than anyone else.

The way a founder builds a new-venture team sends an important signal to potential investors, partners, and employees. Some founders like the feeling of control and are reluctant to involve themselves with partners or hire managers who are more experienced than they are. In contrast, other founders are keenly aware of their own limitations and work hard to find the most experienced people to bring on board. Similarly, some new firms never form an advisory board, whereas others persuade the most important (and influential) people they can find to provide them with counsel and advice. In general, the way to impress

LEARNING OBJECTIVE
1. Explain the concept called *liability of newness.*

LEARNING OBJECTIVE
2. Describe a new-venture team and discuss the primary elements that form such a team.

PARTNERING FOR SUCCESS

To Overcome the Liabilities of Newness, Consider Joining a Start-up Accelerator

Y Combinator: Web: www.ycombinator.com; Facebook: Y Combinator; Twitter: @ycombinator
TechStars: Web: www.techstars.org; Facebook: TechStars; Twitter: @techstars

Start-up Accelerators are fixed-term, cohort-based programs for promising start-ups. The two best-known accelerator programs are Y-Combinator, located in the Silicon Valley, and TechStars, which originated in Boulder, Colorado. Most accelerator programs follow the following format:

- Select a dozen or so start-ups for each class (many have between two and three classes a year)
- Provide each start-up $10,000 to $25,000 in seed funding in exchange for 5 percent to 8 percent equity in its business
- Bring the start-ups together for mentoring over the course of an on-site multiweek mentoring program.
- Host a demo day at the end of the program where the participants pitch their businesses to angel investors, venture capitalists, and others.

Accelerator programs differ from business incubators. Most incubator programs are government-funded, take no equity, charge a modest fee for rent, and focus on a specific industry, such as medical technology or clean tech. They also typically do not have a set duration. In contrast, accelerator programs exemplify the bullet points made above, and can be either privately or publicly funded.

There are four primary benefits to joining an accelerator program, all of which help a start-up overcome the liabilities of newness. The first benefit concerns the network of people you'll meet and with whom you'll become acquainted. You'll be connected to not only mentors and advisers, but to former alumni companies. If a company going through the TechStars program, for example, runs into a technical challenge, those leading the firm can ask the entire TechStars network for help. Engaging successful mentors and alumni companies helps a firm gain legitimacy and support. Both Airbnb and Dropbox, for example, are Y-Combinator graduates. Imagine how helpful it would be for a start-up that is currently going through the Y-Combinator program to get acquainted with people at Airbnb or Dropbox and earn their endorsement and support.

Brand recognition is the second benefit of accelerator programs. The best accelerator programs are hard to get into. As a result, when potential employees, investors, or other companies see that you've graduated from TechStars, Y-Combinator, AngelPad, or one of the other better known accelerator programs, it sets you apart from other start-ups. This factor helps gain legitimacy. It's somewhat akin to having a degree from an academic institution to which it is very difficult to gain admittance. In turn, graduating from a school or a university with high entrance standards sets you apart in some individuals' eyes as a person who is talented and willing to work hard.

The third benefit associated with joining an accelerator program is the opportunity to work side-by-side with other start-ups. As mentioned, most accelerators admit start-ups in classes, ranging from just a few start-ups to 25 at a time. Most participants want to be well-regarded by their peers, which provides an incentive to work hard and succeed. A close bond often develops among the members of an accelerator cohort. The bond remains after the program finishes. As a result, when a company that has been part of an effective accelerator program graduates, it normally already has a group of other companies that are willing to lend it legitimacy and support.

The final benefit is the learning that takes place. Along with providing mentoring and support, most accelerator programs provide training in developing successful business models, raising capital, connecting with potential investors, and protecting intellectual property. A start-up can normally get up to speed on these issues and others faster by participating in an accelerator program than going it alone.

Early research results concerned with accelerator programs are encouraging. A study conducted by Yael Hochberg, a professor at MIT, and Susan Cohen, a professor at the University of Richmond and the University of Virginia's Darden School of Business, found that 59.3 percent of all companies in accelerator programs were able to raise follow-on funding after leaving the program. They also found that start-up founders were almost universally satisfied with their accelerator experience. Roughly 90 percent of the participants in accelerator programs surveyed in Hochberg and Cohen's study said they would repeat their accelerator experience.

Questions for Critical Thinking

1. Find an example of a start-up accelerator in the state in which the college or university you are attending is located. Describe the equity percentage the accelerator takes, how much seed funding is awarded, and in general how the program works.
2. Make a bullet-point list of the ways that participating in a start-up accelerator helps a firm overcome the liabilities of newness.
3. What, if any, are the downsides to participating in a start-up accelerator program?
4. If a college student has a business idea, what should the student do while in college to improve his or her chances of getting accepted by one of the better accelerator programs?

Sources: J. Shieber, "These Are the 15 Best Accelerators in the U.S.," *TechCrunch*, available at http://techcrunch.com/2014/03/10/these-are-the-15-best-accelerators-in-the-u-s/, posted on March 10, 2014, accessed on June 9, 2014; J. Flieger, "The Pros and Cons of Accelerators for Startups," *Forbes*, September 20, 2013.

potential investors, partners, and employees is to put together as strong a team as possible.[4] Investors and others know that experienced personnel and access to good-quality advice contribute greatly to a new venture's success.

The elements of a new-venture team are shown in Figure 9.1. It's important to carefully think through each element. Miscues regarding whether team members are compatible, whether the team is properly balanced in terms of areas of expertise, and how the permanent members of the team will physically work together can be fatal. Conversely, careful attention in each of these areas can help a firm get off to a good start and provide it an advantage over competitors.

There is a common set of mistakes to avoid when putting together a new-venture team. These mistakes raise red flags when a potential investor, employee, or business partner evaluates a new venture. The most common mistakes are shown in Table 9.1.

In the reminder of this chapter, we examine each element shown in Figure 9.1. While reading these descriptions, remember that entrepreneurial ventures vary in how they use the elements.

The Founder or Founders

Founders' characteristics and their early decisions significantly affect the way an entrepreneurial venture is received and the manner in which the new-venture team takes shape. The size of the founding team and the qualities of the founder or founders are the two most important issues in this matter.

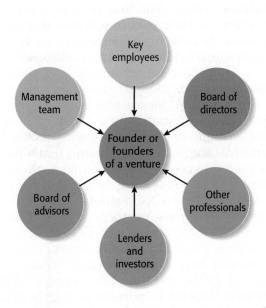

FIGURE 9.1
Elements of a New-Venture Team

TABLE 9.1   Common Mistakes Made in Putting Together a New-Venture Team

- Placing unqualified friends or family members in management positions.
- Assuming that previous success in other industries automatically translates to your industry.
- Presenting a "one person team" philosophy—meaning that one person (or a small group of people) is wearing all hats with no plans to bolster the team.
- Hiring top managers without sharing ownership in the firm.
- Not disclosing or talking dismissively of management team skill or competency gaps.
- Vague or unclear plans for filling the skill or competency gaps that clearly exist.

If a new venture is started by more than one person, it's important that the founders have a good rapport and complement one another rather than duplicate one another in terms of skills and backgrounds. Here, the founders of an educational software company have worked together before and are comfortable with each other's demeanors and work habits. The young man on the far left is a former teacher, the man seated is a software engineer, the woman is a former middle school vice-principal, and the young man on the right is a graphic designer.

Eric Audras/PhotoAlto/Corbis

Size of the Founding Team   The first decision that most founders face is whether to start a firm on their own or whether to build an initial **founding team**. Studies show that 50 to 70 percent of all new firms are started by more than one individual.[5] However, experts disagree about whether new ventures started by a team have an advantage over those started by a sole entrepreneur. Teams bring more talent, resources, ideas, and professional contacts to a new venture than does a sole entrepreneur.[6] In addition, the psychological support that co-founders of a business can offer one another can be an important element in a new venture's success.[7] Conversely, a lot can go wrong in a partnership—particularly one that's formed between people who don't know each other well. Team members can easily differ in terms of work habits, tolerances for risk, levels of passion for the business, ideas on how the business should be run, and similar key issues.[8] If a new-venture team isn't able to reach consensus on these issues, it may be handicapped from the outset.

When a new venture is started by a team, several issues affect the value of the team. First, teams that have worked together before, as opposed to teams that are working together for the first time, have an edge.[9] If people have worked together before and have decided to partner to start a firm together, it usually means that they get along personally and trust one another.[10] They also tend to communicate with one another more effectively than people who are new to one another.[11] Second, if the members of the team are **heterogeneous**, meaning that they are diverse in terms of their abilities and experiences, rather than **homogeneous**, meaning that their areas of expertise are very similar to one another, they are likely to have different points of view about technology, hiring decisions, competitive tactics, and other important activities. Typically, these different points of view generate debate and constructive conflict among the founders, reducing the likelihood that decisions will be made in haste or without the airing of alternative points of view.[12] A founding team can be too big, causing communication problems and an increased potential for conflict. The sweet spot is two to three founders. A founding team larger than four people is typically too large to be practical.[13]

There are three potential pitfalls associated with starting a firm as a team rather than as a sole entrepreneur. First, the team members may not get along. This is the reason investors favor teams consisting of people who have worked together before. It is simply more likely that people who have gotten along with one another in the past will continue to get along in the future. Second, if two or more people start a firm as "equals," conflicts can arise when the firm needs to establish a formal structure and designate one person as the chief executive officer (CEO). If the firm has investors, the investors will usually weigh in on who should be appointed CEO. In these instances, it is easy for the founder that wasn't chosen as the CEO to feel slighted. This problem is exacerbated if multiple founders are involved and they all stay with the firm. At some point, a hierarchy will have to be developed, and the founders will have to decide who reports to whom. Some of these problems can be avoided by developing a formal organizational chart from the beginning, which spells out the roles of each founder. Finally, as illustrated in the "What Went Wrong?" feature, if the founders of a firm have similar areas of expertise, it can be problematic. The founders of Devver were both technically oriented, leaving the firm without a leader on the business side.

Qualities of the Founders The second major issue pertaining to the founders of a firm is the qualities they bring to the table. In the previous several chapters, we described the importance investors and others place on the strength of the firm's founders and initial management team. One reason the founders are so important is that in the early days of a firm, their knowledge, skills, and experiences are the most valuable resource the firm has. Because of this, new firms are judged largely on their "potential" rather than their current assets or current performance. In most cases, this results in people judging the future prospects of a firm by evaluating the strength of its founders and initial management team.

Several features are thought to be significant to a founder's success. The level of a founder's education is important because it's believed that entrepreneurial abilities such as search skills, foresight, creativity, and computer skills are enhanced through obtaining a college degree. Similarly, some observers think that higher education equips a founder with important business-related skills, such as math and communications. In addition, specific forms of education, such as engineering, computer science, management information systems, physics, and biochemistry, provide the recipients of this education an advantage if they start a firm that is related to their area of expertise.[14]

Prior entrepreneurial experience, relevant industry experience, and networking are other attributes that strengthen the chances of a founder's success. Indeed, the results of research studies somewhat consistently suggest that **prior entrepreneurial experience** is one of the most consistent predictors of future entrepreneurial performance.[15] Because launching a new venture is a complex task, entrepreneurs with prior start-up experience have a distinct advantage. The impact of **relevant industry experience** on an entrepreneur's ability to successfully launch and grow a firm has also been studied.[16] Entrepreneurs with experience in the same industry as their current venture will have a more mature network of industry contacts and will have a better understanding of the subtleties of their respective industries.[17] The importance of this factor is particularly evident for entrepreneurs who start firms in technical industries such as biotechnology. The demands of biotechnology are sufficiently intense that it would be virtually impossible for someone to start a biotech firm while at the same time learning biotechnology. The person must have an understanding of biotechnology prior to launching a firm through either relevant industry experience or an academic background. Some entrepreneurs, who come from a nonbusiness background, fear that a lack of business experience will be their Achilles' heel. There are several steps, techniques, or approaches to business that entrepreneurs can utilize

WHAT WENT WRONG?

Devver: How Miscues in Regard to the Composition and Management of a New-Venture Team Can Kill a Start-up

Devver (pronounced like "developer," not "devious") launched in 2008 to help software developers use cloud-based services to "test" their code in a more expedient manner than current practices. The firm started by focusing on Ruby on Rails software applications. One of its flagship products, Caliper, provided quality metrics to Ruby on Rails developers for their Ruby on Rails code. By using Caliper, a Ruby on Rails developer could quickly discover problems such as code duplication, complex code, and code "smells." In computer programming, a code smell is any symptom in the source code of a program that possibly indicates a deeper and potentially more serious problem.

Dan Mayer and Ben Brinckerhoff are Devver's co-founders. The two met in high school and started a Web business before their high school graduations. Both studied computer programming in college, Mayer at the University of Colorado and Brinckerhoff at Washington University in St. Louis. The two reunited in 2008 to launch Devver. They are graduates of TechStars, a Boulder, Colorado-based mentorship-driven seed stage investment fund. Devver operated from early 2008 until early 2010, when it went out of business. In announcing its plans to close, the company indicated that although it had worked hard to achieve its vision—to use the cloud to build tools that would change software developers' lives—it couldn't generate sufficient revenue to sustain and grow the company.

In a thoughtful blog post, Ben Brinckerhoff reflected on the reasons for Devver's failure. While the reasons were varied, the key reasons focused on the composition of the founding team, difficulties in communications, and product development.

In regard to the founding team, both Mayer and Brinckerhoff thought of themselves as geeks. Looking back, Brinckerhoff feels it would have been to their advantage to have had another co-founder who loved the business side of running a start-up. In reflecting on this observation, Mayer challenged the oft-repeated statement that "You can teach a hacker business, but you can't teach a businessman how to hack." This statement is sometimes used by technical founders to justify not needing a businessperson on the team. While Mayer acknowledges that it's possible to teach a hacker business, you can't force a hacker to get excited about it, or give it the proper amount of attention. According to Mayer, what hackers like to do is hack. So they measure progress in lines of code written or use a similar metric. It's equally important to have someone in a start-up measuring progress on business metrics—like number of customers talked to or how well distribution channels are being developed. Not enough of that happened at Devver.

In regard to communication, Devver embraced working remotely. The company started in Boulder, where the two co-founders worked together. Devver's first key hire worked in Pennsylvania, and Mayer later moved to Washington, D.C. The idea was that by embracing working remotely, Devver could hire the best talent available without requiring people to relocate to Colorado. In addition, they felt that by allowing team members to work remotely they would experience minimal distractions, which is important when it comes to effective code writing. Regrettably, achieving these objectives was more difficult than the founders anticipated. Communication was a challenge. It was also an administrative hassle. Mayer and Brinckerhoff found that it was a pain to manage payroll, benefits, and so forth in several states simultaneously. In addition, pair programming was difficult to do remotely—a challenge for which the Devver team never found a good solution.

Finally, Brinckerhoff believes Devver should have spent more time on customer development and finding a minimum viable product. A minimum viable product, which is a staple component of the lean start-up movement, has just those features that allow a product to be deployed, and no more. It's typically deployed to early adopters for testing. The idea is to avoid building bells and whistles into products that customers don't need or want. Instead of doing this, Devver did minimal testing of its first product, the Ruby test accelerator, and then focused intently on building out the product without additional interaction with potential users. As a result, its Ruby test acceleration and additional products never really met market needs before Devver ran out of steam. In retrospect, Brinckerhoff believes Devver should have deployed individual products sooner, and solicited more customer feedback about pricing, market size, and technical challenges. Eventually, they learned that their market was too small and their price point needed to be too low to sustain the company.

Questions for Critical Thinking

1. In retrospect, Brinckerhoff believes that it would have been to Devver's advantage to have had a business-oriented co-founder as part of Devver's new-venture team. Do you think the reverse is true? If two businesspeople are set to launch a technology-oriented firm, do you think it's to their advantage to have a technology-oriented co-founder, or is it sufficient to hire technology-oriented personnel?

2. Make a list of the pluses and minuses of adopting a philosophy of allowing workers to work remotely. Is this philosophy better for some types of start-ups than others? What is your opinion of this philosophy?

3. The "You Be the VC 9.1" feature focuses on The Muse, a job board site that presents companies in a compelling manner, to make job listings interesting and to provide job seekers a better sense of how it would be to work for a particular company. What do you think a minimal viable product would have looked like for The Muse? How could The Muse have used the minimal viable product methodology to get user feedback about its site before committing substantial time and resources to building it out?

4. Do some Internet research to try to determine what Dan Mayer and Ben Brinckerhoff are doing today.

Source: B. Brinckerhoff, "Lessons Learned," *Devver Blog*, http://devver. wordpress.com/2010/04/26/lessons-learned (accessed June 15, 2014, originally posted on April 26, 2010).

to overcome a lack of business experience. These steps and approaches are highlighted in the "Savvy Entrepreneurial Firm" feature.

A particularly important attribute for founders or founding teams is the presence of a mature network of social and professional contacts.[18] Founders must often "work" their social and personal networks to raise money or gain access to critical resources on behalf of their firms.[19] **Networking** is building and maintaining relationships with people whose interests are similar or whose relationship could bring advantages to a firm. The way this might play out in practice is that a founder calls a business acquaintance or friend to ask for an introduction to a potential investor, business partner, or customer. For some founders, networking is easy and is an important part of their daily routine. For others, it is a learned skill.

Table 9.2 shows the preferred attributes of a firm's founder or founders. Start-ups that have founders or a team of founders with these attributes have the best chances of early success. If an individual is starting a company and is looking for a co-founder, there are several websites dedicated to matchmaking co-founders for start-ups. Two of the best sites are CofoundersLab (www. cofounderslab.com) and Founder2Be (www.founder2be.com).

The Management Team and Key Employees

Once the decision to launch a new venture has been made, building a management team and hiring key employees begins. Start-ups vary in terms of how quickly they need to add personnel. In some instances, the founders work alone for a period of time while the business plan is being written and

TABLE 9.2   **Preferred Attributes of the Founder or Founders of an Entrepreneurial Venture**

Attribute	Explanation
Firm started by a team	New ventures that are started by a team can provide greater resources, a broader diversity of viewpoints, and a broader array of other positive attributes than ventures started by individuals.
Higher education	Evidence suggests that important entrepreneurial skills are enhanced through higher education.
Prior entrepreneurial experience	Founders with prior entrepreneurial experience are familiar with the entrepreneurial process and are more likely to avoid costly mistakes than founders new to the rigors of the entrepreneurial process.
Relevant industry experience	Founders with experience in the same industry as their new venture will most likely have better-established professional networks and more applicable marketing and management expertise than founders without relevant industry experience.
Broad social and professional network	Founders with broad social and professional networks have potential access to additional know-how, capital, and customer referrals.

SAVVY ENTREPRENEURIAL FIRM

Overcoming a Lack of Business Experience

Many people who start businesses do not have prior business experience. This is especially true with the recent innovations in IT, where people have started businesses in areas that have never existed before. Some of these new business owners who lack business experience worry that people with experience in accounting, finance, and management will generally have an easier time starting a business than those who are tackling these challenges for the first time.

There are several methods and approaches to starting a business that people can take to compensate for their lack of business experience. However, first let's look at some of the characteristics a new business owner should have. A successful business owner should be:

1. Creative
2. Sure about the business
3. Realistic
4. Fast
5. Honest
6. Firm
7. Friendly
8. Careful
9. Sincere
10. Prepared to face failure

In Malaysia, there are several ways for a person to successfully launch a business even with a lack of prior experience.

Get Business Assistance and Advice

There are many places for business founders to get business assistance and advice. SME Corporation Malaysia (SME Corp. Malaysia), for example, is a government agency that provides management assistance and coaching to business owners. It is a central point of reference for information and advisory services for all small and medium enterprises (SMEs) in Malaysia. You will be able to find your local SME Corp. at www. smecorp.gov.my. You may also find information from SME Toolkit Malaysia, which is a project by Dun & Bradstreet (D&B) Malaysia Sdn Bhd and the Small and Medium Enterprise (SME) Department of the World Bank Group. It is an organization that provides consulting services to small businesses. You can find your local SME Toolkit at www.malaysia.smetoolkit.org. There are also many other organizations that provide coaching, advice, and support to specific groups of business owners and tailor their offerings to fit the groups. An example is the National Association for Women Entrepreneurs of Malaysia (NAWEM), an organization that promotes, develops, and enhances the efforts and activities of women entrepreneurs. You may visit their website at www. nawem.org.my.

If you're looking for a support group in your area and can't find one, check the Meetup website. Meetup (www. meetup.com) is an online platform that allows individuals to organize local groups via the Internet. Once a group is formed, its members "meet up" on a regular basis offline. You may simply follow the directions on Meetup's home page to discover if there is a small business or entrepreneurship Meetup group in your area. The following is a sample of small business Meetup groups that have taken place in Malaysia:

- Business networks
- Social media training
- Discussion and sharing on expanding your business across national borders

Participate in Online Forums and Q&A Sites

There are a growing number of online forums that provide support and advice to business owners. An example is the SMI SME Business Directory (www. smibusinessdirectory.com.my), which sponsors online forums that cover topics such as selecting a business, successful business planning, start-up funding, and financial management. The general tone of forums tends to be supportive and upbeat, which is exactly what business owners with limited experience need. There are also other growing numbers of websites for entrepreneurs that can be very helpful, especially to those who lack business experience.

Pick a Type of Business That Minimizes the Need for Prior Experience

There are also other alternatives for starting a business that minimize the need for prior experience. These alternatives allow people to pursue an opportunity in which fundamentals of the business have already been thought out. Franchising, for example, provides an individual the opportunity to own a business using a tested and refined business system. Other than that, a second alternative would be direct sales or multilevel marketing. These options require minimum experience and have been successful even for those who lack business experience.

Questions for Critical Thinking

1. Identify the sources of business assistance available in your area free of charge.
2. Identify three sources of business assistance or advice, particularly useful for someone who's starting a business without prior business experience, not mentioned in this feature.
3. How valuable do you believe that online forums, like the one mentioned previously, can be to someone who's trying to learn the "business" aspect of starting a business?
4. What other techniques, not mentioned previously, can people who don't have prior business experience utilize to compensate for their lack of experience?

the venture begins taking shape. In other instances, employees are hired immediately.

One technique available to entrepreneurs to help prioritize their hiring needs is to maintain a skills profile. A **skills profile** is a chart that depicts the most important skills that are needed and where skills gaps exist. A skills profile for New Venture Fitness Drinks, the fictitious company introduced in Chapter 3, is shown in Figure 9.2. Along with depicting where a firm's most important skills gaps exist, a skills profile should explain how current skills gaps are being dealt with. For example, two of New Venture Fitness Drink's skills gaps are being covered (on a short-term basis) by members of the board of advisors and the third skills gap does not need to be filled until the firm initiates a franchising program, which is still three to five years in the future.

Evidence suggests that finding good employees (and certainly good key employees) today is not an easy task. According to a 2013 Wells Fargo/Gallop Small Business Index Survey, when it comes to finding qualified employees, 53 percent of small business owners said it is very difficult to do so, 30 percent said it is difficult, and 23 percent said it is somewhat difficult.[20] Similarly, a 2011 survey conducted by the University of Maryland's School of Business and Network Solutions asked small business owners how well they competed with larger companies for good employees; only 46 percent said they were successful with these efforts. Respondents also said that recruiting workers who were comfortable in a small business setting is difficult.[21]

To save money, increase flexibility, and mitigate the difficulty in finding good employees, new ventures use four different sources of labor to get their work done. These are shown in Table 9.3. The first is employees. An **employee**

FIGURE 9.2
Skills Profile for New Venture Fitness Drinks

	Executive Leadership	Store Operations	Supply Chain Management	Marketing and Sales	HR/Recruiting	Accounting and Finance	Community Relations	Information Systems	Franchise Operations
Jack Petty	X								
Peggy Wells		X				X			
Jill Petersen				X					
Cameron Ivey			X						
Gap 1					O				
Gap 2							O		
Gap 3									O

X = position filled
O = position vacant

TABLE 9.3   Sources of Labor That New Ventures Utilize to Get Their Work Done

Type of Labor	Description
Full- or part-time employee	Someone who works for a business, at the business's location, utilizing the business's tools and equipment and according to the business's policies and procedures.
Intern	A person who works for a business as an apprentice or trainee for the purpose of obtaining practical experience.
Freelancer (or contractor)	A person who is in business for themselves, works on their own time with their own tools and equipment, and performs services for a number of different clients.
Virtual assistant	A freelancer who provides administrative, technical, or creative assistance to clients remotely from a home office.

is someone who works for a business, at the business's location or virtually, utilizing the business's tools and equipment and according to the business's policies and procedures.[22] These rules can vary somewhat, particularly as it pertains to working at the business's location. Most businesses bring on employees fairly slowly because of the costs involved. While employees are valuable, they are expensive. An employee who makes $50,000 a year costs a business more than $50,000 a year. Along with an employee's base salary, the employer pays a portion of the employee's Social Security (FICA) and Medicare taxes, provides workers' compensation insurance, pays into an unemployment fund, and provides benefits (such as health insurance and paid vacation) if benefits are part of the job. A general rule of thumb for an employer that offers benefits is that the benefits and taxes cost 33 percent of the base pay. As a result, a $50,000 per year employee would cost the business $66,500 per year.

The second resource that businesses utilize to get their work done is interns. An **intern** is a person who works for a business as an apprentice or trainee for the purpose of obtaining practical experience. For example, TOMS (the focal firm in Case 4.2), used many interns in getting its business up and running and still relies heavily on interns today. Many tech companies, in particular, have formal internship programs. Facebook runs a 12-week internship program (this program is described at www.facebook.com/careers/university). Google sponsors a variety of internship programs, which are detailed at www.google.com/about/careers/students. Many firms run internship programs not only to utilize the help, but as a recruiting tool. It provides them a chance to "look" at a potential hire before making a formal commitment to that person. Many companies also enjoy having interns around because of their vigor, enthusiasm, and tech-savvy skills. For example, a start-up founded by two 50-year-old individuals may learn a lot from college-aged interns about how to use social media platforms such as Facebook and Twitter more effectively in their business.

The third resource that firms utilize to get their work done is freelancers (also called contractors). A **freelancer** is a person who is in business for themselves, works on their own time with their own tools and equipment, and performs services for a number of different clients.[23] For example, a business may hire a freelancer to manage the search engine optimization (SEO) for its website, and pay the freelancer an hourly or monthly fee. Businesses typically find freelancers via word of mouth or through websites such as Odesk or Elance. Odesk and Elance, as explained in the "Partnering for Success" feature in Chapter 4, specialize in matching freelancers with businesses that are looking for specific types of help.

The fourth resource that businesses draw upon to complete their work is virtual assistants. A **virtual assistant** is a freelancer who provides administrative, technical, or creative assistance to clients remotely from a home office.

Businesses use virtual assistants for everything from making customer service calls, to data entry in accounting or bookkeeping platforms, to sending out thank you notes to clients. Similar to freelancers, virtual assistants can be located on online platforms like Odesk and Elance. As of June 2014, Odesk.com had over 17,000 virtual assistants listed that were looking for additional work.

An advantage businesses have in using freelancers and virtual assistants is that they are considered to be "independent contractors." As a result, a business is not responsible for costs (such as Social Security and Medicare taxes, workers' compensation insurance, paying into an unemployment fund, and benefits) beyond their hourly or contracted pay. Businesses have to be careful, however, to not incorrectly categorize an employee as an independent contractor to save money on taxes and benefits. The IRS looks closely at the distinction and can levy severe penalties if workers are misclassified.

Many founders worry about hiring the wrong person for a key role, regardless of whether the person is an employee, an intern, a freelancer, or a virtual assistant. Because most new firms are strapped for cash, everyone who is hired must make a valuable contribution. It's not good enough to hire someone who is well intended but who doesn't precisely fit the job. On some occasions, key hires work out perfectly and fill the exact roles that a firm's founders need. For example, Dave Olsen was one of the first employees hired by Starbucks founder Howard Schultz. At the time of his hiring, Olsen was the owner of a popular coffeehouse in the university district of Seattle, the city where Starbucks was launched. In his autobiography, Schultz recalls the following about the hiring of Olsen:

> On the day of our meeting, Dave and I sat on my office floor and I started spreading the plans and blueprints out and talking about my idea. Dave got it right away. He had spent ten years in an apron, behind a counter, serving espresso drinks. He had experienced firsthand the excitement people can develop about espresso, both in his café and in Italy. I didn't have to convince him that this idea had big potential. He just knew it in his bones. The synergy was too good to be true. My strength was looking outward: communicating the vision, inspiring investors, raising money, finding real estate, designing the stores, building the brand, and planning for the future. Dave understood the inner workings: the nuts and bolts of operating a retail café, hiring and training baristas (coffee brewers), ensuring the best quality coffee.[24]

The fear that an employee will not work out as well as Dave Olsen did for Starbucks is one of the attractions for hiring interns, freelancers, and virtual assistants. These individuals work on strictly an "as needed" basis, or on fairly short-term contracts, and a business can simply move on if the person doesn't work out. In contrast, separating from a full-time or even a part-time employee can be much more difficult.

The Roles of the Board of Directors

If a new venture organizes as a corporation, it is legally required to have a **board of directors**—a panel of individuals who are elected by a corporation's shareholders to oversee the management of the firm.[25] A board is typically made up of both inside and outside directors. An **inside director** is a person who is also an officer of the firm. An **outside director** is someone who is not employed by the firm. A board of directors has three formal responsibilities: (1) appoint the firm's officers (the key managers), (2) declare dividends, and (3) oversee the affairs of the corporation. In the wake of corporate scandals such as Enron, WorldCom, and others, there is a strong emphasis on the board's role in making sure the firm is operating ethically. One outcome of this movement is a trend toward putting more outsiders on boards of directors, because people who do not work for the firm are usually more willing to scrutinize the behavior of management than insiders who work for the company. Most boards meet formally three or four times a year. Large firms pay their directors for their service. New ventures are more likely to pay their directors in company stock or ask them to serve without direct compensation—at least until the company is profitable. The boards for publicly traded companies are required by law to have audit and compensation committees. Many boards also have nominating committees to select stockholders to run for vacant board positions. A list of the most desirable qualities in a board of directors and the most desirable qualities in individual board members is provided in Table 9.4.

If handled properly, a company's board of directors can be an important part of the new-venture team.[26] Providing expert guidance and legitimacy in the eyes of others (e.g., customers, investors, and even competitors) are two ways a board of directors can help a new firm get off to a good start and develop what, it is hoped, will become a sustainable competitive advantage.

Provide Expert Guidance   Although a board of directors has formal governance responsibilities, its most useful role is to provide guidance and support to the firm's managers.[27] Many CEOs interact with their board members frequently and obtain important input. The key to making this happen is to pick board members with needed skills and useful experiences who are willing to give advice and ask insightful and probing questions. The extent to which an effective board can help shape a firm and provide it a competitive advantage in the marketplace is expressed by Ram Charan, an expert on the role of boards of directors in corporations:

> They (effective boards) listen, probe, debate, and become engaged in the company's most pressing issues. Directors share their expertise and wisdom as a matter of course. As they do, management and the board learn together, a collective wisdom emerges, and managerial judgment improves. The on-site coaching and consulting expand the mental capacity of the CEO and the top management team and give the company a competitive edge out there in the marketplace.[28]

TABLE 9.4   Attributes of Effective Boards of Directors and Effective Board Members

Attributes of Effective Boards of Directors

- Strong communication with the CEO
- Customer-focused point of view
- Complementary mix of talents
- Decisiveness
- Mutual respect and regard for each other and the firm's management team
- Ability and willingness to stand up to the CEO and top managers of the firm
- Strong ethics

Attributes of Strong Board Members

- Strong personal and professional networks
- Respected in their field
- Willingness to make personal introductions on behalf of the firm
- Strong interpersonal communication skills
- Pattern recognition skills
- Investment and/or operating experience
- Ability and willingness to mentor the CEO and the firm's top managers

Because managers rely on board members for counsel and advice, the search for outside directors should be purposeful, with the objective of filling gaps in the experience and background of the venture's executives and the other directors. For example, if two computer programmers started a software firm and neither one of them had any marketing experience, it would make sense to place a marketing executive on the board of directors. Indeed, a board of directors has the foundation to effectively serve its organization when its members represent many important organizational skills (e.g., manufacturing, human resource management, and financing) involved with running a company.

Lend Legitimacy Providing legitimacy for the entrepreneurial venture is another important function of a board of directors. Well-known and respected board members bring instant credibility to the firm. For example, just imagine the positive buzz a firm could generate if it could say that Blake Mycoskie of TOMS or Drew Houston of Dropbox had agreed to serve on its board of directors. This phenomenon is referred to as **signaling**. Without a credible signal, it is difficult for potential customers, investors, or employees to identify high-quality start-ups. Presumably, high-quality individuals would be reluctant to serve on the board of a low-quality firm because that would put their reputation at risk. So when a high-quality individual does agree to serve on a firm's board, the individual is in essence "signaling" that the company has potential to be successful.[29]

Achieving legitimacy through high-quality board members can result in other positive outcomes. Investors like to see new-venture teams, including the board of directors, that have people with enough clout to get their foot in the door with potential suppliers and customers. Board members are also often instrumental in helping young firms arrange financing or funding. As we will discuss in Chapter 10, it's almost impossible for an entrepreneurial venture's founders to get an investor's attention without a personal introduction. One way firms deal with this challenge is by placing individuals on their boards that are acquainted with people in the investment community.

Potbelly, which is a restaurant chain that specializes in low-cost sandwiches, cookies, and shakes, is an example of a company with a well-designed board of directors. Its nine-member board consists of two inside directors and seven outsiders. The board members are listed below. Note that the outside members include individuals with backgrounds in real estate, restaurant chain development, hospitality management, finance, and consumer products. Potbelly, which launched an IPO in 2013 and has aggressive growth plans, will benefit from guidance in each of the areas the different board members represent.[30]

1.	AyLwin Lewis	CEO and President of Potbelly
2.	Bryant Keil	Founding Chairman of Potbelly; 2007 Ernst & Young Entrepreneur of the Year Award Recipient
3.	Vann Avedisian	President of Highgate Holdings, a fully-integrated real estate investment firm
4.	Peter Bassi	Retired Chairman of Yum! Restaurants International
5.	Susan Chapman-Hughes	Senior Vice President of American Express
6.	Gerald Gallagher	Venture Capitalist, Oak Investment Partners
7.	Maria Gottschalk	CEO of Pampered Chief
8.	Dan Levitan	Venture Capitalist and Cofounder of Maveron LLC, a VC firm that invests strictly in consumer companies
9.	Dan Ginsberg	CEO of Dermalogica, a U.S.-based skincare brand

Rounding Out the Team: The Role of Professional Advisers

LEARNING OBJECTIVE

3. Identify professional advisers and explain their role with a new-venture team.

Along with the new-venture team members we've already identified, founders often rely on professionals with whom they interact for important counsel and advice. In many cases, these professionals become an important part of the new-venture team and fill what some entrepreneurs call "talent holes."

Next, we discuss the roles that boards of advisers, lenders, investors, and other professionals play in rounding out new-venture teams.

Board of Advisors

Some start-up firms are forming advisory boards to provide them direction and advice.[31] An **advisory board** is a panel of experts who are asked by a firm's managers to provide counsel and advice on an ongoing basis. Unlike a board of directors, an advisory board possesses no legal responsibility for the firm and gives nonbinding advice.[32] As a result, more people are willing to serve on a company's board of advisors than on its board of directors because it requires less time and no legal liability is involved. A board of advisors can be established for general purposes or can be set up to address a specific issue or need. For example, some start-ups set up customer advisory boards shortly after they are founded to help them fine-tune their initial offerings. Similar to a board of directors, the main purpose of a board of advisors is to provide guidance and lend legitimacy to a firm. The most important thing that advisory board members can do is make high-level introductions to early customers, suppliers, and business partners.[33]

Most boards of advisers have between 5 and 15 members. Entrepreneurial firms typically pay the members of their board of advisors a small honorarium for their service either annually or on a per-meeting basis. Boards of advisors interact with each other and with a firm's managers in several ways. Some advisory boards meet three or four times a year at the company's headquarters or in another location. Other advisory boards meet in an online environment. In some cases, a firm's board of advisors will be scattered across the country,

This team of young entrepreneurs is speaking to a member of their Board of Advisors. A board of advisors is a panel of experts who are asked by a firm's founders and managers to provide counsel and advice on an on-going basis.

Hero Images/Corbis

making it more cost-effective for a firm's managers to interact with the members of the board on the telephone, via e-mail, or through a Skype conference call, rather than to bring them physically together. In these situations, board members don't interact with each other at all on a face-to-face basis, yet still provide high levels of counsel and advice.

The fact that a start-up has a board of directors does not preclude it from having one or more boards of advisors. For example, Coolibar, a maker of sun protective clothing, has a board of directors and a medical advisory board. According to Coolibar, its medical advisory board "provides advice to the company regarding UV radiation, sunburn, and the science of detecting, preventing, and treating skin cancer and other UV-related medical disorders, such as lupus."[34] The board currently consists of nine medical doctors, all with impressive credentials. Similarly, Intouch Health, a medical robotics and instruments company, has a board of directors along with a Business & Strategy advisory board, an Applications & Clinical advisory board, and a Scientific & Technical advisory board. Intouch Health says that its "diversified Advisory Board draws on the talents of seasoned executives, clinical and scientific authorities, and pioneers from a variety of technical areas. Their expertise encompasses international business management, robotics, telemedicine, and computer software, hardware and networking."[35]

Several guidelines are followed when organizing a board of advisors. First, a board of advisors should not be organized just so a company can boast of it. Advisers will become quickly disillusioned if they don't play a meaningful role in the firm's development and growth. Second, a firm should look for board members who are compatible and complement one another in terms of experience and expertise. Unless the board is being established for a specific purpose, a board that includes members with varying backgrounds is preferable to a board of people with similar backgrounds. Third, when inviting a person to serve on its board of advisors, a company should carefully spell out to the individual the rules in terms of access to confidential information.[36] Some firms ask the members of their advisory board to sign nondisclosure agreements, which we described in Chapter 7. Finally, firms should caution their advisers to disclose that they have a relationship with the venture before posting positive comments about it or its products on blogs or on social networking sites. A potential conflict of interest surfaces when a person says positive things about a company without disclosing an affiliation with the firm, particularly if there is a financial stake in the company.

Although having a board of advisors is widely recommended in start-up circles, most start-ups do not have one. As a result, one way a start-up can make itself stand out is to have one or more boards of advisors.

Lenders and Investors

As emphasized throughout this book, lenders and investors have a vested interest in the companies they finance, often causing these individuals to become very involved in helping the firms they fund. It is rare that a lender or investor will put money into a new venture and then simply step back and wait to see what happens. In fact, the institutional rules governing banks and investment firms typically require that they monitor new ventures fairly closely, at least during the initial years of a loan or an investment.[37]

The amount of time and energy a lender or investor dedicates to a new firm depends on the amount of money involved and how much help the new firm needs. For example, a lender with a well-secured loan may spend very little time with a client, whereas a venture capitalist may spend an enormous amount of time helping a new venture refine its business model, recruit management personnel, and meet with current and prospective customers and suppliers. In fact, evidence suggests that an average venture capitalist is likely to visit each company in a portfolio multiple times a year.[38] This number of visits denotes a high level of involvement and support.

As with the other nonemployee members of a firm's new-venture team, lenders and investors help new firms by providing guidance and lending legitimacy and assume the natural role of providing financial oversight. In some instances, lenders and investors also work hard to help new firms fill out their management teams. Sometimes this issue is so important that a new venture will try to obtain investment capital not only to get access to money, but also to obtain help hiring key employees.

For example, during its beginning stages, eBay's founders, Pierre Omidyar and Jeff Skoll, decided to recruit a CEO. They wanted someone who was not only experienced, but who also had the types of credentials that are valued by Wall Street investors. They soon discovered that every experienced manager they tried to recruit asked if they had venture capital backing—which at that time they did not. For a new firm trying to recruit a seasoned executive, venture capital backing is a sort of seal of legitimacy. To get this valuable seal, Omidyar and Skoll obtained funding from Benchmark Venture Capital, even though eBay didn't really need the money. Writer Randall Stross recalls this event as follows:

> eBay was an anomaly: a profitable company that was able to self-fund its growth and that turned to venture capital solely for contacts and counsel. No larger lesson can be drawn. When Benchmark wired the first millions to eBay's bank account, the figurative check was tossed into the vault—and there it would sit, unneeded and undisturbed.[39]

This strategy worked for eBay. Soon after affiliating with Benchmark, Bob Kagle, one of Benchmark's general partners, led eBay to Meg Whitman, an executive who had experience working for several top firms, including Procter & Gamble, Disney, and Hasbro. In March 2008, Whitman stepped down as eBay's president and CEO. Her tenure at eBay was considered to be very successful during a critical period in eBay's early development and growth.

Bankers also play a role in establishing the legitimacy of new ventures and their initial management teams. Research evidence rather consistently suggests that the presence of bank loans is a favorable signal to other capital providers.[40] Investors often take a seat on the boards of directors of the firms they fund to provide oversight and advice. It is less common for a banker to take a seat on the board of directors of an entrepreneurial venture, primarily because bankers provide operating capital rather than large amounts of investment capital to new firms.

There are additional ways that lenders and investors add value to a new firm beyond financing and funding. These roles are highlighted in Table 9.5.

TABLE 9.5   Beyond Financing and Funding: Ways Lenders and Investors Add Value to an Entrepreneurial Venture

- Help identify and recruit key management personnel
- Provide insight into the industry and markets in which the venture intends to participate
- Help the venture fine-tune its business model
- Serve as a sounding board for new ideas
- Provide introductions to additional sources of capital
- Recruit customers
- Help to arrange business partnerships
- Serve on the venture's board of directors or board of advisors
- Provide a sense of calm in the midst of the emotional roller-coaster ride that many new-venture teams experience

Other Professionals

At times, other professionals assume important roles in a new venture's success. Attorneys, accountants, and business consultants are often good sources of counsel and advice. The role of lawyers in helping firms get off to a good start is discussed in Chapter 7, and the role of accountants is discussed in Chapter 8. Here, we examine the role a consultant may play.

LEARNING OBJECTIVE

4. Explain why a new-venture team might use consultants to obtain advice.

Consultants

A **consultant** is an individual who gives professional or expert advice. New ventures vary in terms of how much they rely on business consultants for direction. In some ways, the role of the general business consultant has diminished in importance as businesses seek specialists to obtain advice on complex issues such as patents, tax planning, and security laws. In other ways, the role of general business consultant is as important as ever; it is the general business consultant who can conduct in-depth analyses on behalf of a firm, such as preparing a feasibility study or an industry analysis. Because of the time it would take, it would be inappropriate to ask a member of a board of directors or board of advisors to take on one of these tasks on behalf of a firm. These more time-intensive tasks must be performed by the firm itself or by a paid consultant.

Those leading an entrepreneurial venture often turn to consultants for help and advice because while large firms can afford to employ experts in many areas, new firms typically can't. If a new firm needs help in a specialized area, such as building a product prototype, it may need to hire an engineering consulting firm to do the work. Consultants' fees are typically negotiable. If a new venture has good potential and offers a consulting firm the possibility of repeat business, the firm will often be willing to reduce its fee or work out favorable payment arrangements.

Consultants fall into two categories: paid consultants and consultants who are made available for free or at a reduced rate through a nonprofit or government agency. The first category includes large international consulting firms, such as BearingPoint, Accenture, IBM Business Global Services, and Bain & Company. These firms provide a wide array of services but are beyond the reach of most start-ups because of budget limitations. But there are many smaller, localized firms. The best way to find them is to ask around for a referral.

Consultants are also available through nonprofit or government agencies. SCORE, for example, is a nonprofit organization that provides free consulting services to small businesses. SCORE currently has over 11,000 volunteers, 320 local chapters, and provides assistance across 62 industries via one-on-one meetings, workshops, and online webinars. An increasing number of score volunteers, called mentors, assist clients via e-mail rather than face-to-face. Commonly, SCORE mentors are retired business owners who counsel in areas as diverse as cash flow management, operations, and sales.[41] The Small Business Administration, a government agency, provides a variety of consulting services to small businesses and entrepreneurs, primarily through its network of Small Business Development Centers (SBDC), which are spread throughout the United States. There is evidence that these centers are effective in providing advice and helping entrepreneurial ventures get off to a good start. For example, one study found that the rates of survival, growth, and innovation of SBDC-counseled firms are higher than those for the population of start-ups in general.[42]

In summary, putting together a new-venture team is one of the most critical activities that a founder or founders of a firm undertake. Many entrepreneurs suffer by not thinking broadly enough or carefully enough about this process. Ultimately, people must make any new venture work. New ventures benefit by surrounding themselves with high-quality employees and advisers to tackle the challenges involved with launching and growing an entrepreneurial firm.

Chapter Summary

LO1. The liability of newness refers to the fact that entrepreneurial ventures often falter or even fail because the people who start them can't adjust quickly enough to their new roles and because the firm lacks a "track record" with customers and suppliers. These limitations can be overcome by assembling a talented and experienced new-venture team.

LO2. A new-venture team is the group of people who move a new venture from an idea to a fully functioning firm. Company founders, key employees, the board of directors, the board of advisers, lenders and investors, and other professionals are the primary elements involved with forming a new-venture team. A heterogeneous founding team has members with diverse abilities and experiences. A homogeneous founding team has members who are very similar to one another. The personal attributes that affect a founder's chances of launching a successful new firm include level of education, prior entrepreneurial experience, relevant industry experience, and the ability to network. Networking is building and maintaining relationships with people who are similar or whose friendship could bring advantages to the firm.

A skills profile is a chart that depicts the most important skills that are needed in a new venture and where skills gaps exist. Finding good employees and effective new-venture team members is challenging. Founders may draw from their personal networks to find the needed talent or may ask existing employees for referrals.

A board of directors is a panel of individuals who is elected by a corporation's shareholders to oversee the management of the firm. It is typically made up of both inside and outside directors. An inside director is a person who is also an officer of the firm. An outside director is someone who is not employed by the firm. When a

high-quality individual agrees to serve on a company's board of directors, the individual is in essence expressing an opinion that the company has potential (why else would the individual agree to serve?). This phenomenon is referred to as signaling.

LO3. An advisory board is a panel of experts who are asked by a firm's management team to provide counsel and advice on an ongoing basis. Along with lenders and investors and, potentially, consultants, advisory board members are the source of an entrepreneur's efforts to "round out" their new-venture team. We say "round out" because the roles these groups play in a new-venture success is less direct and less frequent compared to the influence of the other elements associated with forming a new-venture team. Most entrepreneurial firms have between 10 and 15 members on a board of advisors. Typically, these individuals are paid a small honorarium for their services.

Lenders and investors have a vested interest in the entrepreneurial firm's success. As the size of their investment increases, lenders and investors tend to be more involved in supporting the new venture's efforts to gain traction in the marketplace as a foundation of organizational success. Helping to recruit key employees, providing information about the industry in which the venture intends to compete, and serving as a sounding board for potential competitive actions are examples of the issues lenders and investors address with new-venture team members.

LO4. The primary reason that new ventures turn to consultants for help and advice is that while large firms can afford to employ experts in many areas, new firms typically can't. Consultants can be paid or can be part of a nonprofit or government agency and provide their services for free or for a reduced rate.

Key Terms

advisory board, **332**
board of directors, **329**
consultant, **335**
employee, **327**
freelancer, **328**
founding team, **322**
heterogeneous, **322**

homogeneous, **322**
inside director, **329**
intern, **328**
liability of newness, **319**
networking, **325**
new-venture team, **318**
outside director, **329**

prior entrepreneurial
   experience, **323**
relevant industry experience,
   323
signaling, **331**
skills profile, **327**
virtual assistant, **328**

Review Questions

9-1. What is a new-venture team?
9-2. Who are the primary participants in a start-up's new-venture team?
9-3. What is liability of newness?
9-4. What can a new venture do to overcome the liability of newness?
9-5. Do new ventures started by a team have an advantage over new ventures started by a sole entrepreneur, or is the opposite the case?
9-6. What are the differences between a heterogeneous and a homogeneous founding team?
9-7. What are the two potential pitfalls of using a team to start a firm?
9-8. What are the personal attributes that affect a founder's chances of launching a successful new firm?
9-9. Why does having relevant industry experience help the founder of a firm?
9-10. What are the attributes that make a founder of a firm successful?
9-11. What are some of the methods used by founders to find good employees?
9-12. What is a board of directors?

9-13. What are the desired attributes of good board members?
9-14. What are the three formal responsibilities of a board of directors?
9-15. How does recruiting a well-known and highly respected board of directors lend legitimacy to a firm?
9-16. How do lenders and investors add value to an entrepreneurial venture?
9-17. What is the purpose of forming an advisory board?
9-18. What are the different ways advisory boards meet and conduct their business?
9-19. What are the guidelines to follow when establishing a board of advisors?
9-20. In what ways do lenders and investors lend legitimacy to a firm?
9-21. Why do new ventures often turn to consultants for advice?
9-22. What is the difference between the two types of consultants available for a new venture?
9-23. What type of advice and counsel do SCORE volunteers provide?

Application Questions

9-24. Emily Jones is in the middle of starting her own business in the advertising industry. She is leaning toward incorporation rather than an LLC because she would like to attract employees by issuing stock. Emily is currently going through all the documents that need to be submitted to the company secretary. One of the requirements for setting up a corporation is the appointment of a board of directors. At the moment, she has no trouble selecting her inside directors. However, she is struggling with the appointment of outside directors.

What should she look out for when making her selection? Advise her.
9-25. According to materials in this chapter, prior entrepreneurial experience, relevant industry experience, and networking are attributes that strengthen a person's chances of launching a successful venture. Think about the type of company you might choose to launch one day. Which of these three attributes do you possess? What steps can you take today to build strengths in the areas where you lack them?

9-26. Greg Mathews has completed his business plan for a ski resort and is ready to put his plan into action. He has been working alone for the past three months to put his venture in place. He needs to start hiring employees for his resort in order to build his management and key employee team. Evidence shows that hiring good employees today is not an easy task. Since you have been in the recruitment services for the last 10 years, he came to seek advice from you on the primary elements of a good team. Assist him.

9-27. Cindy Combs, a professional investor, was having lunch with a colleague recently and said, "Do you remember Peter Kennedy the entrepreneur we met the other day who created an iPhone app that helps busy families keep track of their activities? I checked up on him and concluded that he has all the right personal attributes not only to be an app developer but to be a successful entrepreneur. He's thinking about creating some additional family-focused apps and I'm inclined to invest in his business." Cindy's dinner companion said, "Really, tell me about Peter's characteristics that are so impressive to you." What do you think Cindy said in response to her lunch companion's question about Peter's characteristics?

9-28. In groups of three, visit a corporation in your neighborhood. Make an appointment to interview a human resources manager. Find out if the corporation has an advisory board. If it does, how many members does it have? What are their roles and responsibilities? How are these advisors paid? Are they advisors on a permanent basis or are they called upon from time to time? Try to obtain details such as their background and experience, their role in the corporation, and their appointment terms.

9-29. Lauren Mitchell is achieving some success with the real estate firm she launched two years ago. A rebounding local economy has helped as has the fact that she is well connected with those heading the chamber of commerce in the city in which her firm is located. She feels, however, that she is having to cover too many of the tasks required for her firm to keep running herself. She has asked you for your advice given that she knows you are taking an entrepreneurship course. Use your knowledge about a skills profile to help Lauren understand how to proceed with her labor-related challenges.

9-30. Charlie Berry, Shelly Toombs, Nancy Harder, James Ndofor, Jennifer Atwood, and Cliff Bell are all experienced software engineers. For some time, they've been talking about starting a company—the six of them—around a software solution in which all of them have an interest. Based on materials in this chapter, what challenges do you anticipate these six people will likely encounter cofounding a firm?

9-31. Sunny Newman has always been keen on starting a modeling agency. He has been interested in modeling since he was 10 years old and has been in the profession for over a decade. He recently quit his job as a model and decided to start a model management agency of his own. However, he does not have enough funds to execute his idea. He has been actively seeking an angel investor, and his good friend Josh Smith has agreed to fund his startup initially. In fact, Josh is not only keen to fund Sunny's venture but wants to become involved in the firm as well. How should they proceed and divide the involvement?

9-32. While taking an entrepreneurship course, you heard from several local entrepreneurs who visited your class that in their view, mistakes are easy to make when forming a team to operate a new venture. A friend of yours is interested in opening his own business and wants to effectively establish a team for his new venture. What mistakes would you tell him to try to avoid as he forms his new-venture team?

YOU BE THE VC 9.1 COMPANY: The Muse

• Web: www.themuse.com • Facebook: The Daily Muse • Twitter: @dailymuse

Business Idea: Create a job board site that presents companies in a compelling manner, to make job listings interesting and to provide job seekers a better sense of what it would be like to work for a particular company.

Pitch: Job boards and company profiles on job sites are fairly uninspiring. Usually, there is a boring description of a job, followed by a list of skills and educational background needed and a dull description of the company. Rarely is any insight provided about the culture of a company, what its work environment is like, and what the experiences of the people who work there have been. These types of insights are available if a person is granted an interview and visits the company in which s/he desires to work. But there are occasions when both a company and an applicant spend a considerable amount of time learning about one another, only to go their separate ways when it becomes clear that the applicant isn't a good fit for the culture or the work environment that the company has to offer. Even worse, there are instances where people take jobs and then discover in the first couple of weeks that they aren't a good match with the personality and values of the company.

The Muse solves this problem by providing job applicants much richer detail about a company, its culture, and what it would be like to work there as part of the job solicitation process. It starts by individually selecting the companies that post jobs on its site. Unlike traditional job sites, not all companies that apply are accepted. Once a company is accepted, The Muse sends two employees to the company's headquarters to write the copy for the

job posting, take photos of the company's workspace, and shoot video interviews of employees. The goal is to give job seekers as keen an insight as possible as to the culture of a company and the type of people who work there. This is a level of understanding that isn't available through job sites such as Monster.com and social media platforms like LinkedIn. The reason The Muse sends its own employees to create and gather the content is the belief that a third party can actually be more effective at describing a company than the company itself. Many companies are so steeped in their own culture and idiosyncrasies that they're not good at objectively describing themselves to others. The Muse's goal isn't to make every company sound like the best place in the world to work. Instead, the goal is to give job seekers an honest and realistic look at a company so they will be able to make an informed judgment about whether to pursue a specific job. Companies pay a monthly fee to post jobs on The Muse's website and to recruit Muse users. You can view profiles of companies that are currently recruiting at www.themuse.com.

The Muse offers a variety of complementary services on its website, including career advice.

9-33. Based on the material covered in this chapter, what questions would you ask the firm's founders before making your funding decision? What answers would satisfy you?

9-34. If you had to make your decision on just the information provided in the pitch and on the company's website, would you fund this company? Why or why not?

YOU BE THE VC 9.2 COMPANY: Soma

• Web: www.drinksoma.com • Facebook: Soma Water • Twitter: Soma

Business Idea: Design and produce a drinking water filter for home use that is organic and biodegradable and pair it with a stylish and ergonomic carafe (pitcher) that is elegant enough to be the centerpiece at a formal dinner party. Offer replacement filters on a subscription basis so users never have to worry about running out of filters.

Pitch: Most drinking water filters made for home use are difficult to use and somewhat unappealing. The filters are usually designed to fit on the top of a water pitcher, and if the user isn't careful can easily slip off and spill water on the kitchen counter and floor. In addition, because the filters usually contain charcoal, if the water sits in the refrigerator too long, small flakes of charcoal will be visible in the water. Not too appealing, particularly if you're serving the water at a dinner party.

The Soma drinking water filter and carafe were developed to solve these problems. The filter was designed by David Beeman, a water filtration expert, who created water formulas for Starbucks, Peet's, and other global brands. The filter, which is shaped like a funnel, is made from all-natural Malaysian coconut shells, vegan silk, and food-based plastic. It is 100 percent organic and 100 percent biodegradable. In contrast, most drinking water filters are made from plastic resin and charcoal. Soma filters are paired with an elegant hourglass-shaped carafe that is large enough to serve a family but sleek enough to fit in a refrigerator. It is contoured to fit comfortably in your hand and has a beveled edge for drip-free pouring. The filtration process is simple and quick. You simply fill the carafe with tap water, let the water pass through the filter, and it is ready to drink. The filters last for two months. The combination of the filter and the carafe delivers clean, crisp, pure, good-tasting water. The carafe and filter are also showpieces. Their presence would be appropriate as the centerpiece for a formal dinner party.

To relieve a pain point for its users, Soma offers a subscription service for replacement filters. New filters are delivered every two months. As part of its commitment to pure, clean water, Soma denotes a portion of its sales to Charity: Water. A nonprofit organization, Charity: Water brings clean, safe drinking water to people in developing countries. Soma also contributes to environmental sustainability by providing an alternative to bottled water,

which utilizes plastic bottles that must be recycled or disposed of. Soma launched a Kickstarter campaign in December 2012. The campaign reached its goal of $100,000 in nine days, and raised a total of $147,444 by the end of the campaign.

9-35. Based on the material covered in this chapter, what questions would you ask the firm's founders before making your funding decision? What answers would satisfy you?

9-36. If you had to make your decision on just the information provided in the pitch and on the company's website, would you fund this company? Why or why not?

CASE 9.1

Justin's: The Importance of a Strong New-Venture Team in a Food Start-up's Success

• *Web: www.justins.com* • *Facebook: Justin's* • *Twitter: @justins*

Introduction

After graduating from college in 2000, Justin Gold spent a year in California before settling in Boulder, Colorado. He waited tables to pay the rent, and enjoyed outdoor activities, including hiking, climbing, and exploring. Justin was a vegetarian, and to get the protein he needed he started eating a lot of peanut butter and nut butter. He owned a food processor, and found that making peanut butter was easy. To spice things up, he started making different flavors of peanut butter by adding ingredients such as honey, cinnamon, dried blueberries, and banana chips. The whole idea was to create something for him to eat. Justin's roommates loved the stuff, and kept stealing it from the refrigerator.

To discourage the thievery, Justin, in a good-natured way, scrawled his name—Justin's—across each jar.

Justin's roommates encouraged him to set up a table at the Boulder Farmer's Market to see if his nut butter would sell. He gave it a try and the nut butter was a hit. That experience got Justin thinking. To sell at the Boulder Farmer's Market, he had to make his nut butter in an FDA-approved facility. Today, many states allow small producers to make certain items out of their homes, but that wasn't the case in Colorado at the time. Justin figured that as long as he was going to the trouble of using an FDA-approved kitchen to make his nut butter for the farmer's market, he might approach some stores as well.

An assortment of Justin's products.

The Beginnings of a Business

To educate himself on how to convert his hobby into a business, Justin did two things. First, he spent hours at the University of Colorado's Business School reference library, thumbing through business books. He found a book that contained business plans, and one plan caught his eye. It was for a tomato canning company. Justin used that plan as a model for his first business plan. The second thing he did was reach out to others for advice. At one point, he went to a local grocery store and found the area that featured locally produced products. He wrote down the names and contact information for every area company he could find. He then reached out to the companies for advice. After receiving feedback, he wrote his first business plan in 2002. Based on the strength of the plan, he was able to raise $25,000 from friends and family.

At the same time Justin raised his first funding, he was setting up his manufacturing process. It was hard to find a facility that would take him on. Making peanut butter is messy—it tends to gunk up machines. So Justin bought a used industrial-sized food processer and decided to manufacturer on his own. He found a salsa company in Denver that rented him space. He was finally ready to start cranking out Justin's Nut Butter and Justin's Peanut Butter.

Justin slowly got distribution for his product. His goal was to get into Whole Foods Market. After convincing a local Whole Foods buyer to give him a try, he found out that he'd need to work through Whole Foods's distributor. The distributor was initially reluctant, but Justin persisted, and his product was eventually taken on by Whole Foods stores in the Rocky Mountain region.

Around this time, Justin switched jobs—from working as a waiter to working for REI, a chain of stores that sells outdoors products such as camping and climbing gear. Similar to other outdoors stores, REI sold Power Gels, which were small packages of sugary food that hikers and climbers bought to give them a quick energy boost. On a bike ride one day, Justin wondered whether he could sell his nut butter in small gel packs. He called everyone he could think of that placed products in small squeeze packs, including Heinz, which packages ketchup in small packs (the type of packs you get at a fast-food restaurant). No one offered to help, so he decided to go it alone. At that point, he rewrote his business plan to include the cost of a squeeze-pack machine. Based on his new idea, he was able to raise an additional $120,000 from friends and family.

The peanut butter and nut butter squeeze packs were initially a disappointment, largely as the result of a positioning mistake. They were originally positioned on shelves with protein bars and other energy-boosting gel packs. Justin eventually asked that his squeeze packs be positioned next to his larger jars of Justin's Nut Butter and Peanut Butter. The idea was that consumers, who may be reluctant to try an entire jar of premium-priced peanut butter, might try a 99-cent squeeze pack. The switch did the trick, and Justin's Nut Butter and Peanut Butter squeeze packs starting selling.

It Takes a Qualified Team to Grow a Business

Justin was now at a turning point. He wanted to further grow the business, but needed a sizeable amount of capital to purchase equipment, hire personnel, crank up his marketing, and so forth. He reached out to a number of investors. Despite his successes, they all turned him down. The reasons focused on two issues: first, Justin, himself, had no experience growing a food company, and second, he had never taken serious investor money and returned a profit.

To mitigate these concerns, Justin knew he had to build a team. His first step was finding an experienced executive. He became acquainted with Lance Gentry. Gentry helped build Izzy, a local beverage company, which grew from a start-up to $25 million in sales before it was acquired by Pepsi. The only catch was that Justin couldn't pay Gentry what he was worth. Gentry had a wife and three kids, and he needed an income. Justin asked Gentry what he needed to get by and hired him for a below-the-market salary, but he made up for it by giving Gentry a stake in the firm. The next thing Justin did was put together a board of advisors. He had two criteria in selecting board members: (1) They had to have gray hair—meaning they had to be experienced; and (2) they had to have time to give him. Justin wasn't putting together the advisory board strictly to impress investors. If he was going to take Justin's to the next level, he knew that he'd need to lean on them for advice. Similar to Gentry, to incent the investors to come on board, he offered each a small amount of stock in Justin's.

Justin approached a new set of investors and emphasized three key points. He now had (1) an experienced manager on board, who had grown a successful company, (2) a strong board of advisors, and (3) professional manufacturers lined up to produce his product. The timing wasn't good. It was 2009, which wasn't a good year to raise money. No single investor bit, but Justin was successful in raising $1 million from 50 different people. Justin made sure to retain more than 50 percent of the firm for himself, so he would remain in control of Justin's.

Growing the Business and Expanding the Team

Things progressed smoothly from this point forward. Justin's continued to grow. In 2010, Justin got the idea to make peanut butter cups. His board was against it, but he persevered, later saying that it was the only time he went against the advice of his board. He wanted to produce an organic, all-natural peanut butter cup, as an alternative to Reese's. It took time to find a chocolatier

(continued)

to work with him, but he finally found a small, family-oriented company that would make his product. Justin considered this to be a pivotal juncture for his company. If he could produce and sell another product, Justin's could essentially become a platform from which multiple products could be conceived, produced, and sold. The peanut butter cups were a hit. They quickly became the biggest revenue producer for the company.

To build a team, Justin used the same formula that he used to land Gentry. Each employee he hired was paid a below-average salary but was given stock in Justin's to compensate. Justin maintained that by giving everyone stock, he incented each employee to treat the company as if it were her or his own. The amount of stock varied, depending on the nature of the hire. Stock provided to employees was set up on a multiyear vesting schedule.

Today, Justin's products are available at Whole Foods Markets, Target, Safeway, Kroger, and a number of specialty retailers and coffee shops across the country.

Working at Justin's

Justin's has expanded to 24 employees. The company remains in Boulder. Sadly, in 2012, Lance Gentry, the experienced executive that Justin brought on board in 2008, died of brain cancer. Photos of each team member appear on Justin's website. The company produced a video depicting its culture and featuring some of its employees for *Entrepreneur* magazine's 2012 Entrepreneur of the Year competition. In the video, one of Justin's employees describes the company's culture as follows:

> "We are so innovative. We have so much fun together. We really treat one another as family. We joke around a lot but we get stuff done and it's just such a great environment. Its super fun and Justin is an amazing person and an amazing leader."

While working at Justin's isn't completely dissimilar to other food companies, the company does have some unique quirks. The company takes all of its employees on a vacation each year. A recent trip was a cruise to Mexico. In addition, the company gives back by involving its employees in an initiative to provide aid to the Pine Ridge Native American Reservation in South Dakota.

Merger with VMG Partners

In 2013, Justin's merged with VMG Partners, a California-based private equity firm. The merger netted Justin's $47 million in a combination of equity, options, and securities. When asked to comment on the merger, Justin said, "The company's growing, and the company's growing faster than it knows how to manage." Referring to the move as "smart capital," Justin said that the combined company would provide better resources for Justin's to maintain and further its growth. Justin said that the day-to-day operations of the company's Boulder headquarters would not change.

Discussion Questions

9-37. How did the "liability of newness" affect Justin Gold as he attempted to formally launch his entrepreneurial venture?

9-38. What key employees did Gold recruit to be members of his new-venture team?

9-39. What criteria did Gold establish and use when forming a board of advisors?

9-40. What characteristics describe the new-venture team that Justin Gold has established?

Sources: R. Hofstetter, *Cooking Up Business* (New York: A Perigee Book, 2013); R. Hanley and J. Gold, "Justin Gold: Growing a Food Startup," the DOcast.net podcast, available at www.richardhanleyjr.com/justingold, posted on April 20, 2013, accessed on June 15, 2014; J. Porter, "Spotlight: Justin's Nut Butter's Justin Gold, Entrepreneur of 2012 Finalist," *Entrepreneur*, available at www.entrepreneur.com/blog/224418, posted on September 15, 2012, accessed on June 15, 2014; A. Wallace, "Justin's LLC, Boulder-Based-Nut Butter Maker, Sells Minority Stake to Private Equity Firm," *Daily Camera*, October 17, 2013.

CASE 9.2

Zappos: Making Human Resources the Key to Customer Service

• *Web: Zappos* • *Twitter: zappos* • *Facebook: Zappos.com*

Bruce R. Barringer, *Oklahoma State University*
R. Duane Ireland, *Texas A&M University*

Introduction

Zappos.com is an online shoe and apparel retailer that has built a strong brand and has shown impressive sales growth since its founding. It's based in Las Vegas, Nevada. The company had zero sales in 1999, $370 million in 2005, and over $1 billion in 2008. In 2009, Amazon.com acquired Zappos for $1.2 billion with the agreement that it could operate autonomously and maintain its unique culture. Zappos's formula for success is seemingly simple. It acquires customers through word-of-mouth and search engine marketing (SEM) and then wows them with customer service that keeps them coming back. The popular press often touts Zappos as the classic example of what can be accomplished through exemplary customer service.

But what's really behind Zappos's extraordinary success? Its prices are slightly on the high end. Its website isn't fancy. And it sells shoes and clothing for crying out loud! How does Zappos consistently deliver such a high level of customer service that people are willing to buy shoes, clothing, and a variety of other items to the tune of $1 billion-plus per year? Read on.

Why Shoes?

Zappos was founded by Nick Swinmurn in 1999. Swinmurn had such a hard time finding shoes that he started an e-commerce company to help people just like himself. He was turned away by investors who thought it was crazy to think that people would buy shoes online. Seriously—who buys shoes without trying them on first? Swinmurn persevered, heartened by the fact that over $2 billion in shoes are sold via mail-order catalogs every year—so people do buy shoes without trying them on. Selling shoes is also a fundamentally good business. You don't need to educate people about the product—people know shoes. The brands are strong, and the margins are good. The average order on Zappos.com is over $130. It's also possible to run an effective SEM campaign for shoes. Try this: Search Google for "Nike shoes," "tennis shoes," and "soccer shoes," one by one. How many times do you see search engine ads for Zappos to the right of the results? Many, right?

Zappos's original name was ShoeSite. A few months after the company launched, the name was changed to Zappos. The name "Zappos' is a variation of "zapatos," which is the Spanish name for shoes. Swinmurn decided to abandon the name ShoeSite because he didn't want to limit the company to only selling footwear.

Customer Service

According to reliable reports, customer service is what makes Zappos special. Call center employees don't use scripts and aren't pressed to keep calls short. The longest recorded call was 10 hours and 29 minutes. Shipping and returns are free. The warehouse is open 24/7 so customers can place an order as late as 11 P.M. and still receive quick delivery. Behind the scenes, most orders are upgraded to next-day delivery so customers are pleasantly surprised when their order arrives before expected. Normally, the early arrival is accompanied by an e-mail message from Zappos saying that the order was upgraded to next-day delivery because you are a "valued customer."

Zappos also has a very liberal return policy. It will take returns for up to 365 days, although most returns come within 30 days. About 40 percent of all items ordered are returned. When a customer is on the phone with a Zappos employee and is struggling with which pair of shoes to buy, the Zappos employees will suggest that the customer buy both pairs, and simply return the less desirable shoes. If Zappos's warehouse is out of a pair of shoes a customer wants, Zappos will e-mail the customer links to other websites where the shoes are for sale. Zappos also does little things to help its customers. For example, its toll-free phone number is listed at the top of every page on its website. Employees are given sufficient autonomy so they can do what they believe is "right" for the customer. For example, on one occasion a woman called Zappos to return a pair of boots for her husband because he died in a car accident. The next day she received a flower delivery, which the call center employee had billed to Zappos without checking with her supervisor.

What all this effort has gotten Zappos is a loyal customer base and word-of-mouth advertising. Approximately 75 percent of Zappos's orders come from existing customers.

Tony Hsieh

CEO Tony Hsieh is at the center of everything Zappos does. In his early 20s, Hsieh started a company called LinkExchange, which let small companies barter for

(continued)

banner ads. Hsieh insisted that every e-mail coming into the company was answered promptly and politely. In college, Hsieh made money by selling pizzas out of his Harvard dorm room. A classmate, Alfred Lin, bought whole pizzas from Hsieh and resold them piece by piece, making more money. Hsieh sold LinkExchange to Microsoft for $265 million in 1998 and he and Lin started an angel investment fund. Zappos's founder Nick Swinmurn pitched Hsieh and Lin, trying to raise money. Hsieh was so impressed with Zappos's market opportunity that he invested in the firm and briefly served as Zappos's co-CEO with Swinmurn. It wasn't long before Hsieh and Lin were running Zappos. Hsieh became Zappos's CEO and Lin became the CFO in the early 2000s.

Hsieh isn't the typical CEO, and his values, personality, and approach to doing business have clearly shaped Zappos's culture. Hsieh works in an open space amid a cluster of employee cubicles. He hosts employee parties and barbecues at his home, encourages employees to hang out after work, and spends his spare time studying the science of happiness. Zappos employees are encouraged to decorate their work spaces. Hsieh's desk features jungle vines and an inflatable monkey.

Human Resources

While exemplary customer service may be what keeps Zappos's customers coming back, the root of the company's competitive advantage is its human resource management policies. The company is fiercely protective of its culture, which has been crafted to facilitate its high level of customer service. It's 10 core values, which define its culture, brand, and business strategies, are shown next. Every new employee, regardless of his/her assignment, is required to undergo a four-week customer loyalty training course, which includes at least two weeks of talking on the phone with customers in the call center. Employees enjoy free lunches, no-charge vending machines, a company library, a nap room, and free health care (although employees do pay for their dependents).

Zappos's 10 Core Values

1. Deliver WOW Through Service
2. Embrace and Drive Change
3. Create Fun and a Little Weirdness
4. Be Adventurous, Creative, and Open-Minded
5. Pursue Growth and Learning
6. Build Open and Honest Relationships with Communication
7. Build a Positive Team and Family Spirit
8. Do More with Less
9. Be Passionate and Determined
10. Be Humble

That's not all. After training, each new customer service hire is given what Zappos calls "the offer." The company says to each new hire, "If you quit today, we'll pay you for the amount of time you've worked, plus $3,000." Why would Zappos do this? The answer to this question is simply that the firm wants employees to quit if they don't like the Zappos culture. The $3,000 payoff is small potatoes, Hsieh and his top management team believe, as opposed to having a half-hearted employee on the payroll. Over 97 percent of employees who complete training turn down the offer.

Social Media

Another distinctive aspect of Zappos is its extensive use of social media, which includes Twitter, Facebook, and YouTube. Hsieh encourages his employees to use social media to put a human face on the company. More than 500 Zappos employees have Twitter accounts, one of which is Hsieh, who has over 2.8 million followers. The company's encouragement of Twitter use coincides with core value 6: Build Open and Honest Relationships with Communication. Employees do not use Twitter to spam followers about Zappos's products. Instead, they provide updates about what they're doing and what it's like to work at Zappos. Hsieh himself is very authentic in his tweets. For example, on one occasion, before going onstage for a tech conference, Hsieh tweeted: "Spilled Coke on left leg of jeans, so poured some water on right leg so looks like denim fade." Hsieh also uses Twitter to solicit customer feedback. In his tweets, he frequently refers to something Zappos is doing and asks, "What do you think about this?" The replies he gets are from Zappos employees, customers, and others.

Zappos's Facebook page provides an effective vehicle for feedback and discussions with customers. Its YouTube channel features videos that mostly highlight the work culture at Zappos headquarters, including behind-the-scenes clips. Zappos runs several blogs, covering many topics related to its business.

New Initiatives

Zappos has recently launched two new initiatives in the human resources area. The first is that it's ditching conventional job postings to recruit new hires, instead launching Zappos Insiders, an internal social network design to improve the recruiting process. The site invites job seekers to join a team within the network. They'll receive information about the department they're interested in, including an assessment of the jobs that come open the most frequently. Zappos employees then interact with candidates to ascertain which candidates represent the best fit. You can see how Zappos Insiders works by going to www.zappos.com/choose_your_team.

The second new initiative is a bold one. Zappos is adopting a "holacracy" approach to organizing the company. Zappos will eliminate traditional managers, do away with typical corporate hierarchy, and get rid of job titles, at least internally. The idea is to replace the traditional corporate chain of command with a series of overlapping, self-governing teams. The idea is to give employees more of a voice in the way the company is run, and to keep Zappos lean and nimble as it continues to grow.

What Lies Ahead

By all accounts, Amazon.com has been true to its word and has allowed Zappos to operate independently since it acquired the firm in 2009. Zappos is still quirky, is pushing the boundaries in regard to customer service and human resources management, and is reportedly profitable and growing. It has added to its product line—along with shoes and clothing it now sells bags, housewares, beauty products, eyewear, jewelry, and a number of other categories of products.

Two main challenges lie ahead for Zappos with the first one being competition in its primary categories—shoes and clothing. Zappos is a mainstream online retailer that carries shoes and clothing across the price gamut. Its women's heels, for example, range from $696 Robert Clergerie Divanas to $46.99 Soft Style choices. The challenge with this strategy is that Zappos is now being attacked by niche players at both ends of the price spectrum. In shoes, for example, it's being attacked from the top by high-end online retailers like Bluefly (www.bluefly.com), which have a larger selection of high-end shoes than Zappos does, and from the bottom by low-end online shoe retailers like Payless Shoes (www.payless.com), which sells shoes for as little as $9.99. A similar dynamic exists in online clothing. Zappos also has competition from mainline online shoe and clothing retailers that sell across the price spectrum like it does. Competitors include Shoebuy.com and JCPenny.com.

The second challenge is whether Zappos will be able to maintain its unique culture. Often, the quirky nature of a start-up culture gives way to a more formal culture as a company grows and matures. Zappos seems to be resisting this, in part by implementing the new hiring practices and new way of organizing as described above. A wild card regarding Zappos's culture is whether Tony Hsieh will remain at the helm. There is no indication that Hsieh plans to leave, but if he did, Zappos would lose its spiritual leader. A change in leadership at the top could result in Zappos moving more in the direction of a mainstream company rather than preserving its unusual, yet seemingly effective, corporate culture.

Discussion Questions

9-41. How should Nick Swinmurn, Zappos's founder, be described in terms of the qualities of a founder that are discussed in this chapter?

9-42. How has Zappos gone about recruiting key employees and why are the employees so critical to the firm's ongoing success?

9-43. What steps is Zappos taking to adjust the nature of what has been its new-venture team for many years?

9-44. How might consultants help Zappos deal with two key challenges (as mentioned in the case) the firm faces today?

Sources: Zappos home page, www.zappos.com, accessed June 15, 2014; R. Dragani, "Zappos Gives Old-School Recruitment the Boot," *Ecommerce Times*, available at http://www.ecommercetimes.com/story/80515.html?rss=1, posted on May 28, 2014, accessed on June 14, 2014; J. McGregor, "Zappos Says Goodbye to Bosses," *Washington Post*, January 3, 2014; M. Chafkin, "The Zappos Way of Managing," www.inc.com/magazine/20090501/the-zappos-way-of-managing_pagen_4.html, posted May 1, 2009, accessed June 14, 2014; T. Hsieh, *Delivering Happiness* (New York: Hachette Book Group, 2010).

Endnotes

1. A. Klotz, K. M. Hmieleski, B. H. Bradley, and L. W. Busenitz, "New Venture Teams: A Review of the Literature and Roadmap for Future Research," *Journal of Management*, 40, no. 5 (2013): 1–30.
2. A. Amezcua, M. Grimes, S. Bradley, and J. Wiklund, "Organizational Sponsorship and Founding Environments: A Contingency View on the Survival of Business Incubated Firms, 1994-2007," *Academy of Management Journal*, 56, no. 6 (2013): 1–29; A. Stinchcombe, "Social Structure and Organization," in *Handbook of Organizations*, ed. James G. March (Chicago: Rand McNally, 1965), 142–193.
3. C. Read, J. Ross, J. Dunleavy, D. Schulman, and J. Bramante, *eCFO* (Chichester, UK: John Wiley & Sons, 2001), 117.
4. J. Y.-K. Lim, L. W. Busenitz, and L. Chidambaram, "New Venture Teams and the Quality of Business Opportunities Identified: Faultlines Between Subgroups of Founders and Investors," *Entrepreneurship Theory and Practice* 37, no. 1 (2013): 47–67.
5. D. Miller, I. Le Breton-Miller, and R. H. Lester, "Family and Lone Founder Ownership and Strategic Behaviour: Social Context, Identity, and Institutional Logics," *Journal of Management Studies* 48, no. 1 (2011): 1–25; L. He, "Do Founders Matter? A Study of Executive Compensation, Governance Structure and Firm Performance," *Journal of Business Venturing* 23, no. 3 (2008): 257–279.
6. R. Baptista, M. Karaoz, and J. Mendonca, "The Impact of Human Capital on the Early Success of Necessity versus Opportunity-Based Entrepreneurs," *Small Business Economics* 42, no. 4 (2013): 831–847.
7. P. M. Kreiser, P. C. Patel, and J. O. Fiet, "The Influence of Changes in Social Capital on Firm-Founding Activities," *Entrepreneurship Theory and Practice* 37, no. 3 (2013): 539–568.
8. M. Suster, "The Co-Founder Mythology," Both Sides of the Table blog, www.bothsidesofthetable.com/2011/05/09/the-co-founder-mythology originally posted on May 9, 2011, (accessed May 10, 2011).
9. K. Eisenhardt. "Top Management Teams and the Performance of Entrepreneurial Firms," *Small Business Economics* 40, no. 6 (2013): 805–816.
10. P. H. Kim and K. C. Longest, "You Can't Leave Your Work Behind: Employment Experience and Founding Collaborations," *Journal of Business Venturing*, 2014, in press; M. D. Foo, "Teams Developing Business Ideas: How Member Characteristics and Conflict Affect Member-Rated Team Effectiveness," *Small Business Economics* 36, no. 1 (2011): 33–46.
11. L. Schjoedt, E. Monsen, A. Pearson, T. Barnett, and J. J. Chrisman, "New Venture and Family Business Teams: Understanding Team Formation, Composition, Behaviors, and Performance," *Entrepreneurship Theory and Practice* 37, no. 1 (2013): 1–15.
12. A. Leung, M. D. Foo, and S. Chaturvedi, "Imprinting Effects of Founding Core Teams on HR Values in New Ventures," *Entrepreneurship Theory and Practice* 37, no. 1 (2013): 87–106.
13. B. L. Herrmann, "The 7 Signs of Failure of Internet Startups," VentureBeat, available at http://venturebeat.com/2011/05/30/the-7-signs-of-failure-for-internet-startups/, (posted on May 30, 2011, accessed on June 1, 2014).
14. T. J. Bae, S. Qian, C. Miao, and J. O. Fiet, "The Relationship Between Entrepreneurship Education and Entrepreneurial Intentions: A Meta-Analytic Review," *Entrepreneurship Theory and Practice* 38, no. 2 (2014): 217–254.
15. R. Toft-Kehler, K. Wennberg, and P. H. Kim, "Practice Makes Perfect: Entrepreneurial-Experience Curves and Venture Performance," *Journal of Business Venturing* 29, no. 4 (2014): 453–470; M. Gruber, I. MacMillan, and J. D. Thompson, "From Minds to Markets: How Human Capital Endowments Shape Market Opportunity Identification of Technology Start-Ups," *Journal of Management* 38, no. 5 (2012): 421–449.
16. G. Cassar, "Industry and Startup Experience on Entrepreneur Forecast Performance in New Firms," *Journal of Business Venturing* 29, no. 1 (2014): 137–151.
17. J. C. Dencker and M. Gruber, "The Effects of Opportunities and Founder Experience on New Firm Performance," *Strategic Management Journal*, 2014, in press.
18. D. Grichnik, J. Brinckmann, L. Singh, and S. Manigart, "Beyond Environmental Scarcity: Human and Social Capital as Driving Forces of Bootstrapping Activities," *Journal of Business Venturing* 29, no. 2 (2014): 310–326; J. Brinckmann and M. Hoegl, "Effects of Initial Teamwork Capability and Initial Relational Capability on the Development of New Technology-Based Firms," *Strategic Entrepreneurship Journal* 5, no. 1 (2011): 37–57.
19. D. M. Sullivan and C. M. Ford, "How Entrepreneurs Use Networks to Address Changing Resource Requirements During Early Venture Development," *Entrepreneurship Theory and Practice* 38, no. 5 (2014): 551–574.
20. D. Jacobe, "U.S. Small Businesses Struggle to Find Qualified Employees," available at http://www.gallup.com/poll/160532/small-businesses-struggle-find-qualified-employees.aspx, (originally posted on February 15, 2013, accessed on June 12, 2014).
21. *Small Business Digest*, "Finding the Right Employees Vexes Small-Business Leaders," www.2sbdigest.com/small-business-hires

(originally posted on May 11, 2011, accessed May 11, 2011).

22. B. Barringer, *Launching a Business: The First 100 Days* (New York: Business Expert Press, 2013).

23. B. Barringer, *Launching a Business: The First 100 Days* (New York: Business Expert Press, 2013).

24. H. Schultz, *Pour Your Heart into It* (New York: Hyperion, 1997), 82.

25. N. Wilson, M. Wright, and L. Scholes, "Family Business Survival and the Role of Boards," *Entrepreneurship Theory and Practice* 37, no. 6 (2013): 1369–1389.

26. S. Garg and K. M. Eisenhardt, "Board Level Strategic Decision Making," *Academy of Management Review* 38, no.1 (2013): 90–108.

27. S. A. Lee, M. J. Kroll, and B. A. Walters, "Outside Directors' Experience, TMT Firm-Specific Human Capital, and Firm Performance in Entrepreneurial IPO Firms," *Journal of Business Research* 66, no. 4 (2013): 533–539.

28. R. Charan, *Boards at Work* (San Francisco: Jossey-Bass Publishers, 1998), 3.

29. C. Hopp and C. Lukas, "A Signaling Perspective on Partner Selection in Venture Capital Syndicates," *Entrepreneurship Theory and Practice* 38, no. 3 (2014): 635–670; B. L. Connelly, S. T. Certo, R. D. Ireland, and C. R. Reutzel, "Signaling Theory: An Assessment and Review," *Journal of Management* 36, no. 1 (2011): 39–67.

30. Potbelly home page, www.potbelly.com, (accessed June 12, 2014).

31. A. Pugliese, A. Minichilli, and A. Zattoni, "Integrating Agency and Resource Dependence Theory: Firm Profitability, Industry Regulation, and Board Task Performance," *Journal of Business Research* 67, no. 6 (2014): 1189–1200; P. Devorak, "Board of Advisers Can Help Steer Small Firms to Right Track," *Wall Street Journal*, March 3, 2008, B4.

32. A. Sherman, *Fast-Track Business Growth* (Washington, DC: Kiplinger Books, 2001).

33. S. Blank and B. Dorf, *The Startup Owner's Manual* (Pescadero, CA: K&S Ranch, Inc., 2012).

34. Coolibar home page, www.coolibar.com, (accessed June 12, 2014).

35. Intouch Technologies home page, www.intouchhealth.com, (accessed June 12, 2014).

36. M. Knockaert, E. S. Bjornali, and T. Erikson, "Joining Forces: Top Management Team and Board Chair Characteristics as Antecedents of Board Service Involvement," *Journal of Business Venturing*, 2014, in press.

37. W. Drover, M. S. Wood, and G. T. Payne, "The Effects of Perceived Control on Venture Capitalist Investment Decisions: A Configurational Perspective," *Entrepreneurship Theory and Practice*, 2014, in press; N. Rosenbusch, J. Brinckmann, and V. Muller, "Does Acquiring Venture Capital Pay Off for the Funded Firms? A Meta-Analysis on the Relationship Between Venture Capital Investment and Funded Firm Financial Performance," *Journal of Business Venturing* 28, no. 3 (2013): 335–353.

38. D. Khanin and O. Turel, "Conflicts and Regrets in the Venture Capitalist-Entrepreneurs Relationship," *Journal of Small Business Management*, 2014, in press.

39. R. Stross, *eBoys* (New York: Crown Books, 2000), 29.

40. P. Belleflamme, T. Lambert, and A. Schwienbacher, "Crowdfunding: Tapping the Right Crowd," *Journal of Business Venturing*, 2014, in press; T. W. Moss, D. O. Neubam, and M. Meyskens, "The Effect of Virtuous and Entrepreneurial Orientations on Microfinance Lending and Repayment: A Signaling Theory Perspective," *Entrepreneurship Theory and Practice*, 2014, in press.

41. SCORE home page, www.score.org, (accessed May 14, 2014).

42. J. J. Chrisman and W. E. McMullan, "A Preliminary Assessment of Outsider Assistance as a Knowledge Resource: The Longer-Term Impact of New Venture Counseling," *Entrepreneurship Theory and Practice* 24, no. 1 (2000): 37–53.

Getting Personal with ROOMINATE

Co-Founders

ALICE BROOKS

Master's in Mechanical Engineering Design, Stanford, 2012

BETTINA CHEN

Master's in Electrical Engineering, Stanford, 2012

Dialogue with
Alice Brooks

MY FAVORITE SMARTPHONE APP
Facebook

MY BIGGEST WORRY AS AN ENTREPRENEUR
Prioritizing the right activities

FIRST ENTREPRENEURIAL EXPERIENCE
Lemonade and cookie stand in 3rd grade. It was very successful.

BEST PART OF BEING A STUDENT
Being in an environment where everyone wants to learn

WHAT I DO WHEN I'M NOT WORKING
Sleeping, cooking, or watching TV

MY BIGGEST SURPRISE AS AN ENTREPRENEUR
How supportive our customers have been since the beginning

CHAPTER 10
Getting *Financing* or Funding

OPENING PROFILE

ROOMINATE
Raising Money Carefully and Deliberately

• *Web: www.roominatetoy.com* • *Facebook: Roominate* • *Twitter: @Roominate*

Alice Brooks and Bettina Chen met in 2012, when they were engineering master's students at Stanford University. They both noticed the lack of female classmates. Both had undergraduate degrees in engineering and reflected that females are underrepresented in undergraduate engineering programs too. They set out to try to put their fingers on why more girls aren't attracted to engineering programs. In the accompanying photo, Alice Brooks is on the left and Bettina Chen is on the right.

After giving it some thought, they realized that they had two things in common that might explain why they chose engineering. First, the toys they played with when they were young instilled in them a love for making things. When Brooks was eight she asked for a Barbie Doll for Christmas and got a saw. She used the saw to cut up wood and nail the pieces together to make dolls and animals. She believes that that experience sparked in her a love for making things and for engineering. Similarly, as a young girl Chen spent hours designing things, not with a saw but with Legos. She designed elaborate Lego structures with her older brother, and feels that that instilled in her a love for making things and using her imagination. The second thing the two had in common was a result of the first. They both built skills, as youngsters, that were important to them in sticking with engineering.

Brooks and Chen also found that they both shared an entrepreneurial spirit. They decided to tackle the challenge of encouraging more girls to enter engineering. The idea they came up with was to develop a toy that would provide young girls similar experiences to those they benefited from as children. The toy, they reasoned, had to develop skills such as spatial reasoning, hands-on-problem solving, and self-confidence. The idea they settled on was a kit of pastel-colored pieces that girls could assemble into a building or any other type of structure. Once the building was built, it could be decorated with included paper and other embellishments, and a small motor could be used to add electrical appliances, fans, buzzers, or anything else that uses power. The kit, or toy, would come in a board game–sized box and be called Roominate.

At the same time Brooks and Chen were conceiving Roominate, they were taking a Lean Launchpad class at Stanford taught by Steve Blank. Blank is known for

LEARNING OBJECTIVES

After studying this chapter you should be ready to:

1. Describe the importance of financing for entrepreneurial success.

2. Explain why most entrepreneurial ventures need to raise money during their early life.

3. Identify and describe the three sources of personal financing available to entrepreneurs.

4. Identify and explain the three steps involved in properly preparing to raise debt or equity financing.

5. Explain the three most important sources of equity funding that are available to the entrepreneurial firm.

6. Describe common sources of debt financing entrepreneurial firms use.

7. Describe several creative sources of financing entrepreneurial firms may choose to use.

encouraging students and others to "get out of the building" and talk to as many potential customers as possible while developing a business idea. Brooks and Chen followed Blank's advice. They interacted with over 200 girls in their target age range (ages 6–12) to see what worked best. They also asked young girls to experiment with early prototypes of Roominate at local events and the Children's Creativity Museum in San Francisco. They took time to talk to parents and educators and did a lot of prototyping. Brooks and Chen followed Blank's class with two stints at StartX, which is Stanford's start-up accelerator. Through this program they were put in touch with mentors and subject matter experts, such as attorneys, who helped them develop the business side of Roominate.

The next step was raising funds. Money was needed for two reasons. First, the entrepreneurs needed financial capital so they could scale production through large-quantity orders of wood, electronics, and assembly costs. At this point, Brooks and Chen were assembling Roominate kits by hand, which was unsustainable. Second, because Roominate was designed to be played with by children under the age of 14, money was needed to fulfill the tests required to certify compliance with toy safety standards.

Brooks and Chen decided to launch a Kickstarter campaign. The campaign was launched in mid-2012 with a $25,000 goal. Pause for a moment and go to https://www.kickstarter.com and type "Roominate" into the search box. Although the Roominate campaign is long since over, Kickstarter archives all campaigns indefinitely. You'll be able to view the video pitch, see what the Roominate toy looks like, and examine the specifics of the campaign. The $25,000 goal was easily exceeded, with $85,964 raised from 1,154 backers. The successful Kickstarter campaign was a big plus for Brooks and Chen. Not only did it help fund their initial production run, but the overwhelmingly positive response was a big confidence-builder.

Since the Kickstarter campaign concluded in mid-2012, Roominate has progressed. In defining the first three years of Roominate, Brooks characterizes year one (2012) as developing the product and raising money via Kickstarter, year two (2013) as finding customers and slowly building sales, and year three (2014) as finding retailers and ramping up. In 2013 and 2014, Brooks and Chen raised approximately $1 million from angel investors to fund the buildup. Several things happened along the way that demonstrated momentum, which was important in securing the angel investments. First, Roominate won several toy awards, which provided external validation for the efficacy of the idea and the product. Along with that, it attracted positive PR, including an appearance by Brooks and Chen on the *Today Show* in 2013. Second, sales started to build in 2013, primarily through specialty stores, the Roominate website, and via Amazon.com. Third, mainstream retailers, including Toys"R"Us and Walmart, started showing interest.

The next logical step for Roominate, in terms of funding, would be a Series A round of venture capital. Roominate's ability to get to that point will depend on whether it demonstrates broad product acceptance and is seen as a potential high-growth business.

In this chapter, we focus on the process of getting financing or funding. We begin by discussing why firms raise capital. We follow this with a description of personal financing and the importance of personal funds, capital from friends and family, and bootstrapping in the early life of a firm. We then turn to the different forms of equity, debt, and creative financing available to entrepreneurial ventures. We also emphasize the importance of preparing to secure these types of financing.

The Importance of Getting Financing or Funding

Few people deal with the process of raising investment capital until they need to raise capital for their own firm. As a result, many entrepreneurs go about the task of raising capital haphazardly, because they lack experience in this area and because they don't know much about their choices.[1] This shortfall may cause a business owner to place too much reliance on some sources of capital and not enough on others.[2] Entrepreneurs need to have as full an understanding as possible of the alternatives that are available in regard to raising money. And raising money is a balancing act. Although a venture may need to raise money to survive, its founders usually don't want to deal with people who don't understand or care about their long-term goals.

The need to raise money surprises a number of entrepreneurs, in that many of them launch their firms with the intention of funding all their needs internally. Commonly, though, entrepreneurs discover that operating without investment capital or borrowed money is more difficult than they anticipated. Because of this, it is important for entrepreneurs to understand the role of investment capital in the survival and subsequent success of a new firm.

LEARNING OBJECTIVE

1. Describe the importance of financing for entrepreneurial success.

Why Most New Ventures Need Funding

There are three reasons that most entrepreneurial ventures need to raise money during their early life: cash flow challenges, capital investments, and lengthy product development cycles. These reasons are laid out in Figure 10.1. Let's look at each reason so we can better understand their importance.

LEARNING OBJECTIVE

2. Explain why most entrepreneurial ventures need to raise money during their early life.

Cash Flow Challenges

As a firm grows, it requires an increasing amount of cash to operate as the foundation for serving its customers. Often, equipment must be purchased and new employees hired and trained before the increased customer base generates additional income. The lag between spending to generate revenue and earning income from the firm's operations creates cash flow challenges, particularly for new, often small, ventures, as well as for ventures that are growing rapidly.

If a firm operates in the red, its negative real-time cash flow, usually computed monthly, is called its burn rate. A company's **burn rate** is the rate at which it is spending its capital until it reaches profitability. Although a negative cash flow is sometimes justified early in a firm's life—to build plants and buy equipment, train employees, and establish its brand—it can cause severe complications. A firm usually fails if it burns through all its capital before it becomes profitable. This is why inadequate financial resources is a primary reason new firms fail.[3] A firm can simply run out of money even if it has good products and satisfied customers.

Cash Flow Challenges	Capital Investments	Lengthy Product Development Cycles
Inventory must be purchased, employees must be trained and paid, and advertising must be paid for before cash is generated from sales.	The cost of buying real estate, building facilities, and purchasing equipment typically exceeds a firm's ability to provide funds for these needs on its own.	Some products are under development for years before they generate earnings. The up-front costs often exceed a firm's ability to fund these activities on its own.

FIGURE 10.1

Three Reasons Start-Ups Need Funding

Being an entrepreneur in the biotech industry requires a lot of determination and drive. The path to getting a new drug approved takes up to 10 years. This "tortoise-like pace" of new product development takes substantial up-front investment.

Anyaivanova/Shutterstock

To prevent their firms from running out of money, most entrepreneurs need investment capital or a line of credit from a bank to cover cash flow shortfalls until their firms can begin making money. It is usually difficult for a new firm to get a line of credit from a bank (for reasons discussed later). Because of this, new ventures often look for investment capital, bootstrap their operations, or try to arrange some type of creative financing.

Capital Investments

Firms often need to raise money early on to fund capital investments. Although it may be possible for the venture's founders to fund its initial activities, it becomes increasingly difficult for them to do so when it comes to buying property, constructing buildings, purchasing equipment, or investing in other capital projects. Many entrepreneurial ventures are able to delay or avoid these types of expenditures by leasing space or co-opting the resources of alliance partners. However, at some point in its growth cycle, the firm's needs may become specialized enough that it makes sense to purchase capital assets rather than rent or lease them.

Lengthy Product Development Cycles

In some industries, firms need to raise money to pay the up-front costs of lengthy product development cycles. For example, it typically takes between one and a half and two years to develop an electronic game. In the biotech industry, the path to commercial licensing takes approximately eight years.[4] This tortoise-like pace of product development requires substantial up-front investment before the anticipated payoff is realized. While the biotech industry is an extreme example, lengthy product development cycles are the realities ventures face in many industries.

To meet these challenges, and others described in the chapter and throughout the book, many entrepreneurs like to partner with others to launch their ventures. A fertile place for young entrepreneurs to find potential business partners is to attend a Startup Weekend. A description of what Startup Weekend is and why it represents a fertile place to find a business partner is describe in the "Partnering for Success" feature nearby.

PARTNERING FOR SUCCESS

Startup Weekend: A Fertile Place to Meet Business Cofounders

Startup Weekend: Web: www.startupweekend.com; Facebook: startupweekend; Twitter: @StartupWeekend

Startup Weekend is a not-for-profit organization that organizes weekend events. The purpose is to create a context in which small groups of people conceive and start a business in 54 hours. Startup Weekends are held periodically in local communities and on college campuses across the United States. Since Startup Weekend launched in 2006, the organization has helped local volunteers put on over 1,500 Startup Weekend events in 726 cities. The events have involved over 123,000 entrepreneurs. Over 13,000 businesses have been started during Startup Weekend events.

Here's how it works. Each Startup Weekend is semi-autonomous and is organized by a group of local volunteers. The local volunteers get support through Startup Weekend's events team, which is located in Seattle, Washington. The local volunteers pick the date, find a venue to hold the event, and organize the weekend. A typical Startup Weekend attracts 60-120 people. The ideal mix of participants is 50 percent technical (developers, coders, designers) and 50 percent business (marketing, finance, law). The only requirement for admission (other than a nominal admission fee) is to have a passion for entrepreneurship and a willingness to work with like-minded, motivated people to develop a product or business in one weekend.

Many Startup Weekends are organized around themes. Examples include Fashion & Tech, Mobile, Education, Health & Wellness, and Food. A Startup Weekend is organized as follows.

Friday: Participants arrive between 5 and 7 p.m., begin networking, and eat dinner. After a short ice-breaking exercise, the pitches begin. Anyone is welcome to make a 60-second pitch of a business idea. If the Startup Weekend is a themed weekend (like Fashion & Tech or Health & Wellness), all the pitches must adhere to the theme. After the pitches are finished, all attendees vote on their favorites. The top ideas are selected to be worked on for the weekend. Teams form organically and consolidate, and the work begins.

Saturday: Teams work all day, with the occasional breaks to eat. Mentors and coaches circulate to provide support and advice. Individual team members reach out to people in their networks (typically via text or e-mail) to solicit feedback and advice. The pace is quick and intense, and the business idea may iterate multiple times. A path forward is eventually agreed upon and a rough prototype takes shape. Most teams build a website.

Approximately 95 percent of Startup Weekend ideas are mobile or Web focused (regardless of the theme), thus the need for developers, coders, and designers. The idea is not to conceive an idea for a business. The idea is to build a business.

Sunday: Teams continue their work from morning until mid-afternoon. Around 3 to 4 p.m., they start wrapping things up and practicing their presentations. After the judges arrive, presentations begin. The initial 50-person group is now ten 5-person teams. The judges select the top teams, give out awards, and the event ends—with just 54 hours from first hearing an idea to the birth of a business.

Afterwards: Whether the team stays together after the Startup Weekend concludes is strictly up to the members of the team. About 55 percent of Startup Weekend participants continue working on their idea with their team intact. Approximately 23 percent continue working together with some of their team members. Thus, for participants, Startup Weekend is a fertile place to find a team of people to work with on a business idea. To learn whether a Startup Weekend is being planned for your city or area, simply access the "Upcoming Events" link on Startup Weekend's website.

There is a version of Startup Weekend called 3 Day Startup that is designed specifically for college campuses. It is a for-profit organization, but provides more structure and support than Startup Weekend provides. You can learn more about 3 Day Startup at 3daystartup.org.

Questions for Critical Thinking

1. In referring to Startup Weekend, someone made the comment "It's not a start-up factory, it's an entrepreneur factory." What do you think the person meant by that comment?
2. To what degree do you agree with the basic premise of the feature that Startup Weekends represent a fertile place to meet business co-founders?
3. What can people learn by attending a Startup Weekend, even if they ultimately do not stay together with their team after the weekend ends?
4. Spend some time looking at the website for 3 Day Startup. How do Startup Weekend and 3 Day Startup compare? Are both equally suited for college student entrepreneurs?

Source: Startup Weekend home page, www.startupweekend.com, accessed September 18, 2014.

Sources of Personal Financing

LEARNING OBJECTIVE

3. Identify and describe the three sources of personal financing available to entrepreneurs.

Typically, the seed money that gets a company off the ground comes from the founders' own pockets. There are three categories of sources of money in this area: personal funds, friends and family, and bootstrapping. These sources are depicted in Figure 10.2 and are explained next.

Personal Funds

The vast majority of founders contribute personal funds along with **sweat equity** to their ventures.[5] In fact, according to data complied by Fundable, 57 percent of start-ups are funded by the entrepreneurs' personal savings and credit. The average amount invested is $48,000.[6] Sweat equity, which represents the value of the time and effort that a founder puts into a new venture, is also important. Because many founders do not have a substantial amount of cash to put into their ventures, it is often the sweat equity that makes the most difference.

Friends and Family

Friends and family are the second source of funds for many new ventures. According to the same Fundable data, 38 percent of start-ups are funded by friends and family, with an average investment of $23,000.[7] This type of contribution often comes in the form of loans or investments, but can also involve outright gifts, foregone or delayed compensation (if a friend or family member works for the new venture), or reduced or free rent. For example, Cisco Systems, the giant producer of Internet routers and switches, started in the house of one of its co-founder's parents.

There are three rules of thumb that entrepreneurs should follow when asking friends and family members for money. First, the request should be presented in a businesslike manner, just like one would deal with a banker or investor. The potential of the business along with the risks involved should be carefully and fully described. Second, if the help the entrepreneur receives is in the form of a loan, a promissory note should be prepared, with a repayment schedule, and the note should be signed by both parties. Stipulating the terms of the loan in writing reduces the potential of a misunderstanding and protects both the entrepreneur and the friend or family member providing the funding. Third, financial help should be requested only from those who are in a legitimate position to offer assistance. It's not a good idea to ask certain friends or family members, regardless of how much they may have expressed a willingness to help, for assistance if losing the money would cripple them financially. Entrepreneurs who are unable to repay a loan to a friend or family member risk not only damaging their business relationship with them, but their personal relationship as well.[8]

FIGURE 10.2
Sources of Personal Financing

Personal Funds	Friends and Family	Bootstrapping
Involves both financial resources and sweat equity. Sweat equity represents the value of the time and effort that a founder puts into a firm.	Often comes in the form of loans or investments, but can also involve outright gifts, foregone or delayed compensation, or reduced or free rent.	Finding ways to avoid the need for external financing through creativity, ingenuity, thriftiness, cost-cutting, obtaining grants, or any other means.

LendingKarma (www.lendingkarma.com) helps people involved with friends and family develop loan documents and then track the loans. Following a simple set of online commands, a user can select a loan amount, designate if he or she is the borrower or lender, and set various options such as interest rate, payment frequency, and length of loan. A promissory note, in PDF format, can then be created, along with an amortization schedule. Two tiers of service are available. The premium service, which costs $59.95 per loan, includes all of the above plus online payment tracking and end-of-year reporting, and it allows the parties involved to modify loan documents during repayment. A more basic-service alternative costs $29.95 per loan.[9] For people who only need documents prepared, online document preparation and filing services such as LegalZoom.com and RocketLawyer.com are available. Accountants, attorneys, and bankers can also help individuals structure their loan agreements.

Bootstrapping

Bootstrapping is a third source of seed money for new ventures. **Bootstrapping** is finding ways to avoid the need for external financing or funding through creativity, ingenuity, thriftiness, cost-cutting, or any means necessary.[10] (The term comes from the adage "pull yourself up by your bootstraps.") It is the term attached to the general philosophy of minimizing start-up expenses by aggressively pursuing cost-cutting techniques and money-saving tactics. There are many well-known examples of entrepreneurs who bootstrapped to get their companies started. Legend has it that Steve Jobs and partner Steve Wozniak sold a Volkswagen van and a Hewlett-Packard programmable calculator to raise $1,350, which was the initial seed capital for Apple Computer.

There are many ways entrepreneurs bootstrap to raise money or cut costs. Some of the more common examples of bootstrapping are provided in Table 10.1. A simple example of bootstrapping is that fax machines are no longer an absolute necessity, in most cases. There are several Web-based services that allow businesses to fax documents for free or for a small monthly fee, as long as they have a scanner and are able to scan the document into a word processing program. The document can then be sent to the recipient's fax machine and it will print out as a normal fax. Examples of companies that offer variations of this service are eFax, MyFax, and OnlineFaxes. The overarching point is that a little ingenuity (learning how to fax for free, for example) can save an entrepreneur the cost of purchasing a fax machine.

While bootstrapping and using personal funds are highly recommended actions in almost all start-up situations, there are subtle downsides. Cost-cutting and saving money are admirable practices, but pushing these practices too far can hold a business back from reaching its full potential. For example, renting space in a community incubator or building where other start-ups are

TABLE 10.1 Examples of Bootstrapping Methods

- Buy used instead of new equipment
- Coordinate purchases with other businesses
- Lease equipment instead of buying
- Obtain payments in advance from customers
- Minimize personal expenses
- Avoid unnecessary expenses, such as lavish office space or furniture
- Buy items cheaply, but prudently, through discount outlets or online auctions such as eBay, rather than at full-price stores
- Share office space or employees with other businesses
- Hire interns

located, rather than working from home, may be worth it if it provides entrepreneurs access to a network of people who can be relied on to provide social
support and business advice.[11]

Preparing to Raise Debt or Equity Financing

LEARNING OBJECTIVE

4. Identify and explain the three steps involved in properly preparing to raise debt or equity financing.

Once a start-up's financial needs exceed what personal funds, friends and family, and bootstrapping can provide, debt and equity are the two most common
sources of funds. The most important thing an entrepreneur must do at this
point is determine precisely what the company needs and the most appropriate
source to use to obtain those funds. A carefully planned approach to raising
money increases a firm's chance of success and can save an entrepreneur considerable time.

The steps involved in properly preparing to raise debt or equity financing
are shown in Figure 10.3 and are discussed next.

Step 1   **Determine precisely how much money the company needs.**
Constructing and analyzing documented cash flow statements and
projections for needed capital expenditures are actions taken to
complete this step. This information should already be in the business plan, as described in Chapter 6. Knowing exactly how much
money to ask for is important for at least two reasons. First, a company doesn't want to get caught short, yet it doesn't want to pay for
capital it doesn't need. Second, entrepreneurs talking to a potential
lender or investor make a poor impression when they appear uncertain about the amount of money required to support their venture.

Step 2   **Determine the most appropriate type of financing or funding.**
Equity and debt financing are the two most common alternatives
for raising money. **Equity financing** (or funding) means exchanging
partial ownership of a firm, usually in the form of stock, in return
for funding. Angel investors, private placement, venture capital, and
initial public offerings are the most common sources of equity funding (we discuss all these sources later in the chapter). Equity funding
is not a loan—the money that is received is not paid back. Instead,
equity investors become partial owners of the firm. Some equity investors invest "for the long haul" and are content to receive a return
on their investment through dividend payments on their stock. More
commonly, equity investors have a three- to five-year investment
horizon and expect to get their money back, along with a substantial capital gain, through the sale of their stock. The stock is typically sold following a **liquidity event**, which is an occurrence that
converts some or all of a company's stock into cash. The three most
common liquidity events for a new venture are when it goes public,
finds a buyer, or merges with another company.

FIGURE 10.3
Preparation for Debt or
Equity Financing

Because of the risks involved, equity investors are very demanding and fund only a small percentage of the business plans they consider.[12] An equity investor considers a firm that has a unique business opportunity, high growth potential, a clearly defined niche market, and proven management to be an ideal candidate. In contrast, businesses that don't fit these criteria have a hard time getting equity funding. Many entrepreneurs are not familiar with the standards that equity investors apply and get discouraged when they are repeatedly turned down by venture capitalists and angel investors. Often, the reason they don't qualify for venture capital or angel investment isn't because their business proposal is poor, but because they don't meet the exacting standards equity investors usually apply.[13]

Debt financing is getting a loan. The most common sources of debt financing are commercial banks and Small Business Administration (SBA) guaranteed loans. The types of bank loans and SBA guaranteed loans available to entrepreneurs are discussed later in this chapter. In general, banks lend money that must be repaid with interest. Banks are not investors. As a result, bankers are interested in minimizing risk, properly collateralizing loans, and repayment, as opposed to return on investment and capital gains. The ideal candidate for a bank loan is a firm with a strong cash flow, low leverage, audited financial statements, good management, and a healthy balance sheet. A careful review of these criteria demonstrates why it's difficult for start-ups to receive bank loans. Most start-ups are simply too early in their life cycle to have the set of characteristics bankers want.

Table 10.2 provides an overview of three common profiles of new ventures and the type of financing or funding that is appropriate for each one. This table illustrates why most start-ups must rely on personal funds, friends and family, and bootstrapping at the outset and must wait until later to obtain equity or debt financing. Indeed, most new ventures do not have the characteristics required by bankers or investors until they have proven their product or service idea and have achieved a certain measure of success in the marketplace.

Step 3 **Developing a strategy for engaging potential investors or bankers.** There are three steps to developing a strategy for engaging potential investors or bankers. First, the lead entrepreneurs in a new venture should prepare an **elevator speech (or pitch)**—a brief, carefully constructed statement that outlines the merits of a business opportunity. Why is it called an elevator speech? If an entrepreneur stepped into an elevator on the 25th floor of a building and found that by a stroke of luck a potential investor was in the same elevator, the entrepreneur would have the time it takes to get from the 25th floor to the ground floor to try to get the investor interested in the business opportunity. Most elevator speeches are 45 seconds to 2 minutes long.[14]

There are many occasions when a carefully constructed elevator speech might come in handy. For example, many university-sponsored centers for entrepreneurship hold events that bring investors and entrepreneurs together. Often, these events include social hours and refreshment breaks designed specifically for the purpose of allowing entrepreneurs looking for funding to mingle with potential investors. An outline for a 60-second elevator speech is provided in Table 10.3.

The second step in developing a strategy for engaging potential investors or bankers is more deliberate and requires identifying and contacting the best prospects. First, the new venture should carefully assess the type of financing

TABLE 10.2 **Matching an Entrepreneurial Venture's Characteristics with the Appropriate Form of Financing or Funding**

Characteristics of the Venture	Appropriate Source of Financing or Funding
The business has high risk with an uncertain return:	Personal funds, friends, family, and other forms of bootstrapping
Weak cash flow	
High leverage	
Low to moderate growth	
Unproven management	
The business has low risk with a more predictable return:	Debt financing
Strong cash flow	
Low leverage	
Audited financials	
Good management	
Healthy balance sheet	
The business offers a high return:	Equity
Unique business idea	
High growth	
Niche market	
Proven management	

or funding it is likely to qualify for, as depicted in Table 10.2. Then, a list of potential bankers or investors should be compiled. If venture capital funding is felt to be appropriate, for example, a little legwork can go a long way in pinpointing likely investors. A new venture should identify the venture funds that are investing money in the industry in which it intends to compete and target those firms first. To do this, look to the venture capital firms' websites. These reveal the industries in which the firms have an interest. Sometimes, these sites also provide a list of the companies the firm has funded. For an example, access the website of Sequoia Capital (www.sequoiacap.com), a well-known venture capital firm.

A cardinal rule for approaching a banker or an investor is to get a personal introduction. Bankers and investors receive many business plans, and most of them end up in what often becomes an unread stack of paper in a corner in their offices. To have your business plan noticed, find someone who knows the banker or the investor and ask for an introduction.

The third step in engaging potential investors or bankers is to be prepared to provide the investor or banker a completed business plan and make a presentation of the plan if requested. We looked at how to present a business plan in Chapter 6. The presentation should be as polished as possible and should demonstrate why the new venture represents an attractive endeavor for the lender or investor.

TABLE 10.3 Guidelines for Preparing an Elevator Speech

The elevator speech is a very brief description of your opportunity, product idea, qualifications, and market. Imagine that you step into an elevator in a tall building and a potential investor is already there; you have about 60 seconds to explain your business idea.

Step 1	Describe the opportunity or problem that needs to be solved	20 seconds
Step 2	Describe how your product or service meets the opportunity or solves the problem	20 seconds
Step 3	Describe your qualifications	10 seconds
Step 4	Describe your market	10 seconds
Total		60 seconds

Sources of Equity Funding

LEARNING OBJECTIVE

5. Explain the three most important sources of equity funding that are available to the entrepreneurial firm.

The primary disadvantage of equity funding is that the firm's owners relinquish part of their ownership interest and may lose some control. The primary advantage is access to capital. In addition, because investors become partial owners of the firms in which they invest, they often try to help those firms by offering their expertise and assistance. Unlike a loan, the money received from an equity investor doesn't have to be paid back. The investor receives a return on the investment through dividend payments and by selling the stock.

The three most common forms of equity funding are described next.

Business Angels

Business angels are individuals who invest their personal capital directly in start-ups. The term *angel* was first used in conjunction with finance to describe wealthy New Yorkers who invested in Broadway plays. The prototypical business angel, who invests in entrepreneurial start-ups, is about 50 years old, has high income and wealth, is well educated, has succeeded as an entrepreneur, and invests in companies that are in the region where he or she lives.[15] These investors generally invest between $10,000 and $500,000 in a single company and are looking for companies that have the potential to grow 30 to 40 percent per year before they are acquired or go public.[16] Many well-known firms have received their initial funding from one or more business angels. For example, Apple received its initial investment capital from Mike Markkula, who obtained his wealth as an executive with Intel. In 1977, Markkula invested $91,000 in Apple and personally guaranteed another $250,000 in credit lines. When Apple went public in 1980, his stock in the company was worth more than $150 million.[17] Similarly, in 1998, Google received its first investment from Sun Microsystems's co-founder Andy Bechtolsheim, who gave Larry Page and Sergey Brin (Google's co-founders) a check for $100,000 after they showed him an early version of Google's search engine.[18] Can you imagine what Bechtolsheim's investment was worth when Google went public in 2005?

The number of angel investors in the United States, which is estimated to be around 298,800, has increased dramatically over the past decade.[19] The rapid increase is due in part to the high returns that some angels report. In 2013, angels invested $24.8 billion, an increase of 8.3 percent over 2012. The average deal size was $350,830, which generally included more than one investor.[20] Software accounted for the largest share of angel investment in 2013, with 23 percent of total investment, followed by Media (16 percent), Healthcare Services/Medical Devices and Equipment (14 percent), Biotech (11 percent),

Retail (7 percent), and Financial Services/Business Products and Services (7 percent). The average equity received was 12.5 percent with deal valuation at $2.8 million. According to the Center for Venture Research at the University of New Hampshire, in 2013, 21.6 percent of start-ups that were able to get in front of angel investors received investments. This is a relatively high percentage. Historically, the number has been closer to 15 percent.[21]

Business angels are valuable because of their willingness to make relatively small investments. This gives access to equity funding to a start-up that needs just $75,000 rather than the $1 million minimum investment that most venture capitalists require. Many angels are also motivated by more than financial returns; they enjoy the process of mentoring a new firm. Most angels remain fairly anonymous and are matched up with entrepreneurs through referrals. To find a business angel investor, an entrepreneur should discreetly work a network of acquaintances to see if anyone can make an appropriate introduction. An advantage that college students have in regard to finding business angels is that many angels judge college- or university-sponsored business plan or business model competitions. The number of organized groups of angels continues to grow. Typically, each group consists of 10 to 150 angel investors in a local area that meet regularly to listen to business plan presentations. An example of an angel group is Ann Arbor Angels (www.annarborangels.org) located in Ann Arbor, Michigan. The group invests in early-stage technology companies in Southeast Michigan. Similar to most angel groups, a small committee of members screens investment applications and determines the start-ups that will pitch to the larger group. The group itself does not make investments. Instead, investment decisions are made independently by each member, often in partnership with other members.[22]

According to Fundable, angel investors invest in approximately 61,900 companies per year, which is 16 times the number of investments made by venture capitalists.[23]

Venture Capital

Venture capital is money that is invested by venture capital firms in start-ups and small businesses with exceptional growth potential.[24] There are about 875 venture capital firms in existence, which have approximately $193 billion under management. In 2013, venture capital firms invested $29.6 billion in just over 4,041 deals.[25] The peak year for venture capital investing was 2000, when $98.6 billion was invested at the height of the e-commerce craze. A distinct difference between angel investors and venture capital firms is that angels tend to invest earlier in the life of a company, whereas venture capitalists come in later. The majority of venture capital money goes to follow-on funding for businesses that were originally funded by angel investors, government programs (which are discussed later in the chapter), or by some other means.

Venture capital firms are limited partnerships of money managers who raise money in "funds" to invest in start-ups and growing firms. The funds, or pools of money, are raised from high-net-worth individuals, pension plans, university endowments, foreign investors, and similar sources. In 2013, the average fund size was $110.3 million.[26] The investors who invest in venture capital funds are called **limited partners**. The venture capitalists, who manage the fund, are called **general partners**. The venture capitalists who manage the fund receive an annual management fee in addition to 20 to 25 percent of the profits earned by the fund. The percentage of the profits the venture capitalists get is called the **carry**. So if a venture capital firm raised a $100 million fund and the fund grew to $500 million, a 20 percent carry means that the firm would get, after repaying the original $100 million, 20 percent of the $400

It is always a good idea to practice a pitch to an angel investor or venture capitalist several times before you do it for real. Here, a pair of young entrepreneurs are practicing their pitch in front of a group of friends.

Hero Images/Corbis

million in profits, or $80 million. Some venture capital firms invest in specific areas. For example, Foundry Group invests in information technology start-ups.[27] Similarly, BEV Capital invests exclusively in consumer-oriented businesses, such as 1800diapers and Redfin.[28]

Because of the venture capital industry's lucrative nature and because in the past venture capitalists have funded high-profile successes such as Google, Facebook, Dropbox, and Twitter, the industry receives a great deal of attention. But actually, venture capitalists fund very few entrepreneurial ventures in comparison to business angels and relative to the number of firms seeking funding. According to the 2014 National Venture Capital Yearbook, for every 100 business plans that are submitted to venture capital firms for funding, only 10 get a serious look and only one is funded.[29] As mentioned earlier in this chapter, many entrepreneurs become discouraged when they are repeatedly rejected for venture capital funding, even though they may have an excellent business plan. Venture capitalists are looking for the "home run." The result is that the majority of business plans do not get funded.

Still, for the firms that qualify, venture capital is a viable alternative to equity funding. An advantage to obtaining this funding is that venture capitalists are extremely well connected in the business world (by this we mean that they have a large number of useful contacts with customers, suppliers, government representatives, and so forth) and can offer a firm considerable assistance beyond funding. Firms that qualify typically obtain their money in stages that correspond to their own stage of development. Once a venture capitalist makes an investment in a firm, subsequent investments are made in **rounds** (or stages) and are referred to as **follow-on funding**. Table 10.4 shows the various stages in the venture capital process, from the seed stage to buyout financing.

An important part of obtaining venture capital funding is going through the **due diligence** process, which refers to the process of investigating the merits of a potential venture and verifying the key claims made in the business plan. Firms that prove to be suitable for venture capital funding should conduct their own due diligence of the venture capitalists with whom they are working

TABLE 10.4   Stages (or Rounds) of Venture Capital Funding

Stage or Round	Purpose of the Funding
Seed funding	Investment made very early in a venture's life to fund the development of a prototype and feasibility analysis.
Start-up funding	Investment made to firms exhibiting few if any commercial sales but in which product development and market research are reasonably complete. Management is in place, and the firm has its business model. Funding is needed to start production.
First-stage funding	Funding that occurs when the firm has started commercial production and sales but requires financing to ramp up its production capacity.
Second-stage funding	Funding that occurs when a firm is successfully selling a product but needs to expand both its capacity and its markets.
Mezzanine financing	Investment made in a firm to provide for further expansion or to bridge its financing needs before launching an IPO or before a buyout.
Buyout funding	Funding provided to help one company acquire another.

to ensure that they are a good fit. An entrepreneur should ask the following questions and scrutinize the answers to them before accepting funding from a venture capital firm:

- Do the venture capitalists have experience in our industry?
- Do they take a highly active or passive management role?
- Are the personalities on both sides of the table compatible?
- Does the firm have deep enough pockets or sufficient contacts within the venture capital industry to provide follow-on rounds of financing?
- Is the firm negotiating in good faith in regard to the percentage of our firm they want in exchange for their investment?

Along with traditional venture capital, there is also **corporate venture capital**. This type of capital is similar to traditional venture capital except that the money comes from corporations that invest in start-ups related to their areas of interest. Corporate venture capital firms provide an estimated 10.5 percent of the venture capital invested by all venture groups. Examples of corporate venture capital firms include Intel Capital, Google Ventures, and Time Warner Investments.

Just because a firm receives venture capital funding doesn't mean it's a sure success. In fact, venture-funded firms are under extreme pressure to perform to meet investors' expectations. A firm that received venture capital funding, DrawQuest, and regrettably failed is profiled in the "What Went Wrong?" feature. The feature includes a heartfelt statement by its founder, Chris Poole, which provides unique insight into how failing after taking money from venture capitalists feels.

Initial Public Offering

Another source of equity funding is to sell stock to the public by staging an **initial public offering (IPO)**. An IPO is the first sale of stock by a firm to the public. Any later public issuance of shares is referred to as a **secondary market offering**. When a company goes public, its stock is typically traded on one of the major stock exchanges. Most entrepreneurial firms that go public

WHAT WENT WRONG?

How One Start-up Caught the Attention of VCs, Gained 25,000 Daily Users, and Still Failed

DrawQuest was launched in February 2013 by Christopher Poole. It was a pivot—an earlier version of the product was called Canvas. DrawQuest was an app built for the iPad, iPhone, and iPad Touch. The idea was to encourage creativity through a daily drawing challenge.

Here's how it worked. Each day, a drawing challenge was posted. The DrawQuest screen would display part of a picture and challenge the user to complete it. For example, the screen might show a picture of a child looking out into the water, and the challenge would be "What's in the water?" The user would then complete the picture. Other examples include a screen with a hat at the top, and the challenge would be "Who's wearing the hat?" Similarly the screen might include a person standing on a balcony, and the challenge would be "What can you see from the balcony?" The DrawQuest app provided a basic kit of online drawing tools to complete the picture. The point wasn't to create an elegant drawing. In fact, the tools resulted in the drawings being somewhat cartoonish in nature. The point was to force people to be creative by deciding what to put in the water or what could be seen from the balcony. The app and the basic set of drawing tools were free. DrawQuest made money be selling upgrades to the kit of drawing tools, like better brushes, additional palettes of paint, more vivid colors, and so forth.

The app itself did well. In the short year it was in existence it reached 1.4 million downloads, 550,000 registered users, 400,000 monthly users, and 25,000 daily users. One of the draws was becoming part of the DrawQuest community. You could follow friends and view the drawings that they drew. One of the coolest features was instant replay. You could watch a replay of a friend drawing his or her picture.

To fund the venture, DrawQuest raised money from marquee investors. A $625,000 seed fund was raised in 2010 (when the founders were working on a different app), and $3 million was raised in two subsequent venture rounds from Union Square Ventures, Andreessen Horowitz, Lerer Ventures, Chris Dixon, and several others. Despite all of this, DrawQuest failed. What went wrong?

In a heartfelt bog post titled "Today my startup failed" and in an interview with TechCrunch, Poole outlined the reasons that led to DrawQuest's demise. In short, the company never figured out the business side of the venture. The in-app upgrades, such as better paintbrushes and enhanced palettes of paint, didn't sell as well as anticipated, leaving DrawQuest with insufficient income. Part of the problem was that users didn't feel a sense of urgency to upgrade. A large portion of Candy Crush's success, for example, is that people buy extra lives. DrawQuest didn't have the same emotional "I can't play if I don't pay" urgency. Another problem was that the app was expensive to develop and maintain. In a sobering note to DrawQuest users, explaining that the app would be shut down, Poole wrote:

"While the app and community have come together in a spectacular fashion, the business side of things hasn't gone as well as we had hoped. You may not realize it, but DrawQuest represents of work hours from a very talented seven-person team, who all need to put food on the table and a roof over their heads—not to mention a small army of servers to keep the app running smoothly and Questbot happy."

Another issue DrawQuest encountered was the pivot that Poole and his team executed. Prior to DrawQuest, the team built an app named Canvas that didn't work out. They pivoted to DrawQuest, which resonated better with users and drew a larger audience. The problem is that they spent half their investors' money on Canvas. Referring to that challenge, Poole wrote, "We built this app (DrawQuest) with less than half of our runway remaining. You have to do twice as much with half as much money. It's really freaking hard."

Ultimately, Poole and his team decided to pull the plug. They investigated selling DrawQuest to another company, but no one bit. In the blog post titled "Today my startup failed," Poole provided insight into the human side of business failure. He wrote:

"I'm disappointed that I couldn't produce a better outcome for those who supported me the most— my investors and employees. Few in business will know the pain of what it means to fail as a venture-backed CEO. Not only do you fail your employees, your customers, and yourself, but you fail your investors—partners who helped you bring your idea to life."

Questions for Critical Thinking

1. Examine the problems that DrawQuest encountered. How could the company have avoided or navigated around each problem?
2. What alternatives did DrawQuest have for generating income for its app? Why do you think the company didn't try any of these alternatives before shutting down?
3. Based on what you learned in Chapter 4, complete a Barringer/Ireland Business Model template for DrawQuest. Is there anything that is noticeable in the business model template that may have forecast that DrawQuest would have a hard time surviving?

(continued)

4. The opening features for Chapters 6, 7, and 8 feature student start-ups that have launched smartphone apps. What lessons can these start-ups learn from DrawQuest's experience?

Sources: C. Poole, "Today My Startup Failed," Chris Hates Writing blog, available at http://chrishateswriting.com/post/74083032842/to-day-my-startup-failed, accessed on September 15, 2014; DrawQuest blog, "A Recent Security Breach and the End of DrawQuest," available at http://blog.drawquest.com/, accessed on September 14, 2014; J. Constine, "With Traction but Out of Cash, 4Chan Founder Kills off Canvas/DrawQuest," TechCrunch, available at http://techcrunch.com/2014/01/21/when-goods-not-good-enough/, posted on January 21, 2014, accessed on September 15, 2014; E. Hamburger, "4chan Creator Chris Poole Draws a Future Where Anyone Can Make Art," The Verge, available at http://www.theverge.com/2013/2/8/3942110/drawquest-for-ipad-chris-poole-moot, posted on February 8, 2013, accessed on September 14, 2014.

trade on the NASDAQ, which is weighted heavily toward technology, biotech, and small-company stocks.[30] An IPO is an important milestone for a firm.[31] Typically, a firm is not able to go public until it has demonstrated that it is viable and has a bright future.

Firms decide to go public for several reasons. First, it is a way to raise equity capital to fund current and future operations. Second, an IPO raises a firm's public profile, making it easier to attract high-quality customers, alliance partners, and employees. Third, an IPO is a liquidity event that provides a mechanism for the company's stockholders, including its investors, to cash out their investments. Finally, by going public, a firm creates another form of currency that can be used to grow the company. It is not uncommon for one firm to buy another company by paying for it with stock rather than with cash.[32] The stock comes from "authorized but not yet issued stock," which in essence means that the firm issues new shares of stock to make the purchase. Examples of well-known firms that have gone public in recent years include Facebook, Twitter, GrubHub, Alibaba, and King Digital Entertainment (maker of the popular mobile game Candy Crush Saga).

Although there are many advantages to going public, it is a complicated and expensive process and subjects firms to substantial costs related to SEC reporting requirements. Many of the most costly requirements were initiated by the **Sarbanes-Oxley Act** of 2002. The Sarbanes-Oxley Act is a federal law that was passed in response to corporate accounting scandals involving prominent corporations, such as Enron and WorldCom. This wide-ranging act established a number of new or enhanced reporting standards for public corporations.

The first step in initiating a public offering is for a firm to hire an investment bank. An **investment bank** is an institution that acts as an underwriter or agent for a firm issuing securities.[33] The investment bank acts as the firm's advocate and adviser and walks it through the process of going public. The most important issues the firm and its investment bank must agree on are the amount of capital needed by the firm, the type of stock to be issued, the price of the stock when it goes public (e.g., $20 per share), and the cost to the firm to issue the securities.

There are a number of hoops the investment bank must jump through to assure the Securities and Exchange Commission (SEC) that the offer is legitimate. During the time the SEC is investigating the potential offering, the investment bank issues a **preliminary prospectus** that describes the offering to the general public. The preliminary prospectus is also called the "red herring." After the SEC has approved the offering, the investment bank issues the **final prospectus,** which sets a date and issuing price for the offering.

In addition to getting the offering approved, the investment bank is responsible for drumming up support for the offering. As part of this process, the investment bank typically takes the top management team of the firm wanting to go public on a **road show**, which is a whirlwind tour that consists of meetings in key cities, where the firm presents its business plan to groups of investors.[34] Until December 1, 2005, the presentations made during these road shows were seen only by the investors physically present in the various cities; an SEC regulation went into effect at that time requiring that road show presentations be taped and made available to the public. Road show presentations can be viewed online at www.retailroadshow.com. If enough interest in a potential public offering is created, the offering will take place on the date scheduled in the prospectus. If there isn't, the offering will be delayed or canceled.

Timing and luck play a role in whether a public offering is successful. For example, a total of 332 IPOs raised about $50 billion in 1999, the height of the Internet bubble. When the bubble burst in early 2001, the IPO marketplace all but dried up, particularly for technology and telecom stocks. Since then, the market has recovered. There were 261 IPOs in 2013, which raised a total of $70.5 billion. The first half of 2014 saw 166 IPOs with a busy IPO calendar projected for the second half of the year.[35] The vitality of the IPO market hinges largely on the state of the overall economy and the mood of professional investors. However, even when facing a strong economy and a positive mood toward investing, an entrepreneurial venture should guard itself against becoming caught up in the euphoria and rushing its IPO.

A variation of the IPO is a **private placement**, which is the direct sale of an issue of securities to a large institutional investor. When a private placement is initiated, there is no public offering, and no prospectus is prepared.

Sources of Debt Financing

Debt financing involves getting a loan or selling corporate bonds. Because it is virtually impossible for a new venture to sell corporate bonds, we'll focus on obtaining loans.

LEARNING OBJECTIVE

6. Describe common sources of debt financing entrepreneurial firms use.

There are two common types of loans. The first is a **single-purpose loan**, in which a specific amount of money is borrowed that must be repaid in a fixed amount of time with interest. The second is a **line of credit**, in which a borrowing "cap" is established and borrowers can use the credit at their discretion. Lines of credit require periodic interest payments.

There are two major advantages to obtaining a loan as opposed to equity funding. The first is that none of the ownership of the firm is surrendered—a major advantage for most entrepreneurs. The second is that interest payments on a loan are tax deductible, in contrast to dividend payments made to investors, which are not.

There are two major disadvantages of getting a loan. The first is that it must be repaid, which may be difficult in a start-up venture in which the entrepreneur is focused on getting the company off the ground. Cash is typically "tight" during a new venture's first few months and sometimes for a year or more. The second is that lenders often impose strict conditions on loans and insist on ample collateral to fully protect their investment. Even if a start-up is incorporated, a lender may require that an entrepreneur's personal assets be collateralized as a condition of the loan. In addition, a lender may place a stipulation on a loan, such that the borrower must "maintain a cash balance of $25,000 or more" in its checking account or the loan will become due and payable.

The three common sources or categories of debt financing available to entrepreneurs are described next.

Commercial Banks

Historically, commercial banks have not been viewed as practical sources of financing for start-up firms.[36] This sentiment is not a knock against banks; it is just that banks are risk averse, and financing start-ups is risky business. Instead of looking for businesses that are "home runs," which is what venture capitalists seek to do, banks look for customers who will reliably repay their loans. As shown in Table 10.2, banks are interested in firms that have a strong cash flow, low leverage, audited financials, good management, and a healthy balance sheet. Although many new ventures have good management, few have the other characteristics, at least initially. But banks are an important source of credit for small businesses later in their life cycles.

There are two reasons that banks have historically been reluctant to lend money to start-ups. First, as mentioned previously, banks are risk averse. In addition, banks frequently have internal controls and regulatory restrictions prohibiting them from making high-risk loans. So when an entrepreneur approaches a banker with a request for a $250,000 loan and the only collateral he or she has to offer is the recognition of a problem that needs to be solved, a plan to solve it, and perhaps some intellectual property, there is usually no practical way for the bank to help. Banks typically have standards that guide their lending, such as minimum debt-to-equity ratios that work against start-up entrepreneurs.

The second reason banks have historically been reluctant to lend money to start-ups is that lending to small firms is not as profitable as lending to large firms, which have been the staple clients of commercial banks. If an entrepreneur approaches a banker with a request for a $25,000 loan, it may simply not be worth the banker's time to complete the due diligence necessary to determine the entrepreneur's risk profile. Considerable time is required to digest a business plan and investigate the merits of a new firm. Research shows that a firm's size is an important factor in determining its access to debt capital.[37] The $25,000 loan may be seen as both high risk and marginally profitable (based on the amount of time it would take to do the due diligence involved), making it doubly uninviting for a commercial bank.[38]

Despite these historical precedents, some banks are starting to engage start-up entrepreneurs—although the jury is still out regarding how significant these lenders will become. When it comes to start-ups, some banks are rethinking their lending standards and are beginning to focus on cash flow and the strength of the management team rather than on collateral and the strength of the balance sheet. Entrepreneurs should follow developments in this area closely.

SBA Guaranteed Loans

Approximately 50 percent of the 9,000 banks in the United States participate in the **SBA Guaranteed Loan Program**. The most notable SBA program available to small businesses is the **7(A) Loan Guaranty Program**. This program accounts for 90 percent of the SBA's loan activity. The program operates through private-sector lenders who provide loans that are guaranteed by the SBA. The loans are for small businesses that are unable to secure financing on reasonable terms through normal lending channels. The SBA does not currently have funding for direct loans, other than a program to fund direct loans for businesses in geographic areas that are hit by natural disasters.

Almost all small businesses are eligible to apply for an SBA guaranteed loan. The SBA can guarantee as much as 75 percent (debt to equity) on loans up to $5 million. For loans of $150,000 or under, the guaranteed amount is 85 percent. Guaranteed loan funds can be used for almost any legitimate business purpose. The maximum lengths of the loans are seven years for working capital, 10 years for equipment (or useful life of equipment), and 25 years for real estate purchase. To obtain an SBA guaranteed loan, an application must meet the requirements of both the SBA and the lender. Typically, individuals must pledge all of their assets to secure the loan. Interest rates are negotiated between the borrower and the lender but are subject to SBA maximums.[39]

Although SBA guaranteed loans are utilized more heavily by existing small businesses than start-ups, they should not be dismissed as a possible source of funding. There is a general misconception that the SBA is a "lender of last resort" and only distressed businesses qualify for SBA guaranteed loans. Just the opposite is true. Only viable businesses are eligible under the SBA 7(A) Loan Guaranty Program.[40]

Other Sources of Debt Financing

There are a variety of other avenues business owners can pursue to borrow money or obtain cash. **Vendor credit** (also known as trade credit) is when a vendor extends credit to a business in order to allow the business to buy its products and/or services up front but defer payment until later. The practice is especially common in retail, but it can be seen in other businesses as well. An example of vendor credit is when a retailer orders product from a vendor that ships it on net 30 terms. This means that the retailer has 30 days to submit payment for the product. The idea is that the retailer doesn't have money to pay for the product until it sells it, so the vendor agrees to wait on payment to give the retailer enough time to sell the product and collect the money needed to pay the bill. Some retailers will negotiate up to net 90 terms, meaning that they have 90 days to make payment. Although not really debt financing, factoring is another way that businesses generate cash. **Factoring** is a financial transaction whereby a business sells its account receivable to a third party, called a factor, at a discount in exchange for cash.[41]

There are also alternative lenders who loan money to small businesses and entrepreneurs. These are primarily online firms that offer loans at an escalated interest rate. A common type of alternative lending is the **merchant cash advance**. In a merchant cash advance, the lender provides a business a lump sum of money in exchange for a share of future sales (typically a set percentage of the business's daily credit card sales) that covers the payment amount plus fees. The deals are normally designed for borrowers looking for short-term loans of less than $100,000. The average time for repayment is eight to nine months.[42]

Another type of alternative lending is peer-to-peer loans. **Peer-to-peer lending** is a financial transaction that occurs directly between individuals or "peers." The loans are facilitated by online firms such as Funding Circle, Lending Club, and Dealstruck. The online firms connect businesses with individuals or institutional investors who make the loans. In some cases, such as with Dealstruck, the site itself has money to lend. Borrowers generally must make fixed monthly payments. The thing to watch out for when using alternative lenders is the annual percentage rate (APR), which can run as high as 12 percent to 25 percent.[43]

Creative Sources of Financing and Funding

LEARNING OBJECTIVE
7. Describe several creative sources of financing entrepreneurial firms may choose to use.

Because financing and funding are difficult to obtain, particularly for startups, entrepreneurs often use creative ways to obtain financial resources. Even for firms that have financing or funding available, it is prudent to search for sources of capital that are less expensive than traditional ones. The following sections discuss four of the more common creative sources of financing and funding for entrepreneurial firms.

Crowdfunding

A popular creative source of funding for new businesses is crowdfunding. **Crowdfunding** is the practice of funding a project or new venture by raising monetary contributions from a large number of people, typically via the Internet.

There are two types of crowdfunding sites: rewards-based crowdfunding and equity-based crowdfunding. **Rewards-based crowdfunding** allows entrepreneurs to raise money in exchange for some type of amenity or reward. The most popular rewards-based crowdfunding sites are Kickstarter, Indiegogo, and RocketHub. These sites allow entrepreneurs to create a profile, list their fund-raising goals, and provide an explanation (typically via video) of how the funds will be used. Individuals then pledge money in exchange for some type of amenity, like being one of the first 100 people to obtain the company's product. The site takes a small percentage of the funds raised by the individuals for their service. Once a novelty, rewards-based crowdfunding has become a major source of start-up funds. Two of the student start-ups profiled in this book, LuminAid (Chapter 3) and Roominate (in this chapter), raised money via crowdfunding. In 2014, COOLEST, the subject of the You Be the VC 11.2 feature, raised $13.2 million from 62,642 donors on Kickstarter, which at the time was the all-time crowdfunding record. There are currently over 450 crowdfunding platforms. Some, such as Kickstarter, help fund a wide range of creative projects and business start-ups. Others are narrow in scope. If you're not familiar with how crowdfunding works, go to www.kickstarter.com and type "COOLEST Cooler" into the search engine. Although the campaign is over, Kickstarter leaves the campaign profiles up on its site indefinitely. Looking at COOLEST's campaign will provide you a good sense of how rewards-based crowdfunding campaigns work.

The second type of crowdfunding is equity-based crowdfunding. **Equity-based crowdfunding** helps businesses raise money by tapping individuals who provide funding in exchange for equity in the business. Three of the more popular equity-based crowdfunding sites are FundersClub, Crowdfunder.com, and Circle Up. The catalyst for the advent of equity-based crowdfunding was the JOBS Act, which was passed in April of 2012. The act is still going into effect, so the full set of rules and regulations that will govern equity-based crowdfunding sites are unknown. As of the time this chapter was written (September 2014), it appears that equity-based crowdfunding will be confined to entrepreneurs raising money from accredited investors. An **accredited investor** is a person who is permitted to invest in higher-risk investments such as business start-ups. In the United States, a person must have a net worth of at least $1 million (not including the value of their house) or have an income of at least $200,000 each year for the past two years (or $300,000 together with their spouse if married) and have the expectation to make the same amount in the current year. Still, there is substantial enthusiasm surrounding the potential for equity-based crowdfunding in the future.

Leasing

A **lease** is a written agreement in which the owner of a piece of property allows an individual or business to use the property for a specified period of time in exchange for payments. The major advantage of leasing is that it enables a company to acquire the use of assets with very little or no down payment. Leases for facilities and leases for equipment are the two most common types of leases that entrepreneurial ventures undertake.[44] For example, many new businesses lease computers from Dell Inc. or other PC manufacturers. The advantage for the new business is that it can gain access to the computers it needs with very little money invested up-front.

There are many different players in the leasing business. Some vendors, such as Dell, lease directly to businesses. As with banks, the vendors look for lease clients with good credit backgrounds and the ability to make the lease payments. There are also **venture-leasing firms** that act as brokers, bringing the parties involved in a lease together. These firms are acquainted with the producers of specialized equipment and match these producers with new ventures that are in need of the equipment. One of the responsibilities of these firms is conducting due diligence to make sure that the new ventures involved will be able to keep up with their lease payments.

Most leases involve a modest down payment and monthly payments during the duration of the lease. At the end of an equipment lease, the new venture typically has the option to stop using the equipment, purchase it at fair market value, or renew the lease. Lease deals that involve a substantial amount of money should be negotiated and entered into with the same amount of scrutiny as when getting financing or funding. Leasing is almost always more expensive than paying cash for an item, so most entrepreneurs think of leasing as an alternative to equity or debt financing. Although the down payment is typically lower, the primary disadvantage is that at the end of the lease, the lessee doesn't own the property or equipment.[45] Of course, this may be an advantage if a company is leasing equipment, such as computers or copy machines, which can rather quickly become technologically obsolete.

SBIR and STTR Grant Programs

The Small Business Innovation Research (SBIR) and the Small Business Technology Transfer (STTR) programs are two important sources of early-stage funding for technology firms. These programs provide cash grants to entrepreneurs who are working on projects in specific areas. The main difference between the SBIR and the STTR programs is that the STTR program requires the participation of researchers working at universities or other research institutions. For the purpose of the program, the term *small business* is defined as an American-owned for-profit business with fewer than 500 employees. The principle researcher must also be employed by the business.[46]

The **SBIR Program** is a competitive grant program that provides over $2.5 billion per year to small businesses for early-stage and development projects. Each year, 11 federal departments and agencies are required by the SBIR to reserve a portion of their research and development funds for awards to small businesses. Table 10.5 shows the agencies that participate, along with the types of areas that are funded. Guidelines for how to apply for the grants are provided on each agency's website, along with a description of the types of projects the agencies are interested in supporting. The SBIR is a three-phase program, meaning that firms that qualify have the potential to receive more than one grant to fund a particular proposal. These three phases, along with the amount of funding available for each phase, are as follows:

- **Phase I** is a six-month feasibility study in which the business must demonstrate the technical feasibility of the proposed innovation. Funding available for Phase I research is for up to $150,000.
- **Phase II** awards for up to $1 million are granted for as long as two years to successful Phase I companies. The purpose of a Phase II grant is to develop and test a prototype of Phase I innovations.
- **Phase III** is the period during which Phase II innovations move from the research and development lab to the marketplace. No SBIR funds are involved. At this point, the business must find private funding or financing to commercialize the product or service. In some cases, such as with the Department of Defense, the government may be the primary customer for the product.

Historically, less than 15 percent of all Phase I proposals are funded, and about 30 percent of all Phase II proposals are funded. The payoff for successful proposals, however, is high. The money is essentially free. It is a grant, meaning that it doesn't have to be paid back and no equity in the firm is at stake. The recipient of the grant also retains the rights to the intellectual property developed while working with the support provided by the grant. The real payoff is in Phase III if the new venture can commercialize the research results.

TABLE 10.5 Small Business Innovation Research: Three-Phase Program

Phase	Purpose of Phase	Duration	Funding Available (Varies by Agency)
Phase I	To demonstrate the proposed innovation's technical feasibility.	Up to 6 months	Up to $150,000
Phase II	Available to successful Phase I companies. The purpose of a Phase II grant is to develop and test a prototype of the innovation validated in Phase I.*	Up to 2 years	Up to $1 million
Phase III	Period in which Phase II innovations move from the research and development lab to the marketplace.	Open	No SBIR funding available; however, federal agencies may award non-SBIR-funded follow-on grants or contracts for products or processes that meet the mission needs of those agencies, or for further R&D.

*Some agencies have a fast-track program where applicants can submit Phase I and Phase II applications simultaneously. Government agencies that participate in this program include the following: Department of Agriculture, Department of Commerce, Department of Defense, Department of Education, Department of Energy, Department of Health and Human Services, Department of Homeland Security, Department of Transportation, Environmental Protection Agency, NASA, National Institutes of Health, and National Science Foundation.

The **STTR Program** is a variation of the SBIR for collaborative research projects that involve small businesses and research organizations, such as universities or federal laboratories. In 2010, over $100 million in grants were awarded through the program. More information about the SBIR and STTR programs can be obtained at www.sbir.gov.

Other Grant Programs

There are a limited number of other grant programs available to entrepreneurs. Obtaining a grant takes a little detective work. Granting agencies are, by nature, low-key, so they normally need to be sought out. A typical scenario of a small business that received a grant is provided by Rozalia Williams, the founder of Hidden Curriculum Education, a for-profit company that offers college life skills courses. To kick-start her business, Williams received a $72,500 grant from Miami-Dade Empowerment Trust, a granting agency in Dade County, Florida. The purpose of the Miami-Dade Empowerment Trust is to encourage the creation of businesses in disadvantaged neighborhoods of Dade County. The key to Williams's success, which is true in most grant-awarding situations, is that her business fit nicely with the mission of the granting organization, and she was willing to take her business into the areas the granting agency was committed to improving. After being awarded the grant and conducting her college prep courses in four Dade County neighborhoods over a three-year period, Williams received an additional $100,000 loan from the Miami-Dade Empowerment Trust to expand her business.[47] There are also private foundations that grant money to both existing and start-up firms. These grants are usually tied to specific objectives or a specific project, such as research and development in a specific area.

The federal government has grant programs beyond the SBIR and STTR programs described previously. The full spectrum of grants available is listed at www.grants.gov. State and local governments, private foundations, and philanthropic organizations also post grant announcements on their websites. Finding a grant that fits your business is the key. This is no small task. It is worth the effort, however, if you can obtain some or all of your start-up costs through a granting agency.

SAVVY ENTREPRENEURIAL FIRM

Working Together: How Biotech Firms and Large Drug Companies Bring Pharmaceutical Products to Market

Large firms and smaller entrepreneurial firms play different roles in business and society and can often produce the best results by partnering with each other rather than acting as adversaries. The pharmaceutical industry is an excellent example of how this works.

It is well known that barriers to entry in the pharmaceutical industry are high. The average new product takes between 10 and 15 years from discovery to commercial sale. The process of discovering, testing, obtaining approval, manufacturing, and marketing a new drug is long and expensive. How, then, do biotech start-ups make it? The answer is that few biotech firms actually take their products to market. Here's how it works.

Biotech firms specialize in discovering and patenting new drugs—it's what they're good at. In most cases, however, they have neither the money nor the know-how to bring the products to market. In contrast, the large drug companies, such as Johnson & Johnson, Pfizer, and Merck, specialize in developing and marketing drugs and providing information to doctors about them. It's what they are good at. But these companies typically don't have the depth of scientific talent and the entrepreneurial zeal that the small biotech firms do. These two types of firms need one another to be as successful as possible. Often, but not always, what happens is this. The biotech firms discover and patent new drugs, and the larger drug companies develop them

and bring them to market. Biotech firms earn money through this arrangement by licensing or selling their patent-protected discoveries to the larger companies or by partnering with them in some revenue-sharing way. The large drug companies make money by selling the products to consumers.

The most compelling partnership arrangements are those that help entrepreneurial firms focus on what they do best, which is typically innovation, and that allow them to tap into their partners' complementary strengths and resources.

Questions for Critical Thinking

1. In your opinion, what factors in the business environment encourage firms to partner to compete?
2. What risks do small firms face when partnering with large, successful companies? What risks do large companies take when they rely on small firms as a source of innovation?
3. How might government policies affect partnering actions between small and large firms in the pharmaceutical industry?
4. If you worked for an entrepreneurial venture, what would you want to know about a large company before recommending that your firm form a partnership with that large, established company?

One thing to be careful of is grant-related scams. Business owners often receive unsolicited letters or e-mail messages from individuals or organizations that assure them that for a fee they can help the business gain access to hundreds of business-related grants. The reality is that there aren't hundreds of business-related grants that fit any one business. Most of these types of offers are a scam.

Strategic Partners

Strategic partners are another source of capital for new ventures.[48] Indeed, strategic partners often play a critical role in helping young firms fund their operations and round out their business models.

Biotechnology companies, for example, rely heavily on partners for financial support, as illustrated in this chapter's "Savvy Entrepreneurial Firm" boxed feature. As mentioned in the feature, a small biotech firm would rarely have access to sufficient financial capital and other resources to take a new discovery from the lab all the way to market. It just takes too much time, capital, and other resources to pull off. As a result, they rely on deep-pocketed strategic partners to perform parts of the process. Many strategic partnerships are also formed to gain access to a particular resource or to facilitate speed to market.[49] In exchange for access to plant and equipment and established distribution channels, new ventures bring an entrepreneurial spirit and new ideas to these partnerships. These types of arrangements can help new ventures lessen the need for financing or funding.

Chapter Summary

LO1. Commonly, entrepreneurs discover that trying to operate their business without borrowed funds or invested capital is difficult. Because of this, entrepreneurs need to understand the different approaches available to them to gain access to the amount of capital needed to successfully support their ventures in the pursuit of organizational success.

LO2. For three reasons—cash flow challenges, capital investment needs, and the reality of lengthy product development cycles—most new firms need to raise money at some point during the early part of their life. Firm growth can generate cash flow problems, typically because of the lag between the need to spend capital to generate additional revenue and the time required to earn positive returns from those investments. Founders of entrepreneurial ventures may be able to fund their firm's initial capital investment needs. But, larger investments are required to support firm growth that is the foundation for long-term success. In some instances, the time required for a product to be introduced can be lengthy. When this happens, additional investments are necessary to keep a firm going during what may be a lengthy product development cycle.

LO3. Personal funds, friends and family, and bootstrapping are the three sources of personal financing available to entrepreneurs. It is very common for entrepreneurs to use their own funds to invest in their ventures while simultaneously providing their "sweat equity" (or hard work) to keep the firm going. Entrepreneurs also receive support through funds provided by members of their family and their friends. These investments come in various forms, including loans and gifts. When bootstrapping, entrepreneurs find ways to avoid the need for external funding. Exercising their creativity and ingenuity and finding ways to reduce their firm's costs are examples of what entrepreneurs do to reduce the need for support provided through external funding. Indeed, entrepreneurs are often very creative in finding ways to bootstrap to raise money or cut costs. Additional examples of bootstrapping include minimizing personal expenses and putting all profits back into the business, establishing partnerships and sharing expenses with partners, and sharing office space and/or employees with other businesses.

LO4. The three steps involved in properly preparing to raise debt or equity financing are as follows: Determine precisely how much money is needed, determine the type of financing or funding that is most appropriate, and develop a strategy for engaging potential investors or bankers. Cash flow statements are helpful to efforts to determine the amount of capital a firm requires at a point in time. When deciding how to finance their venture, entrepreneurs commonly choose between equity financing (where partial ownership of the firm is exchanged for financial support) and debt financing (where the entrepreneurs gain access to capital by taking out a loan). Entrepreneurs then develop an elevator pitch (which is a brief, carefully constructed statement outlining a business opportunity's merits), identify the best prospects to contact to seek financing, and prepare themselves to present a potential investor with an effectively developed business plan.

LO5. Business angels, venture capital, and an initial public offering (IPO) are the three most important sources of equity funding available to entrepreneurs. Business angels are individuals who invest their personal capital directly in start-up ventures. These investors tend to be high-net-worth individuals who generally invest between $10,000 and $500.000 in a single company. Venture capital is money that is invested by venture capital firms in start-ups and small businesses with exceptional growth potential. Typically, venture capitalists invest at least $1 million in a single company. An initial public offering (IPO) is an important milestone for a firm for four reasons: It is a way to raise equity capital, it raises a firm's public profile, it is a liquidity event, and it creates another form of currency (company stock) that can be used to grow the company.

LO6. The sources of debt available to entrepreneurs include commercial banks, SBA guaranteed loans, and other sources such as vendor credit, factoring, peer-to-peer lending, and crowdfunding. Historically, commercial banks have been reluctant to loan funds to entrepreneurial ventures, largely because they are risk averse and because lending to smaller firms is less profitable for them compared to lending to large, established organizations. The main SBA program available to small businesses is referred to as the 7(A) Loan Guaranty Program. This program operates through private-sector lenders providing loans that are guaranteed by the SBA. The loans are for small businesses that are unable to secure financing on reasonable terms through normal lending channels. A relatively new source of funding is when entrepreneurs raise money through crowdfunding by generating contributions from a large number of individuals. Commonly, the Internet is used to generate funds in this manner.

LO7. Leasing and SBIR and STTR grant programs, along with other types of grant programs, are examples of creative opportunities entrepreneurs can pursue to obtain financial resources. A lease is a written agreement in which the owner of a piece of property allows an individual or business to use the property for a specified period of time in exchange for payments. The major advantage of leasing is that it enables a company to acquire the use of assets with very little or no down payment. The SBIR and STTR grant programs are important sources of early-stage funding for technology-based ventures.

Key Terms

7(A) Loan Guaranty Program, **366**
accredited investor, **368**
bootstrapping, **355**
burn rate, **351**
business angels, **359**
carry, **360**
corporate venture capital, **362**
crowdfunding, **367**
debt financing, **357**
due diligence, **361**
elevator speech (or pitch), **357**
equity-based crowdfunding, **368**
equity financing, **356**

factoring, **367**
final prospectus, **364**
follow-on funding, **361**
general partners, **360**
initial public offering (IPO), **362**
investment bank, **364**
lease, **368**
limited partners, **360**
line of credit, **365**
liquidity event, **356**
merchant cash advance, **367**
peer-to-peer lending, **367**
preliminary prospectus, **364**
private placement, **365**

rewards-based crowdfunding, **367**
road show, **364**
rounds, **361**
Sarbanes-Oxley Act, **364**
SBA Guaranteed Loan Program, **366**
SBIR Program, **369**
secondary market offering, **362**
single-purpose loan, **365**
STTR Program, **370**
sweat equity, **354**
vendor credit, **367**
venture capital, **360**
venture-leasing firms, **368**

Review Questions

10-1. Why do start-up firms need capital investments? Will they be able to sustain themselves without the capital investment?

10-2. What is meant by the term *burn rate*? What are the consequences of experiencing a negative burn rate for a relatively long period of time?

10-3. What are the different stages involved in venture capital funding? Describe each in brief.

10-4. To what extent do entrepreneurs rely on their personal funds and funds from friends and families to finance their ventures? What are the three rules of thumb that a business owner should follow when asking friends and family members for start-up funds?

10-5. What are the sources of personal financing available to entrepreneurs?

10-6. Describe the three steps involved in properly preparing to raise debt or equity financing.

10-7. What is the difference between equity funding and debt financing?

10-8. What are the most common sources of equity funding?

10-9. Describe the most common sources of debt financing.

10-10. How should an entrepreneur prepare when approaching a potential investor for funding?

10-11. Why is it so important to get a personal introduction before approaching a potential investor or banker?

10-12. What are the three steps required to effectively engage potential investors or bankers?

10-13. What are the three most common forms of equity funding?

10-14. Describe the nature of business angel funding. What types of people typically become business angels, and what is the unique role that business angels play in the process of funding entrepreneurial firms?

10-15. What is meant by the term *venture capital*? Where do venture capital firms get their money? What types of firms do venture capitalists commonly want to fund? Why?

10-16. Describe the purpose of an initial public offering (IPO). Why is an initial public offering considered to be an important milestone for an entrepreneurial firm?

10-17. What is the purpose of the investment bank in the initial public offering process?

10-18. What is the difference between rewards-based crowdfunding and equity-based crowdfunding?

10-19. Briefly describe the SBA's 7(A) Loan Guaranty Program. Do most start-up firms qualify for an SBA guaranteed loan? Why or why not?

10-20. What is a Small Business Innovation Research (SBIR) grant? Why would a firm want to apply for such a grant if it qualifies for it?

Application Questions

10-21. Write a 60-second elevator speech for CareLinx, which is the "You Be the VC 10.1" feature in this chapter.

10-22. Samantha Smith, a friend of yours, was recently telling you about a company that her father is starting in the solar power industry. Samantha's father is using a technology he developed, which has received favorable write-ups in several technical publications. He has been approached by two angel investors who are eager to invest in his proposed venture. He's also been offered a spot in a prestigious technology incubator, where he can maintain an office and a lab to work on his project. Samantha says that her dad has turned away the potential investors and is opting to work out of a shop on some property he owns, rather than move into the incubator. He'll be able to fund the company from personal savings, at least for the first two years. Do you think Samantha's dad is making good decisions? What are the pluses and minuses of his decisions?

10-23. Jim Carter, a classmate of yours, is preparing to launch an e-commerce company to sell home repair guidebooks, tools, how-to videos, and related material for home repair and remodeling projects. He just told you that he talked to his paternal grandmother over the weekend, and she has agreed to lend him $25,000 to launch the firm. When you asked Jim what arrangements he has made with his grandmother to formalize the loan, he looked puzzled and said, "She plans to send me a check in a week or so—she just needs to get the money out of her savings account." Jim seemed concerned by the worried look on your face and said, "Tell me what you're thinking. I really want to do the right thing here." What would you say to Jim?

10-24. Kathy Baker is in the midst of starting a computer hardware firm and thinks she has identified a real problem that her company will be able to solve. She needs investment capital, but doesn't know much about the process and doesn't know where to begin. She's turned to you for advice. Write Kathy a 250- to 300-word e-mail message introducing her to the process of raising investment capital.

10-25. Imagine you invented a new type of car seat for children, which is lighter and safer than the car seats currently on the market. You have a business plan and have won two business plan contests based on your idea. You also have a working prototype. You'd like to find an angel investor to fund the launch of your firm. Describe how you'd go about finding an angel investor in the area in which you live. Make a list of the specific steps you'd take, and the specific people you'd talk to, to try to locate an appropriate angel investor.

10-26. During an entrepreneurship class for final year students, one of the students had presented on a bio-diesel technology that may bring down the cost of a manufacturing firm by half. You feel that this student, if he had the funding, could propose his idea to the government and other private agencies, as it has potential to be developed into a successful product. Being his lecturer, advise him on the SBIR Program, the three phases, along with the amount of funding available for each phase.

10-27. Brenda White has been running a beauty parlor for the last three years. Her beauty parlor has many VIP patrons and is well-known within her neighborhood. Throughout the three years, she has been sustaining her parlor by herself without any financial assistance. However, due to the recent economic downturn, she is finding it difficult to sustain her venture alone and is seeking a funder who is willing to share equity with her. Advise her on the types of funding available for her venture.

10-28. Simon Black is in the middle of starting up a personal gym. At present, his start-up financial needs have exceeded his personal funds, funds from his friends and family, and the funds he obtained from bootstrapping. The most important thing that Simon must do at this point is to determine precisely what his company needs and the most appropriate source to use to obtain the funds. A carefully planned approach to raise money increases the chance of success and can save Simon considerable time. Assist him.

10-29. Steve Peterson has decided to start a café in his neighborhood. He has named his café "The Pitt-Stop" and has many plans to ensure its success. One of his major plans is to purchase a shop-lot and renovate it to accommodate his café. However, he does not have enough funds to complete these two tasks. He has made an appointment to meet you over lunch and ask if you could invest some fund for his startup. You are not too keen to invest in his business but try to advice an alternate option for him. Try to make him understand that it would not be a good idea to purchase a shop-lot right now, instead suggest a creative source of financing that he may choose to use.

YOU BE THE VC 10.1 COMPANY: CareLinx

• Web: www.carelinx.com • Facebook: CareLinx; Twitter: @CareLinx

Business Idea: Design a caregiver marketplace that allows families in need of a caregiver and professional caregivers to connect online.

Pitch: The traditional way families in need of a caregiver have arranged for care is to enlist the services of a brick and mortar agency. The problem with this approach is that it is expensive and the pool of available caregivers is limited to the people that work for the agency. CareLinx's approach is different. It has created an online platform that makes it easy for families in need of caregivers to find professional caregivers online. Via the CareLinx platform, a family is able to find, video interview, read background checks, hire, manage, and pay professional caregivers that match their specific needs and budgetary constraints.

The idea for CareLinx emerged from a personal experience of its founder, Sherwin Sheik. Sheik and his family experienced firsthand the challenges involved with finding and managing professional caregivers for a sister who has multiple sclerosis and an uncle with ALS. They were referred to several local agencies and found the process to be inefficient and costly. To complicate matters, Sheik's mother lived in San Francisco, while the sister that needed help lived in Los Angeles. The distance between the two required Sheik's mother to constantly fly back and forth to coordinate care. There was really no good way for Sheik and his family to manage the care for his sister and uncle efficiently.

CareLinx takes the inefficiency out of the process. A caregiver can be located and interviewed online. All caregivers on the site are prescreened and extensive background checks are provided. CareLinx takes care of the insurance, paperwork, and taxes. Due to the importance of finding the ideal caregiver for an individual who needs care, CareLinx isn't just a website. Once a family goes to the company's website and completes the initial survey, they are contacted by a CareLinx team member, who walks them through the process. Caregivers set their own hourly rate, and salary is negotiated between the caregiver and the family with the need. CareLinx charges the family with the need a 15 percent service fee for the duration of the caregiving relationship. The process typically saves families thousands of dollars, whose alternative is to enlist the services of a traditional bricks-and-mortar caregiving agency.

From the caregiver's point of view, CareLinx provides them an easy way to find clients in their area who need home health care. It also offers flexibility. Caregivers can select clients of their choice, set their hourly pay, and choose clients that fit with their schedules. Caregivers being paid through CareLinx earn up to 25 percent to 30 percent more than those working through a traditional agency.

In short, CareLinx is a win-win for both the caregiver and the family in need. CareLinx's goal is to disrupt the $100 billion-plus home care service delivery industry.

10-30. Based on the material covered in this chapter, what questions would you ask the firm's founders before making your funding decision? What answers would satisfy you?

10-31. If you had to make your decision on just the information provided in the pitch and on the company's website, would you fund this company? Why or why not?

YOU BE THE VC 10.2 COMPANY: PledgeMusic

• Web: www.pledgemusic.com • Twitter: @PledgeMusic • Facebook: PledgeMusic

Business Idea: Provide musicians an online direct-to-fan platform to reach out to their fan base to pre-sell, market, and distribute music projects including recordings, music videos, and concerts.

Pitch: Musicians often have creative ideas for recordings, music videos, or similar projects but can't raise the money to move forward. When their fans hear that they've passed on an album or a creative new approach to offering their music, they often react by saying or thinking to themselves, "Man—I wish there had been a way that I could have helped."

Now there is. PledgeMusic is a direct-to-fan music platform that bears similarities to crowdfunding sites like Kickstarter and Indiegogo. It is focused solely on raising funds for musicians. It allows two distinct types of fundraising campaigns. The first is direct-to-fan campaigns, which are managed like Kickstarter campaigns. The artist sets a target amount to raise (to fund a new album, music video, or similar creative project) and provides amenities in exchange for pledges. Contributors are not charged until the target amount is reached. The second type of campaign is a preorder campaign. Contributors are charged immediately to preorder an album or music video, much like many online music sites. The artist is paid upon project completion. Approximately 90 percent of direct-to-fan campaigns are successful, with most artists raising approximately 140 percent of their goal.

Each direct-to-fan campaign is accompanied by a video pitch from the artist, which explains the project he or she has in mind. PledgeMusic encourages artists to offer a wide range of amenities and exclusive content to contributors in exchange for their contribution. It also encourages artists to include contributions to charity as part of their fund-raising project. An example of a PledgeMusic campaign is a campaign launched by Bobby Long that was ongoing when this feature was written. Long is an indie folk singer-songwriter who organized the campaign to fund the production of his third album. His two-minute video appeal was personal and authentic. In the appeal, he explains that he'll be producing his third album independently and he needs funding for production costs. The album will be produced in Austin, Texas. Long ends the video by promising contributors that they'll be proud of the finished product. A sample of the amenities Long will provide contributors include the following: $10—digital version of the new album; $25—signed copy of his collection of poetry; $75—handwritten rendition of the contributor's favorite Bobby Long song, personalized for the contributor; $250—three guitar lessons via Skype; $1,500—opportunity to spend a day with Bobby Long in New York City visiting his favorite places; $2,500—solo acoustic concert by Bobby Long at the contributor's home.

For its part, PledgeMusic does not take any ownership interest in the projects that are funded through its website, charging a flat 15 percent fee on all money collected.

10-32. Based on the material covered in this chapter, what questions would you ask the firm's founders before making your funding decision? What answers would satisfy you?

10-33. If you had to make your decision on just the information provided in the pitch and on the company's website, would you fund this company? Why or why not?

CASE 10.1

Revolights: Using Multiple Sources of Funding to Bring Its Innovative Bicycle Lighting System to Life

• Revolights: www.revolights.com • Facebook: Revolights • Twitter: @Revolights

Bruce R. Barringer, *Oklahoma State University*

R. Duane Ireland, *Texas A&M University*

Introduction

One evening in October 2010, Kent Frankovich was riding his bike home from work. He was finishing up a research project at Stanford and was running back and forth to the lab a lot at night. The area in front of him was partially illuminated by his handle-mounted bike light. He entered a particularly dark stretch and hit a pothole. It nearly threw him off his bike. It got him thinking that there must be a better way to illuminate the path in front of his bike.

He decided against buying a better handle-mounted light. Why is the light up so high, he thought, if what he's trying to illuminate is directly in front of him? So he decided to do some research. He looked at the lights on cars and the design work that went into them. Many new cars had wraparound lights so the car could be seen from the side as well as the front. In addition, unlike bikes, car headlights are at the front and are fairly low so they can best illuminate the road. Frankovich decided that bike lights should be put where they're needed the most—at the wheel.

This conclusion posed a design challenge. Obviously the wheels on a bike rotate, so a light can't be mounted on the wheel. After giving the matter some thought, Frankovich came up with a solution. He distributed small LED lights all the way around the wheel and timed them so they'd only illuminate when facing forward. Thus, only about a third of the wheel would be illuminated at any given time—the third lighting the path in front of the bike. The whole wheel couldn't be illuminated because the spinning light would interfere with the rider's eyesight.

Frankovich built a prototype and started riding at night. He found that the arch of light not only lit the path in front of him, but made him hugely visible from all sides. That's a big deal. In some archival research Frankovich had done, he found some interesting statistics about bikes. About one third of Americans own bikes, but only 1 percent of trips are made by bike. The top four reasons that people don't ride their bikes more often are (1) car traffic, (2) weather, (3) lack of bike lanes, and (4) darkness. The thing these four reasons have in common is personal safety. Frankovich realized that not only could his solution provide for a better bike light, but it could help people feel safer riding their bike because they would be more visible. According to government surveys, about 70 percent of bike traffic accidents are attributed to a lack of side visibility. In addition, the majority of bike accidents happen between 4:00 p.m. and 4:00 a.m.—which is late afternoon to dusk to darkness.

(continued)

Frankovich used this insight to improve on the initial prototype. To provide for more side visibility at night, he decided to not only mount lights on the front tire but on the back tire as well. To make it not only functional but super cool, the design was for white lights on the front tire and red lights on the back. The result was 360 degrees of illumination, offering not only improved lighting (for the person riding the bike) but improved visibility from all sides.

Next Steps

After settling on the initial design, Frankovich met Adam Pettler at a friend's get-together. Pettler was completing an MBA from the University of California, Davis. According to an interview with Frankovich and Pettler on the Core77 website (Core77 is a site for industrial designers), Frankovich told Pettler about his idea, and pulled out his phone and played a video of the prototype. "Dude," Pettler reportedly said, "We should start a business." Coincidentally, Pettler had to write a business plan for a class and was looking for an idea. The two hit it off and formed a partnership.

Over the next several months, Frankovich and Pettler produced several iterations of the original idea. They formed a company named Revolights. At this point, the Revolights bike lighting system consisted of two narrow rings of LED lights that mounted directly to each bike wheel using a series of rim-specific clips.

They started showing videos of their most recent prototype to bike shop owners. The response was very positive. They felt that they were on to something but still couldn't be absolutely sure that such was the case.

To test the waters in a substantive fashion, they decided to launch a Kickstarter campaign. The campaign launched in mid-2011 with a $43,500 goal. The money would be spent on the final design and development work for the Revolights system and on the first production run. At this juncture, put the case aside for a moment and go to Kickstarter.com. Type "Revolights" into the search bar, and select the Revolights campaign that was funded on September 27, 2011 (Revolights ran two subsequent Kickstarter campaigns). Watch the 2-minute, 50-second video pitch. You'll see Revolights's original pitch. The video also provides a nice demonstration of the Revolights system. The Kickstarter campaign raised $215,621 from 1,442 backers (496 percent of the original goal). That success provided Frankovich and Pettler the confidence to proceed with Revolights and make it an all-out effort.

Funding Journey

Frankovich and Pettler proceeded to build Revolights. Because the Revolights system is a physical product, inventory must be bought and paid for before the product is sold. As a result, scaling the company has required Frankovich and Pettler to raise money. The nearby table shows the funding that has taken place.

Revolights's Funding Journey

Date	Source of Funding	Use of Funds	Amount of Funding
2011	Kickstarter Campaign	Finish design and development work and pay for initial production run	$215,621
2011	SBA Loan	Fund additional production	$250,000
2013	Kickstarter Campaign	Fund the company's second-generation product, Revolights City	$94,793
2013	*Shark Tank*	Fund R&D and production	$300,000
2014	Series A Round Led by Sierra Angels	Expand the team, grow sales and marketing, and expand product line	$1 million (includes $300,000 *Shark Tank* commitment)

As mentioned, the first funding was the initial Kickstarter campaign. Buoyed by a positive response, Frankovich and Pettler decided to expand the production run and took out a $250,000 SBA loan. In early 2013, they ran a second Kickstarter campaign. The $14,500 goal was easily met, in that they raised $94,793 from 233 backers. The differences in the videos that accompanied the 2011 and 2013 Kickstarter campaigns showed how much the company had matured. The purpose of the 2013 campaign was to fund the company's second-generation product, Revolights City. Revolights City fit more bike rims and would make Revolights more widely accessible. The company also announced a partnership with Mission Bike Company, which would start selling a family of bikes with Revolights lights built in.

The next round of funding was a bold one. Frankovich decided to take his chances on *Shark Tank*. The advantages of appearing on *Shark Tank* are threefold: first, the possibility of raising money; second, the potential to get an investment from a high-profile investor, such as Mark Cuban, Barbara Corcoran, or Robert Herjavec; third, the exposure an appearance brings. In 2013, each episode averaged over six million viewers. Appearing on Shark Tank also exposes a product's company, like Revolights, to potential retailers, distributors, and business partners.

The *Shark Tank* episode was filmed in late 2013 and aired on March 7, 2014 (Season 5, Episode 19). A transcript of the episode is available at http://revolights.com/pages/shark-tank. Frankovich asked for $150,000 in exchange for 10 percent of the company. The sharks were impressed with the product and upped the ante. Frankovich received three offers. He eventually said yes to Robert Herjavec's offer of $300,000 for a 10 percent stake in Revolights.

Frankovich and Pettler had one hiccup in their funding journey. They tried to couple the *Shark Tank* appearance with a third Kickstarter campaign. The goal was $100,000. A total of $78,017 was pledged and the campaign failed.

Most recently, Revolights raised a $1 million series A round, which was led by Sierra Angles. Robert Herjavec's $300,000 commitment was folded into the round. The money will be used for expanding the Revolights team, growing sales and marketing, and expanding the product line.

Road Ahead

Like all start-ups, Revolights's road ahead is unclear. All signs are positive; however, the angel round will force Revolights into a more rapid growth mode. In the *Shark Tank* episode, Frankovich indicated that at that time, Revolights had earned $600,000 in sales. He indicated that profits were being reinvested in the company.

As of the time this case was written (September 2014), Revolights's products were for sale in bike shops in 12 states, as well as in Mexico, Thailand, and the United Kingdom. The product was also available via Amazon.com. The key for Revolights will be to win wider acceptance of its product. Price is a challenge. The flagship version of Revolights, which are the arcs of LED lights that clip onto bike wheels, sell for $199 a set. Revolights now sells a product called Revolight Wheels, which are bike wheels with the Revolight lights permanently installed. The wheels sell for $399 a set. It's unclear whether at those price points Revolights's products will become mainstream.

Revolights continues to generate publicity. In 2013, it was a James Dyson Award International Finalist. It also won a Core77 Design Award. In 2013, Frankovich did a TEDx Sacramento talk about Revolights. The talk has generated over 33,000 views.

Frankovich's *Shark Tank* episode was viewed by 7.69 million people.

Discussion Questions

10-34. The following sentence appears early in this chapter: "There are three reasons that most entrepreneurial ventures need to raise money during their early life—cash flow challenges, capital investments, and lengthy product development cycles." Evaluate Revolights's need for capital in terms of each of these reasons.

10-35. In response to a request from Kent Frankovich and Adam Pettler, write a 60-second elevator pitch about Revolights's product.

10-36. Assume that Revolights was interested in working with strategic partners in order to enhance the firm's success. What types of companies might Revolights partner with to become more successful?

10-37. To what degree do you think Revolights is a successful start-up venture? How successful do you believe the firm will be going forward? Justify your answer.

Sources: Revolights website, www.revolights.com, accessed September 19, 2014; L. McCamy, "Innovative Bike Light Company Swims with Sharks and Comes Out a Winner," Intuit Blog, available at http://quickbooks.intuit.com/r/money/innovative-bike-light-company-swims-with-sharks-and-comes-out-a-winner/, posted on July 3, 2014, accessed on September 19, 2014; H. Somerville, "Funding Flash: Revolights Closes $1 Million Series A," available at http://www.siliconbeat.com/2014/05/08/funding-flash-revolights-closes-1-million-series-a/, posted on May 8, 2014, accessed on September 19, 2014; K. Frankovich, "Kickstarting a Bicycle Safety Revolution: Kent Frankovich at TEDx Sacramento TEDx City 2.0," available at https://www.youtube.com/watch?v=axAx_Dq3rn8, posted on November 4, 2013, accessed on September 19, 2014; "Core77 Design Award 2012: The Revolights Bike Lighting System, Professional Winner for Transportation," Core77 website, available at http://www.core77.com/blog/core77_design_awards/core77_design_awards_2012_the_revolights_bike_lighting_system_professional_winner_for_transportation_23048.asp, posted on August 1, 2012, accessed on September 19, 2014.

CASE 10.2

Kickstarter: An Increasingly Important Forum for Raising Seed Capital

• *Web: www.kickstarter.com* • *Facebook: Kickstarter* • *Twitter: @kickstarter*

Bruce R. Barringer, *Oklahoma State University*
R. Duane Ireland, *Texas A&M University*

Introduction

Kickstarter is a crowdfunding platform. The idea behind crowdfunding is to raise money from the public (i.e., the crowd) rather than through traditional means. Kickstarter's stated mission is to bring creative projects to life. The platform was started in April 2009 by Perry Chen, Charles Adler, and Yancy Strickler. Since then, it has reportedly helped raise over $1 billion in pledges from five million donors to fund 60,000 projects. Kickstarter is open to projects based in the United States, Canada, Australia, New Zealand, and the United Kingdom. Backers can come from anywhere in the world. While most people think of Kickstarter as a website, it launched a mobile app in February 2013.

How It Works

Kickstarter funds creative projects. Anyone that meets the company's creator requirements is eligible to launch a project on Kickstarter. A project must fit into one of Kickstarter's 13 categories and 36 subcategories. The 13 categories include Art, Comics, Dance,

Design, Fashion, Film and Video, Food, Games, Music, Photography, Publishing, Technology, and Theater. Business start-ups are eligible if they fit a category. For example, a company that's creating a new type and style of denim jeans would fit into the fashion category. Of the categories, Film and Video and Music are the largest and have raised the most amount of money.

Once accepted, a person uses tools provided by Kickstarter to set up a fund-raising campaign. The campaign, which is displayed on Kickstarter.com and can be accessed via the mobile app, includes a description of the project, a video pitch (not required but recommended), the fund-raising goal, the deadline, and a list of the incentives that are provided in exchange for pledges. If the minimum isn't reached by the deadline, pledgers get their money back. Pledges are tiered ($25, $50, $75, etc.), with each tier earning a certain incentive. Some incentives are merely thank you acknowledgments. For example, a $25 pledge may earn a thank you note from the person running the campaign. In contrast, some pledges result in nice rewards. For example, COOLEST Cooler ran the most successful Kickstarter campaign

This photo depicts an assortment of Pebble Smartwatches. Pebble raised over $10 million on Kickstarter. Pebble smartwatches use Bluetooth technology to connect to smartphones.

Ramin Talaie/Corbis

to date by raising $13.3 million from 62,642 pledgers. A $165 pledge earned the pledger one of the coolers the campaign was designed to help manufacture. The coolers are expected to eventually sell for around $300.

Kickstarter has taken several steps to govern the integrity of its campaigns. Money pledged by donors is collected using Amazon Payments. Kickstarter claims no ownership over the projects and the work they produce. It makes money by retaining 5 percent of the funds raised. An additional 3 percent to 5 percent goes to Amazon Payments. Kickstarter has added requirements for hardware and product design projects, with the most stringent being that a physical prototype of the product must exist and a manufacturing plan must be in place. These requirements help ensure that the device will actually be built and the promised incentives will be delivered to pledgers.

The five most successful Kickstarter projects to date are shown in the table below. You can look at each of the projects by going to Kickstarter's website and typing the project name in the search box. Kickstarter archives all projects indefinitely.

Five Most Successful Kickstarter Projects to Date

Rank	Total Raised	Abbreviated Project Name	Creator	Backers
1	$13,285,226	COOLEST Cooler	Ryan Grepper	62,642
2	$10,266,845	Pebble E-Watch	Pebble Technologies	68,929
3	$8,596,474	Ouya, Inc.	Ouya, Inc.	63,416
4	$6,225,354	PonoMusic Team	PonoMusic Team	18,219
5	$5,702,153	Veronica Mars Movie; LaVar Burton—Reading Rainbow	Rob Thomas; LaVar Burton	91,585

Typical Kickstarter Project

Here's a typical Kickstarter campaign. Memobottle is a company started in 2014 by Jesse Leeworthy and Jonathan Byrt. The idea is to create a series of bottles that resemble the shape of a piece of paper and that conveniently slide into a messenger bag or briefcase alongside a laptop, books, and other valuables. The bottles are filled with tap water and are reusable. A bonus is reducing the number of single-use water bottles that are used and then discarded. In the United States alone, 1,500 plastic bottles are used and discarded every second. This has a damaging effect on both the environment and our bank accounts. Bottled water is 1,400 times more expensive than tap water.

The Memobottle will be produced in three sizes. The bottles are transparent, leak proof, and dishwasher friendly. The Kickstarter campaign, which was going on when this feature was being written, had a goal of $15,000. With 22 days left in the campaign, $183,668 had been pledged. The Memobottle is designed and ready for tooling and production. The purpose of the campaign was to raise the necessary funds for tooling, the first manufacturing and production run, and distribution. The $15,000 figure came from an analysis of the minimum amount of money needed to bring Memobottle to life. To encourage people to participate in its Kickstarter campaign, Memobottle offered tiered incentives. A sample of the incentives, along with the pledge amount required to earn the incentive, are shown in the table below.

Along with financial support, the initiators of Kickstarter campaigns get feedback from the Kickstarter community in the form of "Comments." Memobottle had 120 comments with 22 days to go. The comments often contain thoughtful insights about the product that are helpful to the initiators.

A Sample of the Incentives Offered for Pledging Money to Memobottle's Kickstarter Campaign

Pledge Amount	Incentive
$5 or more	You will receive a Memobottle thank you card and know that you have helped raise support and awareness to reduce single-use bottle consumption. Thank you!
$12 or more	LASER-CUT NECKLACE OR KEY RING! Receive a Memobottle key ring or necklace with either a leather or metal band. You will also receive a thank you card for supporting Memobottle and for helping stop the single-use bottle catastrophe.
$33 or more	One "LETTER Memobottle" with black and white lid—includes recycled paper packaging and a thank you for supporting Memobottle and for helping to stop the single-use bottle disaster.
$88 or more	FOUR x "A5 Memobottles" with black or white lids—includes recycled paper packaging and a thank you for supporting Memobottle and for helping to stop the single-use bottle disaster.

(continued)

Pledge Amount	Incentive
$128 or more	FOUR x "Letter Memobottles" with black or white lids—includes recycled paper packaging and a thank you card for supporting Memobottle and for helping to stop the single-use bottle disaster.
$250 or more	MEMO ONE YEAR WONDER Receive one of every product that Memobottle manufacturers for the next 12 months.
$500 or more	MEMO AMBASSADOR Get your mug featured for 12 months on our website. And of course one of each bottle.
$1,000 or more	MEMO LIFEMEMBER Receive one of every product that Memobottle manufacturers for the next five years!

The Memobottle campaign includes a 3-minute, 16-second video that shows exactly how the Memobottle conveniently slides into a messenger bag and that drives home the negative environmental impact of single-use water bottles.

How to Run a Successful Kickstarter Campaign

There are several things that people who have run successful Kickstarter campaigns learn. First, Kickstarter shouldn't be thought of as a tool for funding one-off projects or events. Instead, it's best to think of it as a mechanism for providing seed capital to help a project or event get up and running, and then grow it from there. Second, it's important that the person or organization that initiates a Kickstarter campaign promote it. Most people who contribute to a specific campaign don't find it by chance. Instead, they go to Kickstarter.com looking for it. In the table shown next, several methods for promoting a Kickstarter campaign are listed.

Third, the majority of donations are made at the beginning and the end of campaigns. As a result, shorter campaigns are typically more effective than longer ones. A Kickstarter campaign can last between one and 60 days. Campaigns lasting less than 30 days have the highest success rates. If a campaign is too long, people lose interest. Fourth, it's important to not set your financial goal too low. If a Kickstarter campaign is successful, it tends to quickly lose momentum once it reaches 100 percent of its goal—even though more money can be collected. Finally, it's imperative that a video pitch be included. It's much easier to donate money to a person or organization's project if you can hear someone talking about it and see the passion in their eyes.

What's Ahead?

Kickstarter has no immediate plans to broaden the scope of its platform. It does have a growing number of competitors. There are now over 450 crowdfunding platforms. Some, such as Indiegogo and RockHub, are broad-based platforms like Kickstarter. Others focus on specific industries, such as PledgeMusic, which helps musicians raise money for albums, concerts, and music DVDs. There are areas in which Kickstarter is becoming more adventurous. For example, it periodically hosts film festivals that feature animations, short films, documentaries, and more, all funded on Kickstarter. In 2014, a Kickstarter film festival was held in Brooklyn in July and Los Angeles in September, and one was in the planning stages for London in the later part of the year.

Techniques for Promoting a Kickstarter Campaign

Platform	Execution
E-mail	Send an e-mail to your e-mail distribution list, describing the campaign. Kickstarter campaigns aren't funded entirely by strangers. Instead, they're often funded largely by the campaign initiator's friends, family, business associates, and so forth.
Twitter and Facebook	Reach out to both your Twitter and Facebook audiences. Provide frequent updates. Try to find the balance between saturating your Twitter followers and Facebook friends with Kickstarter info and providing them with timely reminders.
Blogs and media	Reach out to bloggers and news outlets in the industry that your campaign focuses on. Ask that they mention your campaign and offer support. For example, it would make sense for Memobottle to reach out to bloggers and journalists who write about environmental issues.

Discussion Questions

10-38. Do you think Kickstarter is a viable alternative to raising equity funding or debt financing? If so, under what circumstances?

10-39. Kickstarter is not the first crowdfunding platform, yet it is the most successful. List five reasons that you believe account for Kickstarter's success.

10-40. Cities are able to set up Kickstarter pages that list all the active Kickstarter projects from their community. For example, the Kickstarter page for Oklahoma City, Oklahoma, is available at https://www.kickstarter.com/discover/places/oklahoma-city-ok. Is this a potentially effective way for cities to promote arts and entrepreneurship? How should cities go about promoting their Kickstarter pages?

10-41. To what degree do you believe Kickstarter itself is a successful start-up?

Sources: Kickstarter website, www.kickstarter.com, accessed September 19, 2014; Wikipedia, Kickstarter, www.wikipedia.com, accessed September 19, 2014.

Endnotes

1. M. Nitani and A. Riding, "Fund Size and the Syndication of Venture Capital Investments," *Venture Capital* 15, no. 1 (2013): 53–75.

2. N. Rosenbusch, J. Brinckmann, and V. Muller, "Does Acquiring Venture Capital Pay Off for the Funded Firms? A Meta-Analysis on the Relationship Between Venture Capital Investment and Funded Firm Financial Performance," *Journal of Business Venturing* 26, no. 3 (2013): 335–353.

3. S. Singh, P. D. Corner, and K. Pavlovich, "Failed, Not Finished: A Narrative Approach to Understanding Venture Failure Stigmatization," *Journal of Business Venturing*, 2014, in press.

4. PharmaTech.com. "How Long Does Drug Development Take," http://pharmtech.find-pharma.com/pharmtech/Latest+News/How-long-does-drug-development-take/ArticleStandard/Article/detail/574805?contextCategoryId=45298 (accessed June 1, 2011, originally posted on January 15, 2009).

5. Y. Sarason, D. R. DeTienne, and C. Bently, "Wham-O's Offer to Buy Sprig Toys: Selling in or Selling Out?" *Entrepreneurship Theory and Practice* 38, no. 4 (2014): 959–972.

6. "Where Startup Funding Really Comes From" (Infographic), *Entrepreneur*, November 30, 2013.

7. "Where Startup Funding Really Comes From" (Infographic), *Entrepreneur*, November 30, 2013.

8. B. Barringer, *The Truths About Starting a Business* (Upper Saddle River, NJ: Financial Times Press, 2009).

9. Lending Karma home page, www.lendingkarma.com, (accessed September 13, 2014).

10. D. Grichnik, J. Brinckmann, L. Singh, and S. Manigart, "Beyond Environmental Scarcity: Human and Social Capital As Driving Forces of Bootstrapping Activities," *Journal of Business Venturing* 29, no. 2 (2014): 310–326; M. Malmstrom, "Typologies of Bootstrap Financing Behavior in Small Ventures," *Venture Capital* 16, no. 1 (2014): 27–50.

11. B. Barringer, *The Truth About Starting a Business* (Upper Saddle River, NJ: Financial Times, 2009).

12. A. Schwienbacher, "The Entrepreneur's Investor Choice: The Impact on Later-Stage Firm Development," *Journal of Business Venturing* 28, no. 4 (2013): 528–545.

13. A. N. Link, C. J. Ruhm, and D. S. Siegel, "Private Equity and the Innovation Strategies of Entrepreneurial Firms: Empirical Evidence from the Small Business Innovation Research Program," *Managerial and Decision Economics* 35, no. 2 (2014): 103–113.

14. B. Barringer, *Preparing Effective Business Plans*, 2nd ed. (Upper Saddle River, NJ: Prentice Hall, 2014).

15. A. Parhankangas and M. Ehrlich, "How Entrepreneurs Seduce Business Angels: An Impression Management Approach," *Journal of Business Venturing* 29, no. 4 (2014): 543–564; G. W. Festel and S. H. De Cleyn, "Founding Angels As an Emerging Subtype of the Angel Investment Model in High-Tech Businesses," *Venture Capital* 15, no. 3 (2013): 261–282.

16. D. Khanin and O. Turel, "Conflicts and Regrets in the Venture Capitalist-Entrepreneur Relationship," *Journal of Small Business Management*, 2014, in press.

17. "ASAP," *Forbes*, June 1, 1998, 24.

18. J. Battelle, *The Search* (New York, NY: Portfolio, 2005).

19. "J. Sohl, "The Angel Investor Market in 2013: A Return to Seed Investing," Center for Venture Research, April 30, 2014.

20. Sohl, "The Angel Investor Market in 2013."

21. Sohl, "The Angel Investor Market in 2013."

22. Ann Arbor Angels, www.annarborangels.org, (accessed September 15, 2014).

23. Where Startup Funding Really Comes From" (Infographic), *Entrepreneur*, November 30, 2013.

24. C. B. Moore, G. T. Payne, R. G. Bell, and J. L. Davis, "Institutional Distance and Cross-Border Venture Capital Investment Flows," *Journal of Small Business Management*, 2014, in press.

25. National Venture Capital Association Yearbook 2014, Thomas Reuters, 2014.

26. National Venture Capital Association Yearbook 2014, Thomas Reuters, 2014.

27. Foundry Group home page, www.foundrygroup.com, accessed September 15, 2014.

28. BEV Capital home page, www.bevcapital.com, (accessed September 15, 2014).

29. National Venture Capital Association Yearbook 2014, Thomas Reuters, 2014.

30. A. Carrion, "Very Fast Money: High-Frequency Trading on the NASDAQ," *Journal of Financial Markets* 16, no. 4 (2013): 680–711.

31. J.-S. Michel, "Return on Recent VC Investment and Long-Run IPO Returns," *Entrepreneurship Theory and Practice* 38, no. 3 (2014): 527–549.

32. R. Parrino, D. S. Kidwell, and T. Bates, *Fundamentals of Corporate Finance*, 3rd ed. (New York, NY: John Wiley & Sons, 2014).

33. S. Y. K. Fung, F. A. Gul, and S. Radhakrishnan, "Investment Banks' Entry into New IPO Markets and IPO Underpricing," *Management Science* 60, no. 5 (2014): 1297–1316.

34. T.-K. Chou, J.-C. Cheng, and C.-C. Chien, "How Useful Is Venture Capital Prestige? Evidence from IPO Survivability," *Small Business Economics* 40, no. 4 (2013): 843–863.

35. New York Stock Exchange home page, www.nyse.com, (accessed September 15, 2014).

36. J. C. Leach and R. W. Melicher, *Entrepreneurial Finance*, 5th ed. (Cincinnati, OH: Cengage Learning, 2014).

37. A. P. M. Gama and H. van Auken, "The Interdependence Between Trade Credit and Bank Lending: Commitment in Intermediary Firm Relationships," *Journal of Small Business Management*, 2014, in press.

38. S. Cheng, "Potential Lending Discrimination? Insights from Small Business Financing and New Venture Survival," *Journal of Small Business Management*, 2014, in press.

39. SBA home page, www.sba.gov, (accessed September 16, 2014).

40. M. Eckblad, "Debunking the Myths About SBA Loans," *Wall Street Journal*, May 16, 2011, R2.

41. A. Garcia-Santillan, E. Moreno-Garcia, and A. del C. A. Nunez, "Factoring As a Financial Alternative to Firms," *Journal of Applied Finance & Banking* 4, no. 1 (2014): 193–207.

42. A. Prior, "With Alternative Lenders, Flexibility and Speed Come at a Cost," *Wall Street Journal*, August 25, 2014.

43. A. Prior, "With Alternative Lenders, Flexibility and Speed Come at a Cost," *Wall Street Journal*, August 25, 2014.

44. D. Neuberger and S. Rathke-Doppner, "Leasing by Small Enterprises," *Applied Financial Economics* 23, no. 7 (2013): 535–549.

45. R. C. Moyer, J. McGuigan, and R. Rao, *Contemporary Financial Management*, 13th ed. (Cincinnati, OH: Cengage Learning, 2015).

46. SBA home page, www.sba.gov, (accessed September 14, 2014).

47. B. Barringer and R. D. Ireland, *What's Stopping You! Shatter the 9 Most Common Myths Keeping You from Starting Your Own Business* (New York, NY: Financial Times, 2008).

48. M. Jaaskelainen and M. Maula, "Do Networks of Financial Intermediaries Help Reduce Local Bias? Evidence from Cross-Border Venture Capital Exits," *Journal of Business Venturing* 29, no. 5 (2014): 704–721.

49. D. Li, "Multilateral R&D Alliances by New Ventures," *Journal of Business Venturing* 28, no. 2 (2013): 241–260.

PART 4 Managing and Growing an Entrepreneurial Firm

LuminAID Lab, LLC

CHAPTER 11 **Unique *Marketing* Issues   387**

CHAPTER 12 **The Importance of *Intellectual* Property   403**

CHAPTER 13 **Preparing for and *Evaluating* the Challenges of Growth   441**

CHAPTER 14 **Strategies for *Firm Growth*   473**

CHAPTER 15 **Franchising   507**

Getting Personal with WINK NATURAL COSMETICS

Co-Founders

MEGAN COX

BS, Operations Research, Sloan School of Management, MIT, 2014

MIGUEL SALINAS

BS, Cognitive Science, MIT, Projected 2016

Dialogue with Megan Cox

FIRST ENTREPRENEURIAL EXPERIENCE
I set up shop on my elementary school playground, which landed me my first trip to the principal's office.

BEST PART OF BEING A STUDENT
No rules, no bills.

MY ADVICE FOR NEW ENTREPRENEURS
Think it through, but go with your gut.

BEST ADVICE I'VE RECEIVED
The only person forcing limitations on you is yourself.

MY BIGGEST SURPRISE AS AN ENTREPRENEUR
Immense support I've received from my customers. They're awesome.

FAVORITE PERSON I FOLLOW ON TWITTER
Rihanna (she's always full of surprises)

CHAPTER 11

Unique *Marketing* Issues

OPENING PROFILE

WINK NATURAL COSMETICS
Creating a New Brand in the Cosmetics Industry

• *Web: www.winknaturalcosmetics* • *Facebook: WinkNaturalCosmetics* • *Twitter: @WinkAllNatural*

As a student at MIT, one luxury that Megan Cox afforded herself was eyelash extensions. After a while, however, the experience grew wearisome. The process took up to three hours, included ingredients that she worried about (such as hormones and prostaglandin), and wasn't that effective. The experience prompted Cox to start thinking about creating an eyelash extension product of her own.

In early 2012 Cox, who was a student in the Sloan School of Management at MIT, started studying the eyelash industry and the different options that were available. Although having long eyelashes was a hot new trend, many of the solutions had problems. Applying false eyelashes, one of the solutions, was frustrating for many people. False eyelashes are often sticky and itch and use glues that can cause fungi to grow around the lash lines/eyes. Other options were equally unappealing. In some cases, people's eyelashes grew longer but they still had sparse lashes. Additionally, once a person gained long eyelashes, maintaining them was pricey and time consuming.

Cox proceeded to start experimenting with formulations of her own. The goal was to create an all-natural lash and brow enhancer that would stimulate growth in dormant follicles while strengthening the lashes and brows that a person has. Drawing on her chemistry background, she considered different options before settling on a hypoallergenic formula made from natural ingredients. The product that emerged was an eyelash pen that, when glided along an individual's lash line once a day, was intended to produce longer and healthier eyelashes. The pen, which would eventually retail for $39, contained enough ingredients to last three months.

Rather than rushing forward, Cox tested the product. The results were good. In testing trials, Wink, the name Cox attached to the product, increased eyelash fullness by up to 20 percent (60 lashes) in 100 percent of participants (after 8-10 weeks of product use). In addition, due to Wink's conditioning effectiveness, eyelash length increased by up to 20 percent in 80 percent of the participants. Wink was also effective in regrowing eyebrows in patches where brows had previously stopped growing because of overplucking. Best of all, Wink was a hypoallergenic natural serum. Many cosmetic products cause allergic reactions, something Cox wanted to avoid. A hypoallergenic product causes fewer reactions. Wink was also minimally processed and free of parabens, sulfates, phthalates, horomoes/prostaglandins, artificial fragrances, and artificial dyes.

LEARNING OBJECTIVES

After studying this chapter you should be ready to:

1. Explain the three steps (segmenting the market, selecting a target market, and establishing a unique market position) entrepreneurial firms use to identify their customers.

2. Define a brand and explain why it is important to an entrepreneurial firm's marketing efforts.

3. Identify and explain the 4Ps of marketing activities (product, price, promotion, and place) used by entrepreneurial firms.

4. Describe the seven-step sales process an entrepreneurial firm uses to identify prospects and close sales.

During this time, Cox teamed up with classmate Miguel Salinas. Cox and Salinas met through a mutual friend during Cox's freshman year. The two became partners in Wink Natural Cosmetics. At the time, Cox was studying management science, operations research, entrepreneurship, and finance, and Salinas was studying neuroscience. To determine the formula for Wink, the two looked at research papers and conducted experiments. They formally launched their company, Wink Natural Cosmetics, in July 2013. It was mostly bootstrapped, largely because, as Salinas said in an interview with Dorm Startups, "no one took it seriously."[1] Wink was entering a mature market with established competitors. The product was offered on Wink's website; however, Cox and Salinas knew that salons would be the preferred channel to sell the product. It would be up to Cox and Salinas to convince salon owners to stock Wink Natural Cosmetics and recommend it to their customers.

In terms of marketing, at the start Cox and Salinas were it. They wrote their own press releases, product descriptions, and brochures. To gain visibility, they sent samples to salons and sponsored events. They made contact with catalog companies and got Wink placed in several cosmetic catalogs. All of these efforts were aimed at building Wink's brand. They also reached out to salons by offering risk-free trials. They would send the product to salons in lots of 12, and, if they didn't sell, would take them back. They found that the more they reached out to people in the cosmetics industry, the more people reached out to them in return. They also signed up several salons that agreed to act as distributors and place Wink's products in other salons. Cox and Salinas experienced several surprises along the way, one of which was the target market. As it turned out, the salons that carried Wink's products had the most luck selling to 50- to 60-year-old women. That realization changed Cox and Salinas's marketing tactics some. Wink is not big into social media, for example, because 50- to 60-year-old women are not heavy users of social media.

Wink's products are made in both China and the United States. The bottles and boxes are made in China, while the product itself is manufactured and placed in the bottles in the United States. The manufacturing is done in an FDA approved facility. In terms of future growth, Cox and Salinas plan to grow Wink Natural Cosmetics in two ways. First, they plan to continue to increase the number of salons that carry the product. There are no present plans to place Wink in a mainstream retailer such as Walgreens or CVS. Second, they plan to introduce new complementary products, such as brightening and anti-aging creams.[2]

When talking about her experiences, one thing Cox stresses is to not underestimate yourself. At one point Wink hired a PR firm to write press releases, for example. Cox says that the press releases that she wrote were better than the ones that came from the PR firm. It's also important to get free press. Cox actively reached out to organizations that write about student-initiated companies. Many took an interest in Cox and Salinas and wrote articles or included them in lists of top college start-ups. For example, Wink Natural Cosmetics was included in the list of "America's Coolest College Startups" by *Inc.* magazine in 2014. Cox and Salinas believe that generating positive press is helpful in building a company's brand.

n this chapter, we'll look at the marketing challenges confronting entrepreneurial firms. Marketing is a broad subject, and there are many books and websites dedicated to marketing and its subfields. However, in this chapter, we zero in on the marketing challenges that are most pressing for young entrepreneurial firms. The reason for doing this is that marketing is an essential component to a start-up firm's success.[3]

We begin this chapter by discussing how firms define and select their target markets. Next, we discuss how a firm establishes a brand. We then consider the four key aspects of marketing as they relate to young entrepreneurial firms. These four aspects, commonly referred to as the "4Ps" of marketing, are product, price, promotion, and place (or distribution). We conclude the chapter with a discussion of the sales process, which consists of the steps a company goes through to establish relationships with customers and close sales. Many new ventures do a good job of developing products and defining the size of their markets, but do a poor job of dealing with the practicalities of how the products will be sold. It's imperative that a new business have a plan that details how it will sell its product within the confines of a reasonable budget.

Selecting a Market and Establishing a Position

To succeed, a new firm must know who its customers are and how to reach them. A firm uses a three-step process to determine who its customers are. These steps, which are shown in Figure 11.1, include segmenting the market, selecting a target market, and crafting a unique position within the target market.

As noted in Chapter 3, a firm's target market is the limited group of individuals or businesses that it tries to appeal to. It is important that a new venture choose its target market and position inside in its target market quickly because virtually all of its marketing choices hinge on these critical initial choices. For example, GreatCall makes cell phones designed specifically for older people. If GreatCall had designed a distribution strategy, for example, prior to determining that it would target older people, it might have designed a strategy that placed its phones in retail outlets not frequented by older people. Its decision to target older people will have a bearing on every element of its marketing plan.

LEARNING OBJECTIVE

1. Explain the three steps (segmenting the market, selecting a target market, and establishing a unique market position) entrepreneurial firms use to identify their customers.

Segmenting the Market

The first step in selecting a target market is to study the industry in which the firm intends to compete and determine the different potential target markets in that industry. This process is called **market segmentation**, as explained in Chapter 6. Market segmentation is important because a new firm typically has only enough resources to target one market segment, at least initially.[4] Markets can be segmented in many ways, such as by geography (city, state, country), demographic variables (age, gender, family size, income), psychographic variables (personality, lifestyle, values), behavioral variables (benefits sought, product usage rates, brand loyalty), and product type (varies by product). For example, the computer industry can be segmented by product type (i.e., handheld computers, tablet computers, laptops, PCs, work stations, minicomputers, mainframes, and super computers) or customers served (i.e., individuals, businesses, schools, and government).

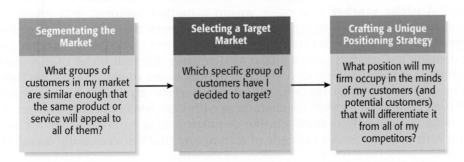

Segmentating the Market	Selecting a Target Market	Crafting a Unique Positioning Strategy
What groups of customers in my market are similar enough that the same product or service will appeal to all of them?	Which specific group of customers have I decided to target?	What position will my firm occupy in the minds of my customers (and potential customers) that will differentiate it from all of my competitors?

FIGURE 11.1
The Process of Selecting a Target Market and Positioning Strategy

Sometimes a firm segments its market on more than one dimension to drill down to a specific market segment that the firm thinks it is uniquely capable of serving. For example, GreatCall probably segmented its market by age and benefits sought. Its ideal customer is someone who is older (age) and is looking for a cell phone that's easy to use (benefits sought).

To test whether you have segmented your market successfully, consider these requirements for successful market segmentation:

- Homogeneity of needs and wants appears within the segment.
- Heterogeneity of needs and wants exists between the segments.
- Differences within the segment should be small compared to differences across segments.
- The segment should be distinct enough so that its members can be easily identified.
- It should be possible to determine the size of the segment.
- The segment should be large enough for the firm to earn profits.

If an entrepreneur is not familiar with how to segment a particular market, IBISWorld, Mintel, and BizMiner, which are online databases often available through large university libraries, provide suggestions. They even show the size of the segments. For example, IBISWorld segments the gym, health, and fitness club industry (NAICS 71394) by service provided. The $26.5 billion industry is 65 percent gyms and fitness centers, 10 percent other, 7 percent dance centers, 7 percent swimming pools, 6 percent ice and roller rinks, and 5 percent tennis centers.[5]

Despite its importance, market segmentation is a process entrepreneurs commonly overlook. Overlooking this step can result in a faulty assessment of the size of the potential market for a new product or service. If a start-up planned to open a chain of tennis centers, for example, it would be incorrect to say that the total market potential is $26.5 billion. Tennis centers are 5 percent of the larger $26.5 billion gym, health, and fitness club industry, which equates to a $1.3 billion market. This doesn't mean that a tennis center business couldn't be profitable or that the new business couldn't expand the market for tennis. It's just that the entrepreneur should enter the business with a realistic assessment of the size of its market.

Selecting a Target Market

Once a firm has segmented the market, the next step is to select a target market. As discussed in previous chapters, the market must be sufficiently attractive, and the firm must be able to serve it well. Typically, a firm (especially a start-up venture) doesn't target an entire segment of a market because many market segments are too large to target successfully. Instead, most firms target a niche market within the segment. For example, within the dance studio market, there are several small niche markets that companies can choose to target. A **niche market** is a place within a market segment that represents a narrow group of customers with similar interests. For example, Broadway Dance Center in New York City targets serious dancers who aspire to earn a living dancing in Broadway plays.[6] That's an entirely different niche than a studio teaching ballroom dancing or a studio teaching ballet to young girls. By focusing on a clearly defined market, a firm can become an expert in that market and then be able to provide its customers with high levels of value and service. Focusing on a clearly defined market requires a firm to know what *not to do* along with what to do. An example of a company that's successfully sorted this out is MailFinch, a company specializing in managing other companies' direct mail campaigns. According to its founder, Paul Singh:

> Looking back at the recent growth of MailFinch, most of the success can be attributed to what the product *can't* do. We do very few things, but we do those things better than anyone else in the game and we make it drop-dead simple to get started (with the MailFinch service).[7]

A firm's choice of target markets must also be in sync with its business model and the backgrounds and skills of its founders and other employees. A firm must also continually monitor the attractiveness of its target market. Societal preferences change, a fact that sometimes causes a target market to lose its attractiveness for a firm and the product or service it has to offer customers.

Crafting a Unique Market Position

After selecting a target market, the firm's next step is to establish a "position" within it that differentiates it from its competitors. As we discussed in Chapter 5, position is concerned with how the firm is situated relative to competitors. For example, in Pittsburgh, Pennsylvania, Art & Style Dance Studio specializes in Latin and Ballroom dancing.[8] That's a different position than the Arthur Murray Dance Studio in Pittsburgh that offers instruction in Fox Trot, Waltz, Tango, Viennese Waltz, Quickstep, and Salsa.[9] A firm's market position is defined by its products or services. Determining which position in a market to occupy and compete in is a strategic call on the part of a company based on its mission, its overall approach to the marketplace, and its competitive landscape.

Once a company has identified its position and primary points of differentiation, a helpful technique is to develop a **product attribute map**, which illustrates a firm's positioning strategy relative to its major rivals. A product attribute map for Snap Fitness is shown in Figure 11.2. Snap Fitness operates small gyms that are located near residential areas and are open 24 hours a day. The centers offer weights, treadmills, and exercise machines. They're

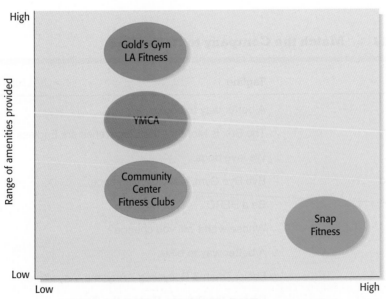

FIGURE 11.2
Product Attribute Map for Snap Fitness

staffed during the day and are available to members at night by swiping a key card at the main door. The equipment is start-of-the-art, and the centers are very clean and secure. They do not offer a wide range of amenities, such as swimming pools, locker rooms, exercise classes, racquetball courts, and massages. The centers offer their members a fast, convenient, and affordable way to develop and maintain fitness. A membership costs around $35 a month for a single membership, $50 for a couple, and $60 for a family.

This firm's product attribute map is based on the two primary attributes that people look for in a fitness center—range of amenities provided and the extent to which the center is both affordable and convenient. The point is to assess Snap Fitness's strengths and/or weaknesses in each of these categories and plot it on the map. The same is done for Snap Fitness's major competitors. The results are shown in Figure 11.2. While Snap Fitness does not rank high in terms of amenities provided, it outranks its competitors by a wide margin in terms of being convenient and affordable. As a result, it stresses its convenience and affordability in its promotions, rather than drawing attention to its lack of amenities. Snap Fitness's tagline is "fast convenient affordable."[10] Any firm can develop a similar product attribute map to illustrate its position in an industry and help direct its marketing plan.

To support their positioning strategy, firms often develop a tagline, just like Snap Fitness has done, to reinforce the position they have staked out in the marketplace. A **tagline** is a catchy phrase that's used consistently in a company's literature, advertisements, stationery, and even invoices, and thus becomes associated with that company—to reinforce the position it has staked out in the market. Table 11.1 is a short matching quiz that asks you to match companies featured in this book with their taglines. A company has created a successful tagline if the message makes you think of its products or services and the position it has established in its market.

Branding

LEARNING OBJECTIVE

2. Define a brand and explain why it is important to an entrepreneurial firm's marketing efforts.

A **brand** is the set of attributes—positive or negative—that people associate with a company. These attributes can be positive, such as trustworthy, innovative, dependable, or easy to deal with. Or they can be negative, such as cheap, unreliable, arrogant, or difficult to deal with. The customer loyalty a company creates through its brand is one of its most valuable assets. Lending support to

TABLE 11.1   Match the Company to Its Tagline

Company	Tagline
GoPro	A better way to cook.
Brain Sentry	The Box is Monthly, the Discoveries are Endless.
Flings Bins	We love dogs.
Giveforward	Bye Bye Gym, Hello Convenience.
Blue Apron	Be a HERO.
Zagster	Whose world will you change?
Birchbox	A better way to bike.
Wello	Easier Trash & Recycling…Anytime, Anywhere.
Rover.com	Protect the Players. Protect the Game.

These two young entrepreneurs just opened a bike shop. They plan to sell bikes, bike accessories and offer repair services through a retail storefront and online. An important task they have ahead of them is building a brand for their company. A brand is the set of attributes that people associate with a company.

Moxie Productions/Blend Images/Corbis

this sentiment, Russell Hanlin, the CEO of Sunkist Growers, said, "An orange is an orange ... is an orange. Unless ... that orange happens to be a Sunkist, a name 80 percent of consumers know and trust."[11] By putting its name on an orange, Sunkist is making a promise to its customers that the orange will be wholesome and fresh. It is important that Sunkist not break this promise. Some companies monitor the integrity of their brands through **brand management**, which is a program used to protect the image and value of an organization's brand in consumers' minds. This means that if Sunkist discovered that some of its oranges weren't fresh, it would take immediate steps to correct the problem.

Table 11.2 lists the different ways people think about the meaning of a brand. All the sentiments expressed in the table are similar, but they illustrate the multifaceted nature of a company's brand.

Start-ups must build a brand from scratch; this process begins with selecting the company's name, as described in Chapter 7's appendix. One of the keys to effective branding is to create a strong personality for a firm, designed to appeal to the chosen target market.[12] Southwest Airlines, for example, has

TABLE 11.2   **What's a Brand? Different Ways of Thinking About the Meaning of a Brand**

- A brand is a promise to serve stakeholders' interests.
- A brand is a firm's guarantee of a level of performance.
- A brand indicates the promises a firm makes to those it serves.
- A brand expresses a firm's reputation.
- A brand presents a firm's credentials.
- A brand is an indicator of trust and reduced risk.
- A brand describes a company's nature.
- A brand serves as a handshake between a firm and its customers.

Source: Adapted from *Emotional Branding* by Daryl Travis, copyright © 2000 by Daryl Travis. Used by permission of Pima Publishing, a division of Random House, Inc.

created a brand that denotes fun. This is a good fit for its historical and current primary target market: people traveling for pleasure rather than business. Similarly, Starbucks and Panera Bread have each created a brand that denotes an experience framed around warmth and hospitality, encouraging people to linger and buy additional products. A company ultimately wants its customers to strongly identify with it—to see themselves as "Southwest Airlines flyers" or as "Panera Bread diners." People won't do this, however, unless they see a company as being different from competitors in ways that create value for them.

So how does a new firm develop a brand? On a philosophical level, a firm must have meaning in its customers' lives. It must create value—something for which customers are willing to pay. Imagine a father shopping for airline tickets so that he can take his three children to see their grandparents for Christmas. If Southwest Airlines can get his family to their destination for $75 per ticket cheaper than its competitors, Southwest has real meaning in the father's life. Similarly, if a young couple invites neighbors to play Cranium, a group board game, and playing the game results in lasting friendships, Cranium will have a special place in their hearts.

On a more practical level, brands are built through a number of techniques, including advertising, public relations, sponsorships, support of social causes, social media, and good performance. A firm's name, logo, website design, Facebook page, and even its letterhead are part of its brand. It's important for start-ups, particularly if they plan to sell to other businesses, to have a polished image immediately so that they have credibility when they approach their potential customers.

Most experts warn against placing an overreliance on advertising to build a firm's brand. A more affordable approach is to rely on word of mouth, the media, and ingenuity to create positive buzz about a company. Creating **buzz** means creating awareness and a sense of anticipation about a company and its offerings.[13] This process can start during feasibility analysis, when a company shows its concept statement or product prototype to prospective buyers or industry experts. Unless a company wants what it is doing to be kept secret (to preserve its proprietary technology or its first-mover advantage), it hopes that people start talking about it and its exciting new product or service. This is certainly the case for movie production studios, as they hope that people talking about a movie they enjoyed watching will encourage others to visit their local theaters.[14] In addition, newspapers, magazines, blogs, and trade journals are always looking for stories about interesting companies. In fact, receiving a favorable review of its products or services in a magazine, trade journal, or highly respected blog lends a sense of legitimacy to a firm that would be hard to duplicate through advertisements.

Focusing too much on the features and benefits of their products is a common mistake entrepreneurs make when trying to gain attention from the media. Journalists are typically skeptical when entrepreneurs start talking about how great their products are relative to those of their competitors. What journalists usually prefer is a human interest story about why a firm was started or a story focused on something that's distinctly unique about the start-up.

Ultimately, a strong brand can be a very powerful asset for a firm. Over 50 percent of consumers say that a known and trusted brand is a reason to buy a product.[15] As a result, a brand allows a company to charge a price for its products that is consistent with its image. A successful brand can also increase the market value of a company by 50 to 75 percent.[16] This increased valuation can be very important to a firm if it is acquired, merges with another firm, or launches an initial public offering (IPO). **Brand equity** is the term that denotes the set of assets and liabilities that are linked to a brand and enable it to raise a firm's valuation.[17] It is important for firms to understand brand equity and how to use it to create value.

Although the assets and liabilities that make up a firm's brand equity will vary from context to context, they usually are grouped into the following five categories:

- Brand loyalty
- Name recognition
- Perceived quality (of a firm's products and services)
- Brand associations in addition to quality (e.g., good service)
- Other proprietary assets, such as patents, trademarks, and high-quality partnerships

One aspect of branding that start-ups should be alert to is the possibility of forming co-branding relationships. Co-branding is when two companies form a partnership to combine their brands. The objective is to combine the strengths of the brands. A co-branding relationship can be short term, to promote a specific event or product launch, or can be long term, such as opening co-branded stores. An example of a co-branding alliance is provided in the "Partnering for Success" feature. In this example two companies, Bruegger's Bagels and Caribou Coffee, are testing a fairly involved co-branding relationship where they're opening new restaurants that will be jointly operated and branded by the two companies.

The 4Ps of Marketing for New Ventures

Once a company decides on its target market, establishes a position within that market, and establishes a brand, it is ready to begin planning the details of its marketing mix. A firm's **marketing mix** is the set of controllable, tactical marketing tools that it uses to produce the response it wants in the target market.[18] Most marketers organize their marketing mix into four categories: product, price, promotion, and place (or distribution). For an obvious reason, these categories are commonly referred to as the 4Ps.

The way a firm sells and distributes its product dramatically affects a company's marketing program. This effect means that the first decision a firm has to make is its overall approach to selling its product or service. Even for similar firms, the marketing mix can vary significantly, depending on the way the firms do business. For example, a software firm can sell directly through its website or through retail stores, or it can license its product to another company to be sold under that company's brand name. A start-up that plans to sell directly to the public would set up its promotions program in a much different way than a firm planning to license its products to other firms. A firm's marketing program should be consistent with its business model and its overall business plan.

Let's look more closely at the 4Ps. Again, these are broad topics on which entire books have been written. In this section, we focus on the aspects of the 4Ps that are most relevant to entrepreneurial ventures.

Product

A firm's **product**, in the context of its marketing mix, is the good or service it offers to its target market. Technically, a product is something that takes on physical form, such as an Apple iPhone, a bicycle, or a solar panel. A **service** is an activity or benefit that is intangible and does not take on a physical form, such as an airplane trip or advice from an attorney. But when discussing a firm's marketing mix, both products and services are lumped together under the label "product."

PARTNERING FOR SUCCESS

How Co-Branding Is Combining the Strengths of Two Already Successful Brands

Caribou Coffee: Web: www.cariboucoffee.com; Facebook: cariboucoffee; Twitter: @caribou_coffee
Bruegger's Bagels: Web: www.brueggers.com; Facebook: Bruegger's Bagels; Twitter: @Brueggers

Co-branding is when two companies form an alliance to work together. The idea is to create marketing synergy. Synergy is the concept of 2 + 2 = 5. Synergy is achieved in a co-branding relationship when two brands working together achieve more than the brands could have cumulatively achieved on their own. This is possible, in a successful co-branding relationship, when each brand benefits from the brand loyalty and the reputation of the other.

Two companies that recently formed a co-branding partnership are Caribou Coffee and Bruegger's Bagels. The idea grew out of a relationship between Caribou CEO Mike Tattersfield and Claude Bergeron, co-CEO of Bruegger's parent company, Le Duff America. It also grew out of a recognition that the two companies do best when located near each other. As of late 2013, Caribou Coffee and Bruegger's Bagels operated stores literally next door to each other in 10 Minneapolis-St. Paul locations, along with an 11th location in Raleigh, North Carolina. Those stores are some of the best performing for both chains. Caribou and Bruegger's have complimentary offerings. People often eat bagels and drink coffee together. So the two executives concluded that trying co-branding was a reasonable decision to reach.

The companies decided to start slowly. As of early 2014, three co-branded stores are open, with more to follow if the initial stores are successful. The co-branded stores project a cohesive brand by incorporating both company's logos. The stores to follow will incorporate design elements of Bruegger's new store prototype. They'll include large glass windows to separate the bakery from the dining room and give customers an unobstructed view of the baking process. They'll also include a full barista system. This is where the co-branded restaurants will create synergy on the customer side. The restaurants will include bakeries where the food products will be made and barista stations where the specialty coffees and other beverages will be prepared, all visible to the customer (to provide a unique experience). This combination will provide the co-branded stores a source of differentiation and a hoped for competitive advantage in the marketplace.

Unseen to the customer, the co-branded stores will have significant synergies in the back of the house as well. In instances where Caribou Coffee and Bruegger's Bagel stores are situated side-by-side, each store has its own manager, its own purchasing system, its own accounting systems, etc. The co-branded stores will operate as a single store and eliminate these redundancies.

So far so good. "We've been thrilled with the performance of our dual operations so far," Judy Kadylak, director of marketing for Bruegger's, said in an article posted on the Foodservice Equipment & Supplies website (http://fesmag.com). If the initial test sites remain successful, the next co-branded stores will open in Raleigh, North Carolina, in Iowa, and in the Minneapolis-St. Paul area.

Along with co-branding stores, like Caribou Coffee and Bruegger's Bagels are doing, co-branding can take on other forms. To learn more about co-branding, go to www.google.com, type the term "co-branding" into the search engine, and select images. You'll see hundreds of example of co-branding. In many instances, companies will co-brand products rather than their entire companies. An example is a co-branding relationship between Element Skateboard and TOMS shoes. The TOMS logo is placed on the underside of Element skateboards. Each brand presumably benefits from the brand loyalty and the reputation of the other.

Questions for Critical Thinking

1. Make a list of the potential pluses and minuses of the co-branding relationship between Caribou Coffee and Bruegger's Bagels. Indicate whether you believe the potential pluses will outweigh the potential minuses for this co-branding relationship. Explain your answer.
2. To what degree do you believe brand management is more difficult in a co-branding setting?
3. Provide three additional examples of co-branding. Describe the rationale behind each co-branding relationship.
4. Examine the You Be the VC 11.2 feature, which focuses on COOLEST, a revolutionary new type of cooler. Suggest some potential co-branding relationships for COOLEST.

Sources: L. White, "Case Study: Bruegger's Bagels Burlington, Vt.," Foodservice Equipment and Supplies website, available at http://fesmag.com/departments/chain-news-profiles/11561-case-study-bruegger%E2%80%99s-bagels-burlington,-vt, posted on March 3, 2014, accessed on September 3, 2014; J. Forgrieve, "Co-Branding Deal Brings Bagels and Coffee Closer Together," Smartblogs, available at http://smartblogs.com/food-and-beverage/2013/11/15/co-branding-deal-brings-bagels-and-coffee-closer-together/, posted on November 15, 2013, accessed on September 3, 2014.

Determining the product or products to be sold is central to the firm's entire marketing effort. As stressed throughout this book, the most important attribute of a product is that it adds value in the minds of its target customers. Let's think about this by comparing vitamins with pain pills, as articulated by Henry W. Chesbrough, a professor at Harvard University:

> We all know that vitamins are good for us and that we should take them. Most of us, though, do not take vitamins on a regular basis, and whatever benefits vitamins provide do not seem to be greatly missed in the short term. People therefore pay relatively very little for vitamins. In contrast, people know when they need a pain killer. And they know they need it now, not later. They can also tell quite readily whether the reliever is working. People will be willing to pay a great deal more for a pain reliever than they pay for a vitamin. In this context, the pain reliever provides a much stronger value proposition than does a vitamin—because the need is felt more acutely, the benefit is greater and is perceived much more quickly.[19]

This example illustrates at least in part why investors prefer to fund firms that potentially have breakthrough products, such as a software firm that is working on a product to eliminate e-mail spam or a biotech firm that is working on a cure for a disease. These products are pain pills rather than vitamins because their benefits would be felt intensely and quickly. In contrast, a new restaurant start-up or a new retail store may be exciting, but these types of firms are more akin to a vitamin than a pain pill. The benefits of these businesses would not be felt as intensely.

As the firm prepares to sell its product, an important distinction should be made between the core product and the actual product. While the core product may be a CD that contains a tax preparation program, the actual product, which is what the customer buys, may have as many as five characteristics: a quality level, features, design, a brand name, and packaging.[20] For example, TurboTax is an actual product. Its name, features, warranty, ability to upgrade, packaging, and other attributes have all been carefully combined to deliver the benefits of the product: helping people prepare their federal and state tax returns while receiving the biggest refund possible. When first introducing a product to the market, an entrepreneur needs to make sure that more than the core product is right. Attention also needs to be paid to the actual product—the features, design, packaging, and so on that constitute the collection of benefits that the customer ultimately buys. Anyone who has ever tried to remove a product from a frustratingly rigid plastic container knows that the way a product is packaged is part of the product itself. The quality of the product should not be compromised by missteps in other areas.

The initial rollout is one of the most critical times in the marketing of a new product. All new firms face the challenge that they are unknown and that it takes a leap of faith for their first customers to buy their products. Some start-ups meet this challenge by using reference accounts. A **reference account** is an early user of a firm's product who is willing to give a testimonial regarding his or her experience with the product. For example, imagine the effect of a spokesperson for Apple Inc. saying that Apple used a new computer hardware firm's products and was pleased with their performance. A testimonial such as this would pave the way for the sales force of this new firm's hardware, and the new firm could use it to reduce fears that it was selling an untested and perhaps ineffective product.

To obtain reference accounts, new firms must often offer their product to an initial group of customers for free or at a reduced price in exchange for their willingness to try the product and for their feedback. There is nothing improper about this process as long as everything is kept aboveboard and the entrepreneur is not indirectly "paying" someone to offer a positive endorsement. Still, many entrepreneurs are reluctant to give away products, even in exchange for a potential endorsement. But there are several advantages to getting a strong set of endorsements: credibility with peers, non-company advocates who are willing to talk to the press, and quotes or examples to use in company brochures and advertisements.

Price

Price is the amount of money consumers pay to buy a product. It is the only element in the marketing mix that produces revenue; all other elements represent costs.[21] Price is an extremely important element of the marketing mix because it ultimately determines how much money a company can earn. The price a company charges for its products also sends a clear message to its target market. For example, Oakley positions its sunglasses as innovative, state-of-the art products that are both high quality and visually appealing. This position in the market suggests the premium price that Oakley charges. If Oakley tried to establish the position described previously and charged a low price for its products, it would send confusing signals to its customers. Its customers would wonder, "Are Oakley sunglasses high quality or aren't they?" In addition, the lower price wouldn't generate the sales revenue Oakley requires to continuously differentiate its sunglasses from competitors' products in ways that create value for customers.

Most entrepreneurs use one of two methods to set the price for their products: cost-based pricing or value-based pricing.

Cost-Based Pricing In **cost-based pricing**, the list price is determined by adding a markup percentage to a product's cost. The markup percentage may be standard for the industry or may be arbitrarily determined by the entrepreneur. The advantage of this method is that it is straightforward, and it is relatively easy to justify the price of a good or service. The disadvantage is that it is not always easy to estimate what the costs of a product will be. Once a price is set, it is difficult to raise it, even if a company's costs increase in an unpredicted manner. In addition, cost-based pricing is based on what a company thinks it should receive rather than on what the market thinks a good or service is worth. It is becoming increasingly difficult for companies to dictate prices to their customers, given customers' ability to comparison shop on the Internet to find what they believe is the best bargain for them.[22]

Value-Based Pricing In **value-based pricing**, the list price is determined by estimating what consumers are willing to pay for a product and then backing off a bit to provide a cushion. What a customer is willing to pay is determined by the perceived value of the product and by the number of choices available in the marketplace. Sometimes, to make this determination, a company has to work backwards by testing to see what its target market is willing to pay. A firm influences its customers' perception of the value through positioning, branding, and the other elements of the marketing mix. Most experts recommend value-based pricing because it hinges on the perceived value of a product or service rather than cost plus markup, which, as stated previously, is a formula that ignores the customer.[23] A gross margin (a company's net sales minus its costs of goods sold) of 60 to 80 percent is not uncommon in high-tech industries. An Intel chip that sells for $300 may cost $50 to $60 to produce. This type of markup reflects the perceived value of the chip. If Intel used a cost-based pricing method instead of a value-based approach, it would probably charge much less for its chips and earn less profit.

Most experts also warn entrepreneurs to resist the temptation to charge a low price for their products in the hopes of capturing market share. This approach can win a sale but generates little profit. In addition, most consumers make a **price-quality attribution** when looking at the price of a product. This means that consumers naturally assume that the higher-priced product is also the better-quality product.[24] If a firm charges a low price for its products, it sends a signal to its customers that the product is low quality regardless of whether it really is.

A vivid example of the association between price and quality is provided by SmugMug (www.smugmug.com), an online photo-sharing site that charges a $40-per-year base subscription fee. According to its website, the company has "Billions of Happy Photos" and "Millions of Happy Customers." What's interesting about the company is that most of its competitors, including Photobucket, Flicker, and Picas Web Albums, offer a similar service for free. Ostensibly, the reason SmugMug is able to charge a fee is that it offers higher levels of customer service and has a more user-friendly interface (in terms of how you view your photos online) than its competitors. But the owners of SmugMug feel that its ability to charge goes beyond these obvious points. Some of the free sites have closed abruptly, and their users have lost photos. SmugMug, because it charges, is seen as more reliable and dependable for the long term. (Who wants to lose their photos?) In addition, the owners believe that when people pay for something, they innately assign a higher value to it. As a result, SmugMug users tend to treat the site with respect, by posting attractive, high-quality photos that are in good taste. SmugMug's users appreciate this facet of the site, compared to the free sites, where unseemly photos often creep in.[25]

The overarching point of this example is that the price a company is able to charge is largely a function of (1) the objective quality of a product or service and (2) the perception of value that is created in the minds of customers relative to competing products in the marketplace. These are issues a firm should consider when developing its positioning and branding strategies.

Price is such an important element of the marketing mix that, if a company gets it wrong, it can be extremely damaging to both the company's short-term profits and future viability. The "What Went Wrong?" feature in this chapter focuses on marketing missteps at JCPenney. In 2011–2012, JCPenney, under the leadership of CEO Ron Johnson, made critical mistakes in the areas of branding, testing (or the lack thereof), and pricing. The mistakes provide lessons for start-ups of marketing miscues they should be particularly on guard to avoid in their own situations.

Promotion

Promotion refers to the activities the firm takes to communicate the merits of its product to its target market. Ultimately, the goal of these activities is to persuade people to buy the product. There are a number of these activities, but most start-ups have limited resources, meaning that they must carefully study promotion activities before choosing the one or ones they'll use. Let's look at the most common activities entrepreneurs use to promote their products.

Advertising **Advertising** is making people aware of a product in hopes of persuading them to buy it. Advertising's major goals are to:

■ Raise customer awareness of a product
■ Explain a product's comparative features and benefits
■ Create associations between a product and a certain lifestyle

These goals can be accomplished through a number of media including direct mail, magazines, newspapers, radio, the Internet, blogs, television, and billboard advertising. The most effective ads tend to be those that are memorable and

WHAT WENT WRONG?

What Start-ups Can Learn About Marketing from Missteps at JCPenney

Web: www.jcpenney.com; Facebook: JCPenney; Twitter: @jcpenney

After successful stretches at Target and Apple, it seemed as though Ron Johnson was a master marketer. But things went sour quickly after JCPenney hired Johnson as its CEO. Johnson's attempt to reinvent JCPenney's brand, change its pricing strategy, and overhaul the way the company did business all fell flat. In fact, during Johnson's 17-month tenure, JCPenney's sales fell quickly, loyal customers deserted the company, and employee morale hit an all-time low.

JCPenney hired Johnson in June 2011. The idea was to bring in a marketing wiz to revitalize JCPenney's tired brand. Johnson seemed to have all the right credentials. At Target, Johnson was vice president of merchandising, where he was responsible for launching the Michael Graves line of consumer products that enhanced Target's image. His most recent job was senior vice president of retail operations at Apple, where he was largely responsible for the sleek look and solid success of Apple stores.

Johnson hit the ground running at JCPenney with bold plans. His goal was to revitalize JCPenney by breathing new life into its stores and brand. When he was brought in, JCPenney was an unremarkable but solid chain of 1,100 stores serving middle America. Sales were around $17.5 billion a year. When he left sales had plummeted to $13 billion and JCPenney was running low on cash. What went wrong?

According to a general consensus, Johnson made three primary mistakes during his stint at JCPenney. The mistakes involve various facets of marketing, and they are mistakes that start-ups can learn from.

Mistake #1—Fair and Square Pricing. In early 2012, Johnson announced that JCPenney would no longer offer merchandise on "sale." Instead, the company would offer "fair and square" everyday low pricing. The idea was to offer a fair price from the get-go, rather than marking a product high and then cutting the price several times before eventually getting to the fair price.

The strategy didn't work. It turns out shoppers like looking for bargains. It's somewhat of a game—shoppers see a new shirt or blouse priced at $50, and then wait for it to go on "sale" for $35 before buying. None of the shirts or blouses sell for $50, so Johnson figured why play games, just list the shirt or blouse for $35 from the outset. But it turns out that shoppers are accustomed to and like playing the game. There is a certain satisfaction in "saving" $15 on a shirt or blouse that a shopper doesn't get paying the same price initially. As a result, loyal JCPenney shoppers left in droves for T.J.Maxx, Kohl's, and Macy's, where the game was ongoing.

Terminology was also a problem. As part of fair and square pricing, JCPenney had two tiers of pricing for a period of time: red tickets indicated that the items were "everyday" merchandise pricing, and clearance items had blue stickers that designated "best price." The result was widespread customer confusion. Shoppers didn't understand what the terms meant. It was another reason to abandon JCPenney and go to a different store.

In fairness to Johnson, fair and square pricing had worked at Apple. Apple doesn't price computers, iPhones, or iPads at one price and then slash the price and offer the product on sale. The mistake Johnson made was to equate the way people buy technology products with the way people buy clothing and other products sold at JCPenney. Consumers are accustomed to paying full freight for technology products, but not for clothing. By the time JCPenney tried to reverse its pricing strategy, significant damage had been done.

Mistake #2—No Testing of Ideas in Advance. The reason Johnson wasn't able to anticipate the negative response to fair and square pricing is because it wasn't tested in advance. When Johnson proposed his bold new strategy, he was asked about the possibility of trying it out on a limited test basis. According to several published reports, Johnson shot down the idea by saying that he didn't test at Apple.

Imagine what could have been learned by simply testing fair and square pricing at a handful of stores before rolling it out system-wide. Surely, much would have been learned. The fact is that JCPenney's loyal customers loved sales and the prospect of finding a "steal" via rounds of markdowns. Also, a simple trial period should have revealed the type of confusion resulting from the new terminology that was put in use.

Mistake #3—A Total Misread of JCPenney's Brand. Perhaps the most damaging mistake was a total misread of JCPenney's brand. Johnson envisioned JCPenney stores having "stores within the stores," which would be boutiques were people could buy specialty merchandise or get their nails done. He wanted JCPenney to be Americans' "favorite place to shop." His goal was for people to show up and hang out at JCPenney stores, like people hang out at Apple stores, and gladly pay a full but fair price. It never happened. JCPenney's core clientele was thrift-minded shoppers who brought impatient kids into the store to buy school clothes. They also tended to move through the stores quickly when shopping alone. The consensus view is that Johnson wanted JCPenney shoppers to be something they weren't. He wanted them to be more like Apple shoppers. Instead, there was more overlap with T.J.Maxx or even Walmart.

The Ron Johnson era ended in January 2013, just 17 months after it began. He was replaced by his predecessor, Mike Ullman.

Questions for Critical Thinking

1. How does a start-up establish a "brand"? What do we learn from JCPenney's miscues about the importance of branding?

2. Although the concept of selecting a target market and establishing a unique position is not specifically mentioned in the feature, what do we learn about these two topics from JCPenney's miscues?

3. What type of testing should a start-up do to ensure that its initial customers see its brand in the way that the company intended?

4. Do a little Internet or gumshoe research on JCPenney today. Where does the company stand in terms of how it prices its products? What does the company's brand mean to consumers today?

Sources: "5 Critical Errors That Triggered Ron Johnson's Removal at JCPenney," *Chief Executive*, available at http://chiefexecutive.net/5-critical-errors-that-triggered-ron-johnsons-removal-at-jc-penney, posted on April 18, 2013, accessed on September 3, 2014; J. Aisner, "What Went Wrong at JC Penney?, *Forbes*, August 21, 2013; Ron Johnson (businessman), Wikipedia, www.wikipedia.org, accessed on September 3, 2014.

support a product's brand. However, advertising has some major weaknesses, including the following:

- Low credibility
- The possibility that a high percentage of the people who see the ad will not be interested
- Message clutter (meaning that after hearing or reading so many ads, people simply tune out)
- Relative costliness compared to other forms of promotions
- The perception that advertising is intrusive[26]

Because of these weaknesses, most start-ups do not advertise their products broadly. Instead, they tend to be very frugal and selective in their advertising efforts or engage in hybrid promotional campaigns that aren't advertising per se, but are designed to promote a product or service.

Along with engaging in hybrid promotional campaigns, many start-ups advertise in trade journals or utilize highly focused pay-per-click advertising provided by Google, Bing, or another online firm to economize the advertising dollars. Pay-per-click advertising represents a major innovation in advertising and has been embraced by firms of all sizes. Google has two pay-per-click programs—AdWords and AdSense. AdWords allows an advertiser to buy keywords on Google's home page (www.google.com), which triggers text-based ads to the side (and sometimes above) the search results when the keyword is used. So, if you type "soccer ball" into the Google search bar, you will see ads that have been paid for by companies that have soccer balls to sell. Many advertisers report impressive results utilizing this approach, presumably because they are able to place their ads in front of people who are already searching for information about their product. Google's other pay-per-click program is called AdSense. It is similar to AdWords, except the advertiser's ads appear on other websites instead of Google's home page. For example, an organization that promotes soccer might allow Google to place some of its client's ads on its website. The advertiser pays on a pay-for-click basis when its ad is clicked on the soccer organization's site. Google shares the revenue generated by the advertisers with the sponsoring site. Table 11.3 provides a summary of the Google AdWords and Google AdSense programs. Yahoo and Microsoft's joint program, which is very similar to Google's, is called the Yahoo Bing Network. The Yahoo Bing Network is a joint venture between Yahoo and Microsoft to sell pay-per-click ads on both the Yahoo and the Microsoft Bing search engines.

As an aside, online advertising in general allows people who know a lot about a particular topic to launch a website, populate it with articles, tips, videos, and other useful information, and make money online by essentially selling access to the people attracted to the website. For example, Tim Carter, a well-known columnist on home repair, has a website named Ask the Builder (www.askthebuilder.com). Information and instructions on all types of home

TABLE 11.3 **Descriptions of Google AdWords and AdSense Programs for Advertisers and Website Owners**

AdWords	AdSense
Allows advertisers to buy keywords on the Google home page.	Allows advertisers to buy ads that will be shown on other websites instead of Google's home page.
Triggers text-based ads to the side (and sometimes above) search results when the keyword is used.	Google selects sites of interest for the advertiser's customers.
Advertisers are charged on a pay-per-click basis.	Advertisers are charged on a pay-per-click or per-thousand-impression basis.
The program includes local, national, and international distribution.	Advertisers are not restricted to text-based ads. Choices include text, image, and video advertisements.
Advertisers specify the maximum amount they are willing to pay per click. The ordering of the paid listings on the search results depends on other advertisers' bids and the historical click-through rates of all ads shown for a given search.	Advertisers benefit because their ads are seen as less intrusive than most banner ads, because the content of the ad is often relevant to the website.
Advertisers have the option of enabling their ads to be displayed on Google's partner network. This network includes AOL, Ask.com, and Netscape.	Website owners benefit by using the service to monetize their websites.
Advertisers benefit because they are able to place their ads in front of people who are already searching for information about their product.	A companion to the regular AdSense program, AdSense for Search lets website owners place the Google search box on their website. Google shares any ad revenues it makes from those searches.

building projects and repair are available on this website, as are links to areas that focus on specific topics, such as air-conditioning, cabinets, deck construction, and plumbing. Clicking any one of these areas brings up online ads that deal with that specific area. All together, the site has hundreds of ads. Carter is able to do this and still attract large numbers of visitors because the information he provides is good and helpful. He might also believe that his ads, in a certain respect, add valuable content to the site. If someone is looking at the portion of his site that deals with how to construct a deck, he or she might actually appreciate seeing ads that point to websites where books and blueprints for building decks are available.

Another medium for advertising, which is growing in popularity, is social media sites, such as Facebook. The advantage of Facebook, in particular, is that it allows companies to deliver highly targeted ads based on where people live and how they describe themselves on their Facebook profiles. For example, a company that sells licensed sports apparel for the Boston Red Sox can deliver a highly targeted ad to the people most likely to buy its products. The company could deliver ads exclusively to men who live in Massachusetts and cite the Boston Red Sox in their Facebook profiles. Any company can identify its ideal potential customer and deliver targeted Facebook ads in the same manner.

The steps involved in putting together an advertisement are shown in Figure 11.3. Typically, for start-up firms, advertisements are the most effective if they're part of a coordinated marketing campaign.[27] For example, a print ad might feature a product's benefits and direct the reader to a website or Facebook page for more information. The website or Facebook page might offer access to coupons or other incentives if the visitor fills out an information request form (which asks for name, address, and phone number). The names collected from the information request form could then be used to make sales calls.

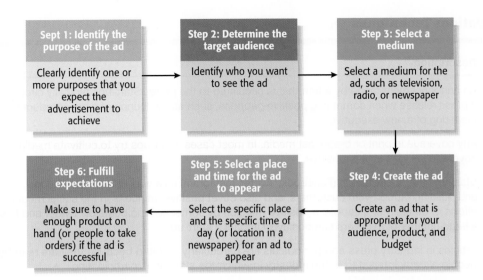

FIGURE 11.3
Steps Involved in
Putting Together
an Advertisement

Public Relations One of the most cost-effective ways to increase the awareness of the products a company sells is through public relations. **Public relations** refers to efforts to establish and maintain a company's image with the public. The major difference between public relations and advertising is that public relations is not paid for directly. The cost of public relations to a firm is the effort it makes to network with journalists, blog authors, and other people to try to interest them in saying or writing good things about the company and its products. Several techniques fit the definition of public relations, as shown in Table 11.4. Airbnb's campaign to reach out to bloggers, chronicled in the "Savvy Entrepreneurial Firm" feature in this chapter, is an example of a public relations campaign.

Many start-ups emphasize public relations over advertising primarily because it's cheaper and helps build the firm's credibility. In slightly different words, it may be better to start with public relations rather than advertising because people view advertising as the self-serving voice of a company that's anxious to make a sale.[28] A firm's public relations effort can be oriented to telling the company's story through a third party, such as a magazine or a newspaper. If a magazine along the lines of *Inc.*, *Entrepreneur*, or *Fortune* publishes a positive review of a new company's products, or a company is profiled in a prominent blog, consumers are likely to believe that those products are at least worth a try. They think that because these magazines and blogs have no vested interest in the company, they have no reason to stretch the truth or lie about the usefulness or value of a company's products. Technology companies, for example, that are featured on TechCrunch or Mashable, two popular technology blogs, typically see an immediate spike in their Web traffic and sales as a result of the mention.

There are many ways in which a start-up can enhance its chances of getting noticed by the press, a blogger, or someone who is influential in social media. As mentioned earlier, journalists and others are typically not interested in overtly helping a firm promote its product. Instead, what they prefer is a human interest story about why a firm was started or a story that focuses on something that is particularly unique about the start-up. The "Savvy Entrepreneurial Firm" feature in this chapter affirms these points. The feature focuses on how Airbnb, which is a marketplace for people to list, discover, and book unique spaces (typically in people's homes or apartments), used blogs as a stepping-stone to generate substantial buzz about its start-up. Another technique is to prepare a **press kit**, which is a folder that contains background information about the company and includes a list of its most recent accomplishments. The

TABLE 11.4 Public Relations Techniques

Technique	Description
Press release	An announcement made by a firm that is circulated to the press. Start-ups typically circulate a press release when something positive happens, such as the launch of a new product or the hiring of a new executive.
Traditional media coverage	Any coverage in print or broadcast media. In most cases, start-ups try to cultivate media coverage, as long as it is positive.
Social media coverage	Start-ups use social media (Facebook, Twitter, Instagram) as a way of communicating and building rapport with customers, and also covet positive mentions in the social media efforts of others. For example, a positive mention by someone who posts on Twitter and has a large number of followers can positively impact a start-up.
Articles in industry press and periodicals	Articles in industry press and periodicals are particularly coveted because they are read by people already interested in the industry in which the start-up is participating.
Blogging	Companies benefit from blogging in three ways: First, by writing their own blog, as a way of building rapport with customers and the general public. Second, by commenting on entries contained in other companies' or people's blogs. Third, by contacting bloggers and asking them to comment on a company's product or service. The general rule of thumb in blogging is that thoughtful and substantive contributions are fine. Outwardly talking about the merits of a company's products is inappropriate, unless it's on the company's own blog.
Monthly newsletter	Many companies stay in touch with their potential target audience by producing and distributing a monthly or quarterly newsletter. Along with containing updates on a firm's products and services, the newsletter should contain more general information of interest to the reader. Companies should avoid sending out newsletters that simply brag about their products. These types of newsletters are often seen as too self-serving.
Civic, social, and community involvement	Start-ups often try to create a positive image of their organization by sponsoring local events or asking their employees to be involved in civic clubs such as the Chamber of Commerce or the Rotary Club.

kit is normally distributed to journalists and made available online. Attending trade shows can also contribute to a firm's visibility. A **trade show** is an event at which the goods or services in a specific industry are exhibited and demonstrated. Members of the media often attend trade shows to get the latest industry news. For example, the largest trade show for consumer electronics is International CES, which is held in Las Vegas every January. Many companies wait until this show to announce their most exciting new products. They do this in part because they have a captive media audience that is eager to find interesting stories to write about. Fitbit's exhibit at a recent International CES show is pictured in Chapter 5.

Social Media   Use of social media consists primarily of blogging and establishing a presence and connecting with customers and others through social networking sites such as Facebook or Twitter. Many of the new ventures featured in this book are active users of social media. A good example is ModCloth, the focus of Case 11.1. ModCloth maintains an active blog, has three separate Twitter accounts (one for general product information, one that is more fashion oriented, and one for recruiting), and maintains an energetic Facebook page.

The idea behind blogs is that they familiarize people with a business and help build an emotional bond between a business and its customers. ModCloth's blog (http://blog.modcloth.com), for example, draws attention to the company's products, but also posts fun, entertaining, and informative articles, features, and photos of interest to ModCloth's target market—18- to 32-year-old women.

SAVVY ENTREPRENEURIAL FIRM

How Airbnb Used Blogs as a Stepping-Stone to Generate Substantial Buzz About Its Service
Web: www.airbnb.com; Twitter: airbnb; Facebook: Airbnb

It's important for entrepreneurial firms to generate press as effectively and inexpensively as possible. One start-up, Airbnb, generated substantial press during its start-up phase at very little cost. Its formula was novel, but it is instructive for any start-up trying to generate buzz and positive PR.

Airbnb is a marketplace for people to list, discover, and book unique spaces (typically in people's homes or apartments) while traveling. It's also useful for people who have space to rent to generate extra income. Founded in late 2007, the firm initially targeted people traveling to conferences and events in the United States. However, Airbnb now offers its services worldwide and has grown to allow people to rent space while traveling for any purpose (instead of business only, which was the initial focus).

Early on, observers were struck by the amount of press that Airbnb generated. In its first two years, the company was featured in *Time* magazine, in the *New York Times*, in the *Washington Post*, on CNN, and in a variety of other places. There wasn't any obvious reason Airbnb (called Air Bed & Breakfast at the time) was getting so much attention. It didn't have celebrity founders, wasn't backed by a venture capital firm, and didn't spend a ton of money. In fact, it was started by three previously unknown entrepreneurs and was bootstrapped until late 2010. So how did they do it? It all started with blogs.

Shortly after the company launched, the firm's founders e-mailed as many design bloggers as they could, explaining the Airbnb concept. The founders were designers, and the site was first used to help people attending design conferences find rooms in local designers' homes for the duration of the conference. Several of the prominent design blogs, including Core77.com, picked up the story and ran articles about the new service. This initial effort prompted a small mention in Mashable, a widely read social media blog. In an interview about how they generated so much press early on, Brian Chesky and Joe Gebbia, two of Airbnb's founders, characterized getting mentions in blogs as a progressive process. If you get mentioned by small blogs, it's easier to get the attention of larger blogs, and a company sort of moves up the ladder. The process wasn't totally efficient. They often had to reach out to several blogs to get a single mention, but overall the strategy worked.

Next, they reached out to newspapers and magazines, which was also a successful effort. Airbnb seemed to resonate with journalists because of the unique aspect of its service. But the blogs played an important role here too. One thing the founders of Airbnb learned is that the first thing a newspaper or magazine writer does, when pitched by a new company, is type the firm's name into Google to see if anyone else has written about them. Fair or unfair, a journalist is much more willing to write about a company if others are writing about it too. That's one of the advantages of being covered by blogs—their stories will show up in Google searches. Even mentions in small blogs, which generally appreciate being reached out to, show up in search engine searches.

Even though Airbnb is much more proven today, its founders still reach out to bloggers. They circle back to the blogs that have already written about them and ask them to write additional stories when there is something exciting to write about.

Questions for Critical Thinking

1. How does an entrepreneur establish a "relationship" with an influential blogger?
2. What's the right way and what's the wrong way to approach a blogger about writing a post about a particular company?
3. How important is generating press and PR for a start-up firm? Is it more important for some types of businesses than others? Explain your answer.
4. Case 11.1 focuses on ModCloth, an online retailer that sells independent designer women's fashion. Make a list of the blogs (minimum of five) that ModCloth's founder could have potentially reached out to when the company was launched.

Source: Airbnb website, www.airbnb.com, accessed September 3, 2014; A. Warner, B. Chesky, and J. Gebbia, "Airbnb," Mixergy, www.mixergy.com, accessed March 28, 2011, posted on January 28, 2010.

The blog also features contests that provide cash prizes, posts photos of customers wearing ModCloth products, and provides behind-the-scenes glimpses of what it's like to work at ModCloth. For example, employees are allowed to bring dogs to work, which are called ModDogs. Periodically, one of the dogs is featured on the blog.

The key to maintaining a successful blog is to keep it fresh and make it informative and fun. It should also engage its readers in the "industry" and

Social media is an increasingly important part of the marketing campaign of many start-up firms. This young entrepreneur is placing videos of customers talking about her products (i.e., reference accounts) on her Facebook page.

Wavebreakmedia/Shutterstock

"lifestyle" that a company promotes as much as a company's products. For example, just after Labor Day 2013, ModCloth posted the following on its blog:

> If the old rule of not wearing white after Labor Day has you rolling your eyes, you're not alone. We too believe that fashion rules were meant to be broken, so we set out to find some post-Labor Day inspiration in the form of street style photos, bloggers, and our ever-stylish Style Gallery community members. If you're on the hunt for the perfect way to mix white into your wardrobe this fall, check out the looks below.[29]

This is the type of feature that ModCloth customers probably enjoy seeing.

Many start-ups also benefit from establishing a presence on social networking sites like Facebook and Twitter. The total number of Facebook accounts is huge, which makes it particularly attractive. Facebook allows anyone in the world that is 13 years old or older to become a registered user. As of September 2012, Facebook had more than one billion active users. The company has also made itself more attractive to businesses since launching a family of social plug-ins in April 2010. **Social plug-ins** are tools that websites can use to provide their users with personalized and social experiences. Facebook's most popular social plug-ins, which a website can install, include the Like button, the Share button, and the Comments box. These social plug-ins allow people to share their experiences off Facebook with their friends on Facebook. The Share button, for example, lets users share pages from a company's website on their Facebook page with one click.[30] As a result, a young woman who just bought a dress from ModCloth's website, because ModCloth has placed the Facebook Share plug-in on its site, can immediately post a picture and description of the dress on her Facebook page and write a comment about the purchase. She might say, "Hey everyone, look at the cool dress I just bought at www.modcloth.com." This is tantamount to free advertising for ModCloth.

Along with taking advantage of social plug-ins, businesses establish a presence on Facebook and Twitter to build a community around their products and services. The benefits include brand building, engaging customers, and getting lead generation and online sales. In regard to branding, a Facebook page or Twitter account can allow a firm to post or tweet material that's consistent with its brand. For example, Beyond Meat, a company that is producing plant-based substitutes for meat products, such as Chicken-Free Strips (which are made from plant-based proteins but taste just like traditional chicken strips), frequently posts material on Twitter that pertains to nutrition, cooking, healthy recipes, plant-based substitutes for meat products, and so on. By doing this, Beyond Meat establishes itself as an expert on healthy eating and healthy lifestyles.

In regard to engagement, many companies use social networks to strengthen their relationships with customers by soliciting feedback, running contests, or posting fun games that pertain to a company's product. For example, ModCloth uses Twitter to do several things. First, the firm posts fun facts, polls, and even recipes that they think their customers will like. Second, they encourage questions from customers, and usually provide a response in a matter of minutes. Third, they post photos of the most popular ModCloth apparel and behind-the-scenes photos of ModCloth employees, offices, and events. What they don't do is overdo promotions. They keep their Twitter account upbeat, fun, and light. In terms of Facebook, ModCloth posts photos and comments about their products to spark conversations with customers. For example in late fall, as winter approaches, they might post a photo of warm-weather ModCloth apparel and accessories and ask, "What cold-weather accessories are the most important to you?" They'll then engage with ModCloth followers, who send in comments just like any Facebook friend would do. ModCloth also makes effective use of Pinterest. Among other things, they post photos of their clothing matched up with accessories and shoes that they sell. It's a great way to show customers how they can buy ModCloth products and mix and match to create multiple outfits and looks.

There is a potpourri of additional social media outlets from which firms can benefit. For example, many businesses post videos on YouTube. YouTube now offers heavy users the ability to create a YouTube channel to archive their videos and to create their own YouTube site. An example is GoPro's YouTube channel at www.youtube.com/gopro. Businesses can also establish a presence on niche social networking sites that are consistent with their mission and product offerings. An example is Care2 (www.care2.com), which is an online community that promotes a healthy and green lifestyle and takes action on social causes.

Other Promotion-Related Activities There are many other activities that help a firm promote and sell its products. Some firms, for example, give away free samples of their products. This technique is used by pharmaceutical companies that give physicians free samples to distribute to their patients as appropriate. A similar technique is to offer free trials, such as a three-month subscription to a magazine or a two-week membership to a fitness club, to try to hook potential customers by exposing them directly to the product or service.

A fairly new technique that has received quite a bit of attention is **viral marketing**, which facilitates and encourages people to pass along a marketing message about a particular product. The most well-known example of viral marketing is Hotmail. When Hotmail first started distributing free e-mail accounts, it put a tagline on every message sent out by Hotmail users that read "Get free e-mail with Hotmail." Within less than a year, the company had several million users. Every e-mail message that passed through the Hotmail system was essentially an advertisement for Hotmail. The success of viral marketing depends on the pass-along rate from person to person. Very few companies have come close to matching Hotmail's success with viral marketing. However, the idea of designing a promotional campaign that encourages a firm's current customers to recommend its product to future customers is well worth considering.

A technique related to both viral marketing and creating buzz is guerrilla marketing. **Guerrilla marketing** is a low-budget approach to marketing that relies on ingenuity, cleverness, and surprise rather than traditional techniques. The point is to create awareness of a firm and its products, often in unconventional and memorable ways. The term was first coined and defined by Jay Conrad Levinson in the 1984 book *Guerrilla Marketing*. Guerrilla marketing is particularly suitable for entrepreneurial firms, which are often on a tight budget but have creativity, enthusiasm, and passion to draw from.

Place (or Distribution)

Place, or distribution, encompasses all the activities that move a firm's product from its place of origin to the consumer. A **distribution channel** is the route a product takes from the place it is made to the customer who is the end user.

The first choice a firm has to make regarding distribution is whether to sell its products directly to consumers or through intermediaries such as wholesalers or distributors. Within most industries, both choices are available, so the decision typically depends on how a firm believes its target market wants to buy its product. For example, it would make sense for a music studio that is targeting the teen market to produce digital recordings and sell the recordings directly over the Web. Most teens have access to a computer or smartphone and know how to download music. In contrast, it wouldn't make nearly as much sense for a recording company targeting retirees to use the same distribution channel to sell its music offerings. A much smaller percentage of the retiree market knows how to download music from the Web. In this instance, it would make more sense to produce CDs and partner with wholesalers or distributors to place them in retail outlets where retirees shop.

Figure 11.4 shows the difference between selling direct and selling through an intermediary. Let's look at the strengths and weaknesses of each approach.

Selling Direct   Many firms sell directly to customers. Being able to control the process of moving their products from their place of origin to the end user instead of relying on third parties is a major advantage of direct selling. Examples of companies that sell direct are Abercrombie & Fitch, which sells its clothing through company-owned stores, and Fitbit, which sells its exercise and sleep monitoring device through its website.

The disadvantage of selling direct is that a firm has more of its capital tied up in fixed assets because it must own or rent retail outlets, must maintain a sales force, and/or must support an e-commerce website. It must also find its own buyers rather than have distributors that are constantly looking for new outlets for the firm's products.

The advent of the Internet has changed how many companies sell their products. Many firms that once sold their products exclusively through retail stores are now also selling directly online. The process of eliminating layers of middlemen, such as distributors and wholesalers, to sell directly to customers is called **disintermediation**.

FIGURE 11.4
Selling Direct versus Selling Through Intermediaries

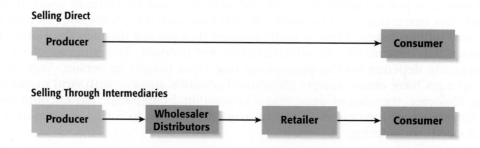

Selling Through Intermediaries Firms selling through intermediaries typically pass off their products to wholesalers or distributors that place them in retail outlets to be sold. An advantage of this approach is that the firm does not need to own as much of the distribution channel. For example, if a company makes car speakers and the speakers are sold through retail outlets such as Best Buy and Walmart, the company avoids the cost of building and maintaining retail outlets. It can also rely on its wholesalers to manage its relationship with Best Buy and Walmart and to find other retail outlets in which to sell its products. The trick to utilizing this approach is to find wholesalers and distributors that will represent a firm's products. A start-up must often pitch wholesalers and distributors much like it pitches an investor for money in order to win their support and cooperation.

The disadvantage of selling through intermediaries is that a firm loses a certain amount of control of its product. Even if a wholesaler or distributor places a firm's products with a top-notch retailer like Best Buy or Walmart, there is no guarantee that Best Buy's or Walmart's employees will talk up the firm's products as much as they would if they were employees in the firm's own stores. Selling via distributors and wholesalers can also be expensive, so it is best to carefully weigh all options. For example, a firm that sells an item for $100 on its website and makes $50 (after expenses) may only make $10 if the exact same item is placed by a distributor into a retail store. The $40 difference represents the profits taken by the distributor and the retailer.

Some firms enter into exclusive distribution arrangements with channel partners. **Exclusive distribution arrangements** give a retailer or other intermediary the exclusive rights to sell a company's products. The advantage to giving out an exclusive distribution agreement is to motivate a retailer or other intermediary to make a concerted effort to sell a firm's products without having to worry about direct competitors. For example, if Nokia granted AT&T the exclusive rights to sell a new type of cell phone, AT&T would be more motivated to advertise and push the phone than if many or all cell phone companies had access to the same phone.

One choice that entrepreneurs are confronted with when selling through intermediaries is how many channels to sell through. The more channels a firm sells through, the faster it can grow. But there are problems associated with selling through multiple channels, particularly early in the life of a firm. A firm can lose control of how its products are being sold. For example, the more retailers through which Ralph Lauren sells its clothing, the more likely it is that one or more retailers will not display the clothes in the manner the company wants.

Sales Process and Related Issues

A firm's **sales process** depicts the steps it goes through to identify prospects and close sales. It doesn't matter whether a firm is selling directly to customers or through intermediaries; it still has a process through which it makes sales. If it's selling through an intermediary, like a distributor, it has to convince the distributor to carry its products and has to offer the distributor varying levels of support.

Some companies simply wing it when it comes to sales, which isn't recommended. It's much better to have a well-thought-out approach to prospecting customers and closing sales. A formal sales process involves a number of identifiable steps. Although the process varies by firm (and industry), it generally includes seven steps, as shown in Figure 11.5. Following a formal or structured process to generate and close sales benefits a firm in two ways. First, it enables a firm to fine-tune its approach to sales and build uniformity into the process. Second, it helps a firm qualify leads, so the firm can spend its time and money

LEARNING OBJECTIVE

4. Describe the seven-step sales process an entrepreneurial firm uses to identify prospects and close sales.

FIGURE 11.5
Sales Process

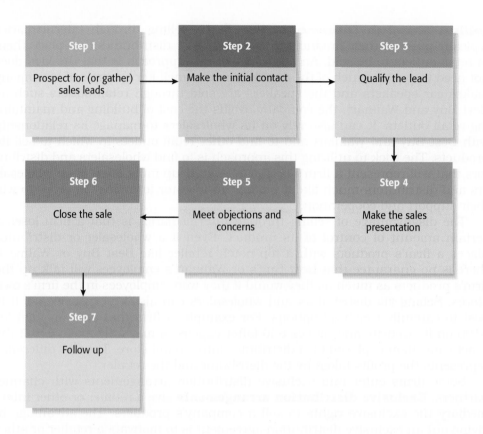

pursuing the most likely buyers of its products or services. The most frustrating thing a salesperson encounters is spending time and effort working with a potential buyer, only to find that the buyer doesn't have the money or the authority to make a purchase. A well-thought-out sales process has triggers in it that help a salesperson discern whether spending time with a particular prospect is a good use of his or her time.

Some firms implement their sales strategy by listing the seven steps in the process, and then writing procedures for how each step will be implemented. In fact, some new ventures include this material in their business plan, to provide the reader confidence that they've thought through how they'll close sales. An example of a sales process, with accompanying action steps, for a fictitious business named Prime Adult Fitness is shown in Table 11.5. The example comes from the book *Preparing Effective Business Plans, Second Edition,* by Bruce R. Barringer (co-author of this book). Prime Adult Fitness is a fitness center for people 50 years old or older. Its mission is to make exercise and fitness a vibrant and satisfying part of the lives of people who are 50 years old and older. The company will start with a single fitness center located in Oviedo, Florida, a suburb of Orlando. The steps shown in Table 11.5 outline the process the company will use to recruit members and is the method that the in-house staff will follow when people walk into the center and inquire about membership. At times the process will take weeks to unfold, for example if Prime Adult Fitness employees have multiple contacts with a prospect, and at times the process will take only a few minutes, such as when an employee provides a prospect a tour of the facility and answers specific questions. Prime Adult's sales process is offered only as an example. Individual firms can use this example as a template for developing a sales process that fits their individual products and circumstances.

TABLE 11.5 Sales Process for Prime Adult Fitness

Stage in Process	Ways Prime Adult Fitness Will Support Each Phase of the Process
1. Prospecting (or sales lead)	▪ Referrals from current members. ▪ Direct mail (targeting households that meet Prime Adult Fitness's demographic profile). ▪ Partnership with Central Florida Health Food. ▪ Partnership with Oviedo Doctor's and Surgeon's Medical Practice. ▪ Downloads from company website. ▪ Responses from the company's radio and print advertisements.
2. Make the initial contact	▪ All employees will be provided training in building rapport with prospects. ▪ Prospects are provided an information packet about Prime Adult Fitness. ▪ Radio and print ads will direct prospects to Prime Adult Fitness's website, which contains a short video and other promotional material.
3. Qualifying the lead	▪ All employees will be trained to assess whether a prospect represents a qualified lead. Prospects that are qualified as good leads will be offered a tour of Prime Adult Fitness's facilities. ▪ If a qualified lead does not join initially, he or she will be contacted by phone as a follow-up three days after the visit.
4. Make the sales presentation	▪ Qualified leads will be provided a facility tour. ▪ Qualified leads will be shown a short film (nine minutes) featuring Prime Adult Fitness's facility and programs and the benefits of fitness for older people. ▪ A packet of testimonials will be developed over time and provided to prospects as part of the sales presentation process.
5. Meeting objections and concerns	▪ Employees will be trained on how to meet the most common and obvious objections and concerns. ▪ In regard to price objections, a brochure has been prepared that compares (1) Prime Adult Fitness's initial (one-time) enrollment fee and monthly membership fee to other fitness centers and (2) the cost of joining and belonging to a fitness center as opposed to other forms of recreation and entertainment (e.g., boating, golfing). ▪ A similar brochure has been prepared to compare Prime Adult Fitness's amenities to the amenities of other fitness centers.
6. Closing the sale	▪ All employees will be trained to ask qualified prospects to join.
7. Follow-up	▪ Each new member will be contacted by phone 30 days after joining as a courtesy to see how things are going. After that, each new member will be contacted by phone once a year. Each phone call will also be used to ask for names of referrals. ▪ Prime Adult Fitness will produce a monthly newsletter that will be mailed to each member. ▪ Prime Adult Fitness's staff and employees will be trained to engage members and to thank them for their membership and solicit suggestions for improvement on a continual basis.

Source: B. R. Barringer, *Preparing Effective Business Plans: An Entrepreneurial Approach* 2e, © 2015. Reprinted by permission of Pearson Education, Inc., Upper Saddle River, NJ (Upper Saddle River, NJ: Pearson Prentice-Hall, 2014).

Mapping the sales process in the manner shown in Table 11.5 provides a standard method for a firm's employees to use, and provides a starting point for careful analysis and continuous improvement. Often, when companies lose an important sale and reflect on what went wrong, they'll find that an important step in the sales process was missed or mishandled. This is where having a well-thought-out sales process, with accompanying action steps and appropriate employee training, can dramatically improve a company's sales performance.

Chapter Summary

LO1. The first step in selecting a target market is to study the industry in which the firm intends to compete and determine the different potential target markets within that industry. This process is called market segmentation. Markets can be segmented in a number of ways, including product type, price point, distribution channels used, and customers served.

After markets are segmented, the firm selects its target market, or the group it intends to serve. The next step is to establish a unique position in that market—one that differentiates the entrepreneurial firm from its competitors. The term *position* was introduced in Chapter 5, where it was emphasized that a firm's position in the marketplace determines how it is situated relative to its competitors. From a marketing perspective, this translates into the image of the way a firm wants to be perceived by its customers. Importantly, position answers the question, "Why should someone in our target market buy our good or service instead of our competitor's?"

Also important to these three steps is the development of a product attribute map, which illustrates a firm's position in its industry relative to its major rivals. It is used as a visual illustration of a firm's positioning strategy and helps a firm develop its marketing plan.

LO2. A company's brand is the set of attributes people associate with it. When positive and effective, a brand can create loyal customers for the entrepreneurial firm. On a philosophical level, a firm builds a brand by having it create meaning in customers' lives. It must create value. On a more practical level, brands are built through advertising, public relations, sponsorships, supporting social causes, and good performance. Creating a strong and identifiable personality for the firm is a key to effectively developing a strong brand.

LO3. A firm's marketing mix is the set of controllable, tactical marketing tools that it uses to produce the response it wants in its target market. Most marketers organize their marketing mix around the 4Ps: product, price, promotion, and place (or distribution). In the context of the marketing mix, a product is a good or service the firm offers in the market it has chosen to serve. Technically, a product is something the firm sells that takes on a physical form, while a service is an activity or a benefit the firm provides that does not take on a physical form. The most important attribute of the product a firm sells is its ability to create value for customers. Price is the amount of money customers are willing to pay to purchase a product. Typically, entrepreneurs use one of two methods to set the price of their product. With cost-based pricing, the list price for a product is determined by adding a markup percentage to the product's cost. When using value-based pricing, the firm determines the price of its product by estimating what consumers are willing to pay for a product and then backing off a bit to provide a cushion. Promotion is concerned with the actions the firm takes to communicate the value its product creates to customers. Several actions are taken to do this. Advertising, for example, is an action taken to make people aware of a good or service the firm hopes to persuade customers to buy. Public relations refers to efforts to establish and maintain a company's image with the public. The major difference between the two is that advertising is paid for and public relations isn't—at least directly. The cost of public relations to a firm is the effort it makes to network with journalists and other people to try to interest them in saying and/or writing good things about the company. Social media consists primarily of blogging and establishing a presence and connecting with people through social networking sites like Facebook and Twitter. Businesses blog and engage in social media to build a community around their products and services. The benefits include brand building, engaging customers, and getting lead generation and online sales.

The first choice a firm makes regarding place or distribution is whether to sell its products directly to consumers or through intermediaries (e.g., wholesalers and retailers). An advantage of selling direct is that it allows a firm to maintain control of its products rather than relying on third parties. The disadvantage is that it ties up more capital in fixed assets because the firm must own (or rent) retail outlets or must field a sales force to sell its products. An advantage of selling through intermediaries is that a firm doesn't have to own much of its distribution channel (e.g., trucks and retail outlets). A disadvantage of this approach is that a firm loses some control of its product, in that there is no guarantee that the retailers it sells through will talk up and push its products as much as

the manufacturer would if it had its own stores.

LO4. A firm's sales process depicts the steps it goes through to identify leads and close sales. The seven-step sales process includes the following steps: Step 1: Prospect for (or gather) sales leads; Step 2: Make the initial contact; Step 3: Qualify the lead; Step 4: Make the sales presentation; Step 5: Meet objections and concerns; Step 6: Close the sale; and Step 7: Follow up.

Key Terms

advertising, **399**
brand, **392**
brand equity, **394**
brand management, **393**
buzz, **394**
cost-based pricing, **398**
disintermediation, **408**
distribution channel, **408**
exclusive distribution arrangements, **409**

guerilla marketing, **408**
market segmentation, **389**
marketing mix, **395**
niche market, **390**
place, **408**
press kit, **403**
price, **398**
price-quality attribution, **399**
product, **395**
product attribute map, **391**

promotion, **399**
public relations, **403**
reference account, **397**
sales process, **409**
service, **395**
social plug-ins, **406**
tagline, **392**
trade show, **404**
value-based pricing, **398**
viral marketing, **407**

Review Questions

11-1. What is a target market? What are the factors that need to be considered when selecting a market?
11-2. Explain the importance of market segmentation. What are several ways markets can be segmented?
11-3. How should a firm go about constructing a product attribute map?
11-4. What is a niche market?
11-5. What is meant by a firm's positioning strategy?
11-6. What is the use of a tagline?
11-7. What is a brand? Provide an example of a brand that you buy frequently and describe the mental image that pops into your mind when you hear or see the brand's name.
11-8. What is the purpose of brand management?

11-9. What is meant by creating "buzz" for a company? Provide an example of a firm that has created effective buzz for its product or service.
11-10. What is meant by the term *brand equity*?
11-11. What are the four elements of a firm's "marketing mix"?
11-12. Describe the difference between a core product and an actual product.
11-13. How can a firm obtain a unique market position?
11-14. Contrast cost-based pricing and value-based pricing.
11-15. What is meant by the phrase "price-quality attribution"? How does an understanding of this phrase help an entrepreneur know how to price a product?
11-16. What are the different ways people think about the meaning of a brand?

11-17. Contrast the roles of advertising and public relations in promoting a firm and its products.

11-18. What is the purpose of writing a blog and establishing a presence on Facebook and Twitter?

11-19. Why do firms focus on promotional activities?

11-20. What is the purpose of having an organized sales process?

Application Questions

11-21. Reread the Opening Profile. After doing this, make a list of all the things that you think that Megan Cox and Miguel Salinas have done well to build an effective marketing program for Wink Natural Cosmetics.

11-22. Brandon Smith has just opened a juice-bar next to the local recreational park. He is planning to promote his product to boost sales. He has noticed that most startups do not advertise their products broadly. What could be the reasons behind small-scale promotional activities of new businesses?

11-23. Imagine you're opening a tutoring service near the college or university you attend. What would be the characteristics of a comprehensive social media strategy that you could employ to build your brand, engage customers, and generate leads and sales revenue?

11-24. Spend some time looking at Red Bull's website (www.redbull.com). Comment on each element of Red Bull's marketing mix (product, price, promotion, and place in terms of distribution and sales). If you need additional information, conduct Internet or library research to obtain it. Using a scale of 1 to 10 (10 is high), what rating would you use to assess the strength of Red Bull's overall marketing plan? What evidence would you provide to support your rating?

11-25. Shannon has developed a new type of space heater that is quieter and safer than previous generations of space heaters and is particularly geared to people who live in small spaces, such as apartments or dorm rooms. Shannon doesn't know how to price this product. Describe to Shannon the two most common methods of pricing as explained in this chapter. Which of these pricing methods would you suggest Shannon use, and why?

11-26. Kelly Andrews has developed a new line of jewelry that has created some positive buzz among friends and some stores in her local community. When asked by a reporter, "Where do you plan to sell your jewelry?" Kelly said, "Hopefully everywhere—jewelry stores, Target, Walmart, gift shops, online, through catalogs, and a dozen other places." How would you evaluate Kelly's approach to selling her products?

11-27. Marie Francis needs to prepare a business plan for her angel investor. She is in the middle of preparing for her new establishment, a yoga and fitness center for women. In her business plan, she needs to include a precise sales process to convince her investor that she has thought everything through. Using Table 11.5 as a base, assist Marie in preparing the seven-step sales process her entrepreneurial firm needs to use to identify prospects and close sales.

11-28. Your friend, Jason Bates has just developed a new application for smartphones and he needs to market the apps. Suggest a viral marketing technique for his new product.

11-29. In a group of three, visit the nearest food outlet in your vicinity. Interview the entrepreneur or manager of the chosen outlet on how they decided the branding. Is the brand important to the firm's marketing efforts?

YOU BE THE VC 11.1 COMPANY: ZinePak

• Web: www.zinepak.com • Facebook: The ZinePak • Twitter: @ZinePak

Business Idea: Create a product for music fans that packages a CD with a fan magazine and other memorabilia tied to the musician, such as posters, guitar picks, and even branded greeting cards and perfume samples.

Pitch: Passionate music fans want more than music. They want to connect with their favorite musicians in deeper ways. Attending a concert achieves that; however, concerts are not only expensive but also few and far between. Many people who are Katy Perry fans, for instance, want to know more about her but may never attend a Katy Perry concert. ZinePak was created for this reason. The company creates custom, interactive content for super fans of music, movies, sports, events, and brands. The content is delivered through ZinePaks, which are physical, limited-edition packets that, when opened, emulate the super-satisfying feeling of opening a new album or a favorite magazine. Each ZinePak pairs a small-format magazine with exclusive merchandise such as posters, magnets, patches, stickers, guitar picks, and other memorabilia into a package. The magazine contains exclusive photos, interviews, games, and behind-the-scenes stories about the subject of the ZinePak. The merchandise is designed to be collectable, special, and fun.

ZinePak was created by Brittany Hodak, who has a background in music, and Kim Kaupe, who has a background in publishing. ZinePak's first distributor was Walmart, which was looking for ways to combat sinking in-store CD sales due to piracy and online downloads. The idea is to enhance audience engagement. Katy Perry fans will presumably be more inclined to buy a Katy Perry CD, rather than purchase her music online or steal it, if the CD is accompanied by the material that's included in a ZinePak. In this respect, ZinePak combats the decline of physical CD sales. ZinePaks are also prepared for athletes, movies, brands, and special events. For example, ZinePak's second project was to put together a ZinePak for the 2012 Academy of Country Music Awards. That particular ZinePak involved putting together a CD featuring all the major acts expected to get awards and an assortment of memorabilia for the performers featured at the show.

Since ZinePak launched in 2011, it has sold more than two million ZinePaks. Its clients have included KIDZ BOP, Justin Bieber, Taylor Swift, KISS, Dove, Dr. Pepper, Selena Gomez, and Toby Keith. In fall 2014, Disney released a ZinePak of the popular Disney film *Frozen*. The ZinePak included a 10-track CD with music from the movie and a 64-page magazine with games, puzzles, comics, and interviews, plus an assortment of memorabilia including collectible stickers, a poster, and a holiday ornament. According to Walmart, the limited-edition ZinePak was available only through Walmart while supplies lasted.

11-30. Based on the material covered in this chapter, what questions would you ask the firm's founders before making your funding decision? What answers would satisfy you?
11-31. If you had to make your decision based only on the information provided in the pitch and on the company's website, would you fund this company? Why or why not?

YOU BE THE VC 11.2 COMPANY: COOLEST

• Web: www.coolestkickstarter.com • Facebook: The CoolestCooler • Twitter: @Coolest_Cooler

Business Idea: Create the world's first rolling cooler with a built-in blender, Bluetooth speakers, tie-down straps (to carry items on top of the cooler), LED lights, oversized tires (great for sandy beaches), built-in USB charger, built-in bottle opener, and built-in storage.

Pitch: The basic design for coolers hasn't changed in 50 years. Most coolers are boring, break easily, are a hassle to move around, and are only good for one thing—keeping food and drinks cool. The COOLEST changed all that. Created by Portland-based product designer Ryan Grepper, the COOLEST is a complete redesign of what a cooler can be. First, it has an 18-volt rechargeable blender. Most coolers already have ice and beverages, so why not blend them up for a tasty smoothie or another drink? Next, it comes with a removable Bluetooth speaker that connects to any smartphone to wirelessly stream music from up to 30 feet away (eight hours on one charge). Also included is a waterproof USB charger, perfect for recharging an iPhone or similar device. At nightfall, the COOLEST's LED lights, embedded in the lid, make looking for a drink easy. Particularly nice are three additional features. It has tie-down straps to help carry gear on top of the cooler, such as lawn chairs or yard toys. It has built-in storage for picnicking or tailgating essentials, like plastic plates, a cutting board, and a rustproof ceramic knife. Finally, the tires are a dream. Regular cooler tires leave much to be desired and sink into the sand. The COOLEST's tires are oversized and perfect for sandy beaches. All in all, the COOLEST is so much fun it encourages people to get outdoors. It is a portable party that is likely to appeal to many groups. It's aesthetically pleasing to boot.

To manufacture the COOLEST, Grepper has lined up a world-class contract manufacturer that has years of experience with top-shelf products. The COOLEST has a 60-quart insulating capacity and is available in several colors. It also has split slides, so ice can be put into one side and drinks and sandwiches into the other. No more soggy sandwiches with the COOLEST.

The COOLEST has generated considerable buzz via its Kickstarter campaign. The campaign ran in the summer of 2014 (savvy timing for an "outdoors" product), and raised $13,285,226 from 62,642 backers, making it the most successful Kickstarter campaign (in terms of money raised) of all time. The Pebble e-watch held the previous record with $10.23 million pledged.

11-32. Based on the material covered in this chapter, what questions would you ask the firm's founders before making your funding decision? What answers would satisfy you?

11-33. If you had to make your decision on just the information provided in the pitch and on the company's website, would you fund this company? Why or why not?

CASE 11.1

ModCloth: The 4Ps of a Successful Online Clothing Retailer

• *Web: www.modcloth.com* • *Facebook: ModCloth* • *Twitter: @ModCloth*

Bruce R. Barringer, *Oklahoma State University*

R. Duane Ireland, *Texas A&M University*

Introduction

ModCloth founders Susan Koger and Eric Koger met in high school. Susan enjoyed shopping for vintage clothing, and over time she accumulated so many outfits that she decided to sell some. Eric, who was her boyfriend at the time, offered to build a website she could use to sell the clothes online. Susan saw this as a way to help pay for college. This initial experience was the foundation for ModCloth's birth.

Susan and Eric both attended Carnegie Mellon in Pittsburgh. ModCloth was a hobby business the first four years. Susan continued to accumulate women's vintage clothing, sell the items on her website, and ship orders from her dorm room. The "customer care" number on the website and boxes was her cell phone number. After graduating in 2006, Susan decided to focus on ModCloth full time. Eric remained at Carnegie Mellon an extra year to earn an MBA. To make ModCloth a full-time pursuit, Susan broadened her thinking. Up until this point, the only clothes that ModCloth sold were vintage clothing that Susan picked out. She started attending trade shows to make contact with independent designers who designed and made vintage-inspired clothing, which is a much larger market than vintage clothing. She knew that to appreciably grow ModCloth, she'd have to move beyond the small vintage clothing niche and broaden her product line.

To make sure she was on the right track, Susan surveyed 100 of her customers to ask if they'd buy vintage-inspired clothing from ModCloth, along with the vintage clothing the company carried. A total of 95 out of 100 customers surveyed said they would. Armed with this information, Susan approached two of her uncles and raised $20,000 in seed funding to buy inventory. She could now expand ModCloth's product offerings to include both vintage clothing and vintage-inspired clothing.

Fast-forward to the present. In the eight years following Susan's ability to raise equity funding from her uncles, ModCloth has grown to a 500-person company. In 2012, it had $100 million in revenue and experienced 40 percent year-over-year growth. It has raised six rounds of funding totaling $63.7 million. Although it focuses exclusively on vintage and vintage-inspired clothing, its product offerings are deep. It currently offers over 7,500 designs from 1,200 designers.

A large part of ModCloth's success is attributed to its marketing program. Although it's strictly an online retailer, the 4Ps—product, price, promotion, and place (distribution)—have played an integral role in its success. The following is a discussion of ModCloth's 4Ps. The discussion highlights elements of the 4Ps that have contributed to ModCloth's success and illustrates future challenges for the firm.

Product

ModCloth offers a full range of vintage and vintage-inspired apparel products for women, including dresses, tops, bottoms, outerwear, swimwear, and intimates. It also sells shoes and accessories. It sources its products from both small designers that create vintage clothing and larger companies, such as BB Dakota, that make vintage-inspired clothing. As a result, its site is populated by a vast assortment of indie designs and one-of-a-kind items as well as larger lots of vintage-inspired clothing. Its target market is 18- to 32-year-old women. Its clothing has been featured in fashion magazines such as *Cosmopolitan, Glamour, InStyle,* and *Seventeen*. A quick perusal of ModCloth's website is the best way to see the fun and unique nature of its products. Each product comes with a descriptive yet somewhat quirky name, along with a colorful description, which adds to the ModCloth shopping experience. A sample of the names of dresses recently for sale on ModCloth's website is shown next. When you look at the dresses and their names, you can see the connection. This is part of ModCloth's efforts to make its shopping experience interesting, engaging, novel, and fun.

Sample of the Names of Dresses for Sale on ModCloth's Website

Address the Room Dress	Flocks of Love Dress
Chocolate Truffles Dress	Elegance & Ease Dress
Windy City Dress in Teal	Morning Moments Dress
Give It Your All Dress	Saved By the Belle Dress

Along with its unique products, ModCloth has a twist to its approach that encourages customer participation in regard to the products that are offered for sale. Its "Be the Buyer" program allows customers to be virtual members of its buying team and invites them to vote on potential clothing designs. ModCloth showcases prospective clothing designs on its site, under the "Be the Buyer" tab, and asks customers to either "Pick It" or "Skip It," which indicates whether they think ModCloth should carry that item. If a design gets enough votes, the style will be carried by ModCloth, and those that voted for the item will be notified by e-mail. This approach, which is referred to as crowdsourcing,

helps ModCloth build an emotional connection with its customers. It also helps it stay fresh and feature items that customers want and will buy. Interestingly, products chosen through the "Be the Buyer" program sell twice as much as similar products. The lifetime spend of "Be the Buyer" customers is three times that of other ModCloth patrons.

Price

It's not exactly known how ModCloth arrives at the price for its products. Products are priced competitively with brick-and-mortar retailers such as Macy's and Dillard's. As we discuss next, the company offers frequent discounts and promotions. The discounts and promotions are typically not visible on ModCloth's website. Instead, they're offered through the company's blog and social media initiatives.

Promotions

ModCloth does not emphasize print and media advertising. Instead, its promotional efforts are geared toward engaging current and prospective customers through its blog, social media, and similar marketing techniques.

ModCloth maintains an active blog, which contains new posts every day. To keep readers coming back, the blog features contests that provide cash prizes and/or features customers wearing ModCloth products. By logging onto the blog (http://blog.modcloth.com) you can get a sense of the types of contests that are run. The blog also provides product updates, along with a behind-the-scenes glimpse of what it's like to work at ModCloth. For example, as mentioned earlier in this chapter, employees are allowed to bring their dogs (affectionately called ModDogs) to work. Periodically, one of the dogs is prominently featured on the blog.

The company is also active on social networks. It has three Twitter accounts. The name, purpose, and number of followers for each account are shown next.

ModCloth Twitter Accounts

Name of Account	Number of Followers	Purpose
@ModCloth	131,000	Provides product information, fun facts, discount coupons, contest updates, and fashion tips. The company also tweets about its employees' favorite books, recipes, movies, and other everyday items.
@ModClothPRBuzz	4,654	More fashion oriented, the site comments frequently on ModCloth products and general fashion trends. It also provides a platform for ModCloth fashion specialists to interact directly with customers, to share ideas and answer questions.
@ModCloth Careers	3,663	For people interested in pursuing a career with ModCloth.

Items posted on ModCloth's blog are frequently referred to on its Twitter accounts. For example, in September 2014, ModCloth announced a Photo Pop-Up in which any customer could stop by a temporary ModCloth location in New York City to have

themselves photographed in ModCloth apparel. ModCloth promised to feature select photos from the photo shoot on its website and across its social media platforms. Plus, each month, one person would receive a full spotlight on its website. The company also runs

(continued)

contests that are promoted across its social media sites. For example, in the summer of 2014, ModCloth ran a contest asking customers to upload a photo of themselves in a summer outfit. Along with the photo, the entrant was asked to submit a 100-word explanation of why the outfit was perfect for summer adventures. At the end of the submission period, ModCloth chose a winner and a runner-up. The winner received a $200 ModCloth gift card and prize pack. The runner-up received a $75 gift card. Of course, both were also recognized on ModCloth's website.

ModCloth is also active on Facebook and has over 1.1 million Facebook likes. Several times a day, ModCloth and its friends post fashion information, fun facts, and a variety of related information on its Facebook wall. Hundreds of pictures of customers wearing ModCloth clothing are also posted. The ModDogs, referred to previously, have their own Facebook page. Simply go to ModDogs (4,564 likes) on Facebook and you'll see what they're up to at ModCloth's headquarters.

ModCloth has other techniques for engaging customers. For example, the company employs fashion experts, called ModStylists, that customers can engage via e-mail, chat, or phone. The ModStylists give advice, answer questions, and interact with customers regarding fashion-related issues. ModCloth also has a YouTube channel (http://www.youtube.com/modcloth) and regularly posts new content.

Place (or Distribution)

ModCloth does not utilize drop shipping or outsource any of its distribution. Instead, products that are made for ModCloth are shipped to the firm's distribution center in Pittsburgh, Pennsylvania. Its Internet orders are fulfilled from this center. In 2013, the company shipped 1,639,275 orders from its distribution center. Its single-day record is 16,268 orders.

ModCloth employs buyers who scour the world for the most interesting and cost-competitive vintage-inspired clothing. Once an article of clothing is selected, it's photographed, and a description of the article is written by ModCloth's creative staff. The creative staff also maintains the company's blog and social network initiatives. ModCloth's IT infrastructure, which enables it to fulfill orders expediently, was built entirely in-house and is maintained by ModCloth IT specialists. It's built on a Ruby on Rails platform. Ruby on Rails platforms tend to attract the most progressive IT specialists.

ModCloth's recent rounds of funding are being used to scale the firm's operations. It has plans to build a new supply chain operation in Los Angeles. It also

recently moved its headquarters from Pittsburgh to San Francisco. Approximately 70 percent of the clothing that ModCloth sells is sourced from companies in California, so the move to San Francisco was motivated to place ModCloth's headquarters closer to its suppliers.

Challenges Ahead

ModCloth has several challenges. The first is to maintain its momentum. It's not known how large the market is for vintage and vintage-inspired women's clothing. So, while the firm has succeeded in its niche, at some point ModCloth may have to move beyond its niche to maintain growth. Maintaining the uniqueness of its social media initiatives is a second challenge. The risk here is that while ModCloth is now seen as cutting-edge in regard to social media, its competitors may catch up, and its social media efforts may no longer be seen as "special," as is currently the case. A third challenge is to satisfy its investors. As mentioned earlier, ModCloth has raised $63.7 million in investment capital. Its investors will want to see ModCloth grow quickly and run up its valuation to justify the investment.

On the positive front, observers give ModCloth high marks for its distinct positioning and for how it engages its customers. The emotional connection it has created between itself and its customers will make it difficult for copycats to make substantial inroads in its vintage and vintage-inspired clothing niche.

Discussion Questions

11-34. In a short paragraph, describe ModCloth's brand. What are the strengths and weaknesses of this firm's brand?

11-35. What is the difference between ModCloth's core product and its actual product? Describe its actual product and your assessment of whether the actual product provides an attractive mix of characteristics.

11-36. In what ways, if any, do you think ModCloth will look different five years from now?

11-37. Follow ModCloth's primary Twitter account (@ ModCloth) for five days. Write a short summary of how ModCloth uses Twitter to engage its customers and promote its products. On a scale of 1 to 10 (10 is high), how effectively does ModCloth use Twitter as a promotional tool?

Sources: ModCloth website, www.modcloth.com, accessed September 6, 2014; CrunchBase, ModCloth, www.crunchbase.com, accessed September 6, 2014; E. Kroger, "The $100 Million Equation: The Art and Science of E-Commerce," slideshare, available at http://www.slideshare.net/500startups/eric-koger-modcloth-32579988, posted on March 21, 2014, accessed on September 6, 2014.

CASE 11.2

Proactiv: How Three Critical Marketing Decisions Shaped a New Venture's Future

• Web: www.proactiv.com • Twitter: @proactiv • Facebook: Proactiv

Bruce R. Barringer, *Oklahoma State University*

R. Duane Ireland, *Texas A&M University*

Introduction

In 1995, two dermatologists, Dr. Katie Rodan and Dr. Kathy Fields, developed what they believed was a medical breakthrough in fighting acne. Their mission: to help millions of people rid themselves of acne and acne-related problems. They named their product Proactiv Solutions. This name was chosen because the product could heal existing blemishes and *proactively* help prevent new ones from forming.

Today, Proactiv is the number-one-selling acne product in the United States. It's a three-part acne treatment kit that includes a cleanser, toner, and treatment. It's not sold in stores. Instead, it is sold via infomercials, the company's website, a subscription service called the "Proactiv Solution Clear Skin Club," and in select upscale boutiques and kiosks. The way Proactiv reached the point it currently occupies is an interesting story. Early in its life, Proactiv was shaped by three critical marketing decisions, from which the company has not wavered, even to this day. This case recounts these decisions and discusses how the decisions shaped this entrepreneurial venture's future.

How It Started

Katie Rodan and Kathy Fields met while they were working summer jobs at a cardiovascular research lab in Los Angeles. The lab was developing a drug to treat post–heart attack patients. Both Rodan and Fields enjoyed the exciting pace of the work as well as the camaraderie they shared with the lab's researchers and doctors. After earning their college degrees, they both went to medical school and became dermatologists. They stayed in touch and often shared with one another how surprised they were at the number of acne patients they were seeing. At the time, the medical research said that only 3 percent of the adult population had acne, but Rodan and Fields became convinced that the number was higher. They were each seeing acne patients on a daily basis, and they weren't just seeing teenagers. They were seeing women in their 20s, 30s, 40s, and even in their 50s who were suffering from acne and acne-related problems.

Rodan and Fields decided to form a partnership to investigate the acne issue further. They started by talking to their patients, asking them a wide range of acne-related questions. What they found was that the vast majority of their patients hated the acne products on the market. The most common complaints were that the products were very drying and they were very irritating. Worst of all, patients told Rodan and Fields, the available products did not work. At this point, the two physicians started thinking there might be an opportunity for them to create a better product.

Rodan and Fields spent the next couple of years thoroughly investigating the acne products on the market. After testing many of the products on their patients, they made what they believed was a shocking discovery. All of the products on the market were designed to spot-treat a pimple—none were designed to stop the pimple from forming in the first place. This just didn't make sense to the two dermatologists—from both a practical and a medical standpoint. By the time you see a pimple, whatever treatment you administer, it's too little too late. In their judgment, not taking steps to prevent acne from developing was akin to not brushing your teeth and instead just going to the dentist to fill cavities. Why not brush your teeth and floss and try to prevent the cavities from developing in the first place?

This revelation motivated Rodan and Fields to start working on a product of their own—one that would be more proactive in preventing acne and acne-related problems. They hired a chemist, and the three worked together for another couple of years. Finally, they had a product they were happy with and that seemed to work and to satisfy their patients.

Important Revelations

To get ideas about how to market and develop their product, which didn't have a name yet, Rodan hosted dinner parties at her house and conducted brainstorming sessions with the guests. The guests included business executives, market researchers, marketing consultants, an FDA regulatory attorney, the chief financial officer of a major company, and others. One of the things the participants in these sessions stressed to Rodan and Fields was the importance of marketing research. In particular, the group urged Rodan and Fields to hire an unbiased third party to validate their findings. Rodan and Fields took this advice to heart and hired an outside consultant. In focus groups that the consultant led, Rodan and Fields learned two important things about older women. First, evidence suggests that many

(continued)

women who *do* have acne as a medical condition refuse to believe that such is the case. Second, people don't like to talk about their acne with others. Rodan and Fields also learned that their product still needed work. There were several aspects of the product that needed improvement, a need that Rodan and Fields fully intended to take care of.

Three Critical Marketing Decisions That Shaped the Future of the Firm

Critical Marketing Decision 1: We're a Skin Care Company

After Rodan and Fields reformulated the product again, they hired another marketing consultant to advise them as to how they should proceed to successfully market their product. The first piece of advice they got from the consultant was to think of their product as a skin care product rather than an acne product. At the time, the acne market in the United States was about $250 million a year, a low number by consumer products standards. In contrast, the skin care market was several billion dollars a year, making it much more attractive. The consultant told Rodan and Fields to think of their product as a skin care system that just happens to treat acne, rather than an acne medication alone. This recommendation obviously caused Rodan and Fields to have a much broader vision for the scope of the market for their product.

Critical Marketing Decision 2: Our Name Is Proactiv

After Rodan and Fields started thinking of their product as part of the skin care market, they got advice from a marketing specialist about what to name their product. The name the specialist recommended was Proactiv (proactive without the *e*). Looking back, Rodan and Fields admit that initially they didn't get the reason for this recommendation. They were hoping for a more cosmetic-sounding name, like Dermo-Beautiful. The name Proactiv turned out to be perfect. It captured the essence of what Rodan and Fields were trying to accomplish—to create a product that would be *proactive* (rather than *reactive*) in dealing with acne and acne-related issues. In other words, the name Proactiv captured the entrepreneurs' interest in signaling to customers that their product was intended to prevent the occurrence of additional acne-related problems for them.

Critical Marketing Decision 3: Infomercials

To get their product on the market, Rodan and Fields initially tried to raise investment capital. They were repeatedly turned down. The biggest objection they encountered was the sentiment that if their product was so good and so obvious, why hadn't Procter & Gamble or Johnson & Johnson already thought of it? "Surely those companies must have dermatologists on their advisory boards telling them what to do," was the comment repeatedly expressed to Rodan and Fields as they talked to those with investment capital. After giving up on raising capital, Rodan and Fields approached Neutrogena to try to get a licensing deal. Neutrogena passed on the deal but did make a suggestion that resonated with Rodan and Fields. Neutrogena said that the most effective way to sell the product would be via infomercials. Initially, Rodan and Fields were shocked, because they had a fairly low opinion of infomercials. But there was one company, according to people at Neutrogena, named Guthy-Renker, that made high-quality infomercials for professional products like Proactiv. Rodan and Fields also got to thinking that an infomercial might be the best way to educate people about their product. The following list lays out the points in favor of using infomercials to sell a product in which Rodan and Fields had a great deal of confidence.

Why Infomercials Have Worked for Proactiv (Infomercials Are 30–60 Minute Programs That Are Paid for by an Advertiser)

- People need to be reeducated about how to treat acne.
- The reeducation can't be done in a 30-second or 60-second television commercial, or in a print ad.
- Acne is an embarrassing problem, so people will be most open to learning about it in the privacy of their homes.
- The demographic group that spends the most time watching infomercials, women in their 20s, 30s, and 40s, are Proactiv's market.
- Infomercials provide Proactiv the opportunity to show heartfelt testimonials of people who have used the product. Showing "before" and "after" pictures of people who have used the product and have experienced dramatic results has been a particularly persuasive tactic.

Guthy-Renker

After being turned down by Neutrogena, Rodan and Fields were about ready to throw in the towel when they met, simply by chance, a person who introduced them to Guthy-Renker, the infomercial company that people at Neutrogena recommended highly. After several meetings, Guthy-Renker offered to license Proactiv and to create an infomercial to sell the product. It also put up the money to buy the media time needed for the infomercial to be televised. The initial infomercial was targeted toward women in the age group most ignored by the present providers of acne products. The 30-minute spot carefully explained what acne is, how it can affect older women, and how Proactiv was the only product available that potentially prevented acne from occurring. It also offered a complete money-back guarantee. The first infomercial sold twice as much Proactiv as expected, and Guthy-Renker and Proactiv remain close partners today.

It was also Guthy-Renker's idea to get celebrity endorsements for Proactiv. The first celebrity endorser was Judith Light. Light was followed by Vanessa Williams, and now a number of other celebrities endorse the product.

Proactiv Today

Today, Proactiv is strong. The first Guthy-Renker infomercial ran in 1994, and the product has steadily gained market share since. The company now sells acne treatment in several varieties, including Gentle Formula, Extra Strength, and Proactiv+. Face masks, body washes, and other skin-care products are also sold under the Proactiv name. Proactive products are now being sold worldwide. Proactiv's marketing strategy has not substantially changed since the company started. The three marketing decisions described in this case set the direction for the company, and the company remains fully committed to taking only the actions suggested by these decisions.

Discussion Questions

11-38. How has Proactiv gone about establishing its brand? To what degree do you believe Proactiv is important in its customers' lives?

11-39. Discuss the things that Rodan and Fields learned, prior to meeting Guthy-Renker, that persuaded them that infomercials were the best way to sell Proactiv. If Proactiv hadn't developed infomercials in partnership with Guthy-Renker, do you think Proactiv would be in existence today? Why were infomercials a better choice than print or media advertising for Proactiv when the company was first being introduced?

11-40. Describe Proactiv's positioning strategy. To what extent did the three critical marketing decisions discussed in the case shape the evolution of Proactiv's positioning strategy?

11-41. What is the difference between Proactiv's core product and its actual product? Describe its actual product and your assessment of whether the actual product provides an attractive mix of characteristics.

Sources: Proactiv home page, www.proactiv.com (accessed May 25, 2011); K. Rodan, Stanford Technology Ventures Entrepreneurial Thought Leaders Podcast, April 2006.

Endnotes

1. Dorm Startups, available at http://www. dormstartups.org/wink-natural-cosmetics/, (accessed on September 3, 2014).

2. Personal conversation with Megan Cox, September 3, 2014.

3. M. A. Abebe and A. Angriawan, "Organizational and Competitive Influences of Exploration and Exploitation Activities in Small Firms," *Journal of Business Research* 67, no. 3 (2014): 339–345; A. O'Donnell, "The Contribution of Networking to Small Firm Marketing," *Journal of Small Business Management* 52, no. 1 (2014): 164–187.

4. C. B. Bingham and S. Kahl, "Anticipatory Learning," *Strategic Entrepreneurship Journal* 8, no. 2 (2014): 101–127.

5. S. Turk, IBISWorld Industry Report 71394 Gym, Health & Fitness Clubs in the US, www.ibisworld. com, June 2014.

6. Broadway Dance Center home page, www.broadwaydancecenter.com, (accessed September 2, 2014).

7. P. Singh, "Startup Market Positioning: Less Is More," Results Junkie Blog, www.resultsjunkies. com/blog/startup-market-positioning-less-is-more, (accessed May 25, 2011, originally posted on May 28, 2010).

8. Art 7 Style Dance Studio home page, www.artandstyledancestudio.com, (accessed September 2, 2014).

9. Arthur Murray Dance Studio (Pittsburgh) home page, www.arthurmurraypgh.com, (accessed September 2, 2014).

10. Snap Fitness home page, www.snapftness.com, (accessed September 3, 2014).

11. P. Kotler, *Marketing Insights from A to Z: 80 Concepts Every Manager Needs to Know* (Hoboken, NJ: John Wiley & Sons, 2009), 65.

12. A. P. Cui, M. Y. Hu, and D. A. Griffith, "What Makes a Brand Manager Effective?" *Journal of Business Research* 67, no. 2 (2014): 144–150; O. Kroll and S. von Wallpach, "Intended Brand Associations: Do They Really Drive Consumer Response?" *Journal of Business Research* 67, no. 7 (2014): 1501–1507.

13. A. J. Kimmel and P. J. Kitchen, "Word of Mouth and Social Media," *Journal of Marketing Communications* 20, no. 1 and no. 2 (2014): 2–4.

14. G. Xiong and S. Bharadwaj, "Prerelease Buzz Evolution Patterns and New Product Performance," *Marketing Science*, 2014, in press; E. Moretti, "Social Learning and Peer Effects in Consumption: Evidence from Movie Sales," *Review of Economic Studies* 78, no. 1 (2010): 356–393.

15. J. Hess, J. Story, and J. Danes, "A Three-Stage Model of Consumer Relationship Investment," *Journal of Product & Brand Management* 20, no. 1 (2011): 14–26; J. Blasberg, V. Vishwanath, and J. Allen, "Tools for Converting Consumers into Advocates," *Strategy & Leadership* 36, no. 2 (2008): 16–23.

16. N. J. Hicks, "From Ben Franklin to Branding: The Evolution of Health Services Marketing," in G. Bashe, N. J. Hicks, and A. Zieegenfuss (Eds.), *Branding Health Services* (Gaithersburg, MD: Aspen Publishers, 2000), 1–18.

17. S. Liao and C. C. J. Cheng, "Brand Equity and the Exacerbating Factors of Product Innovation Failure Evaluations: A Communication Effect Perspective," *Journal of Business Research* 67, no. 1 (2014): 2919–2925.

18. W. Pride and O. C. Ferrell, *Foundations of Marketing*, 6th ed. (Cincinnati, OH: Cengage Learning, 2015).

19. H. W. Chesbrough, *Open Innovation* (Boston, MA: Harvard Business School Press, 2003).

20. P. Kotler and G. Armstrong, *Principles of Marketing*, 15th ed. (Upper Saddle River, NJ: Prentice Hall, 2014).

21. T. C. Flatten, A. Engelen, T. Moller, and M. Brettel, "How Entrepreneurial Firms Profit from Pricing Capabilities: An Examination of Technology-Based Ventures," *Entrepreneurship Theory and Practice*, 2014, in press.

22. K. Jung, Y. C. Cho, and S. Lee, "Online Shoppers' Response to Price Comparison Sites," *Journal of Business Research* 67, no. 10 (2014): 2079–2087; J. Mosteller, N. Donthu, and S. Eroglu, "The Fluent Online Shopping Experience," *Journal of Business Research* 67, no. 11 (2014): 2486–2493.

23. A. Payne and P. Frow, "Deconstructing the Value Proposition of an Innovation Exemplar," *European Journal of Marketing* 48, no. 1 and no. 2 (2014): 237–270; A. Rusetski, J. Andrews, and D. C. Smith, "Unjustified Prices: Environmental Drivers of Managers' Propensity to Overprice," *Journal of the Academy of Marketing Science* 42, no. 4 (2014): 452–469.

24. A. Gneezy, U. Gneezy, and D. O. Lauga, "A Reference-Dependent Model of the Price-Quality Heuristic," *Journal of Marketing Research* 51, no. 2 (2014): 153–164.

25. "Our Story," SmugMug home page, www.smugmug.com (accessed September 3, 2014); N. Kaiser, "Interview with Don MacAskill, CEO of SmugMug," nPost, available at http://www.npost.com/?s=smugmug, posted on January 16, 2007, (accessed on September 2, 2014).

26. B. Gaurav and A. Faraz, "A Comparative Study of TV and Internet Advertising in the Context of Informativeness Parameter," *Asian Journal of Research in Business Economics and Management* 4, no. 3 (2014): 479–487; Z. Mamoon, "Choosing Advertising Media," *Journal of Research in Marketing* 2, no. 2 (2014): 143–150.

27. I. Ater and O. Rigbi, "Price Control and Advertising in Franchising Chains, *Strategic Management Journal*, 2014, in press.

28. E. Fischer and A. R. Reuber, "Online Entrepreneurial Communication: Mitigating Uncertainty and Increasing Differentiation via Twitter," *Journal of Business Venturing* 29, no. 4 (2014): 565–583.

29. ModCloth blog, "Break the Rules: How to Wear White After Labor Day," available at http://blog.modcloth.com/2013/09/03/break-the-rules-how-to-wear-white-after-labor-day/, (posted on September 3, 2013, accessed on September 5, 2014).

30. Facebook, www.facebook.com/press/info.php?statistics (accessed September 5, 2014).

Getting Personal with DRIPCATCH

Founder

ALEXANDRA ABRAHAM

BS, College of Business
Seattle University, expected fall 2015

Dialogue with
Alexandra Abraham

MY FAVORITE SMARTPHONE APP
iTunes

MY BIGGEST WORRY AS AN ENTREPRENEUR
Running out of money to finish and protect my patent.

FAVORITE BAND ON MY SMARTPHONE MUSIC LIST
Dave Matthews & Florence and the Machine

WHAT I DO WHEN I'M NOT WORKING
Spend time with friends and family.

MY BIGGEST SURPRISE AS AN ENTREPRENEUR
SO many people care about you and your dreams, even strangers, and are willing to help you in any way they can.

MY ADVICE FOR NEW ENTREPRENEURS
Recommit yourself every day to the belief that your dream is going to happen.

CHAPTER 12

The Importance of *Intellectual* Property

OPENING PROFILE

DRIPCATCH

The Key Role of Intellectual Property Early in a Firm's Life and Its Ongoing Success

• Web: www.dripcatch.com • Facebook: DripCatch • Twitter: @DripCatch

In 2010, Alexandra Abraham was working for a catering service. One day, while working a job at the Salish Lodge & Spa in Seattle, she slipped on a wet floor and nearly fell to the ground. Although an unsettling experience, it got her thinking. There are often wet spots on the floors of hotel and restaurant kitchens. The main culprit is water that drips from glass-drying racks. Commercial kitchens have square racks that dirty glasses are placed into. The racks are run through a dishwasher, which both washes and dries the glasses. When a rack comes out, some of the glasses typically aren't completely dried. When the rack is moved, water drips to the floor. Abraham knew that the number one cause of injury in commercial kitchens is falling. She went to her manager and asked if there was a way to catch the excess water before it fell to the floor. The response she got was if she could figure out a way to do it, the catering service would be her first customer.

That experience set Abraham on a mission—to design a product that would catch water dripping from glasses in glass-drying racks. She put together some preliminary drawings. Her idea was to create a basin or tray that snaps below glass and dishwasher racks to catch water that might otherwise drip to the floor. Along with water that is still on glasses when they come out of the dishwasher, water is also spilled when servers fill water glasses before they are placed on tables. If glasses were left in a rack, with Abraham's tray below, there wouldn't be a possibility of spilling water at any point in the process. Errant water would be caught by the rack. Abraham showed her drawings around some and got positive feedback. She knew she'd need CAD drawings done if she wanted to show the concept to potential manufacturers and buyers, so she e-mailed the engineering department at Seattle University asking for help. It turned out that there were plenty of students looking for practical experience and she got CAD drawings developed for her concept.

The next step was to see if there was genuine interest for her product in the restaurant industry. Abraham took a chance and sent a blind e-mail to Tom Douglas, one of Seattle's most well-known chefs, asking him to review and endorse her invention. The subject line of the e-mail read "College student seeking Mr. Douglas's

LEARNING OBJECTIVES

After studying this chapter you should be ready to:

1. Define the term *intellectual property* and describe its importance.

2. Explain what a patent is and describe different types of patents.

3. Describe a trademark and explain the process entrepreneurs use to obtain one.

4. Define a copyright and identify what a copyright can protect.

5. Describe a trade secret and understand the common causes of trade secret disputes.

6. Explain what an intellectual property audit is and identify the two primary reasons entrepreneurial firms should complete this type of audit.

help." In two days she had an appointment with Douglas, and showed him an early prototype. She explained to him that DripCatch, the name she gave her product, was a simple device that collects water from glass-drying racks commonly used in restaurants. It prevents slips and falls caused by dripping water. She remembers asking him "What do you think?" "He just shook my hand and said, 'Congratulations, what do you want from me?'"[1] What Abraham wanted was an endorsement, which Douglas provided. There has since been an image of Douglas on DripCatch's website, with a quote that reads:

> "It's great to find a product that makes you smack your head and go 'Perfect! That's just what we need! It keeps our floors drier, our employees and customers safer, the restaurant cleaner and me happier … win, win, win!"[2]

Now that Abraham knew she was on to something, building a company and protecting her intellectual property became a key pursuit. She started by making another cold call, this time to Seattle area entrepreneur Tom Burns. Burns, a long-time Boeing executive, quit his job and became an entrepreneur after he invented a series of small sticks that plug the holes in hot beverage lids, thus eliminating spilling and keeping the beverages hot longer. Burns's company, StixToGo (https://stixtogo.com), has placed its product in more than 30,000 coffee shops, restaurants, and convenience stores worldwide. Abraham connected with Burns, who provided her assistance in filing a provisional patent application on the DripCatch device. Abraham retained a patent agent to file for a utility patent. The patent agent was assisted by an attorney, who also helped Abraham trademark the DripCatch name. The utility patent application is currently pending. Trademarks can be viewed at the U.S. Patent and Trademark's website at www.uspto.gov. Simply go to the website, select trademarks, and place the name of the mark in the search bar. DripCatch's trademark can be viewed at http://tmsearch.uspto.gov/bin/showfield?f=doc&state=4803:nlrmr.2.1.

While waiting for the utility patent to be granted, Abraham has been busy making and marketing her product. She found a local contract manufacturer—Woodinville's Cashmere Molding—to produce the DripCatch tray for less than she could produce them overseas. She signed an agreement with a restaurant-equipment distributor, which is now selling the DripCatch device. She is currently looking for an affiliation with a distributor that has a national reach and representatives in every major city calling on restaurants, hotels, and institutions such as hospitals and schools that could benefit by using DripCatch trays in their kitchens. She is also looking for a manufacturer who has a major presence in her industry.

While the DripCatch device is gaining sales, Abraham says that her exit strategy is probably licensing or a buyout option. "We're more of a product than a company," she acknowledges.[3] In terms of overall potential, Abraham sees the sky as the limit. The problem her DripCatch device solves is a problem that exists in every commercial and industrial kitchen in the world. Once granted, her patent will give her exclusive rights to DripCatch's approach to solving the problem.

Many entrepreneurial firms have valuable intellectual property. In fact, virtually all businesses, including start-ups, have knowledge, information, and ideas that are critical to their success.

For at least three reasons, it is important for businesses to recognize what intellectual property is and how to protect it. First, the intellectual property of a business often represents its most valuable asset.[4] Think of the value of the Facebook and Google trademarks, the Nike "swoosh" logo, or the design of the Apple iPhone. All of these are examples of intellectual property, and because of intellectual property laws, they are the exclusive properties of the firms that own them. Second, it is important to understand what intellectual property is and how to protect it to avoid unintentional violations of intellectual property laws. For example, imagine the hardship facing an entrepreneurial start-up if it selected a name for its business, heavily advertised that name, and was later forced to change the name because it was infringing on a trademark. Finally, intellectual property can be licensed or sold, providing valuable licensing income. This is what Alexandra Abraham may ultimately do with her DripCatch product.

We begin this chapter by defining intellectual property and exploring when intellectual property protection is warranted. There are costs involved with legally protecting intellectual property, and the costs sometimes outweigh the benefits, at least in the short term. We then describe the four key forms of intellectual property. The chapter ends with a discussion of the importance of conducting an intellectual property audit, which is a proactive tool an entrepreneurial firm can use to catalog the intellectual property it owns and determine how its intellectual property should be protected.

The Importance of Intellectual Property

Intellectual property is any product of human intellect that is intangible but has value in the marketplace. It is called "intellectual" property because it is the product of human imagination, creativity, and inventiveness.[5] Traditionally, businesses have thought of their physical assets such as land, buildings, and equipment as their most important assets. Increasingly, however, a company's intellectual assets are the most valuable.[6] In the case of DripCatch, the firm's intellectual property consists of intangible assets such

LEARNING OBJECTIVE

1. Define the term *intellectual property* and describe its importance.

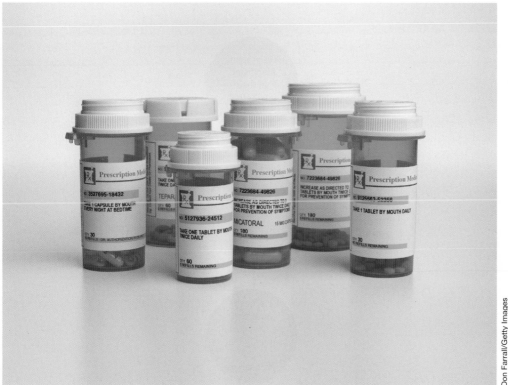

When you purchase prescription medicine, the amount you (and your insurance company) pay is not for the pills themselves. The value you are paying for is the access you now have to the intellectual property that equips the pills to help you feel better.

Don Farrall/Getty Images

as its patent (once granted), its trademark, and its Internet domain name. All these assets can provide a business with a competitive advantage in the marketplace, and the loss of such assets can be just as costly (if not more so) to a business as the loss of physical property or equipment.

Not all firms are as intellectual property savvy as DripCatch. In fact, common mistakes that entrepreneurial firms make are not properly identifying all their intellectual property, not fully recognizing the value of their intellectual property, not using their intellectual property as part of their overall plan of success, and not taking sufficient steps to protect it. These mistakes are presented in Figure 12.1. It can be difficult, however, to determine what qualifies as intellectual property and whether it should be legally protected. Every facet of a company's operations probably owns intellectual property that should be protected. To illustrate this point, Table 12.1 provides examples of the intellectual property that typically resides within the departments of midsize entrepreneurial firms. Intellectual property is also an important part of our nation's economy and its competitive advantage in the world marketplace. "It's a huge issue," former U.S. Commerce Secretary Carlos Gutierrez said. "There is so much of our economy that is linked to branded products, patented products, copyrights. So much of our economy thrives on creativity."[7]

The United States Patent & Trademark Office (USPTO) has several programs designed specifically to help inventors and small businesses protect their intellectual property. The help is motivated in part by The American Invents Act (AIA), which encourages the USPTO to "work with and support intellectual property laws associations across the county in the establishment of pro bono programs designed to assist financially under-resourced independent inventors and small businesses." The first is a pro bono legal assistance program, which is being rolled out state by state. This program provides patent filing assistance to qualified applicants. You can see if the program is available in your state by going to the National Clearinghouse, which is accessible via the USPTO website at www.uspto.gov/inventors/state_resources. The second is the Inventors Assistance Center (www.uspto.gov/inventors/iac), which provides overall patent assistance and support to the general public.

FIGURE 12.1
Common Mistakes
Firms Make in Regard
to Intellectual Property

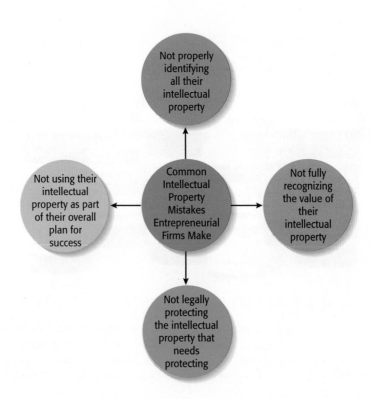

TABLE 12.1 **Examples of Intellectual Property That Typically Reside Within a Midsized Entrepreneurial Firm's Departments**

Department	Forms of Intellectual Property Typically Present	Usual Methods of Protection
Marketing	Names, slogans, logos, jingles, advertisements, brochures, pamphlets, ad copy under development, customer lists, prospect lists, and similar items	Trademark, copyright, and trade secret
Management	Recruiting brochures, employee handbooks, forms and checklists used by recruiters in qualifying and hiring candidates, written training materials, and company newsletters	Copyright and trade secret
Finance	Contractual forms, PowerPoint slides describing the company's financial performance, written methodologies explaining how the company handles its finances, and employee pay records	Copyright and trade secret
Management information systems	Website design, Internet domain names, company-specific training manuals for computer equipment and software, original computer code, e-mail lists, name registry	Copyright, trade secret, and Internet domain
Research and development	New and useful inventions and business processes, improvements to existing inventions and processes, and laboratory notes documenting invention discovery dates and charting the progress on various projects	Patent and trade secret

Determining What Intellectual Property to Legally Protect

There are two primary rules of thumb for deciding if intellectual property protection should be pursued for a particular intellectual asset. First, a firm should determine if the intellectual property in question is directly related to its competitive advantage. For example, Amazon.com has a business method patent on its "one-click" ordering system, which is a nice feature of its website and is arguably directly related to its competitive advantage. Similarly, when PatientsLikeMe launched a social networking platform for people with serious diseases, it would have been foolish for the company not to trademark the PatientsLikeMe name. In contrast, if a business develops a product or business method or produces printed material that isn't directly related to its competitive advantage, intellectual property protection may not be warranted.

The second primary criterion for deciding if intellectual property protection should be pursued is to determine whether an item has value in the marketplace. A common mistake that young companies make is to invent a product, spend a considerable amount of money to patent it, and find that the market for the product does not exist or that the existing market is too small to be worthy of pursuit. As discussed in Chapter 3, business ideas should be properly tested before a considerable amount of money is spent developing and legally protecting them. Owning the exclusive right to something no one wants is of little value. Similarly, if a company develops a logo for a special event, it is probably a waste of money to register it with the USPTO if there is a good chance the logo will not be used again.

The Four Key Forms of Intellectual Property

Patents, trademarks, copyrights, and trade secrets are the four key forms of intellectual property. We discuss each form of intellectual property protection in the following sections. Intellectual property laws exist to encourage creativity and innovation by granting individuals who risk their time and money in creative endeavors exclusive rights to the fruits of their labors for a period of time. Intellectual property laws also help individuals make well-informed choices. For example, when a consumer sees a Panera Bread restaurant, she knows exactly what to expect because only Panera Bread is permitted to use the Panera Bread trademark for soups, signature sandwiches, and bakery products.

One special note about intellectual property laws is that it is up to entrepreneurs to take advantage of them and to safeguard their intellectual property once it is legally protected. Police forces and fire departments are available to quickly respond if an entrepreneur's buildings or other physical assets are threatened, but there are no intellectual property police forces or fire departments in existence. The courts prosecute individuals and companies that break intellectual property laws. However, the individual entrepreneur must understand intellectual property laws, safeguard intellectual property assets, and initiate litigation if intellectual property rights are infringed upon or violated.

There is a government-sponsored website (www.stopfakes.gov) that provides information about how to file a complaint if a business feels that a "knock off" product is infringing on its intellectual property. Increasingly, counterfeit goods are a problem for firms that have spent considerable resources to brand their products in ways that create value for customers. The top five categories of goods that are counterfeited are electronics, shoes, pharmaceutical products, CDs and DVDs, and clothing.[8] Check out the blog IP Law For Startups (www.iplawforstartupcompanies.com) to keep up to date on all aspects of intellectual property law.

While not one of the four *key* forms of intellectual property, Internet domain names are an important form of intellectual property. Having a short, easy-to-spell Internet domain name is becoming increasingly important as the Internet becomes an ever more powerful force in business. An Internet domain name is obtained through a domain name registrar like GoDaddy.com and costs around $13 per year to register. Like other forms of intellectual property, domain names can be bought and sold, and desirable names are valuable. For example, Apple reportedly paid $6 million in 2011 to obtain the domain name www.icloud.com from its previous owner.

Patents

LEARNING OBJECTIVE
2. Explain what a patent is and describe different types of patents.

A **patent** is a grant from the federal government conferring the rights to exclude others from making, selling, or using an invention for the term of the patent.[9] The owner of the patent is granted a legal monopoly for a limited amount of time. However, a patent does not give its owner the right to make, use, or sell the invention; it gives the owner only the right to exclude others from doing so. This is a confusing issue for many entrepreneurs. If a company is granted a patent for an item, it is natural to assume that it could start making and selling the item immediately. But it cannot. A patent owner can legally make or sell the patented invention only if no other patents are infringed on by doing so.[10] For example, if an inventor obtained a patent on a computer chip and the chip needed technology patented earlier by Intel to work, the inventor would need to obtain permission from Intel to make and sell the chip. Intel may refuse permission or ask for a licensing fee for the use of its patented technology. Although this system may seem odd, it is really the only way the system could work. Many inventions are improvements on existing inventions, and the system allows the improvements to be patented, but only with the permission of the original inventors, who usually benefit by obtaining licensing income in exchange for their consent.[11]

Patent protection has deep roots in U.S. history and is the only form of intellectual property right expressly mentioned in the original articles of the U.S. Constitution. The first patent was granted in 1790 for a process of making potash, an ingredient in fertilizer. The patent was signed by George Washington

This woman is an industrial designer who works for an eyeglass start-up. She is working on the prototype of a pair of eyeglasses, using a new material and method for designing the glasses. Her company plans to apply for a utility patent on the new approach and material used to produce the glasses.

Hero Images/Corbis

and was issued to a Vermont inventor named Samuel Hopkins. Patents are important because they grant inventors temporary, exclusive rights to market their inventions. This right gives inventors and their financial backers the opportunity to recoup their costs and earn a profit in exchange for the risks and costs they incur during the invention process. If it weren't for patent laws, inventors would have little incentive to invest time and money in new inventions. "No one would develop a drug if you didn't have a patent," Dr. William Haseltine, former CEO of Human Genome Sciences, a biotech firm, once said.[12]

Since the first patent was granted in 1790, the USPTO has granted 8.7 million patents, including 302,150 in 2013 alone. The number of patents granted in 2013 was 62 percent more than the number granted in 2003, just 10 years earlier. These data suggest that a willingness to invent in the United States is strong. Interestingly, the USPTO, the sole entity responsible for granting patents in the United States, is strained. At the end of 2013, there were 584,998 patent applications pending, and it took an average of 29.1 months to get a patent application approved. Actually, the USPTO has been making strides in this area. The total time required to get a patent application approved reached a high of 35.3 months in 2010.

Some inventors and companies are very prolific and have multiple patents. There is increasing interest in patents, as shown in Table 12.2, as advances in technology spawn new inventions.

TABLE 12.2 **Growth in Patent Applications in the United States**

	2011	2012	2013
Applications received	537,171	565,406	601,317
Patents issued	244,430	270,258	290,083
Average time for approval	33.7 months	32.4 months	29.1 months

Source: United States Patent and Trademark Office, *Performance and Accountability Report for Fiscal Year 2013.*

Types of Patents

There are three types of patents: utility patents, design patents, and plant patents. As shown in Figure 12.2, there are three basic requirements for a patent to be granted: The subject of the patent application must be (1) useful, (2) novel in relation to prior arts in the field, and (3) not obvious to a person of ordinary skill in the field.

Utility patents are the most common type of patent and cover what we generally think of as new inventions. Of the 601,317 patent applications filed in 2013, 94 percent were for utility patents.[13] Patents in this category may be granted to anyone who "invents or discovers any new and useful process, machine, manufacture, or composition of matter, or any new and useful improvement thereof."[14] The term of a utility patent is 20 years from the date of the initial application. After 20 years, the patent expires, and the invention falls into the public domain, which means that anyone can produce and sell the invention without paying the prior patent holder. Consider the pharmaceutical industry. Assume a drug produced by a large firm such as Pfizer Inc. is prescribed for you and that, when seeking to fill the prescription, your pharmacist tells you there is no generic equivalent available. The lack of a generic equivalent typically means that a patent owned by Pfizer protects the drug and that the 20-year term of the patent has not expired. If the pharmacist tells you there is a generic version of the drug available, that typically means the 20-year patent has expired and other companies are now making a drug chemically identical to Pfizer's. The price of the generic version of the drug is generally lower because the manufacturer of the generic version of the drug is not trying to recover the costs Pfizer (in this case) incurred to develop the product (the drug) in question.

A utility patent cannot be obtained for an "idea" or a "suggestion" for a new product or process. A complete description of the invention for which a utility patent is sought is required, including drawings and technical details. In addition, a patent must be applied for within one year of when a product or process was first offered for sale, put into public use, or was described in any printed publication. The requirement that a patent application must be filed within one year of the milestones referred to previously is called the **one year after first use deadline**.

Recently, utility patent law has added business method patents, which have been of particular interest to Internet firms. A **business method patent** is a patent that protects an invention that is or facilitates a method of doing business. Patents for these purposes were not allowed until 1998, when a federal circuit court issued an opinion allowing a patent for a business method, holding that business methods, mathematical algorithms, and software are patentable as long as they produce useful, tangible, and concrete results. This ruling opened a "Pandora's box" and has caused many firms to scramble to try to patent their business methods. Since 1998, the most notable business method patents awarded have been Amazon.com's one-click ordering system, Priceline.com's "name-your-price" business model, and Netflix's method for allowing customers to set up a rental list of movies they

FIGURE 12.2
Three Basic Requirements for a Patent

The subject of the patent application, whether it is an invention, design, or business method, must be . . .

Useful	Novel	Not Obvious
It must have utility.	It must be different from what has come before (i.e., not in the "prior art").	It must not be obvious to a person of ordinary skill in the field.

want mailed to them or that they wish to download for streaming purposes. Activities associated with a business method patent can be an important source of competitive advantage for a firm.

Design patents are the second most common type of patent and cover the invention of new, original, and ornamental designs for manufactured products.[15] Of the 601,317 patent applications filed in 2013, 5.8 percent were for design patents.[16] A design patent is good for 14 years from the grant date. While a utility patent protects the way an invention is used and works, a design patent protects the way it looks. As a result, if an entrepreneur invented a new version of the computer mouse, it would be prudent to apply for a utility patent to cover the way the mouse works and for a design patent to protect the way the mouse looks. Although all computer mice perform essentially the same function, they can be ornamentally designed in an infinite number of ways. As long as each new design is considered by the USPTO to be novel and nonobvious, it is eligible for design patent protection. This is not a trivial issue in that product design is increasingly becoming an important source of competitive advantage for many firms producing many different types of products.

Plant patents protect new varieties of plants that can be reproduced asexually. While only 1,320 of the 601,317 patent applications filed in 2013 were for plant patents, these patents provide essential protection for companies specializing in plant genetics and related areas. Plants that can be reproduced asexually are reproduced by grafting or crossbreeding rather than by planting seeds. The new variety can be different from previous plants in its resistance to disease or drought or in its scent, appearance, color, or productivity. Thus, a new color for a rose or a new type of hybrid vegetable would be eligible for plant patent protection. The term for plant patent protection is 20 years from the date of the original application.

Table 12.3 provides a summary of the three forms of patent protection, the types of inventions the patents cover, and the duration of the patents.

Who Can Apply for a Patent?

Only the inventor of a product can apply for a patent. If two or more people make an invention jointly, they must apply for the patent together. Someone who simply heard about the design of a product or is trying to patent something that is in the public domain may not apply for a patent.

There are notable exceptions to these rules. First, if an invention is made during the course of the inventor's employment, the employer typically is assigned the right to apply for the patent through an **assignment of invention agreement** signed by the employee as part of the employment agreement. A second exception is that the rights to apply for an invention can be sold. This

TABLE 12.3 **Summary of the Three Forms of Patent Protection, the Types of Inventions the Patents Cover, and the Duration of the Patents**

Type of Patent	Types of Inventions Covered	Duration
Utility	New or useful process, machine, manufacture, or composition of material or any new and useful improvement thereof	20 years from the date of the original application
Design	Invention of new, original, and ornamental designs for manufactured products	14 years from the date of the original application
Plant	Any new varieties of plants that can be reproduced asexually	20 years from the date of the original application

option can be an important source of revenue for entrepreneurial firms. If a firm has an invention that it doesn't want to pursue on its own, the rights to apply for a patent on the invention can be sold to another party.

The Process of Obtaining a Patent

Obtaining a patent is a six-step process, as illustrated in Figure 12.3 and as we discuss here. The costs involved include attorney fees, fees for drawings (which are sometimes lumped together with the attorney fees), and USPTO filing and maintenance fees. For a small entity, it costs around $700 to file a utility patent application. An additional $480 fee is assessed when a patent is issued. Maintenance fees of $800, $1,800, and $3,700 are due at the 3 ½ year mark, the 7 ½ year mark, and the 11 ½ year mark, respectively, to keep a patent in force. Additional fees may be assessed depending on the nature of the patent. Attorney fees vary depending on the complexity of the technology involved. An estimate of attorney fees to obtain a patent is provided in Table 12.4.

The inventions that independent inventors create range from relatively simple to moderately complex. Businesses are across the board. For a highly complex technology, such as a semiconductor product, the costs could substantially exceed $15,000.

FIGURE 12.3
The Process of
Obtaining a Patent

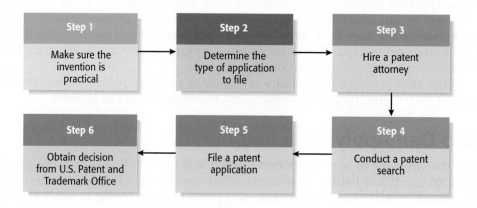

TABLE 12.4   Estimates of Attorney Fees for Obtaining a Patent

Invention Type	Examples of Inventions	Fees for an Attorney's Services
Very simple	Coat hanger, a pencil eraser, a bottle opener	$5,000 to $7,000
Relatively simple	Cup holders for automobiles, retractable dog leash, compact flashlight	$7,000 to $9,000
Somewhat complex	Power hand tool, space heater, compact refrigerator	$9,000 to $10,000
Moderately complex	Basic inventory-tracking systems, sprinkler systems with several capabilities, simple software with business applications	$10,000 to $12,500
Reasonably complex	Hand-held tracking devices, airport security scanning machines, business methods	$12,500 to $15,000
Very complex	Aviation electronics, fuel-efficient engines for commercial aircraft, Internet-based social media systems	$15,000 and up

Source: Based on G. Quinn, "The Cost of Obtaining a Patent in the US," IPWatchDog, http://ipwatchdog.com/2011/01/28/the-cost-of-obtainingpatent/id=14668 (accessed April 29, 2011, posted on January 28, 2011).

The six-step process for obtaining a patent is shown next.

Step 1 **Make sure the invention is practical.** As mentioned earlier, there are two rules of thumb for making the decision to patent. Intellectual property that is worth protecting typically is directly related to the competitive advantage of the firm seeking the protection or has independent value in the marketplace.

Step 2 **Determine what type of application to file.** As mentioned, there are three types of patents: utility patents, design patents, and plant patents. The most common by far is the utility patent.

Step 3 **Hire a patent attorney.** It is highly recommended that an inventor work with a patent attorney. Even though there are "patent-it-yourself" books and websites on the market, it is generally naïve for an entrepreneur to think that the patent process can be successfully navigated without expert help. A correctly prepared patent application with correctly defined claims will provide the best chance for an application to be approved. In addition, a new product may have patentable features that may not be obvious to a novice in the field. As an indication of the difficulty of writing a patent application, the USPTO requires all attorneys and agents to pass a tough exam before they can interact with the agency on behalf of a client.

Step 4 **Conduct a patent search.** To be patentable, an invention must be novel and different enough from what already exists. A patent attorney typically spends several hours searching the USPTO's database (which is available online at www.uspto.gov) to study similar patents. After the search is completed and the patents that are similar to the invention in question have been carefully studied, the patent attorney renders an opinion regarding the probability of obtaining a patent on the new invention.

Step 5 **File a patent application.** The fifth step, if the inventor decides to proceed, is to file a patent application with the USPTO in Washington, DC. Applications can be filed electronically or by mail. Unlike copyright and trademark applications, which can be prepared and filed easily by their owners, patent applications are highly technical and almost always require expert assistance. In terms of priority in filing a patent application, the United States uses a first-to-file system, as is used in all countries. The United States switched to a first-to-file system from a first-to-invent system on March 16, 2013, with the enactment of the America Invents Act. In a first-to-file system, the right to the grant of a patent for an invention lies with the first person to file a patent application for the invention, regardless of the date of the actual invention.

Step 6 **Obtain a decision from the USPTO.** When the USPTO receives a patent application, it is given a serial number, assigned to an examiner, and then waits to be examined. The patent examiner investigates the application and issues a written report ("Office Action") to the applicant's patent attorney, often asking for modifications to the application. Most of the interactions that applicants have with the USPTO are by mail or e-mail. Occasionally, an inventor and a lawyer will meet face to face with a patent examiner to discuss the invention and the written report. There is room to negotiate with the patent office to try to make an invention patentable. Eventually, a yes-or-no decision will be rendered. A rejected application can be appealed, but appeals are rare and expensive.

One provision of patent law that is particularly important to entrepreneurs is that the USPTO allows inventors to file a **provisional patent application** for utility patents, pending the preparation and filing of a complete application. A provisional patent application provides the means to establish an early effective filing date for a nonprovisional patent application, and allows the term "Patent Pending" to be applied. There is often confusion regarding what a provisional patent application is. It's not a provisional patent—there is no such thing. It's merely a provisional *application* for a patent, and is used to establish an early filing date for a subsequently filed full utility patent. It can actually give an entrepreneur a false sense of security if not filed correctly. The ins and outs of filing a provisional patent application are explained in this chapter's "Savvy Entrepreneurial Firm" feature.

In some instances, entrepreneurs license their patents to larger firms, which have nationwide distribution channels to market a product. In fact, consumer product companies like Procter & Gamble (P&G) and General Mills, which at one time relied strictly on their own scientists to develop new products, now have formal programs for inventors and entrepreneurs to submit product ideas, as illustrated in the "Partnering for Success" feature. The arrangements described in the "Partnering for Success" feature represent a win-win for both inventors and larger firms. The inventor receives distribution for his or her product and potential licensing income, and the large firm receives an innovative new product to place in its distribution channels. One requirement most large firms have is that an idea must be patented or a patent must be applied for before they will consider licensing it.

Patent Infringement

Patent infringement takes place when one party engages in the unauthorized use of another party's patent. A typical example of an infringement claim was that initiated by Alacritech, a start-up firm, which claimed that Microsoft violated two of its patents on technology used to speed the performance of computers connected to networks. According to court documents, Alacritech showed its technology to Microsoft, hoping that Microsoft would license it. But Microsoft passed on the offer and later announced a surprisingly similar technology, called Chimney. Alacritech again offered to license the technology to Microsoft but was rebuffed. In response, Alacritech filed suit against Microsoft. Microsoft claimed that its technology was developed independently.[17] After hearing the case, the U.S. District Court in San Francisco sided with Alacritech and filed a preliminary injunction against Microsoft, preventing it from shipping products that contained the contested technology. Later, the suit was settled out of court, with Microsoft agreeing to license Alacritech's technology.[18]

The tough part about patent infringement cases is that they are costly to litigate, which puts start-up firms and their entrepreneurs at quite a disadvantage. While there is no way of knowing how much it cost Alacritech to sue Microsoft, a typical patent-infringement suit, according to *Fortune Small Business*, costs each side at least $500,000 to litigate.[19]

Trademarks

LEARNING OBJECTIVE

3. Describe a trademark and explain the process entrepreneurs use to obtain one.

A **trademark** is any word, name, symbol, or device used to identify the source or origin of products or services and to distinguish those products or services from others. All businesses want to be recognized by their potential clientele and use their names, logos, and other distinguishing features to enhance their visibility. Trademarks also provide consumers with useful information. For example, consumers know what to expect when they see a Macy's store in a mall. Think of how confusing it would be if any retail store could use the name Macy's.

SAVVY ENTREPRENEURIAL FIRM

Knowing the Ins and Outs of Filing a Provisional Patent Application
Web: www.uspto.gov; Facebook: United States Patent and Trademark Office; Twitter: uspto

In start-up circles, it's not uncommon to hear people say that they have a "provisional patent" or that they're protected from someone stealing their invention because a provisional patent has been filed. Neither of these statements can be true, because there is no such thing as a provisional patent. While the people who make those claims are normally well-intentioned, failing to be familiar with the basics of patent law can result in an entrepreneur inadvertently surrendering the patent rights for which he or she has an invention. If this happens, it can cripple a firm that's planning on achieving a sustainable competitive advantage via its exclusive rights on an invention.

Here's an accurate assessment of what takes place for entrepreneurs working in the United States. What's filed with the United States Patent and Trademark Office (USPTO) is a "provisional patent application." It includes specifications (i.e., a description and drawings of an invention), but does not require formal patent claims, inventors' oaths or declarations, or any information disclosure statement. It's not assigned to a patent examiner, and no judgment is made regarding prior art or the patentability of the invention. Its purpose, in the eyes of the USPTO, is to establish an early filing date for a subsequently filed full utility patent. What's meant by this is that if a provisional patent application is filed on December 1, 2014, and the application is done correctly, this becomes the "priority" filing date for that invention. If someone files a utility patent application for an identical invention a month later, that person is out of luck, as long as the inventor who filed the provisional patent application follows through and files for a full utility patent within one year, and both the provisional patent application and the full utility patent application are deemed to be acceptable. A bonus attached to filing a provisional patent application, which costs $149 to file, is that the inventor can legally use the term "patent pending" in relation to the invention. This designation may provide the inventor a significant marketing advantage, if the invention is already for sale, and signal to prospective inventors that the inventor is taking steps to protect his or her patent rights.

There is a catch, however, to this scenario—the provisional patent application must be completed and filed correctly. All patent applications, including provisional patent applications, are subject to three important statutory requirements:

1. It must include an adequate written description of the invention.
2. It should enable one of ordinary skill in the art to make and use the invention.
3. It must set forth the best mode of practicing the invention contemplated by the inventor upon filing.

If any one of these requirements is not met, along with other statutory requirements the USPTO has, it's tantamount to not having filed anything at all. So it's very important that provisional patent applications be sufficiently detailed and filed correctly. Here's what can happen if they're not. Suppose Amy invents a new type of tennis racket. She files a provisional patent application on January 1, 2015, by downloading the application and filing it herself. It's inadequate because it doesn't contain an adequate written description of her invention, but the USPTO doesn't tell Amy it's inadequate because it doesn't examine provisional patent applications until a full utility patent is filed. On July 1, 2015, Amy hires a patent attorney to file for a full utility patent on her invention. After reviewing her file, the USPTO examiner rejects the application, because someone filed a utility patent application for an identical invention a month earlier, on June 1, 2015. The reason for the rejection is that Amy's provisional patent application was deemed to be invalid because the description was inadequate. The fact that Amy filed a provisional patent application on January 1, 2015, five full months before the second party filed for an identical invention, holds no weight because Amy's provisional patent application was deemed to be invalid.

Amy's story illustrates that filing a provisional patent application takes some finesse. Filing a provisional patent application has its place. It's particularly useful for an inventor who invents a new device and wants to lock in a priority filing date while additional prototyping and feasibility analysis are conducted to decide whether it's worth the time and money to file for a full utility patent. It's a balancing act, however. An inventor needs to be far down the road before a provisional patent application makes sense. It may also make sense to hire a patent attorney to file the provisional patent application. Amy's description probably wasn't adequate because she didn't create a prototype of her new tennis racket, and thus was not able to adequately describe it. A patent attorney would have most likely told Amy that her description wasn't adequate, and suggested that more work be completed before the provisional patent application was filed. An idea can't be patented—only the specific expression of an idea, which must contain an adequate description.

The USPTO does allow additional provisional applications for a device to be filed as improvements are made. This protects inventors who are making progress on their device and want to establish priority dates for improved iterations of an invention as progress is made.

Questions for Critical Thinking

1. Briefly describe the difference between a provisional patent application and a utility patent application. If successful, which of the two applications awards an inventor a patent?

(continued)

2. Can a provisional patent application be filed for a design patent? Document your research to arrive at the correct answer to this question.
3. Under what circumstances would you (1) suggest to an inventor that he or she could file a provisional patent application without a patent attorney or (2) suggest to an inventor that he or she needs to hire a patent attorney to file the provisional patent application?
4. Spend some time studying the USPTO's website, or doing some Internet research on patents. Inventor's

Digest (www.inventorsdigest.com) is another good resource for learning about patents. Discuss one fact about patents or the application process you find interesting and isn't included in the material in this chapter.

Sources: USPTO, www.uspto.gov (accessed August 6, 2014); J. H. Muskin, "Pitfalls of Provisional Patent Applications," *Inventors Digest*, www.inventorsdigest.com/archives/4111 (accessed August 6, 2014, posted on July 20, 2010).

As is the case with patents, trademarks have a rich history. Archaeologists have found evidence that as far back as 3,500 years ago, potters made distinctive marks on their articles of pottery to distinguish their work from others. But consider a more modern example. The original name that Jerry Yang and David Filo, the co-founders of Yahoo, selected for their Internet directory service was "Jerry's Guide to the World Wide Web." Not too catchy, is it? The name was later changed to Yahoo, which caught on with early adopters of the Internet.

The Four Types of Trademarks

There are four types of trademarks: trademarks, service marks, collective marks, and certification marks (see Table 12.5). Trademarks and service marks are of the greatest interest to entrepreneurs.

Trademarks, as described previously, include any word, name, symbol, or device used to identify and distinguish one company's products from another's. Trademarks are used to promote and advertise tangible products.

TABLE 12.5   Summary of the Four Forms of Trademark Protection, the Type of Marks the Trademarks Cover, and the Duration of the Trademarks

Type of Trademark	Type of Marks Covered	Duration
Trademark	Any word, name, symbol, or device used to identify and distinguish one company's goods from another Examples: *Apple, d.light, GoPro, DripCatch, Brain Sentry*	Renewable every 10 years, as long as the mark remains in use
Service mark	Similar to trademarks; are used to identify the services or intangible activities of a business, rather than a business's physical products Examples: *1-800-FLOWERS*, Amazon.com, *eBay, Wello, CoachUp, Dropbox*	Renewable every 10 years, as long as the mark remains in use
Collective mark	Trademarks or service marks used by the members of a cooperative, association, or other collective group Examples: *Information Technology Industry Council, International Franchise Association, Rotary International*	Renewable every 10 years, as long as the mark remains in use
Certification mark	Marks, words, names, symbols, or devices used by a person other than its owner to certify a particular quality about a good or service Examples: *100% Napa Valley, Florida Oranges, National Organic Program, Underwriters Laboratories*	Renewable every 10 years, as long as the mark remains in use

PARTNERING FOR SUCCESS

Individual Inventors and Large Firms: Partnering to Bring New Products to Market

Distributing their products is a common problem facing inventors and entrepreneurs. Gary Schwartzberg is a case in point. Schwartzberg, along with a partner, developed a new type of bagel. Dubbed the "Bageler," the bagel was tube-shaped and filled with cream cheese. Schwartzberg was able to get the product into supermarkets and schools in South Florida, where he lived, but couldn't achieve wider distribution. He finally mailed Kraft a box of his cream-cheese-filled bagels with a proposal. He picked Kraft because he wanted to use Philadelphia Cream Cheese (a Kraft product) to fill the bagel.

By coincidence, Kraft had been working on a similar product but couldn't get it right. Schwartzberg had a patented process for "encapsulating" the cream cheese in the center of the bagel without the cream cheese escaping during the baking process. Kraft bit and, after some back and forth, Schwartzberg and Kraft hammered out a deal. Schwartzberg told the *Wall Street Journal* that he couldn't discuss the details of the deal because of a confidentiality agreement with Kraft, but says it's structured as a strategic alliance and he "has skin in the game." Schwartzberg's product, which is now called Bagel-fuls, is sold nationwide by Kraft Foods.

Entrepreneurs and inventors are finding that large consumer products companies are increasingly interested in what they have to offer. For example, Lifetime Brands, the United States' leading resource for nationally branded kitchenware, tabletop, and home décor products, is soliciting ideas from outside inventors. A section of its home page titled "Share your ideas" reads, "Lifetime Brands recognizes that good ideas come from unexpected places. If you have a great idea, we'd love to hear from you." Instructions are then provided for how to submit a product idea.

Companies vary in terms of what stage an idea needs to be at before it can be submitted for consideration. The best way to find out is to study the portion of a company's website that provides instructions for how to submit ideas. Not all companies are open to new ideas, but many are. For example, P&G's idea submission program is titled "P&G Connect + Develop." The program, which vets more than 4,000 submissions annually, has been so successful that P&G credits it with more than half of its new products over the past 10 years. Products that have emerged from the program include Olay Regenerist, Swiffer, and Pulsonic toothbrushes. General Mills's program is titled "G-Win," and has also experienced success, for both inventors and General Mills. Stanley Black & Decker's program is illustrative of how the submission and vetting process works. Simply go to the company's website at www.stanleyblack&decker.com, click on the "Company" tab, and follow the link titled "Submit an Idea."

Questions for Critical Thinking

1. Why do you think companies are increasingly open to ideas from outside inventors?
2. For an inventor or entrepreneur, what are the upsides to working with a company like General Mills or Stanley Black & Decker? What, if any, are the downsides?
3. Find an idea submission site for a company not mentioned in the feature. Describe how to submit an invention to the company. What appear to be the keys to getting an idea accepted by the company?
4. In most cases, do you think inventors and entrepreneurs get a fair shake when they license a product or enter into an alliance with a large firm? What steps should entrepreneurs take to make sure they are getting a fair deal?

Sources: L. Dishman, "How Outsiders Get Their Products to the Innovation Big League at Procter & Gamble, *Fast Company*, July 13, 2012; Stanley Black & Decker home page, www.stanley-blackanddecker.com, accessed August 4, 2014; P&G home page, www.pg.com, accessed August 4, 2014; General Mills home page, www.generalmills.com, accessed August 4, 2014; S. Covel, "My Brain, Your Brawn," *The Wall Street Journal*, October 13, 2008.

Examples here include Apple for smartphones, Nike for athletic shoes, Ann Taylor for women's clothing, and Zynga for online games.

Service marks are similar to ordinary trademarks, but they are used to identify the services or intangible activities of a business rather than a business's physical product. Service marks include *The Princeton Review* for test prep services, eBay for online auctions, and Verizon for cell phone service.

Collective marks are trademarks or service marks used by the members of a cooperative, association, or other collective group, including marks indicating membership in a union or similar organization. The marks belonging to the American Bar Association, The International Franchise Association, and the Entrepreneurs' Organization are examples of collective marks.

Finally, **certification marks** are marks, words, names, symbols, or devices used by a person other than its owner to certify a particular quality about a product or service. The most familiar certification mark is the UL mark, which certifies that a product meets the safety standards established by Underwriters Laboratories. Other examples are the Good Housekeeping Seal of Approval, Stilton Cheese (a product from the Stilton region in England), and 100% Napa Valley (from grapes grown in the Napa Valley of northern California).

What Is Protected Under Trademark Law?

Trademark law, which falls under the **Lanham Act**, passed in 1946, protects the following items:

- **Words:** All combinations of words are eligible for trademark registration, including single words, short phrases, and slogans. Birchbox, Warby Parker, and the National Football League are examples of words and phrases that have been registered as trademarks.

- **Numbers and letters:** Numbers and letters are eligible for registration. Examples include 3M, Boeing 787, and AT&T. Alphanumeric marks are also registerable, such as 1-800-CONTACTS.

- **Designs or logos:** A mark consisting solely of a design, such as the Golden Gate Bridge for Cisco Systems or the Nike swoosh logo, may be eligible for registration. The mark must be distinctive rather than generic. As a result, no one can claim exclusive rights to the image of the Golden Gate Bridge, but Cisco Systems can trademark its unique depiction of the bridge. Composite marks consist of a word or words in conjunction with a design. An example is the trademark for Zephyrhill's bottled water, which includes Zephyrhill's name below a picture of mountain scenery and water.

- **Sounds:** Distinctive sounds can be trademarked, although this form of trademark protection is rare. Recognizable examples of such sounds include MGM's lion's roar, the familiar four-tone sound that accompanies "Intel Inside" commercials, and the Yahoo yodel.

- **Fragrances:** The fragrance of a product may be registerable as long as the product is not known for the fragrance or the fragrance does not enhance the use of the product. As a result, the fragrance of a perfume or room deodorizer is not eligible for trademark protection, whereas stationery treated with a special fragrance in most cases would be.

- **Shapes:** The shape of a product, as long as it has no impact on the product's function, can be trademarked. The unique shape of the Apple iPod has received trademark protection.[20] The Coca-Cola Company has trademarked its famous curved bottle. The shape of the bottle has no effect on the quality of the bottle or the beverage it holds; therefore, the shape is not functional.

- **Colors:** A trademark may be obtained for a color as long as the color is not functional. For example, Nexium, a medicine pill that treats acid reflux disease, is purple and is marketed as "the purple pill." The color of the pill has no bearing on its functionality; therefore, it can be protected by trademark protection.

- **Trade dress:** The manner in which a product is "dressed up" to appeal to customers is protectable. This category includes the overall packaging, design, and configuration of a product. As a result, the overall look of a business is protected as its trade dress. In a famous case in 1992, *Two Pesos, Inc., v. Taco Cabana International Inc.*, the U.S. Supreme Court protected the overall design, colors, and configuration of a chain of Mexican restaurants from a competitor using a similar decor.[21]

Trademark protection is very broad and provides many opportunities for businesses to differentiate themselves from one another. The key for young entrepreneurial firms is to trademark their products and services in ways that draw positive attention to them in a compelling manner.

Exclusions from Trademark Protection

There are notable exclusions from trademark protection that are set forth in the U.S. Trademark Act:

- **Immoral or scandalous matter:** A company cannot trademark immoral or scandalous matter, including profane words.
- **Deceptive matter:** Marks that are deceptive cannot be registered. For example, a food company couldn't register the name "Fresh Florida Oranges" if the oranges weren't from Florida.
- **Descriptive marks:** Marks that are merely descriptive of a product or service cannot be trademarked. For example, an entrepreneur couldn't design a new type of golf ball and try to obtain trademark protection on the words *golf ball*. The words describe a type of product rather than a brand of product, such as Titleist or Taylor Made, and are needed by all golf ball manufacturers to be competitive. This issue is a real concern for the manufacturers of very popular products. At one point, Xerox was in danger of losing trademark protection for the Xerox name because of the common use of the word *Xerox* as a verb (e.g., "I am going to Xerox this").
- **Surnames:** A trademark consisting primarily of a surname, such as Anderson or Smith, is typically not protectable. An exception is a surname combined with other wording that is intended to trademark a distinct product, such as William's Fresh Fish or Smith's Computer Emporium.

The Process of Obtaining a Trademark

As illustrated in Figure 12.4, selecting and registering a trademark is a three-step process. Once a trademark has been used in interstate commerce, it can be registered with the USPTO. It can remain registered forever as long as the trademark stays in use. The first renewal is between the fifth and the sixth year following the year of initial registration. It can be renewed every 10 years thereafter, as long as the trademark stays in use.

Technically, a trademark does not need to be registered to receive protection and to prevent other companies from using confusingly similar marks. Once a mark is used in commerce, such as in an advertisement, it is protected. There are several distinct advantages, however, in registering a trademark with the USPTO: Registered marks are allowed nationwide priority for use of the mark, registered marks may use the federal trademark registration symbol (®), and registered marks carry with them the right to block the importation of infringing goods into the United States. The right to use the trademark registration symbol is particularly important. Attaching the trademark symbol to a product (e.g., My Yahoo!®) provides notice of a trademark owner's registration.

FIGURE 12.4
The Process of Obtaining a Trademark

This posting allows an owner to recover damages in an infringement action and helps reduce an offender's claim that it didn't know that a particular name or logo was trademarked.

There are three steps in selecting and registering a trademark:

Step 1 **Select an appropriate mark.** There are several rules of thumb to help business owners and entrepreneurs select appropriate trademarks. First, a mark, whether it is a name, logo, design, or fragrance, should display creativity and strength. Marks that are inherently distinctive, such as the McDonald's Golden Arches; made-up words, such as *Google* and *eBay*; and words that evoke particular images, such as *Double Delight Ice Cream*, are strong trademarks. Second, words that create a favorable impression about a product or service are helpful. A name such as *Safe and Secure Childcare* for a day care center positively resonates with parents.

Step 2 **Perform a trademark search.** Once a trademark has been selected, a trademark search should be conducted to determine if the trademark is available. If someone else has already established rights to the proposed mark, it cannot be used. There are several ways to conduct a trademark search, from self searches to hiring a firm specializing in trademark clearance checks. The search should include both federal and state searches in any states in which business will be conducted. If the trademark will be used overseas, the search should also include the countries where the trademark will be used.

Although it is not necessary to hire an attorney to conduct a trademark search, it is probably a good idea to do so. As noted above, self searches can also be conducted. The USPTO's website provides a powerful trademark search engine at www.uspto.gov/trademarks. There is a catch. The USPTO's search engine only searches trademarks that are registered. In the United States, you are not required to register a trademark to obtain protection. A trademark attorney can perform a more comprehensive search for you if you think it is necessary. Adopting a trademark without conducting a trademark search is risky. If a mark is challenged as an infringement, a company may have to destroy all its goods that bear the mark (including products, business cards, stationery, signs, and so on) and then select a new mark. The cost of refamiliarizing customers with an existing product under a new name or logo could be substantial.

Step 3 **Create rights in the trademark.** The final step in establishing a trademark is to create rights in the mark. In the United States, if the trademark is inherently distinctive (think of Starbucks, iTunes, or Facebook), the first person to use the mark becomes its owner. If the mark is descriptive, such as "Bufferin" for buffered aspirin, using the mark merely begins the process of developing a secondary meaning necessary to create full trademark protection. **Secondary meaning** arises when, over time, consumers start to identify a trademark with a specific product. For example, the name "chap stick" for lip balm was originally considered to be descriptive, and thus not afforded trademark protection. As people started to think of "chap stick" as lip balm, it met the threshold of secondary meaning, and the name "ChapStick" was able to be trademarked.

There are two ways that the USPTO can offer further protection for firms concerned about maintaining the exclusive rights to their trademarks. First, a person can file an **intent-to-use trademark application**. This is an application based on the applicant's intention to use a trademark. Once this application is filed, the owner obtains the benefits of registration. The benefits are lost, however, if the owner does not use the mark in business within six months of registration. Further protection can be obtained by filing a formal application for a trademark. The application must include a drawing of the trademark and a filing fee, ranging from $275 to $375, depending on how the application is filed. (It's cheaper to file electronically.) After a trademark application is filed, an examining attorney at the USPTO determines if the trademark can be registered. It currently takes about 10 months to get a trademark registered through the USPTO.

Copyrights

A **copyright** is a form of intellectual property protection that grants to the owner of a work of authorship the legal right to determine how the work is used and to obtain the economic benefits from the work.[22] The work must be in a tangible form, such as a book, operating manual, magazine article, musical score, computer software program, or architectural drawing. If something is not in a tangible form, such as a speech that has never been recorded or saved on a computer disk, copyright law does not protect it.

LEARNING OBJECTIVE

4. Define a copyright and identify what a copyright can protect.

Businesses typically possess a treasure trove of copyrightable material, as illustrated earlier in Table 12.1. A work does not have to have artistic merit to be eligible for copyright protection. As a result, things such as operating manuals, advertising brochures, and training videos qualify for protection. The Copyright Revision Act of 1976 governs copyright law in the United States. Under the law, an original work is protected automatically from the time it is created and put into a tangible form, whether it is published or not. The first copyright in the United States was granted on May 31, 1790, to a Philadelphia educator named John Barry for a spelling book.

What Is Protected by a Copyright?

Copyright laws protect "original works of authorship" that are fixed in a tangible form of expression. The primary categories of material that can be copyrighted follow:

- **Literary works:** Anything written down is a literary work, including books, poetry, reference works, speeches, advertising copy, employee manuals, games, and computer programs. Characters found in literary works are protectable if they possess a high degree of distinctiveness. A character that looks and acts like Garfield, the cartoon cat, would infringe on the copyright that protects Garfield.
- **Musical compositions:** A musical composition, including any accompanying words, that is in a fixed form (e.g., a musical score, CD, or an MP3 file) is protectable. The owner of the copyright is usually the composer and possibly a lyricist. **Derivative works**, which are works that are new renditions of something that is already copyrighted, are also copyrightable. As a result of this provision, a musician who performs a unique rendition of a song written and copyrighted by Miley Cyrus, Katy Perry, or Bruno Mars, for example, can obtain a copyright on his or her effort. Of course, each of these artists would have to consent to the infringement on its copyright of the original song before the new song could be used commercially, which is a common way that composers earn extra income.
- **Computer software:** In 1980, Congress passed the **Computer Software Copyright Act**, which amended previous copyright acts. Now, all forms of computer programs are protected.

■ **Dramatic works:** A dramatic work is a theatrical performance, such as a play, comedy routine, newscast, movie, or television show. An entire dramatic work can be protected under a single copyright. As a result, a dramatic work such as a television show doesn't need a separate copyright for the video and audio portions of the show.

■ **Pantomimes and choreographic works:** A pantomime is a performance that uses gestures and facial expressions rather than words to communicate a situation. Choreography is the arrangement of dance movements. Copyright laws in these areas protect ballets, dance movements, and mime works.

■ **Pictorial, graphic, and sculptural works:** This is a broad category that includes photographs, prints, art reproductions, cartoons, maps, globes, jewelry, fabrics, games, technical drawings, diagrams, posters, toys, sculptures, and charts.

Other categories of items covered by copyright law include motion pictures and other audiovisual works, sound recordings, and architectural works.

Copyright law provides broad protection for authors and the creators of other types of copyrightable work. The most common mistake entrepreneurs make in this area is not thinking broadly enough about what they should copyright.

Exclusions from Copyright Protection

There are exclusions from copyright protection. The main exclusion is that copyright laws cannot protect ideas. For example, an entrepreneur may have the idea to open a soccer-themed restaurant. The idea itself is not eligible for copyright protection. However, if the entrepreneur writes down specifically what the soccer-themed restaurant will look like and how it would operate, that description is copyrightable. The legal principle describing this concept is called the **idea–expression dichotomy**. An idea is not copyrightable, but the specific expression of an idea is.

Other exclusions from copyright protection include facts (e.g., population statistics), titles (e.g., *Introduction to Entrepreneurship*), and lists of ingredients (e.g., recipes).

How to Obtain a Copyright

As mentioned, copyright law protects any work of authorship the moment it assumes a tangible form. Technically, it is not necessary to provide a copyright notice or register work with the U.S. Copyright Office to be protected by copyright legislation. The following steps can be taken, however, to enhance the protection offered by the copyright statutes.

First, copyright protection can be enhanced for anything written by attaching the copyright notice, or "**copyright bug**" as it is sometimes called. The bug—a "c" inside a circle—typically appears in the following form: © [first year of publication] [author or copyright owner]. Thus, the notice at the bottom of a magazine ad for Dell Inc.'s computers in 2016 would read, "© 2016 Dell Inc." By placing this notice at the bottom of a document, an author (or company) can prevent someone from copying the work without permission and claiming that they did not know that the work was copyrighted. Substitutes for the copyright bug include the word "Copyright" and the abbreviation "Copr."

Second, further protection can be obtained by registering a work with the U.S. Copyright Office. Filing a simple form and depositing one or two samples of the work with the U.S. Copyright Office completes the registration process. The need to supply a sample depends on the nature of the item involved.

Obviously, one could not supply one or two samples of an original painting. The current cost of obtaining a copyright is $35 if filed electronically and $55 if filed on paper. Although the $35 fee seems modest, in many cases it is impractical for a prolific author to register everything he or she creates. In all cases, however, it is recommended that the copyright bug be attached to copyrightable work and that registration be contemplated on a case-by-case basis. A copyright can be registered at any time, but filing promptly is recommended and makes it easier to sue for copyright infringement.

Copyrights last a long time. According to current law, any work created on or after January 1, 1978, is protected for the life of the author plus 70 years. For works made for hire, the duration of the copyright is 95 years from publication or 120 years from creation, whichever is shorter. For works created before 1978, the duration times vary, depending on when the work was created. After a copyright expires, the work goes into the public domain, meaning it becomes available for anyone's use.

Copyright Infringement

Copyright infringement is a growing problem in the United States and in other countries, with estimates of the costs to owners at more than $25 billion per year. For example, less than a week after the film was released in the United States, bootleg video discs of the original Harry Potter movie were reported to be for sale in at least two Asian countries. Taking this a step further, we note that a recent study showed that as of 2013, Internet infringement in the entertainment industry "accounts for almost one-fourth of all bandwidth in North America, Europe and Asia."[23] **Copyright infringement** occurs when one work derives from another, is an exact copy, or shows substantial similarity to the original work. To prove infringement, a copyright owner is required to show that the alleged infringer had prior access to the copyrighted work and that the work is substantially similar to the owner's.

There are many ways to prevent infringement. For example, a technique frequently used to guard against the illegal copying of software code is to

The rampant illegal downloading and sharing of music—copyright infringement—is a major challenge the music industry continues to struggle with. Hackers are always looking for new ways to skirt the law.

embed and hide in the code useless information, such as the birth dates and addresses of the authors. It's hard for infringers to spot useless information if they are simply cutting and pasting large amounts of code from one program to another. If software code is illegally copied and an infringement suit is filed, it is difficult for the accused party to explain why the (supposedly original) code included the birth dates and addresses of its accusers. Similarly, some publishers of maps, guides, and other reference works will deliberately include bits of phony information in their products, such as fake streets, nonexistent railroad crossings, and so on, to try to catch copiers. Again, it would be pretty hard for someone who copied someone else's copyrighted street guide to explain why the name of a fake street was included.[24]

Current law permits limited infringement of copyrighted material. Consider **fair use**, which is the limited use of copyrighted material for purposes such as criticism, comment, news reporting, teaching, or scholarship. This provision is what allows textbook authors to repeat quotes from magazine articles (as long as the original source is cited), movie critics to show clips from movies, and teachers to distribute portions of newspaper articles. The reasoning behind the law is that the benefit to the public from such uses outweighs any harm to the copyright owner. Other situations in which copyrighted material may be used to a limited degree without fear of infringement include parody, reproduction by libraries, and making a single backup copy of a computer program or a digital music file for personal use. Case 12.2, titled "Protecting Intellectual Property: Elvis's Memory and Intellectual Property Live On," focuses on a copyright infringement case in which the courts ruled that fair use was not being employed appropriately. A more recent case, involving GoldieBlox, a 2012 start-up, and the hip-hop band the Beastie Boys, also involved fair use. The case involved GoldieBlox using a Beastie Boys song in a video ad without obtaining the Beastie Boys' permission, and claiming fair use as justification. The case was closely followed by the media and is profiled in the nearby "What Went Wrong?" feature. It vividly portrays the types of legal entanglements that start-ups can get into if they don't understand or if they push the boundaries of intellectual property laws.

Copyright and the Internet

Every day, vast quantities of material are posted on the Internet and can be downloaded or copied by anyone with a computer and an Internet connection. Because the information is stored somewhere on a computer or Internet server, it is in a tangible form and probably qualifies for copyright protection. As a result, anyone who downloads material from the Internet and uses it for personal purposes should be cautious and realize that copyright laws are just as applicable for material on the Internet as they are for material purchased from a bookstore or borrowed from a library.

Copyright laws, particularly as they apply to the Internet, are sometimes difficult to follow, and it is easy for people to dismiss them as contrary to common sense. For example, say that a golf instructor in Phoenix posted a set of "golf tips" on his website for his students to use as they prepare for their lessons. Because the notes are on a website, anyone can download the notes and use them. As a result, suppose that another golf instructor in a different part of the United States or in a different country ran across the golf tips, downloaded them, and decided to distribute them to his students. Under existing law, the second golf instructor probably violated the intellectual property rights of the first. Arguably, he should have gotten permission from the first golf instructor before using the notes even if the website didn't include any information about how to contact the first instructor. To many people, this scenario doesn't make sense. The first golf instructor put his notes on a public website, didn't include

WHAT WENT WRONG?

GoldieBlox vs. Beastie Boys: The Type of Fight That No Start-up Wants to Be a Part Of

GoldieBlox: Web: www.goldieblox.com; Facebook: GoldieBlox; Twitter: @goldieblox
Beastie Boys: Web: www.beastieboys.com; Facebook: Beastie Boys; Twitter: @beastieboys

GoldieBlox is a toy company, launched in 2012, that introduces girls to the field of engineering. It was started by Debbie Sterling, an engineering student at Stanford, who was troubled by the lack of women in engineering and the lack of encouragement girls receive to go into math and science fields. "Goldie" is a smart young girl that Sterling made up. Each toy in the GoldieBlox series consists of a book, featuring Goldie, and a set of age-appropriate construction items, such as spools and ribbons. Girls play with the toy by helping Goldie solve problems by building things. For example, in GoldieBlox and the Spinning Machine, a toy in the series, players must help Goldie build a belt drive machine to help her dog, Nacho, chase his tail. The idea is to introduce girls to the fundamentals of engineering. GoldieBlox's toys have been picked up by multiple big-name stores, including Toys"R"Us and Target.

In fall 2013, GoldieBlox ran an online advertisement for its game "Princess Machine," featuring three young girls singing an altered version of the Beastie Boys 1987 song "Girls." The advertisement quickly went viral, attracting over eight million views on YouTube. The ad changed the song's lyrics to promote the notion that girls are capable of ambitious tasks. Some of the original lyrics, "Girls do the dishes," "Girls to clean up my room," "Girls to do the laundry," were replaced with "Girls to build a spaceship," "Girls to code the new app," "Girls to grow up knowing." If you'd like to see the ad, go to YouTube and type in GoldieBlox and Beastie Boys, and you can pick from one of many videos that replay and comment on the ad.

The Beastie Boys, who did not know about the ad until it came out, were not happy. When they objected to GoldieBlox's use of their song, claiming copyright infringement, GoldieBlox filed a preemptive lawsuit against the Beastie Boys, saying that the company had created a parody of the song, which constituted fair use. Fair use allows for the limited use of copyrighted material for purposes such as parody, criticism, comment, news reporting, and teaching. Consistent with the nature of parody, GoldieBlox said that it was trying to make fun of the Beastie Boys song for the purpose of breaking down stereotypes and encouraging young girls to engage in activities that challenge their intellect, particularly in the fields of science, technology, engineering, and math.

The Beastie Boys responded by voicing their support for GoldieBlox's overall message and efforts, but outlined, in an open letter, their objections to the video. Their objections were twofold. First, they argued that as creative as the video is, it was made to sell a product. Years ago, according to the letter, the group made a conscious decision not to permit its music or name to be used in product sales. Second, the letter referred to the fact that when they simply asked GoldieBlox how and why their song "Girls" had been used in an ad without their permission, they were sued. GoldixBlox responded to the letter by pulling the video and issuing an open letter of their own. The letter said that the video was made with the best of intentions, with the goal of transforming the song "Girls" into a powerful anthem for young women. They went on to say that although they believe the video falls under fair use, they would honor the Beastie Boys wishes and no longer use the video.

Despite the letter from GoldieBlox, in December 2013, the Beastie Boys filed a countersuit against the company, arguing that the video's use of the song didn't constitute fair use as the ad used "the Beastie Boys" musical composition "Girl" with lyrics modified to become a "jingle" to sell GoldieBlox products.

In March 2014, GoldieBlox and the Beastie Boys reached a settlement, in favor of the Beastie Boys. The settlement included the issuance of an apology by GoldieBlox and a stipulation that GoldieBlox would make payments, based on a percentage of its revenue, to one or more charities selected by the Beastie Boys that support science, engineering, and mathematics education for girls. Along with an apology, the company went on to say that in hindsight, they should have reached out to the Beastie Boys to secure the proper rights to the song bore using it in their ad. A follow-up article published by *The Guardian* reported details of GoldieBlox's settlement with the Beastie Boys. Along with the apology, the settlement requires GoldieBlox to pay $1 million to one or more charities of the Beastie Boys' choice, based on a percentage of yearly earnings, until the $1 million is paid.

(continued)

Questions for Critical Thinking

1. If the case hadn't been settled by GoldieBlox and the Beastie Boys and you had been asked to render a judgment on the case, would you have rendered a judgment in favor of GoldieBlox or the Beastie Boys? Explain your decision.
2. Briefly comment on how both sides handled the dispute.
3. What do we learn about fair use from the GoldieBlox-Beastie Boys dispute?

4. What do we learn about the process of launching and growing a firm, in general, from the GoldieBlox-Beastie Boys dispute?

Sources: S. Dredge, "GoldieBlox Agrees to Pay $1 Million in Beastie Boys Settlement," *The Guardian*, available at www.theguardian.com/technology/2014/may/13/goldieblox-beastie-boys-girls-settlement, posted on May 13, 2014, accessed on August 5, 2014; J. Newman, March 19, 2014, "GoldieBlox Apologizes to Beasties: 'We Have Learned a Valuable Lesson,'" *Rolling Stone*, March 19, 2014; M. Gibson, "Beastie Boys Settle Copyright Dispute with GoldieBlox," *Time*, March 19, 2014.

any information about how to obtain permission to use them, and didn't even include information about how he could be contacted. In addition, he made no attempt to protect the notes, such as posting them on a password-protected Web page. Still, intellectual property rights apply, and the second instructor runs the risk of a copyright infringement suit.

There are a number of techniques available for entrepreneurs and webmasters to prevent unauthorized material from being copied from a website. Password protecting the portion of a site containing sensitive or proprietary information is a common first step. In addition, there are a number of technical protection tools available on the market that limit access to or the use of online information, including selected use of encryption, digital watermarking (hidden copyright messages), and digital fingerprinting (hidden serial numbers or a set of characteristics that tend to distinguish an object from other similar objects).

Trade Secrets

LEARNING OBJECTIVE

5. Describe a trade secret and understand the common causes of trade secret disputes.

Most companies, including start-ups, have a wealth of information that is critical to their success but does not qualify for patent, trademark, or copyright protection. Some of this information is confidential and needs to be kept secret to help a firm maintain its competitive advantage. An example is a company's customer list. A company may have been extremely diligent over time tracking the preferences and buying habits of its customers, helping it fine-tune its marketing message and target past customers for future business. If this list fell into the hands of one or more of the company's competitors, its value would be largely lost, and it would no longer provide the firm a competitive advantage over its competitors.

A **trade secret** is any formula, pattern, physical device, idea, process, or other information that provides the owner of the information with a competitive advantage in the marketplace. Trade secrets include marketing plans, product formulas, financial forecasts, employee rosters, logs of sales calls, and laboratory notebooks. The medium in which information is stored typically has no impact on whether it can be protected as a trade secret. As a result, written documents, computer files, audiotapes, videotapes, financial statements, and even an employee's memory of various items can be protected from unauthorized disclosure.

Unlike patents, trademarks, and copyrights, there is no single government agency that regulates trade secret laws. Instead, trade secrets are governed by a patchwork of various state laws. The federal **Economic Espionage Act**, passed in 1996, does criminalize the theft of trade secrets. The **Uniform Trade Secrets Act**, which a special commission drafted in 1979, attempted to set nationwide standards for trade secret legislation. Although the majority of states have adopted the act, most revised it, resulting in a wide disparity among states in regard to trade secret legislation and enforcement.

What Qualifies for Trade Secret Protection?

Not all information qualifies for trade secret protection. In general, information that is known to the public or that competitors can discover through legal means doesn't qualify for trade secret protection. If a company passes out brochures at a trade show that are available to anyone in attendance, nothing that is in the brochure can typically qualify as a trade secret. Similarly, if a secret is disclosed by mistake, it typically loses its trade secret status. For example, if an employee of a company is talking on a cell phone in a public place and is overheard by a competitor, anything the employee says is generally exempt from trade secret protection. Simply stated, the general philosophy of trade secret legislation is that the law will not protect a trade secret unless its owner protects it first.

Companies can maintain protection for their trade secrets if they take reasonable steps to keep the information confidential. In assessing whether reasonable steps have been taken, courts typically examine how broadly the information is known inside and outside the firm, the value of the information, the extent of measures taken to protect the secrecy of the information, the effort expended in developing the information, and the ease with which other companies could develop the information. On the basis of these criteria, the strongest case for trade secret protection is information that is characterized by the following:

- Is not known outside the company
- Is known only inside the company on a "need-to-know" basis
- Is safeguarded by stringent efforts to keep the information confidential
- Is valuable and provides the company a compelling competitive advantage
- Was developed at great cost, time, and effort
- Cannot be easily duplicated, reverse engineered, or discovered

Trade Secret Disputes

Trade secret disputes arise most frequently when an employee leaves a firm to join a competitor and is accused of taking confidential information along. For example, a marketing executive for one firm may take a job with a competitor and create a marketing plan for the new employer that is nearly identical to the plan being worked on at the previous job. The original employer could argue that the marketing plan on which the departed employee was working was a company trade secret and that the employee essentially stole the plan and took it to the new job. The key factor in winning a trade secret dispute is that some type of theft or misappropriation must have taken place. Trade secrets can be lawfully discovered. For example, it's not illegal for one company to buy another company's products and take them apart to see how they are assembled. In fact, this is a relatively common practice, which is another reason companies continuously attempt to innovate as a means of trying to stay at least one step ahead of competitors.

A company damaged by trade secret theft can initiate a civil action for damages in court. The action should be taken as soon after the discovery of the theft as possible. In denying the allegation, the defendant will typically argue that the information in question was independently developed (meaning no theft took place), was obtained by proper means (such as with the permission of the owner), is common knowledge (meaning it is not subject to trade secret protection), or was innocently received (such as through a casual conversation at a business meeting). Memorization is not a defense. As a result, an employee of one firm can't say that "all I took from my old job to my new one was what's in my head" and claim that just because the information conveyed wasn't in written form, it's not subject to trade secret protection. If the courts rule in favor of the firm that feels its trade secret has been stolen, the firm can stop the offender from using the trade secret and obtain financial damages.

Trade Secret Protection Methods

Aggressive protection of trade secrets is necessary to prevent intentional or unintentional disclosure. In addition, one of the key factors in determining whether something constitutes a trade secret is the extent of the efforts to keep it secret. Companies protect trade secrets through physical measures and written agreements.

Physical Measures There are a number of physical measures firms use to protect trade secrets, from security fences around buildings, to providing employees access to file cabinets that lock, to much more elaborate measures. The level of protection depends on the nature of the trade secret. For example, although a retail store may consider its inventory control procedures to be a trade secret, it may not consider this information vital and may take appropriate yet not extreme measures to protect the information. In contrast, a biotech firm may be on the cusp of discovering a cure for a disease and may take extreme measures to protect the confidentiality of the work being conducted in its laboratories.

The following are examples of commonly used physical measures for protecting trade secrets:

- **Restricting access:** Many companies restrict physical access to confidential material to only the employees who have a "need to know." For example, access to a company's customer list may be restricted to key personnel in the marketing department.

- **Labeling documents:** Sensitive documents should be stamped or labeled "confidential," "proprietary," "restricted," or "secret." If possible, these documents should be secured when not in use. Such labeling should be restricted to particularly sensitive documents. If everything is labeled "confidential," there is a risk that employees will soon lose their ability to distinguish between slightly and highly confidential material.

- **Password protecting confidential computer files:** Providing employees with clearance to view confidential information by using secure passwords can restrict information on a company's computer network, website, or intranet. Companies can also write-protect documents to ensure that employees can read but not modify certain documents.

- **Maintaining logbooks for visitors:** Visitors can be denied access to confidential information by asking them to sign in when they arrive at a company facility, having them wear name badges that identify them as visitors, and always making sure they are accompanied by a company employee.

- **Maintain logbooks for access to sensitive material:** Many companies maintain logbooks for sensitive material and make their employees "check out" and "check in" the material.

- **Maintaining adequate overall security measures:** Commonsense measures are also helpful. Shredders should be provided to destroy documents as appropriate. Employees who have access to confidential material should have desks and cabinets that can be locked and secured. Alarms, security systems, and security personnel should be used to protect a firm's premises.

Some of these measures may seem extreme. On the other hand, we live in an imperfect world and, because of this, companies need to safeguard their information against both inadvertent disclosure and outright theft. Steps such as shredding documents may seem like overkill at first glance but may be very important in ultimately protecting trade secrets. Believe it or not, there have been a number of cases in which companies have caught competitors literally going through the trash bins behind their buildings looking for confidential information.

Written Agreements It is important for a company's employees to know that it is their duty to keep trade secrets and other forms of confidential information secret. For the best protection, a firm should ask its employees to sign nondisclosure and noncompete agreements, as discussed in Chapter 7.

Intellectual property, and the problems that underlie the need for intellectual property to be created, are important enough that firms have been started strictly for the purpose of helping companies solve problems and obtain the intellectual property that they need.

Conducting an Intellectual Property Audit

The first step a firm should take to protect its intellectual property is to complete an intellectual property audit. This is recommended for all firms, regardless of size, from start-ups to mature companies. An **intellectual property audit** is conducted to determine the intellectual property a company owns.

The following sections describe the reasons for conducting an intellectual property audit and the basic steps in the audit process. Some firms hire attorneys to conduct the audit, whereas others conduct the audit on their own. Once an audit is completed, a company can determine the appropriate measures it needs to take to protect the intellectual property that it owns and that is worth the effort and expense of protecting.

LEARNING OBJECTIVE

6. Explain what an intellectual property audit is and identify the two primary reasons entrepreneurial firms should complete this type of audit.

Why Conduct an Intellectual Property Audit?

There are two primary reasons for conducting an intellectual property audit. First, it is prudent for a company to periodically determine whether its intellectual property is being properly protected. As suggested by the contents of Table 12.6, intellectual property resides in every department in a firm, and it is common for firms to simply overlook intellectual property that is eligible for protection.

The second reason for a company to conduct an intellectual property audit is to remain prepared to justify its value in the event of a merger or acquisition. Larger companies purchase many small, entrepreneurial firms primarily because the larger company wants the small firm's intellectual property. When a larger company approaches, the smaller firm should be ready and able to justify its valuation.

The Process of Conducting an Intellectual Property Audit

The first step in conducting an intellectual property audit is to develop an inventory of a firm's existing intellectual property. The inventory should include the firm's present registrations of patents, trademarks, and copyrights. Also included should be any agreements or licenses allowing the company to use someone else's intellectual property rights or allowing someone else to use the focal company's intellectual property.

TABLE 12.6   Types of Questions to Ask When Conducting an Intellectual Property Audit

Patents	Copyrights
■ Are products under development that require patent protection?	■ Is there a policy in place regarding what material needs the copyright bug and when the bug is to be put in place?
■ Are current patent maintenance fees up to date?	■ Is there a policy in place regarding when copyrightable material should be registered?
■ Do we have any business methods that should be patented?	■ Is proper documentation in place to protect the company's rights to use the material it creates or pays to have created?
■ Do we own any patents that are no longer consistent with our business plan that could be sold or licensed?	■ Are we in compliance with the copyright license agreements into which we have entered?
■ Do our scientists properly document key discovery dates?	

Trademarks	Trade Secrets
■ Are we using any names or slogans that require trademark protection?	■ Are internal security arrangements adequate to protect the firm's intellectual property?
■ Do we intend to expand the use of trademarks in other countries?	■ Are employees who do not have a "need to know" routinely provided access to important trade secrets?
■ Do we need additional trademarks to cover new products and services?	■ Is there a policy in place to govern the use of nondisclosure and noncompete agreements?
■ Is anyone infringing on our trademarks?	■ Are company trade secrets leaking out to competitors?

The second step is to identify works in progress to ensure that they are being documented in a systematic, orderly manner. This is particularly important in research and development. As mentioned earlier, if two inventors independently develop essentially the same invention, the right to apply for the patent belongs to the person who invented the product first. Properly dated and witnessed invention logbooks and other documents help prove the date an invention was made.

The third step of the audit is to specify the firm's key trade secrets and describe how they are being protected. Putting this information in writing helps minimize the chance that if a trade secret is lost, someone can claim that it wasn't really a trade secret because the owner took no specific steps to protect it.

Chapter Summary

LO1. Intellectual property is any product of human intellect that is intangible but has value in the marketplace. It is called intellectual property because it is the product of human imagination, creativity, and inventiveness. Patents, trademarks, copyrights, and trade secrets are the major forms of intellectual property. A common mistake companies make is not thinking broadly enough when identifying their intellectual property assets. Almost all companies, regardless of size or age, have intellectual property worth protecting. But to protect this property, firms must first identify it. There are two rules of thumb for determining whether intellectual property is worth the time and expense of protecting. First, a firm should determine whether the intellectual property in question is directly related to its current competitive advantage or could facilitate developing future competitive advantages. Second, it's important to know whether the intellectual property has independent value in the marketplace.

LO2. A patent is a grant from the federal government conferring the right to exclude others from making, selling, or using an invention for the term of the patent. There are three types of patents—utility patents, design patents, and plant patents. The most common of these is the utility patent, which covers what we generally think of as new inventions. Design patents are concerned with the invention of new, original, and ornamental designs for manufactured products. The least common of the three patents—the plant patent—protects new plant varieties that can reproduce asexually. Obtaining a patent is a painstaking, six-step process that usually requires the help of a patent attorney. A patent can be sold or licensed, which is a common strategy for entrepreneurial firms.

LO3. A trademark is any word, name, symbol, or device that is used to identify the source or origin of products or services and to distinguish those items from others. Trademarks, service marks, collective marks, and certification marks are the four types of trademarks. Trademark law is far-reaching, helping businesses be creative in drawing attention to their products and services. Examples of marks that can be protected include words, numbers and letters, designs and logos, sounds, fragrances, shapes, and colors. Immoral or scandalous matter, deceptive matter, descriptive marks, and surnames are ineligible for trademark protection. Entrepreneurs follow three steps to select and register a trademark: (1) select an appropriate trademark, (2) perform a trademark search, and (3) create rights in the trademark.

LO4. A copyright is a form of intellectual property protection that grants to the owner of a work of authorship the legal right to determine how the work is used and to obtain the economic benefits associated with using the work. Thus, copyright law protects original works of authorship that are fixed in a tangible form of expression. This is a broad definition and means that almost anything a company produces that can be written down, recorded, or videotaped or that takes a tangible form itself (such as a sculpture) is eligible for copyright protection. Examples of copyrightable material include literary works, musical compositions, dramatic works, and pictorial, graphic, and sculptural works.

LO5. Unlike patents, trademarks, and copyrights, there is not a single government agency that regulates trade secret laws. Instead, a trade secret (which is any formula, pattern, physical device, idea, process, or other information that provides the owner with a competitive advantage in the marketplace) is governed by a patchwork of various state laws. The federal Economic Espionage Act does criminalize the theft of trade secrets. Trade secret disputes arise most frequently when an employee leaves a firm to join a competitor and is accused of taking confidential information along. Firms protect their trade secrets through both physical measures and written agreements. Firms use a number of physical measures to protect their trade secrets. These include restricting access, labeling documents, password protecting computer files, maintaining logbooks for visitors, and maintaining adequate overall security measures.

LO6. There are two primary reasons for conducting an intellectual property audit. First, it is prudent for a company to periodically assess the intellectual property it owns to determine whether it is being properly protected. Second, a firm should conduct a periodic intellectual property audit to remain prepared to justify its value in the event of a merger or acquisition.

Key Terms

assignment of invention
   agreement, **433**
business method patent, **432**
certification marks, **440**
collective marks, **439**
Computer Software Copyright
   Act, **443**
copyright, **443**
copyright bug, **444**
copyright infringement, **445**
derivative works, **443**
design patents, **433**

Economic Espionage Act, **448**
fair use, **446**
idea–expression dichotomy,
   444
intellectual property, **427**
intellectual property
   audit, **451**
intent-to-use trademark
   application, **442**
Lanham Act, **440**
one year after first use
   deadline, **432**

patent, **430**
patent infringement, **436**
plant patents, **433**
provisional patent application,
   436
secondary meaning, **442**
service marks, **439**
trademark, **436**
trade secret, **448**
Uniform Trade Secrets
   Act, **448**
utility patents, **432**

Review Questions

12-1. What distinguishes intellectual property from other types of property, such as land, buildings, and inventory?

12-2. What are the two primary rules for determining whether intellectual property protection should be pursued for a particular intellectual asset?

12-3. What are the four key forms of intellectual property? What are the common mistakes that firms make with regard to intellectual property?

12-4. What are the major differences between utility patents and design patents? Provide an example of each.

12-5. What is a business method patent? Provide an example of a business method patent. How can having such a patent provide a firm a competitive advantage in the marketplace?

12-6. Give an example of a design patent. How can having a design patent provide a firm a competitive advantage in the marketplace?

12-7. What is a patent infringement? How does this take place? Can you identify a few exclusions from trademark protection?

12-8. What are the six steps in applying for a patent?

12-9. What is a trademark? How can trademarks help a firm establish a competitive advantage in the marketplace?

12-10. What are the three steps involved in selecting and registering a trademark?

12-11. What are the four types of trademarks available to an entrepreneur? What are the items that can be trademarked by firms?

12-12. What is a copyright?

12-13. In the context of copyright law, what is meant by the term *derivative work*?

12-14. What are the categories protected under copyright laws?

12-15. What is a copyright bug? Where would one expect to find the bug, and how is it used?

12-16. What is meant by the phrase *copyright infringement*? Would you characterize copyright infringement as a minor or as a major problem in the United States and in other countries? Explain.

12-17. What is a trade secret? Provide an example of a trade secret. How might the trade secret you identified help a firm establish a competitive advantage in the marketplace?

12-18. Why do trade secret disputes normally take place in an organization?

12-19. What types of physical measures do firms take to protect their trade secrets?

12-20. What are the two primary purposes of conducting an intellectual property audit? What risks does a company run if it doesn't periodically conduct an intellectual property audit?

Application Questions

12-21. Imagine you're about to attend a one-day seminar dealing with intellectual property law, and you contact a friend of yours who is in the process of starting a business to urge her to attend the seminar with you. She says to you, "I'm really busy because I'm just about to launch my start-up, so I'll have to pass. If they offer the same seminar next year, I'll go with you then." How would you respond to your friend?

12-22. In a group of two, list 30 products and services in your university that should be protected under the intellectual property law. Categorize the list under the three forms, namely, patent, copyright, and trademark. Present in class.

12-23. Tyler Simms just invented a new product that he is convinced is unique and will make him wealthy. The product is a toothbrush with a tube of toothpaste attached to the handle. Tyler is anxious to file a patent application on the product, but when he tells you about the idea, you say—"Whoa, let's do a preliminary patent application search first to see if someone else has already patented this idea." What do you find when you help Tyler with the preliminary search?

12-24. You have been appointed as an IP consultant for a shoe manufacturing firm. Recently the managing director, Mr. Elton Grey, emailed to you inquiring about the patent application process. One of the employees in the company has invented a new product for their firm and Mr. Grey is not sure how to apply for the patent. Reply to his email.

12-25. Pam Tarver just opened an information technology consulting company and has thought for a long time about what to name it. She finally settled on the fictitious name Infoxx. Search the USPTO database to determine if the name Infoxx is available. Is it? If it is available, how should Pam go about obtaining a trademark on Infoxx, or any other name?

12-26. Patrick Mitch has recently started an advertising agency with 20 employees. He has prepared resources, such as company brochures, employee handbook, company tagline, training materials, and company website on his own with some help from his employees. When you paid him a visit in the office, he was proudly showing you his hard work and seeking your opinion on the outcome. As you were going through the documents, you noticed that he has not yet registered for any intellectual property protection. What is the common mistake firms make with regard to intellectual property?

12-27. Maggie Simpson has always admired her Grandmother Thompson's cooking and has considered putting together a cookbook titled *Grandma Thompson's Favorite Recipes*. Some of Grandma's recipes are truly original, and before she writes the book, Maggie would like to copyright several of the most original ones. Can she do this?

12-28. You just completed a three-day workshop on intellectual property law. On your way back home, you bumped into your ex-colleague and you mentioned to her that you have just completed an IP workshop. She is very interested as she is looking to know more about protection under the trademark law. She was planning to register the design, logo, name, and number for her laundry shop. How should she do this?

YOU BE THE VC 12.1 COMPANY: KaZAM Balance Bike

• Web: www.kazambikes.com • Facebook: http://www.facebook.com/KaZAM-Bikes • Twitter: @ MyKazambike

Business Idea: Create a bike that teaches kids how to ride without training wheels in a safe, enjoyable, and confidence-building manner.

Pitch: To teach their kids how to ride a bike, most parents choose pedaled bikes with training wheels. While training wheels may seem to be the easiest approach, they do not teach kids balance or proper bicycle steering. A bike with training wheels may even be dangerous since it can tip over if a child turns a corner too quickly or rides on uneven ground. In addition, by not teaching balance, when the training wheels come off a child has yet to learn the most important part of riding a bike.

KaZAM bikes offer a quick, safe, and enjoyable alternative. They are peddle-less bikes that kids propel with their feet on the ground (like a skateboard, but they use both feet). When they build up enough momentum to coast, they pull their feet off the ground and rest them on a patented foot platform. The advantage is that the bike teaches balance and steering. When a child lifts his feet off the ground and places them on the foot platform, he must maintain proper balance and center of gravity, similar to riding a traditional bike. KaZAM bikes teach coordination and balance and prepare kids to ride peddled bikes safely.

The KaZAM bike was created by friends John Lugo and Michael Wagner after Lugo watched his three-year-old try out a wooden European model several years ago. They are designed for three- to six-year-olds, which is the age most kids are when they learn to ride a bike.

While there are other balance bikes on the market, the KaZAM is the only one with the patented foot rest designed to teach perfect balance. Other balance bikes have foot pegs or require kids to drag their feet on the ground. The KaZAM bike has several nice design features. The seat releases quickly, so it can be easily adjusted as a child grows. The handlebars adjust forward and backward as well as up and down. This feature allows a smaller child to better reach the handlebars from a seated position. The bike has a classy look and is available in several colors. The smooth tire tread and steel spokes give the bike a smooth and fast ride.

On May 9, 2013, Mary Beth Lugo (co-creator John Lugo's wife) pitched KaZAM on *Shark Tank* (Season 4, Episode 424). The entertaining episode ended with deals from sharks Mark Cuban and Barbara Corcoran. KaZAM is now branded as a Mark Cuban company. KaZAM bikes are sold online and in a growing number of bike shops and stores. The company has received a number of recognitions and awards, including the National Parent Center Seal of Approval and The Oppenheim Toy Portfolio Gold Seal Award.

12-29. Based on the material covered in this chapter, what questions would you ask the firm's founders before making your funding decision? What answers would satisfy you?

12-30. If you had to make your decision on just the information provided in the pitch and on the company's website, would you fund this company? Why or why not?

YOU BE THE VC 12.2 COMPANY: Wakoopa

• Web: www.wakoopa.com • Facebook: wakoopa • Twitter: @wakoopa

Business Idea: To establish a social network for software users to make it easier to track, share, and find software.

Pitch: Buying computer software online or from a store is often a tricky task, and keeping up to date with the latest releases can be confusing. There are thousands of new software programs every year and dozens of different operating systems. It can be difficult to get a completely impartial view. Although there are many online websites and magazines offering software reviews, there is no way of knowing how long the reviewer has used the program and what kind of program he or she usually likes.

Wakoopa was founded by two Dutch bloggers, Robert Gaal and Wouter Broekhof, to solve these problems and create a social network for software users.

Wakoopa's sign-up process is very simple: Users provide a user name and password and then are given a page with the download links for the Wakoopa tracking software. They then install a small application on their PC or Mac that works by performing a check every 15 minutes to track what software they use for a range of applications such as music players, office software, and photo editing, and how long they use it for. The information gathered can then be shared with friends, and personal profiles are automatically updated with any news, updates, or reviews on each specific application. It helps people decide whether or not to spend money on a program, because they can check out the statistics beforehand and see if the program is a one-hit wonder, or if it has proved its value to many users in the long term.

Wakoopa started as a social network in 2006. They had around 200,000 registered users who called themselves "Wakoopians." In 2010 Wakoopa began selling their tracking software as a market research tool, and as a result they closed down the social network in 2012.

In the first six months following its launch in April 2007, 17,000 people downloaded the Wakoopa tracking program. In the following year, the 17,000 doubled again, helping to generate some 250 million hours of unique and useful data about software, including lists of the most popular and most used software applications on a year-by-year basis. Early adopters of the site are primarily tech-savvy software developers and gamers, although there is evidence that the service is being used more widely by consumers who are happy to see their own desktop behavior become public. The payback is a lively social network for software and the opportunity to test the pulse of the most popular and unpopular new web applications.

In 2014, Wakoopa joined Netquest, the online fieldwork provider for the market research industry. They operate in Spain, Latin America, and Portugal. The goal is to integrate the tracking program with other applications. Wakoopa, however, does remain an independent company.

12-31. Based on the material covered in this chapter, what questions would you ask the firm's founders before making your funding decision? What answers would satisfy you?

12-32. If you had to make your decision on just the information provided in the pitch and on the company's website, would you fund this firm? Why or why not?

CASE 12.1

You Make the Call: Can a Company Patent How It Makes a Peanut Butter and Jelly Sandwich?

• *www.smuckers.com* • *www.albies.com*

Bruce R. Barringer, *Oklahoma State University*
R. Duane Ireland, *Texas A&M University*

Introduction

Here's a question that a panel of judges decided: Can a company patent how it makes a peanut butter and jelly sandwich? More specifically, in this instance, judges considered whether J. M. Smucker's method of making Uncrustables—which is a crustless peanut butter and jelly sandwich sealed inside soft bread—is worthy of legal protection against imitators. While the nature of this case is interesting, the legal rulings resulting from the case have broader implications. At stake is how generous the patent office should be in awarding patents—an issue with solid arguments on both sides.

There were actually two cases leading up to the case that resulted in the final verdict. The three cases are designated Round 1, Round 2, and Round 3 of Smucker's battle to patent the peanut butter and jelly sandwich.

The case involves the Smucker's Uncrustables sandwich. Uncrustables are found in the frozen food section of most grocery stores. They are 2-ounce peanut butter and jelly pockets that are sealed inside soft bread. They come in boxes of 4, 10, or 18 sandwiches. To make an Uncrustables ready to eat, the customer simply needs to let it thaw for 30–60 minutes after being taken out of the freezer.

Uncrustables were developed in 1995 by David Geske, of Fargo, North Dakota, and Len Kretchman, of Fergus Falls, Minnesota. The two started mass-producing them for Midwestern schools. Smucker's took note of their success and bought Geske and Kretchman's company in 1999. The purchase of the company included a general patent on crustless peanut butter and jelly sandwiches (Patent No. 6,004,596) that Geske and Kretchman had obtained.

Round 1: Smucker's Versus Albie's Foods

It wasn't long before Smucker's was defending its turf. In 2001, Smucker's ordered a much smaller firm, Albie's Foods, to stop selling its own crustless peanut butter and jelly sandwich. Albie's was selling the sandwich to a local school district. Albie's fought back, and the case was eventually dismissed. In its arguments, Albie's contended that the "pasty"—a meat pie with crimped edges, which the company saw its crustless peanut butter and jelly sandwich as a variation of—had been a popular food in northern Michigan since the immigration of copper and iron miners from England in the 1800s.

Round 2: Smucker's and the Patent Office

Stung by its experience with the case it brought against Albie's, Smucker's returned to the USPTO to try to get its general patent on crustless peanut butter and jelly sandwiches broadened as a means of being able to better defend the Uncrustables. The patent office rejected the application. The gist of the Smucker's argument

(continued)

was that its sandwich's sealed edge is unique, and its layering approach, which keeps the jelly in the middle of the sandwich, is one-of-a-kind and, as such, should be protected by law. The patent office disagreed with this view. It said that the crimped edge, which was one of the things Smucker's argued was unique about its sandwich, is similar to the crimped edges in ravioli and pie crusts. In addition, the patent office determined that putting jelly in the middle of a peanut butter and jelly sandwich is hardly unique, and as evidence cited a 1994 *Wichita* (Kansas) *Eagle* newspaper article on back-to-school tips that suggested just this approach.

Round 3: Smucker's Appeals

Smucker's appealed the patent office's decision to the U.S. Court of Appeals. During the court hearings the attorney representing Smucker's argued that the method for making the Uncrustables is unique because the two slices of bread are sealed by compression but are not "smashed" as they are in tarts or ravioli. (Recall that the patent office's original decision compared the process of making Uncrustables to that of making ravioli.) Smucker's further argued that it wouldn't be fair to let other companies simply copy the Uncrustables and benefit from the hard work of Smucker's scientists and the money that the company had invested to produce what it believed was a unique product. The Uncrustables is also a big seller for Smucker's. Moreover, sales of the product were up 22 percent at the end of the second quarter of 2013 compared to the same quarter one year earlier.

Broader Issues Involved

The Smucker's case was watched closely because of the broader issues involved. Critics of the U.S. patent process contend that the USPTO is too generous when awarding patents—a generosity that they say stifles innovation and drives up the cost for consumers. In the Smucker's case, the critics would argue that Smucker's shouldn't get the patent, because it will deter other food companies from making their own versions of peanut butter and jelly sandwiches, which will keep the price of the Uncrustables high. Advocates of the U.S. patent process argue the opposite—that patents motivate a company like Smucker's to invest in new-product innovation, and that absent patent protection, a company like Smucker's would have no incentive to develop a product like the Uncrustables.

The Court's Ruling

In mid-April 2005, after listening to all the arguments, the U.S. Court of Appeals ruled on whether Smucker's should get the patent it was requesting. Which way do you think the court ruled?

Discussion Questions

12-33. Go to the USPTO's website (www.uspto.gov) to look up Patent No. 6,004,596. Read the patent. After reading the patent, are you more inclined or less inclined to side with the Smucker's point of view?

12-34. Type "Uncrustables" into the Google search engine and look at the Uncrustables sandwich. Spend a little time reading about the Uncrustables on the Smucker's website. Again, after looking over the website, are you more inclined or less inclined to side with the Smucker's point of view?

12-35. In regard to the arguments espoused by the "critics" of the U.S. patent system and the "advocates" of the U.S. patent system, with which of the points of view do you agree? Thinking as an entrepreneur, use your own words to state why you think the critics or the advocates have a stronger point of view.

12-36. So what do you think happened? Do you think Smucker's did or did not receive the patent it was requesting?

Source: J. Soslan, "Uncrustables Still Growing at Torrid Pace," BakingBusiness.com, August 22, 2013; *Wall Street Journal* (Eastern Edition) by S. Munzo. Copyright 2005 by Dow Jones & Company, Inc.

CASE 12.2

Protecting Intellectual Property: Elvis's Memory and Intellectual Property Live On

• *Web: www.elvis.com* • *Facebook: Elvis Presley* • *Twitter: ElvisPresley*

Bruce R. Barringer, *Oklahoma State University*
R. Duane Ireland, *Texas A&M University*

Introduction

Savvy owners of intellectual property are always on the lookout for people who infringe on their intellectual property and take legal action when necessary. From 2002 to 2005, this scenario played out in a dispute involving a company named Passport Video and the copyright holders of music and videos produced by the late Elvis Presley.

Alleged Copyright Violation

Elvis, affectionately known as "The King" of rock and roll, was a musical icon for more than 20 years until his death on August 16, 1977. During his career Elvis was very prolific, and a wide variety of people own the copyrights to his music, videos, and films. In 2002, Passport Video, a video production company, produced a video documentary of Elvis's life titled *The Definitive Elvis*. The documentary, which included eight DVDs and 16 hours of video, focused on every aspect of Elvis's life and was priced at $99.00. Each episode contained shots of Elvis performing—many of which were taken from sources that are copyrighted and owned by Elvis Presley Enterprises or others. The shots included Presley home movies (owned by Elvis Presley Enterprises), material from *The Ed Sullivan Show*, and portions of *Ed Sullivan Rock & Roll Classics—Elvis Presley* (owned by SOFA Entertainment). Other material included shots from *The Elvis 1968 Comeback Special, Aloha from Hawaii*, and *Elvis in Concert*, which included songs written by Jerry Leiber and Mike Stoller. Passport did not obtain permission to use the material. As a result, the copyright holders, who caught wind of the production of the video, informed Passport Video that they objected to the production of the videos. Passport Video persisted, and in August 2003 the copyright holders sued Passport Video for unauthorized use of footage and copyright violations. They also asked for a preliminary injunction stopping Passport Video from selling any more copies of the documentary, which a U.S. District Court granted.

Passport's Defense

Passport mounted a defense, claiming that its use of the copyrighted material was fair use and that it had spent over $2 million producing and marketing the documentary. Fair use is a doctrine in U.S. copyright law that allows limited use of copyrighted material without requiring permission from the copyright holder. In general, the following uses are protected under this doctrine:

- Quotation of the copyrighted work for review or criticism or in a scholarly or technical work
- Use in a parody or satire
- Brief quotation in a news report
- Reproduction by a teacher or a student of a small part of the work to illustrate a lesson
- Incidental reproduction of a work in a newsreel or broadcast of an event being reported
- Reproduction of a work in a legislative or judicial proceeding

Passport Video also asserted that it interviewed more than 200 people to make the documentary and that only 5 to 10 percent of the length of the videos contained copyright material.

The Initial Decision, the Appeal, and the Final Decision

After listening to both sides, the U.S. District Court ruled in favor of the plaintiffs, saying that fair use didn't apply and Passport Video should have obtained the appropriate copyright permissions. The court stated that Passport Video released the videos with full knowledge that the plaintiffs did not consent to their production, and that Passport Video's documentary would mislead consumers (regarding its legal production) and damage the plaintiffs.

Passport persisted, appealing the decision to the Ninth Circuit Court of Appeals, arguing that its documentary of Elvis's life constituted scholarly research and should therefore be protected under fair use. In a 2005 ruling, the Ninth Circuit Court of Appeals disagreed and affirmed the ruling of the lower court. In its ruling, the court said, "The King is dead. His legacy, and those that wish to profit from it, remain very much alive." The court found that Passport's documentary was for commercial use rather than scholarly research, although the commercial nature of the project was not the deciding factor. Instead, the extent to which the copyrighted material was used tipped the decision

(continued)

for the court, which referred to the lower court's original assessment in its ruling. In its decision, the Ninth Circuit Court of Appeals, quoting from the decision of the lower court, said:

> *Passport's use of clips from television appearances, although in most cases of short duration, were repeated numerous times throughout the tapes. While using a small number of clips to reference an event for biographical purposes seems fair, using a clip over and over will likely no longer serve a biographical purpose. Additionally, some of the clips were not short in length. Passport's use of Elvis' appearance on* The Steve Allen Show *plays for over a minute and many more clips play for more than just a few seconds.*

The ruling barred Passport from selling any additional copies of *The Definitive Elvis*. It also outlined the limits of the fair use defense.

Subsequent to the ruling, the United States District Court in Los Angeles awarded plaintiffs Elvis Presley Enterprises, SOFA Entertainment, and songwriters Leiber and Stoller $2.8 million in monetary damages and attorneys' fees to be paid by Passport Entertainment and its owner, Dante Pugliese. Leiber and Stroller wrote "Hound Dog" and other Elvis hits. The ruling was considered to be a significant monetary judgment for a copyright infringement case.

Takeaways

In this case, the copyright law did exactly what it is designed to do: protect the legal owners of Elvis's material from copyright infringement. It also put publishers on notice that claiming fair use has limits and is not a blanket escape from paying copyright holders appropriate licensing fees. The ruling suggested that arguing fair use is more likely to hold water when used in conjunction with scholarly work or historical analysis than commercial projects.

Discussion Questions

12-37. Do you agree with the Ninth Circuit Court ruling? Why or why not?

12-38. Why do you think the copyright holders of Elvis's work objected to Passport's video series? How were they "harmed" by the production and sale of the videos?

12-39. Do you think Passport Video acted ethically and honestly and believed that its production was protected by fair use, or do you think the firm was simply using fair use as a way of avoiding paying royalties for the copyrighted material it was using?

12-40. What can entrepreneurs who are interested in trademark law learn from this case?

Sources: H. R. Cheeseman, *The Legal Environment of Business and Online Commerce*, 5th ed. (Upper Saddle River, NJ: Prentice Hall, 2007); Ruling by the United States District Court for the Central District of California in the case of *Elvis Presley Enterprises v. Passport Video*, November 6, 2004.

Endnotes

1. V. Bauman, "Kitchen Creativity and Business Savvy Essential Ingredients for Executive of the Year Tom Douglas," *Puget Sound Business Journal*, Dec. 21, 2012.

2. DripCatch home page, www.dripcatch.com, (accessed August 5, 2014).

3. B. Virgin, "Entrepreneurialism in Manufacturing? A College Student Shows How It's Done," *Washington Manufacturing Alert*, August 14, 2012.

4. T. Fischer and P. Ringler, "What Patents Are Used as Collateral? An Empirical Analysis of Patent Reassignment Data," *Journal of Business Venturing* 29, no. 5 (2014): 633–650; H. R. Cheesman, *The Legal Environment of Business and Online Commerce*, 7th ed. (Upper Saddle River, NJ: Prentice Hall, 2012).

5. A. Bhaskarabhalta and D. Hegde, "An Organizational Perspective on Patenting and Open Innovation," *Organization Science* (2014): in press; A. I. Poltorak and P. J. Lerner, *Essentials of Intellectual Property: Law, Economics, and Strategy*, 2nd ed. (New York: Wiley & Sons, 2011).

6. S. A. Abhayawansa, "A Review of Guidelines and Frameworks on External Reporting of Intellectual Capital," *Journal of Intellectual Capital* 15, no. 1 (2014): 100–141; M. Bani, A. Bani, M. Pourbagher, M. Taghavi, and M. Mansourian, "Measuring the Relationship Between Equity and Intellectual Capital," *Management Science Letters* 4, no. 4 (2014): 739–742.

7. A. Murray, "Protecting Ideas Is Crucial for U.S. Businesses," *Wall Street Journal*, November 9, 2005, A2.

8. "Top Ten Counterfeited Goods," available online at http://money.cnn.com/galleries/2012/pf/1202/gallery.counterfeit-goods/4.html, (accessed August 6, 2014).

9. U.S. Patent and Trademark Office, "What Are Patents, Trademarks, Servicemarks, and Copyrights?" www.uspto.gov, accessed August 7, 2014; F.-T. Mousa and R. Reed, "The Impact of Slack Resources on High-Tech IPOs," *Entrepreneurship Theory and Practice* 37, no. 5 (2013): 1123–1147.

10. T. M. Sichelman, "The Vonage Trilogy: A Case Study in 'Patent Bullying'," *Notre Dame Law Review*, 2014: in press.

11. Y. Chen, S. Pan, and T. Zhang, "(When) Do Stronger Patents Increase Continual Innovation?"

Journal of Economic Behavior & Organization 98, no. 1 (2014): 115–124.

12. G. Wolff, *The Biotech Investor's Bible* (New York: John Wiley & Sons, 2001).

13. U.S. Patent and Trademark Office, Performance and Accountability Report for Fiscal Year 2013.

14. U.S. Patent and Trademark Office, www.uspto.gov, (accessed August 8, 2014).

15. R. Stim, *Patent, Copyright & Trademark: An Intellectual Property Desk Reference*, 13th ed. (Berkeley, CA: NOLO, 2014).

16. U.S. Patent and Trademark Office, Performance and Accountability Report for Fiscal Year 2013.

17. P. Thurrott, "Start-Up Cleans Microsoft's Chimney in Court," *WindowsITPro*, April 14, 2005.

18. A. Gilbert, "Microsoft Settles Infringement Suit," *ZDNet*, July 14, 2005.

19. "Protection Money," *Fortune Small Business*, October 2005.

20. D. Orozco and J. Conley, "Shape of Things to Come," *Wall Street Journal*, May 12, 2008, R6.

21. G. Gelb and B. Gelb, "When Appearances Are Deceiving," *Wall Street Journal*, December 1, 2007, B1.

22. InvestorWords.com, "Definition of Copyright," www.investorwords.com, accessed August 7, 2014; C. Bjornskov and N. Foss, "How Strategic Entrepreneurship and the Institutional Context Drive Economic Growth," *Strategic Entrepreneurship Journal* 7, no. 1 (2013): 50–69.

23. T. Johnson, "NBCU-Backed Study: Online Piracy Continues to Rise Dramatically," *Variety*, September 13, 2013.

24. W. S. Strong, *The Copyright Book: A Practical Guide* (Cambridge, MA: MIT Press, 2014).

Getting Personal with BIG FISH PRESENTATIONS

Co-Founders

KENNY NGUYEN
Currently on leave from Louisiana State University

GUS MURILLO
BS, Biology, Louisiana State University, 2014

Dialogue with Kenny Nguyen

BEST ADVICE I'VE RECEIVED
It takes a day to create a bad reputation, but a lifetime to create a good one

MY FAVORITE SMARTPHONE APP
Mailbox

MY BIGGEST SURPRISE AS AN ENTREPRENEUR
Paying taxes. Learning the more you make, the more they take away.

BEST PART OF BEING A STUDENT
The student section for LSU football games

MY ADVICE FOR NEW ENTREPRENEURS
Don't outsource your core competency

MY BIGGEST WORRY AS AN ENTREPRENEUR
Plateauing on creativity

13

Preparing for and *Evaluating* the Challenges of Growth

BIG FISH PRESENTATIONS
Growing in a Cautious, Yet Deliberate Manner

• *Web: www.bigfishpresentations.com* • *Facebook: Big Fish Presentations* • *Twitter: @Bigfishpresco*

In early 2011, Kenny Nguyen and Gus Murillo attended an event taking place at Louisiana State University, the university they were attending. The speaker was the vice president of a *Fortune* 500 firm. Rather than being blown away by the presentation, they were shocked by how boring it was. The speaker plodded through what seemed like 200 PowerPoint slides, and left his audience uninspired. At that moment Nguyen, in particular, saw a niche. Was there an opportunity to start a company to help others create compelling and enriching presentations rather than boring ones? In the accompanying photo, Gus Murillo is on the left while Kenny Nguyen is on the right.

That was the genesis of Big Fish Presentations. Nguyen, who was soon joined by Murillo, got into the presentations training business. The initial service that Big Fish Presentations offered was to provide personalized presentation services on an end-to-end basis. Not only would Nguyen and Murillo help clients define the goals of their presentations and help them develop presentations that would engage and resonate with their specific audiences, but they would also develop the slides that accompanied the presentations and coach clients through practice presentation sessions. The first year Big Fish Presentations generated about $59,000 in revenue. That number was short of Nguyen and Murillo's goal of $100,000, but not bad for a company that started with less than $1,000 in funding.

Initially, Big Fish Presentation's clients came from in and around Baton Rouge, the home of Louisiana State University. Clients included Blue Cross Blue Shield of Louisiana, Raising Cane's, and Voodoo BBQ. From the outset, the company strived towards professionalism. For example, it started in the student incubator at the Louisiana Business and Technology Center on LSU's South Campus, but soon moved out of the incubator to develop its own identity and brand. Similarly, in working with clients, Big Fish Presentations is very focused on helping clients present themselves in new and innovative ways. One way it does this is by selecting the presentation platform that is most appropriate for a particular client, rather than automatically reverting to PowerPoint. As a result, Big Fish Presentation has created slide decks for clients in many different platforms, including Prezi, which builds customized slide presentations with photos, graphics, and other media. In Big Fish Presentation's view, the process of building an effective presentation includes five steps: design, storyboard, copy,

LEARNING OBJECTIVES

After studying this chapter you should be ready to:

1. Describe how firms can properly prepare for growth.

2. Discuss the six most common reasons firms pursue growth.

3. Explain the importance of being able to manage the stages of growth.

4. Describe the challenges of firm growth, particulalry those of adverse selection and moral hazard.

storytelling, and presenting. Big Fish Presentations excels in shepherding its clients through each step of the presentation process.

In regard to growth, Nguyen and Murillo are committed to growing Big Fish Presentations, but have opted to pursue a conservative and patient approach rather than a fast-paced strategy. In its second year of existence, the company's presentation and consulting services were supplemented by video production and design, which now represents 40 percent of the firm's revenue. The company maintains a high degree of self-awareness regarding what it's good at and what lies outside its areas of expertise, and that self-awareness guides its growth-related decisions. For example, the company's creative abilities have garnered some attention and client requests to pursue other graphic design or marketing outlets outside of their core competencies, but Big Fish Presentations does not offer those services. Instead, the company focuses intently on its three core services—presentation design, presentation consulting, and video design and production. The company has passed on some seemingly intriguing possibilities in order to remain true to its core priorities. For example, Nguyen and Murillo had the opportunity to audition for Shark Tank. Ultimately, they turned down the overture based on the recognition that the people who watch Shark Tank aren't part of their target clientele, and that they would rather self-fund Big Fish Presentation's growth than take investment capital to do so. Big Fish Presentations currently has three full-time employees, including Nguyen and Murillo, and seven part-time employees who are utilized on a project-by-project basis. Additional freelancers are employed when demand necessitates. Its client list has expanded considerably since its first year. Its clients now include Paramount Pictures, Cabela's, Mutual of Omaha, and a number of *Fortune* 500 companies.

In regard to managing the day-to-day challenges of growth, Nguyen and Murillo have taken concrete steps to make the process manageable. With respect to cash flow management, the company requires a 50 percent deposit when it retains a client. This practice effectively forces the client to finance half the costs of a project before final payment is received. Big Fish Presentations is also moving to a model where it tries to sell clients "packages" of services rather than a single service. This step is intended to lower the company's administrative overhead and boost sales by generating more income from each client. In regard to price stability, which refers to competitors trying to undercut a company's price, Nguyen and Murillo haven't struggled with this issue. Most of their clients see the value in what they offer, and there aren't many firms that offer the same expertise that Big Fish Presentations is selling. In regard to quality control, there is always a concern that as a company takes on more work, the amount of time they have to devote to each individual project decreases. Nguyen and Murillo have given this aspect of their business a lot of thought. There are two things they're doing to keep quality high as the number of projects grows. First, they've carefully documented the processes they used to produce output, so when they hire a freelancer to work on a job he or she can be brought up to speed quickly, and expectations and quality standards are clear. Second, they never accept a job where they believe, as Gus Murillo puts it, the "odds are stacked against them." What Murillo means by this statement is that they won't accept jobs with unrealistic deadlines, for example. Nguyen and Murillo have learned through experience not to put their company and employees in this type of undesirable situation.

As Big Fish Presentations moves forward, it will face additional challenges preparing for and managing growth. The company is currently contemplating several new initiatives that it feels are consistent with its core competencies and are a good fit for the company moving forward.

The Big Fish Presentations case is encouraging in that the company has gotten off to a good start and has achieved growth in a well-executed manner. Its true test will be whether it is able to achieve **sustained growth**, which is growth in both revenues and profits over a sustained period of time. Evidence shows that relatively few firms generate sustained and outstanding, profitable growth.[1] As evidence of this, consider *Inc.* magazine's Build 100 project. The study entailed collecting data on more than 100,000 U.S. midmarket companies (those with 85 to 999 employees) to study firm growth. Incredibly, the project found that fewer than 1.5 percent of the companies in the study achieve sustained growth, which was measured by increasing their number of employees every year from 2007 to 2012. The study found that a company's growth typically follows one of several patterns: (1) it might burst on the scene with years of expansion and then decelerate and decline, (2) it might grow in fits and starts, possibly in sync with the overall economy, (3) it might enjoy a brief boom and then plateau, or (4) it might achieve steady incremental growth repeated over time. The fourth option is the healthiest and the pattern that leads to sustained growth. "It's akin to Aesop's tortise and hare story," Gary Kunkle, the chief researcher on the project, remarked. "Slow and steady wins the race."[2]

Although challenging, most entrepreneurial ventures try to grow and see it as an important part of their ability to remain successful.[3] This sentiment was expressed by Hewlett-Packard (HP) co-founder David Packard, who wrote that while HP was being built, he and co-founder Bill Hewlett had "speculated many times about the optimum size of a company." The pair "did not believe that growth was important for its own sake" but eventually concluded that "continuous growth was essential" for the company to remain competitive.[4] When HP published a formal list of its objectives in 1996, one of the seven objectives was growth.[5]

The first part of the chapter focuses on preparing for growth, including a discussion of three specific areas on which a firm can focus to equip itself for growth. The second part of the chapter focuses on reasons for growth. Although sustained growth is almost always the result of deliberate intentions, a firm can't always choose its pace of growth. This section lists the seven primary reasons that motivate and stimulate business growth. The chapter's third section focuses on managing growth, which centers on knowing and managing the stages of growth. In the final section, we examine the challenges of growth, including the managerial capacity problem and the day-to-day challenges of growing a firm.

Preparing for Growth

LEARNING OBJECTIVE

1. Describe how firms can properly prepare for growth.

Most entrepreneurial firms want to grow. Especially in the short term, growth in sales revenue is an important indicator of an entrepreneurial venture's potential to survive today and be successful tomorrow. Growth is exciting and, for most businesses, is an indication of success. Many entrepreneurial firms have grown quickly, producing impressive results for their employees and owners as a result of doing so; consider Google, Dropbox, and Warby Parker, among others, as examples of this.

While there is some trial and error involved in starting and growing any business, the degree to which a firm prepares for its future growth has a direct bearing on its level of success.[6] This section focuses on three important things a business can do to prepare for growth.

Appreciating the Nature of Business Growth

The first thing that a business can do to prepare for growth is to appreciate the nature of business growth. Growing a business successfully requires preparation, good management, and an appreciation of the issues involved. The following are issues about business growth that entrepreneurs should appreciate.

Not All Businesses Have the Potential to Be Aggressive Growth Firms   The businesses that have the potential to grow the fastest over a sustained period of time are ones that solve a significant problem or have a major impact on their customers' productivity or lives. This is why the lists of fast-growing firms are often dominated by health care, technology, social media, and entertainment companies. These companies can potentially have the most significant impact on their customers' businesses or lives. This point is affirmed by contrasting the women's clothing store industry with the biotechnology industry. From 2009 to 2014, the average women's clothing store in the United States grew by 2.0 percent while the average biotechnology company grew by 5.5 percent.[7] While there is nothing wrong with starting and owning a women's clothing store, it's important to have a realistic outlook of how fast the business will likely grow. Even though an individual women's clothing store might get off to a fast start, as its gets larger, its annual growth will normally start to reflect its industry norm.[8]

A Business Can Grow Too Fast   Many businesses start fast and never let up, which stresses a business financially and can leave its owners emotionally drained. This sentiment is affirmed by Vipin Jain, the CEO of Retrevo, a consumer electronics company. Jain has started several companies. When asked what lessons he's learned as a serial entrepreneur, Jain replied:

> I think one thing (I've) learned is to not get carried away. Building a startup not only takes a good vision and a good market that you want to go after, but it also requires systematic execution. You can only run at a certain pace. Don't try to overrun yourself. Be conservative in your spending. Don't burn all the cash you have, because you need that. You need to be very, very conscientious about how your business grows and what kind of expenses you have to support your growth.[9]

Sometimes businesses grow at a measured pace and then experience a sudden upswing in orders and have difficulty keeping up. This scenario can transform a business with satisfied customers and employees into a chaotic workplace with people scrambling to push the business's product out the door as quickly as possible. The way to prevent this from happening is to recognize when to put the brakes on and have the courage to do it. This set of circumstances played out early in the life of The Pampered Chef, a company that sells kitchen utensils through home parties. Just about the time the company was gaining serious momentum, it realized that it didn't have a sufficient quantity of products in its inventory to serve the busy Christmas season. This reality posed a serious dilemma. The Pampered Chef couldn't instantly increase its inventory (its vendors were all low in their own inventories and the company was small, so it couldn't make extraordinary demands on its vendors), yet it didn't want to discourage its home consultants from making sales or signing up new consultants. One option was to institute a recruiting freeze (on new home consultants), which would slow the rate of sales. Doris Christopher, the company's founder, remembers asking others for advice. Most advised against instituting a recruiting freeze, arguing that the lifeblood of any direct sales organization is to sign up new recruits. In the end, the company decided to institute the freeze and slowed its sales enough to fill all orders on time during the holiday season. The freeze was lifted the following January, and the number of The Pampered Chef recruits soared. Reflecting on the decision, Doris Christopher later wrote:

> Looking back, the recruiting freeze augmented our reputation with our sales force, customers, and vendors. People saw us as an honest company that was trying to do the right thing and not overestimating our capabilities.[10]

Other businesses have faced similar dilemmas and have sometimes made the right call, and other times haven't. The overarching point is that growth must be handled carefully. As we emphasize throughout this chapter, a business can only grow as fast as its infrastructure allows. Table 13.1 provides a list of 10 warning signs that a business is growing too fast.

One company that almost succumbed to the challenges of rapid growth is Threadless, as chronicled in the nearby "Partnering for Success" feature. At one point early in its life, Threadless was growing so quickly that it's back-end operations couldn't keep up, and it was experiencing multiple problems. Fortunately, the company brought on a strategic partner at just the right time to help correct the problems. The feature is a vivid illustration of how vulnerable even the most seemingly successful firms are to the rigors of rapid growth.

Business Success Doesn't Always Scale   Unfortunately, the very thing that makes a business successful might suffer as the result of growth. This is what business experts often mean when they say growth is a "two-edged sword." For example, businesses that are based on providing high levels of individualized service often don't grow or scale well. For example, an investment brokerage service that initially provided high levels of personalized attention can quickly evolve into providing standard or even substandard service as it adds customers and starts automating its services. Its initial customers might find it harder to get individualized service than it once was and start viewing the company as just another ordinary business.

There is also a category of businesses that sell high-end or specialty products that earn high margins. These businesses typically sell their products through venues where customers prioritize quality over price. These businesses can grow, but only at a measured pace. If they grow too quickly, they can lose the "exclusivity" they are trying to project, or can damage their special appeal. Fashion clothing boutiques often limit the number of garments they sell in a certain size or color for a similar reason. Even though they know they could sell more of a particular blouse or dress, they deliberately limit their sales so their customers don't see each other wearing identical items.

Staying Committed to a Core Strategy

The second thing that a business can do to prepare for growth is to stay committed to a core strategy. As discussed in Chapter 4, an important part of a firm's business model is its core strategy, which defines how it competes relative to its rivals. A firm's core strategy is largely determined by its **core competencies**, or what it does particularly well.[11] While this insight might seem self-evident, it's important that a business not lose sight of its core strategy as it prepares for growth. If a business becomes distracted or starts pursuing every opportunity

TABLE 13.1   10 Warning Signs That a Business Is Growing Too Fast

- Borrowing money to pay for routine operating expenses
- Extremely tight profit margins
- Over-stretched staff
- Declining product quality
- E-mail and text messages start going unanswered
- Customer complaints are up
- Employees dread coming to work
- Productivity is falling
- Operating in a "crisis" mode becomes the norm rather than the exception
- Those working with the business's financial structure are starting to worry

PARTNERING FOR SUCCESS

How Threadless Averted Collapse by Bringing on a Partner with Back-End Operational Expertise

Web: www.threadless.com; Facebook: Threadless; Twitter: @threadless

Threadless is a community-centered T-shirt design site started in 2000 by Jack Nickell and Jacob DeHart with $1,000 of their own money. It's called "Threadless" because it started as a thread on the Dreamlist message board. Dreamlist was a place where designers could exchange information, and in November 2000, Nickell hosted a T-shirt design contest and let fellow designers pick the winner. The contest was such a hit that Nickell and DeHart decided to move it off the Dreamlist message board for the purpose of creating a website where future contests could be hosted.

Threadless was run as a hobby for most of 2001 through 2003, until Nickell and DeHart quit their jobs to start a Web consultancy firm and focus more intently on Threadless. The income they earned from Threadless quickly overshadowed what they were earning from the consultancy business, so in January 2004, they started focusing on Threadless full time. The way Threadless works is that each week about 1,000 designs are submitted online and are put up to a public vote. After seven days the Threadless staff reviews the top-scoring designs. Based on the average score and community feedback, about 10 designs are selected each week. The designs are then printed on clothing and other products and are sold through Threadless's online store and at their retail store in Chicago. Designers whose work is chosen receive $2,000 in cash and $500 in Threadless gift cards. Each time a design is reprinted, the designer received an additional $500.

Threadless grew quickly. In 2005, it sold over one million T-shirts—all designed by the Threadless community. Nickell and DeHart were experiencing difficulties managing the growth. The firm's back-end operations were the main problem. Orders weren't going out on time, the Threadless website was down intermittently, and some months the company would max out the amount it could process through its merchant account and would have to stop taking orders. Worst of all, in 2005, T-shirts that were ordered in anticipation of Christmas weren't delivered until the following January.

Rather than collapsing under the weight of these problems, Nickell and DeHart took bold action. They sold a minority interest in Threadless to Insight Partners, a venture capital firm. They could have hired a consulting firm with operational expertise, but they wanted a partner that would have a long-term interest in Threadless's success. Insight Partners turned out to be an ideal choice. At that time, Insight had a program called Insight Onsight,

where it would send personnel to evaluate its portfolio companies' operations. Insight sent personnel to evaluate Threadless's back-end operations and make recommendations. It moved Threadless's website to a new host, which was better equipped to help Threadless scale its website's traffic and sales. It also helped Threadless improve the functioning of its warehouse and fulfillment operations. Threadless's problems were smoothed out and it moved forward. It hasn't experienced significant technical or order fulfillment glitches since.

In 2008, Threadless was featured on the cover of *Inc.* as "The Most Innovative Small Company in America." It is credited with creating the online buiness model referred to as "crowdsourcing." Crowdsourcing is the process of soliciting ideas or services from a large group of people, called the crowd, rather than from traditional employees. A number of companies now utilize the crowdsourcing model. Many advertise themselves as the "Threadless" of their industry.

Questions for Critical Thinking

1. Do you think Threadless would exist today if Nickell and DeHart hadn't taken decisive action in 2005 and brought Insight Partners into the company as a strategic investor? Why or why not?
2. Why do you think Nickell and DeHart wanted a strategic investor to help Threadless work through its operational problems rather than hire a consulting firm? Hiring a consulting firm wouldn't have required Threadless to surrender any equity.
3. Name at least two companies that are using crowdsourcing business models, similar to the model that Threadless pioneered in the early 2000s. How are the business models and the companies behind them performing?
4. Look at the "You Be the VC" feature at the end of Chapters 13 and 14. Which company do you think has the highest likelihood of experiencing rapid growth? What can that company do to avoid the problems that Threadless experienced?

Sources: Threadless, www.threadless.com (accessed June 25, 2014); A. Warner and J. Nickell, "Threadless: Growing a Design Community. Selling Millions of T-Shirts with Jack Nickell," Mixergy podcast, www.mixergy.com, orginally posted on November 11, 2010, accessed July 3, 2014.

for growth that presents itself, the business can easily stray into areas where it finds itself at a competitive disadvantage. For example, eBags, an online merchant that specializes in selling handbags, luggage, and backpacks, at one point acquired a website that sells shoes. After three years, it sold the site (Shoedini.com) to Zappos after concluding that the shoe business was too far of a stretch from the company's core strategy and its core competencies.

The way most businesses typically evolve is to start by selling a product or service that is consistent with their core strategy and then increase sales by incrementally moving into areas that are different from, but are related to, their strengths and core capabilities. This is how Zappos opeerates. The company started by selling shoes and has gradually expanded into clothing, bags, housewares, and many other products. The success of its new product lines will be determined largely by whether the company's existing core competencies are sufficient to profitably sell these items. If they aren't, then Zappos will have to develop or acquire additional core competencies, or it is likely to struggle to effectively manage its growth.

A parable that helps affirm why sticking to a core strategy is so important is provided by Jim Collins in his book *Good to Great*. In the book, Collins retells the fable of the fox and the hedgehog, which was originally told by Isaiah Berlin. According to the fable, because he is sly, cunning, and strong, everyone thinks the fox is better than the hedgehog. All the lowly hedgehog knows how to do is one thing—curl up in a ball, with its spikes out, to deter intruders. The ironic thing is that whatever the fox does, and no matter how many of its 100 tricks it tries to use, the hedgehog always wins, because it knows how to do one thing well—roll up and stick its spikes out. In *Good to Great*, Collins says businesses that are successful over the long haul are more like hedgehogs than foxes. Rather than moving swiftly in all directions, like foxes, successful businesses keep their heads down and do one thing particularly well. Like the hedgehog, they see what is essential and ignore the rest.[12]

Planning for Growth

The third thing that a firm can do to prepare for growth is to establish growth-related plans.[13] This task involves a firm thinking ahead and anticipating the type and amount of growth it wants to achieve.

The process of writing a business plan, covered in Chapter 6, greatly assists in developing growth-related plans. A business plan normally includes a detailed forecast of a firm's first three to five years of sales, along with an operations plan that describes the resources the business will need to meet its projections. Even though a business will undoubtedly change during its first three to five years, it's still good to have a plan. Many businesses periodically revise their business plans as a foundation for helping them guide their growth-related decisions.

It's also important for a business to determine, as early as possible, the strategies it will choose to employ as a means of pursuing growth. For example, Proactiv, the acne medicine company, is a single-product company and has grown by steadily increasing its domestic sales, introducing its products into foreign countries, and by encouraging nontraditional users of acne medicine, like adult males, to use its product. Proactiv's decision to stick with one product and to avoid growing through initiatives such as acquisitions and licensing has allowed the company to focus on marketing and building its brand. In contrast, uShip, the subject of Case 13.2, has expanded into a number of new product lines since it launched in 2003. It is still primarily an online marketplace for shipping services, but has grown through a variety of avenues. For example, in 2011 eBay Motors began incorporating uShip's Shipping Price Estimator as a vehicle shipping option within all of its U.S. car, motorcycle, and power sports listings.[14]

It is important that a business establish growth-related plans and objectives. Here, the two founders of a young entrepreneurial firm are charting their growth plans for several years in the future.

Ken Seet/Corbis

On a more personal level, a business owner should step back and measure the company's growth plans against his or her personal goals and aspirations. The old adage, "Be careful what you wish for," is as true in business as it is in other areas of life. For example, if a business has the potential to grow rapidly, the owner should know what to expect if the fast-growth route is chosen. Fast growth normally implies a quick pace of activity, a rapidly rising overhead, and a total commitment in terms of time and attention on the part of the business owners. The upside is that if the business is successful, the owner will normally do very well financially. The downside is long hours and time away from family. Commenting on the balancing act that many fast-growth entrepreneurs experience, Felix Lluberes, president and co-founder of Position Logic, a GPS tracking software company, said:

> "The biggest challenge (in growing a company) is keeping your family happy and constantly deciding when to miss important family events because work demands it. Working hard is not a sacrifice as long as you achieve your ultimate objective."[15]

The trade-offs implied by this scenario are acceptable to some business owners and aren't to others.

Reasons for Growth

Although sustained, profitable growth is almost always the result of deliberate intentions and careful planning, firms cannot always choose their pace of growth. A firm's **pace of growth** is the rate at which it is growing on an annual basis. Sometimes firms are forced into a high-growth mode sooner than they would like. For example, when a firm develops a product or service that satisfies a need for many customers and orders roll in very quickly, it must adjust quickly or risk faltering. In other instances, a firm experiences unexpected competition and must grow to maintain its market share.

This section examines the six primary reasons firms try to grow to increase their profitability and valuation, as depicted in Figure 13.1.

- Economies of scale
- Economies of scope
- Market leadership
- Influence, power, and survivability
- Need to accommodate the growth of key customers
- Ability to attract and retain talented employees

FIGURE 13.1
Appropriate Reasons
for Firm Growth

Capturing Economies of Scale

Economies of scale are generated when increasing production lowers the average cost of each unit produced. Economies of scale can be created in service firms as well as traditional manufacturing companies.[16] This phenomenon occurs for two reasons. First, if a company can get a discount by buying component parts in bulk, it can lower its variable costs per unit as it grows larger. **Variable costs** are the costs a company incurs as it generates sales. Second, by increasing production, a company can spread its fixed costs over a greater number of units. **Fixed costs** are costs that a company incurs whether it sells something or not. For example, in a manufacturing setting, it may cost a company $10,000 per month to air-condition its factory. The air-conditioning cost is fixed; cooling the factory will cost the same whether the company produces 10 or 10,000 units per month. In a service setting, a hotel's registration areas, restaurants, and other areas must be air-conditioned regardless of the number of rooms that have been filled for a particular evening.

A related reason firms grow is to make use of unused resources such as labor capacity and a host of others. For example, a firm may need exactly 2.5 full-time salespeople to fully cover its trade area. Because a firm obviously can't hire 2.5 full-time salespeople, it may hire 3 salespeople and expand its trade area.[17]

Capturing Economies of Scope

Economies of scope are similar to economies of scale. With **economies of scope**, the advantage a firm accrues comes through the scope (or range) of a firm's operations rather than from its scale of production.[18] For example, a company's sales force may be able to sell 10 items more efficiently than 5 because the cost of travel and the salesperson's salary is spread out over 10 products rather than 5. Similarly, a company such as TOMS, the focus of Case 4.2, captures economies of scope in its advertising when the same feature is used to advertise TOMS shoes along with TOMS eyewear and TOMS coffee.

Market Leadership

Market leadership occurs when a firm holds the number one or the number two position in an industry or niche market in terms of sales volume. Many firms work hard to achieve market leadership, to realize economies of scale and economies of scope, and to be recognized as the brand leader. Being the market leader also permits a firm to use slogans such as "Number 1 App in the Apple App Store" in its promotions, helping it win customers and attract talented employees as well as business partners.

Influence, Power, and Survivability

Larger businesses usually have more influence and power than smaller firms in regard to setting standards for an industry, getting a "foot in the door" with major customers and suppliers, and garnering prestige. In addition, larger businesses can typically make a mistake yet survive more easily than entrepreneurial ventures. Commenting on this issue, Jack Welch, GE's former CEO, once said, "Size gives us another big advantage; our reach and resources enable us to go to bat more frequently, to take more swings, to experiment more, and unlike a small company, we can miss on occasion and get to swing again."[19]

A firm's capacity for growth affects its survival in additional ways. For example, a firm that stays small and relies on the efforts and motivation of its founder or a small group of people is vulnerable if those people leave the firm or lose their passion for the business. This reason was partly to blame for the failure of Prim, as profiled in Chapter 1. Prim failed in part because its founders lost interest in the business and decided to move on to other things. As a firm grows and adds employees, it's normally not as vulnerable to the loss of a single person or a small group of people's participation or passion for the business.

Need to Accommodate the Growth of Key Customers

Sometimes firms are compelled to grow to accommodate the growth of a key customer. For example, if Intel has a major account with an electronics firm buying a large number of its semiconductor chips, and the electronics firm is growing at a rate of 20 percent per year, Intel may have to add capacity each year to accommodate the growth of its customer or else risk losing some or all of its business.

Ability to Attract and Retain Talented Employees

The final reason that firms grow is to attract and retain high-quality personnel. It is natural for talented employees to want to work for a firm that can offer opportunities for promotion, higher salaries, and increased levels of responsibility. Growth is a firm's primary mechanism to generate promotional opportunities for employees, while failing to retain key employees can be very damaging to a firm's growth efforts. High turnover is expensive, and in knowledge-based industries in particular, such as biotechnology and software development, a company's number-one asset is the combined talent, training, and experience of its employees.[20] In less knowledge-intensive settings, turnover may not be as critical, but it is still costly. The American Management Association estimates that the cost of hiring and training a person earning $8 per hour varies from 25 percent to 200 percent of annual compensation.[21] Entrepreneurial ventures rarely have the excess financial capital needed to support the unfavorable relationship between employee hiring and turnover. However, when talented individuals leave a large company either voluntarily or through layoffs, entrepreneurial ventures have opportunities to hire people with skills the venture did not pay for them to develop.

Managing Growth

LEARNING OBJECTIVE

3. Explain the importance of being able to manage the stages of growth.

Many businesses are caught off guard by the challenges involved with growing their companies. One would think that if a business got off to a good start, steadily increased its sales, and started making money, it would get progressively easier to manage the growth of a firm. In many instances, just the opposite happens. As a business increases its sales, its pace of activity quickens, its resource needs increase, and the founders often find that they're busier than ever. Major challenges can also occur.[22] For example, a business might project its next year's sales and realize it will need more people and additional equipment to handle the increased workload. The new equipment might need to be purchased and the new people hired and trained before the increased business generates additional income. It's easy to imagine serious discussions among the members of a new venture's management team trying to figure out how that will all work out.

The reality is that a company must actively and carefully manage its growth for it to expand in a healthy and profitable manner. As a business grows and becomes better known, there are normally more opportunities that present themselves, but there are more things that can go wrong too. Many potential problems and heartaches can be avoided by prudently managing the growth process. This section focuses on knowing and managing the stages of growth. The final section in this chapter focuses on a related topic—the challenges of growth.

Knowing and Managing the Stages of Growth

The majority of businesses go through a discernable set of stages referred to as the organizational life cycle.[23] The stages, pictured in Figure 13.2, include introduction, early growth, continuous growth, maturity, and decline. Each stage must be managed differently. It's important for an entrepreneur to be familiar with these stages, along with the unique opportunities and challenges that each stage entails.

Introduction Stage This is the start-up phase where a business determines what its strengths and core capabilities are and starts selling its initial product or service. It's a very "hands-on" phase for the founder or founders, who are normally involved in every aspect of the day-to-day life of the business. The business is typically very nonbureaucratic with no (or few) written rules or procedures. The main goal of the business is to get off to a good start and to try to gain momentum in the marketplace.

The main challenges for a business in the introduction stage are to make sure the initial product or service is right and to start laying the groundwork for building a larger organization. It's important to not rush things. This sentiment is affirmed by April Singer, the founder of Rufus, a company that orginally only made high-end shirts for men. Before growing her business beyond the introduction stage, Singer made sure that her unique approach for making men's shirts worked and that it resonated in the marketplace:

> Before growing too much too fast, I wanted to spend two seasons making sure that the concept worked, that I shipped well, and that consumers liked the product. They did.[24]

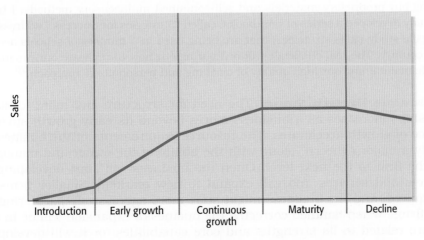

FIGURE 13.2
Organizational Life Cycle

This affirmation gave Singer the confidence to expand her business, add additional product lines, and move into a more aggressive growth mode. In regard to laying the groundwork to build a larger organization, many businesses use the introduction stage to try different concepts to see what works and what doesn't, recognizing that trial and error gets harder as a business grows. It's important to document what works and start thinking about how the company's success can be replicated when the owner isn't present or when the business expands beyond its original location.

Early Growth Stage   A business's early growth stage is generally characterized by increasing sales and heightened complexity. The business is normally still focused on its initial product or service but is trying to increase its market share and might have related products in the works. The initial formation of policies and procedures takes place, and the process of running the business will start to consume more of the founder's or founders' time and attention.

For a business to be successful in this stage, two important things must take place. First, the founder or owner of the business must start transitioning from his or her role as the hands-on supervisor of every aspect of the business to a more managerial role. As articulated by Michael E. Gerber in his excellent book *The E-Myth Revisited*, the owner must start working "on the business" rather than "in the business."[25] The basic idea is that early in the life of a business, the owner typically is directly involved in building the product or delivering the service that the business provides. As the business moves into the early growth stage, the owner must let go of that role and spend more time learning how to manage and build the business. If the owner isn't willing to make this transition or doesn't know it needs to be made, the business will never grow beyond the owner's ability to directly supervise everything that takes place, and the business's growth will eventually stall.

The second thing that must take place for a business to be successful in the early growth stage is that increased formalization must take place. The business has to start developing policies and procedures that tell employees how to run it when the founders or other top managers aren't present. This is how franchise restaurants run so well when they're staffed by what appears to be a group of teenagers. The employees are simply following well-documented policies and procedures. This task was clearly on the mind of Emily Levy, the founder of EBL Coaching, a tutoring service for children who are struggling in school or trying to overcome disabilities, when she was asked by Ladies Who Launch (a support network for female entrepreneurs) early in the life of her business about her growth plans:

> My future goals include continuing to spread EBL Coaching's programs nationally, using our proprietary materials and self-contained multisensory methods. I have already developed a series of workbooks, called "Strategies for Success," addressing specific study skills strategies, that are being used in a number of schools across the country. The real challenge will be figuring out how to replicate our programs while maintaining our high quality of teaching and personalized approach.[26]

Continuous Growth Stage   The need for structure and more formal relationships increases as a business moves beyond its early growth stage and its pace of growth accelerates. The resource requirements of the business are usually a major concern, along with the ability of the owner and manager to take the firm to the next level. Often the business will start developing new products and services and will expand to new markets. Smaller firms may be acquired, and the business might start more aggressively partnering with other firms. When handled correctly, the business's expansion will be in areas that are related to its strengths and core capabilities, or it will develop new strengths and capabilities to complement its activities.

The toughest decisions are typically made in the continuous growth stage. One tough decision is whether the owner of the business and the current management team have the experience and ability to take the firm any further. This scenario played out for Rachel Ashwell, the founder of Shabby Chic, a home furnishing business. Ashwell expanded her company to five separate locations, inked a licensing deal with Target, wrote five how-to books related to her business, and hosted her own television show on the Style Network before concluding that her business had stalled. Her choice was to continue running the business or find more experienced management to grow it further. She opted for the latter, which reignited the company's growth.[27]

The importance of developing policies and procedures increases during the continuous growth stage. It's also important for a business to develop a formal organizational structure and determine clear lines of delegation throughout the business. Well-developed policies and procedures lead to order, which typically makes the process of growing a business more organized and successful.

Maturity Stage A business enters the maturity stage when its growth slows. At this point, the firm typically focuses more intently on efficiently managing the products and services it has rather than expanding in new areas. Innovation slows. Formal policies and procedures, although important, can become an impediment if they are too rigid and strict.[28] It's important that the firm continues to adapt and that the founders, managers, and employees remain passionate about the products and services that are being sold. If this doesn't happen, a firm can easily slip into a no-growth situation.

A well-managed firm that finds its products and services are mature often looks for partnering or acquisition opportunities to breathe new life into the firm. For example, Coca-Cola, a firm in the maturity stage of its life cycle, has a long history of acquisitions. It acquired Minute Made in 1960, the Indian cola brand Thums Up in 1993, the Odwalla brand of fruit juices, smoothies, and bars in 2001, and Fuze Beverages in 2007. In August, 2014, Coca-Cola paid $2.15 billion to take a 16.7 percent ownership stake in Monster Beverage, the energy drink company.

If a company does grow organically while in the maturity stage, it normally focuses on the "next generation" of products it already sells rather than investing in new or related products or services.

Decline Stage It is not inevitable that a business enter the decline stage and either deteriorate or die. Many American businesses have long histories and have thrived by adapting to environmental change and by selling products that remain important to customers. Eventually all businesses' products or services will be threatened by more relevant and innovative products. When this happens, a business's ability to avoid decline depends on the strength of its leadership and its ability to appropriately respond.

A firm can also enter the decline stage if it loses its sense of purpose or spreads itself so thin that it no longer has a competitive advantage in any of its markets. A firm's management team should be aware of these potential pitfalls and guard against allowing them to happen.

A framework that is similar to the organizational life cycle is the technology adoption life cycle, which is suited primarily for technology firms that are introducing disruptive innovations to the market. The technology life cycle is associated with the concept of "crossing the chasm," which explains why some technology products reach mainstream markets while others don't. An explanation of the technology life cycle, the concept of "crossing the chasm," and an example of a start-up that successfully crossed the chasm and reached mainstream markets is provided in the nearby "Savvy Entrepreneurial Firm" feature.

SAVVY ENTREPRENEURIAL FIRM

Safesforce.com Crosses the Chasm

Web: www.salesforce4.com; Facebook: Salesforce; Twitter: @salesforce

In 1991, Geoffrey A. Moore, a lecturer and management consultant, wrote an influential book titled *Crossing the Chasm*. The book became an instant must-read for managers, entrepreneurs, and investors. The book was updated in 2009 and again in 2014. It has been described as the bible for understanding why some technology-oriented start-ups grow into large firms while others stall or languish in terms of adoption and firm growth.

The book's premise is that there is a chasm between the early adopters of a product (the technology enthusiasts and visionaries) and the early majority (the pragmatists). The key insight is that to cross the chasm, firms must first dominate a niche of early adopters and expand from a position of strength. The concept is related to the technology adoption life cycle. The stages in the technology adoption life cycle are innovators, early adopters, early majority, late majority, and laggards. Start-up products initially appeal to "innovators," who are people who like to try new things but are seldom willing to spend much. Then come the early adopters, or visionaries, who are willing to take a chance on a new product if it solves a burning problem. After the early adopters come the early majority, which is the largest segment. The early majority will only buy if a product is complete and is heavily recommended by others. If it's not recommended, they won't buy, regardless of how well a product suits their needs. Next is the late majority, which buys only after a product has become the standard. The laggards, which bring up the rear, rarely buy.

The chasm is hard to cross. Ironically, it is not the early adopters that convince the early majority to buy. In fact, the early majority typically mistrusts the enthusiasm of visionaries. They start buying when credibility is established and momentum within their own group starts to build. In his book, Moore suggests techniques to successfully appeal to the early majority, and cross the chasm, including issues pertaining to a firm's target market, its positioning strategy, its marketing strategy, and a number of other important factors. It's well worth the time to read the book to learn the techniques and capture the subtleties.

Salesforce.com is an example of a company that has crossed the chasm. Prior to Salesforce.com, software was a product that was sold on disks that clients would install on their computers. The software would then need to be integrated into the clients' system, which typically cost more than the software itself. By the time the software was installed, there were often updates available. Many clients would forgo installing the updates, at least for a period of time, to simply avoid the additional hassle and expense of installing them.

Salesforce.com introduced a better way. Its better way was software-as-a-service, later abbreviated as SaaS. The idea was that instead of selling software on disks to be installed on a client's computers, there would be only one copy of the software, running on Salesforce.com computers, which multiple users could access simultaneously via the Internet. The sales pitch was compelling. By adopting Salesforce.com's solution, a client would no longer incur the costs and headaches involved with installing, updating, and maintaining software.

What's interesting is the way Salesforce.com managed the rollout of the product and how the firm eventually crossed the chasm. In regard to the rollout, the company picked a single market to go after, salespeople, and no one else. There was nothing in the product for marketing, customer service, or any other division in a company. Salesforce.com focused exclusively on the United States as its target market, partly to stay close to their customer. The firm also chose to initially target tech-savvy industries. The result was a product designed to achieve a singular objective—helping salespeople make their quota. As a result, salespeople loved it. And because they loved it, they told other salespeople about it, and adoption grew virally. The number of early adopters grew. Credibility was built as the product was displayed at tradeshows and was talked about in mainstream media. Eventually, companies such as Merrill Lynch saw the merits of the service and signed on. Salesforce.com crossed the chasm and started appealing to the early majority and a wider number of users.

The irony of the Salesforce.com story, which is the essence of Moore's insight, is that by picking a single niche market, and establishing sufficient credibility that the early majority took notice, Salesforce.com was able to cross the chasm faster than it would have if it had created a much more robust product initially and tried to appeal to a broader cross-section of markets.

Questions for Critical Thinking

1. Select at least two other firms that you believe have crossed the chasm. Briefly summarize how the firms rolled out their products (or services) and what you believe their key steps were in successfully crossing the chasm.

2. In contrast to question #1, list at least two start-ups that you are familiar with that produced products or services that you believe never crossed the chasm. Briefly describe why you believe they never crossed the chasm.

3. Do you believe consumer products cross the chasm (or fail to cross the chasm) much like technology products?

4. In regard to adopting technology products, do you see yourself as an early adopter or as part of the early majority? How does your answer affect the manner in which you buy technology products?

Sources: Salesforce.com website, www.salescorce.com, accessed July 3, 2014; G. A. Moore, *Crossing the Chasm*, 3rd edition (New York: HarperCollins, 2014).

Challenges of Growth

There is a consistent set of challenges that affect all stages of a firm's growth. The challenges typically become more acute as a business grows, but a business's founder or founders and managers also become more savvy and experienced with the passage of time. The challenges illustrate that no firm grows in a competitive vacuum.[29] As a business grows and takes market share away from rival firms, there will be a certain amount of retaliation that takes place. This is an aspect of competition that a business owner needs to be aware of and plan for. Competitive retaliation normally increases as a business grows and becomes a larger threat to its rivals.

This section is divided into two parts. The first part focuses on the managerial capacity problem, which is a framework for thinking about the overall challenge of growing a firm. The second part focuses on the four most common day-to-day challenges of growing a business.

Managerial Capacity

In her thoughtful and seminal book *The Theory of the Growth of the Firm*, Edith T. Penrose argues that firms are collections of productive resources that are organized in an administrative framework.[30] As an administrative framework, the primary purpose of a firm is to package its resources together with resources acquired outside the firm as a foundation for being able to produce products and services at a profit. As a firm goes about its routine activities, the management team becomes better acquainted with the firm's resources and its markets. This knowledge leads to the expansion of a firm's **productive opportunity set**, which is the set of opportunities the firm feels it's capable of pursuing. The opportunities might include the introduction of new products, geographic expansion, licensing products to other firms, exporting, and so on. The pursuit of these new opportunities causes a firm to grow.

Penrose points out, however, that there is a problem with the execution of this simple logic. The firm's administrative framework consists of two kinds of services that are important to a firm's growth—entrepreneurial services and managerial services. **Entrepreneurial services** generate new market, product, and service ideas, while **managerial services** administer the routine functions of the firm and facilitate the profitable execution of new opportunities. However, the introduction of new product and service ideas requires substantial managerial services (or managerial "capacity") to be properly implemented and supervised. This is a complex problem because if a firm has insufficient managerial services to properly implement its entrepreneurial ideas, it can't quickly hire new managers to remedy the shortfall. It is expensive to hire new employees, and it takes time for new managers to be socialized into the firm's culture, acquire firm-specific skills and knowledge, and establish trusting relationships with other members of their firms.[31] When a firm's managerial resources are insufficient to take advantage of its new product and services opportunities, the subsequent bottleneck is referred to as the **managerial capacity problem**.

As the entrepreneurial venture grows, it encounters the dual challenges of adverse selection and moral hazard. **Adverse selection** means that as the number of employees a firm needs increases, it becomes increasingly difficult for it to find the right employees, place them in appropriate positions, and provide adequate supervision.[32] The faster a firm grows, the less time managers have to evaluate the suitability of job candidates and the higher the chances are that an unsuitable candidate will be chosen. Selecting "ineffective" or "unsuitable" employees increases the venture's costs. **Moral hazard** means that as a firm grows and adds personnel, the new hires typically do not have the same ownership incentives as the original founders, so the new hires may not be as motivated as the founders to put in long hours or may even try to avoid

LEARNING OBJECTIVE

4. Discuss the challenges of firm growth, particularly those of adverse selection and moral hazard.

hard work.[33] To make sure the new hires are doing what they are employed to do, the firm will typically hire monitors (i.e., managers) to supervise the employees. This practice creates a hierarchy that is costly and isolates the top management team from its rank-and-file employees.

The basic model of firm growth articulated by Penrose is shown in Figure 13.3 while Figure 13.4 shows the essence of the growth-limiting managerial capacity problem.[34] Figure 13.4 indicates that the ability to increase managerial services is not friction free. It is constrained or limited by (1) the time required to socialize new managers, (2) how motivated entrepreneurs and/or managers are to grow their firms, (3) adverse selection, and (4) moral hazard.

Wesabe, the focus of this chapter's "What Went Wrong?" feature, suffered as a result of trying to build out its own capabilities or managerial capacity in a key area rather than partnering with a company that was willing to license it the capability. A competitor licensed the technology and sped ahead of Wesabe. Wesabe's own attempt to build out the capability took longer than it thought it would, and it never recovered.

The reality of the managerial capacity problem is one of the main reasons that entrepreneurs and managers worry so much about growth. Growth is a generally positive thing, but it is easy for a firm to overshoot its capacity to manage growth in ways that will diminish the venture's sales revenues and profits.

Day-to-Day Challenges of Growing a Firm

Along with the overarching challenges imposed by the managerial capacity problem, there are a number of day-to-day challenges involved with growing a firm. The following is a discussion of the four most common challenges.

Cash Flow Management As discussed in Chapters 8 and 10, as a firm grows, it requires an increasing amount of cash to service its customers. In

FIGURE 13.3
Basic Model of Firm Growth

FIGURE 13.4
The Impact of Managerial Capacity

Source: Based on material in E. T. Penrose, *The Theory of the Growth of the Firm* (Oxford: Basil Blackwell, 1959).

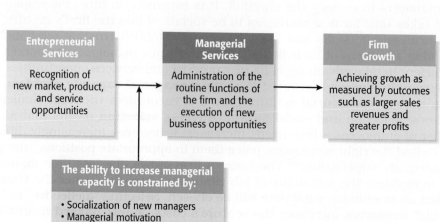

This entrepreneur just opened a fine dining restaurant. His ability to grow his business successfully will hinge largely on how he manages the day-to-day challenges associated with growth.

addition, a firm must carefully manage its cash on hand to make sure it maintains sufficient liquidity to meet its payroll and cover its other short-term obligations. There are many colorful anecdotes about business founders who have had to rush to a bank and get a second mortgage on their houses to cover their business's payroll. This usually occurs when a business takes on too much work, and its customers are slow to pay. A business can literally have $1 million in accounts receivable but not be able to meet a $25,000 payroll. This is why almost any book you pick up about growing a business stresses the importance of properly managing a firm's cash flow.

Growth usually increases rather than decreases the challenges involved with cash flow management because an increase in sales means that more cash will be flowing into and out of the firm. Growth is also expensive, in that it often involves investing more money in operations, marketing, administrative processes (to better track accounts payable and receivable), and personnel. This point is made by Vinny Antonio, president of Victory Marketing Agency:

> "Cash flow management for a rapidly growing, bootstrapped company can be harder than the world's most difficult Sudoku puzzle. It's almost a full-time job staying on top of who owes you what and who you owe, and then priortizing those payments. All the while, you're pushing for more growth, but with that comes additional expenses—most notably, your executive team. Good talent doesn't come cheap, and you often have to find creative ways to lure the right personnel to your team."[35]

Some firms raise the cash needed to fund growth via investors or a line of credit at a bank. Other firms deliberately restrict the pace of their growth to avoid cash flow challenges.

Price Stability   If firm growth comes at the expense of a competitor's market share, price competition can set in. For example, if an entrepreneur opened a fast-casual restaurant near a Panera Bread that started eroding the Panera Bread's market share, Panera Bread would probably fight back by running promotions or lowering prices. This type of scenario places a new firm in a difficult

WHAT WENT WRONG?

How Trying to Build Out Its Own Capabilities in a Key Area Contributed to the Failure of a Promising Firm

In November 2006, Wesabe launched a site to help people manage their personal finances. While it wasn't the first personal finance site on the Web, it was the first to use a Web 2.0 approach. The site automatically aggregated and stored all of its users' financial accounts and, most especially, was able to "learn" from the accumulated data its users uploaded to make recommendations for better financial decisions. Because of its helpful functionality, Wesabe got off to a good start and, until September 2007, was considered the leader in online personal finance. Then Mint.com launched, and from that point forward, Wesabe was in second place at best. Two years later, Mint was acquired by Intuit for $170 million—one of the fastest and most successful exits in software history. In contrast, just short of a year later, Wesabe shut down.

What Went Wrong?

Marc Hedlund, one of Wesabe's co-founders, wrote a thoughtful blog post about Wesabe's failure. While he attributes Wesabe's failure to several factors, two are prominent in Hedlund's opinion. The first speaks to the importance of allowing partners to build some of a firm's capabilities or managerial capacity, while the second focuses on the importance of a first mover remaining sharp and competitive in light of inevitable competition.

The first mistake Wesabe made is that it chose not to partner with Yodlee. Yodlee is a company that provides account aggregation services, which is a highly technical business. If a user is willing to provide his or her account-access information (account numbers, user IDs, and passwords) for bank accounts, credit cards, and investment accounts, Yodlee can "scrape" the appropriate sites and compile all the information in one place. Yodlee was a tough negotiator so Wesabe decided not to tie itself to Yodlee, even though Yodlee could deliver to Wesabe a huge capability it needed. Mint.com partnered with Yodlee out of the gates and, as a result, it was easy for its users to populate their Mint.com accounts with their financial information. Wesabe built its own data acquisition system, which took longer and wasn't as elegant. Wesabe eventually launched a Yodlee-like Web interface, but it didn't come online until six months after Mint.com went live. In retrospect, Hedlund believes that passing on Yodlee was probably enough to kill Wesabe. It should have known that if it didn't use Yodlee, a competitor would come along that would. That would have been

okay if Wesabe had had a solution as capable as Yodlee. But it didn't, and the minute users looked at side-by-side comparisons of Wesabe versus Mint.com, Wesabe was at a disadvantage in that its product's functionality wasn't as solid as what was available from a competitor.

The second mistake Wesabe made was misunderstanding its users. Wesabe deliberately forced people to do some of the data entry and other work on the site themselves, thinking that forcing users to get close to their data would change their financial behavior—for the better. Mint.com did just the opposite. It focused on making the user do almost no work at all, by automating all key processes and giving them instant gratification. As a result, Wesabe's site was perceived as "harder to use" than Mint.com's. While Wesabe's intentions may have been noble, it misread its users. As hard as it is to admit, users were more interested in expediency and an elegant interface than performing the hard work of getting close to their financial data.

The combination of Mint's better data aggregation method (via Yodlee) and the higher amount of work that Wesabe made the user do gave users a better experience on Mint versus Wesabe. Although Wesabe had the first-mover advantage, Mint simply outcompeted Wesabe and gained the upper hand.

Questions for Critical Thinking

1. Why do you think Wesabe opted not to use Yodlee and to build its own account aggregation services? Similarly, why do you think Mint.com jumped at the chance to partner with Yodlee?

2. How does an entrepreneurial firm find the right balance between not "overestimating" its capabilities (i.e., Wesabe thought it could build an account aggregation service faster than it did) and still be willing to do much of the work that needs to be done without paying others to do it?

3. How could Wesabe have avoided misunderstanding its users and allowing Mint.com to obtain the perceived usability advantage it obtained?

4. What can entrepreneurial firms learn about the managerial capacity problem from Wesabe's experience?

Source: M. Hedlund, "Why Wesabe Lost to Mint," Marc Hedlund's blog, http://blog.precipice.org/why-wesabe-lost-to-mint, posted on March 10, 2011, accessed on June 28, 2014.

predicament and illustrates why it's important to start a business by selling a differentiated product to a clearly defined target market. There is no good way for a small firm to compete head-to-head against a much larger rival on price. The best thing for a small firm to do is to avoid price competition by serving a different market and by serving that market particularly well.

Quality Control   One of the most difficult challenges that businesses encounter as they grow is maintaining high levels of quality and customer service. As a firm grows, it handles more service requests and paperwork and contends with an increasing number of prospects, customers, vendors, and other stakeholders. If a business can't build its infrastructure fast enough to handle the increased activity, quality and customer service will usually suffer. What happens to many businesses is that they run into the classic chicken-or-egg quandary. It's hard to justify hiring additional employees or leasing more office space until the need is present, but if the business waits until the need is present, it usually won't have enough employees or office space to properly service new customers.

There is no easy way to resolve this type of quandary other than to recognize that it may take place and to plan for it in the best way possible. Many businesses find innovative ways to expand their capacity to try to avoid shortfalls in quality control or customer service.

Capital Constraints   Although many businesses are started fairly inexpensively, the need for capital is typically the most prevalent in the early growth and continuous growth stages of the organizational life cycle. The amount of capital required varies widely among businesses. Some businesses, like restaurant chains, might need considerable capital to hire employees, construct buildings, and purchase equipment. If they can't raise the capital they need, their growth will be stymied.

Most businesses, regardless of their industry, need capital from time to time to invest in growth-enabling projects. Their ability to raise capital, whether it's through internally generated funds, through a bank, or from investors, will determine in part whether their growth plans proceed.

Chapter Summary

LO1. Sustained growth is defined as growth in both revenues and profits over an extended period of time. Successfully growing a business is a function of preparation, good management, and an appreciation of the issues involved. The three primary things that a business can do to prepare for growth are appreciating the nature of business growth, staying committed to a core strategy, and planning for growth. In this sense, firm growth is not a random or chance event. It is something firms pursue deliberately.

LO2. The six most common reasons that firms grow in an effort to increase their profitability and valuation are to: (1) capture economies of scale (which are generated when increasing production lowers the average cost of each unit produced); (2) capture economies of scope (similar to economies of scale, scope economies are advantages a firm generates through the range of its operations); (3) achieve market leadership (which happens when a firm holds the top or second position in its industry or the segment of an industry in which it competes); (4) maintain influence, power, and survivability (conditions through which a firm is able to affect the setting of an industry's standards as well having the scale and scope that will allow it to make a mistake and continue operating); (5) accommodate the growth of key customers (which is the ability to serve an important customer's expanding demand for the firm's product or service); and (6) maintain an ability to attract and retain talented employees (the most desirable employees want to work for a firm in which learning and growth opportunities will be readily available to them).

LO3. Many businesses are caught off guard by the challenges involved with growing and managing their companies. As a business increases its sales, its pace of activity quickens, its resource needs increase, and the founders often find that they're busier than ever. Evidence indicates that the majority of businesses go through a discernable set of stages referred to as the organizational life cycle. The stages include introduction, early growth, continuous growth, maturity, and decline. The introduction phase is where a business determines what its strengths and core capabilities are and starts selling its initial product or service. The business is typically very nonbureaucratic with no (or few) written rules or procedures. The main goal of the business is to get off to a good start and try to gain momentum in the marketplace. A business's early growth stage is characterized by increasing sales and heightened complexity. For a business to succeed in this stage (1) the founder or owner of the business must start transforming from his or her role as the hands-on supervisor of every aspect of the business to a more managerial role, and (2) increased formalization must take place. The toughest decisions are typically made in the continuous growth stage. One tough decision is whether the owner of the business and the current management team have the experience and ability to take the firm any further. In the maturity stage, the firm's growth slows

and eventually comes to a halt, as does its ability to generate product or service innovations. In the decline stage, the firm's sales begin falling rather dramatically. In addition, the quality of the firm's relationships with stakeholders such as customers, suppliers, employees, and financial institutions begin to suffer.

LO4. There is a consistent set of challenges that affect each and every stage of a firm's growth. The first of these challenges is known as the managerial capacity problem. This particular problem suggests that firm growth is limited by the managerial capacity (i.e., personnel, expertise, and intellectual resources) that firms have available to implement new business ideas. The basic idea is that it does a firm little good to have exciting ideas about growth when it lacks the managerial capacity to implement its ideas. The second core challenge has four parts; collectively, these are categorized as the day-to-day growth-related challenges that firms encounter. The day-to-day challenges of managing growth include cash flow management (the challenge of continuously verifying that the firm has sufficient cash on hand to meet its needs), price stability (this challenge surfaces when a firm competes successfully against larger competitors who respond by making the new venture compete on the basis of price, a competitive dimension on which it is at a disadvantage compared to large, established competitors), quality control (with growth, the entrepreneurial venture may find it increasingly difficult to maintain the quality of its product or service as demanded by customers), and capital constraints (here the challenge is to find the financial capital needed to support early and hopefully continuous firm growth).

Key Terms

adverse selection, **477**
core competencies, **467**
economies of scale, **471**
economies of scope, **471**
entrepreneurial services, **477**

fixed costs, **471**
managerial capacity problem, **477**
managerial services, **477**
market leadership, **471**

moral hazard, **477**
pace of growth, **470**
productive opportunity set, **477**
sustained growth, **465**
variable costs, **471**

Review Questions

13-1. What is sustained growth? Why is it important?

13-2. Can most firms be classified as rapid-growth firms? Explain your answer.

13-3. What are the potential downsides to firm growth?

13-4. Do all firms have the potential to be aggressive-growth firms? Why or why not?

13-5. Is it possible for a firm to grow too fast? If so, what are the potential downsides?

13-6. Why is it difficult for some firms to grow or scale their operations?

13-7. What are the benefits of planning for growth?

13-8. What are the factors that a business needs to keep in mind when preparing for growth? What are the indicators of a business growing too fast?

13-9. Why do firms pursue growth? How can a firm achieve economies of scale?

13-10. How does a firm's growth rate affect its ability to attract and retain talented employees?

13-11. What are the repercussions faced by a firm when it fails to manage growth?

13-12. What is the managerial capacity problem?

13-13. What is adverse selection and how might it affect entrepreneurial firms?

13-14. What is moral hazard and how might it affect entrepreneurial firms?

13-15. Why is cash flow management such an important issue for a firm entering a period of rapid growth?

13-16. How do rapid growth firms deal with potential cash flow shortfalls?

13-17. Why is price stability such an important issue for a firm entering a period of rapid growth?

13-18. According to the chapter, one of the most difficult challenges involved with rapid growth is quality control. Why is this so?

13-19. What are the dual challenges of adverse selection and moral hazard faced by a firm when it grows?

13-20. Why is it expensive for a firm to grow?

Application Questions

13-21. Sean Damsey has been running a budget hotel for the past six months and has been doing quite well. He did a quick survey and found that his town still does not have enough hotels to accommodate the number of tourists that visit their town, especially during weekends and holidays. At the moment, there are only three hotels including Sean's. Hence, Sean is planning to expand and start another hotel in the same area. However, he is afraid that his business might be growing too fast and he would not be able to manage the growth. Advise him.

13-22. Joanna Collins and Pete Stash recently opened a fine dining restaurant in the suburbs. They have been really enthusiastic about this restaurant and have been looking forward to grow their business successfully. Both Joanna and Pete are not experienced restaurateurs. In fact, they are new entrepreneurs and this is their first time doing business. Since their friend Stanley Black has been operating an Italian restaurant for the past five years, Joanna went to Stanley for advice. She knows that there will be many challenges to face while experience growth. What should their expectations be about the day-to-day challenges of a growing firm, as based on Stanley's five years of experience running a restaurant?

13-23. Patty Stone owns an industrial equipment company named Get Smart Industrial that sells three products in the oil services industry. Get Smart's products are sold via a direct sales force. Patty wants to grow the firm by adding new products but has run into resistance from her chief financial officer (CFO), who argues that adding new products will increase inventory costs and place a strain on the company's cash flow. While Patty is sensitive to her CFO's concerns, what arguments can she make in favor of adding new products as a way of effectively growing her firm?

13-24. Three years ago, Chris Dees launched a medical products company that specializes in providing products for people with diabetes. His company is number one in its industry. Recently, a couple of competitors have entered the picture, and Chris is wondering if it is worth the fight to remain number one. In terms of firm growth, what advantages are there to being the market leader?

13-25. Kyle Simms just succeeded his father as the CEO of a consumer products firm in Mission Viejo, California. Prior to returning to the family business, Kyle had spent 11 years at Procter & Gamble in Cincinnati. Kyle's dad built a solid company, but over the past five years, its growth was flat. Kyle wants to grow the company, but at the same time doesn't want to disturb its healthy culture or overshoot its ability to manage its growth. Kyle's question to you is, "How do I manage this careful balance?" What would you tell him?

13-26. Sarah Jeffers lives in Austin, Texas, where she has owned a graphics design company for three years. She spends 12 hours a day at work micromanaging every aspect of her business, yet she still can't get the business to grow. Using materials included in this chapter, what actions would you tell Sarah she needs to take in order for her business to move from the early growth stage to the continuous growth stage of its organizational life cycle?

13-27. Meredith Colella is a food products engineer who has developed an innovative approach for the packaging of meat. Her approach will extend the shelf life of most meat products by about 30 percent. Meredith is getting ready to try to sell the idea to investors. What could Meredith tell the investors that would give them confidence that she is prepared to cope with the challenges of rapid growth?

13-28. As an experienced entrepreneur for the last 25 years operating in cleaning services, Martin Perry has been invited by the local council to give a speech to young entrepreneurs who are keen on starting their own business. As these young entrepreneurs have already attended entrepreneurship workshops before, Mathew's talk may include the organizational life cycle that his business has experienced in the last 25 years.

13-29. Bruce Steven is a renowned entrepreneur in your neighborhood. He has been operating a fitness center for the past 10 years, and everyone in the neighborhood and surrounding areas are loyal members at his center. One evening after your workout at his center, Bruce approached you and invited you to have coffee with him. He was explaining that his center is experiencing slow growth and he is losing his passion for the business. With the knowledge you have, explain to him his next step of action.

13-30. Imagine you have a friend who has created a new board game. A prototyping lab in the College of Engineering where your friend goes to college made a prototype of the game for him, which he took to a trade show; it received an enthusiastic response. He even obtained orders for 2,000 copies of the game. When you asked your friend how he plans to pay for the initial production run of the game, he said that he plans to bootstrap his company and will pay for everything from his profits. Does your friend have a good sense of the financial implications of launching a new product into the marketplace? What scenario is more likely to play out for your friend?

13-31. Look at the website of Scuba Toys (www.scubatoys.com). As you'll see, this firm makes a wide range of products for all types of water sports. Spend some time familiarizing yourself with Scuba Toys's products and its business model. Scuba Toys is about to launch an aggressive growth strategy. Write a one-page set of recommendations for Scuba Toys that outlines some of the issues it should be aware of as it launches its growth initiative.

YOU BE THE VC 13.1 COMPANY: Dollar Shave Club

• Web: www.dollarshaveclub.com • Facebook: Dollar Shave Club • Twitter: @DollarShaveClub

Business Idea: Launch an online subscription service that provides men basic but functional razors at a deep discount from brand-name razors purchased at retail stores.

Pitch: A common irritant for men is buying razor blades. Not only are they costly, but men often run out of serviceable blades at the most inopportune time, which requires a hasty trip to the store. Because razor blades require constant replacement, and are relatively expensive, they are often depicted by marketers as the perfect consumer product. There is even the old joke, which is more than just tongue and cheek, that the razor blade companies would gladly give away razors just to lock more people into buying replacement blades.

Enter the Dollar Shave Club. In March 2012, the Dollar Shave Club debuted in a cheeky video featuring co-founder Mike Dubin walking briskly through a warehouse making wisecracks and encouraging men to quit spending $20 a month on brand-name razors. His alternative—buy razors from him on a monthly subscription plan for as little as $2 per month. The video has now been watched more than 13 million times. It's even won several awards, including the "Best Out-of-Nowhere Video Campaign" at the 2012 AdAge Viral Video Awards.

The Dollar Shave Club has a simple and straightforward premise: manufacture basic but usable razors in Asia and sell them through a monthly subscription service at significant discounts. It has three categories of blades: The Humble Twin, The 4X, and The Executive. The Humble Twin, which is the base model, includes two stainless steel blades, a lubricating strip that smooths and moisturizes the skin, and a shallow pivot head and a handle. A subscriber gets five cartridges a month for $1 (thus, the name Dollar Shave Club). Subscription plans for the 4X and The Executive cost $6 and $9 a month, respectively, and include additional features, such as a more robust blade. Shipping and handling is free. Every member gets a free compatible handle. Subscribers can cancel their subscription at any time. The company's razor blades are not only less expensive than competitors, but also provide men the opportunity for a cleaner shave by using fresher blades more often. Many men, to save money and another trip to a store, milk their blades for as long as possible. Dollar Shave Club blades are delivered directly to a subscriber's doorstep and a subscription includes enough cartridges a month to always be shaving with a relatively new blade.

In 2013, the Dollar Shave Club added two new products: Shave Butter and Wipes for men. The products are sold as add-ons to the company's monthly subscription plans.

13-32. Based on the material covered in this chapter, what questions would you ask the firm's founders before making your funding decision? What answers would satisfy you?

13-33. If you had to make your decision on just the information provided in the pitch and on the company's website, would you fund this company? Why or why not?

YOU BE THE VC 13.2 COMPANY: Class Dojo

• Web: www.classdojo.com • Facebook: Class Dojo • Twitter: @ClassDojo

Business Idea: Create a behavior management tool that makes it easy for elementary and secondary school teachers to keep their students alert and on task.

Pitch: Among the most difficult tasks facing teachers is dealing with disruptive student behavior. In fact, some teachers spend more than 50 percent of their class time improving behavior. Bad behavior in the classroom is not only unsettling, but research shows that unruly classrooms lead to lower test scores, higher dropout rates, and increased behavioral problems outside the classroom.

Class Dojo is a behavior management platform that addresses this pressing problem. Here's how it works. Each student in a classroom has an avatar that receives or loses points throughout the day based on behavior. The classroom is equipped with a public leader board, which shows each avatar's progress throughout the day. All the technology that's needed is a computer hooked up to a projector that projects the avatars and their progress on the leader board. The system is built on a set of categories that reflect positive classroom behaviors. The categories include on task, teamwork, working hard, persistence, participating, helping others, and so forth. Because the categories are framed using positive reinforcement, the system has the ability to do more than just call out good behavior. For example, a teacher might create a category like "was able to disagree with another student without sounding mean or insulting them." Along with advancing a student's avatar, good behavior is recognized on the leader board in written form. For example, during a classroom exercise the sentence "Well done Jeremy +1 for teamwork" might pop up on the leader board. Research suggests the shorter the time period between an action and feedback for that action, the greater is the effect of reinforcement. Continually reinforcing good behavior, and subtracting points for bad behavior, makes a classroom less disruptive and creates a more positive learning environment. Data collected by Class Dojo can be shared with parents and administrators.

Class Dojo can be run from a computer hooked up to the Internet or via a smartphone. The smartphone feature allows teachers to use Class Dojo on the playground and on field trips, in addition to the classroom. Class Dojo is free to the teacher and school district, which lowers the barrier to acceptance. The platform will be monetized through parents who want to use Class Dojo at home and pay a monthly subscription fee.

13-34. Based on the material covered in this chapter, what questions would you ask the firm's founders before making your funding decision? What answers would satisfy you?

13-35. If you had to make your decision on just the information provided in the pitch and on the company's website, would you fund this company? Why or why not?

CASE 13.1

Sir Kensington: Pursuing a Measured, Yet Promising Path to Growth

• *Web: www.sirkensingstons.com* • *Facebook: Sir Kensingston's* • *Twitter: @sirkensingstons*

Bruce R. Barringer, *Oklahoma State University*
R. Duane Ireland, *Texas A&M University*

Introduction

In early 2008, Scott Norton and Mark Ramadan, classmates at Brown University, were having lunch. They got to talking about food and stumbled on an interesting topic. For most types of food there are many choices. Just think of milk. Not only are there different brands of milk, but there is whole milk, 2 percent milk, and skim milk, along with soy milk, rice milk, and almond milk. The same is true for cereal, yogurt, mustard, and sauces. The only product they could think of where there is only one choice is ketchup. Heinz ketchup. They wondered why that was the case and if there was something they could do about it.

For some reason the idea of creating a new brand of ketchup interested them. They started from the premise that they wanted to create something compelling, something that they could create a brand around. They also wanted something that reflected their values. Most ketchup, they learned, is made from tomoto concentrate, corn syrup, vineger, and onion powder. They quickly decided if they made ketchup, it would be made from natural ingredients, such as fresh tomatoes, cane sugar, and real diced onions instead of onion powder. They started tinkering with recipes, mostly in Norton's apartment. To test their early recipes, they invited their friends to a ketchup party. They had eight different ketchups and held a blind taste test. They asked their friends to rate each ketchup on several criteria, including how it tastes, what the texture is like, how similar it is to Heinz, and so forth. There were two ketchups that came out on top—Classic and Spicy. They thought, "Why don't we make these two types of ketchups, put them in jars and see what happens?"

Before they went further, they thought a lot about branding. They instinctively knew that natural ingredients and taste alone wouldn't get the attention they needed. They needed their ketchup to stand out—to jump off the shelf at a grocery store. They imagined the name Sir Kensington, a fictional merchant who would be pictured on their bottles. They also decided to make their bottles and labels unique. Instead of plastic squeeze bottles, they elected to go with squat square bottles with a wide instead of a narrow top (so the ketchup could be spooned rather than squeezed from the bottle). They also designed and printed labels that looked as though they belonged on fine food rather than a ketchup bottle.

In 2009, Norton and Ramadan graduated and took jobs in the business world. They kept the idea of Sir Kensington alive and continued to work part time on the project. In 2010, they both left their traditional jobs to pursue Sir Kensington's full time.

Early Growth

In June 2010, Sir Kensington's debuted at New York's annual Fancy Foods Show. After the show, Norton and Ramadan hit the streets, trying to make sales. Their efforts weren't random. They were aware of the technology adoption life cycle and decided to apply it to their business. The stages in the technology adoption life cycle are innovators, early adopters, early majority, late majority, and laggards. As explained in this chapter, the life cycle is often associated with the concept of "Crossing the Chasm," first introduced in 1991 by Geoffrey A. Moore. In a nutshell, the life cycle concept argues that a firm should start with innovators, and

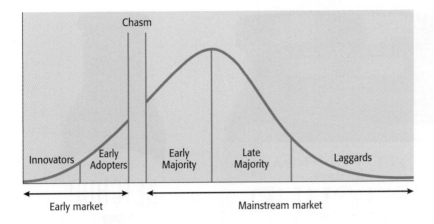

FIGURE 13.5
Technology Adoption
Life Cycle

firmly establish itself in each stage before it moves to the next stage. The hardest transition is from early adopters to the early majority. Innovators and early adopters are people who enjoy trying new things. The early majority are mainstream customers. A firm "crosses the chasm" when it moves from early adopters to the early majority. A diagram of the technology adoption life cycle is shown in Figure 13.5.

Consistent with the theories mentioned above, Norton and Ramadan targeted independent grocery stores as their first adopters of Sir Kensington's ketchup. Independent stores tend to appeal to "innovators," people who are looking for new choices. Norton and Ramadan put a lot of thought into how to appeal to innovators. One important piece was the package. They worked hard to create a bottle and label that looked different and conveyed Sir Kensington's values. They ended up with a bottle and label that looked like nothing else in the ketchup aisle—it was short, squat, had a wide opening at the top, and had Sir Kensington's image prominently displayed on the front. They figured that combination would incent an innovator to pick the bottle up. Once it was in the hands of the innovator, the label took over. The label drew a clear distinction between Sir Kensington's and other ketchups. The label reminded the shopper that Sir Kensington's was made strictly from natural ingredients, with half the sugar and half the salt of traditional ketchup. They figured the label would close the sale. The first store to say yes was Murray's Cheese, an independent grocer in Greenwich Village in New York City. Several other independents quickly followed. Based on this early traction, Norton and Ramadan were able to land Dean & DeLuca, Williams-Sonoma, and Whole Foods. It wasn't easy. Whole Foods, for example, has seasons where they try out different categories of products. Norton and Ramadan established a relationship with a food broker who knew Whole Foods's schedule and made the appropriate introductions. In its first year, 10,000 jars were sold.

Restaurants came next, in the 2012 time frame, and are generally harder than retailers for new food companies to crack. This is particularly true for a product like ketchup. Retailers sell ketchup—it's a product on which

they earn money. Restaurants give ketchup away—it's something that costs them money. Sir Kensington's was a premium-priced product. As a result, it was a tough sell. Eventually, several high-end restaurants signed on, including the Four Seasons Hotels, mostly because they liked the Sir Kensington's product and brand. Once the Four Seasons signed on, it was easier to convince other high-end restaurants to follow suit.

Crossing the Chasm

In 2013, Norton and Ramadan decided it was time for Sir Kensington to cross the chasm. What that meant was finding a way to appeal to mainstream consumers rather than innovators and early adopters. The change was also precipitated by the opportunity to sell in more mainstream stores such as Safeway and Target, and through online outlets such as Amazon.com. As mentioned above, crossing the chasm is not an easy task. The same product, and style, that appeals to innovators and early adopters doesn't necessarily appeal to mainstream consumers. The challenge that Norton and Ramadan faced, which is typical for companies attempting to cross the chasm, was to maintain the integrity and quality of their product while softening it in ways that would incent mainstream consumers to buy.

Several things were changed in preparation for the move. Sir Kensington's image was changed. The original Sir Kensington had a rather stern look with a neatly trimmed fashionable mustache. The new Sir Kensington was happier, with a large bushy mustache. The thinking was that mainstream consumers would be more comfortable bringing the happy Sir Kensington into their homes. Additionally, the taste of the product was tweaked some to make it seem more mainstream. Norton and Ramadan didn't feel as though they were compromising their product or firm's integrity by making these changes. They were just shifting their product to appeal more to mainstream consumers. The nearby photo shows the two Sir Kensington ketchup bottles. Notice how the bottle changed to make it more appealing to mainstream customers.

The shift worked and Sir Kensington's crossed the chasm. By early 2014, it was available in over 3,000

(cont

Original Sir Kensington's bottle (on the left) compared to new Sir Kensington's bottle (on the right). Note how the original Sir Kensington is rather stern while the new Sir Kensington is happier. The company believed that the happier Sir Kensington would better appeal to mainstream consumers.

Kensington & Sons, LLC

stores in the United States and in many restaurants and restaurant chains.

Sir Kensington's Today

While adding new product lines is an obvious path to firm growth, Norton and Ramadan resisted the temptation for some time. They felt that Sir Kensington's Ketchup was successful in part because it offered an alternative to Heinz's near monoploly in the ketchup market. That wasn't true of many products, as Norton and Ramadan had observed that day in 2008 when they first started talking about how few choices consumers had when it came to ketchup. Many times, they later noted, restaurants told them if they only had a matching set of Sir Kensington's Ketchup and Mustard, they would adopt both. But oddly, consumers have many choices for mustard. Everything that Norton and Ramadan felt was to their advantage when it came to selling ketchup would be to their disadvantage is selling mustard.

In 2014, Sir Kensington did expand its product line to include two types of mayonnaise—classic and chipotle. Like ketchup, there aren't many brands of mayonnaise, so Norton and Ramadan are on familiar ground.

Discussion Questions

13-36. There is a discussion early in this chapter of the need to prepare for growth. What actions did Scott Norton and Mark Ramadan take that demonstrate their commitment to trying to fully understand growth and its ramifications for their firm?

13-37. We noted in this chapter that core competencies are essentially what a firm does particularly well. What are the core competencies of the firm Sir Kensington's? How sustainable are these core competencies?

13-38. Look at Figure 13.2, which shows the organizational life cycle. In which of these stages is Sir Kensington's located? To what issues do Sir Kensington's founders need to be particularly sensitive in this stage?

13-39. What are four key lessons about growth potential entrepreneurs could learn by studying how Sir Kensington's has grown?

Sources: Sir Kinginston's website, wwe.sirkinginston.com, accessed June 25, 2014; Sir Kensington's Gourmet Ketchup LORE Workshop, available online at http://www.youtube.com/watch?v=21JjzvXgsD4, posted on October 5, 2012, accessed on July 2, 2014.

CASE 13.2

uShip: Growing Through Helping Individuals and Shippers Move Items More Efficiently

• *Web: www.uship.com* • *Facebook: uShip* • *Twitter: @uShip*

Bruce R. Barringer, *Oklahoma State University*

R. Duane Ireland, *Texas A&M University*

Introduction

In 2001, Matt Chasen graduated from the University of Texas at Austin with an undergraduate degree in mechanical engineering. He moved to Seattle to work for Boeing, but soon found that working for a large corporation wasn't for him. Instead of jumping to another job, he decided to return to UT-Austin to pursue an MBA. Two things happened prior to this move, though, that changed his life. The first was a phone call from his mother. His mom wanted to move an heirloom dresser from Ohio to Houston. She called several shipping companies and concluded that the rates quoted to her were outrageous. She wondered if Matt had any alternative ideas. He did some research, but came up empty. The second was preparing for his move from Seattle to Austin. He rented a 9-foot truck, but when he showed up for the truck all that was available was a 24-footer. He remembers standing in the back of the truck looking at all the unfilled capacity. He thought someone should set up an Internet site that matches people that need things moved, like his mom and her heirloom dresser, with trucks that have unused capacity.

According to Chasen, the drive from Seattle to Austin was a long one for his wife. He went on and on about his idea. Once settled in Austin again, Chasen spent the next two years in his MBA program working on the idea. He picked up two co-founders, Mickey Millsap and Jay Manickam, along the way. They were part of Chasen's MBA cohort. The three would use uShip, which is the name they gave the idea, as a case study in every class they could. Chasen incorporated uShip in 2003 while sitting in the back of one of his business classes.

In 2004, Chasen and his co-founders competed in several business plan competitions, winning first prize at the University of North Texas and scoring runner-up at the University of Texas's MOOT Corp competition (now called the Venture Labs Investment Competition). Participating in MOOT Corp turned out to be particularly fortuitous. One of the judges offered to invest. That particular offer didn't work out, but another investor, Bill Wood, stepped in and offered the three their first round of investment. uShip now had the capacity to become a real company.

uShip

Shortly after Chasen, Millsap, and Manickam graduated, the uShip website went live. The basic idea was to connect people needing things shipped that were bigger or bulkier than UPS or FedEx normally took with shippers that had excess capacity on the same route. The initial plan was to target Texas. Texas was attractive in part because uShip stayed put in Austin, and by servicing Texas the company could be close to its initial customers. It was also attractive because of its triangle of major cities—Dallas, San Antanio, and Houston—and the amount of shipping that took place among the cities. Shortly after the uShip site went live, the company knew it would grow beyond Texas. People from across the country started listing items they needed shipped. In fact, uShip's very first transaction was three beds and a dresser that were shipped from Houston to Pocono Lake, Pennsylvania. The company was up and running.

The way uShip works is as follows. Consumers and businesses post the items they need shipped in one of several categories, including furniture, cars, boats, heavy machinery, and animals. The consumer can let shippers bid on their job, or name their price and see if a shipper bites. On the other side, the transporation service providers, including truckers, movers, and brokers, bid on the jobs or accept the offer price. uShip takes a cut of the total shipping cost.

The beauty of the service is that everyone wins. On the consumer side, a consumer is able to ship a large or bulky item, like a boat, from point A to point B for typically much less than contracting through a freight company direct. On the shipper side, the shippers get access to leads for free. Normally, shippers have to advertise to get jobs. They are only charged by uShip if they win a job and complete the shipment. There are also economic and societal benefits. About 40 percent of the trucks on the road are running partially or completely empty. uShip helps fill the trucks, which makes the overall transportation system more efficient.

Stages of Growth and the Chicken-and-Egg Problem

uShip's growth has progressed in three distinct phases, which are roughly similar to the standard organizatinal life cycle. The organizational life cycle has five phases—introduction, early growth, continuous growth, maturity, and decline. Chasen, in an interview with the first auth

(con

of this case, characterized uShip's growth as having three phases so far: bootstrap, rapid growth, and sustained growth.

Phase 1: Bootstrap.

uShip's first few years were a grind. Although the company achieved some early success, the overarching objectives were to prove product/market fit, show it could make money, and attract a Series A round of venture capital funding. The company also needed substantial traction. Chasen knew that uShip needed to get pretty far before it would attract venture funding. Venture funding would be needed to get to the next level of growth.

A challenge uShip faced straight away was the classic chicken-and-egg problem. Consumers would participate if a large number of shippers were available to bid on their jobs (and move their items), while shippers would participate if a large number of consumers were posting jobs. A critical mass of both is needed. In the industry, this is called "liquidity." Chasen and his small team tackled the challenge with a bootstrap mentality. Its first customers and shippers were driven to its website via guerilla marketing techniques, including using eBay and Craigslist. An interesting tactic was the use of Google AdWords. uShip emerged about the same time that AdWords came online. uShip used AdWords to prove its economic model. It could buy $10 worth of AdWords (i.e., AdWords appear as paid text advertisements that accompany Google search results), and within seven days convert the $10 into $20 in revenue through its transaction process. It was this tactic that convienced Benchmark, a venture capital firm located in Silicon Valley, to sign on. Chasen had met Bill Gurley, a partner at Benchmark, who was a UT alumnus, and started provided him updates about the progress that uShip was making. It wasn't until uShip proved its economic model, however, that Benchmark was willing to make an investment.

Phase 2: Rapid Growth Stage.

After the Benchmark investment, uShip took off. It used the money to bolster its staff, build out its infrastructure, and to enter new markets. The first step was to continue to build its U.S. market position. As the company's visibility grew, people started listing items that Chasen and his team never envisioned. Some of the more unusual items that it has shipped are a 4,000-pound steel horse, an oversized Venus Flytrap (which is a carnivorous plant), and an old English phone booth.

The company also started expanding internationally. From the very beginning, people from foreign ~~countries~~ arranged shipments via uShip. In fact, when ~~it launched~~, it found that people were trying ~~foreign~~ addresses into an online template ~~addresses~~ses. This fact made it neces- ~~sary to~~ quickly modify its site to accom- ~~modate foreign ad~~dresses. As uShip geared up, it ~~was offeri~~ng its service by foreign country,

starting with the most familiar markets, like the United Kingdom, as well as other European Union countries. uShip expanded from these initial positions. As it saw copycat sites pop up across the globe, it felt it was imperative to establish a presence in the most potentially profitable markets.

Partnerships were another key engine of rapid growth. uShip was a perfect partner for an e-commerce site that sold large and bulky items. The site would sell the item, and shipping would be provided via uShip. For example, in 2009, uShip entered into a partnership with Ritchie Brothers Auctioneers, the world's largest auctioneer for heavy equipment, to provide real-time estimates and quotes for the transportation of industrial equipment and vehicles being sold at auction.

uShip also became involved in an effort that led to its Series C round of funding. It establised a partnership with TerraPass. TerraPass is a social enterprise that provides carbon offsetting products to individuals and businesses. uShip created a program that enabled its shippers to become green providers. For every job that they booked through uShip, they agreed to purchase a carbon offset via TerraPass that would make up for the carbon pollution caused by the trip. TerraPass in turn would use the money to invest in clean energy projects, like solar and wind. This program led to a major round of funding through Kleiner Perkins Caufield & Byers, a well-known venture capital firm. Kleiner Perkins had set up a "green fund" and was looking to invest in companies that were attacking environmental issues in innovative ways. The funding round was for $18 million.

Phase 3: Sustained Growth.

uShip is now in a sustained growth phase. It is expanding its international presence, and is now in 18 countries, with an office in Amsterdam. Its partnership network is growing. It now provides customized shipping solutions for Cars.com, iBoats.com, Rock&Dirt, Motorcycle.com, John Deere's MachineFinder.com, and several others. It is also developing a program that will broker full loads of freight, targeted at expanding its presence in the $300 billion truckload freight market in the United States.

In 2012, uShip became the subject of a reality television series aired by A&E called Shipping Wars. The show follows six independent truckers as they compete for jobs on uShip's website, transport the loads, and deal with the challenges that truckers face on the road. Chasen and his team hope the visibility gained through the show will help make uShip a household name.

In early 2014, uShip received a major boost. It announced a partnership with eBay, which is by far the largest partnership in uShip's history. It will become the perferred shipper for all larger-than-parcel items sold via the eBay marketplace.

uShip's Future

Although uShip maintains an entrepreneurial spirit, it is no longer a start-up. It now has 185 employees and operations across the globe. While its future appears bright, it becomes harder to grow as a compay gets larger. Its options include (1) becoming a large private company, (2) staging an IPO and becoming a large public company, (3) being acquired by a larger firm, like eBay, or (4) plateauing and eventually entering the maturity and decline stage of the organizational life cycle. The way to avoid option 4, according to Chasen, is to keep innovating.

Discussion Questions

13-40. Examine the material in the first part of this chapter under the "Preparing for Growth" heading. To what degree has uShip been sensitive to the three issues (appreciating the nature of business growth, staying committed to a core strategy, and planning for growth) under this heading?

13-41. How have partnerships been important to uShip's growth? Why do you think uShip has been able to form so many partnerships with other firms? In slightly different words, why is uShip an attractive partner?

13-42. Refresh your memory of the meaning of the terms *adverse selection* and *moral hazard* as discussed in this chapter. What adverse selection and moral hazard issues does uShip face today and how should the firm deal with those issues?

13-43. uShip's current position is explained at the end of the case. Does this firm face the risk of growing too quickly? Why or why not?

Sources: Personal conversation with Matt Chasen, July 2, 2014; EIR Series, Matt Chasen, Herb Kelleher Center for Entrepreneurship, available at http://www.youtube.com/results?search_query=matt+chasen+uship, posted on April 8, 2014, accessed on July 2, 2014; L. Rao, "Shipping and Transportation Marketplace uShip Raises $18 Million from Kleiner Perkins," TechCrunch, December 19, 2012.

Endnotes

1. F. Bridoux and J. W. Stoelhorst, "Microfoundations for Stakeholder Theory: Managing Stakeholders with Heterogeneous Motives," *Strategic Management Journal* 35, no. 1 (2014): 107–125; L. Naldi and P. Davidsson, "Entrepreneurial Growth: The Role of International Knowledge Acquisitions as Moderated by Firm Age," *Journal of Business Venturing* 29, no. 5 (2014): 687–703.

2. S. Leibs, "Grow, Hire. Repeat," *Inc.*, available at http://www.inc.com/magazine/201403/scott-leibs/sustained-growth-predicts-business-success.html, (posted on February 25, 2014, accessed on June 25, 2014).

3. E. J. Douglas, "Reconstructing Entrepreneurial Intentions to Identify Predisposition for Growth," *Journal of Business Venturing* 28, no. 5 (2013): 633–651; W. J. Baumol and R. J. Strom, "Entrepreneurship and Economic Growth," *Strategic Entrepreneurship Journal* 1, nos. 3–4 (2007): 233–238.

4. D. Packard, *The HP Way: How Bill Hewlett and I Built Our Company*, ed. D. Kirby with Karen Lewis (New York: HarperBusiness, 1996).

5. Packard, *The HP Way*.

6. D. K. Dutta and S. Thornhill, "Venture Cognitive Logics, Entrepreneurial Cognitive Style, and Growth Intentions: A Conceptual Model and an Exploratory Field Study," *Entrepreneurship Research Journal* 4, no. 2 (2014): 147–166; C. Keen and H. Etemad, "The Impact of Entrepreneurial Capital and Rapidly Growing Firms: The Canadian Example," *International Journal of Entrepreneurship and Small Business* 12, no. 3 (2011): 273–289.

7. IBISWorld home page, www.ibisworld.com (accessed April 29, 2014).

8. IBISWorld, available at www.ibisworld.com, 2014.

9. N. Kaiser and V. Jain. "Interview with Vipin Jain, CEO of Retrevo," nPost home page, www.npost.com, originally posted April 9, 2008, accessed June 25, 2014.

10. D. Christopher, *The Pampered Chef* (New York: Doubleday, 2005).

11. M.-J. Chen and D. Miller, "Reconceptualizing Competitive Dynamics: A Multidimensional Framework," *Strategic Management Journal*, 2014, in press.

12. J. Collins, *Good to Great* (New York: Collins Books, 2001).

13. K. A. Eddleston, F. W. Kellermanns, S. W. Floyd, V. L. Crittenden, and W. F. Crittenden, "Planning Growth: Life Stage Differences in Family [...]repreneurship Theory and Practice* 37, [...]77–1202; F. G. Alberti, S. Sciascia, [...] Visconti, "The Entrepreneurial [...] Located in Clusters: A Cross-[...]ternational Journal of Technology* [...]4, no. 1 (2011): 53–79.

14. Wikipedia, uShip, www.wikipedia.org, (accessed June 25, 2014).

15. "12 Challenges Faced by the Fastest-Growing Companies," *Forbes*, November 3, 2013.

16. Y. L. Zhao, M. Song, and G. L. Storm, "Founding Team Capabilities and New Venture Performance: The Mediating Role of Strategic Positional Advantages," *Entrepreneurship Theory and Practice* 37, no. 4 (2013): 789–814.

17. D. Grichnik, J. Brinckmann, L. Singh, and S. Manigart, "Beyond Environmental Scarcity: Human and Social Capital as Driving Forces of Bootstrapping Activities," *Journal of Business Venturing* 29, no. 2 (2014): 310–326; M. Hughes, R. E. Morgan, R. D. Ireland, and P. Hughes, "Network Behaviors, Social Capital, and Organisational Learning in High-Growth Entrepreneurial Firms," *International Journal of Entrepreneurship and Small Business* 12, no. 3. (2011): 257–272.

18. L. Dai, V. Jaksimov, B. A. Gilbert, and S. A. Fernhaber, "Entrepreneurial Orientation and International Scope: The Differential Roles of Innovativeness, Proactiveness, and Risk-Taking," *Journal of Business Venturing* 29, no. 4 (2014): 511–524.

19. J. Welch, "Growth Initiatives," *Executive Excellence* 16, no. 6 (1999): 8–9.

20. M. R. Marvel, "Human Capital and Search-Based Discovery: A Study of High-Tech Entrepreneurship," *Entrepreneurship Theory and Practice* 37, no. 2 (2013): 403–419.

21. "Compilation of Turnover Cost Studies," Sasha Corporation, www.sashacorp.com, (accessed May 2, 2011).

22. A. Rauch and S. A. Rijsdijk, "The Effects of General and Specific Human Capital on Long-Term Growth and Failure of Newly Founded Businesses," *Entrepreneurship Theory and Practice* 37, no. 4 (2013): 923–941.

23. L. Sleuwaegen and J. Onkelinx, "International Commitment, Post-Entry Growth and Survival of International New Ventures," *Journal of Business Venturing* 29, no. 1 (2014): 106–120; J. M. Shulman, R. A. K. Cox, and T. T. Stallkamp, "The Strategic Entrepreneurial Growth Model," *Competitiveness Review* 21, no. 1 (2011): 29–46.

24. Ladies Who Launch, http://www.ladieswholaunch.com/magazine/april-singer/1060, originally posted on December 21, 2004, (accessed on June 25, 2014).

25. M. Gerber, *The E-Myth Revisited* (New York: HarperCollins, 2004).

26. Ladies Who Launch, http://www.ladieswholaunch.com/magazine/emily-levy/1080, originally posted on July 7, 2004, (accessed on June 26, 2014).

27. Entrepreneur, "When Success Isn't Enough," www.entrepreneur.com/article/185574,

(accessed June 25, 2014, originally posted in November 2007).

28. G. N. Chandler, J. C. Broberg, and T. H. Allison, "Customer Value Propositions in Declining Industries: Differences Between Industry Representative and High-Growth Firms," *Strategic Entrepreneurship Journal,* 2014, in press.

29. E. Pahnke, R. McDonald, D. Wang, and B. Hallen, "Exposed: Venture Capital, Competitor Ties, and Entrepreneurial Innovation," *Academy of Management Journal,* 2014, in press.

30. E. T. Penrose, *The Theory of the Growth of the Firm,* 3rd ed. (Oxford: Oxford University Press, 1995).

31. E. T. Penrose, *The Theory of the Growth of the Firm* (New York: John Wiley & Sons, 1959).

32. D. Miller, X. Xu, and V. Mehrotra, "When Is Human Capital a Valuable Resource? The Performance Effects of Ivy League Selection Among Celebrated CEOs," *Strategic Management Journal,* 2014, in press; R. Ragozzino and C. Moschieri, "When Theory Doesn't Meet Practice: Do Firms Really Stage Their Investments?" *Academy of Management Perspective,* 2014, in press.

33. T. W. Moss, D. O. Neubaum, and M. Meyskens, "The Effect of Virtuous and Entrepreneurial Orientations on Microfinance Lending and Repayment: A Signaling Theory Perspective," *Entrepreneurship Theory and Practice,* 2014, in press; A. Croce, J. Marti, and S. Murtinu, "The Impact of Venture Capital on the Productivity Growth of European Entrepreneurial Firms: Screening or Value Added Effect?" *Journal of Business Venturing* 28, no. 4 (2013): 489–510.

34. Penrose, *The Theory of the Growth of the Firm* (1959).

35. "12 Challenges Faced by the Fastest-Growing Companies," *Forbes,* November 3, 2013.

Getting
Personal with SHAKE SMART

Co-Founders

MARTIN REIMAN

BS, College of Business, San Diego State University, 2011

KEVIN GELFAND

BS, College of Business, San Diego State University, 2011

Dialogue with
Martin Reiman

▼

FAVORITE BAND ON MY SMARTPHONE MUSIC LIST
Foster the People

MY ADVICE FOR NEW ENTREPRENEURS
Stay focused

WHAT I DO WHEN I'M NOT WORKING
Stay active and keep my mind off work

FIRST ENTREPRENEURIAL EXPERIENCE
Running a pretty mean lemonade stand as a kid

MY BIGGEST SURPRISE AS AN ENTREPRENEUR
Creativity conquers all problems

BEST ADVICE I'VE RECEIVED
Just go for it

CHAPTER 14

Strategies for *Firm Growth*

OPENING PROFILE

SHAKE SMART
Maintaining Consistent Strategies for Growth

• Web: www.shakesmart.com • Facebook: Shake Smart: • Twitter: @ShakeSmartInc

In late July 2010, Kevin Gelfand had just finished a workout at the Aztec Recreational Center, the gym on the San Diego State University campus. He was dreading the bland protein shake he was about to drink. Rather than repeating this ritual, Gelfand decided to start experimenting with protein shakes of his own. He teamed up with fraternity brother Marin Reiman, and the two started experimenting with shakes that combined fresh fruit, ice, nonfat milk, and other ingredients with the whey protein found in most shakes. The pair came up with more than 60 different blends and recruited friends to do taste tests for them. They finally settled on 15 flavors. In the nearby photo, Martin Reiman is on the left and Kevin Gelfand is on the right.

During this time, Gelfand and Reiman started thinking about their experimentation as a potential business. They decided to call the business Smart Shake, based on the nutritious ingredients they were placing in their shakes. The ideal place to sell the shakes, in their estimation, was right outside the Aztec Center, where students like themselves would be looking for a nutritious snack after a workout. The two raised $50,000 from family and friends, hoping to set up shop near the gym. Getting approval from the university was no easy task. They spent six months planning and jumping through the necessary hoops, and were finally approved. The Shake Smart kiosk opened on January 3, 2011, just outside the Aztec Center, and was the first permanent student-run business to operate on the San Diego State University campus.

To make a go of it, Gelfand and Reiman figured that they would have to sell 60 drinks a day. They averaged 120 a day and within 6 months, were employing 12 people. The shakes were healthy, delicious, and convenient—a rare combination. The shakes had a near ideal combination of protein, fiber, vitamins, minerals, and antioxidants, which made them much more than a snack. They were a meal replacement and at about $5 fit a college student's budget. In August 2011, Gelfand and Reiman made a deal with San Diego State University allowing freshmen to pay using their meal plan.

Like most start-ups, Shake Smart experienced some hiccups early on. At one point they launched a loyalty program with paper punch cards. The punch cards slowed down the line, which wasn't good. Somebody got their hands on a puncher that was similar enough to the puncher Shake Smart was using that they were able to punch cards and redeem them for free shakes. Gelfand and Reiman finally caught on, and they switched to an approach that rewarded customers based on the dollar amount they spent.

LEARNING OBJECTIVES

After studying this chapter you should be ready to:

1. Identify and discuss the core internal growth strategy for entrepreneurial firms.

2. Describe additional internal product-growth strategies entrepreneurial firms can use.

3. Examine international expansion as a growth strategy.

4. Discuss different types of external growth strategies.

In terms of growing the business, Gelfand and Reiman have proceeded steadily but cautiously. In spring 2012, Shake Smart opened a second location, just outside a 24 Hour Fitness Gym in the Horton Plaza mall. The Horton Plaza mall is not far from the San Diego State University campus. Since that time they have added four more locations, bringing the total to six. They now have two locations on the San Diego State University campus, one at Camp Pendleton, a nearby Marine Corps Base, one in an area LA Fitness center, the Horton Plaza location, and the first Shake Smart outside San Diego, in San Francisco's Sports Club. A common theme across the six locations is that they are all in close proximity to people who are actively engaged with fitness. Along with adding to their number of locations, Shake Smart has also bolstered its menu. It now offers three categories of shakes: classic, specialty, and exotic. The ingredient combinations are novel and enticing. For example, one of Shake Smart's exotic shakes, named mea aloha, contains pineapple, banana, acai, apple juice, and protein. Shake Smart also sells smoothies, healthy snacks, and extra toppings for its shakes. One of its snacks, the pb&b sandwich, consists of peanut butter and banana slices on whole wheat bread.

In expanding Shake Smart, Gelfand and Reiman have used their business educations. Reiman graduated in May 2011 with a degree in integrated marketing, while Gelfand graduate in December 2011 with a management/entrepreneurship degree. While managing their first location, they carefully worked out and documented the operational details and made note of what went right and what didn't go right as time progressed. They used those details and knowledge to create a blueprint for subsequent locations. They stayed current on technology, and have a smartphone-based point of sale system that provides them real-time analytics on sales and expenses in all their locations, so they can instantly tell if anything is amiss. They are also active on social media to remain in touch with customers and continue to build the Shake Smart brand. Gelfand and Reiman are comfortable with Shake Smart's pace of growth. They have grown at a pace that they believe has been in step with their ability to properly oversee and operate each additional location. At some point they may consider franchising, but they are not at that point yet.

On several occasions, Gelfand and Reiman have been recognized for their efforts. In November 2012, they won fourth place in the Global Student Entrepreneur Awards, sponsored by the Entrepreneurs' Organization. More than 2,000 individuals from 28 countries entered the competition, which recognizes outstanding student-owned businesses. In 2011, Gelfand and Reiman were recognized by *Forbes* as one of its nine All Star Student Entrepreneurs. The most impressive testament to Gelfand and Reiman's accomplishments is Shake Smart's ongoing success. The company is profitable and employs more than 80 people at its 6 locations.

Shake Smart plans new locations in both Southern and Northern California. If the past is any indication of the future, Gelfand and Reiman will continue to grow Shake Smart by expanding their number of locations and experimenting with new menu combinations.

Shake Smart's experience is not unusual. Many entrepreneurial firms grow by adding to their product lines and by expanding geographically. In this chapter, we discuss the most common strategies firms use to grow. The growth strategies are divided into internal strategies for growth and external strategies for growth, as shown in Figure 14.1.

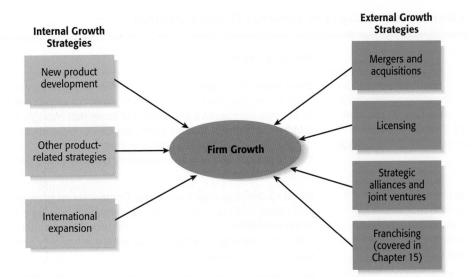

FIGURE 14.1
Internal and External
Growth Strategies

Internal Growth Strategies

Internal growth strategies involve efforts taken within the firm itself, such as new product development, other product-related strategies, and international expansion, for the purpose of increasing sales revenue and profitability. Many businesses, such as Modcloth, Sir Kensington's, and Zappos, are growing through internal growth strategies. The distinctive attribute of internally generated growth is that a business relies on its own competencies, expertise, business practices, and employees. Internally generated growth is often called **organic growth** because it does not rely on outside intervention. Almost all companies grow organically during the early stages of their organizational life cycles.

Effective though it can be, there are limits to internal growth. As a company enters the middle and later stages of its life cycle, sustaining growth strictly through internal means becomes more challenging. Because of this, the concern is that a company will "hit the wall" in terms of growth and will experience flat or even declining sales. This can happen when a company has the same product or service that it's trying to sell to the same list of potential buyers. Companies in this predicament need to either expand their client list, add new products or services to complement their existing ones, or find new avenues to growth. Sometimes companies face this challenge through no fault of their own.

Some start-ups, to avoid quickly hitting the wall in terms of growth, configure their initial products or services in ways that have built-in growth potential. This tactic is illustrated in this chapter's "Savvy Entrepreneurial Firm" feature. SwitchFlops is an example of a company that has "built-in" avenues for future growth as a result of the unique nature of its product and how it's configured.

We list the distinct advantages and disadvantages of internal growth strategies in Table 14.1.

New Product Development

New product development involves designing, producing, and selling new products (or services) as a means of increasing firm revenues and profitability. In many fast-paced industries, new product development is a competitive necessity. For example, the average product life cycle in the computer software industry is 14 to 16 months, at the most. Just thinking of how quickly we are introduced to new computers, new smartphones, and related products

LEARNING OBJECTIVE

1. Identify and discuss the core internal growth strategy for entrepreneurial firms.

TABLE 14.1   Advantages and Disadvantages of Internal Growth Strategies

Advantages	Disadvantages
Incremental, even-paced growth. A firm that grows at an even pace can continually adjust to changing environmental conditions to fine-tune its strategies over time. In contrast, a firm that doubles its size overnight through a merger or acquisition is making a much larger commitment at a single point in time.	**Slow form of growth.** In some industries, an incremental, even-paced approach toward growth does not permit a firm to develop competitive economies of scale fast enough. In addition, in some industries it may not be possible for a firm to develop sufficient resources to remain competitive. A high level of merger and acquisition activity typically characterizes these industries.
Provides maximum control. Internal growth strategies allow a firm to maintain control over the quality of its products and services during the growth process. In contrast, firms that grow through collaborative forms of growth, such as alliances or joint ventures, must share the oversight function with their business partners.	**Need to develop new resources.** Some internal growth strategies, such as new product development, require a firm to be innovative and develop new resources. While internal innovation has many positive attributes, it is typically slow, expensive, and risky.
Preserves organizational culture. Firms emphasizing internal growth are not required to blend their organizational culture with another organization. As a result, the venture can grow under the auspices of a clearly understood, unified corporate culture.	**Investment in a failed internal effort can be difficult to recoup.** Internal growth strategies, such as new product development, run the risk that a new product or service idea may not sell, making it difficult to recoup the development cost the firm incurred.
Encourages internal entrepreneurship. Firms that grow via internal growth strategies are looking for new ideas from within the business rather than from outsiders. This approach encourages a climate of internal entrepreneurship and innovation.	**Adds to industry capacity.** Some internal growth strategies add to industry capacity, and this can ultimately help force industry profitability down. For example, a restaurant chain that grows through geographic expansion may ultimately force industry profitability down by continuing to open new restaurants in an already crowded market.
Allows firms to promote from within. Firms emphasizing internal growth strategies have the advantage of being able to promote within their own organizations. The availability of promotional opportunities within a firm is a powerful tool for employee motivation.	

This young entrepreneur is hoping to grow her organic food start-up via a smartphone app for her store. Here, she is checking out some reviews that customers posted on her app.

SAVVY ENTREPRENEURIAL FIRM

SwitchFlops: How to Create Built-in Avenues for Future Growth

Web: www.lindsay-phillips.com; Facebook: Lindsay Phillips SwitchFlops; Twitter: @SwitchFlops

One thing that savvy, growth-minded start-ups do is configure their products or services in ways that have built-in growth potential. Producing "one-off" products or services leads to limited growth potential. Instead, it's best to produce products and services that, if successful, provide natural segues to complementary products and services that can be added later.

SwitchFlops are sandals with interchangeable straps. Lindsay Phillips developed the original idea for these products when enrolled in high school, as part of an art project, when she was 16. Amazed by the response, Phillips continued with the project. She started designing functional flops with colorful straps, each adorned by a unique button. She realized that by using a hook-and-loop fastener on each flop, she could create a shoe that accommodated interchangeable straps. This was the birth of SwitchFlops. A shopper buys one pair of SwitchFlops sandals, and can then purchase interchangeable straps.

During her college years, Phillips fine-tuned her design, merchandising, and manufacturing skills working summers at Polo Ralph Lauren's leather goods division in New York City. She also traveled to Europe for classes and enrolled in the Semester at Sea program. These last two experiences exposed her to a variety of colors, cultures, and patterns that helped her fashion unique strap designs. A patent on her unique approach was granted in 2004. SwitchFlops made its retail debut in January 2007 at the Surf Expo Trade Show in Orlando, Florida, where it was showcased as a new, creative product.

SwitchFlops started with several basic sandal designs and 10 straps. Most customers bought more than one pair of sandals and several straps, allowing them to "customize" their look by trading out sandals and straps. Most customers seemed to enjoy this experience. SwitchFlops's value proposition was both versatility and value.

Today, SwitchFlops sandals cost between $24.05 and $59.95, and the straps cost between $7.50 and $16.95 each. To make it fun, the sandals and straps all have names. Sandals include Rosie Neutral Snakeskin, Lulu Flop Gray, and Brenna Brown Wedge. Straps include Arlene Snap, Dhana Strap, Franny Snap, and Joanie Snap. There are now multiple SwitchFlops sandals and straps to choose from. Phillips has evolved her footwear line and currently sells ballet flats, wedges, and espadrilles along with sandals and has added shopping bags, scarves, and sandals for children to her firm's product lines.

SwitchFlops sandals benefit from being both fashion-conscious and economical. Instead of owning 10 pairs of sandals, a customer can own two or three, and have multiple "looks" by changing out straps. By making a product (sandals) that is based on buying add-ons (straps), the strategy has also benefited SwitchFlops and helped fuel its growth.

Questions for Critical Thinking

1. As an up-and-coming entrepreneur, what things did Lindsay Phillips do to equip herself to lead a growth-oriented firm?
2. Think of a company that sells a product or service that's similar to SwitchFlops, in that the product or service provides a natural segue to add-on products or services. Briefly explain the product and its built-in avenues for future growth.
3. Of the companies profiled in the "You Be the VC" features in the book, which company has a product or service that is best positioned for natural segues for future growth? Explain your answer.
4. Why do you think SwitchFlops has been so successful? Draw lessons from several chapters of the book to formulate your answer.

Sources: Lindsay Phillips website, www.lindsay-phillips.com, accessed July 14, 2014; Business Pundit Blog, "SwitchFlops: A Smart, Successful Fashion Startup," available at www.businesspundit.com/switchflops-a-smart-successful-fashion-startup, posted on September 8, 2010, accessed on July 14, 2014.

highlights for us how rapidly products change in this industry. Because of these rapid changes, to remain competitive, software companies must always have new products in their pipelines. For some companies, continually developing new products is the essence of their existence.

Although developing new products can result in substantial rewards, it is a high-risk strategy. The key is developing innovative new products that aren't simply "me-too" products that are entering already crowded markets. When properly executed though, there is tremendous upside potential to developing new products and/or services. Many biotech and pharmaceutical companies, for example, have developed products that not only improve the quality of life for their customers but also provide reliable revenue streams. In many cases, the products are patented, meaning that no one else can make them, at least until the patents expire. Successful new products can also provide sufficient cash flow to fund a company's operations and provide resources to support developing additional new products. For example, Amgen, a large and historically profitable biotech company, has several stellar pharmaceutical products, including Enbrel and Neupogen. Enbrel is a tumor necrosis factor (TNF) blocker that is used to treat rheumatoid arthritis as well as some related conditions, and Neupogen helps prevent infection in cancer patients undergoing certain types of chemotherapy. These products have provided the company sufficient revenue to cover its overhead, fund new product development, and generate profits for an extended period of time.[1]

The keys to effective new product and service development, which are consistent with the material on opportunity recognition (Chapter 2) and feasibility analysis (Chapter 3), follow:

- ■ **Find a need and fill it:** Most successful new products fill a need that is presently unfilled. "Saturated" markets should be avoided. For example, in the United States as well as in most developed countries, consumers have a more-than-adequate selection of appliances, tires, credit cards, and cell phone plans. These are crowded markets with low profit margins. The challenge for entrepreneurs is to find unfilled needs in attractive markets and then find a way to fill those needs.

- ■ **Develop products that add value:** In addition to finding a need and fulfilling it, the most successful products are those that "add value" for customers in some meaningful way.

- ■ **Get quality and pricing right:** Every product represents a balance between quality and pricing. If the quality of a product and its price are not compatible, the product may fail and have little chance for recovery. To put this in slightly different terms, customers are willing to pay higher prices for higher-quality products and are willing to accept lower quality when they pay lower prices.

- ■ **Focus on a specific target market:** Every new product and service should have a specific target market in mind, as we have highlighted throughout this book. This degree of specificity gives the innovating entrepreneurial venture the opportunity to conduct a focused promotional campaign and select the appropriate distributors. The notion that "it's a good product, so somebody will by it" is a naïve way to do business and often contributes to failure.

- ■ **Conduct ongoing feasibility analysis:** Once a product or service is launched, the feasibility analysis and marketing research should not end. The initial market response should be tested in focus groups and surveys, and incremental adjustments should be made when appropriate.

There is also a common set of reasons that new products fail, as articulated by eSeller Media and shown in Table 14.2.[2] It behooves entrepreneurs to

TABLE 14.2   The Top 5 Reasons New Products Fail

1. The potential market was overestimated.

2. Customers saw the product as too expensive.

3. The product was poorly designed.

4. The product was no different than the competition's ("me too" products).

5. The costs of developing the product line were too high.

be aware of these reasons and to work hard to prevent new product failures as a result of poor execution in these areas.

This discussion is a reminder that to achieve healthy growth, whether via the development of new products or another means, a firm must sell a product or service that legitimately creates value and has the potential to generate profits along with sales.

Additional Internal Product-Growth Strategies

Along with developing new products, firms grow by improving existing products or services, increasing the market penetration of an existing product or service, or pursuing a product extension strategy.

LEARNING OBJECTIVE

2. Describe additional internal product-growth strategies entrepreneurial firms can use.

Improving an Existing Product or Service

A business can often increase its revenue by **improving an existing product or service**—enhancing quality, making it larger or smaller, making it more convenient to use, improving its durability, or making it more up-to-date. Improving an item means increasing its value and price potential from the customer's perspective. For example, smartphone companies routinely increase revenues by coming out with "new" versions of their existing phones.

A mistake many businesses make is not remaining vigilant enough regarding opportunities to improve existing products and services. It is typically much less expensive for a firm to modify an existing product or service and extend its life than to develop a new product or service from scratch. For example, many women have set aside the flat irons that they've used for years to do their hair and have bought a ceramic flat iron because they're safer and do a better job. Selling "improved" flat irons is a much less expensive way for curling iron manufacturers to grow sales than to develop a completely new product.

Increasing the Market Penetration of an Existing Product or Service

A **market penetration strategy** involves actions taken to increase the sales of a product or service through greater marketing efforts or through increased production capacity and efficiency.[3] An increase in a product's market share is typically accomplished by increasing advertising expenditures, offering sales promotions, lowering the price, increasing the size of the sales force, or increasing a company's social media efforts. Consider Proactiv, the skincare company. Since its inception in 1994, Proactiv has relied on celebrity endorsers to demonstrate and promote its product. Actress Judith Light and actress/singer Vanessa Williams were the firm's first celebrity endorsers. Over the years, the company has added additional celebrity endorsers to appeal to a broader and more diverse clientele. The additions include actress Jane Seymour, music artists Katy Perry, Jenna Fischer, and Justin Bieber, and tennis player Caroline Wozniacki.[4] Dr. Katie Rodan, a cofounder of Proactiv, points to the celebrity endorser program as one of the savviest actions the company has taken to build market share.[5]

Another example is the prepaid card, like the Starbucks Card, that almost all restaurants and retailers now offer. By making it more convenient for customers to purchase its products, restaurants and retailers boost their revenues. Prepaid cards also make it easier to give a restaurant's or retailer's offering as a gift. Think of how many people buy Target, Macy's, or Pottery Barn prepaid (gift) cards as birthday or holiday gifts. A benefit to those receiving these cards is the opportunity to use them to buy a product that fulfills a true need.

Increased market penetration can also occur through increased capacity or efficiency, which permits a firm to have a greater volume of product or service to sell. In a manufacturing context, an increase in product capacity can occur by expanding plant and equipment or by outsourcing a portion of the production process to another company. **Outsourcing** is work that is done for a company by people other than the company's full-time employees.[6] For example, a firm that previously manufactured and packaged its product may outsource the packaging function to another company and as a result free up factory space to increase production of the basic product. Additionally, a firm might outsource its information technology function to free up resources that could be invested in product development efforts.

Extending Product Lines

A **product line extension strategy** involves making additional versions of a product so that it will appeal to different clientele or making related products to sell to the same clientele.[7] For example, a company may make another version of a low-end product that is a little better and then make another version of it that represents the top of the line to appeal to different clientele. This is a strategy that allows a firm to take one product and extend it into several products without incurring significant additional development expense. Computer manufacturers provide a good example of how to execute a product line extension strategy. Each manufacturer sells several versions of its desktop and laptop computers. The different versions of the same computer typically represent good, better, and best alternatives based on processor speed, memory capacity, monitor size, graphic capabilities, and other features. In regard to making related products to sell to the same clientele, many firms start by offering one product or service and then expand into related areas.

Firms also pursue product extension strategies as a way of leveraging their core competencies into related areas. For example, Zipcar, the popular car sharing service, has applied the expertise it developed through its consumer car sharing service to launch Zipcar for business, an initiative that allows businesses to use Zipcar's services in the same way that individuals do. Similarly, it recently launched FastFleet, a service to help cities more efficiently use cars in their fleet. An account of the history of Oracle, a computer database software company, provides a particularly interesting example of the potential payoff of a product extension strategy. The example demonstrates that product extension strategies can take time and patience to pay off but can lead to breakthrough growth strategies:

> As Ellison [Oracle's CEO] recognized that he had sold a database to almost every one of the biggest companies in the world, he knew he would need new products to sell. That is how he came up with the idea of applications. Oracle applications would sit on top of and use Oracle databases to perform functions such as inventory management, personnel record keeping, and sales tracking. The proof of his thinking took almost seven years, but by 1995, the company generated nearly $300 million in license revenues from application products and an additional $400 million in applications-related services.[8]

Geographic Expansion

Geographic expansion is another internal growth strategy. Many entrepreneurial businesses grow by simply expanding from their original location to additional geographic sites. This type of expansion is most common in retail settings. For example, a small business that has a successful retail store in one location may expand by opening a second location in a nearby community. Gap Inc., Walgreens, and Panera Bread are examples of firms that have grown through geographic expansion. Of course, McDonald's, which now has over 35,000 worldwide locations, is the classic example of incredibly successful growth through geographic expansion. Interestingly, Subway, another firm achieving a significant level of success through geographic expansion, now has more locations worldwide than does McDonald's. The keys to successful geographic expansion follow:

- **Perform successfully in the initial location:** Additional locations can learn from the initial location's success.

- **Establish the legitimacy of the business concept in the expansion locations:** For example, a particular type of fitness center may be well accepted in its original location because it has been there a long time and has a loyal clientele. However, potential clientele in a neighboring community may be completely unfamiliar with its unique products and services. A common mistake an entrepreneurial venture makes when it expands from one community to another is to assume that if something works in one community, it will automatically work in another.

- **Don't isolate the expansion location:** Sometimes the employees in an expansion location feel isolated and that they are not receiving adequate training and oversight from the headquarters location. It is a mistake to believe that an expansion location can excel without the same amount of attention and nurturing that it took to build the business in the original location.

Product-related strategies, regardless of the form they take, work best when a company remains vigilant about making sure the product remains in demand and consumer trends aren't turning against it. A lack of vigilance in this area contributed to the failure of Crumbs Bake Shop, a company that at one time was the most popular cupcake-focused bake shop in the United States. A description of why Crumbs failed, which is an example all entrepreneurial firms can learn from, is provided in the nearby "What Went Wrong?" feature.

International Expansion

International expansion is another common form of growth for entrepreneurial firms.[9] According to a 2011 survey conducted by the Small Business & Entrepreneurship Council (SBE) and the Financial Services Roundtable, 21 percent of small businesses said that expanding into overseas markets factored into their business plans over the next five years.[10] A look at the world's population and purchasing power statistics affirms the importance of international markets for growth-oriented firms. Approximately 96 percent of the world's population and 70 percent of its total purchasing power are located outside the United States. Influenced by these data, an increasing number of the new firms launched in the United States today are international new ventures.

International new ventures are businesses that, from inception, seek to derive competitive advantage by using their resources to sell products or services in multiple countries.[11] From the time they are started, these firms, which are sometimes called "global start-ups" or "born globals," view the world as their marketplace rather than confining themselves to a single country. ASOS, for example, which is a European fashion website, was an international firm from its inception. It now generates over 67 percent of its revenues from overseas sales.[12] Similarly, some start-ups become international firms because overseas customers request their product or service. This is what happened to uShip, an Austin, Texas, company, as reported in Case 13.2. Shortly

LEARNING OBJECTIVE
3. Examine international expansion as a growth strategy.

WHAT WENT WRONG?

Lessons for Growth-Minded Start-ups from Crumbs Bake Shop's Failure

Crumbs Bake Shop was founded in 2003 by Jason and Mia Bauer, a husband-and-wife team. The idea was to sell gourmet cupcakes. The cupcakes came in an assortment of sizes and fillings. Most of the cupcakes were familiar flavors, such as cookie dough, tiramisu, and caramel apple. There were also cupcakes named after celebrities like Elvis Presley and Artie Lange. The cupcakes came in three main sizes: the mini "taste" size, the "classic" size, and the "signature" size. The signature size cupcakes, which were nearly double the size of standard cupcakes, cost anywhere from $3.50 to $4.50. Crumbs placed small signs in front of each cupcake or baked good reporting the price and calorie count. The blackbottom cheesecake brownie cupcake was reported to have 1,090 calories. In its latter years, Crumbs made a $42 "Colossal" cupcake that served as many as eight people.

Crumbs expanded quickly and soon became the largest cupcake chain in the United States. At its peak it had expanded to 79 locations with plans for many more. It broadened its approach some but primarily stuck to selling cupcakes. In early 2011, Crumbs was sold to a shell company, which took it public that June. For the first time, its same-store sales started to decline. The company's new CEO, Edward Slezak, tried a new approach to growth—striking licensing deals to sell Crumbs-branded products in other stores. He also started closing unprofitable locations. In mid-2013, Crumbs announced a partnership with David Burke, a well-known chef and restaurateur, to begin marketing a new line of gourmet sandwiches and salads at select Crumbs locations. The partnership ended roughly a month later due to poor sales. In late 2013, Crumbs opened a gluten-free store in downtown Manhattan in New York City.

On July 8, 2014, Crumbs announced that it planned to close all of its stores. The company's stock had been delisted several days earlier by the NASDAQ Stock Exchange. The company warned that the delisting would cause it to default on up to $14 million in debt. A sad ending. At one time Crumbs was proud and growing. Now it was closing. What went wrong? Several things— all of which provide valuable lessons for growing entrepreneurial firms.

First, an increasingly crowded market. When Crumbs opened in 2003, it was unique. There were only a handful of bakeries devoted to cupcakes nationwide. By 2011, the year Crumbs's same-day sales started to decline, there were many. Some were bakeries and some were simple kiosks. In addition, almost any bakery could add gourmet cupcakes to its product offerings if it wanted to do so.

Second, consumers started losing interest in cupcakes. When Crumbs opened, cupcakes were hot. Consumers eventually moved on. To illustrate this point, the *Wall Street Journal* ran an article in early 2013 titled "Forget Gold, the Gourmet-Cupcake Market is Crashing," in which it reported Crumbs's declining sales. While its drop in sales was attributed in part to Hurricane Sandy (many of Crumbs's restaurants were in the New York City area), the *Wall Street Journal* article said Crumbs was suffering from a larger problem: "gourmet-cupcake burnout."

Third, high real estate costs. Crumbs had nice stores. Many were large for a single-product company. Its shops averaged about 1,000 square feet. One Crumbs Bake Shop near Chicago, according to a 2014 *Business Insider* article, measured 3,300 square feet. That's about the same size as a generous four-bedroom home.

Fourth, no pivot or change in strategy. Despite falling same-store sales, Crumbs kept opening new locations. It added 35 locations from mid-2011 to 2013 alone. This was during a period in which it knew its same-store sales were declining. It also maintained its focus on cupcakes, with no serious attempt to diversify. A challenge with selling a product like cupcakes is that it's an occasional rather than a regular purchase. While people might eat at the same restaurant every day or buy bread from the same bakery several times a week, very few people buy items like gourmet cupcakes more than occasionally.

Questions for Critical Thinking

1. What are three lessons that other start-ups can learn from Crumbs's failure?
2. To what degree do you think Crumbs should have been able to anticipate a decline in interest in gourmet cupcakes?
3. Why do you think Crumbs doggedly stuck to its singular focus on selling cupcakes, in light of declining same-store sales?
4. Was Crumbs's failure preventable? What, if anything, could have been done to save Crumbs? Based on the material in the chapter, what types of growth could Crumbs have pursued that it didn't go after?

Sources: H. Peterson, "4 Reasons Why Crumbs Bake Shop Massively Failed," *Business Insider*, available at http://www.businessinsider.com/4-reasons-why-crumbs-bake-shop-closed-2014-7, posted on July 8, 2014, accessed on July 8, 2014; Wikipedia, Crumbs Bake Shop, www.wikipedia.com, accessed July 7, 2014; E. Maltby and S. Needleman, "Forget Gold, the Gourmet-Cupcake Market is Crashing," *Wall Street Journal*, April 17, 2013.

after it launched in 2003, overseas customers started arranging shipments via uShip's website. uShip is now in 18 countries and has an office in Amsterdam.

Although there is vast potential associated with selling overseas, it is a fairly complex form of firm growth. Of course, alert entrepreneurs should carefully observe any changes in purchasing power among the world's societies that may result from a financial crisis like the one the world experienced in 2008 and 2009. Let's look at the most important issues that entrepreneurial firms should consider in pursuing growth via international expansion.

Assessing a Firm's Suitability for Growth Through International Markets

Table 14.3 provides a review of the issues that should be considered, including management/organizational issues, product and distribution issues, and financial and risk management issues, when a venture considers expanding

TABLE 14.3 Evaluating a Firm's Overall Suitability for Growth Through International Markets

Management/Organizational Issues

Depth of management commitment. A firm's first consideration is to test the depth of its management commitment to entering international markets. Although a firm can "test the waters" by exporting with minimal risk, other forms of internationalization involve a far more significant commitment. A properly funded and executed international strategy requires top management support.

Depth of international experience. A firm should also assess its depth of experience in international markets. Many entrepreneurial firms have no experience in this area. As a result, to be successful, an inexperienced entrepreneurial firm may have to hire an export management company to familiarize itself with export documentation and other subtleties of the export process. Many entrepreneurial firms err by believing that selling and servicing a product or service overseas is not that much different than doing so at home. It is.

Interference with other firm initiatives. Learning how to sell in foreign markets can consume a great deal of entrepreneurs' or managers' time. Overseas travel is often required, and selling to buyers who speak a different language and live in a different time zone can be a painstaking process. Overall, efforts must be devoted to understanding the culture of the international markets the venture is considering. Thus, a firm should weigh the advantages of involvement in international markets against the time commitment involved and the potential interference with other firm initiatives.

Product and Distribution Issues

Product issues. A firm must first determine if its products or services are suitable for overseas markets. Many pertinent questions need to be answered to make this determination. For example, are a firm's products subject to national health or product safety regulations? Do the products require local service, supplies, or spare parts distribution capability? Will the products need to be redesigned to meet the specifications of customers in foreign markets? Will foreign customers find the products desirable? All these questions must have suitable answers before entering a foreign market. A firm can't simply "assume" that its products are salable and easily serviceable in foreign countries.

Distribution issues. How will the product be transported from the United States to a foreign country? Alternatively, how would an entrepreneurial firm transport a product produced in Sweden to a market in the United States? Is the transportation reliable and affordable? Can the product be exported from the venture's home operation, or will it have to be manufactured in the country of sale?

Financial and Risk Management Issues

Financing export operations. Can the foreign initiative be funded from internal operations, or will additional funding be needed? How will foreign customers pay the firm? How will the firm collect bad debts in a foreign country? Informed answers to these questions must be obtained before the firm initiates overseas sales.

Foreign currency risk. How will the firm manage fluctuations in exchange rates? If the entrepreneurial firm is located in the United States and it sells to a buyer in Japan, will it be paid in U.S. dollars or in Japanese yen?

into international markets. If these issues can be addressed successfully, growth through international markets may be an excellent choice for an entrepreneurial firm. The major impediment in this area is not fully appreciating the challenges involved.

Foreign Market Entry Strategies

The majority of entrepreneurial firms first enter foreign markets as exporters, but firms also use licensing, joint ventures, franchising, turnkey projects, and wholly owned subsidiaries to start international expansion.[13] These strategies, along with their primary advantages and disadvantages, are explained in Table 14.4.

Selling Overseas

Many entrepreneurial firms first start selling overseas by responding to an unsolicited inquiry from a foreign buyer. It is important to handle the inquiry appropriately and to observe protocols when trying to serve the needs of

TABLE 14.4 **Primary Advantages and Disadvantages of Various Foreign-Market Entry Strategies**

Foreign-Market Entry Strategy	Primary Advantage	Primary Disadvantage
Exporting. Exporting is the process of producing a product at home and shipping it to a foreign market. Most entrepreneurial firms begin their international involvement as exporters.	Exporting is a relatively inexpensive way for a firm to become involved in foreign markets.	High transportation costs can make exporting uneconomical, particularly for bulky products.
Licensing. A licensing agreement is an arrangement whereby a firm with the proprietary rights to a product grants permission to another firm to manufacture that product for specified royalties or other payments. Proprietary services and processes can also be licensed.	The licensee puts up most of the capital needed to establish the overseas operation.	A firm in effect "teaches" a foreign company how to produce its proprietary product. Eventually, the foreign company will probably break away and start producing a variation of the product on its own.
Joint ventures. A joint venture involves the establishment of a firm that is jointly owned by two or more otherwise independent firms. Fuji-Xerox, founded in 1962, for example, is a joint venture between an American and a Japanese firm.	Gaining access to the foreign partner's knowledge of local customs and market preferences.	A firm loses partial control of its business operations.
Franchising. A franchise is an agreement between a franchisor (the parent company that has a proprietary product, service, or business method) and a franchisee (an individual or firm that is willing to pay the franchisor a fee for the right to sell its product, service, and/or use its business method). U.S. firms can sell franchises in foreign markets, with the reverse being true as well.	The franchisee puts up the majority of capital needed to operate in the foreign market.	Quality control.
Turnkey projects. In a turnkey project, a contractor from one country builds a facility in another country, trains the personnel that will operate the facility, and *turns* over the *keys* to the project when it is completed and ready to operate.	Ability to generate revenue.	It is usually a one-time activity, and the relationships that are established in a foreign market may not be valuable to facilitate future projects.
Wholly owned subsidiary. A firm that establishes a wholly owned subsidiary in a foreign country has typically made the decision to manufacture in the foreign country and establish a permanent presence.	Provides a firm total control over its foreign operations.	The cost of setting up and maintaining a manufacturing facility and permanent presence in a foreign country can be high.

customers in foreign markets. The following are several rules of thumb for selling products in foreign markets:

- Answer requests promptly and clearly. Do not ignore a request just because it lacks grammatical clarity and elegance. Individuals using a nonnative language to contact a business located outside their home nation often are inexperienced with a second language.

- Replies to foreign inquires, other than e-mail or fax, should be communicated through some form of airmail or overnight delivery. Ground delivery is slow in some areas of the world.

- A file should be set up to retain copies of all foreign inquiries. Even if an inquiry does not lead to an immediate sale, the names of firms that have made inquiries will be valuable for future prospecting.

- Keep promises. The biggest complaint from foreign buyers about U.S. businesses is failure to ship on time (or as promised). The first order is the most important in that it sets the tone for the ongoing relationship.

- All correspondence should be personally signed. Form letters are offensive in some cultures.

- Be polite, courteous, friendly, and respectful. This is simple common sense, but politeness is particularly important in some Asian cultures. In addition, avoid the use of business slang that is indigenous to the United States, in that the slang terms lack meaning in many other cultures. Stated simply, be sensitive to cultural norms and expectations.

- For a personal meeting, always make sure to send an individual who is of equal rank to the person with whom he or she will be meeting. In some cultures, it would be seen as inappropriate for a salesperson from a U.S. company to meet with the vice president or president of a foreign firm.

External Growth Strategies

External growth strategies rely on establishing relationships with third parties. Mergers, acquisitions, strategic alliances, joint ventures, licensing, and franchising are examples of external growth strategies. Each of these strategic options is discussed in the following sections, with the exception of franchising, which we consider separately in Chapter 15.

LEARNING OBJECTIVE
4. Discuss different types of external growth strategies.

An emphasis on external growth strategies typically results in a more fast-paced, collaborative approach toward growth than the slower-paced internal strategies, such as new product development and expanding to foreign markets. External growth strategies level the playing field between smaller firms and larger companies.[14] For example, Pixar, the small animation studio that produced the animated hits *Toy Story, Finding Nemo,* and *Up,* had a number of key strategic alliances with Disney, before Disney acquired Pixar in 2006. By partnering with Disney, Pixar effectively co-opted a portion of Disney's management savvy, technical expertise, and access to distribution channels. The relationship with Disney helped Pixar grow and enhance its ability to effectively compete in the marketplace, to the point where it became an attractive acquisition target.

There are distinct advantages and disadvantages to emphasizing external growth strategies, as shown in Table 14.5.

Mergers and Acquisitions

Many entrepreneurial firms grow through mergers and acquisitions. A **merger** is the pooling of interests to combine two or more firms into one. An **acquisition** is the outright purchase of one firm by another. In an acquisition, the

TABLE 14.5 Advantages and Disadvantages of Emphasizing External Growth Strategies

Advantages	Disadvantages
Reducing competition. Competition is lessened when a firm acquires a competitor. This step often helps a firm establish price stability by eliminating the possibility of getting in a price war with at least one competitor. By turning potential competitors into partners and through alliances and franchises, the firm can also reduce the amount of competition it experiences.	**Incompatibility of top management.** The top managers of the firms involved in an acquisition, an alliance, a licensing agreement, or a franchise organization may clash, making the implementation of the initiative difficult.
Getting access to proprietary products or services. Acquisitions or alliances are often motivated by a desire on the part of one firm to gain legitimate access to the proprietary property of another.	**Clash of corporate cultures.** Because external forms of growth require the combined effort of two or more firms, corporate cultures often clash, resulting in frustration and subpar performance.
Gaining access to new products and markets. Growth through acquisition, alliances, or franchising is a quick way for a firm to gain access to new products and markets. Licensing can also provide a firm an initial entry into a market.	**Operational problems.** Another problem that firms encounter when they acquire or collaborate with another company is that their equipment and business processes may lack full compatibility.
Obtaining access to technical expertise. Sometimes, businesses acquire or partner with other businesses to gain access to technical expertise. In franchise organizations, franchisors often receive useful tips and suggestions from their franchisees.	**Increased business complexity.** Although the vast majority of acquisitions and alliances involve companies that are in the same or closely related industries, some entrepreneurial firms acquire or partner with firms in unrelated industries. This approach vastly increases the complexity of the combined business. The firm acquiring a brand or partnership with another company to gain access to its brand may subsequently fail to further develop its own brand and trademarks. This failure can lead to an increased dependency on acquired or partnered brands, reducing the firm's ability to establish and maintain a unique identity in the marketplace.
Gaining access to an established brand name. A growing company that has good products or services may acquire or partner with an older, more established company to gain access to its trademark and name recognition.	
Economies of scale. Combining two or more previously separate firms, whether through acquisition, partnering, or franchising, often leads to greater economies of scale for the combined firms.	**Loss of organizational flexibility.** Acquiring or establishing a partnership with one firm may foreclose the possibility of acquiring or establishing a partnership with another one.
Diversification of business risk. One of the principal driving forces behind all forms of collaboration or shared ownership is to diversify business risk.	**Antitrust implications.** Acquisitions and alliances are subject to antitrust review. In addition, some countries have strict antitrust laws prohibiting certain business relationships between firms.

surviving firm is called the **acquirer**, and the firm that is acquired is called the **target**. This section focuses on acquisitions rather than mergers because entrepreneurial firms are more commonly involved with acquisitions than mergers.

Acquiring another business can fulfill several of a company's needs, such as expanding its product line, gaining access to distribution channels, achieving economies of scale, gaining access to technology that will enhance its current offerings, or gaining access to talented employees. In most cases, a firm acquires a competitor or a company that has a product line or core competence that it needs. For example, in 2012 Facebook acquired Instagram as a way of enhancing its photo sharing capabilities. Similarly, in 2014 Twitter acquired a company called TapCommerce to bolster its capabilities in mobile advertising.

Although it can be advantageous, the decision to grow the entrepreneurial firm through acquisitions should be approached with caution.[15] Many firms

One thing that often surprises entrepreneurs is that growing a firm is as challenging as starting one. Here, a young entrepreneur is checking her monthly expenses against her budget at the end of a long day.

Jetta Productions/Blend Images/Corbis

have found that the process of assimilating another company into their current operation is not easy and can stretch finances to the brink.

Finding an Appropriate Acquisition Candidate If a firm decides to grow through acquisition, it is very important for it to exercise extreme care in finding acquisition candidates. Many acquisitions fail not because the companies involved lack resolve, but because they were a poor match to begin with. There are typically two steps involved in finding an appropriate target firm. The first step is to survey the marketplace and make a "short list" of promising candidates. The second is to carefully screen each candidate to determine its suitability for acquisition. The key areas to focus on in accomplishing these two steps are as follows:

- The target firm's openness to the idea of being acquired and its ability to receive consent for its acquisition from key third parties. The third parties from whom consent may be required include bankers, investors, suppliers, employees, and key customers.
- The strength of the target firm's management team, its industry, and its physical proximity to the acquiring firm's headquarters.
- The perceived compatibility of the target company's top management team and corporate culture with the acquiring firm's top management team and corporate culture.
- The target firm's past and projected financial performance.
- The likelihood the target firm will retain its key employees and customers if acquired.
- The identification of any legal complications that might impede the purchase of the target firm and the extent to which patents, trademarks, and copyrights protect the firm's intellectual property.
- The extent to which the acquiring firm understands the business and industry of the target firm.

The screening should be as comprehensive as possible to provide the acquiring firm sufficient data to determine realistic offering prices for the firms under consideration. A common mistake among acquiring firms is to pay too much for the businesses they purchase. Firms can avoid this mistake by basing their bids on hard data rather than on guesses or intuition.

Steps Involved in an Acquisition   Completing an acquisition is a nine-step process, as illustrated in Figure 14.2.

Step 1   **Schedule a meeting with the target firm's executives:** The acquiring firm should have legal representation at this point to help structure the initial negotiations and help settle any legal issues. The acquiring firm should also have a good idea of what it thinks the acquisition target is worth.

Step 2   **Evaluate the feelings of the target firm's executives about the acquisition:** If the target is in a "hurry to sell," it works to the acquiring firm's advantage. If the target starts to get cold feet, the negotiations may become more difficult.

Step 3   **Determine how to most appropriately finance the acquisition:** The acquiring firm should be financially prepared to complete the transaction if the terms are favorable.

Step 4   **Actively negotiate with the target firm:** If a purchase is imminent, obtain all necessary shareholder and third-party consents and approvals.

Step 5   **Make an offer if negotiations indicate that doing so is appropriate:** Both parties should have the offer reviewed by attorneys and certified public accountants (CPAs) that represent their interests. Determine how payment will be structured.

Step 6   **Develop a noncompete agreement with key target firm employees who will be retained:** This agreement, as explained in Chapter 7, limits the rights of the key employees of the acquired firm to start the

FIGURE 14.2
The Process of Completing the Acquisition of Another Firm

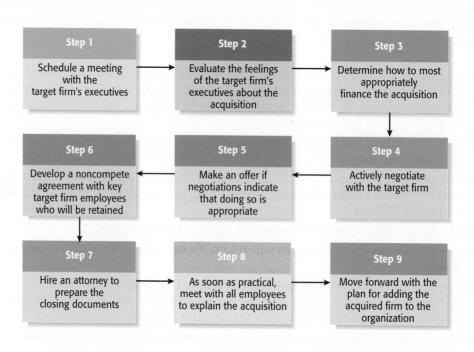

same type of business in the acquiring firm's trade area for a specific amount of time.

Step 7 **Hire an attorney to prepare the closing documents:** Complete the transaction.

Step 8 **As soon as practical, meet with all employees to explain the acquisition:** A meeting should be held as soon as possible with the employees of both the acquiring firm and the target firm. Articulate a vision for the combined firm and ease employee anxiety where possible.

Step 9 **Move forward with the plan for adding the acquired firm to the organization:** In some cases, the acquired firm is immediately assimilated into the operations of the acquiring firm. In other cases, the acquired firm is allowed to operate in a relatively autonomous manner.

Along with acquiring other firms to accelerate their growth, entrepreneurial firms are often the targets of larger firms that are looking to enter a new market or acquire proprietary technology. Selling to a large firm is often the goal of an investor-backed company, as a way of creating a liquidity event to allow investors to monetize their investment. Some entrepreneurs allow their companies to be bought by larger firms as a way of accelerating their growth. For example, in 2008 Honest Tea sold a large stake of itself to Coca-Cola, primarily as a means of integrating itself into Coke's worldwide distribution channels. Coke is now providing Honest Tea access to markets it could have never penetrated on its own.

Licensing

Licensing is the granting of permission by one company to another company to use a specific form of its intellectual property under clearly defined conditions. Virtually any intellectual property a company owns that is protected by a patent, trademark, or copyright can be licensed to a third party. Licensing also works well for firms that create novel products but do not have the resources to build manufacturing capabilities or distribution networks, which other firms may already have in place.

Entrepreneurial firms can also benefit by licensing technology from larger companies. For example Mint.com, the subject of Case 14.2, licenses technology from Yodlee, a larger firm. Yodlee's technology enables Mint.com to access its members' account information, such as credit card balances and payment due dates. A firm named Wesabe, the subject of the "What Went Wrong?" feature in Chapter 13, tried to build a personal financial management website similar to Mint.com and decided to build its own capabilities for scraping bank websites rather than license the technology from Yodlee. Marc Hedlund, one of Wesabe's co-founders, identified this decision as one of the reasons Wesabe failed.

The terms of a license are spelled out through a **licensing agreement**, which is a formal contract between a licensor and a licensee. The **licensor** is the company that owns the intellectual property; the **licensee** is the company purchasing the right to use it. A license can be exclusive, nonexclusive, for a specific purpose, and for a specific geographic area.[16] In almost all cases, the licensee pays the licensor an initial payment plus an ongoing royalty for the right to use the intellectual property. There is no set formula for determining the amount of the initial payment or the royalties—these are issues that are part of the process of negotiating a licensing agreement.[17] Entrepreneurial firms often press for a relatively large initial payment as a way of generating immediate cash to fund their operations.

There are two principal types of licensing: technology licensing and merchandise and character licensing.

Technology Licensing **Technology licensing** is the licensing of proprietary technology that the licensor typically controls by virtue of a utility patent.[18] This type of licensing agreement commonly involves one of two scenarios. First, firms develop technologies to enhance their own products and then find noncompetitors to license the technology to spread out the costs and risks involved. Second, companies that are tightly focused on developing new products pass on their new products through licensing agreements to companies that are more marketing oriented and that have the resources to bring the products to market.

Striking a licensing agreement with a large firm can involve tough negotiations. An entrepreneur should carefully investigate potential licensees to make sure they have a track record of paying licensing fees on time and are easy to work with. To obtain this information, it is appropriate to ask a potential licensee for references. It is also important that an entrepreneur not give away too much in regard to the nature of the proprietary technology in an initial meeting with a potential licensee. This challenge means finding the right balance of piquing a potential licensee's interest without revealing too much. Nondisclosure agreements, described in Chapter 7, should be used in discussing proprietary technologies with a potential licensee.

Merchandise and Character Licensing **Merchandise and character licensing** is the licensing of a recognized trademark or brand that the licensor typically controls through a registered trademark or copyright. For example, Harley-Davidson licenses its trademark to multiple companies that place the Harley trademark on T-shirts, jackets, collectibles, gift items, jewelry, watches, bike accessories, and so on. By doing this, Harley not only generates licensing income but also promotes the sale of Harley-Davidson motorcycles. Similarly, entrepreneurial firms such as eBay and Starbucks license their trademarks not only to earn licensing income, but also to promote their products or services to a host of current and potential customers.

The key to merchandise and character licensing is to resist the temptation to license a trademark too widely and to restrict licensing to product categories that have relevance and that appeal to a company's customers. If a company licenses its trademark too broadly, it can lose control of the quality of the products with which its trademark is identified. This outcome can diminish the strength of a company's brand. For example, a company such as ModCloth, which is a U.S. based online retailer specializing in vintage and vintage-inspired clothing, accessories, and décor, might license its trademark to a watch manufacturer that is interested in producing a line of ModCloth women's watches. ModCloth would want to make sure that the watches bearing its trademark were fashionable, were of similar quality to its clothing and other products, and were appealing to its clientele. ModCloth can enforce these standards through the terms of its licensing agreements.

Strategic Alliances and Joint Ventures

The increase in the popularity of strategic alliances and joint ventures has been driven largely by a growing awareness that firms can't "go it alone" and succeed.[19] As with all forms of firm growth, strategic alliances and joint ventures have advantages and disadvantages. We present these points in Table 14.6.

TABLE 14.6 **Advantages and Disadvantages of Participating in Strategic Alliances and Joint Ventures**

Advantages	Disadvantages
Gain access to a particular resource. Firms engage in strategic alliances and joint ventures to gain access to a particular resource, such as capital, employees with specialized skills, or modern production facilities.	**Loss of proprietary information.** Proprietary information can be lost to a partner who is already a competitor or will eventually become one. This is a common worry.
Economies of scale. In many industries, high fixed costs require firms to find partners to expand production volume as a means of developing economies of scale.	**Management complexities.** Because strategic alliances and joint ventures require the combined effort of two or more firms, managing them can be challenging. Frustrations and costly delays often occur as a result.
Risk and cost sharing. Strategic alliances and joint ventures allow two or more firms to share the risk and cost of a particular business endeavor.	**Financial and organizational risks.** The failure rate for strategic alliances and joint ventures is high.
Gain access to a foreign market. Partnering with a local company is often the only practical way to gain access to a foreign market.	**Risk becoming dependent on a partner.** A power imbalance arises if one partner becomes overly dependent on the other. This situation increases the potential for opportunism on the part of the stronger partner. Opportunistic behavior takes advantage of a partner.
Learning. Strategic alliances and joint ventures often provide the participants the opportunity to learn from their partners.	**Partial loss of decision autonomy.** Joint planning and decision making may result in a loss of decision autonomy.
Speed to market. Firms with complementary skills, such as one firm being technologically strong and another having strong market access, partner to increase speed to market in hopes of capturing first-mover advantages.	**Partners' cultures may clash.** The corporate cultures of alliance partners may clash, making the implementation and management of the alliance difficult.
Neutralizing or blocking competitors. Through strategic alliances and joint ventures, firms can gain competencies and market power that can be used to neutralize or block a competitor's actions.	**Loss of organizational flexibility.** Establishing a partnership with one firm may foreclose the possibility of establishing a partnership with another firm.

Source: Based on B. R. Barringer and J. S. Harrison, "Walking a Tightrope: Creating Value Through Interorganizational Relationships," *Journal of Management* 26, no. 3 (2002): 367–403.

Strategic Alliances A **strategic alliance** is a partnership between two or more firms that is developed to achieve a specific goal. Various studies show that participation in alliances can boost a firm's rate of patenting,[20] product innovation,[21] and foreign sales.[22] Alliances tend to be informal and do not involve the creation of a new entity (such as in a joint venture). Although engaging in alliances can be tremendously helpful for an entrepreneurial firm, setting up an alliance and making it work can be tricky. This dimension of alliances is highlighted in this chapter's "Partnering for Success" feature.

Technological alliances and marketing alliances are two of the most common forms of alliances.[23] **Technological alliances** feature cooperation in research and development, engineering, and manufacturing. Research-and-development alliances often bring together entrepreneurial firms with specific technical skills and larger, more mature firms with experience in development and marketing. By pooling their complementary assets, these firms can typically produce a product and bring it to market faster and cheaper than either firm could alone.[24] Pfizer's blockbuster drug Celebrex, for example, was created via a technological alliance. Celebrex is a prescription arthritis medicine. **Marketing alliances** typically match a company that has a distribution system with a company that has a product to sell in order to increase sales of a product or service. For example, an American food company may initiate an alliance with Nestlé (a Swiss food company) to gain access to Nestlé's distribution channels in Europe. The strategic logic of this type of alliance for both partners is simple. By finding

PARTNERING FOR SUCCESS

Three Steps to Alliance Success

Although alliances are an increasingly popular way for entrepreneurial firms to accelerate growth, they should be approached strategically and carefully. A failed alliance can cause a firm to lose money and can be very time consuming and frustrating to exit. Alliances are often compared to marriages and other close relationships: easy to get into but very hard to get out of—at least gracefully.

There are three key steps in setting up and executing a successful alliance relationship. The following are the three steps, along with words of advice on how to handle each one.

Selecting a Partner

Any company or group of companies that has something a firm needs is a potential alliance partner. For example, small food companies often partner with large food companies to gain access to their distribution channels. But a company should remember that a potential partner is looking for a leg up too, in the form of some type of advantage, while competing in the marketplace. If the small food company has to give the large food company "exclusive" distribution rights to its best products to get the deal, it may not be worth it. Entering into an alliance should improve a company's situation—it shouldn't be a jump ball. Alliances take a great deal of effort to manage and certainly to manage successfully. If each company in an alliance breaks even in terms of outcomes, the alliance is not usually worth it, because of the time and effort it takes from other activities.

Also, a firm should always investigate the reputation of the companies it is thinking about partnering with. Asking for references of other businesses the company is partnering with is appropriate, even if the company is well known. If a company is reluctant or unwilling to provide references, look elsewhere.

According to Guy Kawasaki, a respected Silicon Valley entrepreneur and venture capitalist, most companies form alliances for the wrong reason: to make the press and analysts happy. Kawasaki says this is foolish. Alliances should be formed for one of two reasons in Kawasaki's opinion: to either increase revenues or decrease costs.

Cutting the Deal

Negotiating an alliance can take multiple meetings, conference calls, and e-mail messages. So it's best to cut to the chase, as early as possible, to discern if a deal is possible. It's easy for a small firm to get sucked into months of negotiations with a large company like Facebook or Google, only to have the deal fall through. It probably won't hurt Facebook or Google if a handful of its employees lose time failing to negotiate an alliance agreement with a small firm. The lost time on the part of the small firm may be much more damaging.

The most important consideration in cutting a deal is to make sure the potential partners truly have synergies (i.e., $2 + 2 = 5$), and that the synergies are sustainable. Otherwise, experts agree, "no contract will hold them together." Also, firms should be leery of entering into an alliance if there is any hint that the people who will actually implement the alliance aren't totally on board. The worst-case scenario is two CEOs who meet at a conference and start talking about their two firms "working together." If they start kicking around alliance ideas that don't make sense, the mid-level people in an organization need to be empowered to hold their ground. The people who have to implement the alliance, for both organizations, should be heard. If they're less than enthused about an alliance proposal, it should be scrapped.

If an alliance agreement is struck, it should be accompanied by a set of operating principles that guide its day-to-day operation. It's also smart to include an "out" clause, which allows each party in the alliance to terminate its involvement relatively easily.

Making It Work

The biggest obstacle to making an alliance work is that the corporate cultures of organizations often vary in substantially important ways. As a result, the first thing that should be determined when deciding how to manage an alliance is how decisions are made. A start-up may be used to making decisions on the fly, while a large-company partner may route decisions through several committees before a final decision is made. Unless the partners know what to expect, frustrations can result.

Each alliance partner should also appoint an internal "champion" who has direct responsibility for the alliance's health and progress. "A bunch of people helping out when they can" doesn't cut it. An alliance should have a boss inside each involved organization, just as employees have bosses.

The individuals who will make the alliance work for all the parties involved should also meet face to face. It's normally easier for people to trust one another and work together across distances if they've met at least one time and have had an opportunity to get to know one another as individuals.

Questions for Critical Thinking

1. In what ways is it easy for the founder of a firm to get caught up in the potential advantages of participating in alliances without remaining equally focused on the potential disadvantages?

2. Think about the partnership arrangements you've been involved with, even if your experience has been limited to working with other students in team settings in classes. What are some of the challenges in making alliances work that are not mentioned in the feature?

3. Do some Internet research and find an example of an alliance between a small firm and a large firm that seems to be working well. Briefly describe the nature of the alliance and explain its success.
4. The "You Be the VC 14.1" feature focuses on Barnana, a start-up that's producing a healthy snack that consists of bite-sized morsels of partially de-hydrated bananas, which are easy to carry and are potassium-rich. Brainstorm three to five likely alliance partners for Barnana. Explain how each partner can help Barnana either increase its revenue or decrease its costs.

Sources: "Inc. Guidebook, Build Business Alliances," *Inc*, June 1, 2010; Guy Kawasaki, "The Art of Partnering," How to Change the World, available at http://blog.guykawasaki.com/2006/02/the_art_of_part.html#axzz1IOLXJ1Sv, posted on February 6, 2006, accessed on July 14, 2014.

more outlets for its products, the partner that is supplying the product can increase economies of scale and reduce per-unit cost. The partner that supplies the distribution channel benefits by adding products to its product line, increasing its attractiveness to those wanting to purchase a wide array of products from a single supplier.

Both technological and marketing alliances allow firms to focus on their specific area of expertise and partner with others to fill their expertise gaps. This approach is particularly attractive to entrepreneurial firms, which often lack the financial resources or time to develop all the competencies they need to bring final products to market quickly. Michael Dell describes the early years of Dell Inc.:

As a small start-up, we didn't have the money to build the components [used to make up a PC] ourselves. But we also asked, "Why should we want to?" Unlike many of our competitors, we actually had an option: to buy components from the specialists, leveraging the investments they had already made and allowing us to focus on what we did best—designing and delivering solutions and systems directly to customers. In forging these early alliances with suppliers, we created exactly the right strategy for a fast-growing company.[25]

Joint Ventures A **joint venture** is an entity created when two or more firms pool a portion of their resources to create a separate, jointly owned organization.[26] An example is Beverage Partners Worldwide, which is a joint venture between Coca-Cola and Nestlé. Formed in 1991, the joint venture markets ready-to-drink chilled teas based on green tea and black tea in more than 50 countries worldwide.

Gaining access to a foreign market is a common reason to form a joint venture.[27] In these cases, the joint venture typically consists of the firm trying to reach a foreign market and one or more local partners. Joint ventures created for reasons other than foreign market entry are typically described as either scale or link joint ventures.[28] In a **scale joint venture**, the partners collaborate at a single point in the value chain to gain economies of scale in production or distribution. This type of joint venture can be a good vehicle for developing new products or services. In a **link joint venture**, the position of the parties is not symmetrical, and the objectives of the partners may diverge. For example, many of the joint ventures between American and Canadian food companies provide the American partner with access to Canadian markets and distribution channels and the Canadian partner with the opportunity to add to its product line.

A hybrid form of joint venture that some larger firms utilize is to take small equity stakes in promising young companies. In these instances, the large companies act in the role of corporate venture capitalists, as explained in Chapter 10. Google established a venture capital program in 2009, named Google Ventures. Investing in private companies, this program seeks to help start-up ventures grow from their initial stages to a point of either issuing an initial public offering or being acquired. Notable investments include Nest

Labs, Rocker Lawyer, HomeAway, Uber, 23andMe, and Namo Media.[29] Firms typically make investments of this nature in companies with the potential to be suppliers, customers, or acquisition targets in the future. The equity stake provides the large company a "say" in the development of the smaller firm. On occasion, the larger firm that has a small equity stake will acquire the smaller firm. These transactions are called **spin-ins**. The opposite of a spin-in is a **spin-out**, which occurs when a larger company divests itself of one of its smaller divisions and the division becomes an independent company. Hewlett-Packard, for example, spun off its test-and-measurement equipment division as Agilent Technologies, which advertises itself as the "world's premiere measurement company."

Chapter Summary

LO1. Internal growth strategies rely on efforts generated within the firm itself, such as new product development, other product-related strategies, international expansion, and Internet-driven strategies. External growth strategies rely on establishing relationships with third parties, such as mergers, acquisitions, licensing, strategic alliances, joint ventures, and franchising. The keys to effective new product development, which is the core internal growth strategy, are as follows: find a need and fill it, develop products that add value, get quality and pricing right, focus on a specific target market, and conduct an ongoing feasibility analysis. The reasons that new products fail include an inadequate feasibility analysis, overestimation of market potential, bad timing (i.e., introducing a product at the wrong time), inadequate advertising and promotion, and poor service.

LO2. Improving an existing product or service, increasing the market penetration of an existing product or service, extending product lines, and geographic expansion are additional internal product growth strategies entrepreneurial firms use. Improving an existing product finds a firm creating more value for the customer in the form of additional product functionality. With a market penetration strategy, the firm seeks to increase the sales of a product or service through greater marketing efforts or through increased production capacity and efficiency. To extend a product line, a firm typically creates additional versions of its product that will appeal to a different—that is, new—set of customers. Through geographic expansion, a firm

seeks growth by expanding its operations from an initial site to additional locations.

LO3. International new ventures are businesses that, from inception, seek to derive significant competitive advantage from the use of resources and the sale of outputs in multiple countries. To successfully use this growth strategy, firms must master the complexity of profitably selling their product or service outside their home, domestic market.

LO4. Through external growth strategies, an entrepreneurial firm establishes relationships with third parties. Mergers, acquisitions, strategic alliances, joint ventures, licensing, and franchising are examples of external growth strategies. We concentrate on acquisitions in this chapter given their frequency with entrepreneurial firms compared to mergers. Acquiring another business can fulfill several of a company's needs, such as expanding its product line, gaining access to distribution channels, achieving competitive economies of scale, or expanding the company's geographic reach. A promising acquisition candidate has the following characteristics: operates in a growing industry, has proprietary products and/or processes, has a well-defined and established market position, has a good reputation, is involved in very little, if any, litigation, is open to the idea of being acquired by another firm, is positioned to readily obtain key third-party consent to an acquisition, and is located in a geographic area that is easily accessible from the acquiring firm's headquarters location. Licensing is the granting of permission by one company to another company to use a specific form of its intellectual property under clearly defined conditions. Virtually any intellectual property a company owns can be licensed to a third party. Licensing can be a very effective way of earning income, particularly for intellectual property–rich firms, such as software and biotech companies. A strategic alliance is a partnership between two or more firms that is developed to achieve a specific objective or goal. Technological alliances involve cooperating in areas such as research and development, engineering, and manufacturing.

Marketing alliances typically match one firm with a partner's distribution system that is attractive to the company trying to increase sales of its products or services. A joint venture is an entity that is created when two or more firms pool a portion of their resources to create a separate, jointly owned organization. In a scale joint venture, the partners collaborate at a single point in the value chain to gain economies of scale in production or distribution by combining their expertise. In a link joint venture, the position of the parties is not symmetrical and the objectives of the partners may diverge.

Key Terms

acquirer, **486**
acquisition, **485**
external growth strategies, **485**
geographic expansion, **480**
improving an existing product or service, **479**
internal growth strategies, **475**
international new ventures, **481**
joint venture, **493**
licensee, **489**

licensing, **489**
licensing agreement, **489**
licensor, **489**
link joint venture, **493**
marketing alliances, **491**
market penetration strategy, **479**
merchandise and character licensing, **490**
merger, **485**
new product development, **475**

organic growth, **475**
outsourcing, **480**
product line extension strategy, **480**
scale joint venture, **493**
spin-ins, **494**
spin-outs, **494**
strategic alliance, **491**
target, **486**
technological alliances, **491**
technology licensing, **490**

Review Questions

14-1. What is the difference between an internal and an external growth strategy?

14-2. What are the advantages and disadvantages of internal growth strategies?

14-3. How can a business increase its revenue by improving an existing product or service?

14-4. What is a market penetration strategy? Provide an example of a market penetration strategy and describe how using it effectively might increase a firm's sales.

14-5. What is a product line extension strategy? Provide an example of a product line extension strategy and describe how its effective use might increase a firm's sales.

14-6. What is an international expansion strategy? What are the keys to implementing this strategy successfully in an entrepreneurial firm?

14-7. What is an international new venture? Why might it be to the benefit of an entrepreneurial start-up to position itself as an international new venture from the outset?

14-8. What are the six foreign-market entry strategies and what are the key characteristics of each one?

14-9. What rules of thumb should an entrepreneurial venture follow to successfully sell its products overseas?

14-10. What is the difference between a merger and an acquisition? How can acquisitions help firms fill their needs?

14-11. What are some of the methods of identifying new products and services?

14-12. What is the difference between a licensor and a licensee?

14-13. Why do acquisitions fail sometimes? What is the main reason behind their failure?

14-14. What would make a firm suitable for growth in international markets?

14-15. What is the difference between technology licensing and merchandise and character licensing? Provide examples of both types of licensing and how they can increase a firm's sales.

14-16. Over the past several years, why have strategic alliances and joint ventures become increasingly prevalent growth strategies for entrepreneurial firms?

14-17. What is the difference between technological alliances and marketing alliances? Provide examples of both types of alliances and how they can increase a firm's sales.

14-18. What is a joint venture?

14-19. How does a joint venture differ from a strategic alliance?

14-20. What is the difference between a scale joint venture and a link joint venture? Provide examples of both types of joint ventures and how their effective use can increase a firm's sales.

Application Questions

14-21. Spend some time studying Barnana, the focus of the "You Be the VC 14.1" feature. Is it more likely that Barnana will grow through internal or external growth strategies? What internal growth strategies and/or external growth strategies make sense for Barnana?

14-22. Jessica Martin, a classmate of yours, just returned from an entrepreneurship boot camp that your university's technology incubator sponsored. The boot camp consisted of three days of intense focus on how to successfully launch a firm. You overheard Jessica telling another classmate that the boot camp was extremely helpful and she's already signed up for another three-day boot camp that will focus on how to successfully grow a firm. The classmate looked at Jessica and said, "How in the world can you spend three days talking about how to successfully grow a firm?" Jessica opened her notebook and showed the classmate the 10-item agenda for the upcoming three-day boot camp. What do you think the 10 items consist of? (Consider the material in Chapter 13 and this chapter in formulating your answer.)

14-23. Visit a local business in your vicinity. With permission from the owner or the manager, assess the business's suitability for growth using internal growth strategies. You may also discuss with him the internal growth strategies adopted by the business, if any.

14-24. Spend some time studying Chipotle, the popular Mexican food restaurant chain. What growth strategies has this firm used? What challenges to you think Chipotle faces today in terms of its future growth potential?

14-25. Zynga is a social network game developer that develops browser-based games that work both as stand-alone games and as application widgets on social networking sites like Facebook. What are the pluses and minuses of Zynga's approach to launching games that rely on another company's platform (i.e., Facebook) to reach its intended audience? Is Zynga growing primarily via internal or external growth strategies?

14-26. Cisco Systems, Microsoft, and IBM often acquire small, technology-based entrepreneurial firms. Why would Cisco Systems, Microsoft, and IBM, which each employ hundreds of product development specialists and engineers, buy other firms to acquire technology and add to their product lines, rather than developing the technology and new products in-house?

14-27. Shana Adams needs to prepare an outline of a lecture for her class on foreign market entry strategies. Explain the advantages and disadvantages of each strategy. Shana has to highlight the foreign entry strategies that have the highest and lowest risk.

14-28. Arthur Drake is looking at expanding his bakery business. He has been in this line of business for the last six years and feels that it is the right time for him to grow. He has looked at many options for growth, such as growing through a merger or an acquisition. After thorough investigation, he has finally decided to proceed with acquisition. It is very important for him now to exercise care in finding the right acquisition candidates and completing the whole process. What steps should he take to complete the acquisition?

14-29. Rupert Dwine has been selling fruit juice and is planning on expanding his business. For the past one month, he has been looking for new ideas for his

growth. Suggest some internal growth strategies that may help him pursue his dream.

14-30. Study the popular social networking site LinkedIn. What growth strategies has the company employed? What are the most appropriate growth strategies for this firm to use going forward? Why?

14-31. Which of the growth strategies discussed in the chapter are the most risky? Which are the least risky? What role should risk play in a company's decision to pursue a particular growth strategy?

YOU BE THE VC 14.1 COMPANY: Barnana

• Web: www.barnana.com • Facebook: Barnana • Twitter: @barnana

Business Idea: Produce a healthy snack that consists of bite-sized morsels of partially dehydrated bananas, which are easy to carry and are potassium-rich.

Pitch: In 2001, Caue Suplicy moved to the United States to pursue a career as a professional triathlete. He often carried with him small squares of dehydrated bananas, made from a family recipe he learned in Brazil. The small squares were an excellent source of potassium and other nutrients. After 10 years of competing at an elite level, he retired from his professional racing career. In 2010, Suplicy created Barnana to share his special snack with others.

Barnana is the perfect snack for athletes or anyone with an interest in healthy food. As an alternative to traditional snacks, Barnana is pioneering the use of the banana's naturally occurring nutritional content. Grown in soil alive with nutrients and free of chemicals, Barnana has no additives or preservatives and is naturally sweet.

The Barnana treats are bit-sized morsels that can be popped into one's mouth. They are packaged in resealable plastic bags, and are easy to carry on a run, a bike ride, or simply for an afternoon snack. They are available in four varieties—Organic Original Chewy Banana Bites, Organic Chocolate Chewy Barnana Bites, Organic Coconut Chewy Barnana Bites, and Organic Peanut Butter Chewy Barnana Bites. The small morsels are partially dehydrated bananas that are soft and chewy and taste like banana bread. With only one ingredient, pure organic banana, they are an exceptional source of potassium and fiber and have over 20 vitamins and minerals. Each variety is dairy free, gluten free, non-GMO, Kosher, and vegan. Barnana Bites are perfect for people with Celiac Disease. Because of their fiber content, they aid in digestion, which is a property that people with Celiac Disease are generally looking for. Extreme care is taken in the growing of the bananas that Barnana Bites are made from. The bananas are grown on sustainable, organic farms in South America.

Barnana Bites are also delicious. They have a chewy texture that makes them satisfying for snacking. Each morsel is flavorful and is dusted in banana powder with no added sugar. The Organic Chocolate Chewy Banana Bites are covered in 54 percent organic cacao, which contains the nutritional benefits of dark chocolate.

Barnana snacks are available across the United States at a variety of stores, including Whole Foods Markets, Wegmans, Sprouts, PCC Markets, and other local outlets. They are also available via Amazon.com and on Barnana's website.

14-32. Based on the material covered in this chapter, what questions would you ask the firm's founders before making your funding decision? What answers would satisfy you?

14-33. If you had to make your decision on just the information provided in the pitch and on the company's website, would you fund this company? Why or why not?

YOU BE THE VC 14.2 COMPANY: Double Robotics

• Web: www.doublerobotics.com • Facebook: Double Robotics • Twitter: @doublerobotics.com

Business Idea: Design and manufacture a telepresence robot that allows someone to remotely inhabit the body of the robot and have the freedom to roam around an office building or facility even through the person inhabiting the body of the robot is hundreds or thousands of miles away.

Pitch: There are many circumstances that would cause someone to want to be virtually present in one location even though they are physically present in another. An example would be a scientist or engineer in one location wanting to spend a day interacting with colleagues in another location. Short-term discussions can be facilitated by video-conferencing tools such as Skype. But Skype limits participants to a single location where they each have access to a monitor that is projecting the Skype call. What if someone in one location wants to be virtually present in a second location, and wants to be able to move from office to office or lab to lab to interact with a variety of colleagues?

Double Robotics has created a solution that facilitates this type of interaction. The solution is a robot, named Double, which has two wheels at its base and a poll that extends upwards to eye level. An iPad is mounted on top of the poll. You can log onto the iPad from a computer, iPad, or iPhone from anywhere in the world and drive the robot around while streaming two-way audio and video that allows you to interact with anyone who is present. There are multiple photos of the Double on Double Robotic's website. It is sleek with a futuristic, minimalist design. The poll with the iPad on top is adjustable so it can be placed at eye level with people sitting or standing. The Segway-style base uses high-efficiency motors to zip around for up to eight hours on a single charge. A touch-based interface makes controlling the Double a breeze, while an accelerometer and gyroscope work to keep the device stable until you're done moving it, at which point dual kickstands pop out to let the batteries take a rest. The Double's initial price tag is $2,500.

The Double has a number of potential applications. It is first and foremost the ultimate tool for colleagues working in separate locations that need to interact with one another. Most workers know how difficult it can be to schedule a call or ask someone to set up a computer or a laptop for a video chat. With Double one engineer or executive can be in Chicago, for example, and if the company has a second facility in New York City that has a Double robot available, the engineer or executive in Chicago can log onto the Double in New York City and literally roam from office to office, interacting with his or her colleagues who are in a different location. There are other potential uses. For example, museums or art galleries could offer virtual tours utilizing Double. The

person taking the tour could log onto one of the museum or gallery Double robots, and then follow the person giving the tour by steering the robot from location to location. The same approach could be used in providing prospective students tours of colleges or universities.

Several large corporations, including Johnson & Johnson and the Coca-Cola Company, are reportedly testing Double for telecommuters and for employees who need to interact with one another but are situated in different geographic locations.

14-34. Based on the material covered in this chapter, what questions would you ask the firm's founders before making your funding decision? What answers would satisfy you?

14-35. If you had to make your decision on just the information provided in the pitch and on the company's website, would you fund this company? Why or why not?

CASE 14.1

Uber: Will It Maintain Its Sizzling Pace of Growth?

• *Web: www.uber.com* • *Facebook: Uber* • *Twitter: @uber*

Bruce R. Barringer, *Oklahoma State University*

R. Duane Ireland, *Texas A&M University*

Introduction

Uber is a San Francisco-based start-up that connects riders with safe, reliable transportation providers at a variety of price points in cities across the world. It is growing at a rapid pace. It has expanded from a start-up in 2009 to over 60 cities in early 2014. Some observers say that Uber may be more valuable than Facebook someday. Here's why.

Problem and Solution

Problem. Just in case you're not familiar with Uber, here are the basics. For most people, hailing a cab isn't a pleasant experience. You either stand outside and wave your hand until you catch the eye of a cabbie, or you call a taxi dispatch (if you have their number) and wait for what seems like forever until a cab arrives. You ride to your destination in a vanilla cab. You then have to scramble to count out the right amount of cash plus a tip. The driver never seems to have the right change. Very few people see this as an enjoyable experience.

Solution. With Uber, you download an app to your smartphone and enter your credit card information. When you need a ride, you access the app, and

choose one of several grades of cars, from a luxury SUV to a Toyota Prius. You indicate where you want to be picked up. Drivers in Uber's network are circling the surrounding area, waiting for a fare. The app is integrated with Google maps so that you can see how far the nearest drivers are from you. The app will identify the driver that will pick you up, and you can watch the car approach. While you wait, you can look at your driver's information, including his or her name, ratings, and license plate number. The driver will usually send a text to confirm the reservation. When the car arrives, you hop in and are taken to your destination. When the trip is over, the app charges your credit card. Uber drivers are not allowed to accept tips. Uber's pricing is similar to metered taxis. Most trips are priced based on the distance traveled.

There are two classes of Uber cars. The regular Uber service features upscale cars and SUVs such as Lincoln Town Cars, Cadillac Escalades, and Mercedes-Benz S550 sedans. In 2013 Uber introduced a less expensive tier of cars called UberX. UberX cars are Toyota Priuses and similar models. Uber doesn't employ drivers. It acts as a liaison between people who need rides and drivers who qualify to be part of its network. Uber conducts background checks on all of its drivers and provides them with a smartphone preloaded with the

(continued)

Uber app. For an example $30 fare, Uber keeps about $6.00 (20 percent) and the driver gets the rest. All Uber rides are protected by the driver's insurance policy as well as Uber's corporate policy.

The attractiveness of Uber is that it has completely taken the friction out of the experience of buying a ride. No more hailing cabs, no more plain-vanilla cars, no more fumbling for change to pay. The ride is an enjoyable experience rather than a hassle.

Uber

Uber was founded by Garrett Camp and Travis Kalanick. Kalanick is the driving force behind the company's design and growth. It launched in San Francisco in 2009, and arranged its first rides in June 2010. Six months later, it had more than 3,000 users and had facilitated between 10,000 and 20,000 rides. Its initial target market was the tech community, which is typically quick to embrace new things. San Francisco is also known for a spotty taxi industry, so an alternative garnered attention. Uber grew largely via word of mouth. It had a certain "cool" factor in that early adopters could impress their friends with the ability to call a certain type of car from their phone with a couple of taps. The firm also benefited from the fact that many of its early users talked up the service on social media. According to some reports, 95 percent of Uber riders heard about the service from other Uber riders.

Although Uber has grown rapidly, there are methodical aspects to its growth. It grows city by city. Each new city has a launch team, which forges partnerships with local organizations, creates events that promote Uber's service, and reaches out to local businesses. It typically offers one to two weeks of free rides in a new community, to kick-start its service. In each new city, Uber has the challenge of building a two-sided marketplace. It has to recruit both riders and drivers. On the driver side, it actively recruits both independent operators and car service owners to participate in its service, offering sign-on bonuses and ongoing incentives. It does not require an exclusive arrangement. As a result, a car service owner can maintain his or her service and drive for Uber too.

Uber has stirred up controversy. As it enters new cities, it has been sued numerous times, primarily by taxi-industry advocates and local governments, trying to protect their existing taxi cab industry. In most cases, it has successfully fought off the suits, but not everywhere. Uber is currently banned in Miami, Florida, and Austin, Texas. It was forced to shut down in Vancouver, Canada. A Vancouver regulatory agency ruled that Uber was a limousine service, and the minimum charge for a limousine ride was $75, regardless of the distance of the trip. That made Uber uncompetitive. In most cases, Uber has prevailed because of public support for its service. In Washington, D.C., for example, a regulatory agency tried to pass a law to prohibit on-demand sedan services, which was an attack on Uber. Uber users raised such an uproar on social media that the objection was quickly dropped. In some European cities, taxi cab drivers have picketed airports and deliberately tied up traffic to object to Uber entering their communities.

Uber has made one strategic move that has irritated riders. It recently implemented a policy referred to as surge pricing. During rush hour and other times of peak ridership (like Halloween or New Year's Eve), it increases its prices. In some instances, fares increase to several times their normal level. The idea behind surge pricing is to reach an economic equilibrium by attracting more drivers. In many cities, it's difficult to get a cab at peak times. There are just too many riders seeking a fixed number of drivers. Surge pricing encourages a larger number of Uber drivers to make themselves available at peak times, because they can make more money. Uber feels the practice is necessary and works, but some customers see it as price gouging.

A tragic incident happened in December 2013. An Uber driver accidently struck and killed a six-year-old girl, and injured several others. Although the driver was not carrying Uber-arranged passenger at the time, the girl's family filed a wrongful death suit against Uber, claiming the driver was using Uber's mobile app at the time of the accident. The accident and lawsuit have provided additional ammunition to those that oppose Uber, arguing that the service is inherently dangerous.

Uber has not had difficulty raising money. It has all the ingredients that professional investors look for, including a disruptive business idea, rapid growth, a large potential market, and aggressive plans for expansion. According to Crunchbase, Uber has raised the following rounds of funding:

- $200,000 seed funding (Aug. 2009)
- $1.3 million angel round (Oct. 2010)
- $11 million Series A round (Feb. 14, 2011)
- $37 million Series B round (Dec. 7, 2011)
- $258 million Series C round (Aug. 23, 2013)
- $1.2 billion Series D round (Jun. 6, 2014)

Its stable of investors is also impressive, including Amazon CEO Jeff Bezos, Goldman Sachs, Google Ventures, Fidelity Investments, and Benchmark Venture Capital.

Uber's Aggressive Plans for Growth

The size of the investments in Uber, and the bold prediction that Uber may someday have a larger market capitalization value than Facebook, are driven by its aggressive growth plans. The consensus is that Uber is hoping for three distinct phases of growth, each of which is bolder and more ambitious than its predecessor. Phases 1 and 2 have already begun, with Phase 3 hopefully to follow. The three phases are depicted in the figure below.

Phase 1: Disrupt the taxi industry. Uber is out to disrupt or kill the taxi industry. It simply sees itself as a better solution for getting people from point A to point B quickly and safely than taxicabs. At the time this case was written in the summer of 2014, the firm was operating in 22 countries and 60 cities—an amazing feat for a company that launched in 2009. By all accounts it is well-run, well-funded, and is growing its infrastructure at a pace consistent with its growth. It's also extremely

Phase 1	Phase 2	Phase 3
Disrupt the taxi industry	Make it increasingly unnecessary to own a car	Start delivering everything

Uber's Three "Hoped For" Phases of Growth

smart. For example, Uber has lined up $2.5 billion in outside financing for low-interest car loans for UberX drivers. That will make it possible for up to 200,000 drivers to buy their own cars at very low interest rates, under the condition that they use the cars on the Uber network for the duration of the loan. If they drop out of the Uber network, their interest rate will balloon for the remainder of the loan. This strategy helps Uber in two important ways. It will add to Uber's supply of drivers and will enhance the stability of its driver force. If this experiment works, Uber may repeat it and add even more drivers. The more Uber drivers, the more cities Uber can expand to, the shorter the wait times for Uber riders, the lower the cost per ride, and the more efficient and profitable the entire system becomes.

Phase 2: Make it Increasingly Unnecessary to Own a Car. As Uber becomes more ubiquitous, and the cost per ride goes down, there will be less and less need for people to own cars. In areas where Uber is present and pickup times are quick, this is already starting to happen. While Uber's most obvious competitor is taxis, interestingly a large number of Uber users never take taxis. They use Uber instead of driving their car, particularly when they think parking will be a hassle or will be exorbitantly expensive. Some observers see Uber as part of an overall movement called the "death of the ownership society." The problem with owning a car, advocates of this view would say, is that it sits idle most of the time, so it is uneconomical to own. Uber would like people to eventually think in terms of "buying a ride" to get from Point A to Point B rather than owning and driving a car to cover the same distance. To make this work, Uber will need to have a dense enough presence that people can get rides quickly and reliably to cover the distance they need to travel.

Phase 3: Start Delivering Everything. The third phase of growth is the most exciting. Uber would like to grow beyond providing rides, and become a transportation network for all kinds of deliveries, including food, prescription drugs, retail products, etc. Uber is often compared to Amazon. Amazon started as a bookseller in 1994, and quickly realized that the efficient warehousing and shipping infrastructure that it had built could be used to sell all kinds of things to consumers. So the firm branched out, and it now sells items as diverse as kitchen utensils, tools, and paper towels. Uber could theoretically do the same. Once its network of drivers is sufficiently dense, along with transporting people, it could start delivering nearly anything. This ambition is the reason Uber recently changed its tagline from "Everyone's private driver" to "Where lifestyle meets logistics."

There are also futuristic versions of what Uber may someday look like, which surpass Phase 3. One of Uber's principle investors is Google Ventures. Google is working on self-driving cars. Use your imagination to envision a world that would combine self-driving cars with Uber's ability to dispatch and track vehicles efficiently and effectively.

Challenges Ahead

Uber is not without compelling challenges. The popularity of its service has attracted competitors. Sidecar and Lyft are well-funded rivals that are competing toe-to-toe with Uber in many markets. The taxi industry, which Uber is bent on killing, will not go down without a fight. In many areas, regulators and advocates of the traditional taxi industry are upping their legal challenges to Uber and its service. How this will ultimately play out is unknown. The press is currently on Uber's side, primarily because the company is pro-consumer and delivers a high-quality product. If it becomes too disruptive, however, and starts killing off local delivery services, local courier services, etc., along with taxies, how the press and public in general will react is anyone's bet.

Discussion Questions

14-36. Uber's organic or internal growth to this point in the firm's life is quite dramatic. The following statement appears in this chapter: "Effective though it can be, there are limits to internal growth." Given its striking internal growth to date, does the statement from the chapter apply to Uber? Why or why not?

14-37. The top five reasons new products fail are presented in Table 14.2. If Uber were to fail, which of these five reasons would be most likely to explain the firm's failure? Why?

14-38. Some firms might find Uber to be an attractive acquisition candidate. Why would this be the case? What type of firm or firms might be interested in acquiring Uber?

14-39. If Uber were to consider participating in a strategic alliance, what type of firm might be an appropriate partner for Uber and why? If you were a consultant, would you advise Uber to form a strategic alliance as part of its growth efforts? Why or why not?

Sources: Wikipedia, Uber, www.uber.com, accessed July 7, 2014; K. Roose, "Uber Might Be More Valuable Than Facebook Someday. Here's Why," *New York Magazine,* available at http://nymag.com/daily/intelligencer/2013/12/uber-might-be-more-valuable-than-facebook.html, posted on December 6, 2013, accessed on July 7, 2014; GrowthHackers, "Uber—What's Fueling Uber's Growth Engine?," available at http://growthhackers.com/companies/uber/, posted on October 22, 2013, accessed on July 7, 2014.

CASE 14.2

How Mint.com Went from Launch to a $170 Million Acquisition in 24 Months

• *Web: www.mint.com* • *Facebook: Mint.com* • *Twitter: @mint*

Bruce R. Barringer, *Oklahoma State University*

R. Duane Ireland, *Texas A&M University*

Introduction

How did Mint.com go from launch to a $170 million acquisition in 24 months? The answer isn't as spectacular as you might think. Using a football metaphor, Mint.com did it more through blocking and tackling than through big plays. Mint.com's story is one of how a start-up that solves a real problem, and executes very well, can overcome obstacles and win the support of others. It's also a story of how a small company can take on a big rival, and by positioning itself for the future rather than the past, can motivate the rival to acquire it rather than trying to put it out of business through aggressive competition. Let's see how all of this took place.

Aaron Patzer

Aaron Patzer started Mint.com when he was just 25. After earning degrees from Duke and Princeton, he took a job with Nascentric, a Silicon Valley start-up. During this time, he was managing his personal finances with Quicken and Microsoft Money, and became increasingly frustrated with his experiences. He asked around and found others who were aggravated with these products and personal finance in general. He started thinking about how to build a product that would not only be an improvement on Quicken and Microsoft Money, but would make the entire process of managing money more efficient and potentially rewarding.

Patzer struggled with whether to act on his instincts and eventually decided to move forward. His thought process during this period is best illustrated through his own words. In an interview with Carson McComas, the creator of WorkHappy.net, a popular blog, Patzer reflected on how he made the decision to quit his job and focus on Mint.com full time:

> I began to think about the business nights and weekends. But it's hard to find time when you've got a full-time (and very demanding) job. One day I said to myself, "If you give it 100% and fail, I can live with that. But I can't live with going half-way, part-time." So on March 1, [2006], I quit my job and began working on Mint. The first few months were tough, and I basically oscillated day to day between thinking "This is the greatest idea ever" and "This will never work." Who am I to take on Intuit (the maker of Quicken) and Microsoft? If this was a good idea, someone would have done it before.

Patzer went on to say that the thing that gave him the most inner confidence was that he knew he was exceptionally good at one thing: algorithms—the key to computer programming. He also knew he was persistent and extremely passionate about his idea.

Prelaunch Stage—March 2006 until September 2007

Patzer worked 14 to 16 hours a day, almost 7 days per week, from March 2006 to the fall of the same year banging out the early prototype of Mint.com. Needing money to make key hires, improve on Mint.com's consumer interface, and buy servers, Patzer approached several investors. None bit. The problem was the way Mint.com was set up. Quicken and Microsoft Money were software products that people bought and then installed on their computers. Mint.com was an online dashboard. When you signed up for a Mint.com account, it asked you to provide all of your bank, credit card, and investment account information, user IDs, and passwords. Mint.com, through a partnership with a financial services firm named Yodlee, could then "scrape" the sites of your bank and credit card details, and provide a real-time update of your financial information. It could also e-mail you due date reminders, low-balance alerts, unusual activity alerts, and the like. A user could log onto his or her Mint.com account at any time and see all of his or her account information on a single screen. This is the better experience that Patzer was looking for. The average American has 11 separate bank, credit card, loan, and investment accounts. Patzer's idea was that having a single place where all the account information is displayed and updated on a consistent basis would be a superior customer experience.

The investors all said the same thing. People will not trust a start-up with their account information—let alone their user IDs and passwords. Patzer persisted. In September 2006 he found an investor that believed in his vision and was able to persuade a venture capital firm to go along. Mint.com's first round of funding was $750,000, with $325,000 from First Round Capital and $425,000 from other investors.

Two things helped Mint.com raise more money. The first was carefully explaining the security aspects of its service, not only to potential investors but to literally anyone who would listen. Mint.com is a read-only system. What this means is that even if someone broke into its system, they couldn't steal someone's money or even move it around. They could just look at account balances and how people spent their money. In addition, Mint.com had bank-level security in place from the outset. It had the same level of encryption and back-end protections that a bank did. Mint.com also did something very smart. It turned the security issue on its head. It argued that rather than putting people at risk, it actually protected people's finances. By allowing its customers to view all of their financial information at a single site, customers could quickly log on to their account and scan their financial information to see if anything seemed out of place. In addition, it sent its customers low-balance and unusual activity alerts.

The second thing that helped Mint.com raise additional money is that it won TechCrunch40, a high-profile business plan competition, in the fall of 2007. TechCrunch40, which was later named TechCrunch50, was a prestigious business plan competition that ran from 2007 to 2009. Looking back, Patzer says that the seven minutes he had to pitch Mint.com at the competition were the seven most important minutes of his life. The conference was an enormous platform. It was well attended by press, investors, and large companies looking for strategic partners. Over 700 companies applied for the 2007 competition. The top 40 were chosen to present. Winning gave Mint.com the outside validation it needed to move beyond the small group of investors that believed in it to a larger group that was now willing to give it a second look. It also explains Mint.com's fast start with users. The enormous press generated by the TechCrunch40 win placed Mint.com's name in front of an untold number of people in a very positive manner.

During this time, Mint.com was intently focused on execution. One of the rules of TechCrunch40 was that the competitors had to be at the prelaunch stage, so Mint.com was still in a testing mode. Patzer made his first key hires. His first hire was Jason Putori, the designer who had built Apple.com, to plan and design Mint.com's customer interface. According to Patzer, Putori cared about every pixel, and it showed in the beauty and functionality of the site. Putori brought people into Mint.com offices, literally right off the street, to test the site and see where the rough spots were. He brought in young people, old people, men, women—as diverse of a group as he could find. Patzer's third hire was David Michaels, VP of Engineering. Michaels had 15 years of experience in security, including financial Web services.

Two Years as an Independent Company— September 2007 until September 2009

Mint.com formally launched in September 2007, just after TechCrunch40. The skeptics were wrong. In its first four months it signed up 100,000 people, all of whom entered their financial information, including account numbers, user IDs, and passwords, into Mint.com. Mint.com didn't have a single security breach. Its numbers accelerated through the end of 2007 and into 2008.

Mint.com is free to the user. Its revenue model is to make referrals to its users, and then collect affiliate fees when its users follow through. For example, if Mint.com sees that a specific user is paying 16.9 percent interest on a credit card, and the user is financially sound, it will suggest a lower-interest rate credit card. If the user takes the offer, Mint.com makes a small commission.

Buoyed by its TechCrunch40 win and steady growth, Mint.com raised $31 million through several venture capital rounds from September 2007 until mid-2009. The purpose of the capital was to build out the company's infrastructure to accommodate its growth. During this period, Patzer remained Mint.com's primary spokesperson and evangelist. He would accept almost any opportunity to talk about Mint.com and its story. As a result, Mint.com's growth was paralleled by persistent public relations efforts on the part of the company to keep itself in the news and on the minds of journalists and bloggers.

In late 2009, just prior to the Intuit acquisition, Mint.com had 1.5 million users tracking nearly $50 billion in assets. It was also widely considered to be one of the up-and-coming Web 2.0 companies.

The Intuit Acquisition—September 2009

Intuit acquired Mint.com in September 2009, just 24 months after Mint.com launched. That's a quick run-up to an acquisition. Venture capitalists, for example, typically have a three- to five-year investment horizon, meaning they'd like to see the companies they invest in get acquired or launch an IPO sometime during that period. Most of the Mint.com investors monetized their investment in 24 months or less.

For its part, Intuit was a strong company in 2009, with over $1.1 billion in sales and several marquee products, including Quicken, Quick Books, and TurboTax. But it was also a boxed software company, struggling to gain a footing on the Web. Its fear was that Web-based services like Mint.com represented the future, while boxed software products like Quicken represented the past. In June 2009, Microsoft contributed to this fear by discontinuing sales of Microsoft Money, its boxed financial software product. In the end, many analysts believe it was a no-brainer for Intuit to buy Mint.com. It gave Intuit a quick entry into the Web-based side of personal financial management.

The acquisition was also good timing for Mint.com. Patzer and his team were interested in continuing to accelerate Mint.com's growth. Intuit had the financial resources to do that, and by being part of a large company, Patzer could focus solely on product development rather than raising funds. One of the conditions of the deal was that Patzer was able to continue to operate Mint.com in an autonomous manner. He was also named general manager of Intuit's personal finance division. As an added bonus for Intuit, Patzer's charge was not only to continue to build Mint.com, but to instill some of its Web savvy into other Intuit products.

(continued)

Discussion Questions

14-40. If you had been a venture capitalist at the time Patzer was originally pitching Mint.com, would you have had the same concerns as the venture capitalists at that time did? Why do you think the venture capitalists weren't more forward thinking? Why do you think Patzer didn't see the initial reaction to Mint.com as reason to either give up or to significantly modify his service?

14-41. Evaluate how effectively Mint.com prepared for its launch and early growth. What specific steps did the company take to prepare for and stimulate its early growth?

14-42. Do you think Intuit's acquisition of Mint.com was a win for both Intuit and Mint.com? In what ways does an acquisition by a large firm potentially accelerate the growth of a small firm, beyond what the small firm could have accomplished on its own?

14-43. Why do you think Intuit didn't create an online site similar to Mint.com, rather than choosing to spend $170 million to acquire Mint.com?

Sources: Mint.com website, www.mint.com, accessed July 14, 2014; C. McComas, "Interview with Aaron Patzer, founder of Mint.com," Workhappy.net, available at http://www.workhappy.net/2008/02/interview-wit-1.html, posted on Feb 19, 2008, accessed on July 14, 2014; Intuit Press Release, "Intuit to Acquire Mint.com," available at http://about.intuit.com/about_intuit/press_room/press_release/articles/2009/IntuitToAcquireMint.html, posted on September 14, 2009, accessed on July 14, 2014.

Endnotes

1. Amgen home page, www.amgen.com, (accessed July 5, 2014).

2. D. Matthews, "Why New Product Lines Fail or Succeed," eSeller Media, available at http://esellermedia.com/2012/10/31/why-new-product-lines-fail-or-succeed/, (posted on October 31, 2012, accessed on July 6, 2014).

3. A. C. Godley, "Entrepreneurial Opportunities, Implicit Contracts, and Market Making for Complex Consumer Goods," *Strategic Entrepreneurship Journal* 7, no. 4 (2013): 273–287.

4. Proactiv home page, www.proactiv3.com, (accessed July 6, 2014).

5. K. Rodan, "Stanford Technology Ventures," Entrepreneurial Thought Leaders Podcast, April 20, 2006.

6. S. M. Handley and C. M. Angst, "The Impact of Culture on the Relationship Between Governance and Opportunism in Outsourcing Relationships," *Strategic Management Journal*, 2014, in press.

7. K. Rahman and C. S. Areni, "Generic, Genuine, or Completely New? Branding Strategies to Leverage New Products," *Journal of Strategic Marketing* 22, no. 1 (2014): 3–15.

8. F. M. Stone, *The Oracle of Oracle* (New York: AMACOM Books, 2002), 125.

9. A. Al-Aali and D. J. Teece, "International Entrepreneurship and the Theory of the (Long-Lived) International Firm: A Capabilities Perspective," *Entrepreneurship Theory and Practice* 38, no. 1 (2014): 95–116; J.-F. Hennart, "The Accidental Internationalists: A Theory of Born Globals," *Entrepreneurship Theory and Practice* 38, no. 1 (2014): 117–135.

10. SBE Council, "Business Success Strategies Q&A with Laurel Delaney: Going Global for Business Growth," available at http://www.sbecouncil.org/2014/02/11/business-success-strategies-qa-with-laurel-delaney-going-global-for-small-business-growth/, (posted on February 22, 2014, accessed on July 7, 2014).

11. P. McDougall-Covin, M. V. Jones, and M. G. Serapio, "High-Potential Concepts, Phenomena, and Theories for the Advancement of International Entrepreneurship Research," *Entrepreneurship Theory and Practice* 38, no. 1 (2014): 1–10; L. Sleuwaegen and J. Onkelinx, "International Commitment, Post-Entry Growth and Survival of International New Ventures," *Journal of Business Venturing* 29, no. 1 (2014): 106–120.

12. "Asos Boosted by Increase in International Sales," BBC News, available at http://www.bbc.com/news/business-22867759, (posted on June 12, 2013, accessed on July 7, 2014).

13. S. A. Feernhaber and D. Li, "International Exposure Through Network Relationships: Implications for New Venture Internationalization," *Journal of Business Venturing* 28, no. 2 (2013): 316–334; C. N. Pitelis and D. J. Teece, "Cross-Border Market Co-Creation, Dynamic Capabilities and the Entrepreneurial Theory of the Multinational Enterprise," *Industrial and Corporate Change* 19, no. 4 (2010): 1247–1270.

14. L. Naldi and P. Davidsson, "Entrepreneurial Growth: The Role of International Knowledge Acquisition as Moderated by Firm Age," *Journal of Business Venturing* 29, no. 5 (2014): 687–703.

15. S. Arvanitis and T. Stucki, "How Swiss Small and Medium-Sized Firms Assess the Performance Impact of Mergers and Acquisitions," *Small Business Economics* 42, no. 2 (2014): 339–360.

16. A. Bhaskarabhatla and D. Hegde, "An Organizational Perspective on Patenting and Open Innovation," *Organization Science*, 2014, in press.

17. J. Li-Ying, and Y. Wang, "Find Them Home or Abroad? The Relative Contribution of International Technology In-Licensing to Indigenous Innovation in China," *Long Range*

Planning, 2014, in press; I. M. Cockburn, M. J. MacGarvie, and E. Muller, "Patent Thickets, Licensing and Innovative Performance," *Industrial and Corporate Change* 19, no. 1 (2010): 899–925.

18. T. Fischer and P. Ringler, "What Patents Are Used as Collateral? An Empirical Analysis of Patent Reassignment Data," *Journal of Business Venturing* 29, no. 5 (2014): 633–650.

19. D. Li, "Multilateral R&D Alliances by New Ventures," *Journal of Business Venturing* 28, no. 2 (2013): 241–260.

20. P.-H. Soh and A. M. Subramanian, "When Do Firms Benefit from University-Industry R&D Collaborations? The Implications of Firm R&D Focus on Scientific Research and Technological Recombination," *Journal of Business Venturing*, 2014, in press.

21. Y. K. Lew and R. R. Sinkovics, "Crossing Borders and Industry Sectors: Behavioral Governance in Strategic Alliances and Product Innovation for Competitive Advantage," *Long Range Planning* 46, no. 1 and 2 (2013): 13–38; N. Rosenbusch, J. Brinckmann, and A. Bausch, "Is Innovation Always Beneficial? A Meta-Analysis of the Relationship Between Innovation and Performance in SMEs," *Journal of Business Venturing* (2010): 441–457.

22. H. Milanov and S. A. Fernhaber, "When Do Domestic Alliances Help Ventures Abroad? Direct and Moderating Effects from a Learning Perspective," *Journal of Business Venturing* 29, no. 3 (2014): 377–391; N. Evers, "Exploring Market Orientation in New Export Ventures," *International Journal of Entrepreneurship and Innovation Management* 13, nos. 3–4 (2010): 357–376.

23. T. C. Flatten, A. Engelen, T. Moller, and M. Brettel, "How Entrepreneurial Firms Profit from Pricing Capabilities: An Examination of Technology-Based Ventures," *Entrepreneurship Theory and Practice*, 2014, in press; H. Yang, Y. Zheng, and X. Zhao, "Exploration or Exploitation? Small Firms' Alliances Strategies with Large Firms," *Strategic Management Journal* 35, no. 1 (2014): 146–157; R. E. Hoskisson, J. Covin, H. W. Volberda, and R. A. Johnson, "Revitalizing Entrepreneurship: The Search for New Research Opportunities," *Journal of Management Studies* 48, no. 6 (2011): 1141–1168.

24. V. Gilsing, W. Vanhaverbeke, and M. Pieters, "Mind the Gap: Balancing Alliance Network and Technology Portfolios During Periods of Technological Uncertainty," *Technological Forecasting and Social Change* 81, no. 4 (2014): 351–362; U. Wassmer, "Alliance Portfolios: A Review and Research Agenda," *Journal of Management* 38, no. 6 (2010): 141–171.

25. M. Dell, *Direct from Dell* (New York: HarperBusiness, 1999), 50.

26. S.-J. Chang, J. Chung, and J. J. Moon, "When Do Wholly Owned Subsidiaries Perform Better than Joint Ventures," *Strategic Management Journal* 34, no. 3 (2013): 317–337.

27. R. Ragozzino and C. Moschieri, "When Theory Doesn't Meet Practice: Do Firms Really Stage Their Investments?" *Academy of Management Perspectives*, 2014, in press; C. E. Stevens and B. J. Dykes, "The Home Country Cultural Determinants of Firms' Foreign Market Entry Timing Strategies," *Long Range Planning* 46, nos. 4–5 (2013): 387–410.

28. T. W. Tong and J. J. Reuer, "Competitive Consequences of Interfirm Collaboration: How Joint Ventures Shape Industry Profitability," *Journal of International Business Studies* 41, no. 8 (2010): 1056–1073.

29. Google Ventures home page, www.gv.com, (accessed July 8, 2014).

Getting Personal

Co-Founders

CHELSEA SLOAN
BYU, 2012, BS in Business Management

SCOTT SLOAN
University of Utah, 2008, BS in Marketing

Dialogue with
Chelsea Sloan

BEST ADVICE I'VE RECEIVED
Being an entrepreneur means that you can make other people's lives better. Do that.

FIRST ENTREPRENRIAL EXPERIENCE
Sloan Spook Alley: Admission $.50 (age 8)

FAVORITE BAND ON MY SMARTPHONE MUSIC LIST
Tchaikovsky, the Imagine Dragons

MY FAVORITE SMARTPHONE APP
Airbnb

WHAT I DO WHEN I'M NOT WORKING
Wakeboard and read

MY BIGGEST SURPRISE AS AN ENTREPRENEUR
Not every franchisee follows direction

CHAPTER 15

Franchising

UPTOWN CHEAPSKATE
Franchising as a Form of Business Ownership and Growth

• Web: www.uptowncheapskate.com • Facebook: Uptown Cheapskate

When Chelsea Sloan was young she lived with her family for a period of time in Ohio where her father was a shopping center redevelopment manager. Her mother shopped resale stores to help clothe her four children, all of whom were under age ten (two additional children came later). One store that caught the attention of Sloan's parents was Once Upon a Child, a store that bought and sold gently used children's clothing. Her parents considered buying a Once Upon a Child franchise, but thought they could improve upon the concept. So they moved the family to Utah to develop a children's clothing franchise organization of their own. In 1992, they opened the first Kid to Kid resale store with fixtures they made themselves. Although initial sales were modest, they quickly developed a successful business model, and have grown Kid to Kid to over 100 franchise locations in the United States and Portugal.

By the time Sloan was 10 she was working in Kid to Kid stores, helping tag merchandise, cleaning toys, and doing odd jobs. As the child of entrepreneurs, she participated in numerous dinnertime conversations that centered on franchising and related topics. By 2006, Sloan was a student at Brigham Young University, and she had already helped open and run multiple Kid to Kid stores. At the University of Utah, her older brother Scott was finishing his degree in marketing and was working for Kid to Kid. The two knew they wanted to own their own company, and they decided to work together. They kicked around several ideas and settled on an upscale resale store for gently used men's and women's clothing. They would differentiate themselves by creating a store atmosphere that felt like the mall, not like a thrift shop. They would hand select their product so that the clothing was clean, fresh, and stylish as well.

The business didn't come together immediately. Sloan took a one-and-a-half-year break to do a mission in Alaska. While she was gone, she and her brother Scott corresponded frequently, sharing ideas about the potential business. One thing that took some time was choosing a name. It had to be a name that was catchy, was trademarkable, and had an available URL. After considering hundreds of alternatives, they settled on Uptown Cheapskate. They also talked about their growth strategy, long before opening their first (or pilot) location. They wanted to grow

LEARNING OBJECTIVES

After studying this chapter you should be ready to:

1. Explain franchising and how this form of business ownership works.

2. Describe steps entrepreneurs can take to establish a franchise system.

3. Become familiar with the advantages and disadvantages of establishing a franchise system.

4. Describe actions and issues associated with a decision to buy a franchise.

5. Explain the steps an entrepreneur goes through to buy a franchise.

6. Identify and explain the various legal aspects associated with the franchise relationship.

7. Discuss two additional issues—franchise ethics and international franchising—entrepreneurs should think about when considering franchising.

quickly without having to make huge investments in store locations. They settled on franchising.

When Sloan returned from her mission, she arrived in Salt Lake City at 10:00 A.M. and was working on Uptown Cheapskate with her brother by 2:00 P.M. the same day. They knew that to become a successful franchise organization, they had to consistently deliver as much value to their franchisees as the franchisees paid them in franchise fees and royalties. As a result, Sloan and her brother spent the next eight months fine-tuning the Uptown Cheapskate concept. They focused on the critical aspects of building both the front end and the back end of a unique retail offering. One of the first things they worked on was creating a proprietary software platform that would allow their franchisees to quickly determine what to pay for an item brought into the store. The trick in developing this type of system is to pay people fairly for items brought in while leaving room to price the items competitively for shoppers and make a profit. The platform also had to be populated with the current brands, clothing selections, and reasonable price ranges. Building this platform took months, but it was completed. A lot of thought was also put into the Uptown Cheapskate brand, store layout, and sales reporting mechanisms for franchisees.

The first Uptown Cheapskate opened in mid-2009 in Salt Lake City, Utah. The first franchise was sold later that year to an individual in Greensboro, North Carolina. The company has grown steadily since, with two stores after Year 1, six stores after Year 2, 14 stores after Year 3 and upwards of 40 stores today. The average store earns a net profit of over six figures, which is excellent in the retail store industry. As a result of these numbers, many of the company's franchisees are opening multiple locations. Sloan and her brother credit much of their success to the upfront work they did in fleshing out the Uptown Cheapskate concept and the support they offer their franchisees. The following is a partial list of the types of support that Uptown Cheapskate offers to their franchisees:

■ Proprietary Software Platform. Referred to above, the platform allows a franchisee's buyer to quickly determine what to pay for items brought into the store. Over time, the platform has become very robust. It now contains over 4,000 brands and nearly 300 subcategories. If a seller brings in a pair of gently worn size-five Abercrombie & Fitch women's jeans, for example, the platform will instantly provide a price range to offer for the garment. This feature allows a single buyer to purchase hundreds of pieces of merchandise per day, and pay an intelligent price for each piece of merchandise acquired.

■ Franchise in a Box. Uptown Cheapskate helps franchisees configure their stores. Based on a description of the available space, the franchisee is provided a plan for exactly how to build out the store, arrange the fixtures, and display the merchandise. This service allows a franchisee to get up and running quickly.

■ Buyer Training. Franchisees are provided substantial support in terms of knowing what fashions and articles of clothing are hot and are likely to sell well and which aren't. The training is provided in the form of monthly podcasts, training videos, and other forms of support.

■ Marketing Materials. Uptown maintains an in-house marketing team that develops everything from in-store signage to radio ads to billboards and mass media.

■ Back-end Systems to Track Sales and Other Metrics. Uptown owners have access to back-end reports that update store numbers in live time. For example, a franchisee can compare their sales and other metrics against the other stores. The company has found that this functionality results in healthy competition among franchisees. A suite of back-end systems has been developed, which track sales and other metrics.

Uptown Cheapskate continues to grow with the goal of having 100 franchises by the end of 2016. The firm is routinely listed in *Entrepreneur* magazine's Franchise 500 along with its sister company, Kid to Kid. Sloan enjoys talking about franchising, and says that one of her most enjoyable experiences is sharing her story with college students. In November 2012, Sloan became the first female to win the Entrepreneurs' Organization's Global Student Entrepreneur Award. The competition included 1,700 candidates from 20 countries. In 2013, Sloan was named as one of *Inc.* magazine's 30 under 30.

As with Uptown Cheapskate, many retail and service organizations find franchising to be an attractive form of business ownership and growth.[1] In some industries, such as automotive and retail food, franchising is a dominant business ownership. Franchising is less common in other industries, although it is used in industries as diverse as Internet service providers, furniture restoration, personnel staffing, and senior care.

There are instances in which franchising is not appropriate. For example, new technologies are typically not introduced through franchise systems, particularly if the technology is proprietary or complex. Why? Because by its nature, franchising involves sharing of knowledge between a franchisor and its franchisees; in large franchise organizations, thousands of people may be involved in doing this. The inventors of new technologies typically involve as few people as possible in the process of rolling out their new products or services because they want to keep their trade secrets secret. They typically reserve their new technologies for their own use or license them to a relatively small number of companies, with strict confidentiality agreements in place.[2]

Still, franchising is a common method of business expansion and is growing in popularity. In 2014, there were 770,368 individual franchise outlets operating in the United States. These operations accounted for 8.5 million jobs and a combined economic output of $839 billion. These numbers have grown steadily since 2010.[3] You can even go to a website (www.franchising.com) to examine the array of franchises available for potential entrepreneurs to consider. This website groups franchising opportunities by industry, state, investment required, and several other criteria. These categorizations highlight the breadth of franchising opportunities now available for consideration.[4]

Unfortunately, not all the news about franchising is positive. Some entire franchise systems fail. In addition, some individual franchisees fail, even if they are a part of an otherwise successful system. Franchising is also a relatively poorly understood form of business ownership and growth. While most students and entrepreneurs generally know what franchising is and what it entails, the many subtle aspects of franchising can be learned only through experience or careful study.

We begin this chapter, which is dedicated to franchising as an important potential path to entrepreneurship and subsequent venture growth, with a description of franchising and when to use it. We then explore setting up a franchise system from the franchisor's perspective and buying a franchise from the franchisee's point of view. Next, we look at the legal aspects of franchising. We close this chapter by considering a few additional topics related to the successful use of franchising.

What Is Franchising and How Does It Work?

LEARNING OBJECTIVE

1. Explain franchising and how this form of business ownership works.

Franchising is a form of business organization in which a firm that already has a successful product or service (**franchisor**) licenses its trademark and method of doing business to other businesses (**franchisees**) in exchange for an initial franchise fee and an ongoing royalty.[5] Some franchisors are established firms; others are first-time enterprises that entrepreneurs are launching. This section explores the origins of franchising and how franchising works.

What Is Franchising?

The word *franchise* comes from an old dialect of French and means "privilege" or "freedom." Franchising has a long history. In the Middle Ages kings and lords granted franchises to specific individuals or groups to hunt on their land or to conduct certain forms of commerce. In the 1840s, breweries in Germany granted franchises to certain taverns to be the exclusive distributors of their beer for the region. Shortly after the U.S. Civil War, the Singer Sewing Machine Company began granting distribution franchises for its sewing machines and pioneered the use of written franchise agreements. Many of the most familiar franchises in the United States, including Kentucky Fried Chicken (1952), McDonald's (1955), Burger King (1955), Midas Muffler (1956), and H&R Block (1958), started in the post–World War II era of the 1940s and 1950s.

The franchise organization Comfort Keepers demonstrates how franchises are started. A year before the company was founded, Kristina Clum, a registered nurse, noticed that her parents were having trouble with ordinary daily chores. She wanted someone to come into their home to help them but was unable to find people willing to do so. So Kristina and her husband Jerry founded a business dedicated to helping seniors cope with everyday nonmedical tasks, such as meal preparation, light housekeeping, grocery shopping, laundry, and errands. The first Comfort Keepers office was opened in Springfield, Ohio, in March 1998, and the second was opened in Dayton a year later.

Comfort Keepers is a timely idea that addresses a need for a particular target market. As we've discussed in earlier chapters, having a solid business idea is critical to achieving firm growth. In 2013, 14.1 percent of the U.S. population, or 44.6 million people, were 65 years old or older.[6] That number is expected to steadily increase. Comfort Keepers's services may provide some seniors the option of staying in their homes as opposed to entering more costly assisted living centers. In August 1999, the company began franchising, and by 2014 it had over 700 franchise outlets throughout the United States, Canada, Ireland, Australia, France, Portugal, and Singapore.[7]

The Comfort Keepers business idea lends itself to franchising because the company has a good trademark and a good business method. Moreover, because the nature of the business keeps the cost of starting a Comfort Keepers franchise relatively low, there is a substantial pool of people available to purchase the franchise. For Comfort Keepers and its franchisees, franchising is a win-win proposition. Comfort Keepers wins because it is able to use its franchisees' money to quickly grow its business and strengthen its brand. The franchisees win because they are able to start a business in a growing industry relatively inexpensively and benefit by adopting the Comfort Keepers trademark and method of doing business.

How Does Franchising Work?

There is nothing magical about franchising. It is a form of growth that allows a business to get its products or services to market through the efforts of business

Many fast-food and casual dining restaurants are business format franchises. Here, a family is enjoying some time together and some smoothies in a business format franchise.

Andresr/Shutterstock

partners or "franchisees." As described previously, a franchise is an agreement between a franchisor (the parent company, such as Uptown Cheapskate or Comfort Keepers) and a franchisee (an individual or firm that is willing to pay the franchisor a fee for the right to sell its product, service, and/or business method).[8] Planet Smoothie, for example, is a very successful franchise system. The franchisor (Planet Smoothie, Inc.) provides the rights to individual businesspersons (the local franchisees) to use the Planet Smoothie trademark and business methods. In turn, the franchisees pay Planet Smoothie a franchise fee and an ongoing royalty for these privileges and agree to operate their Planet Smoothie restaurants according to Planet Smoothie Inc.'s standards.

There are two distinctly different types of franchise systems: the product and trademark franchise and the business format franchise. A **product and trademark franchise** is an arrangement under which the franchisor grants to the franchisee the right to buy its products and use its trade name. This approach typically connects a single manufacturer with a network of dealers or distributors. For example, General Motors has established a network of dealers that sell GM cars and use the GM trademark in their advertising and promotions. Similarly, ExxonMobil has established a network of franchisee-owned gasoline stations to distribute its gasoline. Product and trademark franchisees are typically permitted to operate in a fairly autonomous manner. The parent company, such as GM or ExxonMobil, is generally concerned more with maintaining the integrity of its products than with monitoring the day-to-day activities of its dealers or station owners. Other examples of product and trademark franchise systems include agricultural machinery dealers, soft-drink bottlers, and beer distributorships. Rather than obtaining a royalty or franchise fee, the product and trademark franchisor obtains the majority of its income from selling its products to its dealers or distributors at a markup.

The second type of franchise, the **business format franchise**, is by far the more popular approach to franchising and is more commonly used by entrepreneurs and entrepreneurial ventures. In a business format franchise, the franchisor provides a formula for doing business to the franchisee along with training, advertising, and other forms of assistance. Table 15.1 shows 10 industries in which business format franchises predominate. While a business

TABLE 15.1   10 Industries in Which Business Format Franchises Predominate

- Automotive
- Business Services
- Commercial & Residential Services
- Lodging
- Personal Services
- Quick Service Restaurants
- Real Estate
- Retail Food
- Retail Products & Services
- Table/Full Service Restaurants

Source: Based on International Franchise Organization, "Franchise Business Economic Outlook for 2014," January 13, 2014.

format franchise provides a franchisee a formula for conducting business, it can also be very rigid and demanding. For example, fast-food restaurants such as McDonald's and Burger King teach their franchisees every detail of how to run their restaurants, from how many seconds to cook french fries to the exact words their employees should use when they greet customers (such as "Will this be dining in or carry out?"). Business format franchisors obtain the majority of their revenues from their franchisees in the form of royalties and franchise fees.

For both product and trademark franchises and business format franchises, the franchisor–franchisee relationship takes one of three forms of a franchise agreement (see Figure 15.1). The most common type of franchise arrangement is an individual franchise agreement. An **individual franchise agreement** involves the sale of a single franchise for a specific location. For example, an individual may purchase a Play It Again Sports franchise to be constructed and operated at 901 Pearl Street in Boulder, Colorado. An **area franchise agreement** allows a franchisee to own and operate a specific number of outlets in a particular geographic area. For example, a franchisee may purchase the rights to open five Play It Again Sports franchises within the city limits of Sioux Falls, South Dakota. This is a very popular franchise arrangement, because in most cases it gives the franchisee exclusive rights for a given area. Finally, a **master franchise agreement** is similar to an area franchise agreement, with one major difference. A master franchisee, in addition to having the right to open and operate a specific number of locations in a particular area, also has the right to offer and sell the franchise to other people in its area. For example, ProntoWash is a mobile car washing service that uses environmentally friendly soaps, waxes, and other products. The company sells master franchise agreements that provide a master franchisee the right to open a certain number of ProntoWash outlets in a defined geographic area. After its own outlets have been opened, the master franchisee can then sell the rights to open additional ProntoWash locations in the same area to other individuals.[9] The people who buy franchises from master franchisees are typically called **subfranchisees**.

A person who owns and operates more than one outlet of the same franchisor, whether through an area or a master franchise agreement, is called a **multiple-unit franchisee**. For the franchisee, there are advantages and disadvantages to multiple-unit franchising. By owning more than one unit, a multiple-unit franchisee can capture economies of scale and reduce its administrative overhead per unit of sale. The disadvantages of multiple-unit franchising are that the franchisor takes more risk and makes a deeper commitment to a single franchisee. In general, franchisors encourage multiple-unit franchising. By selling an additional franchise to an existing franchisee, a franchisor

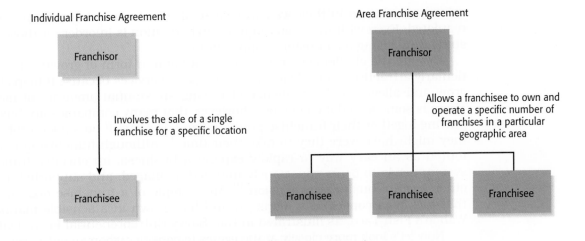

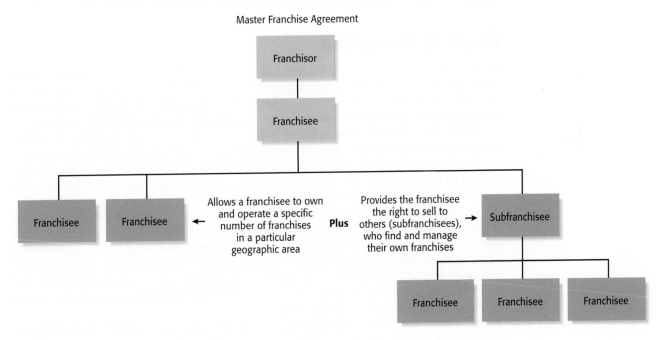

FIGURE 15.1
Different Types of Franchise Systems

can grow its business without adding to the total number of franchisees with whom it must maintain a relationship to conduct its business.

Establishing a Franchise System

Establishing a franchise system should be approached carefully and deliberately. While the process is a familiar one to a company such as McDonald's, which at the end of 2013 had 35,429 restaurants in 119 countries,[10] franchising is an unfamiliar process to a new franchise organization. Franchising is a complicated business endeavor, which means that an entrepreneur must look closely at all of its aspects before deciding to franchise. Indeed, franchising often involves the managerially demanding tasks of training, supporting, supervising, and nurturing franchisees.

An entrepreneur should also be aware that over the years a number of fraudulent franchise organizations have come and gone and left financially

LEARNING OBJECTIVE

2. Describe steps entrepreneurs can take to establish a franchise system.

ruined franchisees in their wake. Because of this, franchising is fairly heavily regulated. Even with this regulation, though, caution is in order for those pursuing franchising as a business opportunity.

Despite the challenges, franchising is a popular form of growth. It is particularly attractive to new firms in retailing and services because it helps firms grow and alleviates the challenge of raising substantial amounts of money. There is some anecdotal evidence, however, that many companies are hasty in putting together their franchise programs and as a result do a poorer job than they might have were they to take their time.[11] Although franchising is often touted as an easy way to rapidly expand a business, an effective franchise system needs to be as consciously initiated, managed, and supported as any other form of business expansion.[12] An example of a franchise organization that has been consciously managed and has grown in a sensible manner is Wahoo's Fish Taco, as illustrated in the "Savvy Entrepreneurial Firm" feature.

Now let's look more closely at the issues to consider when an entrepreneur is trying to decide if franchising is an appropriate approach to growing a business.

When to Franchise

Retail firms grow when two things happen: first, when the attractiveness of a firm's products or services become well known, whether it is a new restaurant or a fitness center, and, second, when a firm has the financial capability to build the outlets needed to satisfy the demand for its products or services.

There are at least two options firms have as a means to grow. Building company-owned outlets is one of these options. However, this choice presents a company with the challenge of raising the money to fund its expansion. As discussed in Chapter 10, this option is typically pursued through debt, investment capital, or earnings, none of which is easy to achieve for a start-up venture.

Franchising is a second growth alternative available to firms. Franchising is perhaps especially attractive to young firms in that the majority of the money needed for expansion comes from the franchisees. Franchising is appropriate when a firm has a strong or potentially strong trademark, a well-designed business model, and a desire to grow. A franchise system will ultimately fail if the franchisee's brand doesn't create value for customers and its business model is flawed or poorly developed.

In some instances, franchising is simply not appropriate. For example, franchising works for Burger King but would not work for Walmart. While Burger King has a large number of franchise outlets, each individual outlet is relatively small and has a limited menu, and policies and procedures can be written to cover almost any contingency. In contrast, although Walmart is similar to Burger King in that it, too, has a strong trademark and thousands of outlets, Walmart stores are much larger, more expensive to build, and more complex to run compared to the complexity of running a Burger King restaurant. It would be nearly impossible for Walmart to find an adequate number of qualified people who would have the financial capital and expertise to open and successfully operate a Walmart store.

Steps to Franchising a Business

Let's assume that as an entrepreneur you have decided to use franchising as a means of growing your venture. What steps should you take to develop a franchise system? As illustrated in Figure 15.2, you, as an entrepreneur, should take nine steps in order to successfully set up a franchise system.

Step 1   **Develop a franchise business plan:** The franchise business plan should follow the format of a conventional business plan, which we

SAVVY ENTREPRENEURIAL FIRM

Wahoo's Fish Taco: A Moderate-Growth Yet Highly Successful Franchise Organization

Web: www.wahoos.com; Facebook: Wahoo's Fish Taco; Twitter: @WahoosFish Taco

Wahoo's Fish Taco is a franchise organization that offers Mexican food mixed with Brazilian and Asian flavors. It is a "fast-casual" restaurant that was founded in Costa Mesa, California, in 1988 by Chinese-Brazilian brothers Eduardo Lee, Mingo Lee, and Wing Lam, who mixed traditional Chinese and Brazilian flavors with dishes they encountered traveling in Mexico. The first Wahoo's Fish Taco restaurant was launched to combine the brothers' love for surfing and food.

Wahoo's is now just over 25 years old and has about 60 locations, located in California, Texas, Colorado, Nevada, Nebraska, and Hawaii. It's known for its specialty charbroiled fish, steak, and chicken tacos and burritos. Although it's been very successful, it couldn't be characterized as a "rapid growth" franchise system. Instead, the founders have elected to make Wahoo's Fish Taco a relatively slow growth system, focusing on branding and service quality rather than rapid growth. This philosophy has been an entrenched part of the way Wahoo's Fish Taco has done business since the beginning. It started with a single restaurant in 1988; the second unit was added only when the founders had saved enough money to build it debt free. This pattern has characterized the company's growth. Early on, it only added one new restaurant a year, then two, then three, and so on. Despite its success, it has averaged only about 2.5 restaurants per year since its founding. For many years, the company only sold franchises to people the founders personally knew and trusted.

Wahoo's pace of expansion has picked up some in recent years, but not dramatically. Its brand has been built around its enthusiasm for surfing and other extreme sports. More than half of its restaurants are in California, and its locations in other states are largely in college towns or "hip" communities. The company does not have international locations, although there are some indications that it plans to expand to Japan.

Along with its staple dishes, Wahoo's Fish Taco offers many vegetarian and vegan options, such as tofu, banzai veggies, and brown rice. Its restaurants are very attractive inside and out, and offer a relaxed environment with a definite "surfer" feel. Buying a Wahoo Fish Taco franchise requires a major financial commitment. The initial franchise fee is $35,000. The ongoing royalty is 5 percent of gross sales plus an additional 2 percent for marketing. The cost to build a Wahoo Fish Taco restaurant runs from $425,000 to $715,000 depending on location, size of restaurant, landscaping, and local ordinances.

Questions for Critical Thinking

1. What are the advantages and disadvantages of Wahoo's Fish Taco's slow growth philosophy of franchise expansion?
2. Spend some time looking at Wahoo's Fish Taco's website, focusing particularly on its menu and its store layout. Do you think the business is well positioned or poorly positioned to take advantage of current trends in the types of restaurants that are doing well and in light of today's food preferences? Explain your answer.
3. To what degree do you think Wahoo's Fish Taco has been too conservative in its expansion?
4. Spend some time studying the cost of becoming a Wahoo's Fish Taco franchisee compared to similar franchise organizations. Is the cost of acquiring and owning a Wahoo Fish Taco franchise on the high end, in the middle, or on the low end compared to its closest competitors? To what degree do you believe your answer has affected Wahoo's pace of growth?

Sources: Wahoo's Fish Taco's website, www.wahoos.com (accessed August 15, 2015); Wikipedia, Wahoo's Fish Taco, www.wikipedia.org, accessed August 15, 2014.

discussed in Chapter 6, and should fully describe the rationale for franchising the business and act as a blueprint for rolling out the franchise operation. Particular attention should be paid to the location of the proposed franchise outlet. For example, a Baskin-Robbins franchise that is successful in the food court of a mall in an upscale area doesn't mean that it will be successful in a less heavily trafficked strip mall in an average-income neighborhood.

Step 2 **Get professional advice:** Before going too far, a potential franchisor should seek advice from a qualified franchise attorney, consultant, or certified public accountant. If the business cannot be realistically turned into a franchise, then a qualified professional can save a potential franchisor a lot of time, money, and frustration by urging that the

FIGURE 15.2
Nine Steps in Setting
Up a Franchise System

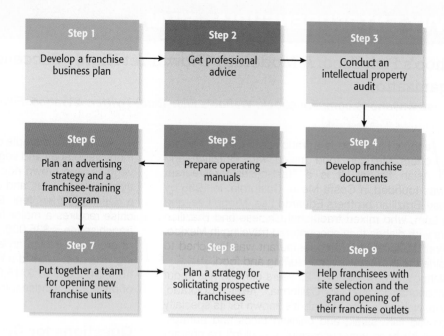

process be stopped. If the business can be turned into a franchise, then it is advisable to get professional advice to help direct the entire process.

Step 3 **Conduct an intellectual property audit:** As we discussed in Chapter 12, this step is necessary to determine the intellectual property a company owns and to ensure that the property is properly registered and protected. All original written, audio, and visual material, including operating manuals, training videos, advertising brochures, and similar matter, should be afforded copyright protection. If a firm has a unique business model that includes a unique business method, it should consider obtaining a patent for its business method. These protective measures are vital because once a company begins franchising, its trademarks and business model and any unique business methods are disseminated, making them more visible to customers and competitors. In addition, a franchisor should make sure that its trademark is not infringing on the trademark of any other firm.

Step 4 **Develop franchise documents:** Later in the chapter, we discuss the documents that are required to franchise a business. Here, we can note that at the beginning of the franchise evaluation process, a prospective franchisor should prepare the Franchise Disclosure Document (formally called the Uniform Franchise Offering Circular) and the franchise agreement. A franchise attorney can provide specific information regarding the content and format of these documents.

Step 5 **Prepare operating manuals:** Businesses that are suitable for franchising typically have a polished business system that can be fairly easily taught to qualified franchisees. The franchisor should prepare manuals that document all aspects of its business model.

Step 6 **Plan an advertising strategy and a franchisee training program:** Prospective franchisees will want to see an advertising strategy and a franchisee training program in place. The scope of each program should match the speed at which the franchisor wants to grow its business.

Step 7 **Put together a team for opening new franchise units:** A team should be developed and prepared to help new franchisees open their franchise units. The team should be well trained and equipped to provide the franchisee a broad range of training and guidance.

Step 8 **Plan a strategy for soliciting prospective franchisees:** There are many channels available to franchisors to solicit and attract potential franchisees. Franchise trade fairs, newspaper ads, franchise publications, social media platforms, and Internet advertising are examples of these channels.

Step 9 **Help franchisees with site selection and the grand opening of their franchise outlets:** Location is very important to most retail businesses, so a franchisor should be heavily involved in the site selection of its franchisees' outlets. The franchisor should also help the franchisee with the grand opening of the franchise outlet.

Along with the specific steps shown in Figure 15.2, it is important for a franchisor to remember that the quality of the relationships it maintains with its franchisees often defines the ultimate success of the franchise system. It is to the franchisor's advantage to follow through on all promises and to establish an exemplary reputation. This is an ongoing commitment that a franchisor should make to its franchisees.

Selecting and Developing Effective Franchisees

The franchisor's ability to select and develop effective franchisees strongly influences the degree to which a franchise system is successful. For most systems, the ideal franchisee is someone who has solid ideas and suggestions but is willing to work within the franchise system's rules. Bold, aggressive entrepreneurs typically do not make good franchisees. Franchisees must be team players to properly fit within the context of a successful franchise system.

Once franchisees are selected, it is important that franchisors work to develop their franchisees' potential. Table 15.2 contains a list of the qualities that franchisors look for in prospective franchisees and the steps that franchisors can take to develop their franchisees' potential.

TABLE 15.2 Selecting and Developing Effective Franchisees

Qualities to Look for in Prospective Franchisees

- Good work ethic
- Ability to follow instructions
- Ability to operate with minimal supervision
- Team oriented
- Experience in the industry in which the franchise competes
- Adequate financial resources and a good credit history
- Ability to make suggestions without becoming confrontational or upset if the suggestions are not adopted
- Represents the franchisor in a positive manner

Ways Franchisors Can Develop the Potential of Their Franchisees

- Provide mentoring that supersedes routine training
- Keep operating manuals up-to-date
- Keep product, services, and business systems up-to-date
- Solicit input from franchisees to reinforce their importance in the larger system
- Encourage franchisees to develop a franchise association
- Maintain the franchise system's integrity

Advantages and Disadvantages of Establishing a Franchise System

LEARNING OBJECTIVE

3. Become familiar with the advantages and disadvantages of establishing a franchise system.

There are two primary advantages to franchising. First, early in the life of an organization, capital is typically scarce, and rapid growth is needed to achieve brand recognition and economies of scale. Franchising helps a venture grow quickly because franchisees provide the majority of the capital.[13] For example, if Comfort Keepers were growing via company-owned outlets rather than franchising, it would probably have only a handful of outlets rather than the more than 700 it has today. Many franchisors even admit that they would have rather grown through company-owned stores but that the capital requirements needed to grow their firms dictated franchising. This sentiment is affirmed by an executive at Hardee's, who wrote the following about the growth of this fast-food chain:

> Hardee's would have preferred not to have franchised a single location. We prefer company-owned locations. But due to the heavy capital investment required, we could only expand company-owned locations to a certain degree—from there we had to stop. Each operation represents an investment in excess of $100,000; therefore, we entered the franchise business.[14]

Second, a concept called **agency theory** argues that for organizations with multiple units (such as restaurant chains), it is more effective for the units to be run by franchisees than by managers who run company-owned stores. The theory is that managers, because they are usually paid a salary, may not be as committed to the success of their individual units as franchisees, who are in effect the owners of the units they manage.[15]

The primary disadvantage of franchising is that an organization allows others to profit from its trademark and business model. For example, each time Comfort Keepers sells a franchise it receives a $32,500 initial franchise fee and an ongoing royalty, which is 3 to 4 percent of gross sales. However, if Comfort Keepers had provided its service itself in the same location, it would be getting 100 percent of the gross sales and net profits from the location. This is the main reason some organizations that are perfectly suitable for franchising grow through company-owned stores rather than franchising. An example is Darden Restaurants Inc., the parent company of Olive Garden, Bahama Breeze, LongHorn Steakhouse, The Capital Grille, Seasons 52, Eddie V's, and Yard House. With over 1,500 locations, the firm employs more than 150,000 people and serves more than 320 million meals a year.[16] All of Darden's units are company owned. Starbucks is another company that is suitable for franchising but has only a small number of franchise outlets. We provide a more complete list of the advantages and disadvantages of franchising as a means of business expansion in Table 15.3.

When a company decides to investigate franchising as a means of growth, it should ensure that it and its product or service meet several criteria. Businesses that fail to satisfy these criteria are less likely to make effective franchise systems. Before deciding to franchise, a firm should consider the following:

■ **The uniqueness of its product or service:** The business's product or service should be unique along some dimension that creates value for customers. Businesses with a unique product or service typically have the best potential to expand.

■ **The consistent profitability of the firm:** The business should be consistently profitable, and the future profitability of the business should be fairly easy to predict. When developing a franchise system, a company

TABLE 15.3 **Advantages and Disadvantages of Franchising as a Method of Business Expansion**

Advantages	Disadvantages
Rapid, low-cost market expansion. Because franchisees provide most of the cost of expansion, the franchisor can expand the size of its business fairly rapidly	**Profit sharing.** By selling franchises instead of operating company-owned stores, franchisors share the profits derived from their proprietary products or services with their franchisees. For example, before being acquired by FedEx, Kinko's did not sell franchises, allowing it to retain all its profits.
Income from franchise fees and royalties. By collecting franchise fees, the franchisor gets a fairly quick return on the proprietary nature of its products/services and business model. The franchisor also receives ongoing royalties from its franchisees without incurring substantial risk.	**Loss of control.** It is typically more difficult for a franchisor to control its franchisees than it is for a company to control its employees. Franchisees, despite the rules governing the franchise system, still often view themselves as independent businesspeople.
Franchisee motivation. Because franchisees put their personal capital at risk, they are highly motivated to make their franchise outlets successful. In contrast, the managers of company-owned outlets typically do not have their own capital at risk. As a result, these managers may not be prone to work as hard as franchisees or be as attentive to cost savings.	**Friction with franchisees.** A common complaint of franchisors is dealing with the friction that often develops between franchisors and franchisees. Friction can develop over issues such as the payment of fees, hours of operation, caveats in the franchise agreement, and surprise inspections.
Access to ideas and suggestions. Franchisees represent a source of intellectual capital and often make suggestions to their franchisors. By incorporating these ideas into their business model, franchisors can in effect leverage the ideas and suggestions of their individual franchisees.	**Managing growth.** Franchisors that are in growing industries and have a strong trademark often grow quickly. Although this might seem like an advantage, rapid growth can be difficult to manage. A franchisor provides each of its franchisees a number of services, such as site selection and employee training. If a franchise system is growing rapidly, the franchisor will have to continually add personnel to its own staff to properly support its growing number of franchisees.
Cost savings. Franchisees share many of the franchisors' expenses, such as the cost of regional and national advertising.	**Differences in required business skills.** The business skills that made a franchisor successful in the original business are typically not the same skills needed to manage a franchise system. For example, Sam Jones may be a very effective owner/manager of a seafood restaurant. That does not necessarily mean, however, that he will be an effective manager of a franchise system if he decided to franchise his seafood restaurant concept.
Increased buying power. Franchisees provide franchisors increased buying power by enlarging the size of their business, allowing them to purchase larger quantities of products and services when buying those items.	**Legal expenses.** Many states have specific laws pertaining to franchising. As a result, if a franchisor sells franchises in multiple states, legal expenses can be high to properly interpret and comply with each state's laws. Unfortunately, from the franchisor's point of view, some of the toughest laws are in the most populated states.

should have several prototype outlets up and running to test and ensure the viability of the business idea. Remember, a franchisee is supposed to be buying a way of doing business (in the form of a business model) that is "proven"—at least to a certain extent. Franchisors that learn how to run their businesses through the trial and error of their franchisees have typically franchised their businesses prematurely (especially from the franchisees' point of view).

■ **The firm's year-round profitability:** The business should be profitable year-round, not only during specific seasons. For example, a lawn and garden care franchise in North Dakota should be set up to provide the franchisee supplemental products and services to sell during off-peak seasons. Otherwise, owning the franchise may not be an attractive form of business ownership. This issue is particularly problematic for some ice cream and smoothie franchises in northern states, which experience a significant decline in sales during winter months.

■ **The degree of refinement of the firm's business systems:** The systems and procedures for operating the business should be polished and the procedures documented in written form. The systems and procedures should also be fairly easy to teach to qualified candidates.

■ **The clarity of the business proposition:** The business proposition should be crystal clear so that prospective franchisees fully understand the business proposition to which they are committing. The relationship between the franchisor and the franchisee should be completely open, and communication between them should be candid.

After determining that the firm satisfies these criteria, the entrepreneur should step back and review all the alternatives for business expansion. No single form of business expansion is the best under all circumstances. For any entrepreneurial venture, the best form of expansion is the one that increases the likelihood that the venture will reach its objectives.

One franchise organization that started fast but is now faltering is Curves International, as depicted in this chapter's "What Went Wrong?" feature.

Buying a Franchise

LEARNING OBJECTIVE

4. Describe actions and issues associated with a decision to buy a franchise.

Now let's look at franchising from the franchisee's perspective. Purchasing a franchise is an important business decision involving a substantial financial commitment. Potential franchise owners should strive to be as well informed as possible before purchasing a franchise and should be well aware that it is often legally and financially difficult to exit a franchise relationship. Indeed, an individual franchise opportunity should be meticulously scrutinized. Close scrutiny of a potential franchise opportunity includes activities such as meeting with the franchisor and carefully reading the Franchise Disclosure Document, soliciting legal and financial advice, and talking to former franchisees that have dropped out of the system one is considering. In particularly heavily franchised industries, such as fast food and automobile repair, a prospective franchisee may have 20 or more franchisors from which to make a selection. It is well worth franchisees' time to carefully select the franchisor that best meets their individual needs.[17]

Some franchise organizations are designed to provide their franchisees a part-time rather than a full-time income, which is attractive to some people. An example is Fit4Mom, a company that gathers new mothers together to do 45-minute power walks with their babies in strollers. The initial franchise fee ranges between $5,000 and $50,000, depending on several factors, including how densely populated the area is in which the franchise will be located. Owning a Fit4Mom franchise is ideal for a woman who wants to work two to three hours a day rather than eight, and who is passionate about fitness.

Franchising may be a particularly good choice for someone who wants to start a business but has no prior business experience. Along with offering a refined business system, well-run franchise organizations provide their franchisees training, technical expertise, and other forms of ongoing support.

Is Franchising Right for You?

Entrepreneurs should weigh the possibility of purchasing a franchise against the alternatives of buying an existing business or launching their own venture from scratch. Answering the following questions will help determine whether

WHAT WENT WRONG?

Trouble at Curves International
Web: www.curves.com; Facebook: Curves; Twitter: @CurvesNews

Curves International, whose 30-minute workout and singular focus on women made it among the world's fastest-growing franchise organizations, seems to be losing a lot of steam.

According to a May 27, 2014, article in *Forbes*, since 2006 Curves has shed more than 4,000 locations, from a peak of 10,000 in 2006 to 6,000 today. Its North American locations dropped 65 percent during a similar period. That drop ranked Curves seventh worst among franchises with an initial investment of up to $150,000.

While opinions vary about what went wrong with Curves, a consensus has emerged on four points: (1) the company failed to keep up with changing trends, including more flexible hours for busy working women, (2) cheaper competition, (3) the poor economy, and (4) the company sold too many franchises that are located too close together. Of the four reasons, a failure to keep up with changing trends may be the biggest culprit. Some Curves locations are open for limited hours, causing patrons to look elsewhere for their workouts. Also, 24-hour fitness centers, including Anytime Fitness and Snap Fitness, have opened in many areas, providing busy women even more flexibility than Curves. Some members may have also tired of Curves's bare-boned approach and gravitated to fitness centers that offer aerobics classes, Yoga, Pilates, and dressing rooms with showers.

Founded in 1992, Curves was an instant hit, largely because it targeted an underserved part of the market: busy and unfit women. Curves's founders believed that many women 30 years old and older cared deeply about their health and appearance but didn't want to join a fitness center full of people who were already fit. So they created a fitness center "just for them" that was convenient, affordable, and restricted to females. The Curves "concept" was structured on a stripped-down version of the traditional fitness center, based on a tightly structured 30-minute workout using 8 to 12 exercise machines. Curves fitness centers do not have locker rooms, showers, aerobic classes, or juice bars. Instead they're designed to be convenient and quick. Members pay $99 up front to join, through the fee is often discounted. Monthly dues vary, averaging about $44 per month.

In 2012, Curves was acquired by North Castle Partners, a private equity firm. Its new owners disagree with the critics and blame Curves's troubles on franchisees. The gist of their argument, which is laid out in the *Forbes* magazine article mentioned above, is that people who bought multiple Curves franchises were the wrong owners for Curves. "If you aren't there working it and working in the community to try to bring new people in and providing great service to your members ... often those locations are not going to do very well," Jon Canarick, managing director of North Central Partners, was quoted as saying. The inference is that failed franchisees were motivated primarily as investors rather than owners.

In regard to turning Curves around, North Castle Partners has several things in mind. The plans involve strengthening the company's existing fitness and weight-loss programs, as well as pushing nutrition bars and apparel. There may also be some cross-initiatives with Jenny Craig, a company that sells weight-loss and diet programs and is also owned by North Castle Partners. Curves also hopes for a lift from its new spokesperson, Jillian Michaels, who became known as a result of her appearances on NBC's *The Biggest Loser.*

Questions for Critical Thinking

1. Why do you think Curves failed to respond to changing trends? To what degree do you think this single factor contributes to Curves's recent troubles?

2. To what degree do you believe that Curves's former owners (the franchisor) is culpable in the failure of so many Curves franchise locations? What is your opinion of North Castle Partners's turnaround plans for Curves? Do you believe that Curves will continue losing franchises, or do you think the company will recover and start growing again?

3. If you were thinking about buying a franchise, write three questions that you'd ask a franchise organization you were thinking about buying into as a direct result of reading this feature.

4. The "You Be the VC 15.1" feature focuses on IceBorn, a rapidly growing franchise organization that furnishes its franchisees state-of-the art, 24-hour, on-demand ice and water vending machines. If you were the CEO of IceBorn, what lessons would you learn by studying Curves's troubles?

Source: Curves home page, www.curves.com, accessed August 15, 2014; L. Jackson, "Crash Diet: After Shedding Thousands of Locations, Can Curves Get Back in Shape," *Forbes*, May 27, 2014; R. Gibson, "Curves Loses Stamina, Closing Fitness Clubs," *Wall Street Journal*, July 7, 2010.

This man just purchased an auto repair franchise. Prospective franchise owners should carefully determine whether they're willing to be part of a structured franchise system before buying in.

Minerva Studio/Shutterstock

franchising is a good fit for people thinking about starting their own entrepreneurial venture:

■ Are you willing to take orders? Franchisors are typically very particular about how their outlets operate. For example, McDonald's and other successful fast-food chains are very strict in terms of their restaurants' appearance and how each unit's food is prepared. Franchising is typically not a good fit for people who like to experiment with their own ideas or are independent minded.

■ Are you willing to be part of a franchise "system" rather than an independent businessperson? For example, as a franchisee you may be required to pay into an advertising fund that covers the costs of advertising aimed at regional or national markets rather than the market for your individual outlet. Will it bother you to have someone use your money to develop ads that benefit the "system" rather than only your outlet or store? Are you willing to lose creative control over how your business is promoted?

■ How will you react if you make a suggestion to your franchisor and your suggestion is rejected? How will you feel if you are told that your suggestion might work for you but can be put in place only if it works in all parts of the system?

■ What are you looking for in a business? How hard do you want to work?

■ How willing are you to put your money at risk? How will you feel if your business is operating at a net loss but you still have to pay royalties on your gross income?

None of these questions is meant to suggest that franchising is not an attractive method of business ownership for entrepreneurs. It is important, however, that a potential franchisee be fully aware of the subtleties involved with franchising before purchasing a franchise outlet.

The Cost of a Franchise

The initial cost of a business format franchise varies, depending on the franchise fee, the capital needed to start the business, and the strength of the franchisor. For example, some franchisors, such as McDonald's, own the land and buildings that their franchisees use, and lease the property to the franchisees. In contrast, other organizations require their franchisees to purchase the land, buildings, and equipment needed to run their franchise outlets. Table 15.4 shows the total costs of buying into several franchise organizations. As you can see, the total initial cost varies from a low of $10,250 for a Coffee News franchise up to $6.6 million for a Hampton Inn Hotel franchise.

Also shown in Table 15.4 is a breakdown of the number of company-owned units and the number of franchise units maintained by different organizations. Company-owned units are managed and operated by company personnel, and there is no franchisee involved. Franchise organizations vary in their philosophies regarding company-owned versus franchised units. As we noted earlier in this chapter, some companies (e.g., Budget Blinds) are strictly franchisors and have no company-owned units. Other companies, such as Qdoba Mexican Grill, have roughly the same number of franchises and company owned stores. In addition, some U.S.-based franchise systems have more foreign franchises than domestic franchises. For example, of the 18,875 franchises in KFC's system, 4,491 are in the United States and 14,384 are in foreign countries. In fact, there are more KFC franchises in China (4,563) than there are in the United States.

When evaluating the cost of a franchise, prospective franchisees should consider all the costs involved. Franchisors are required by law to disclose all their costs in a document called the Franchise Disclosure Document and send it to the franchisee. (We'll talk about this document in more detail later in this chapter.) To avoid making a hasty judgment, a franchisee may

TABLE 15.4 **Initial Costs to the Franchisee of a Sample of Franchise Organizations**

Franchise Organization	Year Started Franchising	Company-Owned Units	Franchised Units	Franchise Fee	Ongoing Royalty Fee	Total Initial Investment
Anytime Fitness	2002	28	2,511	$22,500 varies	$549/ month	$78,700–$371,175
Budget Blinds	1994	0	929	$14,950	Varies	$89,240–$187,070
Coffee News	1994	5	819	$9,000	$25–$80/ week	$10,250–$11,250
Edible Arrangements	2001	3	1,150	$30,000	5%	$155,999–$276,984
Hampton Inn Hotels	1984	1	1,943	$75,000	6%	$3.7–$6.6 million
Liberty Tax Service	1973	180	4,226	$40,000	14%	$56,800–$69,900
Papa John's	1986	724	2,616	$25,000 varies	5%	$129,910–$644,210
Qdoba Mexican Grill	1997	284	313	$30,000	5%	$594,000–$795,000
The UPS Store	2001	0	4,789	$29,950	8.5%	$150,152–$420,299
Wetzel's Pretzels	1996	12	284	$35,000	7%	$156,300–$370,950

Source: Based on Entrepreneur.com, www.entrepreneur.com (accessed August 15, 2014).

not purchase a franchise for 14 days from the time the circular is received. The following costs are typically associated with buying a business format franchise:[18]

- **Initial franchise fee:** The initial franchise fee varies, depending on the franchisor, as shown in Table 15.4. High-overhead brick-and-mortar franchises charge less (4 to 5 percent of gross sales), while low-overhead home-based and service business charge more (8 to 10 percent of gross sales).

- **Capital requirements:** These costs vary, depending on the franchisor, but may include the cost of buying real estate, the cost of constructing a building, the purchase of initial inventory, and the cost of obtaining a business license. Some franchisors also require a new franchisee to pay a "grand opening" fee for its assistance in opening the business.

- **Continuing royalty payment:** In the majority of cases, a franchisee pays a royalty based on a percentage of weekly or monthly gross income. Note that because the fee is typically assessed on gross income rather than net income, a franchisee may have to pay a monthly royalty even if the business is losing money. Royalty fees are usually around 5 percent of gross income.[19]

- **Advertising fees:** Franchisees are often required to pay into a national or regional advertising fund, even if the advertisements are directed at goals other than promoting the franchisor's product or service. (For example, advertising could focus on the franchisor's attempt at attracting new franchisees.) Advertising fees are typically less than 3 percent of gross income.

- **Other fees:** Other fees may be charged for various activities, including training additional staff, providing management expertise when needed, providing computer assistance, or providing a host of other items or support services.

Although not technically a fee, many franchise organizations sell their franchisee products that they use in their businesses, such as restaurant supplies for a restaurant franchise. The products are often sold at a markup and may be more expensive than those the franchisee could obtain on the open market.

The most important question a prospective franchisee should consider is whether the fees and royalties charged by a franchisor are consistent with the franchise's value or worth. If they are, then the pricing structure may be fair and equitable. If they are not, then the terms should be renegotiated or the prospective franchisee should look elsewhere.

An increasingly common way that franchise organizations decrease costs and increase sales is by partnering with one another through co-branding relationships. This practice is discussed in this chapter's "Partnering for Success" feature.

Finding a Franchise

There are thousands of franchise opportunities available to prospective franchisees. The most critical step in the early stages of investigating franchise opportunities is for the entrepreneur to determine the type of franchise that is the best fit. For example, it is typically unrealistic for someone who is not a mechanic to consider buying a muffler repair franchise. A franchisor teaches a franchisee how to use the contents of a business model, not a trade. Before buying a franchise, a potential franchisee should imagine operating the prospective franchise or, better yet, should spend a period of time working in one of the franchisor's outlets. After working in a print shop for a week, for example, someone who thought she might enjoy running a print shop might find out that she hates it. This type of experience could help avoid making a mistake that is costly both to the franchisee and to the franchisor.

PARTNERING FOR SUCCESS

Using Co-Branding to Reduce Costs and Boost Sales

Have you ever stopped at a gas station and caught a quick lunch at an Arby's or a Blimpie sub sandwich inside? Or have you ever noticed that Baskin-Robbins and Dunkin' Donuts often share the same building? If either of these two scenarios applies to you, then you have witnessed co-branding firsthand.

Co-branding takes place when two or more businesses are grouped together. Co-branding is becoming increasingly common among franchise organizations that are looking for new ways to increase sales and reduce expenses. As we describe next, there are two primary types of co-branding arrangements that apply to franchise organizations.

Two Franchises Operating Side by Side

The first type of co-branding arrangement involves two or more franchises operating side by side in the same building or leased space. This type of arrangement typically involves a franchise like a donut shop that is busiest in the morning and a taco restaurant that is busiest at lunch and dinner. By locating side by side, these businesses can increase their sales by picking up some business from the traffic generated by their co-branding partner and can cut costs by sharing rent and other expenses.

Side-by-side co-branding arrangements are not restricted to restaurants. Sometimes the benefit arises from the complementary nature of the products involved, rather than time of day. For example, a franchise that sells exercise equipment could operate side by side with a business that sells vitamins. By locating side by side, these two businesses could realize the same types of benefits as the donut shop and the taco restaurant.

Two Franchises Occupying the Exact Same Space

The second type of co-branding arrangement involves two franchises occupying essentially the same space. For example, it is increasingly common to see sub shops inside gasoline stations and other retail outlets. The relationship is meant to benefit both parties. The sub shop benefits by opening another location without incurring the cost of constructing a freestanding building or leasing expensive shopping mall space. The gasoline station benefits by having a quality branded food partner to help it attract road traffic and by collecting lease income. Having a sub shop inside its store also helps a gasoline station become a "destination stop" for regular customers rather than simply another gas station serving passing cars.

Important Considerations

Although co-branding can be an excellent way for franchise organizations to partner for success, a firm should consider three questions before entering into a co-branding relationship:

- Will the co-branding arrangement maintain or strengthen my brand image?
- Do I have adequate control over how my partner will display or use my brand?
- Are there tangible benefits associated with attaching my brand to my partner's brand? For example, will my partner's brand have a positive effect on my brand and actually increase my sales?

If the answer to each of these questions is yes, than a co-branding arrangement may be a very effective way for a franchise organization to boosts sales and reduce expenses.

Questions for Critical Thinking

1. Do you think co-branding will continue to gain momentum, or do you think it is a fad that will wane in terms of its popularity? Explain your answer.
2. What are the potential downsides of co-branding? What might make a franchise hesitant to enter into a co-branding relationship with another franchise organization?
3. Consider the Uptown Cheapskate opening profile. Suggest some co-branding relationships that Uptown Cheapskate might consider forming.
4. Make a list of the types of businesses that might work well together in a co-branding relationship. Several initial examples include (a) a quick oil change and a tire store, (b) a bakery and a coffeehouse, and (c) a florist and a candy store.

There are many periodicals, websites, and associations that provide information about franchise opportunities. Every Thursday and Saturday, for example, ads for franchise opportunities appear in special sections of the *Wall Street Journal*. Similar ads appear every Wednesday in *USA Today*. Periodicals featuring franchise opportunities include *Inc.* and *Entrepreneur*, and franchise-specific magazines to review include *The Franchise Handbook* and *Franchise Times*. Prospective franchisees should also consider attending franchise opportunity shows that are held periodically in major U.S. cities and the International Franchise Expo, which is held annually in different cities across the United

States. The U.S. Small Business Administration is another good source of franchise information. There are also several excellent franchise-focused individuals and organizations that post frequently on Twitter. Examples include Franchise Expert (@FranchiseBiz), Franchising.com (@Franchising_com), and Franchise Direct USA (@topfranchises). Because of the risks involved in franchising, the selection of a franchisor should be a careful, deliberate process. One of the smartest moves a potential franchise owner can make is to talk to current franchisees and inquire if they are making money and if they are satisfied with their franchisor. Reflecting on how this approach helped ease her inhibitions about buying a franchise, Carleen Peaper, the owner of a Cruise Planner franchise, said:

> I was really apprehensive about making an investment of my time and money into a franchise, so I e-mailed 50 Cruise Planner agents with a set of questions, asking for honest feedback. Everyone responded. That was a big thing and helped me determine that I wanted to join them.[20]

Table 15.5 contains a list of sample questions to ask a franchisor and some of its current franchisees before investing. Potential entrepreneurs can expect to learn a great deal by studying the answers they receive in response to these questions.

Advantages and Disadvantages of Buying a Franchise

There are two primary advantages to buying a franchise over other forms of business ownership. First, franchising provides an entrepreneur the opportunity to own a business using a tested and refined business model. This attribute lessens the probability of business failure. In addition, the trademark that comes with the franchise often provides instant legitimacy for a business.[21] For example, an entrepreneur opening a new Gold's Gym would likely

TABLE 15.5 Questions to Ask Before Buying a Franchise

Questions to Ask a Franchisor

- What is the background of the company and its performance record?
- What is the company's current financial status?
- What are the names, addresses, and phone numbers of existing franchisees in my trade area?
- How do you train and mentor your franchisees?
- If at some point I decide to exit the franchise relationship, how does the exit process work?
- In what ways do you work with a franchisee who is struggling?

Questions to Ask Current Franchisees

- How much does your franchise gross per year? How much does it net? Are the procedures followed to make royalty payments to the franchisee burdensome?
- Are the financial projections of revenues, expenses, and profits that the franchisor provided me accurate in your judgment?
- Does the franchisor give you enough assistance in operating your business?
- How many hours, on average, do you work per week?
- How often are you able to take a vacation?
- Have you been caught off-guard by any unexpected costs or expectations?
- Does your franchisor provide ongoing training and support to you?
- If you had to do it all over again, would you purchase a franchise in this system? Why or why not?

attract more customers than an entrepreneur opening a new, independently owned fitness center because many people who are a part of the target market of Gold's Gym have already heard of the firm and have a positive impression of it. Second, when an individual purchases a franchise, the franchisor typically provides training, technical expertise, and other forms of support. For example, many franchise organizations provide their franchisees periodic training both at their headquarters location and in their individual franchise outlets.

The cost involved is the main disadvantage of buying and operating a franchise. As mentioned earlier, the franchisee must pay an initial franchise fee. The franchisee must also pay the franchisor an ongoing royalty as well as pay into a variety of funds, depending on the franchise organization. Thus, franchisees have both immediate (i.e., the initial franchise fee) and long-term (i.e., continuing royalty payments) costs. By opening an independent business, an entrepreneur can keep 100 percent of the profits if it is successful.

Table 15.6 contains a list of the advantages and disadvantages of buying a franchise.

TABLE 15.6 Advantages and Disadvantages of Buying a Franchise

Advantages	Disadvantages
A proven product or service within an established market. The most compelling advantage to buying a franchise is that the franchise offers a proven product or service within an established market.	**Cost of the franchise.** The initial cost of purchasing and setting up a franchise operation can be quite high, as illustrated in Table 15.4.
An established trademark or business system. The purchase of a franchise with an established trademark provides franchisees with considerable market power. For example, the purchaser of a McDonald's franchise has a trademark with proven market power.	**Restrictions on creativity.** Many franchise systems are very rigid and leave little opportunity for individual franchisees to exercise their creativity. This is an often-cited frustration of franchisees.
Franchisor's training, technical expertise, and managerial experience. Another important attribute of franchising is the training, technical expertise, and managerial experience that the franchisor provides the franchisee.	**Duration and nature of the commitment.** For a variety of reasons, many franchise agreements are difficult to exit. In addition, virtually every franchise agreement contains a noncompete clause. These clauses vary in terms of severity, but a typical clause prevents a former franchisee from competing with the franchisor for a period of two years or more.
An established marketing network. Franchisees who buy into a powerful franchise system are part of a system that has tremendous buying power and substantial advertising power and marketing prowess.	**Risk of fraud, misunderstandings, or lack of franchisor commitment.** Along with the many encouraging stories of franchise success, there are also many stories of individuals who purchase a franchise only to be disappointed by the franchisor's broken promises.
Franchisor's ongoing support. One of the most attractive advantages of purchasing a franchise rather than owning a store outright is the notion that the franchisor provides the franchisee ongoing support in terms of training, product updates, management assistance, and advertising. A popular slogan in franchising is that people buy franchises to "be in business for themselves but not by themselves."	**Problems of termination or transfer.** Some franchise agreements are very difficult and expensive to terminate or transfer. Often, a franchisee cannot terminate a franchise agreement without paying the franchisor substantial monetary damages.
Availability of financing. Some franchisors offer financing to their franchisees, although these cases are the exception rather than the rule. This information is available in section 10 of the Franchise Disclosure Document.	**Poor performance on the part of other franchisees.** If some of the franchisees in a franchise system start performing poorly and make an ineffective impression on the public, that poor performance can affect the reputation and eventually the sales of a well-run franchise in the same system.
Potential for business growth. If a franchisee is successful in the original location, the franchisee is often provided the opportunity to buy additional franchises from the same franchisor. For many franchisees, this prospect offers a powerful incentive to work hard to be as successful as possible.	**Potential for failure.** Some franchise systems simply fail to reach their objectives. When this happens, franchisees' wealth can be negatively affected. Indeed, when a franchise system fails, it commonly brings its franchisees down with it.

Steps in Purchasing a Franchise

Purchasing a franchise system is a seven-step process, as illustrated in Figure 15.3. The first rule of buying a franchise is to avoid making a hasty decision. Again, owning a franchise is typically costly and labor-intensive, and the purchase of a franchise should be a careful, deliberate decision. Once the decision to purchase a franchise has been nearly made, however, the following steps should be taken. If at any time prior to signing the franchise agreement the prospective franchisee has second thoughts, the process should be stopped until the prospective franchisee's concerns are adequately addressed.

Step 1 **Visit several of the franchisor's outlets:** Prior to meeting with the franchisor, the prospective franchisee should visit several of the franchisor's outlets and talk with their owners and employees. During the visits, the prospective franchisee should continually ask, "Is this the type of business I would enjoy owning and operating or managing?"

Step 2 **Meet with a franchise attorney:** Prospective franchisees should have an attorney who represents their interests, not the franchisor's. The attorney should prepare the prospective franchisee for meeting with the franchisor and should review all franchise documents before they are signed. If the franchisor tries to discourage the prospective franchisee from retaining an attorney, this is a red flag.

Step 3 **Meet with the franchisor and check the franchisor's references:** The prospective franchisee should meet with the franchisor, preferably at the franchisor's headquarters. During the meeting, the prospective franchisee should compare what was observed firsthand in the franchised outlets with what the franchisor is saying. Additional references should also be checked. The Franchise Disclosure Document is a good source for references. In section 20 of this document, there is a list of all the franchisees that have dropped out of the system in the past three years along with their contact information. Several of these should be called. Although it may seem to be overkill, the mantra for prospective franchisees is to check, double-check, and triple-check a franchisor's references.

FIGURE 15.3
Seven Steps in
Purchasing a Franchise

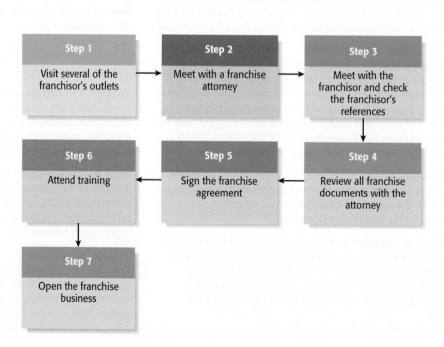

Step 4 **Review all franchise documents with the attorney:** The franchise attorney should review all the franchise documents, including the Franchise Disclosure Document and the franchise agreement.

Step 5 **Sign the franchise agreement:** If everything is a go at this point, the franchise agreement can be signed. The franchise agreement is the document in which the provisions of the franchisor–franchisee relationship are outlined. We discuss this agreement in greater detail later in this chapter.

Step 6 **Attend training:** Almost all franchise organizations provide training for their franchisees. For example, Comfort Keepers requires each of its new franchisees to attend Comfort Keeper's Academy, the company's training center, for 40 hours of training before they open their Comfort Keepers franchise.

Step 7 **Open the franchise business:** For many franchises, particularly restaurants, the first two to three weeks after the business is opened may be its busiest period, as prospective customers "try it out." This is why many franchise organizations send experienced personnel to help the franchisee open the business as smoothly as possible. One goal of a franchisee is generating positive word of mouth about the business right from the start.

Watch Out! Common Misconceptions About Franchising

Despite the abundance of advice available to them, many franchisees make false assumptions about franchising. Part of the explanation for this is that franchising has an attractive lure. It is easy to become enthralled with the promise of franchising and not spend an adequate amount of time examining the potential pitfalls. The following is a list of misconceptions franchisees often have about franchising:

- **Franchising is a safe investment:** Franchising, in and of itself, is no safer as an investment than is any other form of business ownership.

- **A strong industry ensures franchise success:** Although it is generally important to operate in a growing industry, the strength of an industry does not make up for a poor product, a poor business model, poor management, or inappropriate advertising. There are many firms that fail in growing industries just as there are firms that succeed in unattractive ones.

- **A franchise is a "proven" business system:** A franchisor sells a franchisee the right to use a particular business model. Whether the model is proven or not is subject to the test of time. Obviously, companies such as Subway, Papa John's Pizza, and H&R Block are using models that are polished and that have worked well over time. Most prospective franchisees, however, cannot afford a Papa John's Pizza or a Subway unit and will be considering a lesser-known franchise. All too frequently, companies start selling franchises before their systems are anywhere close to being proven—a fact that should cause entrepreneurs to be wary.

- **There is no need to hire a franchise attorney or an accountant:** Professional advice is almost always needed to guide a prospective franchisee through the franchise purchase process. A prospective franchisee should never give in to the temptation to save money by relying solely on the franchisor's advice.

- ■ **The best systems grow rapidly, and it is best to be a part of a rapid-growth system:** While some franchise systems grow rapidly because they have a good trademark and a polished business model, other franchise systems grow quickly because their major emphasis is on selling franchises. It is to a franchisee's benefit to be part of a system that has a solid trademark and business system—as that trademark and system will attract more customers—but some franchise systems grow so quickly that they outrun their ability to provide their franchisees adequate support.

- ■ **I can operate my franchise outlet for less than the franchisor predicts:** The operation of a franchise outlet usually costs just as much as the franchisor predicts.

- ■ **The franchisor is a nice person—he'll help me out if I need it:** Although it may be human nature to rely on the goodwill of others, don't expect anything from your franchisor that isn't spelled out in the franchise agreement.

Because these misconceptions are often hard to detect, some prospective franchisees attend seminars or franchise "boot camps" that teach them the ins and outs of franchising, including the things to watch out for when they talk to prospective franchisors. These types of seminars and boot camps are regularly offered by organizations such as Women in Franchising, the United States Hispanic Chamber of Commerce, and the International Franchising Organization.

Legal Aspects of the Franchise Relationship

LEARNING OBJECTIVE

6. Identify and explain the various legal aspects associated with the franchise relationship.

According to the Federal Trade Commission (FTC), a franchise exists any time that the operations of a business involve (1) the selling of goods or services that bear a trademark, (2) the retention of significant control or assistance by the holder of the trademark on the operation of the business, and (3) royalty payments by the purchaser of the business to the owner of the trademark for the right to use the trademark in the business.

The legal and regulatory environment surrounding franchising is based on the premise that the public interest is served if prospective franchisees are as informed as possible regarding the characteristics of a particular franchisor. The offer and sale of a franchise is regulated at both the state and the federal level. The legal aspects of the franchise relationship are unique enough that some attorneys specialize in franchise law.

Federal Rules and Regulations

Except for the automobile and petroleum industries, federal laws do not directly address the franchisor–franchisee relationship. Instead, franchise disputes are matters of contract law and are litigated at the state level. During the 1990s, Congress considered several proposals for federal legislation to govern franchise relationships, but none became law.

However, the offer and sale of a franchise is regulated at the federal level. Under the Franchise Rule, which is enforced by the Federal Trade Commission (FTC), franchisors must furnish potential franchisees with written disclosures that provide information about the franchisor, the franchised business, and the franchise relationship. The disclosures must be supplied at least 14 business days before a franchise agreement can be signed or the franchisee pays the franchisor any money.[22] In most cases, the disclosures are made through a lengthy document referred to as the Franchise Disclosure Document, which is accepted in all 50 states and parts of Canada. The **Franchise Disclosure**

Document (FDD) contains 23 categories of information that give a prospective franchisee a broad base of information about the background and financial health of the franchisor. A summary of the information contained in the FDD is provided in Table 15.7. A prospective franchisee should fully understand all the information contained in the FDD before a franchise agreement is signed.

The FDD requires the franchisor to attach a copy of the franchise agreement and any other related contractual documents to the circular. The **franchise agreement**, or contract, is the document that consummates the sale of a franchise. Franchise agreements vary, but each agreement typically contains two sections: the purchase agreement and the franchise or license agreement. The purchase agreement typically spells out the price, the services to be provided by the franchisor to the franchisee, and the "franchise package," which refers to all the items the franchisee has been told to expect. The franchise or license agreement typically stipulates the rights granted to the franchisee (including the right to use the franchisor's trademark), the obligations and duties of the franchisor, the obligations and duties of the franchisee, trade restrictions, rights and limitations regarding the transfer or termination of the franchise agreement, and who is responsible for attorney fees if disputes arise. Most states have enacted a statute of frauds that requires franchise agreements to be in writing.

The federal government does not require franchisors to register with the FTC. The offer of a franchise for sale does not imply that the FTC has examined the franchisor and has determined that the information contained in the franchisor's FDD is accurate. The franchisor is responsible for voluntarily complying with the law, and it is the responsibility of prospective franchisees to exercise due diligence in investigating franchise opportunities. Although most franchisor–franchisee relationships are conducted in an entirely ethical manner, it is a mistake to assume that a franchisor has a fiduciary obligation to its franchisees. What this means is that if a franchisor had a **fiduciary obligation** to its franchisees, it would always act in their best interest, or be on the franchisees' "side." Commenting on this issue, Robert Purvin, an experienced franchise attorney, wrote:

> While the conventional wisdom talks about the proactive relationship of the franchisor to its franchisees, virtually every court case decided in the U.S. has ruled that a franchisor has no fiduciary obligation to its franchisees. Instead, U.S. courts have agreed with franchisors that franchise agreements are "arms length" business transactions.[23]

Purvin's statement suggests that a potential franchisee should not rely solely on the goodwill of a franchisor when negotiating a franchise agreement. A potential franchisee should have a lawyer who is fully acquainted with franchise law and should closely scrutinize all franchise-related legal documents.

State Rules and Regulations

In addition to the FTC disclosure requirements, 15 states have franchise investment laws that provide additional protection to potential franchisees.[24] The states are California, Hawaii, Illinois, Indiana, Maryland, Michigan, Minnesota, New York, North Dakota, Oregon, Rhode Island, South Dakota, Virginia, Washington, and Wisconsin. The franchise investment laws require franchisors to provide presale disclosures, known as "offering circulars," to potential franchisees. Thirteen of the states have laws that treat the sale of a franchise like the sale of a security. These states require that a franchisor's FDD be filed with a designated state agency and be placed into public record.

By requiring franchisors to file their FDDs with a state agency, these states provide franchise purchasers important legal protection, including the right to sue a franchisor for violation of state disclosure requirements (if the franchise purchaser feels that full disclosure in the offering circular was not made). For

TABLE 15.7 **Information Contained in the Franchise Disclosure Document (FDD) Along with Explanations of Their Meanings**

Section and Item	Explanation
1. The franchisor, its predecessors, and affiliates 2. Business experience of the franchisor 3. Litigation experience of the franchisor 4. Bankruptcy on the part of the franchisor	These items provide information about the franchisor's operating history, business affiliations, and past litigation and bankruptcy experience, if any. It is not uncommon for a large company to have experienced some litigation. It would be a red flag, however, if a disproportionate percentage of the litigation involved suits with current or former franchisees.
5. Initial franchise fee 6. Other fees 7. Initial investment	These items specify the fees that the franchisee is subject to along with the franchisees' initial investment, which can be quite substantial. The "other fees" section should be carefully studied to avoid any surprises.
8. Restrictions on sources of products and services 9. Franchisee's obligations	These items stipulate the franchisee's obligations, along with restrictions pertaining to where the franchisee is permitted to purchase supplies and services. Some franchise agreements require the franchisee to purchase supplies from the franchisor.
10. Financing available 11. Franchisor's obligations	These items spell out the franchisor's obligations, along with a description of the financing (if any) that the franchisor offers to the franchisee. The franchisor's obligations typically include providing assistance in opening the franchisee's unit, ongoing training, and advertising.
12. Territory 13. Trademarks 14. Patents, copyrights, and proprietary information	These items describe the territorial rights granted the franchisee (if any) and the franchisor's right to grant other franchises and open company-owned outlets. In addition, items 13 and 14 specify the principal trademarks, patents, and copyrights and other proprietary information owned by the franchisor and the extent to which these items can be used by the franchisee.
15. Obligation to participate in the actual operation of the franchise business	This section addresses the franchisee's obligation to participate personally in the operation of the franchise. Franchisors typically do not want absentee franchisees.
16. Restrictions on what the franchisee may sell 17. Renewal, termination, transfer, and dispute resolution	These sections deal with what the franchisee may sell and how the franchisor resolves disputes with its franchisees. Item 17 also contains important information about the manner in which franchisees can renew, terminate, and/or transfer their franchise.
18. Public figures	This section lists public figures affiliated with the franchise through advertising and other means.
19. Earnings claim	If a franchisor makes an earnings claim in connection with an offer of a franchise, then certain past and projected earnings information must be provided.
20. List of outlets	This section is quite exhaustive and contains (1) the number of franchises sold by the franchisor, (2) the number of company-owned outlets, (3) the names of all franchisees and the addresses and telephone numbers of all their outlets (within certain limitations), (4) an estimate of the number of franchises to be sold in the next year, and (5) a list of all franchisees (covering the past three years) who have dropped out of the system, including their last-known home addresses and telephone numbers.
21. Financial statements	This section contains the franchisor's previous two years of independently audited financial statements.
22. Contracts	These last two sections contain copies of the documents that franchisees have to sign.
23. Receipt	These are the common exhibits attached to the FDD.

Attachments:
Franchise Agreement (or contract)
Equipment Lease
Lease for Premises
Loan
Agreement

example, if someone purchased a franchise in one of the states fitting the profile described previously and six months later discovered that the franchisor did not disclose an issue required by the FDD (and, as a result, felt that he or she had been damaged), that person could seek relief by suing the franchisor in state court. All 15 states providing additional measures of protection for franchisees also regulate some aspect of the termination process. Although the provisions vary by state, they typically restrict a franchisor from terminating the franchise before the expiration of the franchise agreement, unless the franchisor has "good cause" for its action.

Although not as comprehensive as in the United States, at least 24 countries now have laws regulating franchising in some manner. Australia, Brazil, Romania, South Korea, and Spain are five of these countries.[25]

More About Franchising

There are a number of additional issues pertaining to the franchisor–franchisee relationship. Three important topics, for both franchisors and franchisees, are franchise ethics, international franchising, and the future of franchising as a method of business ownership and growth.

Franchise Ethics

The majority of franchisors and franchisees are highly ethical individuals who are interested only in making a fair return on their investment. In fact, instances of problems between franchisors and their franchisees tend to be isolated occurrences rather than prevalent practices.[26] There are certain features of franchising, however, that make it subject to ethical abuse. An understanding of these features can help franchisors and franchisees guard against making ethical mistakes. These features are the following:

- **The get-rich-quick mentality:** Some franchisors see franchising as a get-rich-quick scheme and become more interested in selling franchises than in using franchising as a legitimate means of distributing their product or service. These franchisors have a tendency to either oversell the potential of their franchise or overpromise the support they will offer to their franchisees.

- **The false assumption that buying a franchise is a guarantee of business success:** Buying a franchise, as with all other business investments, involves risk. Any statement to the contrary is typically misleading or unethical. A franchisor must steer clear of claims that it has the "key" to business success, and a franchisee needs to be wary of all such claims.

- **Conflicts of interest between franchisors and their franchisees:** The structure of the franchise relationship can create conflicts of interest between franchisors and their franchisees. For example, franchisees benefit from the profits of a unit, while franchisors benefit from increased revenues (recall that a franchisor's royalty is typically paid on a percentage of gross profits rather than net profits). This anomaly in the franchise arrangement can motivate franchisors to take steps that boost revenues for the entire system but hurt profits for individual franchisees. For example, a franchisor might insist that a franchisee sell a product that has high revenue but low margins (or net income). Similarly, a franchisor might sell several franchises in a given geographic area to maximize the revenue potential of the area regardless of the effect on each individual franchisee's net income. These actions can at times be ethically questionable and can often lead to contentious conflicts of interest in franchise systems.

LEARNING OBJECTIVE

7. Discuss two additional issues—franchise ethics and international franchising—entrepreneurs should think about when considering franchising.

Despite the protection of law and the advocacy of franchise associations, individual franchisors and franchisees must practice due diligence in their relationships. "Buyer beware" is a good motto for franchisors selecting franchisees and prospective franchisees selecting franchisors. Entering into a franchise relationship is a major step for both parties and should be treated accordingly. The metaphor used frequently to describe the franchisor–franchisee relationship is marriage. Similar to marriage, the franchisor–franchisee relationship is typically close, long-term, and painful to terminate. Each side of the franchise partnership should scrutinize the past ethical behavior of the other before a franchise agreement is executed.

International Franchising

International opportunities for franchising are becoming more prevalent as the markets for certain franchised products in the United States have become saturated.[27] Indeed, heavily franchised companies, such as McDonald's, KFC, and Century 21 Real Estate, are experiencing much of their growth in international markets. The trend toward globalization in many industries is also hastening the trend toward international franchising, and the growing middle classes in many countries are creating large populations of consumers eager for American-style goods. In fact, to illustrate how global many familiar franchise systems have become, there is a Papa John's pizzeria in Karachi, Pakistan, a Denny's in Christchurch, New Zealand, and a Chili's Grill and Bar on a riverboat on the Egyptian Nile.

A U.S. citizen who is thinking about buying a franchise abroad may be confronted with the choice of buying from an American company or a foreign company, regardless of the location in the world. For U.S. citizens, these are some of the steps to take before buying a franchise in a foreign country:

- **Consider the value of the franchisor's name in the foreign country:** There are very few franchise systems whose names are known worldwide. Beyond a select few—McDonald's, Coca-Cola, and KFC come to mind—the majority of trademarks well known to Americans may be known to only a small percentage of the population of a foreign country. When considering the purchase of a U.S.-based franchise in a foreign country, carefully evaluate the value of the trademark in that country.

- **Work with a knowledgeable lawyer:** Many of the legal protections afforded to prospective franchisees in the United States are unavailable in foreign countries, highlighting the need for the purchaser of a franchise in a foreign country to obtain excellent legal advice. All the hazards involved with purchasing a domestic franchise are magnified when purchasing a franchise in a foreign country.

- **Determine whether the product or service is salable in a foreign country:** Just because a product or service is desirable to Americans is no guarantee of success in a foreign culture. Before buying a franchise in a foreign country, determine if sufficient marketing research has been conducted to ensure that the product or service will have a sufficient market in the foreign country.

- **Uncover whether the franchisor has experience in international markets:** It is typically not a good idea to be a franchisor's "test case" to see if the franchisor wants to operate in foreign markets. Be leery of franchisors with aggressive expansion plans but little international experience.

- **Find out how much training and support you will receive from the franchisor:** If your franchise unit will be in a foreign country and the franchisor remains headquartered in the United States, make sure you fully understand the amount of training and support you can expect. Will the franchisor have an area representative in your country? If not, do you have to make an international phone call each time you want to talk to your franchisor? Will your franchisor be willing to travel to the foreign country to offer you training and support? Who pays for the international travel of the franchisor's training staff? Who is responsible for advertising in the foreign country, the franchisor or the franchisee?

■ **Evaluate currency restrictions:** Evaluate any restrictions that the foreign country places on the convertibility of its currency into U.S. dollars.

To avoid some of the potential problems alluded to here, U.S. franchisors typically structure their expansion into a foreign country through the following:

■ **Direct franchising arrangement:** Under a direct franchise arrangement, the U.S. franchisor grants the rights to an individual or a company (the developer) to develop multiple franchised businesses within a country or territory. For example, if Play It Again Sports decided to sell franchises for the first time in Spain, Play It Again Sports may grant the rights to a Spanish company to develop multiple Play It Again Sports franchises there.

■ **Master franchise agreement:** Under a master franchise arrangement, the U.S. firm grants the right to an individual or company (the master franchisee) to develop one or more franchise businesses and to license others to develop one or more franchise businesses within the country or territory.

■ **Other agreements:** Combinations of other arrangements are also employed by franchisors expanding to foreign markets. Examples include joint-venture arrangements, direct-sales arrangements, or straight franchising agreements.

The Future of Franchising

The future of franchising appears bright. Franchising represents a large and growing segment of the retail and service sectors of U.S. businesses and is in some cases replacing more traditional forms of business ownership. More and more college graduates are choosing careers in industries that are heavily dominated by franchising. Franchising is also becoming more popular among seniors. At the same time, the number of franchises focusing on "senior care" is increasing. Aging Excellence, FirstLight HomeCare, and Visiting Angels are examples of senior care franchises, as is Comfort Keepers, which we discussed previously in this chapter.[28]

There are also innovations taking place today in franchising, such as the extensive use of social media that is occurring in many franchise organizations.[29] There are additional innovations as well, such as the extensive use of instant couponing to encourage people to drop in and make a purchase. Many restaurant franchises are revamping their menus to appeal to health-conscious consumers. There are a growing number of Internet-based franchise organizations. An example is My Destination (www.mydestination.com), which is an Internet franchise opportunity. The franchisor sells exclusive rights to franchisees for specific destinations, such as Vienna, Austria, Auckland, New Zealand, or Orlando, Florida. The franchisee then develops comprehensive information about the destination, with unique travel articles and guides, insider tips, videos, and panoramic virtual tours, all designed to be posted online. The franchisees make money in a number of ways, including by selling their content to business directories and local businesses. Franchisees are carefully selected, and they must have a unique passion and love for the destination they are purchasing.

Chapter Summary

LO1. A franchise is an agreement between a franchisor (the parent company, such as McDonald's) and a franchisee (an individual or firm that is willing to pay the franchisor a fee for the right to sell its product or service). There are two distinctly different types of franchise systems: the product trademark franchise and the business format franchise. A product trademark franchise is an arrangement under which the franchisor grants to the franchisee the right to buy its products and use its trade name. Automobile dealerships and soft-drink distributorships are examples of product trademark franchises. In a business format franchise, the franchisor provides a formula for doing business to the franchisee along with training, advertising, and other forms of assistance. Curves and Comfort Keepers are examples of this type of franchise system. An individual franchise agreement involves the sale of a single franchise for a specific location. An area franchise agreement allows a franchisee to own and operate a specific number of outlets in a particular geographic area. A master franchise agreement is similar to an area franchise agreement with one major exception: In addition to having the right to operate a specific number of locations in a particular area, the franchisee also has the right to offer and sell the franchise to other people in the area.

LO2. Entrepreneurs take the following nine steps to establish a franchise system: (1) develop a franchise business plan, (2) get professional advice, (3) conduct an intellectual property audit, (4) develop franchise documents, (5) prepare operating manuals, (6) plan an advertising strategy and a franchise training program, (7) put together a team for opening new franchise units, (8) plan a strategy for soliciting prospective franchisees, and (9) help franchisees with site selection and the grand opening of their franchise outlets.

LO3. The advantages of setting up a franchise system include rapid, low-cost market expansion; income from franchise fees and royalties; franchisee motivation; access to ideas and suggestions; cost savings; and increased buying power. The disadvantages of setting up a franchise system include sharing profits with franchisees, loss of control, friction with franchisees, managing growth, differences in required business skills, and legal expenses.

LO4. Preparing answers to the following questions helps the entrepreneur determine if buying a franchise is a good or effective decision for him or her. Questions for which the entrepreneur should prepare carefully thought out answers are: (1) Are you willing to take orders? (2) Are you willing to be part of a franchise system rather than to seek to operate primarily independently? (3) How will you react if you make a suggestion to your franchisor and your suggestion is rejected? (4) What are you looking for in a business? And (5) How willing are you to put your money at risk?

LO5. Once an entrepreneur has decided to buy a franchise as part of an ongoing franchise system, s/he should expect to take the following steps to complete the purchase transaction: (1) visit several of the franchisor's outlets, (2) meet with a franchise attorney, (3) meet with the franchisor and check the franchisor's references, (4) review all franchise documents with the attorney, (5) sign the franchise agreement, (6) attend training, and (7) open the franchise business unit.

LO6. In the United States, there are a number of rules and regulations at both the federal and individual state levels that pertain to franchising. The premise behind all of these rules and regulations is that the public interest is best served when prospective franchisees have as much accurate information as possible about the characteristics of individual franchisors. The offer and sale of a franchise is regulated at the federal level. Increasingly, franchising is being regulated in some form or fashion in countries outside the United States. The Franchise Disclosure Document (FDD) is a document with 23 categories of information that is used prominently in the United States. This document provides a prospective franchisee a broad base of information about a franchisor's background and financial health. The FDD must be provided by the franchisor to a prospective franchisee at least 10 business days before a franchise contract can be signed or the franchisee pays the franchisor any money.

LO7. Entrepreneurs considering franchising also need to be aware of the role of ethics within franchising relationships. Evidence suggests that most franchisors and franchisees are ethical parties who want to support each other in the pursuit of profit-generating business transactions. On the other hand, entrepreneurs should understand that three features of franchising—a get-rich-quick mentality, a false assumption that purchasing a franchise is a guarantee of entrepreneurial success, and potential conflicts of interest between the franchisee and the franchisor—have the potential to create ethical issues. Entrepreneurs thinking of franchising should also recognize that franchising is not a strictly U.S. phenomenon. In fact, opportunities to engage in international franchising are becoming more and more prevalent. Although potentially attractive, entrepreneurs from any country thinking of buying a franchise in a different country should carefully examine all local rules and regulations, as well as the franchisor itself, prior to deciding to purchase a franchise.

Key Terms

agency theory, **540**

area franchise agreement, **534**

business format franchise, **533**

fiduciary obligation, **553**

franchise agreement, **553**

Franchise Disclosure Document (FDD), **552**

franchisees, **532**

franchising, **532**

franchisor, **532**

individual franchise agreement, **534**

master franchise agreement, **534**

multiple-unit franchisee, **534**

product and trademark franchise, **533**

subfranchisees, **534**

Review Questions

15-1. What is franchising?

15-2. How does franchising differ from other forms of business ownership?

15-3. What are the differences between a product and trademark franchise and a business format franchise? Provide at least two examples of both types of franchise arrangements.

15-4. What are the differences among an individual franchise agreement, an area franchise agreement, and a master franchise agreement?

15-5. What are the steps involved in setting up a franchise system?

15-6. What are the advantages and disadvantages of establishing a franchise system?

15-7. What are the qualities to look for in a prospective franchisee?

15-8. What is an example of a business that wouldn't be suitable for franchising?

15-9. What are the advantages and disadvantages of buying a franchise?

15-10. What are the costs involved in purchasing a business format franchise? Are these costs similar across franchise systems, or do they vary widely? Which costs are one-time costs and which costs continue indefinitely?

15-11. What is the meaning of fiduciary obligation?

15-12. What are the innovations taking place in franchising today?

15-13. What are the principal advantages and disadvantages of buying a franchise?

15-14. Why is it important for a prospective franchisee to retain his or her own franchise attorney?

15-15. "Franchising is a safe investment." What would you think if you saw this statement in a book or magazine?

15-16. What is the purpose of the Franchise Disclosure Document (FDD)? Are there any regulations regarding when the FDD must be provided to a prospective franchisee? If so, what are they?

15-17. What is the purpose of a franchise agreement?

15-18. What are some aspects of franchising that make it subject to ethical abuses?

15-19. For U.S. citizens, what are the main issues that should be considered before buying a franchise in a foreign country?

15-20. What are the main reasons that many U.S. franchise systems are expanding into global markets? Do you think this expansion will continue to gain momentum or decline over time? Why or why not?

Application Questions

15-21. A friend of yours heard her roommates talking about different kinds of franchises. Before she could ask questions, they left for a team meeting to work on a class project. Your friend knows that you are taking an entrepreneurship course. She asks you: What are the differences between a product and trademark franchise and a business format franchise? For a first-time entrepreneur, she wonders, is there an advantage to one of these types of franchise agreements compared to the other one? If so, which one is more advantageous for the first-time entrepreneur to pursue and why?

15-22. Identify a franchise location near where you live and ask to talk to the owner. Show the owner one of the two "You Be the VC" features at the end of this chapter and ask the person whether he or she thinks the company will be successful. Write a brief summary of the owner's response.

15-23. Andrew Simmons is a young, energetic entrepreneur who is enthusiastic about developing his business venture. He has established a good, reputable name for his fast-food outlet. "The Crunchies," Andrew's outlet, has been a household name among patrons in his neighborhood. There is scope to expand his business, especially since his outlet has a potentially strong trademark and a well-designed business model, and Andrew has a strong desire to grow. He should consider franchising his business. How should he do this?

15-24. As a lead trainer in the "How to Create a Successful Franchise" seminar, you need to address your audience on the do's and don'ts of franchising. One particular participant approached you at the end of the seminar. He was still confused about the legal aspects of franchising and needed personal tutoring. Guide him.

15-25. Look at Table 15.4. If you were offered the opportunity to buy into any one of the franchise organizations listed in Table 15.4, which one would it be? Explain the rationale for your selection.

15-26. A friend of yours owns a carpet installation and cleaning business, which is a full-time job. To increase his income, he's thinking about buying a 1-800-Water Damage franchise, which is a franchise that helps home owners and businesses restore property that has been damaged by a flood or water leak. His thinking is that he already has most of the equipment he needs to perform this type of service and has an experienced crew. Is your friend a good candidate for a 1-800-Water Damage franchise? If not, what type of franchise could he buy that would be a good fit with his current business?

15-27. Suppose you ran into an old friend who is just about to buy into a replacement batteries retail franchise. He tells you that he is excited about the opportunity because the system he is about to buy into (1) is in an industry that virtually guarantees its success, (2) has a "proven" business model, and (3) is operated by people who are so honest that he can skip the expense of hiring a franchise attorney to review the documents he has to sign. If your friend asked you, "What do you think? Am I approaching this opportunity correctly?" how would you respond?

15-28. Jane Simmons attended a two-day seminar about owning a franchise. At the end of the seminar, she decided to invest in an online cosmetics franchise that would cost her almost $500,000 to start the business. She mentioned this to her friend Beth, who was shocked that Jane decided on the investment based on promises made during the seminar. Though some of the promises might hold true, Beth needs to advise Jane before she makes a hasty decision.

15-29. Brandon Steel is planning to start a franchise business in Cambodia. Recently he approached "Fast & Fury Pizza," an American-based franchise, and had a thorough discussion with the franchisor on his expansion plans in Cambodia. However, the franchisor was hesitant about Brandon's plans as the expansion plan involved a foreign country. How can the franchisor and Brandon come to an agreement?

YOU BE THE VC 15.1 COMPANY: IceBorn

• Web: www.ice-born.com • Facebook: Iceborn • Twitter: @MyIceBorn

Business Idea: Develop a 24-hour-a-day, convenient, on-demand ice vending destination offering fresh, clean ice at a competitive price.

Pitch: Think about the experience of buying ice. You go to a supermarket or convenience store, reach into a freezer department, and pull out a bag of ice that is partially stuck to other bags. You then bring the bag home, and have to slam it on the counter several times to break the pieces of ice apart. If you're lucky, you don't think about how the ice was made. It's normally made at a central location, bagged, loaded on a truck, and carried into the store on a cart. The bags have tiny holes which allow them to "breathe." Unfortunately, the holes can also allow germs and other contaminants to be transferred to the ice. This is the ice that you put in the glasses of your family members and guests.

IceBorn offers an alternative that's a game-changer. It's a franchise organization that manufactures state-of-the-art, 24-hour, on-demand ice and water vending machines. The machines come in several sizes, and they dispense filtered water and both bagged and straight-to-the-cooler ice. The largest machine, the Ice House, can dispense more than 12,000 pounds of ice a day, which is the equivalent of six hundred 20-pound bags. It normally sits in a parking lot, and takes up the space of about two parking places. The ice is produced fresh using municipal-supplied water that is filtered on site. The company's proprietary system, which is protected by five U.S. patents, can be monitored and controlled by franchisees remotely via a computer or smartphone. Ice is made continuously throughout the day and is stored in sanitary internal bins. As a result, it is always fresh and clean. No one touches the ice other than the buyer.

IceBorn began franchising in May 2012. Depending on the IceBorn model, the initial investment ranges from $18,995 to $130,000 plus fees for site preparation, shipping, and installation. As of summer 2014, the company had commitments for more than 1,800 units in 19 states. IceBorn has been around for about 10 years. Prior to franchising, the company sold units, and there are about 2,700 individually-owned IceBorn units located in the United States, primarily in the South. IceBorn is currently looking for franchisees across the United States to install its machines in well-trafficked areas.

Ice is a $4 billion-per-year industry. In just 10 years, the ice vending business has captured 4 percent of the market, and it is expected by some industry experts to increase by 3 percent to 5 percent each year for the next 10 years. IceBorn feels that it is perfectly positioned to capture the lion's share of the growth.

15-30. Based on the material covered in this chapter, what questions would you ask the firm's founders before making your funding decision? What answers would satisfy you?

15-31. If you had to make your decision on just the information provided in the pitch and on the company's website, would you fund this company? Why or why not?

YOU BE THE VC 15.2 COMPANY: Engineering for Kids

• Web: www.engineeringforkids.net • Facebook: Engineering for Kids • Twitter: @EFKCorp

Business Idea: Launch a franchise organization that acquaints kids ages 4 to 14 with STEM concepts via hands-on workshops. STEM is an acronym that stands for Science, Technology, Engineering, and Math.

Pitch: The U.S. Department of Commerce projects that STEM jobs will grow by 17 percent from now until 2018, creating 2.4 million jobs. In contrast, overall job growth is expected to be 10 percent during the same period. Ironically, a recent study by Intel Corp reported that 63 percent of teenagers have never considered a job in engineering. Many young people also don't realize the social good that engineers can do. By building dams, finding solutions that provide people in developing countries with clean water, or building better medical devices, engineers can positively impact the lives of millions of people.

Engineering for Kids, which is a franchise organization, was founded to bring this message to 4- to 14-year-old students. It conveys the message and helps build requisite skills, primarily through six-week after-school programs that last for about 90 minutes and meet once a week. The programs are divided into three different age groups—Junior Engineers (Pre-K to 2nd grade), Apprentice Engineers (3rd to 5th grade) and Master Engineers (6th to 8th grade). Each class is given an engineering problem that the kids are asked to address. The classes have different names and different subject matters, so the same child can repeat the program and work on a different problem each class. For example, in the Junior Engineer category one class is titled "Taking to the Skies." In the class for pre-K to 2nd graders they are introduced to fundamental concepts of aircraft and spacecraft designs and, through hands-on instruction, the students design and construct model airplanes, rockets, hot air balloons, and more. An example of a more advanced course in the Master Engineering category, which is for kids from 6th to 8th grade, is a class titled "Rescue Robots." In the class students design and program robots to respond to simulated disaster situations such as removing rubble from a house or a building destroyed by an earthquake, tornado, or similar natural disaster. Each class is hands-on with a low instructor-to-student ratio. The participants pay a fee for attending the classes.

Along with after-school classes, Engineering for Kids franchises also offer home-school programs, Scouts workshops, birthday parties, summer camps, and the like. Some franchises partner with public schools, YMCAs, and city parks and recreation departments during the summer months. In certain circumstances, the programs can be funded through Title 1 grants. An Engineering for Kids franchise costs between $31,850 and $88,050 to start. The ongoing royalty is 7 percent of sales.

15-32. Based on the material covered in this chapter, what questions would you ask the firm's founders before making your funding decision? What answers would satisfy you?

15-33. If you had to make your decision on just the information provided in the pitch and on the company's website, would you fund this firm? Why or why not?

CASE 15.1

School of Rock: Filling a Gap in Music Education and Growing Via Franchising

- Web: www.schoolofrock.com • Facebook: School of Rock • Twitter: SchoolofRockUSA

Bruce R. Barringer, *Oklahoma State University*

R. Duane Ireland, *Texas A&M University*

Introduction

In 1996 Paul Green, a University of Pennsylvania philosophy graduate, started giving guitar lessons in his home. At one point, he invited a group of his students to sit in, or "jam," with his own band. The results were initially disappointing. But over time, he found that the students who played in a group did better than the students who received only individual instruction. As a result, he modified his teaching methods to supplement individual lessons with group practices. He compared it to the difference between shooting hoops and playing basketball.

Green continued combining individual instruction with group jam sessions. In 1998, he decided to expand beyond his home, and opened the Paul Green School of Rock Music in Philadelphia. The building he chose had a number of small rooms for individual lessons along with a larger space for jam sessions and concerts. He also started organizing students, with similar skill levels, into bands. His top students were put into what he called the school's AllStars band. The band started getting gigs in the Philadelphia area, and attracted media attention. In 2003, filmmakers Sheena M. Joyce and Don Argott attended a concert by the students, and decided to make a documentary about the Paul Green School of Rock and how it transformed high school students into performing musicians. A film crew followed a class of students through a nine-month school year and produced a documentary titled *Rock School*. Shortly after the documentary was released, Paramount released a fictional film called *School of Rock*, which featured an aspiring musician teaching kids to play rock music. Many observers felt the film was based on Green and the way he worked with students.

Early Growth

By 2002, Green had more than 100 students, and decided to open an additional location in Dowingtown, Pennsylvania, which is 35 miles west of Philadelphia. Expansion continued in counties around Philadelphia and then in New Jersey and Delaware. Along the way Green's dentist, Dr. Joseph Roberts, became interested in what Green was doing, and provided funding to open School of Rock locations in several additional states, including California, New York, and Texas. At some point along the way Green shortened the name of his business from the Paul Green School of Rock Music to the School of Rock.

In 2009, Green sold the School of Rock to Sterling Partners, a private equity firm. Sterling has kept the original vision for the School of Rock intact and has used its financial resources to fuel further expansion.

How It Works

Each School of Rock location provides a place for kids with a passion for rock music to either learn how to play a rock instrument or sharpen their existing skills. It's also a wholesome and safe place for kids to learn to play rock music and become part of a rock band. Kids 7 to 19 of all different skill levels spend 12 weeks in sessions learning to play the guitar, bass, keyboards, or drums. Voice

(continued)

High school students with an interest in the guitar, like this teenager, are ideal candidates for the School of Rock's program.

Michaeljung/Shutterstock

lessons are also provided. The students receive both group and individual lessons. Tuition varies across School of the Rock locations, averaging $300 a month for the basic program. The most skilled students in each location form a band and play concerts in their city. The top students in each school become members of an AllStars band and tour nationally. A recent School of Rock AllStars band completed a 27-city tour, which kicked off at the Knitting Factory in Hollywood, California. As a result of experiences like this, a number of School of Rock graduates are now performing musicians or are making a living in the music industry in other ways.

Most School of Rock instructors are music teachers who also play in an active band. From time to time, prominent rock musicians make guest appearances at School of Rock locations. The instructors help students hone their musical skills and inspire them with tales of their own successes and recoveries from failures. The company's foundational belief is that the best way to learn or do something is by doing it, so students are handed instruments and are playing rock music from the minute they enroll. The curriculum is formulaic, depending on a particular student's skill level, and is driven by the added motivation that students will be placed in bands and play in front of live audiences. The schools are set up much like a club, where students are encouraged to visit to jam, work on their songs with other students, form bands, or write original music. The school becomes a community for its participants, where they not only learn music but also form lasting friendships. Many students enroll for multiple 12-week sessions, where their skills are allowed to advance and flourish. The schools operate year-round. During the summer, winter, and spring breaks from school, many School of Rock locations offer day camps for intensive instruction.

Franchising

The School of Rock is a franchise organization. It currently has 16 company-owned units and 118 franchise locations, located in the United States, Mexico, Canada, Brazil, Australia, and the Philippines. According to *Entrepreneur* magazine, purchasing a franchise costs between $147,850 and $334,600, depending on the location and the size of the facility. The costs include a $49,500 initial franchise fee. The ongoing royalty is 8 percent of gross income.

In exchange for the fees and royalties, the franchisees receive training in how to run a School of Rock location, along with IT support including a website, assistance with real estate selection, help with facility design, and ongoing marketing support. One third of all School of Rock franchisees own more than one location. To obtain a School of Rock franchise, you must commit to actively running and managing the location you acquire (i.e., no absentee ownership).

New Programs

Along with its staple 12-week music instruction programs for 7- to 19-year-olds, the School of Rock is adding additional programs. It now has a program in early childhood music education called Little Wing, after the Jimi Hendrix song by the same name. Children participate in 45-minute music-related activities by age group. There is now a program for adult amateur musicians called "Grad School." Two additional offerings include a career development program for working musicians and a corporate team building program. In the corporate team building program, School of Rock instructors divide the participants into two groups. Each group learns how to play a classic rock song. At the end of the experience, the two groups come together for an old-fashioned battle of the bands.

School of Rock Future

There are two factors to suggest a strong future for the School of Rock. The first is a reduction in music programs in public schools. Regrettably, as a result of tight budgets, a growing number of schools across the United States are cutting back on music programs. The School of Rock is poised to fill the gap. It is already the largest after-school

music program in the United States. Second, there are currently 33.5 million teenagers in the United States, all looking for a place to fit in and shine. The School of Rock offers a one-of-a-kind experience for 7- to 19-year-olds willing to commit to the rigors and joys of becoming successful musicians.

Discussion Questions

15-34. What types of characteristics do you anticipate School of Rock looks for in franchisees?

15-35. Look at Table 15.2. Of the ways mentioned in this table for franchisors to develop franchisees, which ones are the most important for School of Rock to emphasize to support its franchisees?

15-36. If you were to consider buying a School of Rock franchise, what issues would concern you the most about your ability to be successful as a franchisee for this company?

15-37. Over the next 10 years, what do you think lies ahead for School of Rock? What are some things that could go "right" for the firm and some of the things that could go "wrong" as the firm continues selling franchise locations as a means of growth?

Sources: School of Rock home page (www.schoolofrock.com), accessed August 18, 2014; Wikipedia, School of Rock, www.wikipedia.com, accessed August 18, 2014; W. Boast, "A School for Brooklyn's Youngest Hipsters," *New Yorker,* May 12, 2014; Entrepreneur, School of Rock, available at http://www.entrepreneur.com/franchises/schoolofrock/333874-0.html, accessed August 18, 2014.

CASE 15.2

GameTruck: Bringing Multiplayer Gaming to Its Customers' Homes

• *Web: www.GameTruckpartyfranchise.com* • *Facebook: GameTruck HQ* • *Twitter: @GameTruckHQ*

Bruce R. Barringer, *Oklahoma State University*

R. Duane Ireland, *Texas A&M University*

Introduction

The idea for GameTruck first came to Scott Novis at his son's fourth birthday party. They were at a pizza arcade and the noise, expense, and frustration caused him to think about a better alternative. What's more, he knew that the electronic games he was working on at his job were better than anything in the arcade. That experience led to an epiphany. Instead of taking kids to an arcade for birthday parties or similar events, why not bring the arcade to their homes? And what if, instead of making something "kiddy," the arcade featured the best video

games available on the latest consoles? And what if it was something that people of all ages could enjoy?

These thoughts were the foundation for the launching of GameTruck, Novis's entrepreneurial venture. GameTruck is the world's first mobile video game theater. The basic idea was to create a mobile arcade or truck that contained the latest video games, video game consoles, and large screens for people to play multiplayer video games. By making the arcade mobile, it could be taken anywhere for people to enjoy.

(continued)

There are several different models of the mobile arcade or truck, from a tow-behind trailer to a "top of the line" all-in-one unit that looks like a large tour bus. The mobile theater will travel to any location that has a large enough parking area for it to set up. Once it arrives, it is entirely self-sufficient and provides its own power. It can accommodate up to 20 players, who can engage in multiplayer video games aided by ultra-modern consoles and 54-inch screens. The atmosphere inside the truck is super cool, with neon green lighting, spacious leather couches, and air-conditioning. GameCoaches are available to help participants learn new games or troubleshoot any problems that occur. Along with providing a venue for a fun birthday party or another occasion, a staple concept of the GameTruck experience is to encourage people to play electronic games with one another. GameTruck finds themselves as a solution to the common complaint by parents that computer games isolate their children and cause them to focus on playing against their computer rather than socializing with other kids. The GameTruck experience is designed to bring kids, their friends, and their families together to participate in multiplayer games in a fun and highly engaging environment. Founded in 2006, GameTruck now has over 70 franchisees that are making GameTruck parties available on a weekly basis in cities across the United States. A total of 40 percent of the company's franchisees run multi-rig operations.

Sound simple enough? It is, but as straightforward as the GameTruck concept is, it took a great deal of effort and hard work to get off the ground. And there are also questions regarding how GameTruck will continue to grow and evolve its offering.

with kids and their families. The first GameTruck prototype was built in Novis's garage in Tempe, Arizona. To see how the prototype would perform, Novis and his brother Chris threw the first GameTruck party for a friend and neighbor. Novis and GameTruck benefited from a fortunate convergence of technologies, which took place at about the time Novis's ideas for GameTruck came together. The three technologies, each of which is instrumental to GameTruck's offering, are shown in the figure nearby.

Franchise Setup and GameTruck Offering

A GameTruck franchise costs between $122,500 and $310,500 to open, depending on the location and the model of the GameTruck trailer or mobile unit acquired. The initial franchise fee is $12,500. The ongoing royalty is 7 percent of gross sales. There are additional marketing and operational support fees.

GameTruck offers its franchisees multiple levels of assistance and support. The size of a franchisee's territory is determined by taking into consideration factors such as number of schools in a particular area, the average family income level of the area, and other demographic factors. Each GameTruck franchisee is provided training in regard to how to book parties, how to operate the GameTruck trailer, and how to set up a local marketing plan. Because the training program is so comprehensive, no prior experience is necessary to own and operate a GameTruck franchise. The company is establishing a strong brand recognition. Its trailers and mobile units are painted a bright

Technologies Instrumental to GameTruck's Founding

Inexpensive portable power	Cost efficient flat screen TVs	Arrival of high definition video game consoles

Scott Novis

GameTruck's founder, Scott Novis, is no stranger to electronic games. He has nearly a decade of video game development experience, working for several companies. His two stops prior to GameTruck were particularly instrumental. At one point, he was the VP for Development for Rainbow Studios, which is one of the largest video game development studios in the Southwestern United States. During Novis's tenure, Rainbow Studios was responsible for some of the most successful games of the PS2 era. His stop just prior to GameTruck was with Walt Disney Corporation, where he developed a new kind of video game studio, dubbed the Walt Disney Nintendo Center for Excellence.

Novis's vision for GameTruck was to create a physical, mobile space where people could play the best video games on the latest consoles with their friends in an effortless, affordable, and fun atmosphere. It also had to be operable by virtually anyone with a passion for video games and a desire to work

green with the GameTruck name and fireball logo prominently featured. Once a franchise agreement is in place, a GameTruck franchisee can be up-and-running within 12 weeks.

The cost of GameTruck parties varies. On weekends the Des Moines, Iowa, franchise, for example, charges $295 for the first two hours and $95 for each additional hour. The rates drop some for weekdays. In contrast, the weekend rates in Chicago are $425 for the first two hours and $125 for each additional hour. Parents choose the games that will be played. For example, M (mature) rated games can be removed from parties for younger children. One unique aspect of GameTruck's offering to its franchisees is that because most parties are held on weekends, a GameTruck franchisee can be owned and operated by someone who has another job.

One aspect of its business that GameTruck points to as a positive indicator for continued success is that its Phoenix, Arizona, headquarters serves as a base for ongoing refinement of the GameTruck experience. The company remains laser focused on bringing people

Super cool interior of a GameTruck mobile theater. A GameTruck mobile theater can accommodate up to 20 players who can engage in multiplayer video games.

GameTruck Licensing

together in a multiplayer gaming context in the most innovative, cutting-edge, and cost-effective manner possible. GameTruck has received some recognition along the way. In January 2013, *Entrepreneur* magazine ranked GameTruck #218 on its list of the 500 fastest growing franchises in the United States. Later in the year, *Entrepreneur* ranked GameTruck the #7 top new franchise and the #55 top home based franchise.

Challenges Ahead

As GameTruck evaluates future growth and the ongoing viability of its basic concept, several questions will need to be answered. First, is there a market for its mobile game studios beyond the staple kid's party market? Some GameTruck franchisees are now offering laser-tag on-site adventures and corporate events. There may be other possibilities. Second, although many observers see the electronic games market as recession-proof, there is always the possibility that downturns in the economy may deter parents and other potential users from booking a GameTruck party, which costs a minimum of $295 for two hours. What can GameTruck do to minimize that possibility? Finally, is GameTruck's business model scalable utilizing the franchise concept? Will GameTruck be successful in its efforts to find a sufficient number of future franchisees who are passionate about gaming, have the financial ability to own and operate a GameTruck franchise, and are able to either operate the franchise

successfully on a part-time basis or book sufficient parties to make it a full-time pursuit? There is a possibility that some GameTruck franchisees may find themselves caught in the middle—it's too much work to operate as a part-time business but it doesn't provide enough income to justify doing it full-time. How GameTruck resolves these challenges will be instrumental to its future success.

Discussion Questions

15-38. What do you think of GameTruck's basic concept?

15-39. Would you characterize GameTruck's potential nationwide market as small, medium, or large? Would the concept work in the town where your college or university is located? Explain your answer.

15-40. What qualities do you think GameTruck looks for in prospective franchisees? If you were a prospective franchisee, what questions would you ask the company as part of your due diligence process?

15-41. Address each of the rhetorical questions at the end of the case. Add two challenges GameTruck may face that are not mentioned in the case. Comment on how problematic each challenge is and if you think the company will successfully deal with both challenges.

Sources: GameTruck home page, www.GameTruck.com, accessed August 20, 2014; *Entrepreneur,* available at www.entrepreneur.com/franchises/GameTruckLicensingllc/333684-0.html, accessed August 20, 2014.

Endnotes

1. I. Ater and O. Rigbi, "Price Control and Advertising in Franchising Chains," *Strategic Management Journal*, 2014: in press.

2. D. H. Hsu and R. H. Ziedonis, "Resources As Dual Sources of Advantage: Implications for Valuing Entrepreneurial-Firm Patents," *Strategic Management Journal* 34, no. 7 (2013): 761–781.

3. M. Hailer, "Franchise Businesses Projected to Grow Faster Than the Rest of the Economy in 2014," available at www.franchise.org/Franchise-News-Detail.aspx?id=61661, (posted on January 13, 2014, accessed on August 15, 2014).

4. Franchising.com home page, www.franchising.com, (accessed August 15, 2014).

5. J.-S. Chiou and C. Droge, "The Effects of Standardization and Trust on Franchisee's Performance and Satisfaction: A Study on Franchise Systems in the Growth Stage," *Journal of Small Business Management*, 2014 in press; J. G. Combs, D. J. Ketchen, Jr., C. L. Shook, and J. C. Short, "Antecedents and Consequences of Franchising: Past Accomplishments and Future Challenges," *Journal of Management* 37, no. 1 (2011): 99–126.

6. CIA World Factbook, www.cia.gov/library/publications/the-world-factbook/geos/us.html, (accessed August 10, 2014).

7. Comfort Keepers home page, www.comfortkeepers.com, (accessed August 15, 2014).

8. W. E. Gillis, J. G. Combs, and D. J. Ketchen, Jr., "Using Resource-Based Theory to Help Explain Plural Form Franchising," *Entrepreneurship Theory and Practice* 38, no. 3 (2014): 449–472.

9. ProntoWash, www.prontowash.com/franchising_master_faq.php#2, (accessed August 11, 2014).

10. McDonalds 10K report, 2013.

11. L. Altinay, M. Brookes, M. Madanoglu, and G. Aktas, "Franchisees' Trust in and Satisfaction with Franchise Partnerships," *Journal of Business Research* 67, no. 5 (2014): 722–728.

12. H. Cori, O. Harmen, and T. Civilai, "Determinants of Franchise Conversion: A Franchisee Perspective," *European Journal of Marketing* 47, no. 10 (2013): 1544–1575; A. Watson and R. Johnson, "Managing the Franchisor-Franchisee Relationship: A Relationship Marketing Perspective," *Journal of Marketing Channels* 17, no. 1 (2010): 51–68.

13. B. L. Fernandez, B. Gonzalez-Buston, and Y. A. Castano, "The Dynamics of Growth in Franchising," *Journal of Marketing Channels* 20, no. 1 and no. 2 (2013): 2–24.

14. R. Bennett, "To Franchise or Not: How to Decide," in C. L. Vaughn and D. B. Slater (Eds.), *Franchising Today: 1966–1967* (New York, NY: Matthew Bender and Company, 1967), 20.

15. R. P. Dant, S. K. Weaven, B. L. Baker, and H. J. J. Jeon, "An Introspective Examination of Single-Unit Versus Multi-Unit Franchisees,"

Journal of the Academy of Marketing Science 41, no. 4 (2013): 473–496; W. E. Gillis, E. McEwan, T. R. Crook, and S. C. Michael, "Using Tournaments to Reduce Agency Problems: The Case of Franchising," *Entrepreneurship Theory and Practice* 35, no. 3 (2011): 427–447.

16. "Darden home page, www.darden.com, (accessed August 15, 2014).

17. E. Calderon-Monge and P. Huerta-Zavala, "Brand and Performance Signals in the Choice of Franchise Opportunities," *The Service Industries Journal* 34, no. 9 and no. 10 (2014): 772–787; D. Grewal, G. R. Iyer, R. G. Javalgi, and L. Radulovich, "Franchise Partnership and International Expansion: A Conceptual Framework and Research Propositions," *Entrepreneurship Theory and Practice* 35, no. 3 (2011): 533–557.

18. Federal Trade Commission, Consumers Guide to Buying a Franchise (Washington, DC: U.S. Government Printing Office, 2014).

19. S. Jayachandran, P. Kaufman, V. Kumar, and K. Hewett, "Brand Licensing: What Drives Royalty Rates," *Journal of Marketing* 77, no. 5 (2013): 108–122; I. Kotliarov, "Royalty Rate Structure in Case of Franchising," *Annals of Economics and Finance* 12, no. 1 (2011): 139–156.

20. J. Bennett, "Cruise Franchisee Says It's Been Smooth Sailing," *StartupJournal*.com, www.startupjournal.com, (accessed May 30, 2006).

21. F. A. Zafeiropoulou and D. N. Koufopoulos, "The Influence of Relational Embeddedness on the Formation and Performance of Social Franchising," *Journal of Marketing Channels* 20, no. 1 and no. 2 (2013): 73–98; J. G. Combs, D. J. Ketchen, Jr., and J. C. Short, "Franchising Research: Major Milestones, New Directions, and Its Future Within Entrepreneurship," *Entrepreneurship Theory and Practice* 35, no. 3 (2011): 413–425.

22. Bureau of Consumer Protection, "Buying a Franchise: A Consumer Guide," http://business.ftc.gov/documents/inv05-buying-franchise-consumer-guide#2, (accessed August 10, 2014).

23. R. L. Purvin, *The Franchise Fraud* (New York, NY: John Wiley & Sons, 1994), 7.

24. Federal Trade Commission, www.ftc.gov/bcp/franchise/netdiscl.shtm, (accessed August 15, 2014).

25. Franchise Regulation, Franchise Direct, https://www.franchisedirect.com, (accessed August 20, 2014).

26. M. Freedman and R. Kosova, "Agency and Compensation: Evidence from the Hotel Industry," *Journal of Law, Economics, and Organization* 30, no. 1 (2014): 72–103.

27. V. Baena and J.Cervino, "International Franchising Decision-Making: A Model for Country Choice," *Latin American Business Review*

15, no. 1 (2014): 13–43; R. Perrigot, B. Lopez-Fernandez, and S. Eroglu, "Intangible Resources and Plural Form As Drivers of Franchise Internationalization: Examination Within a Two-Country Perspective," *Journal of Small Business Management* 51, no. 4 (2013): 557–577.

28. Senior Care Franchises, Entrepreneur.com, http://www.entrepreneur.com, (accessed August 20, 2014); All Business, "Hot Trend: Seniors Buying Franchises," www.allbusiness.com/franchises/buying-a-franchise/14572171-1.html, (accessed May 19, 2011).

29. M. Hummel, "How Franchises Are Using Social Media to Grow Their Business," Blogpost, https://www.linkedin.com, (accessed August 20, 2014).

Glossary

7(A) loan guaranty program. The main Small Business Administration (SBA) program available to small businesses operating through private sector lenders providing loans that are guaranteed by the SBA; loan guarantees reserved for small businesses that are unable to secure financing through normal lending channels. (366)

10-K. A report that is similar to the annual report, except that it contains more detailed information about the company's business. (287)

accounts receivable. The money owed to a firm by its customers. (284)

accredited investor. A person who is permitted to invest in high-risk investments such as business start-ups. (368)

acquirer. The surviving firm in an acquisition. (508)

acquisition. The outright purchase of one firm by another. (507)

adverse selection. The challenge a firm must face as it grows such that as the number of employees a firm needs increases, it becomes more difficult to find the right employees, place them in appropriate positions, and provide adequate supervision. (477)

advertising. Making people aware of a product or service in hopes of persuading them to buy it. (399)

advisory board. A panel of experts who are asked by a firm's managers to provide counsel and advice on an ongoing basis; unlike a board of directors, an advisory board possesses no legal responsibilities for the firm and gives nonbinding advice. (332)

agency theory. A management concept that argues that managers, because they are paid a salary, may not be as committed to the success of the businesses they manage as the owners, who capture the business's profits. This theory supports the notion of franchising, because franchisees are in effect the owners of the units they manage. (540)

area franchise agreement. Agreement that allows a franchisee to own and operate a specific number of outlets in a particular geographic area. (534)

articles of incorporation. Documents forming a legal corporation that are filed with the secretary of state's office in the state of incorporation. (262)

assignment of invention agreement. A document signed by an employee as part of the employment agreement that assigns the employer the right to apply for the patent of an invention made by the employee during the course of his or her employment. (433)

assumptions sheet. An explanation in a new firm's business plan of the sources of the numbers for its financial forecast and the assumptions used to generate them. (223, 295)

balance sheet. A snapshot of a company's assets, liabilities, and owner's equity at a specific point in time. (289)

barrier to entry. Conditions that create disincentives for a new firm to enter an industry. (178)

basis of differentiation. What causes consumers to pick one company's products over another's. (144)

board of advisors. A panel of experts asked by a firm's management to provide counsel and advice on an ongoing basis. (222)

board of directors. A panel of individuals who are elected by a corporation's shareholders to oversee the management of the firm. (222, 329)

bootstrapping. Using creativity, ingenuity, or any means possible to obtain resources other than borrowing money or raising capital from traditional sources. (355)

brainstorming. A technique used to quickly generate a large number of ideas and solutions to problems; conducted to generate ideas that might represent product or business opportunities. (81)

brand. The set of attributes—positive or negative—that people associate with a company. (392)

brand equity. The set of assets and liabilities that is linked to a brand and enables it to raise a firm's valuation. (394)

brand management. A program that protects the image and value of an organization's brand in consumers' minds. (393)

break-even point. The point where total revenue received equals total costs associated with the output. (297)

budgets. Itemized forecasts of a company's income, expenses, and capital needs that are also important tools for financial planning and control. (285)

bug report. A popular technique that is used in classrooms to teach brainstorming. (82)

burn rate. The rate at which a company is spending its capital until it reaches profitability. (351)

business angels. Individuals who invest their personal capital directly in new ventures. (359)

business format franchise. By far the most popular approach to franchising in which the franchisor provides a formula for doing business to the franchisee along with training, advertising, and other forms of assistance. (533)

business method patent. A patent that protects an invention that is or facilitates a method of doing business. (432)

business model. A company's plan for how it competes, uses its resources, structures its relationships, interfaces with customers, and creates value to sustain itself on the basis of the profits it generates. (47, 134)

business plan. A written document describing all the aspects of a business venture, which is usually necessary to raise money and attract high quality business partners. (47, 204)

buyback clause. A clause found in most founders' agreements that legally obligates the departing founder to sell to the remaining founders his or her interest in the firm if the remaining founders are interested. (250)

buzz. An awareness and sense of anticipation about a company and its offerings. (394)

C corporation. A legal entity that in the eyes of the law is separate from its owners. (261)

carry. The percentage of profits that the venture capitalist gets from a specific venture capital fund. (360)

certification marks. Marks, words, names, symbols, or devices used by a person other than its owner to certify a particular quality about a product or service. (440)

channels. A company's description of how it delivers its product or service to its customers. (152)

churn. The number of subscribers. (137)

closely held corporation. A corporation in which the voting stock is held by a small number of individuals and is very thinly or infrequently traded. (262)

code of conduct. A formal statement of an organization's values on certain ethical and social issues. (245)

collective marks. Trademarks or service marks used by the members of a cooperative, association, or other collective group, including marks indicating membership in a union or similar organization. (439)

common stock. Stock that is issued more broadly than preferred stock and that gives the stockholders voting rights to elect the firm's board of directors. (261)

competitive analysis grid. A tool for organizing the information a firm collects about its competitors to see how it stacks up against its competitors, provide ideas for markets to pursue, and identify its primary sources of competitive advantage. (190)

competitive intelligence. The information that is gathered by a firm to learn about its competitors. (188)

competitor analysis. A detailed evaluation of a firm's direct, indirect, and future competitors. (173, 218)

Computer Software Copyright Act. In 1980, Congress passed this act, which amended previous copyright acts; now, all forms of computer programs are protected. (443)

concept statement. A preliminary description of a business that includes descriptions of the product or service being offered, the intended target market, the benefits of the product or service, the product's position in the market, and how the product or service will be sold and distributed. (101)

concept test. A representation of the product or service to prospective users to gauge customer interest, desirability, and purchase intent. (101)

constant ratio method of forecasting. A forecasting approach using the percent of sales method in which expense items on a firm's income statement are expected to grow at the same rate as sales. (297)

consultant. An individual who gives professional or expert advice. Consultants fall into two categories: paid consultants and consultants who are made available for free or at a reduced rate through a nonprofit or governmental agency. (335)

contribution margin. The amount per unit of sale that is left over and is available to "contribute" to covering the firm's fixed costs and producing a profit. (219)

copyright. A form of intellectual property protection that grants to the owner of a work of authorship the legal right to determine how the work is used and to obtain the economic benefits of the work. (443)

copyright bug. The letter c inside a circle with the first year of publication and the author copyright owner (e.g., © 2007 Dell Inc). (444)

copyright infringement. Violation of another's copyright that occurs when one work derives from another work or is an exact copy or shows substantial similarity to the original copyrighted work. (445)

core competency. A unique skill or capability that transcends products or markets, makes a significant contribution to the customer's perceived benefit, is difficult to imitate, and serves as a source of a firm's competitive advantage over its rivals. (146, 467)

core strategy. The overall manner in which a firm competes relative to its rivals. (142)

corporate entrepreneurship. Behavior orientation exhibited by established firms with an entrepreneurial emphasis that is proactive, innovative, and risk taking. (29)

corporate venture capital. A type of capital similar to traditional venture capital, except that the money comes from corporations that invest in new ventures related to their areas of interest. (362)

corporation. A separate legal entity organized under the authority of a state. (261)

cost-based pricing. A pricing method in which the list price is determined by adding a markup percentage to the product's cost. (398)

cost of goods sold. The materials and direct labor needed to produce firm's revenue. (218)

cost of sales. All of the direct costs associated with producing or delivering a product or service, including the material costs and direct labor costs (also cost of goods sold). (288)

cost reduction strategy. A marketing strategy that is accomplished through achieving lower costs than industry incumbents through process improvements. (186)

cost structure. A description of the most important costs a business incurs to support its business model. (149)

creative destruction. The process by which new products and technologies developed by entrepreneurs over time make current products and technologies obsolete; stimulus of economic activity. (44)

creativity. The process of generating a novel or useful idea. (79)

crowdfunding. A method of funding in which people pool their money and other resources, usually via the Internet, to support efforts initiated by other people or organizations. (367)

current assets. Cash plus items that are readily convertible to cash, such as accounts receivable, inventories, and marketable securities. (289)

current liabilities. Obligations that are payable within a year, including accounts payable, accrued expenses, and the current portion of long-term debt. (291)

current ratio. A ratio that equals the firm's current assets divided by its current liabilities. (291)

customer advisory boards. A panel of individuals set up by some companies to meet regularly to discuss needs, wants, and problems that may lead to new product, service, or customer service ideas. (84)

day-in-the-life research. A form of anthropological research used by companies to make sure customers are satisfied and to probe for new product ideas by sending researchers to the customers' homes or business. (84)

debt financing. Getting a loan; most common sources of debt financing are commercial banks and the Small Business Administration's (SBA's) guaranteed loan program. (357)

debt-to-equity ratio. A ratio calculated by dividing the firm's long-term debt by its shareholders' equity. (284)

declining industry. An industry that is experiencing a reduction in demand. (186)

derivative works. Works that are new renditions of something that is already copyrighted, which are also copyrightable. (443)

design patents. The second most common type of patent covering the invention of new, original, and ornamental designs for manufactured products. (433)

disintermediation. The process of eliminating layers of intermediaries, such as distributors and retailers, to sell directly to customers. (408)

disruptive business models. Business models, which are rare, that do not fit the profile of a standard business model, and are impactful enough that they disrupt or change the way business is conducted in an industry or an important niche within an industry. (140)

distribution channel. The route a product takes from the place it is made to the customer who is the end user. (408)

double taxation. Form of taxation in which a corporation is taxed on its net income. When the same income is distributed to shareholders in the form of dividends, it is taxed again on shareholders' personal income tax returns. (262)

due diligence. The process of investigating the merits of a potential venture and verifying the key claims made in the business plan. (361)

Economic Espionage Act. Passed in 1996, an act that makes the theft of trade secrets a crime. (448)

economies of scale. A phenomenon that occurs when mass producing a product results in lower average costs. (178, 471)

economies of scope. The advantage a firm accrues through the scope (or range) of its operations rather than from the scale of its production. (471)

efficiency. How productively a firm utilizes its assets relative to its rate of return. (284)

elevator speech (or pitch). A brief, carefully constructed statement that outlines the merits of a business opportunity. (357)

emerging industry. A new industry in which standard operating procedures have yet to be developed. (185)

employee. Someone who works for a business, at the business's location or virtually, utilizing the business's tools and equipment and according to the business's policies and procedures. (327)

entrepreneurial alertness. The ability to notice things without engaging in deliberate search. (78)

entrepreneurial firms. Companies that bring new products and services to market by creating and seizing opportunities. (40)

entrepreneurial intensity. The position of a firm on a conceptual continuum that ranges from highly conservative to highly entrepreneurial. (29)

entrepreneurial services. Those services that generate new market, product, and service ideas. (477)

entrepreneurship. The process by which individuals pursue opportunities without regard to resources they currently control. (28)

equity-based crowdfunding. This type of funding helps businesses raise money by tapping individuals who provide funding in exchange for equity in the business. (368)

equity financing. A means of raising money by exchanging partial ownership in a firm, usually in the form of stock, for funding. (356)

ethical dilemma. A situation that involves doing something that is beneficial to oneself or the organization, but may be unethical. (246)

ethics training programs. Programs designed to teach employees how to respond to the types of ethical dilemmas that might arise on their jobs. (246)

exclusive distribution arrangements. An agreement that gives a retailer or other intermediary the exclusive rights to sell a company's products in a specific area for a specific period of time. (409)

execution intelligence. The ability to fashion a solid business idea into a viable business is a key characteristic of successful entrepreneurs. (35)

executive summary. A quick overview of the entire business plan that provides a busy reader everything that he or she needs to know about the distinctive nature of the new venture. (212)

external growth strategies. Growth strategies that rely on establishing relationships with third parties, such as mergers, acquisitions, strategic alliances, joint ventures, licensing, and franchising. (507)

factoring. A financial transaction whereby a business sells its accounts receivable to a third party, called a factor, at a discount in exchange for cash. (367)

fair use. The limited use of copyright material for purposes such as criticism, comment, news reporting, teaching, or scholarship. (446)

feasibility analysis. A preliminary evaluation of a business idea to determine if it is worth pursuing. (99)

Federal employee identification number (EIN). A tax identification number; is used when filing various tax returns. (257)

fictitious business name permit. A permit that's required for businesses that plan to use a fictitious name, which is any name other than the business owner's name (also called dba or doing business as). (257)

fiduciary obligation. The obligation to always act in another's best interest; it is a mistake to assume that a franchisor has a fiduciary obligation to its franchisees. (553)

final prospectus. Documents issued by the investment bank after the Securities and Exchange Commission (SEC) has approved the offering that sets a date and issuing price for the offering. (364)

financial feasibility analysis. A preliminary financial assessment of a new venture that considers the total start up cash needed, financial performance of similar businesses, and the overall financial attractiveness of the proposed venture. (114)

financial management. The process of raising money and managing a company's finances in a way that achieves the highest rate of return. (283)

financial ratios. Ratios showing the relationships between items on a firm's financial statements that are used to discern whether a firm is meeting its financial objectives and how it stacks up against industry peers. (286)

financial statement. Written reports that quantitatively describe a firm's financial health. (284)

financing activities. Activities that raise cash during a certain period by borrowing money or selling stock, and/or use cash during a certain period by paying dividends, buying back outstanding stock, or buying back outstanding bonds. (293)

first-mover advantage. A sometimes significant advantage, created by the opportunity to establish brand recognition and/or market power, gained by the first company to produce a product or service or the first company to move into a market. (185)

fixed assets. Assets used over a longer time frame, such as real estate, buildings, equipment, and furniture. (289)

fixed costs. The costs that a company incurs in operating a business whether it sells something or not (e.g., overhead). (150, 219, 471)

focus group. A gathering of five to ten people who have been selected based on their common characteristics relative to the issue being discussed; conducted to generate ideas that might represent product or business opportunities. (82)

follow-on funding. Additional funding for a firm following the initial investment made by investors. (361)

forecasts. Estimates of a firm's future income and expenses, based on its past performance, its current circumstances, and its future plans. (285, 295)

founders' agreement. A written document that deals with issues such as the relative split of the equity among the founders of a firm, how individual founders will be compensated for the cash or the "sweat equity" they put into the firm, and how long the founders will have to remain with the firm for their shares to fully vest (also shareholders' agreement). (250)

founding team. A team of individuals chosen to start a new venture; has an advantage over firms started by an individual because a team brings more talent, resources, ideas, and professional contacts to a new venture than does a sole entrepreneur. (322)

fragmented industry. An industry characterized by a large number of firms approximately equal in size. (185)

franchise agreement. The document that consummates the sale of a franchise, which typically contains two sections: (1) the purchase agreement and (2) the franchise or license agreement. (553)

Franchise Disclosure Document (FDD). Accepted in all 50 states and part of Canada, a lengthy document that contains 23 categories of information that give a prospective franchisee a broad base of information about the background and financial health of the franchisor. (552)

franchisee. An individual or firm that enters into a franchise agreement and pays an initial fee and an ongoing royalty to an franchisor in exchange for using the franchisor's trademark and method of doing business. (532)

franchising. A form of business organization in which a firm that already has a successful product or service (franchisor) licenses its trademark and method of doing businesses to other businesses (franchisees) in exchange for an initial franchise fee and an ongoing royalty. (532)

franchisor. A firm with a successful product or service that enters into a franchising agreement to license its trademark and method of doing business to other businesses in exchange for fee and royalty payments. (532)

freelancer. A person who is in business for themselves, works on their own time with their own tools and equipment, and performs services for a number of different clients. (328)

full business plan. A document that spells out a company's operations and plans in much more detail than a summary business plan; the format that is usually used to prepare a business plan for an investor. (210)

general partners. The venture capitalists who manage a venture capital fund. (360)

general partnership. A form of business organization in which two or more people pool their skills, abilities, and resources to run a business. (260)

geographic expansion. An internal growth strategy in which an entrepreneurial business grows by simply expanding from its original location to additional geographical sites. (502)

geographic roll-up strategy. When one firm starts acquiring similar firms that are located in different geographic areas. (185)

global industry. An industry that is experiencing significant international sales. (187)

global strategy. An international expansion strategy in which firms compete for market share by using the same basic approach in all foreign markets. (187)

guerilla marketing. A low budget approach to marketing that relies on ingenuity, cleverness, and surprise rather than traditional techniques. (408)

heterogeneous team. A team whose individual members are diverse in terms of their abilities and experiences. (322)

historical financial statements. Reflect past performance and are usually prepared on a quarterly and annual basis. (287)

homogenous team. A team whose individual members' experiences and areas of expertise are very similar to one another. (322)

idea. A thought, impression, or notion. (66)

idea bank. A physical or digital repository for storing ideas. (84)

idea–expression dichotomy. The legal principle describing the concept that although an idea is not able to be copyrighted, the specific expression of an idea is. (444)

illiquid. Describes stock in both closely held and private corporations, meaning that it typically isn't easy to find a buyer for the stock. (262)

improving an existing product or service. Enhancing a product or service's quality by making it larger or smaller, making it easier to use, or making it more up-to-date, thereby increasing its value and price potential. (501)

income statement. A financial statement that reflects the results of the operations of a firm over a specified period of time: prepared on a monthly, quarterly, or annual basis. (288)

individual franchise agreement. The most common type of franchise agreement, which involves the sale of a single franchise for a specific location. (534)

industry. A group of firms producing a similar product or service, such as airlines, fitness drinks, or electronic games. (107, 172)

industry analysis. Business research that focuses on the potential of an industry. (172)

industry/target market feasibility. An assessment of the overall appeal of the industry and target market for the product or service being proposed. (107)

initial public offering (IPO). The first sale of a company's stock to the public and an important milestone for a firm for four reasons: it is a way to raise equity capital; it raises a firm's public profile; it is a liquidity event; and it creates another form of currency (company stock) that can be used to grow the company. (362)

innovation. The process of creating something new, which is central to the entrepreneurial process. (46)

inside director. A person on a firm's board of directors who is also an officer of the firm. (329)

intellectual property. Any product of human intellect, imagination, creativity, or inventiveness that is intangible but has value in the marketplace and can be protected through tools such as patents, trademarks, copyrights, and trade secrets. (427)

intellectual property audit. A firm's assessment of the intellectual property it owns. (451)

intent-to-use trademark application. An application based on the applicant's intention to register and use a trademark. (442)

internal growth strategies. Growth strategies that rely on efforts generated within the firm itself, such as new product development, other product related strategies, or international expansion. (497)

international new ventures. Businesses that, from inception, seek to derive significant competitive advantage by using their resources to sell products or services in multiple countries. (503)

intern. A person who works for a business as an apprentice or trainee for the purpose of obtaining practical experience. (328)

intranet. A privately maintained Internet site that can be accessed only by authorized users. (84)

inventory. A company's merchandise, raw materials, and products waiting to be sold. (284)

investing activities. Activities that include the purchase, sale, or investment in fixed assets, such as real estate and buildings. (293)

investment bank. A financial institution that acts as an underwriter or agent for a firm issuing securities. (364)

joint venture. An entity created when two or more firms pool a portion of their resources to create a separate, jointly owned organization. (515)

key assets. The assets that a firm owns that enable its business model to work. (147)

landing page. A single Web page that typically provides direct sales copy, like "click here to buy a Hawaiian vacation." (106)

Lanham Act. An act of Congress, passed in 1946, that spells out what is protected under trademark law. (440)

leadership strategy. A competitive strategy in which the firm tries to become the dominant player in the industry. (186)

lease. A written agreement in which the owner of a piece of property allows an individual or business to use the property for a specified period of time in exchange for regular payments. (368)

liability of newness. Situation that often causes new firms to falter because the people who start the firms can't adjust quickly enough to their new roles, and because the firm lacks a "track record" with customers and suppliers. (319)

licensee. A company that purchases the right to use another company's intellectual property. (511)

licensing. The granting of permission by one company to another company to use a specific form of its intellectual property under clearly defined conditions. (506)

licensing agreement. The formal contract between a licensor and licensee. (511)

licensor. The company that owns the intellectual property in a licensing agreement. (511)

lifestyle firms. Businesses that provide their owners the opportunity to pursue a particular lifestyle and earn a living while doing so (e.g., ski instructors, golf pros, and tour guides). (40)

limited liability company (LLC). A form of business organization that combines the limited liability advantage of the corporation with the tax advantages of the partnership. (264)

limited partners. Participants in a partnership, such as a venture capital fund, which have limited liability, meaning that they are only liable up to the amount of their investment and have no management authority. (360)

limited partnership. A modified form of a general partnership that includes two classes of owners: general partners and limited partners. The general partners are liable for the debts and obligations of the partnership, but the limited partners are liable only up to the amount of their investment. The limited partners may not exercise any significant control over the organization without jeopardizing their limited liability status. (261)

limited partnership agreement. Sets forth the rights and duties of the general and limited partners, along with the details of how the partnership will be managed and eventually dissolved. (261)

line of credit. A borrowing "cap" is established and borrowers can use the credit at their discretion; requires periodic interest payments. (365)

link joint venture. A joint venture in which the position of the parties is not symmetrical and the objectives of the partners may diverge. (515)

liquid market. A market in which stock can be bought and sold fairly easily through an organized exchange. (262)

liquidity. The ability to sell a business or other asset quickly at a price that is close to its market value; also, a company's ability to meet its short-term financial obligations. (258, 284)

liquidity event. An occurrence such as a new venture going public, finding a buyer, or being acquired by another company that converts some or all of a company's stock into cash. (356)

long-term liabilities. Notes or loans that are repayable beyond one year, including liabilities associated with purchasing real estate, buildings, and equipment. (291)

low-end market disruption. A type of disruption that is possible when the firms in an industry continue to improve products or services to the point where they are actually better than a sizable portion of their clientele needs or desires. (140)

managerial capacity problem. The problem that arises when the growth of a firm is limited by the managerial capacity (i.e., personnel, expertise, and intellectual resources) that a firm has available to investigate and implement new business ideas. (477)

managerial services. The routine functions of the firm that facilitate the profitable execution of new opportunities. (477)

market analysis. An analysis that breaks the industry into segments and zeros in on the specific segment (or target market) to which the firm will try to appeal. (216)

market leadership. The position of a firm when it is the number one or the number two firm in an industry or niche market in terms of sales volume. (471)

market penetration strategy. A strategy designed to increase the sales of a product or service through greater marketing efforts or through increased production capacity and efficiency. (501)

market segmentation. The process of studying the industry in which a firm intends to compete to determine the different potential target markets in that industry. (216, 389)

marketing alliance. Typically matches a company with a distribution system with a company with a product to sell in order to increase sales of a product or service. (513)

marketing mix. The set of controllable, tactical marketing tools that a firm uses to produce the response it wants in the target market; typically organized around the four Ps—product, price, promotion, and place (or distribution). (395)

marketing strategy. A firm's overall approach for marketing its products and services. (219)

master franchise agreement. Similar to an area franchise agreement, but in addition to having the right to operate a specific number of locations in a particular area, the franchisee also has the right to offer and sell the franchise to other people in the area. (534)

mature industry. An industry that is experiencing slow or no increase in demand, has numerous (rather than new) customers, and has limited product innovation. (185)

mediation. A process in which an impartial third party (usually a professional mediator) helps those involved in a dispute reach an agreement. (253)

mentor. Someone who is more experienced than you and is willing to by your counselor, confidant, and go-to person for advice. (85)

merchandise and character licensing. The licensing of a recognized trademark or brand, which the licensor typically controls through a registered trademark or copyright. (512)

merchant cash advance. A common type of alternative lending. (367)

merger. The pooling of interests to combine two or more firms into one. (507)

milestone. In a business plan context, a noteworthy event in the past or future development of a business. (216)

mission statement. A statement that describes why a firm exists and what its business model is supposed to accomplish. (143, 216)

moderate risk takers. Entrepreneurs who are often characterized as willing to assume a moderate amount of risk in business, being neither overly conservative nor likely to gamble. (37)

moral hazard. A problem a firm faces as it grows and adds personnel; the assumption is that new hires will not have the same ownership incentives or be as motivated to work as hard as the original founders. (477)

multidomestic strategy. An international expansion strategy in which firms compete for market share on a country by country basis and vary their product or services offerings to meet the demands of the local market. (187)

multiple-unit franchisee. An individual who owns and operates more than one outlet of the same franchisor, whether through an area or a master franchise agreement. (534)

net sales. Total sales minus allowances for returned goods and discounts. (288)

network entrepreneurs. Entrepreneurs who identified their idea through social contacts. (79)

networking. Building and maintaining relationships with people whose interests are similar or whose relationship could bring advantages to a firm. (325)

new market disruption. A market disruption that addresses a market that previously wasn't served. (140)

new product development. The creation and sale of new products (or services) as a means of increasing a firm's revenues. (497)

new-venture team. The group of founders, key employees, and advisors that move a new venture from an idea to a fully functioning firm. (111, 318)

niche market. A place within a large market segment that represents a narrow group of customers with similar interests. (390)

niche strategy. A marketing strategy that focuses on a narrow segment of the industry. (186)

noncompete agreement. An agreement that prevents an individual from competing against a former employer for a specific period of time. (253)

nondisclosure agreement. A promise made by an employee or another party (such as a supplier) to not disclose a company's trade secrets. (253)

one year after first use deadline. Requirement that a patent must be filed within one year of when a product or process was first offered for sale, put into public use, or was described in any printed publication. If this requirement is violated, the right to apply for a patent is forfeited. (432)

operating activities. Activities that affect net income (or loss), depreciation, and changes in current assets and current liabilities other than cash and short-term debt. (293)

operating expenses. Marketing, administrative costs, and other expenses not directly related to producing a product or service. (289)

operating leverage. An analysis of the firm's fixed costs versus its variable costs. (219)

operational business plan. A blueprint for a company's operations; primarily meant for an internal audience. (210)

operations. Activities that are both integral to a firm's overall business model and represent the day-to-day heartbeat of a firm. (151)

opportunity. A favorable set of circumstances that creates a need for a new product, service, or business. (65)

opportunity gap. An entrepreneur recognizes a problem and creates a business to fill it. (65)

opportunity recognition. The process of perceiving the possibility of a profitable new business or a new product or service. (76)

organic growth. Internally generated growth within a firm that does not rely on outside intervention. (497)

organizational chart. A graphic representation of how authority and responsibility are distributed within a company. (222)

organizational feasibility analysis. A study conducted to determine whether a proposed business has sufficient management expertise, organizational competence, and resources to be successful. (111)

other assets. Miscellaneous assets including accumulated goodwill. (289)

outside director. Someone on a firm's board of directors who is not employed by the firm. (329)

outsourcing. Work that is done for a company by people other than the company's full-time employees. (502)

owner's equity. The equity invested in the business by its owner(s) plus the accumulated earnings retained by the business after paying dividends. (291)

pace of growth. The rate at which a firm is growing on an annual basis. (470)

partnership agreement. A document that details the responsibility and the ownership shares of the partners involved with an organization. (260)

passion for their business. An entrepreneur's belief that his or her business will positively influence people's lives; one of the characteristics of successful entrepreneurs. (31)

patent. A grant from the federal government conferring the rights to exclude others from making, selling, or using an invention for the term of the patent. (430)

patent infringement. This is when one party engages in the unauthorized use of another's patent. (436)

peer-to-peer lending. A category of financial transactions which occur directly between individuals or "peers." (367)

percent of sales method. A method for expressing each expense item as a percent of sales. (297)

piercing the corporate veil. The chain of effects that occurs if the owners of a corporation don't file their yearly payments, neglect to pay their annual fees, or commit fraud, which may result in the court ignoring the fact that a corporation has been established, and the owners could be held personally liable for actions for the corporation. (262)

place. The marketing mix category that encompasses all of the activities that move a firm's product from its place of origin to the consumer (also distribution). (408)

plant patents. Patents that protect new varieties of plants that can be reproduced asexually by grafting or cross-breeding rather than by planting seeds. (433)

position. How the entire company is situated relative to its competitors. (173, 216)

preferred stock. Stock that is typically issued to conservative investors, who have preferential rights over common stockholders in regard to dividends and to the assets of the corporation in the event of liquidation. (261)

preliminary prospectus. A document issued by an investment bank that describes the potential offering to the general public while the SEC is conducting an investigation of the offering (also red-herring). (364)

press kit. A folder typically distributed to journalists and made available online that contains background information about a company and includes a list of the company's most recent accomplishments. (403)

price. The amount of money consumers pay to buy a product; one of the four Ps in a company's marketing mix. (398)

price/earnings (P/E) ratio. A simple ratio that measures the price of a company's stock against its earnings. (289)

price-quality attribution. The assumption consumers naturally make that the higher priced product is also the better quality product. (399)

primary research. Research that is original and is collected firsthand by the entrepreneur by, for example, talking to potential customers and key industry participants. (100)

prior entrepreneurial experience. Prior start up experience; this experience has been found to be one of the most consistent predictors of future entrepreneurial performance. (323)

private corporation. A corporation in which all of the shares are held by a few shareholders, such as management or family members, and the stock is not publicly traded. (262)

private placement. A variation of the IPO in which there is a direct sale of an issue of securities to a large institutional investor. (365)

product. The element of the marketing mix that is the good or service a company offers to its target market; often thought of as something having physical form. (395)

product and trademark franchise. An arrangement under which the franchisor grants to the franchisee the right to buy its product and use its trade name. (533)

product attribute map. A map that illustrates a firm's positioning strategy relative to it's major rivals. (391)

product/customer focus. A defining characteristic of successful entrepreneurs that emphasizes producing good products with the capability to satisfy customers. (34)

product line extension strategy. A strategy that involves making additional versions of a product so they will appeal to different clientele. (502)

product/market scope. A range that defines the products and markets on which a firm will concentrate. (145)

product prototype. The first physical manifestation of a new product, often in a crude or preliminary form. (220)

product/service feasibility analysis. An assessment of the overall appeal of the product or service being proposed. (100)

productive opportunity set. The set of opportunities the firm feels it is capable of pursuing. (477)

pro forma balance sheet. Financial statements that show a projected snapshot of a company's assets, liabilities, and owner's equity at a specific point in time. (301)

pro forma financial statements. Projections for future periods, based on a firm's forecasts, and typically completed for two to three years in the future. (287)

pro forma income statement. A financial statement that shows the projected results of the operations of a firm over a specific period. (300)

pro form (or projected) financial statements. Statements that are at the heart of the financial section of a business plan. (223)

pro forma statement of cash flows. A financial statement that shows the projected flow of cash into and out of a company for a specific period. (302)

profit margin. A measure of a firm's return on sales that is computed by dividing net income by average net sales. (289)

profitability. The ability to earn a profit. (284)

promotion. The marketing mix category that includes the activities planned by a company to communicate the merits of its product to its target market with the goal of persuading people to buy the product. (399)

provisional patent application. A part of patent law that grants "provisional rights" to an inventor for up to one year, pending the filing of a complete and final application. (436)

public corporation. A corporation that is listed on a major stock exchange, such as the New York Stock Exchange or the NASDAQ, in which owners can sell their shares at almost a moment's notice. (262)

public relations. The efforts a company makes to establish and maintain a certain image with the public through networking with journalists and others to try to interest them in saying or writing good things about the company and its products. (403)

ratio analysis. Ratios showing the relationships between items on a firm's financial statements that are used to discern whether a firm is meeting its financial objectives and how it stacks up against industry peers. (223)

reference account. An early user of a firm's product who is willing to give a testimonial regarding his or her experience with the product. (397)

regression analysis. A statistical technique used to find relationships between variables for the purpose of predicting future values. (296)

relevant industry experience. Experience in the same industry as an entrepreneur's current venture that includes a network of industry contacts and an understanding of the subtleties of the industry. (323)

resources. The inputs a firm uses to produce, sell, distribute, and service a product or service. (146)

revenue streams. A description of how a firm makes money. (148)

rewards-based crowdfunding. This type of funding allows entrepreneurs to raise money in exchange for some type of amenity or reward. (367)

road show. A whirlwind tour taken by the top management team of a firm wanting to go public; consists of meetings in key cities where the firm presents its business plan to groups of investors. (364)

rounds. Stages of subsequent investments made in a firm by investors. (361)

salary-substitute firms. Small firms that yield a level of income for their owner or owners that is similar to what they would earn when working for an employer (e.g., dry cleaners, convenience stores, restaurants, accounting firms, retail stores, and hairstyling salons). (40)

sales forecast. A projection of a firm's sales for a specified period (such as a year); most firms though forecast their sales for two to five years into the future. (295)

Sarbanes-Oxley Act. A federal law that was passed in response to corporate accounting scandals involving prominent corporations, like Enron and WorldCom. (364)

sales process. The systematic process a business engages in to identify prospects and close sales. (409)

SBA Guaranteed Loan Program. An important source of funding for small businesses in general in which approximately 50 percent of the 9,000 banks in the United States participate. (366)

SBIR Program. Small Business Innovation Research (SBIR) competitive grant program that provides over $1 billion per year to small businesses for early stage and development projects. (369)

scale joint venture. A joint venture in which the partners collaborate at a single point in the value chain to gain economies of scale in production or distribution. (515)

secondary market offering. Any later public issuance of shares after the initial public offering. (362)

secondary meaning. This arises when, over time, consumers start to identify a trademark with a specific product. For example, the name CHAP STICK for lip balm was originally considered to be descriptive, and thus not afforded trademark protection. (442)

secondary research. Data collected previously by someone else for a different purpose. (100)

service. An activity or benefit that is intangible and does not take on a physical form, such as an airplane trip or advice from an attorney. (395)

service marks. Similar to ordinary trademarks but used to identify the services or intangible activities of a business rather than a business's physical product. (439)

shareholders. Owners of a corporation who are shielded from personal liability for the debts and obligations of the corporation. (261)

signaling. The act of a high-quality individual agreeing to serve on a company's board of directors, which indicates that the individual believes that the company has the potential to be successful. (331)

single-purpose loan. One common type of loan in which a specific amount of money is borrowed that must be repaid in a fixed amount of time with interest. (365)

skills profile. A chart that depicts the most important skills that are needed and where skills gaps exist. (327)

social plug-ins. Tools that Web sites use to provide its users with personalized and social experiences. (406)

Solo entrepreneurs. Entrepreneurs who identified their business idea on their own. (79)

sole proprietorship. The simplest form of business organization involving one person, in which the owner maintains complete control over the business and business losses can be deducted against the owner's personal tax return. (258)

sources and uses of funds statement. A document, usually included in the financial section of a business plan, that lays out specifically how much money a firm needs, where the money will come from, and what the money will be used for. (223)

spin-ins. A transaction that takes place when a large firm that has a small equity stake in a small firm, decided to acquire a 100% interest in the firm. (516)

spin-out. The opposite of a spin-in that occurs when a larger company divests itself of one of its smaller divisions. (516)

stability. The strength and vigor of the firm's overall financial posture. (284)

standard business models. Models that depict existing plans or recipes firms can use to determine how they will create, deliver, and capture value for their stakeholders. (137)

statement of cash flows. A financial statement summarizing the changes in a firm's cash position for a specified period of time and detailing why the changes occurred. Similar to a month end bank statement, it reveals how much cash is on hand at the end of the month as well as how the cash was acquired and spent during the month. (292)

stock options. Special form of incentive compensation providing employees the option or right to buy a certain number of shares of their company's stock at a stated price over a certain period of time. (262)

strategic alliance. A partnership between two or more firms that is developed to achieve a specific goal. (513)

strong-tie relationships. Relationships characterized by frequent interaction that form between like-minded individuals such as coworkers, friends, and spouses; these relationships tend to reinforce insights and ideas the individuals already have and, therefore, are not likely to introduce new ideas. (79)

STTR Program. A government grant program, similar to the SBIR program, which requires the participation of a research organization, such as a research university or a federal laboratory. (370)

subchapter S corporation. A form of business organization that combines the advantages of a partnership and C corporation; similar to a partnership, in that the profits and losses of the business are not subject to double taxation, and similar to a corporation, in that the owners are not subject to personal liability for the behavior of the business. (263)

subfranchisees. The people who buy franchises from master franchisees. (534)

summary business plan. A business plan 10 to 15 pages long that works best for companies very early in their development that are not prepared to write a full plan. (210)

supplier. A company that provides parts or services to another company. (152)

sustained growth. Growth in both revenues and profits over an extended period of time. (465)

sweat equity. The value of the time and effort that a founder puts into a new firm. (354)

tagline. A phrase that is used consistently in a company's literature, advertisements, promotions, stationery, and even invoices to develop and to reinforce the position the company has staked out in its market. (216, 392)

target. In an acquisition, the firm that is acquired. (508)

target market. The limited group of individuals or businesses that a firm goes after or tries to appeal to at a certain point in time. (107, 144)

technological alliances. Business alliances that cooperate in R&D, engineering, and manufacturing. (513)

technology licensing. The licensing of proprietary technology, which the licensor typically controls by virtue of a utility patent. (512)

trademark. Any work, name, symbol, or device used to identify the sources or origin of products or services and to distinguish those products and services from others. (436, 438)

trade secret. Any formula, pattern, physical device, idea, process, or other information that provides the owner of the information with a competitive advantage in the marketplace. (448)

trade show. An event at which the goods or services in a specific industry are exhibited and demonstrated. (404)

triggering event. The event that prompts an individual to become an entrepreneur (e.g., losing a job, inheriting money, accommodating a certain lifestyle). (47)

Uniform Trade Secrets Act. Drafted in 1979 by a special commission in an attempt to set nationwide standards for trade secret legislation; although the majority of states have adopted the act, most revised it, resulting in a wide disparity among states in regard to trade secret legislation and enforcement. (448)

utility patents. The most common type of patent covering what we generally think of as new inventions that must be useful, must be novel in relation to prior arts in the field, and must not be obvious to a person of ordinary skill in the field. (432)

value. Relative worth, importance, or utility. (40)

value-based pricing. A pricing method in which the list price is determined by estimating what consumers are willing to pay for a product and then backing off a bit to provide a cushion. (398)

variable costs. The costs that are not fixed that a company incurs as it generates sales. (150, 219, 471)

vendor credit. A form of credit in which a vendor extends credit to a business in order to allow the business to buy its products and/or services upfront but defer payment until later. (367)

venture capital. The money that is invested by venture capital firms in start ups and small businesses with exceptional growth potential. (360)

venture-leasing firms. Firms that act as brokers, bringing the parties involved in a lease together (e.g., firms acquainted with the producers of specialized equipment match these producers with new ventures that are in need of the equipment). (368)

viral marketing. A new marketing technique that facilitates and encourages people to pass along a marketing message about a particular product or service. (407)

virtual assistant. A freelancer who provides administrative, technical, or creative assistance to clients remotely from a home office. (328)

virtual prototype. A computer generated 3-D image of an idea. (220)

weak tie relationships. Relationships characterized by infrequent interaction that form between casual acquaintances who do not have a lot in common and, therefore, may be the source of completely new ideas. (79)

window of opportunity. The time period in which a firm or an entrepreneur can realistically enter a new market. (65)

working capital. A firm's current assets minus its current liabilities. (291)

Name Index

A

Abraham, Alexandra, 424–427
Adler, Charles, 75, 380–383
Algard, Alex, 34
Altman, Sam, 139
Angle, Colin, 38
Antonio, Vinny, 479
Argott, Don, 563
Ariav, Yuval, 310–312
Ashwell, Rachel, 475

B

Bagley, Constance E., 254–255
Barna, Hayley, 144–145, 232–234
Barringer, Bruce R., 410
Bauer, Jason, 504
Bauer, Mia, 504
Baxter, Amy, 231
Beastie Boys, 446, 447–448
Beauchamp, Katia, 144–145,
    232–234
Bechtolsheim, Andy, 359
Beeman, David, 339–340
Bergeron, Claude, 396
Bezos, Jeff, 30, 35, 65, 221, 522
Bieber, Justin, 274, 501
Blank, Steve, 122, 349–350
Blumenthal, Neil, 199
Branson, Richard, 29, 31
Brin, Sergey, 30, 359
Brinckerhoff, Ben, 324–325
Broekhof, Wouter, 456
Brooks, Alice, 348–350
Burke, David, 504
Burns, Tom, 426
Byrt, Jonathan, 381–382

C

Calagione, Sam, 78
Callahan, T. J., 197
Camp, Garrett, 521–523
Canarick, Jon, 543
Cao, Xuwen, 33
Carter, Tim, 401–402
Charan, Ram, 330
Chasen, Matt, 489–491
Chen, Bettina, 348–350
Chen, Jane, 124–126
Chen, Mollie, 233
Chen, Perry, 75, 380–383
Chesbrough, Henry W., 397
Chesky, Brian, 405
Christensen, Clayton, 140, 233
Christopher, Doris, 466
Ciravolo, Tish, 75, 217
Clark, Maxine, 252–253, 254
Clum, Jerry, 532
Clum, Kristina, 532
Cohen, Susan, 320
Collins, Jim, 469
Cooper, Matt, 103
Coover, Gary, 122–123
Corcoran, Barbara, 456
Cox, Megan, 386–388
Creelman, Bill, 309
Cuban, Mark, 71, 456

D

Dana, Neil, 55
DeFeudis, Wendy, 29
DeHart, Jacob, 468
Dell, Michael, 515
Demos, Steve, 186
Dickerson, Chad, 160
Doherty, Fraser, 24
Douglas, Tom, 425–426
Dr. Oz, 274
Dubin, Mike, 485

E

Ebert-Zavos, Benny, 202–204
Ellison, Larry, 502
Elton, John, 112
Estrade, Erica, 235

F

Fan, Wayne, 77
Feld, Brad, 211
Ferdowsi, Arash, 90–92
Fields, Kathy, 419–421
Filo, David, 438
Fischer, Jenna, 501
Fishman, Michael, 24
Fliegel, Jordan, 274
Forsythe, Al, 62–64
Franklin, Sam, 170
Frankovich, Kent, 377–379
Friedman, Thomas, 313

G

Gaal, Robert, 456
Gallaer, Jodi, 35
Gates, Bill, 286
Gatzen, Phil, 202–204
Gebbia, Joe, 405
Gelfand, Kevin, 494–496
Gentry, Lance, 341, 342
Gerber, Michael E., 474
Geske, David, 457
Gilboa, David, 199
Goff, Greg, 75
Goh, Zenton, 121
Goizueta, Roberto, 188
Gold, Justin, 340–342
Goldman, Sam, 235–237
Gottesman, Greg, 92–94
Graham, Paul, 90
Green, Paul, 563–565
Grepper, Ryan, 415–416
Gross, Bill, 108
Gurley, Bill, 490
Gutierrez, Carlos, 428

H

Hanger, Windsor, 132–135
Hanlin, Russell, 393
Harden, Dan, 242
Harden, John, 240–242
Harrison, Scott, 274
Haseltine, William, 431
Hawk, Tony, 274
Haywood, Ben, 57

Haywood, Jamie, 57
Hedlund, Marc, 480, 511
Henikoff, Troy, 317
Herjavec, Robert, 379
Hewlett, Bill, 465
Hill, Austin, 112
Hochberg, Yael, 320
Hodak, Brittany, 415
Hoffman, David, 316–318
Hogarth, Ian, 213
Houston, Drew, 90–92, 210
Hsieh, Fu-Hung, 196
Hsieh, Tony, 343–345
Huff, Harold, 196
Hunt, Andrew, 199

J

Jain, Vipin, 466
Jobs, Steven, 34, 355
Johnson, Don, 74
Johnson, Ron, 400–401
Jones, Sarah, 270–272
Joyce, Sheena M., 563

K

Kadylak, Judy, 396
Kagle, Bob, 334
Kalanick, Travis, 521–523
Kalin, Rob, 159–162
Kaplan, Stephanie,
    132–135
Kaufman, Ben, 136
Kaupe, Kim, 415
Kawasaki, Guy, 514
Ketler, Lorna, 75–76
Kiesel, Jason, 74
Klaus, Sharelle, 82
Koger, Eric, 416–418
Koger, Susan, 416–418
Kotler, Philip, 73
Kretchman, Len, 457
Krieger, Mike, 213
Kristof, Greg, 274
Kunkle, Gary, 465
Kutscher, Hesky, 74

L

Lam, Wing, 537
Latour, Pierre-Olivier, 77
Lee, Eduardo, 537
Lee, Mingo, 537
Leeworthy, Jesse, 381–382
Leiber, Jerry, 459–460
Leider, Josh, 202–204
Levinson, Conrad, 408
Levitt, Susie, 73
Levy, Emily, 474
Liang, Linus, 124–125
Light, Judith, 420
Lin, Alfred, 344
Linehan, Sean, 123
Liu, Jimmy, 280–282
Lluberes, Felix, 470
Long, Bobby, 377
Lugo, John, 456
Lugo, Mary Beth, 456

M

Manickam, Jay, 489–491
Markkula, Mike, 359
Marsh, Roger, 75
Martin, Anthony, 62–64
Mayer, Dan, 324–325
McComas, Carson, 524
Mendelson, Jason, 317–318
Michael, Tomer, 310–312
Michaels, David, 525
Michaels, Jillian, 543
Millsap, Mickey, 489–491
Moore, Geoffrey A., 476, 486–487
Morgan, Howard, 139
Mullins, John W., 99
Murillo, Gus, 462–464
Murty, Naganand, 125
Mycoskie, Blake, 163–166

N

Neeleman, David, 276
Ngo, Fred, 112
Nguyen, Kenny, 462–464
Nickell, Jack, 468
Nicols, Susan, 74
Norton, Scott, 486–488
Novis, Scott, 565–567

O

Okun, Sally, 58
Olsen, Dave, 329
Omidyar, Pierre, 334
Osterwalder, Alexander, 142

P

Packard, David, 465
Page, Larry, 28, 30, 359
Pak, James, 248
Panicker, Rahul, 124–126
Parag, Ashil, 123
Parker, J., 269–270
Patelli, Jim, 235
Patzer, Aaron, 524–526
Peaper, Carleen, 548
Penrose, Edith T., 477–478
Perry, Katy, 501
Peterson, Barbara, 276
Peterson, Jack, 270–272
Pettler, Adam, 378
Phillips, Lindsay, 499
Picariello, Jim, 301
Pickering, Melissa, 30
Pigneur, Yves, 142
Poole, Christopher, 362, 363–364

Porter, Michael, 176
Presley, Elvis, 446, 459–460
Proschk, Adam, 202–204
Purvin, Robert, 553
Putori, Jason, 525

Q

Quennesson, Kevin, 77

R

Raider, Jeffrey, 199
Ramadan, Mark, 486–488
Rayani, Samir, 316–318
Reiman, Martin, 494–496
Ries, Eric, 91, 122
Roberts, Joseph, 563
Rodan, Katie, 82, 419–421, 501
Rose, Kevin, 192
Rovner, Michael, 227
Rue, Alison Johnson, 74
Ryan, Kris, 165

S

Salinas, Miguel, 386–388
Schau, Jordan, 24
Schau, Zach, 28
Schultz, Howard, 35, 329
Schumpeter, Joseph, 44
Schwartz, Aaron, 83, 122–124
Schwartz, Johathan, 69
Schwartzberg, Gary, 439
Seymour, Jane, 501
Shea, Katie, 73
Sheik, Sherwin, 376
Shinar, Eyal, 310–312
Simmons, Russel, 34–35
Singer, April, 473–474
Singh, Paul, 391
Skoll, Jeff, 334
Slezak, Edward, 504
Sloan, Chelsea, 528–531
Sloan, Scott, 528–531
Smith, Pete, 213
Sorensen, Jay, 73
Sreshta, Andrea, 96–98, 215–216
Sterling, Debbie, 447–448
Stoffers, Austin, 24
Stoller, Mike, 459–460
Stoppelman, Jerry, 34–35
Stork, Anna, 96–98, 215–216
Strickler, Yancey, 75, 380–383
Stross, Randall, 334

Sun Tzu, 173, 187
Suplicy, Caue, 520
Swinmurn, Nick, 343–345
Systrom, Kevin, 213

T

Tan, Garry, 33
Tattersfield, Mike, 396
Theron, Charlize, 165
Tozun, Ned, 235–237
Tung, Peter, 309–310
Turner, Ted, 38

U

Udall, Laura, 144
Ullman, Mike, 400

W

Waaden, Mark von, 198
Wagner, Michael, 456
Walton, Sam, 38–39
Wang, Annie, 132–135
Washington, George, 430–431
Weiner, Jonathan, 57
Welch, Jack, 472
White, Alex, 316–318
White, Shaun, 56
Whiting, Gwen, 205–206
Whitman, Meg, 334
Wieber, Lindsey, 205–206
Wilkins, Barb, 75–76
Williams, Rozalia, 370
Williams, Vanessa, 420
Wilson, Fred, 28
Wood, Bill, 489
Wood, John, 31–32
Woodman, Nick, 54–56
Wozniacki, Caroline, 501
Wozniak, Steve, 355
Wu, Xian, 235
Wu, Yin Yin, 33

Y

Yang, Jerry, 438
Yang, Michael, 66
Yauch, Adam, 447
Yoskovitz, Ben, 112
You, Michelle, 213
Yung, Yuen, 309–310

Z

Zhang, Jiangyang, 280–282
Zuckerberg, Mark, 30

Company Index

A

Abercrombie & Fitch, 408
ABI Research, 69–70
Accenture, 277, 335
Administaff, 217
ADP, 217
Agilent Technologies, 516
Aging Excellence, 557
AHeirloom, 159–160
Airbnb, 139, 320, 403, 405
Alacritech, 436
Albie's Foods, 457–458
Alibaba, 364
ALS Therapy Development Foundation, 57
Alta Bicycle Share, 69
Amazon.com, 30, 70, 137, 147, 152, 188, 221, 343, 345, 350, 379, 381, 429, 432, 487, 520, 523
American Bar Association, 439
American Management Association, 472
American Veterinary Medical Association, 92–94
American Watchmakers-Clockmakers Institute, 175
Amgen, 29, 46, 180, 500
Anderson Consulting, 277
Andreessen Horowitz, 363
AngelPad, 320
Anheuser-Busch InBev, 178
Ann Arbor Angels, 360
Ann Taylor, 439
Anytime Fitness, 276, 543
Apple, Inc., 29, 46, 70, 91, 92, 138, 178, 282, 283, 314, 355, 359, 400, 430, 439
Arby's, 547
Art & Style Dance Studio, 391
Arthur Murray Dance Studio, 391
ASOS, 503
AT&T, 440
Au Bon Pain Co., 197
Audax Health, 70
August Smart Lock, 121–122
AV Labs, 227

B

Bahama Breeze, 540
Bain & Company, 335
Barnana, 520
Barnes & Noble, 188
Baskin-Robbins, 547
Baxters, 26
BB Dakota, 416
BearingPoint, 335
Become.com, 66
Bed Bath & Beyond, 276
Benchmark Venture Capital, 334, 490, 522
BenchPrep, 189–190
Benefits, 233
Best Buy, 56, 152, 312
Betaworks, 192
BEV Capital, 361
Beverage Partners Worldwide, 515
Beyond Meat, 186, 196, 407
Big Fish Presentations, 462–464
BioTechniques, 175
Birchbox, 137, 145, 148–149, 150, 232–234, 440

BizMiner, 110, 115, 294, 390
BlackJet, 139
Blue Cross Blue Shield of Louisiana, 463
Bluefly, 345
Bodacious, 75–76
Borders, 188
Box.net, 71
Brain Sentry, 53–54, 185
Brandbury Lewis, 200
Broadway Dance Center, 390
Bruegger's Bagels, 395, 396
Budget Blinds, 545
Build-A-Bear Workshop, 252–253, 254
Burbn, 213
Burger King, 532, 534, 536
Business Insider, 504
Buzzy, 185, 231

C

Cabela's, 464
CADI Scientific, 121
The Capital Grille, 540
Care2, 407
CareLinx, 376
CareZone, 69
Caribou Coffee, 395, 396
Cars.com, 490
Century 43 Real Estate, 556
Character Training International (CTI), 246–247
Charity:Water, 274–275
Charles Schwab, 276
Chili's Grill and Bar, 556
Chipotle Mexican Grill, 185
Circle Up, 368
Cirque du Soleil, 180, 185, 186
Cisco Systems, 354, 440
CitySlips, 73
Class Dojo, 485–486
CNNMoney, 33
CoachUp, 274
Coca-Cola Company, 188, 440, 475, 511, 515, 521, 556
Coffee News, 545
CofoundersLab, 113, 325
Coleman, 56
Comfort Keepers, 532, 540, 551
Compaq, 183
COOLEST, 368, 380–381, 415–416
Coolibar, 333
Core77.com, 379, 405
Costco, 75
Count Me In, 42
Craigslist, 490
Crowdfunder.com, 368
Cruise Planner, 548
Crumbs Bake Shop, 503, 504
Curves International, 542, 543

D

Daisy Rock, 75, 217
Darden Restaurants Inc., 540
Dealstruck, 367
Dean & DeLuca, 487
Dell Inc., 141, 183, 312–314, 368, 515
Delta Airlines, 277
Denny's, 556
Devver, 323, 324–325

Dick's Sporting Goods, 55
Digg, 191, 192
Digital Media Association, 106
d.light, 185, 235–237
Dogfish Head Craft Brewery, 78
Dollar Shave Club, 485
Dorm Room Fund, 44
Double Robotics, 520–521
DrawQuest, 362, 363–364
Dripcatch, 424–428
Dropbox, 28, 90–92, 134–135, 145–146, 210, 320, 361, 465
Dry Soda, 82
Dun & Bradstreet, 326
Dunkin' Donuts, 547

E

eBags, 217, 469
eBay, 137, 277, 334, 439, 490, 512
eBay Motors, 469
EBL Coaching, 474
Eddie V's, 540
Edible Arrangement, 545
eFax, 355
Elance, 154, 328–329
Element Bars, 189
Element Skateboard, 396
Elvis Presley Enterprises, 459–460
Embrace, 124–126
Engineering for Kids, 562–563
Enron, 329, 364
Entrepreneur, 248, 342, 403, 531, 547, 564, 567
Entrepreneurs' Organization, 439, 496, 531
eSeller Media, 500
Etsy, 159–162
EventVue, 223, 224
Everpix, 76, 77
Evite, 171, 172
ExxonMobil, 533

F

Facebook, 28, 30, 72, 91, 123, 148, 150, 180, 192, 213, 318, 328, 344, 361, 364, 402, 404, 406–407, 418, 508
Fast Company, 92
FastFleet, 502
Fidelity Investments, 522
Financial Services Roundtable, 503
Firefly Mobile, 73–74
FirstLight HomeCare, 557
First Round Capital, 524
First Screen Marketing, 116–117, 126–128t
Fit4Mom, 542
Fitbit, 247, 248, 277
Flicker, 399
Flings Bins, 185, 231–232
Forbes, 38–39, 123, 496, 543
Fortune, 403
Fortune Small Business, 436
Founder2Be, 113, 325
Foundry Group, 317–318, 361
Four Seasons Hotels, 487
Foursquare, 213
Franchise Direct USA, 548
The Franchise Handbook, 547
Franchise Times, 547
Fresh Healthy Vending, 173

Fundable, 354, 360
Fundbox, 310–312
FundersClub, 368
Funding Circle, 367
Fuze Beverages, 475

G

GameTruck, 565–567
Gap Inc., 503
GasBuddy, 68
GasPriceWatch.com, 68
G Asset Management, 188
General Electric (GE), 283
General Mills, 436, 439
General Motors (GM), 276, 533
Get Satisfaction, 83
The Giving Partners, 165
Glaukos, 69
Global Entrepreneurship Monitor
    (GEM), 27
GoDaddy.com, 270, 277, 430
GoldieBlox, 219–220, 446, 447–448
Goldman Sachs, 522
Gold's Gym, 548–549
Google, 28, 30, 44, 65–66, 68, 106, 114,
    123, 140, 141, 183, 245–246, 277,
    282, 328, 359, 361, 401, 465,
    515–516
Google Ventures, 362, 522, 523
GoPro, 54–56, 152, 407
Gowalla, 213
GreatCall, Inc., 73, 216, 390
GreenJob Spider, 75
Green Mountain Coffee Roasters, 29
Greenvelope, 170–172, 179, 183, 191
GrubHub, 213, 364
Guru.com, 154
Guthy-Renker, 420–421
GymFlow, 280–282

H

Hampton Inn Hotel, 545
H&R Block, 532, 551
Hardee's, 540
Harley-Davidson, 512
Harry's, 199
The Hartford, 205
Hasbro, 153, 334
Heinz, 486, 488
Her Campus Media, 132–135, 137–138,
    146, 147
HerUni.com, 134
Hewlett-Packard, 183, 312, 313, 516
Hidden Curriculum Education, 370
Hipmunk, 189
HomeAway, 516
Home Depot, 136, 276, 283
Honest Tea, 511
Hoovers, 115, 294
How Do You Roll? 309–310

I

IBISWorld, 83, 107, 110, 115, 173, 174,
    176, 390
IBM, 183
IBM Business Global Services, 335
iBoats.com, 490
IceBorn, 562
iCracked, 62–64
iCreate to Educate, 30
Idealab, 108
Inc., 205, 388, 403, 457, 465, 468, 547
Indiegogo, 98, 367–368, 382
iNovia Capital, 112

Insight Partners, 468
Instagram, 213, 508
Intel, 178, 181, 440, 562
Intel Capital, 362
International Franchise Association, 439
International Franchising Organization,
    552
Intouch Health, 333
Intuit, 29, 84, 480, 525
Inventors Assistance Center, 428
Irn Bru, 26
iRobot, 38
iUser Accessories, 270–272, 277
Izzy, 341

J

Java Jacket, 73
Jawbone, 248
JCDecaux, 269
JCPenny, 345, 399, 400–401
Jenny Craig, 543
JetBlue, 185, 276
Jiffy Print, 276
John Deere, 490
Johnson & Johnson, 46, 371, 521
JolieBox, 234
Jones's and Boylan's, 309
JumpStart, 108
Justin's, 185, 340–342

K

Kabbage, 311
KaZAM, 456
Keihl's, 233
Kentucky Fried Chicken, 532,
    545, 556
Kickstarter, 98, 123, 340, 350, 367–368,
    378–379, 380–383, 416
Kid to Kid, 529, 531
King Digital Entertainment, 364
Kleiner Perkins Caufield & Byers, 490
Knowledge Adventure, 108
Kohl's, 400
Kraft Foods, 439
Kroger, 342

L

Ladies Who Launch, 205–206, 326
La Petite Femme, 275
LaunchRock, 106
The Laundress, 205
Le Duff America, 396
LegalZoom, 249, 355
Lemonade Day, 44
Lending Club, 311, 367
LendingKarma, 355
LensCrafters, 199
Lerer Ventures, 363
Liberty Tax Service, 545
LinkedIn, 72, 85, 339
LinkExchange, 343–344
Liz Claiborne, 276
Local Dirt, 275–276
LongHorn Steakhouse, 540
LuminAID, 96–98, 215–216, 368
Luxottica, 199
Lyft, 139, 523

M

Macy's, 400, 501
Magic Johnson Enterprises, 276
MailFinch, 390–391
Major League Baseball, 123, 124

Malaysia Sdn Bhd, 326
Mango Health, 158–159
McDonald's, 254–255, 442, 503, 532,
    534, 535, 545, 556
Meetup, 326
Memobottle, 381–382
Merck, 217, 371
Merrill Lynch, 476
MGM, 440
Miami-Dade Empowerment
    Trust, 370
MicroMentor.org, 85
Microsoft, 66, 181, 401, 436, 525
Midas Muffler, 532
Mint.com, 480, 511, 524–526
Mintel, 110, 115, 176, 390
Minute Maid, 475
ModCloth, 75, 185, 404–406, 407,
    416–418, 497, 512
Modify Watches, 83, 122–124, 208
Monster Beverage, 475
Monster.com, 339
Mophie, 136
Motorcycle.com, 490
Mountains to Sound, 172
Murray's Cheese, 487
The Muse, 339
Mutual of Omaha, 464
MyFax, 355

N

Namo Media, 516
Napkin Labs, 83, 123
Nars, 233
NASDAQ, 28–29, 39, 262
National Association for Women
    Business Owners (NAWBO), 85
National Association for Women
    Entrepreneurs of Malaysia
    (NAWEM), 326
National Basketball Association
    (NBA), 90
National Clearinghouse, 428
National Football League (NFL), 440
National Hockey Association
    (NHL), 90
National Institutes of Health
    (NIH), 231
NatureBox, 89
Neighborrow.com, 139
Neiman Marcus, 110
Nest Labs, 68, 515–516
Nestlé, 515
Netflix, 146, 180, 432–433
Neutrogena, 420
New Venture Fitness Drinks, 327
New York Stock Exchange, 262
Next Big Sound, 316–318
Nike, 248, 439, 440
Nolo, 249
Nordstrom, 162
North Castle Partners, 543
Nucor Steel, 185, 186

O

Oakley, 199, 398
Odesk, 154, 328–329
Odesk.com, 242
Odwalla, 475
Olive Garden, 540
OnDeck, 311
1-800-CONTACTS, 440
1-800-FLOWERS, 187, 276
1-800-GOT-JUNK, 185

1800contacts.com, 180
1800diapers, 361
OnlineFaxes, 355
OpenTable. com, 70
Oracle, 502

P

The Pampered Chef, 466
Pandora, 35, 36, 318
Panera Bread, 183, 197–198, 394, 430, 503
Papa John's Pizza, 545, 551, 556
Paperless Post, 172
Paramount Pictures, 464
Parking Panda, 89–90
Passport Video, 459–460
Patagonia, 253, 254
PatientsLikeMe, 57–58, 69, 429
Paul Green School of Rock Music, 563
Paychex, 217
Payless Shoes, 345
PCC Markets, 520
Pearle Vision, 199
Pebble, 380, 416
Peet's, 339
Pepsi, 341
Persol, 199
PetCare.com, 92
PetCo, 94
Pfizer, 217, 371, 513
PharmaJet, 185
Photobucket, 399
Picas Web Albums, 399
PillPack, 269–270
Pine Ridge Native American Reservation, 342
Pinterest, 407
Pixar, 507
Planet Smoothie, 533
Play It Again Sports, 534, 557
PledgeMusic, 376–377, 382
PopCap Games, 76
Position Logic, 470
Potbelly, 331
Pottery Barn, 501
Priceline.com, 432
Prim, 32–33
The Princeton Review, 439
Proactiv, 82, 419–421, 469, 501
Procter & Gamble, 334, 436, 439
ProntoWash, 534

Q

Qdoba Mexican Grill, 545
Quirky, 135, 136

R

Raising Cane's, 463
Ray-Ban, 199
RedBrick Health, 70
Redfin, 361
Reference USA, 115
Refill Revolution, 122
REI, 55, 341
Revolights, 377–379
Ridjoy, 139
Ritchie Brothers Auctioneers, 490
Rock&Dirt, 490
RocketHub, 367–368, 382
RocketLawyer, 249, 355, 516

Rokit, 70
Roominate, 348–350, 368
Room to Read, 31–32
Rover.com, 92, 151
Rufus, 473
Ryanair, 140

S

SafetyWeb, 74
Safeway, 342, 487
Saint Louis Bread Company, 197
Salesforce.com, 141, 476
Samsung, 46
School of Rock, 563–565
Sears Optical, 199
Sears Roebuck and Company, 137
Seasons 74, 540
Secret Recipe Cakes and Café, 158
Sequoia Capital, 358
Service Corps of Retired Executives (SCORE), 115, 335
Seva Foundation, 164
Shabby Chic, 475
Shake Smart, 494–496
Shoebuy.com, 345
Sidecar, 523
Sierra Angels, 379
Singer Sewing Machine Company, 532
Sir Kensington, 486–488, 497
Small Business & Entrepreneurship Council (SBE), 503
Small Business Development Center (SBDC), 271, 335
SME Corporation Malaysia, 326
Smuckers, 457–458
SmugMug, 399
Snap Fitness, 391–392, 543
SOFA Entertainment, 459–460
Soggy Bottom Canoe and Kayak Rental, 103
Soma, 339–340
Songkick, 213
Sony, 56
Southpaw Guitars, 75
Southwest Airlines, 140, 284, 393–394
SpeakLike, 46–47
Spotify, 318
Sprig Toys, 106
Sprindrift Soda, 309
Sprouts, 520
Square, 180
Standard & Poor's NetAdvantage, 176
Standout Jobs, 111, 112
Stanley Black & Decker, 439
Staples, 312
Starbucks, 35, 177–178, 329, 339, 394, 501, 512, 540
Startup America, 123
Startup Weekend, 44, 92, 113, 352–353
StartX, 350
Sterling Partners, 563
StixToGo, 426
Subway, 551
Sunglass Hut, 199
Sunkist Growers, 393
SuperJam, 25–26, 150, 152, 185
Swann, 56
SwitchFlops, 497, 499

T

Talent Technology, 112
TapCommerce, 508

Target, 136, 342, 400, 447, 475, 487, 501
Target Optical, 199
TechStars, 41, 317–318, 320, 324
TEDMED, 58
Tempered Mind, Inc., 240–242
TempoRun, 202–204
TerraPass, 490
Tesla, 178
Threadless, 468
3 Day Startup, 353
3D Robotics, 70
Thums Up, 475
Time Warner Investments, 362
T.J.Maxx, 400
Tommy John, 110
TOMS, 163–166, 328, 396, 471
Total, 236
Toys"R"Us, 220, 350, 447
Toymaster Group, 285
Tunnock, 26
TriNet, 217
Tumblr, 72
23andMe, 516
Twitter, 72, 192, 318, 344, 361, 364, 404, 406–407, 508, 548

U

Uber, 139, 141, 147, 516, 521–523
Ubersense, 70, 196–197
Union Square Ventures, 363
United National Foods, 301
United Nations, 235
United States Hispanic Chamber of Commerce, 552
UPS Store, 545
Uptown Cheapskate, 528–531
USA Today, 547
U.S. Census Bureau, 42
U.S. Consumer Products Safety Commission (CPSC), 248
U.S. Copyright Office, 444
U.S. Department of Commerce, 562
U.S. Department of Health and Human Services, 70
U.S. Federal Trade Commission (FTC), 552–553
U.S. Internal Revenue Service (IRS), 255, 257, 329
U.S. Minority Business Development Agency (MBDA), 43
U.S. Patent and Trademark Office (USPTO), 426, 428, 431, 433, 434–437, 457–458
U.S. Securities and Exchange Commission (SEC), 190, 364
U.S. Small Business Administration (SBA), 46, 85, 115, 357, 366–367, 548
UserVoice, 83
uShip, 469, 489–491, 503, 505

V

Velib, 269
Verizon, 277, 439
VeryWendy, 29
Victory Marketing Agency, 479
Virerbi Startup Garage, 282
Virgin Group, 29
Virgin Records, 31
VisionSpring, 199
Visiting Angels, 557
VMG Partners, 342
Voodoo BBQ, 463

W

Wahoo's Fish Taco, 536, 537
Wakoopa, 456
Walgreens, 503
Wall Street Journal, 504, 547
Walmart, 75, 312, 350, 415, 536
Walt Disney Corporation, 30, 276, 334, 415, 507, 566
Warby Parker, 149–150, 152, 199–200, 440, 465
WaterSmart Software, 68
Weebly.com, 122
Wegmans, 301, 520
Wello, 53, 216, 277
Wesabe, 478, 480, 511
West Elm, 162

Wetzel's Pretzels, 545
WhitePages.com, 34
White Wave, 186
Whole Food Markets, 147, 301, 341, 487, 520
Williams-Sonoma, 487
Windspire, 185
Wink Natural Cosmetics, 386–388
Wise Acre Frozen Treats, 300, 301
Women in Franchising, 552
Woodinville's Cashmere Molding, 426
WorldCom, 329, 364

Y

Yahoo! 65, 140, 183, 401, 438, 440
Yard House, 540

Y Combinator, 33, 41, 64, 90, 320
Yelp, 34–35
Yodlee, 480, 511, 524
Yogitoes, 74
YouTube, 91, 233, 318, 407

Z

Zappos, 146, 152, 343–345, 469, 497
Zephyrhill, 440
ZinePak, 415
Zipcar, 69, 502
ZUCA, 144
Zynga, 69, 143, 144–145, 147–148, 153

Subject Index

Page references with "f" refer to figures and page references with "t" refer to tables.

A

accelerator programs, 41, 282, 319, 320, 350
accounts receivable, 284
accredited investors, 368
acquirer, 508
acquisitions, 507–511
AdAge Viral Video Awards, 485
adverse selection, 477
advertising, 399, 401–402, 402t, 403f
advisory boards, 332–333
Affordable Care Act, 58, 70
agency theory, 540
alliances, 514–515
American Express OPEN study, 42
American Invents Act, 428
angel investors, 344, 359–360
area franchise agreements, 534
articles of incorporation, 262
The Art of War (Sun Tzu), 173
assignment of invention agreements, 433–434
assumptions sheet, 223, 295
attorneys, 242, 247, 249, 249t, 434t
audits, of intellectual property, 451–452, 452t, 538

B

baby boomers, 68
backward integration, 182
balance sheets, 289, 291–292
barrier to entry, 178, 180t
Barringer/Ireland Business Model Template, 135, 141–146, 143f, 167–168
basis of differentiation, 144
Best Brand Food & Beverage Café Award, 158
biotech firms, 371
blogs, 72, 403, 404–407.
    See also specific blogs
Blue Streak (Peterson), 276
board of advisors, 222, 332–333
board of directors, 222, 329–331, 330t
bookkeeping software, 311
bootstrapping, 355–356, 355t
brainstorming, 81–82, 81t, 82t
brand equity, 394–395
branding, 392–395, 393t
brand management, 393
brands, 392, 393t
break-even point, 297, 299
budgets, 285
bug reports, 82
burn rate, 351
business angels, 344, 359–360
business format franchise, 533–534
business licenses and permits, 255–257, 256t
business method patents, 432–433
Business Model Canvas, 142
Business Model Generation (Osterwalder and Pigneur), 142
business models, 47, 132–169
    Barringer/Ireland Template, 135, 141–146, 143f, 167–168
    core strategy, 142–146

disruptive type, 140–141, 141t
financials, 148–151, 149t
importance of, 135
operations, 151–153
resources, 146–148
standard type, 137–138, 138t, 140
types of partnerships, 153t
business names, 275–277
business plans, 47–48, 202–238, 209t
    content of, 209–211
    employees, 207
    estimating initial sales in, 218, 218t
    financial projections, 223–225
    investors/external stakeholders, 207–208
    oral presentations to investors, 225–227, 226t
    outline of, 211–225, 212t
    purpose of, 205–207, 225t
    structure of, 208–209
business trends, 174
buyback clauses, 250, 251
buyers, in five forces model, 181–182
buzz, 394

C

carry, 360
cash flow shortfalls, 310–312
C corporations, 261–263
certification marks, 438t, 440
channels, 152
Chris Dixon (blog), 363
churn, 137
closely held corporations, 262
co-branding, 395, 396, 547
code of conduct, 245–246, 245–246t
collective marks, 438t, 439
commercial banks, 357, 358t, 365–366
common stock, 261–262
Competitive Advantage (Porter), 176
competitive analysis grids, 190–191, 191t
competitive intelligence, 188, 190, 190t
competitor analysis, 173, 187–191.
    See also industry analysis
    in business plans, 218
    competitive analysis grids, 190–191, 191t
    identifying competitors, 187–188, 188f
    sources of competitive intelligence, 188, 190, 190t
Computer Software Copyright Act, 443–444
concept statement, 101–102, 102f
concept test, 101
constant ratio method of forecasting, 297
consultants, 335
contribution margin, 219
copyright bug, 444
copyright infringement, 445–446
Copyright Revision Act, 443
copyrights, 429–430, 443–448
    infringement of, 445–446
    internet and, 446, 448
    legal protections, 443–444
    process for obtaining, 444–445

Core77 Design Award, 379
core competencies, 146–147, 467
core strategy, 142–146
    basis of differentiation, 144
    mission statement, 143–144
    product/market scope, 145–146
    target markets, 144–145
corporate entrepreneurship, 29
corporate venture capital, 362
corporations, 261–264
cost-based pricing, 398
cost of sales/goods sold, 218, 288–289
cost reduction strategy, 186
cost structure, in business models, 149–150
creative destruction, 44
creativity
    for identifying opportunities and ideas, 79–81, 84, 86, 86t
    stages of, 79f, 80
Crossing the Chasm (Moore), 476, 486–487, 487f
crowdfunding, 367–368
current assets, 289
current liabilities, 291
current ratio, 291
customer advisory boards, 84
customers, in feasibility analysis, 105–106, 106t

D

day-in-the-life research, 84
debt financing, 356–359, 358–359t, 365–367
debt-to-equity ratio, 284
declining industries, 185t, 186
derivative works, 443
design patents, 433, 433t
disintermediation, 408
disruptive business models, 140–141, 141t
distribution channels, 408
"Does Anyone in Healthcare Want to Be Understood?" (Okun), 58
double taxation, 262
Draper Fisher Jurvetson Venture Challenge, 236
drones, 70
due diligence, 208, 361–362

E

Economic Espionage Act, 448
economic impacts, 44, 46
economies of scale, 178, 471
economies of scope, 471
efficiency, 284
elevator speeches (pitch), 357, 359t
emerging industries, 185, 185t
employee benefits, 328
Employee Identification Number (EIN), 257
employees, 327–328, 328t
The E-Myth Revisited (Gerber), 474
entrepreneurial alertness, 78
entrepreneurial firms, 40, 40f
entrepreneurial intensity, 29

entrepreneurial process, 47–48f, 47–49
entrepreneurial services, 477–478, 478f
entrepreneurship, 28
entrepreneurship and entrepreneurs, overview, 23–60
  changing demographics and, 42–44
  characteristics of, 31–35, 31f, 32t
  common myths, 36–40, 38–39t
  explanation of, 28
  introduction, 27–28, 27t
  positive effects of, 44–47
  process of, 47–48f, 47–49
  rationale for, 28–31
  types of start-up firms, 40, 40f
  young entrepreneurs, 45t
environmental trends, 174
equity-based crowdfunding, 368
equity financing
  preparing for, 356–359, 358–359t
  sources of, 359–365, 362t
ethical cultures, 243–247, 247f
  code of conduct, 245–246, 245–246t
  franchising and, 555–556
  implementing ethics training programs, 246–247
  leading by example, 244
  misconduct/unethical behavior survey, 244t
ethical dilemmas, 246
ethics training programs, 246–247
exclusive distribution arrangements, 409
execution intelligence, 35
executive summary, 212, 214
external growth strategies, 507–516, 508t

F

factoring, 367
fair use, 446, 459
feasibility analysis, 96–131
  explanation of, 99–100, 99f, 100t
  financial assessment, 114–116, 114t
  First Screen Marketing survey, 126–128t
  of industry/target markets, 107–111, 109t
  of management prowess, 111
  online tools for, 103–104t, 128–130t
  of product/service demand, 105–107, 105t
  of product/service desirability, 100–104, 103–104t
  of resource sufficiency, 111, 113–114
  template for, 116–117, 116t
Federal Employee Identification Number (EIN), 257
fictitious business name permits, 257, 258
fiduciary obligation, 553
final prospectus, 364
financial feasibility analysis
  explanation of, 114
  nonfinancial resources, 114t
  overall financial attractiveness, 116
  performance of similar businesses, 115–116
  start-up cash, 114–115
financial management, 283, 284–286
financial objectives, 284, 284f
financial projections, 223–225
financial ratios, 286
financials, in business models, 148–151
  cost structure, 149–150
  financing and funding, 150–151
  revenue streams, 148–149, 149t

financial statements, 284–285
financial statements, historical.
    See historical financial statements
financing activities, 293
financing and funding, 348–384
  accelerator programs, 41
  in business models, 150–151
  crowdfunding, 367–368
  importance of, 351
  leasing, 368–369
  other grant programs, 370–371
  preparing for debt or equity financing, 356–359, 358–359t
  SBIR and STTR grant programs, 369–370
  sources of debt financing, 365–367
  sources of equity funding, 359–365
  sources of personal financing, 354–356, 355t
  for startups, 351–353
  strategic partners, 371
first-mover advantage, 185
five forces model (Porter), 176–183, 176f
  for assessing new ventures, 182–183, 182t, 184f
  bargaining power of buyers, 181–182
  bargaining power of suppliers, 180–181
  rivalry among existing firms, 179–180
  threat of new entrants, 178–179
  threat of substitutes, 177–178
fixed assets, 289
fixed costs, 150, 219, 471
focus groups, 82–83
follow-on funding, 361
forecasts, 285, 295–299
forward integration, 181
founders
  new-venture teams and, 321–325
  qualities of, 323, 325, 325t
founders' agreements, 250, 250t
founding teams, 322
fragmented industries, 185, 185t
franchise agreements, 553
Franchise Disclosure Document (FDD), 538, 545, 550, 552–555, 554t
franchises, 532
franchising, 528–569
  criteria for, 539, 539t
  ethics and, 555–556
  explanation of, 528–534
  federal rules and regulations for, 552–553, 554t
  future trends, 557
  industries for, 534t
  international, 556–557
  misconceptions about, 551–552
  pros and cons of, 540–542, 541t
  purchasing of, 542, 544–551, 545t, 548–549t
  state rules and regulations, 553, 555
  steps for establishing, 535–539
  types of systems, 534–535, 535f
franchisors, 532
freelancers, 154, 328
freemium model, 91, 134–135
full business plans, 210, 210f

G

general partners, 360
general partnerships, 260

geographic expansion, 502–503
geographic roll-up strategy, 185
global industries, 185t, 187
global strategy, 187
Good to Great (Collins), 469
Google AdSense, 401, 402t
Google AdWords, 106, 171, 401, 402t, 490
government regulation
  as basis for opportunities and ideas, 70–71, 71t
  of franchises, 552–553, 554t, 555
  Stopfakes.gov, 430
grant programs, 369–371
growth, challenges of, 462–493
  capital constraints, 481
  cash flow management, 478–479
  challenges of, 467t, 477–481
  core strategy and, 467, 469
  managerial capacity, 477–478
  managing stages of, 472–475, 473f
  planning for, 469–470
  preparing for, 465–467
  price stability, 479, 481
  quality control, 481
  rationale for, 470–472
growth, strategies for, 494–527.
    See also franchising
  geographic expansion, 502–503
  international expansion, 503–507, 505–506t
  licensing, 511–512
  market penetration strategy, 501–502
  mergers and acquisitions, 507–511, 510f
  new product development, 497, 500–501
  product line extension strategy, 502
  product/service improvement, 501
  strategic alliances and joint ventures, 512–513, 513t, 515–516
guerilla marketing, 408
Guerilla Marketing (Levinson), 408

H

The Hartford's 2013 Small Business Success Study, 38
heterogeneous, 322
His Brother's Keeper (Weiner), 57
historical financial statements, 287–295
  balance sheets, 289, 291–292
  comparison to industry norms, 294
  income statements, 288–289
  ratio analysis, 293–294
  statement of cash flows, 292–293
holacracy (Zappos), 344
homogenous, 322

I

idea, 66
idea banks, 84
idea-expression dichotomy, 444
idea generation. *See* opportunities and ideas
illiquid, 262
improving an existing product or service, 501
income statement forecasts, 297, 299
income statements, 288–289
incubators, 41
individual franchise agreements, 534

industry, 107, 172
industry analysis, 173–187. *See also* competitor analysis
  in business plans, 214–215
  explanation of, 173–174
  five forces model, 176–183, 176f, 182t, 184f
  industry types, 184–187, 185t
industry attractiveness, 109–110, 109t, 182–183, 182t
industry/target market feasibility, 107–111, 109t
industry trends, 174
infomercials, 420–421
initial public offering (IPO), 362, 364–365
innovation, 46
The Innovator's Dilemma (Christensen), 140
inside directors, 329
intellectual property, 424–461
  conducting audits of, 451–452, 452t
  copyrights, 429–430, 443–448
  criteria for protection of, 429
  importance of, 427–430
  patents, 429–436, 433t
  trademarks, 429–430, 436–443, 438t
  trade secrets, 448–451
intellectual property audits, 451–452, 452t
intent-to-use trademark applications, 442–443
internal growth strategies, 497–503, 498t
International CES, 404
International Consumer Electronics Trade Show, 175
International Franchise Expo, 547–548
international new ventures, 503, 505, 505–506t
internet. *See also* library and internet research
  copyrights and, 446, 448
  domain names, 277, 430
interns, 328
intranets, 84
inventory, 284
investing activities, 293
investment banks, 364
investors
  accredited, 368
  business angels, 344, 359–360
  new-venture teams and, 333–334, 334t
  presentation of business plans to, 225–227, 226t
IP Law For Startups (blog), 430

J

job creation, 46
JOBS Act, 368
joint ventures, 153, 515–516

K

The Kauffman Foundation and LegalZoom 2102 Startup Environment Index, 39, 39t, 43
key assets, 147–148

L

labor sources, 327–329, 328t
landing page, 106
Lanham Act, 440
leadership strategy, 186
Lean Startup movement, 122, 211

leases, 368–369
Leaving Microsoft to Change the World (Wood), 31
legal issues, 247–265
  avoiding legal disputes, 250–255
  business licenses and permits, 255–257, 256t
  business names, 276–277
  choosing attorneys, 247, 249, 249t
  choosing form of business organization, 257–265, 259t
  copyrights, 443–444
  drafting founders' agreements, 250, 250t
  trademarks, 440–441
lenders, 333–334, 334t
LexisNexis Academic, 115
liability of newness, 319
library and internet research
  for feasibility analysis, 103–104t, 106–107, 128–130t
  for identifying opportunities and ideas, 83–84
licensees, 511
licenses. *See* business licenses and permits
licensing, 511–512
licensing agreements, 511, 512
licensors, 511
lifestyle firms, 40, 40f
limited liability company (LLC), 264–265
limited partners, 360
limited partnership agreements, 261
limited partnerships, 261
line of credit, 365
link joint ventures, 515
liquidity, 258, 284
liquidity events, 356
liquid market, 262
long-term liabilities, 291
low-end market disruption, 140

M

management prowess, 111
management team
  in business plans, 222
  new-venture teams and, 325, 327–329, 328t
managerial capacity problem, 477
managerial services, 477–478, 478f
market analysis, 216
marketing, 386–423
  branding, 392–395, 393t
  creating unique market position, 391–392, 392t
  market segmentation, 389–390
  place/distribution, 408–409
  price and, 398–399
  product, 395, 397–398
  promotion activities, 399, 401–408, 402t, 403f, 404t
  sales process issues, 409–412, 410f
  selecting target markets, 390–391
marketing alliances, 513, 515
marketing mix, 395
marketing plans, 219–220
marketing strategy, 219
market leadership, 471
market penetration strategy, 501–502
marketplace gaps, 75, 76t
market segmentation, 216, 389–390
Mashable (blog), 403
master franchise agreements, 534
mature industries, 185–186, 185t

mediation, 253
mentors, 85
merchandise and character licensing, 512
merchant cash advance, 367
mergers, 507–511
milestone, 216
minority entrepreneurs, 43
misconduct/unethical behavior, 244t
mission statements, 143–144, 216
moderate risk takers, 37–38
moral hazard, 477–478
multidomestic strategy, 187
multiple-unit franchisees, 534–535

N

naming businesses. *See* business names
National Business Ethics Survey, 244t
National Parent Center Seal of Approval, 456
National Venture Capital Yearbook (2014), 361
net sales, 288
network entrepreneurs, 79
Network for Teaching Entrepreneurship (NFTE), 43–44
networking, 325
The New Business Road Test (Mullins), 99
new market disruption, 140
new product development, 497, 500–501
new ventures, assessment of, 280–315
  financial management, 283, 284–286, 286f
  financial objectives, 284, 284f
  financial statements, 284, 287–295
  forecasts, 285, 295–299
  pro forma (or projected) financial statements, 287, 299–305
new-venture teams, 111, 316–347
  building process, 319, 321
  consultants and, 335
  founders and, 321–325, 325t
  lenders and investors, 333–334, 334t
  liability of newness, 319
  management team/key employees and, 325, 327–329, 328t
  role of board of advisors, 332–333
  role of board of directors, 329–331, 330t
niche markets, 390–391
niche strategy, 186
noncompete agreements, 253, 253f
nondisclosure agreements, 253, 253f

O

one year after first use deadline, 432
online forums, 326
online surveys, 106
online tools, for feasibility analysis, 103–104t, 128–130t
operating activities, 293
operating expenses, 289
operating leverage, 219
operational business plans, 210, 210f
operations, in business models, 151–153
  channels, 152
  key partners, 152–153, 153t
  product/service production, 151
operations plans, 221
Oppenheim Toy Portfolio Gold Seal Award, 456

opportunities and ideas, 62–95, 80f
  brainstorming, 81–82, 81t, 82t
  characteristics of entrepreneurs, 76, 78
  cognitive factors, 78
  creativity, 79–81, 79f, 84, 86, 86t
  differences between, 65–66
  essential qualities of, 65f
  focal points for, 84
  focus groups, 82–83
  identifying, 66–76, 67f, 71t, 74–76t
  library and internet research, 83–84
  marketplace gaps, 75, 76t
  prior experience, 78
  problem solving approach, 72–74, 74–75t
  social networks, 79
opportunity, 65
opportunity gap, 65
opportunity recognition, 76, 78, 80f
organic growth, 497
organizational charts, 222
organizational feasibility analysis, 111–114
other assets, 289
outside directors, 329–330
outsourcing, 502
owners' equity, 291

P

pace of growth, 467t, 470
partners, 113
partnership agreements, 260
partnerships, 153t, 217, 259t, 260–261
passion for their business, 31–33, 32t
patent infringement, 436
patent research, 114
patents, 429–436
  attorney fees for, 434t
  eligibility for, 433–434
  growth in applications for, 431, 431t
  infringement of, 436
  process for obtaining, 434–436
  types of, 432–433, 433t
pay-per-click advertising, 401
peer-to-peer business models, 139
peer-to-peer lending, 367
percent-of-sales method, 297
permits. *See* business licenses and permits
personal financing, 354–356
piercing the corporate veil, 262
place (marketing), 408
plant patents, 433, 433t
position
  in industry analysis, 173
  of product/service, 216
PowerPoint, 207, 208, 226t
preferred stock, 261
preliminary prospectus, 364
prepaid gift cards, 501–502
Preparing Effective Business Plans (Barringer), 410
press kits, 403–404
price, 398–399
price-quality attribution, 398–399
price-to-earnings (P/E) ratio, 289
primary research, 100
prior entrepreneurial experience, 323
private corporations, 262
private placement, 365
problem solving approach, 72–74, 74–75t
product, 395
product and trademark franchise, 533

product attribute maps, 391–392
product/customer focus, 34
productive opportunity set, 477
product line extension strategy, 502
product/market scope, 145–146
product prototypes, 220
products, and marketing, 395, 397–398
product/service demand, 105–107, 105t
product/service desirability, 100–104, 103–104t
product/service feasibility analysis, 100
professional employer organizations (PEOs), 217
profitability, 284
profit margin, 289
pro forma (or projected) financial statements, 223, 287, 299–305
pro forma balance sheets, 301–302
pro forma income statements, 300
pro forma statement of cash flows, 302–305
promotion, 399
promotion activities, 399, 401–408
  advertising, 399, 401–402, 402t, 403f
  guerilla marketing, 408
  public relations, 403–404, 404t
  social media, 404–407
  viral marketing, 407
ProQuest, 115
provisional patent applications, 436, 437–438
public corporations, 262
public relations, 403–404, 404t
Putra Brand Award, 158

R

ratio analysis, 223, 293–294, 305
reference accounts, 397
registered marks, 441–442
regression analysis, 296–297
relevant industry experience, 323
resources, in business models, 146–148
resource sufficiency, 111, 113–114
revenue streams, 148–149, 149t
rewards-based crowdfunding, 367–368
road shows, 364–365
Rock School (documentary), 563
rounds (venture capital), 361, 362t

S

salary-substitute firms, 40, 40f
sales forecasts, 295–297, 296f
sales process, 409–412, 410f
sales tax permits, 256
Sarbanes-Oxley Act, 364
SBA Guaranteed Loan Program, 357, 366–367
SBIR Program, 369, 370t
scale joint ventures, 515
School of Rock (film), 563
search engines, 65–66
secondary market offering, 362
secondary meaning, of trademarks, 442
secondary research, 100
senior entrepreneurs, 43
service, 395
service marks, 438t, 439
7(A) Loan Guaranty Program, 366–367
shareholders, 261–262

Shark Tank (tv show), 310, 378–379, 456, 464
Shipping Wars (tv show), 490
signaling, 331
Simple Internet, 115
single-purpose loans, 365
skills profiles, 327
Small Business Innovation Research (SBIR), 369, 370t
Small Business Technology Transfer (STTR), 370
small and medium enterprises (SMEs), 326
smartphones, 69–70, 73–74
social media
  identifying emerging trends via, 72
  popularity of, 68, 69
  for product sales, 56, 344
  promotion activities and, 404–407
social networks, 79
social plug-ins, 406
software
  for bookkeeping, 311
  for writing business plans, 209
sole proprietorship, 258–260, 259t
solo entrepreneurs, 79
So Much So Fast (film), 57
sources and uses of funds statement, 223
South by Southwest Music and Media Conference, 203–204
spin-ins, 516
spin-outs, 516
stability, 284
standard business models, 137–138, 138t, 140
start-up cash, 114–115
start-up incubators, 41
statement of cash flows, 292–293
stock options, 262–263
Stopfakes.gov, 430
strategic alliances, 153, 513, 515
strategic partners, 371
strong-tie relationships, 79
STTR Program, 370
subchapter S corporations, 263–264
subfranchisees, 534
summary business plans, 210, 210f
suppliers, 152–153, 180–181
sustained growth, 465
sweat equity, 354
switching costs, 181

T

taglines, 216, 392, 392t
target markets, 107, 109, 110–111, 144–145, 390–391
targets, 508
teams. *See* new-venture teams
TechCrunch (blog), 311, 363, 403
TechCrunch40 (competition), 525
technological advances, 69–70, 71t
technological alliances, 513, 515
technology adoption life cycle (Moore), 486–487, 487f
technology licensing, 512
10-K, 287
The Theory of Economic Development (Schumpeter), 44
The Theory of the Growth of the Firm (Penrose), 477–478, 478f
trade associations, 106, 175
trade journals, 175
Trademark Act, 441

trademarks, 277, 429–430, 436–443
  legal protections, 440–441
  process for obtaining, 441–443
  types of, 438–440, 438t
trade secrets, 179, 448–451
  disputes, 449–450
  eligibility for, 449
  protection methods, 450–451
Trade Show News Network, 175
trade shows, 175, 404
trends, 66–71, 67f, 71t
  business, 174
  economic forces and, 67–68
  environmental, 174
  in franchising, 557
  identifying via social media, 72
  industry, 174
  political and regulatory changes and, 70–71
  social forces and, 68–69
  technological advances and, 69–70
triggering events, 47
Two Pesos, Inc., v. Taco Cabana International Inc. (1992), 440

U

Uniform Trade Secrets Act, 448
utility patents, 432, 433t

V

value, 40
value-based pricing, 398
variable costs, 150, 219, 471
vendor credit, 367
venture capital, 360–362, 362t
venture capitalists, 333
venture-leasing firms, 368
vesting ownership, 250–251
videoconferencing, 177
viral marketing, 407
virtual assistants, 328–329
virtual prototypes, 220

W

Wakoopians, 457
weak-tie relationships, 79
window of opportunity, 65
Women Owned Business report, 42
WorkHappy.net (blog), 524
working capital, 291
The World Is Flat (Friedman), 313

Y

Year Best Sales Growth Award, 158
young entrepreneurs, 43–44, 45t